Rules for Categorical Syllogisms

Rule 1: **The middle term must be distributed at least once.**

Fallacy: Undistributed middle

Rule 2: **If a term is distributed in the conclusion, then it must be distributed in a premise.**

Fallacy: Illicit major; illicit minor

Rule 3: **Two negative premises are not allowed.**

Fallacy: Exclusive premises

Rule 4: **A negative premise requires a negative conclusion, and a negative conclusion requires a negative premise.**

Fallacy: Drawing an affirmative conclusion from a negative premise; drawing a negative conclusion from affirmative premises

Rule 5: **If both premises are universal, the conclusion cannot be particular.**

Fallacy: Existential fallacy

NOTE: If only Rule 5 is broken, the syllogism is valid from the Aristotelian standpoint if the critical term denotes actually existing things.

Truth Tables for the Propositional Operators

p	q	$\sim p$	$p \cdot q$	$p \vee q$	$p \supset q$	$p \equiv q$
T	T	F	T	T	T	T
T	F	F	F	T	F	F
F	T	T	F	T	T	F
F	F	T	F	F	T	T

D1450108

Rules for the Probability Calculus

1. $P(A \text{ or not } A) = 1$
2. $P(A \text{ and not } A) = 0$
3. $P(A \text{ and } B) = P(A) \times P(B)$ (when A and B are independent)
4. $P(A \text{ and } B) = P(A) \times P(B \text{ given } A)$
5. $P(A \text{ or } B) = P(A) + P(B)$ (when A and B are mutually exclusive)
6. $P(A \text{ or } B) = P(A) + P(B) - P(A \text{ and } B)$
7. $P(A) = 1 - P(\text{not } A)$

A CONCISE INTRODUCTION TO

LOGIC

Thirteenth Edition

PATRICK J. HURLEY
University of San Diego

LORI WATSON
University of San Diego

CENGAGE
Learning·

Australia • Brazil • Mexico • Singapore • United Kingdom • United States

CENGAGE
Learning®

A Concise Introduction to Logic,
13th Edition
Patrick J. Hurley, Lori Watson

Product Director: Paul Banks

Product Manager: Joseph Potvin

Senior Content Developer: Florence Kilgo

Product Assistant: Staci Eckenroth

Marketing Manager: Sean Ketchem

Senior Content Project Manager:
Margaret Park Bridges

Senior Art Director: Marissa Falco

Manufacturing Planner: Julio Esperas

IP Analyst: Alex Ricciardi

IP Project Manager: Nick Barrows

Production Service: Greg Hubit Bookworks

Copy Editor: Marne Evans

Proofreader: Debra Nichols

Compositor: MPS Limited

Text and Cover Designer: Deborah Dutton

Cover Images: iStockphoto.com/pavlen;
Route55/Shutterstock.com

For product information and technology assistance, contact us at
Cengage Learning Customer & Sales Support, 1-800-354-9706

For permission to use material from this text or product,
submit all requests online at **www.cengage.com/permissions**
Further permissions questions can be emailed to
permissionrequest@cengage.com

Library of Congress Control Number: 2016941673

Student Edition:
ISBN: 978-1-305-95809-8

Loose-leaf Edition:
ISBN: 978-1-305-95976-7

Cengage Learning
20 Channel Center Street
Boston, MA 02210
USA

Cengage Learning is a leading provider of customized learning solutions with employees residing in nearly 40 different countries and sales in more than 125 countries around the world. Find your local representative at **www.cengage.com**

Cengage Learning products are represented in Canada by Nelson Education, Ltd.

To learn more about Cengage Learning Solutions, visit **www.cengage.com**

Purchase any of our products at your local college store or at our preferred online store **www.cengagebrain.com**

Unless otherwise noted, all content is © Cengage Learning 2018.

Printed in the United States of America
Print Number: 01   Print Year: 2016

It is wrong always, everywhere, and for anyone,
to believe anything upon insufficient evidence.

—W. K. Clifford

Nothing can be more important than the art of
formal reasoning according to true logic.

—Gottfried Wilhelm Leibniz

Brief Contents

Contents

PART III INDUCTIVE LOGIC

Preface

Logic: The key to all learning

The most immediate benefit derived from the study of logic is the skill needed to construct sound arguments of one's own and to evaluate the arguments of others. In accomplishing this goal, logic instills a sensitivity for the formal component in language, a thorough command of which is indispensable to clear, effective, and meaningful communication. On a broader scale, by focusing attention on the requirement for reasons or evidence to support our views, logic provides a fundamental defense against the prejudiced and uncivilized attitudes that threaten the foundations of our democratic society. Finally, through its attention to inconsistency as a fatal flaw in any theory or point of view, logic proves a useful device in disclosing ill-conceived policies in the political sphere and, ultimately, in distinguishing the rational from the irrational, the sane from the insane. This book is written with the aim of securing these benefits.

About *A Concise Introduction to Logic*

The new edition of *A Concise Introduction to Logic* maintains the text's tradition of careful sequencing, precision, elegance, and clarity, by retaining a number of signature features:

- Chapters are organized so that earlier sections provide the foundation for later ones. Later sections can be skipped by instructors opting to do so.

- The main points are always presented up front so students cannot possibly miss them.

- Relevant and up-to-date examples are used extensively.

- Key terms are introduced in boldface type and defined in the Glossary/Index.

- Central concepts are illustrated in graphic boxes.

- Numerous exercises, many drawn from real-life sources such as newspapers, textbooks, and magazines, are included to perfect student skills—the current edition includes over 2,700 exercises.

- Biographical vignettes of prominent logicians are included to give logic a human face.

- Dialogue exercises illustrate the application of logical principles to real-life situations.

- Venn diagrams for syllogisms are presented in a novel and more effective way, using color to identify the relevant areas.

- End-of-chapter summaries facilitate student review.

- The solution to every third exercise is provided in the Answer section, so students can easily check their work.

- Important rules and tables are printed on the inside covers for ready access, and they are also presented on a tear-out card.

New to This Edition

New to MindTap

MindTap Important to this revision is the introduction of several new features in MindTap. MindTap is a personalized, fully online digital learning platform that offers an interactive eBook, a tutorial program, and homework all in one place. We have enhanced the resources in MindTap and added to them.

Revised Learning Path In response to user and reviewer feedback, we have modified the MindTap learning path. The *Concise Introduction to Logic* MindTap for this edition still includes the prized tools that contribute to this product's popularity, including

- The interactive version of some of the textbook's exercise sets

- Aplia™

- *Learning Logic* tutorials

- Video lectures

In addition, the revised learning path incorporates improvements and new resources to help guide students and instructors.

- Each chapter opens with stated Learning Objectives.

- The section folders now include the reading, with video lectures when available, along with the interactive version of most of the text's exercise sets, and an online writing exercise—see the more detailed description of this new addition that follows.

- The *Learning Logic* tutorials and Aplia are now found at the chapter level, with all their respective sections in a folder.

- The new Living Logic activity, the Chapter Review (the textbook's Chapter Summary), and the Chapter Test (now available as an online gradable activity) round out the new learning path's offerings.

How Logical Are You? These short, real-life scenarios, which replace the Previews of the prior edition, engage students creatively with the themes of the chapter. The questions posed in these scenarios are answered online in MindTap.

Annotated Answers We have added explanations to the exercise answers, detailing why the answer is correct, for most sections of Chapter 1 (Sections 1.1–1.4) and Chapter 3 (Sections 3.1–3.4).

Writing Exercises Any set of exercises that did not already include a writing activity now does. These new writing activities require students to create a short example of a concept presented in the section, such as an explanation, a deductive argument, or a dispute. In performing this activity, students are further engaged and retention is reinforced.

Living Logic This integrative digital activity helps students apply their logic skills to a current real-world problem: climate change. It offers exercises targeted to the content of Chapters 1 through 7, bringing to life the practical and relevant nature of this content.

Chapter Tests These multiple-choice questions, offered as PDFs in the prior edition of MindTap, are now available, at the end of each chapter, as gradable interactive quizzes.

Visualizing Inferences This new technique, introduced in Chapter 7 (Natural Deduction in Propositional Logic) uses geometrical shapes in the place of "p" and "q" to help students visually understand the rules of inference. The technique is introduced in the textbook and expanded in MindTap. We have also added exercises that offer practice in creating instances of the rules of inference.

Well-Formed Formulas A more detailed account of this subject supplements the account found in Chapter 6 of the textbook.

New Text Features

- A feature entitled "How Logical Are You?" replaces the prior edition "Preview" and occurs at the beginning of every section of the textbook (except for Chapters 9–14, where it occurs at the beginning of every chapter). These prompts are intended to get the students thinking about the content of the pertinent section before they actually start reading that material. The questions presented in these selections are answered in MindTap.

- Every exercise set now includes a writing component—an activity to engage the student's creativity. These usually involve creating arguments of various kinds, definitions, fallacies, and symbolized expressions.

- "Why Study Logic?" has been added to the front material. This section aims to motivate the study of logic by emphasizing its importance across a variety of activities. Among other things, it compares studying logic to going to the gym for your brain.

New Chapter Content

As you proceed through the textbook, you will encounter numerous improvements. For example, many exercises have been rewritten and updated. A more detailed list of the substantive changes follows:

Chapter 3

- Slippery slope has been expanded by noting that the fallacy is usually committed to defend the status quo and by pointing to the importance of identifying the precise causal link where the reasoning fails.

Chapter 4

- New exercises have been added to Sections 4.1 and 4.2.

- A subsection entitled "Boole, Venn, and Existential Import" has been written to address student questions about the Boolean standpoint, which makes no assumption as to whether the things referred to actually exist. Students often ask about the utility of a logic that deals with nonexisting things. This subsection also sketches the history of the Boolean standpoint in the nineteenth century.

- The concept of vacuous falsity is introduced in Section 4.3.

- A note, added to Section 4.5, addresses the truth value of statements such as "All unicorns are two-horned animals," and "Some unicorns are one-horned animals."

Chapter 6

- Truth tables are now introduced using the technique of writing the truth values of the simple propositions to the left of the truth table and using those truth values to generate the truth values of the compound propositions. The presentation of this technique is followed by the abbreviated technique whereby truth values are entered initially beneath the simple components of the compound propositions.

- New exercises for using truth tables to test arguments for validity have been added to Section 6.4.

- Section 6.6 has been reorganized so that the valid argument forms are introduced in the same order as the inference forms in Section 7.1. Also, the invalid forms (affirming the consequent and denying the antecedent) are assigned to a separate subsection to help prevent their being confused with the valid forms.

Chapter 7

- A new way of visualizing *modus ponens* and disjunctive syllogism, using squares and circles, is introduced to aid students who learn best through visual imagery. This technique is expanded in MindTap.

- In Section 7.3 a dialogue entitled "New Cradle" replaces "With This Ring."

Chapter 10

- A simpler characterization of the joint method of agreement and difference is given to ease students through the more complicated definition of this method.

Chapter 11

- A brief account is given of recent applications of Bayes's theorem. These include the attempt to use Bayes's theorem to locate Malaysia Airlines Flight 370.

Chapter 12

- A paragraph has been added to show how samples become biased in clinical trials intended to disclose drug side effects.

- A brief explanation is given as to how pharmaceutical companies use tricks with percentages to mislead customers.

- An account is given explaining how large corporations undermine the integrity of science by enlisting the services of university scientists to sway public opinion regarding the safety of their products.

Note to the Student

Imagine that you are interviewing for a job. The person across the desk asks about your strengths, and you reply that you are energetic, enthusiastic, and willing to work long hours. Also, you are creative and innovative, and you have good leadership skills. Then the interviewer asks about your weaknesses. You hadn't anticipated this question, but after a moment's thought you reply that your reasoning skills have never been very good.

The interviewer quickly responds that this weakness could create big problems.

"Why is that?" you ask.

"Because reasoning skills are essential to good judgment. And without good judgment your creativity will lead to projects that make no sense. Your leadership skills will direct our other employees in circles. Your enthusiasm will undermine everything we have accomplished up until now. And your working long hours will make things even worse."

"But don't you think there is some position in your company that is right for me?" you ask.

The interviewer thinks for a moment and then replies, "We have a competitor on the other side of town. I hear they are hiring right now. Why don't you apply with them?"

The point of this brief dialogue is that good reasoning skills are essential to doing anything right. The business person uses reasoning skills in writing a report or preparing a presentation; the scientist uses them in designing an experiment or clinical trial, the department manager uses them in maximizing worker efficiency, the lawyer uses them in composing an argument to a judge or jury. And that's where logic comes in. The chief purpose of logic is to develop good reasoning skills. In fact, logic is so important that when the liberal arts program of studies was formulated fifteen hundred years ago, logic was selected as one of the original seven liberal arts. Logic remains to this day a central component of a college or university education.

From a more pragmatic angle, logic is important to earning a good score on any of the several tests required for admission to graduate professional schools—the LSAT, GMAT, MCAT, GRE, and so on. Obviously, the designers of these tests recognize that the ability to reason logically is a prerequisite to success in these fields. Also, logic is a useful tool in relieving what has come to be called math anxiety. For whatever reason, countless students today are terrified of any form of reasoning that involves abstract symbols. If you happen to be one of these students, you should find it relatively easy to master the use of logical symbols, and your newly found comfort with these symbols will carry over into the other, more difficult fields.

In addition to the existing and new features described in the "New to This Edition" section of this preface, MindTap also includes the following supplements. *Critical*

Thinking and Writing offers practice in writing arguments about real-life topics; *Truth Trees* presents a standard introduction to the method of truth trees, which can be used as a supplement or alternative to the truth-table method; and *Logic and Graduate-Level Admission Tests* shows how the principles learned in studying logic can be used to answer questions on the LSAT, GMAT, MCAT, and GRE. Finally, *Existential Import* traces the history of existential import through the logic of Aristotle and George Boole.

Among the MindTap offerings that I would especially urge you to investigate is *Learning Logic*. This interactive tutorial program teaches the basics of the entire course in a very user-friendly way. It tracks the textbook chapter by chapter, but your computer must be equipped with speakers or headphones, because the audio component is essential.

Note to the Instructor

The image on the front cover is intended to convey the message that logic is the key to all learning. Keys open doors. Logic is the key that opens the door to reasoned discourse and dialogue, unlocking an important opportunity for learning. Through logic, students learn to support their views with reasons and to open their minds to the reasons of others. Logic creates a common foundation upon which individuals who hold opposing points of view can learn from each other. What might otherwise devolve into a shouting match of conflicting opinions becomes a venue for the rational exchange of ideas.

To promote the achievement of this goal, this new edition features selections entitled "How Logical Are You?" at the beginning of chapter sections, that are designed to get students thinking, activate prior learning, and induce the students to read the section that follows. The instructor can also use these selections as springboards for in-class lectures. While the inclusion of these selections is probably the most visible change in the new edition, as you proceed through the book you will encounter numerous less-visible improvements. Many of them are listed previously in "New Chapter Content," and a complete list is given in the Instructor's Manual.

The online resource, MindTap, continues to be a central component of this new edition. One of the more noteworthy offerings on MindTap is *Learning Logic*. This tutorial program teaches the fundamentals of the whole course, and it is especially helpful for students who have difficulty mastering logical principles directly from the textbook or from classroom lectures alone. The program is multimedia, which means that students learn not only by seeing but also by hearing. In addition, it incorporates easy-to-use forward and reverse buttons, so students who have failed to understand something the first time can easily go back to hear the lesson repeated. *Learning Logic* contains over two thousand practice problems not contained in the textbook, and students get immediate feedback for correct and incorrect answers.

Another great product available on MindTap is Aplia, an online homework program that improves student comprehension by increasing effort and engagement. Students get immediate feedback on their work—not only what they got right or wrong—but *why*; and they can choose to see another set of related problems if they want further practice. Aplia's simple-to-use course management interface allows instructors to post announcements, host student discussions, e-mail students, and manage the grade book. Personalized help is available from a knowledgeable and friendly support team. To learn more, ask your Cengage Learning sales representative for a demonstration, or view a specific demonstration for this book at www.aplia.com.

Also note that the Instructor's Companion Website contains the Instructor's Manual and the Test Bank. The Instructor's Manual includes answers to all the book's exercises and a complete list of the improvements introduced in this edition. The 600-page author-generated Test Bank includes numerous tests for each chapter in the book, and most of them are in easily gradable multiple-choice format.

This thirteenth edition marks a break with its predecessors in that it has a coauthor, Lori Watson. One of Professor Watson's contributions has been to ensure that the new edition engages the interests of today's students. When we began our collaboration we split up the work so that Professor Watson would focus mainly on the online material, while Professor Hurley would revise the hard-copy book. But as work progressed, it turned out that each of us contributed to both areas. For example, Watson wrote the piece on the value of studying logic following this preface, and she contributed to many of the new exercises and the "How Logical Are You?" selections, while Hurley contributed to some of the online annotated answers to the exercises and the Living Logic activity.

Type of Course

	Traditional logic course	Informal logic course, critical-reasoning course	Course emphasizing modern formal logic
Recommended material	Chapter 1 Chapter 3 Chapter 4 Chapter 5 Chapter 6 Sections 7.1–7.4	Chapter 1 Chapter 2 Chapter 3 Chapter 4 Sections 5.1–5.3 Sections 5.5–5.6 Sections 6.1–6.4 Section 6.6 Chapter 9 Chapter 12 Chapter 13 Chapter 14 *Critical Thinking and Writing* supplement	Chapter 1 Sections 4.1–4.3 Section 4.7 Sections 6.1–6.5 Chapter 7 Chapter 8 *Truth Trees* supplement
Optional material	Chapter 2 Sections 7.5–7.7 Chapters 9–14	Section 5.4 Section 5.7 Section 6.5 Chapter 10 Chapter 11	Chapter 3 Sections 4.4–4.6 Sections 5.1–5.2 Section 5.7 Section 6.6

Let us now turn to alternate ways of approaching the textbook. In general, the material in each chapter is arranged so that certain later sections can be skipped without affecting subsequent chapters. For example, those wishing a brief treatment of natural deduction in both propositional and predicate logic may want to skip the last three sections of Chapter 7 and the last four (or even five) sections of Chapter 8. Chapter 2 can be skipped altogether, although some may want to cover the first section of that chapter as an introduction to Chapter 3. Finally, Chapters 9 through 14 depend only slightly on earlier chapters, so these can be treated in any order one chooses. However, Chapter 14 does depend in part on Chapter 13.

Digital Options

A Concise Introduction to Logic is available in multiple formats, including as a printed textbook that can be bought alone [ISBN: 9781305958098], and it can be combined with digital solutions in a variety of ways, including the following:

1. **MindTap (alone) [ISBN: 9781305959644].** Available with the interactive eBook (MindTap Reader), this option includes *Learning Logic* (the tutorial), Aplia quizzing assignments, videos (covering difficult-to-master topics), chapter learning path activities, quizzing, and appendices. Available only at www.cengagebrain.com, this option can be a cost-saving choice for students.

2. **Aplia (alone) [ISBN: 9781305959712].** Available with the interactive eBook (MindTap Reader), this option includes everything in Option 2 except the printed textbook. Available only at www.cengagebrain.com, this option can be a cost-saving choice for students.

Contact your personal Learning Consultant, http://www.cengage.com/repfinder/, for more information about all available options, pricing, and assistance in selecting the best solutions for your students and your course.

Acknowledgments

For their reviews and suggestions leading to this thirteenth edition I want to thank the following:

Karl Aho, Baylor University; Benjamin Arah, Bowie State University; Peter Barry, Saginaw Valley State University; Jeff Broome, Arapahoe Community College; Louis Colombo, Bethune-Cookman University; Rosibel Cruz, Harold Washington College; Benjamin Easton, Azusa Pacific University; Samantha Emswiler, John Tyler Community College; William Ferraiolo, San Joaquin Delta College; Albert Filice, Mesa Community College; Paul Gass, Coppin State University; Dimitria Gatzia, University of Akron Wayne College; Douglas Hill, Saddleback College and Golden West College; Ron Jackson, Clayton State University; Stephen Leach, University of Texas–Pan American; Chris Lorkowski, Kent State University–Trumbull Campus; Leemon McHenry, California State University Northridge; Daniel Metz, Metropolitan State College of Denver (Program chair at CCCOnline); Mike Monge, Orange Coast College; Tim O'Neill, Rochester Community and Technical College; Christopher Pallotti, Los Angeles Valley College/CSUN; Sean Stidd, Wayne State University; Corine Sutherland, Cerritos College; Catherine S. Sutton, Virginia Commonwealth University; Michael Thune, Joliet Junior College; Dennis Weiss, York College of Pennsylvania; Elaine Yoshikawa, Arizona State University; Xiaoyu Zhu, Antelope Valley College.

Of course any errors or omissions that may remain are the result of my own oversight.

Those who have contributed reviews and suggestions leading to the twelve previous editions, and to whom I express my continued thanks, are the following:

James T. Anderson, University of San Diego; Carol Anthony, Villanova University; Joseph Asike, Howard University; Harriet E. Baber, University of San Diego; Kent Baldner, Western Michigan University; James Baley, Mary Washington College; Jerome Balmuth, Colgate University; Victor Balowitz, State University of New York, College at Buffalo; Ida Baltikauskas, Century College; Gary Baran, Los Angeles City College; Robert Barnard, University of Mississippi; Peter Barry, Saginaw Valley State University; Gregory Bassham, Kings College; Thora Bayer, Xavier University of Louisiana; David Behan, Agnes Scott College; John Bender, Ohio University, Athens; James O. Bennett, University of Tennessee, Knoxville; Victoria Berdon, IUPU Columbus; Robert Berman, Xavier University of Louisana; Kevin Berry, Ohio University; Joseph Bessie, Normandale Community College; John R. Bosworth, Oklahoma State University; Andrew Botterell, University of Toronto; Jeff Broome, Arapahoe Community College; Tom Browder, University of Nevada, Las Vegas; Harold Brown, Northern Illinois University; Kevin Browne, Indiana University Southeast; Ken Buckman, University of Texas, Pan American; Robert Burch, Texas A&M University; Keith Burgess-Jackson, University of Texas, Arlington; Michael Byron, Kent State University; Scott Calef, Ohio Wesleyan University; Gabriel Camacho, El Paso Community College; James Campbell, University of Toledo; Joseph Keim Campbell, Washington State University; Loren Cannon, Humboldt State University; Charles Carr, Arkansas State University; William Carroll, Coppin State University; Jennifer Caseldine-Bracht, IUPU Fort Wayne; John Casey, Northern Illinois University; Robert Greg Cavin, Cypress College; Ping-Tung Chang, University of Alaska; Prakash Chenjeri, Southern Oregon University; Drew Christie, University of New Hampshire; Timothy Christion, University of North Texas; Ralph W. Clarke, West Virginia University; David Clowney, Rowan University; Darryl Cohen, Mesa Community College; Michael Cole, College of William and Mary; Michael Coledu, Reedley College; Louis Colombo, Bethune-Cookman University; Michael J. Colson, Merced College; William F. Cooper, Baylor University; William Cornwell, Salem State College; Victor Cosculluela, Polk Community College; Mike Coste, Front Range Community College; Ronald R. Cox, San Antonio College; Houston A. Craighead, Winthrop University; Donald Cress, Northern Illinois University, DeKalb; Jack Crumley, University of San Diego; Drew Dalton, Florida Southern College; Linda Damico, Kennesaw State University; Ray Darr, Southern Illinois University; William J. DeAngelis, Northeastern University; Joseph DeMarco, Cleveland State University; Paul DeVries, Wheaton College; Jill Dieterle, Eastern Michigan University; Mary Domski, University of New Mexico; Beverly R. Doss and Richard W. Doss, Orange Coast College; Paul Draper, Purdue University; William A. Drumin, King's College, Pennsylvania; Clinton Dunagan, Saint Philips College; Jeffrey Easlick, Saginaw Valley State University; Paul Eckstein, Bergen Community College; Anne M. Edwards, Austin Peay State University; Michael Epperson, California State University, Sacramento; Lenore Erickson, Cuesta College; Cassandra Evans, San Diego City College; Frank Fair, Sam Houston State University; Evan Fales, University of Iowa; Thompson Faller, University of Portland; William Ferraiolo, San Joaquin Delta College; Albert Filice, Mesa Community College; Lewis S. Ford, Old Dominion University; Gary Foulk, Indiana State University, Terre Haute; Timothy C. Fout, University of Louisville; LeAnn Fowler, Slippery Rock University; Craig Fox, California University of Pennsylvania; Thomas H. Franks, Eastern Michigan University; Bernard D. Freydberg, Slippery Rock University; Thomas J. Frost, Biola University/Long Beach City College; Dick Gaffney, Siena College; George Gale, University of Missouri–Kansas City; Pieranna Garavaso, University of Minnesota at Morris; Paul Gass, Coppin State University; Dimitria Gatzia, The University of Akron Wayne College; Joseph Georges, El Camino College; Kevin Gibson, University of Colorado;

James Granitto, Santiago Canyon College; Victor Grassian, Los Angeles Harbor College; Catherine Green, Rockhurst University; James Greene, Northern Michigan University; Harold Greenstein, SUNY Brockport; J. Randall Groves, Ferris State University; Shahrokh Haghighi, California State University; Alexander W. Hall, Clayton State University; Dean Hamden, Montclair State University; Courtney Hammond, Cuyamaca College; Ken Hanly, Brandon University; Anthony Hanson, West Valley College; Merle Harton, Edward Waters College; Larry Hauser, Alma College; Deborah Heikes, University of Alabama in Huntsville; Ryan Hickerson, Western Oregon University; Ronald Hill, University of San Diego; Lawrence Hinman, University of San Diego; Lynn Holt, Mississippi State University; Jeremy Hovda, Minneapolis Community & Technical College; John B. Howell, III, Southwestern Baptist Theological Seminary; R. I. G. Hughes, University of South Carolina, Columbia; Peter Hutcheson, Texas State University; Debby Hutchins, Gonzaga University; William H. Hyde, Golden West College; Ron Jackson, Clayton State University; William Jamison, University of Alaska Anchorage; Sandra Johanson, Green River Community College; Gary Jones, University of San Diego; Richard A. Jones, Howard University; Russel Jones, University of Oklahoma; Glenn C. Joy, Texas State University, San Marcos; Olin Joynton, North Harris County College; Grant Julin, St. Francis University; Patrick Kenny, Onondaga Community College; Glen Kessler, University of Virginia; Charles F. Kielkopf, Ohio State University; Moya Kinchla, Bakersfield College; Kristin Klamm-Doneen, Anoka Ramsey Community College; Bernard W. Kobes, Arizona State University; Keith W. Krasemann, College of DuPage; Richard La Croix, State University College at Buffalo; Sandra LaFave, West Valley College, Saratoga, California; William Lawhead, University of Mississippi; Stephen Leach, UTPA; Richard Lee, University of Arkansas; Lory Lemke, University of Minnesota, Morris; Robert Levis, Pasadena City College; Chenyang Li, Monmouth College, Monmouth, Illinois; Chris M. Lorkowski, Kent State University; Keane Lundt, Massachusetts College of Liberal Arts; Ardon Lyon, City University of London; Scott MacDonald, University of Iowa; Ian MacKinnon, The University of Akron; Krishna Mallick, Salem State College; Thomas Manig, University of Missouri–Columbia; James Manns, University of Kentucky; Dalman Mayer, Bellevue Community College; Larry D. Mayhew, Western Kentucky University; Leemon McHenry, California State University Northridge; Robert McKay, Norwich University; Rick McKita, Colorado State University; Phillip McReynolds, Pennsylvania State University; Erik Meade, Southern Illinois University–Edwardsville; Noel Merino, Humboldt State University; Kenneth R. Merrill, University of Oklahoma; Daniel Metz, Metropolitan State College of Denver; Thomas Michaud, Wheeling Jesuit College; Alexander Miller, Piedmont Technical College; Dolores Miller, University of Missouri–Kansas City; George D. Miller, DePaul University; Richard Miller, East Carolina University; Frederick Mills, Bowie State University; Jeff Mitchell, Arkansas Tech University; John Mize, Long Beach City College; Allyson Mount, Keene State College; Seyed Mousavian, University of Alberta; Dwayne Mulder, California State University, Fresno; John D. Mullen, Dowling College; Madeline Muntersbjorn, University of Toledo; Henry Nardone, Kings College; Nathaniel Nicol, Washington State University; Theresa Norman, South Texas Community College; David O'Connor, Seton Hall University; Len Olsen, Georgia Southern University; Tim O'Neill, Rochester Community and Technical College; Elane O'Rourke, Moorpark College; Brendan O'Sullivan, Rhodes College; Stephen Pacheco, University of San Diego; Joseph Pak, Los Angeles City College; Christopher Pallotti, Los Angeles Valley College/CSUN; Christopher Pearson, Southern Illinois University Edwardsville; Rodney Peffer, University of San Diego; Linda Peterson, University of San Diego; Robert G. Pielke, El Camino College; Cassandra Pinnick, Western Kentucky University; Nelson Pole, Cleveland State University; Norman Prigge, Bakersfield State University; Gray Prince, West Los Angeles College; R. Puligandla, University of Toledo; T. R. Quigley, Oakland University; Nani Rankin, Indiana University at Kokomo; Robert Redmon, Virginia Commonwealth University; Bruce Reichenbach, Augsburg College; Herminia Reyes, San Diego State University; Fernando Rincon-Tellez,

Piedmont Technical College; David Ring, Southern Methodist University; Tony Roark, Boise State University; Matthew Roberts, Patrick Henry College; Michael Rooney, Pasadena City College; Phyllis Rooney, Oakland University; Beth Rosdatter, University of Kentucky; Michelle M. Rotert, Rock Valley College; Paul A. Roth, University of Missouri–Saint Louis; Daniel Rothbart, George Mason University; Robert Rupert, University of Colorado, Boulder; Sam Russo, El Camino College; Frank Ryan, Kent State University; Eric Saidel, George Washington University; Kelly Salsbery, Stephen F. Austin State University; Paul Santelli, Siena College; Stephen Satris, Clemson University; Philip Schneider, George Mason University; James D. Schumaker, University of North Carolina at Charlotte; Stephanie Semler, Radford University; Pat Sewell, University of North Texas; Elizabeth Shadish, El Camino College; Joseph G. Shay, Boston College; Candice Shelby, University of Colorado Denver; Janet Simpson, Suffolk County Community College; Robert Skipper, St. Mary's University; Aeon Skoble, Bridgewater State College; Matthew Slater, Bucknell University; Kent Slinker, Pima Community College; Dennis L. Slivinski, California State University, Channel Islands; Arnold Smith, Youngstown State University; John-Christian Smith, Youngstown State University; Joshua Smith, Central Michigan University; Paula Smithka, University of Southern Mississippi; Eric W. Snider, University of Toledo; Bob Snyder, Humboldt University; Joseph Snyder, Anne Arundel Community College; Lynne Spellman, University of Arkansas; David Stern, University of Iowa; James Stuart, Bowling Green State University; Paul Studtmann, Davidson College; Krys Sulewski, Edmonds Community College; John Sullins, Sonoma State University; Weimin Sun, California State University, Northridge; Corine Sutherland, Cerritos College; Robert Sutton, Cape Fear Community College; John Sweigart, James Madison University; Clarendon Swift, Moorpark College; Wayne Swindall, California Baptist College; Mojgan Taheri, California State University, Northridge; Brian Tapia, Foothill College; Bangs Tapscott, University of Utah; J. Ramon Tello, Shasta College; Mark Thames, El Centro College; Jan Thomas, University of Arkansas at Little Rock; Phil Thompson, Eastern Illinois University; Michael Thune, Joliet Junior College; Richard Tieszen, San Jose State University; Larry Udell, West Chester University; Ted Ulrich, Purdue University; Robert Urekew, University of Louisville; William Uzgalis, Oregon State University; William Vanderburgh, Wichita State University; Michael Ventimiglia, Sacred Heart University; Susan Vineberg, Wayne State University; Mark Vopat, Youngstown State University; Thomas H. Warren, Solano College; Andrew J. Waskey, Dalton State University; Roy Weatherford, University of South Florida; Chris Weigand, Our Lady of the Lake University; David Weinburger, Stockton State College; Paul Weirich, University of Missouri–Columbia; David Weise, Gonzaga University; Dennis Weiss, York College of Pennsylvania; Robert Wengert, University of Illinois at Urbana–Champaign; Shannon Grace Werre, Edmonds Community College; Gerald Joseph Williams, Seton Hall University; Derrick Willis, Temple College; Frank Wilson, Bucknell University; W. Kent Wilson, University of Illinois, Chicago; Katherine D. Witzig, Southwestern Illinois College; Sandra Woien, Mesa Community College; Stephen Wykstra, Calvin College; Julie Yoo, California State University, Northridge; Marie Zaccaria, Georgia Perimeter College; Jeffrey Zents, University of Texas; Xiaoyu Zhu, Antelope Valley College.

Finally, it has been a pleasure working with philosophy editor Debra Matteson, product director Paul Banks, content developer Florence Kilgo, production supervisor Greg Hubit, copy editor Marne Evans, and proofreader Debra Nichols. Most of all, I want to thank my wife, Linda Peterson, for her countless suggestions and support.

Why Study Logic?

Logic can be a challenging subject for beginners. Much like learning a new language, it takes patience and hard work to master the skills necessary to truly excel at logic. Given that challenging work can sometimes prove frustrating, students often wonder why logic is a required course for their major, or what the real value of learning logic truly is. This latter concern is often expressed as: How does logic help me in the "real" world? Given that students raise this question over and over, it's worthwhile to provide an answer right at the beginning of this textbook.

On the first day of any logic class, we ask our students if they regularly go to the gym. The majority say that they do. We then ask them what they do at the gym; many reply that they walk or run on a treadmill and that they lift weights. We ask them "why do you do this?" After all, they are not likely to encounter a treadmill in "real" life or to bench press weights in any other than a gym setting. As the dialogue continues, students eventually reveal that the reason they do these specific activities in the gym is because by doing so they build or maintain the muscles they need for other activities they enjoy doing, such as, surfing, hiking, biking, skateboarding, or just going for a walk on the beach.

We tell them that doing logic is, in many ways, like going to the gym for your brain. While you may never be called upon to do a formal logic proof in the context of your everyday activities, learning how to construct such a proof hones the skills needed for those routine activities. If asked what distinguishes human beings from the rest of the animal kingdom, one common answer is that humans have the ability to reason in a particular way. Learning the various techniques of logic improves and perfects that very reasoning ability that is so essential to our being human.

Moreover, recognizing that logic is primarily concerned with distinguishing good reasoning from bad reasoning may lessen some of the anxiety you have with learning this new material. It should soon become clear that you already engage in the kind of reasoning that you will learn in this textbook all the time. Studying logic will just make explicit the rules of inference (reasoning) that are already a part of your everyday life.

For example, consider the kinds of inferences you made today just to arrive at class on time: Last night, you may have set your alarm clock to wake you up in the morning. You may have reasoned, "If I want to arrive at class on time, I need to get up by 8:00 a.m. I do want to arrive at class on time, so I will set my alarm for 8:00 a.m." That is a basic form of reasoning that logicians call *modus ponens*. We will study this particular rule of inference and many others in later chapters of the book. While calling it *modus ponens* and representing it symbolically may seem intimidating at first, remember that you already know and understand how to make this inference and you do it all the time.

To the point, if you didn't understand this rule already or couldn't draw the correct conclusion, you would likely not be alive. That is, you would have walked off a cliff or strolled in front of a speeding car or succumbed to some other tragedy. But, you stop walking when you get to the edge of a cliff, you pause at a red light and look both ways before crossing the street, and you do many other such things because you realize the importance of making inferences that are necessary to preserve your life. You are "doing logic"!

Whatever your college major or career plans, a strong foundation in making good inferences (doing logic) will improve your performance. If you are interested in science—designing an experiment, testing hypotheses, drawing warranted conclusions from the evidence, all of these involve making basic logical inferences. If you are interested in business, economics, or finance, making sound financial decisions requires knowing how to make correct inferences. If you are interested in marketing, you will do well to understand the kinds of tactics that convince people to purchase the products you are trying to promote. Sometimes this will involve asking *them* to make good inferences; for example, if you are marketing products or medications that claim to improve their lives.

However, sometimes marketing involves appealing to the emotions of consumers or to their vanity, or convincing the potential buyer that your product is necessary in some way. While such appeals are not grounded in logic, they reflect common mistakes of reasoning we call "fallacies." Chapter 3 of the textbook will introduce many of these common mistakes of reasoning. If you are a marketer you may want to draw on such appeals, for they often work! If you are a consumer, you may hope to arm yourself against such appeals so you aren't taken in by advertising claims that lead you to buy products you don't need. Either way, you are using logic.

If you are interested in computer science, you will quickly realize how necessary logic is to computer programing. In fact, the first person to invent a computer was a logician and mathematician! All the technology we have come to rely on as a part of our daily lives—our mobile phones, our iPads, our computers, and so on—are made possible by logic.

If you are interested in the humanities, philosophy, literature, the arts, or history, you too rely on logic as a fundamental part of your engagement with these subjects. There is a reason that logic is taught in philosophy departments, and that is because philosophers make and evaluate arguments across a wide range of subjects, including what gives value and meaning to life, whether it is rational to believe in a God, and what counts as having knowledge as opposed to mere belief or opinion on these and other topics. If you study literature, engaging with a text critically means evaluating its coherence, its development of characters and their motivations, and many other things, almost all of which involve logic. In short, logic teaches and improves the kinds of knowledge and basic skills that are relevant to almost everything you do or want to study.

Finally, it's worth saying that logic can also be fun! Undertaking any new form of study can, of course, prove frustrating and challenging at times, but with patience and hard work the material gets easier and clearer. We think you will find that mastering some of these skills is rewarding in itself, and once you become good at it, you will see just how much fun it can be to identify a fallacy, point out someone else's poor argument, and even construct a proof.

1 Basic Concepts

1.1 Arguments, Premises, and Conclusions

HOW LOGICAL ARE YOU? After a momentary absence, you return to your table in the library only to find your smartphone is missing. It was there just minutes earlier. You suspect the student sitting next to you took it. After all, she has a guilty look. Also, there is a bulge in her backpack about the size of your phone, and one of the pouches has a loose strap. Then you hear a "ring" come from the backpack—and it's the same ringtone that you use on your phone. Which of these pieces of evidence best supports your suspicion?

Find the answer on MindTap.

Logic may be defined as the organized body of knowledge, or science, that evaluates arguments. All of us encounter arguments in our day-to-day experience. We read them in books and newspapers, hear them on television, and formulate them when communicating with friends and associates. The aim of logic is to develop a system of methods and principles that we may use as criteria for evaluating the arguments of others and as guides in constructing arguments of our own. Among the benefits to be expected from the study of logic is an increase in confidence that we are making sense when we criticize the arguments of others and when we advance arguments of our own.

MindTap® Read, study, reflect, and prepare for exams online, anytime, anywhere.

An **argument**, in its simplest form, is a group of statements, one or more of which (the premises) are claimed to provide support for, or reasons to believe, one of the others (the conclusion). Every argument may be placed in either of two basic groups: those in which the premises really do support the conclusion and those in which they do not, even though they are claimed to. The former are said to be good arguments (at least to that extent), the latter bad arguments. The purpose of logic, as the science that evaluates arguments, is thus to develop methods and techniques that allow us to distinguish good arguments from bad.

As is apparent from the given definition, the term *argument* has a very specific meaning in logic. It does not mean, for example, a mere verbal fight, as one might have with one's parent, spouse, or friend. Let us examine the features of this definition in greater detail. First of all, an argument is a group of statements. A **statement** is a sentence that is either true or false—in other words, typically a declarative sentence or a sentence component that could stand as a declarative sentence. The following sentences are statements:

> Chocolate truffles are loaded with calories.
> Melatonin helps relieve jet lag.
> Political candidates always tell the complete truth.
> No wives ever cheat on their husbands.
> Tiger Woods plays golf and Maria Sharapova plays tennis.

The first two statements are true, the second two false. The last one expresses two statements, both of which are true. Truth and falsity are called the two possible **truth values** of a statement. Thus, the truth value of the first two statements is true, the truth value of the second two is false, and the truth value of the last statement, as well as that of its components, is true.

Unlike statements, many sentences cannot be said to be either true or false. Questions, proposals, suggestions, commands, and exclamations usually cannot, and so are not usually classified as statements. The following sentences are not statements:

> Where is Khartoum?   (question)
> Let's go to a movie tonight.   (proposal)
> I suggest you get contact lenses.   (suggestion)
> Turn off the TV right now.   (command)
> Fantastic!   (exclamation)

The statements that make up an argument are divided into one or more premises and exactly one conclusion. The **premises** are the statements that set forth the reasons or evidence, and the **conclusion** is the statement that the evidence is claimed to support or imply. In other words, the conclusion is the statement that is claimed to follow from the premises. Here is an example of an argument:

> All film stars are celebrities.
> Halle Berry is a film star.
> Therefore, Halle Berry is a celebrity.

The first two statements are the premises; the third is the conclusion. (The claim that the premises support or imply the conclusion is indicated by the word "therefore.") In this argument the premises really do support the conclusion, and so the argument is a good one. But consider this argument:

> Some film stars are men.
> Cameron Diaz is a film star.
> Therefore, Cameron Diaz is a man.

In this argument the premises do not support the conclusion, even though they are claimed to, and so the argument is not a good one.

One of the most important tasks in the analysis of arguments is being able to distinguish premises from conclusions. If what is thought to be a conclusion is really a premise, and vice versa, the subsequent analysis cannot possibly be correct. Many arguments contain indicator words that provide clues in identifying premises and conclusion. Some typical **conclusion indicators** are

therefore	accordingly	entails that
wherefore	we may conclude	hence
thus	it must be that	it follows that
consequently	for this reason	implies that
we may infer	so	as a result

Whenever a statement follows one of these indicators, it can usually be identified as the conclusion. By process of elimination the other statements in the argument are the premises. Example:

> Tortured prisoners will say anything just to relieve the pain. Consequently, torture is not a reliable method of interrogation.

The conclusion of this argument is "Torture is not a reliable method of interrogation," and the premise is "Tortured prisoners will say anything just to relieve the pain."

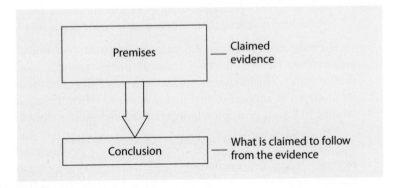

If an argument does not contain a conclusion indicator, it may contain a premise indicator. Some typical **premise indicators** are

since	in that	seeing that
as indicated by	may be inferred from	for the reason that
because	as	inasmuch as
for	given that	owing to

Any statement following one of these indicators can usually be identified as a premise. Example:

> Expectant mothers should never use recreational drugs, since the use of these drugs can jeopardize the development of the fetus.

The premise of this argument is "The use of these drugs can jeopardize the development of the fetus," and the conclusion is "Expectant mothers should never use recreational drugs."

In reviewing the list of indicators, note that "for this reason" is a conclusion indicator, whereas "for the reason that" is a premise indicator. "For this reason" (except when followed by a colon) means for the reason (premise) that was just given, so what follows is the conclusion. On the other hand, "for the reason that" announces that a premise is about to be stated.

Sometimes a single indicator can be used to identify more than one premise. Consider the following argument:

> It is vitally important that wilderness areas be preserved, for wilderness provides essential habitat for wildlife, including endangered species, and it is a natural retreat from the stress of daily life.

The premise indicator "for" goes with both "Wilderness provides essential habitat for wildlife, including endangered species," and "It is a natural retreat from the stress of daily life." These are the premises. By method of elimination, "It is vitally important that wilderness areas be preserved" is the conclusion.

Some arguments contain no indicators. With these, the reader/listener must ask such questions as: What single statement is claimed (implicitly) to follow from the others? What is the arguer trying to prove? What is the main point in the passage? The answers to these questions should point to the conclusion. Example:

> We must get serious about modernizing our nation's crumbling infrastructure. Many of our bridges are practically falling down, and our transit system is in dire need of repair. Furthermore, making these improvements would create jobs for millions of workers.

The conclusion of this argument is the first statement, and all of the other statements are premises. The argument illustrates the pattern found in most arguments that lack indicator words: The intended conclusion is stated first, and the remaining statements are then offered in support of this first statement. When the argument is restructured according to logical principles, however, the conclusion is always listed *after* the premises:

P_1: Many of our bridges are practically falling down.
P_2: Our transit system is in dire need of repair.
P_3: . Making these improvements would create jobs for millions of workers.
C: We must get serious about modernizing our nation's crumbling infrastructure.

When restructuring arguments such as this, one should remain as close as possible to the original version, while at the same time attending to the requirement that premises and conclusion be complete sentences that are meaningful in the order in which they are listed.

Note that the first two premises are included within the scope of a single sentence in the original argument. For the purposes of this chapter, compound arrangements of statements in which the various components are all claimed to be true will be considered as separate statements.

Passages that contain arguments sometimes contain statements that are neither premises nor conclusions. Only statements that are actually intended to support the conclusion should be included in the list of premises. If, for example, a statement serves merely to introduce the general topic, or merely makes a passing comment, it should not be taken as part of the argument. Examples:

> The claim is often made that malpractice lawsuits drive up the cost of health care. But if such suits were outlawed or severely restricted, then patients would have no means of recovery for injuries caused by negligent doctors. Hence, the availability of malpractice litigation should be maintained intact.

> Massive federal deficits push up interest rates for everyone. Servicing the debt gobbles up a huge portion of the federal budget, which lowers our standard of living. And big deficits also weaken the value of the dollar. For these reasons, Congress must make a determined effort to cut overall spending and raise taxes. Politicians who ignore this reality imperil the future of the nation.

In the first argument, the opening statement serves merely to introduce the topic, so it is not part of the argument. The premise is the second statement, and the conclusion is the last statement. In the second argument, the final statement merely makes a passing comment, so it is not part of the argument. The premises are the first three statements, and the statement following "for these reasons" is the conclusion.

Closely related to the concepts of argument and statement are those of inference and proposition. An **inference**, in the narrow sense of the term, is the reasoning process expressed by an argument. In the broad sense of the term, "inference" is used interchangeably with "argument." Analogously, a **proposition**, in the narrow sense, is the meaning or information content of a statement. For the purposes of this book, however, "proposition" and "statement" are used interchangeably.

Note on the History of Logic

The person who is generally credited as the father of logic is the ancient Greek philosopher Aristotle (384–322 B.C.E.). Aristotle's predecessors had been interested in the art of constructing persuasive arguments and in techniques for refuting the arguments of others, but it was Aristotle who first devised systematic criteria for analyzing and evaluating arguments.

Aristotle's chief accomplishment is called **syllogistic logic**, a kind of logic in which the fundamental elements are *terms,* and arguments are evaluated as good or bad depending on how the terms are arranged in the argument. Chapters 4 and 5 of this textbook are devoted mainly to syllogistic logic. But Aristotle also deserves credit for originating **modal logic**, a kind of logic that involves such concepts as possibility, necessity, belief, and doubt. In addition, Aristotle catalogued several informal fallacies, a topic treated in Chapter 3 of this book.

After Aristotle's death, another Greek philosopher, Chrysippus (280–206 B.C.E.), one of the founders of the Stoic school, developed a logic in which the fundamental elements were *whole propositions.* Chrysippus treated every proposition as either true or false and developed rules for determining the truth or falsity of compound propositions from the truth or falsity of their components. In the course of doing so, he laid the foundation for the truth-functional interpretation of the logical connectives presented in Chapter 6 of this book and introduced the notion of natural deduction, treated in Chapter 7.

For thirteen hundred years after the death of Chrysippus, relatively little creative work was done in logic. The physician Galen (C.E. 129–ca. 199) developed the theory of the compound categorical syllogism, but for the most part philosophers confined themselves to writing commentaries on the works of Aristotle and Chrysippus. Boethius (ca. 480–524) is a noteworthy example.

The first major logician of the Middle Ages was Peter Abelard (1079–1142). Abelard reconstructed and refined the logic of Aristotle and Chrysippus as communicated by Boethius, and he originated a theory of universals that traced the universal character of general terms to concepts in the mind rather than to "natures" existing outside the mind, as Aristotle had held. In addition, Abelard distinguished arguments that are valid because of their form from those that are valid because of their content, but he held that only formal validity is the "perfect" or conclusive variety. This textbook follows Abelard on this point.

After Abelard, the study of logic during the Middle Ages flourished through the work of numerous philosophers. A logical treatise by William of Sherwood (ca. 1200–1271) contains the first expression of the "Barbara, Celarent . . ." poem quoted in Section 5.1 of this book, and the *Summulae Logicales* of Peter of Spain (ca. 1205–1277) became the standard textbook in logic for three hundred years. However, the most original contributions from this period were made by William of Ockham (ca. 1285–1347). Ockham extended the theory of modal logic, conducted an exhaustive study of the forms of valid and invalid syllogisms, and further developed the idea of a metalanguage, a higher-level language used to discuss linguistic entities such as words, terms, and propositions.

Toward the middle of the fifteenth century, a reaction set in against the logic of the Middle Ages. Rhetoric largely displaced logic as the primary focus of attention; the logic of Chrysippus, which had already begun to lose its unique identity in the Middle Ages, was ignored altogether, and the logic of Aristotle was studied only in highly simplistic presentations. A reawakening did not occur until two hundred years later through the work of Gottfried Wilhelm Leibniz (1646–1716).

Leibniz, a genius in numerous fields, attempted to develop a symbolic language or "calculus" that could be used to settle all forms of disputes, whether in theology, philosophy, or international relations. As a result of this work, Leibniz is sometimes credited with being the father of symbolic logic. Leibniz's efforts to symbolize logic were carried into the nineteenth century by Bernard Bolzano (1781–1848).

In the middle of the nineteenth century, logic commenced an extremely rapid period of development that has continued to this day. Work in symbolic logic was done by many philosophers and mathematicians, including Augustus De Morgan (1806–1871), George Boole (1815–1864), William Stanley Jevons (1835–1882), and John Venn (1834–1923). The rule bearing De Morgan's name is used in Chapter 7 of this book. Boole's interpretation of categorical propositions and Venn's method for diagramming them are covered in Chapters 4 and 5. At the same time a revival in inductive logic was initiated by the British philosopher John Stuart Mill (1806–1873), whose methods of induction are presented in Chapter 10.

Across the Atlantic, the American philosopher Charles Sanders Peirce (1839–1914) developed a logic of relations, invented symbolic quantifiers, and suggested the truth-table method for formulas in propositional logic. These topics are covered in Chapters 6 and 8 of this book. The truth-table method was completed independently by Emil Post (1897–1954) and Ludwig Wittgenstein (1889–1951).

Toward the end of the nineteenth century, the foundations of modern mathematical logic were laid by Gottlob Frege (1848–1925). His *Begriffsschrift* sets forth the theory of quantification presented in Chapter 8 of this text. Frege's work was continued into the twentieth century by Alfred North Whitehead (1861–1947) and Bertrand Russell (1872–1970), whose monumental *Principia Mathematica* attempted to reduce the whole of pure mathematics to logic. The *Principia* is the source of much of the symbolism that appears in Chapters 6, 7, and 8 of this text.

During the twentieth century, much of the work in logic focused on the formalization of logical systems and on questions dealing with the completeness and consistency of such systems. A now-famous theorem proved by Kurt Gödel (1906–1978) states that in any formal system adequate for number theory there exists an undecidable formula—that is, a formula such that neither it nor its negation is derivable from the axioms of the system. Other developments included multivalued logics and the formalization of modal logic. Most recently, logic has made a major contribution to technology by providing the conceptual foundation for the electronic circuitry of digital computers.

EXERCISE 1.1

I. Each of the following passages contains a single argument. Using the letters "P" and "C," identify the premises and conclusion of each argument, writing premises first and conclusion last. List the premises in the order in which they make the most sense (usually the order in which they occur), and write both premises and conclusion in the form of separate declarative sentences. Indicator words may be eliminated once premises and conclusion have been appropriately labeled. The exercises marked with a star are answered in the back of the book.

★1. Carbon monoxide molecules happen to be just the right size and shape, and happen to have just the right chemical properties, to fit neatly into cavities within hemoglobin molecules in blood that are normally reserved for oxygen molecules. Consequently, carbon monoxide diminishes the oxygen-carrying capacity of blood.

(Nivaldo J. Tro, *Chemistry: A Molecular Approach*, 2nd ed.)

MindTap® Complete exercises online for immediate feedback.

2. Since the good, according to Plato, is that which furthers a person's real interests, it follows that in any given case when the good is known, men will seek it.

(Avrum Stroll and Richard Popkin, *Philosophy and the Human Spirit*)

3. As the denial or perversion of justice by the sentences of courts, as well as in any other manner, is with reason classed among the just causes of war, it will follow that the federal judiciary ought to have cognizance of all causes in which the citizens of other countries are concerned.

(Alexander Hamilton, *Federalist Papers*, No. 80)

★4. When individuals voluntarily abandon property, they forfeit any expectation of privacy in it that they might have had. Therefore, a warrantless search or seizure of abandoned property is not unreasonable under the Fourth Amendment.

(Judge Stephanie Kulp Seymour, *United States v. Jones*)

5. Artists and poets look at the world and seek relationships and order. But they translate their ideas to canvas, or to marble, or into poetic images. Scientists try to find relationships between different objects and events. To express the order they find, they create hypotheses and theories. Thus the great scientific theories are easily compared to great art and great literature.

(Douglas C. Giancoli, *The Ideas of Physics*, 3rd ed.)

6. The fact that there was never a land bridge between Australia and mainland Asia is evidenced by the fact that the animal species in the two areas are very different. Asian placental mammals and Australian marsupial mammals have not been in contact in the last several million years.

(T. Douglas Price and Gary M. Feinman, *Images of the Past*)

★7. It really does matter if you get enough sleep. We need sleep to think clearly, react quickly, and create memories. Studies show that people who are taught mentally challenging tasks do better after a good night's sleep. Other research suggests that sleep is needed for creative problem solving.

(U.S. National Institutes of Health, "Your Guide to Healthy Sleep")

8. The classroom teacher is crucial to the development and academic success of the average student, and administrators simply are ancillary to this effort. For this reason, classroom teachers ought to be paid at least the equivalent of administrators at all levels, including the superintendent.

(Peter F. Falstrup, letter to the editor)

9. An agreement cannot bind unless both parties to the agreement know what they are doing and freely choose to do it. This implies that the seller who intends to enter a contract with a customer has a duty to disclose exactly what the customer is buying and what the terms of the sale are.

(Manuel G. Velasquez, "The Ethics of Consumer Production")

★10. Punishment, when speedy and specific, may suppress undesirable behavior, but it cannot teach or encourage desirable alternatives. Therefore, it is crucial to use positive techniques to model and reinforce appropriate behavior that the person can use in place of the unacceptable response that has to be suppressed.

(Walter Mischel and Harriet Mischel, *Essentials of Psychology*)

11. Profit serves a very crucial function in a free-enterprise economy, such as our own. High profits are the signal that consumers want more of the output of the industry. High profits provide the incentive for firms to expand output and for more firms to enter the industry in the long run. For a firm of above-average efficiency, profits represent the reward for greater efficiency.

(Dominic Salvatore, *Managerial Economics*, 3rd ed.)

12. Cats can think circles around dogs! My cat regularly used to close and lock the door to my neighbor's doghouse, trapping their sleeping Doberman inside. Try telling a cat what to do, or putting a leash on him—he'll glare at you and say, "I don't think so. You should have gotten a dog."

(Kevin Purkiser, letter to the editor)

★13. Since private property helps people define themselves, since it frees people from mundane cares of daily subsistence, and since it is finite, no individual should accumulate so much property that others are prevented from accumulating the necessities of life.

(Leon P. Baradat, *Political Ideologies, Their Origins and Impact*)

14. To every existing thing God wills some good. Hence, since to love any thing is nothing else than to will good to that thing, it is manifest that God loves everything that exists.

(Thomas Aquinas, *Summa Theologica*)

15. Women of the working class, especially wage workers, should not have more than two children at most. The average working man can support no more and the average working woman can take care of no more in decent fashion.

(Margaret Sanger, *Family Limitations*)

★16. Radioactive fallout isn't the only concern in the aftermath of nuclear explosions. The nations of planet Earth have acquired nuclear weapons with an explosive power equal to more than a million Hiroshima bombs. Studies suggest that explosion of only half these weapons would produce enough soot, smoke, and dust to blanket the earth, block out the sun, and bring on a nuclear winter that would threaten the survival of the human race.

(John W. Hill and Doris K. Kolb, *Chemistry for Changing Times*, 7th ed.)

17. An ant releases a chemical when it dies, and its fellows then carry it away to the compost heap. Apparently the communication is highly effective; a healthy ant painted with the death chemical will be dragged to the funeral heap again and again.

(Carol R. Ember and Melvin Ember, *Cultural Anthropology*, 7th ed.)

18. Every art and every inquiry, and similarly every action and pursuit, is thought to aim at some good; and for this reason the good has rightly been declared to be that at which all things aim.

(Aristotle, *Nicomachean Ethics*)

★19. Poverty offers numerous benefits to the nonpoor. Antipoverty programs provide jobs for middle-class professionals in social work, penology, and public health. Such workers' future advancement is tied to the continued growth of bureaucracies dependent on the existence of poverty.

(J. John Palen, *Social Problems*)

20. Corn is an annual crop. Butcher's meat, a crop which requires four or five years to grow. As an acre of land, therefore, will produce a much smaller quantity of the one species of food than the other, the inferiority of the quantity must be compensated by the superiority of the price.

(Adam Smith, *The Wealth of Nations*)

21. Neither a borrower nor lender be
For loan oft loses both itself and friend,
And borrowing dulls the edge of husbandry.

(William Shakespeare, *Hamlet* I, 3)

★22. The stakes in whistleblowing are high. Take the nurse who alleges that physicians enrich themselves in her hospital through unnecessary surgery; the engineer who discloses safety defects in the braking systems of a fleet of new rapid-transit vehicles; the Defense Department official who alerts Congress to military graft and overspending: all know that they pose a threat to those whom they denounce and that their own careers may be at risk.

(Sissela Bok, "Whistleblowing and Professional Responsibility")

23. If a piece of information is not "job relevant," then the employer is not entitled qua employer to know it. Consequently, since sexual practices, political beliefs, associational activities, etc., are not part of the description of most jobs, that is, since they do not directly affect one's job performance, they are not legitimate information for an employer to know in the determination of the hiring of a job applicant.

(George G. Brenkert, "Privacy, Polygraphs, and Work")

24. Many people believe that a dark tan is attractive and a sign of good health, but mounting evidence indicates that too much sun can lead to health problems. One of the most noticeable effects is premature aging of the skin. The sun also contributes to certain types of cataracts, and, what is most worrisome, it plays a role in skin cancer.

(Joseph M. Moran and Michael D. Morgan, *Meteorology*, 4th ed.)

★25. Contrary to the tales of some scuba divers, the toothy, gaping grin on the mouth of an approaching shark is not necessarily anticipatory. It is generally accepted that by constantly swimming with its mouth open, the shark is simply avoiding suffocation. This assures a continuous flow of oxygen-laden water into their mouths, over their gills, and out through the gill slits.

(Robert A. Wallace et al., *Biology: The Science of Life*)

26. Not only is the sky blue [as a result of scattering], but light coming from it is also partially polarized. You can readily observe this by placing a piece of Polaroid (for example, one lens of a pair of Polaroid sunglasses) in front of

your eye and rotating it as you look at the sky on a clear day. You will notice a change in light intensity with the orientation of the Polaroid.

(Frank J. Blatt, *Principles of Physics*, 2nd ed.)

27. Since the secondary light [from the moon] does not inherently belong to the moon and is not received from any star or from the sun, and since in the whole universe there is no other body left but the earth, what must we conclude? What is to be proposed? Surely we must assert that the lunar body (or any other dark and sunless orb) is illuminated by the earth.

(Galileo Galilei, *The Starry Messenger*)

★28. Anyone familiar with our prison system knows that there are some inmates who behave little better than brute beasts. But the very fact that these prisoners exist is a telling argument against the efficacy of capital punishment as a deterrent. If the death penalty had been truly effective as a deterrent, such prisoners would long ago have vanished.

("The Injustice of the Death Penalty," *America*)

29. Though it is possible that REM sleep and dreaming are not necessary in the adult, REM deprivation studies seem to suggest otherwise. Why would REM pressure increase with deprivation if the system is unimportant in the adult?

(Herbert L. Petri, *Motivation: Theory and Research*, 2nd ed.)

30. We say that an end pursued in its own right is more complete than an end pursued because of something else, and that an end that is never choiceworthy because of something else is more complete than ends that are choiceworthy both in their own right and because of this end. Hence, an end that is always choiceworthy in its own right, and never because of something else, is complete without qualification.

(Aristotle, *Nicomachean Ethics*)

II. The following arguments were taken from magazine and newspaper editorials and letters to the editor. In most instances the main conclusion must be rephrased to capture the full intent of the author. Write out what you interpret the main conclusion to be.

★1. University administrators know well the benefits that follow notable success in college sports: increased applications for admissions, increased income from licensed logo merchandise, more lucrative television deals, postseason game revenue, and more successful alumni fund drives. The idea that there is something ideal and pure about the amateur athlete is self-serving bunk.

(Michael McDonnell, letter to the editor)

2. In a nation of immigrants, people of diverse ethnic backgrounds must have a common bond through which to exchange ideas. How can this bond be accomplished if there is no common language? It is those who shelter the immigrant from learning English by encouraging the development of a multilingual society who are creating a xenophobic atmosphere. They allow the immigrant to surround himself with a cocoon of language from which he cannot escape and which others cannot penetrate.

(Rita Toften, letter to the editor)

3. The health and fitness of our children has become a problem partly because of our attitude toward athletics. The purpose of sports, especially for children, should be to make healthy people healthier. The concept of team sports has failed to do this. Rather than learning to interact and cooperate with others, youngsters are taught to compete. Team sports have only reinforced the notion that the team on top is the winner, and all others are losers. This approach does not make sports appealing to many children, and some, especially among the less fit, burn out by the time they are twelve.

(Mark I. Pitman, "Young Jocks")

★4. College is the time in which a young mind is supposed to mature and acquire wisdom, and one can only do this by experiencing as much diverse intellectual stimuli as possible. A business student may be a whiz at accounting, but has he or she ever experienced the beauty of a Shakespearean sonnet or the boundless events composing Hebrew history? Most likely not. While many of these neoconservatives will probably go on to be financially successful, they are robbing themselves of the true purpose of collegiate academics, a sacrifice that outweighs the future salary checks.

(*Robert S. Griffith*, "Conservative College Press")

5. History has shown repeatedly that you cannot legislate morality, nor does anyone have a right to. The real problem is the people who have a vested interest in sustaining the multibillion-dollar drug industry created by the laws against drugs. The legalization of drugs would remove the thrill of breaking the law; it would end the suffering caused by unmetered doses, impurities, and substandard paraphernalia. A huge segment of the underground and extra-legal economy would move into a legitimate economy, taking money away from criminals, eliminating crime and violence, and restoring many talented people to useful endeavor.

(Thomas L. Wayburn, letter to the editor)

6. Infectious disease is no longer the leading cause of death in this country, thanks to antibiotics, but there are new strains of bacteria that are resistant to—and others that grow only in the presence of—antibiotics. Yet Congress wants to cut the National Institutes of Health budget. Further cuts would leave us woefully unprepared to cope with the new microbes Mother Nature has cooking in her kitchen.

(Valina L. Dawson, letter to the editor)

★7. A person cannot reject free will and still insist on criminality and codes of moral behavior. If people are compelled by forces beyond their control (genes or environment), then their actions, no matter how vile, are excusable. That means the Nuremberg trials of Nazi murderers were invalid, and all prison gates should be flung open. The essence of our humanity is the ability to choose between right and wrong, good and evil, and act accordingly. Strip that from us and we are mere animals.

(Rabbi Gilbert S. Rosenthal, letter to the editor)

8. Ideally, decisions about health care should be based on the doctor's clinical judgment, patient preference, and scientific evidence. Patients should always be presented with options in their care. Elective cesarean section, however, is not used to treat a problem but to avoid a natural process. An elective surgery like this puts the patient at unnecessary risk, increases the risk for complications in future deliveries, and increases health-care costs.

(Anne Foster-Rosales, M.D., letter to the editor)

9. Parents who feel guilty for the little time they can (or choose to) spend with their children "pick up" after them—so the children don't learn to face the consequences of their own choices and actions. Parents who allow their children to fail are showing them greater love and respect.

(Susan J. Peters, letter to the editor)

★10. Most of the environmental problems facing us stem, at least in part, from the sheer number of Americans. The average American produces three quarters of a ton of garbage every year, consumes hundreds of gallons of gasoline, and uses large amounts of electricity (often from a nuclear power plant, coal burning, or a dam). The least painful way to protect the environment is to limit population growth.

(Craig M. Bradley, letter to the editor)

III. Define the following terms:

logic	premise	inference
argument	conclusion	proposition
statement	conclusion indicator	syllogistic logic
truth value	premise indicator	modal logic

IV. Answer "true" or "false" to the following statements:

1. The purpose of the premise or premises is to set forth the reasons or evidence given in support of the conclusion.

2. Some arguments have more than one conclusion.

3. All arguments must have more than one premise.

4. The words "therefore," "hence," "so," "since," and "thus" are all conclusion indicators.

5. The words "for," "because," "as," and "for the reason that" are all premise indicators.

6. In the strict sense of the terms, *inference* and *argument* have exactly the same meaning.

7. In most (but not all) arguments that lack indicator words, the conclusion is the first statement.

8. Any sentence that is either true or false is a statement.

9. Every statement has a truth value.

10. Aristotle is the person usually credited with being the father of logic.

V. Create the following arguments:

1. An argument having one or more premise indicators and the conclusion: "Uniforms should/should not be required in high schools."

2. An argument having a conclusion indicator and the conclusion: "The legal drinking age should/should not be lowered to 18."

3. An argument having no indicator words and the conclusion: "Renewable forms of energy should/should not be subsidized by the government."

MindTap® Master concepts and improve outcomes with Aplia, at the end of the chapter, in the Aplia folder.

1.2   Recognizing Arguments

HOW LOGICAL ARE YOU? Suppose a friend tells you that he believes life exists on other planets and it's just a matter of time before someone proves it. You ask him why he believes this, and he replies, "This is my opinion, and I'm entitled to it. I have always held this view, and I have the right to think whatever I choose. You have your opinions, and I have mine. Yours are no better than mine." Has your friend given you an argument? Why or why not?

Find the answer on MindTap.

Not all passages contain arguments. Because logic deals with arguments, it is important to be able to distinguish passages that contain arguments from those that do not. In general, a passage contains an argument if it purports to prove something; if it does not do so, it does not contain an argument.

In the previous section of this book we learned that every argument has at least one premise and exactly one conclusion. The premise or premises set forth the alleged evidence or reasons, and the conclusion asserts what is claimed to follow from the alleged evidence or reasons. This definition of an argument expresses what is needed for a passage to contain an argument:

1. At least one of the statements must claim to present evidence or reasons.
2. There must be a claim that the alleged evidence supports or implies something—that is, a claim that something follows from the alleged evidence or reasons.

It is not necessary that the premises present actual evidence or true reasons nor that the premises actually support the conclusion. But at least the premises must *claim* to present evidence or reasons, and there must be a *claim* that the evidence or reasons support or imply something. Also, you should recognize that the second claim is not equatable with the intentions of the arguer. Intentions are subjective and, as such, are usually not accessible to the evaluator. Rather, this claim is an objective feature of an argument grounded in its language or structure.

Aristotle 384–322 B.C.E.

Mansell/Time Life Pictures/Getty Images

Aristotle was born in Stagira, a small Greek town situated on the northern coast of the Aegean Sea. His father was a physician in the court of King Amyntas II of Macedonia, and the young Aristotle was a friend of the king's son Philip, who was later to become king himself and the father of Alexander the Great. When he was about seventeen, Aristotle was sent to Athens to further his education in Plato's Academy, the finest institution of higher learning in the Greek world. After Plato's death Aristotle left for Assos, a small town on the coast of Asia Minor, where he married the niece of the local ruler.

Six years later Aristotle accepted an invitation to return to Macedonia to serve as tutor of the young Alexander. When Alexander ascended the throne following his father's assassination, Aristotle's tutorial job was finished, and he departed for Athens where he set up a school near the temple of Apollo Lyceus. The school came to be known as the Lyceum, and Alexander supported it with contributions of money and specimens of flora and fauna derived from his far-flung conquests. After Alexander's death, an anti-Macedonian rebellion forced Aristotle to leave Athens for Chalcis, about thirty miles to the north, where he died one year later at the age of sixty-two.

Aristotle is universally recognized as the originator of logic. He defined *logic* as the study of the process by which a statement follows by necessity from one or more other statements. The most fundamental kind of statement, he thought, is the categorical proposition, and he classified the four kinds of categorical propositions in terms of their being universal, particular, affirmative, and negative. He also developed the square of opposition, which shows how one such proposition implies the truth or falsity of another,

and he identified the relations of conversion, obversion, and contraposition, which provide the basis for various immediate inferences.

His crowning achievement is the theory of the categorical syllogism, a kind of argument consisting of three categorical propositions. He showed how categorical syllogisms can be catalogued in terms of mood and figure, and he developed a set of rules for determining the validity of categorical syllogisms. Also, he showed how the modal concepts of possibility and necessity apply to categorical propositions. In addition to the theory of the syllogism, Aristotle advanced the theory of definition by genus and difference, and he showed how arguments could be defective in terms of thirteen forms of informal fallacy.

Aristotle made profound contributions to many areas of human learning including biology, physics, metaphysics, epistemology, psychology, aesthetics, ethics, and politics. However, his accomplishments in logic were so extensive and enduring that two thousand years after his death, the great philosopher Immanuel Kant said that Aristotle had discovered everything that could be known about logic. His logic was not superseded until the end of the nineteenth century when Frege, Whitehead, and Russell developed modern mathematical logic.

In deciding whether a passage contains an argument, the claim that the alleged reasons or evidence supports or implies something is usually the more important of the two. Such a claim can be either explicit or implicit. An *explicit* claim is usually asserted by premise or conclusion indicator words ("thus," "since," "because," "hence," "therefore," and so on). Example:

> The Ebola virus has yet to be eradicated, and it kills on average 50 percent of those it infects. Thus, Ebola remains a threat to human health.

The word "thus" expresses the claim that something is being inferred, so the passage is an argument.

An *implicit* claim exists if there is an inferential relationship between the statements in a passage, but the passage contains no indicator words. Example:

> The genetic modification of food is risky business. Genetic engineering can introduce unintended changes into the DNA of the food-producing organism, and these changes can be toxic to the consumer.

The inferential relationship between the first statement and the other two constitutes an implicit claim that evidence supports something, so we are justified in calling the passage an argument. The first statement is the conclusion, and the other two are the premises.

In deciding whether there is a claim that evidence supports or implies something, keep an eye out for (1) premise and conclusion indicator words and (2) the presence of an inferential relationship between the statements. In connection with these points, however, a word of caution is in order. First, the mere occurrence of an indicator word by no means guarantees the presence of an argument. For example, consider the following passages:

> Since Edison invented the phonograph, there have been many technological innovations.

> Since Edison invented the phonograph, he deserves credit for a major technological innovation.

In the first passage the word "since" is used in a *temporal* sense. It means "from the time that." Thus, the first passage is not an argument. In the second passage "since" is used in a *logical* sense, and so the passage *is* an argument.

The second cautionary point is that it is not always easy to detect the occurrence of an inferential relationship between the statements in a passage, and one may have to review a passage several times before making a decision. In reaching such a decision, one may find it helpful to mentally insert the word "therefore" before the various statements to see whether it makes sense to interpret one of them as following from the others. Even with this mental aid, however, the decision whether a passage contains an inferential relationship (as well as the decision about indicator words) often involves a heavy dose of interpretation. As a result, not everyone will agree about every passage. Sometimes the only answer possible is a conditional one: "*If* this passage contains an argument, then these are the premises and that is the conclusion."

To assist in distinguishing passages that contain arguments from those that do not, let us now investigate some typical kinds of nonarguments. These include simple noninferential passages, expository passages, illustrations, explanations, and conditional statements.

Simple Noninferential Passages

Simple noninferential passages are unproblematic passages that lack a claim that anything is being proved. Such passages contain statements that could be premises or conclusions (or both), but what is missing is a claim that any potential premise supports a conclusion or that any potential conclusion is supported by premises. Passages of this sort include warnings, pieces of advice, statements of belief or opinion, loosely associated statements, and reports.

A **warning** is a form of expression that is intended to put someone on guard against a dangerous or detrimental situation. Examples:

> Watch out that you don't slip on the ice.

> Whatever you do, never confide personal secrets to Blabbermouth Bob.

If no evidence is given to prove that such statements are true, then there is no argument.

A **piece of advice** is a form of expression that makes a recommendation about some future decision or course of conduct. Examples:

> You should keep a few things in mind before buying a used car. Test drive the car at varying speeds and conditions, examine the oil in the crankcase, ask to see service records, and, if possible, have the engine and power train checked by a mechanic.

> Before accepting a job after class hours, I would suggest that you give careful consideration to your course load. Will you have sufficient time to prepare for classes and tests, and will the job produce an excessive drain on your energies?

As with warnings, if there is no evidence that is intended to prove anything, then there is no argument.

A **statement of belief** or **opinion** is an expression about what someone happens to believe or think about something. Examples:

> We believe that our company must develop and produce outstanding products that will perform a great service or fulfill a need for our customers. We believe that our business must be run at an adequate profit and that the services and products we offer must be better than those offered by competitors.
>
> (Robert D. Hay and Edmund R. Gray, "Introduction to Social Responsibility")

> When I can read the latte menu through the hole in my server's earlobe, something is seriously out of whack. What happened to an earring, maybe two, in each lobe? Now any surface is game. Brow, lip, tongue, cheek, nose. I've adjusted to untied shoelaces and pants that make mooning irrelevant. But when it comes to piercings, I just can't budge.
>
> (Debra Darvick, "Service with a Smile, and Plenty of Metal")

Because neither of these statements asserts any claim that a belief or opinion is supported by evidence, or that it supports some conclusion, there is no argument.

Loosely associated statements may be about the same general subject, but they lack a claim that one of them is proved by the others. Example:

> Not to honor men of worth will keep the people from contention; not to value goods that are hard to come by will keep them from theft; not to display what is desirable will keep them from being unsettled of mind.
>
> (Lao-Tzu, *Thoughts from the Tao Te Ching*)

Because there is no claim that any of these statements provides evidence or reasons for believing another, there is no argument.

A **report** consists of a group of statements that convey information about some topic or event. Example:

> The period of 1648–1789 was one of competition among the primary monarchs of Europe. Wars among the great powers were frequent but limited. France made major efforts to become paramount, but the balance of power operated to block French expansion.
>
> (Steven L. Spiegel, *World Politics in a New Era*)

These statements could serve as the premises of an argument, but because the author makes no claim that they support or imply anything, there is no argument. Another type of report is the news report:

> Witnesses said they heard a loud crack before a balcony gave way at a popular nightspot, dropping dozens of screaming people fourteen feet. At least eighty people were injured at the Diamond Horseshoe casino when they fell onto broken glass and splintered wood. Investigators are waiting for an engineer's report on the deck's occupancy load.
>
> (Newspaper clipping)

Again, because the reporter makes no claim that these statements imply anything, there is no argument.

One must be careful, though, with reports *about* arguments:

> "The Air Force faces a serious shortage of experienced pilots in the years ahead, because repeated overseas tours and the allure of high-paying jobs with commercial airlines are winning out over lucrative bonuses to stay in the service," says a prominent Air Force official.
>
> (Newspaper clipping)

Properly speaking, this passage is not an argument, because the author of the passage does not claim that anything is supported by evidence. Rather, the author reports the claim by the Air Force official that something is supported by evidence. If such passages are interpreted as "containing" arguments, it must be made clear that the argument is not the author's but one made by someone about whom the author is reporting.

Expository Passages

An **expository passage** is a kind of discourse that begins with a topic sentence followed by one or more sentences that develop the topic sentence. If the objective is not to prove the topic sentence but only to expand it or elaborate it, then there is no argument. Examples:

> There are three familiar states of matter: solid, liquid, and gas. Solid objects ordinarily maintain their shape and volume regardless of their location. A liquid occupies a definite volume, but assumes the shape of the occupied portion of its container. A gas maintains neither shape nor volume. It expands to fill completely whatever container it is in.
>
> (John W. Hill and Doris K. Kolb, *Chemistry for Changing Times*, 7th ed.)

There is a stylized relation of artist to mass audience in the sports, especially in baseball. Each player develops a style of his own—the swagger as he steps to the plate, the unique windup a pitcher has, the clean-swinging and hard-driving hits, the precision quickness and grace of infield and outfield, the sense of surplus power behind whatever is done.

(Max Lerner, *America as a Civilization*)

In each passage the topic sentence is stated first, and the remaining sentences merely develop and flesh out this topic sentence. These passages are not arguments, because they lack an inferential claim. However, expository passages differ from simple noninferential passages (such as warnings and pieces of advice) in that many of them can also be taken as arguments. If the purpose of the subsequent sentences in the passage is not only to flesh out the topic sentence but also to prove it, then the passage is an argument. Example:

Skin and the mucous membrane lining the respiratory and digestive tracts serve as mechanical barriers to entry by microbes. Oil-gland secretions contain chemicals that weaken or kill bacteria on skin. The respiratory tract is lined by cells that sweep mucus and trapped particles up into the throat, where they can be swallowed. The stomach has an acidic pH, which inhibits the growth of many types of bacteria.

(Sylvia S. Mader, *Human Biology*, 4th ed.)

In this passage the topic sentence is stated first, and the purpose of the remaining sentences is not only to *show how* the skin and mucous membranes serve as barriers to microbes but also to *prove* that they do this. Thus, the passage can be taken as both an expository passage and an argument.

In deciding whether an expository passage should be interpreted as an argument, try to determine whether the purpose of the subsequent sentences in the passage is merely to develop the topic sentence or also to prove that it is true. In borderline cases, ask yourself whether the topic sentence makes a claim that everyone accepts or agrees with. If it does, the passage is probably not an argument. In real-life situations authors rarely try to prove something is true when everyone already accepts it. However, if the topic sentence makes a claim that many people do not accept or have never thought about, then the purpose of the remaining sentences may be both to prove the topic sentence is true as well as to develop it. If this is so, the passage is an argument.

Finally, if even this procedure yields no definite answer, the only alternative may be to say that *if* the passage is taken as an argument, then the first statement is the conclusion and the others are the premises.

Illustrations

An **illustration** is an expression involving one or more examples that is intended to show what something means or how it is done. Illustrations are often confused with arguments because many illustrations contain indicator words such as "thus." Examples:

Chemical elements, as well as compounds, can be represented by molecular formulas. Thus, oxygen is represented by "O_2," water by "H_2O," and sodium chloride by "NaCl."

A deciduous tree is any tree that loses its leaves during the winter. For example, maples are deciduous. And so are elms, poplars, hawthorns, and alders.

These selections are not arguments, because they make no claim that anything is being proved. In the first selection, the word "thus" indicates how something is done—namely, how chemical elements and compounds can be represented by formulas. In the second, the examples cited are intended to illustrate the meaning of the word "deciduous." It pins down the meaning by providing concrete instances.

However, as with expository passages, many illustrations can be taken as arguments. Such arguments are often called **arguments from example**. Here is an instance of one:

> Although most forms of cancer, if untreated, can cause death, not all cancers are life threatening. For example, basal cell carcinoma, the most common of all skin cancers, can produce disfigurement, but it almost never results in death.

In this passage the example given is intended to prove the truth of "Not all cancers are life threatening." Thus, the passage is best interpreted as an argument.

In deciding whether an illustration should be interpreted as an argument, determine whether the passage merely shows how something is done or what something means, or whether it also purports to prove something. In borderline cases it helps to note whether the claim being illustrated is one that practically everyone accepts or agrees with. If it is, the passage is probably not an argument. As already noted, in real-life situations authors rarely attempt to prove what everyone already accepts. But if the claim being illustrated is one that many people do not accept or have never thought about, then the passage may be interpreted as an argument.

Thus, in reference to the first two examples we considered, most people are aware that elements and compounds can be expressed by formulas—practically everyone knows that water is H_2O—and most people have at least a vague idea of what a deciduous tree is. But they may not have ever considered whether some forms of cancer are not life threatening. This is one of the reasons for evaluating the first two examples as mere illustrations and the last one as an argument.

Explanations

One of the most important kinds of nonargument is the explanation. An **explanation** is an expression that purports to shed light on some event or phenomenon. The event or phenomenon in question is usually accepted as a matter of fact. Examples:

> The sky appears blue from the earth's surface because light rays from the sun are scattered by particles in the atmosphere.

> Golf balls have a dimpled surface because the dimples reduce air drag, causing the ball to travel farther.

> Navel oranges are called by that name because they have a growth that resembles a human navel on the end opposite the stem.

Every explanation is composed of two distinct components: the explanandum and explanans. The **explanandum** is the statement that describes the event or phenomenon to be explained, and the **explanans** is the statement or group of statements that purports to do the explaining. In the first example, the explanandum is the statement "The sky appears blue from the earth's surface" and the explanans is "Light rays from the sun are scattered by particles in the atmosphere."

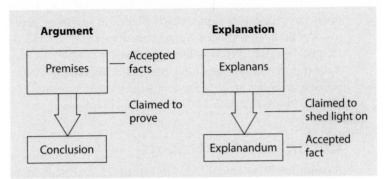

Explanations are sometimes mistaken for arguments because they often contain the indicator word "because." Yet explanations are not arguments, because in an explanation the purpose of the explanans is to shed light on, or to make sense of, the explanandum event—not to prove that it occurred. In other words, the purpose of the explanans is to show *why* something is the case, whereas in an argument, the purpose of the premises is to prove *that* something is the case.

In the first example given, the fact that the sky is blue is readily apparent to everyone. The statement that light rays from the sun are scattered by particles in the atmosphere is not intended to prove *that* the sky is blue, but rather to show *why* it is blue. In the second example, practically everyone knows that golf balls have a dimpled surface. The purpose of the passage is to explain *why* they have a dimpled surface—not to prove *that* they do. Similarly, in the third example, it is obvious that naval oranges are called naval oranges. The purpose of the passage is to shed light on why they have this name.

Thus, to distinguish explanations from arguments, identify the statement that is either the explanandum or the conclusion (usually this is the statement that precedes the word "because"). If this statement describes an accepted matter of fact, and if the remaining statements purport to shed light on this statement, then the passage is an explanation.

This method usually works to distinguish arguments from explanations. However, some passages can be interpreted as both explanations and arguments. Examples:

> Women become intoxicated by drinking a smaller amount of alcohol than men because men metabolize part of the alcohol before it reaches the bloodstream, whereas women do not.

> Household bleach should never be mixed with ammonia because the combination releases chlorine gas, which is highly poisonous.

The purpose of these passages could be to prove the first statement to those who do not accept it as fact, and to shed light on that fact to those who do accept it. Alternately, the passage could be intended to prove the first statement to a person who accepts its truth on blind faith or incomplete experience, and simultaneously to shed light on this truth. Thus, these passages can be correctly interpreted as both an explanation and an argument.

Perhaps the greatest problem confronting the effort to distinguish explanations from arguments lies in determining whether something is an accepted matter of fact. Obviously, what is accepted by one person may not be accepted by another. Thus, the effort often involves determining which person or group of people the passage is directed to—the intended audience. Sometimes the source of the passage (textbook, newspaper, technical journal, etc.) will decide the issue. But when the passage is taken totally out of context, ascertaining the source may prove impossible. In those circumstances the only possible answer may be to say that *if* the passage is an argument, then such-and-such is the conclusion and such-and-such are the premises.

Conditional Statements

A **conditional statement** is an "if ... then ..." statement; for example:

> If professional football games incite violence in the home, then the widespread approval given to this sport should be reconsidered.

> If Roger Federer has played in more Grand Slam finals than any other contender, then he rightfully deserves the title of world's greatest tennis player.

Every conditional statement is made up of two component statements. The component statement immediately following the "if" is called the **antecedent**, and the one following the "then" is called the **consequent**. (Occasionally, the word "then" is left out, and occasionally the order of antecedent and consequent is reversed.) In the first example, the antecedent is "Professional football games incite violence in the home," and the consequent is "The widespread approval given to this sport should be reconsidered." In both of these examples, there is a meaningful relationship between antecedent and consequent. However, such a relationship need not exist for a statement to count as conditional. The statement "If Taylor Swift is a singer, then Denver is in Colorado" is just as much a conditional statement as those about professional football and Roger Federer.

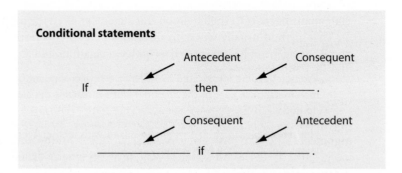

Conditional statements are not arguments, because they fail to meet the criteria given earlier. In an argument, at least one statement must claim to present evidence, and there must be a claim that this evidence implies something. In a conditional statement, there is no claim that either the antecedent or the consequent presents evidence. In other words, there is no assertion that either the antecedent or the consequent is true. Rather, there is only the assertion that *if* the antecedent is true, then so is the consequent. Of course, a conditional statement as a whole may present evidence because it asserts a relationship between statements. Yet when conditional statements are taken in this sense, there is still no argument, because there is then no separate claim that this evidence implies anything.

Some conditional statements are similar to arguments, however, in that they express the outcome of a reasoning process. As such, they may be said to have a certain inferential content. Consider the following:

> If sugary drinks cause heart disease and diabetes, then sugary drinks should be regulated.

The link between the antecedent and consequent resembles the inferential link between the premises and conclusion of an argument. Yet there is a difference because the premises of an argument are claimed to be true, whereas no such claim is made for the antecedent of a conditional statement. Accordingly, conditional statements are not arguments.* Yet their inferential content may be reexpressed to form arguments:

> Sugary drinks cause heart disease and diabetes.
> Therefore, sugary drinks should be regulated.

Finally, while no single conditional statement is an argument, a conditional statement may serve as either the premise or the conclusion (or both) of an argument, as the following examples illustrate:

> If North Korea is developing nuclear weapons, then North Korea is a threat to world peace.
> North Korea is developing nuclear weapons.
> Therefore, North Korea is a threat to world peace.

> If our borders are porous, then terrorists can enter the country at will.
> If terrorists can enter the country at will, then all of us are less secure.
> Therefore, if our borders are porous, then all of us are less secure.

The relation between conditional statements and arguments may now be summarized as follows:

1. A single conditional statement is not an argument.
2. A conditional statement may serve as either the premise or the conclusion (or both) of an argument.
3. The inferential content of a conditional statement may be reexpressed to form an argument.

The first two rules are especially pertinent to the recognition of arguments. According to the first rule, if a passage consists of a single conditional statement, it is not an argument. But if it consists of a conditional statement together with some other statement, then, by the second rule, it *may* be an argument, depending on such factors as the presence of indicator words and an inferential relationship between the statements.

---

*In saying this we are temporarily ignoring the possibility of these statements being enthymemes. As we shall see in Chapter 5, an enthymeme is an argument in which a premise or conclusion (or both) is implied but not stated. If, to this example, we add the premise "Sugary drinks cause heart disease and diabetes" and the conclusion "Therefore, sugary drinks should be regulated," we have a complete argument. To decide whether a conditional statement is an enthymeme, we must be familiar with the context in which it occurs.

Conditional statements are especially important in logic (and many other fields) because they express the relationship between necessary and sufficient conditions. *A* is said to be a **sufficient condition** for *B* whenever the occurrence of *A* is all that is needed for the occurrence of *B*. For example, being a dog is a sufficient condition for being an animal. On the other hand, *B* is said to be a **necessary condition** for *A* whenever *A* cannot occur without the occurrence of *B*. Thus, being an animal is a necessary condition for being a dog.

The difference between sufficient and necessary conditions is a bit tricky. So, to clarify the idea further, suppose you are given a large, closed cardboard box. Also, suppose you are told there is a dog in the box. Then you know for sure there is an animal in the box. No additional information is needed to draw this conclusion. This means that being a dog is sufficient for being an animal. However, being a dog is not necessary for being an animal, because if you are told that the box contains a cat, you can conclude with equal certainty that it contains an animal. In other words, it is not necessary for the box to contain a dog for it to contain an animal. It might equally well contain a cat, a mouse, a squirrel, or any other animal.

On the other hand, suppose you are told that whatever might be in the box, it is not an animal. Then you know for certain there is no dog in the box. The reason you can draw this conclusion is that being an animal is necessary for being a dog. If there is no animal, there is no dog. However, being an animal is not sufficient for being a dog, because if you are told that the box contains an animal, you cannot, from this information alone, conclude that it contains a dog. It might contain a cat, a mouse, a squirrel, and so on.

These ideas are expressed in the following conditional statements:

If *X* is a dog, then *X* is an animal.
If *X* is not an animal, then *X* is not a dog.

The first statement says that being a dog is a sufficient condition for being an animal, and the second that being an animal is a necessary condition for being a dog. However, a little reflection reveals that these two statements say exactly the same thing. Thus, each expresses in one way a necessary condition and in another way a sufficient condition. The terminology of sufficient and necessary conditions will be used in later chapters to express definitions and causal connections.

Summary

In deciding whether a passage contains an argument, you should look for three things: (1) indicator words such as "therefore," "since," "because," and so on; (2) an inferential relationship between the statements; and (3) typical kinds of nonarguments. But remember that the mere occurrence of an indicator word does not guarantee the presence of an

MindTap Need help? See the Learning Logic folder at the end of the chapter: The self-paced tutorial walks you through any section.

argument. You must check to see that the statement identified as the conclusion is claimed to be supported by one or more of the other statements. Also keep in mind that in many arguments that lack indicator words, the conclusion is the first statement. Furthermore, it helps to mentally insert the word "therefore" before the various statements before deciding that a statement should be interpreted as a conclusion. The typical kinds of nonarguments that we have surveyed are as follows:

warnings	reports
pieces of advice	expository passages
statements of belief	illustrations
statements of opinion	explanations
loosely associated statements	conditional statements

Keep in mind that these kinds of nonargument are not mutually exclusive, and that, for example, one and the same passage can sometimes be interpreted as both a report and a statement of opinion, or as both an expository passage and an illustration. The precise kind of nonargument a passage might be is nowhere near as important as correctly deciding whether or not it is an argument.

After working the exercises in this section, you may, if you wish, proceed directly to Section 1.6 ["Extended Arguments"].

EXERCISE 1.2

I. Determine which of the following passages are arguments. For those that are, identify the conclusion. For those that are not, determine the kind of nonargument.

★1. The turkey vulture is called by that name because its red featherless head resembles the head of a wild turkey.

2. If public education fails to improve the quality of instruction in both primary and secondary schools, then it is likely that it will lose additional students to the private sector in the years ahead.

3. Freedom of the press is the most important of our constitutionally guaranteed freedoms. Without it, our other freedoms would be immediately threatened. Furthermore, it provides the fulcrum for the advancement of new freedoms.

★4. A mammal is a vertebrate animal that nurses its offspring. Thus, cats and dogs are mammals, as are sheep, monkeys, rabbits, and bears.

5. It is strongly recommended that you have your house inspected for termite damage at the earliest possible opportunity.

6. Mosquito bites are not always the harmless little irritations most of us take them to be. For example, some mosquitoes carry West Nile virus, and people who are infected can become very sick or even die.

MindTap® Complete exercises online for immediate feedback.

★ 7. If stem-cell research is restricted, then future cures will not materialize. If future cures do not materialize, then people will die prematurely. Therefore, if stem-cell research is restricted, then people will die prematurely.

8. Fictional characters behave according to the same psychological probabilities as real people. But the characters of fiction are found in exotic dilemmas that real people hardly encounter. Consequently, fiction provides us with the opportunity to ponder how people react in uncommon situations, and to deduce moral lessons, psychological principles, and philosophical insights from their behavior.

(J. R. McCuen and A. C. Winkler, *Readings for Writers*, 4th ed.)

9. I believe that it must be the policy of the United States to support free peoples who are resisting attempted subjugation by armed minorities or by outside pressures. I believe that we must assist free peoples to work out their own destinies in their own way. I believe that our help should be primarily through economic and financial aid, which is essential to economic stability and orderly political processes.

(President Truman, Address to Congress, 1947)

★ 10. Five college students who were accused of sneaking into the Cincinnati Zoo and trying to ride the camels pleaded no contest to criminal trespass yesterday. The students scaled a fence to get into the zoo and then climbed another fence to get into the camel pit before security officials caught them, zoo officials said.

(Newspaper clipping)

11. Mortality rates for women undergoing early abortions, where the procedure is legal, appear to be as low as or lower than the rates for normal childbirth. Consequently, any interest of the state in protecting the woman from an inherently hazardous procedure, except when it would be equally dangerous for her to forgo it, has largely disappeared.

(Justice Blackmun, *Roe v. Wade*)

12. The pace of reading, clearly, depends entirely upon the reader. He may read as slowly or as rapidly as he can or wishes to read. If he does not understand something, he may stop and reread it, or go in search of elucidation before continuing. The reader can accelerate his pace when the material is easy or less than interesting, and can slow down when it is difficult or enthralling. If what he reads is moving he can put down the book for a few moments and cope with his emotions without fear of losing anything.

(Marie Winn, *The Plug-In Drug*)

★ 13. Any unit of length, when cubed, becomes a unit of volume. Thus, the cubic meter, cubic centimeter, and cubic millimeter are all units of volume.

(Nivaldo J. Tro, *Chemistry: A Molecular Approach*, 2nd ed.)

14. Lions at Kruger National Park in South Africa are dying of tuberculosis. "All of the lions in the park may be dead within ten years because the disease is

incurable, and the lions have no natural resistance," said the deputy director of the Department of Agriculture.

(Newspaper clipping)

15. Economics is of practical value in business. An understanding of the overall operation of the economic system puts the business executive in a better position to formulate policies. The executive who understands the causes and consequences of inflation is better equipped during inflationary periods to make more-intelligent decisions than otherwise.

(Campbell R. McConnell, Economics, 8th ed.)

★16. Bear one thing in mind before you begin to write your paper: Famous literary works, especially works regarded as classics, have been thoroughly studied to the point where prevailing opinion on them has assumed the character of orthodoxy.

(J. R. McCuen and A. C. Winkler, Readings for Writers, 4th ed.)

17. Young people at universities study to achieve knowledge and not to learn a trade. We must all learn how to support ourselves, but we must also learn how to live. We need a lot of engineers in the modern world, but we do not want a world of modern engineers.

(Winston Churchill, A Churchill Reader, ed. Colin R. Coote)

18. No business concern wants to sell on credit to a customer who will prove unable or unwilling to pay his or her account. Consequently, most business organizations include a credit department which must reach a decision on the credit worthiness of each prospective customer.

(Walter B. Meigs and Robert F. Meigs, Accounting)

★19. For organisms at the sea surface, sinking into deep water usually means death. Plant cells cannot photosynthesize in the dark depths. Fishes and other animals that descend lose contact with the main surface food supply and themselves become food for strange deep-living predators.

(David H. Milne, Marine Life and the Sea)

20. Since the 1950s a malady called whirling disease has invaded U.S. fishing streams, frequently attacking rainbow trout. A parasite deforms young fish, which often chase their tails before dying, hence the name.

("Trout Disease—A Turn for the Worse," National Geographic)

21. Dachshunds are ideal dogs for small children, as they are already stretched and pulled to such a length that the child cannot do much harm one way or the other.

(Robert Benchley, quoted in Cold Noses and Warm Hearts)

★22. Atoms are the basic building blocks of all matter. They can combine to form molecules, whose properties are generally very different from those of the constituent atoms. Table salt, for example, a simple chemical compound formed from chlorine and sodium, resembles neither the poisonous gas nor the highly reactive metal.

(Frank J. Blatt, Principles of Physics, 2nd ed.)

23. The coarsest type of humor is the *practical joke:* pulling away the chair from the dignitary's lowered bottom. The victim is perceived first as a person of consequence, then suddenly as an inert body subject to the laws of physics: authority is debunked by gravity, mind by matter; man is degraded to a mechanism.

(Arthur Koestler, Janus: A Summing Up)

24. If a man holding a belief which he was taught in childhood or persuaded of afterwards keeps down and pushes away any doubts which arise about it in his mind, purposely avoids the reading of books and the company of men that call in question or discuss it, and regards as impious those questions which cannot easily be asked without disturbing it—the life of that man is one long sin against mankind.

(W. K. Clifford, The Ethics of Belief)

★25. It is usually easy to decide whether or not something is alive. This is because living things share many common attributes, such as the capacity to extract energy from nutrients to drive their various functions, the power to actively respond to changes in their environment, and the ability to grow, to differentiate, and to reproduce.

(Donald Voet and Judith G. Voet, Biochemistry, 2nd ed.)

26. Words are slippery customers. The full meaning of a word does not appear until it is placed in its context.... And even then the meaning will depend upon the listener, upon the speaker, upon their entire experience of the language, upon their knowledge of one another, and upon the whole situation.

(C. Cherry, On Human Communication)

27. Haydn developed the string quartet from the eighteenth-century *divertimento,* giving more substance to the light, popular form and scoring it for two violins, a viola, and a cello. His eighty-three quartets, written over the course of his creative lifetime, evolved slowly into a sophisticated form. Together they constitute one of the most important bodies of chamber-music literature.

(Robert Hickok, Exploring Music)

★28. A person never becomes truly self-reliant. Even though he deals effectively with things, he is necessarily dependent upon those who have taught him to do so. They have selected the things he is dependent upon and determined the kinds and degrees of dependencies.

(B. F. Skinner, Beyond Freedom and Dignity)

29. There is no doubt that some businessmen conspire to shorten the useful life of their products in order to guarantee replacement sales. There is, similarly, no doubt that many of the annual model changes with which American (and other) consumers are increasingly familiar are not technologically substantive.

(Alvin Toffler, Future Shock)

30. The brain and the nervous system are composed of two types of cells— neurons and glial cells. Neurons are responsible for information transmission throughout the nervous system. Glial cells constitute the support system for

the neurons. For example, glial cells take away the waste products of neurons, keep the neurons' chemical environment stable, and insulate them, allowing neurons to do their work more efficiently.

(Richard Griggs, *Psychology: A Concise Introduction*)

★31. In areas where rats are a problem, it is very difficult to exterminate them with bait poison. That's because some rats eat enough poison to die but others eat only enough to become sick and then learn to avoid that particular poison taste in the future.

(Rod Plotnik, *Introduction to Psychology*, 4th ed.)

32. Although it is customary to think of human population as increasing continuously without declines or fluctuations, population growth has not been a steady march. For example, great declines occurred during the time of the Black Death, during the fourteenth century. Entire towns were abandoned, production of food declined, and in England, one-third of the population died within a single decade.

(Daniel B. Botkin and Edward A. Keller, *Environmental Science*)

33. If someone avoids and is afraid of everything, standing firm against nothing, he becomes cowardly; if he is afraid of nothing at all and goes to face everything, he becomes rash. Similarly, if he gratifies himself with every pleasure and abstains from none, he becomes intemperate; if he avoids them all, he becomes some sort of insensible person. Temperance and bravery, then, are ruined by excess and deficiency, but preserved by the mean.

(Aristotle, *Nicomachean Ethics*)

★34. Nations are made in two ways, by the slow working of history or the galvanic force of ideas. Most nations are made the former way, emerging slowly from the mist of the past, gradually coalescing within concentric circles of shared sympathies, with an accretion of consensual institutions. But a few nations are formed and defined by the citizens' assent to a shared philosophy.

(George Will, "Lithuania and South Carolina")

35. One form of energy can be converted to another. For example, when an electric motor is connected to a battery, chemical energy is converted to electrical energy, which in turn is converted to mechanical energy.

(Raymond A. Serway, *Physics for Scientists and Engineers*, 4th ed.)

II. The following selections were originally submitted as letters to the editor of newspapers and magazines. Determine which of them can, with good reason, be considered arguments. In those that can, identify the conclusion.

★1. What this country needs is a return to the concept of swift and certain justice. If we need more courts, judges and prisons, then so be it. And as for capital punishment, I say let the punishment fit the crime. When criminals behave more like humans, then we can start to treat them more humanely. In the meantime, I would like to see the Night Stalkers of our society swiftly executed rather than coddled by our courts and prisons.

(John Pearson)

2. Social security is not merely a retirement program. Six and a half million children in the United States are kept out of poverty each year because of assistance from Social Security's survivors benefits program—which protects virtually all American children in the tragic event of the death of a parent. Beneficiaries include spouses and children of workers who have died or become disabled; grandparents raising grandchildren; severely disabled children; and families of fallen service members.

(Donna Butts)

3. Is there any country in the world that worries more about its kids having fun in school, making lessons exciting and relevant, and then is more disappointed with the result than the United States? We think learning is like buying a car or smoking a cigarette. Just get into the thing or draw a breath and you will be effortlessly transported to lands of pleasure and excitement.

(Charles M. Breinin)

★4. After reading your cover story, I find that cable TV has simply flooded our airwaves with more sex, violence, and teenage punk junk. Now our children can spend even less time studying and we can spend more time in blank-space stares at the idiot box. Cable would be fine with more educational channels—and fewer cheap thrills aimed at narrow-minded bubble brains.

(Jacqueline Murray)

5. Once the basic necessities have been achieved, future income is only lightly connected to well-being. Democrats generally seek to tax future income to finance programs that meet basic needs, including food, clothing shelter, retirement security, and health care. Republicans, in contrast, seek to protect future income from taxation, often at the expense of meeting the basic needs of the less fortunate. So which of our two main political parties is more concerned with achieving broad happiness, and which party is more concerned with fulfilling selfishness?

(Jonathan Carey)

6. Animal abusers are cowards who take their issues out on "easy victims"—and their targets often include their fellow humans. I cannot begin to say how many incidents I've seen involving animal abusers who commit violent acts against humans, and animal neglecters who have neglected their children or other human dependents. Treating cruelty to animals with the seriousness it deserves doesn't only protect animals, it also makes the entire community safer.

(Martin Mersereau)

★7. The creation of a third political party—the independent party—would allow Congressional aspirants who desire to think for themselves to claim a high ground that is currently vacant. The new party would provide a more effective forum to discuss the right course for this country and might compel the other two parties to do likewise. The pressure such a movement would put on those now stagnating in cozy sinecures would, at the least, prove entertaining for a weary, frustrated public.

(Bill Cannon)

8. I agree that when religious institutions exclude woman from their hierarchies and rituals, the inevitable implication is that females are inferior. But it is important to note that when women's voices are silenced, it is not only the message that such discrimination sends that is damaging. The institutions themselves suffer. By disempowering women, religious institutions, and the broader societies in which they operate, lose the invaluable input of 51 percent of their constituents.

(Jessie Cronan)

9. It looks like India and China are going to compete for a manned landing on the moon by 2020 while America is muddling along with no real future space plan. Let's do something significant in space—say, go to Mars by 2020. We could have done it 30 years ago. Planning for a Mars mission was well along. But the nation turned away from space after we landed on the moon, even canceling the three remaining flights to the moon. These Saturn 5 rockets now sit in museums.

(Bill Ketchum)

★10. Teenage bullying is all about power. One person has it, one person does not. Reluctant to seek help, victims feel ashamed and powerless, and they fear retaliation should they "rat out" the bully. Strong anti-bullying programs are needed to provide a means to report bullying anonymously, to train all school personnel to take reports of bullying seriously, and to offer workshops for children on how to respond to being bullied.

(Karen Schulte O'Neill)

III. The following statements represent conclusions for arguments. Each is expressed in the form of two alternatives. Select one of the alternatives for each conclusion, and then jot down several reasons that support it. Finally, incorporate your reasons into a written argument of at least 100 words that supports the conclusion. Include premise and conclusion indicators in some of your arguments, but not in all of them.

1. A constitutional amendment that outlaws flag burning should/should not be adopted.

2. Street drugs should/should not be legalized.

3. The death penalty should/should not be abolished.

4. Sanctions should/should not be imposed on students for using speech that is offensive to minorities.

5. Free health care should/should not be guaranteed to all citizens.

6. Same-sex marriages should/should not be recognized by the state.

7. The possession, ownership, and sale of handguns should/should not be outlawed.

8. Cigarettes should/should not be regulated as an addictive drug.

9. Affirmative action programs should/should not be abolished.

10. Doctors should/should not be allowed to assist terminally ill patients in committing suicide.

IV. Define the following terms:

expository passage   conditional statement
illustration   antecedent
argument from example   consequent
explanation   sufficient condition
explanandum   necessary condition
explanans

V. Answer "true" or "false" to the following statements:

1. Any passage that contains an argument must contain a claim that something is supported by evidence or reasons.

2. In an argument, the claim that something is supported by evidence or reasons is always explicit.

3. Passages that contain indicator words such as "thus," "since," and "because" are always arguments.

4. In deciding whether a passage contains an argument, we should always keep an eye out for indicator words and the presence of an inferential relationship between the statements.

5. Some expository passages can be correctly interpreted as arguments.

6. Some passages containing "for example" can be correctly interpreted as arguments.

7. In deciding whether an expository passage or an illustration should be interpreted as an argument, it helps to note whether the claim being developed or illustrated is one that is accepted by everyone.

8. Some conditional statements can be reexpressed to form arguments.

9. In an explanation, the explanandum usually describes an accepted matter of fact.

10. In an explanation, the explanans is the statement or group of statements that does the explaining.

VI. Fill in the blanks with "necessary" or "sufficient" to make the following statements true. After the blanks have been filled in, express the result in terms of conditional statements.

★1. Being a tiger is a _____ condition for being an animal.

2. Being an animal is a _____ condition for being a tiger.

3. Drinking a glass of water is a _____ condition for quenching one's thirst.

★4. Having a racket is a _____ condition for playing tennis.

5. Heating water is a _____ condition for brewing coffee.

6. Stepping on a cat's tail is a _____ condition for making the cat yowl.

★7. Burning leaves is a _____ condition for producing smoke.

8. Paying attention is a _____ condition for understanding a lecture.

9. Being exactly divisible by 4 is a _____ condition for a number being even.

★10. Intending to deceive someone is a _____ condition for telling a lie.

VII. Page through a book, magazine, or newspaper and find two arguments, one with indicator words, the other without. Copy the arguments as written, giving the appropriate reference. Then identify the premises and conclusion of each.

VIII. Create the following nonarguments:

1. A conditional statement about a topic in astronomy. Identify the antecedent and the consequent.

2. An explanation about a topic in history. Explain why your explanation is not an argument.

3. An expository passage about a topic in chemistry. Explain why your expository passage is not an argument.

4. An illustration about a topic in mathematics. Explain why your illustration is not an argument from example.

MindTap® Master concepts and improve outcomes with Aplia, at the end of the chapter, in the Aplia folder.

1.3   Deduction and Induction

HOW LOGICAL ARE YOU? Recreational marijuana is not legal in your state, but there is a referendum coming up that would make it legal. You do some research and find that every state that has legalized recreational marijuana up to that date is a politically "blue" state. But your state is "red"—and becoming even more so. You conclude that your state will not be legalizing marijuana any time soon. Does your conclusion follow with certainty? If not, does it follow with probability?

Find the answer on MindTap.

The idea that arguments come in two forms, deductive and inductive, was first asserted by Aristotle. In the intervening centuries, deduction and induction have become a settled fixture not only in logic but in our intellectual culture. Countless books, both fiction and nonfiction, have referred to it. Einstein wrote a paper on it. And a huge number of textbooks ranging from philosophy to education, business to psychology, and chemistry to anthropology explore the subject. So what is the difference between a deductive and an inductive argument? Briefly we can say that deductive arguments are those that rest on *necessary* reasoning, while inductive arguments are those that rest on *probabilistic* reasoning.

Ruth Barcan Marcus 1921–2012

Courtesy Michael Marsland

Ruth Barcan was born in New York City in 1921. Her mother was a homemaker, and her father a typesetter at, and contributor to, the *Jewish Daily Forward*. After completing her primary and secondary education at public schools, she enrolled in New York University, where, in addition to her academic pursuits, she won praise as an outstanding fencer. In 1941 she earned a bachelor's degree in mathematics and philosophy, and five years later she received a PhD in philosophy from Yale University. In 1942 she married Jules Alexander Marcus, a physicist, and the couple had four children, two boys and two girls.

After graduating from Yale, Barcan Marcus's early career was spent holding several postdoctoral fellowships (including a Guggenheim) and visiting professorships. In 1959 she accepted a position at Roosevelt University, followed by positions at the University of Illinois, Chicago (where she was founding department chair) and Northwestern University. In 1973 she returned to Yale as professor of philosophy.

Commencing early in her career, Barcan Marcus made pioneering contributions to the area of quantified modal logic. She proposed, as an axiom, the widely discussed Barcan formula, which asserts, in symbols, $(x)\Box Fx \supset \Box(x) Fx$. In English, this means that if everything is necessarily F, then it is necessary that everything is F. The formula is controversial because it implies that all objects that exist in every possible world exist in the actual world. This could be taken to imply that nothing new can be created.

Personally, Ruth Barcan Marcus was fearless, down to earth, unpretentious, and a constant supporter of others. She had a great sense of humor—and she was also endearingly absentminded. On one occasion, while in the midst of a frantic search, she received a call from the local supermarket informing her that her final exams had been found amid the frozen meats.

Stated more precisely, a **deductive argument** is an argument incorporating the claim that it is *impossible* for the conclusion to be false given that the premises are true. On the other hand, an **inductive argument** is an argument incorporating the claim that it is *improbable* that the conclusion be false given that the premises are true. Two examples:

> The meerkat is closely related to the suricat.
> The suricat thrives on beetle larvae.
> Therefore, probably the meerkat thrives on beetle larvae.

> The meerkat is a member of the mongoose family.
> All members of the mongoose family are carnivores.
> Therefore, it necessarily follows that the meerkat is a carnivore.

The first of these arguments is inductive, the second deductive.

In deciding whether an argument is inductive or deductive, we look to certain objective features of the argument. These features include (1) the occurrence of special indicator words, (2) the *actual* strength of the inferential link between premises and conclusion, and (3) the form or style of argumentation. However, we must acknowledge at the outset that many arguments in ordinary language are incomplete, and because of this, deciding whether the argument should best be interpreted as deductive or inductive may be impossible.

The occurrence of special indicator words is illustrated in the examples we just considered. The word "probably" in the conclusion of the first argument suggests that the argument should be taken as inductive, and the word "necessarily" in the conclusion of the second suggests that the second argument be taken as deductive. Additional inductive indicators are "improbable," "plausible," "implausible," "likely," "unlikely," and "reasonable to conclude." Additional deductive indicators are "certainly," "absolutely," and "definitely." (Note that the phrase "it must be the case that" is simply a conclusion indicator that can occur in either deductive or inductive argments.)

Inductive and deductive indicator words often suggest the correct interpretation. However, if they conflict with one of the other criteria (discussed shortly), we should probably ignore them. Arguers often use phrases such as "it certainly follows that" for rhetorical purposes to add impact to their conclusion and not to suggest that the argument be taken as deductive. Similarly, some arguers, not knowing the distinction between inductive and deductive, will claim to "deduce" a conclusion when their argument is more correctly interpreted as inductive.

The second factor that bears on our interpretation of an argument as inductive or deductive is the *actual* strength of the inferential link between premises and conclusion. If the conclusion actually does follow with strict necessity from the premises, the argument is clearly deductive. In such an argument it is impossible for the premises to be true and the conclusion false. On the other hand, if the conclusion does not follow with strict necessity but does follow probably, it is often best to consider the argument inductive. Examples:

> All entertainers are extroverts.
> Stephen Colbert is an entertainer.
> Therefore, Stephen Colbert is an extrovert.

> The vast majority of entertainers are extroverts.
> Stephen Colbert is an entertainer.
> Therefore, Stephen Colbert is an extrovert.

In the first example, the conclusion follows with strict necessity from the premises. If we assume that all entertainers are extroverts and that Stephen Colbert is an entertainer, then it is impossible that Stephen Colbert not be an extrovert. Thus, we should interpret this argument as deductive. In the second example, the conclusion does not follow from the premises with strict necessity, but it does follow with some degree of probability. If we assume that the premises are true, then based on that assumption it is probable that the conclusion is true. Thus, it is best to interpret the second argument as inductive.

Occasionally, an argument contains no special indicator words, and the conclusion does not follow either necessarily or probably from the premises; in other words, it does not follow at all. This situation points to the need for the third factor to be taken into account, which is the character or form of argumentation the arguer uses.

Deductive Argument Forms

Many arguments have a distinctive character or form that indicates that the premises are supposed to provide absolute support for the conclusion. Five examples of such forms or kinds of argumentation are arguments based on mathematics, arguments from definition, and categorical, hypothetical, and disjunctive syllogisms.

An **argument based on mathematics** is an argument in which the conclusion depends on some purely arithmetic or geometric computation or measurement. For example, a shopper might place two apples and three oranges into a paper bag and then conclude that the bag contains five pieces of fruit. Or a surveyor might measure a square piece of land and, after determining that it is 100 feet on each side, conclude that it contains 10,000 square feet. Since all arguments in pure mathematics are deductive, we can usually consider arguments that depend on mathematics to be deductive as well. However, arguments that depend on statistics are a noteworthy exception. As we will see shortly, such arguments are usually best interpreted as inductive.

An **argument from definition** is an argument in which the conclusion is claimed to depend merely on the definition of some word or phrase used in the premise or conclusion. For example, someone might argue that because Claudia is mendacious, it follows that she tells lies, or that because a certain paragraph is prolix, it follows that it is excessively wordy. These arguments are deductive because their conclusions follow with necessity from the definitions of "mendacious" and "prolix."

A *syllogism,* in general, is an argument consisting of exactly two premises and one conclusion. Categorical syllogisms will be treated in greater depth in Chapter 5, but for now we will say that a **categorical syllogism** is a syllogism in which each statement begins with one of the words "all," "no," or "some." Example:

> All ancient forests are sources of wonder.
> Some ancient forests are targets of the timber industry.
> Therefore, some sources of wonder are targets of the timber industry.

Arguments such as these are nearly always best treated as deductive.

A **hypothetical syllogism** is a syllogism having a conditional ("if ... then") statement for one or both of its premises. Examples:

> If estate taxes are abolished, then wealth will accumulate disproportionately.
> If wealth accumulates disproportionately, then democracy will be threatened.
> Therefore, if estate taxes are abolished, then democracy will be threatened.

> If Fox News is a propaganda machine, then it misleads its viewers.
> Fox News is a propaganda machine.
> Therefore, Fox News misleads its viewers.

Later in this book, the first of these arguments will be given the more specific name of pure hypothetical syllogism because it is composed exclusively of conditional (hypothetical) statements. The second argument is called a mixed hypothetical syllogism because only one of its component statements is a conditional. Later in this book, the second argument will be given the more specific Latin name *modus ponens.*

A **disjunctive syllogism** is a syllogism having a disjunctive ("either ... or ...") statement. Example:

> Either global warming will be arrested, or hurricanes will become more intense.
> Global warming will not be arrested.
> Therefore, hurricanes will become more intense.

As with hypothetical syllogisms, such arguments are usually best taken as deductive. Hypothetical and disjunctive syllogisms will be treated in greater depth in Chapter 6.

Inductive Argument Forms

In general, inductive arguments are such that the content of the conclusion is in some way intended to "go beyond" the content of the premises. The premises of such an argument typically deal with some subject that is relatively familiar, and the conclusion then moves beyond this to a subject that is less familiar or that little is known about. Such an argument may take any of several forms: predictions about the future, arguments from analogy, inductive generalizations, arguments from authority, arguments based on signs, and causal inferences, to name just a few.

A **prediction** is an argument that proceeds from our knowledge of the past to a claim about the future. For example, someone might argue that because certain meteorological phenomena have been observed to develop over a certain region of central Missouri, a storm will occur there in six hours. Or again, one might argue that because certain fluctuations occurred in the prime interest rate on Friday, the value of the dollar will decrease against foreign currencies on Monday. Nearly everyone realizes that the future cannot be known with certainty; thus, whenever an argument makes a prediction about the future, one is usually justified in considering the argument inductive.

An **argument from analogy** is an argument that depends on the existence of an analogy, or similarity, between two things or states of affairs. Because of the existence of this analogy, a certain condition that affects the better-known thing or situation is concluded to affect the similar, lesser-known thing or situation. For example, someone might argue that because Christina's Porsche is a great-handling car, it follows that Angela's Porsche must also be a great-handling car. The argument depends on the existence of a similarity, or analogy, between the two cars. The certitude attending such an inference is probabilistic at best.

A **generalization** is an argument that proceeds from the knowledge of a selected sample to some claim about the whole group. Because the members of the sample have a certain characteristic, it is argued that all the members of the group have that same characteristic. For example, one might argue that because three oranges selected from a certain crate were especially tasty and juicy, all the oranges from that crate are especially tasty and juicy. Or again, one might argue that because six out of a total of nine members sampled from a certain labor union intend to vote for Johnson for union president, two-thirds of the entire membership intend to vote for Johnson. These examples illustrate the use of statistics in inductive argumentation.

An **argument from authority** is an argument that concludes something is true because a presumed expert or witness has said that it is. For example, a person might argue that earnings for Hewlett-Packard Corporation will be up in the coming quarter because of a statement to that effect by an investment counselor. Or a lawyer might argue that Mack the Knife committed the murder because an eyewitness testified to that effect under oath. Because the investment counselor and the eyewitness could be either mistaken or lying, such arguments are essentially probabilistic.

An **argument based on signs** is an argument that proceeds from the knowledge of a sign to a claim about the thing or situation that the sign symbolizes. The word "sign," as it is used here, means any kind of message (usually visual) produced by an intelligent being. For example, when driving on an unfamiliar highway one might see a sign indicating that the road makes several sharp turns one mile ahead. Based on this information, one might argue that the road does indeed make several sharp turns one mile ahead. Because the sign might be misplaced or in error about the turns, the conclusion is only probable.

A **causal inference** is an argument that proceeds from knowledge of a cause to a claim about an effect, or, conversely, from knowledge of an effect to a claim about a cause. For example, from the knowledge that a bottle of wine had been accidentally left in the freezer overnight, someone might conclude that it had frozen (cause to effect). Conversely, after tasting a piece of chicken and finding it dry and tough, one might conclude that it had been overcooked (effect to cause). Because specific instances of cause and effect can never be known with absolute certainty, one may usually interpret such arguments as inductive.

Further Considerations

It should be noted that the various subspecies of inductive arguments listed here are not intended to be mutually exclusive. Overlaps can and do occur. For example, many causal inferences that proceed from cause to effect also qualify as predictions. The purpose of this survey is not to demarcate in precise terms the various forms of induction but rather to provide guidelines for distinguishing induction from deduction.

Keeping this in mind, we should take care not to confuse arguments in geometry, which are always deductive, with arguments from analogy or inductive generalizations. For example, an argument concluding that a triangle has a certain attribute (such as a right angle) because another triangle, with which it is congruent, also has that attribute might be mistaken for an argument from analogy. Similarly, an argument that concludes that all triangles have a certain attribute (such as angles totaling two right angles) because any particular triangle has that attribute might be mistaken for an inductive generalization. Arguments such as these, however, are always deductive, because the conclusion follows necessarily and with complete certainty from the premises.

One broad classification of arguments not listed in this survey is scientific arguments. Arguments that occur in science can be either inductive or deductive, depending on the circumstances. In general, arguments aimed at the *discovery* of a law of nature are usually considered inductive. Suppose, for example, that we want to discover a law that governs the time required for a falling body to strike the earth. We drop bodies of various weights from various heights and measure the time it takes them to fall. Comparing our measurements, we notice that the time is approximately proportional to the square root of the distance. From this we conclude that the time required for any body to fall is proportional to the square root of the distance through which it falls. Such an argument is best interpreted as an inductive generalization.

Another type of argument that occurs in science has to do with the *application* of known laws to specific circumstances. Scientific laws are widely considered to be generalizations that hold for all times and all places. As so understood, their application to a specific situation is always deductive, even though it might relate to the future. Suppose, for example, that we want to apply Boyle's law for ideal gases to a container of gas in our laboratory. Boyle's law states that the pressure exerted by a gas on the walls of its container is inversely proportional to the volume. Applying this law, we conclude that when we reduce the volume of our laboratory sample by half, the pressure will double. This application of Boyle's law is deductive, even though it pertains to the future.

A final point needs to be made about the distinction between inductive and deductive arguments. There is a tradition extending back to the time of Aristotle that holds that inductive arguments are those that proceed from the particular to the general, while deductive arguments are those that proceed from the general to the particular. (A **particular statement** is one that makes a claim about one or more particular members of a class, while a **general statement** makes a claim about *all* the members of a class.) It is true, of course, that many inductive and deductive arguments do work in this way; but this fact should not be used as a criterion for distinguishing induction from deduction. As a matter of fact, there are deductive arguments that proceed from the general to the general, from the particular to the particular, and from the particular to the general, as well as from the general to the particular; and there are inductive arguments that do the same. For example, here is a deductive argument that proceeds from the particular to the general:

> Three is a prime number.
> Five is a prime number.
> Seven is a prime number.
> Therefore, all odd numbers between two and eight are prime numbers.

And here is one that proceeds from the particular to the particular:

> Gabriel is a wolf.
> Gabriel has a tail.
> Therefore, Gabriel's tail is the tail of a wolf.

Here is an inductive argument that proceeds from the general to the particular:

> All emeralds previously found have been green.
> Therefore, the next emerald to be found will be green.

The other varieties are easy to construct. Thus, the progression from particular to general, and vice versa, cannot be used as a criterion for distinguishing induction from deduction.

Summary

To distinguish deductive arguments from inductive arguments, we attempt to evaluate the strength of the argument's inferential claim—how strongly the conclusion is claimed to follow from the premises. This claim is an objective feature of an argument, and it may or may not be related to the subjective intentions of the arguer.

MindTap   Need help? See the Learning Logic folder at the end of the chapter: The self-paced tutorial walks you through any section.

To interpret an argument's inferential claim we look at three factors: special indicator words, the actual strength of the inferential link between premises and conclusion, and the form or style of argumentation. Given that we have more than one factor to look at, it is possible in a single argument for the occurrence of two of these factors to conflict with each other, leading to opposite interpretations. For example, in drawing a conclusion to a categorical syllogism (which is clearly deductive), an arguer might say "It probably follows that . . ." (which suggests induction). To help alleviate this conflict we can list the factors in order of importance:

1. Arguments in which the premises provide absolute support for the conclusion. Such arguments are always deductive.

2. Arguments having a specific deductive character or form (e.g., categorical syllogism). This factor is often of equal importance to the first, and, when present, it provides a clear-cut indication that the argument is deductive.

3. Arguments having a specific inductive character or form (e.g., a prediction). Arguments of this sort are nearly always best interpreted as inductive.

4. Arguments containing inductive indicator language (e.g., "It probably follows that . . ."). Since arguers rarely try to make their argument appear weaker than it really is, such language can usually be trusted. But if this language conflicts with one of the first two factors, it should be ignored.

5. Arguments containing deductive indicator language (e.g., "It necessarily follows that . . ."). Arguers occasionally use such language for rhetorical purposes, to make their argument appear stronger than it really is, so such language should be evaluated carefully.

6. Arguments in which the premises provide only probable support for the conclusion. This is the least important factor, and if it conflicts with any of the earlier ones, it should probably be ignored.

Unfortunately, many arguments in ordinary language are incomplete, so it often happens that none of these factors are clearly present. Determining the inductive or deductive character of such arguments may be impossible.

EXERCISE 1.3

I. Determine whether the following arguments are best interpreted as being inductive or deductive. Also state the criteria you use in reaching your decision (i.e., the presence of indicator words, the nature of the inferential link between premises and conclusion, or the character or form of argumentation).

MindTap® Complete exercises online for immediate feedback.

★1. Because triangle A is congruent with triangle B, and triangle A is isosceles, it follows that triangle B is isosceles.

2. The plaque on the Leaning Tower of Pisa says that Galileo performed experiments there with falling objects. It must be the case that Galileo did indeed perform those experiments there.

3. The rainfall in Seattle has been more than 15 inches every year for the past thirty years. Therefore, the rainfall next year will probably be more than 15 inches.

★4. No e-mail messages are eloquent creations. Some love letters are eloquent creations. Therefore, some love letters are not e-mail messages.

5. Amoco, Exxon, and Texaco are all listed on the New York Stock Exchange. It must be the case that all major American oil companies are listed on the New York Stock Exchange.

6. The longer a pendulum is, the longer it takes to swing. Therefore, when the pendulum of a clock is lengthened, the clock slows down.

★7. Paying off terrorists in exchange for hostages is not a wise policy, since such action will only lead them to take more hostages in the future.

8. The Matterhorn is higher than Mount Whitney, and Mount Whitney is higher than Mount Rainier. The obvious conclusion is that the Matterhorn is higher than Mount Rainier.

9. Although both front and rear doors were found open after the burglary, there were pry marks around the lock on the rear door and deposits of mud near the threshold. It must be the case that the thief entered through the rear door and left through the front.

★10. The *Wall Street Journal* has an article on the new banking regulations. The *Financial Times,* like the *Wall Street Journal,* is a highly respected business publication. Therefore, the *Financial Times* probably also has an article on the new banking regulations.

11. Cholesterol is endogenous with humans. Therefore, it is manufactured inside the human body.

12. Either classical culture originated in Greece, or it originated in Egypt. Classical culture did not originate in Egypt. Therefore, classical culture originated in Greece.

★13. World-renowned physicist Stephen Hawking says that the condition of the universe at the instant of the big bang was more highly ordered than it is today. In view of Hawking's stature in the scientific community, we should conclude that this description of the universe is correct.

14. If Elon Musk is right about artificial intelligence, then artificial intelligence poses a risk to human survival. Elon Musk is right about artificial intelligence. Therefore, artificial intelligence poses a risk to human survival.

15. Crater Lake, the deepest lake in the United States, was caused by a huge volcanic eruption 7,700 years ago. Since human beings have lived around the mountain for more than 10,000 years, it is likely that people witnessed that eruption.
(National Park Service, "Crater Lake—Its History")

★16. Each element, such as hydrogen and iron, has a set of gaps—wavelengths that it absorbs rather than radiates. So if those wavelengths are missing from the spectrum, you know that that element is present in the star you are observing.
(Rick Gore, "Eyes of Science")

17. Because the apparent daily movement which is common to both the planets and the fixed stars is seen to travel from the east to the west, but the far-slower single movements of the single planets travel in the opposite direction from west to east, it is therefore certain that these movements cannot depend on the common movement of the world but should be assigned to the planets themselves.
(Johannes Kepler, *Epitomy of Copernican Astronomy*)

18. Contrary to the common notion that women tend to be chatty compared to men, little difference exists between the sexes in terms of talkativeness. Over a five-year period researchers placed unobtrusive microphones on 396 college students in various fields, at campuses in Mexico as well as in the United States. They found that both men and women spoke about 16,000 words per day.
(Richard T. Schaefer, *Sociology: A Brief Introduction*, 8th ed.)

★19. When the Romans occupied England, coal was burned. Since coal produces quite a bit of soot and sulfur dioxide, there must have been days almost 2,000 years ago when the air in the larger towns was badly polluted.
(Stanley Gedzelman, *The Science and Wonders of the Atmosphere*)

20. The graphical method for solving a system of equations is an approximation, since reading the point of intersection depends on the accuracy with which the lines are drawn and on the ability to interpret the coordinates of the point.
(Karl J. Smith and Patrick J. Boyle, *Intermediate Algebra for College Students*)

21. That [the moons of Jupiter] revolve in unequal circles is manifestly deduced from the fact that at the longest elongation from Jupiter it is never possible to see two of these moons in conjunction, whereas in the vicinity of Jupiter they are found united two, three, and sometimes all four together.
(Galileo Galilei, *The Starry Messenger*)

★22. Lenses function by refracting light at their surfaces. Consequently, their action depends not only on the shape of the lens surfaces, but also on the indices of refraction of the lens material and the surrounding medium.
(Frank J. Blatt, *Principles of Physics*, 2nd ed.)

23. Given present growth rates in underdeveloped countries, the limited practice of birth control, and the difficulty of slowing the current growth momentum, it can be said with virtual certainty that none of the people now reading this book will ever live in a world where the population is not growing.
(J. John Palen, *Social Problems*)

24. The interpretation of the laws is the proper and peculiar province of the courts. A constitution is, in fact, and must be regarded by the judges, as a fundamental law. It therefore belongs to them to ascertain its meaning, as well as the meaning of any particular act proceeding from the legislative body.

(Alexander Hamilton, *Federalist Papers,* No. 78)

★25. The Simpson incident had shown me that a dog was kept in the stables, and yet, though someone had been in and had fetched out a horse, he had not barked enough to arouse the two lads in the loft. Obviously the midnight visitor was someone whom the dog knew well.

(A. Conan Doyle, *Memoirs of Sherlock Holmes*)

26. Eternity is simultaneously whole. But time has a before and an after. Therefore time and eternity are not the same thing.

(Thomas Aquinas, *Summa Theologica*)

27. Ordinary things that we encounter every day are electrically neutral. Therefore, since negatively charged electrons are a part of everything, positively charged particles must also exist in all matter.

(James E. Brady and Gerard E. Humiston, *General Chemistry*)

★28. Animals that live on plant foods must eat large quantities of vegetation, and this consumes much of their time. Meat eaters, by contrast, have no need to eat so much or so often. Consequently, meat-eating hominines [early humans] may have had more leisure time available to explore and manipulate their environment; like lions and leopards, they would have time to spend lying around and playing.

(William A. Haviland, *Cultural Anthropology*, 8th ed.)

29. We tell people not to speed, but equip cars with air bags in case they do. So what's wrong with telling kids not to have sex, but making Plan B available in case they do?

(Susan Beck, letter to the editor)

30. Because the moon moves relative to the earth so that it returns to the same position overhead after about 25 hours, there are two high and two low tides at any point every 25 hours.

(Douglas C. Giancoli, *The Ideas of Physics*, 3rd ed.)

II. Define the following terms:

deductive argument	prediction
inductive argument	argument from analogy
argument based on	generalization
mathematics	argument from authority
argument from definition	argument based on signs
categorical syllogism	causal inference
hypothetical syllogism	particular statement
disjunctive syllogism	general statement

III. Answer "true" or "false" to the following statements:

1. In an inductive argument, it is intended that the conclusion contain more information than the premises.

2. In a deductive argument, the conclusion is not supposed to contain more information than the premises.

3. The form of argumentation the arguer uses may allow one to determine whether an argument is inductive or deductive.

4. The actual strength of the link between premises and conclusion may allow one to determine whether an argument is inductive or deductive.

5. A geometrical proof is an example of an inductive argument.

6. Most arguments based on statistical reasoning are deductive.

7. If the conclusion of an argument follows merely from the definition of a word used in a premise, the argument is deductive.

8. An argument that draws a conclusion about a thing based on that thing's similarity to something else is a deductive argument.

9. An argument that draws a conclusion that something is true because someone has said that it is, is a deductive argument.

10. An argument that presents two alternatives and eliminates one, leaving the other as the conclusion, is an inductive argument.

11. An argument that proceeds from knowledge of a cause to knowledge of an effect is an inductive argument.

12. If an argument contains the phrase "it definitely follows that," then we know for certain that the argument is deductive.

13. An argument that predicts what will happen in the future, based on what has happened in the past, is an inductive argument.

14. Inductive arguments always proceed from the particular to the general.

15. Deductive arguments always proceed from the general to the particular.

IV. Page through a book, magazine, or newspaper and find two arguments, one inductive and the other deductive. Copy the arguments as written, giving the appropriate reference. Then identify the premises and conclusion of each.

V. Create the following deductive and inductive arguments:

1. A categorical syllogism involving groups of people

2. A disjunctive syllogism dealing with corporations

3. A hypothetical syllogism relating to the environment

4. A prediction relating to the economy

5. A generalization relating to students in a math class

6. An argument from analogy relating to two individual people

7. A causal inference about a car accident

MindTap® Master concepts and improve outcomes with Aplia, at the end of the chapter, in the Aplia folder.

Validity, Truth, Soundness, Strength, Cogency

HOW LOGICAL ARE YOU? Instagram does not allow the posting of photos. Therefore, you will not be allowed to post any of your selfies on Instagram, and you will not be able to see any photos of your friends on Instagram. Does this conclusion follow from the premise? Why or why not?

Find the answer on MindTap.

This section introduces the central ideas and terminology needed to evaluate arguments—to distinguish good arguments from bad arguments. Regardless of the type of argument, whether deductive or inductive, the evaluation of any argument involves answering two distinct questions: (1) Do the premises support the conclusion? (2) Are all the premises true? The answer to the first question is the more important one, because if the premises fail to support the conclusion (that is, if the reasoning is bad), the argument is worthless. The material that follows first considers deductive arguments and then inductive.

Deductive Arguments

The previous section defined a deductive argument as one incorporating the claim that it is impossible for the conclusion to be false given that the premises are true. If this claim is true, the argument is said to be valid. Thus, a **valid deductive argument** is an argument in which it is impossible for the conclusion to be false given that the premises are true. In these arguments the conclusion follows with strict necessity from the premises. Conversely, an **invalid deductive argument** is a deductive argument in which it *is* possible for the conclusion to be false given that the premises are true. In these arguments the conclusion does not follow with strict necessity from the premises, even though it is claimed to.

An immediate consequence of these definitions is that there is no middle ground between valid and invalid. There are no arguments that are "almost" valid and "almost" invalid. If the conclusion follows with strict necessity from the premises, the argument is valid; if not, it is invalid.

To test an argument for validity we begin by assuming that all the premises are true, and then we determine if it is possible, in light of that assumption, for the conclusion to be false. Here is an example:

> All television networks are media companies.
> NBC is a television network.
> Therefore, NBC is a media company.

In this argument both premises are actually true, so it is easy to *assume* that they are true. Next we determine, in light of this assumption, if it is possible for the conclusion to be false. Clearly this is not possible. If NBC is included in the group of television networks (second premise) and if the group of television networks is included in the group of media companies (first premise), it necessarily follows that NBC is included in the group of media companies (conclusion). In other words, assuming the premises to be true and the conclusion false entails a strict *contradiction*. Thus, the argument is valid.

Here is another example:

> All automakers are computer manufacturers.
> United Airlines is an automaker.
> Therefore, United Airlines is a computer manufacturer.

In this argument, both premises are actually false, but it is easy to assume that they are true. Every automaker could have a corporate division that manufactures computers. Also, in addition to flying airplanes, United Airlines could make cars. Next, in light of these assumptions, we determine if it is possible for the conclusion to be false. Again, we see that this is not possible, by the same reasoning as the previous example. Assuming the premises to be true and the conclusion false entails a contradiction. Thus, the argument is valid.

Another example:

> All banks are financial institutions.
> Wells Fargo is a financial institution.
> Therefore, Wells Fargo is a bank.

As in the first example, both premises of this argument are true, so it is easy to assume they are true. Next we determine, in light of this assumption, if it is possible for the conclusion to be false. In this case it *is* possible. If banks were included in one part of the group of financial institutions and Wells Fargo were included in another part, then Wells Fargo would *not* be a bank. In other words, assuming the premises to be true and the conclusion false does not involve any contradiction, and so the argument is invalid.

In addition to illustrating the basic idea of validity, these examples suggest an important point about validity and truth. In general, validity is not something that is uniformly determined by the actual truth or falsity of the premises and conclusion. Both the NBC example and the Wells Fargo example have actually true premises and an actually true conclusion, yet one is valid and the other invalid. The United Airlines example has actually false premises and an actually false conclusion, yet the argument is valid. Rather, validity is something that is determined by the *relationship* between premises and conclusion. The question is not whether the premises and conclusion are true or false, but whether the premises *support* the conclusion. In the examples of valid arguments the premises do support the conclusion, and in the invalid case they do not.

Nevertheless, there is *one* arrangement of truth and falsity in the premises and conclusion that does determine the issue of validity. Any deductive argument having actually true premises and an actually false conclusion is invalid. The reasoning behind this fact is fairly obvious. If the premises are actually true and the conclusion is actually false, then it certainly is *possible* for the premises to be true and the conclusion false. Thus, by the definition of invalidity, the argument is invalid.

The idea that any deductive argument having actually true premises and a false conclusion is invalid may be the most important point in all of deductive logic. The entire system of deductive logic would be quite useless if it accepted as valid any inferential process by which a person could start with truth in the premises and arrive at falsity in the conclusion.

Table 1.1 presents examples of categorical syllogisms (deductive arguments) that illustrate the various combinations of truth and falsity in the premises and conclusion. In the examples having false premises, both premises are false, but it is easy to construct other examples having only one false premise. When examining this table, note that the only combination of truth and falsity that does not allow for *both* valid and invalid arguments is true premises and false conclusion. As we have just seen, any argument having this combination is necessarily invalid.

TABLE 1.1 Deductive Arguments

	Valid	Invalid
True premises **True conclusion**	All flowers are plants. All daisies are flowers. Therefore, all daisies are plants. **[sound]**	All flowers are plants. All daisies are plants. *plants* Therefore, all daisies are flowers. **[unsound]**
True premises **False conclusion**	None exist	All roses are flowers. All daisies are flowers. Therefore, all daisies are roses. **[unsound]**
False premises **True conclusion**	All flowers are dogs. All poodles are flowers. Therefore, all poodles are dogs. **[unsound]**	All dogs are flowers. All poodles are flowers. Therefore, all poodles are dogs. **[unsound]**
False premises **False conclusion**	All flowers are dogs. All tigers are flowers. Therefore, all tigers are dogs. **[unsound]**	All roses are cats. All daisies are cats. Therefore, all daisies are roses. **[unsound]**

The relationship between the validity of a deductive argument and the truth or falsity of its premises and conclusion, as illustrated in Table 1.1, is summarized as follows:

Premises	Conclusion	Validity
T	T	?
T	F	Invalid
F	T	?
F	F	?

This short summary table reinforces the point that merely knowing the truth or falsity of the premises and conclusion tells us nothing about validity except in the one case of true premises and false conclusion. Any deductive argument having true premises and a false conclusion is necessarily invalid.

A **sound argument** is a deductive argument that is *valid* and has *all true premises.* Both conditions must be met for an argument to be sound; if either is missing the argument is unsound. Thus, an **unsound argument** is a deductive argument that is invalid, has one or more false premises, or both. Because a valid argument is one such that it is impossible for the premises to be true and the conclusion false, and because a sound argument does in fact have true premises, it follows that every sound argument, by definition, will have a true conclusion as well. A sound argument, therefore, is what is meant by a good, or successful, deductive argument in the fullest sense of the term.

In connection with this definition of soundness, a single proviso is required: For an argument to be unsound, the false premise or premises must actually be needed to support the conclusion. An argument having a conclusion that is validly supported by true premises but having a superfluous false premise would still be sound. By similar reasoning, no addition of a false premise to an originally sound argument can make the argument unsound. Such a premise would be superfluous and should not be considered part of the argument. Analogous remarks, incidentally, extend to induction.

Since (at least from the standpoint of logic) every premise is either true or false, and every deductive argument is either valid or invalid, it follows that every deductive argument is either sound or unsound. However, given that many, if not most, premises have truth values that are unknown or impossible to determine, it is not always possible to determine the soundness of a deductive argument. But that does not mean that soundness is unimportant in logic. It is crucially important that soundness be recognized as a criterion of evaluation that is distinct from validity and that the evaluator be ever vigilant never to confuse soundness with validity.

Inductive Arguments

Section 1.3 defined an inductive argument as one incorporating the claim that it is improbable that the conclusion be false given that the premises are true. If this claim is true, the argument is said to be strong. Thus, a **strong inductive argument** is an inductive argument in which it is improbable that the conclusion be false given that the premises are true. In such arguments, the conclusion does in fact follow probably from the premises. Conversely, a **weak inductive argument** is an argument in which the conclusion does not follow probably from the premises, even though it is claimed to.

All inductive arguments depend on what philosophers call the uniformity of nature. According to this principle, the future tends to replicate the past, and regularities that prevail in one spatial region tend to prevail in other regions. For example, in the past, sugar has always tasted sweet. According to the uniformity of nature, sugar will continue to taste sweet in the future. Also, just as sugar tastes sweet in Los Angeles, so does it in New York, London, and everywhere else. The uniformity of nature is the ultimate basis for our judgments about what we naturally expect to occur. Good inductive arguments are those that accord with the uniformity of nature. They have conclusions that we naturally expect to turn out true. If the conclusion of such an argument should turn out to be false, in violation of our expectations, this occurrence would cause us to react with surprise.

The procedure for testing the strength of inductive arguments runs parallel to the procedure for deduction. First we assume the premises are true, and then we determine whether, based on that assumption, the conclusion is probably true. This determination is accomplished by linking up the premises with regularities that exist in our experiential background. For example, if the argument is a causal inference, we link the information in the premises with known causal patterns. If the argument is an argument from signs, we connect the information in the premises with what we know about signs: some kinds of signs are trustworthy, others are not. If the argument is a generalization, we connect the information in the premises with what we know about a sample being representative of a population. All of these regularities are instances of the uniformity of nature. Here is an example of a prediction:

> All dinosaur bones discovered to this day have been at least 50 million years old. Therefore, probably the next dinosaur bone to be found will be at least 50 million years old.

In this argument the premise is actually true. Given that all dinosaur bones discovered to date have been over 50 million years old (and that thousands of such bones have been discovered), the uniformity of nature dictates that the next one to be discovered will also be over 50 million years old. This is what we would naturally expect, and anything to the contrary would be highly surprising. Thus, the conclusion is probably true, and so the argument is strong.

Here is another example:

> All meteorites found to this day have contained salt. Therefore, probably the next meteorite to be found will contain salt.

The premise of this argument is clearly false; but if we assume it to be true, then we would naturally expect that the next meteorite to be found would contain salt. Thus, the argument is strong.

The next example is an argument from analogy:

> Dom Pérignon champagne, which is made in France, sells for over $100 per bottle. Marquis de la Tour is also a French champagne. Therefore probably it, too, sells for over $100 per bottle.

In this argument the premises are actually true, but our background experience tells us that the mere fact that two wines come from the same country does not imply that they sell for the same price. Thus, the argument is weak. The conclusion, incidentally, happens to be false.

Another example:

> During the past fifty years, inflation has consistently reduced the value of the American dollar. Therefore, industrial productivity will probably increase in the years ahead.

In this argument, the premise is actually true and the conclusion is probably true in the actual world, but the probability of the conclusion is in no way based on the assumption that the premise is true. Because there is no direct connection between inflation and increased industrial productivity, the premise is irrelevant to the conclusion and it provides no probabilistic support for it. The conclusion is probably true independently of the premise. As a result, the argument is weak.

This last example illustrates an important distinction between strong inductive arguments and valid deductive arguments. As we will see in later chapters, if the conclusion of a deductive argument is necessarily true independently of the premises, the argument is still considered valid. But if the conclusion of an inductive argument is probably true independently of the premises, the argument is weak.

These four examples show that in general the strength or weakness of an inductive argument results not from the actual truth or falsity of the premises and conclusion, but from the probabilistic support the premises give to the conclusion. The dinosaur-bone argument has a true premise and a probably true conclusion, and the meteorite argument has a false premise and a probably false conclusion; yet both are strong because the premise of each provides probabilistic support for the conclusion. The industrial productivity argument has a true premise and a probably true conclusion, but the argument is weak because the premise provides no probabilistic support for the conclusion. As in the evaluation of deductive arguments, the only arrangement of truth and falsity that establishes anything is true premises and probably false conclusion (as in the Dom Pérignon argument). Any inductive argument having true premises and a probably false conclusion is weak.

TABLE 1.2 Inductive Arguments

	Strong	Weak
True premise **Probably true conclusion**	Every previous U.S. president was older than 40. Therefore, probably the next U.S. president will be older than 40. **[cogent]**	A few U.S. presidents were lawyers. Therefore, probably the next U.S. president will be older than 40. **[uncogent]**
True premise **Probably false conclusion**	None exist	A few U.S. presidents were unmarried. Therefore, probably the next U.S. president will be unmarried. **[uncogent]**
False premise **Probably true conclusion**	Every previous U.S. president was a TV debater. Therefore, probably the next U.S. president will be a TV debater. **[uncogent]**	A few U.S. presidents were dentists. Therefore, probably the next U.S. president will be a TV debater. **[uncogent]**
False premise **Probably false conclusion**	Every previous U.S. president died in office. Therefore, probably the next U.S. president will die in office. **[uncogent]**	A few U.S. presidents were dentists. Therefore, probably the next U.S. president will be a dentist. **[uncogent]**

Before proceeding further, however, we must qualify and explain this last statement. When we speak of the premises being true, we mean "true" in a complete sense. The premises must not exclude or overlook some crucial piece of evidence that undermines the stated premises and requires a different conclusion. This proviso is otherwise called the *total evidence requirement*. If the total evidence requirement is not met, an argument might have literally true premises and a probably false conclusion and still be strong. Also, when we speak of the conclusion being probably false, we mean probably false in the actual world in light of all the known evidence.

Table 1.2 presents several predictions (inductive arguments) that illustrate the various combinations of truth and falsity in the premises and conclusion. Note that the only arrangement of truth and falsity that is missing for strong arguments is true premises and probably false conclusion.

The relationship between the strength of an inductive argument and the truth or falsity of its premises and conclusion, as illustrated in Table 1.2, is summarized as follows:

Premises	Conclusion	Strength
T	probably T	?
T	probably F	Weak
F	probably T	?
F	probably F	?

Like the summary table for deduction, this brief table reinforces the point that merely knowing the truth values of the premises and conclusion tells us nothing about the strength of an argument except in the one case of true premises and probably false conclusion. Any inductive argument having true premises (in the sense just explained) and a probably false conclusion is weak.

Unlike the validity and invalidity of deductive arguments, the strength and weakness of inductive arguments allow for degrees. To be considered strong, an inductive argument must have a conclusion that is more probable than improbable. In other words, given that the premises are true, the likelihood that the conclusion is true must be more than 50 percent, and as the probability increases, the argument becomes stronger. For this purpose, consider the following pair of arguments:

> This barrel contains 100 apples.
> Three apples selected at random were found to be ripe.
> Therefore, probably all 100 apples are ripe.

> This barrel contains 100 apples.
> Eighty apples selected at random were found to be ripe.
> Therefore, probably all 100 apples are ripe.

The first argument is weak and the second is strong. However, the first is not absolutely weak nor the second absolutely strong. Both arguments would be strengthened or weakened by the random selection of a larger or smaller sample. For example, if the size of the sample in the second argument were reduced to seventy apples, the argument would be weakened. The incorporation of additional premises into an inductive argument will also generally tend to strengthen or weaken it. For example, if the premise "One unripe apple that had been found earlier was removed" were added to either argument, the argument would be weakened.

A **cogent argument** is an inductive argument that is *strong* and has *all true premises*. Also, the premises must be true in the sense of meeting the *total evidence requirement*. If any one of these conditions is missing, the argument is *uncogent*. Thus, an **uncogent argument** is an inductive argument that is weak, has one or more false premises, fails to meet the total evidence requirement, or any combination of these. A cogent argument is the inductive analogue of a sound deductive argument and is what is meant by a good, or successful, inductive argument without qualification. Because the conclusion of a cogent argument is genuinely supported by true premises, it follows that the conclusion of every cogent argument is probably true in the actual world in light of all the known evidence.

As an illustration of the need for the total evidence requirement, consider the following argument:

> Swimming in the Caribbean is usually lots of fun. Today the water is warm, the surf is gentle, and on this beach there are no dangerous currents. Therefore, it would be fun to go swimming here now.

If the premises reflect all the important factors, then the argument is cogent. But if they ignore the fact that several large dorsal fins are cutting through the water (suggesting sharks), then obviously the argument is not cogent. Thus, for cogency the premises must not only be true but also not overlook some important fact that requires a different conclusion.

Finally, just as it is not always possible to determine the soundness of a deductive argument, it is not always possible to determine the cogency of an inductive argument. And this follows for two reasons. Many inductive arguments, especially those about complex real-life subjects, are not susceptible to being evaluated as clearly strong or clearly weak. And many premises have truth values that are unknown or impossible to determine. Yet, it remains important that cogency be recognized as a criterion for evaluating inductive arguments and that it not be confused with strength and weakness.

MindTap Strengthen your understanding of the topic with the section's **Video Lectures**.

Summary

For both deductive and inductive arguments, two separate questions need to be answered: (1) Do the premises support the conclusion? (2) Are all the premises true? To answer the first question we begin by *assuming* the premises to be true. Then, for deductive arguments we determine whether, in light of this *assumption*, it necessarily follows that the conclusion is true. If it does, the argument is valid; if not, it is invalid. For inductive arguments we determine whether it probably follows that the conclusion is true. If it does, the argument is strong; if not, it is weak. For inductive arguments we keep in mind the requirements that the premises actually support the conclusion and that they not ignore important evidence. Finally, if the argument is either valid or strong, we turn to the second question and determine whether the premises are actually true. If all the premises are true, the argument is sound (in the case of deduction) or cogent (in the case of induction). All invalid deductive arguments are unsound, and all weak inductive arguments are uncogent.

The various alternatives open to statements and arguments may be diagrammed as follows. Note that in logic one never speaks of an argument as being "true" or "false," and one never speaks of a statement as being "valid," "invalid," "strong," or "weak."

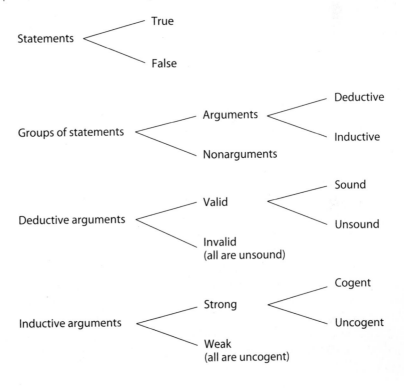

MindTap° See the Learning Logic folder at the end of the chapter: The self-paced tutorial walks you through any section.

Chrysippus was born in Soli, a city located on the southeast coast of Asia Minor. Early in life he moved to Athens, where he studied under the Stoic philosopher Cleanthes, who in turn was a student of Zeno of Citium, the founder of Stoicism. Upon Cleanthes' death in 232 B.C.E., Chrysippus took over as leader of the school, and he produced over 700 treatises that systematized Stoic teaching. All of these works have been lost, but fragments survive in the writings of Cicero, Seneca, and others. Because of his extraordinary contribution, Chrysippus is considered to be the second founder of Stoicism.

Stoicism derives its name from the Greek word *stoa*, which means porch; Stoic philosophers used to gather on a porch in the Agora (public square) in Athens to discuss their views. The Stoics prized the virtue of self-sufficiency, and they emphasized the importance of not allowing oneself to be carried away by emotions or passions such as fear or love. The Stoics considered emotions to be false judgments about the goodness or badness of something. The proper therapy for those victimized by emotions is to persuade them that these judgments are indeed false because they constitute obstacles to true happiness.

Chrysippus is often considered to be the originator of propositional logic. Unlike Aristotelian logic, where the fundamental components are terms, in propositional logic the fundamental components are whole propositions or statements. Aristotle had overlooked this kind of logic, but his close friend and successor Theophrastus worked out some of the logic of the pure hypothetical syllogism (If A then B; If B, then C; therefore, If A, then C). Also, Philo of Megara introduced the truth-functional interpretation of the material conditional (If A, then B). Beginning at this point, Chrysippus advanced propositional logic to a high level of development.

Science Source

Chrysippus divided propositions into simple and compound, and he introduced a set of connectives that were used to produce compound propositions from one or more simple propositions. The compound propositions included negation, conjunction, exclusive disjunction, and implication, and Chrysippus showed how the truth value of a compound statement is a function of the truth values of its simple components. Chrysippus also introduced a set of rules of inference including what is today called *modus ponens, modus tollens,* disjunctive syllogism, and a rule similar to De Morgan's rule. Finally, he introduced the theory of natural deduction by which the conclusion of an argument can be derived from its premises through a series of discrete steps.

The broader philosophy of Chrysippus is characterized by monism and determinism. While most of us think that the universe is made up of millions of discrete entities, Chrysippus argued that in fact only one substance exists, and what appear to be individual substances are really parts of this one primary substance. Furthermore, everything that occurs is strictly governed by fate. Yet, in the face of this rigid causal determinism Chrysippus held that humans are responsible for their actions, and he tried in many ways to prove that the two viewpoints are in fact compatible with each other.

I. The following arguments are deductive. Determine whether each is valid or invalid, and note the relationship between your answer and the truth or falsity of the premises and conclusion. Finally, determine whether the argument is sound or unsound.

valid

★1. Since *Moby Dick* was written by Shakespeare, and *Moby Dick* is a science-fiction novel, it follows that Shakespeare wrote a science-fiction novel.

2. Since London is north of Paris and south of Edinburgh, it follows that Paris is south of Edinburgh.

3. If George Washington was beheaded, then George Washington died. George Washington died. Therefore, George Washington was beheaded.

valid

★4. The longest river in South America is the Amazon, and the Amazon flows through Brazil. Therefore, the longest river in South America flows through Brazil.

5. Since the Spanish-American War occurred before the U.S. Civil War, and the U.S. Civil War occurred after the Korean War, it follows that the Spanish-American War occurred before the Korean War.

6. The Empire State Building is taller than the Statue of Liberty, and the Statue of Liberty is taller than the Eiffel Tower. Therefore, the Empire State Building is taller than the Eiffel Tower.

invalid

★7. All leopards with lungs are carnivores. Therefore, all leopards are carnivores.

8. Chicago is a city in Michigan and Michigan is part of the United States. Therefore, Chicago is a city in the United States.

9. If Queen Elizabeth was born in Los Angeles, then she is a California native. Queen Elizabeth is not a California native. Therefore, Queen Elizabeth was not born in Los Angeles.

valid

★10. Every province in Canada has exactly one city as its capital. Therefore, since there are thirty provinces in Canada, there are thirty provincial capitals.

11. Since the Department of Defense Building outside Washington, D.C., has the shape of a hexagon, it follows that it has seven sides.

12. Since Winston Churchill was English, and Winston Churchill was a famous statesman, we may conclude that at least one Englishman was a famous statesman.

valid

★13. Since some fruits are green, and some fruits are apples, it follows that some fruits are green apples.

14. All physicians are individuals who have earned degrees in political science, and some lawyers are physicians. Therefore, some lawyers are persons who have earned degrees in political science.

MindTap® Complete exercises online for immediate feedback.

15. The United States Congress has more members than there are days in the year. Therefore, at least two members of Congress have the same birthday.

II. The following arguments are inductive. Determine whether each is strong or weak, and note the relationship between your answer and the truth or falsity of the premise(s) and conclusion. Then determine whether each argument is cogent or uncogent.

★1. The grave marker at Arlington National Cemetery says that John F. Kennedy is buried there. It must be the case that Kennedy really is buried in that cemetery.

2. The ebb and flow of the tides has been occurring every day for millions of years. But nothing lasts forever. Therefore, probably the motion of the tides will die out within a few years.

3. The vast majority of Rose Bowl games (in Pasadena, California) have been played in freezing-cold weather. Therefore, probably the next Rose Bowl game will be played in freezing-cold weather.

★4. Franklin Delano Roosevelt said that we have nothing to fear but fear itself. Therefore, people have no reason to fear serial killers.

5. Most popular film stars are millionaires. Shailene Woodley is a popular film star. Therefore, probably Shailene Woodley is a millionaire.

6. Constructing the great pyramid at Giza required lifting massive stone blocks to great heights. Probably the ancient Egyptians had some antigravity device to accomplish this feat.

★7. People have been listening to rock and roll music for over a hundred years. Probably people will still be listening to it a year from now.

8. Paleontologists have unearthed the fossilized bones of huge reptiles, which we have named dinosaurs. Tests indicate that these bones are more than 50 million years old. Therefore, probably dinosaurs really did roam the earth more than 50 million years ago.

9. The Declaration of Independence says that all men are endowed by their creator with certain unalienable rights. Therefore it probably follows that a creator exists.

★10. Coca-Cola is an extremely popular soft drink consumed all over the world. Therefore, probably someone, somewhere, is drinking a Coke right this minute.

11. Every map of the United States shows that Alabama is situated on the Pacific coast. Therefore, Alabama must be a western state.

12. When Neil Armstrong landed on the moon, he left behind a gold-plated Schwinn bicycle, which he used to ride around on the moon's surface. Probably that bicycle is still up there on the moon.

★13. Children love green M&M's. But brussels sprouts are green, too. Therefore, it must be the case that children love brussels sprouts.

14. Unlike monkeys, today's humans have feet that are not suited for grasping objects. Therefore, a thousand years from now, probably humans will still have feet that are not suited for grasping objects.

15. A random sample of twenty-five famous country singers, which included Taylor Swift and Blake Shelton, revealed that every single one of them studied music in Tasmania. Therefore, probably the majority of famous country singers studied music in Tasmania.

III. Determine whether the following arguments are inductive or deductive. If an argument is inductive, determine whether it is strong or weak. If it is deductive, determine whether it is valid or invalid.

★1. Since Tom is the brother of Agatha, and Agatha is the mother of Raquel, it follows that Tom is the uncle of Raquel.

2. When a cook cannot recall the ingredients in a recipe, it is appropriate that she refresh her memory by consulting the recipe book. Similarly, when a student cannot recall the answers during a final exam, it is appropriate that she refresh her memory by consulting the textbook.

3. The Broadway Theater marquee says that *The Phantom of the Opera* is playing nightly. Therefore, it must be that case that *Phantom* is playing there tonight.

★4. Since Christmas is always on a Thursday, it follows that the day after Christmas is always a Friday.

5. Suppose figure A is a triangle having two equal angles. It follows that figure A has two equal sides.

6. By accident Karen baked her brownies two hours longer than she should have. Therefore, they have probably been ruined.

★7. After taking LSD, Alice said she saw a flying saucer land in the shopping center parking lot. Since Alice has a reputation for always telling the truth, we must conclude that a flying saucer really did land there.

8. Since Phyllis is the cousin of Denise, and Denise is the cousin of Harriet, it follows necessarily that Harriet is the cousin of Phyllis.

9. The picnic scheduled in the park for tomorrow will most likely be cancelled. It's been snowing for six days straight.

★10. Circle A has exactly twice the diameter of circle B. From this we may conclude that circle A has exactly twice the area of circle B.

11. Robert has lost consistently at blackjack every day for the past several days. Therefore, it is very likely that he will win today.

12. Since John loves Nancy and Nancy loves Peter, it follows necessarily that John loves Peter.

★13. This cash register drawer contains over 100 coins. Three coins selected at random were found to have dates earlier than 1960. Therefore, probably all of the coins in the drawer have dates earlier than 1960.

14. The Japanese attack on Pearl Harbor happened in either 1941 or 1951. But it didn't happen in 1941. Therefore, it happened in 1951.

15. Harry will never be able to solve that difficult problem in advanced calculus in the limited time allowed. He has never studied anything beyond algebra, and in that he earned only a C−.

★16. Since $x + y = 10$, and $x = 7$, it follows that $y = 4$.

17. If acupuncture is hocus pocus, then acupuncture cannot relieve chronic pain. But acupuncture can relieve chronic pain. Therefore, acupuncture is not hocus pocus.

18. If inflation heats up, then interest rates will rise. If interest rates rise, then bond prices will decline. Therefore, if inflation heats up, then bond prices will decline.

★19. Statistics reveal that 86 percent of those who receive flu shots do not get the flu. Jack received a flu shot one month ago. Therefore, he should be immune, even though the flu is going around now.

20. Since Michael is a Pisces, it necessarily follows that he was born in March.

IV. Define the following terms:

valid deductive argument	strong inductive argument
invalid deductive argument	weak inductive argument
sound argument	cogent argument
unsound argument	uncogent argument

V. Answer "true" or "false" to the following statements:

1. Some arguments, while not completely valid, are almost valid.

2. Inductive arguments allow for varying degrees of strength and weakness.

3. Invalid deductive arguments are basically the same as inductive arguments.

4. If a deductive argument has true premises and a false conclusion, it is necessarily invalid.

5. A valid argument may have a false premise and a false conclusion.

6. A valid argument may have a false premise and a true conclusion.

7. A sound argument may be invalid.

8. A sound argument may have a false conclusion.

9. A strong argument may have false premises and a probably false conclusion.

10. A strong argument may have true premises and a probably false conclusion.

11. A cogent argument may have a probably false conclusion.

12. A cogent argument must be inductively strong.

13. If an argument has true premises and a true conclusion, we know that it is a perfectly good argument.

14. A statement may legitimately be spoken of as "valid" or "invalid."

15. An argument may legitimately be spoken of as "true" or "false."

VI. Create the following sound and cogent arguments:

1. A sound argument about musicians

2. A valid unsound argument about painters

3. An invalid argument about writers

4. A cogent argument relating to politics

5. A weak argument relating to cooking

MindTap® Master concepts and improve outcomes with Aplia, at the end of the chapter, in the Aplia folder.

1.5 Argument Forms: Proving Invalidity

HOW LOGICAL ARE YOU? Your friend Joe argues that climate change as a result of human activity doesn't exist because climates have always been changing. Your friend Claudia replies that Joe's argument is like saying that smoking doesn't cause cancer because people got cancer long before smoking existed. Is Claudia correct?

Find the answer on MindTap.

This section explores the idea that the validity of a deductive argument is determined by its form. This idea was suggested by the arguments in Table 1.1 in the previous section. All the arguments in the Valid column have the same valid form, and all the arguments in the Invalid column have the same invalid form. The form of an argument illustrates the argument's internal structure or pattern of reasoning. If the pattern of reasoning is good, the argument will be valid; if not, it will be invalid.

In reference to Table 1.1, all the valid arguments have this form:

> All A are B.
> All C are A.
> All C are B.

If A, B, and C are thought of as referring to groups of things, it is easy to see that this form is valid. Assume, by the second premise, that the Cs (whatever they might be) are included in the As, and, by the first premise, that the As (whatever they might be) are included in the Bs. Then it necessarily follows that the Cs are included in the Bs, which is what the conclusion asserts.

We can use this example to define what we mean by an argument form. An **argument form**, for the present purpose, is an arrangement of letters (in this case *A*, *B*, and *C*) and words (in this case "all" and "are") such that the uniform substitution of words or phrases in the place of the letters results in an argument. For this form, the words or phrases being substituted must refer to groups of things. Thus, if we substitute "sporting events," "engaging pastimes," and "baseball games" in the place of *A*, *B*, and *C*, respectively, in the argument form (left), we obtain the following argument (right):

All *A* are *B*.	All sporting events are engaging pastimes.
All *C* are *A*.	All baseball games are sporting events.
All *C* are *B*.	All baseball games are engaging pastimes.

This argument is called a **substitution instance** of the argument form. Any substitution instance of a valid argument form is a valid argument.

Before proceeding to invalid arguments, we must briefly consider valid arguments in which the form is not apparent. Many of the arguments in the previous set of exercises were like this. How can we reconcile the existence of such arguments with the claim that validity is determined by form? The answer is that these arguments are incomplete, so the form is not explicit. But once such arguments are completed and correctly phrased (which we address later in this book), the form becomes apparent. For example, consider the following valid argument:

Geese are migratory waterfowl, so they fly south for the winter.

This argument is missing a premise:

Migratory waterfowl fly south for the winter.

The argument can now be rephrased to make its form apparent:

All migratory waterfowl are birds that fly south for the winter.
All geese are migratory waterfowl.
Therefore, all geese are birds that fly south for the winter.

The form of the argument is

All *A* are *B*.
All *C* are *A*.
All *C* are *B*.

This form is identical to the form we just considered and is valid.
Let us now consider an invalid argument form:

All *A* are *B*.
All *C* are *B*.
All *A* are *C*.

In this argument form, if we assume that the *A*s are in the *B*s and that the *C*s are in the *B*s, it does not *necessarily* follow that the *A*s are in the *C*s. It would not follow if the *A*s were in one part of the *B*s and the *C*s were in another part, as the following diagram illustrates:

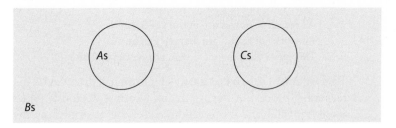

This diagram suggests that we can prove the form invalid if we can find a substitution instance having actually true premises and an actually false conclusion. In such a substitution instance the *A*s and the *C*s would be separated from each other, but they would both be included in the *B*s. If we substitute "cats" for *A,* "animals" for *B,* and "dogs" for *C,* we have such a substitution instance:

All *A* are *B*.	All cats are animals.	True
All *C* are *B*.	All dogs are animals.	True
All *A* are *C*.	Therefore, all cats are dogs.	False

This substitution instance proves the form invalid, because it provides a concrete example of a case where the *A*s are in the *B*s, the *C*s are in the *B*s, but the *A*s are *not* in the *C*s.

Now, since the form is invalid, can we say that any argument that has this form is invalid? Unfortunately, the situation with invalid forms is not quite as simple as it is with valid forms. Every substitution instance of a valid form is a valid argument, but it is not the case that every substitution instance of an invalid form is an invalid argument. The reason is that some substitution instances of invalid forms are also substitution instances of valid forms.* However, we can say that any substitution instance of an invalid form is an invalid argument *provided* that it is not a substitution instance of any valid form. Thus, we will say that an argument actually *has* an invalid form if it is a substitution instance of that form and it is not a substitution instance of any valid form.

The fact that some substitution instances of invalid forms are also substitution instances of valid forms means simply that we must exercise caution in identifying the form of an argument. However, cases of ordinary language arguments that can

---

For example, the following valid argument is a substitution instance of the invalid form we have been discussing:

All bachelors are persons.
All unmarried men are persons.
Therefore, all bachelors are unmarried men.

However, because "bachelors" is equivalent in meaning to "unmarried men," the argument is also a substitution instance of this valid form:

All *A* are *B*.
All *A* are *B*.
All *A* are *A*.

be interpreted as substitution instances of both valid and invalid forms are so rare that this book chooses to ignore them. With this in mind, consider the following argument:

> All romantic novels are literary pieces.
> All works of fiction are literary pieces.
> Therefore, all romantic novels are works of fiction.

This argument clearly has the invalid form just discussed. This invalid form captures the reasoning process of the argument, which is obviously defective. Therefore, the argument is invalid, and it is invalid precisely because it has an invalid form.

Counterexample Method

A substitution instance having true premises and a false conclusion (like the cats-and-dogs example just constructed) is called a counterexample, and the method we have just used to prove the romantic-novels argument invalid is called the **counterexample method**. It consists of isolating the form of an argument and then constructing a substitution instance having true premises and a false conclusion. This proves the form invalid, which in turn proves the argument invalid. The counterexample method can be used to prove the invalidity of any invalid argument, but it cannot prove the validity of any valid argument. Thus, before the method is applied to an argument, the argument must be known or suspected to be invalid in the first place. Let us apply the counterexample method to the following invalid categorical syllogism:

> Since some employees are not social climbers and all vice presidents are employees, we may conclude that some vice presidents are not social climbers.

This argument is invalid because the employees who are not social climbers might not be vice presidents. Accordingly, we can *prove* the argument invalid by constructing a substitution instance having true premises and a false conclusion. We begin by isolating the form of the argument:

> Some E are not S.
> All V are E.
> ———————
> Some V are not S.

Next, we select three terms to substitute in place of the letters that will make the premises true and the conclusion false. The following selection will work:

> E = animals
> S = mammals
> V = dogs

The resulting substitution instance is this:

> Some animals are not mammals.
> All dogs are animals.
> Therefore, some dogs are not mammals.

The substitution instance has true premises and a false conclusion and is therefore, by definition, invalid. Because the substitution instance is invalid, the form is invalid, and therefore the original argument is invalid.

In applying the counterexample method to categorical syllogisms, it is useful to keep in mind the following set of terms: "cats," "dogs," "mammals," "fish," and "animals." Most invalid syllogisms can be proven invalid by strategically selecting three of these terms and using them to construct a counterexample. Because everyone agrees about these terms, everyone will agree about the truth or falsity of the premises and conclusion of the counterexample. Also, in constructing the counterexample, it often helps to begin with the conclusion. First, select two terms that yield a false conclusion, and then select a third term that yields true premises. Another point to keep in mind is that the word "some" in logic always means "at least one." For example, the statement "Some dogs are animals" means "At least one dog is an animal"—which is true. Also note that this statement does not imply that some dogs are not animals.

Not all deductive arguments, of course, are categorical syllogisms. Consider, for example, the following hypothetical syllogism:

> If the government imposes import restrictions, the price of automobiles will rise. Therefore, since the government will not impose import restrictions, it follows that the price of automobiles will not rise.

This argument is invalid because the price of automobiles might rise even though import restrictions are not imposed. It has the following form:

> If G, then P.
> Not G.
> _____
> Not P.

This form differs from the previous one in that its letters stand for complete statements. G, for example, stands for "The government imposes import restrictions." If we make the substitution

> G = Abraham Lincoln committed suicide.
> P = Abraham Lincoln is dead.

we obtain the following substitution instance:

> If Abraham Lincoln committed suicide, then Abraham Lincoln is dead.
> Abraham Lincoln did not commit suicide.
> Therefore, Abraham Lincoln is not dead.

Since the premises are true and the conclusion false, the substitution instance is clearly invalid. Therefore, the form is invalid, and this proves the original argument invalid.

When applying the counterexample method to an argument having a conditional statement as a premise (such as the one just discussed), it is recommended that the statement substituted in place of the conditional statement express some kind of necessary connection. In the Lincoln example, the first premise asserts the necessary connection between suicide and death. There can be no doubt about the truth of such a statement. Furthermore, if it should turn out that the conclusion is a conditional statement, note that one sure way of producing a false conditional statement is by joining a true antecedent with a false consequent. For example, the conditional statement "If Lassie is a dog, then Lassie is a cat" is clearly false.

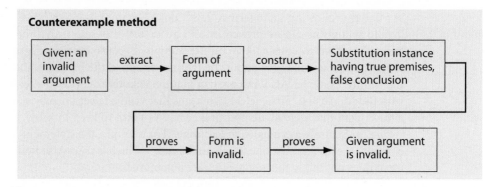

Being able to identify the form of an argument with ease requires a familiarity with the basic deductive argument forms. The first task consists in distinguishing the premises from the conclusion. Always write the premises first and the conclusion last. The second task involves distinguishing what we may call "form words" from "content words." To reduce an argument to its form, leave the form words as they are, and replace the content words with letters. For categorical syllogisms, the words "all," "no," "some," "are," and "not" are form words, and for hypothetical syllogisms the words "if," "then," and "not" are form words. Additional form words for other types of arguments are "either," "or," "both," and "and." For various kinds of hybrid arguments, a more intuitive approach may be needed. Here is an example:

> All movie stars are actors who are famous, because all movie stars who are famous are actors.

If we replace "movie stars," "actors," and "famous" with the letters *M, A,* and *F,* this argument has the following form:

> All *M* who are *F* are *A.*
> All *M* are *A* who are *F.*

Here is one possible substitution instance for this form:

> All humans who are fathers are men.
> Therefore, all humans are men who are fathers.

Because the premise is true and the conclusion false, the form is invalid and so is the original argument.

Using the counterexample method to prove arguments invalid requires a little ingenuity because there is no rule that will automatically produce the required term or statement to be substituted into the form. Any term or statement will work, of course, provided that it yields a substitution instance that has premises that are indisputably true and a conclusion that is indisputably false. Ideally, the truth value of these statements should be known to the average individual; otherwise, the substitution instance cannot be depended on to prove anything. If, for example, *P* in the earlier hypothetical syllogism had been replaced by the statement "George Wilson is dead," the substitution instance would be useless, because nobody knows whether this statement is true or false.

The counterexample method is useful only for proving invalidity, because the only arrangement of truth and falsity that proves anything is true premises and false conclusion. If a substitution instance is produced having true premises and a true conclusion, it does *not* prove that the argument is valid. Furthermore, the method is useful only for deductive arguments because the strength and weakness of inductive arguments is only partially dependent on the form of the argument. Accordingly, no method that relates exclusively to the form of an inductive argument can be used to prove the argument weak.

EXERCISE 1.5

I. Use the counterexample method to prove the following categorical syllogisms invalid. In doing so, follow the suggestions given in the text.

★1. All galaxies are structures that contain black holes in the center, so all galaxies are quasars, since all quasars are structures that contain black holes in the center.

2. Some evolutionists are not people who believe in the Bible, for no creationists are evolutionists, and some people who believe in the Bible are not creationists.

3. No patents are measures that discourage research and development, and all patents are regulations that protect intellectual property. Thus, no measures that discourage research and development are regulations that protect intellectual property.

★4. Some farmworkers are not people who are paid decent wages, because no undocumented individuals are people who are paid decent wages, and some undocumented individuals are not farmworkers.

5. Some politicians are people who will stop at nothing to win an election, and no people who will stop at nothing to win an election are true statesmen. Hence, no politicians are true statesmen.

6. All meticulously constructed timepieces are true works of art, for all Swiss watches are true works of art and all Swiss watches are meticulously constructed timepieces.

★7. No patrons of fast-food restaurants are health-food addicts. Consequently, no patrons of fast-food restaurants are connoisseurs of fine desserts, since no connoisseurs of fine desserts are health-food addicts.

MindTap® Complete exercises online for immediate feedback.

8. Some toxic dumps are sites that emit hazardous wastes, and some sites that emit hazardous wastes are undesirable places to live near. Thus, some toxic dumps are undesirable places to live near.

9. All persons who assist others in suicide are people guilty of murder. Accordingly, some individuals motivated by compassion are not persons guilty of murder, inasmuch as some people who assist others in suicide are individuals motivated by compassion.

★10. Some school boards are not groups that oppose values clarification, because some school boards are not organizations with vision, and some groups that oppose values clarification are not organizations with vision.

11. All super PACs are unlimited spenders. For this reason, some big-time power brokers are not super PACs, inasmuch as some unlimited spenders are big-time power brokers.

12. No movie producers are uncompetitive business executives, and some Hollywood moguls are movie producers. It follows that no Hollywood moguls are uncompetitive business executives.

★13. Some improvers of humankind are not exploiters of personal information. As a result, some corporate social networks are not improvers of humankind, seeing that all corporate social networks are exploiters of personal information.

14. Some drone attacks are assaults on human life, given that some stealth operations are assaults on human life and all drone attacks are stealth operations.

15. Some near-death experiences are supernatural phenomena, and no near-death experiences are easily forgotten happenings. Consequently some easily forgotten happenings are not supernatural phenomena.

II. Use the counterexample method to prove each of the following arguments invalid.

★1. If animal species are fixed and immutable, then evolution is a myth. Therefore, evolution is not a myth, since animal species are not fixed and immutable.

2. If carbon dioxide is present in the atmosphere, then plants have a source of carbon. Hence, since plants have a source of carbon, carbon dioxide is present in the atmosphere.

3. If human rights are recognized, then civilization flourishes. If equality prevails, then civilization flourishes. Thus, if human rights are recognized, then equality prevails.

★4. If energy taxes are increased, then either the deficit will be reduced or conservation will be taken seriously. If the deficit is reduced, then inflation will be checked. Therefore, if energy taxes are increased, then inflation will be checked.

5. All homeless people who are panhandlers are destitute individuals. Therefore, all homeless people are destitute individuals.

6. Some wrestlers are colorful hulks, since some wrestlers are colorful and some wrestlers are hulks.

★7. All community colleges with low tuition are either schools with large enrollments or institutions supported by taxes. Therefore, all community colleges are institutions supported by taxes.

8. All merchandisers that are retailers are businesses that are inventory rotators. Therefore, all merchandisers are inventory rotators.

9. All diabetes victims are either insulin takers or glucose eliminators. Accordingly, some diabetes victims are glucose eliminators, since some diabetes victims are insulin takers.

★10. All FHA loans are living-standard enhancers for the following reasons. All reverse mortgages that are FHA loans are either living-standard enhancers or home-equity depleters, and all reverse mortgages are home-equity depleters.

III. Create the following arguments:

1. Two valid arguments, having the same form, about jobs.

2. Two invalid arguments, having the same form, about fast food.

MindTap Master concepts and improve outcomes with Aplia, at the end of the chapter, in the Aplia folder.

1.6 Extended Arguments

HOW LOGICAL ARE YOU? Suppose, to graduate you must take either a life science or a physical science course. Either algebra or statistics is a prerequisite for enrolling in a life science course, and both calculus and data management are prerequisites for signing up for a physical science course. Also, algebra is a prerequisite for calculus. Draw a diagram illustrating your path to graduation. Based on this diagram, must you take algebra to graduate?

Find the answer on MindTap.

The logical analysis of extended arguments, such as those found in editorials, essays, and lengthy letters to newspaper editors, involves numerous difficulties. Such arguments are often mixed together with fragments of reports, pieces of expository writing, illustrations, explanations, and statements of opinion. Proper analysis involves weeding out the extraneous material and isolating premises and conclusions. Another problem stems from the fact that lengthy arguments often involve complex arrangements of subarguments that feed into the main argument in various ways. Distinguishing one subargument from another is often a complicated task. And then there are some argumentative passages that involve completely separate strands of argumentation leading to separate conclusions. Again, distinguishing the strands and assigning premises to the right conclusion is not only problematic but often involves an element of creativity on the part of the analyst.

To facilitate the analysis of extended arguments, we will assign numerals to the various statements in the passage and use arrows to represent the inferential links. Example:

> ① The contamination of underground aquifers represents a pollution problem of catastrophic proportions. ② Half the nation's drinking water, which comes from these aquifers, is being poisoned by chemical wastes dumped into the soil for generations.

This argument is diagrammed as follows:

The diagram says that statement ②, the premise, supports statement ①, the conclusion.

In extended arguments we can identify two distinct patterns of argumentation, which we will name the vertical pattern and the horizontal pattern. The *vertical pattern* consists of a series of arguments in which a conclusion of a logically prior argument becomes a premise of a subsequent argument. Example:

> ① The selling of human organs, such as hearts, kidneys, and corneas, should be outlawed. ② Allowing human organs to be sold will inevitably lead to a situation in which only the rich will be able to afford transplants. This is so because ③ whenever something scarce is bought and sold as a commodity, the price always goes up. ④ The law of supply and demand requires it.

This argument is diagrammed as follows:

Vertical pattern

The diagram says that statement ①, which is the main conclusion, is supported by ②, which in turn is supported by ③, which in turn is supported by ④.

The *horizontal pattern* consists of a single argument in which two or more premises provide independent support for a single conclusion. If one of the premises were omitted, the other(s) would continue to support the conclusion in the same way. Example:

> ① The selling of human organs, such as hearts, kidneys, and corneas, should be outlawed. ② If this practice is allowed to get a foothold, people in desperate financial straits will start selling their own organs to pay their bills. Alternately, ③ those with a criminal bent

will take to killing healthy young people and selling their organs on the black market. ④ In the final analysis, the buying and selling of human organs comes just too close to the buying and selling of life itself.

The diagram for this argument is as follows:

Horizontal pattern

This diagram says that statements ②, ③, and ④ support ①, independently.

Two variations on the horizontal and vertical patterns occur when two or more premises support a conclusion *conjointly,* and when one or more premises support *multiple* conclusions. The first variation occurs when the premises depend on one another in such a way that if one were omitted, the support that the others provide would be diminished or destroyed. The following argument illustrates the occurrence of conjoint premises:

> ① Getting poor people off the welfare rolls requires that we modify their behavior patterns. ② The vast majority of people on welfare are high school dropouts, single parents, or people who abuse alcohol and drugs. ③ These behavior patterns frustrate any desire poor people may have to get a job and improve their condition in life.

Statement ① is the conclusion. Taken separately, statements ② and ③ provide little or no support for ①, but taken together they do provide support. That is, ② and ③ support ① *conjointly.* This relationship between the premises is illustrated by the use of the brace in the following diagram:

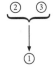

Conjoint premises

The next example illustrates the occurrence of a multiple conclusion:

> ① Dropping out of school and bearing children outside of marriage are two of the primary causes of poverty in this country. Therefore, ② to eliminate poverty we must offer incentives for people to get high school diplomas. Also, ③ we must find some way to encourage people to get married before they start having children.

In this passage statement ① supports both ② and ③. Since no single argument can have more than one conclusion, the passage is correctly evaluated as consisting of two arguments. For our purposes, however, we will treat it as if it were a single argument by joining the two conclusions with a bracket:

Multiple conclusion

Our symbolism is now sufficiently developed to analyze most arguments found in editorials and letters to the editor of newspapers and magazines. Consider the following argument, taken from a newspaper editorial:

> ① Antibiotic resistant bacteria cost the economy $20 billion annually. ② We need new antibiotics to combat these bacteria, but ③ developing new antibiotics is not profitable. ④ Antibiotics tend to be given for only a short time, and ⑤ antibiotics are used sparingly under controlled circumstances. ⑥ Thus, to encourage the development of new antibiotics, a government prize of $2 billion should be given to any company that develops an effective one.
>
> (Ezekiel J. Emanuel, "How to Develop New Antibiotics")

The main conclusion is ⑥, which is supported independently by ① and conjointly by ② and ③. Then, ③ is supported independently by ④ and ⑤. The argument pattern is as follows:

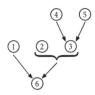

The next argument is taken from a letter to the editor:

> ① Rhinos in Kenya are threatened with extinction because ② poachers are killing them for their horn. Since ③ the rhino has no natural predators, ④ it does not need its horn to survive. Thus ⑤ there should be an organized program to capture rhinos in the wild and remove their horn. ⑥ Such a program would eliminate the incentive of the poachers.
>
> (Pamela C. Wagner, "Rhino Poaching")

First we search for the final conclusion. We select ⑤, because it is the ultimate point that the passage attempts to establish. Next we survey the premise and conclusion indicators. From this, we see that ② supports ① and ③ supports ④. Finally, we see that ①, ④, and ⑥ support ⑤. Yet these supporting statements depend on one another for their effect. Thus, they support the final conclusion conjointly. The argument pattern is as follows:

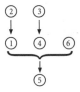

The next argument is taken from a magazine article:

> ① Skating is a wonderful form of exercise and relaxation, but ② today's rollerbladers are a growing menace and ③ something should be done to control them. ④ Rollerbladers are oblivious to traffic regulations as ⑤ they breeze through red lights and ⑥ skim down the wrong way on one-way streets. ⑦ They pose a threat to pedestrians because ⑧ a

collision can cause serious injury. ⑨ Rollerbladers are even a hazard to shopkeepers as ⑩ they zoom through stores and ⑪ damage merchandise.

(Joan Schmidt, "Hell—On Wheels")

After reading the argument, we see that ① is merely an introductory sentence, and ②. and ③ together compose the main conclusion. Also, ④, ⑦, and ⑨ support the main conclusion independently, while ⑤ and ⑥ support ④ independently, ⑧ supports ⑦, and ⑩ and ⑪ support ⑨ independently. The diagram is as follows:

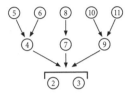

The next argument is taken from the science column of a newspaper:

① We can expect small changes to occur in the length of our calendar year for an indefinite time to come. ② This is true for two reasons. ③ First, the rotation of the earth exhibits certain irregularities. ④ And why is this so? ⑤ The rotation of any body is affected by its distribution of mass, and ⑥ the earth's mass distribution is continually subject to change. For example, ⑦ earthquakes alter the location of the tectonic plates. Also, ⑧ the liquid core of the earth sloshes as the earth turns, and ⑨ rainfall redistributes water from the oceans. The second reason is that ⑩ the motion of the tides causes a continual slowing down of Earth's rotation. ⑪ Tidal motion produces heat, and ⑫ the loss of this heat removes energy from the system.

(Isaac Asimov, "As the World Turns")

Preliminary analysis reveals that the final conclusion is ①. Also, ② tells us that the supporting statements are divided into two basic groups, but since ② does not add any support, we can leave it out of the diagram. In the first group, ⑤ and ⑥ support ③ conjointly, while ⑦, ⑧, and ⑨ support ⑥ independently. ④ will not appear in the diagram, because it serves merely as a premise indicator. In the second group, ⑪ and ⑫ support ⑩ conjointly. Thus, the argument pattern is as follows:

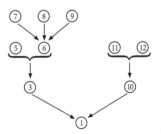

Our last example is taken from a letter to the editor of a newspaper:

① Community college districts save a great deal of money by hiring untenured part-time instructors, but ② the extensive use of these instructors is a disadvantage to the students. ③ Most part-time instructors are paid only 60 percent of what a full-time teacher earns, and as a result, ④ they are forced to teach five or six courses just to survive. ⑤ This detracts from the opportunity to consult with students outside the classroom. To make matters worse, ⑥ many part-timers are not even given office space. Furthermore, ⑦ the lower pay demoralizes the part-timer, and ⑧ the lack of tenure makes for constant financial insecurity. ⑨ Obviously these conditions render the instructor less receptive to student needs. Lastly, because ⑩ these part-timers are burning the candle from both ends, ⑪ they have no spare energy to improve their courses, and ⑫ many lack the enthusiasm to motivate their students. As a result, ⑬ the educational process is impaired.

(Gordon Dossett et al., "Part-Time College Instructors")

Preliminary analysis reveals that the main conclusion is not ① but ②. Also, we see three main reasons why part-timers are a disadvantage to students: They have little opportunity to consult with students, they are less receptive to student needs, and the educational process is impaired by ⑪ and ⑬. In the first main branch, the indicator "as a result" shows that ③ supports ④, and ④ and ⑥ independently support ⑤. In the second branch, ⑦ and ⑧ independently support ⑨. In the third, ⑩ supports both ⑪ and ⑫, which in turn support ⑬ independently. Here is the argument pattern:

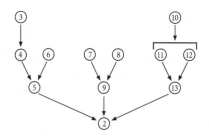

I. The following arguments were abstracted from newspaper articles, editorials, and letters to the editor. Use the method presented in this section to construct argument patterns. If a statement is redundant or plays no role in the argument, do not include it in the pattern.

★1. ① The conditions under which many food animals are raised are unhealthy for humans. ② To keep these animals alive, large quantities of drugs must be administered. ③ These drugs remain in the animals' flesh and are passed on to the humans who eat it.

(Philip D. Oliver, "We Can Eat Ribs and Still Be Humane")

2. ① The development of carbon-embedded plastics, otherwise called "composits," is an important new technology because ② it holds the key for new

MindTap Complete exercises online for immediate feedback.

aircraft and spacecraft designs. This is so because ③ these composits are not only stronger than steel but lighter than aluminum.

(Thomas H. Maugh II, "Composits—The Lightweight Champs of
Aircraft Industry")

3. ① Homework stifles the thrill of learning in the mind of the student. ② It instills an oppressive learn-or-else discipline. ③ It quenches the desire for knowledge and the love of truth. For these reasons ④ homework should never be assigned.

(Colman McCarthy, "Homework's Tyranny Hobbles
Promising Minds")

★4. ① When parents become old and destitute, the obligation of caring for them should be imposed on their children. ② Clearly, children owe a debt to their parents. ③ Their parents brought them into the world and cared for them when they were unable to care for themselves. ④ This debt could be appropriately discharged by having grown children care for their parents.

(Gary Jones, "The Responsibility of Parents")

5. ① Defending the war on drugs may not be fashionable, but the fact remains that ② hard-core drugs should remain illegal. ③ As long as hard-core drugs are illegal, they are harder to get, and ④ the social stigma of being arrested deters many users.

(Charles Van DeVenter, "I'm Proof: The War on Drugs Is Working")

6. ① The rain forest of Brazil produces oxygen for the whole world, yet ② it yields no monetary return to that country. Given that ③ the industrialized nations consume the most oxygen, ④ those nations ought to pay Brazil an annual fee for the use of its rain forest.

(Diane B. Robinson, letter to the editor)

★7. ① It appears that animals may be able to predict earthquakes. ② Prior to a major quake in China, hundreds of snakes suddenly appeared from hibernation and froze to death in the snow, ③ fish were seen leaping from rivers and lakes, and ④ cows and horses refused to enter barns. Also, ⑤ prior to a quake in Fremont, California, a flood of callers reported strange behavior from their pets and domestic animals.

(Michael Bowker, "Can Animals Really Predict Earthquakes?")

8. ① Contributions to relief organizations are often wasted. ② Food sent to war-torn countries rarely reaches its destination, because ③ food distribution is controlled by the warring groups, and ④ these groups sell the food to buy weapons and ammunition.

(Michael Maren, "The Faces of Famine")

9. ① Research leading to the development of a scramjet engine is worthwhile. ② Commercial aircraft incorporating such an engine could cross the Pacific in as little as two hours. ③ This would relieve the fatigue of flights from New York to Tokyo. Also, ④ such an engine could power future orbiting spacecraft.

(T. A. Heppenheimer, "A Plane for Space")

★**10.** ① There is a lot of pressure on untenured college teachers to dumb down their courses. ② Administrators tend to rehire teachers who bring in more money, and ③ teachers who dumb down their classes do precisely this. Why? Because ④ easier classes attract more students, and ⑤ more students means more money for the school.

(Lynne Drury Lerych, "Meeting the Bottom Line in the College Biz")

11. ① The use of ethanol as an additive in gasoline is really a bad idea. ② Ethanol is produced from corn, and ③ when 40 percent of the annual corn crop is burned up in car engines, that obviously raises the price of corn for food. ④ Also, adding ethanol to gasoline is highly inefficient. ⑤ Ethanol yields about 30 percent less energy than gasoline, and ⑥ it's more expensive to transport and handle than gasoline.

(Colin A. Carter and Henry I. Miller, "Corn for Food, Not Fuel")

12. ① Unscrupulous for-profit colleges are not only cheating their students but ② they are also ripping off the American taxpayer to the tune of billions of dollars. ③ Ninety-six percent of the students who attend these colleges are forced to take out loans. ④ Most of these students leave without degrees. ⑤ And the students then default on their loans, leaving a $32 billion annual debt to the taxpayer.

(Newspaper editorial, "False Promises")

★**13.** ① Numerous cancer patients on chemotherapy suffer from constant nausea, loss of appetite, and inability to sleep. ② For many of these patients, inhaled marijuana is the only medicine that provides relief. ③ Also, it causes no harmful side effects. ④ For these reasons, medical marijuana should be legalized and made available to these patients. ⑤ This is not a law and order issue; it is a medical and human-rights issue.

(Gustin L. Reichbach, "A Judge's Plea for Pot")

14. ① The United States is currently experiencing the greatest economic inequality since the 1920s, and ② this inequality is depressing the economy. ③ The true sustainers of the economy are the bottom 99 percent of households, but ④ the top 1 percent takes in 93 percent of the growth in income. Also, ⑤ economic inequality is undercutting tax receipts, which are vital for infrastructure, education, and research. This is because ⑥ income earned by the rich is taxed at a far lower rate than income earned by the middle class.

(Joseph E. Stiglitz, "Inequality Is Holding Back the Recovery")

15. ① Programs to develop clean energy have seen some early notable successes. ② The price of solar and wind power have both fallen sharply in recent years. ③ The nation's largest wind farm, sprawling across eastern Oregon, is now open and running, and ④ there is even good news from the natural gas front. ⑤ The use of natural gas, which is far cleaner than coal, to generate electricity has jumped substantially in the last few years, and ⑥ thanks to government-sponsored research, energy companies are now able to extract much more gas from a tract of land than once seemed possible.

(David Leonhardt, "There's Still Hope for the Planet")

II. The following arguments gradually increase in difficulty. Use the method presented in this section to construct argument patterns. If a statement is redundant or plays no role in the argument, do not include it in the pattern.

★1. ① Many people believe that the crime of bribery cannot extend to campaign contributions. ② From a legal standpoint, however, countless campaign contributions are in fact bribes. ③ A bribe is anything of value or advantage given with the intent to unlawfully influence the person to whom it is given in his official capacity. ④ A campaign contribution is certainly something of value or advantage. Furthermore, ⑤ every contribution from a lobbyist or special interest group is given with the intent to influence voting, and ⑥ thousands of such contributions are made in every important election.

(Daniel Hays Lowenstein, "Can Candidates Run for Political Office Without Taking Bribes?")

2. ① America's farm policy desperately needs revamping. ② Seventy-three cents of every farm-program dollar ends up in the pockets of the nation's super-farmers. As a result, ③ the mid-sized family farms are being squeezed out of existence. Also, ④ our farm policy courts environmental disaster. ⑤ Federal subsidies encourage farmers to use enormous amounts of fertilizer and pesticides. ⑥ These chemicals percolate down through the soil and pollute limited groundwater.

(Osha Gray Davidson, "Rise of America's Rural Ghetto")

3. ① Society values white lives more than black lives. This is clear from the fact that ② killers of whites are much more likely to be sentenced to death than killers of blacks. ③ Of the 1,788 people currently on death row, 1,713 were convicted of killing a white person. Yet ④ blacks are six times more likely to be murder victims than whites are. ⑤ In Florida, no one has ever been executed for murdering a black person, but ⑥ dozens have been executed for murdering white people.

(Los Angeles Times editorial, "Death and Race")

★4. ① Powerful new particle accelerators are important in high-energy physics, and ② they are worth their cost because ③ they will allow scientists to produce and capture significant quantities of Z particles. ④ Z particles result from the collision of positrons and electrons, and ⑤ particle accelerators are needed to achieve significant numbers of these collisions. ⑥ Z particles are thought to be the bearers of the weak nuclear force, and ⑦ learning the nature of this force may lead to the development of entirely new sources of energy.

(Lee Dye, "Linear Collider: Bold Gamble in Atomic Physics")

5. ① Although Thomas Jefferson's contributions to the foundation of the country were profound, ② as the master of Monticello, Jefferson was a monster. ③ Simultaneously with his writing the Declaration of Independence, which announced the self-evident truth that all men are created equal, he owned 175 slaves. ④ Clearly the man was a creepy hypocrite. ⑤ But Jefferson was

also cruel. ⑥ He sometimes punished slaves by selling them away from their family and friends, and ⑦ for slaves and free blacks who ran afoul of the law, he advocated harsh, almost barbaric forms of punishment.

(Paul Finkelman, "The Monster of Monticello")

6. ① All men crave material success because ② it serves as an insurance policy against sexual rejection. This is true because ③ women love men who are successful. ④ Both men and women want power, and ⑤ success is the form of power women feel most deprived of. Thus, ⑥ women try to achieve it vicariously through men. ⑦ As the 5-foot 6-inch Dustin Hoffman once put it, "When I was in high school, women wouldn't touch me with a 10-foot pole. Now I can't keep them away with a 10-foot pole."

(Warren Farrell, "Success Story: From Frog to Prince")

★7. ① Cigarette consumption could be easily reduced by simply outlawing tailor-made cigarettes. ② The manufacture of tailor-made cigarettes to American standards is a high-tech industry. ③ It cannot be done in small illicit labs like the processing of PCP, cocaine, or heroin. ④ The availability of quality tobacco for hand rolling would discourage the development of an illegal tailor-made market. ⑤ Most people would not pay the premium prices demanded by an illicit market for a product of unknown quality. ⑥ They could roll a high-quality product for themselves. ⑦ Truly addicted persons would continue to smoke no matter how inconvenient. But ⑧ most would give it up as too much bother before it became a deeply ingrained habit.

(Richard Sand, "An Easy Way to Reduce Cigarette Consumption")

8. ① Flesh food is not a necessity in the human diet, as ② nutritionally adequate alternatives are readily available. ③ Many people in the world thrive on a non-meat diet. ④ Indeed, vegetarian Seventh-Day Adventists in this country live an average of six years longer than their meat-eating counterparts. ⑤ The National Academy of Science warns that our fat-laden diet is directly responsible for much of the heart disease and cancer that afflict so many. ⑥ At a time when people are starving in certain parts of the world, it should be noted that a steer must consume sixteen pounds of grain and soy to produce one pound of meat. ⑦ The grain and soybeans we feed our meat-producing animals would feed every hungry mouth in the world many times over. ⑧ Cattle are competing with humans for food. ⑨ Clearly, a reassessment of the whole concept of killing and eating animals is in order.

(Suzanne Sutton, "Killing Animals for Food—Time for a Second Look")

9. ① The argument has been made that to cut down on teenage drunk driving we should increase the federal excise tax on beer. ② Such a measure, however, would almost certainly fail to achieve its intended result. ③ Teenagers are notoriously insensitive to cost. ④ They gladly accept premium prices for the latest style in clothes or the most popular albums. And then, ⑤ those who drink and drive already risk arrest and loss of driving privileges. ⑥ They would not think twice about paying a little more for a six-pack. Finally, ⑦ the situation is not as

bleak as it has been made to appear. ⑧ The fatality rate for teenage drivers is lower today than it has been in years.

(James C. Sanders, "Increased U.S. Tax on Beer")

★10. ① It has been widely acknowledged that the quality of undergraduate education in this country is diminishing. ② An often unrecognized cause of this malady is the exploitative way that universities as employers treat their part-time and temporary faculty members. ③ In many universities there are no formal guidelines for evaluating the work of these instructors. As a result, ④ poor instructors who solicit the favor of the department chairman are often retained over better ones who do not. ⑤ Another factor is the low pay given to these instructors. ⑥ In order to survive, many of them must accept heavy teaching loads spread out over three or four institutions. ⑦ The quality of instruction can only suffer when faculty members stretch themselves so thin. Lastly, because ⑧ part-time and temporary faculty are rarely members of the faculty senate, ⑨ they have no voice in university governance. But ⑩ without a voice, the shoddy conditions under which they work are never brought to light.

(Michael Schwalbe, "Part-Time Faculty Members Deserve a Break")

11. ① Doctors who attend elderly people in nursing homes often prescribe tranquilizers to keep these people immobile. ② This practice is often unwarranted, and ③ it often impairs the health of the patients. ④ These tranquilizers often have damaging side effects in that ⑤ they accentuate the symptoms of senility, and ⑥ they increase the likelihood of a dangerous fall because ⑦ they produce unsteadiness in walking. Furthermore, since ⑧ these medications produce immobility, ⑨ they increase the risk of bedsores. ⑩ Doctors at the Center for Aging and Health say that physicians who care for the elderly are simply prescribing too much medication.

(Hal Willard, "At 90, the Zombie Shuffle")

12. ① All of us have encountered motorists who will go to any length to get a parking spot within 20 feet of the door they expect to enter. ② This obsession with good parking spots transcends all logic. ③ It might take 5 minutes to secure the ideal spot in a store parking lot, ④ while a more distant spot that is immediately available is only a 40-second walk from the door. ⑤ Waiting for that ideal spot also results in frenzied nerves and skyrocketing blood pressure. ⑥ Inevitably the occupant of the desired space will preen her hair before departing, and ⑦ all the while the cars backed up behind the waiting driver are blaring their horns. ⑧ Parking a little farther away is usually easier and safer because ⑨ you can pull out more quickly, and ⑩ it avoids damage to car doors by adjacent parkers.

(Gwinn Owens, "A Ridiculous Addiction")

★13. ① The state has a right to intervene on behalf of unborn children, and ② this right should be implemented immediately. ③ While it may be true that a mere fetus has no rights, ④ surely a born child does have rights, and ⑤ these rights project backward to the time it was in the womb. This is true because ⑥ what happens to the child in the womb can have an impact throughout the child's life. ⑦ It is well known that alcohol and drug abuse by expectant mothers cause birth defects, and ⑧ these defects are not correctable after birth. ⑨ Granted, an expectant mother has the right to treat her own body as she chooses, but ⑩ this right does not extend to her unborn child. ⑪ Once a pregnant woman decides to give birth, she effectively transfers part of her rights over to her unborn child. ⑫ Unfortunately, however, the unborn child is incapable of securing these rights for itself. Thus, ⑬ the intervention of a higher power is justified.

(Alan Dershowitz, "Drawing the Line on Prenatal Rights")

14. ① A manned trip to Mars is a justified scientific goal because ② it affords a unique opportunity to explore the origins of the solar system and the emergence of life. However, ③ from a scientific standpoint, an initial landing on the tiny Martian moons, Phobos and Deimos, would be more rewarding than a landing on the planet itself. Because ④ the Martian terrain is rugged, ⑤ humans would not be able to venture far, ⑥ nor could they operate a robot vehicle for great distances, since ⑦ Mars's mountains would block their view. ⑧ Explorers on Phobos and Deimos could easily send robot vehicles to the planet's surface. ⑨ Using Mars's moons as a base would also be better than unmanned exploration directed from the Houston space center. Because ⑩ the distance is so great, ⑪ radio signals to and from Mars can take as long as an hour. Thus, ⑫ driving an unmanned rover from Earth, step by step, would be a time-consuming operation. ⑬ Sample returns to Earth would take months instead of hours, and ⑭ follow-on missions would be years apart instead of days, further slowing the process of exploration.

(S. Fred Singer, "The Case for Going to Mars")

15. ① A small group of people still believe in nuclear weapons, but ② the facts dictate that nuclear weapons not only should be eliminated but ③ they can be eliminated. ④ The opposing arguments are that nuclear weapons hastened the end of World War II, they deter nations from going to war, they have kept the peace, and nuclear technology is irreversible. But ⑤ nuclear weapons did not persuade the Japanese to surrender. ⑥ New research shows that the real reason Japan surrendered is because the Soviets renounced neutrality and entered the war. And ⑦ before losing two cities to nuclear weapons, Japan had already lost sixty-six to conventional weapons. ⑧ Two more made little difference. Also, ⑨ history shows that nuclear weapons are ineffective as a deterrent. ⑩ They did not deter the United States during the Cuban missile crisis, and ⑪ they did not deter Argentina in the conflict with Britain over the Falklands. Furthermore, ⑫ there is no good reason to think that nuclear weapons cause peace. ⑬ Peace means the absence of war, but ⑭ the absence of something can be explained in countless ways. Lastly, ⑮ the argument that you can't stuff the nuclear genie back in the bottle is specious. ⑯ The question is not whether nuclear weapons can be disinvented but whether they are useful. ⑰ This is doubtful given that ⑱ not one has been used since 1945 and ⑲ the trend in modern warfare is toward smaller, more effective precision-guided weapons. ⑳ Banning nuclear weapons will not be easy, but ㉑ the existing ban on chemical and biological weapons shows that it can be done.

(Ward Wilson, "The Myth of Nuclear Necessity")

III. Turn to the editorial pages of a newspaper and select an editorial that contains an argument. Keep in mind that some editorials are really reports and contain no arguments at all. Also, few editorials are as neat and straightforward as the selections presented in Parts I and II of this exercise. Guest editorials on the opinion–editorial page (usually opposite the editorial page) are often better written than those on the editorial page. Analyze the argument (or arguments) according to the method presented in this section. Begin by placing a numeral at the beginning of each statement. Compound statements having components that are claimed to be true may be broken up into parts and the parts enumerated accordingly. Numerals should usually be placed after genuine premise and conclusion indicators even when they occur in the middle of a statement. Do *not*, however, break up conditional statements into antecedent and consequent. Proceed to identify the main conclusion (or conclusions) and determine how the other statements provide support. Any statement that does not play a direct role in the argument should be left out of the final argument pattern.

IV. Create an extended argument, containing at least six statements, about climate change.

MindTap® Master concepts and improve outcomes with Aplia, at the end of the chapter, in the Aplia folder.

Summary

Logic: The science that evaluates arguments

Argument: A group of statements comprising one or more premises and one conclusion

Premises: The statements that set forth the reasons or evidence

Conclusion: The statement that is claimed to follow from the premises

To distinguish premises from conclusion, look for:

- Indicator words ("hence," "therefore," "since," "because," etc.)
- An inferential relationship among the statements

Not all groups of statements are arguments. To distinguish arguments from nonarguments, look for:

- Indicator words ("hence," "since," etc.)
- An inferential relationship among the statements
- Typical kinds of nonarguments (warnings, reports, expository passages, etc.)

MindTap® Need help? See the Learning Logic folder at the end of the chapter: the self-paced tutorial walks you through any section.
Prepare for exams with the Chapter Test.

The most problematic kinds of nonarguments:

- Expository passages (Is the topic sentence proved by the other statements?)
- Illustrations (Could the passage be an argument from example?)
- Explanations (Could the explanandum also be a conclusion?)

Conditional statements express the relation between sufficient conditions and necessary conditions:

- A is a sufficient condition for B: The occurrence of A is all that is needed for the occurrence of B.
- A is a necessary condition for B: A cannot occur without the occurrence of B.

Arguments are traditionally divided into deductive and inductive:

- Deductive argument: The conclusion is claimed to follow necessarily from the premises.
- Inductive argument: The conclusion is claimed to follow probably from the premises.

To distinguish deductive arguments from inductive arguments, look for:

- Special indicator phrases ("it necessarily follows that," "it probably follows that," etc.)
- The actual strength of the inferential relationship between premises and conclusion
- Typical forms or styles of argumentation:
  - Deductive forms: Arguments based on mathematics; arguments from definition; and categorical, hypothetical, and disjunctive syllogisms
  - Inductive forms: Predictions, arguments from analogy, generalizations, arguments from authority, arguments based on signs, and causal inferences

Evaluating an argument (either deductive or inductive) involves two steps:

- Evaluating the link between premises and conclusion
- Evaluating the truth of the premises

Deductive arguments are valid, invalid, sound, or unsound.

- Valid: The conclusion actually follows from the premises.
- Sound: The argument is valid and has all true premises.

Inductive arguments are strong, weak, cogent, or uncogent.

- Strong: The conclusion actually follows from the premises.
- Cogent: The argument is strong and has all true premises.

The validity of a deductive argument is determined by the argument's form. An invalid form allows for a substitution instance having true premises and a false conclusion.

- Counterexample method:
  - Is used to prove invalidity.
  - Consists in identifying the form of a given invalid argument and producing a substitution instance having true premises and a false conclusion.
  - This proves the form invalid, which proves the given argument invalid.

The structure of longer arguments can be disclosed by a diagramming method. Four basic argument patterns are:

- Vertical pattern
- Horizontal pattern
- Conjoint premises
- Multiple conclusion

2 Language: Meaning and Definition

2.1 Varieties of Meaning
2.2 The Intension and Extension of Terms
2.3 Definitions and Their Purposes
2.4 Definitional Techniques
2.5 Criteria for Lexical Definitions

2.1 Varieties of Meaning

HOW LOGICAL ARE YOU? Compare the statements: (1) Physician-assisted suicide, which is often confused with mercy killing, is always at the request of the patient, and is legally permissible only with the patient's consent. (2) Physician-assisted suicide is a terrifying, intolerable practice in which doctors, who are sworn to preserve human life, end up destroying it by murdering their patients. In what basic way do these two statements differ?

Find the answer on MindTap.

Ordinary language, as most of us are at least vaguely aware, serves various functions in our day-to-day lives. The twentieth-century philosopher Ludwig Wittgenstein thought the number of these functions to be virtually unlimited. Thus, among many other things, language is used to

ask questions	tell jokes
tell stories	flirt with someone
tell lies	give directions
guess at answers	sing songs
form hypotheses	issue commands
launch verbal assaults	greet someone

MindTap® Read, study, reflect, and prepare for exams online, anytime, anywhere.

For our purpose, two linguistic functions are particularly important: (1) to convey information and (2) to express or evoke feelings. Consider, for example, the following statements:

> The death penalty, which is legal in thirty-one states, has been carried out most often in Virginia; however, since 1977 Texas holds the record for the greatest number of executions.

> The death penalty is a cruel and inhuman form of punishment in which hapless prisoners are dragged from their cells and summarily slaughtered only to satiate the bloodlust of a vengeful public.

The first statement is intended primarily to convey information about the death penalty, whereas the second is intended to persuade us that the death penalty is bad. The second accomplishes this function by engaging our feelings and not, as in an argument, by establishing the truth of a claim.

These statements accomplish their respective functions through the distinct kinds of terminology in which they are phrased. Terminology that conveys information is said to have **cognitive meaning**, and terminology that expresses or evokes feelings is said to have **emotive meaning**. Thus, in the first statement the words "legal," "thirty-one," "most often," "Virginia," "record," and so on have primarily a cognitive meaning, while in the second statement the words "cruel," "inhuman," "hapless," "dragged," "slaughtered," "bloodlust," and "vengeful" have a strong emotive meaning. Of course, these latter words have cognitive meaning as well. "Cruel" means tending to hurt others, "inhuman" means inappropriate for humans, "hapless" means unfortunate, and so on.

The emotively charged statement about the death penalty illustrates two important points. The first is that statements of this sort usually have *both* cognitive meaning and emotive meaning. Therefore, since logic is concerned chiefly with cognitive meaning, we must be able to distinguish and disengage the cognitive meaning of such statements from the emotive meaning. The second point is that part of the cognitive meaning of such statements is a value claim. A **value claim** is a claim that something is good, bad, right, wrong, better, worse, more important, or less important than some other thing. For example, the statement about the death penalty asserts the value claim that the death penalty is wrong or immoral. Such value claims are often the most important part of the cognitive meaning of emotive statements. Thus, for the purposes of logic, we must be able to disengage the value claims of emotively charged statements from the emotive meaning and treat these claims as separate statements.

These observations suggest the reason that people use emotive terminology as often as they do: Value claims as such normally require evidence to support them. For example, the claim that the death penalty is immoral cannot simply stand by itself. It cries out for reasons to support it. But when value claims are couched in emotive terminology, the emotive "clothing" tends to obscure the fact that a value claim is being made, and it simultaneously gives psychological momentum to that claim. As a result, readers and listeners are inclined to swallow the value claim whole without any evidence. Furthermore, the intellectual laziness of many speakers and writers, combined with their inability to supply supporting reasons for their value claims, reinforces the desirability of couching such claims in emotive terminology.

Many people, for example, will refer to someone as "crazy," "stupid," or "weird" when they want to express the claim that what that person is doing is bad or wrong and when they are unable or unwilling to give reasons for this claim. Also, many people will use such words as "awesome" or "fantastic" to express the claim that something is good. Those who happen to be listening, especially if they are friendly with the speaker, will often accept these claims without hesitation.

The use of emotive terminology in advertising often results in huge profits for companies that sponsor the ads. The pharmaceutical industry is a prime example. Nowadays, instead of pitching their ads to the doctors who prescribe the drugs, pharmaceutical companies go directly to the patients, and they select names for their drugs that are easy to recall and convey a positive, though often subtle, emotional message. For example, lunesta, a drug for insomnia, suggests a peaceful sleep bathed in moonlight (recall that *luna* means "moon"). Boniva, a drug for osteoporosis, suggests giving new life to one's bones ("bone" + *vita*). Viagra suggests vigor and growth. Celebrex, a drug for arthritis, suggests celebrating. Abilify, a drug for depression, "abilifies" you to be happy and productive. Enablex, a drug for overactive bladder, enables you to regain control. These are just a few.

For another example of emotive terminology, consider the word "harvest." This word evokes feelings associated with honest, hardworking farmers being rewarded for their labor in planting and tending their crops. To capitalize on this positive feeling, wood products companies speak of harvesting the trees in 200-year-old forests, even though they had nothing to do with planting them, and surgeons speak of harvesting the organs from the bodies of donors and the tissue from aborted fetuses. In all of these cases, the use of the word "harvest" is specifically calculated to elicit a favorable or agreeable response from the listener.

Let us now consider emotive terminology as it occurs in arguments. In arguments, emotive terminology accomplishes basically the same function as it does in statements. It allows the arguer to make value claims about the subject matter of the argument without providing evidence, and it gives the argument a kind of steamroller quality by which it tends to crush potential counterarguments before the reader or listener has a chance to think of them. This steamroller quality also tends to paralyze the logical thought processes of readers or listeners so that they are not able to see illogical arguments in their true light. These effects of emotive terminology can be avoided if the reader or listener will disengage the value claims and other cognitive meanings from the emotive meaning of the language and reexpress them as distinct premises.

Consider, for example, the following emotively charged argument taken from the letters to the editor section of a newspaper:

> Now that we know that the rocks on the moon are similar to those in our backyard and that tadpoles can exist in a weightless environment, and now that we have put the rest of the world in order, can we concentrate on the problems here at home? Like what makes people hungry and why is unemployment so elusive?
>
> (Robert J. Boland)

The conclusion of this argument is that our government should take money that has been spent on the space program and on international police actions and redirect it to solving domestic problems. The author minimizes the importance of the space program by covertly suggesting that it amounts to nothing more than work on ordinary rocks and tadpoles (which by themselves are relatively insignificant), and he exaggerates the scope of the international effort by covertly suggesting that it has solved every problem on earth but our own. Also, the phrase "put . . . in order" suggests that the international effort has been no more important than restoring order to a room in one's house. We might rephrase the argument in emotively neutral language, making the implicit suggestions and value claims explicit, as follows:

The space program has been confined to work on ordinary rocks and tadpoles.

Ordinary rocks and tadpoles are less important than domestic hunger and unemployment.

Our international efforts have restored order to every nation on earth but our own.

These efforts have been directed to problems that are less important than our own domestic problems.

Therefore, our government should redirect funds that have been spent on these projects to solving our own domestic problems.

By restructuring the argument in this way, we can more easily evaluate the degree to which the premises support the conclusion. Inspection of the premises reveals that the first, third, and possibly fourth premises are false. Thus, the actual support provided by the premises is less than what we might have first expected. If the argument were to be rephrased a second time so that the premises turned out true (for example, the first premise might read "*Part* of the space program has been devoted to research on ordinary rocks and tadpoles"), the support given to the conclusion would still be weaker than the author intended.

Now that we have distinguished emotive meaning from cognitive meaning, let us explore some of the ways that language having cognitive meaning can be defective. Two of them are vagueness and ambiguity. A **vague expression** is one that allows for borderline cases in which it is impossible to tell if the expression applies or does not apply. Vague expressions often allow for a continuous range of interpretations. The meaning is hazy, obscure, and imprecise. For example, words such as "love," "happiness," "peace," "excessive," "fresh," "rich," "poor," "normal," "conservative," and "polluted" are vague. We can rarely tell with any precision whether they apply to a given situation or not. How fresh does something have to be in order to be called "fresh"?

Vagueness can also affect entire statements. Such vagueness may arise not so much from the individual words as from the way in which the words are combined. For example, suppose someone were to say, "Today our job situation is more transparent." First, what is the meaning of "job situation"? Does it refer to finding a job, keeping a job, filling a job, completing a job, or bidding on a job? And what exactly does it mean for a job situation to be "transparent"? Does it mean that the job is more easily perceived or comprehended? That the job is more easily completed? That we can anticipate our future job needs more clearly? Or what else?

Not all cases of vagueness, however, are problematic. To describe an acquaintance as "tall" or "thin" often causes no trouble in ordinary conversation. Indeed, it may be burdensome to describe this person in more precise language. Trouble arises only when the language is not sufficiently precise for what the situation demands.

The other way in which cognitive meanings can be defective is ambiguity. An **ambiguous expression** is one that can be interpreted as having more than one clearly distinct meaning in a given context. For example, words such as "light," "proper," "critical," "stress," "mad," "inflate," "chest," "bank," "sound," and "race" can be used ambiguously. Thus, if one were to describe a beer as a light pilsner, does this mean that the beer is light in color, light in calories, or light in taste? If one were to describe an action as proper, does this mean proper in a moral sense or proper in the sense of being socially acceptable? Or if one were to describe a person as critical, does this mean that the person is essential for a certain task or that the person tends to criticize others?

As is the case with vagueness, ambiguity can also affect entire statements. Such ambiguity often results from the way in which certain words are combined. For example, there was a newspaper headline that read, "Tuna are biting off the Washington coast." Does this mean that the tuna are nibbling away at the coastline or that fishermen are catching them off the coast? Presumably it means the latter. Another headline read, "College students are turning to vegetables." Does this mean that the students are metamorphosing into vegetables or that they are incorporating more vegetables into their diet? Again, the intended meaning is probably the latter.

The difference between ambiguity and vagueness is that vague terminology allows for a relatively continuous range of interpretations, whereas ambiguous terminology allows for multiple discrete interpretations. A vague expression creates a blur of meaning, whereas an ambiguous expression mixes up otherwise clear meanings. However, many forms of expression are ambiguous in one context and vague in another. For example, the word "slow" in one context could mean either mentally challenged or physically slow, but when the word refers to physical slowness, it could be vague. How slow is slow? Similar remarks apply to "light," "fast," and "rich."

Ambiguity and vagueness are important in logic because there are countless occasions in which the evaluation of an argument leads to the observation, "Well, that depends on what you mean by . . ." Certain phraseology in the argument is vague or ambiguous, and its meaning must be clarified before any evaluation can proceed. For example, Scientologists argue that their organization should be exempt from paying taxes because, they claim, Scientology is a religion. Evaluating their argument requires that we clarify the meaning of "religion." Pro-life advocates argue that abortion is wrong because it results in the killing of human beings. But what is the meaning of "human being"? And some feminists argue that leering glances constitute sexual harassment. To evaluate their arguments we must clarify the meaning of "leering glances" and "sexual harassment."

The role of vagueness and ambiguity in arguments may be conveniently explored in the context of conflicting arguments between individuals. Such conflicts are called disputes:

> CLAUDIA: Mrs. Wilson abuses her children. And how do I know that? I saw her spank one of her kids the other day after the kid misbehaved.

> JANE: Don't be silly. Kids need discipline, and by disciplining her children, Mrs. Wilson is showing that she loves them.

Here the problem surrounds the vagueness of the words "abuse" and "discipline." When does discipline become abuse? The line separating the two is hazy at best, but unless it is clarified, disputes of this sort will never be resolved.

Another example:

> BRENDA: I'm afraid that Smiley is guilty of arson. Last night he confided to me that he was the one who set fire to the old schoolhouse.

> WARREN: No, you couldn't be more mistaken. In this country no one is guilty until proven so in a court of law, and Smiley has not yet even been accused of anything.

In this case the dispute arises over the ambiguity of the word "guilty." Brenda is using the word in the moral sense. Given that Smiley has admitted to setting fire to the old schoolhouse, it is very likely that he did indeed set fire to it and therefore is guilty of arson in the moral sense of the term. Warren, on the other hand, is using the word in the legal sense. Because Smiley has not been convicted in a court of law, he is not legally guilty of anything.

Disputes that arise over the meaning of language are called *verbal disputes.* But not all disputes are of this sort. Some disputes arise over a disagreement about facts, and these are called *factual disputes.* Example:

> KEITH: I know that Freddie stole a computer from the old schoolhouse. Barbara told me that she saw Freddie do it.

> PHYLLIS: That's ridiculous! Freddie has never stolen anything in his life. Barbara hates Freddie, and she is trying to pin the theft on him only to shield her criminal boyfriend.

Here the dispute centers on the factual issues of whether Barbara told the truth and whether Freddie stole the computer.

In dealing with disputes, the first question is whether the dispute is factual, verbal, or some combination of the two. If the dispute is verbal, then the second question to be answered is whether the dispute concerns ambiguity or vagueness.

EXERCISE 2.1

I. The following selection is taken from a speech delivered by George C. Wallace, former governor of Alabama, on July 4, 1964. In this speech Wallace attacked Lyndon Johnson's signing of the Civil Rights Act. The speech is liberally sprinkled with emotive terminology. Make a list of what you consider to be the twenty-five most highly charged words or phrases, and then indicate whether they are intended to evoke a favorable or an unfavorable attitude from the listener.

We come here today in deference to the memory of those stalwart patriots who on July 4, 1776, pledged their lives, their fortunes, and their sacred honor to establish and

MindTap® Complete exercises online for immediate feedback.

defend the proposition that governments are created by the people, empowered by the people, derive their just powers from the consent of the people, and must forever remain subservient to the will of the people.

Today, 188 years later, we celebrate that occasion and find inspiration and determination and courage to preserve and protect the great principles of freedom enunciated in the Declaration of Independence.

It is therefore a cruel irony that the president of the United States has only yesterday signed into law the most monstrous piece of legislation ever enacted by the United States Congress.

It is a fraud, a sham, and a hoax.

This bill will live in infamy. To sign it into law at any time is tragic. To do so upon the eve of the celebration of our independence insults the intelligence of the American people.

It dishonors the memory of countless thousands of our dead who offered up their very lives in defense of principles which this bill destroys.

Never before in the history of this nation have so many human and property rights been destroyed by a single enactment of the Congress. It is an act of tyranny. It is the assassin's knife stuck in the back of liberty.

With this assassin's knife and a blackjack in the hand of the federal force-cult, the left-wing liberals will try to force us back into bondage. Bondage to a tyranny more brutal than that imposed by the British monarchy which claimed power to rule over the lives of our forefathers under sanction of the omnipotent black-robed despots who sit on the bench of the United States Supreme Court.

This bill is fraudulent in intent, in design, and in execution.

It is misnamed. Each and every provision is mistitled. It was rammed through the Congress on the wave of ballyhoo, promotions, and publicity stunts reminiscent of P. T. Barnum.

It was enacted in an atmosphere of pressure, intimidation, and even cowardice, as demonstrated by the refusal of the United States Senate to adopt an amendment to submit the bill to a vote of the people.

To illustrate the fraud—it is not a civil rights bill. It is a federal penal code. It creates federal crimes which would take volumes to list and years to tabulate because it affects the lives of 192 million American citizens. Every person in every walk and station of life and every aspect of our daily lives become subject to the criminal provisions of this bill.

It threatens our freedom of speech, of assembly, of association, and makes the exercise of these freedoms a federal crime under certain conditions.

It affects our political rights, our right to trial by jury, our right to the full use and enjoyment of our private property, the freedom from search and seizure of our private property and possessions, the freedom from harassment by federal police and, in short, all the rights of individuals inherent in a society of free men.

Ministers, lawyers, teachers, newspapers, and every private citizen must guard his speech and watch his actions to avoid the deliberately imposed booby traps put into this bill. It is designed to make federal crimes of our customs, beliefs, and traditions. Therefore, under the fantastic powers of the federal judiciary to punish for contempt of court and under their fantastic powers to regulate our most intimate aspects of our lives by injunction, every American citizen is in jeopardy and must stand guard against these despots.

II. The following selections were taken from the letters-to-the-editor section of a newspaper. Each can be interpreted as expressing one or more arguments. Begin by identifying the conclusion of each. Then disengage the covert assumptions, value claims, and other cognitive assertions from the emotive language and translate them into emotively neutral premises. Use the two examples in the text as models. Finally, evaluate the restructured arguments. Some may turn out to be good ones.

★1. Why don't animal lovers do something about these dog sled races? Have you ever witnessed a race on television? Talk about torture. It's sickening to watch the dogs, panting and their tongues hanging out, pull a heavily laden sled with a driver through snow and ice in bitter cold.

(Joe Shapiro)

2. How anyone who has seen even one photo of the fly-covered, starving children in Somalia can still believe in a loving, everpresent, omnipotent God is beyond intelligent reasoning.

(William Blanchard)

3. The creationists have no right to impose their mistaken, ignorant, superstitious beliefs on others. They claim the constitutional right to the free exercise of religion. How about the rights of the majority of people who want their children taught the scientific truth about evolution—not fallacious myths and superstitions from primitive societies.

(Andrew M. Underhill Jr.)

★4. God, guts, and guns made this great country of ours free, and you can bet your buns it will take more of the same to keep it that way. One of the very last things in this world we need is handgun control.

(R. Kinzie)

5. The insanity plea should be done away with; criminals should lose this easy way out. Killers can theoretically spend as little as six months in a mental hospital, then be released. It's time to take a stand for safety and put psychotic killers in prison.

(Keith Aikens)

6. Until now, the protest against the holocaust in our own nation has been vocal but far too small. The massacre of an unwanted generation through abortion and infanticide has sounded an alarm that should wake up every Christian. Helpless and guiltless little infants are mercilessly butchered daily in hospitals and clinics across our land. For the love of God, let us all urge the passage of the Human Life Bill, now before Congress.

(Jim Key)

★7. It's time to challenge all this nonsense about the "celebration of diversity" in our society. The more the schizophrenics preach the glories of diversity, the more we pull apart. This is not to deny appreciation of the ethnic roots, rituals, and foods, which add color to life. But to lay undue emphasis upon diversification results in destruction of the "social glue" that binds us together. Our forefathers framed one nation, indivisible. In the misguided effort to "celebrate" the uniqueness of every disparate culture and subculture, we betray our heritage and dilute our identities as Americans.

(Ruth M. Armstrong)

8. A kind and loving God surely favors the pro-choice attitude. He wants his world inhabited by happy, well-fed children with parents who love and care for them.

Our burgeoning population in Third World nations with constant famine and disease, and many other human miseries, could be relieved if the Catholic Church were to adjust more of its ancient policies to our current civilization.

(Art Bates)

9. Thousands of years of organized religion have done nothing to solve any problems and have almost always exacerbated them by promoting fear, superstition, and irrational mythologies. Kneeling in prayer to some supernatural entity seeking "divine guidance" or, even more implausibly, "divine intervention," is not only a waste of time, it is counterproductive because it lulls the supplicant into inactivity.

We must stand up, open our eyes, and face life's challenges head-on in a problem-solving approach that is reality-based, empirical, and above all, rational.

(James W. Baugh)

★10. Liberalism has turned our welfare system from a social safety net into a hammock. We hand out money with few questions asked. When welfare recipients are asked for some contribution to our society in return, liberals scream that it's unconstitutional.

Liberalism has transformed our criminal justice system into one that cares more about the criminal's past childhood problems than for the victim. Liberalism in its never-ending quest for "social justice" has sacrificed the rights of the majority while continuing to push the rights of a few to new limits.

Liberalism has turned our school system from one of excellence to one where condoms and metal detectors are more important than prayer.

(Marc Sexton)

III. Visit a drug store and find the aisle that displays hair-care products (shampoos, conditioners, etc.). Identify five items whose names have emotional meaning. Then, for each one, explain how its name is supposed to elicit a favorable response from the consumer.

IV. Determine whether the following disputes are verbal, factual, or some combination of the two. If verbal, discuss whether the dispute arises from vagueness or ambiguity.

★1. FRANK: Look at that huge tree that fell last night. It must have made a tremendous crash when it came down.
SHIRLEY: No, I'm afraid you're quite wrong. Sound is a perception, and perceptions depend on a perceiver. Therefore, since nobody was around here last night, there was no crash.

2. VICKIE: Yesterday I visited the exhibition of the work of Jean Michel Basquiat at the Central Gallery. What an interesting artist he is!
BARBARA: Don't be ridiculous! That's not art—it's just graffiti.

3. PHIL: That was a great basketball game last night. Stephen Curry scored 37 points.
ARTHUR: Your statistics are all wet. Curry scored only 34 points.

★4. ROGER: I think modern society is becoming more and more violent every day. Just look at the increase in murder, rape, and robbery. Violence is clearly an evil that must be eradicated.
MARK: You might be right about the increase in crime, but the idea that violence is an evil is nonsense. Violence is quite natural. The universe was created in a tremendously violent big bang, the nuclear reactions that bring us sunlight are extremely violent, and insects and animals kill and devour one another all the time.

5. KATHY: I was saddened to hear about the death of your uncle. He was such a wonderful man. You must be consoled knowing that he's enjoying his heavenly reward.
ANNE: Thanks, but I'm afraid I don't know what you mean. If death is the end of life, how could my uncle be alive right now in heaven?

6. HEIDI: This morning I heard a lecture on the life of Jane Austen. She was such a wonderfully educated woman.
DAVID: That's not true at all. Jane Austen dropped out of school when she was only eleven, and she never even attended high school, much less college or graduate school.

★7. LESLIE: Your friend Paul told us that he would be visiting his parents in Knoxville this weekend. Therefore, he must not be at home.
DIANA: I agree that Paul is probably not at home, but you didn't hear him right. He said that his parents live in Nashville.

8. KARL: There's a euthanasia measure on the ballot today, and I think I'll vote for it. It seems reasonable that terminally ill patients should be allowed to be disconnected from life-support systems so that they can die peacefully and naturally.
SERGIO: You must be crazy! Euthanasia means giving people lethal injections, and that's clearly murder.

9. CHERYL: Tomorrow I'm going to the Metallica concert. Their music is fabulous.
OLIVER: You call that music? Really it's just noise, and incredibly loud noise at that.

★10. CAROL: Nelson could not have fought in the battle of Trafalgar, because that battle occurred in 1806, and Nelson died in 1804.
JUSTIN: Your knowledge of history is atrocious! Nelson did fight in Trafalgar, and the date was October 21, 1805.

11. ERIC: I've just signed up for Philosophy 502—Dr. Peterson's class in metaphysics. I know I'm going to enjoy it because I've always been fascinated by magic and ghosts.
    LEAH: I'm afraid you're in for a surprise.

12. HAROLD: Professor Steinbeck is the most intelligent man I know. His lecture series on matter and consciousness was simply brilliant.
    JOYCE: Steinbeck is actually an idiot. Yesterday I watched while he tried to get his car started. When it wouldn't start, he opened the hood, and he didn't even notice that someone had stolen the battery.

★13. THOMAS: George Foreman committed those crimes of child abuse through his own free choice. Nobody put a gun to his head. Therefore, he should be punished for them.
    EMILIE: That's not true. It's been established that Foreman was severely abused himself when he was a child, and such children have an irresistible obsession to abuse others when they grow up.

14. ANTHONY: The sun is much smaller than the earth. You see, it's just a small thing up there in the sky. Therefore, since the sun's gravitational attraction is proportional to its mass, the sun's gravity is less than the earth's.
    CINDY: You are as stupid as they come. I agree the mass of the sun is less than that of the earth, but its volume is greater. Therefore, since gravitational attraction is proportional to volume, the sun's gravity is greater than the earth's.

15. MINDY: Blue Mango is a terrific three-piece band.
    FRED: That's impossible. No band is terrific if it can only play three pieces.

★16. FRED: Today's professional athletes are overpaid. Many of them make millions of dollars a year.
    SHAWN: I don't think they are overpaid at all. Just look at the owners of some of these teams. They make ten times as much as the athletes do.

17. BRIAN: All of us have a right to life, and that means to the things necessary to sustain life. Therefore, that penniless, hungry person had a right to steal food from the grocery store.
    ELAINE: You're wrong about that. Rights are created by laws, and there is no law that says we have a right to steal.

18. PENNY: In my mind, the use of marijuana should be legalized. After all, caffeine and alcohol are no less of a drug than marijuana, and it's not illegal to enjoy a glass of beer or drink a cup of coffee.
    SAM: Your conclusion is way off. Beer and coffee are not drugs; they're foods.

★19. JERRY: In spite of the great strides technology has made in this country, poverty remains a terrible problem. Why, some people earn less than $10,000 per year. The government should do something about it.
    FRANKIE: I hardly think that $10,000 per year constitutes poverty. Why, in many Third World countries the majority of inhabitants earn less than $1,000 per year.

2

20. JOSEPH: My friend Jarvis, who plays for the NFL, told me that he has never taken any performance-enhancing drugs.
STEPHEN: That can't be true. I know Jarvis too, and he told me that he has taken Viagra for years.

V. Create the following disputes:

1. A dispute focusing on the vagueness of the word "awesome"

2. A dispute focusing on the ambiguity of the word "tip"

3. A factual dispute focusing on the date of some historical event

MindTap® Master concepts and improve outcomes with Aplia, at the end of the chapter, in the Aplia folder.

2.2   The Intension and Extension of Terms

HOW LOGICAL ARE YOU? Suppose you invite a friend to dine at a local restaurant, but she refuses to go to that restaurant because, she says, "it is so ghetto." What does your friend mean by this assertion? What is the origin of the expression? What attributes does the expression call to mind? Is the expression in any way offensive?

Find the answer on MindTap.

The main task of logic is the evaluation of arguments. However, as we saw in the previous section, there are countless arguments in which this task leads to the observation, "Well, that depends on what you mean by . . ." Such an observation usually indicates that the meaning of certain words in the argument is vague or ambiguous. Clearing up the problem often involves supplying a definition. Thus, the study of meaning and definition is closely related to the main task of logic. In this section we continue our inquiry into aspects of linguistic meaning, and the results of this inquiry provide the basis for the theory of definition in the next section.

The basic units of any ordinary language are *words*. Our main concern in this chapter, however, is not with words in general but with terms. A **term** is any word or arrangement of words that may serve as the subject of a statement. Terms consist of proper names, common names, and descriptive phrases. Here are some examples:

Proper names	Common names	Descriptive phrases
Napoleon	animal	first president of the United States
North Dakota	restitution	author of *Hamlet*
The United States	house	books in my library
Senate	activity	officers in the Swiss Navy
Toni Morrison	person	blue things
Robinson Crusoe		those who study hard

Words that are not terms include verbs, nonsubstantive adjectives, adverbs, prepositions, conjunctions, and all nonsyntactic arrangements of words. The following words or phrases are not terms; none can serve as the subject of a statement:

dictatorial	moreover
runs quickly	craves
above and beyond	cabbages into again the forest

The last example is a nonsyntactic arrangement.

At this point it is important to distinguish the *use* of a word from the *mention* of a word. Without this distinction any word can be imagined to serve as the subject of a statement and, therefore, to count as a term. The word "wherever," for example, is not a term, but "wherever" (in quotes) can serve as the subject of a statement, such as "'Wherever' is an eight-letter word." But in this statement, it is not the word itself that is the subject but rather the *quoted* word. The word is said to be *mentioned*—not *used*. On the other hand, "wherever" is *used* in this statement: "I will follow you wherever you go." In distinguishing terms from nonterms one must be sure that the word or group of words can be *used* as the subject of a statement.

The previous section of this chapter explored the cognitive meaning of language in general. The cognitive meaning of terms comprises two kinds: intensional and extensional. The **intensional meaning**, or **intension**, consists of the qualities or attributes that the term *connotes,* and the **extensional meaning**, or **extension**, consists of the members of the class that the term *denotes.* For example, the intensional meaning of the term "cat" consists of the attributes of being furry, of having four legs, of moving in a certain way, of emitting certain sounds, and so on, while the extensional meaning consists of cats themselves—all the cats in the universe. The term connotes the attributes and denotes the cats.

The intensional meaning of a term is otherwise known as the **connotation**, and the extensional meaning is known as the **denotation**. *Intension* and *extension* are roughly equivalent to the more modern terms *sense* and *reference*, respectively. Also, note that logic uses the terms *connotation* and *denotation* differently from the way they are used in grammar. In grammar, *connotation* refers to the subtle nuances of a word, whereas *denotation* refers to the word's direct and specific meaning.

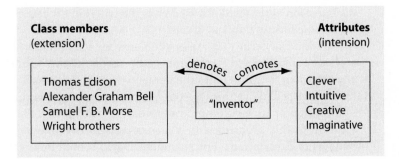

Class members
(extension)

Attributes
(intension)

Thomas Edison
Alexander Graham Bell
Samuel F. B. Morse
Wright brothers

denotes connotes

"Inventor"

Clever
Intuitive
Creative
Imaginative

Exactly how a term connotes a set of attributes allows for at least two different interpretations. Some philosophers take an objective approach and hold that a term connotes whatever attributes something must have in order to be denoted by the term. Others take what might be called a subjective approach and hold that a term connotes the attributes that occur in the minds of the people who use that term. This text takes the latter approach.

In connection with this approach, however, we encounter the problem of terms connoting different things to different people. Thus, to a cat lover the term "cat" might connote the attributes of being cuddly and adorable, while to someone who hates cats it might connote the attributes of being obnoxious and disgusting. To avoid this problem, we restrict the meaning of connotation to what is usually called the conventional connotation. The **conventional connotation** of a term includes the attributes that the term *commonly* calls forth in the minds of competent speakers of the language. Under this interpretation, the connotation of a term remains more or less the same from person to person and from time to time.

The denotation of a term also typically remains the same from person to person, but it may change over time. The denotation of "currently living cat," for example, is constantly fluctuating as some cats die and others are born. The denotation of the term "cat," on the other hand, is presumably constant because it denotes all cats—past, present, and future.

Sometimes the denotation of a term can change radically with the passage of time. The terms "currently living dodo bird" and "current king of France," for example, at one time denoted actually existing entities, but today all such entities have perished. Accordingly, these terms now have what is called **empty extension**. They are said to denote the empty (or "null") class, the class that has no members. Other terms with empty extension include "unicorn," "leprechaun," "gnome," "elf," and "griffin." While these terms have empty extension, however, they do not have empty intension. "Currently living dodo bird" and "current king of France," as well as "unicorn," "elf," and "griffin," connote a variety of intelligible attributes.

The fact that some terms have empty extension leads us to an important connection between extension and intension—namely, that *intension determines extension*. The intensional meaning of a term serves as the criterion for deciding what the extension consists of. Because we know the attributes connoted by the term "unicorn," for example, we know that the term has empty extension. That is, we know that there are no four-legged mammals having a single straight horn projecting from their forehead. Similarly, the intension of the word "cat" serves as the criterion for determining what is and what is not a member of the class of cats.

One kind of term that raises problems for the intension-determines-extension rule is proper names. For example, the name "David" might not appear to have any intension, but it denotes the person who has this name. Although philosophers have disagreed about this, it would seem that proper names must have some kind of intension or we would not know what persons, if any, they denote. One possible solution to this problem is that names are shorthand symbols for descriptions or bundles of descriptions. For example, "David" could be shorthand for "the person who lives next door" or "the person who works at the corner store and who drives a green Chevy."

Another possible solution to the problem of proper names is that the intension of proper names consists of the causal chain of events leading from the point at which the name is first assigned to the point at which a certain person learns about the name. Thus, the first link in such a chain might be the baptismal event at which the name "David" is given to a certain infant, the second link would be the event in which a certain third party is informed of the first event, and so on. This entire chain of events extending through the linguistic community would then constitute the intension of "David." Thus, we conclude that for all terms, including proper names, intension determines extension.

The distinction between intension and extension may be further illustrated by comparing the way in which these concepts can be used to give order to random sequences of terms. Terms may be put in the order of increasing intension, increasing extension, decreasing intension, and decreasing extension. A series of terms is in the order of **increasing intension** when each term in the series (except the first) connotes more attributes than the one preceding it. In other words, each term in the series after the first is *more specific* than the one preceding it. (A term is specific to the degree that it connotes more attributes.) The order of **decreasing intension** is the reverse of that of increasing intension.

A series of terms is in the order of **increasing extension** when each term in the series (except the first) denotes a class having more members than the class denoted by the term preceding it. In other words, the class size gets larger with each successive term. **Decreasing extension** is, of course, the reverse of this order. Examples:

increasing intension:	animal, mammal, feline, tiger
increasing extension:	tiger, feline, mammal, animal
decreasing intension:	tiger, feline, mammal, animal
decreasing extension:	animal, mammal, feline, tiger

These examples illustrate a fact pertaining to most such series: The order of increasing intension is usually the same as that of decreasing extension. Conversely, the order of decreasing intension is usually the same as that of increasing extension. There are some exceptions, however. Consider the following series:

unicorn; unicorn with blue eyes; unicorn with blue eyes and green horn; unicorn with blue eyes, green horn, and a weight of over 400 pounds

Each term in this series has empty extension; so, while the series exhibits the order of increasing intension, it does not exhibit the order of decreasing extension. Here is another, slightly different, example:

living human being; living human being with a genetic code; living human being with a genetic code and a brain; living human being with a genetic code, a brain, and a height of less than 100 feet

In this series none of the terms has empty extension, but each term has exactly the *same* extension as the others. Thus, while the intension increases with each successive term, once again the extension does not decrease.

2

I. The following exercises deal with words and terms.

1. Determine which of the following words or groups of words are terms and which are nonterms.

extortion	Thomas Jefferson
laborious	Empire State Building
cunningly	annoy
practitioner	render satisfactory
seriousness	graceful dancer
forever	wake up
whoever studies	not only
interestingly impassive	tallest man on the squad
scarlet	mountaintop
reinvestment	between
therefore	since

2. Name some of the attributes connoted by the following terms. Express your answer with adjectives or adjectival phrases. Example: The term "elephant" connotes the attributes of being large, having tusks, having a trunk.

drum	wolf	fanatic	riot
politician	Mona Lisa	carrot	piano
devil	Statue of Liberty		

3. In the following, name three items denoted by the terms in the left-hand column and all items denoted by the terms in the right-hand column:

newspaper	tallest mountain on earth
scientist	prime number less than 10
manufacturer	governor of New York
river	language of Canada
opera	Scandinavian country

4. Put the following sequences of terms in the order of increasing intension:

★a. conifer, Sitka spruce, tree, spruce, plant

b. Italian sports car, car, vehicle, Maserati, sports car

c. doctor of medicine, person, brain surgeon, professional person, surgeon

d. wallaby, marsupial, mammal, animal, kangaroo

e. parallelogram, polygon, square, rectangle, quadrilateral

MindTap   Complete exercises online for immediate feedback.

5. Construct a series of four terms that exhibits increasing intension but non-decreasing extension.

II. Answer "true" or "false" to the following statements:

1. All words have an intensional meaning and an extensional meaning.

2. The intensional meaning of a term consists of the attributes connoted by the term.

3. The extensional meaning of a term consists of the members of the class denoted by the term.

4. The extension of a term always remains the same with the passage of time.

5. Some terms have empty intension.

6. Some terms have empty extension.

7. The intension of a term determines the extension.

8. The intension of a term determines how specific the term is.

9. The order of increasing intension is always the same as that of decreasing extension.

10. "Leprechaun" and "unicorn" have the same extension.

III. Create the following series of terms:

1. A series of four terms, relating to music, that are in the order of increasing intension

2. A series of four terms, relating to beverages, that are in the order of increasing extension

---

MindTap   Master concepts and improve outcomes with Aplia, at the end of the chapter, in the Aplia folder.

<table>
<tr><td>2.3</td><td>Definitions and Their Purposes</td></tr>
</table>

HOW LOGICAL ARE YOU? Two friends are discussing the relative merits of a new dictionary. One of them speaks approvingly, noting that the dictionary contains the words "emoji" and "selfie." The other disagrees, arguing that it is ridiculous to include such words in a dictionary because they are simply "made-up words." The first friend then counters by observing that many people use these words regularly, and nearly everybody knows what they mean. Whom do you agree with, and why?

Find the answer on MindTap.

Over the years philosophers have held various conflicting views about the purpose of definitions. For example, Plato claimed that definitions were intended to explicate the meaning of certain eternal essences or forms, such as justice, piety, and virtue. For most logicians today, however, definitions are intended exclusively to explicate the meaning of *words*. In conformity with this latter position, we may define **definition** as a group of words that assigns a meaning to some word or group of words. Accordingly, every definition consists of two parts: the definiendum and the definiens. The **definiendum** is the word or group of words that is supposed to be defined, and the **definiens** is the word or group of words that does the defining. For example, in the definition "'Tiger' means a large, striped, ferocious feline indigenous to the jungles of India and Asia," the word "tiger" is the definiendum, and everything after the word "means" is the definiens. The definiens is not itself the meaning of the definiendum; rather, it is the group of words that symbolizes (or that is supposed to symbolize) the *same* meaning as the definiendum. Because we presumably know in advance what the definiens symbolizes, we are led, via the definition, to understand what the definiendum symbolizes. It is in this way that the definition "assigns" a meaning to its definiendum.

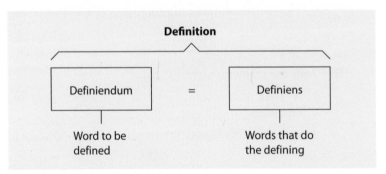

Once it has been decided that definitions explicate the meaning of words, other disagreements emerge among the philosophers. Some argue that since a definition is merely a rule that allows one set of words (the definiens) to be used in place of another set (the definiendum), definitions communicate no information at all about the subject matter of the definiendum. Others take the opposite tack and argue that since definitions result in a clarification of language, they provide a means for the discovery of deeper philosophical truths. It seems, however, that neither of these approaches is able to make good sense of all the various kinds of definitions that are actually employed in ordinary usage. As a result, instead of beginning their analysis of definitions with a set of a priori criteria, many logicians take a pragmatic approach and begin with a survey of the various kinds of definitions that are actually used and of the functions that they actually serve. This is the approach taken here.

Stipulative Definitions

A **stipulative definition** assigns a meaning to a word for the first time. This may involve either coining a new word or giving a new meaning to an old word. The purpose of a stipulative definition is usually to replace a more complex expression with a simpler one.

The need for a stipulative definition is often occasioned by some new phenomenon or development. For example, many years ago lions were crossbred with tigers. The word "tigon" was selected to name the offspring of male tiger and a female lion, and "liger" was selected to name the offspring of a male lion and a female tiger. When a zebra was crossbred with a donkey, the offspring was called a "zeedonk." Crossbreeding a lime with a kumquat produced a fruit that was called a "limequat," and crossbreeding a plum with an apricot produced a fruit called a "plumcot" and a "plout." All of these words were first assigned their meanings through stipulative definitions.

Another use for stipulative definitions is to set up secret codes. For example, during World War II, "Tora! Tora! Tora!" was the Japanese code name that triggered the attack on Pearl Harbor. "Wotan" was the German code name for a radar system; "Golfplatz" signified Great Britain; and "Operation Sealion" was the plan to invade Great Britain. "Operation Crossbow" was the British code name for countermeasures against the V-2 rocket; "Manhattan Project" signified the American effort to develop the atomic bomb; and "Operation Overlord" was the code name for the planned invasion of Normandy. More recently, corporations have employed code names to keep their projects secret from competitors. Intel has named its central processing units "Willamette," "Deschutes," and "Clackamas"—all of them pertinent to Oregon, where the units were designed. And Apple has named its operating systems after big cats: "Snow Leopard," "Lion," and "Mountain Lion."

Because people are continually coming up with new creations, whether it be food concoctions, inventions, modes of behavior, or kinds of apparel, stipulative definitions are continually being introduced to name them. The invention of computers provides a prime example. Today we have dozens of new terms or new uses of old terms that did not exist a few years ago: "cyberspace," "e-mail," "browser," "hacker," "dot-com," "hardware," "software," "download," "website," "webmaster," "server," "boot," "bar code," "mouse," "modem," "cookies," "spam," "Blackberry," "iPhone," "Bluetooth," "iPad," "Twitter," "tweet," "texting," and "sexting"—to name just a few. Earlier, in the area of biology, when a certain excretion of the pancreas was refined to its pure form, the word "insulin" was chosen to name it, and the word "penicillin" was chosen for an antibacterial substance produced by certain *Penicillium* molds. In mathematics, the symbol "10^5" was chosen as a simple substitute for "$10 \times 10 \times 10 \times 10 \times 10$."

Because a stipulative definition is a completely arbitrary assignment of a meaning to a word for the first time, there can be no such thing as a "true" or "false" stipulative definition. Furthermore, for the same reason, a stipulative definition cannot provide any new information about the subject matter of the definiendum. The fact that the word "tigon" was selected to replace "offspring of a male tiger and a female lion" tells us nothing new about the nature of the animal in question. One stipulative definition may, however, be more or less convenient or more or less appropriate than another.

Stipulative definitions are misused in verbal disputes when one person covertly uses a word in a peculiar way and then proceeds to assume that everyone else uses that word in the same way. Under these circumstances that person is said to be using the word "stipulatively." In such cases the assumption that other persons use the word in the same way is rarely justified.

Lexical Definitions

A **lexical definition** is used to report the meaning that a word already has in a language. Dictionary definitions are all instances of lexical definitions. Thus, in contrast with a stipulative definition, which assigns a meaning to a word for the first time, a lexical definition may be true or false depending on whether it does or does not report the way a word is actually used. Because words are frequently used in more than one way, lexical definitions have the further purpose of eliminating the ambiguity that would otherwise arise if one of these meanings were to be confused with another. Here are two lexical definitions:

> Light: (1) Something that makes things visible; (2) Electromagnetic radiation; (3) Of little weight; (4) Having fewer calories than the standard product.

> Bank: (1) The slope bordering a stream or river; (2) The inclination of an aircraft during a turn; (3) An institution for receiving, lending, and safeguarding money.

Because a lexical definition lists the various meanings that a word can have, a person who consults such a definition is better prepared to avoid ambiguous constructions of his or her own and to detect those of others. Undetected ambiguity causes the most trouble. In many cases the problem lies not with the obvious differences in meaning that words such as "light" and "bank" may have but with the subtle shadings of meaning that are more likely to be confused with one another. For example, if a woman is described as "nice," any number of things could be intended. She could be fastidious, refined, modest, pleasant, attractive, or even lewd. A good lexical definition will distinguish these various shadings and thereby guard against the possibility that two such meanings will be unconsciously jumbled together.

Precising Definitions

The purpose of a **precising definition** is to reduce the vagueness of a word. As we saw in the first section of this chapter, an expression is *vague* if there are borderline cases in which it is impossible to tell if the word applies or does not apply. Words such as "fresh," "rich," and "poor" are vague. Once the vagueness of such words is reduced by a precising definition, one can reach a decision as to the applicability of the word to a specific situation. For example, if legislation were ever introduced to give direct financial assistance to the poor, a precising definition would have to be supplied specifying exactly who is poor and who is not. The definition "'Poor' means having an annual income of less than $10,000 and a net worth of less than $20,000" is an example of a precising definition.

Whenever words are taken from ordinary usage and used in a highly systematic context, such as science, mathematics, medicine, or law, they must always be clarified by means of a precising definition. The terms "force," "energy," "acid," "element," "number," "equality," "contract," and "agent" have all been given precising definitions by specific disciplines.

Sometimes the substance of a court trial may revolve around the precise usage of a term. A recent harassment case before the U.S. Court of Appeals depended on whether a certain person qualified as a supervisor. The court ruled that a supervisor was one who had "the power to hire, fire, demote, promote, transfer, or discipline" an employee. This ruling amounted to a precising definition of the word "supervisor."

eminentlogicians

Peter Abelard 1079–1142

Hulton Archive/Getty Images

Generally considered the greatest logician of the Middle Ages, Peter Abelard was born in the village of Le Pallet in the Brittany region of France. His parents were members of the French nobility, and as their eldest son, Abelard was slated to inherit substantial wealth and noble standing. However, he gave up claim to this inheritance and the knighthood that went with it, choosing instead the life of a scholar.

When he was only a teenager, Abelard went off to Paris to study philosophy with William of Champeaux at the cathedral school of Notre-Dame. He proved to be a brilliant student and arrogant to a fault. He openly challenged the views of his teacher and seized on every opportunity to debate William in public. Later, he set up a rival school, describing its founder as the "only remaining philosopher in the world." Gradually, he became renowned throughout all of Europe, and he was eventually appointed to the faculty of Notre-Dame, where he attracted hundreds of students eager to learn from this illustrious master.

Around this time Abelard's attentions were drawn to Heloise, the beautiful and brilliant young niece of a prominent Parisian canon named Fulbert. Making the acquaintance of Fulbert's young protégé proved a daunting task, since her uncle kept her closely guarded. Nonetheless, Abelard persuaded Fulbert to allow him to move into his house and tutor the gifted niece, who, though only in her teens, had already mastered Greek and Hebrew. Fulbert saw this as a way of providing Heloise with a first-rate higher education, but for Abelard it provided quite a different opportunity. He later compared Fulbert's credulity in allowing him access to his charge as akin to placing a lamb in the care of a devouring wolf.

The tutoring sessions rapidly turned toward seduction, with Heloise a receptive student. Before long Heloise became pregnant and gave birth to a son whom she named Astrolabe (after the astronomical device). A public marriage might have abated the ensuing scandal, but scholars and clerics were not supposed to marry. The couple decided to marry secretly, and Heloise fled to a convent to shield herself from the scandal mongers who persecuted her for being ostensibly unwed. Meanwhile, a furious Fulbert plotted to punish Abelard, and he hired a gang of marauders to break into Abelard's lodgings in the middle of the night and castrate him.

After the castration, Abelard took refuge in one monastery after another. However his arrogance made him ill suited for monastic life, as he went out of his way to provoke the other monks. Much later, he returned to Paris where he taught until he was silenced by the church for alleged heresy. At one point he was forced to burn one of his own books. Throughout all of these calamities, Abelard remained devoted to his scholarly endeavors. He developed a truth-functional propositional logic and a theory of entailment, and he wrote prolifically in the areas of metaphysics, ethics, and philosophy of language. He is buried alongside Heloise in the Père-Lachaise Cemetery in Paris. Today, their grave site is visited by people seeking solace from the frustrations of love.

Another example involves the practice of surgical transplantation of vital organs. Before a heart transplant can be conducted, the donor must be dead; otherwise, the surgeon will be accused of murder. If the donor is dead for too long, however, the success of the transplant will be imperiled. But exactly when is a person considered to be dead? Is it when the heart stops beating, when the person stops breathing, when rigor mortis sets in, or some other time? The question involves the meaning of the term "moment of death." The courts have decided that "moment of death" should be taken to mean the moment the brain stops functioning, as measured by an electro-encephalograph. This decision amounts to the acceptance of a precising definition for "moment of death."

A precising definition differs from a stipulative definition in that the latter involves a purely arbitrary assignment of meaning, whereas the assignment of meaning in a precising definition is not at all arbitrary. A great deal of care must be taken to ensure that the assignment of meaning in a precising definition is appropriate and legitimate for the context within which the term is to be employed.

Theoretical Definitions

A **theoretical definition** assigns a meaning to a word by suggesting a theory that gives a certain characterization to the entities that the term denotes. Such a definition provides a way of viewing or conceiving these entities that suggests deductive consequences, further investigation (experimental or otherwise), and whatever else would be entailed by the acceptance of a theory governing these entities. The definition of the term "heat" found in texts dealing with the kinetic theory of heat provides a good example: "'Heat' means the energy associated with the random motion of the molecules of a substance." This definition does more than merely assign a meaning to a word; it provides a way of conceiving the physical phenomenon that is heat. In so doing, it suggests the deductive consequence that as the molecules of a substance speed up, the temperature of the substance increases. In addition, it suggests a number of experiments—experiments investigating the relationship between molecular velocity and the phenomena of radiation, gas pressure, molecular elasticity, and molecular configuration. In short, this definition of "heat" provides the impetus for an entire theory about heat.

Other examples of theoretical definitions are the definition of "light" as a form of electromagnetic radiation and the definition of "force," "mass," and "acceleration" in Newton's second law of motion as expressed in the equation "$F = MA$." The latter is a kind of contextual definition in which each term is defined in terms of the other two. Both definitions entail numerous deductive consequences about the phenomena involved and suggest numerous avenues of experimental investigation.

Not all theoretical definitions are associated with science. Many terms in philosophy, such as "substance," "form," "cause," "change," "idea," "good," "mind," and "God," have been given theoretical definitions. In fact, most of the major philosophers in history have given these terms their own peculiar theoretical definitions, and this fact accounts in part for the unique character of their respective philosophies. For example, Gottfried

Wilhelm Leibniz's definition of "substance" in terms of what he called "monads" laid the foundation for his metaphysical theory, and John Stuart Mill's definition of "good" as the greatest happiness of the greatest number provided the underpinnings for his utilitarian theory of ethics.

Like stipulative definitions, theoretical definitions are neither true nor false, strictly speaking. The reason is that theoretical definitions function as proposals to see or interpret some phenomenon in a certain way. Since proposals have no truth value, neither do theoretical definitions. They may, however, be more or less interesting or more or less fruitful, depending on the deductive consequences they entail and on the outcome of the experiments they suggest.

Persuasive Definitions

The purpose of a **persuasive definition** is to engender a favorable or unfavorable attitude toward what is denoted by the definiendum. This purpose is accomplished by assigning an emotionally charged or value-laden meaning to a word while making it appear that the word really has (or ought to have) that meaning in the language in which it is used. Thus, persuasive definitions amount to a certain synthesis of stipulative, lexical, and, possibly, theoretical definitions backed by the rhetorical motive to engender a certain attitude. As a result of this synthesis, a persuasive definition masquerades as an honest assignment of meaning to a term while condemning or blessing with approval the subject matter of the definiendum. Here are some examples of opposing pairs of persuasive definitions:

> "Abortion" means the ruthless murdering of innocent children.
> "Abortion" means a safe and established surgical procedure whereby a woman is relieved of an unwanted burden.
>
> "Liberal" means a drippy-eyed do-gooder obsessed with giving away other people's money.
> "Liberal" means a genuine humanitarian committed to the goals of adequate housing and health care and of equal opportunity for all of our citizens.
>
> "Capitalism" means the economic system in which individuals are afforded the God-given freedom to own property and conduct business as they choose.
> "Capitalism" means the economic system in which humanity is sacrificed to the wanton quest for money, and mutual understanding and respect are replaced by alienation, greed, and selfishness.
>
> "Taxation" means the procedure by means of which our commonwealth is preserved and sustained.
> "Taxation" means the procedure used by bureaucrats to rip off the people who elected them.

The objective of a persuasive definition is to influence the attitudes of the reader or listener; thus, such definitions may be used with considerable effectiveness in political speeches and editorial columns. While persuasive definitions may, like lexical definitions, be evaluated as either true or false, the primary issue is neither truth nor falsity but the effectiveness of such definitions as instruments of persuasion.

I. Determine whether the following definitions are stipulative, lexical, precising, theoretical, or persuasive.

★1. "Blind" means, for federal income-tax purposes, either the inability to see better than 20/200 in the better eye with glasses or having a field of vision of 20 degrees or less.

2. "Football" means a sport in which modern-day gladiators brutalize one another while trying to move a ridiculously shaped "ball" from one end of the playing field to the other.

3. "Dogbomber" means an inconsiderate person who does not clean up the messes his dog leaves on other people's lawns.

★4. "Diffident" means lacking confidence in oneself; characterized by modest reserve.

5. "Magnetism" means a property of certain substances such as iron, cobalt, and nickel that arises from the spin of the electrons in the unfilled inner shell of the atoms that compose the substance.

6. "Fiduciary" means having to do with a confidence or trust; a person who holds something in trust.

★7. "Politician" means a person of unquestioned honesty and integrity whom the people, in their collective wisdom, have duly elected to guide the ship of state and protect it from the reefs and shoals that threaten it on every side.

8. "Intoxicated," for purposes of driving a car in many states, means having a blood-alcohol content of 0.08 percent (.0008) or greater.

9. "Femikin" means a female manikin.

★10. "Sound" means a compression wave, in air or some other elastic medium, having a frequency ranging (for humans) from 20 to 20,000 vibrations per second.

11. "Radioactive area" means, for purposes of the U.S. Nuclear Regulatory Commission, any area accessible to individuals in which there exists radiation at such levels that a major portion of the body could receive in any one hour a dose in excess of 5 millirems or in any five consecutive days a dose in excess of 100 millirems.

12. "Neurosis" means a chronic emotional disturbance that arises from suppressed or forgotten emotional stress (such as resentment, hostility, aggression, or guilt) experienced in early childhood.

★13. "Petrograb" means invading a country to steal its oil.

MindTap® Complete exercises online for immediate feedback.

14. "Smoker" means a rude and disgusting individual who callously emits noxious tobacco fumes into the air, threatening the health and comfort of everyone in the vicinity.

15. "Diadem" means an ornamental headband worn as a badge of royalty; a crown.

★16. "Psychiatry" means the fortuitous melding of modern medicine with psychology that promises relief to thousands of poor, desperate souls who suffer the pains of emotional disorder.

17. "Gene" means the hereditary unit that occupies a fixed chromosomal locus, which through transcription has a specific effect on phenotype and which can mutate to various allelic forms.

18. "Ramster" means an animal produced by crossbreeding a rat with a hamster.

★19. "Intractable" means not easily governed; obstinate; unruly; not disposed to be taught.

20. "Recession" means, for purposes of the National Bureau of Economic Research, two consecutive quarters of negative growth in real GNP or in aggregate output for the entire economy.

21. "Gravity" means a force that results from the universal attraction that every particle of matter has for every other particle, and which varies directly with the mass of the particles and inversely with the square of the distance between them.

★22. "Assault" means, for legal purposes, an intentional and unprivileged act resulting in the apprehension of an immediate harmful or offensive contact.

23. "Television" means the electronic medium that keeps an entire nation of viewers in a state of seminarcosis by feeding them a steady stream of inane drivel.

24. "Obelisk" means an upright, four-sided pillar that terminates in a pyramid; a dagger.

★25. "Bimboy" means a boy who is a total airhead.

II. The following exercises involve constructing definitions:

1. Invent stipulative definitions for two new words that you wish to introduce into the language for the first time.

2. Construct lexical definitions for "capital" and "depression," and indicate two different meanings for each.

3. Construct precising definitions for "middle-aged" and "alcoholic." Interpret both words as relating to people and specify the purpose for which the definitions are to be used.

4. Construct theoretical definitions for "energy" and "atom."

5. Construct opposing pairs of persuasive definitions for "conservative" and "socialism."

III. Answer "true" or "false" to the following statements:

1. From the standpoint of logic, many definitions are concerned not with words but with things.
2. The definiendum is the word or term that is supposed to be defined.
3. The definiens is the word or group of words that assigns a meaning to the word being defined.
4. A stipulative definition is either true or false.
5. A lexical definition reports the way a word is actually used in a language.
6. One of the purposes of a lexical definition is to guard against the ambiguous use of a word.
7. The meaning given to a word by a precising definition is completely arbitrary.
8. Theoretical definitions are either true or false, just as are lexical definitions.
9. Theoretical definitions provide a theoretical characterization of the entity or entities denoted by the word being defined.
10. The purpose of a persuasive definition is to influence attitudes.

IV. Create the following definitions:

1. A stipulative definition for a new word you have invented
2. A precising definition for the word "loud"
3. A persuasive definition for the word "terrorist"
4. A theoretical definition for the word "atom"

MindTap® Master concepts and improve outcomes with Aplia, at the end of the chapter, in the Aplia folder.

2.4   Definitional Techniques

HOW LOGICAL ARE YOU? Suppose you are involved in a discussion with a friend as to whether there is really any difference between Republicans and Democrats. You ask your friend to define these words and he says "Republican" means a person such as Dwight D. Eisenhower, Ronald Reagan, and Richard Nixon, and "Democrat" means a person such as Sarah Jessica Parker, Gwyneth Paltrow, and Ashley Judd. Do you see any problem with these definitions? If so, what is it?

Find the answer on MindTap.

In the previous section we presented a survey of some of the kinds of definitions actually in use and the functions they are intended to serve. In this section we will investigate some of the techniques used to produce these definitions. These techniques may be classified in terms of the two kinds of meaning, intensional and extensional, discussed in Section 2.2.

Extensional (Denotative) Definitions

An **extensional (denotative) definition** is one that assigns a meaning to a term by indicating the members of the class that the definiendum denotes. There are at least three ways of indicating the members of a class: pointing to them, naming them individually, and naming them in groups. The three kinds of definitions that result are called, respectively, demonstrative or ostensive definitions, enumerative definitions, and definitions by subclass.

Demonstrative (ostensive) definitions are probably the most primitive form of definition. All one need know to understand such a definition is the meaning of pointing. As the following examples illustrate, such definitions may be either partial or complete, depending on whether all or only some of the members of the class denoted by the definiendum are pointed to:

> "Chair" means this and this and this—as you point to several chairs, one after the other.

> "Washington Monument" means that—as you point to it.

If you were attempting to teach a foreigner your own native language, and neither of you understood a word of each other's language, demonstrative definition would almost certainly be one of the methods you would use.

Because demonstrative definitions are the most primitive, they are also the most limited. In addition to the limitations affecting all extensional definitions (which will be discussed shortly), there is the obvious limitation that the required objects be available for being pointed at. For example, if one wishes to define the word "sun" and it happens to be nighttime, or the word "dog" and none happens to be in the vicinity, a demonstrative definition cannot be used.

Demonstrative definitions differ from the other kinds of definitions in that the definiens is constituted at least in part by a gesture—the gesture of pointing. Since the definiens in any definition is a group of words, however, a gesture, such as pointing, must count as a word. While this conclusion may appear strange at first, it is supported by the fact that the "words" in many sign languages consist exclusively of gestures.

Enumerative definitions assign a meaning to a term by naming the members of the class the term denotes. Like demonstrative definitions, they may also be either partial or complete. Examples:

> "Actress" means a person such as Reese Witherspoon, Blake Lively, or Emma Stone.

> "Baltic state" means Estonia, Latvia, or Lithuania.

Complete enumerative definitions are usually more satisfying than partial ones because they identify the definiendum with greater assurance. Relatively few classes, however, can be completely enumerated. Many classes, such as the class of real numbers greater than 1 but less than 2, have an infinite number of members. Others, such as the class of stars and the class of persons, while not infinite, have still too many members to enumerate. Therefore, anything approximating a complete enumerative definition of terms denoting these classes is virtually impossible. Then there are others—the class of insects and the class of trees, for example—the vast majority of whose members have no names. For terms that denote these classes, either a demonstrative definition or a definition by subclass is the more appropriate choice.

A **definition by subclass** assigns a meaning to a term by naming subclasses of the class denoted by the term. Such a definition, too, may be either partial or complete, depending on whether the subclasses named, when taken together, include all the members of the class or only some of them. Examples:

"Tree" means an oak, pine, elm, spruce, maple, and the like.

"Flower" means a rose, lily, daisy, geranium, zinnia, and the like.

"Cetacean" means either a whale, a dolphin, or a porpoise.

"Fictional work" means either a poem, a play, a novel, or a short story.

The first two are partial, the second two complete. As with definitions by enumeration, complete definitions by subclass are more satisfying than partial ones; but because relatively few terms denote classes that admit of a conveniently small number of subclasses, complete definitions by subclass are often difficult, if not impossible, to provide.

Extensional definitions are chiefly used as techniques for producing lexical and stipulative definitions. Lexical definitions are aimed at communicating how a word is actually used, and one of the ways of doing so is by identifying the members of the class that the word denotes. Dictionaries frequently include references to the individual members (or to the subclasses) of the class denoted by the word being defined. Sometimes they even include a kind of demonstrative definition when they provide a picture of the object that the word denotes. Not all lexical definitions have to occur in dictionaries, however. A lexical definition can just as well be spoken, as when one person attempts to explain orally to another how a word is used in a language. Such attempts, incidentally, often have recourse to all three kinds of extensional definition.

Stipulative definitions are used to assign a meaning to a word for the first time. This task may be accomplished by all three kinds of extensional definition. For example, a biologist engaged in naming and classifying types of fish might assign names to the specific varieties by pointing to their respective tanks (demonstrative definition), and then she might assign a class name to the whole group by referring to the names of the specific varieties (definition by subclass). An astronomer might point via his telescope to a newly discovered comet and announce, "That comet will henceforth be known as 'Henderson's Comet'" (demonstrative definition). The organizer of a children's game might make the stipulation: "John, Mary, and Billy will be called 'Buccaneers,' and Judy, George, and Nancy will be 'Pirates'" (enumerative definition).

Although it is conceivable that extensional definitions could also serve as techniques for theoretical and persuasive definitions (though this would be highly unusual), extensional definitions by themselves cannot properly serve as precising definitions for the following reason. The function of a precising definition is to clarify a vague word, and vagueness is a problem affecting intensional meaning. Because the intension is imprecise, the extension is indefinite. To attempt to render the intension precise by exactly specifying the extension (as with an extensional definition) would be tantamount to having extension determine intension—which cannot be done.

The principle that intension determines extension, whereas the converse is not true, underlies the fact that all extensional definitions suffer serious deficiencies. For example, in the case of the demonstrative definition of the word "chair," if all the chairs pointed to are made of wood, observers might get the idea that "chair" means "wood" instead of something to sit on. Similarly, they might get the idea that "Washington Monument" means "tall" or "pointed" or any of a number of other things. From the definition of "actress," readers or listeners might think that "actress" means "woman"—which would include countless individuals who have nothing to do with the stage or screen. From the definition of "tree" they might get the idea that "tree" means "firmly planted in the ground," which would also include the pilings of a building. And they might think that "cetacean" means "aquatic animal," which includes salmon, tuna, squid, manatees, and so on. In other words, it makes no difference how many individuals or subclasses are named in an extensional definition, there is no assurance that listeners or readers will get the *intensional* meaning. Extensions can *suggest* intensions, but they cannot *determine* them.

Intensional (Connotative) Definitions

An **intensional definition** is one that assigns a meaning to a word by indicating the qualities or attributes that the word connotes. Because at least four strategies may be used to indicate the attributes a word connotes, there are at least four kinds of intensional definitions: synonymous definition, etymological definition, operational definition, and definition by genus and difference.

A **synonymous definition** is one in which the definiens is a single word that connotes the same attributes as the definiendum. In other words, the definiens is a synonym of the word being defined. Examples:

> "Physician" means doctor.
>
> "Intentional" means willful.
>
> "Voracious" means ravenous.
>
> "Observe" means see.

When a single word can be found that has the same intensional meaning as the word being defined, a synonymous definition is a highly concise way of assigning a meaning. Many words, however, have subtle shades of meaning that are not connoted by any other single word. For example, the word "wisdom" is not exactly synonymous with either "knowledge," "understanding," or "sense"; and "envious" is not exactly synonymous with either "jealous" or "covetous."

An **etymological definition** assigns a meaning to a word by disclosing the word's ancestry in both its own language and other languages. Most ordinary English words have ancestors either in Old or Middle English or in some other language such as Greek, Latin, or French, and the current English meaning (as well as spelling and pronunciation) is often closely tied to the meaning (and spelling and pronunciation) of these ancestral words. For example, the English word "license" is derived from the Latin verb *licere,* which means to be permitted, and the English word "captain" derives from the Latin noun *caput,* which means head.

Etymological definitions have special importance for at least two reasons. The first is that the etymological definition of a word often conveys the word's root meaning or seminal meaning from which all other associated meanings are derived. Unless one is familiar with this root meaning, one often fails to place other meanings in their proper light or to grasp the meaning of the word when it is used in its most proper sense. For example, the word "principle" derives from the Latin word *principium,* which means beginning or source. Accordingly, the "principles of physics" are those fundamental laws that provide the "source" of the science of physics. The English word "efficient" derives from the Latin verb *efficere,* which means to bring about. Thus, the "efficient cause" of something (such as the motion of a car) is the agent that actually brings that thing about (the engine).

The second reason for the importance of etymological definitions is that if one is familiar with the etymology of one English word, one often has access to the meaning of an entire constellation of related words. For example, the word "orthodox" derives from the two Greek words *ortho,* meaning right or straight, and *doxa,* meaning belief or opinion. From this, one might grasp that "orthopedic" has to do with straight bones (originally in children—*pais* in Greek means child), and that "orthodontic" has to do with straight teeth (*odon* in Greek means tooth). Similarly, if one is familiar with the etymological definition of "polygon" (from the Greek words *poly,* meaning many, and *ganos* meaning angle), one might grasp the meanings of "polygamy" (from *gamos,* meaning marriage) and "polygraph" (from *graphein,* meaning to write). A polygraph is a lie detector that simultaneously records pulse rate, blood pressure, respiration, and so on.

An **operational definition** assigns a meaning to a word by specifying certain experimental procedures that determine whether or not the word applies to a certain thing. Examples:

> One substance is "harder than" another if and only if one scratches the other when the two are rubbed together.
>
> "Brain activity" means that an electroencephalograph shows oscillations when attached to a patient's head.
>
> A "potential difference" exists between two conductors if and only if a voltmeter shows a reading when connected to the two conductors.
>
> A solution is an "acid" if and only if litmus paper turns red when dipped into it.

Each of these definitions prescribes an operation to be performed. The first prescribes that the two substances in question be rubbed together, the second that the electro-encephalograph be connected to the patient's head and observed for oscillations, the third that the voltmeter be connected to the two conductors and observed for deflection, and the fourth that the litmus paper be placed in the solution and observed for color change. Unless it specifies such an operation, a definition cannot be an operational definition.

For example, the definition "A solution is an 'acid' if and only if it has a pH of less than 7," while good in other respects, is not an operational definition, because it prescribes no operation.

Operational definitions were invented for the purpose of tying down relatively abstract scientific concepts to the solid ground of empirical reality. In this they succeed fairly well; yet, from the standpoint of ordinary language usage, they involve certain deficiencies. One of these deficiencies concerns the fact that operational definitions usually convey only *part* of the intensional meaning of a term. Certainly "brain activity" means more than oscillations on an electroencephalograph, just as "acid" means more than litmus paper turning red. This deficiency becomes more acute when one attempts to apply operational definitions to terms outside the framework of science. For example, no adequate operational definition could be given for such words as "love," "respect," "freedom," and "dignity." Within their proper sphere, however, operational definitions are quite useful and important. Interestingly Einstein developed his special theory of relativity in partial response to the need for an operational definition of simultaneity.

A **definition by genus and difference** assigns a meaning to a term by identifying a genus term and one or more difference words that, when combined, convey the meaning of the term being defined. Definition by genus and difference is more generally applicable and achieves more adequate results than any of the other kinds of intensional definition. To explain how it works, we must first explain the meanings of the terms *genus*, *species*, and *specific difference*.

In logic, *genus* and *species* have a somewhat different meaning than they have in biology. In logic, *genus* simply means a relatively larger class, and *species* means a relatively smaller subclass of the genus. For example, we may speak of the genus animal and the species mammal, or of the genus mammal and the species feline, or of the genus feline and the species tiger, or the genus tiger and the species Bengal tiger. In other words, genus and species are merely relative classifications.

The *specific difference*, or *difference*, is the attribute or attributes that distinguish the various species within a genus. For example, the specific difference that distinguishes tigers from other species in the genus feline would include the attributes of being large, striped, ferocious, and so on. Because the specific difference is what distinguishes the species, when a genus is qualified by a specific difference, a species is identified. Definition by genus and difference is based on this fact. It consists of combining a term denoting a genus with a word or group of words connoting a specific difference so that the combination identifies the meaning of the term denoting the species.

Let us construct a definition by genus and difference for the word "ice." The first step is to identify a genus of which ice is the species. The required genus is water. Next we must identify a specific difference (attribute) that makes ice a special form of water. The required difference is frozen. The completed definition may now be written out:

Species		Difference	Genus
"Ice"	means	frozen	water.

A definition by genus and difference is easy to construct. Simply select a term that is more general than the term to be defined, then narrow it down so that it means the same thing as the term being defined. Examples:

Species		Difference	Genus
"Daughter"	means	female	offspring.
"Husband"	means	married	man.
"Doe"	means	female	deer.
"Fawn"	means	very young	deer.
"Skyscraper"	means	very tall	building.

Other examples are more complex:

> "Tent" means a collapsible shelter made of canvas or other material that is stretched and sustained by poles.

"Tent" is the species, "shelter" is the genus, and "collapsible" and "made of canvas . . ." the difference.

Definition by genus and difference is the most effective of the intensional definitions for producing the five kinds of definition discussed in Section 2.3. Stipulative, lexical, precising, theoretical, and persuasive definitions can all be constructed according to the method of genus and difference. Lexical definitions are typically definitions by genus and difference, but they also often include etymological definitions. Operational definition can serve as the method for constructing stipulative, lexical, precising, and persuasive definitions, but because of the limitations we have noted, it typically could not be used to produce a *complete* lexical definition. Other techniques would have to be used in addition. Synonymous definition may be used to produce only lexical definitions. Since, in a synonymous definition, the definiendum must have a meaning before a synonym can be found, this technique cannot be used to produce stipulative definitions, and the fact that the definiens of such a definition contains no more information than the definiendum prohibits its use in constructing precising, theoretical, and persuasive definitions.

This account of definitions is inevitably incomplete. At the beginning of the chapter we saw that all words—not just terms—stand in need of definitions, but the account given here is based on the intension and extension of *terms*. Nevertheless, many of the techniques developed here can be applied to words in general, and even to symbols. For example, Chapters 6 and 8 will present definitions of various symbols that are used in modern logic to connect one statement with another and to translate ordinary language statements into symbolic form. When logicians introduced these symbols many years ago, they did it through stipulative definitions. Also, as we will see in Chapter 6, some of these symbols are defined by certain tables, called *truth tables,* which establish each symbol's meaning under all possible arrangements of truth values. These definitions are probably best described as extensional, and they are similar in some ways to demonstrative definitions and enumerative definitions.

The applicability of the seven definitional techniques in producing the five kinds of definition is summarized in Table 2.1.

TABLE 2.1 Correlation of Definitional Techniques with Types of Definitions

| This Technique | Can Produce This Type of Definition | | | | |
	Stipulative	Lexical	Precising	Theoretical	Persuasive
Demonstrative	yes	yes	no	(unusual)	(unusual)
Enumerative	yes	yes	no	(unusual)	(unusual)
Subclass	yes	yes	no	(unusual)	(unusual)
Synonymous	no	yes	no	no	no
Etymological	yes	yes	no	no	no
Operational	(limited)	yes	yes	(unusual)	(unusual)
Genus and Difference	yes	yes	yes	yes	yes

EXERCISE 2.4

I. Determine whether the following are demonstrative definitions, enumerative definitions, definitions by subclass, synonymous definitions, etymological definitions, operational definitions, or definitions by genus and difference.

★1. "Plant" means something such as a tree, a flower, a vine, or a cactus.

2. "Hammer" means a tool used for pounding.

3. A triangle is "equilateral" if and only if a compass, when placed sequentially on two vertices and properly adjusted, strikes through the other two vertices.

★4. "State" means something such as Ohio, Arkansas, Minnesota, and Tennessee.

5. "Angel" is a word that originates from the Greek word *angelos,* which means messenger.

6. "Neophyte" means beginner.

★7. "House" means this:

8. "Painting" means something like da Vinci's *Mona Lisa,* van Gogh's *Starry Night,* Botticelli's *Birth of Venus,* or Rembrandt's *Night Watch.*

9. "Dessert" means something such as pie, cake, cookies, or ice-cream sundaes.

★10. "Hot" means, for an electric iron, that your wetted finger sizzles when placed momentarily in contact with it.

MindTap® **Complete exercises online for immediate feedback.**

11. "Universe" originates from the Latin word *universus,* which means whole or entire.

12. "Mountain" means something such as Everest, Rainier, Whitney, or McKinley.

★13. "Hurricane" means a storm having constant winds of at least 74 miles per hour that originates at sea.

14. A substance is "translucent" if and only if when held up to a strong light some of the light comes through.

15. "Insect" means something such as a fly, an ant, a wasp, or a caterpillar.

★16. "Poignant" is a word derived from the Latin word *pungere,* which means prick, pierce, or sting.

17. "Facade" means face.

18. "Prime number" means a number greater than one that is divisible only by itself and one.

★19. "Language" means something such as French, German, Spanish, or English.

20. "Tree" means this, and this, and this (as you point to several trees).

21. "Oak" means a tree that bears acorns.

★22. "Rapier" means sword.

23. An "electric current" flows in a circuit if and only if an ammeter connected in series with the circuit shows a reading.

24. "Philosopher" means someone such as Plato, Aristotle, Descartes, or Kant.

★25. "Professional person" means a person such as a doctor, a lawyer, a professor, or an architect.

26. "Error" means mistake.

27. "Tale" is a word that derives from the Old English word *talu,* which means talk.

★28. "Truck" means a vehicle used for hauling.

29. "Done" means, in reference to a baking cake, that a wooden toothpick poked into the center comes out clean.

30. "Musical composition" means something such as a symphony, a concerto, a sonata, or a toccata.

II. The following exercises involve constructing definitions:

1. Construct a partial enumerative definition for the following terms by naming three members of the class the term denotes. Then find a nonsynonymous term that these members serve equally well to define. Example: "Poet" means a person such as Wordsworth, Coleridge, or Shelley. A nonsynonymous term is "Englishman."

   ★a. skyscraper

   b. corporation

  c. island

  d. composer

  e. novel

2. Construct a complete enumerative definition for the following terms:

  a. ocean

  b. continent

3. Construct a definition by subclass for the following terms by naming three subclasses of the class the term denotes. Then find a nonsynonymous term that these subclasses serve equally well to define.

 ★a. animal

  b. fish

  c. vehicle

  d. gemstone

  e. polygon

4. Construct a complete definition by subclass for the following terms:

  a. quadrilateral

  b. circulating American coin

5. Construct synonymous definitions for the following terms:

 ★a. intersection

  b. fabric

  c. nucleus

  d. abode

  e. wedlock

  f. cellar

  g. summit

  h. apparel

6. Construct operational definitions for the following words:

 ★a. genius

  b. ferromagnetic

  c. fluorescent

  d. alkaline

  e. polarized (light)

7. Construct definitions by genus and difference for the following terms. In each definition identify the genus term.

★a. drake

b. biologist

c. felony

d. widow

e. library

8. Consult a dictionary to find the etymological roots of the following words, and then explain how they relate to the conventional meaning of these words.

★a. morphology

b. isomorphic

c. isotropic

d. phototropic

e. photography

f. lithography

g. lithology

h. psychology

III. Answer "true" or "false" to the following statements:

1. The technique of extensional definition may be used to produce precising definitions.

2. The technique of extensional definition may be used to produce stipulative and lexical definitions.

3. Most extensional definitions convey the precise intensional meaning of a term.

4. An intensional definition conveys the meaning of a term by indicating the members of the class the term denotes.

5. In a synonymous definition the definiens must be a single word.

6. The technique of synonymous definition may be used to construct precising definitions.

7. Operational definitions typically convey the entire intensional meaning of a word.

8. The species is a subclass of the genus.

9. The specific difference is an attribute or set of attributes that identifies a species.

10. Definition by genus and difference may be used to produce stipulative, lexical, precising, theoretical, and persuasive definitions.

IV. Create the following definitions:

1. A demonstrative definition for the word "sky"

2. An enumerative definition for the word "novel"

3. A synonymous definition for the word "bumbershoot"

4. A definition by subclass for the word "sport"

5. An etymological definition for the word "telephone"

6. An operational definition for the word "solid"

7. A definition by genus and difference for the word "fawn"

2.5 Criteria for Lexical Definitions

HOW LOGICAL ARE YOU? Suppose you were to look in a dictionary and find these definitions: "Beaver: a furry animal"; Oligarchy: a terrible form of government"; "Art: whatever is produced by an artist." Do you think these definitions are appropriate in a dictionary? Why or why not?

Find the answer on MindTap.

Because the function of a lexical definition is to report the way a word is actually used in a language, lexical definitions are the ones we most frequently encounter and are what most people mean when they speak of the "definition" of a word. Accordingly, it is appropriate that we have a set of rules that we may use in constructing lexical definitions of our own and in evaluating the lexical definitions of others. While some of these rules apply to the other kinds of definitions as well, the unique functions that are served by stipulative, precising, theoretical, and persuasive definitions prescribe different sets of criteria.

Rule I: A Lexical Definition Should Conform to the Standards of Proper Grammar

A definition, like any other form of expression, should be grammatically correct. Examples of definitions that are grammatically *incorrect* are as follows:

Vacation is when you don't have to go to work or school.

Furious means if you're angry at someone.

Cardiac is like something to do with the heart.

The corrected versions are these:

"Vacation" means a period during which activity is suspended from work or school.

"Furious" means a condition of being very angry.

"Cardiac" means pertaining to, situated near, or acting on the heart.

Technically the definiendum should be put in quotation marks or italics, but this convention is not always followed.

Rule 2: A Lexical Definition Should Convey the Essential Meaning of the Word Being Defined

The word "human" is occasionally defined as featherless biped. Such a definition fails to convey the essential meaning of "human" as the word is used in ordinary English. It says nothing about the important attributes that distinguish humans from the other animals—namely, the capacity to reason and to use language on a sophisticated level. A more adequate definition would be "'Human' means the animal that has the capacity to reason and to speak."

If a lexical definition is to be given in terms of an operational definition or in terms of any of the forms of extensional definition, it should usually be supplemented by one of the other forms of intensional definition, preferably definition by genus and difference. As noted, from the standpoint of ordinary language usage, an operational definition often conveys only part of the intensional meaning of a word, and this part frequently misses the essential meaning altogether. As for extensional definitions, at best they can only *suggest* the essential meaning of a word; they cannot *determine* it precisely. As a result, no adequate lexical definition can consist exclusively of extensional definitions.

Rule 3: A Lexical Definition Should Be Neither Too Broad nor Too Narrow

If a definition is too broad, the definiens includes too much; if it is too narrow, the definiens includes too little. If, for example, "bird" were defined as any warm-blooded animal having wings, the definition would be too broad because it would include bats, and bats are not birds. If, on the other hand, "bird" were defined as any warm-blooded, feathered animal that can fly, the definition would be too narrow because it would exclude ostriches and penguins, which cannot fly.

The only types of lexical definitions that tend to be susceptible to either of these deficiencies are synonymous definitions and definitions by genus and difference. With synonymous definitions, one must be careful that the definiens really is a synonym of the definiendum. For example, the definition "'king' means ruler" is too broad because many rulers are not kings. "Ruler" is not genuinely synonymous with "king." As for definitions by genus and difference, one must ensure that the specific difference narrows the genus in exactly the right way. Both of the given definitions of "bird" are definitions by genus and difference in which the specific difference fails to restrict the genus in exactly the right manner.

Rule 4: A Lexical Definition Should Avoid Circularity

A definition is *circular* when the definiendum is defined in terms of itself, or virtually in terms of itself. Sometimes the problem of circularity appears in connection with *pairs* of definitions. The following pair is circular:

> "Science" means the activity engaged in by scientists.

> "Scientist" means anyone who engages in science.

At other times a definition may be intrinsically circular. Of the following, the first is a synonymous definition, the second a definition by genus and difference:

> "Soporific" means soporiferous.

> "Jewelers' rouge" means rouge used by a jeweler.

In the first example, the definiendum is virtually the same word as the definiens. As a result, anyone who does not already know the meaning of "soporofic" would probably not know the meaning of "soporiferous," either. In the second example, "jewelers' rouge" is clearly defined in terms of itself. The corrected definitions are as follows:

> "Soporific" means tending to cause sleep.

> "Jewelers' rouge" means a very fine polishing compound.

Certain operational definitions also run the risk of circularity:

> "Time" means whatever is measured by a clock.

Arguably a person would have to know what "time" means before he or she could understand the purpose of a clock.

Rule 5: A Lexical Definition Should Not Be Negative When It Can Be Affirmative

Of the following two definitions, the first is affirmative, the second negative:

> "Concord" means harmony.

> "Concord" means the absence of discord.

Some words, however, have meanings that are are intrinsically negative. For them, a negative definition is quite appropriate. Examples:

> "Bald" means lacking hair.

> "Darkness" means the absence of light.

Rule 6: A Lexical Definition Should Avoid Figurative, Obscure, Vague, or Ambiguous Language

A definition is *figurative* if it involves metaphors or tends to paint a picture instead of exposing the essential meaning of a term. Examples:

> "Architecture" means frozen music.

> "Camel" means a ship of the desert.

A definition is *obscure* if its meaning is hidden as a result of defective or inappropriate language. One source of obscurity is overly technical language. Compare these two definitions:

> "Bunny" means a mammalian of the family Leporidae of the order Lagomorpha whose young are born furless and blind.

> "Bunny" means a rabbit.

The problem lies not with technical language as such but with *needlessly* technical language. Because "bunny" is very much a nontechnical term, no technical definition is needed. On the other hand, some words are intrinsically technical, and for them only a technical definition will suffice. Example:

> "Neutrino" means a quasi-massless lepton obeying Fermi-Dirac statistics and having one-half quantum unit of spin.

A definition is *vague* if it lacks precision or if its meaning is blurred—that is, if there is no way of telling exactly what class of things the definiens refers to. Example:

> "Democracy" means a kind of government where the people are in control.

This definition fails to identify the people who are in control, how they exercise their control, and what they are in control of.

A definition is *ambiguous* if it lends itself to more than one distinct interpretation. Example:

> "Triangle" means a figure composed of three straight lines in which all the angles are equal to two right angles.

Does this mean that each angle separately is equal to two right angles or that the angles taken together are equal to two right angles? Either interpretation is possible given the ambiguous meaning of "all the angles are equal to two right angles."

Rule 7: A Lexical Definition Should Avoid Affective Terminology

Affective terminology is any kind of word usage that plays on the emotions of the reader or listener. It includes sarcastic and facetious language and any other kind of language that could influence attitudes. Examples:

> "Communism" means that "brilliant" invention of Karl Marx and other foolish political visionaries in which the national wealth is supposed to be held in common by the people.

> "Theism" means belief in that great Santa Claus in the sky.

The second example also violates Rule 6 because it contains a metaphor.

Rule 8: A Lexical Definition Should Indicate the Context to Which the Definiens Pertains

This rule applies to any definition in which the context of the definiens is important to the meaning of the definiendum. For example, the definition "'Deuce' means a tie in points toward a game or in games toward a set" is practically meaningless without any reference to tennis. Whenever the definiendum is a word that means different things in different contexts, a reference to the context is important. Examples:

"Strike" means (in baseball) a pitch at which a batter swings and misses.

"Strike" means (in bowling) the act of knocking down all the pins with the first ball of a frame.

"Strike" means (in fishing) a pull on a line made by a fish in taking the bait.

It is not always necessary to make *explicit* reference to the context, but at least the phraseology of the definiens should indicate the context.

EXERCISE 2.5

I. Criticize the following definitions in light of the eight rules for lexical definitions:

★1. A sculpture is a three-dimensional image made of marble.

2. "Elusory" means elusive.

3. "Birdie" means sinking the ball in one stroke under par.

★4. A cynic is a person who knows the price of everything and the value of nothing.

(Oscar Wilde)

5. "Semantics" is when somebody studies words.

6. "iPhone" means a handheld electronic device having an LCD screen and a single toggle button at the bottom of the face.

★7. A theist is anyone who is not an atheist or an agnostic.

8. "Intelligence" means whatever is measured by an IQ test.

9. A symphony is a musical piece written for full orchestra.

★10. Feminism is a militant movement originated by a group of deviant women for the purpose of undermining the natural distinction between the sexes.

11. "Wood" means fibrous, lignified cellulose.

12. Logic is the study of arguments including definitions.

★13. "Truculent" is if you're cruel or fierce.

14. A house is a structure made of wood or stone intended for human habitation.

MindTap® Complete exercises online for immediate feedback.

15. Satire is a kind of glass, wherein beholders do generally discover everybody's face but their own.

(Jonathan Swift)

★16. A carpenter's square is a square used by a carpenter.

17. "Safety" means a play in which a player grounds the ball behind his own goal line when the ball was caused to cross the goal line by his own team.

18. Puberty: the time in life in which the two sexes begin first to be acquainted.

(Johnson's Dictionary)

★19. "Normal" means an attribute possessed by people who are able to get on in the world.

20. An organic substance is any substance that is not inorganic.

21. Faith is the bird that sings when the dawn is still dark.

(Rabindranath Tagore)

★22. "Schooner" means sort of like a sailboat.

23. "Faith" means reason succumbing to insecurity.

24. "Gammon" means, in backgammon, a victory in which one player defeats another before he can remove any of his men from the board.

★25. A cello is a stringed musical instrument played with a bow.

26. Tobacco is a plant grown in the southeastern United States that, when enjoyed in the form of cigars and cigarettes, produces a most delightful and satisfying taste and aroma.

27. History is the unfolding of miscalculations.

(Barbara Tuchman)

★28. "Clock" means a manufactured device featuring two pointers that rotate past a set of numerals ranging from 1 to 12.

29. "Soap" means saponified glyceride.

30. Mackerel: a sea-fish.

(Johnson's Dictionary)

★31. "Anchorperson" means an electronic media guru who has great looks but less-than-average intelligence and who brings canned news to people incapable of reading a newspaper.

32. "Diet" means like when you cut back on your calories.

33. Animal: a living creature corporeal, distinct, on the one side, from pure spirit, on the other, from pure matter.

(Johnson's Dictionary)

★34. "Pen" means an instrument used for writing on paper.

35. Wine is an alcoholic beverage made from grapes.

II. Create the following defective lexical definitions:

    1. A definition of "hexagon" that is too broad

    2. A definition of "scarf" that is too narrow

    3. A definition of "corporeal" that is negative

    4. A definition of "butcher knife" that is circular

2

MindTap®   Master concepts and improve outcomes with Aplia, at the end of the chapter, in the Aplia folder.

Summary

Linguistic expressions can have different kinds of meaning:

- Cognitive meaning: Conveys information
- Emotive meaning: Expresses or evokes feelings

Statements having emotive meaning often make value claims. When such statements occur in arguments, the value claims should be disengaged from the emotive terminology and expressed as separate premises.

Cognitive meanings can be defective in two ways:

- Vagueness: The meaning is blurred.
- Ambiguity: More than one clearly distinct meaning is possible.

A term is a word or phrase that can serve as the subject of a statement. Terms include:

- Proper names (Napoleon, North Dakota, etc.)
- Common names (animal, house, etc.)
- Descriptive phrases (author of *Hamlet*, books in my library, etc.)

Terms can have different kinds of meaning:

- Intensional meaning (or intension): The attributes that the term connotes
- Extensional meaning (or extension): The members of the class that the term denotes

Terms that refer to nonexistent things have empty extension.

A definition is a word or group of words that assigns a meaning to a word or group of words:

- Definiendum: The word or group of words being defined
- Definiens: The word or group of words that does the defining

MindTap®   **Need help?** See the Learning Logic folder at the end of the chapter: the self-paced tutorial walks you through any section.

Prepare for exams with the Chapter Test.

Definitions can serve different purposes, so there are different kinds of definitions:

- Stipulative definitions assign a meaning to a word when it first comes into use.
- Lexical definitions report the meaning a word has within a community of users.
- Precising definitions reduce the vagueness of a word.
- Theoretical definitions appeal to a theory to characterize whatever the term denotes.
- Persuasive definitions influence the attitudes of the community of users regarding whatever the word denotes.

Intensional meaning and extensional meaning provide a basis for constructing definitions:

- Extensional definitions assign a meaning by identifying the things the word denotes:
  - Demonstrative definitions "point" to these things.
  - Enumerative definitions name individuals that the word denotes.
  - Definitions by subclass identify subclasses of these things.

- Intensional definitions assign a meaning by identifying the attributes the word connotes:
  - Synonymous definitions equate the word being defined with another word that connotes the same attributes.
  - Etymological definitions disclose the word's ancestry.
  - Operational definitions specify experimental procedures for determining whether the word applies to a certain thing.
  - Definitions by genus and difference identify a genus term and one or more difference words that, when combined, convey the meaning of the definiendum.

Lexical definitions are governed by eight rules. They should:

- Conform to the standards of proper grammar.
- Convey the essential meaning of the word being defined.
- Be neither too broad nor too narrow.
- Avoid circularity.
- Not be negative when they can be affirmative.
- Avoid figurative, obscure, vague, or ambiguous language.
- Avoid affective terminology.
- Indicate the context to which the definiens pertains.

3 Informal Fallacies

3.1 Fallacies in General

HOW LOGICAL ARE YOU? Suppose a friend is doing badly in a class, and she asks for advice on how to speak to the professor. Her plan is to plead with the professor to raise her grade because she must work full time to afford tuition, and she spends every free moment caring for her sick mother. Would you encourage your friend to make this argument, or would you suggest a different kind of argument?

Find the answer on MindTap.

A **fallacy** is a defect in an argument that arises from either a mistake in reasoning or the creation of an illusion that makes a bad argument appear good. The fallacies that appear in this chapter involve errors that occur so often that they have been given specific names. The term *non sequitur* ("it does not follow") is another name for fallacy. Both deductive and inductive arguments may contain fallacies; if they do, they are either unsound or uncogent, depending on the kind of argument. Conversely, if an argument is unsound or uncogent, it has one or more false premises or it contains a fallacy (or both).

Fallacies are usually divided into two groups: formal and informal. A **formal fallacy** is one that may be identified by merely examining the form or structure of an argument. Fallacies of this kind are found only in deductive arguments that have identifiable forms. Chapter 1 presented some of these forms: categorical syllogisms,

MindTap® Read, study, reflect, and prepare for exams online, anytime, anywhere.

disjunctive syllogisms, and hypothetical syllogisms. The following categorical syllo-gism contains a formal fallacy:

> All bullfights are grotesque rituals.
> All executions are grotesque rituals.
> Therefore, all bullfights are executions.

This argument has the following form:

> All A are B.
> All C are B.
> All A are C.

By merely examining this form, one can see that it is invalid. The fact that A, B, and C stand respectively for "bullfights," "grotesque rituals," and "executions" is irrelevant in detecting the fallacy. The problem may be traced to the second premise. If the letters C and B are interchanged, the form becomes valid, and the original argument, with the same change introduced, also becomes valid (but unsound).

Here is an example of a formal fallacy that occurs in a hypothetical syllogism:

> If apes are intelligent, then apes can solve puzzles.
> Apes can solve puzzles.
> Therefore, apes are intelligent.

This argument has the following form:

> If A then B.
> B.
> A.

In this case, if A and B are interchanged in the first premise, the form becomes valid, and the original argument, with the same change, also becomes valid. This fallacy and the one that precedes it will be discussed in later chapters.

In distinguishing formal from informal fallacies, remember that formal fallacies occur only in deductive arguments. Thus, if a given argument is inductive, it cannot contain a formal fallacy. Also, keep an eye out for standard deductive argument forms such as categorical syllogisms and hypothetical syllogisms. If such an argument is invalid because of an improper arrangement of terms or statements, it commits a formal fallacy. Section 1.5 investigated some of these forms and gave instruction on distinguishing the form from the content of an argument. All of the exercises at the end of that section commit formal fallacies.

Informal fallacies are those that can be detected only by examining the content of an argument. Consider the following example:

> The Brooklyn Bridge is made of atoms.
> Atoms are invisible.
> Therefore, the Brooklyn Bridge is invisible.

To detect this fallacy one must know something about bridges—namely, that they are large visible objects, and even though their atomic components are invisible, this does not mean that the bridges themselves are invisible.

Or consider this example:

A chess player is a person.
Therefore, a bad chess player is a bad person.

To detect this fallacy one must know that the meaning of the word "bad" depends on what it modifies, and that being a bad chess player is quite different from being a bad person.

The various informal fallacies accomplish their purpose in so many different ways that no single umbrella theory covers them all. Some fallacies work by getting the reader or listener to feel various emotions, such as fear, pity, or camaraderie, and then attaching a certain conclusion to those emotions. Others attempt to discredit an opposing argument by associating it with certain pejorative features of its author. And then there are those that appeal to various dispositions on the part of the reader or listener, such as superstition or mental laziness, to get him or her to accept a conclusion. By studying the typical ways in which arguers apply these techniques, one is less likely to be fooled by the fallacious arguments posed by others or to stumble blindly into fallacies when constructing arguments for one's own use.

Since the time of Aristotle, logicians have attempted to classify the various informal fallacies. Aristotle himself identified thirteen and separated them into two groups. The work of subsequent logicians has produced dozens more, rendering the task of classifying them even more difficult. The presentation that follows divides twenty-two informal fallacies into five groups: fallacies of relevance, fallacies of weak induction, fallacies of presumption, fallacies of ambiguity, and fallacies of illicit transference. The final section of the chapter considers the related topics of detecting and avoiding fallacies in the context of ordinary language.

EXERCISE 3.1

I. Determine whether the fallacies committed by the following arguments are formal fallacies or informal fallacies.

★1. If Rasputin was really mad, then he deceived Czar Nicholas II. Rasputin was not really mad. Therefore, he did not deceive Czar Nicholas II.

2. Everything that runs has feet. The Columbia River runs very swiftly. Therefore, the Columbia River has feet.

3. All people who believe we create our own reality are people who lack social responsibility. All people governed by selfish motives are people who lack social responsibility. Therefore, all people who believe we create our own reality are people governed by selfish motives.

MindTap Complete exercises online for immediate feedback.

★4. The ship of state is like a ship at sea. No sailor is ever allowed to protest orders from the captain. For the same reason, no citizen should ever be allowed to protest presidential policies.

5. Renowned violinist Pinchas Zukerman has said, "When it comes to vodka, Smirnoff plays second fiddle to none." We must therefore conclude that Smirnoff is the best vodka available.

6. If the Chinese government systematically kills its unwanted orphans, then the Chinese government is immoral. The Chinese government is indeed immoral. Therefore, the Chinese government systematically kills its unwanted orphans.

★7. Sarah Jessica Parker, Ben Affleck, and Julia Roberts are Democrats. Therefore, it must be the case that all Hollywood stars are Democrats.

8. Mark Zuckerberg, cofounder of Facebook, argues in favor of opening up the Arctic National Wildlife Refuge to oil drilling. But consider this: Zuckerberg is just a moneygrubbing capitalist who only cares about inflating his already bloated bank account. Clearly his arguments are ridiculous.

9. If plastic guns are sold to the public, then terrorists will carry them aboard airliners undetected. If plastic guns are sold to the public, then airline hijackings will increase. Therefore, if terrorists carry plastic guns aboard airliners undetected, then airline hijackings will increase.

★10. Some corporate mergers are arrangements that produce layoffs. Some arrangements that produce layoffs are social catastrophes. Therefore, some corporate mergers are social catastrophes.

II. Create the following formal and informal fallacies:

1. A hypothetical syllogism that contains a formal fallacy (see the "apes" argument given earlier in this section)

2. An informal fallacy similar to the Brooklyn Bridge argument given earlier in this section

MindTap® Master concepts and improve outcomes with Aplia, at the end of the chapter, in the Aplia folder.

3.2   Fallacies of Relevance

HOW LOGICAL ARE YOU? Suppose your parents are urging you to spend more time on your studies and less time on social activities. You reply by pointing out that each of them had a C average upon graduation from college, and each was a member of multiple social organizations on campus. So, why should you listen to them? Do you think this rebuttal is sufficient to dismiss their recommendations?

Find the answer on MindTap.

The **fallacies of relevance** share the common characteristic that the arguments in which they occur have premises that are *logically* irrelevant to the conclusion. Yet the premises may appear to be *psychologically* relevant, so the conclusion may *seem* to follow from the premises, even though it does not follow logically. In a good argument the premises provide genuine evidence in support of the conclusion. In an argument that commits a fallacy of relevance, on the other hand, the connection between premises and conclusion is emotional. To identify a fallacy of relevance, therefore, one must be able to distinguish genuine evidence from various forms of emotional appeal.

1. Appeal to Force (*Argumentum ad Baculum*: Appeal to the "Stick")

The fallacy of **appeal to force** occurs whenever an arguer presents a conclusion to another person and tells that person either implicitly or explicitly that some harm will come to him or her if he or she does not accept the conclusion. The fallacy always involves a threat by the arguer to the physical or psychological well-being of the listener or reader, who may be either an individual or a group of people. Obviously, such a threat is logically irrelevant to the subject matter of the conclusion, so any argument based on such a procedure is fallacious. The *ad baculum* fallacy often occurs when children argue with one another:

> *Child to playmate: Sesame Street* is the best show on TV; and if you don't believe it, I'm going to call my big brother over here and he's going to beat you up.

But it occurs among adults as well:

> *Lobbyist to senator:* Senator Casey, of course you support our bill to reduce inheritance taxes. After all, you wouldn't want the press to find out about all the contributions you receive from the Ku Klux Klan.

The first example involves a physical threat, the second a psychological one. While neither threat provides any genuine evidence that the conclusion is true, both provide evidence that someone might be injured. If the two types of evidence are confused with each other, both arguer and listener may be deluded into thinking that the conclusion is supported by evidence, when in fact it is not.

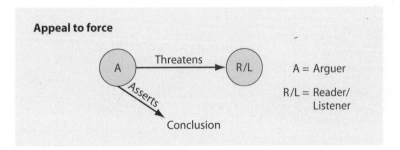

The appeal to force fallacy usually accomplishes its purpose by psychologically impeding the reader or listener from acknowledging a missing premise that, if acknowledged, would be seen to be false or at least questionable. The two examples just given can be interpreted as concealing the following premises, both of which are most likely false:

> If my brother forces you to admit that *Sesame Street* is the best show on TV, then *Sesame Street* is in fact the best show.

> If I succeed in threatening you, then you support the bill to reduce inheritance taxes.

The conclusion of the first argument is that *Sesame Street* is the best show on TV. But just because someone is forced into saying that it is does not mean that such is the case. Similarly, the conclusion of the second argument is that the senator supports the bill to reduce inheritance taxes. But just because the lobbyist succeeds in threatening the senator does not mean that the senator supports the bill. Many of the other informal fallacies can be interpreted as accomplishing their purpose in this way.

2. Appeal to Pity (*Argumentum ad Misericordiam*)

The **appeal to pity** fallacy occurs when an arguer attempts to support a conclusion by merely evoking pity from the reader or listener. This pity may be directed toward the arguer or toward some third party. Example:

> *Taxpayer to judge:* Your Honor, I admit that I declared thirteen children as dependents on my tax return, even though I have only two. But if you find me guilty of tax evasion, my reputation will be ruined. I'll probably lose my job, my poor wife will not be able to have the operation that she desperately needs, and my kids will starve. Surely I am not guilty.

The conclusion of this argument is "Surely I am not guilty." Obviously, the conclusion is not *logically* relevant to the arguer's set of pathetic circumstances, although it is *psychologically* relevant. If the arguer succeeds in evoking pity from the listener or reader, the latter is likely to exercise his or her desire to help the arguer by accepting the argument. In this way the reader or listener may be fooled into accepting a conclusion that is not supported by any evidence. The appeal to pity is quite common and is often used by students on their instructors at exam time and by lawyers on behalf of their clients before judges and juries.

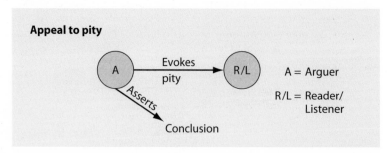

Of course, some arguments that attempt to evoke sympathetic feelings from the reader or listener are not fallacious. We might call them *arguments from compassion*. Such arguments differ from the fallacious appeal to pity in that, in addition to evoking compassion on behalf of some person, they supply information about why that person is genuinely deserving of help or special consideration. Whenever possible these non-fallacious arguments should show that the person in question is a victim of circumstances and not responsible for the dire straits he finds himself in, that the recommended help or special consideration is not illegal or inappropriate, and that it will genuinely help the person in question. In contrast to such arguments, the appeal to pity proceeds by ignoring all of these considerations and attempts to support a conclusion by merely evoking pity from the reader or listener.

3. Appeal to the People (*Argumentum ad Populum*)

Nearly everyone wants to be loved, esteemed, admired, valued, recognized, and accepted by others. The **appeal to the people** uses these desires to get the reader or listener to accept a conclusion. Two approaches are involved: one of them direct, the other indirect.

The *direct approach* occurs when an arguer, addressing a large group of people, excites the emotions and enthusiasm of the crowd to win acceptance for his or her conclusion. The objective is to arouse a kind of mob mentality. This is the strategy used by nearly every propagandist and demagogue. Adolf Hitler was a master of the technique, but speech makers at Democratic and Republican national conventions also use it with some measure of success. Waving flags and blaring music add to the overall effect. Because the individuals in the audience want to share in the camaraderie, the euphoria, and the excitement, they find themselves accepting a variety of conclusions with ever-increasing fervor.

An appeal to negative emotions can also generate a mob mentality. The **appeal to fear**, also known as fear mongering, is a variety of the direct form of the appeal to the people that occurs when an arguer trumps up a fear of something in the mind of the crowd and then uses that fear as a premise for some conclusion. Of course many fears that we experience in daily life are supported by solid evidence, such as the fear of getting mugged in a dark alley when several muggings have occurred there recently. In the appeal to fear fallacy, the fear is not supported by any solid evidence, and it usually rests on nothing more than irrational suspicion created by repeating a message or rumor over and over again. As the message gradually sinks in it causes the crowd to feel uneasy, and this alone may be enough to get a large number to accept the arguer's conclusion.

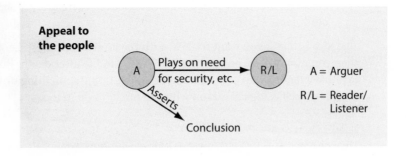

Fear mongering has played at least a minor role in nearly every presidential election. A famous example was the so-called Daisy Commercial* used in 1964 by the Lyndon Johnson campaign to defeat Barry Goldwater. The commercial raised the specter of Goldwater's possible use of nuclear weapons in Vietnam if he were to become president. What if Goldwater were elected? Could this lead to an all-out nuclear confrontation with the Soviet Union? No one could be sure of the answer. Even though the commercial was pulled after its first airing, countless news shows picked it up and repeated it over and over again. The effect was to plant the fear of nuclear annihilation in the minds of millions of voters, and in the end it swayed many of them to side with President Johnson.

Practically any social or political change is fertile ground for appeals to fear. When Darwin's theory of evolution began to be taught in the schools, William Jennings Bryan argued that it would increase the number of wars, undermine morality, convert love into hate, and destroy civilization. His speeches were a driving force in the movement to ban the teaching of evolution. When the nation was debating whether women should be allowed to vote, Elihu Root argued that suffrage would make women "hard, harsh, unlovable, repulsive." When the Soviet Union developed the atomic bomb and became a threat to world peace, Senator Joseph McCarthy argued that Soviet spies or sympathizers had infiltrated many branches of the government including the State Department and the U.S. Army. The resulting atmosphere of fear wrecked the lives of many innocent victims.

As these examples illustrate, the direct approach of appeal to the people is often accomplished through oral communication. However, writing can also produce the same effect. By using such emotionally charged phrases as "champion of the free-enterprise system," "defender of the working man," "bleeding-heart liberal," and "profligate spender," polemicists can awaken the same kind of mob mentality in their writings as they would if they were speaking.

In the *indirect approach* of appeal to the people, the arguer aims his or her appeal not at the crowd as a whole but at one or more individuals separately, focusing on some aspect of those individuals' relationship to the crowd. The indirect approach includes such specific forms as the bandwagon argument, the appeal to vanity, the appeal to snobbery, and the appeal to tradition.

The **bandwagon argument** has this general structure: Everybody believes such-and-such or does such-and-such; therefore, you should believe or do such-and-such, too. Examples:

> Everyone nowadays is on a low-carb diet. Therefore, you should go on a low-carb diet, too.

> Practically everybody believes in life after death. Therefore, you should believe in life after death, too.

The idea is that if you want to fit in with the crowd and not stick out like a sore thumb, then you, too, will go on the diet and believe in life after death. But of course the mere fact that a large group of people happen to be doing something or believe in something is not, by itself, a logical reason why you ought to do it, too.

This commercial, in its entirety, is readily available on the Internet.

The **appeal to vanity** is another form of the indirect approach, and it often involves linking the love, admiration, or approval of the crowd with some famous figure who is loved, admired, or approved of. This version of the fallacy is often used by advertisers, parents, and people in general.

> Of course you want to look as fresh and beautiful as Ellen DeGeneres. That means you will want to buy and use Cover Girl cosmetics.

> Daniel Craig wears an Omega wristwatch. Thus, if you want to be like him, you will buy and wear an Omega watch, too.

> *Mother to child:* You want to grow up and be just like Wonder Woman, don't you? Then eat your liver and carrots.

The idea is that if you succeed in becoming like DeGeneres, Craig, or Wonder Woman, then you will win the love and approval of the crowd; but to become like them you must buy the advertised product or, in the case of the little girl, eat the liver and carrots. Incidentally, these examples show how the appeal to vanity can overlap the false cause fallacy (presented in Section 3.3), because they might be interpreted to mean that using Cover Girl cosmetics will *cause* a person to look like Ellen DeGeneres, and so on. Of course, any such causal connection is unlikely.

In the **appeal to snobbery** the crowd that the arguer appeals to is a smaller group that is supposed to be superior in some way—more wealthy, more powerful, more culturally refined, more intelligent, and so on. As the argument goes, if the listener wants to be part of this group, then he or she will do a certain thing, think in a certain way, or buy a certain product. Example:

> The Lexus 400 series is not for everyone. Only those with considerable means and accomplishment will acquire one. To show the world that you are among the select few, you will want to purchase and drive one of these distinguished automobiles.

Even if a group of snobs might happen to think or feel something, this is not a logical reason for why you should act in conformity.

The **appeal to tradition** is yet another variety of the indirect appeal to the people. It occurs when an arguer cites the fact that something has become a tradition as grounds for some conclusion. The claim that something is a tradition is basically synonymous with the claim that a lot of people have done it that way for a long time. Examples:

> Traditionally, professional sporting events have been preceded by the national anthem. Therefore, professional sporting events should continue to be preceded by the national anthem.

> Serving turkey on Thanksgiving Day is a long-standing tradition. Therefore, we should serve turkey next Thanksgiving Day.

The mere fact that something has been done in a certain way for a long time does not by itself justify its being repeated in the future. Yet, there are some appeals to tradition that have conclusions that are true for other reasons, and this may trick a reader or listener into thinking that the argument is a good one. Example:

> Traditionally, guests have worn elegant clothing to Mrs. Channing's annual cocktail party. Therefore, it would not be a good idea for you to go naked to her party this year.

This argument is just as fallacious as the previous two. The conclusion is clearly true, but the reason why it is true is not because of any tradition but because the purpose of a cocktail party is to foster a feeling of conviviality among the guests. One of the guests showing up naked would threaten to destroy this purpose to the detriment of the host and all the other guests.

Incidentally, this final point about appeals to tradition with true conclusions applies to the other forms of *ad populum* as well. If such arguments have true conclusions, those conclusions are true for reasons other than the fact that the crowd believes something or feels something.

Both the direct and indirect approaches of the *ad populum* fallacy have the same basic structure:

> You want to be accepted/included in the group/loved/esteemed....Therefore, you should accept XYZ as true.

In the direct approach the arousal of a mob mentality produces an immediate feeling of belonging, even if it relates to something feared. Each person feels united with the crowd, and this feeling evokes a sense of strength and security. When the crowd roars its approval of the conclusions that are then offered, anyone who does not accept them automatically cuts himself or herself off from the crowd and risks the loss of his or her security, strength, and acceptance. The same thing happens in the indirect approach, but the context and technique are somewhat subtler.

4. Argument Against the Person (*Argumentum ad Hominem*)

This fallacy always involves two arguers. One of them advances (either directly or implicitly) a certain argument, and the other then responds by directing his or her attention not to the first person's argument but to the first person *himself*. When this occurs, the second person is said to commit an **argument against the person**.

The argument against the person occurs in three forms: the *ad hominem* abusive, the *ad hominem* circumstantial, and the *tu quoque*. In the **ad hominem abusive**, the second person responds to the first person's argument by verbally abusing the first person. Example:

> Television entertainer Bill Maher argues that religion is just a lot of foolish nonsense. But Maher is an arrogant, shameless, self-righteous pig. Obviously his arguments are not worth listening to.

The author of this argument ignores the substance of Maher's argument and instead attacks Maher himself. However, because Maher's personal attributes are irrelevant to whether the premises of his religion argument support the conclusion, the argument attacking him is fallacious.

Not all cases of the *ad hominem* abusive are so blunt, but they are just as fallacious. Example:

> Dr. Phil argues that mutual self-esteem is essential to a good marriage. But Dr. Phil is not terribly well educated, and he never attended an Ivy League college. Thus, his arguments are worthless.

A very common form of the *ad hominem* abusive occurs when the responding arguer's retort is to suggest that the opposing arguer consider going somewhere else—such as out of the country ("America—love it or leave it"), switching to a different religion or political party, or doing something ridiculous (such as jumping in a lake or flying a kite). Example:

> Billionaire investor Warren Buffet argues that wealthy people should be required to pay more taxes. I would remind Mr. Buffett that he is free to send a check to the Department of the Treasury any time he likes.

This argument commits an *ad hominem* because instead of replying to Mr. Buffet's argument, the second arguer directs his attention to Mr. Buffet himself and suggests that if he is so concerned about the inflow of tax dollars, he can increase the amount of his own taxes. The aim is to show that Mr. Buffet is insincere.

The **ad hominem circumstantial** begins the same way as the *ad hominem* abusive, but instead of heaping verbal abuse on his or her opponent, the respondent attempts to discredit the opponent's argument by alluding to certain circumstances that affect the opponent. By doing so the respondent hopes to show that the opponent is predisposed to argue the way he or she does and should therefore not be taken seriously. Here is an example:

> The Dalai Lama argues that China has no business in Tibet and that the West should do something about it. But the Dalai Lama just wants the Chinese to leave so he can return as leader. Naturally he argues this way. Therefore, we should reject his arguments.

The author of this argument ignores the substance of the Dalai Lama's argument and attempts to discredit it by calling attention to certain circumstances that affect the Dalai Lama—namely, that he wants to return to Tibet as its leader. But the fact that the Dalai Lama happens to be affected by these circumstances is irrelevant to whether his premises support a conclusion. The *ad hominem* circumstantial is easy to recognize because it always takes this form: "Of course Mr. X argues this way; just look at the circumstances that affect him."

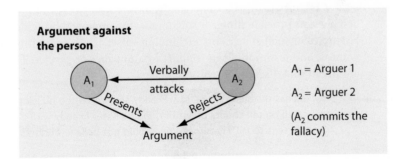

The **tu quoque** ("you too") fallacy begins the same way as the other two varieties of the *ad hominem* argument, except that the second arguer attempts to make the first appear to be hypocritical or arguing in bad faith. The second arguer usually accomplishes this by citing features in the life or behavior of the first arguer that conflict with the latter's conclusion. The fallacy often takes the form, "How dare you argue that I should stop doing X; why, you do (or have done) X yourself." Example:

> Kim Kardashian argues that women should not have children out of wedlock. But who is she to talk? She gave birth to her daughter North without being married. Clearly Kardashian's argument is not worth listening to.

Again, the fact that Kim Kardashian gave birth to a daughter out of wedlock is irrelevant to whether her premises support her conclusion. Thus, the argument is fallacious.

Keep in mind that the purpose of an *ad hominem* argument is to discredit another person's argument by placing its author in a bad light. Thus, for the fallacy to be committed, there must always be two arguers (at least implicitly). If it should turn out that the person being attacked is not an arguer, then the personal comments made by the attacker may well be relevant to the conclusion that is drawn. In general, personal observations are relevant to conclusions about what kind of person someone is (good, bad, stingy, trustworthy, and so forth) and whether a person has done something. Example:

> North Korean dictator Kim Jong-un has murdered political opponents and their entire families, and he has committed other crimes including extermination, enslavement, torture, and rape. Also, he has threatened U. S. cities with nuclear annihilation. Kim Jong-un is therefore a thoroughly despicable and disgusting human being.

The conclusion is not that Kim Jong's argument is bad but that Kim Jong himself is bad. Because the premises give relevant support to this conclusion, the argument commits no fallacy. Another example:

> Shakespeare cannot possibly have written the thirty-six plays attributed to him, because the real Shakespeare was a two-bit country businessman who barely finished the fourth grade in school and who never left the confines of his native England.

The conclusion is not that some argument of Shakespeare's is bad but that Shakespeare did not write certain plays. Again, since the premises are relevant to this conclusion, the argument commits no *ad hominem* fallacy.

Determining what kind of person someone is includes determining whether that person is trustworthy. Thus, personal comments are often relevant in evaluating whether a person's proclamations or statements, unsupported by evidence, warrant our belief. Examples of such statements include promises to do something, testimony given by a witness, and testimonials in support of a product or service. Here is an example of an argument that discredits a witness:

> Mickey has testified that he saw Freddy set fire to the building. But Mickey was recently convicted on ten counts of perjury, and he hates Freddy with a passion and would love to see him sent to jail. Therefore, you should not believe Mickey's testimony.

This argument commits no fallacy. The conclusion is not that you should reject Mickey's argument but rather that you should reject his testimony. Testimony is not argument, and the fact that the witness is a known liar and has a motive to lie now is relevant to whether we should believe him. Furthermore, note that the conclusion is not that Mickey's statement is literally false but rather that we should not *believe* the statement. It is quite possible that Mickey really did see Freddy set fire to the building and that Mickey's statement to that effect is true. But if our only reason for believing this statement is the mere fact that Mickey has made it, then given the circumstances, we are not justified in that belief. Personal factors are never relevant to truth and falsity as such, but they are relevant to believability.

Yet there is often a close connection between truth and believability, and this provides one of the reasons why *ad hominem* arguments are often effective. In evaluating any argument there are always two issues to be considered: the quality of the reasoning and the truth of the premises. As noted, both are irrelevant to the personal characteristics of the arguer. But whether we *accept* the premises as true may depend on the credibility of the arguer. Knowing that the arguer is biased or has a motive to lie may provide good grounds for distrusting the premises. Another reason why *ad hominem* arguments are effective is that they engage the emotions of readers and listeners and thereby motivate them to transfer their negative feelings about the arguer onto the argument.

5. Accident

The fallacy of **accident** is committed when a general rule is applied to a specific case it was not intended to cover. Typically, the general rule is cited (either directly or implicitly) in the premises and then wrongly applied to the specific case mentioned in the conclusion. Two examples:

> Freedom of speech is a constitutionally guaranteed right. Therefore, John Q. Radical should not be arrested for his speech that incited the riot last week.

> Zoe promised to meet Ethan for coffee, but while she was walking to the local Starbucks, a pedestrian collapsed on the sidewalk right in front of her and she stopped to administer CPR. Since people are obligated to keep their promises, it was wrong for Zoe to miss her appointment with Ethan.

In the first example, the general rule is that freedom of speech is normally guaranteed, and the specific case is the speech made by John Q. Radical. Because the speech incited a riot, the rule does not apply. In the second example, the general rule is that people are obligated to keep their promises, and the specific case is the promise that Zoe made to Ethan. The rule does not apply because saving a human life is more important than keeping a coffee appointment.

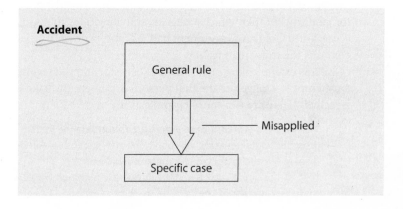

The fallacy of accident gets its name from the fact that one or more accidental features of the specific case make it an exception to the rule. In the first example the accidental feature is that the speech incited a riot; in the second example the accidental feature is that while Zoe was en route to meeting Ethan, someone collapsed on the sidewalk right in front of her.

6. Straw Man

The **straw man** fallacy is committed when an arguer distorts an opponent's argument for the purpose of more easily attacking it, demolishes the distorted argument, and then concludes that the opponent's real argument has been demolished. By so doing, the arguer is said to have set up a straw man and knocked it down, only to conclude that the real "man" (opposing argument) has been knocked down as well. Example:

> Mr. Goldberg has argued against prayer in the public schools. Obviously Mr. Goldberg advocates atheism. But atheism is what they used to have in Russia. Atheism leads to the suppression of all religions and the replacement of God by an omnipotent state. Is that what we want for this country? I hardly think so. Clearly Mr. Goldberg's argument is nonsense.

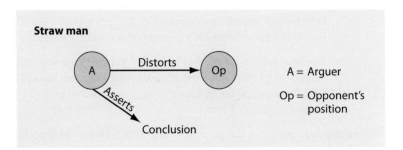

Straw man, along with argument against the person, are called refutational fallacies because they involve one arguer refuting another. These are the only fallacies presented in this chapter that always involve two arguers. In the Goldberg argument, Mr. Goldberg, who is the first arguer, has presented an argument against prayer in the public schools. The second arguer then attacks Goldberg's argument by equating it with an argument for atheism. He then attacks atheism and concludes that Goldberg's argument is nonsense. Since Goldberg's argument had nothing to do with atheism, the second argument commits the straw man fallacy.

As this example illustrates, the kind of distortion the second arguer resorts to is often an attempt to exaggerate the first person's argument or make it look more extreme than it really is. Here are two more examples:

> The garment workers have signed a petition arguing for better ventilation on the work premises. Unfortunately, air-conditioning is expensive. Air ducts would have to be run throughout the factory, and a massive heat exchange unit installed on the roof. Also, the cost of operating such a system during the summer would be astronomical. In view of these considerations the petition must be rejected.

The student status committee has presented us with an argument favoring alcohol privileges on campus. What do the students want? Is it their intention to stay boozed up from the day they enter as freshmen until the day they graduate? Do they expect us to open a bar for them? Or maybe a chain of bars all over campus? Such a proposal is ridiculous!

In the first argument, the petition is merely for better ventilation in the factory—maybe a fan in the window during the summer. The arguer exaggerates this request to mean an elaborate air-conditioning system installed throughout the building. He then points out that this is too expensive and concludes by rejecting the petition. A similar strategy is used in the second argument. The arguer distorts the request for alcohol privileges to mean a chain of bars all over campus. Such an idea is so patently outlandish that no further argument is necessary.

7. Missing the Point (*Ignoratio Elenchi*)

All the fallacies we have discussed thus far have been instances of cases where the premises of an argument are irrelevant to the conclusion. **Missing the point** illustrates a special form of irrelevance. This fallacy occurs when the premises of an argument support one particular conclusion, but then a different conclusion, often vaguely related to the correct conclusion, is drawn. Whenever one suspects that such a fallacy is being committed, he or she should be able to identify the *correct* conclusion, the conclusion that the premises *logically* imply. This conclusion must be significantly different from the conclusion that is actually drawn. Examples:

Crimes of theft and robbery have been increasing at an alarming rate lately. The conclusion is obvious: We must reinstate the death penalty immediately.

Abuse of the welfare system is rampant nowadays. Our only alternative is to abolish the system altogether.

At least two correct conclusions are implied by the premise of the first argument: either "We should provide increased police protection in vulnerable neighborhoods" or "We should initiate programs to eliminate the causes of the crimes." Reinstating the death penalty is not a logical conclusion at all. Among other things, theft and robbery are not capital crimes. In the second argument the premises logically suggest some systematic effort to eliminate the cheaters rather than eliminating the system altogether.

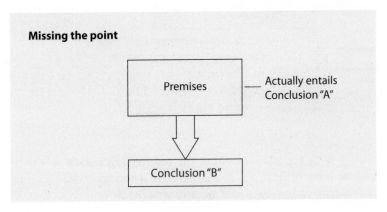

Missing the point

Premises ———— Actually entails Conclusion "A"

Conclusion "B"

Ignoratio elenchi means "ignorance of the proof." The arguer is ignorant of the logical implications of his or her own premises and, as a result, draws a conclusion that misses the point entirely. The fallacy has a distinct structure all its own, but in some ways it serves as a catchall for arguments that are not clear instances of one or more of the other fallacies. An argument should not be identified as a case of missing the point, however, if one of the other fallacies fits.

8. Red Herring

This fallacy is closely associated with missing the point (*ignoratio elenchi*). The **red herring** fallacy is committed when the arguer diverts the attention of the reader or listener by changing the subject to a different but sometimes subtly related one. He or she then finishes by either drawing a conclusion about this different issue or by merely presuming that some conclusion has been established. By so doing, the arguer purports to have won the argument. The fallacy gets its name from a procedure used to train hunting dogs to follow a scent. A red herring (or bag of them) is dragged across the trail with the aim of leading the dogs astray. Since red herrings have an especially potent scent (caused in part by the smoking process used to preserve them), only the best dogs will follow the original scent.

To use the red herring fallacy effectively, the arguer must change the original subject of the argument without the reader or listener noticing it. One way of doing this is to change the subject to one that is subtly related to the original subject. Here are two examples of this technique:

> Environmentalists are continually harping about the dangers of nuclear power. Unfortunately, electricity is dangerous no matter where it comes from. Every year hundreds of people are electrocuted by accident. Since most of these accidents are caused by carelessness, they could be avoided if people would just exercise greater caution.

> There is a good deal of talk these days about the need to eliminate pesticides from our fruits and vegetables. But many of these foods are essential to our health. Carrots are an excellent source of vitamin A, broccoli is rich in iron, and oranges and grapefruit have lots of vitamin C.

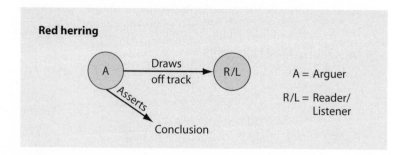

Both arguments commit the red herring fallacy. In the first, the original issue is whether nuclear power is dangerous. The arguer changes this subject to the danger of electrocution and proceeds to draw a conclusion about that. The new subject is clearly different from the possibility of nuclear explosion or meltdown, but the fact that both are related to electricity facilitates the arguer's goal of leading someone off the track. In the second argument, the original issue is pesticides, and the arguer changes it to the value of fruits and vegetables in one's diet. Again, the fact that the second topic is related to the first assists the arguer in committing the fallacy. In neither case does the arguer draw a conclusion about the original topic, but by merely diverting the attention of the reader or listener, the arguer creates the presumption of having won the argument.

A second way of using the red herring effectively is to change the subject to some flashy, eye-catching topic that is virtually guaranteed to distract the listener's attention. Topics of this sort include sex, crime, scandal, immorality, death, and any other topic that might serve as the subject of gossip. Here is an example of this technique:

> Professor Conway complains of inadequate parking on our campus. But did you hear that Conway's eldest son, Jasper, was convicted a year ago of embezzlement? Jasper managed to steal half a million dollars from the First National Bank before officials figured out what was going on. It's really important that bank officials be constantly vigilant. Okay, let's move on to the next topic.

The red herring fallacy can be confused with the straw man fallacy because both have the effect of drawing the reader/listener off the track. This confusion can usually be avoided by remembering the unique ways in which they accomplish this purpose. In the straw man, the arguer begins by distorting an opponent's argument and concludes by knocking down the distorted argument. In the red herring, the arguer ignores the opponent's argument (if there is one) and subtly changes the subject. Thus, to distinguish the two fallacies, one should attempt to determine whether the arguer has knocked down a distorted argument or simply changed the subject. Also keep in mind that straw man always involves two arguers, at least implicitly, whereas a red herring often does not.

Both the red herring and straw man fallacies are susceptible of being confused with missing the point, because all three involve a similar kind of irrelevancy. To avoid this confusion, one should note that both red herring and straw man proceed by generating a new set of premises, whereas missing the point does not. Straw man draws a conclusion from new premises that are obtained by distorting an earlier argument, and red herring, if it draws any conclusion at all, draws one from new premises obtained by changing the subject. Missing the point, however, draws a conclusion from the original premises. Also, in the red herring and straw man, the conclusion, if there is one, is *relevant* to the premises from which it is drawn; but in missing the point, the conclusion is *irrelevant* to the premises from which it is drawn. Finally, remember that missing the point serves in part as a kind of catchall fallacy, and a fallacious argument should not be identified as a case of missing the point if one of the other fallacies clearly fits.

MindTap Strengthen your understanding of the topic with the section's **Video Lecture**.

I. Identify the fallacies of relevance committed by the following arguments, giving a brief explanation for your answer. If no fallacy is committed, write "no fallacy."

★**1.** The position open in the accounting department should be given to Frank Thompson. Frank has six hungry children to feed, and his wife desperately needs an operation to save her eyesight.

2. Erica Evans, who takes orders at the local Taco Bell, argues persuasively in favor of increasing the minimum wage. But this is exactly what you would expect. Erica is paid the minimum wage, and if the minimum wage is increased, then her own salary will go up. Obviously Erica's arguments are worthless.

3. The school board argues that our schools are in desperate need of repair. But the real reason our students are falling behind is that they spend too much time on their smartphones. Becoming educated means a lot more than learning how to scroll up and down. The school board should send a letter to the parents urging them to confiscate their kids' smartphones.

★**4.** Whoever thrusts a knife into another person should be arrested. But surgeons do precisely this when operating. Therefore, surgeons should be arrested.

5. You should read Irving Stone's latest novel right away. It's sold over a million copies, and practically everyone in the Manhattan cocktail circuit is talking about it.

6. Friedrich Nietzsche's philosophy is not worth the paper it's printed on. Nietzsche was an immoral reprobate who went completely insane from syphilis before he died.

★**7.** Surely you welcome the opportunity to join our protective organization. Think of all the money you will lose from broken windows, overturned trucks, and damaged merchandise in the event of your not joining.

8. Senator Barrow advocates increased Social Security benefits for the poor. It is regrettable that the senator finds it necessary to advocate socialism. Socialism defeats initiative, takes away promised rewards, and leads directly to inefficiency and big government. It was tried for years in Eastern Europe, and it failed miserably. Clearly, socialism is no good.

9. Something is seriously wrong with high school education these days. After ten years of decline, SAT scores are still extremely low, and high school graduates are practically incapable of reading and writing. The obvious conclusion is that we should close the schools.

★**10.** Giving ridiculous reasons, the editors of the *Daily Register* have accused our company of being one of the city's worst water polluters. But the *Daily Register* is responsible for much more pollution than we are. After all, they own

MindTap   Complete exercises online for immediate feedback.

the Western Paper Company, and that company discharges tons of chemical residue into the city's river every day.

11. If 20 percent of adult Americans are functionally illiterate, then it's no wonder that morons get elected to public office. In fact, 20 percent of adult Americans *are* functionally illiterate. Therefore, it's no wonder that morons get elected to public office.

12. Ladies and gentlemen, today the lines of battle have been drawn. When the din of clashing armor has finally died away, the Republican party will emerge victorious! We are the true party of the American people! We embody the values that all real Americans hold sacred! We cherish and protect our founding fathers' vision that gave birth to the Constitution! We stand for decency and righteousness; for self-determination and the liberty to conduct our affairs as each of us freely chooses! In the coming election, victory will be ours, so help us God!

★13. We've all heard the argument that too much television is the reason our students can't read and write. Yet many of today's TV shows are excellent. *Madam Secretary* offers a look at the personal and professional life of a secretary of state, *The Big Bang Theory* serves up lots of laughs in a highbrow setting, and *The Voice* presents vocalists from across the country competing with help from coaches. Today's TV is just great!

14. Surely architect Norris is not responsible for the collapse of the Central Bank Tower. Norris has had nothing but trouble lately. His daughter eloped with a child molester, his son committed suicide, and his alcoholic wife recently left for Las Vegas with his retirement savings.

15. The First Amendment to the Constitution prevents the government from interfering with the free exercise of religion. The liturgical practice of the Religion of Internal Enlightenment involves human sacrifice. Therefore, it would be wrong for the government to interfere with this religious practice.

★16. U.S. Senator Elizabeth Warren argues that big banks have been ripping off the American consumer for years. It's clear, however, that Warren says this only to scratch up more campaign contributions from those very consumers. Thus, you shouldn't take her arguments seriously.

17. Professor Pearson's arguments in favor of the theory of evolution should be discounted. Pearson is a cocaine-snorting sex pervert and, according to some reports, a member of the Communist party.

18. Rudolf Höss, commandant of the Auschwitz concentration camp, confessed to having exterminated 1 million people, most of whom were Jews, in the Auschwitz gas chamber. We can only conclude that Höss was either insane or an extremely evil person.

★19. TV commentator Larry Kudlow argues that government should get off the back of the American businessman. Obviously, Kudlow wants to abolish government altogether. Yet without government there would be no defense, no judicial system, no Social Security, and no health and safety regulations. None of us wants to forgo these benefits. Thus, we can see that Kudlow's argument is absurd.

20. I know that some of you oppose the appointment of David Cole as the new sales manager. On further consideration, however, I am confident you will find him well qualified for the job. If Cole is not appointed, it may become necessary to make severe personnel cutbacks in your department.

21. Animal rights activists say that animals are abused in biomedical research labs. But consider this: Pets are abused by their owners every day. Probably 25 percent of pet owners should never get near animals. Some cases of abuse are enough to make you sick.

★22. Of course you want to buy a pair of Slinky fashion jeans. Slinky jeans really show off your figure, and all the Hollywood starlets down on the Strip can be seen wearing them these days.

23. Marie Osmond says on TV that Nutrisystem is the best way to get rid of belly fat. But this is exactly what you would expect given that Nutrisystem pays her millions of dollars to make these ads. Thus, you shouldn't take her testimonials too seriously.

24. Dr. Morrison has argued that smoking is responsible for the majority of health problems in this country and that every smoker who has even the slightest concern for his or her health should quit. Unfortunately, however, we must consign Dr. Morrison's argument to the trash bin. Only yesterday I saw none other than Dr. Morrison himself smoking a cigar.

★25. Mr. Rhodes is suffering from amnesia and has no recollection whatever of the events of the past two weeks. We can only conclude that he did not commit the crime of murdering his wife a week ago, as he has been accused of doing.

II. Answer "true" or "false" to the following statements:

1. In the appeal to force, the arguer physically attacks the listener.

2. In the direct variety of the appeal to the people, the arguer attempts to create a kind of mob mentality.

3. If an arguer attempts to discredit courtroom testimony or a promise by pointing out that the witness or the person making the promise is a liar, then the arguer commits an *argumentum ad hominem* (argument against the person) fallacy.

4. The *argumentum ad hominem* always involves two arguers.

5. In the *argumentum ad hominem* circumstantial, the circumstances cited by the second arguer are intended precisely to malign the character of the first arguer.

6. In the *tu quoque* fallacy, the arguer threatens the reader or listener.

7. In the fallacy of accident, a general rule is applied to a specific case where it does not fit.

8. In the straw man fallacy, an arguer often distorts another person's argument by making it look more extreme than it really is.

9. Whenever one suspects that a missing the point fallacy is being committed, one should be able to state the conclusion that is logically implied by the premises.

10. In the red herring fallacy, the arguer attempts to lead the reader or listener off the track.

III. Identify the fallacies committed in the following dialogue. You should be able to find at least one case of each fallacy presented in this section.

Food for Thought

"Let's hit the produce section first," Curtis says to his fiancée Talia, as they enter Payless grocery store.

"Okay," she says.

"Oh, look," says Curtis. "The corn is on sale. Let's get some for dinner."

"I don't know," says Talia. "Did you see that sign over the display? The corn is genetically modified. I know we've never paid much attention to that sign in the past, but now I'm thinking that maybe we should."

"Why's that?" asks Curtis.

"I read an article the other day about foods containing genetically modified organisms— they call them GMO foods—and now I know what's behind this GMO business," Talia replies.

"And what is behind it?" Curtis asks.

Talia picks up an ear and sniffs it. "For starters," she says, "one of the reasons they modify corn is to make it resistant to herbicides like Roundup—you know, the stuff you spray on the weeds in the garden. So with GMO corn the farmer can spray the whole field with Roundup, the weeds will die, and the cornstalks will be unaffected."

"Sounds like a great way to grow corn," Curtis says.

"Yes," replies Talia, "but that means the corn contains a residue of Roundup. That's definitely not good. Roundup is a probable cause of cancer."

"Good grief," says Curtis. "If what you say is right, I think there is only one conclusion: We must ban the sale of Roundup immediately."

After pausing to scratch his head, he continues, "On the other hand, look at all the people who are buying this corn. If everyone is buying it, then I think we should, too."

"You're right that everyone is buying it," says Talia. "Nearly 90 percent of the corn sold in this country is genetically modified. But that doesn't mean that we should buy it. Look, there's a small display of organic corn over there. Let's get some of that."

"Now wait just a minute," says Curtis. "You better not be going organic on me. That would be too much. You know I like to eat out at least once a week, and most restaurants don't serve organic food. If you insist on organic, then you will stay at home cooking your own food, while I go out."

"Well, maybe I could eat conventional restaurant food once in a while," says Talia. "But organic food has become really appealing these days. That actor Christian Slater promotes it in magazine ads. And some of my friends say that he is really sexy and that you look like him! Maybe you should think about switching to organic."

"I look like Christian Slater?" asks Curtis, looking flattered. "Wow! Maybe you're right. But now that you've raised the issue, that reminds me of something. Didn't you tell me a while back that you had an uncle who grew organic food? If he makes a lot of money, you might inherit it. I bet that's what's behind this organic thing of yours."

"Not at all," says Talia. "But I'm glad you mentioned the farmers. Some of these people have invested every cent they have in growing organic food. If consumers don't buy it, these poor, hardworking farmers will all go broke. We really can't let that happen. They've put their heart and soul into growing really healthy food for people like you and me. We can't let them down."

"And here's another consideration," continues Talia. "A basic principle of morality says that we should help others in need. The owner of this grocery store needs for people to buy his organic produce. Thus, I think we have an obligation to buy it."

"Ha, ha," Curtis laughs. "According to that argument we also have a moral obligation to buy the GMO food. I don't think we have a moral obligation to buy anything. But now that I think of it, you've always been a bit resistant to anything new. When smartphones came out, you didn't want one, you didn't want a flat-screen TV, and now you don't want GMO corn. You should be more open to scientific developments."

Talia smirks. "And what about you?" she asks. "You seem to think technology can solve all our problems. By that line of reasoning, we should have robots serving our every need. Robot doctors, robot lawyers, robot cooks, robot grade-school teachers. But robots will never replace human beings. Human beings have feelings. They have hopes and fears and they love each other. Robots don't love anything."

"I know nothing about robots," says Curtis, "but getting back to corn, just compare this GMO corn with the organic corn in the other bin. The GMO corn looks larger and more appetizing than the organic. In fact, we do lots of things these days to make vegetables look more appetizing and grow better. For example, we add fertilizer to the soil. Nitrogen is an important ingredient in these fertilizers, and so is phosphorus and potassium."

"I didn't realize you knew so much about fertilizer," Talia says. "I need some fertilizer for my flower garden. Could you recommend something?"

"Yes, I could. But in the meantime, shall we get some corn?" Curtis asks as he selects two ears from the GMO bin.

Talia takes one ear from his hand and puts it back. She then crosses over to the organic bin, tucks an ear under her arm, and smiles at Curtis. "One for you, one for me," she says.

IV. Create the following informal fallacies:

1. An appeal to force dealing with an automobile collision

2. An appeal to pity about hiring someone for a job

3. An appeal to fear related to immigration

4. A bandwagon argument dealing with alcoholic beverages

5. An *ad hominem* abusive related to politics

6. An *ad hominem* circumstantial about gender identity

7. A *tu quoque* connected with diet and exercise

8. A red herring dealing with climate change

MindTap Master concepts and improve outcomes with Aplia, at the end of the chapter, in the Aplia folder.

Fallacies of Weak Induction

HOW LOGICAL ARE YOU? Suppose, while visiting Las Vegas for the weekend, that you spend all of your allotted gambling money ($100) on a single slot machine. You remark to a friend that you would love to win your money back, and he urges you to withdraw another $100 from a nearby ATM. After all, he argues, you have put so much money into that one machine that you are due for a big win. Has your friend given you good advice?

Find the answer on MindTap.

The **fallacies of weak induction** occur not because the premises are logically irrelevant to the conclusion, as is the case with the eight fallacies of relevance, but because the connection between premises and conclusion is not strong enough to support the conclusion. In each of the following fallacies, the premises provide at least a shred of evidence in support of the conclusion, but the evidence is not nearly good enough to cause a reasonable person to believe the conclusion. Like the fallacies of relevance, however, the fallacies of weak induction often involve emotional grounds for believing the conclusion.

9. Appeal to Unqualified Authority (*Argumentum ad Verecundiam*)

We saw in Chapter 1 that an argument from authority is an inductive argument in which an arguer cites the authority or testimony of another person in support of some conclusion. The **appeal to unqualified authority** fallacy is a variety of the argument from authority and occurs when the cited authority or witness lacks credibility. There are several reasons why an authority or witness might lack credibility. The person might lack the requisite expertise, might be biased or prejudiced, might have a motive to lie or disseminate "misinformation," or might lack the requisite ability to perceive or recall. The following examples illustrate these reasons:

> Dr. Bradshaw, our family physician, has stated that the creation of muonic atoms of deuterium and tritium hold the key to producing a sustained nuclear fusion reaction at room temperature. In view of Dr. Bradshaw's expertise as a physician, we must conclude that this is indeed true.

This conclusion deals with nuclear physics, and the authority is a family physician. Because it is unlikely that a physician would be an expert in nuclear physics, the argument commits an appeal to unqualified authority.

> David Duke, former Grand Wizard of the Ku Klux Klan, has stated, "Jews are not good Americans. They have no understanding of what America is." On the basis of Duke's authority, we must therefore conclude that the Jews in this country are un-American.

As an authority, David Duke is clearly biased, so his statements cannot be trusted.

> James W. Johnston, former Chairman of R. J. Reynolds Tobacco Company, testified before Congress that tobacco is not an addictive substance and that smoking cigarettes does not produce any addiction. Therefore, we should believe him and conclude that smoking does not in fact lead to any addiction.

If Mr. Johnston had admitted that tobacco is addictive, it would have opened the door to government regulation, which could put his company out of business. Thus, because Johnston had a clear motive to lie, we should not believe his statements.

> Old Mrs. Furguson (who is practically blind) has testified that she saw the defendant stab the victim with a bayonet while she was standing in the twilight shadows 100 yards from the incident. Therefore, members of the jury, you must find the defendant guilty.

Here the witness lacks the ability to perceive what she has testified to, so her testimony is untrustworthy.

Of course if an authority is credible, the resulting argument will contain no fallacy. Example:

> The county tax collector issued a press release stating that property tax revenues are higher this year than last. Therefore, we conclude that these revenues are indeed higher this year.

Normally a county tax collector would be considered a qualified expert in the area of tax revenues, so assuming the tax collector has no reason to lie, this argument is inductively strong.

In deciding whether a person is a qualified authority, one should keep two important points in mind. First, the person might be an authority in more than one field. For example, a chemist might also be an authority in biology, or an economist might also be an authority in law. The second point is that there are some areas in which practically no one can be considered an authority. Such areas include politics, morals, and religion. For example, if someone were to argue that abortion is immoral because a certain philosopher or religious leader has said so, the argument would be weak regardless of the authority's qualifications. Many questions in these areas are so hotly contested that there is no conventional wisdom an authority can depend on.

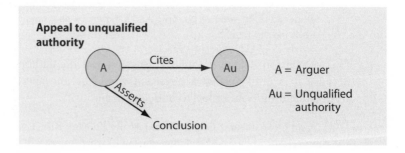

Appeal to unqualified authority

A — Cites → Au

A = Arguer
Au = Unqualified authority

A — Asserts → Conclusion

10. Appeal to Ignorance
(*Argumentum ad Ignorantiam*)

When the premises of an argument state that nothing has been proved one way or the other about something, and the conclusion then makes a definite assertion about that thing, the argument commits an **appeal to ignorance**. The issue usually involves something that is incapable of being proved or something that has not yet been proved. Example:

> People have been trying for centuries to provide conclusive evidence for the claims of astrology, and no one has ever succeeded. Therefore, we must conclude that astrology is a lot of nonsense.

Conversely, the following argument commits the same fallacy.

> People have been trying for centuries to disprove the claims of astrology, and no one has ever succeeded. Therefore, we must conclude that the claims of astrology are true.

The premises of an argument are supposed to provide positive evidence for the conclusion. The premises of these arguments, however, tell us nothing about astrology; rather, they tell us about what certain unnamed and unidentified people have tried unsuccessfully to do. This evidence may provide some slight reason for believing the conclusion, but certainly not sufficient reason.

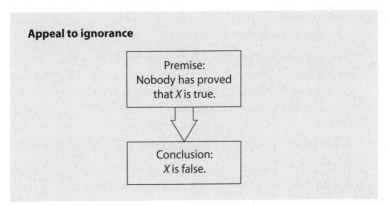

Appeal to ignorance

Premise:
Nobody has proved
that *X* is true.

Conclusion:
X is false.

These examples do, however, lead us to the first of two important exceptions to the appeal to ignorance. The first stems from the fact that if qualified researchers investigate a certain phenomenon within their range of expertise and fail to turn up any evidence that the phenomenon exists, this fruitless search by itself constitutes positive evidence about the question. Consider, for example, the following argument:

> Teams of scientists attempted over several decades to detect the existence of the luminiferous aether, and all failed to do so. Therefore, the luminiferous aether does not exist.

The premises of this argument are true. Given the circumstances, it is likely that the scientists in question would have detected the aether if in fact it did exist. Since they did not detect it, it probably does not exist. Thus, we can say that the given argument is inductively strong (but not deductively valid).

As for the two arguments about astrology, if the attempts to prove or disprove the astrological claims had been done in a systematic way by qualified experts, the arguments would more likely be good. Exactly what is required to qualify someone to investigate astrological claims is, of course, difficult to say. But as these arguments stand, the premises state nothing about the qualifications of the investigators, and so the arguments remain fallacious.

It is not always necessary, however, that the investigators have *special* qualifications. The kinds of qualifications needed depend on the situation. Sometimes the mere ability to see and report what one sees is sufficient. Example:

> No one has ever seen Mr. Andrews drink a glass of wine, beer, or any other alcoholic beverage. Probably Mr. Andrews is a nondrinker.

Because it is highly probable that if Mr. Andrews were a drinker, somebody would have seen him drinking, this argument is inductively strong. No special qualifications are needed to be able to see someone take a drink.

The second exception to the appeal to ignorance relates to courtroom procedure. In the United States and a few other countries, a person is presumed innocent until proven guilty. If the prosecutor in a criminal trial fails to prove the guilt of the defendant beyond reasonable doubt, counsel for the defense may justifiably argue that his or her client is not guilty. Example:

> Members of the jury, you have heard the prosecution present its case against the defendant. Nothing, however, has been proved beyond a reasonable doubt. Therefore, under the law, the defendant is not guilty.

This argument commits no fallacy because "not guilty" means, in the legal sense, that guilt beyond a reasonable doubt has not been proved. The defendant may indeed have committed the crime of which he or she is accused, but if the prosecutor fails to prove guilt beyond a reasonable doubt, the defendant is considered "not guilty."

11. Hasty Generalization (Converse Accident)

Hasty generalization is a fallacy that affects inductive generalizations. In Chapter 1 we saw that an inductive generalization is an argument that draws a conclusion about all members of a group from evidence that pertains to a selected sample. The fallacy occurs when there is a reasonable likelihood that the sample is not representative of the group. Such a likelihood may arise if the sample is either too small or not randomly selected. Here are two examples:

> Today's money managers are a pack of thieves, every last one of them. Look at Bernie Madoff and Robert Allen Stanford. They ripped off billions of dollars from thousands of trusting clients. And Raj Rajaratnam profited to the tune of millions of dollars through illegal insider trading.

> The mass shooting in a Colorado movie theater was carried out by a young, white male. The school shootings in Roseburg, Santa Barbara, and Newtown were all carried out by young, white males. The evidence is clear. Young, white males are a serious threat to public safety.

In these arguments a conclusion about a whole group is drawn from premises that mention only a few instances. Because such small, atypical samples are not sufficient to support a general conclusion, each argument commits a hasty generalization.

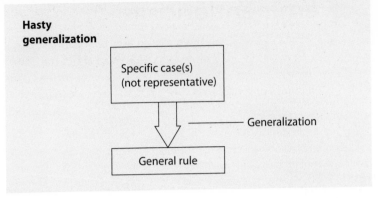

Hasty generalization

Specific case(s) (not representative)

Generalization

General rule

The mere fact that a sample is small, however, does not necessarily mean that it is atypical. On the other hand, the mere fact that a sample is large does not guarantee that it is typical. In the case of small samples, various factors may intervene that render such a sample typical of the larger group. Examples:

> Ten milligrams of substance Z was fed to four mice, and within two minutes all four went into shock and died. Probably substance Z, in this amount, is fatal to mice in general.

> On three separate occasions I drank a bottle of Figowitz beer and found it flat and bitter. Probably I would find every bottle of Figowitz beer flat and bitter.

Neither of these arguments commits the fallacy of hasty generalization, because in neither case is there any likelihood that the sample is atypical of the group. In the first argument the fact that the mice died in only two minutes suggests the existence of a causal connection between eating substance Z and death. If there is such a connection, it would hold for other mice as well. In the second example the fact that the taste of beer typically remains constant from bottle to bottle causes the argument to be strong, even though only three bottles were sampled.

In the case of large samples, if the sample is not random, it may not be typical of the larger group. Example:

> One hundred thousand voters from Orange County, California, were surveyed on their choice for governor, and 68 percent said they intend to vote for the Republican candidate. Clearly the Republican candidate will be elected.

Even though the sample cited in this argument is large, the argument commits a hasty generalization. The problem is that Orange County is overwhelmingly Republican, so the mere fact that 68 percent intend to vote for the Republican candidate is no indication of how others in the state intend to vote. In other words, the survey was not conducted randomly, and for this reason the sample is biased. The need for randomness in samples is discussed further in Chapter 12 of this book.

Hasty generalization is otherwise called "converse accident" because it proceeds in a direction opposite to that of accident. Whereas accident proceeds from the general to the particular, converse accident moves from the particular to the general. The premises cite some characteristic affecting one or more atypical instances of a certain class, and the conclusion then applies that characteristic to all members of the class.

The English philosopher and theologian, William of Ockham, was born in or near the village of Ockham not far from London. Little is known about his childhood, and his biographers are not even certain about the year of his birth, with estimates running from 1280 to 1290. However, they are certain that while Ockham was still a small boy, his parents delivered him to the nearest Franciscan monastery to be brought up in the monastic way of life. His parents' intentions were realized when he entered the Franciscan Order and was ordained in 1306.

Ockham studied theology at Oxford, possibly under Duns Scotus, and he lectured there. He also studied and taught at the University of Paris, where he wrote extensively on theology and philosophy. Ockham's theological views generated controversy among theologians of the day, some of whom vehemently opposed him. In 1324, he was called to Avignon, then the location of the papal court, to answer charges of heresy.

A panel of scholars had been appointed to review the charges made against Ockham, and he was obliged to remain at a Franciscan house in Avignon throughout the investigation, which lasted four years. During this time, the Franciscan minister general, Michael of Cesena, was called to Avignon, because he had become embroiled in a controversy with Pope John XXII over the issue of the poverty of Jesus and the apostles. Michael held that Jesus and the apostles did not own property but instead survived through goodwill offerings of people in the community. The Franciscans regarded themselves as emulating the model set by Jesus and the apostles, but the pope, who lived in luxury, obviously disagreed.

Though Ockham had more than enough problems of his own, the minister general asked him to research the issue to see which position was right—the pope's or the minister general's. Ockham ultimately came out on the side of the minister general, claiming that the pope was a heretic and had no business even being

The Granger Collection, NYC

pope. This got the Avignon Franciscans into a great deal of trouble, and to extricate themselves they purloined several horses and rode out of town in the middle of the night. Ludwig of Bavaria, the Holy Roman Emperor, gave them protection, and Ockham lived out the rest of his life in Munich. While there he turned his attention to politics and political philosophy. He was a staunch advocate of the separation of church and state, claiming that the pope had no right to intervene in state affairs. The pope retaliated by excommunicating him.

Ockham is best known for endorsing a principle of parsimony that has come to be called "Ockham's razor." This principle states that, among alternative explanations, the simplest one is the best. Ockham emphasized the importance of keeping the number of entities hypothesized in an explanation to an absolute minimum. In the area of logic, he is known for his theory of truth conditions for categorical propositions, for work in the foundations of inductive reasoning, for preliminary work on a three-valued logic, and for developing a close approximation to what would later come to be known as De Morgan's rule.

12. False Cause

The fallacy of **false cause** occurs whenever the link between premises and conclusion depends on some imagined causal connection that probably does not exist. Whenever an argument is suspected of committing the false cause fallacy, the reader or listener should be able to say that the conclusion depends on the supposition that X causes Y, whereas X probably does not cause Y at all. Examples:

> During the past two months, every time that the cheerleaders have worn blue ribbons in their hair, the basketball team has been defeated. Therefore, to prevent defeats in the future, the cheerleaders should get rid of those blue ribbons.

> Successful business executives are paid salaries in excess of $100,000. Therefore, the best way to ensure that Ferguson will become a successful executive is to raise his salary to at least $100,000.

> There are more laws on the books today than ever before, and more crimes are being committed than ever before. Therefore, to reduce crime we must eliminate the laws.

The first argument depends on the supposition that the blue ribbons caused the defeats, the second on the supposition that a high salary causes success, and the third on the supposition that laws cause crime. In no case is it likely that any causal connection exists.

The first argument illustrates a variety of the false cause fallacy called *post hoc ergo propter hoc* ("after this, therefore on account of this"). This variety of the fallacy presupposes that just because one event precedes another event, the first event causes the second. Obviously, mere temporal succession is not sufficient to establish a causal connection. Nevertheless, this kind of reasoning is quite common and lies behind most forms of superstition. (Example: "A black cat crossed my path and later I tripped and sprained my ankle. It must be that black cats really are bad luck.")

The second and third arguments illustrate a variety of the false cause fallacy called *non causa pro causa* ("not the cause for the cause"). This variety is committed when what is taken to be the cause of something is not really the cause at all and the mistake is based on something other than mere temporal succession. In reference to the second argument, success as an executive causes increases in salary—not the other way around—so the argument mistakes the cause for the effect. In reference to the third argument, the increase in crime is, for the most part, only coincidental with the increase in the number of laws. Obviously, the mere fact that one event is coincidental with another is not sufficient reason to think that one caused the other.

A third variety of the false cause fallacy, and one that is probably committed more often than either of the others in their pure form, is *oversimplified cause*. This variety occurs when a multitude of causes is responsible for a certain effect but the arguer selects just one of these causes and represents it as if it were the sole cause. Here are some examples:

> The quality of education in our grade schools and high schools has been declining for years. Clearly, our teachers just aren't doing their job these days.

> Today, all of us can look forward to a longer life span than our parents and grandparents. Obviously we owe our thanks to the millions of dedicated doctors who expend every effort to ensure our health.

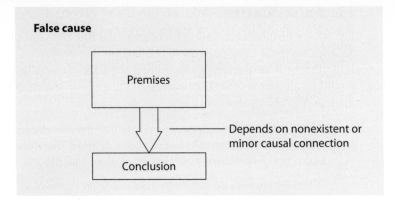

False cause

Premises

Depends on nonexistent or minor causal connection

Conclusion

In reference to the first argument, the decline in the quality of education is caused by many factors, including lack of discipline in the home, lack of parental involvement, too much television, too much time spent on video games, and drug use by students. Poor teacher performance is only one of these factors and probably a minor one at that. In the second argument, the efforts of doctors are only one among many factors responsible for our longer life span. Other, more important factors include a better diet, more exercise, reduced smoking, safer highways, and more-stringent occupational safety standards.

The oversimplified cause fallacy is usually motivated by self-serving interests. Sometimes the arguer wants to take undeserved credit for himself or herself or give undeserved credit to some movement with which he or she is affiliated. At other times, the arguer wants to heap blame on an opponent or shift blame from himself or herself onto some convenient occurrence. Instances of the fallacy can resemble either the *post hoc* or the *non causa pro causa* varieties in that the alleged cause can occur either prior to or concurrently with the effect. It differs from the other varieties of false cause fallacy in that the single factor selected for credit or blame is often partly responsible for the effect, but responsible to only a minor degree.

The last variety of false cause we will consider is called the *gambler's fallacy*. This fallacy is committed whenever the conclusion of an argument depends on the supposition that independent events in a game of chance are causally related. Here is an example:

> A fair coin was flipped five times in a row, and each time it came up heads. Therefore, it is extremely likely that it will come up tails on the next flip.

In fact, it is no more likely that the coin will come up tails on the next flip than it was on the first flip. Each flip is an independent event, so earlier flips have no causal influence on later ones. Thus, the fact that the earlier flips came up heads does not increase the likelihood that the next flip will come up tails.

For the gambler's fallacy to be committed, the events must be independent or nearly independent. Such events include rolls of a pair of fair (unloaded) dice, spins of a fair roulette wheel, and selections of lottery winning numbers. Events are not completely independent whenever the skill of the gambler affects the outcome. Thus, poker, blackjack, and horse-race betting provide less-than-perfect candidates for the gambler's fallacy.

The false cause fallacy is often convincing because it is often difficult to determine whether two phenomena are causally related. A lengthy time lapse between the operation of the cause and the occurrence of the effect can exacerbate the problem. For example, the thirty-year interval between exposure to asbestos and the onset of asbestosis impeded the recognition of a causal connection. Also, when two events are causally related, determining the degree of relatedness may be hard. Thus, there may be some connection between the electromagnetic field produced by high-voltage transmission lines and leukemia, but the connection may be extremely slight. Finally, when a causal connection is recognized, it may be difficult to determine which is the cause and which is the effect. For example, an allergic reaction may be connected with an episode of anxiety, but it may be hard to tell if the reaction causes the anxiety or if the anxiety causes the reaction.

The realm of human action constitutes another area in which causal connections are notoriously difficult to establish. For example, the attorneys for accused murderer Dan White argued that Twinkies, Coke, and potato chips caused him to kill San Francisco mayor George Moscone. Other attorneys have blamed their clients' crimes on PMS, rap music, childhood abuse, mental retardation, and hallucinations. The complex nature of human motivation renders all such causal claims difficult to evaluate. The situation may become even worse when a whole nation of people are involved. Thus, the recent drop in crime rates has been attributed to "three strikes" laws, but it is difficult to say whether this or some other factor is really responsible.

One point that should be kept in mind when establishing causal connections is that statistical correlations by themselves often reveal little about what is actually going on. For example, if all that we knew about smoking and lung cancer was that the two frequently occur together, we might conclude any number of things. We might conclude that both have a common cause, such as a genetic predisposition, or we might conclude that lung cancer is a disease contracted early in life and that it manifests itself in its early stages by a strong desire for tobacco. Fortunately, in this case we have more evidence than a mere statistical correlation. This additional evidence inclines us to believe that the smoking is a cause of the cancer.

13. Slippery Slope

The fallacy of **slippery slope** is a variety of the false cause fallacy. It occurs when the conclusion of an argument rests on an alleged chain reaction and there is not sufficient reason to think that the chain reaction will actually take place. Here is an example:

> Immediate steps should be taken to outlaw pornography once and for all. The continued manufacture and sale of pornographic material will almost certainly lead to an increase in sex-related crimes such as rape and incest. This in turn will gradually erode the moral fabric of society and result in an increase in crimes of all sorts. Eventually a complete disintegration of law and order will occur, leading in the end to the total collapse of civilization.

Because there is no good reason to think that the mere failure to outlaw pornography will result in all these dire consequences, this argument is fallacious. An equally fallacious counterargument is as follows:

> Attempts to outlaw pornography threaten basic civil rights and should be summarily abandoned. If pornography is outlawed, censorship of newspapers and news magazines is

only a short step away. After that there will be censorship of textbooks, political speeches, and the content of lectures delivered by university professors. Complete mind control by the central government will be the inevitable result.

Both arguments attempt to persuade the reader or listener that the welfare of society rests on a "slippery slope" and that a single step in the wrong direction will result in an inevitable slide all the way to the bottom.

The slippery slope fallacy can involve various kinds of causality. For example, someone might argue that removing a single brick from a building would set off a chain reaction leading to the destruction of the building, or that chopping down a tall tree would set off a cascade of falling trees leading to the destruction of the forest. These arguments depend on pure physical causality. On the other hand, someone might argue that starting a rumor about the health of the economy would set off a chain reaction leading to the collapse of the stock market. Such an argument would depend on the kind of causality found in interpersonal communications.

The following example involves a chain reaction of mental causes where wanting one thing leads to wanting another.

> Professor Fallon has asked us to purchase a coffeemaker for her office. But we shouldn't do that because next she'll want a microwave, and then a convection oven. Then she'll want a full-sized refrigerator, a sink with hot and cold water, a dishwasher, and a complete set of expensive china. This will exhaust the budget of our department.

Two points to keep in mind about slippery slope are first, in real-life situations, the fallacy is almost always used to defend the status quo against some kind of attack. The strategy is to make the reader and listener fear change—to fear it so much that they will cling rigidly to the prevailing state of affairs even if it is thoroughly immoral. For example, prior to the Civil War slippery slope arguments were used over and over again to shut down opposing arguments in favor of abolishing slavery. In a famous debate in Cincinnati in 1845, N. L. Rice, a Presbyterian minister, invited his listeners to imagine what would happen if slavery were abolished forthright. In no time former slaves would be given the right to vote:

> Then a colored man might be the next governor [of states having a black majority]; and colored men might constitute their Legislature, and sit on the bench as judges in their courts. Thus the entire administration in those States would be placed in the hands of degraded men, wholly ignorant of the principles of law and government.[*]

As a result, Mr. Rice wants us to believe, the government will collapse.

The second point to keep in mind is that in every case of a slippery slope fallacy the chain of causes is neither inevitable nor necessary. Somewhere along the line there are one or more links that are likely to fail. In the case of the anti-abolitionist argument, one weak link was the supposition that freed slaves, once given the right to vote, would actually be allowed to vote. As it turned out, they were not. There were poll taxes, literacy tests, threats, and intimidation. Another weak link was the supposition that slaves, once given the right to vote, would run for public office. They did not.

---

*N. L. Rice, A Debate on Slavery (New York, Wm. H. Moore & Co., 1846), p. 33.

A similar critique applies to contemporary slippery slope arguments used to crush support for physician-assisted suicide. Example:

> Allowing a physician to assist a terminally ill patient to end his life may seem innocent enough to start with. But if this practice is allowed to get a foothold, death at the hands of a physician will become commonplace. Physicians will think nothing of administering a lethal injection, and in no time patients will be killed against their will. For these reasons, physician-assisted suicide should never be allowed.

This argument is probably fallacious because the chain of causes leading from the innocent first step to the final calamity is far from assured. If physician-assisted suicide were made lawful and the abuses envisioned by this argument began to occur, there is reason to believe that the medical community would step in and call for corrective measures. Also, as suspicious deaths began to mount up, law enforcement would step in. Thus, in critiquing slippery slope arguments it is always important to examine carefully the chain of causes and look for weak links.

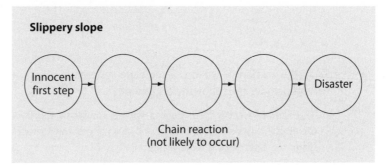

14. Weak Analogy

This fallacy affects inductive arguments from analogy. As we saw in Chapter 1, an argument from analogy is an argument in which the conclusion depends on the existence of an analogy, or similarity, between two things or situations. The fallacy of **weak analogy** is committed when the analogy is not strong enough to support the conclusion that is drawn. Example:

> Amber's dog is similar in many ways to Kyle's cat. Both like being petted, they enjoy being around people, they beg for food at the dinner table, and they sleep with their owners. Amber's dog loves to romp on the beach with Amber. Therefore, Kyle's cat probably loves to romp on the beach with Kyle.

In this argument the similarities cited between Amber's dog and Kyle's cat probably have nothing to do with the cat's attitude toward romping on the beach. Thus, the argument is fallacious.

The basic structure of an argument from analogy is as follows:

> Entity A has attributes $a, b, c,$ and z.
> Entity B has attributes a, b, c.
> Therefore, entity B probably has attribute z also.

Evaluating an argument having this form requires a two-step procedure: (1) Identify the attributes $a, b, c, \ldots$ that the two entities A and B share, and (2) determine how the attribute z, mentioned in the conclusion, relates to the attributes a, b, c, ... If some causal or systematic relation exists between z and a, b, or c, the argument is strong; otherwise, it is weak. In the given example, the two entities share the attributes of liking to be petted, enjoying people, begging for food, and sleeping with their owners. Because it is highly probable that none of these attributes is systematically or causally related to romping on the beach, the argument is fallacious.

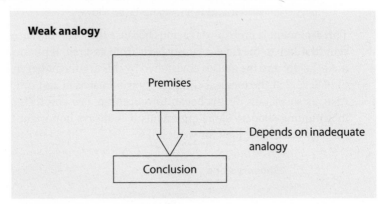

As an illustration of when the requisite systematic or causal relation does and does not exist, consider the following arguments:

> The flow of electricity through a wire is similar to the flow of water through a pipe. Obviously a large-diameter pipe will carry a greater flow of water than a pipe of small diameter. Therefore, a large-diameter wire should carry a greater flow of electricity than a small-diameter wire.

> The flow of electricity through a wire is similar to the flow of water through a pipe. When water runs downhill through a pipe, the pressure at the bottom of the hill is greater than it is at the top. Thus, when electricity flows downhill through a wire, the voltage should be greater at the bottom of the hill than at the top.

The first argument is good and the second is fallacious. Both arguments depend on the similarity between water molecules flowing through a pipe and electrons flowing through a wire. In both cases there is a systematic relation between the diameter of the pipe/wire and the amount of flow. In the first argument this systematic relation provides a strong link between premises and conclusion, and so the argument is a good one. But in the second argument a causal connection exists between difference in elevation and increase in pressure that holds for water but not for electricity. Water molecules flowing through a pipe are significantly affected by gravity, but electrons flowing through a wire are not. Thus, the second argument is fallacious.

The theory and evaluation of arguments from analogy is one of the most complex and elusive subjects in all of logic. Additional material on arguments from analogy appears in Section 3.5 and Chapter 9 of this text.

MindTap® Strengthen your understanding of the topic with the section's **Video Lecture**.

I. Identify the fallacies of weak induction committed by the following arguments, giving a brief explanation for your answer. If no fallacy is committed, write "no fallacy."

★1. The *Daily News* carried an article this morning about three local teenagers who were arrested on charges of drug possession. Teenagers these days are nothing but a bunch of junkies.

2. If a car breaks down on the freeway, a passing mechanic is not obligated to render emergency road service. For similar reasons, if a person suffers a heart attack on the street, a passing physician is not obligated to render emergency medical assistance.

3. There must be something to psychical research. Three famous physicists—Oliver Lodge, James Jeans, and Arthur Stanley Eddington—took it seriously.

★4. The secretaries have asked us to provide lounge areas where they can spend their coffee breaks. This request will have to be refused. If we give them lounge areas, next they'll be asking for spas and swimming pools. Then it will be racquetball courts, tennis courts, and fitness centers. Expenditures for these facilities will drive us into bankruptcy.

5. The accumulation of pressure in a society is similar to the buildup of pressure in a boiler. If the pressure in a boiler increases beyond a critical point, the boiler will explode. Accordingly, if a government represses its people beyond a certain point, the people will rise up in revolt.

6. A few minutes after Governor Harrison finished his speech on television, a devastating earthquake struck southern Alaska. For the safety of the people up there, it is imperative that Governor Harrison make no more speeches.

★7. No one has ever been able to prove the existence of extrasensory perception. We must therefore conclude that extrasensory perception is a myth.

8. Lester Brown, universally respected author of the yearly *State of the World* report, has said that the destruction of tropical rain forests is one of the ten most serious worldwide problems. Thus, it must be the case that this is indeed a very serious problem.

9. George Clooney and Angelia Jolie give large sums of money to charitable causes every year. It must be the case that all movie stars give large amounts of money to charity every year.

★10. There is substantial evidence that units of the Chinese military hack into the computers of American technology companies to steal intellectual property and trade secrets. But Chinese Premier Li Keqiang denies that this happens. Therefore, given Mr. Li's intimate knowledge of the Chinese military, we must conclude that the Chinese military does not engage in hacking.

MindTap® Complete exercises online for immediate feedback.

11. Probably no life exists on Venus. Teams of scientists have conducted exhaustive studies of the planet's surface and atmosphere, and no living organisms have been found.

12. We don't dare let the animal-rights activists get their foot in the door. If they sell us on the idea that dogs, cats, and dolphins have rights, next it will be chickens and cows. That means no more chicken Kiev or beef Wellington. Next it will be worms and insects. This will lead to the decimation of our agricultural industry. The starvation of the human race will follow close behind.

★13. No one should buy clothing at a department store without first trying it on. Accordingly, no one should buy food at a grocery store without first tasting it.

14. No one has proved conclusively that America's nuclear power plants constitute a danger to people living in their immediate vicinity. Therefore, it is perfectly safe to continue to build nuclear power plants near large metropolitan centers.

15. There are more churches in New York City than in any other city in the nation, and more crimes are committed in New York City than anywhere else. So, if we are to eliminate crime, we must abolish the churches.

II. Answer "true" or "false" to the following statements:

1. If an arguer cites a statement by a recognized expert in support of a conclusion and the statement falls within the expert's range of expertise, then the arguer commits an appeal to unqualified authority.

2. If an arguer cites a statement in support of a conclusion and the statement reflects the strong bias of its author, then the arguer commits an appeal to unqualified authority.

3. In the appeal to ignorance, the arguer accuses the reader or listener of being ignorant.

4. If an attorney for the defense in an American or Canadian criminal trial argues that the prosecution has proved nothing beyond a reasonable doubt about the guilt of the defendant, then the attorney commits an appeal to ignorance.

5. Hasty generalization always proceeds from the particular to the general.

6. The *post hoc ergo propter hoc* variety of the false cause fallacy presumes that X causes Y merely because X happens before Y.

7. If an argument concludes that X causes Y simply because X and Y occur over the same time interval, then the argument commits the *non causa pro causa* variety of the false cause fallacy.

8. If the conclusion of an argument depends on the occurrence of a chain reaction of events, and there is good reason to believe that the chain reaction will actually occur, the argument commits a slippery slope fallacy.

9. The fallacy of weak analogy always depends on an alleged similarity between two things or situations.

10. If an argument from analogy depends on a causal or systematic relationship between certain attributes, and there is good reason to believe that this relationship exists, then the argument commits no fallacy.

III. Identify the fallacies of relevance and weak induction committed by the following arguments. If no fallacy is committed, write "no fallacy."

★1. I bumped into my friend Andy the other day, and the first thing his German shepherd did was rush up to me and sniff that spot about ten inches beneath my navel. When I visited Lucy at her home, her Irish setter made a beeline for . . . yep, the same spot. Dogs are all alike. The only thing they like to do is annoy you by sniffing.

2. Tagging by graffiti artists has become a terrible problem in recent years. Obviously our schools are stifling the creative spirit of these young people.

3. These equal rights ordinances that supposedly protect gays and transexuals from discrimination are the work of the devil! Once these ordinances are enacted, sexual deviants, lurking in the shadows of public restrooms and locker rooms, will spring upon unsuspecting girls and women and perpetrate all forms of molestation and rape. For the sake of your daughters, your wives, your mothers and your grandmothers, never say yes to these innocent-sounding pieces of legislation.

★4. Todd Burpo, the best-selling author, argues in his book that heaven is real and that his son Colton met Jesus and John the Baptist in a near-death experience. But it's clear that Burpo says these things only to sell lots of books. Therefore, his arguments have no merit.

5. What the farmer sows in the spring he reaps in the fall. In the spring he sows $8-per-bushel soybeans. Therefore, in the fall he will reap $8-per-bushel soybeans.

6. World-renowned physicist Stephen Hawking claims that black holes do not gobble up everything that falls into them without leaving a trace, but that something is always left behind. Given Hawking's stature as a scientist and the many years he has worked on this problem, we should conclude that this is indeed the case.

★7. Emily has bought over 100 tickets on the weekly state lottery, and she has never won anything. Therefore, the likelihood increases every week that she will win something if she continues to buy tickets.

8. Johnny, of course I deserve the use of your bicycle for the afternoon. After all, I'm sure you wouldn't want your mother to find out that you played hooky today.

9. Practically everyone has a fake ID card these days. Therefore, you should have no qualms about getting one yourself.

★10. Ellen Quinn has argued that logic is not the most important thing in life. Apparently Ellen advocates irrationality. It has taken two million years for the human race to achieve the position that it has, and Ellen would throw the whole thing into the garbage. What utter nonsense!

11. When water is poured on the top of a pile of rocks, it always trickles down to the rocks on the bottom. Similarly, when rich people make lots of money, we can expect this money to trickle down to the poor.

12. Extensive laboratory tests have failed to prove any deleterious side effects of the new painkiller lexaprine. We conclude that lexaprine is safe for human consumption.

★13. Environmentalists accuse us of blocking the plan to convert Antarctica into a world park. In fact, nothing could be further from the truth. Antarctica is a huge continent teeming with life. It is the home of millions of penguins, seals, sea birds, and sea lions. Also, great schools of finfish and whales inhabit its coastal waters.

14. Michael Moore, the documentary filmmaker, argues that capitalist institutions are ravaging America's middle class and walking away with billions of dollars in their pockets. But Moore is just a big, fat, populist rabble-rouser, and a multimillionaire to boot. He should keep his mouth shut.

15. The operation of a camera is similar in many ways to the operation of an eye. If you are to see anything in a darkened room, the pupils of your eyes must first dilate. Accordingly, if you are to take a photograph (without flash) in a darkened room, the aperture of the camera lens must first be increased.

★16. Student loan debt is becoming a national crisis. Clearly, we should provide free textbooks to all college students.

17. James Dobson, founder of Focus on the Family, says that men have the divine obligation to lead their families, and women have the divine obligation to submit to their husband's authority. Given Dobson's apparent ability to receive messages from God, we must conclude that this statement is absolutely true.

18. Dear Internal Revenue Service: I received a notice that my taxes are being audited for last year. But you have no right to do this. The deadline for filing a return was April 15, and I filed my tax return on April 12—a full three days before the deadline.

★19. To prevent dangerous weapons from being carried aboard airliners, those seeking to board must pass through a magnetometer or X-ray device and submit to a possible pat-down search. Therefore, to prevent alcohol and drugs from being carried into rock concerts, those entering should submit to similar search procedures.

20. Mr. Flemming's arguments against the rent-control initiative on the September ballot should be taken with a grain of salt. As a landlord he would naturally be expected to oppose the initiative.

21. India is suffering a serious drought, thousands of children are dying of starvation in their mothers' arms, and homeless beggars line the streets of the major

cities. Surely we must give these poor downtrodden people the chance of bettering their condition in America, the land of wealth and opportunity.

★22. Members of the jury, you have heard Jack Fix testify that the defendant is not in fact a drug dealer. But Mr. Fix is a known drug dealer himself, and a close friend of the defendant. Also, only a year ago, he was convicted of five counts of perjury. Therefore, you should discount Fix's testimony.

23. It is ridiculous to hear that man from Peru complaining about America's poverty. Peru has twice as much poverty as America has ever had.

24. Folks who argue in favor of amnesty for undocumented immigrants are dead wrong. Homeland security is of vital importance. National security is necessary for a healthy economy and the psychological well-being of all our citizens. We must work to secure our nation from all threats, domestic or foreign.

★25. Nobody has ever proved that immoral behavior by elected officials erodes public morality. Therefore, we must conclude that such behavior does not erode public morality.

26. Freedom of speech is guaranteed by the First Amendment. Therefore, your friend was acting within his rights when he shouted "Fire! Fire!" in that crowded theater, even though it was only a joke.

27. No one, on encountering a wristwatch lying on a forest trail, would expect that it had simply appeared there without having been made by someone. For the same reason, no one should expect that the universe simply appeared without having been made by some intelligent being.

★28. On Monday I drank ten rum and Cokes, and the next morning I woke up with a headache. On Wednesday I drank eight gin and Cokes, and the next morning I woke up with a headache. On Friday I drank nine bourbon and Cokes, and the next morning I woke up with a headache. Obviously, to prevent further headaches I must give up Coke.

29. Radio entertainer Rush Limbaugh claims there is not a shred of evidence to prove that nicotine is addictive or that cigarettes cause emphysema, lung cancer, or any other disease. Given Limbaugh's apparent expertise in medical science, we can only conclude that what he says about nicotine and cigarettes is true.

30. Some of the parents in our school district have asked that we provide bilingual education in Spanish. This request will have to be denied. If we provide this service, then someone will ask for bilingual education in Greek. Then it will be German, French, and Hungarian. Polish, Russian, Chinese, Japanese, and Korean will follow close behind. We certainly can't accommodate all of them.

IV. Identify the fallacies committed in the following dialogue. You should be able to find at least one case of each fallacy presented in this section and one case of a fallacy presented in the previous section.

Gun Love

Holly and her friend Ben have just attended a panel discussion in response to a recent shooting on a college campus. As they leave the auditorium and head for the parking lot, Holly asks, "Do you agree with any of the panelists?"

"I agree with the panelist who said that guns should be banned on every campus," Ben replies. "And I would even go a step further and say that we need strict gun control throughout the U.S. The simple fact is that guns are way too available in this country."

"Sounds like you're saying that the availability of guns leads to violent crime," Holly says. "Is that what you're saying?"

"Yes, I do think guns lead to crime," Ben replies.

"Well, let me ask you this," Holly says. "Has anybody ever proved that? Has anybody ever proved that the mere availability of guns leads to violent crime? The answer is no. So until somebody proves that it does, we should conclude that gun availability does not lead to violence."

"Well, you heard what one of the panelists said about England, didn't you?" Ben asks. "England has strict limitations on gun possession, and practically no gun-related crime. I think that proves that guns do cause crime. If the U.S. would adopt the English law, crime in this country would drop like a rock."

"In fact," Holly counters, "the England example proves nothing of the sort. There's no reason to think that what works in England would also work in the U.S."

"Why do you think that?" Ben asks.

"Well," Holly responds, "you recall what the other panelist said about gun control in this country. When Evanston, Illinois, banned guns altogether a few years back, that led to no reduction at all in violent crime. That shows that gun availability does not cause crime. If every city in the country followed Evanston's example, they would get the same result."

"Sounds like you're pretty negative on gun control," Ben observes.

"Yes, I am," Holly replies. "As soon as we have gun registration, the next thing you know we'll need a license to buy a gun. And that will lead the government to impose a tax on gun ownership. Taxes always increase, and when gun owners are no longer able to pay the tax, that will lead to gun confiscation. Finally, when guns are completely removed from the hands of the public, there will be nothing to prevent some wild-eyed fanatic from taking over the government. Complete totalitarianism will follow in no time."

"Do you really think that could happen in this country?" Ben asks.

"If it happened in Nazi Germany, it could happen here," she replies. "And, as one of the panelists said, it did happen in Nazi Germany, and Fascist Italy, too."

"So, do you think you have a right to own a gun?" Ben asks.

"Absolutely," Holly replies. "The current president of the NRA—his name escapes me at the moment—says that the right to own a gun, even an assault weapon, is guaranteed by the Constitution. Given that he knows a lot about guns, what he says about them is certainly true."

"I'll withhold judgment on that," says Ben. "But here's what I think you should do. You should take a couple deep breaths and calm down. You've turned into a gun nut. If people see what's happened to you, they won't take any of your arguments seriously."

"Think what you want about me," Holly says. "But the next time you're robbed at gunpoint, don't come crying in my direction."

Ben laughs. "Okay, I promise I won't. Well, see you around . . . if I survive!"

"See you!" she says.

V. Create the following informal fallacies:

1. An appeal to unqualified authority relating to a psychic

2. An appeal to ignorance about life on other planets

3. A hasty generalization dealing with ageism

4. A *post hoc ergo propter hoc* connected with getting sick

5. A gambler's fallacy about playing the lottery

6. A slippery slope fallacy dealing with credit card use

7. A weak analogy connected with caring for a pet

MindTap® Master concepts and improve outcomes with Aplia, at the end of the chapter, in the Aplia folder.

3.4 Fallacies of Presumption, Ambiguity, and Illicit Transference

HOW LOGICAL ARE YOU? Suppose you are pulled over for speeding. Upon walking up to your car, the officer asks you, "Where have you hidden the drugs?" Is there a flaw in the officer's question? If so, what is it? How would you reply to the officer?

Find the answer on MindTap.

The **fallacies of presumption** include begging the question, complex question, false dichotomy, and suppressed evidence. These fallacies arise not because the premises are irrelevant to the conclusion or provide insufficient reason for believing the conclusion but because the premises presume what they purport to prove. *Begging the question* presumes that the premises provide adequate support for the conclusion when in fact they do not, and *complex question* presumes that a question can be answered by a simple "yes," "no," or other brief answer when a more sophisticated answer is needed. *False dichotomy* presumes that an "either . . . or . . ." statement presents jointly exhaustive alternatives when in fact it does not, and *suppressed evidence* presumes that no important evidence has been overlooked by the premises when in fact it has.

The **fallacies of ambiguity** include *equivocation* and *amphiboly*. These fallacies arise from the occurrence of some form of ambiguity in either the premises or the conclusion (or both). As we saw in Section 2.1, an expression is ambiguous if it is susceptible to different interpretations in a given context. The words "light" and "bank" are ambiguous, as is the statement "Tuna are biting off the Washington coast." When the conclusion of an argument depends on a shift in meaning of an ambiguous word or phrase or on the wrong interpretation of an ambiguous statement, the argument commits a fallacy of ambiguity.

The **fallacies of illicit transference** include *composition* and *division*. Arguments that commit these fallacies involve the incorrect transference of an attribute from the parts of something onto the whole, or from the whole onto the parts.

15. Begging the Question (*Petitio Principii*)

The fallacy of **begging the question** is committed whenever the arguer creates the illusion that inadequate premises provide adequate support for the conclusion by leaving out a possibly false (shaky) key premise, by restating a possibly false premise as the conclusion, or by reasoning in a circle. The Latin name for this fallacy, *petitio principii,* means "request for the source." The actual source of support for the conclusion is not apparent, and so the argument is said to beg the question. After reading or hearing the argument, the observer is inclined to ask, "But how do you know X?" where X is the needed support.

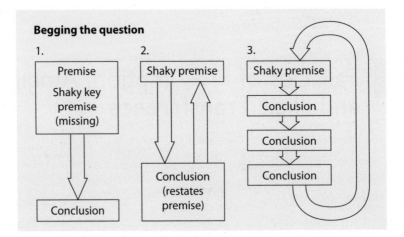

The first, and most common, way of committing this fallacy is by leaving a possibly false key premise out of the argument while creating the illusion that nothing more is needed to establish the conclusion. Examples:

Murder is morally wrong. This being the case, it follows that abortion is morally wrong.

We know that humans are intended to eat lots of fruit because the human hand and arm are perfectly suited for picking fruit from a tree.

It's obvious that the poor in this country should be given handouts from the government. After all, these people earn less than the average citizen.

Clearly, terminally ill patients have a right to doctor-assisted suicide. After all, many of these people are unable to commit suicide by themselves.

The first of these arguments begs the question "How do you know that abortion is a form of murder?" The second begs the question "Does the structure and function of the human hand and arm tell us what humans should eat?" And the third and fourth beg the questions "Just because the poor earn less than the average citizen, does this imply that the government should give them handouts?" and "Just because terminally ill patients cannot commit suicide by themselves, does it follow that they have a right to a doctor's assistance?"

These questions indicate that something has been left out of the original arguments. Thus, the first argument is missing the premise "Abortion is a form of murder"; the second is missing the premise "The structure and function of the human hand and arm tell us what humans should eat"; and so on. These premises are crucial for the soundness of the arguments. If the arguer is unable to establish the truth of these premises, then the arguments prove nothing. However, in most cases of begging the question, this is precisely the reason why such premises are left unstated. The arguer is *not* able to establish their truth, and by employing rhetorical phraseology such as "of course," "clearly," "this being the case," and "after all," the arguer hopes to create the illusion that the stated premise, by itself, provides adequate support for the conclusion when in fact it does not.

The same form of begging the question often appears in arguments concerning religious topics to justify conclusions about the existence of God, the immortality of the soul, and so on. Example:

> The world in which we live displays an amazing degree of organization. Obviously this world was created by an intelligent God.

This argument begs the question "How do you know that the organization in the world could only have come from an intelligent creator?" Of course the claim that it did come from an intelligent creator may well be true, but the burden is on the arguer to prove it. Without supporting reasons or evidence, the argument proves nothing. Yet most people who are predisposed to believe the conclusion are likely to accept the argument as a good one. The same can be said of most arguments that beg the question, and this fact suggests another reason why arguers resort to this fallacy: Such arguments tend to reinforce preexisting inclinations and beliefs.

The second form of *petitio principii* occurs when the conclusion of an argument merely restates a possibly false premise in slightly different language. In such an argument, the premise supports the conclusion, and the conclusion tends to reinforce the premise. Examples:

> Capital punishment is justified for the crimes of murder and kidnapping because it is quite legitimate and appropriate that someone be put to death for having committed such hateful and inhuman acts.

> Anyone who preaches revolution has a vision of the future for the simple reason that if a person has no vision of the future he could not possibly preach revolution.

In the first argument, saying that capital punishment is "justified" means the same thing as saying that it is "legitimate and appropriate," and in the second argument the premise and the conclusion say exactly the same thing. However, by repeating the same thing in slightly different language, the arguer creates the illusion that independent evidence is being presented in support of the conclusion, when in fact it is not. Both arguments contain rhetorical phraseology ("hateful and inhuman," "simple reason," and "could not possibly") that help effect the illusion. The first argument begs the question "How do you know that capital punishment really is legitimate and appropriate?" and the second begs the question "How do you know that people who preach revolution really do have a vision of the future?"

The third form of *petitio principii* involves circular reasoning in a chain of inferences having a first premise that is possibly false. Example:

> Verizon has the best wireless service. After all, their phones have the clearest sound. And we know this is so because customers hear better on Verizon phones. And this follows from the fact that Verizon has digital technology. But this is exactly what you would expect given that Verizon has the best wireless service.

On encountering this argument, the attentive reader is inclined to ask, "Where does this reasoning begin? What is its source?" Since the argument goes in a circle, it has no beginning or source, and as a result it proves nothing. Of course, in this example the circularity is rather apparent, so the argument is not likely to convince anyone. Cases in which circular reasoning may convince involve long and complex arguments having premises that depend on one another in subtle ways and a possibly false key premise that depends on the conclusion.

In all cases of begging the question, the arguer uses some linguistic device to create the illusion that inadequate premises provide adequate support for a conclusion. Without such an illusion, the fallacy is not committed. Thus, the following arguments commit no fallacy:

> No dogs are cats.
> Therefore, no cats are dogs.

> London is in England and Paris is in France.
> Therefore, Paris is in France and London is in England.

In both of these examples, the premise amounts to little more than a restatement of the conclusion. Yet both arguments are sound because they are valid and have true premises. No fallacy is committed, because no illusion is created to make inadequate premises appear as adequate. We will study arguments of this sort in Chapters 4 and 7.

Here is another example:

> Rome is in Germany or Rome is in Germany.
> Therefore, Rome is in Germany.

This argument is valid, but it is unsound because it has a false premise. However, it commits no fallacy because, again, no illusion is created to cover anything up. Arguments having this form also appear in Chapter 7.

As with these examples, arguments that beg the question are normally valid. This is easy to see. Any argument that includes the conclusion as one of the premises is clearly valid, and those forms of the fallacy that leave a key premise out of the argument become valid when that key premise is introduced. The problem with arguments that beg the question is that they are usually unsound, or at least not clearly sound, because the premise needed to provide adequate support for the conclusion is, at best, of uncertain truth value. Because such arguments presume the truth of this premise, begging the question is called a fallacy of presumption.

16. Complex Question

The fallacy of **complex question** is committed when two (or more) questions are asked in the guise of a single question and a single answer is then given to both of them. Every complex question presumes the existence of a certain condition. When the respondent's answer is added to the complex question, an argument emerges that establishes the presumed condition. Thus, although not an argument as such, a complex question involves an implicit argument. This argument is usually intended to trap the respondent into acknowledging something that he or she might otherwise not want to acknowledge. Examples:

> Have you stopped cheating on exams?
>
> Where did you hide the marijuana you were smoking?

Let us suppose the respondent answers "yes" to the first question and "under the bed" to the second. The following arguments emerge:

> You were asked whether you have stopped cheating on exams. You answered, "Yes." Therefore, it follows that you have cheated in the past.
>
> You were asked where you hid the marijuana you were smoking. You replied, "Under the bed." It follows that you were in fact smoking marijuana.

On the other hand, let us suppose that the respondent answers "no" to the first question and "nowhere" to the second. We then have the following arguments:

> You were asked whether you have stopped cheating on exams. You answered, "No." Therefore, you continue to cheat.
>
> You were asked where you hid the marijuana you were smoking. You answered, "Nowhere." It follows that you must have smoked all of it.

Obviously, each of the questions is really two questions:

> Did you cheat on exams in the past? If you did cheat in the past, have you stopped now?
>
> Were you smoking marijuana? If you were smoking it, where did you hide it?

If respondents are not sophisticated enough to identify a complex question when one is put to them, they may answer quite innocently and be trapped by a conclusion that is supported by no evidence at all; or, they may be tricked into providing the evidence themselves. The correct response lies in resolving the complex question into its component questions and answering each separately.

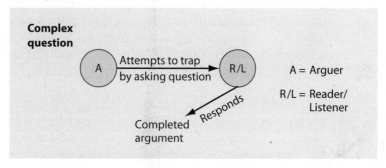

The fallacy of complex question should be distinguished from another kind of question known in law as a leading question. A *leading question* is one in which the answer is in some way suggested in the question. Whether or not a question is a leading one is important in the direct examination of a witness by counsel. Example:

Tell us, on April 9, did you see the
defendant shoot the deceased?   (leading question)
Tell us, what did you see on April 9?   (straight question)

Leading questions differ from complex questions in that they involve no logical fallacies—that is, they do not attempt to trick the respondent into admitting something he or she does not want to admit. To distinguish between the two, however, one sometimes needs to know whether prior questions have been asked. Here are some additional examples of complex questions:

Are you going to be a good little boy and eat your hamburger?
Is George Hendrix still telling lies?
How long must I put up with your snotty behavior?
When are you going to stop talking nonsense?

17. False Dichotomy

The fallacy of **false dichotomy** is committed when a disjunctive ("either . . . or . . .") premise presents two unlikely alternatives as if they were the only ones available, and the arguer then eliminates the undesirable alternative, leaving the desirable one as the conclusion. Such an argument is clearly valid, but since the disjunctive premise is false, or at least probably false, the argument is typically unsound. The fallacy is often committed by children when arguing with their parents, by advertisers, and by adults generally. Here are three examples:

Either you let me attend the P!nk concert or I'll be miserable for the rest of my life. I know you don't want me to be miserable for the rest of my life, so it follows that you'll let me attend the concert.

Either you use Ultra Guard deodorant or you risk the chance of perspiration odor. Surely you don't want to risk the chance of perspiration odor. Therefore, you will want to use Ultra Guard deodorant.

Either we adopt a one-world government, or regional wars will continue forever. We certainly can't tolerate constant war. Therefore, we must adopt a one-world government.

In none of these arguments does the disjunctive premise present the only alternatives available, but in each case the arguer tries to convey that impression. For example, in the first argument, the arguer tries to convey the impression that he or she either goes to the concert or faces a lifetime of misery, and that no other alternatives are possible. Clearly, however, this is not the case.

The fallacious nature of false dichotomy lies in the creation of an illusion that the disjunctive premise presents jointly exhaustive alternatives. If it did, the premise would be true of necessity. For example, the statement "Either Reno is in Nevada, or it is not in Nevada" presents jointly exhaustive alternatives and is true of necessity. But in the fallacy of false dichotomy, not only do the two alternatives fail to be jointly exhaustive, but they are not even likely. As a result, the disjunctive premise is false, or at least probably false. Thus, the fallacy amounts to making a false or probably false premise appear true.

Also, if one of the alternatives in the disjunctive premise is factually true beyond any doubt, then the fallacy is not committed. For example, the following argument is valid and sound:

> Either Seattle is in Washington, or it is in Oregon.
> Seattle is not in Oregon.
> Therefore, Seattle is in Washington

False dichotomy is otherwise called "false bifurcation" and the "either-or fallacy." Also, in most cases the arguer expresses only the disjunctive premise and leaves it to the reader or listener to supply the missing statements:

> Either you buy me a new mink coat, or I'll freeze to death when winter comes.

> Either I continue smoking, or I'll get fat and you'll hate to be seen with me.

The missing premise and conclusion are easily introduced.

18. Suppressed Evidence

Chapter 1 explained that a cogent argument is an inductive argument with good reasoning and true premises. The requirement of true premises includes the proviso that the premises not ignore some important piece of evidence that outweighs the presented evidence and entails a very different conclusion. If an inductive argument does indeed ignore such evidence, then the argument commits the fallacy of **suppressed evidence**. Consider, for example, the following argument:

> Most dogs are friendly and pose no threat to people who pet them. Therefore, it would be safe to pet the little dog that is approaching us now.

If the arguer ignores the fact that the little dog is excited and foaming at the mouth (which suggests rabies), then the argument commits a suppressed evidence fallacy. This fallacy is classified as a fallacy of presumption because it works by creating the presumption that the premises are both true and complete when in fact they are not.

Perhaps the most common occurrence of the suppressed evidence fallacy appears in inferences based on advertisements. Nearly every ad neglects to mention certain negative features of the product advertised. As a result, an observer who sees or hears an advertisement and then draws a conclusion from it may commit the fallacy of suppressed evidence. Example:

> The ad for Kentucky Fried Chicken says, "Buy a bucket of chicken and have a barrel of fun!" Therefore, if we buy a bucket of that chicken, we will be guaranteed to have lots of fun.

The ad fails to state that the fun does not come packaged with the chicken but must be supplied by the buyer. Also, of course, the ad fails to state that the chicken is loaded with fat and that the buyer's resultant weight gain and clogged arteries may not amount to a barrel of fun. By ignoring these facts, the argument based on the ad is fallacious.

Another rich source of the suppressed evidence fallacy is the biennial U.S. general election in which two candidates, usually a Republican and a Democrat, compete with each other for a single office. During the campaign leading up to the election countless speech makers (including the candidates themselves) tear down the policies and accomplishments of the candidate they oppose only to conclude that the candidate they favor should be elected. Example:

> Ladies and gentlemen, Mr. Smith has supported policies that will bankrupt Medicare and Social Security, his budgetary recommendations increase the federal deficit, and his approach to foreign policy will destabilize the Middle East. Therefore, you should vote to elect Jones to this office.

What the speaker fails to mention are the many undisputed successes that Smith has achieved. Also, he fails to mention that Jones is even less qualified than Smith for the office, and that Jones's policies bode even worse for Medicare, Social Security, the federal deficit, and the Middle East. When these unmentioned facts are taken into account it becomes clear that it is actually Smith who should be elected.

Another way that an arguer can commit the suppressed evidence fallacy is by ignoring important events that have occurred with the passage of time that render an inductive conclusion improbable.

The following argument resembles one that Mitt Romney used in a presidential debate with Barack Obama:

> The U.S. military has fewer battleships, M1 rifles, and horse-drawn howitzers today than it did in 1940. Therefore, the U.S. military is a less effective fighting force today than it was in 1940.

The argument ignores that fact that battleships, M1 rifles, and horse-drawn howitzers became obsolete long ago and have been replaced by more-effective ships and weaponry. Thus, it is not true that the U.S. military is less effective today than it was in 1940.

Suppressed evidence

Premises —— Ignores stronger evidence that supports a different conclusion

Conclusion

Yet another form of suppressed evidence is committed by arguers who quote passages out of context from sources such as the Bible, the Constitution, and the Bill of

Rights to support a conclusion that the passage was not intended to support. Consider, for example, the following argument against gun control:

> The Second Amendment to the Constitution states that the right of the people to keep and bear arms shall not be infringed. But a law controlling handguns would infringe the right to keep and bear arms. Therefore, a law controlling handguns would be unconstitutional.

In fact, the Second Amendment reads, "A well regulated militia being necessary to the security of a free state, the right of the people to keep and bear arms shall not be infringed." In other words, the constitutional right to keep and bear arms is in some way related to the preservation of a well-regulated militia. Arguably a law controlling handguns that is unrelated to the preservation of a well-regulated militia could be constitutional.

The suppressed evidence fallacy is similar to the form of begging the question in which the arguer leaves a key premise out of the argument. The difference is that suppressed evidence leaves out a premise that requires a *different* conclusion, while that form of begging the question leaves out a premise that is needed to support the *stated* conclusion. However, because both fallacies proceed by leaving a premise out of the argument, there are cases where the two fallacies overlap.

19. Equivocation

The fallacy of **equivocation** occurs when the conclusion of an argument depends on the fact that a word or phrase is used, either explicitly or implicitly, in two different senses in the argument. Such arguments are either invalid or have a false premise, and in either case they are unsound. Examples:

> Some triangles are obtuse. Whatever is obtuse is ignorant. Therefore, some triangles are ignorant.

> Any law can be repealed by the legislative authority. But the law of gravity is a law. Therefore, the law of gravity can be repealed by the legislative authority.

> We have a duty to do what is right. We have a right to speak out in defense of the innocent. Therefore, we have a duty to speak out in defense of the innocent.

> A mouse is an animal. Therefore, a large mouse is a large animal.

In the first argument "obtuse" is used in two different senses. In the first premise it describes a certain kind of angle, whereas in the second it means dull or stupid. The second argument equivocates on the word "law." In the first premise it means statutory law, and in the second it means law of nature. The third argument uses "right" in two senses. In the first premise "right" means morally correct, but in the second it means a just claim or power. The fourth argument illustrates the ambiguous use of a relative word. The word "large" means different things depending on the context. Other relative words that are susceptible to this same kind of ambiguity include "small," "good," "bad," "light," "heavy," "difficult," "easy," "tall," and "short."

To be convincing, an argument that commits an equivocation must use the equivocal word in ways that are subtly related. Of the examples just given, only the third might

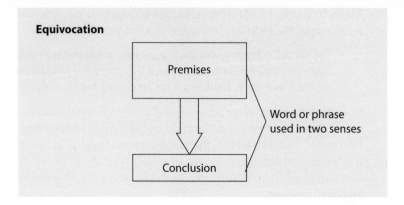

Equivocation

Premises

Word or phrase used in two senses

Conclusion

fulfill this requirement. Since both uses of the word "right" are related to ethics, the unalert observer may not notice the shift in meaning. Another technique is to spread the shift in meaning out over the course of a lengthy argument. Political speech makers often use phrases such as "equal opportunity," "gun control," "national security," and "environmental protection" in one way at the beginning of a speech and in quite another way at the end. A third technique consists in using such phrases one way in a speech to one group and in a different way in a speech to an opposing group. If the same people are not present at both speeches, the equivocation is not detected.

20. Amphiboly

The fallacy of **amphiboly** occurs when the arguer misinterprets an ambiguous statement and then draws a conclusion based on this faulty interpretation. The original statement is usually asserted by someone other than the arguer, and the ambiguity usually arises from a mistake in grammar or punctuation—a missing comma, a dangling modifier, an ambiguous antecedent of a pronoun, or some other careless arrangement of words. Because of this ambiguity, the statement may be understood in two clearly distinguishable ways. The arguer typically selects the unintended interpretation and proceeds to draw a conclusion based on it. Here are some examples:

> The tour guide said that standing in Greenwich Village, the Empire State Building could easily be seen. It follows that the Empire State Building is in Greenwich Village.

> John told Henry that he had made a mistake. It follows that John has at least the courage to admit his own mistakes.

> Professor Johnson said that he will give a lecture about heart failure in the biology lecture hall. It must be the case that a number of heart failures have occurred there recently.

The premise of the first argument contains a dangling modifier. Is it the observer or the Empire State Building that is supposed to be standing in Greenwich Village? The factually correct interpretation is the former. In the second argument the pronoun "he" has an ambiguous antecedent; it can refer either to John or to Henry. Perhaps John told Henry that *Henry* had made a mistake. In the third argument the ambiguity concerns

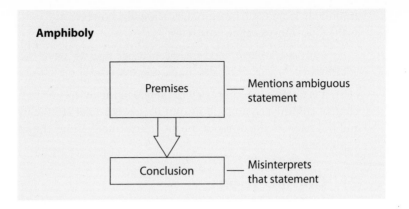

Amphiboly

Premises — Mentions ambiguous statement

Conclusion — Misinterprets that statement

what takes place in the biology lecture hall; is it the lecture or the heart failures? The correct interpretation is probably the former. The ambiguity can be eliminated by inserting commas ("Professor Johnson said that he will give a lecture, about heart failure, in the biology lecture hall") or by moving the ambiguous modifier ("Professor Johnson said that he will give a lecture in the biology lecture hall about heart failure"). Ambiguities of this sort are called *syntactical ambiguities.*

Two areas where cases of amphiboly cause serious problems involve contracts and wills. The drafters of these documents often express their intentions in terms of ambiguous statements, and alternate interpretations of these statements then lead to different conclusions. Examples:

> Mrs. Hart stated in her will, "I leave my 500-carat diamond necklace and my pet chinchilla to Alice and Theresa." Therefore, we conclude that Alice gets the necklace and Theresa gets the chinchilla.

> Mr. James signed a contract that reads, "In exchange for painting my house, I promise to pay David $5,000 and give him my new Cadillac only if he finishes the job by May 1." Therefore, since David did not finish until May 10, it follows that he gets neither the $5,000 nor the Cadillac.

In the first example the conclusion obviously favors Alice. Theresa is almost certain to argue that the gift of the necklace and chinchilla should be shared equally by her and Alice. Mrs. Hart could have avoided the dispute by adding either "respectively" or "collectively" to the end of the sentence. In the second example, the conclusion favors Mr. James. David will argue that the condition that he finish by May 1 affected only the Cadillac and that he therefore is entitled to the $5,000. The dispute could have been avoided by properly inserting a comma in the language of the promise.

Amphiboly differs from equivocation in two important ways. First, equivocation is always traced to an ambiguity in the meaning of a *word* or *phrase*, whereas amphiboly involves a syntactical ambiguity in a *statement.* The second difference is that amphiboly usually involves a mistake made by the arguer in interpreting an ambiguous statement made by someone else, whereas the ambiguity in equivocation is typically the arguer's own creation. If these distinctions are kept in mind, it is usually easy to distinguish amphiboly from equivocation. Occasionally, however, the two fallacies occur together, as the following example illustrates:

> The *Great Western Cookbook* recommends that we serve the oysters when thoroughly stewed. Apparently the delicate flavor is enhanced by the intoxicated condition of the diners.

First, it is unclear whether "stewed" refers to the oysters or to the diners, and so the argument commits an amphiboly. But if "stewed" refers to the oysters it means "cooked," and if it refers to the diners it means "intoxicated." Thus, the argument also involves an equivocation.

21. Composition

The fallacy of **composition** is committed when the conclusion of an argument depends on the erroneous transference of an attribute from the parts of something onto the whole. In other words, the fallacy occurs when it is argued that because the parts have a certain attribute, it follows that the whole has that attribute, too, and the situation is such that the attribute in question cannot be legitimately transferred from parts to whole. Examples:

> Maria likes anchovies. She also likes chocolate ice cream. Therefore, it is certain that she would like a chocolate sundae topped with anchovies.

> Each player on this basketball team is an excellent athlete. Therefore, the team as a whole is excellent.

> Each atom in this teacup is invisible. Therefore, this teacup is invisible.

> Sodium and chlorine, the atomic components of salt, are both deadly poisons. Therefore, salt is a deadly poison.

In these arguments the attributes that are transferred from the parts onto the whole are designated by the words "Maria likes," "excellent," "invisible," and "deadly poison," respectively. In each case the transference is illegitimate, and so the argument is fallacious.

Not every such transference is illegitimate, however. Consider the following arguments:

> Every atom in this teacup has mass. Therefore, this teacup has mass.

> Every component in this picket fence is white. Therefore, the whole fence is white.

In each case an attribute (having mass, being white) is transferred from the parts onto the whole, but these transferences are quite legitimate. Indeed, the fact that the atoms have mass is the very reason *why* the teacup has mass. The same reasoning extends to the fence. Thus, the acceptability of these arguments is attributable, at least in part, to the *legitimate* transference of an attribute from parts onto the whole.

These examples illustrate the fact that the fallacy of composition is indeed an informal fallacy. It cannot be discovered by a mere inspection of the form of an argument—that is, by the mere observation that an attribute is being transferred from parts onto the whole. In addition, detecting this fallacy requires a general knowledge of the situation and of the nature of the attribute being transferred. The critic must be certain that, given the situation, the transference of this particular attribute is incorrect.

Further caution is required by the fact that composition is sometimes confused with hasty generalization. The only time this confusion is possible is when the "whole" is a

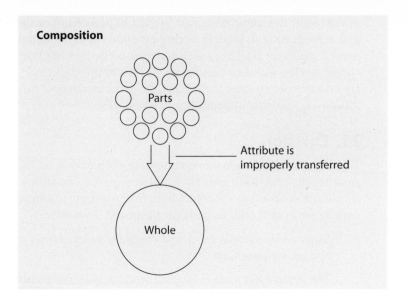

Composition

Parts

Whole

Attribute is improperly transferred

class (such as the class of people in a city or the class of trees in a forest), and the "parts" are the members of the class. In such a case composition proceeds from the members of the class to the class itself. Hasty generalization, on the other hand, proceeds from the specific to the general. Because it is sometimes easy to mistake a statement about a class for a general statement, composition can be mistaken for hasty generalization. Such a mistake can be avoided if one is careful to keep in mind the distinction between these two kinds of statements. This distinction falls back on the difference between the **collective** and the **distributive predication** of an attribute. Consider the following statements:

Fleas are small.
Fleas are numerous.

The first statement is a general statement. The attribute of being small is predicated distributively; that is, it is assigned (or distributed) to each and every flea in the class. Each and every flea in the class is said to be small. The second statement, on the other hand, is a statement about a class as a whole, or what we will call a "class statement." The attribute of being numerous is predicated collectively; in other words, it is assigned not to the individual fleas but to the *class* of fleas. The meaning of the statement is not that each and every flea is numerous but that the class of fleas is large.

To distinguish composition from hasty generalization, therefore, the following procedure should be followed. Examine the conclusion of the argument. If the conclusion is a general statement—that is, a statement in which an attribute is predicated distributively to each and every member of a class—the fallacy committed is hasty generalization. But if the conclusion is a class statement—that is, a statement in which an attribute is predicated collectively to a class as a whole—the fallacy is composition. Example:

Less fuel is consumed by a car than by a fire truck. Therefore, less fuel is consumed in the United States by cars than by fire trucks.

At first sight this argument might appear to proceed from the specific to the general and, consequently, to commit a hasty generalization. But in fact the conclusion is not a general statement at all but a class statement. The conclusion states that the whole class of cars uses less fuel than does the whole class of fire trucks (which is false, because there are many more cars than fire trucks). Since the attribute of using less fuel is predicated collectively, the fallacy committed is composition.

22. Division

The fallacy of **division** is the exact reverse of composition. As composition goes from parts to whole, division goes from whole to parts. The fallacy is committed when the conclusion of an argument depends on the erroneous transference of an attribute from a whole (or a class) onto its parts (or members). Examples:

> Salt is a nonpoisonous compound. Therefore, its component elements, sodium and chlorine, are nonpoisonous.

> This airplane was made in Seattle. Therefore, every component part of this airplane was made in Seattle.

> The Royal Society is over 300 years old. Professor Thompson is a member of the Royal Society. Therefore, Professor Thompson is over 300 years old.

In each case the attribute, designated respectively by the terms "nonpoisonous," "made in Seattle," and "over 300 years old," is illegitimately transferred from the whole or class onto the parts or members. As with the fallacy of composition, however, this kind of transference is sometimes legitimate. The following arguments contain no fallacy:

> This teacup has mass. Therefore, the atoms that compose this teacup have mass.

> This field of poppies is uniformly orange. Therefore, the individual poppies are orange.

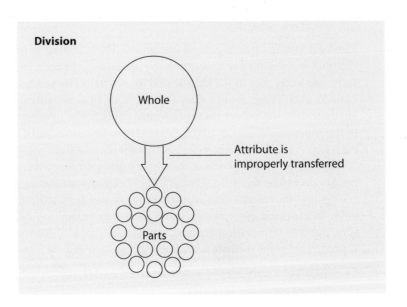

Division

Whole

Attribute is improperly transferred

Parts

Obviously, one must be acquainted with the situation and the nature of the attribute being transferred to decide whether the fallacy of division is actually committed.

Just as composition can sometimes be confused with hasty generalization (converse accident), division can sometimes be confused with accident. As with composition, this confusion can occur only when the "whole" is a class. In such a case, division proceeds from the class to the members, whereas accident proceeds from the general to the specific. Thus, if a class statement is mistaken for a general statement, division may be mistaken for accident. To avoid such a mistake, one should analyze the premises of the argument. If the premises contain a general statement, the fallacy committed is accident; but if they contain a class statement, the fallacy is division. Example:

> Stanley Steamers have almost disappeared.
> This car is a Stanley Steamer.
> Therefore, this car has almost disappeared.

The first premise is not a general statement but a class statement. The attribute of having almost disappeared is predicated collectively. Accordingly, the fallacy committed is division, not accident.

This example also illustrates how cases of division that involve class statements can include a subtle form of equivocation. In the conclusion, the word "disappeared" means fading from vision, as when the lights are turned down; but in the first premise it means rarely seen. The equivocation is a kind of secondary fallacy that results from the primary fallacy, which is division.

The next example shows how division turns up in arguments dealing with averages.

> The average American family has 2.5 children.
> The Jones family is an average American family.
> Therefore, the Jones family has 2.5 children.

The statement "The average American family has 2.5 children" is not a general statement, but rather a class statement. The sense of the statement is not that each and every family has 2.5 children, but that the class of families having two parents is reducible to about 55 percent children and 45 percent adults. Thus, once again, the fallacy is division, and not accident.

MindTap Strengthen your understanding of the topic with the section's **Video Lecture**.

EXERCISE 3.4

I. Identify the fallacies of presumption, ambiguity, and illicit transference committed by the following arguments, giving a brief explanation for your answer. If no fallacy is committed, write "no fallacy."

MindTap Complete exercises online for immediate feedback.

★1. Either we require forced sterilization of Third World peoples or the world population will explode and all of us will die. We certainly don't want to die, so we must require forced sterilization.

2. Every sentence in this paragraph is well written. Therefore, the paragraph is well written.

3. An athlete is a human being. Therefore, a good athlete is a good human being.

★4. James said that he saw a picture of a beautiful girl stashed in Stephen's locker. We can only conclude that Stephen has broken the rules, because girls are not allowed in the locker room.

5. Why is it so difficult for you to reach a decision?

6. Water will quench one's thirst. Water is composed of hydrogen and oxygen. Therefore, hydrogen will quench one's thirst, and so will oxygen.

★7. People who lack humility have no sense of beauty, because everyone who has a sense of beauty also has humility.

8. Butane is combustible. Therefore, it burns.

9. Twenty years ago, Kung Fong, the great sumo wrestler, could have yanked up one of the fir trees in the new municipal arboretum with a single pull. Therefore, since Mr. Fong is as strong today as he was then, he could just as easily pull up one of those trees today.

★10. If Thomas gives Marie a ring, then Thomas and Marie will be engaged. Thomas did give Marie a ring. In fact, he phoned her just the other night. Therefore, Thomas and Marie are engaged.

11. Alex, I heard your testimony in court earlier today. Tell me, why did you lie on the witness stand?

12. Johnson is employed by the General Services Administration, and everyone knows that the GSA is the most inefficient branch of the government. Therefore, Johnson must be an inefficient worker.

★13. All men are mortal. Therefore, someday man will disappear from the earth.

14. Each and every cell in this carrot is 90 percent water. Therefore, the entire carrot is 90 percent water.

15. George said that he was interviewing for a job drilling oil wells in the supervisor's office. We can only conclude that the supervisor must have an awfully dirty office.

★16. During the fifty years that Mr. Jones worked, he contributed $90,000 to Social Security. Now that he is retired, he stands to collect $200,000 from the system. Obviously he will collect a much greater monetary value than he contributed.

17. Either you major in business administration, or you have no chance at a successful career. You told me that you aren't majoring in business administration. It's sad that you haven't chosen a path that will lead to success.

18. Either James Franco or Miley Cyrus is a popular singer. James Franco is not a popular singer. Therefore, Miley Cyrus is a popular singer.

★19. Switzerland is 48 percent Protestant. Heidi Gilsing is a Swiss. Therefore, Heidi Gilsing is 48 percent Protestant.

20. Picasso is the greatest artist of the twentieth century. We know that this is so because art critics have described him in these terms. These art critics are correct in their assessment because they have a more keenly developed sense of appreciation than the average person. This is true because it takes a more keenly developed sense of appreciation to realize that Picasso is the greatest artist of the twentieth century.

21. An atomic bomb causes more damage than a conventional bomb. Therefore, during World War II more damage was caused by atomic bombs than by conventional bombs.

★22. Sylvia, I saw you shopping for wine the other day. Incidentally, are you still drinking excessively?

23. The author warns about numerous computational errors in his accounting text. Therefore, he must have written it very carelessly.

24. Emeralds are seldom found in this country, so you should be careful not to misplace your emerald ring.

★25. Of course abortion is permissible. After all, a woman has a right to do as she pleases with her own body.

II. Answer "true" or "false" to the following statements:

1. Arguments that commit the fallacy of begging the question are normally valid.

2. The effect of begging the question is to hide the fact that a premise may not be true.

3. The correct way of responding to a complex question is to divide the question into its component questions and answer each separately.

4. False dichotomy always involves an "either . . . or . . ." statement, at least implicitly.

5. The fallacy of equivocation arises from a syntactical defect in a statement.

6. The fallacy of amphiboly usually involves the ambiguous use of a single word.

7. Amphiboly usually arises from the arguer's misinterpreting a statement made by someone else.

8. The fallacy of composition always proceeds from whole to parts.

9. The fallacy of division always proceeds from parts to whole.

10. A general statement makes an assertion about each and every member of a class.

11. A class statement makes an assertion about a class as a whole.

12. In the statement "Divorces are increasing," an attribute is predicated distributively.

13. In the statement "Waistlines are increasing," an attribute is predicated distributively.

14. Composition and division involve the distributive predication of an attribute.

15. Equivocation and amphiboly are classified as fallacies of ambiguity.

III. Identify the fallacies of relevance, weak induction, presumption, ambiguity, and illicit transference committed by the following arguments, giving a brief explanation for your answer. If no fallacy is committed, write "no fallacy."

★1. In his *History of the American Civil War*, Jeffry Noland argues that the war had little to do with slavery. However, as a historian from Alabama, Noland could not possibly present an accurate account. Therefore, his arguments should be discounted.

2. Mr. Wilson said that on July 4 he went out on the veranda and watched the fireworks go up in his pajamas. We conclude that Mr. Wilson must have had an exciting evening.

3. Oregon State Representative Dennis Richardson says that the reason the Newtown school massacre occurred is because the teachers were not armed. Thus, to prevent future shootings of this sort we must make sure that every teacher in the United States is armed with a gun.

★4. A crust of bread is better than nothing. Nothing is better than true love. Therefore, a crust of bread is better than true love.

5. Every member of the Delta Club is over seventy years old. Therefore, the Delta Club must be over seventy years old.

6. Of course you should eat Wheaties. Wheaties is the breakfast of champions, you know.

★7. Surely it's morally permissible to kill animals for food. If God didn't want us to eat animals, he wouldn't have made them out of meat.

8. The idea that black people in this country live in poverty is ridiculous. Look at LeBron James. He's a millionaire. And so are Sean Combs, Samuel L. Jackson, and Michael Jordan.

9. No one has ever proved that the human fetus is not a person with rights. Therefore, abortion is morally wrong.

★10. Giant pandas are rapidly disappearing. This animal is a giant panda. Therefore, this animal should disappear any minute now.

11. When a car breaks down so often that repairs become pointless, the car is thrown on the junk heap. Similarly, when a person becomes old and diseased, he or she should be mercifully put to death.

12. The twenty-story Carson Building is constructed of concrete blocks. Each and every concrete block in the structure can withstand an earthquake of 9.5 on

the Richter scale. Therefore, the building can withstand an earthquake of 9.5 on the Richter scale.

★13. Childhood obesity is a major problem these days. Obviously our public health officials have not been doing their job.

14. This administration is not anti-German, as it has been alleged. Germany is a great country. It has contributed immensely to the world's artistic treasury. Goethe and Schiller made magnificent contributions to literature, and Bach, Beethoven, Wagner, and Brahms did the same in music.

15. Paul, it was great to see you at the party the other night. Everyone there was doing crack. Incidentally, how long have you been dealing that stuff?

★16. Texas oilman T. Boone Pickens says that natural-gas fracking is perfectly safe and poses no threat to the nation's drinking water. Therefore we must conclude that fracking is just as safe as he claims it is.

17. Senator Chris Murphy's arguments for the protection of wilderness areas should be ignored. Murphy is just another one of those tree-hugging liberals who supports such legislation only to please the environmental nuts in his home state of Connecticut.

18. Professor Andrews, surely I deserve a B in logic. I know that I have gotten F's on all the tests, but if you give me an F for my final grade, I will lose my scholarship. That will force me to drop out of school, and my poor, aged parents, who yearn to see me graduate, will be grief stricken for the rest of their lives.

★19. Molecules are in constant random motion. The Statue of Liberty is composed of molecules. Therefore, the Statue of Liberty is in constant random motion.

20. Either we have prayer in our public schools or the moral fabric of society will disintegrate. The choice should be obvious.

21. White sheep eat more than black sheep (because there are more of them). Therefore, this white sheep eats more than that black sheep.

★22. If someone rents a piece of land and plants crops on it, the landlord is never permitted to come and take those crops for himself when harvest time arrives. Similarly, if couples enlist the services of a surrogate mother to provide them with a baby, the mother should never be allowed to renege on the deal and keep the baby for herself once it is born.

23. Motives and desires exert forces on people, causing them to choose one thing over another. But force is a physical quantity, governed by the laws of physics. Therefore, human choices are governed by the laws of physics.

24. Each and every brick in the completely brick-faced Wainright Building has a reddish-brown color. Therefore, the Wainright Building has a reddish-brown color.

★25. Humanitarian groups have argued in favor of housing for the poor. Unfortunately, these high-density projects have been tried in the past and have failed. In no time they turn into ghettos with astronomical rates of crime and delinquency. Clearly, these humanitarian arguments are not what they seem.

26. Pauline said that after she had removed her new mink coat from the shipping carton she threw it into the trash. We conclude that Pauline has no appreciation for fine furs.

27. We know that induction will provide dependable results in the future because it has always worked in the past. Whatever has consistently worked in the past will continue to work in the future, and we know that this is true because it has been established by induction.

★28. What goes up must come down. The price of food has been going up for years. Therefore, it will surely come down soon.

29. Mr. Prime Minister, I am certain you will want to release the members of our National Liberation Group whom you currently hold in prison. After all, I'm sure you will want to avoid having car bombs go off in the centers of your most heavily populated cities.

30. Recent studies have shown that conventional food has the same vitamins, minerals, proteins, and other nutrients as organic food. Therefore, it's just as good to eat conventional food as organic food.

★31. We've all heard the complaint that millions of Americans are without adequate health care. But America's doctors, nurses, and hospitals are among the best in the world. Thousands of people come from abroad every year to be treated here. Clearly there is nothing wrong with our health-care system.

32. Real estate mogul Donald Trump argues that good management is essential to any business. But who is he to talk? Trump's own mismanagement drove Trump Entertainment Resorts into bankruptcy three times in eighteen years.

33. The farmers of our state have asked that we introduce legislation to provide subsidies for soybeans. Unfortunately, we will have to turn down their request. If we give subsidies to the soybean farmers, then the corn and wheat growers will ask for the same thing. Then it will be the cotton growers, citrus growers, truck farmers, and cattle raisers. In the end, the cost will be astronomical.

★34. The travel brochure states that walking up O'Connell Street, the statue of Parnell comes into view. Apparently that statue has no trouble getting around.

35. Criminals are basically stupid, because anyone who isn't basically stupid wouldn't be a criminal.

36. Professor Glazebrooks's theory about the origin of the Martian craters is undoubtedly true. Rudolph Orkin, the great concert pianist, announced his support of the theory in this morning's newspaper.

★37. Mr. Franklin has lost at the craps table for the last ten throws of the dice. Therefore, it is extremely likely that he will win on the next throw.

38. Raising a child is like growing a tree. Sometimes violent things, such as cutting off branches, have to be done to force the tree to grow straight. Similarly, corporal punishment must sometimes be inflicted on children to force them to develop properly.

39. Good steaks are rare these days, so don't order yours well done.

★40. The Book of Mormon is true because it was written by Joseph Smith. Joseph Smith wrote the truth because he was divinely inspired. We know that Joseph Smith was divinely inspired because the Book of Mormon says that he was, and the Book of Mormon is true.

41. The students attending Bradford College come from every one of the fifty states. Michelle attends Bradford College. Therefore, Michelle comes from every one of the fifty states.

42. Rhubarb pie is a dessert. Therefore, whoever eats rhubarb pie eats a dessert.

★43. The vast majority of car accidents occur within twenty miles of one's home. Apparently it is much more dangerous to drive close to home than far away from home.

44. Either you buy me a new BMW, or I won't be able to get back and forth to school. I know you want me to go to school, so the choice is clear.

45. Nobody has ever proved that using cell phones causes brain tumors. Therefore, using cell phones does not cause brain tumors.

★46. When I visited Dr. Ames about my cholesterol, she insisted that I go on a statin drug. She says everybody should be on a statin. And when I saw Dr. Collins for depression, he prescribed Prozac. And when the Prozac gave me nausea, he prescribed Zofran to stop the nausea. Doctors are all the same. They all take their orders from the pharmaceutical industry.

47. Dozens of species of plants and animals are being wiped out every year, even though we have laws to prevent it. Clearly, we should repeal the Endangered Species Act.

48. People are driving their cars like maniacs tonight. There must be a full moon.

★49. A line is composed of points. Points have no length. Therefore, a line has no length.

50. Are you in favor of the ruinous economic policy of the Democratic Platform Committee?

IV. Identify the fallacies committed in the following dialogue. You should be able to find at least one case of each fallacy presented in this section and a few of the fallacies presented in the two previous sections.

Personal Paper Mill

Carly catches sight of Brad as the two head for their class in sociology. "Hi!" she says as she joins him. "Did you get your paper finished?"

"Yes," he replies. "And given that first-rate work deserves an A, I deserve an A for this paper."

"That's great!" she says.

"But just between you and me, I had my girlfriend write my paper."

"Don't tell me that." Carly looks disgusted. "Do you think that's moral?"

"Beats me. Why do you always insist on giving moral advice to everyone?"

"The real question is, why do you always ignore moral advice?" she asks.

"Well, the way I see it," Brad says, "there's really nothing wrong with plagiarism. After all, students who plagiarize their work usually get better grades. Anyway, I'm just following in the footsteps of most U.S. presidents. They have speechwriters who write most of their speeches. Why shouldn't I get someone to write my papers?"

"You are so stupid!" Carly replies. "Honestly, I really think everyone should stop listening to you."

"Okay, how about this?" he asks. "Either I get someone to write this paper for me, or I'll get an F in the class. I can't afford to get an F; thus, I get someone to write the paper for me."

"That's not much better," Carly replies. "But you should realize that plagiarism is really dangerous. If you get caught, it could destroy your reputation."

"I doubt many students would think badly of me," he says. "Practically everyone plagiarizes their work nowadays, and if they do it, so can I."

"It's not true that all students plagiarize their work," Carly replies. "In fact, I am quite certain that none of them do. I certainly don't, and all of the students I know don't."

"Ah, but you do plagiarize your work," Brad insists.

"What do you mean?" Carly asks.

"Well, every word of your paper appears in the dictionary, so it's clear that you plagiarized it from the dictionary."

"Very funny," Carly says. "But here's what I think. I think you should ask Professor Halvorson for an extension on your paper and write it yourself. She really takes plagiarism seriously, and she insists that all work submitted to her be original."

"But this paper is original work," Brad insists, as they enter the social sciences building. "My girlfriend has never written a paper like this before, and she didn't copy it from anyone."

Carly laughs. "I don't think that's what she means by 'original.'" Incidentally, did you remember to attach a copy of the integrity pledge to the front of your paper? The academic integrity policy says that all instructors must direct their students to sign their full name on the integrity pledge, which asserts that the work being submitted has not been plagiarized."

"Yes, I have attached a copy of the pledge document to the paper, and I signed it 'Professor Judy Halvorson,' just as the rule says."

"How dense can you get?" Carly asks. "You're not supposed to sign the professor's name! You're supposed to sign your *own* name."

"Oh," says Brad. For the first time he looks concerned. "But that means I would be lying."

"Yes, it would," Carly agrees, "but I don't see why that should bother you. Still, I can assure you of this: If you hand in the paper, you won't graduate."

"You're wrong about that," Brad counters. "Consider this. I'm a member of the senior class, and the senior class graduates in May. That means I'll graduate in May."

"I wouldn't bet on it," Carly says, as they approach their classroom. "You forget that I'm on the Academic Integrity Committee, and I've sworn to uphold the policy on plagiarism."

"Uh oh." Brad looks concerned again. "That had slipped my mind. But you won't rat on me, will you? Please, please don't. All my life I have struggled with my sense of self-esteem, and if I get an F on this paper, I will feel absolutely crushed."

"Rat on you? Well, that depends," says Carly.

They enter the classroom, and Brad gives Carly a tense smile. "On what?"

Carly smiles grimly back. "On whether you hand in the paper your girlfriend wrote."

V. Create the following informal fallacies:

1. A begging the question connected with religion

2. A complex question dealing with cyberstalking

3. A false dichotomy related to a Tiffany watch

4. An equivocation involving the word "fan"

5. An amphiboly depending on the ambiguous use of a pronoun

6. A composition fallacy dealing with a church choir

MindTap® Master concepts and improve outcomes with Aplia, at the end of the chapter, in the Aplia folder.

3.5 Fallacies in Ordinary Language

HOW LOGICAL ARE YOU? While on the topic of student loans, your friend argues that she should not be required to pay back her loan because it's unfair. She's been poor all of her life, and all her friends are rich. They don't need loans. Also, she hasn't gotten her money's worth from her education. All she has earned in college are rotten grades. After graduation, she must either default on the loan or forget about any future happiness. How would you assess your friend's reasoning?

Find the answer on MindTap.

This section addresses two topics. The first concerns the challenge of detecting the fallacies of others in ordinary language, and the second relates to the goal of avoiding fallacies in one's own arguments.

Detecting Fallacies

Most of the informal fallacies that we have seen thus far have been clear-cut, easily recognizable instances of a specific mistake. When fallacies occur in ordinary usage, however, they are often neither clear-cut nor easily recognizable. The reason is that there are innumerable ways of making mistakes in arguing, and variations inevitably occur that may not be exact instances of any specifically named fallacy. In addition, one fallacious mode of arguing may be mixed with one or more others, and the strands of reasoning may have to be disentangled before the fallacies can be named. Yet another problem arises from the fact that arguments in ordinary language are rarely presented in complete form. A premise or conclusion often is left unexpressed, which may obscure the nature of the evidence that is presented or the strength of the link between premises and conclusion.

Consider, for example, the following letter that appeared in a newspaper:

> God, I am sick of "women's rights"! Every time one turns on the news we hear about some form of discrimination against some poor female who wants to be a fireman—or some "remark" that suggests or implies women are inferior to men.
>
> I, for one, do not want to be rescued by a "woman fireman," especially if I am a 6-foot-2 male and she is a 5-foot-6 female.
>
> Why is it that women find their "role" so degrading? What is wrong with being a wife and mother, staying home while the male goes out and "hunts for food" and brings it home to his family?
>
> I don't think women have proven themselves to be as inventive, as capable (on the average) of world leadership, as physically capable, or as "courageous" as men. Most of us have yet to fight a war (the average American woman) and let's face it ladies, who wants to?
>
> Whether a person is female, black, white, handicapped—whatever—*ability* is what counts in the final analysis. Women cannot demand "equality"—no one can—unless it is earned.
>
> When push comes to shove and a damsel is in distress, she is hard-pressed to protect herself and usually has to be rescued by a man. Until I can move a piano, beat off a potential robber or rapist, or fight a war, I am quite content to be a woman, thank you.
>
> (Patricia Kelley)

This letter presents numerous fallacies. The phrase "poor female who wants to be a fireman" suggests a mild *ad hominem* abusive, and equating women's rights in general with the right to be a firefighter suggests a straw man. The second paragraph commits another straw man fallacy by supposing that the job of firefighter inevitably entails such activities as climbing up ladders and rescuing people. Surely there are many male firefighters who cannot do this. The same paragraph also can be interpreted as begging the question: Do women who want to be firefighters want the specific job of rescuing tall men?

The third paragraph throws out a red herring. The issue is whether women have the right to be considered for a job of their choice and whether they must be paid as much as a man in the same situation. Whether there is something wrong with being a wife and mother is quite a different issue. Also, the reference to men hunting for food suggests a possible begging of the question: Are we still locked into a "hunter-gatherer" social structure?

The paragraph about whether women have proved themselves to be as inventive, capable, and courageous as men begs yet another question: Assuming, for the sake of argument, that this is true, have women been allowed to occupy roles in society where such inventiveness, capability, and courageousness can be demonstrated? Furthermore, this paragraph commits a red herring fallacy and/or misses the point: Even if women have not proved this, what does that have to do with the issue? Most jobs do not require any high degree of inventiveness or courage or a capacity for world leadership.

The paragraph about ability begs yet another question: Is it in fact the case that women have less ability? I am not aware that anything of the sort has ever been proved. Finally, the last paragraph throws out another red herring. What does moving pianos and beating off rapists have to do with most jobs or the question of equal pay for equal work?

Probably the single most important requirement for detecting fallacies in ordinary language is alertness. The reader or listener must pay close attention to what the arguer is saying. What is the conclusion? What are the reasons given in support of the conclusion? Are the reasons relevant to the conclusion? Do the reasons support the conclusion? If the reader or listener is half asleep or lounging in that passive, drugged-out state that attends much television viewing, then none of these questions will receive answers. Under those circumstances the reader or listener will never be able to detect informal fallacies, and he or she will accept even the worst reasoning without the slightest hesitation.

Avoiding Fallacies

Why do people commit informal fallacies? Unfortunately, this question allows for no simple, straightforward answer. The reasons underlying the commission of fallacies are complex and interconnected. However, we can identify three factors that lead to most of the informal mistakes in reasoning. The first is intent. Many fallacies are committed intentionally. The arguer may know full well that his or her reasoning is defective but goes ahead with it anyway because of some benefit for himself or herself or some other person. All of the informal fallacies we have studied can be used for that purpose, but some of them are particularly well suited to it. These include the appeal to force, appeal to pity, appeal to the people, straw man, *ad hominem,* complex question, false dichotomy, and suppressed evidence. Here is such a case of appeal to force:

> I deserve a chocolate sundae for dessert, and if you don't buy me one right now, I'll start screaming and embarrass you in front of all of the people in this restaurant.

And here is a case of false dichotomy that conveys the appearance of being intentionally committed:

> Either you take me on a Caribbean cruise, or I'll have a nervous breakdown. It's up to you.

The key to avoiding fallacies that are intentionally committed probably lies in some form of moral education. The arguer must come to realize that using intellectually dishonest means in order to acquire something he or she does not deserve is just another form of cheating.

The situation becomes more complicated, however, when the sought-after goal is morally justified. Arguers sometimes use fallacious reasoning intentionally to trick a person into doing something that is really for that person's own good. Here is a false dichotomy of that sort:

> Either you control your eating and get regular exercise, or you'll have a heart attack and die. The choice is yours.

Given the beneficial consequences of controlled eating and regular exercise, some moral philosophers will find nothing wrong with this argument. Others will contend that manipulating someone into doing something violates human dignity. In either case, such arguments are logically unacceptable.

The second factor that leads to the commission of informal fallacies is a careless mental posture combined with an emotional disposition favoring or opposing some person or thing. The careless mental posture opens the door, so to speak, to fallacious reasoning, and the emotional disposition pushes the arguer through it. Even people who are thoroughly versed in the informal fallacies occasionally succumb to the deadly combination of mental carelessness and emotional impetus. For example, arguments such as the following *ad hominem* abusive can sometimes be heard in the halls of university philosophy departments:

> Professor Ballard's argument in favor of restructuring our course offering isn't worth a hoot. But what would you expect from someone who publishes in such mediocre journals? And did you hear Ballard's recent lecture on Aristotle? It was total nonsense.

When people who should know better are confronted with the fact that their argument commits a common fallacy, they often admit with embarrassment that they have not been thinking and then revise their argument according to logical principles. In contrast, people who are not familiar with the distinction between good and fallacious reasoning will likely deny that there is anything wrong with their argument. Thus, the key to avoiding fallacies that arise from mental carelessness lies in developing a thorough familiarity with the informal fallacies, combined with a habitual realization of how emotions affect people's reasoning. Everyone should realize that unchecked emotions are an open invitation to illogical reasoning, and they can lead a person to commit quite blindly every one of the fallacies we have studied thus far.

The third factor that leads to the commission of informal fallacies is far more difficult to contend with than the first two. It consists in the influence of what we might call the "worldview" of the arguer. By worldview we mean a cognitive network of beliefs, attitudes, habits, memories, values, and other elements that conditions and renders meaningful the world in which we live. Beginning in infancy, our worldview emerges quietly and unconsciously from enveloping influences—culture, language, gender, religion, politics, and social and economic status. As we grow older, it continues to develop through the shaping forces of education and experience. Once it has taken root, our worldview determines how each of us sizes up the world in which we live. Given a set of circumstances, it indicates what is reasonable to believe and what is unreasonable.

In connection with the construction and evaluation of arguments, an arguer's worldview determines the answer to questions about importance, relevance, causal connections, the qualifications of authorities, whether a sample is typical or atypical of a group, what can and cannot be taken for granted, and other factors. However, because these determinations inevitably involve unexamined presuppositions, the arguer's worldview can lead to the commission of informal fallacies. All of the fallacies we have studied so far are likely candidates, but the ones especially susceptible are appeal to pity, straw man, missing the point, appeal to unqualified authority, hasty generalization, false cause, slippery slope, weak analogy, begging the question, false dichotomy, and suppressed evidence.

Thus, a person with a victim mentality may think that his pathetic circumstances really justify some favorable treatment; an uncritical conservative may cite with complete confidence the authority of Rush Limbaugh; a person with a racist worldview may conclude that the errant behavior of a handful of Asians, African Americans, or Hispanics really is typical of the larger class; a person with a liberal worldview may quite innocently distort an opponent's argument by equating it with fascism; a pro-life arguer may consider it obvious that the fetus is a person with rights, while a pro-choice arguer may take it for granted that the fetus is not a person with rights, and so on. Consider, for example, the following argument from analogy:

> A court trial is like a professional football game. In a professional football game, the most important thing is winning. Similarly, in a trial, the most important thing is winning.

This argument is consistent with the worldview of many, if not most, lawyers. Lawyers are trained as advocates, and when they enter a courtroom they see themselves going into battle for their clients. In any battle, winning is the most important objective. But this viewpoint presupposes that truth and justice are either unattainable in the courtroom or of secondary importance. Thus, while many lawyers would evaluate this argument as nonfallacious, many nonlawyers would reject it as a weak analogy.

For another example, consider the following causal inference:

> After enslaving most of Eastern Europe for nearly fifty years, the evil Soviet empire finally collapsed. Obviously God listened to our prayers.

This argument reflects the worldview of many theists. It presupposes that there is a God, that God listens to prayers, that God is influenced by prayers, that God has the power to alter the course of history, and that God does alter the course of history. While the theist is likely to consider this argument a good one, the atheist will reject it as a blatant case of false cause.

To avoid fallacies that arise from the influence of worldviews, the arguer must acknowledge and critique his or her presuppositions. Doing so inclines the arguer to couch his or her arguments in language that takes those presuppositions into account. The result is nearly always an argument that is more intelligently crafted and, it is hoped, more persuasive. However, the task of recognizing and critiquing one's presuppositions is not easy. Presuppositions are intrinsically linked to one's worldview, and many people are not even aware that they have a worldview. The reason is that worldviews are formed through a process that is largely unconscious. Thus, the arguer must first recognize that he or she has a worldview and must then exercise constant vigilance over the presuppositions it comprises.

Even after one's presuppositions have been exposed and thoroughly critiqued, however, there is no guarantee that one's arguments will agree with the arguments of others who have critiqued their worldviews. This is because a person's worldview reflects the unique perspective that person has on the world. No two people share exactly the same perspective. Nevertheless, disclosing and critiquing the presuppositions in one's worldview lays a foundation for meaningful communication with other reasonable arguers, and it provides a context of reasonableness for working out disagreements.

In summary, the three factors that are probably responsible for most informal fallacies are intent, mental carelessness combined with emotional dispositions, and unexamined presuppositions in the arguer's worldview. However, these factors rarely occur in isolation. In the vast majority of cases, two or all three conspire to produce fallacious reasoning. This fact exacerbates the difficulty in avoiding informal fallacies in one's own arguments and in detecting fallacies in the arguments of others.

Now let us consider some cases of real-life arguments in light of the factors we have just discussed. All are taken from letters-to-the-editor columns of newspapers and magazines. The first relates to affirmative action programs:

> I'm a nonracist, nonsexist, white male born in 1969, who has never owned a slave, treated anyone as inferior because of his or her race, or sexually harassed a female co-worker. In other words, I don't owe women or minorities a thing. Since when are people required to pay for the sins of their predecessors simply because they belong to the same race or gender?
>
> (Ben Gibbons)

The author of this argument presupposes that racist and sexist patterns in society have not benefited him in any way. Among other things, he presupposes that his white ancestors in no way benefited from their being white and that none of these benefits passed down to him. On the other hand, given that he has received such benefits, he may presuppose that he is not obligated to pay any of them back. Of course, none of these things may have occurred, but the author should at least address these issues. Because he does not address them, the argument begs the question.

The next argument relates to secondhand smoke from cigarettes:

> Now, besides lung cancer and other nasty business, secondhand smoke causes deafness and impotence. Was secondhand smoke a problem when people heated their homes solely by fireplaces? How about those romantic teepees with the smoke hole at the top? And what about fireplaces in new homes? Let's have some research about the problems caused by these as well as barbecues. A little cancer with your hot dog, anyone?
>
> (Pat Sharp)

This argument seems to commit the fallacy of equivocation. The arguer begins by using "secondhand smoke" to refer to the smoke from burning tobacco, and then uses the term to refer to the smoke from fireplaces, teepee fires, and barbecues. Smoke from burning tobacco is clearly not the same thing as smoke from burning wood or charcoal. Alternately, the argument might be seen to beg the question: "But do people burn tobacco in their fireplaces and barbecues?" These fallacies probably arise either from the intentions of the author or from carelessness in failing to distinguish the two kinds of secondhand smoke. In either event, the author is probably hostile to government efforts to control secondhand tobacco smoke in confined areas.

The next argument deals with gun control:

> Detroit, the seventh largest city and one with strict gun laws, had 596 homicides last year. In the same year Phoenix, the ninth largest city and one that at the time did not require gun owners to be licensed, had 136 homicides. Criminals don't fear the toothless criminal-justice system, but they do fear armed citizens.
>
> (Paul M. Berardi)

This argument commits a false cause fallacy. The author presupposes that the availability of guns caused Phoenix to have a lower homicide rate than Detroit. The arguer also presupposes that Detroit and Phoenix are comparable as to homicide rate merely because they are roughly the same size. As a result, the argument involves a weak analogy and also begs the question. The additional factors of emotion and intent may also be present. The arguer probably hates the prospect of gun control, and he may be fully aware of the fact that Phoenix and Detroit are not comparable for his purpose, but he went ahead with the comparison anyway.

The next argument deals with religious fundamentalism:

> If we compromise God's word, we compromise the truth. To say that the fundamentalist is a loud shrill voice drowning out religious moderation implies that diluted truth is better than absolute truth.
>
> (Gerald Gleason)

This argument begs the question. The arguer presupposes that there is a God, that God has spoken, that God has revealed his intentions to fundamentalist preachers, and that those preachers accurately report the word of God. The argument also seems to reflect an emotional disposition in favor of religious fundamentalism.

The last argument we will consider relates to English as the official U.S. language:

> This great country has been held together for more than 200 years because of one simple thing: the English language. There are two things we must do: Make English the official language of the United States and do away with bilingual education.
>
> (David Moisan)

This argument misses the point. The arguer presupposes that making English the official language would guarantee that all citizens speak it and that doing away with bilingual education would accelerate the learning process of immigrant children. The argument may also reflect the fear that many feel in connection with the changes U.S. society is experiencing as a result of recent immigration.

EXERCISE 3.5

I. Most of the following selections were taken from letters-to-the-editor columns of newspapers and magazines. Identify any fallacies that may be committed, giving a brief explanation for your answer. Then, if a fallacy is identified, discuss the possible factors that led the arguer to commit the fallacy.

★1. Exporting cigarettes [to Asia] is good business for America; there is no reason we should be prohibited from doing so. Asians have been smoking for decades; we are only offering variety in their habit. If the Asians made

MindTap® Complete exercises online for immediate feedback.

tobacco smoking illegal, that would be a different situation. But as long as it is legal, the decision is up to the smokers. The Asians are just afraid of American supremacy in the tobacco industries.

(Pat Monohan)

2. When will these upper-crust intellectuals realize that the masses of working people are not in cozy, cushy, interesting, challenging, well-paying jobs, professions and businesses? My husband is now fifty-one; for most of the last thirty-three years he has worked in the same factory job, and only the thought of retiring at sixty-two has sustained him. When he reaches that age in eleven years, who will tell him that his aging and physically wracked body must keep going another two years? My heart cries out for all the poor souls who man the assembly lines, ride the trucks or work in the fields or mines, or in the poorly ventilated, hot-in-summer, cold-in-winter factories and garages. Many cannot afford to retire at sixty-two, sixty-five, or even later. Never, never let them extend the retirement age. It's a matter of survival to so many.

(Isabel Fierman)

3. Women in military combat is insane. No society in its right mind would have such a policy. The military needs only young people and that means the only women who go are those in their childbearing years. Kill them off and society will not be able to perpetuate itself.

(Jack Carman)

★4. Dear Ann: I've read that one aspirin taken every other day will reduce the risk of heart attack. Why not take two and double the protection?

(Boston)

5. The American Civil Liberties Union did a study that found that in the last eighty years it believes twenty-five innocent people have been executed in the United States. This is unfortunate. But, there are innocent people who die each year in highway accidents. Out of 40,000 deaths, how many deaths are related to driving while intoxicated? How many more thousands are injured and incur financial ruin or are invalids and handicapped for the remainder of their lives?

(Mahlon R. Braden)

6. Mexico's president expresses legitimate concern when he questions supplying oil to Americans who are unwilling to apply "discipline" in oil consumption. In view of the fact that his country's population is expected to double in only twenty-two years, isn't it legitimate for us to ask when Mexicans will apply the discipline necessary to control population growth and quit dumping their excess millions over our borders?

(Wayne R. Bartz)

★7. A parent would never give a ten-year-old the car keys, fix him or her a martini, or let him or her wander at night through a dangerous part of town. The same holds true of the Internet. Watch what children access, but leave the Net alone. Regulation is no substitute for responsibility.

(Bobby Dunning)

8. How would you feel to see your children starving and have all doors slammed in your face? Isn't it time that all of us who believe in freedom and human rights stop thinking in terms of color and national boundaries? We should open our arms and hearts to those less fortunate and remember that a time could come when we might be in a similar situation.

(Lorna Doyle)

9. A capital gains tax [reduction] benefits everyone, not just the "rich," because everyone will have more money to invest or spend in the private economy, resulting in more jobs and increasing prosperity for all. This is certainly better than paying high taxes to a corrupt, self-serving, and incompetent government that squanders our earnings on wasteful and useless programs.

(David Miller)

★10. After reading "Homosexuals in the Churches," I'd like to point out that I don't know any serious, capable exegetes who stumble over Saint Paul's denunciation of homosexuality. Only a fool (and there seem to be more and more these days) can fail to understand the plain words of Romans, Chapter one. God did not make anyone "gay." Paul tells us in Romans 1 that homosexuals become that way because of their own lusts.

(LeRoy J. Hopper)

11. When will they ever learn—that the Republican party is not for the people who voted for it?

(Alton L. Stafford)

12. Before I came to the United States in July 1922, I was in Berlin where I visited the famous zoo. In one of the large cages were a lion and a tiger. Both respected each other's strength. It occurred to me that it was a good illustration of "balance of power." Each beast followed the other and watched each other's moves. When one moved, the other did. When one stopped, the other stopped.

In today's world, big powers or groups of powers are trying to maintain the status quo, trying to be as strong as or stronger than the other. They realize a conflict may result in mutual destruction. As long as the countries believe there is a balance of power we may hope for peace.

(Emilie Lackow)

★13. Doctors say the birth of a baby is a high point of being a doctor. Yet a medical survey shows one out of every nine obstetricians in America has stopped delivering babies.

Expectant mothers have had to find new doctors. In some rural areas, women have had to travel elsewhere to give birth.

How did this happen? It's part of the price of the lawsuit crisis.

The number of lawsuits Americans file each year is on the rise. Obstetricians are among the hardest hit—almost three out of four have faced a malpractice claim. Many have decided it isn't worth the risk.

(Magazine ad by the Insurance Information Institute)

14. The conservative diatribe found in campus journalism comes from the mouths of a handful of affluent brats who were spoon-fed through the '90s. Put them on an ethnically more diverse campus, rather than a Princeton or a Dartmouth, and then let us see how long their newspapers survive.

(David Simons)

15. I see that our courts are being asked to rule on the propriety of outlawing video games as a "waste of time and money."

It seems that we may be onto something here. A favorable ruling would open the door to new laws eliminating show business, spectator sports, cocktail lounges, the state of Nevada, public education and, of course, the entire federal bureaucracy.

(A. G. Dobrin)

★**16.** The death penalty is the punishment for murder. Just as we have long jail terms for armed robbery, assault and battery, fraud, contempt of court, fines for speeding, reckless driving and other numerous traffic violations, so must we have a punishment for murder. Yes, the death penalty will not deter murders any more than a speeding ticket will deter violating speed laws again, but it is the punishment for such violation!

(Lawrence J. Barstow)

17. Would you rather invest in our nation's children or Pentagon waste? The choice is yours.

(Political ad)

18. My gun has protected me, and my son's gun taught him safety and responsibility long before he got hold of a far more lethal weapon—the family car. Cigarettes kill many times more people yearly than guns and, unlike guns, have absolutely no redeeming qualities. If John Lennon had died a long, painful and expensive death from lung cancer, would you have devoted a page to a harangue against the product of some of your biggest advertisers—the cigarette companies?

(Silvia A. DeFreitas)

★**19.** If the advocates of prayers in public schools win on this issue, just where will it end? Perhaps next they will ask for prayers on public transportation? Prayers by government workers before they start their job each day? Or maybe, mandatory prayers in public restaurants before starting each meal might be a good idea.

(Leonard Mendelson)

20. So you want to ban smoking in all eating establishments? Well, you go right ahead and do that little thing. And when the 40 percent of smokers stop eating out, the restaurants can do one of two things: close, or raise the price of a $25 dinner 40 percent to $35.

(Karen Sawyer)

21. Pigeons are forced to leave our city to battle for life. Their struggle is an endless search for food. What manner of person would watch these hungry creatures suffer from want of food and deny them their survival? These helpless birds are too often ignored by the people of our city, with not the least bit of compassion shown to them. Pigeons are God's creatures just as the so-called human race is. They need help.

(Leslie Ann Price)

★22. You take half of the American population every night and set them down in front of a screen watching people getting stabbed, shot and blown away. And then you expect them to go out into the streets hugging each other?

(Mark Hustad)

23. So you think that putting the worst type of criminal out of his misery is wrong. How about the Americans who were sent to Korea, to Vietnam, to Beirut, to the Middle East? Thousands of good men were sacrificed supposedly for the good of our country. At the same time we were saving and protecting Charles Manson, Sirhan Sirhan [Robert Kennedy's murderer], and a whole raft of others too numerous to mention.

(George M. Purvis)

24. The fact is that the hype over "acid rain" and "global warming" is just that: hype. Take, for example, Stephen Schneider, author of *Global Warming*. In his current "study" he discusses a "greenhouse effect of catastrophic proportions," yet twenty years ago Schneider was a vocal proponent of the theory of a "new ice age."

(Urs Furrer)

★25. Just as our parents did for us, my husband and I rely solely on Christian Science for all the health needs of our four sons and find it invaluable for the quick cure of whatever ailments and contagions they are subject to. One particular healing that comes to mind happened several years ago when our youngest was a toddler. He had a flu-type illness that suddenly became quite serious. We called a Christian Science practitioner for treatment and he was completely well the next morning.

(Ellen Austin)

26. As somebody who has experienced the tragedy of miscarriage—or spontaneous abortion—at eight weeks, I greatly resent the position that a fetus is not a baby. I went through the grief of losing a baby, and no one should tell me otherwise.

(Ann Fons)

27. How can we pledge allegiance to the flag of the United States of America and not establish laws to punish people who burn the flag to make a statement? We are a people who punish an individual who libels another person but will not seek redress from an individual who insults every citizen of this great country by desecrating the flag.

(William D. Lankford)

★28. The notion of "buying American" is as misguided as the notion of buying Wisconsin, or Oshkosh, Wisconsin, or South Oshkosh, Wisconsin. For the same reasons that Wisconsin increases its standard of living by trading with the rest of the nation, America increases its standard of living by trading with the rest of the world.

(Phillip Smith)

29. We've often heard the saying, "Far better to let 100 guilty men go free than to condemn one innocent man." What happens then if we apply the logic of this argument to the question, "Is a fetus an unborn human being?" Then is it not better to let 100 fetuses be born rather than to mistakenly kill one unborn human being? This line of reasoning is a strictly humanist argument against abortion.

(James Sebastian)

30. In our society it is generally considered improper for a man to sleep, shower, and dress amid a group of women to whom he normally would be sexually attracted. It seems to me, then, to be equally unacceptable that a gay man sleep, shower, and dress in a company of men to whom, we assume, he would be no less sexually attracted.

(Mark O. Temple)

★31. I say "bravo" and "right on!" Now we have some real-life humane heroes to look up to! These brave people [a group of animal liberators] went up against the insensitive bureaucratic technology, and won, saving former pet animals from senseless torture.

    If researchers want to experiment, let them use computers, or themselves—but not former pet animals! I know it's bad enough they use monkeys and rats, but if those animals are bred knowing nothing else but these Frankensteins abusing them it's different (but not better) than dogs or cats that have been loved and petted all their lives to suddenly be tortured and mutilated in the name of science. End all animal research! Free all research animals!

    Right on, animal liberators!

(Linda Magee)

32. Dear Ann: Recently I was shopping downtown in 20-below-zero weather. A stranger walked up to me and said, "I wonder how many beautiful rabbits died so you could have that coat?" I noticed she was wearing a down coat, so I asked if the geese they got the down from to make her coat were still alive. She looked surprised. Obviously she had never given it a thought.

    If people are so upset about cruelty to animals, why don't they go after the folks who refuse to spend the money to have their pets neutered and spayed? Thousands of dogs are put to death every year because the animal pounds can't feed and house them. Talk about cruelty to animals—that's the best example there is.

("Baby It's Cold Outside")

33. I prayed for the U.S. Senate to defeat the prayer amendment—and it did. There is a God.

(Richard Carr)

★34. People of the Philippines, I have returned! The hour of your redemption is here! Rally to me! Let the indomitable spirit of Bataan and Corregidor lead on! As the lines of battle roll forward to bring you within the zone of operations, rise and strike! For future generations of your sons and daughters, strike! Let no heart be faint! Let every arm be steeled! The guidance of divine God points the way! Follow in his name to the Holy Grail of righteous victory!

(General Douglas MacArthur)

35. As the oldest of eleven children (all married), I'd like to point out our combined family numbers more than 100 who vote only for pro-life candidates. Pro-lifers have children, pro-choicers do not.

(Mrs. Kitty Reickenback)

36. I am twelve years old. My class had a discussion on whether police used unnecessary force when arresting the people from Operation Rescue.

My teacher is an ex-cop, and he demonstrated police holds to us. They don't hurt at all unless the person is struggling or trying to pull away. If anybody was hurt when they were arrested, then they must have been struggling with the officers trying to arrest them.

(Ben Torre-Bueno)

★37. As corporate farms continue to gobble up smaller family farms, they control a larger percentage of the grain and produce raised in the United States. Some have already reached a point in size where, if they should decide to withhold their grain and produce from the marketplace, spot shortages could occur and higher prices would result. The choice is to pay us family farmers now or pay the corporations later.

(Delwin Yost)

38. If you buy our airline ticket now you can save 60 percent, and that means 60 percent more vacation for you.

(Radio ad)

39. Why all the flap about atomic bombs? The potential for death is always with us. Of course, if you just want something to worry about, go ahead. Franklin D. Roosevelt said it: "The only thing we have to fear is fear itself."

(Lee Flemming Reese)

★40. September 17 marked the anniversary of the signing of the U.S. Constitution. How well have we, the people, protected our rights? Consider what has happened to our private-property rights.

"Property has divine rights, and the moment the idea is admitted into society that property is not as sacred as the laws of God, anarchy and tyranny begin." John Quincy Adams, 1767–1848, Sixth President of the United States.

Taxes and regulations are the two-edged sword which gravely threatens the fabric of our capitalistic republic. The tyranny of which Adams speaks is with us today in the form of government regulators and regulations which have all but destroyed the right to own property. Can anarchy be far behind?

(Timothy R. Binder)

41. Evolution would have been dealt serious setbacks if environmentalists had been around over the eons trying to save endangered species.

Species are endangered because they just do not fit the bigger picture any more as the world changes. That's not bad. It's just life.

In most cases we have seen the "endangered species" argument is just a ruse; much deeper motives usually exist, and they are almost always selfish and personal.

(Tom Gable)

42. The problem that I have with the pro-choice supporters' argument is that they make "choice" the ultimate issue. Let's face facts. No one has absolute freedom of choice sanctioned by the law. One can choose to rob a bank, but it's not lawful. Others can choose to kill their one-year-old child, but it is not legal. Why then should a woman have the legal right to take the life of her unborn child?

(Loretta S. Horn)

★43. If a car or truck kills a person, do politicians call for car control or truck control? And call in all cars/trucks?

If a child burns down a house do we have match control or child control and call in all of each?

Gun control and confiscation is equally as pathetic a thought process in an age of supposed intelligence.

(Pete Hawes)

44. I was incensed to read in your article about the return of anti-Semitism that New York City Moral Majority Leader Rev. Dan C. Fore actually said that "Jews have a God-given ability to make money, almost a supernatural ability . . ." I find it incredibly ironic that he and other Moral Majority types conveniently overlook the fact that they, too, pack away a pretty tidy sum themselves through their fund-raising efforts. It is sad that anti-Semitism exists, but to have this prejudice voiced by leaders of religious organizations is deplorable. These people are in for quite a surprise come Judgment Day.

(John R. Murks)

45. I couldn't help but compare the ducks in Fairbanks, Alaska, who refuse to fly south for the winter, to our welfare system. Instead of going south, four ducks have set up housekeeping there because people keep feeding them. The biologist dealing with the ducks said that while it's nice that people are concerned, in the long run it isn't good for the ducks because it conditions them to stay when they need to get to warmer temperatures. Our welfare system, in many instances, conditions people to stay on welfare. Compassion is a wonderful virtue, and we need to help people who need help, but is it compassionate to keep people on welfare who should be developing and using their God-given abilities to do for themselves what the government is doing for them?

(Donna Symes)

★46. Why are people so shocked that Susan Smith apparently chose to kill her children because they had become an inconvenience? Doesn't this occur every day in abortion clinics across the country? We suspect Smith heard very clearly the message many feminists have been trying to deliver about the expendable nature of our children.

(Kevin and Diana Cogan)

47. What's wrong with kids today? Answer: nothing, for the majority of them. They are great.

Witness the action of two San Diego teenage boys recently, when the Normal Heights fire was at its worst. They took a garden hose to the roof of a threatened house—a house belonging to four elderly sisters, people they didn't even know. They saved the house, while neighboring houses burned to the ground.

In the Baldwin Hills fire, two teenage girls rescued a blind, retired Navy man from sure death when they braved the flames to find him, confused, outside his burning house. He would probably have perished if they hadn't run a distance to rescue him.

(Theodore H. Wickham)

48. Now that Big Brother has decided that I must wear a seatbelt when I ride in a car, how long will it take before I have to wear an inner tube when I swim in my pool, a safety harness when I climb a ladder, and shoes with steel-reinforced toecaps when I carry out the garbage?

(G. R. Turgeon)

★49. Dear Ann: I was disappointed in your response to the girl whose mother used the strap on her. The gym teacher noticed the bruises on her legs and backside and called it "child abuse." Why are you against strapping a child when the Bible tells us in plain language that this is what parents should do?

The Book of Proverbs mentions many times that the rod must be used. Proverbs 23:13 says: "Withhold not correction from the child for if thou beatest him with the rod he shall not die." Proverbs 23:14 says: "Thou shalt beat him with the rod and shalt deliver his soul from death."

There is no substitute for a good whipping. I have seen the results of trying to reason with kids. They are arrogant, disrespectful and mouthy. Parents may wish for a more "humane" way, but there is none. Beating children is God's way of getting parents to gain control over their children.

(Davisville, W.Va.)

50. The Fourth Amendment guarantees our right to freedom from unreasonable search and seizure. It does not prohibit *reasonable* search and seizure. The matter of sobriety roadblocks to stop drunk drivers boils down to this: Are such roadblocks reasonable or unreasonable? The majority of people answer: "Reasonable." Therefore, sobriety roadblocks should not be considered to be unconstitutional.

(Haskell Collier)

51. The Supreme Court recently ruled that a police department in Florida did not violate any rights of privacy when a police helicopter flew over the backyard of a suspected drug dealer and noticed marijuana growing on his property. Many people, including groups like the Anti-Common Logic Union, felt that the suspect's right to privacy outweighed the police department's need to protect the public at large.

   The simple idea of sacrificing a right to serve a greater good should be allowed in certain cases. In this particular case the danger to the public wasn't extremely large; marijuana is probably less dangerous than regular beer. But anything could have been in that backyard—a load of cocaine, an illegal stockpile of weapons, or other major threats to society.

   (Matt Cookson)

★52. I am seventy-nine and have been smoking for sixty years. My husband is ninety and has inhaled my smoke for some fifty years with no bad effects.

   I see no reason to take further steps to isolate smokers in public places, other than we now observe.

   Smokers have taken punishment enough from neurotic sniffers, some of whom belong in bubbles. There are plenty of injudicious fumes on our streets and freeways.

   (Helen Gans)

53. The mainstream press finds itself left behind by talk radio, so they try to minimize its importance. Americans are finding the true spirit of democracy in community and national debate. Why should we be told what to believe by a news weekly or the nightly news when we can follow public debate as it unfolds on talk radio?

   (Adam Abbott)

54. The issue is not whether we should subsidize the arts, but whether anyone should be able to force someone else to subsidize the arts. You and I are free to *give* any amount of our money to any artistic endeavor we wish to support. When the government gets involved, however, a group of bureaucrats is given the power to *take* our money and give it to the arts they wish to support. We are not consulted. That is not a way to promote a responsible culture. That is tyranny.

   (Jerry Harben)

★55. Who are these Supreme Court justices who have the guts to OK the burning of our flag?

   If the wife or daughter of these so-called justices were raped, could the rapist be exonerated because he took the First Amendment? That he was just expressing himself? How about murder in the same situation?

   (Robert A. Lewis)

56. I have one question for those bleeding hearts who say we should not have used the atomic bomb: If the nation responsible for the Rape of Nanking, the Manchurian atrocities, Pearl Harbor, and the Bataan Death March had invented the bomb first, don't you think they would have used it? So do I.

   (Bill Blair)

57. Since when did military service become a right, for gays or anyone else? The military has always been allowed to discriminate against people who don't meet its requirements, including those who are overweight or too tall or too short. There is an adequate supply of personnel with the characteristics they need. And there is no national need for gays in the military.

(William R. Cnossen)

★58. There is something very wrong about the custom of tipping. When we go to a store, we don't decide what a product is worth and pay what we please; we pay the price or we leave. Prices in coffee bars and restaurants should be raised, waiters should be paid a decent wage, and the words "no tipping" should be clearly visible on menus and at counters.

(George Jochnowitz)

59. Most Americans do not favor gun control. They know that their well-being depends on their own ability to protect themselves. So-called "assault rifles" are used in few crimes. They are not the weapon of choice of criminals, but they are for people trying to protect themselves from government troops.

(Larry Herron)

60. Holding a gun, a thief robs John Q. Public of thousands of dollars. Holding a baby, an unmarried mother robs taxpayers of thousands of dollars. If one behavior is considered a crime, then so should the other.

(Louis R. Ward)

II. Turn to the editorial pages of a newspaper or the letters column of a magazine and find an instance of a fallacious argument in the editorials or letters to the editor. Identify the premises and conclusion of the argument and write an analysis at least one paragraph in length identifying the fallacy or fallacies committed and the factors that may have led the arguer to commit them.

III. Select a topic that you are familiar with, and write a brief argument about that topic that contains at least three fallacies.

MindTap Master concepts and improve outcomes with Aplia, at the end of the chapter, in the Aplia folder.

Summary

Fallacy: A defect in an argument that arises from a mistake in reasoning or the creation of an illusion that makes a bad argument appear good. There are two kinds of fallacy:

- Formal fallacy: Detectable by analyzing the form of an argument
- Informal fallacy: Detectable only by analyzing the content of an argument

MindTap Need help? See the Learning Logic folder at the end of the chapter: the self-paced tutorial walks you through any section.
Prepare for exams with the Chapter Test.

Fallacies of Relevance: The premises are not relevant to the conclusion:

- Appeal to force: Arguer threatens the reader/listener.
- Appeal to pity: Arguer elicits pity from the reader/listener.
- Appeal to the people: Arguer incites a mob mentality (direct form) or appeals to our desire for security, love, or respect (indirect form). This fallacy includes appeal to fear, the bandwagon argument, appeal to vanity, appeal to snobbery, and appeal to tradition.
- Argument against the person: Arguer personally attacks an opposing arguer by verbally abusing the opponent (*ad hominem* abusive), presenting the opponent as predisposed to argue as he or she does (*ad hominen* circumstantial), or by presenting the opponent as a hypocrite (*tu quoque*).

  Note: For this fallacy to occur, there must be two arguers.

- Accident: A general rule is applied to a specific case it was not intended to cover.
- Straw man: Arguer distorts an opponent's argument and then attacks the distorted argument.

  Note: For this fallacy to occur, there must be two arguers.

- Missing the point: Arguer draws a conclusion different from the one supported by the premises.

  Note: Do not cite this fallacy if another fallacy fits.

- Red herring: Arguer leads the reader/listener off the track.

Fallacies of Weak Induction: The premises may be relevant to the conclusion, but they supply insufficient support for the conclusion:

- Appeal to unqualified authority: Arguer cites an untrustworthy authority.
- Appeal to ignorance: Premises report that nothing is known or proved about some subject, and then a conclusion is drawn about that subject.
- Hasty generalization: A general conclusion is drawn from an atypical sample.
- False cause: Conclusion depends on a nonexistent or minor causal connection. This fallacy has four forms: *post hoc ergo propter hoc, non causa pro causa,* oversimplified cause, and the gambler's fallacy.
- Slippery slope: Conclusion depends on an unlikely chain reaction of causes.
- Weak analogy: Conclusion depends on a defective analogy (similarity).

Fallacies of Presumption: The premises presume what they purport to prove:

- Begging the question: Arguer creates the illusion that inadequate premises are adequate by leaving out a key premise, restating the conclusion as a premise, or reasoning in a circle.
- Complex question: Multiple questions are concealed in a single question.
- False dichotomy: An "either . . . or . . ." premise presents two unlikely alternatives as if they were the only ones available.
- Suppressed evidence: Arguer ignores important evidence that requires a different conclusion.

Fallacies of Ambiguity: An ambiguous word, phrase, or statement leads to an incorrect conclusion:

- Equivocation: Conclusion depends on a shift in meaning of a word or phrase.
- Amphiboly: Conclusion depends on an incorrect interpretation of an ambiguous statement made by someone other than the arguer.

Fallacies of Illicit Transference: An attribute is incorrectly transferred from the parts of something onto the whole or from the whole onto the parts:

- Composition: An attribute is incorrectly transferred from the parts to the whole.
- Division: An attribute is incorrectly transferred from the whole to the parts.

Fallacies that occur in real-life argumentation may be hard to detect:

- They may not exactly fit the pattern of the named fallacies.
- They may involve two or more fallacies woven together in a single passage.

Three factors underlie the commission of fallacies in real-life argumentation:

- The intent of the arguer (the arguer may intend to mislead someone).
- Mental carelessness combined with unchecked emotions.
- Unexamined presuppositions in the arguer's worldview.

3

4 Categorical Propositions

4.1 The Components of Categorical Propositions

4.2 Quality, Quantity, and Distribution

4.3 Venn Diagrams and the Modern Square of Opposition

4.4 Conversion, Obversion, and Contraposition

4.5 The Traditional Square of Opposition

4.6 Venn Diagrams and the Traditional Standpoint

4.7 Translating Ordinary Language Statements into Categorical Form

4.1 The Components of Categorical Propositions

HOW LOGICAL ARE YOU? Consider these two statements: (1) No pianists are engineers; (2) All pianists are engineers. In reference to the group of pianists (all the pianists in the world) and the group of engineers (all the engineers in the world), what do these statements say about the group of pianists and the group of engineers?

Find the answer on MindTap.

In Chapter 1 we saw that a proposition (or statement—here we are ignoring the distinction) is a sentence that is either true or false. A proposition that relates two classes, or categories, is called a **categorical proposition**. The classes in question are denoted respectively by the **subject term** and the **predicate term**, and the proposition asserts that either all or part of the class denoted by the subject term is included in or excluded from the class denoted by the predicate term. Here are some examples of categorical propositions:

> Reality TV stars hope for recognition.
> Junk foods do not belong in school cafeterias.
> Many of today's unemployed have given up on finding work.
> Not all romances have a happy ending.
> Oprah Winfrey publishes magazines.

MindTap® Read, study, reflect, and prepare for exams online, anytime, anywhere.

The first statement asserts that the entire class of reality TV stars is included in the class of people who hope for recognition, the second that the entire class of junk foods is excluded from the class of things that belong in school cafeterias, and the third that part of the class of today's unemployed people is included in the class of people who have given up on finding work. The fourth statement asserts that part of the class of romances is excluded from the class of things that have a happy ending, and the last statement asserts that the class that has Oprah Winfrey as its single member is included in the class of people who publish magazines.

Since any categorical proposition asserts that either all or part of the class denoted by the subject term is included in or excluded from the class denoted by the predicate term, it follows that there are exactly four types of categorical propositions: (1) those that assert that the whole subject class is included in the predicate class, (2) those that assert that part of the subject class is included in the predicate class, (3) those that assert that the whole subject class is excluded from the predicate class, and (4) those that assert that part of the subject class is excluded from the predicate class. A categorical proposition that expresses these relations with complete clarity is called a **standard-form categorical proposition**. A categorical proposition is in standard form if and only if it is a substitution instance of one of the following four forms:

All S are P.
No S are P.
Some S are P.
Some S are not P.

Many categorical propositions, of course, are not in standard form because, among other things, they do not begin with the words "all," "no," or "some." In the final section of this chapter we will develop techniques for translating categorical propositions into standard form, but for now we may restrict our attention to those that are already in standard form.

The words "all," "no," and "some" are called **quantifiers** because they specify how much of the subject class is included in or excluded from the predicate class. The first form asserts that the whole subject class is included in the predicate class, the second that the whole subject class is excluded from the predicate class, and so on. (Incidentally, in formal deductive logic the word "some" always means at least one.) The letters S and P stand respectively for the subject and predicate terms, and the words "are" and "are not" are called the **copula** because they link (or "couple") the subject term with the predicate term.

Consider the following example:

All members of the American Medical Association are people holding degrees from recognized academic institutions.

This standard-form categorical proposition is analyzed as follows:

quantifier:	all
subject term:	members of the American Medical Association
copula:	are
predicate term:	people holding degrees from recognized academic institutions

In resolving standard-form categorical propositions into their four components, one must keep these components separate. They do not overlap. In this regard, note that

Alice Ambrose 1906–2001

Alice Ambrose was born in 1906 in Lexington, Illinois. She was orphaned at age 13, but still managed to attend Millikin University in Decatur and graduate with a major in mathematics and philosophy. After earning a PhD in philosophy from the University of Wisconsin, where she worked on Whitehead and Russell's *Principia Mathematica*, she entered a postdoctoral program at Cambridge University. There she studied under, and became a close disciple of, the famous philosopher Ludwig Wittgenstein. (She received a second PhD from that university in 1938.) In 1937 she accepted a teaching position in philosophy at Smith College, where she remained until her retirement in 1972.

Within a year after arriving at Smith, Ambrose met and married the philosopher Morris Lazerowitz, with whom she coauthored several books and articles. One was a textbook in symbolic logic, commonly called "Ambrose and Lazerowitz" that was used by a generation of young philosophers. Other subjects on which Ambrose did important work include the foundations of mathematics, finitism in

Courtesy Pat Safford

mathematics, logical impossibility, the justification of induction, and Wittgenstein's theory of proof. Ambrose was a particularly lucid writer, and this, combined with her keen insight, won widespread recognition by philosophers and logicians.

From 1975 to 1976 Ambrose served as president of the American Philosophical Association (Eastern Division). Interestingly, in that office she was immediately preceded by John Rawls, and immediately succeeded by Hillary Putnam. Ambrose was also a dedicated supporter of peace and social justice, and she remained active as a speaker and writer until her death in 2001 at the age of 94. Today Smith College sponsors an annual address in her honor.

"subject term" and "predicate term" do not mean the same thing in logic that "subject" and "predicate" mean in grammar. The *subject* of the example statement includes the quantifier "all," but the *subject term* does not. Similarly, the *predicate* includes the copula "are," but the *predicate term* does not.

Two additional points should be noted about standard-form categorical propositions. The first is that the form "All S are not P" is *not* a standard form. This form is ambiguous and can be rendered as either "No S are P" or "Some S are not P," depending on the content. The second point is that there are exactly three forms of quantifiers and two forms of copulas. Other texts allow the various forms of the verb "to be" (such as "is," "is not," "will," and "will not") to serve as the copula. For the sake of uniformity, our discussion will always restrict the copula to "are" and "are not." The last section of this chapter describes techniques for translating these alternate forms into the two accepted ones.

Originated by Aristotle, the theory of categorical propositions has constituted one of the core topics in logic for over 2,000 years. It remains important even today because many of the statements we make in ordinary discourse are either categorical propositions as they stand or are readily translatable into them. Standard-form categorical propositions represent an ideal of clarity in language, and a familiarity with the relationships that prevail among them provides a backdrop of precision for all kinds of linguistic usage. In Chapter 5 we will see how categorical propositions may be combined to produce *categorical syllogisms*, a kind of argumentation that is closely related to the most basic forms of human reasoning.

EXERCISE 4.1

I. In the following categorical propositions identify the quantifier, subject term, copula, and predicate term.

★1. Some executive-pay packages are insults to ordinary workers.

2. No stressful jobs are occupations conducive to a healthy lifestyle.

3. All oil-based paints are products that contribute to photochemical smog.

★4. Some preachers who are intolerant of others' beliefs are not television evangelists.

5. All trials in which a coerced confession is read to the jury are trials in which a guilty verdict can be reversed.

6. Some artificial hearts are mechanisms that are prone to failure.

★7. No sex-education courses that are taught competently are programs that are currently eroding public morals.

8. Some universities that emphasize research are not institutions that neglect undergraduate education.

9. All occasions of civil disobedience are protests that should be tolerated.

★10. No fast-food restaurants are establishments that promote public health.

11. Some cases of road rage are episodes that end in tragedy.

12. Some asylum seekers are not travelers who will reach their destinations.

★13. All animal-rights activists are individuals motivated by empathy.

14. No foods that are loaded with antibiotics are meals suitable for humans.

15. Some school uniforms are useful tools for social conditioning.

★16. Some presidential candidates are not threats to the establishment.

II. Create two new examples of each of the four kinds of standard-form categorical propositions. Make sure each has a quantifier, subject term, copula, and predicate term.

MindTap® Complete exercises online for immediate feedback.
Master concepts and improve outcomes with Aplia, at the end of the chapter, in the Aplia folder.

4

Suppose there is a remote tribe of jungle dwellers in which immunity to malaria is distributed uniformly among all the members who have this characteristic: both of their parents are also members of the tribe. Based on this information alone, can you conclude that every member of the tribe is immune to malaria? If not, what additional information must you have to draw such a conclusion?

Find the answer on MindTap.

Quality and quantity are attributes of categorical propositions. In order to see how these attributes pertain, it is useful to rephrase the meaning of categorical propositions in class terminology:

Proposition	Meaning in class notation
All S are P.	Every member of the S class is a member of the P class; that is, the S class is included in the P class.
No S are P.	No member of the S class is a member of the P class; that is, the S class is excluded from the P class.
Some S are P.	At least one member of the S class is a member of of the P class.
Some S are not P.	At least one member of the S class is not a member of of the P class.

The **quality** of a categorical proposition is either affirmative or negative depending on whether it affirms or denies class membership. Accordingly, "All *S* are *P*" and "Some *S* are *P*" have **affirmative** quality, and "No *S* are *P*" and "Some *S* are not *P*" have **negative** quality. These are called **affirmative propositions** and **negative propositions**, respectively.

The **quantity** of a categorical proposition is either universal or particular, depending on whether the statement makes a claim about *every* member or just *some* member of the class denoted by the subject term. "All *S* are *P*" and "No *S* are *P*" each assert something about every member of the *S* class and thus are **universal propositions**. "Some *S* are *P*" and "Some *S* are not *P*" assert something about one or more members of the *S* class and hence are **particular propositions**.

Note that the quantity of a categorical proposition may be determined through mere inspection of the quantifier. "All" and "no" immediately imply universal quantity, while "some" implies particular. But categorical propositions have no "qualifier." In universal propositions the quality is determined by the quantifier, and in particular propositions it is determined by the copula.

Particular propositions mean no more and no less than the meaning assigned to them in class notation. The statement "Some *S* are *P*" does *not* imply that some *S* are not P, and the statement "Some S are not P" does *not* imply that some S are P. It often *happens*, of course, that substitution instances of these statement forms are both true. For example, "Some apples are red" is true, as is "Some apples are not red." But the fact that one is true does not *necessitate* that the other be true. "Some zebras are animals" is true (because at least one zebra is an animal), but "Some zebras are not animals" is false. Similarly, "Some turkeys are not fish" is true, but "Some turkeys are fish" is false. Thus, the fact that one of these statement forms is true does not *logically imply* that the other is true, as these substitution instances clearly prove.

Since the early Middle Ages the four kinds of categorical propositions have commonly been designated by letter names corresponding to the first four vowels of the Roman alphabet: **A, E, I, O.** The universal affirmative is called an **A proposition**, the universal negative an **E proposition**, the particular affirmative an **I proposition**, and the particular negative an **O proposition**. Tradition has it that these letters were derived from the first two vowels in the Latin words *affirmo* ("I affirm") and *nego* ("I deny"), thus:

		n
Universal	**A**	**E**
	f	
	f	g
Particular	**I**	**O**
	r	
	m	
	o	

The material presented thus far in this section may be summarized as follows:

Proposition	Letter name	Quantity	Quality
All S are P.	**A**	universal	affirmative
No S are P.	**E**	universal	negative
Some S are P.	**I**	particular	affirmative
Some S are not P.	**O**	particular	negative

Unlike quality and quantity, which are attributes of *propositions,* **distribution** is an attribute of the *terms* (subject and predicate) of propositions. A term is said to be distributed if the proposition makes an assertion about every member of the class denoted by the term; otherwise, it is undistributed. Stated another way, a term is distributed if and only if the statement assigns (or distributes) an attribute to every member of the class denoted by the term. Thus, if a statement asserts something about every member of the S class, then S is distributed; if it asserts something about every member of the P class, then P is distributed; otherwise S and P are undistributed.

Let us imagine that the members of the classes denoted by the subject and predicate terms of a categorical proposition are contained respectively in circles marked with the letters "S" and "P." The meaning of the statement form "All S are P" may then be represented by the following diagram:

The S circle is contained in the P circle, which represents the fact that every member of S is a member of P. (Of course, should S and P represent terms denoting identical classes, the two circles would overlap exactly.) As the diagram shows, "All S are P" makes a claim about every member of the S class, since the statement says that every member of S is in the P class. But the statement does not make a claim about every member of the P class, since there may be some members of P that are outside of S. Thus, by the definition of "distributed term" given above, S is distributed and P is not. In other words, for any universal affirmative (**A**) proposition, the subject term, whatever it may be, is distributed, and the predicate term is undistributed.

Let us now consider the universal negative (**E**) proposition. "No S are P" states that the S and P classes are separate, which may be represented as follows:

This statement makes a claim about every member of S and every member of P. It asserts that every member of S is separate from every member of P, and also that every member of P is separate from every member of S. Accordingly, by our definition, both the subject and predicate terms of universal negative (**E**) propositions are distributed.

The particular affirmative (**I**) proposition states that at least one member of S is a member of P. If we represent this one member of S that we are certain about by an asterisk, the resulting diagram looks like this:

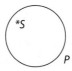

Since the asterisk is inside the P class, it represents something that is simultaneously an S and a P; in other words, it represents a member of the S class that is also a member of the P class. Thus, the statement "Some S are P" makes a claim about one member (at least) of S and also one member (at least) of P, but not about all members of either class. Hence, by the definition of distribution, neither S nor P is distributed.

The particular negative (**O**) proposition asserts that at least one member of *S* is not a member of *P*. If we once again represent this one member of *S* by an asterisk, the resulting diagram is as follows:

Since the other members of *S* may or may not be outside of *P*, it is clear that the statement "Some *S* are not *P*" does not make a claim about every member of *S*, so *S* is not distributed. But, as may be seen from the diagram, the statement does assert that every member of *P* is separate and distinct from this one member of *S* that is outside the *P* circle. Thus, in the particular negative (**O**) proposition, *P* is distributed and *S* is undistributed.

At this point the notion of distribution may be somewhat vague and elusive. Unfortunately, there is no simple and easy way to make the idea graphically clear. The best that can be done is to repeat some of the things that have already been said. First of all, distribution is an attribute or quality that the subject and predicate terms of a categorical proposition may or may not possess, depending on the kind of proposition. If the proposition in question is an **A** type, then the subject term, whatever it may be, is distributed. If it is an **E** type, then both terms are distributed; if an **I** type, then neither; and if an **O** type, then the predicate term. If a certain term is *distributed* in a proposition, this simply means that the proposition says something about every member of the class that the term denotes. If a term is *undistributed,* the proposition does not say something about every member of the class.

An easy way to remember the rule for distribution is to keep in mind that universal (**A** and **E**) statements distribute their subject terms and negative (**E** and **O**) statements distribute their predicate terms. As an aid to remembering this arrangement, the following mnemonic may be useful: "Unprepared Students Never Pass." Attending to the first letter in these words may help one recall that Universals distribute Subjects, and Negatives distribute Predicates. Another mnemonic that accomplishes the same purpose is "Any Student Earning B's Is Not On Probation." In this mnemonic the first letters may help one recall that **A** statements distribute the Subject, **E** statements distribute Both terms, **I** statements distribute Neither term, and **O** statements distribute the Predicate.

Two mnemonic devices for distribution

"<u>U</u>nprepared <u>S</u>tudents <u>N</u>ever <u>P</u>ass"

<u>U</u>niversals distribute <u>S</u>ubjects.

<u>N</u>egatives distribute <u>P</u>redicates.

"<u>A</u>ny <u>S</u>tudent <u>E</u>arning <u>B</u>'s <u>I</u>s <u>N</u>ot <u>O</u>n <u>P</u>robation"

A distributes **S**ubject.

E distributes **B**oth.

I distributes **N**either.

O distributes **P**redicate.

Finally, note that the attribute of distribution, while not particularly important to subsequent developments in this chapter, is essential to the evaluation of syllogisms in the next chapter.

The material of this section may now be summarized as follows:

Proposition	Letter name	Quantity	Quality	Terms distributed
All S are P.	A	universal	affirmative	S
No S are P.	E	universal	negative	S and P
Some S are P.	I	particular	affirmative	none
Some S are not P.	O	particular	negative	P

EXERCISE 4.2

I. For each of the following categorical propositions identify the letter name, quantity, and quality. Then state whether the subject and predicate terms are distributed or undistributed.

★1. No vampire movies are films without blood.

2. All governments that bargain with terrorists are governments that encourage terrorism.

3. Some symphony orchestras are organizations on the brink of bankruptcy.

★4. Some Chinese leaders are not thoroughgoing opponents of capitalist economics.

5. All human contacts with benzene are potential causes of cancer.

6. No labor strikes are events welcomed by management.

★7. Some hospitals are organizations that overcharge the Medicare program.

8. Some affirmative action plans are not programs that result in reverse discrimination.

II. Change the quality but not the quantity of the following categorical propositions:

★1. All drunk drivers are threats to others on the highway.

2. No wildlife refuges are locations suitable for condominium developments.

3. Some slumlords are people who eventually wind up in jail.

★4. Some CIA operatives are not champions of human rights.

5. All identity thieves are criminals who deserve jail time.

6. No college athletes are students who can be paid by equipment manufacturers.

MindTap® Complete exercises online for immediate feedback.

★7. Some stay-at-home moms are workers who deserve Social Security.

8. Some news media are not disseminators of accurate information.

III. Change the quantity but not the quality of the following categorical propositions:

★1. All owners of pit bull terriers are people who can expect expensive lawsuits.

2. No tax proposals that favor the rich are fair proposals.

3. Some grade-school administrators are people who choke the educational process.

★4. Some residents of Manhattan are not people who can afford to live there.

5. All hate crimes are offenses deserving enhanced sentencing.

6. No suicide bombers are individuals with moral sensibilities.

★7. Some prescription medicines are substances hazardous to human health.

8. Some shelter animals are not good prospects for adoption.

IV. Change both the quality and the quantity of the following categorical propositions:

★1. All oil spills are events catastrophic to the environment.

2. No alcoholics are people with a healthy diet.

3. Some Mexican vacations are episodes that end with gastrointestinal distress.

★4. Some corporate lawyers are not people with a social conscience.

5. All coal-fired electric plants are major sources of pollution.

6. No fashion shows are celebrations of normal clothing.

★7. Some economic forums are venues for airing financial fears.

8. Some paparazzi are not welcome guests at celebrity functions.

V. Create four categorical propositions, having different letter names, about your favorite food, and identify their quality, quantity, and distributed terms.

MindTap® Master concepts and improve outcomes with Aplia, at the end of the chapter, in the Aplia folder.

4.3 Venn Diagrams and the Modern Square of Opposition

HOW LOGICAL ARE YOU? Suppose your child (or niece or nephew) comes excitedly to you and asks, "Do you know that all vampires have fangs that allow them to suck your blood?" You reply that you do know this is true of vampires. How would you explain your reasoning?

Find the answer on MindTap.

Existential Import

The primary goal of our inquiry into categorical propositions is to disclose the role that such propositions play in the formation of arguments. However, it turns out that we can interpret universal (**A** and **E**) propositions in two different ways, and according to one of these interpretations an argument might be valid, while according to the other it might be invalid. Thus, before turning to the evaluation of arguments, we must explore the two possible interpretations of universal propositions. Our investigation will focus on what is called **existential import**. To illustrate this concept, consider the following pair of propositions:

> All Tom Cruise's movies are hits.
>
> All unicorns are one-horned animals.

In ordinary conversation the first proposition implies that Tom Cruise has indeed made some movies. In other words, the statement has existential import. It implies that one or more things denoted by the subject term actually exist. On the other hand, no such implication is made by the statement about unicorns. The statement might be said to be true, because unicorns, by definition, have a single horn. But the statement does not imply that unicorns actually exist.

Thus, the question arises: Should universal propositions be interpreted as implying that the things talked about actually exist? Or should they be interpreted as implying no such thing? In response to this question, logicians have taken two different approaches. Aristotle held that universal propositions about existing things have existential import. In other words, such statements imply the existence of the things talked about:

Aristotelian standpoint

All pheasants are birds.	Implies the existence of pheasants.
No pine trees are maples.	Implies the existence of pine trees.
All satyrs are vile creatures.	Does not imply the existence of satyrs.

The first two statements have existential import because their subject terms denote actually existing things. The third statement has no existential import, because satyrs do not exist.

On the other hand, according to the theory developed by the nineteenth-century logician George Boole (as perfected by John Venn), no universal propositions have existential import. Such statements never imply the existence of the things talked about:

Boolean standpoint

All trucks are vehicles.	Does not imply the existence of trucks.
No roses are daisies.	Does not imply the existence of roses.
All werewolves are monsters.	Does not imply the existence of werewolves.

We might summarize these results by saying that the Aristotelian standpoint is "open" (or receptive) to existence.* When things exist, the Aristotelian standpoint recognizes

---

*In general, we interpret this openness to existence as extending to the subject class, the predicate class, and the complements of these classes. However, in the present account we confine our attention to the subject class. The concept of class complement is discussed in Section 4.4 (Obversion).

their existence, and universal statements about those things have existential import. In other words, existence counts for something. On the other hand, the Boolean standpoint is "closed" (unreceptive) to existence. When things exist, the Boolean standpoint does not recognize their existence, and universal statements about those things have no existential import. Conversely, when things do not exist, neither the Aristotelian nor the Boolean standpoint recognizes any existence. Under these circumstances, the Aristotelian standpoint merges with the Boolean.*

The Aristotelian standpoint differs from the Boolean standpoint only with regard to universal (**A** and **E**) propositions. The two standpoints are identical with regard to particular (**I** and **O**) propositions. Both the Aristotelian and the Boolean standpoints recognize that particular propositions make a positive assertion about existence. For example, from both standpoints, the statement "Some cats are animals" asserts that at least one cat exists that is an animal. Also, from both standpoints, "Some fish are not mammals" asserts that at least one fish exists that is not a mammal. Thus, from both standpoints, the word "some" implies existence.†

Adopting either the Aristotelian or the Boolean standpoint amounts to accepting a set of ground rules for interpreting the meaning of universal propositions. Either standpoint can be adopted for any categorical proposition or any argument composed of categorical propositions. Taking the Aristotelian standpoint amounts to recognizing that universal statements about existing things convey evidence about existence. Conversely, for a statement to convey such evidence, the Aristotelian standpoint must be taken and the subject of the statement must denote actually existing things. Taking the Boolean standpoint, on the other hand, amounts to ignoring any evidence about existence that universal statements might convey.

Because the Boolean standpoint is closed to existence, it is simpler than the Aristotelian standpoint, which recognizes existential implications. For this reason, we will direct our attention first to arguments considered from the Boolean standpoint. Later, in Section 4.5, we will extend our treatment to the Aristotelian standpoint.

Venn Diagrams

From the Boolean standpoint, the four kinds of categorical propositions have the following meaning. Notice that the first two (universal) propositions imply nothing about the existence of the things denoted by S:

All S are P. = No members of S are outside P.
No S are P. = No members of S are inside P.
Some S are P. = At least one S exists that is a P.
Some S are not P. = At least one S exists that is not a P.

---

*For a more complete account of the relation between the Aristotelian and the Boolean standpoints, see "Existential Import: Historical Background," by Patrick J. Hurley. This article is available on MindTap.

†In ordinary language, the word "some" occasionally implies something less than actual existence. For example, the statement "Some unicorns are tenderhearted" does not seem to suggest that unicorns actually exist, but merely that among the group of imaginary things called "unicorns," there is a subclass of tenderhearted ones. In the vast majority of cases, however, "some" in ordinary language implies existence. The logical "some" conforms to these latter uses.

George Boole 1815–1864

The English mathematician and philosopher George Boole is known primarily for the development of Boolean algebra—a type of logic based on the three fundamental operations of *and, or,* and *not.* The American philosopher and logician Charles Sanders Peirce was captivated by Boole's ideas, and he saw a possible application in the area of electrical circuitry. Fifty years later, the American mathematician and engineer Claude Shannon put theory to practice by showing how Boole's system could be used in designing telephone routing switches. This innovation subsequently led to the development of electronic digital computers.

Boole's early years were marked by struggle. His father, John, was a cobbler, and his mother, Mary Ann, a lady's maid. They could afford only the most basic education for their son, which John supplemented by teaching mathematics and science to young George and by hiring a Latin tutor for him. Boole taught himself Greek, French, and German. His father, a leading member of the Mechanics Institute, was intrigued by the application of mathematics in making instruments, and he passed this interest to his son. Though poverty limited the resources available to him, Boole used mathematics journals borrowed from the institute to further his mathematics education on his own.

When George was only sixteen, his father's shoe-making business folded, and it fell to him to support the family by working as an assistant teacher. When he was twenty-two, he took over the operation of a boarding school after its former director had died, and his whole family assisted him in running it. Throughout this period, Boole continued his study of mathematics, and at age twenty-nine he published a paper on the use of algebraic methods in solving differential equations. In recognition of this work he received the Royal Society Medal, which brought him considerable fame in the mathematical world.

Three years later Boole published *The Mathematical Analysis of Logic,* which brought to fruition some of Leibniz's earlier speculations on the relationship between mathematics and logic. It also showed how the symbolism of mathematics could be imported into logic. This work won him a professorship at Queens College, in Cork, Ireland, where he remained for the rest of his life. Seven years later he published a much larger and more mature work on the same subject, *An Investigation of the Laws of Thought, on Which Are Founded the Mathematical Theories of Logic and Probabilities.* This later work presented a complete system of symbolic reasoning.

Boole married Mary Everest (the niece of Sir George Everest, after whom Mt. Everest is named). He met her when she came to visit her famous uncle in Cork, and the relationship developed through his giving her lessons on differential equations. The couple had five daughters, but when Boole was only forty-nine his life was cut short from what was probably pneumonia. Boole had walked two miles in the pouring rain to lecture at Queens, and he delivered the lecture in wet clothing. After he developed a high fever and became desperately ill, his wife, thinking that a good cure always mirrors the cause, poured cold water on him as he lay in bed. He died shortly thereafter.

Adopting this interpretation of categorical propositions, the nineteenth-century logician John Venn developed a system of diagrams to represent the information they express. These diagrams have come to be known as **Venn diagrams**.

A Venn diagram is an arrangement of overlapping circles in which each circle represents the class denoted by a term in a categorical proposition. Because every categorical proposition has exactly two terms, the Venn diagram for a single categorical proposition consists of two overlapping circles. Each circle is labeled so that it represents one of the terms in the proposition. Unless otherwise required, we adopt the convention that the left-hand circle represents the subject term, and the right-hand circle the predicate term. Such a diagram looks like this:

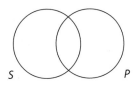

The members of the class denoted by each term should be thought of as situated inside the corresponding circle. Thus, the members of the S class (if any such members exist) are situated inside the S circle, and the members of the P class (if any such members exist) are situated inside the P circle. If any members are situated inside the area where the two circles overlap, then such members belong to both the S class and the P class. Finally, if any members are situated outside both circles, they are members of neither S nor P.

Suppose, for example, that the S class is the class of Americans and the P class is the class of farmers. Then, if we use numerals to identify the four possible areas, the diagram looks like this:

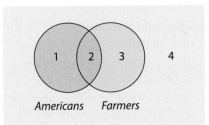

Anything in the area marked "1" is an American but not a farmer, anything in the area marked "2" is both an American and a farmer, and anything in the area marked "3" is a farmer but not an American. The area marked "4" is the area outside both circles; thus, anything in this area is neither a farmer nor an American.

We can now use Venn diagrams to represent the information expressed by the four kinds of categorical proposition. To do this we make a certain kind of mark in a diagram. Two kinds of marks are used: shading an area and placing an X in an area. Shading an area means that the shaded area is empty,* and placing an X in an area means

---

*In many mathematics texts, shading an area of a Venn diagram indicates that the area is not empty. The significance of shading in logic is exactly the opposite.

that at least one thing exists in that area. The X may be thought of as representing that one thing. If no mark appears in an area, this means that nothing is known about that area; it may contain members or it may be empty. Shading is always used to represent the content of universal (**A** and **E**) propositions, and placing an X in an area is always used to represent the content of particular (**I** and **O**) propositions. The content of the four kinds of categorical propositions is represented as follows:

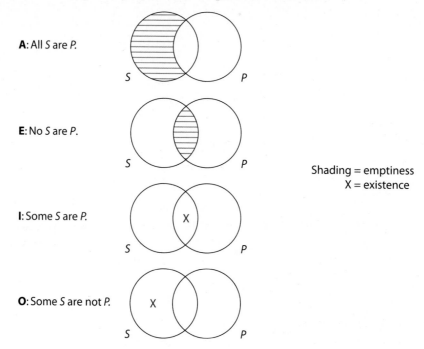

A: All S are P.

E: No S are P.

Shading = emptiness
X = existence

I: Some S are P.

O: Some S are not P.

Recall that the **A** proposition asserts that no members of S are outside P. This is represented by shading the part of the S circle that lies outside the P circle. The **E** proposition asserts that no members of S are inside P. This is represented by shading the part of the S circle that lies inside the P circle. The **I** proposition asserts that at least one S exists and that S is also a P. This is represented by placing an X in the area where the S and P circles overlap. This X represents an existing thing that is both an S and a P. Finally, the **O** proposition asserts that at least one S exists, and that S is not a P. This is represented by placing an X in the part of the S circle that lies outside the P circle. This X represents an existing thing that is an S but not a P.

Because there is no X in the diagrams that represent the universal propositions, these diagrams say nothing about existence. For example, the diagram for the **A** proposition merely asserts that nothing exists in the part of the S circle that lies outside the P circle. The area where the two circles overlap and the part of the P circle that lies outside the S circle contain no marks at all. This means that something might exist in these areas, or they might be completely empty. Similarly, in the diagram for the **E** proposition, no marks appear in the left-hand part of the S circle and the right-hand part of the P circle. This means that these two areas might contain something or, on the other hand, they might not.

The Modern Square of Opposition

Let us compare the diagram for the **A** proposition with the diagram for the **O** proposition. The diagram for the **A** proposition asserts that the left-hand part of the *S* circle is empty, whereas the diagram for the **O** proposition asserts that this same area is not empty. These two diagrams make assertions that are the exact opposite of each other. As a result, their corresponding statements are said to contradict each other. Analogously, the diagram for the **E** proposition asserts that the area where the two circles overlap is empty, whereas the diagram for the **I** proposition asserts that the area where the two circles overlap is not empty. Accordingly, their corresponding propositions are also said to contradict each other. This relationship of mutually contradictory pairs of propositions is represented in a diagram called the **modern square of opposition**. This diagram, which arises from the modern (or Boolean) interpretation of categorical propositions, is represented as follows:

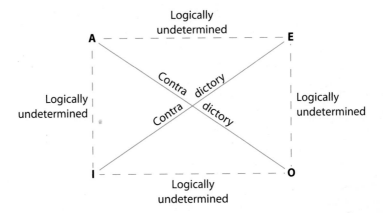

If two propositions are related by the **contradictory relation**, they necessarily have opposite truth value. Thus, if a certain **A** proposition is given as true, the corresponding **O** proposition must be false. Similarly, if a certain **I** proposition is given as false, the corresponding **E** proposition must be true. But no other inferences are possible. In particular, given the truth value of an **A** or **O** proposition, nothing can be determined about the truth value of the corresponding **E** or **I** propositions. These propositions are said to have **logically undetermined truth value**. Like all propositions, they do have a truth value, but logic alone cannot determine what it is. Similarly, given the truth value of an **E** or **I** proposition, nothing can be determined about the truth value of the corresponding **A** or **O** propositions. They, too, are said to have logically undetermined truth value.

Finally, suppose we should be given a set of four propositions about nonexisting things, such as flying zebras. The **A** proposition, which asserts that there are no flying zebras outside the predicate class will be true because there are no flying zebras at all, and the **E** proposition, which asserts that there are no flying zebras inside the predicate class will be true for the same reason. These propositions are said to be **vacuously true**, because their truth value results solely from the fact that the subject class is empty, or void of members. Furthermore, the truth value of these propositions does not violate the "logically undetermined" relation between the **A** and the **E** because it results not from any relation between these propositions but from the fact the subject class is empty. The same can be said about the false truth values of the **I** and the **O**. As the contradictories of the **A** and **E** propositions, these propositions can be said to be **vacuously false**.

Testing Immediate Inferences

Since the modern square of opposition provides logically necessary results, we can use it to test certain arguments for validity. We begin by assuming the premise is true, and we enter the pertinent truth value in the square. We then use the square to compute the truth value of the conclusion. If the square indicates that the conclusion is true, the argument is valid; if not, the argument is invalid. Here is an example:

> Some trade spies are not masters at bribery.
> Therefore, it is false that all trade spies are masters at bribery.

Arguments of this sort are called **immediate inferences** because they have only one premise. Instead of reasoning from one premise to the next, and then to the conclusion, we proceed immediately from the single premise to the conclusion. To test this argument for validity, we begin by assuming that the premise, which is an **O** proposition, is true, and we enter this truth value in the square of opposition. We then use the square to compute the truth value of the corresponding **A** proposition. By the contradictory relation, the **A** proposition is false. Since the conclusion claims that the **A** proposition is false, the conclusion is true, and therefore the argument is valid. Arguments that are valid from the Boolean standpoint are said to be **unconditionally valid** because they are valid regardless of whether their terms refer to existing things.

Note that the conclusion of this argument has the form "It is false that all *S* are *P*." Technically, statements of this type are not standard-form categorical propositions because, among other things, they do not begin with a quantifier. To remedy this difficulty we adopt the convention that statements having this form are equivalent to "'All *S* are *P*' is false." Analogous remarks apply to the negations of the **E**, **I**, and **O** statements.

Here is another example:

> It is false that all meteor showers are common spectacles.
> Therefore, no meteor showers are common spectacles.

We begin by assuming that the premise is true. Since the premise claims that an **A** proposition is false, we enter "false" into the square of opposition. We then use the square to compute the truth value of the corresponding **E** proposition. Since there is no relation that links the **A** and **E** propositions, the **E** proposition has undetermined truth value. Thus, the conclusion of the argument has undetermined truth value, and the argument is invalid.

We can also use Venn diagrams to test immediate inferences for validity. However, using this technique often requires that we diagram statements beginning with the phrase "It is false that." Let us begin by showing how to diagram such statements. Here are two examples:

> It is false that all *A* are *B*.

> It is false that some *A* are *B*.

The first statement claims that "All A are B" is false. Thus, to diagram it, we do the exact opposite of what we would do to diagram "All A are B." To diagram "All A are B," we shade the left-hand part of the A circle:

All A are B.

To diagram "It is false that all A are B," we enter an X in the left-hand part of the A circle. Entering an X in an area is the opposite of shading an area:

4

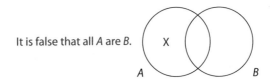

It is false that all A are B.

Any statement that is diagrammed by entering an X in an area is a particular proposition. Thus, as the diagram shows, "It is false that all A are B" is actually a particular proposition. By similar reasoning, "It is false that no A are B" is also a particular proposition.

To diagram "It is false that some A are B," we do the exact opposite of what we would do to diagram "Some A are B." For "Some A are B," we would enter an X in the overlap area. Thus, to diagram "It is false that some A are B," we shade the overlap area:

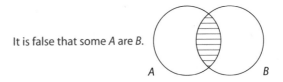

It is false that some A are B.

Any statement that is diagrammed by shading an area is a universal proposition. Thus, "It is false that some A are B" is actually a universal proposition. By similar reasoning, "It is false that some A are not B" is also a universal proposition.

Now let us use Venn diagrams to test an immediate inference. To do so we begin by using letters to represent the terms, and we then draw Venn diagrams for the premise and conclusion. If the information expressed by the conclusion diagram is contained in the premise diagram, the argument is valid; if not, it is invalid. Here is the symbolized form of the trade spies inference that we tested earlier.

> Some T are not M.
> Therefore, it is false that all T are M.

The next step is to draw two Venn diagrams, one for the premise and the other for the conclusion. For the premise we enter an X in the left-hand part of the T circle, and for the conclusion, as we have just seen, we enter an X in the left-hand part of the *T* circle:

Some *T* are not *M*.

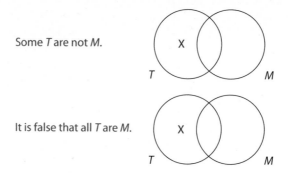

It is false that all *T* are *M*.

To evaluate the inference, we look to see whether the information expressed by the conclusion diagram is also expressed by the premise diagram. The conclusion diagram asserts that something exists in the left-hand part of the *T* circle. Since this information is also expressed by the premise diagram, the inference is valid. In this case, the diagram for the conclusion is identical to the diagram for the premise, so it is clear that premise and conclusion assert exactly the same thing. However, as we will see in Sections 4.5 and 4.6, for an immediate inference to be valid, it is not necessary that premise and conclusion assert exactly the same thing. It is only necessary that the premise assert *at least as much* as the conclusion.

Here is the symbolized version of the meteor shower inference evaluated earlier:

> It is false that all *M* are *C*.
> Therefore, no *M* are *C*.

To diagram the premise, we enter an X in the left-hand part of the *M* circle, and for the conclusion we shade the overlap area:

It is false that all *M* are *C*.

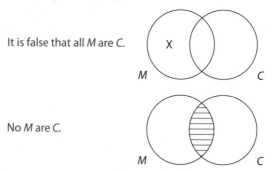

No *M* are *C*.

Here, the conclusion diagram asserts that the overlap area is empty. Since this information is not contained in the premise diagram, the inference is invalid.

We conclude with a special kind of inference:

> All smartphones are wireless devices.
> Therefore, some smartphones are wireless devices.

The completed Venn diagrams are as follows:

All S are W.

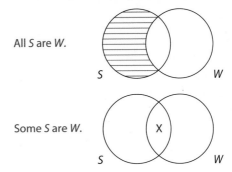

Some S are W.

The information of the conclusion diagram is not contained in the premise diagram, so the inference is invalid. However, if the premise were interpreted as having existential import, then the S circle in the premise diagram would not be empty. Specifically, there would be members in the overlap area. This would make the inference valid.

Arguments of this sort are said to commit the existential fallacy. From the Boolean standpoint, the **existential fallacy** is a formal fallacy that occurs whenever an argument is invalid merely because the premise lacks existential import. Such arguments always have a universal premise and a particular conclusion. The fallacy consists in attempting to derive a conclusion having existential import from a premise that lacks it.

The existential fallacy is easy to detect. Just look for a pair of diagrams in which the premise diagram contains shading and the conclusion diagram contains an X. If the X in the conclusion diagram is in the same part of the left-hand circle that is unshaded in the premise diagram, then the inference commits the existential fallacy. In the smartphone example we just considered, the premise diagram contains shading, and the conclusion diagram contains an X. Also, the X in the conclusion diagram is in the overlap area, and this area is unshaded in the premise diagram. Thus, the inference commits the existential fallacy.

There are exactly eight inference forms that commit the existential fallacy. Four of them are as follows. (The other four are left for an exercise.) Among these forms, recall that any proposition asserting that a particular (**I** or **O**) proposition is false is a universal proposition, and any proposition asserting that a universal (**A** or **E**) proposition is false is a particular proposition. With this in mind, you can see that all of these forms proceed from a universal premise to a particular conclusion.

Existential fallacy

All A are B.
Therefore, some A are B.

It is false that some A are not B.
Therefore, it is false that no A are B.

No *A* are *B*.
Therefore, it is false that all *A* are *B*.

It is false that some *A* are *B*.
Therefore, some *A* are not *B*.

Finally, while all of these forms proceed from a universal premise to a particular conclusion, it is important to see that not every inference having a universal premise and a particular conclusion commits the existential fallacy. For example, the inference "All *A* are *B*; therefore, some *A* are not *B*" does not commit this fallacy. This inference is invalid because the conclusion contradicts the premise. Thus, to detect the existential fallacy, one must ensure that the invalidity results merely from the fact that the premise lacks existential import. This can easily be done by constructing a Venn diagram.

Note on Boole, Venn, and Existential Import

Students occasionally ask about the motivation behind Boole's elimination of existential import from universal propositions. What is to be gained by this move, they ask? What's the point? To answer this question, we begin with a clarification: It was not Boole who took this step, it was Venn. That Boole interpreted universal statements as having existential import is clear from the fact that he allows for inferences that move from the universal to the particular. One of these inferences is what is called conversion by limitation: "All *A* are *B*" implies "Some *B* are *A*."[1] The other (which will be treated in Section 4.5 of this chapter) is called subalternation: "All *A* are *B*" implies "Some *A* are *B*."[2] The only way these inferences can be valid is if the class *A* is considered to have at least one member.

The first logician who confronted head-on the issue of the existential import of universal propositions was John Venn. In his *Symbolic Logic,* Venn defended the logic of Boole, but at the same time he insisted that universal propositions should be interpreted as having no existential import. This modification of Boole's logic came to be accepted as the official Boolean position. Thus, when we speak today of the *Boolean standpoint* or the *Boolean interpretation* of universal propositions, what we mean is Boole's position as amended by Venn.

Venn's work can be considered as launching a two-pronged attack on existential import. According to the first prong, insisting that all universal propositions have existential import results in "numerous perplexities." One of these perplexities arises from contraposing **A** type propositions (see Section 4.4 of this chapter). Suppose, for example, we are given the true statement "All *A* are *B*." According to the position Venn is attacking, both *A* and *B* represent non-empty classes. When we contrapose this statement, we get the true statement "All non-*B* are non-*A*," where both non-*B* and non-*A* represent non-empty classes.[3] Now, most of the time this operation is unproblematic, but suppose you are given the presumably true statement "All measurable things are finite things." When we contrapose

[1]G. Boole, The Mathematical Analysis of Logic *(Cambridge: Macmillan, Barclay, and Macmillan, 1847), 27–28.*

[2]*Ibid, 28. Boole reiterates both of these inferences in* The Laws of Thought *(London: Macmillan, 1854), 229.*

[3]*J. Venn,* Symbolic Logic *(London: Macmillan, 1881), 137–138.*

it, we get the true statement "All infinite things are immeasurable things," and this implies that there is at least one infinite thing (God?). Many logicians would reject this result.

Another perplexity relates to complex groups of statements and single statements having complex terms. In the case of complex groups of statements, Venn shows how existential import can result in inconsistencies, where not all the members of the group can be true.[4] For single statements having complex terms, the components can combine in ways that render existential import problematic.[5] For example, the statement "All *A* who are *B* are *C*" is generally acceptable. But if *A*, *B*, and *C* are replaced by "basketball players," "20 feet tall," and "formidable athletes,"[6] insisting on existential import implies there is at least one basketball player who is 20 feet tall. Again, most logicians would reject this outcome. And the problem is exacerbated as the complexity of the terms increases. In some cases it may be very difficult to see exactly what happens when the statement is given existential import.

The second prong of Venn's attack consists in resolutely adhering to Boole's interpretation of the meaning of universal propositions. According to this interpretation, universal propositions say nothing about where class members exist. They simply say where class members do *not* exist. Venn invites us to consider this pair of propositions: "All *A* are *B*" and "No *A* are *B*."[7] These propositions are said to be contraries, and if they are interpreted as having existential import, they cannot both be true (see Section 4.5 of this chapter). But if they are given the Boolean interpretation, there is no reason to think they cannot both be true. According to the first, nothing exists in the part of *A* that lies outside *B*, and according to the second, nothing exists in the part of *A* that lies inside *B*. Now there is nothing inconsistent at all about these two interpretations. Clearly they can both be true. But, taken together, they imply that there is nothing in *A* at all. Thus, the Boolean interpretation of universal propositions, pure and simple, without anything else being added, implies there are propositions that have no existential import. Boole himself apparently did not notice this.

In summary, eliminating existential import does away immediately with the perplexities that Venn identifies. Without existential import, we need not be concerned whether there are infinite things that actually exist, or whether there really are such things as basketball players who are 20 feet tall. Also, we need not worry whether existential import causes inconsistencies in complex groups of statements. Finally, abandoning existential import harmonizes perfectly with Boole's interpretation of universal statements whereby such statements merely say where class members do not exist, and not where they do exist. The result is a system of logic that is simpler and more elegant than one that allows for existential import. However, from a practical standpoint, a logical system having existential import is more widely applicable to real-life situations than one that lacks it. We will explore this idea further in Section 4.5 of this chapter.

---

[4]*The example Venn uses is: All x is either y and z, or not-y; All xy is w or not z; No wx is zx. J. Venn*, Symbolic Logic *(London: Macmillan, 1881), 139–140, 147.*

[5]*Ibid., 139.*

[6]*This example, and the "infinite things" example are mine.*

[7]*J. Venn*, Symbolic Logic *(London: Macmillan, 1881), 145–146.*

I. Draw Venn diagrams for the following propositions.

★1. No life decisions are happenings based solely on logic.

2. All electric motors are machines that depend on magnetism.

3. Some political campaigns are mere attempts to discredit opponents.

★4. Some rock-music lovers are not fans of Jay-Z.

5. All redistricting plans are sources of controversy.

6. No tax audits are pleasant experiences for cheaters.

★7. Some housing developments are complexes that exclude children.

8. Some cruise ships are not steam-driven vessels.

II. Use the modern square of opposition to determine whether the following immediate inferences are valid or invalid from the Boolean standpoint.

★1. No sculptures by Rodin are boring creations.
   Therefore, all sculptures by Rodin are boring creations.

2. It is false that some lunar craters are volcanic formations.
   Therefore, no lunar craters are volcanic formations.

3. All trial lawyers are people with stressful jobs.
   Therefore, some trial lawyers are people with stressful jobs.

★4. All dry martinis are dangerous concoctions.
   Therefore, it is false that some dry martinis are not dangerous concoctions.

5. It is false that no jazz musicians are natives of New Orleans.
   Therefore, some jazz musicians are not natives of New Orleans.

6. Some country doctors are altruistic healers.
   Therefore, some country doctors are not altruistic healers.

★7. No fertility drugs are solutions to every problem.
   Therefore, it is false that all fertility drugs are solutions to every problem.

8. It is false that no credit cards are things that contain holograms.
   Therefore, some credit cards are things that contain holograms.

9. It is false that some stunt pilots are not colorful daredevils.
   Therefore, it is false that some stunt pilots are colorful daredevils.

★10. No vampires are avid connoisseurs of garlic bread.
   Therefore, it is false that some vampires are avid connoisseurs of garlic bread.

MindTap® Complete exercises online for immediate feedback.

11. No talk radio shows are accurate sources of information.
    Therefore, some talk radio shows are not accurate sources of information.

12. Some stellar constellations are spiral-shaped objects.
    Therefore, no stellar constellations are spiral-shaped objects.

★13. It is false that some soap bubbles are not occasions of glee.
    Therefore, some soap bubbles are occasions of glee.

14. It is false that all weddings are light-hearted celebrations.
    Therefore, some weddings are not light-hearted celebrations.

15. It is false that some chocolate soufflés are desserts containing olives.
    Therefore, it is false that all chocolate soufflés are desserts containing olives.

III. Use Venn diagrams to evaluate the immediate inferences in Part II of this exercise. Identify any that commit the existential fallacy.

IV. This section of Chapter 4 identified four forms of the existential fallacy. Use Venn diagrams to identify the other four. In doing so, keep in mind that all forms of this fallacy have a universal premise and a particular conclusion, that "It is false that some *A* are *B*" and "It is false that some *A* are not *B*" are universal propositions, and "It is false that all *A* are *B*" and "It is false that no *A* are *B*" are particular.

V. Create five new immediate inferences composed of standard-form categorical propositions. Then test each for validity.

MindTap   Master concepts and improve outcomes with Aplia, at the end of the chapter, in the Aplia folder.

4.4 Conversion, Obversion, and Contraposition

HOW LOGICAL ARE YOU? Suppose you have a friend who is considering rushing a fraternity or sorority. You warn your friend that some students in Greek organizations are persons who drink irresponsibly. Your friend replies that based on your warning it follows that some students who drink responsibly are not members of Greek organizations. Is your friend right about this argument?

Find the answer on MindTap.

For a preliminary glimpse into the content of this section, consider the statement "No dogs are cats." This statement claims that the class of dogs is separated from the class of cats. But the statement "No cats are dogs" claims the same thing. Thus, the two statements have the same meaning and the same truth value. For another example, consider the statement "Some dogs are not retrievers." This statement claims there is at least one dog outside the class of retrievers. But the statement "Some dogs are non-retrievers" claims the same thing, so again, the two statements have the same meaning and the same truth value.

Conversion, obversion, and contraposition are operations that can be performed on a categorical proposition, resulting in a new statement that may or may not have the same meaning and truth value as the original statement. Venn diagrams are used to determine how the two statements relate to each other.

Conversion

The simplest of the three operations is **conversion**, and it consists of switching the subject term with the predicate term. For example, if the statement "No foxes are hedgehogs" is converted, the resulting statement is "No hedgehogs are foxes." This new statement is called the *converse* of the given statement. To see how the four types of categorical propositions relate to their converse, compare the following sets of Venn diagrams:

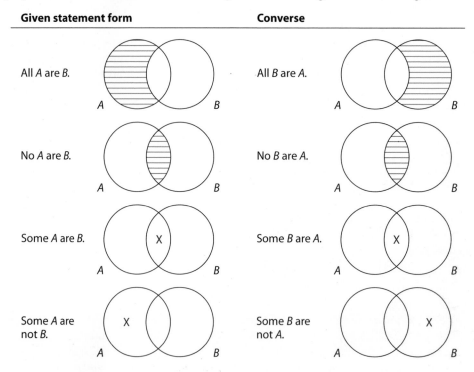

Given statement form	Converse
All *A* are *B*.	All *B* are *A*.
No *A* are *B*.	No *B* are *A*.
Some *A* are *B*.	Some *B* are *A*.
Some *A* are not *B*.	Some *B* are not *A*.

If we examine the diagram for the **E** statement, we see that it is identical to that of its converse. Also, the diagram for the **I** statement is identical to that of its converse. This means that the **E** statement and its converse are logically equivalent, and the **I** statement and its converse are logically equivalent. Two statements are said to be **logically equivalent statements** when they necessarily have the same truth value (as we will see again in Chapter 6). Thus, converting an **E** or **I** statement gives a new statement that always has the same truth value (and the same meaning) as the given statement. These equivalences are strictly proved by the Venn diagrams for the **E** and **I** statements.

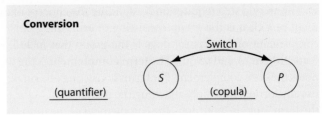

Conversion

Switch

S   P

(quantifier)   (copula)

On the other hand, the diagram for the **A** statement is clearly not identical to the diagram for its converse, and the diagram for the **O** statement is not identical to the diagram for its converse. Also, these pairs of diagrams are not the exact opposite of each other, as is the case with contradictory statements. This means that an **A** statement and its converse are logically unrelated as to truth value, and an **O** statement and its converse are logically unrelated as to truth value. In other words, converting an **A** or **O** statement gives a new statement whose truth value is logically undetermined in relation to the given statement. The converse of an **A** or **O** statement does have a truth value, of course, but logic alone cannot tell us what it is.

Because conversion yields necessarily determined results for **E** and **I** statements, it can be used as the basis for immediate inferences having these types of statements as premises. The following inference forms are valid:

No A are B.
Therefore, no B are A.

Some A are B.
Therefore, some B are A.

Since the conclusion of each inference form necessarily has the same truth value as the premise, if the premise is assumed true, it follows necessarily that the conclusion is true. On the other hand, the next two inference forms are invalid. Each commits the fallacy of **illicit conversion**:

All A are B.
Therefore, all B are A.

Some A are not B.
Therefore, some B are not A.

Here are two examples of inferences that commit the fallacy of illicit conversion:

All cats are animals.   (True)
Therefore, all animals are cats.   (False)

Some animals are not dogs.   (True)
Therefore, some dogs are not animals.   (False)

Obversion

More complicated than conversion, **obversion** requires two steps: (1) changing the quality (without changing the quantity), and (2) replacing the predicate with its term complement. The first part of this operation was treated in Exercise 4.2. It consists in changing "No *S* are *P*" to "All *S* are *P*" and vice versa, and changing "Some *S* are *P*" to "Some *S* are not *P*" and vice versa.

The second step requires understanding the concept of *class complement*. The complement of a class is the group consisting of everything outside the class. For example, the complement of the class of dogs is the group that includes everything that is not a dog (cats, fish, trees, and so on). The **term complement** is the word or group of words that denotes the class complement. For terms consisting of a single word, the term complement is usually formed by simply attaching the prefix "non" to the term. Thus, the complement of the term "dog" is "non-dog," the complement of the term "book" is "non-book," and so on.

The relationship between a term and its complement can be illustrated by a Venn diagram. For example, if a single circle is allowed to represent the class of dogs, then everything outside the circle represents the class of non-dogs:

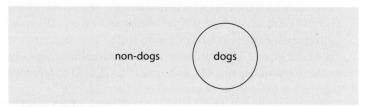

We now have everything we need to form the *obverse* of categorical propositions. First we change the quality (without changing the quantity), and then we replace the predicate term with its term complement. For example, if we are given the statement "All horses are animals," then the obverse is "No horses are non-animals"; and if we are given the statement "Some trees are maples," then the obverse is "Some trees are not non-maples." To see how the four types of categorical propositions relate to their obverse, compare the following sets of Venn diagrams:

Given statement form	Obverse
All *A* are *B*.	No *A* are non-*B*.
No *A* are *B*.	All *A* are non-*B*.
Some *A* are *B*.	Some *A* are not non-*B*.
Some *A* are not *B*.	Some *A* are non-*B*.

To see how the obverse diagrams are drawn, keep in mind that "non-B" designates the area outside the B circle. Thus, "No A are non-B" asserts that the area where A overlaps non-B is empty. This is represented by shading the left-hand part of the A circle. "All A are non-B" asserts that all members of A are outside B. This means that no members of A are inside B, so the area where A overlaps B is shaded. "Some A are not non-B" asserts that at least one member of A is not outside B. This means that at least one member of A is inside B, so an X is placed in the area where A and B overlap. Finally, "Some A are non-B" asserts that at least one member of A is outside B, so an X is placed in the left-hand part of the A circle.

If we examine these pairs of diagrams, we see that the diagram for each given statement form is identical to the diagram for its obverse. This means that each of the four types of categorical proposition is logically equivalent to (and has the same meaning as) its obverse. Thus, if we obvert an **A** statement that happens to be true, the resulting statement will be true; if we obvert an **O** statement that happens to be false, the resulting statement will be false, and so on.

It is easy to see that if a statement is obverted and then obverted again, the resulting statement will be identical to the original statement. For example, the obverse of "All horses are animals" is "No horses are non-animals." To obvert the latter statement we again change the quality ("no" switches to "all") and replace "non-animals" with its term complement. The term complement is produced by simply deleting the prefix "non." Thus, the obverse of the obverse is "All horses are animals."

When a term consists of more than a single word, more ingenuity is required to form its term complement. For example, if we are given the term "animals that are not native to America," it would not be appropriate to form the term complement by writing "non-animals that are not native to America." Clearly it would be better to write "animals native to America." Even though this is technically not the complement of the given term, the procedure is justified if we allow a reduction in the scope of discourse. This can be seen as follows. Technically the term complement of "animals that are not native to America" denotes all kinds of things such as ripe tomatoes, battleships, gold rings, and so on. But if we suppose that we are talking *only* about animals (that is, we reduce the scope of discourse to animals), then the complement of this term is "animals native to America."

As is the case with conversion, obversion can be used to supply the link between the premise and the conclusion of immediate inferences. The following inference forms are valid:

All A are B.   Some A are B.
Therefore, no A are non-B.   Therefore, some A are not non-B.

No A are B.   Some A are not B.
Therefore, all A are non-B.   Therefore, some A are non-B.

Because the conclusion of each inference form necessarily has the same truth value as its premise, if the premise is assumed true, it follows necessarily that the conclusion is true.

Contraposition

Like obversion, **contraposition** requires two steps: (1) switching the subject and predicate terms and (2) replacing the subject and predicate terms with their term complements. For example, if the statement "All goats are animals" is contraposed, the resulting statement is "All non-animals are non-goats." This new statement is called the contrapositive of the given statement. To see how all four types of categorical propositions relate to their contrapositive, compare the following sets of diagrams:

Given statement form		Contrapositive	
All A are B.		All non-B are non-A.	
No A are B.		No non-B are non-A.	
Some A are B.		Some non-B are non-A.	
Some A are not B.		Some non-B are not non-A.	

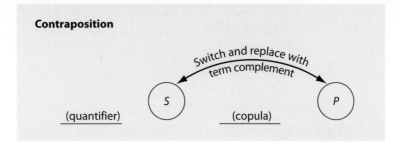

Contraposition

Switch and replace with term complement

(quantifier) S (copula) P

To see how the first diagram on the right is drawn, remember that "non-*A*" designates the area outside *A*. Thus, "All non-*B* are non-*A*" asserts that all members of non-*B* are outside *A*. This means that no members of non-*B* are inside *A*. Thus, we shade the area where non-*B* overlaps *A*. "No non-*B* are non-*A*" asserts that the area where non-*B* overlaps non-*A* is empty. Since non-*B* is the area outside the *B* circle and non-*A* is the area outside the *A* circle, the place where these two areas overlap is the area outside both circles. Thus, we shade this area. "Some non-*B* are non-*A*" asserts that something exists in the area where non-*B* overlaps non-*A*. Again, this is the area outside both circles, so we place an X in this area. Finally, "Some non-*B* are not non-*A*" asserts that at least one member of non-*B* is outside non-*A*. This means that at least one member of non-*B* is inside *A*, so we place an X in the area where non-*B* overlaps *A*.

Now, inspection of the diagrams for the **A** and **O** statements reveals that they are identical to the diagrams of their contrapositive. Thus, the **A** statement and its contrapositive are logically equivalent (and have the same meaning), and the **O** statement and its contrapositive are logically equivalent (and have the same meaning). On the other hand, the diagrams of the **E** and **I** statements are neither identical to nor the exact opposite of the diagrams of their contrapositives. This means that contraposing an **E** or **I** statement gives a new statement whose truth value is logically undetermined in relation to the given statement.

> To help remember when conversion and contraposition yield logically equivalent results, note the second and third vowels in the words. Conversion works for **E** and **I** propositions, contraposition works for **A** and **O** propositions.
>
> C O N V E R S I O N
>
> C O N T R A P O S I T I O N

As with conversion and obversion, contraposition may provide the link between the premise and the conclusion of an immediate inference. The following inference forms are valid:

All *A* are *B*.
Therefore, all non-*B* are non-*A*.

Some *A* are not *B*.
Therefore, some non-*B* are not non-*A*.

On the other hand, the following inference forms are invalid. Each commits the fallacy of **illicit contraposition**:

> Some A are B.
> Therefore, some non-B are non-A.

> No A are B.
> Therefore, no non-B are non-A.

Here are two examples of inferences that commit the fallacy of illicit contraposition:

No dogs are cats.	(True)
Therefore, no non-cats are non-dogs.	(False)

Some animals are non-cats.	(True)
Therefore, some cats are non-animals.	(False)

In regard to the first inference, an example of something that is both a non-cat and a non-dog is a pig. Thus, the conclusion implies that no pigs are pigs, which is false. In regard to the second inference, if both premise and conclusion are obverted, the premise becomes "Some animals are not cats," which is true, and the conclusion becomes "Some cats are not animals," which is false.

Both illicit conversion and illicit contraposition are formal fallacies: They can be detected through mere examination of the form of an argument.

Finally, note that the Boolean interpretation of categorical propositions has prevailed throughout this section. This means that the results obtained are unconditional, and they hold true regardless of whether the terms in the propositions denote actually existing things. Thus, they hold for propositions about unicorns and leprechauns just as they do for propositions about dogs and animals. These results are summarized in the following table.

Conversion: Switch Subject and Predicate Terms

Given Statement	Converse	Truth Value
E: No A are B.	No B are A.	Same truth value as given statement
I: Some A are B.	Some B are A.	
A: All A are B.	All B are A.	Undetermined truth value
O: Some A are not B.	Some B are not A.	

Obversion: Change Quality; Replace Predicate with Term Complement

Given Statement	Obverse	Truth Value
A: All A are B.	No A are non-B.	Same truth value as given statement
E: No A are B.	All A are non-B.	
I: Some A are B.	Some A are not non-B.	
O: Some A are not B.	Some A are non-B.	

Contraposition: Switch Subject and Predicate Terms; Replace Each with Its Term Complement

Given Statement	Contrapositive	Truth Value
A: All A are B.	All non-B are non-A.	Same truth value as given statement
O: Some A are not B.	Some non-B are not non-A.	
E: No A are B.	No non-B are non-A.	Undetermined truth value
I: Some A are B.	Some non-B are non-A.	

4

EXERCISE 4.4

I. Exercises 1 through 6 provide a statement, its truth value in parentheses, and an operation to be performed on that statement. Supply the new statement and the truth value of the new statement. (*Hint*: For number 1, first obtain the converse of "No A are non-B"; then, since the given statement is a true E proposition, use this information to calculate the truth value of the converse.)

Exercises 7 through 12 provide a statement, its truth value in parentheses, and a new statement. Determine how the new statement was derived from the given statement and supply the truth value of the new statement. (*Hint*: For number 7, first compare the terms in the given statement with the terms in the new statement. This will tell you the operation. Then, since the given statement is a false E proposition, use this information together with the operation to calculate the truth value of the new statement.)

Given statement	Operation	New statement	Truth value
★1. No A are non-B. (T)	conv.	_____	_____
2. Some A are B. (T)	contrap.	_____	_____
3. All A are non-B. (F)	obv.	_____	_____
★4. All non-A are B. (F)	contrap.	_____	_____
5. Some non-A are not B. (T)	conv.	_____	_____
6. Some non-A are non-B. (T)	obv.	_____	_____
★7. No non-A are non-B. (F)	_____	No B are A.	_____
8. Some A are not non-B. (T)	_____	Some A are B.	_____
9. All A are non-B. (F)	_____	All non-B are A.	_____
★10. No non-A are B. (F)	_____	All non-A are non-B.	_____

11. Some non-*A* are not *B*. (T) _____ Some non-*B* are not *A*. _____

12. Some *A* are non-*B*. (F) _____ Some non-*B* are *A*. _____

II. Perform the operations of conversion, obversion, and contraposition as indicated.

   1. Convert the following propositions and state whether the converse is logically equivalent or not logically equivalent to the given proposition.

    ★a. All hurricanes are storms intensified by global warming.

    b. No cosmetic surgeries are completely successful procedures.

    c. Some murals by Diego Rivera are works that celebrate the revolutionary spirit.

    d. Some forms of carbon are not substances with a crystalline structure.

   2. Obvert the following propositions and state whether the obverse is logically equivalent or not logically equivalent to the given proposition.

    ★a. All radically egalitarian societies are societies that do not preserve individual liberties.

    b. No cult leaders are people who fail to brainwash their followers.

    c. Some college football coaches are people who do not slip money to their players.

    d. Some budgetary cutbacks are not actions fair to the poor.

   3. Contrapose the following propositions and state whether the contrapositive is logically equivalent or not logically equivalent to the given proposition.

    ★a. All physicians whose licenses have been revoked are physicians ineligible to practice.

    b. No unpersecuted migrants are migrants granted asylum.

    c. Some politicians who do not defend Social Security are politicans who do not want to increase taxes.

    d. Some opponents of gay marriage are not opponents of civil unions.

III. Use conversion, obversion, and contraposition to determine whether the following arguments are valid or invalid. For those that are invalid, name the fallacy committed.

   ★1. All commodity traders are gamblers who risk sudden disaster.
     Therefore, all gamblers who risk sudden disaster are commodity traders.

   2. No child abusers are people who belong in day-care centers.
     Therefore, all child abusers are people who do not belong in day-care centers.

   3. Some states having limited powers are not slave states.
     Therefore, some free states are not states having unlimited powers.

   ★4. Some insane people are illogical people.
     Therefore, some logical people are sane people.

   5. Some organ transplants are not sensible operations.
     Therefore, some organ transplants are senseless operations.

   6. No individuals who laugh all the time are people with a true sense of humor.
     Therefore, no people with a true sense of humor are individuals who laugh all the time.

★7. All periods when interest rates are high are times when businesses tend not to expand.
Therefore, all times when businesses tend to expand are periods when interest rates are low.

8. Some swimsuits are not garments intended for the water.
Therefore, some garments intended for the water are not swimsuits.

9. No promises made under duress are enforceable contracts.
Therefore, no unenforceable contracts are promises made in the absence of duress.

★10. All ladies of the night are individuals with low self-esteem.
Therefore, no ladies of the night are individuals with high self-esteem.

11. Some graffiti writers are artists relieving pent-up frustrations.
Therefore, some artists relieving pent-up frustrations are graffiti writers.

12. Some peaceful revolutions are episodes that erupt in violence.
Therefore, some episodes that do not erupt in violence are non-peaceful revolutions.

★13. Some insurance companies are not humanitarian organizations.
Therefore, some humanitarian organizations are not insurance companies.

14. Some fossil fuels are unrenewable energy sources.
Therefore, some fossil fuels are not renewable energy sources.

15. All hired killers are criminals who deserve the death penalty.
Therefore, all criminals who deserve the death penalty are hired killers.

★16. No nonprescription drugs are medicines without adverse effects.
Therefore, no medicines with adverse effects are prescription drugs.

17. All fire-breathing dragons are lizards that languish in soggy climates.
Therefore, no fire-breathing dragons are lizards that flourish in soggy climates.

18. Some distant galaxies are not structures visible to the naked eye.
Therefore, some structures visible to the naked eye are not distant galaxies.

★19. All unpleasant experiences are things we do not like to remember.
Therefore, all things we like to remember are pleasant experiences.

20. Some pro-lifers are not people concerned with child welfare.
Therefore, some pro-lifers are people unconcerned with child welfare.

IV. Create a new categorical proposition for each of the four forms (**A, E, I, O**). Then convert, obvert, and contrapose each one, and state whether the resulting proposition is logically equivalent to the original proposition.

MindTap® Master concepts and improve outcomes with Aplia, at the end of the chapter, in the Aplia folder.

4

In Section 4.3 we adopted the Boolean standpoint, and we saw how the modern square of opposition applies regardless of whether the propositions refer to actually existing things. In this section, we adopt the Aristotelian standpoint, which recognizes that universal propositions about existing things have existential import. For such propositions the traditional square of opposition becomes applicable. Like the modern square, the **traditional square of opposition** is an arrangement of lines that illustrates logically necessary relations among the four kinds of categorical propositions. However, because the Aristotelian standpoint recognizes the additional factor of existential import, the traditional square supports more inferences than does the modern square. It is represented as follows:

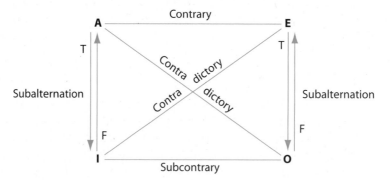

The four relations in the traditional square of opposition may be characterized as follows:

Contradictory	=	opposite truth value
Contrary	=	at least one is false (not both true)
Subcontrary	=	at least one is true (not both false)
Subalternation	=	truth flows downward, falsity flows upward

The **contradictory relation** is the same as that found in the modern square. Thus, if a certain **A** proposition is given as true, the corresponding **O** proposition is false, and vice versa, and if a certain **A** proposition is given as false, the corresponding **O** proposition is true, and vice versa. The same relation holds between the **E** and **I** propositions. The contradictory relation thus expresses complete opposition between propositions.

The **contrary relation** differs from the contradictory in that it expresses only partial opposition. Thus, if a certain **A** proposition is given as true, the corresponding **E** proposition is false (because at least one must be false), and if an **E** proposition is given as true, the corresponding **A** proposition is false. But if an **A** proposition is given as false, the corresponding **E** proposition could be *either* true or false without violating the "at least one is false" rule. In this case, the **E** proposition has logically undetermined truth value. Similarly, if an **E** proposition is given as false, the corresponding **A** proposition has logically undetermined truth value.

These results are borne out in ordinary language. Thus, if we are given the actually true **A** proposition "All cats are animals," the corresponding **E** proposition "No cats are animals" is false, and if we are given the actually true **E** proposition "No cats are dogs," the corresponding **A** proposition "All cats are dogs" is false. Thus, the **A** and **E** propositions cannot both be true. However, they can both be false. "All animals are cats" and "No animals are cats" are both false.

The **subcontrary relation** also expresses a kind of partial opposition. If a certain **I** proposition is given as false, the corresponding **O** proposition is true (because at least one must be true), and if an **O** proposition is given as false, the corresponding **I** proposition is true. But if either an **I** or an **O** proposition is given as true, then the corresponding proposition could be either true or false without violating the "at least one is true" rule. Thus, in this case the corresponding proposition would have logically undetermined truth value.

Again, these results are borne out in ordinary language. If we are given the actually false **I** proposition "Some cats are dogs," the corresponding **O** proposition "Some cats are not dogs" is true, and if we are given the actually false **O** proposition "Some cats are not animals," the corresponding **I** proposition "Some cats are animals" is true. Thus, the **I** and **O** propositions cannot both be false, but they can both be true. "Some animals are cats" and "Some animals are not cats" are both true.

The **subalternation relation** is represented by two arrows: a downward arrow marked with the letter T (true), and an upward arrow marked with an F (false). These arrows can be thought of as pipelines through which truth values "flow." The downward arrow "transmits" only truth, and the upward arrow only falsity. Thus, if an **A** proposition is given as true, the corresponding **I** proposition is true also, and if an **I** proposition is given as false, the corresponding **A** proposition is false. But if an **A** proposition is given as false, this truth value cannot be transmitted downward, so the corresponding **I** proposition will have logically undetermined truth value. Conversely, if an **I** proposition is given as true, this truth value cannot be transmitted upward, so the corresponding **A** proposition will have logically undetermined truth value. Analogous reasoning prevails for the subalternation relation between the **E** and **O** propositions. To remember the direction of the arrows for subalternation, imagine that truth "trickles down," and falsity "floats" up.

Now that we have examined these four relations individually, let us see how they can be used together to determine the truth values of corresponding propositions. The first rule of thumb that we should keep in mind when using the square to compute more than one truth value is always to use contradiction first. Now, let us suppose that we are told that the nonsensical proposition "All adlers are bobkins" is true.

Suppose further that adlers actually exist, so we are justified in using the traditional square of opposition. By the contradictory relation, "Some adlers are not bobkins" is false. Then, by either the contrary or the subalternation relation, "No adlers are bobkins" is false. Finally, by either contradictory, subalternation, or subcontrary, "Some adlers are bobkins" is true.

Next, let us see what happens if we assume that "All adlers are bobkins" is false. By the contradictory relation, "Some adlers are not bobkins" is true, but nothing more can be determined. In other words, given a false **A** proposition, both contrary and subalternation yield undetermined results, and given a true **O** proposition (the one whose truth value we just determined), subcontrary and subalternation yield undetermined results. Thus, the corresponding **E** and **I** propositions have logically undetermined truth value. This result illustrates two more rules of thumb. Assuming that we always use the contradictory relation first, if one of the remaining relations yields a logically undetermined truth value, the others will as well. The other rule is that whenever one statement turns out to have logically undetermined truth value, its contradictory will also. Thus, statements having logically undetermined truth value will always occur in pairs, at opposite ends of diagonals on the square.

Testing Immediate Inferences

Next, let us see how we can use the traditional square of opposition to test immediate inferences for validity. Here is an example:

> All Rolex watches are works of art.
> Therefore, it is false that no Rolex watches are works of art.

We begin, as usual, by assuming the premise is true. Since the premise is an **A** proposition, by the contrary relation the corresponding **E** proposition is false. But this is exactly what the conclusion says, so the argument is valid.

Here is another example:

> Some viruses are structures that attack T cells.
> Therefore, some viruses are not structures that attack T cells.

Here the premise and conclusion are linked by the subcontrary relation. According to that relation, if the premise is assumed true, the conclusion has logically undetermined truth value, and so the inference is invalid. It commits the formal fallacy of **illicit subcontrary**. Analogously, inferences that depend on an incorrect application of the contrary relation commit the formal fallacy of **illicit contrary**, and inferences that depend on an illicit application of subalternation commit the formal fallacy of **illicit subalternation**. Some forms of these fallacies are as follows:

Illicit contrary

> It is false that all A are B.
> Therefore, no A are B.

> It is false that no A are B.
> Therefore, all A are B.

Illicit subcontrary

> Some A are B.
> Therefore, it is false that some A are not B.

> Some A are not B.
> Therefore, some A are B.

Illicit subalternation

> Some A are not B.
> Therefore, no A are B.

> It is false that all A are B.
> Therefore, it is false that some A are B.

Cases of the incorrect application of the contradictory relation are so infrequent that an "illicit contradictory" fallacy is not usually recognized.

As we saw at the beginning of this section, for the traditional square of opposition to apply, the Aristotelian standpoint must be adopted, and the propositions to which it is applied must assert something about actually existing things. The question may now be asked, What happens when the Aristotelian standpoint is adopted but the propositions are about things that do not exist? The answer is that under these conditions the traditional square reverts to the modern square (see Section 4.3). Inferences that are based on a correct application of the contradictory relation are valid, but inferences that are based on an otherwise correct application of the other three relations are invalid and commit the existential fallacy.

The reason for this result is easy to see. The modern square of opposition rests on the Boolean standpoint, and the traditional square rests on the Aristotelian standpoint. But the Aristotelian standpoint differs from the Boolean only with respect to universal propositions about existing things. The Aristotelian standpoint interprets these propositions as having existential import, while the Boolean standpoint does not. But universal propositions about things that do not exist have no existential import from the Aristotelian standpoint. In other words, the Aristotelian standpoint interprets these propositions in exactly the same way as does the Boolean. Thus, for universal propositions about things that do not exist, the traditional square reverts to the modern square.*

Accordingly, the **existential fallacy** is committed from the Aristotelian standpoint when and only when contrary, subcontrary, and subalternation are used (in an otherwise correct way) to draw a conclusion from a premise about things that do not exist. All such inferences begin with a universal proposition, which has no existential import, and they conclude with a particular proposition, which has existential import. The existential fallacy is never committed in connection with the contradictory relation, nor is it committed in connection with conversion, obversion, or contraposition, all of which

---

*Following on this result, from the Aristotelian standpoint "All unicorns are X" is vacuously true, as is "No unicorns are X." Thus, their contradictories, "Some unicorns are not X" and "Some unicorns are X" are vacuously false. It makes no difference what X stands for.

hold regardless of existence. The following inferences commit the existential fallacy from the Aristotelian standpoint:

All witches who fly on broomsticks are fearless women.
Therefore, some witches who fly on broomsticks are fearless women.

No wizards with magical powers are malevolent beings.
Therefore, it is false that all wizards with magical powers are malevolent beings.

The first depends on an otherwise correct use of the subalternation relation, and the second on an otherwise correct use of the contrary relation. If flying witches and magical wizards actually existed, both arguments would be valid. But since they do not exist, both arguments are invalid and commit the existential fallacy. In regard to the second example, recall that the conclusion, which asserts that an **A** proposition is false, is actually a particular proposition. Thus, this example, like the first one, proceeds from the universal to the particular.

Existential fallacy examples: Two standpoints

All cats are animals.   }   Boolean: Invalid, existential fallacy
Some cats are animals.   }   Aristotelian: Valid

All unicorns are animals.   }   Boolean: Invalid, existential fallacy
Some unicorns are animals. }   Aristotelian: Invalid, existential fallacy

---

The phrase **conditionally valid** applies to an inference after the Aristotelian standpoint has been adopted and we are not certain if the subject term of the premise denotes actually existing things. For example, the following inference is conditionally valid:

All students who failed the exam are students on probation.
Therefore, some students who failed the exam are students on probation.

The validity of this inference rests on whether there were in fact any students who failed the exam. The inference is either valid or invalid, but we lack sufficient information about the meaning of the premise to tell which is the case. Once it becomes known that there are indeed some students who failed the exam, we can assert that the inference is valid from the Aristotelian standpoint. But if there are no students who failed the exam, the inference is invalid because it commits the existential fallacy.

Similarly, all inference *forms* that depend on valid applications of contrary, subcontrary, and subalternation are conditionally valid because we do not know if the letters in the propositions denote actually existing things. For example, the following inference form, which depends on the contrary relation, is conditionally valid:

All A are B.
Therefore, it is false that no A are B.

If "dogs" and "animals" are substituted in place of *A* and *B,* respectively, the resulting inference is valid. But if "unicorns" and "animals" are substituted, the resulting inference is invalid because it commits the existential fallacy. In Section 4.3, we noted that all inferences (and inference forms) that are valid from the Boolean standpoint are *unconditionally valid.* They are valid regardless of whether their terms denote actually existing things.

In testing an inference for validity, we are never concerned with the actual truth of the premise. Regardless of whether the premise is actually true or false, we always begin by assuming it to be true, and then we determine how this assumption bears on the truth or falsity of the conclusion. The actual truth of the premise affects only the soundness of the argument. So let us now turn to the question of soundness. Recall from Section 1.4 that a sound argument is one that is valid and has all true premises, and consider the following example:

> All cats are dogs.
> Therefore, some cats are dogs.

The premise is obviously false; but if we assume it to be true, then it follows necessarily by subalternation that the conclusion is true. Thus, the inference is valid. However, because the premise is false, the inference is unsound.

Here is another example:

> No rabbits are toads.
> Therefore, it is false that all rabbits are toads.

This inference is sound. By the contrary relation it is valid, and it also has a true premise.

Here is a final example:

> Some unicorns are not gazelles.
> Therefore, it is false that all unicorns are gazelles.

This inference differs from the others in that the premise asserts the existence of something that does not actually exist (namely, unicorns). In other words, the premise seems to be self-contradictory. Nevertheless, the inference can be evaluated in the usual way. If the premise is assumed true, then it necessarily follows that the conclusion is true by the contradictory relation. Thus, the inference is valid. But the inference is unsound because it has a false premise. The premise asserts the existence of something that does not actually exist.

Now that we have seen how the traditional square of opposition, by itself, is used to test inferences for validity and soundness, let us see how it can be used together with the operations of conversion, obversion, and contraposition to prove the validity of inferences that are given as valid. Suppose we are given the following valid inference:

> All inappropriate remarks are faux pas.
> Therefore, some faux pas are not appropriate remarks.

To prove this inference valid, we select letters to represent the terms, and then we use some combination of conversion, obversion, and contraposition together with the traditional square to find the intermediate links between premise and conclusion:

All non-*A* are *F*.	(assumed true)
Some non-*A* are *F*.	(true by subalternation)
Some *F* are non-*A*.	(true by conversion)
Therefore, some *F* are not *A*.	(true by obversion)

The premise is the first line in this proof, and each succeeding step is validly derived from the one preceding it by the relation written in parentheses at the right. Since the conclusion (which is the last step) follows by a series of three necessary inferences, the inference is valid.

Various strategies can be used to construct proofs such as this, but one useful procedure is first to concentrate on obtaining the individual terms as they appear in the conclusion, then to attend to the order of the terms, and finally to use the square of opposition to adjust quality and quantity. As the faux pas proof illustrates, however, variations on this procedure are sometimes necessary. The fact that the predicate of the conclusion is "*A*," while "non-*A*" appears in the premise, leads us to think of obversion. But using obversion to change "non-*A*" into "*A*" requires that the "non-*A*" in the premise be moved into the predicate position via conversion. The latter operation, however, is valid only on **E** and **I** statements, and the premise is an **A** statement. The fact that the conclusion is a particular statement suggests subalternation as an intermediate step, thus yielding an **I** statement that can be converted.

EXERCISE **4.5**

I. Use the traditional square of opposition to find the answers to these problems. When a statement is given as false, simply enter an "F" into the square of opposition and compute (if possible) the other truth values.

★1. If "All fashion fads are products of commercial brainwashing" is true, what is the truth value of the following statements?
   a. No fashion fads are products of commercial brainwashing.
   b. Some fashion fads are products of commercial brainwashing.
   c. Some fashion fads are not products of commercial brainwashing.

2. If "All fashion fads are products of commercial brainwashing" is false, what is the truth value of the following statements?
   a. No fashion fads are products of commercial brainwashing.
   b. Some fashion fads are products of commercial brainwashing.
   c. Some fashion fads are not products of commercial brainwashing.

MindTap Complete exercises online for immediate feedback.

3. If "No sting operations are cases of entrapment" is true, what is the truth value of the following statements?
   a. All sting operations are cases of entrapment.
   b. Some sting operations are cases of entrapment.
   c. Some sting operations are not cases of entrapment.

★4. If "No sting operations are cases of entrapment" is false, what is the truth value of the following statements?
   a. All sting operations are cases of entrapment.
   b. Some sting operations are cases of entrapment.
   c. Some sting operations are not cases of entrapment.

5. If "Some assassinations are morally justifiable actions" is true, what is the truth value of the following statements?
   a. All assassinations are morally justifiable actions.
   b. No assassinations are morally justifiable actions.
   c. Some assassinations are not morally justifiable actions.

6. If "Some assassinations are morally justifiable actions" is false, what is the truth value of the following statements?
   a. All assassinations are morally justifiable actions.
   b. No assassinations are morally justifiable actions.
   c. Some assassinations are not morally justifiable actions.

★7. If "Some obsessive-compulsive behaviors are not curable diseases" is true, what is the truth value of the following statements?
   a. All obsessive-compulsive behaviors are curable diseases.
   b. No obsessive-compulsive behaviors are curable diseases.
   c. Some obsessive-compulsive behaviors are curable diseases.

8. If "Some obsessive-compulsive behaviors are not curable diseases" is false, what is the truth value of the following statements?
   a. All obsessive-compulsive behaviors are curable diseases.
   b. No obsessive-compulsive behaviors are curable diseases.
   c. Some obsessive-compulsive behaviors are curable diseases.

II. Use the traditional square of opposition to determine whether the following immediate inferences are valid or invalid. Name any fallacies that are committed.

★1. All advocates of school prayer are individuals who insist on imposing their views on others.
Therefore, some advocates of school prayer are individuals who insist on imposing their views on others.

2. It is false that no jailhouse informants are people who can be trusted.
Therefore, some jailhouse informants are not people who can be trusted.

3. All homemakers are people with real jobs.
Therefore, it is false that no homemakers are people with real jobs.

★4. It is false that some trolls are not creatures who live under bridges.
Therefore, it is false that no trolls are creatures who live under bridges.

5. Some campus romances are episodes plagued by violence.
   Therefore, some campus romances are not episodes plagued by violence.

6. Some pornographic publications are materials protected by the First Amendment.
   Therefore, it is false that no pornographic publications are materials protected by the First Amendment.

★7. It is false that all mainstream conservatives are people who support free legal services for the poor.
   Therefore, no mainstream conservatives are people who support free legal services for the poor.

8. It is false that some forms of human creativity are activities amenable to mathematical analysis.
   Therefore, it is false that all forms of human creativity are activities amenable to mathematical analysis.

9. It is false that some tooth fairies are daytime visitors.
   Therefore, some tooth fairies are not daytime visitors.

★10. It is false that some orthodox psychoanalysts are not individuals driven by a religious fervor.
   Therefore, it is false that some orthodox psychoanalysts are individuals driven by a religious fervor.

11. Some school busses manufactured on the moon are not plasma-powered vehicles.
   Therefore, it is false that all school busses manufactured on the moon are plasma-powered vehicles.

12. It is false that some network news programs are exercises in mediocrity.
   Therefore, it is false that no network news programs are exercises in mediocrity.

★13. No flying reindeer are animals who get lost in the fog.
   Therefore, it is false that all flying reindeer are animals who get lost in the fog.

14. It is false that no leveraged buyouts are deals unfair to workers.
   Therefore, all leveraged buyouts are deals unfair to workers.

15. It is false that some wood ticks are not carriers of Lyme disease.
   Therefore, some wood ticks are carriers of Lyme disease.

III. Use the traditional square of opposition to determine whether the following immediate inferences are valid or invalid and sound or unsound. Name any fallacies that are committed.

★1. All dolphins are polar bears.
   Therefore, it is false that no dolphins are polar bears.

2. It is false that some recessions are not periods of economic decline.
   Therefore, it is false that no recessions are periods of economic decline.

3. It is false that some suicide survivors are comeback kids.
   Therefore, some suicide survivors are not comeback kids.

★4. It is false that some ruby earrings are not pieces of jewelry.
Therefore, some ruby earrings are pieces of jewelry.

5. It is false that all visitors to Rio are Carnival addicts.
Therefore, no visitors to Rio are Carnival addicts.

6. Some tax cheats are not honest citizens.
Therefore, no tax cheats are honest citizens.

★7. All truthful lies are curious assertions.
Therefore, some truthful lies are curious assertions.

8. It is false that no bankrupt hair salons are thriving enterprises.
Therefore, all bankrupt hair salons are thriving enterprises.

9. It is false that some functional skateboards are not devices equipped with wheels.
Therefore, all functional skateboards are devices equipped with wheels.

★10. Some film directors are artistic visionaries.
Therefore, some film directors are not artistic visionaries.

IV. Exercises 1 through 10 provide a statement, its truth value in parentheses, and an operation to be performed on that statement. Supply the new statement and the truth value of the new statement. Exercises 11 through 20 provide a statement, its truth value in parentheses, and a new statement. Determine how the new statement was derived from the given statement and supply the truth value of the new statement. Take the Aristotelian standpoint in working these exercises and assume that the terms refer to actually existing things.

Given statement	Operation/ relation	New statement	Truth value
★1. All non-A are B. (T)	contrap.	_____	_____
2. Some A are non-B. (F)	subalt.	_____	_____
3. No A are non-B. (T)	obv.	_____	_____
★4. Some non-A are not B. (T)	subcon.	_____	_____
5. No A are non-B. (F)	contradic.	_____	_____
6. No A are B. (T)	contrap.	_____	_____
★7. All non-A are B. (T)	contrary	_____	_____
8. Some A are not non-B. (F)	obv.	_____	_____
9. No A are non-B. (F)	conv.	_____	_____
★10. Some non-A are non-B. (F)	subcon.	_____	_____
11. Some non-A are not B. (T)	_____	All non-A are B.	_____
12. Some A are non-B. (T)	_____	Some non-B are A.	_____
★13. All non-A are B. (F)	_____	No non-A are non-B.	_____

14. Some non-*A* are not *B*. (T) _____ No non-*A* are *B*. _____

15. All *A* are non-*B*. (F) _____ All non-*B* are *A*. _____

★16. Some non-*A* are non-*B*. (F) _____ No non-*A* are non-*B*. _____

17. Some *A* are not non-*B*. (T) _____ Some *B* are not non-*A*. _____

18. No non-*A* are *B*. (T) _____ Some non-*A* are not *B*. _____

★19. No *A* are non-*B*. (F) _____ All *A* are non-*B*. _____

20. Some non-*A* are *B*. (F) _____ Some non-*A* are not *B*. _____

V. Use either the traditional square of opposition or conversion, obversion, or contraposition to determine whether the following immediate inferences are valid or invalid. For those that are invalid, name the fallacy committed.

★1. It is false that some jogging events are not aerobic activities.
Therefore, it is false that no jogging events are aerobic activities.

2. No meat-eating vegetarians are individuals with a high-protein diet.
Therefore, no individuals with a high-protein diet are meat-eating vegetarians.

3. Some jobs in health care are not glamorous occupations.
Therefore, some jobs in health care are glamorous occupations.

★4. Some terminally ill patients are patients who do not want to live.
Therefore, some patients who want to live are recovering patients.

5. All Barbie dolls are toys that engender a false sense of values.
Therefore, no Barbie dolls are toys that engender a true sense of values.

6. All flying elephants are jolly pachyderms.
Therefore, some flying elephants are jolly pachyderms.

★7. It is false that some international terrorists are political moderates.
Therefore, some international terrorists are not political moderates.

8. No pet hamsters are animals that need much attention.
Therefore, it is false that all pet hamsters are animals that need much attention.

9. Some hedge-fund managers are not responsible investors.
Therefore, some responsible investors are not hedge-fund managers.

★10. It is false that all substances that control cell growth are hormones.
Therefore, no substances that control cell growth are hormones.

11. Some cases of whistle-blowing are actions disloyal to employers.
Therefore, some cases of whistle-blowing are not actions loyal to employers.

12. No stolen computer chips are easy items to trace.
Therefore, no difficult items to trace are computer chips that are not stolen.

★13. Some economists are followers of Ayn Rand.
Therefore, some economists are not followers of Ayn Rand.

14. All porcelain figurines are fragile artifacts.
    Therefore, it is false that some porcelain figurines are not fragile artifacts.

15. Some pleasant recollections are not missed opportunities.
    Therefore, some availed opportunities are not unpleasant recollections.

VI. Use the traditional square of opposition together with conversion, obversion, and contraposition to prove that the following immediate inferences are valid. Show each intermediate step in the deduction.

★1. All insurance policies are cryptically written documents.
    Therefore, some cryptically written documents are insurance policies.

2. No gemstones that do not contain chromium are emeralds.
   Therefore, some stones that are not emeralds are not gemstones that contain chromium.

3. It is false that some *Ficus benjaminas* are untemperamental house plants.
   Therefore, all *Ficus benjaminas* are temperamental house plants.

★4. All exogenous morphines are addictive substances.
    Therefore, it is false that all addictive substances are endogenous morphines.

5. No people who do not advocate free-enterprise economics are fundamentalist Christians.
   Therefore, it is false that some fundamentalist Christians are not people who advocate free-enterprise economics.

6. It is false that some Gothic cathedrals are buildings that do not feature pointed arches.
   Therefore, some buildings that feature pointed arches are Gothic cathedrals.

★7. Some people who recognize paranormal events are not non-scientists.
    Therefore, it is false that no scientists are people who recognize paranormal events.

8. It is false that no unhealthy things to ingest are food additives.
   Therefore, some food additives are not healthy things to ingest.

9. It is false that some illegal searches are not sobriety checkpoints.
   Therefore, some sobriety checkpoints are not legal searches.

★10. It is false that some feminists are not advocates of equal pay for equal work.
    Therefore, it is false that all advocates of equal pay for equal work are non-feminists.

VII. Create a new categorical proposition for each of the four forms (**A, E, I, O**). Then, for each one, write out the three categorical propositions related to it by the traditional square of opposition (similar to Part I of this exercise). Finally, assuming the original propositions are true, use the traditional square to determine the truth value of the other three propositions.

MindTap Master concepts and improve outcomes with Aplia, at the end of the chapter, in the Aplia folder.

Venn Diagrams
and the Traditional Standpoint

HOW LOGICAL ARE YOU? Suppose a friend makes the claim that it is wrong to drink bottled water when it is perfectly safe to drink water from the tap. When you see your friend chugging a bottle of water, you remind him of what he said earlier. He replies that he is doing nothing wrong. Is he contradicting himself? What does it mean for two statements to contradict each other? What circumstances could your friend cite to avoid a contradiction?

Find the answer on MindTap.

Earlier in this chapter we saw how Venn diagrams can be used to represent the content of categorical propositions from the Boolean standpoint. With a slight modification they can also be used to represent the content of categorical propositions from the traditional, or Aristotelian, standpoint. These modified Venn diagrams can then be used to prove the relationships of the traditional square of opposition, and also to test the validity of immediate inferences from the traditional standpoint.

The difference between the Boolean standpoint and the Aristotelian standpoint concerns only universal (**A** and **E**) propositions. From the Boolean standpoint, universal propositions have no existential import, but from the Aristotelian standpoint they do have existential import when their subject terms refer to actually existing things. For example, from the Boolean standpoint the statement "All raccoons are pests" does not imply the existence of anything, but from the Aristotelian standpoint it implies the existence of raccoons. Thus, if we are to construct a Venn diagram to represent such a statement from the Aristotelian standpoint, we need to use some symbol that represents this implication of existence.

The symbol that we will use for this purpose is an X surrounded by a circle. Like the X's that we have used up until now, this circled X signifies that something exists in the area in which it is placed. However, the two symbols differ in that the uncircled X represents the positive claim of existence made by particular (**I** and **O**) propositions, whereas the circled X represents an implication of existence made by universal propositions about actually existing things. For the purpose at hand, a circled X is placed inside the *S* circle as follows:

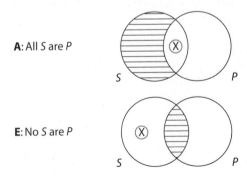

A: All *S* are *P*

E: No *S* are *P*

In the diagram for the **A** statement, the left-hand part of the *S* circle is shaded, so if there are any members of *S*, they must be in the area where the two circles overlap. Thus, a circled X is placed in the overlap area. In the diagram for the **E** statement, the overlap area is shaded, so if there are any members of *S* they must be in the left-hand part of the *S* circle. Thus, a circled X is placed in this area.

The diagrams for the **I** and **O** statements are the same from the Aristotelian standpoint as they are from the Boolean:

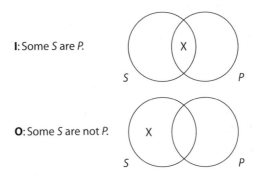

I: Some *S* are *P.*

O: Some *S* are not *P.*

Proving the Traditional Square of Opposition

We can now use this modified Venn diagram technique to prove the relations of the traditional square of opposition.* Having such a proof is important because up until now these relations have only been illustrated with various examples; they have not been proved. The accompanying figure reproduces the traditional square of opposition together with Venn diagrams that represent the Aristotelian interpretation of the four standard-form categorical propositions.

Let us begin with the contradictory relation. If the **A** statement is given as true, then the left-hand part of the *S* circle is empty. This makes the **O** statement false, because it claims that the left-hand part of the *S* circle is not empty. And if the **O** statement is given as true, then the left-hand part of the *S* circle is not empty, which makes the **A** statement false. On the other hand, if the **O** statement is given as false, then the left-hand part of the *S* circle is empty. However, given that some members of *S* exist, they must be in the overlap area. This double outcome makes the **A** statement true. Also, if the **A** statement is given as false, then either the left-hand part of the *S* circle is not empty, or the overlap area is empty (or both). If the left-hand part of the *S* circle is not empty, then the **O** statement is true. Alternately, if the overlap area is empty, then, given that some members of *S* exist, they must be in the left-hand part of the *S* circle,

---

*The modified Venn diagram technique can also be used to prove the validity of conversion, obversion, and contraposition from the Aristotelian standpoint, but to do so a circled X must be entered in the unshaded part of both the S and P circles and also in the unshaded area outside both circles.

and, once again, the **O** statement is true. Analogous reasoning applies for the relation between the **E** and **I** statements.

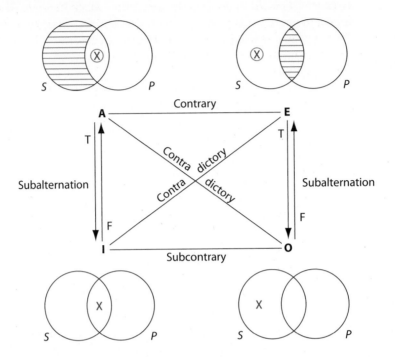

Next, we turn to the contrary relation. If the **A** statement is given as true, then the overlap area is not empty, which makes the **E** statement false. By analogous reasoning, if the **E** statement is given as true, the overlap area is empty, which makes the **A** statement false. However, if the **A** statement is given as false (making the **O** statement true), then the **E** statement could be either true or false depending on whether or not the overlap area is empty. Thus, in this case the **E** statement would have logically undetermined truth value. By analogous reasoning, if the **E** statement is given as false (making the **I** statement true), the **A** statement could be either true or false depending on whether or not the left-hand part of the *S* circle is empty. Thus, the **A** statement would have logically undetermined truth value.

Turning next to the subcontrary relation, if the **I** statement is given as false, then the area where the *S* and *P* circles overlap is empty. Given that at least one *S* exists, there must be something in the left-hand part of the *S* circle, which makes the **O** statement true. By analogous reasoning, if the **O** statement is given as false, there must be something in the overlap area, making the **I** statement true. But if the **I** statement is given as true, then the **O** statement could be either true or false depending on whether something exists in the left-hand part of the *S* circle. Thus, the **O** statement would have undetermined truth value. Similarly, if the **O** statement is given as true, then the **I** statement could be either true or false depending on whether something exists in the overlap area. Thus, the **I** statement would have undetermined truth value.

Finally, we consider subalternation. If the **A** statement is given as true, then something exists in the area where the *S* and *P* circles overlap, which makes the **I** statement true as well. And if the **I** statement is given as false, then the overlap area is empty, making the **A** statement false. But if the **A** statement is given as false (making the **O** statement true), then the **I** statement could be either true or false depending on whether something exists in the overlap area. Thus, the **I** statement would have logically undetermined truth value. And if the **I** statement is given as true, then the **A** statement could be either true or false depending on whether or not the left-hand part of the *S* circle is empty. Thus, the **A** statement would have logically undetermined truth value. Analogous reasoning applies for the subalternation relation between the **E** and **O** statements.

Testing Immediate Inferences

From the Aristotelian standpoint, the modified Venn diagram technique involving circled X's can be used to test immediate inferences. The only requirement is that the subject and predicate terms of the conclusion be the same as those of the premise. Such inferences depend on the square of opposition and do not involve the operations of conversion, obversion, and contraposition. Venn diagrams can also be used to test inferences involving these latter operations, but a further modification must be introduced.

Since any inference that is valid from the Boolean standpoint is also valid from the Aristotelian standpoint, testing the inference from the Boolean standpoint is often simpler. If the inference is valid, then it is valid from both standpoints. But if the inference is invalid from the Boolean standpoint and has a particular conclusion, then it may be useful to test it from the Aristotelian standpoint. Let us begin by testing an inference *form* for validity:

> All *A* are *B*.
> Therefore, some *A* are *B*.

First, we draw Venn diagrams from the Boolean standpoint for the premise and conclusion:

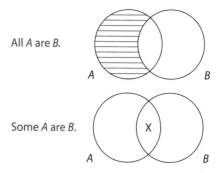

The information of the conclusion diagram is not represented in the premise diagram, so the inference form is not valid from the Boolean standpoint. Thus, noting that the conclusion is particular, we adopt the Aristotelian standpoint and assume for the moment that the subject of the premise (A) denotes at least one existing thing. This thing is represented by placing a circled X in the open area of that circle:

All A are B.

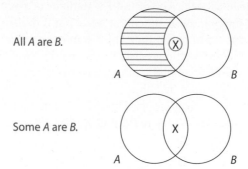

Some A are B.

Now the information of the conclusion diagram *is* represented in the premise diagram. Thus, the inference form is conditionally valid from the Aristotelian standpoint. It is valid on condition that the circled X represents at least one existing thing.

To test a complete inference we begin by testing its form. Here is an example:

No penguins are birds that can fly.
Therefore, it is false that all penguins are birds that can fly.

First, we reduce the immediate inference to its form and test it from the Boolean standpoint:

No P are B.

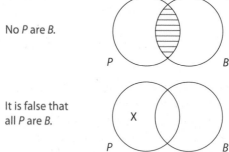

It is false that
all P are B.

Since the inference form is not valid from the Boolean standpoint, we adopt the Aristotelian standpoint and assume for the sake of this test that the subject of the premise (P) denotes at least one existing thing:

No P are B.

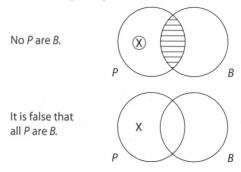

It is false that
all P are B.

The Venn diagrams show that the inference form is conditionally valid from the Aristotelian standpoint. It is valid on condition that the circled X represents at least one existing thing. Since the circled X is in the *P* circle, the final step is to see if the term in the inference corresponding to *P* denotes something that exists. The term in question is "penguins," and at least one penguin actually exists. Thus, the condition is fulfilled, and the inference is valid from the Aristotelian standpoint.

Another example:

> All sugarplum fairies are delicate creatures.
> Therefore, some sugarplum fairies are delicate creatures.

This immediate inference has the same form as the first one we tested. The form is not valid from the Boolean standpoint, but it is conditionally valid from the Aristotelian standpoint:

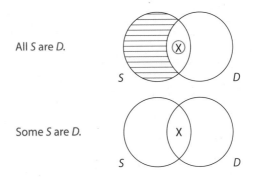

All *S* are *D*.

Some *S* are *D*.

The final step is to see if the circled X represents at least one existing thing. The circled X is in the *S* circle and *S* stands for "sugarplum fairies," which do not exist. Thus, the requisite condition is not fulfilled, and the inference is not valid from the Aristotelian standpoint. The inference commits the existential fallacy from the Aristotelian standpoint.

The steps involved in testing an immediate inference from the Aristotelian standpoint may now be summarized:

1. Reduce the inference to its form and test it from the Boolean standpoint. If the form is valid, proceed no further. The inference is valid from both standpoints.

2. If the inference form is invalid from the Boolean standpoint and has a particular conclusion, then adopt the Aristotelian standpoint and look to see if the left-hand premise circle is partly shaded. If it is, enter a circled X in the unshaded part and retest the form.

3. If the inference form is conditionally valid, determine if the circled X represents something that exists. If it does, the condition is fulfilled, and the inference is valid from the Aristotelian standpoint. If it does not, the inference is invalid, and it commits the existential fallacy from the Aristotelian standpoint.

I. Use the modified Venn diagram technique to determine if the following immediate inference forms are valid from the Boolean standpoint, conditionally valid from the Aristotelian standpoint, or invalid.

★1. Some *A* are not *B*.
Therefore, no *A* are *B*.

2. It is false that some *A* are *B*.
Therefore, it is false that all *A* are *B*.

3. It is false that no *A* are *B*.
Therefore, some *A* are *B*.

★4. All *A* are *B*.
Therefore, it is false that no *A* are *B*.

5. Some *A* are *B*.
Therefore, it is false that some *A* are not *B*.

6. Some *A* are not *B*.
Therefore, it is false that all *A* are *B*.

★7. It is false that some *A* are *B*.
Therefore, no *A* are *B*.

8. It is false that some *A* are not *B*.
Therefore, some *A* are *B*.

9. It is false that all *A* are *B*.
Therefore, no *A* are *B*.

★10. No *A* are *B*.
Therefore, some *A* are not *B*.

II. Use the modified Venn diagram technique to determine if the following immediate inferences are valid from the Boolean standpoint, valid from the Aristotelian standpoint, or invalid. Identify any inferences that commit the existential fallacy from either standpoint.

★1. No summer romances are banal pastimes.
Therefore, it is false that some summer romances are banal pastimes.

2. It is false that some people who hunger for wealth are not victims of their obsession.
Therefore, some people who hunger for wealth are victims of their obsession.

MindTap® Complete exercises online for immediate feedback.

3. No lamps containing genies are ordinary sources of light.
   Therefore, some lamps containing genies are not ordinary sources of light.

★4. It is false that some duck hunters are animal-rights activists.
   Therefore, some duck hunters are not animal-rights activists.

5. All repressive political regimes are insults to human dignity.
   Therefore, no repressive political regimes are insults to human dignity.

6. It is false that all skating rinks are playgrounds for amateurs.
   Therefore, some skating rinks are not playgrounds for amateurs.

★7. All pixies who slide down moonbeams are fun-loving daredevils.
   Therefore, it is false that no pixies who slide down moonbeams are fun-loving daredevils.

8. It is false that some graduate teaching assistants are not underpaid laborers.
   Therefore, it is false that no graduate teaching assistants are underpaid laborers.

9. Some housing projects are developments riddled with crime.
   Therefore, it is false that no housing projects are developments riddled with crime.

★10. It is false that some thunderstorms are quiescent phenomena.
   Therefore, all thunderstorms are quiescent phenomena.

11. No flower gardens are creations that feature skunkweed.
   Therefore, it is false that all flower gardens are creations that feature skunkweed.

12. It is false that no incendiary devices are contraptions that misfire.
   Therefore, some incendiary devices are not contraptions that misfire.

★13. It is false that some pet lovers are people who think that animals are mere machines.
   Therefore, it is false that all pet lovers are people who think that animals are mere machines.

14. No werewolves are creatures who lurk about in the daytime.
   Therefore, it is false that all werewolves are creatures who lurk about in the daytime.

15. Some soccer games are not thrilling events to watch.
   Therefore, no soccer games are thrilling events to watch.

III. Create five new immediate inferences composed of standard-form categorical propositions. Then use the modified Venn diagram technique to test each for validity.

MindTap® Master concepts and improve outcomes with Aplia, at the end of the chapter, in the Aplia folder.

Translating Ordinary Language Statements into Categorical Form

4

Although few statements that occur in ordinary written and oral expression are categorical propositions in standard form, many of them can be translated into standard-form propositions. Such translation has two chief benefits. The first is that the operations and inferences pertinent to standard-form categorical propositions (contrary, subcontrary, etc.) become applicable to these statements. The second is that such statements, once translated, are completely clear and unambiguous as to their meaning. Many statements in ordinary language are susceptible to multiple interpretations, and each interpretation represents one possible mode of translation. The effort to translate such statements discloses the various interpretations and thus helps prevent misunderstanding and confusion.

Translating statements into categorical form is like any other kind of translation in that no set of specific rules will cover every possible form of phraseology. Yet, one general rule always applies: Understand the *meaning* of the given statement, and then reexpress it in a new statement that has a quantifier, subject term, copula, and predicate term. Some of the forms of phraseology that are typically encountered are terms without nouns, nonstandard verbs, singular propositions, adverbs and pronouns, unexpressed and nonstandard quantifiers, conditional statements, exclusive propositions, "the only," and exceptive propositions.

1. Terms Without Nouns

The subject and predicate terms of a categorical proposition must contain either a plural noun or a pronoun that serves to denote the class indicated by the term. Nouns and pronouns denote classes, while adjectives (and participles) connote attributes. If a term consists of only an adjective, a plural noun or pronoun should be introduced to make the term genuinely denotative. Examples:

Some roses are red.   Some roses are red *flowers*.

All tigers are carnivorous.   All tigers are carnivorous *animals*.

2. Nonstandard Verbs

According to the position adopted earlier in this chapter, the only copulas that are allowed in standard-form categorical propositions are "are" and "are not." Statements in ordinary usage, however, often incorporate other forms of the verb "to be." Such statements may be translated as the following examples illustrate:

Some college students will
become educated.

Some college students *are people who*
will become educated.

Some dogs would rather bark
than bite.

Some dogs *are animals that* would rather
bark than bite.

In other statements no form of the verb "to be" occurs at all. These may be translated as the following examples indicate:

Some birds fly south during the
winter.

Some birds *are animals that* fly south
during the winter.

All ducks swim.

All ducks *are swimmers.*

or

All ducks *are animals that* swim.

3. Singular Propositions

A **singular proposition (statement)** is a proposition that makes an assertion about a specific person, place, thing, or time. Singular propositions are typically translated into universals by means of a parameter. A **parameter** is a phrase that, when introduced into a statement, affects the form but not the meaning. Some parameters that may be used to translate singular propositions are these:

people identical to
places identical to
things identical to
cases identical to
times identical to

For example, the statement "Socrates is mortal" may be translated as "All people identical to Socrates are people who are mortal." Because only one person is identical to Socrates, namely Socrates himself, the term "people identical to Socrates" denotes the class that has Socrates as its only member. In other words, it simply denotes Socrates. Such a translation admittedly leaves some of the original information behind, because singular statements usually have existential import, whereas universal statements do not—at least from the Boolean standpoint. But if such translations are interpreted from the Aristotelian standpoint, the existential import is preserved. Here are some examples:

George went home.

All *people identical to* George are *people
who* went home.

Sandra did not go shopping.

No *people identical to* Sandra are *people
who* went shopping.

There is a TV in the bedroom.

All *places identical to* the bedroom
are *places* there is a TV.

or

Some TVs are *things* in the bedroom.

The moon is full tonight.	All *things identical to* the moon are *things that* are full tonight.
	or
	All *times identical to* tonight are *times* the moon is full.
I hate gin.	All *people identical to* me are *people who* hate gin.
	or
	All *things identical to* gin are *things that* I hate.

In translating singular statements, note that the parameter "people identical to" is *not* the same as "people similar to" or "people like." There may be many people *like* Socrates, but there is only one person *identical to* Socrates. Also note that parameters should *not* be used when the term in question already has a plural noun (or pronoun) that denotes the intended class. Such use is not wrong, technically, but it is redundant. Example:

| Diamonds are carbon allotropes. | *Correct:* | All diamonds are carbon allotropes. |
| | *Redundant:* | All things identical to diamonds are things identical to carbon allotropes. |

4. Adverbs and Pronouns

When a statement contains a spatial adverb such as "where," "wherever," "anywhere," "everywhere," or "nowhere," or a temporal adverb such as "when," "whenever," "anytime," "always," or "never," it may be translated in terms of "places" or "times," respectively. Statements containing pronouns such as "who," "whoever," "anyone," "what," "whatever," or "anything" may be translated in terms of "people" or "things," respectively. Examples:

He always wears a suit to work.	All *times* he goes to work are *times* he wears a suit.
He is always clean shaven.	All *times* are *times* he is clean shaven.
She never brings her lunch to school.	No *times* she goes to school are *times* she brings her lunch.
Nowhere on earth are there any unicorns.	No *places* on earth are *places* there are unicorns.
Whoever works hard will succeed.	All *people* who work hard are *people* who will succeed.
Whenever he wins he celebrates.	All *times* he wins are *times* he celebrates.

She goes where she chooses.	All *places* she chooses to go are *places* she goes.
She does what she wants.	All *things* she wants to do are *things* she does.

Notice the order of the subject and predicate terms in the last four examples. When translating statements such as these it is often easy to confuse the subject term with the predicate term. However, since these statements are all translated as **A** type categorical propositions, such a mix-up amounts to committing the fallacy of illicit conversion. To prevent it from happening, keep this rule in mind: For "W" words ("who," "what," "when," "where," "whoever," "whatever," "whenever," "wherever"), the language following the "W" word goes into the subject term of the categorical proposition.

5. Unexpressed Quantifiers

Many statements in ordinary usage have quantifiers that are implied but not expressed. In introducing the quantifiers one must be guided by the most probable meaning of the statement. Examples:

Emeralds are green gems.	*All* emeralds are green gems.
There are lions in the zoo.	*Some* lions are animals in the zoo.
A tiger is a mammal.	*All* tigers are mammals.
A fish is not a mammal.	*No* fish are mammals.
A tiger roared.	*Some* tigers are animals that roared.
Children are human beings.	*All* children are human beings.
Children live next door.	*Some* children are people who live next door.

6. Nonstandard Quantifiers

In some ordinary language statements, the quantity is indicated by words other than the three standard-form quantifiers. Such words include "few," "a few," "not every," "anyone," and various other forms. Another problem occurs when the quantifier "all" is combined with the copula "are not." As we have already seen, statements of the form "All S are not P" are *not* standard-form categorical propositions. Depending on their meaning, they should be translated as either "No S are P" or "Some S are not P." When the intended meaning is "Some S are not P," the meaning may be indicated by placing oral emphasis on the word "all." For example, "*All* athletes are not superstars" means "Some athletes are not superstars." Here are some additional examples:

A few soldiers are heroes.	*Some* soldiers are heroes.
Anyone who votes is a citizen.	*All* voters are citizens.
Not everyone who votes is a Democrat.	*Some* voters are not Democrats.

Not a single dog is a cat.	*No* dogs are cats.
All newborns are not able to talk.	*No* newborns are people able to talk.
All prisoners are not violent.	*Some* prisoners are not violent people.
Many entertainers are comedians	*Some* entertainers are comedians.
Several demonstrators were arrested.	*Some* demonstrators are people who were arrested.
Few sailors entered the regatta.	*Some* sailors are people who entered the regatta *and some* sailors are not people who entered the regatta.

Notice that this last statement beginning with "few" cannot be translated as a single categorical proposition. Such statements (and some beginning with "a few") must be translated as a compound arrangement of an **I** proposition and an **O** proposition. Statements beginning with "almost all" and "not quite all" must be handled in the same way. When these statements occur in arguments, the arguments must be treated in the same way as those containing exceptive propositions, which will be discussed shortly.

7. Conditional Statements

When the antecedent and consequent of a conditional statement refer to the same class of things, the statement can usually be translated into categorical form. Such statements are always translated as universals. Language following the word "if" goes in the subject term of the categorical proposition, and language following "only if" goes in the predicate term. Examples:

If it's a mouse, then it's a mammal.	All mice are mammals.
If a bear is hungry, then it is dangerous.	All hungry bears are dangerous animals.
Jewelry is expensive if it is made of gold.	All pieces of jewelry made of gold are expensive things.
A car is a Camry only if it's a Toyota.	All Camrys are Toyotas.

Conditional statements having a negated consequent are usually best translated as **E** propositions. Examples:

If it's a turkey, then it's not a mammal.	No turkeys are mammals.
If an animal has four legs, then it is not a bird.	No four-legged animals are birds.
A knife will cut only if it isn't dull.	No knives that cut are dull knives.

The word "unless" means "if not." Since language following the word "if" goes in the subject, statements containing "unless" are translated as categorical propositions having negated subject terms. Examples:

Tomatoes are edible unless they are spoiled.	All unspoiled tomatoes are edible tomatoes.

| Unless a boy misbehaves he will be treated decently. | All boys who do not misbehave are boys who will be treated decently. |

8. Exclusive Propositions

Many propositions that involve the words "only," "none but," "none except," and "no . . . except" are exclusive propositions. Efforts to translate them into categorical propositions often lead to confusing the subject term with the predicate term. To avoid such confusion keep in mind that language following "only," "none but," "none except," and "no . . . except" goes in the predicate term of the categorical proposition. For example, the statement "Only executives can use the silver elevator" is translated "All people who can use the silver elevator are executives." If it were translated "All executives are people who can use the silver elevator," the translation would be incorrect. Examples:

Only elected officials will attend the convention.	All people who will attend the convention are elected officials.
None but the brave deserve the fair.	All people who deserve the fair are brave people.
No birds except peacocks are proud of their tails.	All birds proud of their tails are peacocks.
He owns only blue-chip stocks.	All stocks he owns are blue-chip stocks.
She invited only wealthy socialites.	All people she invited are wealthy socialites.

For a statement involving "only," "none but," "none except," and "no . . . except" to be a genuinely exclusive proposition, the word that follows these words must be a *plural* noun or pronoun. If the word that follows "only," "none but," or the like designates an *individual*, the statement really asserts two things. For example, the statement "Only Megan painted a picture" asserts that Megan painted a picture *and* that no other person painted a picture. Thus it would be translated as two statements: "All people identical to Megan are people who painted a picture, *and* all people who painted a picture are people identical to Megan." This section of the text will ignore cases where the word following "only," "none but," or the like designates an individual.

Also note that many English statements containing "only" are ambiguous because "only" can be interpreted as modifying alternate words in the statement. Consider, for example, the statement "He only jogs after sunset." Does this mean "He is the only person who jogs after sunset" or "He jogs and does not walk after sunset" or "The only time he jogs is after sunset"? If the statement's context does not provide an answer, the translator is free to pick any of these senses for translation. This same ambiguity, incidentally, affects the last two examples in the earlier list. Accordingly, they might also be translated "All things he owns are blue-chip stocks" and "All socialites she invited are wealthy people."

9. "The Only"

Statements beginning with the words "the only" are translated differently from those beginning with "only." For example, the statement "The only cars that are available are Chevrolets" means "If a car is available, then it is a Chevrolet." This in turn is translated as "All cars that are available are Chevrolets." In other words, language following "the only" goes in the subject term of the categorical proposition. Examples:

The only animals that live in this canyon are skunks.	All animals that live in this canyon are skunks.
Accountants are the only ones who will be hired.	All those who will be hired are accountants.

Statements involving "the only" are similar to those involving "only" in this one respect: When the statement is about an *individual*, two statements are needed to translate it. For example, "The only person who painted a picture is Megan" means that Megan painted a picture, *and* no other person painted a picture. The statement is equivalent in meaning to "Only Megan painted a picture." Thus, it is translated "All people identical to Megan are people who painted a picture, *and* all people who painted a picture are people identical to Megan." Statements involving "the only" that refer to individuals are ignored throughout the remainder of this chapter.

10. Exceptive Propositions

Propositions of the form "All except S are P" and "All but S are P" are exceptive propositions. They must be translated not as single categorical propositions but as pairs of conjoined categorical propositions. Statements that include the phrase "none except," on the other hand, are exclusive (not exceptive) propositions. "None except" is synonymous with "none but." Here are some examples of exceptive propositions:

All except students are invited.	No students are invited people, and all nonstudents are invited people.
All but managers must report to the president.	No managers are people who must report to the president, and all nonmanagers are people who must report to the president.

Because exceptive propositions cannot be translated into single categorical propositions, many of the simple inferences and operations pertinent to categorical propositions cannot be applied to them. Arguments that contain exceptive propositions as premises or conclusion can be evaluated only through the application of extended techniques. This topic is taken up in the next chapter.

Key word (to be eliminated)	Translation hint
whoever, wherever, always, anyone, never, etc.	use "all" together with people, places, times
a few, several, many	use "some"
if . . . then	use "all" or "no"
unless	use "if not"
only, none but, none except, no . . . except	use "all"
the only	use "all"
all but, all except, few	two statements required
not every, not all	use "some . . . are not"
there is, there are	use "some"

Rule for A propositions

Language following these words goes in the subject term: "if," "the only," and "W" words ("who," "what," "when," "where," "whoever," "whatever," "whenever," "wherever").

Language following these words goes in the predicate term: "only if," "only," "none but," "none except," and "no . . . except."

MindTap® Strengthen your understanding of the topic with the section's **Video Lectures**.

EXERCISE 4.7

I. Translate the following into standard-form categorical propositions.

★1. Any bank that makes too many risky loans will fail.

2. Temporary workers are not eligible for fringe benefits.

3. Terrorist attacks succeed whenever security measures are lax.

★4. Bromine is extractable from seawater.

5. Not all guilt feelings are psychological aberrations.

MindTap® Complete exercises online for immediate feedback.

6. Every jazz fan admires Duke Ellington.

★7. If it's a halogen, then it isn't chemically inert.

8. A television show that depicts violence incites violence.

9. Manipulators do not make good marriage partners.

★10. None but pirate ships fly the Jolly Roger.

11. She gains weight whenever she's depressed.

12. She's depressed whenever she gains weight.

★13. A man is a bachelor only if he is unmarried.

14. Warmth always relieves pain.

15. Joseph J. Thomson discovered the electron.

★16. A few organic silicones are used as lubricants.

17. Only nuclear-powered vehicles are suitable for deep-space exploration.

18. Comets are the only heavenly bodies with tails.

★19. There is a giant star in the Tarantula Nebula.

20. If an activity emits methane, then it contributes to climate change.

21. No shellfish except oysters make pearls.

★22. Only diabetics require insulin treatments.

23. The electroscope is a device for detecting static electricity.

24. Occasionally there are concerts in Central Park.

★25. Berlin was the setting for the 1936 Olympic Games.

26. The Kentucky Derby is never run in January.

27. The only way to get rid of a temptation is to yield to it.

★28. Where there's smoke, there's fire.

29. Lunar eclipses do not occur unless the moon is full.

30. Radio transmissions are disrupted whenever sunspot activity increases.

★31. If an ore isn't radioactive, then it isn't pitchblende.

32. All but the rats left the sinking ship.

33. A pesticide is dangerous if it contains DDT.

★34. John Grisham writes only novels about lawyers.

35. He who hesitates is lost.

36. Modern corporations are all run in the interest of their managers.

★37. Unless the sun is shining, a rainbow cannot occur.

38. Whoever suffers allergic reactions has a weakened immune system.

39. All fruits except pineapples ripen after they are picked.

★40. Few corporate raiders are known for their integrity.

41. Monkeys are found in the jungles of Guatemala.

42. Monkeys are mammals.

★43. I like strawberries.

44. All passengers are not allowed to smoke on board the aircraft.

45. All flowers are not fragrant.

★46. Cynthia travels where she wants.

47. Bats are the only true flying mammals.

48. Not every river runs to the sea.

★49. Physicists do not understand the operation of superconductors.

50. Many apartment dwellers are victimized by noise.

51. There are forced labor camps in China.

★52. Whatever increases efficiency improves profitability.

53. Dolphins are swimming between the breakers.

54. Feathers are not heavy.

★55. Few picnics are entirely free of ants.

56. A civil right is unalienable if it is a human right.

57. She says what she pleases.

★58. Several contestants won prizes.

59. An animal is a feline only if it is a cat.

60. Renee does whatever she is told to do.

II. The following exercises contain typical mistakes that students make in attempting to translate statements into standard form. Correct the errors and redundancies in these attempted translations.

★1. Some of the figure-skating finalists are performers who are athletes that may win medals.

2. All cars identical to BMWs are the only cars that young lawyers drive.

3. All vertebrates except cartilaginous fishes are animals with a bony skeleton.

★4. No downhill skiers are effective competitors if they suffer from altitude sickness.

5. All substances like cobalt are things that are substances identical to ferromagnetic metals.

6. No people identical to nuclear pacifists are people who believe a just war is possible.

★7. All people identical to matadors are not performers who succumb easily to fear.

8. All companies identical to Google are looking forward to a bright future.

9. No toxic dumps are ecological catastrophes unless they leak.

★10. All crocodiles are things identical to dangerous animals when they are hungry.

III. Translate the premise and conclusion of the following immediate inferences into standard-form categorical propositions. Then use conversion, obversion, contraposition, or the traditional square of opposition to determine whether each is valid or invalid. For those that are invalid, name the fallacy committed.

★1. Flu vaccines are never completely effective.
Therefore, not every flu vaccine is completely effective.

2. Only diamonds are a girl's best friend.
Therefore, every diamond is a girl's best friend.

3. A child destined to succeed in life has high self-esteem.
Therefore, a child with low self-esteem is not destined to succeed in life.

★4. If a date is a good dinner companion, then she does not spend every minute texting. Therefore, if a date does not spend every minute texting, then she is not a bad dinner companion.

5. There are banks that engage in money laundering.
Therefore, there are banks that do not engage in money laundering.

6. Not a single major storm fails to cause flight cancellations.
Therefore, every major storm causes flight cancellations.

★7. Tax cuts never please everyone.
Therefore, every tax cut pleases everyone.

8. Military exercises are sometimes condemned by opponents.
Therefore, any military exercise is condemned by opponents.

9. It is false that not a single charter school is an academic underperformer.
Therefore, several charter schools are academic underperformers.

★10. Fake artworks are sold on eBay.
Therefore, a few items sold on eBay are fake artworks.

IV. Create a total of fifteen new categorical propositions (not in standard form) that may be described as follows:

1. One contains a term without a noun.

2. One contains the nonstandard verb "will."

3. One begins with the name "Margie."

4. One contains the adverb "never."

5. One contains the pronoun "whoever."

6. One contains an unexpressed quantifier.

7. One begins with the words "not everyone."

8. One begins with the word "few."

9. One begins with the words "a few."

10. One is a conditional (if . . . then) statement.

11. One contains the word "unless."

12. One begins with the word "only."

13. One begins with the words "no . . . except."

14. One begins with the words "the only."

15. One begins with the words "all except."

Finally, translate each of these new statements into one or more standard-form categorical propositions.

4

MindTap® Master concepts and improve outcomes with Aplia, at the end of the chapter, in the Aplia folder.

Summary

Categorical Proposition: A proposition that relates two classes (or categories). Standard-form categorical propositions occur in four forms and are identified by letter names:

- **A**: All S are P.
- **E**: No S are P.
- **I**: Some S are P.
- **O**: Some S are not P.

Every standard-form categorical proposition has four components:

- Quantifier ("all," "no," "some")
- Subject term
- Copula ("are," "are not")
- Predicate term

The *quality* of a categorical proposition:

- Affirmative (All S are P, Some S are P.)
- Negative (No S are P, Some S are not P.)

The *quantity* of a categorical proposition:

- Universal (All S are P, No S are P.)
- Particular (Some S are P, Some P are not P.)

MindTap® Need help? See the Learning Logic folder at the end of the chapter: the self-paced tutorial walks you through any section.
Prepare for exams with the Chapter Test.

The subject and predicate terms are distributed if the proposition makes an assertion about every member of the class denoted by the term; otherwise, undistributed:

- **A**: Subject term is distributed.
- **E**: Subject and predicate terms are distributed.
- **I**: Neither term is distributed.
- **O**: Predicate term is distributed.

Universal (**A** and **E**) propositions allow for two different interpretations:

- Aristotelian: Universal propositions about existing things have existential import.
- Boolean: Universal propositions have no existential import.

The modern square of opposition is a diagram that represents necessary inferences from the Boolean standpoint:

- **A** and **O** propositions contradict each other.
- **E** and **I** propositions contradict each other.

The content of categorical propositions may be represented by two-circle Venn diagrams:

- Shading an area indicates that the area is empty.
- Entering an X in an area means that the area is not empty.

Using Venn diagrams to test an immediate inference:

- Enter the content of the premise and conclusion in separate Venn diagrams.
- See if the content of the conclusion diagram is contained in the premise diagram.

Three operations that sometimes yield logically equivalent results:

- Conversion: Switch *S* and *P*. Logically equivalent results for **E**, **I**.
- Obversion: Change the quality, replace *P* with its term complement. Logically equivalent results for **A**, **E**, **I**, **O**.
- Contraposition: Switch *S* and *P*, replace *S* and *P* with term complements. Logically equivalent results for **A**, **O**.

Two formal fallacies may occur when these operations are used to derive conclusions:

- Illicit conversion: Performing conversion on an **A** or **O** premise.
- Illicit contraposition: Performing contraposition on an **E** or **I** premise.

The traditional square of opposition applies to categorical propositions when the Aristotelian standpoint is adopted and the subject term refers to existing things:

- Contrary: Holds between **A** and **E**. At least one is false.
- Subcontrary: Holds between **I** and **O**. At least one is true.
- Subalternation: Holds between **A** and **I** and between **E** and **O**. Truth flows downward and falsity flows upward.
- Contradiction: Holds as in the modern square.

Three formal fallacies may occur when the traditional square is used to derive conclusions:

- Illicit contrary: Results from an incorrect application of Contrary.
- Illicit subcontrary: Results from an incorrect application of Subcontrary.
- Illicit subalternation: Results from an incorrect application of Subalternation.

Existential fallacy: Occurs when Contrary, Subcontrary, or Subalternation are used on premises whose subject terms refer to nonexistent things.

Venn diagrams may be modified to apply to the Aristotelian standpoint:
- For **A** and **E**: Enter a circled X in the unshaded part of the subject circle.
- The circled X represents the temporary assumption of existence.
- May be used to prove the traditional square and test immediate inferences.

Translation: Propositions not in standard form may be put into standard form.
- Translation must have a proper quantifier, subject term, copula, predicate term.
- Translate singular propositions by using a parameter.
- Translate adverbs and pronouns by using "persons," "places," "things," "times."
- For **A** propositions:
  - Language following "if," "the only," and "W" words goes in the subject term.
  - Language following "only if," "only," "none but," "none except," and "no ... except" goes in the predicate term.

5 Categorical Syllogisms

- **5.1** Standard Form, Mood, and Figure
- **5.2** Venn Diagrams
- **5.3** Rules and Fallacies
- **5.4** Reducing the Number of Terms
- **5.5** Ordinary Language Arguments
- **5.6** Enthymemes
- **5.7** Sorites

5.1 Standard Form, Mood, and Figure

HOW LOGICAL ARE YOU? Consider these four groups of words:

1. Lion, lion, bear
2. Dog, dog, cat
3. Snake, spider, snake
4. Mouse, mouse, rabbit

Which one of these groups can be considered "wrong"? Why is it wrong?

Find the answer on MindTap.

In the general sense of the term, a **syllogism** is a deductive argument consisting of two premises and one conclusion. Provisionally we will define a *categorical syllogism* as a syllogism consisting of three categorical propositions and containing a total of three different terms, each of which appears twice in distinct propositions. (We will give a more precise definition shortly.) The following argument is a categorical syllogism:

> All soldiers are patriots.
> No traitors are patriots.
> Therefore, no traitors are soldiers.

MindTap   Read, study, reflect, and prepare for exams online, anytime, anywhere.

Each of the three terms in a categorical syllogism has its own name depending on its position in the argument. The **major term**, by definition, is the predicate of the conclusion, and the **minor term** is the subject of the conclusion. The **middle term**, which provides the middle ground between the two premises, is the one that occurs once in each premise and does not occur in the conclusion. Thus, for the argument just given, the major term is "soldiers," the minor term is "traitors," and the middle term is "patriots."

The premises of a categorical syllogism also have their own names. The **major premise**, by definition, is the one that contains the major term, and the **minor premise** is the one that contains the minor term. Thus, in the syllogism just given the major premise is "All soldiers are patriots," and the minor premise is "No traitors are patriots." Now that we are supplied with these definitions, we may proceed to the idea of standard form. A **standard-form categorical syllogism** is one that meets the following four conditions:

1. All three statements are standard-form categorical propositions.

2. The two occurrences of each term are identical.

3. Each term is used in the same sense throughout the argument.

4. The major premise is listed first, the minor premise second, and the conclusion last.

The first condition requires that each statement have a proper quantifier, subject term, copula, and predicate term. The second condition is clear. The third rules out the possibility of equivocation. For example, if a syllogism containing the word "men" used that term in the sense of human beings in one statement and in the sense of male human beings in another statement, the syllogism would really contain more than three terms and would therefore not be in standard form. Finally, the fourth condition merely requires that the three statements be listed in the right order.

The syllogism about soldiers is in standard form because all four conditions are fulfilled. However, the following syllogism is not in standard form, because the fourth condition is violated:

All watercolors are paintings.
Some watercolors are masterpieces.
Therefore, some paintings are masterpieces.

To put this syllogism into standard form the order of the premises must be reversed. The major premise (the one containing "masterpieces," which is the predicate term in the conclusion) must be listed first, and the minor premise (the one containing "paintings," which is the subject term in the conclusion) must be listed second.

Standard form of a syllogism

1. Quantifier _____ copula _____ { Major premise (contains major term)
2. Quantifier _____ copula _____ { Minor premise (contains minor term)
3. Quantifier _____ copula _____ { Conclusion
       Minor   Major
       term   term

Now that we have a definition of standard-form categorical syllogism, we can give a more precise definition of categorical syllogism. A **categorical syllogism** is a deductive argument consisting of three categorical propositions that is capable of being translated into standard form. For an argument to qualify as a categorical syllogism, all three statements need not be standard-form categorical propositions; but if they are, the analysis is greatly simplified. For this reason, all of the syllogisms presented in the first four sections of this chapter will consist of statements that are in standard form. In later sections, techniques will be developed for translating non-standard-form syllogisms into equivalent arguments that are in standard form.

After a categorical syllogism has been put into standard form, its validity or invalidity may be determined through mere inspection of the form. The individual form of a syllogism consists of two factors: mood and figure. The **mood** of a categorical syllogism consists of the letter names of the propositions that make it up. For example, if the major premise is an **A** proposition, the minor premise an **O** proposition, and the conclusion an **E** proposition, the mood is **AOE**. To determine the mood of a categorical syllogism, one must first put the syllogism into standard form; the letter name of the statements may then be noted to the side of each. The mood of the syllogism is then designated by the order of these letters, reading the letter for the major premise first, the letter for the minor premise second, and the letter for the conclusion last.

The **figure** of a categorical syllogism is determined by the location of the two occurrences of the middle term in the premises. Four different arrangements are possible. If we let S represent the subject of the conclusion (minor term), P the predicate of the conclusion (major term), and M the middle term, and leave out the quantifiers and copulas, the four possible arrangements may be illustrated as follows:

Figure 1		Figure 2		Figure 3		Figure 4	
Ⓜ	P	P	Ⓜ	Ⓜ	P	P	Ⓜ
S	Ⓜ	S	Ⓜ	Ⓜ	S	Ⓜ	S
S	P	S	P	S	P	S	P

In the first figure the middle term is top left, bottom right; in the second, top right, bottom right, and so on. Example:

> No painters are sculptors.
> Some sculptors are artists.
> Therefore, some artists are not painters.

This syllogism is in standard form. The mood is **EIO** and the figure is four. The form of the syllogism is therefore designated as **EIO-4**.

To remember how the four figures are defined, imagine the four possible arrangements of the middle term as depicting the outline of a shirt collar:

The only problem with this device is that it may lead you to confuse the second figure with the third. To avoid this confusion, keep in mind that for these two figures the S and P terms go on the same "collar flap" as the middle term. These terms are represented by the X's in the diagram. Thus, for Figure 2, the occurrences of the middle term are on the right side of the syllogism, and for Figure 3 they are on the left.

Since there are four kinds of categorical propositions and there are three categorical propositions in a categorical syllogism, there are 64 possible moods ($4 \times 4 \times 4 = 64$). And since there are four different figures, there are 256 different forms of categorical syllogisms ($4 \times 64 = 256$).

Once the mood and figure of a syllogism is known, the validity of the syllogism can be determined by checking the mood and figure against a list of valid syllogistic forms. To do this, first adopt the Boolean standpoint and see if the syllogism's form appears in the following table of unconditionally valid forms. If it does, the syllogism is valid from the Boolean standpoint. In other words, it is valid regardless of whether its terms denote actually existing things.

Unconditionally Valid Forms

Figure 1	Figure 2	Figure 3	Figure 4
AAA	EAE	IAI	AEE
EAE	AEE	AII	IAI
AII	EIO	OAO	EIO
EIO	AOO	EIO	

If the syllogism does not appear on the list of unconditionally valid forms, then adopt the Aristotelian standpoint and see if the syllogism's form appears in the following table of conditionally valid forms. If it does, the syllogism is valid from the Aristotelian standpoint on condition that a certain term (the "critical" term) denotes actually existing things. The required condition is stated in the last column.

Conditionally Valid Forms

Figure 1	Figure 2	Figure 3	Figure 4	Required condition
AAI	AEO		AEO	S exists
EAO	EAO			
		AAI	EAO	M exists
		EAO		
			AAI	P exists

For example, the **AAI**-1 is valid from the Aristotelian standpoint if the subject of the conclusion (the minor term) denotes actually existing things. The **EAO**-3 is valid if the middle term denotes actually existing things. Thus, if we are given an **AAI**-1 syllogism and the minor term is "cats," then the syllogism is valid from the Aristotelian standpoint. But if the minor term is "unicorns," then the syllogism is invalid. On the other hand, if the minor term is "students who failed the exam" and we are not certain if there are any such students, then the syllogism is conditionally valid.

The relationship between the Aristotelian standpoint and the Boolean standpoint is illustrated in the following bar graph:

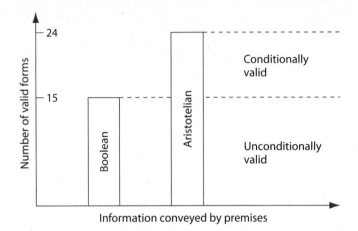

The graph shows that when the premises of a syllogistic form are recognized as conveying information about existence, an additional nine forms become valid.

Interestingly, during the Middle Ages logic students used to memorize a little poem that served as a rule of thumb for distinguishing valid from invalid syllogisms. The vowels in the words identified the mood, and the words "prioris," "secundae," and so on the figure.*

> Barbara, Celarent, Darii, Ferioque prioris;
> Cesare, Camestres, Festino, Baroco secundae;
> Tertia, Darapti, Disamis, Datisi, Felapton,
> Bocardo, Ferison habet: quarta insuper addit
> Bramantip, Camenes, Dimaris, Fesapo, Fresison.

For example, the "Barbara" syllogism (this designation is still encountered today) is **AAA**-1, "Celarent" is **EAE**-1, and so on. This poem conforms substantially to the two tables given earlier, except that five forms have been left out. The reason these forms were left out is that the logicians of that time considered them weak: They draw a particular conclusion from premises that would support a (stronger) universal conclusion. For example, the weaker **AAI**-1 is left out in favor of the stronger **AAA**-1. Needless to say, few students today depend on this poem to distinguish valid from invalid syllogisms.

We have seen how, given the syllogism, we can obtain the mood and figure. But sometimes we need to go in the reverse direction: from the mood and figure to the

---

*This poem appears for the first time in William of Sherwood's Introductiones in Logicam, written ca. 1260, but it was probably not originally composed by him. See William Kneale and Martha Kneale, Development of Logic (Oxford: Clarendon Press, 1962), 232.

syllogistic form. Suppose we are given the form **EIO**-4. To reconstruct the syllogistic form is easy. First use the mood to determine the skeleton of the form:

E	No _____ are _____.
I	Some _____ are _____.
O	Some _____ are not _____.

Then use the figure to determine the arrangement of the middle terms:

E	No _____ are M.
I	Some M are _____.
O	Some _____ are not _____.

Finally, supply the major and minor terms, using the letters S and P to designate the subject and predicate of the conclusion. The predicate of the conclusion is always repeated in the first premise, and the subject of the conclusion is repeated in the second premise:

E	No P are M.
I	Some M are S.
O	Some S are not P.

5

EXERCISE 5.1

I. The following syllogisms are in standard form. Identify the major, minor, and middle terms, as well as the mood and figure of each. Then use the two lists of valid syllogistic forms to determine whether each is valid from the Boolean standpoint, valid from the Aristotelian standpoint, or invalid.

★1. All neutron stars are things that produce intense gravity.
All neutron stars are extremely dense objects.
Therefore, all extremely dense objects are things that produce intense gravity.

2. No insects that eat mosquitoes are insects that should be killed.
All dragonflies are insects that eat mosquitoes.
Therefore, no dragonflies are insects that should be killed.

3. No environmentally produced diseases are inherited afflictions.
Some psychological disorders are not inherited afflictions.
Therefore, some psychological disorders are environmentally produced diseases.

★4. No people who mix fact with fantasy are good witnesses.
Some hypnotized people are people who mix fact with fantasy.
Therefore, some hypnotized people are not good witnesses.

MindTap® Complete exercises online for immediate feedback.

5. All ozone molecules are good absorbers of ultraviolet rays.
   All ozone molecules are things destroyed by chlorine.
   Therefore, some things destroyed by chlorine are good absorbers of ultraviolet rays.

II. Put the following syllogisms into standard form, using letters to represent the terms, and name the mood and figure. Then use the two lists of valid syllogistic forms to determine whether each is valid from the Boolean standpoint, valid from the Aristotelian standpoint, or invalid.

★1. No Republicans are Democrats, so no Republicans are big spenders, since all big spenders are Democrats.

2. Some latchkey children are not kids who can stay out of trouble, for some youngsters prone to boredom are latchkey children, and no kids who can stay out of trouble are youngsters prone to boredom.

3. No rent-control proposals are regulations welcomed by landlords, and all regulations welcomed by landlords are measures that allow a free hand in raising rents. Therefore, some rent-control proposals are measures that allow a free hand in raising rents.

★4. Some insects that feed on milkweed are not foods suitable for birds, inasmuch as no monarch butterflies are foods suitable for birds and all monarch butterflies are insects that feed on milkweed.

5. No undocumented individuals are people who have a right to welfare payments, and some migrant workers are undocumented individuals. Thus, some people who have a right to welfare payments are migrant workers.

6. Some African nations are not countries deserving military aid, because some African nations are not upholders of human rights, and all countries deserving military aid are upholders of human rights.

★7. All pranksters are exasperating individuals, consequently some leprechauns are exasperating individuals, since all leprechauns are pranksters.

8. Some racists are not people suited to be immigration officials, given that some humanitarians are not people suited to be immigration officials, and no humanitarians are racists.

9. No people who respect human life are terrorists, and all airline hijackers are terrorists. Hence, no airline hijackers are people who respect human life.

★10. Some silicates are crystalline substances, because all silicates are oxygen compounds, and some oxygen compounds are not crystalline substances.

III. Reconstruct the syllogistic forms from the following combinations of mood and figure:

★1. OAE-3

2. EIA-4

3. AII-3

★4. **IAE**-1

5. **AOO**-2

6. **EAO**-4

★7. **AAA**-1

8. **EAO**-2

9. **OEI**-3

★10. **OEA**-4

IV. Construct the following syllogisms.

★1. An **EIO**-2 syllogism with these terms—*major*—dogmatists; *minor*—theologians; *middle*—scholars who encourage freethinking.

2. An unconditionally valid syllogism in the first figure with a particular affirmative conclusion and these terms: *major*—people incapable of objectivity; *minor*—Supreme Court justices; *middle*—lockstep ideologues.

3. An unconditionally valid syllogism in the fourth figure having two universal premises and these terms: *major*—teenage suicides; *minor*—heroic episodes; *middle*—tragic occurrences.

★4. A valid syllogism having mood **OAO** and these terms: *major*—things capable of replicating by themselves; *minor*—structures that invade cells; *middle*—viruses.

5. A valid syllogism in the first figure having a universal negative conclusion and these terms: *major*—guarantees of marital happiness; *minor*—prenuptial agreements; *middle*—legally enforceable documents.

V. Answer "true" or "false" to the following statements:

1. Every syllogism is a categorical syllogism.

2. Some categorical syllogisms cannot be put into standard form.

3. The statements in a categorical syllogism need not be expressed in standard form.

4. The statements in a standard-form categorical syllogism need not be expressed in standard form.

5. In a standard-form categorical syllogism the two occurrences of each term must be identical.

6. The major premise of a standard-form categorical syllogism contains the subject of the conclusion.

7. To determine its mood and figure, a categorical syllogism must first be put into standard form.

8. In a standard-form syllogism having Figure 2, the two occurrences of the middle term are on the right.

9. The unconditionally valid syllogistic forms are valid from both the Boolean and the Aristotelian standpoints.

10. The conditionally valid syllogistic forms are invalid if the requisite condition is not fulfilled.

MindTap® Master concepts and improve outcomes with Aplia, at the end of the chapter, in the Aplia folder.

5.2   Venn Diagrams

HOW LOGICAL ARE YOU? Imagine you are preparing a pizza for a group of individuals. Some want only cheese. Some want only pepperoni. Some want only veggies. Some want cheese and pepperoni. Some want cheese and veggies. Draw a diagram illustrating the simplest arrangement of these toppings.

Find the answer on MindTap.

Venn diagrams provide the most intuitively evident and, in the long run, easiest to remember technique for testing the validity of categorical syllogisms. The technique is basically an extension of the one developed in Chapter 4 to represent the informational content of categorical propositions. Because syllogisms contain three terms, whereas propositions contain only two, the application of Venn diagrams to syllogisms requires three overlapping circles.

These circles should be drawn so that seven areas are clearly distinguishable within the diagram. The second step is to label the circles, one for each term. The precise order of the labeling is not critical, but we will adopt the convention of always assigning the lower-left circle to the subject of the conclusion, the lower-right circle to the predicate of the conclusion, and the top circle to the middle term. This convention is easy to remember because it conforms to the arrangement of the terms in a standard-form syllogism: The subject of the conclusion is on the lower left, the predicate of the conclusion is on the lower right, and the middle term is in the premises, above the conclusion.*

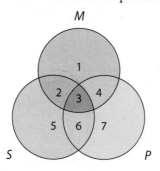

Some textbooks present three-circle Venn diagrams with two circles on the top and one on the bottom. In our discussions we will present them the way John Venn himself drew them, with two circles on the bottom and one on the top. See his Symbolic Logic (London: Macmillan, 1881), 105, 114, 116.

Anything in the area marked "1" is an *M* but neither an *S* nor a *P*, anything in the area marked "2" is both an *S* and an *M* but not a *P*, anything in the area marked "3" is a member of all three classes, and so on.

The test procedure consists of transferring the information content of the premises to the diagram and then inspecting the diagram to see whether it necessarily implies the truth of the conclusion. If the information in the diagram does do this, the argument is valid; otherwise it is invalid.

The use of Venn diagrams to evaluate syllogisms usually requires a little practice at first. Perhaps the best way of learning the technique is through illustrative examples, but a few pointers are needed first:

1. Marks (shading or placing an X) are entered only for the premises. No marks are made for the conclusion.

2. If the argument contains one universal premise, this premise should be entered first in the diagram. If there are two universal premises, either one can be done first.

3. When entering the information contained in a premise, one should concentrate on the circles corresponding to the two terms in the statement. While the third circle cannot be ignored altogether, it should be given only minimal attention.

4. When inspecting a completed diagram to see whether it supports a particular conclusion, one should remember that particular statements assert two things. "Some *S* are *P*" means "At least one *S* exists *and* that *S* is a *P*"; "Some *S* are not *P*" means "At least one *S* exists *and* that *S* is not a *P*."

5. When shading an area, one must be careful to shade *all* of the area in question. Examples:

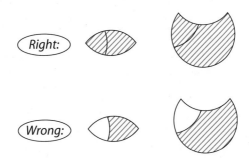

6. The area where an X goes is always initially divided into two parts. If one of these parts has already been shaded, the X goes in the unshaded part. Examples:

John Venn 1834–1923

John Venn is known mainly for his circle diagrams, which have contributed to work in many areas of mathematics and logic, including computer science, set theory, and statistics. His book *The Logic of Chance* (1866) advanced probability theory by introducing the relative frequency interpretation of probability; it significantly influenced later developments in statistical theory as well. In *Symbolic Logic* (1881) he defended George Boole against various critics and rendered the new logic intelligible to nonmathematical thinkers. Finally, in *The Principles of Empirical and Inductive Logic* (1889) he criticized Mill's methods of induction as being of limited application as an engine of discovery in science.

John Venn was born in Hull, England, the son of Henry Venn, the Drypool parish rector, and Martha Sykes Venn, who died when John was a child. The Venns were prominent members of the evangelical movement within the Church of England. John Venn's grandfather had been an evangelical leader, as was his father, whom his contemporaries regarded as the head of the evangelical movement. His father served for many years in an administrative capacity for the Church Missionary Society, and John was expected to follow in the family tradition. In 1858, after graduating from Gonville and Caius (pronounced "keys") College, Cambridge, he was ordained and served for a time as a curate in parishes near London.

Perhaps owing to his contact with Henry Sidgwick and other Cambridge agnostics, Venn's confidence in the Thirty-Nine Articles of the Church of England began to erode. Also, as a result of his reading the works of De Morgan, Boole, and Mill, his interest shifted almost totally from theological matters to issues related to logic. At age twenty-eight, Venn returned to Cambridge to become a lecturer in logic and probability theory. Five years later, he married Susanna Carnegie Edmonstone,

the daughter of an Anglican cleric, and they had one child, John Archibald Venn. In 1883, at age forty-nine, Venn became a fellow of the Royal Society and received the degree of Doctor of Science.

The greater part of Venn's life centered completely on his association with Cambridge. In 1857 he became a fellow of Caius, and he remained a member of the college foundation for sixty-six years, until his death. During the last twenty years of his life he served as college president, during which time he wrote a history of the college. Also, in collaboration with his son, he completed Part 1 of the massive *Alumni Cantabrigienses*, which contains short biographies of 76,000 graduates and office-holders ranging from the university's earliest days through 1751.

John Venn's son said of his father that he was a "fine walker and mountain climber." Also, in keeping with his view that abstract subjects such as logic and mathematics ought to serve practical utility, Venn loved to use this knowledge to build machines. He invented a cricket bowling machine that was used against the best batsman of an Australian team. The machine "clean bowled" this batsman four times. Today Venn is memorialized by a stained-glass window in the dining hall of Caius College that contains a representation of a Venn diagram.

If one of the two parts is not shaded, the X goes on the line separating the two parts. Examples:

This means that the X may be in either (or both) of the two areas—but it is not known which one.

7. An X should never be placed in such a way that it dangles outside of the diagram, and it should never be placed on the intersection of two lines.

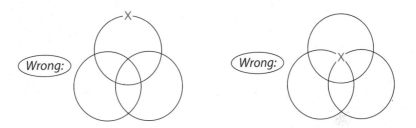

Boolean Standpoint

Because the Boolean standpoint does not recognize universal premises as having existential import, its approach to testing syllogisms is simpler and more general than that of the Aristotelian standpoint. Hence, we will begin by testing syllogisms from that standpoint and later proceed to the Aristotelian standpoint. Here is an example:

> 1. No *P* are *M*.   **EAE**-2
>   All *S* are *M*.
>   No *S* are *P*.

Since both premises are universal, it makes no difference which premise we enter first in the diagram. To enter the major premise, we concentrate our attention on the *M* and *P* circles, which are highlighted with color:

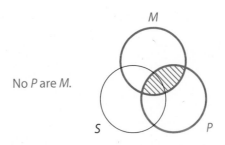

No *P* are *M*.

We now complete the diagram by entering the minor premise. In doing so, we concentrate our attention on the *S* and *M* circles, which are highlighted with color:

All *S* are *M*.

The conclusion states that the area where the *S* and *P* circles overlap is shaded. Inspection of the diagram reveals that this area is indeed shaded, so the syllogistic form is valid. Because the form is valid from the Boolean standpoint, it is *unconditionally valid*. In other words, it is valid regardless of whether its premises are recognized as having existential import.

Here is another example:

2. All *M* are *P.*   **AEE-1**
    No *S* are *M.*
    No *S* are *P.*

Again, both premises are universal, so it makes no difference which premise we enter first in the diagram. To enter the major premise, we concentrate our attention on the *M* and *P* circles:

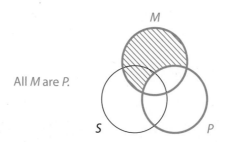

All *M* are *P.*

To enter the minor premise, we concentrate our attention on the *M* and *S* circles:

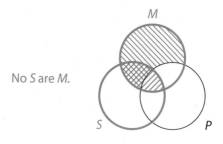

No *S* are *M.*

Again, the conclusion states that the area where the *S* and *P* circles overlap is shaded. Inspection of the diagram reveals that only part of this area is shaded, so the syllogistic form is invalid.

Another example:

3. Some *P* are *M*.   **IAI**-4
   All *M* are *S*.
   Some *S* are *P*.

We enter the universal premise first. To do so, we concentrate our attention on the *M* and *S* circles:

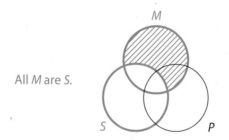

All *M* are *S*.

To enter the particular premise, we concentrate our attention on the *M* and *P* circles. This premise tells us to place an X in the area where the *M* and *P* circles overlap. Because part of this area is shaded, we place the X in the remaining area:

Some *P* are *M*.

The conclusion states that there is an X in the area where the *S* and *P* circles overlap. Inspection of the diagram reveals that there is indeed an X in this area, so the syllogistic form is valid.

The examples that follow are done in a single step.

4. All *P* are *M*.   **AOO**-2
   Some *S* are not *M*.
   Some *S* are not *P*.

The universal premise is entered first. The particular premise tells us to place an X in the part of the S circle that lies outside the M circle. Because part of this area is shaded, we place the X in the remaining area. The conclusion states that there is an X that is inside the S circle but outside the P circle. Inspection of the diagram reveals that there is indeed an X in this area, so the syllogistic form is valid.

5. Some *M* are *P.*   **IAI**-1
   All *S* are *M.*
   Some *S* are *P.*

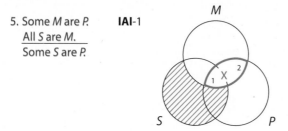

As usual, we enter the universal premise first. In entering the particular premise, we concentrate on the area where the M and P circles overlap. (For emphasis, this area is colored in the diagram.) Because this overlap area is divided into two parts (the areas marked "1" and "2"), we place the X on the line (arc of the S circle) that separates the two parts. The conclusion states that there is an X in the area where the S and P circles overlap. Inspection of the diagram reveals that the single X is dangling outside of this overlap area. We do not know if it is in or out. Thus, the syllogistic form is invalid.

6. All *M* are *P.*   **AOO**-1
   Some *S* are not *M.*
   Some *S* are not *P.*

In entering the particular premise, we concentrate our attention on the part of the S circle that lies outside the M circle (colored area). Because this area is divided into two parts (the areas marked "1" and "2"), we place the X on the line (arc of the P circle) separating the two areas. The conclusion states that there is an X that is inside the S circle but outside the P circle. There *is* an X in the S circle, but we do not know whether it is inside or outside the P circle. Hence, the syllogistic form is invalid.

7. All *M* are *P.*   **AAA**-1
   All *S* are *M.*
   All *S* are *P.*

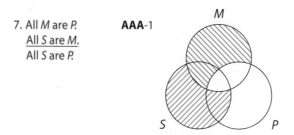

This is the "Barbara" syllogism. The conclusion states that the part of the S circle that is outside the P circle is empty. Inspection of the diagram reveals that this area is indeed empty. Thus, the syllogistic form is valid.

8. Some M are not P. **OIO**-1
   Some S are M.
   Some S are not P.

In this diagram no areas have been shaded, so there are two possible areas for each of the two X's. The X from the first premise goes on the line (arc of the S circle) separating areas 1 and 2, and the X from the second premise goes on the line (arc of the P circle) separating areas *a* and *b*. The conclusion states that there is an X that is inside the S circle but outside the P circle. We have no certainty that the X from the first premise is inside the S circle, and while the X from the second premise is inside the S circle, we have no certainty that it is outside the P circle. Hence, the syllogistic form is invalid.

> **When entering an X . . .**
> Look at the general area where the X goes. If neither of the sub-areas is shaded, put the X on the line (arc of circle) separating the two sub-areas.

We have yet to explain the rationale for placing the X on the boundary separating two areas when neither of the areas is shaded. Consider this syllogistic form:

No P are M.
Some S are not M.
Some S are P.

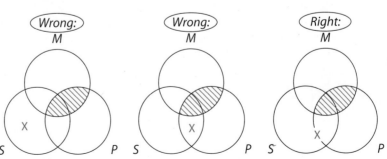

In each of the three diagrams the content of the first premise is represented correctly. The problem concerns placing the X from the second premise. In the first diagram the X is placed inside the S circle but outside both the M circle and the P circle. This diagram asserts: "At least one S is not an M and it is also not a P." Clearly the diagram says more than the premise does, and so it is incorrect. In the second diagram the X is placed inside the S circle, outside the M circle, and inside the P circle. This diagram asserts: "At least one S is not an M, but it is a P." Again, the diagram says more than the premise says, and so it is incorrect. In the third diagram, which is done correctly, the X is placed on the boundary between the two areas. This diagram asserts: "At least one S is not an M, and it may or may not be a P." In other words, nothing at all is said about P, and so the diagram represents exactly the content of the second premise.

Aristotelian Standpoint

For the syllogistic forms tested thus far, we have adopted the Boolean standpoint, which does not recognize universal premises as having existential import. We now shift to the Aristotelian standpoint, where existential import can make a difference to validity. To test a syllogism from the Aristotelian standpoint, we follow basically the same procedure we followed in Section 4.6 to test immediate inferences:

1. Reduce the syllogism to its form and test it from the Boolean standpoint. If the form is valid, proceed no further. The syllogism is valid from both standpoints.

2. If the syllogistic form is invalid from the Boolean standpoint and has universal premises and a particular conclusion, then adopt the Aristotelian standpoint and look to see if there is a Venn circle that is completely shaded except for one area. If there is, enter a circled X in that area and retest the form.

3. If the syllogistic form is conditionally valid, determine if the circled X represents something that exists. If it does, the condition is fulfilled, and the syllogism is valid from the Aristotelian standpoint.

In regard to step 2, if the diagram contains no Venn circle completely shaded except for one area, then the syllogism is invalid from the Aristotelian standpoint. However, if it does contain such a Venn circle and the syllogism has a particular conclusion, then we place a circled X in the one unshaded area. This circled X represents the temporary assumption that the Venn circle in question is not empty.

In regard to step 3, if the circled X does not represent something that exists, then the syllogism is invalid. As we will see in Section 5.3, such syllogisms commit the existential fallacy from the Aristotelian standpoint.

The table of conditionally valid syllogistic forms presented in Section 5.1 names nine forms that are valid from the Aristotelian standpoint if a certain condition is fulfilled. The following syllogism has one of those forms:

> 9. No fighter pilots are tank commanders.
>   All fighter pilots are courageous individuals.
>   Therefore, some courageous individuals are not tank commanders.

First, we replace the terms with letters and test the syllogism from the Boolean standpoint:

No *F* are *T*.
All *F* are *C*.
Some *C* are not *T*.

EAO-3

The conclusion asserts that there is an X that is inside the *C* circle but outside the *T* circle. Inspection of the diagram reveals no X's at all, so the syllogism is invalid from the Boolean standpoint. Proceeding to step 2, we adopt the Aristotelian standpoint and, noting that the conclusion is particular and that the *F* circle is all shaded except for one area, we enter a circled X in that area:

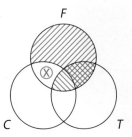

The diagram now indicates that the syllogism is conditionally valid, so we proceed to step 3 and determine whether the circled X represents something that actually exists. Since the circled X represents an *F*, and since *F* stands for fighter pilots, the circled X does represent something that exists. Thus, the condition is fulfilled, and the syllogism is valid from the Aristotelian standpoint.

The *F* circle in this diagram represents the critical term, first mentioned in connection with the table of conditionally valid forms in Section 5.1. The critical term is the term listed in the farthest right-hand column of that table. As the diagram shows, if the circle for the critical term has at least one member, then this member is necessarily also in the circle representing the subject of the conclusion (in this case *C*). This fact provides the basis for a definition of *critical term*. The **critical term** is the term in a categorical syllogism which, when it denotes at least one existing thing, guarantees that the subject of the conclusion denotes at least one existing thing.

Here is another example:

10. All reptiles are scaly animals.
    All currently living tyrannosaurs are reptiles.
    Therefore, some currently living tyrannosaurs are scaly animals.

First we test the syllogism from the Boolean standpoint:

All *R* are *S.*   **AAI**-1
All *C* are *R.*
Some *C* are *S.*

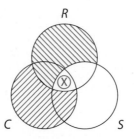

The conclusion asserts that there is an X in the area where the *C* and *S* circles overlap. Since the diagram contains no X's at all, the syllogism is invalid from the Boolean standpoint. Proceeding to step 2, we adopt the Aristotelian standpoint. Then, after noticing that the conclusion is particular and that the *C* circle is all shaded except for one area, we enter a circled X in that area:

The diagram now indicates that the syllogism is conditionally valid, so we proceed to the third step and determine whether the circled X represents something that actually exists. Since the circled X represents a *C,* and *C* stands for currently living tyrannosaurs, the circled X does not represent something that actually exists. Thus, the condition is not fulfilled, and the syllogism is invalid. As we will see in the next section of this chapter, the syllogism commits the existential fallacy from the Aristotelian standpoint.

In determining whether the circled X stands for something that exists, we always look to the Venn circle that is all shaded except for one area. If the term corresponding to that circle denotes existing things, then the circled X represents one of those things. In some diagrams, however, there may be two Venn circles that are all shaded except for one area, and each may contain a circled X in the unshaded area. In these cases we direct our attention only to the circled X needed to draw the conclusion. If that circled X stands for something that exists, the argument is valid; if not, it is invalid.

MindTap   Strengthen your understanding of the topic with the section's **Video Lecture**.

I. Use Venn diagrams to determine whether the following standard-form categorical syllogisms are valid from the Boolean standpoint, valid from the Aristotelian standpoint, or invalid. Then, identify the mood and figure, and cross-check your answers with the tables of valid syllogisms found in Section 5.1.

★**1.** All corporations that overcharge their customers are unethical businesses.
Some unethical businesses are investor-owned utilities.
Therefore, some investor-owned utilities are corporations that overcharge their customers.

2. No fossil fuels are renewable forms of energy.
Some combustible gases are fossil fuels.
Therefore, some combustible gases are not renewable forms of energy.

3. No individuals truly concerned with the plight of suffering humanity are people motivated primarily by self-interest.
All television evangelists are people motivated primarily by self-interest.
Therefore, some television evangelists are not individuals truly concerned with the plight of suffering humanity.

★**4.** All high-fat diets are diets high in cholesterol.
Some diets high in cholesterol are not healthy food programs.
Therefore, some healthy food programs are not high-fat diets.

5. No engineering majors are candidates for nightly hookups.
No candidates for nightly hookups are deeply emotional individuals.
Therefore, no deeply emotional individuals are engineering majors.

6. All impulse buyers are consumers with credit cards.
All shopaholics are impulse buyers.
Therefore, all shopaholics are consumers with credit cards.

★**7.** No pediatricians are individuals who jeopardize the health of children.
All faith healers are individuals who jeopardize the health of children.
Therefore, no faith healers are pediatricians.

8. Some individuals prone to violence are not men who treat others humanely.
Some police officers are individuals prone to violence.
Therefore, some police officers are not men who treat others humanely.

9. Some ATM locations are places criminals lurk.
All places criminals lurk are places to avoid at night.
Therefore, some places to avoid at night are ATM locations.

MindTap   Complete exercises online for immediate feedback.

★10. No corporations that defraud the government are organizations the government should deal with.
Some defense contractors are not organizations the government should deal with.
Therefore, some defense contractors are not corporations that defraud the government.

11. All circular triangles are plane figures.
All circular triangles are three-sided figures.
Therefore, some three-sided figures are plane figures.

12. All supernovas are objects that emit massive amounts of energy.
All quasars are objects that emit massive amounts of energy.
Therefore, all quasars are supernovas.

★13. No people who profit from the illegality of their activities are people who want their activities legalized.
All drug dealers are people who profit from the illegality of their activities.
Therefore, no drug dealers are people who want their activities legalized.

14. Some individuals who risk heart disease are people who will die young.
Some smokers are individuals who risk heart disease.
Therefore, some smokers are people who will die young.

15. Some communications satellites are rocket-launched failures.
All communications satellites are devices with antennas.
Therefore, some devices with antennas are rocket-launched failures.

★16. All currently living dinosaurs are giant reptiles.
All giant reptiles are ectothermic animals.
Therefore, some ectothermic animals are currently living dinosaurs.

17. All survivalists are people who enjoy simulated war games.
No people who enjoy simulated war games are soldiers who have tasted the agony of real war.
Therefore, all soldiers who have tasted the agony of real war are survivalists.

18. No spurned lovers are Valentine's Day fanatics.
Some moonstruck romantics are Valentine's Day fanatics.
Therefore, some moonstruck romantics are not spurned lovers.

★19. No theocracies are regimes open to change.
All theocracies are governments that rule by force.
Therefore, some governments that rule by force are not regimes open to change.

20. Some snowflakes are not uniform solids.
All snowflakes are six-pointed crystals.
Therefore, some six-pointed crystals are not uniform solids.

II. Use Venn diagrams to obtain the conclusion that is validly implied by each of the following sets of premises. If no conclusion can be validly drawn, write "no conclusion."

★1. No *P* are *M.*
   All *S* are *M.*

2. Some *P* are not *M.*
   Some *M* are *S.*

3. Some *M* are *P.*
   All *S* are *M.*

★4. Some *M* are not *P.*
   All *M* are *S.*

5. Some *P* are *M.*
   All *M* are *S.*

6. No *M* are *P.*
   Some *S* are not *M.*

★7. All *M* are *P.*
   All *S* are *M.*

8. All *P* are *M.*
   All *S* are *M.*

9. No *P* are *M.*
   Some *M* are *S.*

★10. No *P* are *M.*
   No *M* are *S.*

III. Answer "true" or "false" to the following statements:

   1. In the use of Venn diagrams to test the validity of syllogisms, marks are sometimes entered in the diagram for the conclusion.

   2. When an X is placed on the arc of a circle, it means that the X could be in either (or both) of the two areas that the arc separates.

   3. If an X lies on the arc of a circle, the argument cannot be valid.

   4. When representing a universal statement in a Venn diagram, one always shades two of the seven areas in the diagram (unless one of these areas is already shaded).

   5. If a completed diagram contains two X's, the argument cannot be valid.

   6. If the conclusion asserts that a certain area is shaded, and inspection of the diagram reveals that only half that area is shaded, the argument is valid.

   7. If the conclusion asserts that a certain area contains an X and inspection of the diagram reveals that only half an X appears in that area, the argument is valid.

   8. If the conclusion is in the form "All *S* are *P*," and inspection of the diagram reveals that the part of the *S* circle that is outside the *P* circle is shaded, then the argument is valid.

   9. If, in a completed diagram, three areas of a single circle are shaded, and placing a circled X in the one remaining area would make the conclusion true, then the argument is valid from the Aristotelian standpoint but not from the Boolean standpoint.

   10. If, in a completed diagram, three areas of a single circle are shaded, but the argument is not valid from the Boolean standpoint, then it must be valid from the Aristotelian standpoint.

IV. Create a standard-form categorical syllogism relating to each of the following topics: clean energy, motion pictures, military drones, immigration, money in professional sports. Then, test each of your syllogisms with a Venn diagram.

MindTap® Master concepts and improve outcomes with Aplia, at the end of the chapter, in the Aplia folder.

HOW LOGICAL ARE YOU? Suppose you hear the following argument: No adults are children; some teenagers are not adults; therefore, some teenagers are not children. How would you explain the flaw in this reasoning? Use a diagram consisting of two circles and an asterisk to assist in the explanation.

Find the answer on MindTap.

The idea that valid syllogisms conform to certain rules was first expressed by Aristotle. Many such rules are discussed in Aristotle's own account, but logicians of today generally settle on five or six.* If any one of these rules is violated, a specific formal fallacy is committed and, accordingly, the syllogism is invalid. Conversely, if none of the rules is broken, the syllogism is valid. These rules may be used as a convenient cross-check against the method of Venn diagrams. We will first consider the rules as they apply from the Boolean standpoint, and then shift to the Aristotelian standpoint.

Boolean Standpoint

Of the five rules presented in this section, the first two depend on the concept of distribution, the second two on the concept of quality, and the last on the concept of quantity. In applying the first two rules, you may want to recall either of the two mnemonic devices presented in Chapter 4: "Unprepared Students Never Pass" and "Any Student Earning B's Is Not On Probation." These mnemonics help one remember that the four categorical propositions distribute their terms as follows:

Statement type	Terms distributed
A	subject
E	subject, predicate
I	none
O	predicate

Here is the first rule.

Rule 1: The Middle Term Must Be Distributed at Least Once.

Fallacy: **Undistributed middle**

Example: All sharks are fish.
All salmon are fish.
All salmon are sharks.

---

*Some texts include a rule stating that the three terms of a categorical syllogism must be used in the same sense throughout the argument. In our discussion, this requirement is included as part of the definition of standard-form categorical syllogism and is subsequently incorporated into the definition of categorical syllogism. See Section 5.1.

In this standard-form categorical syllogism the middle term is "fish." In both premises "fish" occurs as the predicate of an **A** proposition and therefore it is not distributed in either premise. Thus, the syllogism commits the fallacy of undistributed middle and is invalid. If the major premise were rewritten to read "All fish are sharks," then "fish" would be distributed in that premise and the syllogism would be valid. But, of course, it would still be unsound because the rewritten premise would be false.

The logic behind Rule 1 may be explained by recounting how the middle term accomplishes its intended purpose, which is to provide a common ground between the subject and predicate terms of the conclusion. Let us designate the minor, major, and middle terms by the letters S, P, and M, respectively, and let us suppose that M is distributed in the major premise. By definition, P is related to the *whole* of the M class. Then, when the M class is related either in whole or in part to S, S and P necessarily become related. Analogous reasoning prevails if we suppose that M is distributed in the minor premise. But if M is undistributed in both premises, S and P may be related to *different parts* of the M class, in which case there is no common ground for relating S and P. This is exactly what happens in our fish example. The terms "salmon" and "sharks" are related to different parts of the fish class, so no common ground exists for relating them.

Rule 2: If a Term Is Distributed in the Conclusion, Then It Must Be Distributed in a Premise.

Fallacies:	**Illicit major; illicit minor**
Examples:	All horses are animals.
	<u>Some dogs are not horses.</u>
	Some dogs are not animals.
	All tigers are mammals.
	<u>All mammals are animals.</u>
	All animals are tigers.

In the first example the major term, "animals," is distributed in the conclusion but not in the major premise, so the syllogism commits the fallacy of illicit major, or, more precisely, "illicit process of the major term." In the second example the minor term, "animals," is distributed in the conclusion but not in the minor premise. The second example therefore commits the fallacy of illicit minor, or "illicit process of the minor term."

In applying this rule, one must always examine the conclusion first. If no terms are distributed in the conclusion, Rule 2 cannot be violated. If one or both terms in the conclusion are distributed, then the appropriate premise must be examined. If the term distributed in the conclusion is also distributed in the premise, then the rule is not violated. But, if the term is not distributed in the premise, the rule is violated and the syllogism is invalid. In applying Rule 2 (and also Rule 1), you may find it helpful to begin by marking all the distributed terms in the syllogism—either by circling them or by labeling them with a superscript letter "d."

The logic behind Rule 2 is easy to understand. Let us once again designate the minor, major, and middle terms by the letters S, P, and M, respectively, and let us suppose that a certain syllogism commits the fallacy of illicit major. The conclusion of that syllogism then makes an assertion about every member of the *P* class, but the major premise makes an assertion about only some members of the *P* class. Because the minor premise, by itself, says nothing at all about the *P* class, the conclusion clearly contains information not contained in the premises, and the syllogism is therefore invalid. Analogous reasoning applies to the fallacy of illicit minor.

Rule 2 becomes intuitively plausible when it is recognized that distribution is a positive attribute. Granting this, an argument that has a term distributed in the conclusion but not in the premises has *more* in the conclusion than it does in the premises and is therefore invalid. Of course, it is always permissible to have more in a premise than appears in the conclusion, so it is perfectly all right for a term to be distributed in a premise but not in the conclusion.

Rule 3: Two Negative Premises Are Not Allowed.

Fallacy: **Exclusive premises**

Example: No fish are mammals.
Some dogs are not fish.
Some dogs are not mammals.

This syllogism may be seen as invalid because it has true premises and a false conclusion. The defect stems from the fact that it has two negative premises.

On reflection, Rule 3 should be fairly obvious. Let *S*, *P*, and *M* once again designate the minor, major, and middle terms. Now, if the *P* class and the *M* class are separate either wholly or partially, and the *S* class and the *M* class are separate either wholly or partially, nothing is said about the relation between the *S* class and the *P* class. These two classes may be either distinct or identical in whole or in part. Venn diagrams may be used effectively to illustrate the fact that no conclusion can be validly drawn from two negative premises.

Rule 4: A Negative Premise Requires a Negative Conclusion, and a Negative Conclusion Requires a Negative Premise.

Fallacy: **Drawing an affirmative conclusion from a negative premise**

or

Drawing a negative conclusion from affirmative premises

Examples: All crows are birds.
Some wolves are not crows.
Some wolves are birds.

All triangles are three-angled polygons.
All three-angled polygons are three-sided polygons.
Some three-sided polygons are not triangles.

These arguments may be seen as invalid because each has true premises and a false conclusion. The first draws an affirmative conclusion from a negative premise, and the second draws a negative conclusion from affirmative premises.

The logic behind Rule 4 may be seen as follows. If *S*, *P*, and *M* once again designate the minor, major, and middle terms, an affirmative conclusion always states that the *S* class is contained either wholly or partially in the *P* class. The only way that such a conclusion can follow is if the *S* class is contained either wholly or partially in the *M* class, and the *M* class wholly in the *P* class. In other words, it follows only when both premises are affirmative. But if, for example, the *S* class is contained either wholly or partially in the *M* class, and the *M* class is separate either wholly or partially from the *P* class, such a conclusion will never follow. Thus, an affirmative conclusion cannot be drawn from negative premises.

Conversely, a negative conclusion asserts that the *S* class is separate either wholly or partially from the *P* class. But if both premises are affirmative, they assert class inclusion rather than separation. Thus, a negative conclusion cannot be drawn from affirmative premises.

As a result of the interaction of these first four rules, it turns out that no valid syllogism can have two particular premises. This result is convenient to keep in mind, because it allows us to identify as invalid any standard-form syllogism in which both premises start with "some." Because it is logically derivable from the first four rules, a separate rule to this effect is not given here.

Rule 5: If Both Premises Are Universal, the Conclusion Cannot Be Particular.

Fallacy: **Existential fallacy**

Example: All mammals are animals.
All tigers are mammals.
Some tigers are animals.

The example has two universal premises and a particular conclusion, so it violates Rule 5. It commits the existential fallacy from the Boolean standpoint. The reason the syllogism is invalid from the Boolean standpoint is that the conclusion asserts that tigers exist, whereas the premises make no such assertion. From the Boolean standpoint, universal premises have no existential import.

In applying Rule 5, keep in mind that the existential fallacy is a fallacy that occurs when a syllogism is invalid merely because the premises lack existential import. Thus, if a syllogism is invalid for some other reason (that is, if it commits some other fallacy), it does not commit the existential fallacy. Hence, before deciding that a syllogism breaks Rule 5, make certain that no other rule is violated. If a syllogism does break one of the other four rules, Rule 5 does not apply.

Aristotelian Standpoint

Any categorical syllogism that breaks one of the first four rules is invalid from the Aristotelian standpoint. However, if a syllogism breaks only Rule 5, it is valid from the Aristotelian standpoint on condition that the critical term denotes at least one existing thing. (The critical term is the term listed in the farthest right-hand column of the table of conditionally valid syllogistic forms presented in Section 5.1.) In the example given in connection with Rule 5, the critical term is "tigers," and the syllogism breaks no other rules, so it is valid from the Aristotelian standpoint. The conclusion asserts that tigers exist, and from the Aristotelian standpoint the premises imply their existence. On the other hand, consider the following example:

> All mammals are animals.
> All unicorns are mammals.
> Some unicorns are animals.

In this example, the critical term is "unicorns." Since unicorns do not exist, the premises have no existential import from the Aristotelian standpoint. Thus, the syllogism is invalid from the Aristotelian standpoint, and it commits the existential fallacy from that standpoint. Of course, it also commits the existential fallacy from the Boolean standpoint.

In addition to consulting the table of conditionally valid forms, one way of identifying the critical term is to draw a Venn diagram. The critical term is the one that corresponds to the circle that is all shaded except for one area. In the case of two such circles, it is the one that corresponds to the Venn circle containing the circled X on which the conclusion depends. Another way of identifying the critical term is through examination of the distributed terms in the syllogism. The critical term is the one that is *superfluously distributed*. In other words, it is the term that, in the premises, is distributed in more occurrences than is necessary for the syllogism to obey the first two rules. Here are three examples:

All M^d are P.	No M^d are P^d.	All P^d are M.
All S^d are M.	All M^d are S.	All M^d are S.
Some S are P.	Some S are not P^d.	Some S are P.

The distributed terms are tagged with a superscript "d." In the first syllogism, M must be distributed to satisfy Rule 1, but S, in the second premise, need not be distributed to satisfy any rule. Thus, by the *superfluous distribution rule,* S is the term that must denote actually existing things for the syllogism to be valid from the Aristotelian standpoint. In the second syllogism, P must be distributed in the first premise to satisfy Rule 2, and M must be distributed once to satisfy Rule 1; but M is distributed twice. Thus, M is the term that must denote existing things for the syllogism to be valid from the Aristotelian standpoint. In the third syllogism, M must be distributed to satisfy Rule 1, but P need not be distributed to satisfy any rule. Thus, in this syllogism, P is the critical term.

You may recall that the existential fallacy from the Boolean standpoint first appeared in Section 4.3, where it arose in connection with the modern square of opposition. Also, the existential fallacy from the Aristotelian standpoint first appeared in Section 4.5, where it arose in connection with the traditional square of opposition. The two versions of the existential fallacy that appear in connection with Rule 5 stem from the same mistake as it relates to categorical syllogisms.

Finally, if you turn to the table of conditionally valid forms in Section 5.1, you will see that all of the forms listed there break Rule 5. All of them have universal premises and a particular conclusion, and they break no other rule. Thus, all of them commit the existential fallacy from the Boolean standpoint. But if the Aristotelian standpoint is adopted and the critical term refers to something that does not exist, the Aristotelian standpoint gives exactly the same results as the Boolean. (See Section 4.3.) Thus, under these conditions, all of the syllogistic forms in the conditionally valid table commit the existential fallacy from the Aristotelian standpoint as well.

Proving the Rules

The foregoing discussion has shown that if a syllogism breaks any one of the five rules, it cannot be valid from the Boolean standpoint. Thus, we have shown that each of the rules is a *necessary* condition for validity. The question remains, however, whether a syllogism's breaking none of the rules is a *sufficient* condition for validity. In other words, does the fact that a syllogism breaks none of the rules guarantee its validity? The answer to this question is "yes," but unfortunately there appears to be no quick method for proving this fact. Therefore, if you are willing to take your instructor's word for it, you may stop reading this section now and proceed to the exercises. The proof that follows is somewhat tedious, and it proceeds by considering four classes of syllogisms having **A**, **E**, **I**, and **O** propositions for their conclusions.

Let us first suppose we are given a valid syllogism having an **A** proposition for its conclusion. Once again, suppose that *P*, *S*, and *M* designate the major, minor, and middle terms, respectively. Then, by Rules 1 and 2, both *M* and *S* are distributed in the premises. Further, by Rule 4, both premises are affirmative. Now, since **I** propositions distribute neither term, and **A** propositions distribute only one term, both premises must be **A** propositions, and *S* must be distributed in one and *M* in the other. Accordingly, the premises are "All *S* are *M*" and "All *M* are *P*." If we now combine these premises with the conclusion, "All *S* are *P*," we can determine by simple reasoning or a Venn diagram that the syllogism is valid. Note that only Rules 1, 2, and 4 were used in producing this first step in our proof, but the resulting syllogism obeys the unused rules as well. A similar process applies to the steps that follow.

Next, we consider a syllogism having an **E** proposition for its conclusion. By Rules 1 and 2, all three terms are distributed in the premises, and by Rules 3 and 4, one premise is negative and the other affirmative. Because three terms are distributed in the premises and there are only two premises, one of the premises must distribute two terms. Accordingly, this premise must be an **E** proposition. Furthermore, the other premise, which is affirmative and which distributes the third term, must be an **A** proposition. From this we conclude that there are four possible sets of premises: "All *S* are *M*" and "No *M* are *P*" (or its converse), and "All *P* are *M*" and "No *M* are *S*" (or its converse). Since converting an **E** proposition has no effect on validity, we may ignore the converse of these propositions. If we now combine the two given sets of premises with the conclusion, "No *S* are *P*," simple reasoning or a pair of Venn diagrams will establish the validity of the two resulting syllogisms.

Next, consider a syllogism having an **I** proposition for its conclusion. By Rule 1, *M* is distributed in at least one premise, and by Rule 4, both premises are affirmative. Further, by Rule 5, both premises cannot be universal. Thus, at least one premise is an **I** proposition. However, since the other premise distributes a term, that premise must be an **A** proposition. Accordingly, the four possible sets of premises are "All *M* are *S*" and "Some *M* are *P*" (or its converse), and "All *M* are *P*" and "Some *M* are *S*" (or its converse). Again, since converting an **I** proposition has no effect on validity, we may ignore the converse of these propositions. Then if we combine the two given pairs of premises with the conclusion, "Some *S* are *P*," simple reasoning or a pair of Venn diagrams will establish the validity of the two resulting syllogisms.

Last, we consider a syllogism having an **O** proposition for its conclusion. By Rules 1 and 2, both *M* and *P* are distributed in the premises. Also, by Rules 3 and 4, one premise is negative and the other affirmative, and by Rule 5, both premises cannot be universal. However, both premises cannot be particular (**I** and **O**), because then only one term would be distributed. Therefore, the premises are either **A** and **O** or **E** and **I**. In regard to the first of these alternatives, either *M* is the subject of the **A** statement and *P* is the predicate of the **O**, or *P* is the subject of the **A** statement and *M* is the predicate of the **O**. This gives the premises as "All *M* are *S*" and "Some *M* are not *P*," and "All *P* are *M*" and "Some *S* are not *M*." When these pairs of premises are combined with the conclusion, "Some *S* are not *P*," simple reasoning or a pair of Venn diagrams will establish the validity of the two resulting syllogisms. Finally, considering the other alternative (**E** and **I**), the resulting four sets of premises are "No *M* are *P*" (or its converse) and "Some *M* are *S*" (or its converse). Again ignoring the converted propositions, simple reasoning or a Venn diagram will establish the validity of the single resulting syllogism.

This procedure proves that the five rules collectively provide a sufficient condition for the validity of any syllogism from the Boolean standpoint. Since eight distinct inferences or Venn diagrams were needed to accomplish it, this shows that there are really only eight significantly distinct syllogisms that are valid from the Boolean standpoint. The other seven are variations of these that result from converting one of the premises. For syllogisms having particular conclusions and universal premises about existing things, an analogous procedure can be used to prove that the first four rules collectively provide a sufficient condition for the validity of any syllogism from the Aristotelian standpoint.

MindTap® Strengthen your understanding of the topic with the section's **Video Lectures**.

EXERCISE **5.3**

I. Reconstruct the following syllogistic forms and use the five rules for syllogisms to determine if they are valid from the Boolean standpoint, conditionally valid from the Aristotelian standpoint, or invalid. For those that are conditionally valid, identify the condition that must be fulfilled. For those that are invalid from either the Boolean or Aristotelian standpoint, name the fallacy or fallacies committed. Check your answers by constructing a Venn diagram for each.

MindTap® Complete exercises online for immediate feedback.

★1. AAA-3	11. AII-2
2. IAI-2	12. AIO-3
3. EIO-1	★13. AEE-4
★4. AAI-2	14. EAE-4
5. IEO-1	15. EAO-3
6. EOO-4	★16. EEE-1
★7. EAA-1	17. EAE-1
8. AII-3	18. OAI-3
9. AAI-4	★19. AOO-2
★10. IAO-3	20. EAO-1

II. Use the five rules to determine whether the following standard-form syllogisms are valid from the Boolean standpoint, valid from the Aristotelian standpoint, or invalid. For those that are invalid from either the Boolean or Aristotelian standpoint, name the fallacy or fallacies committed. Check your answer by constructing a Venn diagram for each.

★1. Some nebulas are clouds of gas.
Some clouds of gas are objects invisible to the naked eye.
Therefore, some objects invisible to the naked eye are nebulas.

2. No individuals sensitive to the difference between right and wrong are people who measure talent and success in terms of wealth.
All corporate take-over experts are people who measure talent and success in terms of wealth.
Therefore, no corporate take-over experts are individuals sensitive to the difference between right and wrong.

3. No endangered species are creatures loved by the timber industry.
All spotted owls are endangered species.
Therefore, some spotted owls are not creatures loved by the timber industry.

★4. Some cases of affirmative action are not measures justified by past discrimination.
No cases of affirmative action are illegal practices.
Therefore, some illegal practices are not measures justified by past discrimination.

5. All transparent metals are good conductors of heat.
All transparent metals are good conductors of electricity.
Therefore, some good conductors of electricity are good conductors of heat.

6. All members of the National Rifle Association are people opposed to gun control.
All members of the National Rifle Association are law-abiding citizens.
Therefore, all law-abiding citizens are people opposed to gun control.

★7. No searches based on probable cause are violations of Fourth Amendment rights.
Some warrantless searches are violations of Fourth Amendment rights.
Therefore, some warrantless searches are not searches based on probable cause.

8. All war zones are places where abuse of discretion is rampant.
   Some places where abuse of discretion is rampant are international borders.
   Therefore, some international borders are war zones.

9. All inside traders are people subject to prosecution.
   Some executives with privileged information are not people subject to prosecution.
   Therefore, some executives with privileged information are inside traders.

★10. All successful flirts are masters at eye contact.
   All masters at eye contact are people genuinely interested in others.
   Therefore, some people genuinely interested in others are successful flirts.

III. Answer "true" or "false" to the following statements:

1. If a standard-form categorical syllogism violates one of the first four rules, it may still be valid.

2. If a valid standard-form syllogism has an **E** statement as its conclusion, then both the major and minor terms must be distributed in the premises.

3. If a standard-form syllogism has two **I** statements as premises, then it is invalid.

4. If a standard-form syllogism has an **E** and an **O** statement as premises, then no conclusion follows validly.

5. If a standard-form syllogism has an **I** statement as its conclusion, then Rule 2 cannot be violated.

6. If a valid standard-form syllogism has an **O** statement as its conclusion, then its premises can be an **A** and an **I** statement.

7. If a valid standard-form syllogism has an **E** statement as a premise, then its conclusion can be an **A** statement.

8. If a standard-form syllogism breaks only Rule 5 and its three terms are "dogs," "cats," and "animals," then the syllogism is valid from the Boolean standpoint.

9. If a standard-form syllogism breaks only Rule 5 and its three terms are "dogs," "cats," and "animals," then the syllogism is valid from the Aristotelian standpoint.

10. If a standard-form syllogism breaks only Rule 5 and its three terms are "elves," "trolls," and "gnomes," then the syllogism is valid from the Aristotelian standpoint.

IV. Create five standard-form categorical syllogisms about flowers, each of which breaks one of the five rules for syllogisms.

MindTap® Master concepts and improve outcomes with Aplia, at the end of the chapter, in the Aplia folder.

304 **CHAPTER 5** CATEGORICAL SYLLOGISMS

5.4   Reducing the Number of Terms

Categorical syllogisms, as they occur in ordinary spoken and written expression, are seldom phrased according to the precise norms of the standard-form syllogism. Sometimes quantifiers, premises, or conclusions are left unexpressed, chains of syllogisms are strung together into single arguments, and terms are mixed together with their negations in a single argument. The final four sections of this chapter are concerned with developing techniques for reworking such arguments in order to render them testable by Venn diagrams or by the rules for syllogisms.

In this section we consider arguments that contain more than three terms but that can be modified to reduce the number of terms to three. Consider the following:

> All photographers are non-writers.
> Some editors are writers.
> Therefore, some non-photographers are not non-editors.

This syllogism is clearly not in standard form because it has six terms: "photographers," "editors," "writers," "non-photographers," "non-editors," and "non-writers." But because three of the terms are complements of the other three, the number of terms can be reduced to a total of three, each used twice in distinct propositions. To accomplish the reduction, we can use the three operations of conversion, obversion, and contraposition discussed in Chapter 4. But, of course, since the reworked syllogism must be equivalent in meaning to the original one, we must use these operations only on the kinds of statements for which they yield logically equivalent results. That is, we must use conversion only on **E** and **I** statements and contraposition only on **A** and **O** statements. Obversion yields logically equivalent results for all four kinds of categorical statements.

Let us rewrite our six-term argument using letters to represent the terms, and then obvert the first premise and contrapose the conclusion in order to eliminate the negated letters:

Symbolized argument	Reduced argument
All *P* are non-*W*.	No *P* are *W*.
Some *E* are *W*.	Some *E* are *W*.
Some non-*P* are not non-*E*.	Some *E* are not *P*.

Because the first premise of the original argument is an **A** statement and the conclusion an **O** statement, and because the operations performed on these statements yield logically equivalent results, the reduced argument is equivalent in meaning to the original

Saul Kripke 1940–

Steve Pyke/Premium Archive /Getty Images

As a child, Saul Kripke demonstrated prodigious intellectual abilities. By the age of ten he had read all the plays of Shakespeare, and he discovered algebra, which he said he could have invented on his own. By fourteen he had mastered geometry and calculus and became deeply involved in philosophy. At seventeen he wrote a paper, published in the prestigious *Journal of Symbolic Logic*, that introduced a completeness theorem for modal logic. Legend has it that when this paper reached the attention of the Harvard mathematics department, someone there invited him to apply for a teaching position. He replied, "My mother said that I should finish high school and go to college first." Today Kripke is considered by many to be the world's greatest living philosopher and logician.

Saul Kripke was born the son of a rabbi in Bay Shore, New York, in 1940. He attended public grade school and high school in Omaha, Nebraska, and then Harvard University where, during his sophomore year, he taught a graduate-level course at MIT. In 1962 he graduated *summa cum laude* with a bachelor's degree in mathematics. After that, instead of going to graduate school, he simply began teaching—first at Harvard, then Rockefeller University, then Princeton University, and finally CUNY Graduate Center. He has received honorary degrees from several universities, and in 2001 he received the Schock Prize (comparable to the Nobel Prize) in Logic and Philosophy.

Kripke is universally hailed for his work in modal logic where, in addition to proving its formal completeness, he created a semantics, now called Kripke semantics, in which a proposition is said to be necessarily true when it holds in all possible worlds and possibly true when it holds in some possible world. Also, his book *Naming and Necessity* made groundbreaking contributions to the philosophy of language by introducing a new theory of reference for proper names.

argument. The reduced argument is in standard syllogistic form and may be evaluated either with a Venn diagram or by the five rules for syllogisms. The application of these methods indicates that the reduced argument is valid. We conclude, therefore, that the original argument is also valid.

It is not necessary to eliminate the negated terms in order to reduce the number of terms. It is equally effective to convert certain non-negated terms into negated ones. Thus, instead of obverting the first premise of the example argument and contraposing the conclusion, we could have contraposed the first premise and converted and then obverted the second premise. The operation is performed as follows:

Symbolized argument	**Reduced argument**
All *P* are non-*W*.	All *W* are non-*P*.
Some *E* are *W*.	Some *W* are not non-*E*.
Some non-*P* are not non-*E*.	Some non-*P* are not non-*E*.

The reduced argument is once again equivalent to the original one, but now we must reverse the order of the premises to put the syllogism into standard form:

Some W are not non-E.
All W are non-P.
Some non-P are not non-E.

When tested with a Venn diagram or by means of the five rules, this argument will, of course, also be found valid, and so the original argument is valid. When using a Venn diagram, no unusual method is needed; the diagram is simply lettered with the three terms "W," "non-E," and "non-P."

The most important point to remember in reducing the number of terms is that conversion and contraposition must never be used on statements for which they yield undetermined results. That is, conversion must never be used on **A** and **O** statements, and contraposition must never be used on **E** and **I** statements. The operations that are allowed are summarized as follows:

Conversion:	No A are B.	No B are A.
	Some A are B.	Some B are A.
Obversion:	All A are B.	No A are non-B.
	No A are B.	All A are non-B.
	Some A are B.	Some A are not non-B.
	Some A are not B.	Some A are non-B.
Contraposition:	All A are B.	All non-B are non-A.
	Some A are not B.	Some non-B are not non-A.

5

EXERCISE 5.4

I. Rewrite the following arguments using letters to represent the terms, reduce the number of terms, and put the arguments into standard form. Then test the new forms with Venn diagrams or by means of the five rules for syllogisms to determine the validity or invalidity of the original arguments.

★1. Some intelligible statements are true statements, because all unintelligible statements are meaningless statements and some false statements are meaningful statements.

2. Some people who do not regret their crimes are convicted murderers, so some convicted murderers are people insusceptible of being reformed, since all people susceptible of being reformed are people who regret their crimes.

3. All Peace Corps volunteers are people who have witnessed poverty and desolation, and all people insensitive to human need are people who have failed to

MindTap® Complete exercises online for immediate feedback.

witness poverty and desolation. Thus, all Peace Corps volunteers are people sensitive to human need.

★4. Some unintentional killings are not punishable offenses, inasmuch as all cases of self-defense are unpunishable offenses, and some intentional killings are cases of self-defense.

5. All aircraft that disintegrate in flight are unsafe planes. Therefore, no poorly maintained aircraft are safe planes, because all well-maintained aircraft are aircraft that remain intact in flight.

6. No objects that sink in water are chunks of ice, and no objects that float in water are things at least as dense as water. Accordingly, all chunks of ice are things less dense than water.

★7. Some proposed flights to Mars are inexpensive ventures, because all unmanned space missions are inexpensive ventures, and some proposed flights to Mars are not manned space missions.

8. All schools driven by careerism are institutions that do not emphasize liberal arts. It follows that some universities are not institutions that emphasize liberal arts, for some schools that are not driven by careerism are universities.

9. No cases of encephalitis are infections easily curable by drugs, since all diseases that infect the brain are infections not easily curable by drugs, and all diseases that do not infect the brain are cases other than encephalitis.

★10. Some foreign emissaries are people without diplomatic immunity, so some people invulnerable to arrest and prosecution are foreign emissaries, because no people with diplomatic immunity are people vulnerable to arrest and prosecution.

II. Create a categorical syllogism about people that contains two negated terms. Then reduce the number of terms so the syllogism is in standard form. Finally, test the syllogism for validity using either the Venn-diagram method or the rules method.

MindTap Master concepts and improve outcomes with Aplia, at the end of the chapter, in the Aplia folder.

5.5   Ordinary Language Arguments

HOW LOGICAL ARE YOU? Suppose you are afraid you might not pass your communications studies class, so you decide to speak to the instructor. The instructor tells you: "You won't pass the course unless you pass the final exam. But surely you will pass the final exam; it's fairly easy. Thus, you will pass the course." Should this response from the instructor allow you to rest more easily? Why or why not?

Find the answer on MindTap.

Many arguments that are not standard-form categorical syllogisms as written can be translated into standard-form syllogisms. In doing so we often use techniques developed in the last section of Chapter 4—namely, inserting quantifiers, modifying subject and predicate terms, and introducing copulas. The goal, of course, is to produce an argument consisting of three standard-form categorical propositions that contain a total of three different terms, each of which occurs twice in distinct propositions. Once translated, the argument can be tested by means of a Venn diagram or the rules for syllogisms.

Since the task of translating arguments into standard-form syllogisms involves not only converting the component statements into standard form but adjusting these statements one to another so that their terms occur in matched pairs, a certain amount of practice may be required before it can be done with facility. In reducing the terms to three matched pairs it is often helpful to identify some factor common to two or all three propositions and to express this common factor through the strategic use of parameters. For example, if all three statements are about people, the term "people" or "people identical to" might be used; or if they are about times or places, the term "times" or "times identical to" or the term "places" or "places identical to" might be used. Here is an example:

> Whenever people put off marriage until they are older, the divorce rate decreases. Today, people are putting off marriage until they are older. Therefore, the divorce rate is decreasing today.

The temporal adverbs "whenever" and "today" suggest that "times" should be used as the common factor. Following this suggestion, we have this:

> All times people put off marriage until they are older are times the divorce rate decreases. All present times are times people put off marriage until they are older. Therefore, all present times are times the divorce rate decreases.

This is a standard-form categorical syllogism. Notice that each of the three terms is matched with an exact duplicate in a different proposition. To obtain such a match, it is sometimes necessary to alter the wording of the original statement just slightly. Now if we adopt the convention

> M = times people put off marriage until they are older
> D = times the divorce rate decreases
> P = present times

the syllogism may be symbolized as follows:

> All M are D.
> All P are M.
> All P are D.

This is the so-called "Barbara" syllogism and is, of course, valid. Here is another example:

> Boeing must be a manufacturer because it hires riveters, and any company that hires riveters is a manufacturer.

For this argument the parameter "companies" suggests itself:

> All companies identical to Boeing are manufacturers, because all companies identical to Boeing are companies that hire riveters, and all companies that hire riveters are manufacturers.

The first statement, of course, is the conclusion. When the syllogism is written in standard form, it will be seen that it has, like the previous syllogism, the form **AAA**-1.

Here is another example:

> If a piece of evidence is trustworthy, then it should be admissible in court. Polygraph tests are not trustworthy. Therefore, they should not be admissible in court.

To translate this argument, using a single common factor is not necessary:

> All trustworthy pieces of evidence are pieces of evidence that should be admissible in court. No polygraph tests are trustworthy pieces of evidence. Therefore, no polygraph tests are pieces of evidence that should be admissible in court.

This syllogism commits the fallacy of illicit major and is therefore invalid.

As was mentioned in Section 4.7, arguments containing an exceptive proposition must be handled in a special way. Let us consider one that contains an exceptive proposition as a premise:

> All of the jeans except the Levi's are on sale. Therefore, since the Calvin Klein jeans are not Levi's, they must be on sale.

The first premise is translated as two conjoined categorical propositions: "No Levi's are jeans on sale," and "All jeans that are not Levi's are jeans on sale." These give rise to two syllogisms:

> No Levi's are jeans on sale.
> No Calvin Klein jeans are Levi's.
> Therefore, all Calvin Klein jeans are jeans on sale.

> All jeans that are not Levi's are jeans on sale.
> No Calvin Klein jeans are Levi's.
> Therefore, all Calvin Klein jeans are jeans on sale.

The first syllogism, which is in standard form, is invalid because it has two negative premises. The second one, on the other hand, is not in standard form, because it has four terms. If the second premise is obverted, so that it reads "All Calvin Klein jeans are jeans that are not Levi's," the syllogism becomes an **AAA**-1 standard-form syllogism, which is valid.

Each of these two syllogisms may be viewed as a pathway in which the conclusion of the original argument might follow necessarily from the premises. Since it does follow via the second syllogism, the original argument is valid. If both of the resulting syllogisms turned out to be invalid, the original argument would be invalid.

I. Translate the following arguments into standard-form categorical syllogisms, then use Venn diagrams or the rules for syllogisms to determine whether each is valid or invalid. See Section 4.7 for help with the translation.

★1. Physicists are the only scientists who theorize about the nature of time, and Stephen Hawking certainly does that. Therefore, Stephen Hawking must be a physicist.

2. Whenever suicide rates decline, we can infer that people's lives are better adjusted. Accordingly, since suicide rates have been declining in recent years, we can infer that people's lives have been better adjusted in recent years.

3. Environmentalists purchase only fuel-efficient cars. Hence, Jeep Wranglers must not be fuel efficient, since environmentalists do not purchase them.

★4. Whoever wrote the Declaration of Independence had a big impact on civilization, and Thomas Jefferson certainly had that. Therefore, Thomas Jefferson wrote the Declaration of Independence.

5. There are public schools that teach secular humanism. Therefore, since secular humanism is a religion, there are public schools that teach religion.

6. Any city that has excellent art museums is a tourist destination. Therefore, Paris is a tourist destination, because it has excellent art museums.

★7. Miranda Lambert sings what she wants. Hence, since Miranda sings country songs, it follows that she must want to sing country songs.

8. Not all interest expenses are tax deductible. Home-mortgage payments are interest expenses. Thus, they are not tax deductible.

9. If a marriage is based on a meshing of neuroses, it allows little room for growth. If a marriage allows little room for growth, it is bound to fail. Therefore, if a marriage is based on a meshing of neuroses, it is bound to fail.

★10. TV viewers cannot receive scrambled signals unless they have a decoder. Whoever receives digital satellite signals receives scrambled signals. Therefore, whoever receives digital satellite signals has a decoder.

11. Wherever icebergs are present, threats to shipping exist. Icebergs are not present in the South Pacific. Hence, there are no threats to shipping in the South Pacific.

12. According to surveys, there are college students who think that Africa is in North America. But anyone who thinks that has no knowledge of geography. It follows that there are college students who have no knowledge of geography.

★13. Diseases carried by recessive genes can be inherited by offspring of two carriers. Thus, since cystic fibrosis is a disease carried by recessive genes, it can be inherited by offspring of two carriers.

14. All of the movies except the romantic comedies were exciting. Hence, the action films were exciting, because none of them is a romantic comedies.

MindTap® Complete exercises online for immediate feedback.

15. Autistic children are occasionally helped by aversion therapy. But aversion therapy is sometimes inhumane. Thus, autistic children are sometimes helped by inhumane therapy.

II. Create two arguments—one about desserts, the other about beverages—each of which contains two or more of the following words: "whoever," "whenever," "only," "the only," "not every," "if," "any," "only if," "a few," "there is," "none but." Then, translate your arguments into standard-form syllogisms and test each for validity using a Venn diagram or the rules method.

MindTap® Master concepts and improve outcomes with Aplia, at the end of the chapter, in the Aplia folder.

5

| 5.6 | # Enthymemes |

HOW LOGICAL ARE YOU? Given the following argument: "The number of campus shootings has increased sharply in recent years. Therefore, if we want to address this kind of gun violence, we must enact stricter gun-control laws." This argument is missing a premise. What is it?

Find the answer on MindTap.

An **enthymeme** is an argument that is expressible as a categorical syllogism but that is missing a premise or a conclusion. Examples:

> The corporate income tax should be abolished; it encourages waste and high prices.

> Animals that are loved by someone should not be sold to a medical laboratory, and lost pets are certainly loved by someone.

The first enthymeme is missing the premise "Whatever encourages waste and high prices should be abolished," and the second is missing the conclusion "Lost pets should not be sold to a medical laboratory."

Enthymemes occur frequently in ordinary spoken and written English for several reasons. Sometimes it is simply boring to express every statement in an argument. The listener or reader's intelligence is called into play when he or she is required to supply a missing statement, thereby sustaining his or her interest. On other occasions the arguer may want to slip an invalid or unsound argument past an unwary listener or reader, and this aim may be facilitated by leaving a premise or conclusion out of the picture.

Many enthymemes are easy to convert into syllogisms. The reader or listener must first determine what is missing, whether it is a premise or conclusion, and then introduce the missing statement with the aim of converting the enthymeme into a good argument. Attention to indicator words will often provide the clue as to the nature of the missing statement, but a little practice can render this task virtually automatic. The missing statement need not be expressed in categorical form; expressing it in the general context of the other statements is sufficient and is often the easier alternative. Once this is done, the entire argument may be translated into categorical form and then tested with a Venn diagram or by the rules for syllogisms. Example:

> Venus completes its orbit in less time than the earth, because Venus is closer to the sun.
>
> *Missing premise:* Any planet closer to the sun completes its orbit in less time than the earth.

Translating this argument into categorical form, we have

> All planets closer to the sun are planets that complete their orbit in less time than the earth.
> All planets identical to Venus are planets closer to the sun.
> All planets identical to Venus are planets that complete their orbit in less time than the earth.

This syllogism is valid (and sound).

Any enthymeme (such as the one about Venus) that contains an indicator word is missing a premise. This may be seen as follows. If an enthymeme contains a conclusion indicator, then the conclusion follows it, which means that the missing statement is a premise. On the other hand, if the enthymeme contains a premise indicator, then the conclusion precedes it, which means, again, that the missing statement is a premise.

If, however, an enthymeme contains no indicator words at all (such as the two enthymemes at the beginning of this section), then the missing statement could be either a premise or a conclusion. If the two given statements are joined by a word such as "and," "but," "moreover," or some similar conjunction, the missing statement is usually a conclusion. If not, the first statement is usually the conclusion, and the missing statement is a premise. To test this latter alternative, it may help to mentally insert the word "because" between the two statements. If this insertion makes sense, the missing statement is a premise.

After the nature of the missing statement has been determined, the next task is to write it out. To do so, one must first identify its terms. This can be done by taking account of the terms that are given. Two of the terms in the given statements will match up with each other. Once this pair of terms is found, attention should be focused on the other two terms. These are the ones that will be used to form the missing statement. In constructing the missing statement, attention to the rules for syllogisms may be helpful (if the resulting syllogism is to be valid). For example, if the missing statement is a conclusion and one of the given premises is negative, the missing conclusion must be negative. Or if the missing statement is a premise and the stated conclusion is universal, the missing premise must be universal.

The enthymemes that we have considered thus far have been fairly straightforward. The kinds of enthymemes that occur in letters-to-the-editor columns of magazines and newspapers often require a bit more creativity to convert into syllogisms. Consider the following:

> The motorcycle has served as basic transportation for the poor for decades. It deserves to be celebrated.
>
> (William B. Fankboner)

The conclusion is the last statement, and the missing premise is that any vehicle that has served as basic transportation for the poor for decades deserves to be celebrated. The enthymeme may be written as a standard-form syllogism as follows:

> All vehicles that have served as basic transportation for the poor for decades are vehicles that deserve to be celebrated.
> All vehicles identical to the motorcycle are vehicles that have served as basic transportation for the poor for decades.
> Therefore, all vehicles identical to the motorcycle are vehicles that deserve to be celebrated.

The syllogism is valid and arguably sound. Here is another example:

> I know several doctors who smoke. In a step toward my own health, I will no longer be their patient. It has occurred to me that if they care so little about their own health, how can they possibly care about mine?
>
> (Joan Boyer)

In this argument the author draws three connections: the connection between doctors' smoking and doctors' caring about their own health, between doctors' caring about their own health and doctors' caring about the author's health, and between doctors' caring about the author's health and doctors who will have the author as a patient. Two arguments are needed to express these connections:

> All doctors who smoke are doctors who do not care about their own health.
> All doctors who do not care about their own health are doctors who do not care about my health.
> Therefore, all doctors who smoke are doctors who do not care about my health.

And,

> All doctors who smoke are doctors who do not care about my health.
> All doctors who do not care about my health are doctors who will not have me as a patient.
> Therefore, all doctors who smoke are doctors who will not have me as a patient.

Notice that the conclusion of the first argument becomes a premise in the second argument. To put these arguments into final standard form, the order of the premises must be reversed. Both arguments are valid, but probably not sound.

EXERCISE 5.6

I. In the following enthymemes, determine whether the missing statement is a premise or a conclusion. Then supply the missing statement, attempting whenever possible to convert the enthymeme, into a valid argument. The missing statement need not be expressed as a standard-form categorical proposition.

MindTap® Complete exercises online for immediate feedback.

★1. Some police chiefs undermine the evenhanded enforcement of the law, because anyone who fixes parking tickets does that.

2. Any form of cheating deserves to be punished, and plagiarism is a form of cheating.

3. Carrie Underwood is a talented singer. After all, she's won several Grammy awards.

★4. A few fraternities have dangerous initiation rites, and those that do have no legitimate role in campus life.

5. Only nonprofit organizations are exempt from paying taxes, so churches must be exempt.

6. All of the operas except Mozart's were well performed, and *Carmen* was not written by Mozart.

★7. Not all text messages are welcome, but those from friends are.

8. Higher life-forms could not have evolved through merely random processes, because no organized beings could have evolved that way.

9. None but great novels are timeless, and *The Brothers Karamazov* is a great novel.

★10. Attempts to reduce tuition have failed in recent years because administrative salaries have exploded.

11. Wherever water exists, human life can be sustained, and water exists on the moon.

12. If a symphony orchestra has effective fund-raisers, it will survive; and the Cleveland symphony has survived for years.

★13. Mechanistic materialists do not believe in free will, because they think that everything is governed by deterministic laws.

14. A contract to buy land is not enforceable unless it's in writing, but our client's contract to buy land *is* in writing.

15. The only telescopes that are unaffected by the atmosphere are orbiting telescopes, and the Hubble telescope is in orbit.

II. Translate the enthymemes in Part I of this exercise into standard-form categorical syllogisms and test them for validity.

III. The following enthymemes were originally submitted in letters to the editor of various magazines and newspapers. Convert them into valid standard-form syllogisms. In some cases two syllogisms may be required.

★1. If the Defense Department is so intent on fighting alcohol abuse, why does it make alcohol so readily available and acceptable? Alcohol is tax free at post liquor stores, and enlisted men's and officers' clubs make drinking almost a mandatory facet of military life.

(Diane Lynch)

2. All aid to Israel should be stopped at once. Why should the American taxpayer be asked to send billions of dollars to Israel when every city in the United States is practically broke and millions of people are out of work?

(Bertha Grace)

3. Suicide is not immoral. If a person decides that life is impossible, it is his or her right to end it.

(Donald S. Farrar)

★4. The best way to get people to read a book is to ban it. The fundamentalist families in Church Hill, Tennessee, have just guaranteed sales of *Macbeth, The Diary of Anne Frank, The Wizard of Oz,* and other stories.

(Paula Fleischer)

5. The budget deficit will not be brought under control because to do so would require our elected leaders in Washington to do the unthinkable—act courageously and responsibly.

(Bruce Crutcher)

6. The Constitution bans any law that is so vague that "men of common intelligence must necessarily guess at its meaning." Sexual harassment laws, however, are so vague that no one knows what they mean.

(Hans Bader)

★7. College students of today are the higher-income taxpayers of tomorrow. Congress should consider financial aid as an investment in the financial future of our country.

(Carol A. Steimel)

8. Our genes and our environment control our destinies. The idea of conscious choice is ridiculous. Yes, prisons should be designed to protect society, but they should not punish the poor slobs who were headed for jail from birth.

(Paul R. Andrews)

9. Encouraging toy-gun play gives children a clear message that the best way to deal with frustration and conflict is with a gun. Is this the message that we want to be sending our kids?

(Patricia Owen)

★10. The U.S. surgeon general's latest report on cigarettes and cancer is an interesting example of natural selection. The intelligent members of our species will quit smoking, and survive. The dummies will continue to puff away.

(Kelly Kinnon)

IV. Page through a magazine or newspaper and identify five topics of current interest. Construct an enthymeme involving each topic.

V. Translate the arguments in the following dialogue into standard-form categorical syllogisms. The dialogue contains more than twenty arguments, and most are expressed in the form of enthymemes. The first translated syllogism may be found in the answer section.

Do Kids Make Parents Happy?

Tad and Lara, his fiancée, are walking in the park. Tad pauses a moment to look at some children playing in the grass. Lara stops beside him.

"I know we've talked about this before," she says, "but I wish you'd get over this idea about us having a bunch of kids."

"I'll think about it," Tad says. "But could you tell me once again about why you don't want any?"

"I think most couples believe that kids automatically bring happiness," Lara says. "But that's simply not the case. I've read some recent studies about this. They show that childless couples experience higher levels of emotional well-being than couples with kids. Thus, childless couples are happier than couples with kids."

"I've read those studies of yours," Tad says, "but I don't know what to make of them. Consider this. Kids make you laugh, and laughter is essential to happiness. So kids do make you happy. Plus, in a way, having kids makes you immortal."

"How do you figure *that?*"

"Okay, not immortal exactly, but I mean that they make you participate in a kind of immortality. Your children grow up and have children, and those children have children, and on it goes. This feeling of contributing to the perpetuation of the human race makes you happy, don't you think?"

"Frankly," Lara replies, "that's all a bit too removed from the 'now' to suit me. Maybe at the beginning when a couple is expecting their first child, they tend to be happy. But once the baby arrives, the honeymoon ends. The newborn has to be fed every couple of hours, the parents aren't getting any sleep, and those parents aren't happy."

"Well, very tired, yes, but unhappy?" says Tad. "Plus, it's temporary and only lasts for the first few months."

"And after the first few months, you have toys and food all over the house and sticky stuff on all the furniture. How happy is living in a constant mess going to make you?"

"Not very, I guess. But there's more to life than a neat house. Having kids will force us not to be selfish, and no one who's selfish is truly happy. Also, kids promote an atmosphere of growth. Watching kids learn, change, and grow makes parents happy. Don't you think that's true?"

"Sure," Lara says, "in theory. In reality, growing means infants become toddlers who scream, whine, and throw tantrums. Having to listen to all that racket makes no one happy. And then, life just gets more hectic. Kids constantly have to be driven to and from school, dancing lessons, little league, the mall—all detracting from the happiness of the parents. Right?"

"Right," Tad says, "but kids are fun. They're constantly playing; and having playful children around you brings happiness. Plus some kids grow up to accomplish extraordinary things. How could one not be happy at witnessing the success of one's child?"

"Okay," says Lara, "but kids take up a tremendous amount of time. Couples who have kids often have no time for vacations—I know that wouldn't make you happy. And some couples with kids don't even have time for sex. How would you like that?"

"I wouldn't," Tad admits. "But maybe we could learn to manage our time better than those other couples. Which leads me to something else: Having kids will force us to work together as a couple. That will deepen our relationship, and deeper relationships are happier relationships. And don't forget unconditional love. Kids love you for who you are. They don't care what you look like, whether you're overweight, or what kind of car you drive. Being loved like that makes you happy."

"Well, of course it does," says Lara. "But what about money? Kids cost a fortune. Food, clothing, medical bills, and a college education will leave us constantly broke. Can we be happy like that? And what about my career? I have goals, just like you. If I'm constantly pregnant or taking care of little kids, I'll never achieve them. I can't possibly be happy if that happens."

"No," Tad says. "We'd have to work that out. As we grow older, though, think about what our lives will be like without any children. We'll be lonely and cut off, with no one to call us and no grandchildren to visit us. Does that sound like happiness to you?"

"Ha!" Lara says. "You assume that the kids will eventually leave the house. You forget that we live in the age of boomerang offspring. After they finish school, they come back home to live, and you never get rid of them. How does that grab you?"

"Well, we didn't stay around long after college. I think when we decided to leave the nest and get married, we made our parents truly happy."

"Yeah," Lara replies. "I think we did. So maybe we've proved your case. Some kids, at least, end up making their parents happy."

MindTap® Master concepts and improve outcomes with Aplia, at the end of the chapter, in the Aplia folder.

5.7   Sorites

HOW LOGICAL ARE YOU? The following activities are components of a familiar task. List them in the order in which they are usually performed to accomplish the intended result: Remove flat tire from hub. Remove lug nuts from hub bolts. Place flat tire in trunk. Engage emergency brake. Replace lug nuts on hub bolts. Jack up car. Use jack to lower car. Install inflated tire on hub. Working a sorites involves a similar organizing procedure.

Find the answer on MindTap.

A **sorites** is a chain of categorical syllogisms in which the intermediate conclusions have been left out. The name is derived from the Greek word *soros*, meaning "heap," and is pronounced "sōrītēz," with the accent on the second syllable. The plural form is also "sorites." Here is an example:

> All bloodhounds are dogs.
> All dogs are mammals.
> No fish are mammals.
> Therefore, no fish are bloodhounds.

The first two premises validly imply the intermediate conclusion "All bloodhounds are mammals." If this intermediate conclusion is then treated as a premise and put together with the third premise, the final conclusion follows validly. The sorites is thus composed of two valid categorical syllogisms and is therefore valid. The rule in evaluating a sorites is based on the idea that a chain is only as strong as its weakest link. If any of the component syllogisms in a sorites is invalid, the entire sorites is invalid.

A **standard-form sorites** is one in which each of the component propositions is in standard form, each term occurs twice, the predicate of the conclusion is in the first premise, and each successive premise has a term in common with the preceding one.* The sorites in the example is in standard form. Each of the propositions is in standard form, each term occurs twice; the predicate of the conclusion, "bloodhounds," is in the first premise; the other term in the first premise, "dogs," is in the second premise, and so on.

We will now introduce two techniques for testing a sorites for validity. The first technique involves three steps: (1) put the sorites into standard form, (2) introduce the intermediate conclusions, and (3) test each component syllogism for validity. If each component is valid, the sorites is valid. Consider the following sorites form:

No B are C.
Some E are A.
All A are B.
All D are C.
———————
Some E are not D.

To put the sorites form into standard form, the premises must be rearranged. To do this find the premise that contains the predicate of the conclusion and write it first. Then find the premise that contains the other term in the first premise and write it second. Continue in this way until all the premises are listed:

All D are C.
No B are C.
All A are B.
Some E are A.
———————
Some E are not D.

Next, the intermediate conclusions are drawn. Venn diagrams are useful in performing this step, and they serve simultaneously to check the validity of each component syllogism:

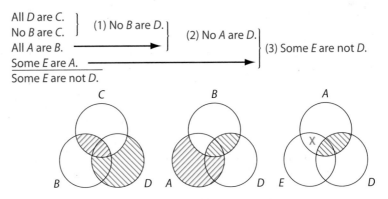

———————

*Actually, there are two definitions of standard-form sorites: the Goclenian and the Aristotelian. The one given here is the Goclenian. In the Aristotelian version, the premises are arranged so that the subject of the conclusion occurs in the first premise.

The first intermediate conclusion, "No B are D," is drawn from the first two premises. The second, "No A are D," is drawn from the first intermediate conclusion and the third premise. And the third conclusion, which is identical to the final conclusion, is drawn from the second intermediate conclusion and the fourth premise. Since all conclusions are drawn validly, the sorites is valid. On the other hand, if at some step in the procedure no conclusion can be drawn, the sorites is invalid.

The second technique for testing the validity of a sorites is faster and simpler than the first one because it does not require that the intermediate conclusions be derived. This second technique consists in applying five rules that closely resemble the rules for syllogisms. The rules are as follows:

Rule 1: Each of the middle terms must be distributed at least once.
Rule 2: If a term is distributed in the conclusion, then it must be distributed in a premise.
Rule 3: Two negative premises are not allowed.
Rule 4: A negative premise requires a negative conclusion, and a negative conclusion requires a negative premise.
Rule 5: If all the premises are universal, the conclusion cannot be particular.

Rule 1 refers to the "middle terms" in the sorites. These are the terms that occur in matched pairs in the premises. The conclusion referred to in Rules 2, 4, and 5 is the final conclusion of the sorites. Also, as with categorical syllogisms, if a sorites breaks only Rule 5, it is valid from the Aristotelian standpoint on condition that its critical term refers to at least one existing thing.

The critical term can be identified in the same way as it is for categorical syllogisms. There are three possible approaches. By entering the mood and figure of the last component syllogism of the sorites into the table of conditionally valid forms in Section 5.1, the critical term is given in the farthest right-hand column. Applying the superfluous distribution rule, the critical term is the term in the premises that is distributed in more occurrences than is necessary for the sorites to obey the first two rules. And in the Venn diagram for the final component syllogism of the sorites, the critical term is the one that corresponds to the circle that is all shaded except for one area. In the case of two such circles, it is the one that corresponds to the Venn circle containing the circled X on which the conclusion depends.

Before applying the rules, it helps to put the sorites into standard form; in either event the sorites must be written so that the terms occur in matched pairs. The following sorites is in standard form, and the distributed terms are marked with a superscript "d." As is apparent, there are three middle terms: M, K, and R.

All S^d are M.
All K^d are M.
No K^d are R^d.
Some F are R.
Some F are not S^d.

This sorites breaks Rule 1 because neither occurrence of M in the first two premises is distributed. Thus, the sorites is invalid. Note that no other rule is broken. Both of the K's in lines 2 and 3 are distributed, one of the R's in lines 3 and 4 is distributed, S is distributed in the conclusion and also in the first premise, there is a negative conclusion and only one negative premise, and while the conclusion is particular so is one of the premises.

The logic behind the five rules is as follows. For Rule 1, each of the middle terms in the sorites is also a middle term in one of the component syllogisms. Thus, if Rule 1 is broken, one of the component syllogisms has an undistributed middle, making the entire sorites invalid.

For Rule 2, when the sorites is in standard form, the predicate of the conclusion must appear in each of the intermediate conclusions. Thus, if the predicate of the conclusion is distributed, it must also be distributed in each of the intermediate conclusions, and also in the first premise. Otherwise, one of the component syllogisms would have either an illicit major or an illicit minor, making the entire sorites invalid. Analogously, if the subject of the conclusion is distributed, it must also be distributed in the last premise. Otherwise, the last component syllogism would have an illicit minor, making the entire sorites invalid.

For Rule 3, when a negative premise appears in the list of premises, the conclusion derived from that premise must be negative, as must all subsequent conclusions. Otherwise, one of the component syllogisms would break Rule 4 for syllogisms. If a second negative premise should appear, the syllogism consisting of that premise and the prior intermediate conclusion would commit the fallacy of exclusive premises, making the entire sorites invalid.

Similarly, for Rule 4, when a negative premise appears in the list of premises, all subsequent conclusions must be negative. Otherwise, one of the component syllogisms would break Rule 4 for syllogisms. Conversely, if the conclusion of the sorites is negative, either the last premise or the last intermediate conclusion must be negative. Otherwise, the last component syllogism would break Rule 4 for syllogisms. If the last intermediate conclusion is negative, then either the prior premise or the prior intermediate conclusion must be negative. If we continue this reasoning, we see that some prior premise must be negative.

For Rule 5, a particular conclusion has existential import, while universal premises (from the Boolean standpoint) do not. Thus, if all the premises are universal and the conclusion is particular, the sorites as a whole commits the existential fallacy.

One of the advantages of the rules method for testing a sorites is that invalidity can often be detected through immediate inspection. Once a sorites has been put into standard form, any sorites having more than one negative premise is invalid, and any sorites having a negative premise and an affirmative conclusion (or vice versa) is invalid. Also, as with syllogisms, any sorites having more than one particular premise is invalid. This last requirement is implied by the other rules.

EXERCISE 5.7

I. Rewrite the following sorites in standard form, reducing the number of terms when necessary. Then supply the intermediate conclusions and test with Venn diagrams.

MindTap® Complete exercises online for immediate feedback.

★1. No *B* are *C*.
Some *D* are *C*.
All *A* are *B*.
Some *D* are not *A*.

2. No *C* are *D*.
All *A* are *B*.
Some *C* are not *B*.
Some *D* are not *A*.

3. No *S* are *M*.
All *F* are *S*.
Some *M* are *H*.
All *E* are *F*.
Some *H* are not *E*.

★4. Some *T* are *K*.
No *K* are *N*.
Some *C* are *Q*.
All *T* are *C*.
Some *Q* are not *N*.

5. All *B* are *C*.
No *C* are *D*.
All *E* are *A*.
All *A* are *B*.
Some *E* are not *D*.

6. All *M* are non-*P*.
Some *M* are *S*.
All *K* are *P*.
Some non-*K* are not non-*S*.

★7. All non-*U* are non-*V*.
No *U* are non-*W*.
All *V* are *Y*.
No *X* are *W*.
All *Y* are non-*X*.

8. All *D* are non-*C*.
All non-*B* are non-*A*.
Some *E* are *D*.
All *B* are *C*.
Some non-*A* are not non-*E*.

9. All non-*L* are non-*K*.
Some *K* are *M*.
All *P* are non-*L*.
No non-*N* are *M*.
No *Q* are non-*P*.
Some *N* are not *Q*.

★10. All *R* are *S*.
No non-*V* are *T*.
No *Q* are non-*R*.
No non-*Q* are *P*.
All *T* are non-*S*.
All *V* are non-*P*.

II. For the sorites in Part I above, rewrite each in standard form, reducing the number of terms when necessary. Then use the five rules for sorites to test each for validity.

III. The following sorites are valid. Rewrite each sorites in standard form, using letters to represent the terms and reducing the number of terms whenever necessary. Then use Venn diagrams or the rules method to prove each one valid.

★1. Whatever produces oxygen supports human life.
Rain forests produce oxygen.
Nothing that supports human life should be destroyed.
Rain forests should not be destroyed.

2. No restrictive trade policies fail to invite retaliation.
Trade wars threaten our standard of living.
Some Chinese trade policies are restrictive.
Policies that invite retaliation lead to a trade war.
Some Chinese trade policies threaten our standard of living.

3. Anything that poisons drinking water causes disease and death.
Chemicals percolating through the soil contaminate aquifers.

Dumped chemicals percolate through the soil.
Whatever contaminates aquifers poisons drinking water.
Dumped chemicals cause disease and death.

★4. Nothing that is brittle is ductile.
Superconductors are all ceramics.
Only ductile things can be pulled into wires.
Ceramics are brittle.
Superconductors cannot be pulled into wires.

5. Some college students purchase their term papers.
Any cheat is expelled from college.
No one will achieve his career goals who is expelled.
No one who purchases term papers is other than a cheat.
Some college students will not achieve their career goals.

6. Creation science does not favor the teaching of evolution.
Nothing should be taught that frustrates the understanding of life.
Whatever opposes the teaching of evolution impedes the learning of biology.
Anything that enhances the understanding of life fosters the learning of biology.
Creation science should not be taught.

★7. Whoever gives birth to crack babies increases future crime rates.
Some pregnant women use crack.
None but criminals increase future crime rates.
Pregnant crack users never give birth to anything but crack babies.
Some pregnant women are criminals.

8. Whatever retards population growth increases food availability.
Anything that prevents starvation enhances life.
Birth-control measures never accelerate population growth.
Anything that enhances life should be encouraged.
Whatever increases food availability prevents starvation.
Birth-control measures should not be discouraged.

9. A few countries allow ivory trading.
Whatever country resists elephant killing discourages poachers.
Any country that allows ivory trading encourages poachers.
No country that promotes the extinction of elephants should escape the condemnation of the civilized world.
Any country that supports elephant killing promotes the extinction of elephants.
A few countries should be condemned by the civilized world.

★10. Anything that promotes skin cancer causes death.
Whatever preserves the ozone layer prevents the release of CFCs.
Nothing that resists skin cancer increases UV radiation.
Anything that destroys the ozone layer increases UV radiation.
There are packaging materials that release CFCs.
Nothing that causes death should be legal.
Some packaging materials should be illegal.

IV. The following sorites are taken from Lewis Carroll's *Symbolic Logic*. All are valid. Rewrite each sorites in standard form, using letters to represent the terms and reducing the number of terms whenever necessary. Then use Venn diagrams or the rules method to prove each one valid.

★1. No ducks waltz.
No officers ever decline to waltz.
All my poultry are ducks.
My poultry are not officers.

2. No experienced person is incompetent.
Jenkins is always blundering.
No competent person is always blundering.
Jenkins is inexperienced.

3. No terriers wander among the signs of the zodiac.
Nothing that does not wander among the signs of the zodiac is a comet.
Nothing but a terrier has a curly tail.
No comet has a curly tail.

★4. All hummingbirds are richly colored.
No large birds live on honey.
Birds that do not live on honey are dull in color.
All hummingbirds are small.

5. All unripe fruit is unwholesome.
All these apples are wholesome.
No fruit grown in the shade is ripe.
These apples were grown in the sun.

6. All my sons are slim.
No child of mine is healthy who takes no exercise.
All gluttons who are children of mine are fat.
No daughter of mine takes any exercise.
All gluttons who are children of mine are unhealthy.

★7. The only books in this library that I do not recommend for reading are unhealthy in tone.
The bound books are all well written.
All the romances are healthy in tone.
I do not recommend you to read any of the unbound books.
All the romances in this library are well written.

8. No interesting poems are unpopular among people of real taste.
No modern poetry is free from affectation.
All your poems are on the subject of soap bubbles.
No affected poetry is popular among people of real taste.
No ancient poem is on the subject of soap bubbles.
All your poems are uninteresting.

5

9. All writers who understand human nature are clever.
No one is a true poet unless he can stir the hearts of men.
Shakespeare wrote *Hamlet*.
No writer who does not understand human nature can stir the hearts of men.
None but a true poet could have written *Hamlet*.

Shakespeare was clever.

★10. I trust every animal that belongs to me.
Dogs gnaw bones.
I admit no animals into my study unless they beg when told to do so.
All the animals in the yard are mine.
I admit every animal that I trust into my study.
The only animals that are really willing to beg when told to do so are dogs.

All the animals in the yard gnaw bones.

V. Create a sorites having four premises about trees; then put it into standard form and test it for validity using Venn diagrams or the rules method.

MindTap® Master concepts and improve outcomes with Aplia, at the end of the chapter, in the Aplia folder.

Summary

Categorical syllogism:

- A deductive argument consisting of three categorical propositions
- Containing three different terms
- Each term occurs twice in distinct propositions

Terms in a categorical syllogism:

- Major term: The term that occurs in the predicate of the conclusion
- Minor term: The term that occurs in the subject of the conclusion
- Middle term: The term that occurs twice in the premises

Premises of a categorical syllogism:

- Major premise: The premise that contains the major term
- Minor premise: The premise that contains the minor term

Standard-form categorical syllogism:

- All three propositions are in standard form.
- The two occurrences of each term are identical.

MindTap® Need help? See the Learning Logic folder at the end of the chapter: the self-paced tutorial walks you through any section.
Prepare for exams with the Chapter Test.

- Each term is used in the same sense throughout the argument.
- The major premise is listed first, minor premise second, conclusion last.

The validity of a categorical syllogism is determined by its mood and figure:
- Mood: Consists of the letter names of the propositions in the syllogism
- Figure: Is determined by how the occurrences of the middle term are arranged

Tables for categorical syllogisms:
- Unconditionally valid: Lists all forms valid from the Boolean standpoint
- Conditionally valid: Lists additional forms valid from the Aristotelian standpoint
- Critical term: The term listed in the farthest right-hand column of the conditionally valid table

Venn diagrams: To test a syllogism:
- Enter the information from the premises into the diagram.
- Look at the completed diagram to see if it supports the conclusion.
- If a syllogism having universal premises and a particular conclusion is not valid from the Boolean standpoint, test it from the Aristotelian standpoint.

Rules for syllogisms: For a syllogism to be valid from the Boolean standpoint:
- The middle term must be distributed in at least one premise;
- A term distributed in the conclusion must also be distributed in a premise;
- At least one premise must be affirmative;
- A negative conclusion requires a negative premise, and vice versa;
- A particular conclusion requires a particular premise.

If only the last rule is broken, a syllogism is valid from the Aristotelian standpoint on condition that the critical term refers to at least one existing thing.

Some syllogisms having more than three terms can be reduced to standard form:
- Each additional term must be a complement of one of the others.
- Conversion, obversion, and contraposition must be applied only when they yield logically equivalent results.

Ordinary language syllogisms: The component propositions are not in standard form.
- Can be converted into standard-form syllogisms by applying the techniques presented in Section 4.7.

Enthymemes: Syllogisms that are missing a premise or conclusion:
- Can be converted into standard-form syllogisms by supplying the missing statement.

Sorites: A chain of syllogisms in which the intermediate conclusions are missing

Testing a sorites:
- Using the five rules:
  - Put the sorites into standard form.
  - Apply the rules.
  - If only the last rule is broken, a sorites is valid from the Aristotelian standpoint on condition that the critical term refers to at least one existing thing.
- Using Venn diagrams
  - Put the sorites into standard form.
  - Supply the missing intermediate conclusions.
  - Test each component syllogism.

6 Propositional Logic

6.1 Symbols and Translation

HOW LOGICAL ARE YOU? While strolling on a remote island you encounter what appears to be a treasure chest. On top of the chest are four buttons labeled A, B, C, D. According to a local legend, pressing the correct buttons will open the chest, but pressing the wrong buttons will set off a bomb. Beneath the buttons there is a code that reads: $(B \cdot D) \cdot \sim(A \vee C)$. Since you studied logic in college, you know that • means "and," ~ means "not," and ∨ means "or." So, which buttons do you push?

Find the answer on MindTap.

Earlier chapters showed that the validity of a deductive argument is purely a function of its form. By knowing the form of an argument, we can often tell immediately whether it is valid or invalid. Unfortunately, however, ordinary linguistic usage often obscures the form of an argument. To dispel this obscurity, logic introduces various simplifying procedures. In Chapter 5, letters were used to represent the terms in a syllogism, and techniques were developed to reduce syllogisms to what is called standard form. In this chapter, form recognition is facilitated through the introduction of special symbols called **operators**, or **connectives**. When arguments are expressed in terms of these symbols, determining validity often becomes a matter of mere visual inspection.

In the two previous chapters, the fundamental elements were terms. In **propositional logic**, however, the fundamental elements are whole statements (or propositions). Statements are represented by letters, and these letters are then combined by means of the operators to form more-complex symbolic representations.

MindTap® Read, study, reflect, and prepare for exams online, anytime, anywhere.

To understand the symbolic representation used in propositional logic, we must distinguish simple statements from compound statements. A **simple statement** is one that does not contain any other statement as a component. Here are some examples:

Fast foods tend to be unhealthy.
James Joyce wrote *Ulysses*.
Parakeets are colorful birds.
The bluefin tuna is threatened with extinction.

Any convenient uppercase letter may be selected to represent each statement. Thus, *F* might be selected to represent the first, *J* the second, *P* the third, and *B* the fourth. As will be explained shortly, lowercase letters are reserved for use as statement variables.

A **compound statement** is one that contains at least one simple statement as a component. Here are some examples:

It is not the case that al-Qaeda is a humanitarian organization.
Dianne Reeves sings jazz, and Christina Aguilera sings pop.
Either people get serious about conservation or energy prices will skyrocket.
If nations spurn international law, then future wars are guaranteed.
The Broncos will win if and only if they run the ball.

Using uppercase letters to stand for the simple statements, these compound statements may be represented as follows:

It is not the case that *A*.
D and *C*.
Either *P* or *E*.
If *N* then *F*.
B if and only if *R*.

In the first example, note that the statement is compound even though it contains only a single component (*A*). In general, negative statements are interpreted as compound units consisting of an affirmative statement and the phrase "it is not the case that."

The expressions "it is not the case that," "and," "or," "if . . . then . . . ," and "if and only if" are translated by logical operators. The five logical operators* are as follows:

Operator	Name	Logical function	Used to translate
~	tilde	negation	not, it is not the case that
•	dot	conjunction	and, also, moreover
∨	wedge	disjunction	or, unless
⊃	horseshoe	implication	if . . . then . . . , only if
≡	triple bar	equivalence	if and only if

Saying that logical operators are used to "translate" these English expressions does not mean that the expressions and the operators are identical. As in any translation

---

Some textbooks use the ampersand, &, in place of the dot; the arrow, →, in place of the horseshoe; and the double arrow, ↔, in place of the triple bar.

(from English to French, for example), a certain distortion of meaning occurs. The meaning of such English expressions as "and," "or," and "if and only if" is often vague and may vary with context, whereas the meaning of the logical operators is clear, precise, and invariable. Thus, when we say that the logical operators may be used to translate expressions in ordinary language, we mean that the operators capture a certain aspect of their correlative English expressions. The precise character of this aspect is spelled out in the next section of this chapter. The purpose of the current section is to develop a familiarity with the logical operators through practice in translation.

When we use the operators to translate the previous examples of compound statements, the results are as follows:

It is not the case that A.	$\sim A$
D and C.	$D \cdot C$
Either P or E.	$P \vee E$
If N then F.	$N \supset F$
B if and only if R.	$B \equiv R$

The statement $\sim A$ is called a **negation**. The statement $D \cdot C$ is called a **conjunctive statement** (or a **conjunction**), and the statement $P \vee E$ is called a **disjunctive statement** (or a **disjunction**); in the conjunctive statement, the components D and C are called **conjuncts**, and in the disjunctive statement the components P and E are called **disjuncts**. The statement $N \supset F$ is called a **conditional statement** (or a **conditional**), and it expresses the relation of **material implication**. Its components are called **antecedent** (N) and **consequent** (F). Lastly, $B \equiv R$ is called a **biconditional statement** (or a **biconditional**), and it expresses the relation of **material equivalence**.

Let us now use the logical operators to translate additional English statements. The tilde symbol is used to translate any negated simple proposition:

Rolex does not make computers.	$\sim R$
It is not the case that Rolex makes computers.	$\sim R$
It is false that Rolex makes computers.	$\sim R$

As these examples show, the tilde is always placed *in front* of the proposition it negates. All of the other operators are placed *between* two propositions. Also, unlike the other operators, the tilde cannot be used to connect two propositions. Thus, $G \sim H$ is not a proper expression. But the tilde is the only operator that can immediately follow another operator. Thus, it would be proper to write $G \cdot \sim H$. In the Rolex examples, the tilde is used to negate a simple proposition, but it can also be used to negate a compound proposition—for example $\sim(G \cdot F)$. In this case the tilde negates the entire expression inside the parentheses.

These statements are all **negations**. The main operator is a tilde.

$\sim B$

$\sim(G \supset H)$

$\sim[(A \equiv F) \cdot (C \equiv G)]$

At this point we should define what is called the main operator in a compound statement. The **main operator** is the operator that has as its scope everything else in the statement. If there are no parentheses in the statement, the main operator will either be the only operator or, if there is more than one, it will be the operator that is not a tilde. If there are parentheses, brackets, or braces in the statement, the main operator will be the operator that lies outside all parentheses, brackets, and braces; if there is more than one such operator, the main operator will be the one that is not a tilde.

For example, in the statement $H \cdot (J \lor K)$, the main operator is the dot, because its scope extends to everything else in the statement, whereas the scope of the wedge extends only to the J and K. In the statement $\sim(K \cdot M)$, the main operator is the tilde because its scope extends to everything else. In the statement $K \supset \sim(L \cdot M)$, the main operator is the horseshoe, because, once again, its scope extends to everything else in the statement. Excluding the tilde, it is the only operator outside the parentheses.

The dot symbol is used to translate such conjunctions as "and," "also," "but," "however," "yet," "still," "moreover," "although," and "nevertheless":

Tiffany sells jewelry, and Gucci sells cologne.	$T \cdot G$
Tiffany sells jewelry, but Gucci sells cologne.	$T \cdot G$
Tiffany sells jewelry; however, Gucci sells cologne.	$T \cdot G$
Tiffany and Ben Bridge sell jewelry.	$T \cdot B$

Note that the last example is equivalent in meaning to "Tiffany sells jewelry, and Ben Bridge sells jewelry." To translate such a statement as a conjunction of two simple statements, the original statement must be equivalent to a compound statement in English. For example, the statement "Mary and Louise are friends" is *not* equivalent in meaning to "Mary is a friend, and Louise is a friend," so this statement cannot be translated as $M \cdot L$.

These statements are all **conjunctions**. The main operator is a dot.

$K \cdot \sim L$

$(E \lor F) \cdot \sim(G \lor H)$

$[(R \supset T) \lor (S \supset U)] \cdot [(W \equiv X) \lor (Y \equiv Z)]$

The wedge symbol is used to translate "or" and "unless." A previous chapter explained that "unless" is equivalent in meaning to "if not." This equivalence holds in propositional logic as well, but in propositional logic it is usually simpler to equate "unless" with "or." For example, the statement "You won't graduate unless you pass freshman English" is equivalent to "Either you pass freshman English or you won't graduate" and also to "If you don't pass freshman English, then you won't graduate." As the next section demonstrates, the wedge symbol has the meaning of "and/or"—that is, "or" in the inclusive sense. Although "or" and "unless" are sometimes used in an exclusive sense, the wedge is usually used to translate them as well.

The word "either," which is often used to introduce disjunctive statements, has primarily a punctuational meaning. The placement of this word often tells us where parentheses and brackets must be introduced in the symbolic expression. If parentheses or brackets are not needed, "either" does not affect the translation. A similar point applies to the word "both," which is often used to introduce conjunctive statements. Here are some disjunctive statements:

Aspen allows snowboards or Telluride does.	$A \lor T$
Either Aspen allows snowboards or Telluride does.	$A \lor T$
Aspen allows snowboards unless Telluride does.	$A \lor T$
Unless Aspen allows snowboards, Telluride does.	$A \lor T$

From the English sense of these statements, it should be clear that $A \lor T$ is logically equivalent to $T \lor A$. Also $T \cdot G$ is logically equivalent to $G \cdot T$. Logically equivalent propositions necessarily have the same truth value.

> These statements are all **disjunctions**. The main operator is a wedge.
>
> $\sim C \lor \sim D$
> $(F \cdot H) \lor (\sim K \cdot \sim L)$
> $\sim [S \cdot (T \supset U)] \lor \sim [X \cdot (Y \equiv Z)]$

6

The horseshoe symbol is used to translate "if . . . then . . . ," "only if," and similar expressions that indicate a conditional statement. The expressions "in case," "provided that," "given that," and "on condition that" are usually translated in the same way as "if." By customary usage, the horseshoe symbol is also used to translate "implies." Although "implies" is used most properly to describe the relationship between the premises and conclusion of an argument, we may accept this translation as an alternate meaning for "implies." According to this alternate meaning, A implies B is translated $A \supset B$.

The function of "only if" is, in a sense, just the reverse of "if." For example, the statement "You will catch a fish only if your hook is baited" does not mean "If your hook is baited, then you will catch a fish." If it meant this, then everyone with a baited hook would catch a fish. Rather, the statement means "If your hook is not baited, then you will not catch a fish," which is logically equivalent to "If you catch a fish, then your hook was baited." To avoid mistakes in translating "if" and "only if" remember this rule: The statement that follows "if" is always the antecedent, and the statement that follows "only if" is always the consequent. Thus, "C only if H" is translated $C \supset H$, whereas "C if H" is translated $H \supset C$. Additional examples:

If Purdue raises tuition, then so does Notre Dame.	$P \supset N$
Notre Dame raises tuition if Purdue does.	$P \supset N$
Purdue raises tuition only if Notre Dame does.	$P \supset N$
Cornell cuts enrollment provided that Brown does.	$B \supset C$
Cornell cuts enrollment on condition that Brown does.	$B \supset C$
Brown's cutting enrollment implies that Cornell does.	$B \supset C$

In translating conditional statements, it is essential not to confuse antecedent with consequent. Just as 6 ÷ 3 is not equal to 3 ÷ 6, the statement $A \supset B$ is not logically equivalent to $B \supset A$.

These statements are all **conditionals** (material implications). The main operator is a horseshoe.

$H \supset \sim J$

$(A \vee C) \supset \sim(D \cdot E)$

$[K \vee (S \cdot \sim T)] \supset [\sim F \vee (M \cdot O)]$

The horseshoe symbol is also used to translate statements phrased in terms of sufficient conditions and necessary conditions. Event A is said to be a **sufficient condition** for event B whenever the occurrence of A is all that is required for the occurrence of B. On the other hand, event A is said to be a **necessary condition** for event B whenever B cannot occur without the occurrence of A. For example, having the flu is a sufficient condition for feeling miserable, whereas having air to breathe is a necessary condition for survival. Other things besides having the flu might cause a person to feel miserable, but that by itself is sufficient; other things besides having air to breathe are required for survival, but without air, survival is impossible. In other words, air is necessary.

To translate statements involving sufficient and necessary conditions into symbolic form, place the statement that names the sufficient condition in the antecedent of the conditional and the statement that names the necessary condition in the consequent. The mnemonic device "SUN" may be conveniently used to keep this rule in mind. Turning the U sideways creates $S \supset N$, wherein S and N designate sufficient and necessary conditions, respectively. Whatever is given as a sufficient condition goes in the place of the S, and whatever is given as a necessary condition goes in the place of the N:

| Hilton's opening a new hotel is a sufficient condition for Marriott's doing so. | $H \supset M$ |

| Hilton's opening a new hotel is a necessary condition for Marriott's doing so. | $M \supset H$ |

The triple-bar symbol is used to translate the expressions "if and only if" and "is a sufficient and necessary condition for":

| JFK tightens security if and only if O'Hare does. | $J \equiv O$ |

| JFK's tightening security is a sufficient and necessary condition for O'Hare's doing so. | $J \equiv O$ |

Analysis of the first statement reveals that $J \equiv O$ is logically equivalent to $(J \supset O) \cdot (O \supset J)$. The statement "JFK tightens security only if O'Hare does" is translated $J \supset O$, and "JFK tightens security if O'Hare does" is translated $O \supset J$. Combining the two English statements, we have $(J \supset O) \cdot (O \supset J)$, which is just a longer way of writing

$J \equiv O$. A similar analysis applies to the second statement. Because the order of the two conjuncts can be reversed, $J \equiv O$ is logically equivalent to $O \equiv J$. However, when translating such statements, we adopt the convention that the letter representing the first English statement is written to the left of the triple bar, and the letter representing the second English statement is written to the right of the triple bar. Thus, the examples given are translated $J \equiv O$, and not $O \equiv J$.

> These statements are all **biconditionals** (material equivalences).
> The main operator is a triple bar.
>
> $M \equiv {\sim}T$
> ${\sim}(B \vee D) \equiv {\sim}(A \cdot C)$
> $[K \vee (F \supset I)] \equiv [{\sim}L \cdot (G \vee H)]$

Whenever more than two letters appear in a translated statement, we must use parentheses, brackets, or braces to indicate the proper range of the operators. The statement $A \cdot B \vee C$, for example, is ambiguous. When parentheses are introduced, this statement becomes either $(A \cdot B) \vee C$ or $A \cdot (B \vee C)$. These two statements are not logically equivalent. Thus, with statements such as these, some clue must be found in the English statement that indicates the correct placement of the parentheses in the symbolic statement. Such clues are usually given by commas and semicolons, by such words as "either" and "both," and by the use of a single predicate in conjunction with two or more subjects. The following examples illustrate the correct placement of parentheses and brackets:

Prozac relieves depression and Allegra combats allergies, or Zocor lowers cholesterol.	$(P \cdot A) \vee Z$
Prozac relieves depression, and Allegra combats allergies or Zocor lowers cholesterol.	$P \cdot (A \vee Z)$
Either Prozac relieves depression and Allegra combats allergies or Zocor lowers cholesterol.	$(P \cdot A) \vee Z$
Prozac relieves depression and either Allegra combats allergies or Zocor lowers cholesterol.	$P \cdot (A \vee Z)$
Prozac relieves depression or both Allegra combats allergies and Zocor lowers cholesterol.	$P \vee (A \cdot Z)$
Prozac relieves depression and Allegra or Zocor lowers cholesterol.	$P \cdot (A \vee Z)$
If Merck changes its logo, then if Pfizer increases sales, then Lilly will reorganize.	$M \supset (P \supset L)$
If Merck's changing its logo implies that Pfizer increases sales, then Lilly will reorganize.	$(M \supset P) \supset L$

If Schering and Pfizer lower prices or Novartis downsizes,
then Warner will expand production. $\qquad$ $[(S \cdot P) \vee N] \supset W$

Do not confuse these three statement forms:

A if B	$B \supset A$
A only if B	$A \supset B$
A if and only if B	$A \equiv B$

When a tilde appears in a symbolic expression, by convention it is considered to affect only the unit that immediately follows it. For example, in the expression $\sim K \vee M$ the tilde affects only the K; in the expression $\sim(K \vee M)$ it affects the entire expression inside the parentheses. In English, the expression "It is not the case that K or M" is ambiguous, because the range of the negating words is indefinite. To eliminate this ambiguity, we now adopt the convention that the negating words are considered to affect only the unit that follows them. Thus, "It is not the case that K or M" is translated $\sim K \vee M$.

The statement "Not both S and T" is translated $\sim(S \cdot T)$. By an important rule called *De Morgan's rule*, this statement is logically equivalent to $\sim S \vee \sim T$. For example, the statement "Not both Steven and Thomas were fired" is equivalent in meaning to "Either Stephen was not fired or Thomas was not fired." Because the former statement is *not* equivalent in meaning to "Stephen was not fired and Thomas was not fired," $\sim(S \cdot T)$ is *not* logically equivalent to $\sim S \cdot \sim T$. Analogously, the statement "Not either S or T" is translated $\sim(S \vee T)$, which by De Morgan's rule is logically equivalent to $\sim S \cdot \sim T$. For example, "Not either Steven or Thomas was fired" is equivalent in meaning to "Steven was not fired and Thomas was not fired." Thus, $\sim(S \vee T)$ is *not* logically equivalent to $\sim S \vee \sim T$. The following examples illustrate these points:

Megan is not a winner, but Kathy is.	$\sim M \cdot K$
Not both Megan and Kathy are winners.	$\sim(M \cdot K)$
Either Megan or Kathy is not a winner.	$\sim M \vee \sim K$
Both Megan and Kathy are not winners.	$\sim M \cdot \sim K$
Not either Megan or Kathy is a winner.	$\sim(M \vee K)$
Neither Megan nor Kathy is a winner.	$\sim(M \vee K)$

Notice the function of "either" and "both":

Not either A or B.	$\sim(A \vee B)$
Either not A or not B.	$\sim A \vee \sim B$
Not both A and B.	$\sim(A \cdot B)$
Both not A and not B.	$\sim A \cdot \sim B$

The symbolic expressions that we have used throughout this section to translate meaningful, unambiguous English statements are called **well-formed formulas**

Gottfried Wilhelm Leibniz 1646–1716

Gottfried Wilhelm Leibniz was a polymath who knew virtually everything that could be known at the time about nearly every area of intellectual endeavor. He also made important contributions to many of them, including physics, engineering, philosophy, theology, history, law, politics, and philology. In mathematics Leibniz invented differential and integral calculus (independently of Newton) and the theory of differential equations. He also discovered the binary number system (used by all of today's digital computers), and he created the first calculating machine that could add, subtract, multiply, and divide. In metaphysics he created the famous theory of monads which, among other things, explained the relation between the soul and the body.

Leibniz was born in Leipzig to prominent parents. His father (who died when Leibniz was six) was a professor of moral philosophy at the city's university, and his mother was the daughter of a famous lawyer. As a child Leibniz proved himself a prodigy. By age twelve he was fluent in Latin and had a passing knowledge of Greek, both of which he had learned by himself. By thirteen he was deep into the works of Aristotle and scholastic philosophy, and at fourteen he entered the University of Leipzig, where he studied philosophy, mathematics, and law. After completing that program he began a doctoral program in law; however, when he applied for the degree at age twenty, he was refused because of his youth. Not to be outdone, Leibniz presented his thesis to the University of Altdorf, and the professors there were so impressed that they immediately awarded him the degree of Doctor of Laws and offered him a professorship.

Quite early in life Leibniz developed a taste for the finer things in life, including expensive clothing; long, flowing wigs; fancy carriages; and luxurious accommodations. However, following the death of his mother when he was eighteen, an uncle received what should have been Leibniz's inheritance. When this happened Leibniz figured that the best way of satisfying his expensive tastes was to attach

himself to the wealthy and the powerful, which he did with great success. He entered the employment of the elector of Mainz, and by the age of twenty-four he held the rank of privy counselor of justice, one of the highest positions in the government. His work as a diplomat allowed him the opportunity to travel widely and meet most of the prominent figures in Europe. Later he worked for the Duke of Hanover, a position that also allowed much time for travel and independent study.

Leibniz is sometimes called the father of symbolic logic for his work in developing the *universal characteristic,* a symbolic language in which any item of information can be represented in a natural and systematic way, together with the *calculus ratiocinator,* a deductive system for manipulating the symbols and deriving consequences. Given the dispassionate nature of this enterprise, Leibniz thought that it would serve to resolve differences of opinion in religion, theology, and philosophy. However, at age seventy he died in Hanover before completing the project.

6

(WFFs). "WFFs" is usually pronounced "woofs." A well-formed formula is a *syntactically* correct arrangement of symbols. In English, for example, the expression "there is a cat on the porch" is syntactically correct, but "Porch on the is cat a there" is not syntactically correct. Some examples of symbolic arrangements that are *not* well-formed formulas are "$A \supset \vee B$," "$A \bullet B (\vee C)$," and "$\sim \vee B \equiv \supset C$."

A few informal cues for constructing well-formed formulas follow. In these cues, the term *statements* includes simple statements and compound statements. Remember, $\sim A$ is a compound statement.

- Statements cannot be combined without an operator occurring between them.

  Not WFFs: AB, $A(B \supset C)$, $(A \supset B)(B \vee C)$
  WFFs: $A \supset B$, $A \vee \sim B$, $A \bullet (B \equiv C)$

- A tilde cannot immediately follow a statement, but it can immediately precede any statement (except when it immediately follows a statement).

  Not WFFs: $A\sim$, $A\sim B$, $(A \bullet B)\sim$
  WFFs: $\sim A$, $\sim(A \bullet B)$, $\sim\sim A$

- A tilde cannot immediately precede any other operator.

  Not WFFs: $\sim\bullet A$, $A\sim\vee B$

- A dot, wedge, horseshoe, or triple bar must go immediately between statements.

  Not WFFs: $\bullet A$, $A \vee$, $A \bullet \supset B$
  WFFs: $A \bullet B$, $A \supset \sim B$, $A \vee (B \bullet C)$

- Parentheses, brackets, and braces must be inserted to prevent ambiguity.

  Not WFFs: $A \supset B \vee C$, $A \bullet B \equiv C$
  WFFs: $A \supset (B \vee C)$, $(A \bullet B) \supset C$

Summary	Operator
not, it is not the case that, it is false that	$\sim$
and, yet, but, however, moreover, nevertheless, still, also, although, both, additionally, furthermore	$\bullet$
or, unless	$\vee$
if . . . then, only if, implies, given that, in case, provided that, on condition that, sufficient condition for, necessary condition for (Note: Do not confuse antecedent with consequent!)	$\supset$
if and only if, is equivalent to, sufficient and necessary condition for	$\equiv$

MindTap Strengthen your understanding of the topic with the section's **Video Lectures**.

I. Translate the following statements into symbolic form using uppercase letters to represent affirmative English statements. Example: Suppose you are given the statement "If Facebook makes us narcissistic, then either Twitter or LinkedIn relieves our loneliness." This would be translated $F \supset (T \lor L)$.

★1. Cartier does not make cheap watches.

2. Arizona has a national park but Nebraska does not.

3. Either Stanford or Tulane has an architecture school.

★4. Both Harvard and Baylor have medical schools.

5. If Chanel has a rosewood fragrance, then so does Lanvin.

6. Chanel has a rosewood fragrance if Lanvin does.

★7. Maureen Dowd writes incisive editorials if and only if Paul Krugman does.

8. Reese Witherspoon wins best actress only if Martin Scorsese wins best director.

9. Armani will launch a leather collection given that Gucci rejects skinny models.

★10. The Packers' winning most of their games implies that Aaron Rodgers is a great quarterback.

11. Bill Gates does not support malaria research unless Warren Buffet does.

12. Mercedes will introduce a hybrid model only if Lexus and BMW do.

★13. Mariah Carey sings pop and either Elton John sings rock or Diana Krall sings jazz.

14. Either Mariah Carey sings pop and Elton John sings rock or Diana Krall sings jazz.

15. Not both Jaguar and Porsche make motorcycles.

★16. Both Jaguar and Porsche do not make motorcycles.

17. Either Apple or Samsung makes smartphones.

18. Not either Ferrari or Maserati makes economy cars.

★19. Neither Ferrari nor Maserati makes economy cars.

20. Either Ferrari or Maserati does not make economy cars.

21. If Bill O'Reilly spins the news, then if Chris Matthews fights back, then Rachel Maddow tells it straight.

★22. If Bill O'Reilly's spinning the news implies that Chris Matthews fights back, then Rachel Maddow tells it straight.

6

MindTap® Complete exercises online for immediate feedback.

23. Tommy Hilfiger celebrates casual if and only if neither Ralph Lauren nor Calvin Klein offers street chic.

24. If Saks promotes gift cards, then either Macy's or Bloomingdale's puts on a fashion show.

★25. Either Rado does not make a sapphire watch or if Movado makes one then so does Pulsar.

26. If either Lockheed Martin or Raytheon floods the world with weapons of war, then neither General Dynamics nor Boeing reduces the likelihood of armed conflict.

27. If Electronic Arts and Activision Blizzard sell extremely violent video games, then either Colt or Smith & Wesson can expect increased profits.

★28. Mercury is a planet given that both Pluto and Ceres are not.

29. Saturn has rings, and Neptune is windy or Jupiter is massive.

30. Saturn has rings and Neptune is windy, or Jupiter is massive.

★31. Tiffany and Ben Bridge will release an emerald collection unless Zales and Kay do not.

32. Chevron continues to pollute provided that British Petroleum does, but Koch Industries and Exxon Mobil deny climate change.

33. Either Pablo Picasso or Salvador Dali ignored perspective, but it is not the case that both of them did.

★34. South Korea supports diplomacy; but if North Korea starts a war, then either China or Japan will be involved.

35. It is not the case that both Iran gives up its nuclear program and Sudan or Pakistan combats terrorism.

36. It is not the case that either Hezbollah will renounce violence or al-Qaeda and ISIS will be defeated.

★37. If Monsanto poisons the entire human race, then if Nestlé buries us in bottles, then Smithfield and Tyson load us up with antibiotics.

38. If Maria Cantwell promotes alternative energy, then if Patty Murray supports wilderness areas, then Dianne Feinstein's advocating gun control implies that Susan Collins does so, too.

39. It is not the case that either Tiger Woods and Maria Sharapova play professional football or Drew Brees and Serena Williams play professional baseball.

★40. It is not the case that both Lindsey Vonn or Kevin Durant plays professional tennis and Tom Brady or Matt Ryan plays professional basketball.

41. Israel's abandoning its settlements is a sufficient condition for the Palestinians' declaring an end to hostilities.

42. Israel's abandoning its settlements is a necessary condition for the Palestinians' declaring an end to hostilities.

★43. Israel's abandoning its settlements is a sufficient and necessary condition for the Palestinians' declaring an end to hostilities.

44. The Taliban's being defeated is a sufficient condition for Pakistan's winning the war on terror only if Afghanistan's securing its borders is a necessary condition for the UN's stopping the opium trade.

45. Katie Couric and Brooke Baldwin report international news if and only if Erica Hill and Norah O'Donnell cover political developments.

★46. It is not the case that both Walmart's jeopardizing worker safety implies that Target does and Costco's treating workers decently implies that Kmart does.

47. Cameron Diaz promotes environmental causes if Ben Affleck supports civil liberties, provided that Sean Penn opposes the death penalty.

48. JP Morgan's getting another bailout implies that Goldman Sachs cheats its clients, given that Bank of America's foreclosing on more homes implies that neither Morgan Stanley nor Citigroup curtails obscene bonuses.

★49. If Christina Aguilera's singing soul and Justin Timberlake's singing pop are sufficient and necessary conditions for Kelly Clarkson's singing rock, then neither Beyoncé nor Shakira will sing rap.

50. Nassau's advertising sizzling night clubs is a necessary condition for Puerto Vallarta's offering luxury hotels; moreover, Cancun's having turquoise waters and Acapulco's promising powder-white beaches is a sufficient condition for Jamaica's offering reggae music.

II. Translate the following statements into symbolic form using uppercase letters to represent affirmative English statements. Use the letters given in parentheses to form the translations.

★1. Unless we reduce the incidence of child abuse, future crime rates will increase. (R, F)

2. If pharmaceutical makers conceal test results, they are subject to substantial fines. (P, S)

3. African safaris are amazing, but they are also expensive. (A, E)

★4. Cigarette manufacturers are neither honest nor socially responsible. (H, S)

5. Psychologists and psychiatrists do not both prescribe antidepressant drugs. (O, I)

6. If health maintenance organizations cut costs, then either preventive medicine is emphasized or the quality of care deteriorates. (H, P, Q)

★7. A necessary condition for a successful business venture is good planning. (S, G)

8. If heroin is legalized, then its use may increase but criminal activity will decline. (L, U, C)

9. Ozone depletion in the atmosphere is a sufficient condition for increased cancer rates. (*O, I*)

★10. If affirmative action programs are dropped, then if new programs are not created, then minority applicants will suffer. (*A, N, M*)

11. If Internet use continues to grow, then more people will become cyber addicts and normal human relations will deteriorate. (*I, M, N*)

12. Human life will not perish unless either we poison ourselves with pollution or a large asteroid collides with the earth. (*H, P, L*)

★13. Cooling a group of atoms to absolute zero and keeping them bunched together is a necessary and sufficient condition for producing a Bose–Einstein condensate. (*C, K, P*)

14. If motion pictures contain subliminal sex messages or if they challenge the traditional family, then conservative politicians call for censorship. (*M, C, P*)

15. Either clear-cutting in national forests is halted and old-growth trees are allowed to stand, or salmon runs will be destroyed and bird habitats obliterated. (*C, O, S, B*)

★16. Three-strikes laws will be enforced and longer sentences imposed only if hundreds of new prisons are built, and that will happen only if taxes are increased. (*T, L, H, I*)

17. The Ebola virus is deadly, but it will become a major threat to humanity if and only if it becomes airborne and a vaccine is not developed. (*E, M, A, V*)

18. If evolutionary biology is correct, then higher life-forms arose by chance, and if that is so, then it is not the case that there is any design in nature and divine providence is a myth. (*E, H, D, P*)

★19. If banks charge fees for teller-assisted transactions, then more people will use ATMs; and if that happens and ATM fees increase, then banks will close branches and profits will skyrocket. (*B, M, F, C, P*)

20. If corporate welfare continues, then taxpayer interests will be ignored and billions of tax dollars will go to giant corporations; and if the latter occurs, then there will not be anything left for the poor and the budget will not be balanced. (*C, T, B, A, U*)

III. Determine which of the following are *not* well-formed formulas.

1. $(S \cdot {\sim}T) \vee ({\sim}U \cdot W)$

2. ${\sim}(K \vee L) \cdot (\supset G \vee H)$

3. $(E {\sim} F) \vee (W \equiv X)$

4. $(B \supset {\sim}T) \equiv {\sim}({\sim}C \supset U)$

5. $(F \equiv {\sim}Q) \cdot (A \supset E \vee T)$

6. ${\sim}D \vee {\sim}[(P \supset Q) \cdot (T \supset R)]$

7. $[(D \cdot \vee Q) \supset (P \vee E)] \vee [A \supset (\cdot H)]$

8. $M(N \supset Q) \vee (\sim C \cdot D)$

9. $\sim(F \vee \sim G) \supset [(A \equiv E) \cdot \sim H]$

10. $(R \equiv S \cdot T) \supset \sim(\sim W \cdot \sim X)$

IV. Construct compound propositions involving at least three simple propositions about the following topics. Then, symbolize your propositions as per Parts I and II of this exercise.

1. Political figures

2. NFL teams

3. Corporations

4. Brands of automobiles

5. Music or film celebrities

MindTap® Master concepts and improve outcomes with Aplia, at the end of the chapter, in the Aplia folder.

6.2   Truth Functions

HOW LOGICAL ARE YOU? Suppose your instructor makes this promise: If you get an A on the final exam, then you will get an A for the course. This is a conditional statement. Since there are two possible truth values for the antecedent (true and false) and two possible truth values for the consequent (true and false), there are four possible combinations in all. Under what combination of truth values would you say your instructor had lied?

Find the answer on MindTap.

The truth value of a compound proposition expressed in terms of one or more logical operators is said to be a function of the truth values of its components. This means that the truth value of the compound proposition is completely determined by the truth values of its components. If the truth values of the components are known, then the truth value of the compound proposition can be calculated from the definitions of the logical operators. Accordingly, a **truth function** is any compound proposition whose truth value is completely determined by the truth values of its components.

Many compound propositions in ordinary language are not truth functions. For example, the statement "Mary believes that Paul is dishonest" is compound because it contains the statement "Paul is dishonest" as a component. Yet the truth value of the compound statement is not determined by the truth value of the component, because Mary's beliefs about Paul are not compelled by any attribute that Paul may or may not possess.

The first part of this section presents the definitions of the five logical operators, the second part shows how they are used to compute the truth values of more-complicated propositions, and the third examines further the degree to which symbolized expressions match the meaning of expressions in ordinary language.

Definitions of the Logical Operators

The definitions of the logical operators are presented in terms of **statement variables**, which are lowercase letters (p, q, r, s) that can stand for any statement. For example, the statement variable p could stand for the statements A, $A \supset B$, $B \vee C$, and so on.

Statement variables are used to construct statement forms. A **statement form** is an arrangement of statement variables and operators such that the uniform substitution of statements in place of the variables results in a statement. For example, $\sim p$ and $p \supset q$ are statement forms because substituting the statements A and B in place of p and q, respectively, results in the statements $\sim A$ and $A \supset B$. For a slightly more complicated example, $(p \cdot q) \supset (q \vee r)$ is a statement form, because substituting A, B, and C in the place of p, q, and r, respectively, results in the statement $(A \cdot B) \supset (B \vee C)$. These statements are substitution instances of the respective statement forms.

A compound statement is said to have a certain form if it can be produced by substituting statements in place of the letters in that form. Thus, $\sim A$, $\sim(A \vee B)$, and $\sim[A \cdot (B \vee C)]$ are negations because they can be produced by substituting statements in place of p in the form $\sim p$.

Now let us consider the definition of the tilde operator (negation). This definition is given by a **truth table**, an arrangement of truth values that shows in every possible case how the truth value of a compound proposition is determined by the truth values of its simple components. The truth table for negation shows how any statement having the form of a negation ($\sim p$) is determined by the truth value of the statement that is negated (p):

	Negation	p	$\sim p$
		T	F
		F	T

The truth table shows that $\sim p$ is false when p is true and that $\sim p$ is true when p is false. This is exactly what we would expect, because it perfectly matches ordinary English usage. Examples:

It is not the case that McDonald's makes hamburgers. $\sim M$

It is not the case that Starbucks makes hamburgers. $\sim S$

The first statement is false because M is true, and the second is true because S is false.

Let us now consider the definition of the dot operator (conjunction). The truth table that follows shows how any statement having the form of a conjunction ($p \cdot q$) is determined by the truth values of its conjuncts (p, q):

Conjunction

p	q	$p \cdot q$
T	T	T
T	F	F
F	T	F
F	F	F

This truth table shows that a conjunction is true when its two conjuncts are true and is false in all other cases. This definition reflects ordinary language usage almost as perfectly as negation. Consider the following conjunctive statements:

Ferrari and Maserati make sports cars.	$F \cdot M$
Ferrari and GMC make sports cars.	$F \cdot G$
GMC and Jeep make sports cars.	$G \cdot J$

The first statement is true, because both conjuncts are true; but the second and third statements are false, because at least one of their conjuncts is false.

Turning now to the definition of the wedge operator (disjunction), the truth table is as follows:

Disjunction

p	q	$p \vee q$
T	T	T
T	F	T
F	T	T
F	F	F

The truth table indicates that the disjunction is true when at least one of the disjuncts is true and that otherwise it is false. The truth-functional interpretation of "or" is that of *inclusive* disjunction: Cases in which the disjunction is true include the case when both disjuncts are true. This inclusive sense of "or" corresponds to many instances of ordinary usage, as the following examples illustrate:

Either Steven King or Cate Blanchett is a novelist.	$S \vee C$
Either Steven King or Danielle Steel is a novelist.	$S \vee D$
Either Kobe Bryant or Tiger Woods is a novelist.	$K \vee T$

The first two statements are true, because in each case at least one of the disjuncts is true. The third is false, because both disjuncts are false.

The match between the truth-functional definition of disjunction and ordinary usage is not perfect, however. Sometimes the sense of a statement in ordinary language is that of *exclusive* disjunction. Examples:

The Orient Express is on either track A or track B.

You can have either soup or salad with this meal.

Tammy is either ten or eleven years old.

The sense of these statements excludes the possibility of both alternatives being true. Thus, if these statements were translated using the wedge, a portion of their ordinary meaning would be lost. If the exclusive aspect of these "either . . . or . . ." statements is essential, the symbolic equivalent of "but not both" can be attached to their translations. Thus the first statement could be translated $(A \lor B) \cdot {\sim}(A \cdot B)$.

Let us now consider the horseshoe operator (material implication, or conditional). Its truth table is as follows:

Conditional
(material implication)

p	q	$p \supset q$
T	T	T
T	F	F
F	T	T
F	F	T

The truth table shows that a conditional statement is false when the antecedent is true and the consequent false and is true in all other cases. This truth-functional interpretation of conditional statements conforms in part with the ordinary meaning of "if . . . then . . ." and in part it diverges. Consider the following examples:

If Nicole Kidman is an actor, then so is Meryl Streep.	$N \supset M$
If Nicole Kidman is an actor, then so is Wolf Blitzer.	$N \supset W$
If Wolf Blitzer is an actor, then so is Jennifer Aniston.	$W \supset J$
If Wolf Blitzer is an actor, then so is Anderson Cooper.	$W \supset A$

In these statements N, M, and J are true and W and A are false. Thus, according to the truth-functional interpretation, the first statement is true and the second false. This result conforms in large measure to our expectations. But the truth-functional interpretation of the last two statements is true. Although this result may not conflict with our expectations, it is not at all clear why these statements should be considered true.

For an intuitive approach to this problem, imagine that your logic instructor made the following statement: "If you get an A on the final exam, then you will get an A for the course." Under what conditions would you say that your instructor had lied to you? Clearly, if you got an A on the final exam but did not get an A for the course, you would say that she had lied. This outcome corresponds to a true antecedent and a false consequent. On the other hand, if you got an A on the final exam and also got an A for the course, you would say that she had told the truth (true antecedent, true consequent). But what if you failed to get an A on the final exam? Two alternatives are then possible: Either you got an A for the course anyway (false antecedent, true consequent) or you did not get an A for the course (false antecedent, false consequent). In neither case, though, would you say that your instructor had lied to you. Giving her the benefit of the doubt, you would say that she had told the truth.

Lastly, let us consider the definition of the triple-bar operator (material equivalence, or biconditional). Its truth table is as follows:

Biconditional

(material equivalence)

p	q	$p \equiv q$
T	T	T
T	F	F
F	T	F
F	F	T

The truth table shows that the biconditional is true when its two components have the same truth value and that otherwise it is false. These results are required by the fact that $p \equiv q$ is simply a shorter way of writing $(p \supset q) \cdot (q \supset p)$. If p and q are either both true or both false, then $p \supset q$ and $q \supset p$ are both true, making their conjunction true. But if p is true and q is false, then $p \supset q$ is false, making the conjunction false. Similarly, if p is false and q is true, then $q \supset p$ is false, again making the conjunction false. Thus, $p \equiv q$ is true when p and q have the same truth value and false when they have opposite truth values.

The truth-table definition of the triple-bar symbol conforms quite closely with ordinary usage, as the following examples illustrate:

Bill Maher is a show host if and only if Jimmy Fallon is.	$B \equiv J$
Bill Maher is a show host if and only if Emma Watson is.	$B \equiv E$
Emma Watson is a show host if and only if Matt Damon is.	$E \equiv M$

In these statements, B and J are true and E and M false. Thus, from the truth-functional standpoint, the first is true and the second false. This is what we would ordinarily expect. The third statement, however, turns out to be true because both of its components are false. While this result may not be what we would expect, it does not violate our expectations either. Other biconditional statements having false components are more obviously true. Example:

The Equal Rights Amendment is law if and only if thirty-eight states have approved it.

This statement asserts what is required to ratify any amendment to the U.S. Constitution, and so it is clearly true.

In summary, the definitions of the five logical operators conform reasonably well with ordinary linguistic usage. However, as the last part of this section shows, the match is less than perfect. Before considering this question, though, let us use the operator definitions to compute the truth values of more-complicated statements.

Computing the Truth Value of Longer Propositions

To compute the truth value of a more-complicated expression, use this procedure: Enter the truth values of the simple components directly beneath the letters. Then use these truth values to compute the truth values of the compound components. The truth value of a compound statement is written beneath the operator representing it. Let us suppose, for example, that we are told in advance that the simple propositions A, B, and C are true and D, E, and F are false. We may then compute the truth value of the following compound proposition:

$(A \vee D) \supset E$

First, we write the truth values of the simple propositions immediately below the respective letters and bring the operators and parentheses down:

$(A \vee D) \supset E$

$(T \vee F) \supset F$

Next, we compute the truth value of the proposition in parentheses and write it beneath the operator to which it pertains:

$(A \vee D) \supset E$

$(T \vee F) \supset F$

$\quad T \quad \supset F$

Finally, we use the last-completed line to obtain the truth value of the conditional, which is the main operator in the proposition:

$(A \vee D) \supset E$

$(T \vee F) \supset F$

$\quad T \quad \supset F$

$\quad \quad \textcircled{F}$

The final answer is circled. This is the truth value of the compound proposition given that A is true and D and E are false.

The general strategy is to build the truth values of the larger components from the truth values of the smaller ones. In general, the order to be followed in entering truth values is this:

1. Individual letters representing simple propositions
2. Tildes immediately preceding individual letters
3. Operators joining letters or negated letters
4. Tildes immediately preceding parentheses
5. And so on

Here are some additional examples. As before, let A, B, and C be true, D, E, and F false. Note that the computed truth values are written beneath the operators to which they pertain. The final answers, which are written beneath the main operators, are circled.

1. $(B \cdot C) \supset (E \supset A)$
   $(T \cdot T) \supset (F \supset T)$
   $\quad T \quad \supset \quad T$
   $\quad \quad \textcircled{T}$

2. $\sim (C \vee \sim A) \supset \sim B$
   $\sim (T \vee \sim T) \supset \sim T$
   $\sim (T \vee F) \quad \supset F$
   $\sim \quad T \qquad \supset F$
   $F \qquad\qquad \supset F$
   $\qquad\qquad\qquad \textcircled{T}$

3. $[\sim (D \vee F) \cdot (B \vee \sim A)] \supset \sim (F \supset \sim C)$
   $[\sim (F \vee F) \cdot (T \vee \sim T)] \supset \sim (F \supset \sim T)$
   $[\sim (F \vee F) \cdot (T \vee F) \quad] \supset \sim (F \supset F \quad)$
   $[\sim \quad F \quad \cdot \quad T \qquad] \supset \sim \quad T$
   $[T \qquad \cdot \quad T \qquad] \supset F$
   $\qquad\qquad T \qquad\qquad \supset F$
   $\qquad\qquad\qquad \textcircled{F}$

If preferred, the truth values of the compound components may be entered directly beneath the operators, without using the line-by-line approach illustrated in these examples. The following examples illustrate this second approach, which is used in the next section:

1. $[(D \equiv \sim A) \cdot \sim (C \cdot \sim B)] \equiv \sim [(A \supset \sim D) \vee (C \equiv E)]$
   F T F T T T   T F F T $\textcircled{F}$ F   T T T F T T F F

2. $\sim \{[(C \cdot \sim E) \supset \sim (A \cdot \sim B)] \supset [\sim (B \vee D) \equiv (\sim C \vee E)]\}$
   $\textcircled{F}$ T T T F T T T F F T T F T T F T F T F F

Further Comparison with Ordinary Language

The first part of this section showed that the definitions of the five logical operators conform reasonably well with ordinary linguistic usage. This part further examines the extent of this match in meaning.

In regard to the dot operator, which is used to translate "and" and "but," the match is often good; but it fails, at least in part, when the meaning of a conjunctive statement depends on the order of the conjuncts. Consider the following statements:

She got married and had a baby. $M \cdot B$

She had a baby and got married. $B \cdot M$

The first statement implies that the marriage occurred first, and the baby came later, while the second statement implies that the baby came first. This implied meaning is lost in the truth-functional interpretation, because $M \cdot B$ is logically equivalent to $B \cdot M$.

Another kind of mismatch between the truth-functional meaning of conjunctive statements and their ordinary language meaning occurs when the order of the conjuncts implies a causal connection. Example:

He fell off a ladder and broke his arm. $F \cdot B$

He broke his arm and fell off a ladder. $B \cdot F$

The first statement implies that the fall caused the broken arm, but the second statement implies no such thing. However, the truth-functional meanings of the two statements are logically equivalent.

For yet another example, consider the following:

This car is ugly, but it's economical to drive. $U \cdot E$

This car is economical to drive, but it's ugly. $E \cdot U$

The first statement subtly implies that we should buy this car, while the second implies that we should not buy it. But once again, the truth-functional interpretations are logically equivalent.

Another instance where the truth-functional interpretation of "and" differs from the ordinary linguistic meaning is offered by slang statements like this one:

You go for that gun, and you'll regret it.

The sense of this statement is not that you will in fact go for the gun but rather that, *if* you go for that gun, then . . . Accordingly, if this statement were interpreted as a truth-functional conjunction, its meaning would be distorted.

In regard to the wedge operator, which is used to translate "or" and "unless," we saw that the wedge is defined as inclusive disjunction, but we observed that the English word "or" sometimes has the sense of exclusive disjunction. This same observation applies to "unless." In the following statements, "unless" has an inclusive sense:

You won't win the lottery unless you buy a ticket.

It will not rain unless there are clouds in the sky.

The meaning of the first statement includes the case of buying a ticket and not winning, and the meaning of the second includes the case of there being clouds and no rain. In statements like these, where "unless" has an inclusive sense, using the wedge symbol to translate "unless" results in no loss of meaning.

On the other hand, in the following statements "unless" is used in the exclusive sense:

Pork is not properly cooked unless the meat is white.

These logs will make a nice campfire unless they are wet.

The first statement suggests that the meat cannot be white and at the same time not be properly cooked, and the second suggests that the logs cannot be wet and at the same time be used to make a nice campfire. Thus, if these statements are translated using the wedge operator, part of the meaning will be left out. If this additional part is essential, it can be included by adding the symbolic equivalent of "but not both" to the translation.

In connection with the horseshoe operator, we saw that a question arose when the antecedent of a conditional statement turned out to be false. Why, under this circumstance, should the conditional statement be said to be true? For an example of some conditional statements that conform to the truth-functional interpretation, consider the following:

If the temperature rises above 32°F, then the snow will begin to melt.

If Figure A is a triangle, then Figure A has three sides.

If all *A* are *B* and all *B* are *C*, then all *A* are *C*.

In all three examples the statement remains true even though the antecedent might be false. In the first, even though the temperature does not rise above 32°F at any particular moment, the law that governs the melting point of snow holds true. In other words, the statement (which expresses this law) is true regardless of the truth value of the antecedent. In the second, the mere fact that Figure A might not be a triangle does not affect the fact that a triangle, by definition, has three sides. Thus, the statement (which expresses this fact) is true regardless of the truth value of the antecedent. The third statement expresses a logical relationship between statements. This logical relationship remains unchanged regardless of what the terms A, B, and C are taken to represent. Thus, if A, B, and C represent "dogs," "cats," and "birds," respectively, both antecedent and consequent turn out to be false, but the conditional statement remains true.

As these examples illustrate, the definition of the horseshoe operator matches the meaning of some conditional statements in ordinary language very well. However, in general, the match is far from perfect. The source of the mismatch stems from the fact that the horseshoe operator designates the *material* conditional, or *truth-functional* conditional. The material conditional is a kind of conditional statement whose truth value depends purely on the truth or falsity of the antecedent and consequent and not on any inferential connection *between* antecedent and consequent. Since many conditional statements in ordinary language express such an inferential connection, when the horseshoe operator is used to translate them, part of their meaning is left out. For example, compare the following two statements:

> If Shakespeare wrote *Hamlet*, then the sun rises in the east.

> If ice is lighter than water, then ice floats in water.

The first statement expresses no inferential connection between antecedent and consequent, so using the horseshoe operator to translate it results in no loss of meaning. However, the second statement does express such a connection. The fact that ice is lighter than water is the reason why it floats. Accordingly, when the horseshoe operator is used to translate the second statement, this special meaning is lost.

The fact that the material conditional ignores inferential connections between antecedent and consequent allows for conflicts between the truth-functional interpretation of a conditional statement and the ordinary interpretation. Consider, for example, the following:

> If Kristen Gillibrand advocates the use of cocaine, then she is a good senator.

> If Chicago is in Michigan, then Chicago is very close to Miami.

According to their ordinary language interpretation, both of these statements are false. Good senators do not advocate the use of cocaine, and Michigan is far from Miami. Yet, when these statements are interpreted as material conditionals, both turn out to be true, because their antecedents are false. In cases like these, when the truth-functional interpretation of a conditional statement conflicts with the ordinary language interpretation, using the horseshoe operator to translate it may not be appropriate.

While inferential relations between antecedent and consequent often play some role in conditionals expressed in the indicative mood (such as those we just considered), they play a dominant role in conditional statements expressed in the subjunctive mood. Consider, for example, the following:

> If I were Dr. Dre, then I would be rich.
>
> If dolphins were fish, then they would be cold blooded.
>
> If the Washington Monument were made of lead, then it would be lighter than air.
>
> If President Kennedy had committed suicide, then he would be alive today.

Subjunctive conditionals are often called counterfactual conditionals because their antecedents are typically false. As a result, the *only* way of determining their truth value in ordinary language is through some kind of inference. Thus, from our knowledge that Dr. Dre is rich, we reason that if I were he, then I would be rich. Similarly, from our knowledge that all fish are cold blooded, we conclude that if dolphins were fish, then they would be cold blooded. On the other hand, we reason that the second two are false from our knowledge that lead is heavier than air and our knowledge that suicide results in death. Because the truth value of subjunctive conditionals is so closely tied to inferences like these and is so unrelated to the truth or falsity of the components, subjunctive conditionals are generally not considered to be truth functional at all, and the horseshoe operator is not used to translate them. But if they were interpreted truth-functionally, note that all four of these statements would turn out true, because they have false antecedents.

These observations about conditional statements apply equally to biconditionals. Just as the horseshoe operator expresses *material* implication, the triple-bar operator expresses *material* equivalence. As such, it ignores any inferential connection between its component statements, and, as a result, conflicts can arise between the ordinary meaning of a biconditional and its truth-functional meaning. Here are two examples of biconditionals expressed in the indicative mood that illustrate such a conflict:

> Mount Everest is easy to climb if and only if it is twenty-five miles high.
>
> The Department of Defense building is a hexagon if and only if it has eight sides.

According to the ordinary interpretation, these statements are false. Mountains that are twenty-five miles high are not easy to climb, and hexagons, by definition, have six sides, not eight. Yet, when these statements are interpreted as expressing material biconditionals, both are true, because in each case the component statements are false. In cases like these, when the ordinary meaning of a biconditional conflicts with the truth-functional meaning, using the triple-bar operator to translate it may not be appropriate. Furthermore, as with subjunctive conditionals, subjunctive biconditionals are generally not considered to be truth functional at all, so the triple-bar operator is not used to translate them.

I. Identify the main operator in the following propositions.

★1. $\sim(A \lor M) \cdot \sim(C \supset E)$

2. $(G \cdot \sim P) \supset \sim(H \lor \sim W)$

3. $\sim[P \cdot (S \equiv K)]$

★4. $\sim(K \cdot \sim O) \equiv \sim(R \lor \sim B)$

5. $(M \cdot B) \lor \sim[E \equiv \sim(C \lor I)]$

6. $\sim[(P \cdot \sim R) \supset (\sim E \lor F)]$

★7. $\sim[(S \lor L) \cdot M] \supset (C \lor N)$

8. $[\sim F \lor (N \cdot U)] \equiv \sim H$

9. $E \cdot [(F \supset A) \equiv (\sim G \lor H)]$

★10. $\sim[(X \lor T) \cdot (N \lor F)] \lor (K \supset L)$

II. Write the following compound statements in symbolic form, then use your knowledge of the historical events referred to by the simple statements to determine the truth value of the compound statements.

★1. It is not the case that Hitler ran the Third Reich.

2. Nixon resigned the presidency and Lincoln wrote the Gettysburg Address.

3. France bombed Pearl Harbor, or Lindbergh crossed the Atlantic.

★4. Hitler ran the Third Reich and Nixon did not resign the presidency.

5. Edison invented the telephone, or Custer was killed by the Indians.

6. Julius Caesar conquered America if Napoleon ruled France.

★7. Washington was assassinated only if Edison invented the telephone.

8. Lincoln wrote the Gettysburg Address if and only if France bombed Pearl Harbor.

9. It is not the case that either Julius Caesar conquered America or Washington was assassinated.

★10. If Hitler ran the Third Reich, then either Custer was killed by the Indians or Einstein discovered aspirin.

11. Either Lindbergh crossed the Atlantic and Edison invented the telephone or both Nixon resigned the presidency and it is false that Edison invented the telephone.

MindTap® Complete exercises online for immediate feedback.

12. Lincoln's having written the Gettysburg Address is a sufficient condition for Julius Caesar's having conquered America if and only if Washington's being assassinated is a necessary condition for Custer's having been killed by the Indians.

★13. Both Hitler ran the Third Reich and Lindbergh crossed the Atlantic if neither Einstein discovered aspirin nor France bombed Pearl Harbor.

14. It is not the case that Custer was killed by the Indians unless both Nixon resigned the presidency and Edison invented the telephone.

15. Custer was killed by the Indians, and Lincoln wrote the Gettysburg Address only if either Washington was assassinated or Julius Caesar conquered America.

III. Determine the truth values of the following symbolized statements. Let A, B, and C be true and X, Y, and Z be false. Circle your answer.

★1. $A \cdot X$

2. $B \cdot \sim Y$

3. $X \vee \sim Y$

★4. $\sim C \vee Z$

5. $B \supset \sim Z$

6. $Y \supset \sim A$

★7. $\sim X \supset Z$

8. $B \equiv Y$

9. $\sim C \equiv Z$

★10. $\sim (A \cdot \sim Z)$

11. $\sim B \vee (Y \supset A)$

12. $A \supset \sim (Z \vee \sim Y)$

★13. $(A \cdot Y) \vee (\sim Z \cdot C)$

14. $\sim (X \vee \sim B) \cdot (\sim Y \vee A)$

15. $(Y \supset C) \cdot \sim (B \supset \sim X)$

★16. $(C \equiv \sim A) \vee (Y \equiv Z)$

17. $\sim (A \cdot \sim C) \supset (\sim X \supset B)$

18. $\sim [(B \vee \sim C) \cdot \sim (X \vee \sim Z)]$

★19. $\sim [\sim (X \supset C) \equiv \sim (B \supset Z)]$

20. $(X \supset Z) \supset [(B \equiv \sim X) \cdot \sim (C \vee \sim A)]$

21. $[(\sim X \vee Z) \supset (\sim C \vee B)] \cdot [(\sim X \cdot A) \supset (\sim Y \cdot Z)]$

★22. $\sim[(A \equiv X) \vee (Z \equiv Y)] \vee [(\sim Y \supset B) \cdot (Z \supset C)]$

23. $[(B \cdot \sim C) \vee (X \cdot \sim Y)] \supset \sim[(Y \cdot \sim X) \vee (A \cdot \sim Z)]$

24. $\sim\{ \sim[(C \vee \sim B) \cdot (Z \vee \sim A)] \cdot \sim[\sim(B \vee Y) \cdot (\sim X \vee Z)]\}$

★25. $(Z \supset C) \supset \{[(\sim X \supset B) \supset (C \supset Y)] \equiv [(Z \supset X) \supset (\sim Y \supset Z)]\}$

IV. When possible, determine the truth values of the following symbolized statements. Let A and B be true, Y and Z false. P and Q have unknown truth values. If the truth value of the statement cannot be determined, write "undetermined."

★1. $A \vee P$

  2. $Q \vee Z$

  3. $Q \cdot Y$

★4. $Q \cdot A$

  5. $P \supset B$

  6. $Z \supset Q$

★7. $A \supset P$

  8. $P \equiv \sim P$

  9. $(P \supset A) \supset Z$

★10. $(P \supset A) \equiv (Q \supset B)$

  11. $(Q \supset B) \supset (A \supset Y)$

  12. $\sim(P \supset Y) \vee (Z \supset Q)$

★13. $\sim(Q \cdot Y) \equiv \sim(Q \vee A)$

  14. $[(Z \supset P) \supset P] \supset P$

  15. $[Q \supset (A \vee P)] \equiv [(Q \supset B) \supset Y]$

V. Create three simple propositions that you know to be true, and three simple propositions that you know to be false. Then select letters to represent these six simple propositions, and combine these letters in various ways to produce five compound propositions. Finally, use the rules for the logical operators to determine the truth value of the five compound propositions (as in Part III of this exercise).

MindTap®   Master concepts and improve outcomes with Aplia, at the end of the chapter, in the Aplia folder.

HOW LOGICAL ARE YOU? Suppose your boss says to you, "I will give you a raise only if your performance improves." You reply, "So, if my performance doesn't improve, you won't give me a raise?" Have you interpreted your boss correctly?

Find the answer on MindTap.

As we saw in Section 6.2, a truth table is an arrangement of truth values that shows, in every possible case, how the truth value of a compound proposition is determined by the truth value of its simple components.* To construct a truth table, the first step is to determine the number of lines (or rows). Because each line represents one possible arrangement of truth values, the total number of lines is equal to the number of possible combinations of truth values for the simple propositions. If there is only one simple proposition, p, the number of lines in the truth table is two, because there are only two possible truth values for p: true, and false. If there are two simple propositions, p and q, there are four lines, because there are four combinations of truth values: p true and q true, p true and q false, p false and q true, and p false and q false. The relationship between the number of different simple propositions and the number of lines in the truth table is expressed as follows:

Number of different simple propositions	Number of lines in truth table
1	2
2	4
3	8
4	16
5	32
6	64

The relationship between these two columns of numbers is expressed by the formula,

$$L = 2^n$$

where L designates the number of lines in the truth table, and n the number of *different* simple propositions.

Let us now construct a truth table for a compound proposition. We may begin with a fairly simple one:

$$(A \vee \sim B) \supset B$$

The number of different simple propositions is two. Thus the number of lines in the truth table is four. We begin by writing the simple propositions (A, B) to the left of the

---

*An alternate technique, called Truth Trees, is presented in MindTap.

compound proposition, separated by a vertical line. Then, beneath this arrangement, we write the four lines for the truth table:

A	B	(A ∨ ~ B) ⊃ B

The next step is to enter truth values for the two letters on the left. For *A*, we divide the total number of lines (four) in half. This gives us two, so we write two T's and two F's beneath *A*:

A	B	(A ∨ ~ B) ⊃ B
T		
T		
F		
F		

Next, we take the number we obtained for *A*, namely two, and divide that in half, which gives us one. So, beneath *B*, we write one true, one false, one true, and one false:

A	B	(A ∨ ~ B) ⊃ B
T	T	
T	F	
F	T	
F	F	

This arrangement gives us all possible combinations of truth values for *A* and *B*: *A* true, *B* true; *A* true, *B* false; *A* false, *B* true; and *A* false, *B* false.

To complete the truth table, we use the columns of truth values beneath the letters on the left to compute the column of truth values for the given proposition. Beginning inside the parentheses, we compute the truth value of ~*B* on each line, which is the negation of the truth value of *B*:

A	B	(A ∨ ~ B) ⊃ B
T	T	F
T	F	T
F	T	F
F	F	T

Next, we look at the column beneath *A*, on the left, and the column beneath the tilde, to produce the column beneath the wedge:

A	B	(A ∨ ~ B) ⊃ B
T	T	T F
T	F	T T
F	T	F F
F	F	T T

Lastly, we look at the column beneath the wedge, and the column beneath *B* on the left, to produce the column beneath the horseshoe. Since the horseshoe is the main operator, we place a box around the column beneath it to indicate that it represents the entire compound proposition:

```
A   B │ (A ∨ ~ B) ⊃ B
T   T │    T F      T
T   F │    T T      F
F   T │    F F      T
F   F │    T T      F
```

The truth table tells us that the truth value of the compound proposition is true when *B* is true and false when *B* is false, regardless of the truth value of *A*.

Next, let us construct a truth table for a proposition containing three simple components:

$$(C \cdot \sim D) \supset E$$

Since there are three simple components, there are eight lines in the truth table. We begin by writing the three simple components (*C, D, E*) on the left, and we separate them from the compound proposition with a vertical line:

```
C   D   E │ (C • ~ D) ⊃ E
──────────│──────────────
          │
──────────│──────────────
          │
──────────│──────────────
          │
──────────│──────────────
          │
```

First, we enter truth values for the three letters on the left. Since there are eight lines in the truth table, we divide that number in half and enter four T's and four F's beneath *C*. Then we enter two T's, two F's, two T's, and two F's beneath *D*, and one T, one F, and so forth, beneath *E*:

```
C   D   E │ (C • ~ D) ⊃ E
T   T   T │
T   T   F │
T   F   T │
T   F   F │
F   T   T │
F   T   F │
F   F   T │
F   F   F │
```

Then we look at the column beneath D on the left to compute the truth value for $\sim D$, and we use that column together with the column beneath C on the left to produce the column beneath the dot:

C	D	E	(C	•	~ D)	⊃ E
T	T	T		F	F	
T	T	F		F	F	
T	F	T		T	T	
T	F	F		T	T	
F	T	T		F	F	
F	T	F		F	F	
F	F	T		F	T	
F	F	F		F	T	

Lastly, we look at the column beneath the dot and the column beneath E on the left to produce the column beneath the horseshoe. We outline the column beneath the horseshoe to indicate that it represents the entire compound proposition:

C	D	E	(C	•	~ D)	⊃	E
T	T	T		F	F	T	
T	T	F		F	F	T	
T	F	T		T	T	T	
T	F	F		T	T	F	
F	T	T		F	F	T	
F	T	F		F	F	T	
F	F	T		F	T	T	
F	F	F		F	T	T	

The truth table shows that the truth value of the compound proposition is false when C is true, D is false, and E is false, and otherwise it is true.

An alternate method for constructing truth tables can be shorter than the conventional method just presented. Let us return to the compound proposition considered at the beginning of this section. For this alternate method, we dispense with the two columns of truth values on the left-hand side, and we begin by entering truth values directly beneath the A and B in the compound proposition:

(A	v ~	B)	⊃	B
T				T
T				F
F				T
F				F

Then we enter the truth values beneath the tilde:

(A	v	~	B)	⊃	B
T		F	T		
T		T	F		
F		F	T		
F		T	F		

Next, we use the column of truth values beneath *A* and beneath the tilde to produce the column beneath the wedge:

```
(A  v  ~  B) ⊃ B
 T  T  F  T
 T  T  T  F
 F  F  F  T
 F  T  T  F
```

Lastly, we use the column beneath the wedge and the column beneath *B* inside the parentheses to produce the column beneath the horseshoe. We place a box around this final column to indicate that it represents the entire compound proposition:

```
(A  v  ~  B)  ⊃  B
 T  T  F  T    T
 T  T  T  F    F
 F  F  F  T    T
 F  T  T  F    F
```

Again, the truth table shows that the truth value of the compound proposition is true when *B* is true and false when *B* is false, without regard to the truth value of *A*. This alternate method will be used to produce truth tables later in this chapter.

Classifying Statements

Truth tables may be used to determine whether the truth value of a compound statement depends solely on its form or whether it also depends on the specific truth values of its components. A compound statement is said to be a **logically true** or **tautologous statement** if it is true regardless of the truth values of its components. It is said to be a **logically false** or **self-contradictory statement** if it is false regardless of the truth values of its components. And it is said to be a **contingent statement** if its truth value varies depending on the truth values of its components. By inspecting the column of truth values under the main operator, we can determine how the compound proposition should be classified:

Column under main operator	Statement classification
all true	tautologous (logically true)
all false	self-contradictory (logically false)
at least one true, at least one false	contingent

As the truth table we developed earlier indicates, $(C \cdot \sim D) \supset E$ is a contingent proposition. The column under the main operator contains at least one T and at least one F. In other words, the truth value of the compound proposition is "contingent" on the truth values of its components. Sometimes it is true, sometimes false, depending on the truth values of the components.

On the other hand, consider the following truth tables:

```
[(G ⊃ H) • G] ⊃ H        (G v H)  ≡  (~ G • ~ H)
 T T T  T T  T  T          T T T   F   F T F F T
 T F F  F T  T  F          T T F   F   F T F T F
 F T T  F F  T  T          F T T   F   T F F F T
 F T F  F F  T  F          F F F   F   T F T T F
```

The proposition on the left is tautologous (logically true or a **tautology**) because the column under the main operator is all true. The one on the right is self-contradictory (logically false) because the main operator column is all false. In neither case is the truth value of the compound proposition contingent on the truth values of the components. The one on the left is true regardless of the truth values of its components—in other words, *necessarily* true. The one on the right is *necessarily* false.

If a proposition is either logically true or logically false, its truth value depends merely on its form and has nothing to do with its content. As a result, such statements do not make any genuine assertions about things in the world. For example, the tautologous statement "It is either raining or it is not raining" provides no information about the weather. Similarly, the self-contradictory statement "It is raining and it is not raining" provides no information about the weather. On the other hand, the contingent statement "It is raining in the mountains" does provide information about the weather.

Comparing Statements

Truth tables may also be used to determine how two propositions are related to each other. Two propositions are said to be **logically equivalent statements** if they have the same truth value on each line under their main operators, and they are **contradictory statements** if they have opposite truth values on each line under their main operators. If neither of these relations hold, the propositions are either consistent or inconsistent. Two (or more) propositions are **consistent statements** if there is at least one line on which both (or all) of them turn out to be true, and they are **inconsistent statements** if there is no line on which both (or all) of them turn out to be true. By comparing the main operator columns, one can determine which is the case. However, because the first two relations are stronger than (and may overlap) the second two, the first two relations should be considered first.

Columns under main operators	Relation
same truth value on each line	logically equivalent
opposite truth value on each line	contradictory
there is at least one line on which the truth values are both true	consistent
there is no line on which the truth values are both true	inconsistent

For example, the following two propositions are logically equivalent. The main operator columns of their respective truth tables are identical. Note that for proper comparison the columns under K must be identical and the columns under L must be identical.

$K \supset L$	$\sim L \supset \sim K$	
T T T	F T T F T	
T F F	T F F F T	**Logically equivalent**
F T T	F T T T F	
F T F	T F T T F	

For any two propositions that are logically equivalent, the biconditional statement formed by joining them with a triple bar is tautologous. Thus, $(K \supset L) \equiv (\sim L \supset \sim K)$ is tautologous. This is easy to see because the columns under the main operators of $K \supset L$ and $\sim L \supset \sim K$ are identical.

The next two propositions are contradictory:

$K \supset L$	$K \cdot \sim L$	
T T T	T F F T	
T F F	T T T F	**Contradictory**
F T T	F F F T	
F T F	F F T F	

The next two propositions are consistent. On the first line of each truth table the column under the main operator turns out true. This means that it is possible for both propositions to be true, which is the meaning of consistency:

$K \vee L$	$K \cdot L$	
T T T	T T T	
T T F	T F F	**Consistent**
F T T	F F T	
F F F	F F F	

Finally, the next two propositions are inconsistent. There is no line in the columns under the main operators where the truth values are both true:

$K \equiv L$	$K \cdot \sim L$	
T T T	T F F T	
T F F	T T T F	**Inconsistent**
F F T	F F F T	
F T F	F F T F	

Any pair of propositions is either consistent or inconsistent. Furthermore, some consistent propositions are also logically equivalent, and some inconsistent propositions are either contradictory or logically equivalent. Because of this partial overlap, pairs of propositions are usually first classified in terms of the stronger of these relations, which are logical equivalence and contradiction. If neither of these stronger relations applies, then the pair of propositions is classified in terms of the weaker relations, consistency and inconsistency.

Unlike logical equivalence and contradiction, which usually relate exactly two propositions, consistency and inconsistency often apply to larger groups of propositions. For consistency, the only requirement is that there be at least one line in the group of truth tables where all of the propositions are true, and for inconsistency the only requirement is that there be no such line. As a result of these requirements, the statement consisting of the conjunction of a group of inconsistent propositions will always be self-contradictory, whereas the statement consisting of the conjunction of a group of consistent propositions will never be self-contradictory.

Consistency and inconsistency are important because, among other things, they can be used to evaluate the overall rationality of a person's stated position on something. If the statements expressing such a position are consistent, then there is at least a possibility that the position makes sense. This is so because there will be at least one line in the group of truth tables where all of the person's statements are true. On the other hand, if the statements are inconsistent, then there is no possibility that the position makes sense. In this case there is no line in the truth tables where all of the statements are true. Conjoining the statements results in a self-contradiction.

The truth tables for consistency and logical equivalence also illustrate the important difference between two propositions being factually true and their being logically equivalent. For example, the statements "Water boils at 100°C" and "The current population of the United States is over 300 million" are both true in the present actual world. This real-world situation conforms to the one truth-table line on which both statements are true. As a result of this line, the two statements are consistent. However, they are not logically equivalent, because their truth values are not *necessarily* the same. The truth value of the second proposition might change in the future, while that of the first would remain the same. An analogous distinction, incidentally, holds between two statements having actually opposite truth values and their being contradictory.

6

EXERCISE 6.3

I. Use truth tables to determine whether the following symbolized statements are tautologous, self-contradictory, or contingent.

★1. $N \supset (N \supset N)$

2. $(G \supset G) \supset G$

3. $(S \supset R) \cdot (S \cdot {\sim}R)$

★4. $[(E \supset F) \supset F] \supset E$

5. $({\sim}K \supset H) \equiv {\sim}(H \vee K)$

6. $(M \supset P) \vee (P \supset M)$

★7. $[(Z \supset X) \cdot (X \vee Z)] \supset X$

8. $[(C \supset D) \cdot {\sim}C] \supset {\sim}D$

MindTap® Complete exercises online for immediate feedback.

9. $[X \supset (R \supset F)] \equiv [(X \supset R) \supset F]$

★10. $[G \supset (N \supset \sim G)] \cdot [(N \equiv G) \cdot (N \vee G)]$

11. $[(Q \supset P) \cdot (\sim Q \supset R)] \cdot \sim (P \vee R)$

12. $[(H \supset N) \cdot (T \supset N)] \supset [(H \vee T) \supset N]$

★13. $[U \cdot (T \vee S)] \equiv [(\sim T \vee \sim U) \cdot (\sim S \vee \sim U)]$

14. $\{[(G \cdot N) \supset H] \cdot [(G \supset H) \supset P]\} \supset (N \supset P)$

15. $[(F \vee E) \cdot (G \vee H)] \equiv [(G \cdot E) \vee (F \cdot H)]$

II. Use truth tables to determine whether the following pairs of symbolized statements are logically equivalent, contradictory, consistent, or inconsistent. First, determine whether the pairs of propositions are logically equivalent or contradictory; then, if these relations do not apply, determine if they are consistent or inconsistent.

★1. $\sim D \vee B$ $\sim (D \cdot \sim B)$

2. $F \cdot M$ $\sim (F \vee M)$

3. $\sim K \supset L$ $K \supset \sim L$

★4. $R \vee \sim S$ $S \cdot \sim R$

5. $\sim A \equiv X$ $(X \cdot \sim A) \vee (A \cdot \sim X)$

6. $H \equiv \sim G$ $(G \cdot H) \vee (\sim G \cdot \sim H)$

★7. $(E \supset C) \supset L$ $E \supset (C \supset L)$

8. $N \cdot (A \vee \sim E)$ $\sim A \cdot (E \vee \sim N)$

9. $M \supset (K \supset P)$ $(K \cdot M) \supset P$

★10. $W \equiv (B \cdot T)$ $W \cdot (T \supset \sim B)$

11. $G \cdot (E \vee P)$ $\sim (G \cdot E) \cdot \sim (G \cdot P)$

12. $R \cdot (Q \vee S)$ $(S \vee R) \cdot (Q \vee R)$

★13. $H \cdot (K \vee J)$ $(J \cdot H) \vee (H \cdot K)$

14. $Z \cdot (C \equiv P)$ $C \equiv (Z \cdot \sim P)$

15. $Q \supset \sim (K \vee F)$ $(K \cdot Q) \vee (F \cdot Q)$

III. Use truth tables to obtain the answers to the following exercises. The letters to be used in constructing the truth tables are given in parentheses.

★1. Renowned economist Harold Carlson makes the following prediction: "The balance of payments will decrease if and only if interest rates remain steady; however, it is not the case that either interest rates will not remain steady or the balance of payments will decrease." What can we say about Carlson's prediction? (B, I)

2. A high school principal made this statement to the school board: "Either music is not dropped from the curriculum or the students will become cultural

philistines; furthermore, the students will not become cultural philistines if and only if music is dropped from the curriculum." Assuming the principal is correct, what has she told us about music and the students? (*Hint*: Construct a truth table for the principal's statement and examine the line on which the statement turns out true.) (*M, C*)

3. Christina and Thomas are having a discussion about their plans for the evening. Christina: "If you don't love me, then I'm certainly not going to have sex with you." Thomas: "Well, that means that if I do love you, then you will have sex with me, right?" Is Thomas correct? (*Hint*: Construct a truth table for each statement and compare them.) (*L, S*)

★4. Two astronomers are discussing supernovas. Dr. Frank says, "Research has established that if a supernova occurs within ten light-years of the earth, then life on Earth will be destroyed." Dr. Harris says, "Research has also established that either a supernova will not occur within ten light-years of the earth or life on Earth will not be destroyed." Is it possible that both astronomers are correct? If so, what can we determine about the occurrence of a supernova? (*S, L*)

5. Antonia Martinez, who is running for the state senate, makes this statement: "Either a tax reduction is feasible only if both educational costs do not increase and the welfare program is abolished, or a tax reduction is feasible and either the welfare program will not be abolished or educational costs will increase." What has Martinez told us about taxes, educational costs, and welfare? (*T, E, W*)

6. Automotive expert Frank Goodbody has this to say about Japanese imports: "If Mitsubishi is the sportiest, then both Toyota is the most trouble-free and Isuzu is not the lowest priced. If Isuzu is the lowest priced, then both Toyota is not the most trouble-free and Mitsubishi is the sportiest." Is it possible that Goodbody is correct in his assessment? If so, what may we conclude about Mitsubishi, Toyota, and Isuzu? (*M, T, I*)

★7. Two stockbrokers are having a discussion. One claims that Netmark will introduce a new product if and only if both Datapro cuts its workforce and Compucel expands production. The other claims that Datapro will cut its workforce, and Compucel will expand production if and only if Netmark introduces a new product. Is it possible that both stockbrokers are right? If so, what have they told us about these companies? (*N, D, C*)

8. Eric Carson sums up his beliefs about God as follows: "God exists if and only if either life is meaningful or the soul is not immortal. God exists and the soul is immortal. If God exists, then life is not meaningful." Is it possible that Eric's beliefs make sense? (*G, L, S*)

9. Cindy, Jane, and Amanda witnessed a bank robbery. At trial, Cindy testified that Lefty did not enter the bank, and if Howard pulled a gun, then Conrad collected the money. Jane testified that if Howard did not pull a gun, then Lefty entered the bank. Amanda testified that if Conrad collected the money, then Howard pulled a gun. Is it possible that all three witnesses told the truth? If so, what can we conclude about Lefty, Howard, and Conrad? (*L, H, C*)

★10. Nicole Evans expresses her philosophy as follows: "If the mind is identical to the brain, then personal freedom does not exist and humans are not responsible for their actions. If personal freedom does not exist, then the mind is identical to the brain. Either humans are responsible for their actions or the mind is not identical to the brain. If personal freedom exists, then humans are responsible for their actions." Is it possible that Nicole's philosophy makes sense? If so, what does it say about the mind, personal freedom, and responsibility? (*M*, *P*, *H*)

IV. Did you work Exercise 6.1, IV? If not, work it now. Then take the symbolized compound statements you created for this exercise and construct a truth table for each. Finally, categorize each statement as tautologous, self-contradictory, or contingent.

MindTap° Master concepts and improve outcomes with Aplia, at the end of the chapter, in the Aplia folder.

6.4   Truth Tables for Arguments

HOW LOGICAL ARE YOU? Imagine that you enter a race and you are faster than all the other runners but you still don't win. Or, you live an upstanding life and never lie or cheat but you end up on death row. Or, you always drive your car within the speed limit but still get speeding tickets. Or, you work hard and do a great job but don't get paid. Do you see a similarity between these situations and being given what you are told is a good argument that has true premises and yet has a false conclusion?

Find the answer on MindTap.

Truth tables provide the standard technique for testing the validity of arguments in propositional logic. To construct a truth table for an argument, follow these steps:

1. Symbolize the arguments using letters to represent the simple propositions.
2. Write out the symbolized argument, placing a single slash between the premises and a double slash between the last premise and the conclusion.
3. Draw a truth table for the symbolized argument as if it were a proposition broken into parts, outlining the columns representing the premises and conclusion.
4. Look for a line in which all of the premises are true and the conclusion is false. If such a line exists, the argument is invalid; if not, it is valid.

For example, let us test the following argument for validity:

> If juvenile killers are as responsible for their crimes as adults are, then execution is a justifiable punishment.
> Juvenile killers are not as responsible for their crimes as adults are.
> Therefore, execution is not a justifiable punishment.

The first step is to symbolize the argument:

$$J \supset E$$
$$\underline{\sim J}$$
$$\sim E$$

Now a truth table may be constructed. Since the symbolized argument contains two different letters, the truth table has four lines. Make sure that identical letters have identical columns beneath them. Here are the columns for the individual letters:

J	⊃	E	/	~	J	//	~	E
T		T			T			T
T		F			T			F
F		T			F			T
F		F			F			F

The truth table is now completed, and the columns representing the premises and conclusion are outlined:

J	⊃	E	/	~	J	//	~	E
T	T	T		F	T		F	T
T	F	F		F	T		T	F
F	T	T		T	F		F	T
F	T	F		T	F		T	F

Inspection of the third line reveals that both of the premises are true and the conclusion is false. The argument is therefore invalid.

Another example:

> If insider trading occurs, then investors will not trust the securities markets. If investors do not trust the securities markets, then business in general will suffer. Therefore, if insider trading occurs, then business in general will suffer.

The completed truth table is this:

O	⊃	~	T	/	~	T	⊃	B	//	O	⊃	B
T	F	F	T		F	T	T	T		T	T	T
T	F	F	T		F	T	T	F		T	F	F
T	T	T	F		T	F	T	T		T	T	T
T	T	T	F		T	F	F	F		T	F	F
F	T	F	T		F	T	T	T		F	T	T
F	T	F	T		F	T	T	F		F	T	F
F	T	T	F		T	F	T	T		F	T	T
F	T	T	F		T	F	F	F		F	T	F

Inspection of the truth table reveals that there is no line on which both premises are true and the conclusion is false. The argument is therefore valid.

The logic behind the method of truth tables is easy to understand. By definition, a valid argument is one in which it is not possible for the premises to be true and the

Ada Byron, Countess of Lovelace 1815–1852

Ada Byron, born in 1815, was the only child of the English poet George Gordon (Lord Byron) and Annabella Milbanke. By the time Ada was born, Lady Byron had grown to detest her husband, and she did everything in her power to ensure that Ada would grow up to be as much unlike him as possible. Lady Byron had a talent for mathematics, which her husband did not share in the least, so she hired a series of tutors to instruct young Ada in that discipline. One of those tutors was the famous mathematician and logician Augustus De Morgan, with whom Ada became a close friend.

In 1835 Ada Byron married William King, and when King was elevated to Earl of Lovelace three years later, Ada became Countess of Lovelace. The couple had three children, but the duties of wife and mother did not interrupt Ada's study of mathematics and logic. Two years prior to her marriage Ada met Charles Babbage, an early inventor of mechanical computers, and when she was first shown Babbage's Difference Engine, she immediately grasped all the intricacies of its operation.

A few years later, when Babbage proposed a design for the Analytic Engine, Ada wrote a lengthy program for the new machine, and she envisioned how it could be used not only to solve problems in mathematics, but to produce music and graphics as well. Because of this work, Ada Byron is usually credited with being the first computer programmer.

ARPL/HIP/The Image Works

Ada had suffered problems with her health ever since childhood, and as she grew older, these problems were aggravated by alcohol abuse. In 1852 she died from cancer at the relatively young age of thirty-six.

conclusion false. A truth table presents every possible combination of truth values that the components of an argument may have. Therefore, if no line exists on which the premises are true and the conclusion false, then it is not possible for the premises to be true and the conclusion false, in which case the argument is valid. Conversely, if there *is* a line on which the premises are true and the conclusion false, then it *is* possible for the premises to be true and the conclusion false, and the argument is invalid. Accordingly, to test the validity of an argument, use this procedure:

Look for a line that has all true premises and a false conclusion. If you find such a line, the argument is invalid. If not, the argument is valid.

Truth tables provide a convenient illustration of the fact that any argument having inconsistent premises is valid regardless of what its conclusion may be, and any argument having a tautologous conclusion is valid regardless of what its premises may be. Example:

The sky is blue.
The sky is not blue.
Therefore, Paris is the capital of France.

S / ∼ S // P

S	∼ S	P
T	F T	T
T	F T	F
F	T F	T
F	T F	F

Since the premises of this argument are inconsistent, there is no line on which the premises are both true. Accordingly, there is no line on which the premises are both true and the conclusion false, so the argument is valid. Of course, the argument is unsound, because it has a false premise. Another example:

Bern is the capital of Switzerland. Therefore, it is either raining or it is not raining.

B // R ∨ ∼ R

B	R	∨	∼	R
T	T	T	F	T
T	F	T	T	F
F	T	T	F	T
F	F	T	T	F

The conclusion of this argument is a tautology. Accordingly, there is no line on which the premise is true and the conclusion false, and so the argument is valid. Incidentally, it is also sound, because the premise is true.

The conditional statement having the conjunction of an argument's premises as its antecedent and the conclusion as its consequent is called the argument's **corresponding conditional**. For example, the corresponding conditional of the second argument tested in this section is $[(O \supset {\sim}T) \cdot ({\sim}T \supset B)] \supset (O \supset B)$. For any valid argument (such as this one), the corresponding conditional is a tautology. This is easy to see. In any valid argument, there is no line on which the premises are all true and the conclusion false. Thus, in the corresponding conditional, there is no line on which the antecedent is true and the consequent false, so the corresponding conditional is true on every line.

EXERCISE 6.4

I. Translate the following arguments into symbolic form. Then determine whether each is valid or invalid by constructing a truth table for each. The letters to be used in constructing the truth tables are given in parentheses.

★1. If national elections deteriorate into TV popularity contests, then smooth-talking morons will get elected. Therefore, if national elections do not deteriorate into TV popularity contests, then smooth-talking morons will not get elected. (N, S)

MindTap® Complete exercises online for immediate feedback.

2. Brazil has a huge foreign debt. Therefore, either Brazil or Argentina has a huge foreign debt. (B, A)

3. If fossil-fuel combustion continues at its present rate, then a greenhouse effect will occur. If a greenhouse effect occurs, then world temperatures will rise. Therefore, if fossil-fuel combustion continues at its present rate, then world temperatures will rise. (F, G, W)

★4. If there are dried-up riverbeds on Mars, then water once flowed on the Martian surface. There are dried-up riverbeds on Mars. Therefore, water once flowed on the Martian surface. (D, W)

5. If high school graduates are deficient in reading, they will not be able to compete in the modern world. If high school graduates are deficient in writing, they will not be able to compete in the modern world. Therefore, if high school graduates are deficient in reading, then they are deficient in writing. (R, C, W)

6. The disparity between rich and poor is increasing. Therefore, political control over economic equality will be achieved only if restructuring the economic system along socialist lines implies that political control over economic equality will be achieved. (D, P, R)

★7. Einstein won the Nobel Prize either for explaining the photoelectric effect or for the special theory of relativity. But he did win the Nobel Prize for explaining the photoelectric effect. Therefore, Einstein did not win the Nobel Prize for the special theory of relativity. (P, S)

8. If microchips are made from diamond wafers, then computers will generate less heat. Computers will not generate less heat and microchips will be made from diamond wafers. Therefore, synthetic diamonds will be used for jewelry. (M, C, S)

9. Either the USS *Arizona* or the USS *Missouri* was not sunk in the attack on Pearl Harbor. Therefore, it is not the case that either the USS *Arizona* or the USS *Missouri* was sunk in the attack on Pearl Harbor. (A, M)

★10. If racial quotas are adopted for promoting employees, then qualified employees will be passed over; but if racial quotas are not adopted, then prior discrimination will go unaddressed. Either racial quotas will or will not be adopted for promoting employees. Therefore, either qualified employees will be passed over or prior discrimination will go unaddressed. (R, Q, P)

II. Determine whether the following symbolized arguments are valid or invalid by constructing a truth table for each.

★1. $\dfrac{K \supset \sim K}{\sim K}$

2. $\dfrac{R \supset R}{R}$

3. $\dfrac{P \equiv \sim N}{N \vee P}$

★4. $\begin{array}{l} \sim(G \cdot M) \\ \underline{M \vee \sim G} \\ \sim G \end{array}$

5. $K \equiv \sim L$
$\sim (L \cdot \sim K)$
$\overline{K \supset L}$

6. Z
$\overline{E \supset (Z \supset E)}$

★7. $\sim (W \cdot \sim X)$
$\sim (X \cdot \sim W)$
$\overline{X \vee W}$

8. $C \equiv D$
$E \vee \sim D$
$\overline{E \supset C}$

9. $A \equiv (B \vee C)$
$\sim C \vee B$
$\overline{A \supset B}$

★10. $J \supset (K \supset L)$
$K \supset (J \supset L)$
$\overline{(J \vee K) \supset L}$

11. $\sim (K \equiv S)$
$S \supset \sim (R \vee K)$
$\overline{R \vee \sim S}$

12. $E \supset (F \cdot G)$
$F \supset (G \supset H)$
$\overline{E \supset H}$

★13. $A \supset (N \vee Q)$
$\sim (N \vee \sim A)$
$\overline{A \supset Q}$

14. $G \supset H$
$R \equiv G$
$\sim H \vee G$
$\overline{R \equiv H}$

15. $L \supset M$
$M \supset N$
$N \supset L$
$\overline{L \vee N}$

★16. $S \supset T$
$S \supset \sim T$
$\sim T \supset S$
$\overline{S \vee \sim T}$

17. $W \supset X$
$X \supset W$
$X \supset Y$
$Y \supset X$
$\overline{W \equiv Y}$

18. $K \equiv (L \vee M)$
$L \supset M$
$M \supset K$
$K \vee L$
$\overline{K \supset L}$

★19. $A \supset B$
$(A \cdot B) \supset C$
$A \supset (C \supset D)$
$\overline{A \supset D}$

20. $\sim A \vee R$
$\sim (N \cdot \sim C)$
$R \supset C$
$C \supset \sim N$
$\overline{A \vee C}$

21. $(G \vee S) \supset S$
$S \equiv (G \vee S)$
$(G \cdot \sim S) \supset \sim G$
$(S \cdot \sim G) \supset \sim S$
$\sim G \vee \sim S$
$\overline{G \cdot S}$

★22. $(Q \cdot E) \supset (F \vee H)$
$F \supset H$
$H \supset E$
$Q \cdot \sim F$
$\overline{E \vee F}$

23. $(N \cdot \sim T) \equiv K$
$T \supset \sim K$
$(N \vee K) \supset T$
$(K \cdot T) \supset N$
$T \vee \sim N$
$\overline{N \supset K}$

24. $C \supset (P \vee E)$
    $P \supset \sim C$
    $E \supset (C \cdot P)$
    $P \supset E$
    $(C \vee E) \supset P$
    _____
    $C \vee \sim E$

★25. $D \equiv (R \supset J)$
     $J \supset \sim D$
     $D \vee \sim R$
     $R \supset (D \cdot J)$
     $(J \vee R) \supset D$
     _____
     $\sim (R \vee J)$

III. The following dialogue contains eleven arguments. Translate each into symbolic form, and then use truth tables to determine whether each is valid or invalid.

Android Rights

"I just came from Professor Shaw's class on the philosophy of human nature," Nick says to his friend Erin, as he meets her in the hallway. "We discussed the question of whether an android could be a person and whether they have rights."

"Sounds like an interesting class," Erin replies, "but an android could never be a person."

"Why is that?" Nick asks.

"It's really quite simple," she says. "If an android is a person, then it's rational. But no android is rational, so it's not a person."

"But wait," Nick says. "Androids can solve problems, and they can also deliberate. And if they can either deliberate or solve problems, then they're rational. Right? So androids are rational, after all."

"No they're not," Erin says. "If an android is rational, then it's conscious, and if it's conscious, then it has reflective mental activity—it can reflect on its own act of thinking. But no android can do that, so it's not rational."

"How do you know that no android has reflective mental activity?" he asks.

"Because an android has reflective mental activity only if it has a soul," Erin says. "And it's ridiculous to think that an android could have a soul. Hence it has no reflective mental activity."

"But consider this," Nick says. "Either a soul is a material entity or it's a nonmaterial entity. You would agree with that, wouldn't you?"

"Of course," Erin replies.

"Okay," says Nick. "Now let me finish the argument. If a soul is a material entity, then if an android is material, it could easily have a soul. But if a soul is a nonmaterial entity, then if God could infuse a soul into it, then it could have a soul. Now an android is material and God could infuse a soul into an android—after all, God can do anything. Thus, an android could have a soul."

"Well, I know that Descartes considered humans to be machines with souls, but to me it's crazy to think that God would infuse a soul into a computer. He might as well infuse a soul into a pile of rocks. Anyway, let me try another approach," Erin says. "If an android is a person, then it has free will. But if androids are programmed, then they have no free will. Androids are just computers made to appear like humans, and every computer is programmed. Hence, once again, an android is not a person. What do you think of that?"

"By your reasoning," Nick replies, "even humans may not be free."

"How is that?" Erin asks.

"Well," he says, "whatever we do is caused by our biological makeup or by our social conditioning. If it's caused by our biological makeup, then it's determined. If it's caused by our social conditioning, then it's determined, too. And if it's determined, then it's not free. Thus, whatever we do is not free."

"Not so," Erin objects. "Our actions may be influenced by our biological makeup and our social conditioning, but they're not caused by them. Not strictly. And if they're not strictly caused by them, they're not determined by them, and if they're not determined by them, then they're free. Thus, our actions are free."

"Well, I don't know what it means for our actions to be influenced by something yet not be determined," Nick replies. "If X is influenced by Y, then X is caused by Y, and if X is caused by Y, then X is determined by Y. Thus, if X is influenced by Y, then X is determined by Y."

"I think you're equivocating on the meaning of cause," Erin replies. "But if you're unconvinced, how about this: If an android is a person, then it has feelings. And if it has feelings, then it can feel love or compassion. But no android loves anything. Just imagine two computers in love. The very thought is absurd. So is one android feeling compassion for another. Thus, an android cannot be a person."

"Well, look at it this way," Nick replies. "Feelings are either mental or they're physical. If they're mental, then they're brain states, and if they're brain states then androids could have them—because all brain states are just arrangements of atoms. If feelings are physical, then androids could have them—because, once again, all physical things are just arrangements of atoms. Thus, androids can have feelings."

Erin laughs. "That's the worst reasoning I've ever heard in my life. Sure, feelings may be accompanied by physical states, but they're not identical with them. Anyway, before I have to head off to class, tell me this: Do you really think that androids could be persons?"

"I think it's possible," Nick replies.

"So, would you say that an android has rights? Say the right to vote?"

"That depends," he says.

"On what?" Erin asks.

"On whether it's a Democrat or Republican," he replies.

"Uh-huh." She sighs. "Well, I'm off to class. Bye."

IV. Construct five symbolized arguments having at least two premises each. Then determine whether each is valid or invalid by constructing a truth table.

MindTap   Master concepts and improve outcomes with Aplia, at the end of the chapter, in the Aplia folder.

6.5   Indirect Truth Tables

HOW LOGICAL ARE YOU? Suppose you are given an argument having $P \vee Q$ as the conclusion. The only line on the truth table that you are really interested in is the line having true premises and false conclusion. This line, if it exists, can be produced easily and quickly. What truth values do you enter for P and Q in the premises and conclusion to produce this line?

Find the answer on MindTap.

Indirect truth tables provide a shorter and faster method for testing the validity of arguments than do ordinary truth tables. This method is especially applicable to arguments that contain a large number of different simple propositions. For example, an argument containing five different simple propositions would require an ordinary truth table having thirty-two lines. The indirect truth table for such an argument, on the other hand, would usually require only a single line and could be constructed in a fraction of the time required for the ordinary truth table.

Indirect truth tables can also be used to test a series of statements for consistency. In Section 6.3 we showed how ordinary truth tables are used to test pairs of statements for consistency and we noted that consistency was a relation that applied to any group of propositions. In this section we use indirect truth tables to test groups of three, four, five, and six propositions for consistency. Given the abbreviated nature of indirect truth tables, this evaluation can usually be done much more quickly than it can with ordinary truth tables.

Preliminary Skills

Using indirect truth tables requires developing the skill to work backward from the truth value of the main operator of a compound statement to the truth values of its simple components. Suppose, for example, that you are given a conjunctive statement that is true:

A • B
  T

Because a conjunctive statement can be true in only one way, you know immediately that both A and B are true:

A • B
T T T

Suppose, on the other hand, that you are given a conditional statement that is false:

A ⊃ B
  F

Since a conditional statement can be false in only one way, you know that A is true and B is false:

A ⊃ B
T F F

But suppose you are given a conditional statement that is true:

A ⊃ B
  T

Since a conditional statement can be true in three ways, you cannot compute the truth values of A and B. It could be the case that A is true and B is true, or A is false and B is true, or *A* is false and *B* is false. But let us suppose, in relation to this example, that you have one more piece of information. Suppose you know that *B* is false:

A ⊃ B
   T F

Then you know immediately that *A* is false. If *A* were true, then the truth value under the horseshoe would have to be false. But since this truth value is given as true, *A* must be false:

A ⊃ B
F T F

Similarly, suppose you are given a disjunctive statement with these truth values:

A ∨ B
F T

Then you know immediately that *B* is true, because if a disjunctive statement is true, at least one of the disjuncts must be true:

A ∨ B
F T T

Computing the truth values for the simple components of a compound proposition, as we have just done, requires a thorough knowledge of the truth-table definitions of the five operators given in Section 6.2. But after a little practice with examples such as these, this skill becomes almost automatic.

Testing Arguments for Validity

To construct an indirect truth table for an argument, we begin by assuming that the argument is invalid. That is, we assume that it is possible for the premises to be true and the conclusion false. Truth values corresponding to true premises and false conclusion are entered beneath the main operators for the premises and conclusion. Then, working backward, the truth values of the separate components are derived. If no contradiction is obtained in the process, this means that it is indeed possible for the premises to be true and the conclusion false, as originally assumed, so the argument is therefore invalid. If, however, the attempt to make the premises true and the conclusion false necessarily leads to a contradiction, it is not possible for the premises to be true and the conclusion false, in which case the argument is valid. Consider the following symbolized argument:

~A ⊃ (B ∨ C)
~B

C ⊃ A

We begin as before by writing the symbolized argument on a single line, placing a single slash between the premises and a double slash between the last premise and the conclusion. Then we assign T to the premises and F to the conclusion:

~ A ⊃ (B ∨ C) / ~ B // C ⊃ A
    T   T   F

We can now derive the truth values of *B*, *C*, and *A*, as follows:

~ A ⊃ (B ∨ C) / ~ B // C ⊃ A
   T   T F   T F F

These truth values are now transferred to the first premise:

~ A ⊃ (B ∨ C) / ~ B // C ⊃ A
T F T F T T   T F   T F F

We thus have a perfectly consistent assignment of truth values, which makes the prem-ises true and the conclusion false. The argument is therefore invalid. If an ordinary truth table were constructed for this argument, it would be seen that the argument fails on the line on which *A* is false, *B* is false, and *C* is true. This is the exact arrangement found in the indirect truth table we just finished.

    Here is another example. As always, we begin by assigning T to the premises and F to the conclusion:

A ⊃ (B ∨ C) / B ⊃ D / A // ~ C ⊃ D
 T   T   T   F

From the conclusion we can now derive the truth values of *C* and *D*, which are then transferred to the first two premises:

A ⊃ (B ∨ C) / B ⊃ D / A // ~ C ⊃ D
 T   F   T F T   T F F F

The truth value of *B* is now derived from the second premise and transferred, together with the truth value of *A*, to the first premise:

A ⊃ (B ∨ C) / B ⊃ D / A // ~ C ⊃ D
(T T F F) F   F T F T   T F F F

A contradiction now appears in the truth values assigned to the first premise, since T ⊃ F is F. The inconsistent truth values are circled. Because every step was strictly necessitated by some prior step, we have shown that it is impossible for the premises to be true and the conclusion false. The argument is therefore valid.

    Sometimes a single row of truth values is not sufficient to prove an argument valid. Example:

~ A ⊃ B / B ⊃ A / A ⊃ ~ B // A • ~ B
    T   T   T   F

Since a conditional statement can be true in any one of three ways, and a conjunctive statement can be false in any one of three ways, merely assigning truth to the premises and falsity to the conclusion of this argument is not sufficient to obtain the truth values of any of the component statements. When faced with a situation such as this, the best way of proceeding is either to list all of the possible ways that one of the premises can be true or all of the possible ways that the conclusion can be false, and to proceed from there. For this argument, let us select the conclusion. Since the conclusion is a false conjunctive statement, the first conjunct can be true and the other false, the first can be false and the other true, or they can both be false. Thus, we obtain the following:

```
~ A ⊃ B / B ⊃ A / A ⊃ ~ B // A • ~ B
    T         T        T        T F F T
    T         T        T        F F T F
    T         T        T        F F F T
```

Extending the truth values of A and B to the premises, we obtain the following result:

```
~ A ⊃ B / B ⊃ A / A ⊃ ~ B // A • ~ B
    T       T    (T  T  F) T   T F F T
(T F T  F)  T           T      F F T F
    T     (T  T  F)     T      F F F T
```

Since each line necessarily leads to a contradiction, the argument is valid. If a contradiction had been avoided on some line, the argument would, of course, be invalid, because it would be possible for the premises to be true and the conclusion false. Note that in this argument it is not necessary to fill out all the truth values on any one line to be forced into a contradiction. On each line the contradiction is necessarily derived within the context of a single premise.

If an indirect truth table requires more than one line, the method to be followed is this: Either select one of the premises and compute all of the ways it can be made true, or select the conclusion and compute all of the ways it can be made false. This selection should be dictated by the requirement of simplicity. For example, if the conclusion can be made false in only two ways, while each of the premises can be made true in three ways, then select the conclusion. On the other hand, if one of the premises can be made true in only two ways while the conclusion can be made false in three ways, then select that premise. If neither of these situations prevails, then select the conclusion.

Having made your selection, proceed to compute the truth values of each line, beginning with the first. If no contradiction is derived on this line, stop! The argument has been proved invalid. If a contradiction *is* derived on the first line, proceed to the second line. If no contradiction is derived on this line, then, again, the argument has been proved invalid. If a contradiction *is* derived, proceed to the third line, and so on. Remember, the objective is to produce a line having no contradiction. Once such a line is produced, the argument has been proved invalid, and no further work need be done. If, on the other hand, each line necessarily leads to a contradiction, the argument is valid.

Three final points need to be made about indirect truth tables for arguments. First, if a contradiction is obtained in the assignment of truth values, every step leading to it must be logically implied by some prior step. In other words, the contradiction must be unavoidable. If a contradiction is obtained after truth values are assigned haphazardly or by guessing, then nothing has been proved. The objective is not to produce a contradiction but to *avoid* one (if possible).

For example, in the following indirect truth table a contradiction is apparent in the first premise:

```
A ⊃ B / C ⊃ B // A ⊃ C
(T T F)  F T F   T F F
```

Yet the argument is invalid. The contradiction that appears is not *required* by the assignment of truth to the premises and falsity to the conclusion. The following indirect truth table, which is done correctly, proves the argument invalid:

A ⊃ B / C ⊃ B // A ⊃ C
T T T   F T T   T F F

The second point is that for valid arguments the order in which the truth values are assigned may affect where the contradiction turns up. That is, depending on the order of assignment, the contradiction may appear in the first premise, second premise, third premise, and so on. But, of course, the order of assignment does not affect the final determination of validity.

The last point is that it is essential that identical letters be assigned identical truth values. For example, if the letter *A* appears three times in a certain symbolized argument and the truth value T is assigned to it in one occurrence, then the same truth value must be assigned to it in the other occurrences as well. After the truth table has been completed, each letter should be rechecked to ensure that one and the same truth value has been assigned to its various occurrences.

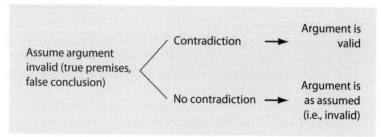

Testing Statements for Consistency

The method for testing a series of statements for consistency is similar to the method for testing arguments. We begin by writing the statements on a line, separating each with a single slash mark. (Since we have no conclusion, we use no double slash marks.) Then we assume that the statements are consistent. We assign a T to the main operator of each, and we then compute the truth values of the components. If this computation leads necessarily to a contradiction, the statements are not as we assumed them to be. That is, they are inconsistent. But if no contradiction is reached, the statements are consistent. Here is an example:

A ∨ B
B ⊃ (C ∨ A)
C ⊃ ~ B
~A

First, we write the statements on a single line separated by a single slash mark; we then assign T to each of the main operators:

A ∨ B / B ⊃ (C ∨ A) / C ⊃ ~ B / ~ A
   T   T   T   T

Next, we compute the truth values of the components. First we compute the truth value of *A*. Next, we enter this truth value in the first statement and compute the truth value of *B*. Next, we enter the truth value of *B* in the second statement and compute the truth value of *C*. Finally, the truth values of *C* and *B* are carried to the third statement:

```
A ∨ B / B ⊃ (C ∨ A) / C ⊃ ~ B / ~ A
F T T   T T  T T F    T T F T    T F
```

Since this computation leads necessarily to a contradiction (third statement), the group of statements is inconsistent.

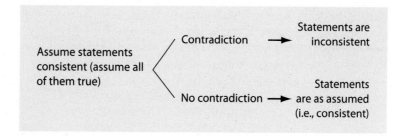

Here is another example. The statements are written on a single line, and a T is assigned to each of the main operators:

```
A ⊃ (B • C) / C ⊃ ~ A / B ∨ A / B ⊃ C
T               T           T        T
```

Since all of the statements can be true in three ways, we select one of them (the fourth) and figure all of the ways it can be true:

```
A ⊃ (B • C) / C ⊃ ~ A / B ∨ A / B ⊃ C
T               T          T     T T T
                                 F T T
                                 F T F
```

Filling out the first line leads to no contradiction, so the statements are consistent:

```
A ⊃ (B • C) / C ⊃ ~ A / B ∨ A / B ⊃ C
F T  T T T    T T  T F   T T F   T T T
                                 F T T
                                 F T F
```

As with testing arguments, the objective is to *avoid* a contradiction. As soon as no contradiction is reached, we stop. The statements are consistent. Only if all three lines had led to a contradiction would these statements be inconsistent.

Rule for all multiline indirect truth tables
Contradiction is derived ⟶ Go to next line (if there is one).
No contradiction is derived ⟶ Stop. Argument is invalid/ Statements are consistent.

Augustus De Morgan 1806–1871

The English logician and mathematician Augustus De Morgan is famous for the development of predicate quantification and the invention of relational algebra—an algebra fundamental to the work of Russell and Whitehead in their *Principia Mathematica*. He is known to all students of symbolic logic owing to his formulation of what came to be known as De Morgan's rule of inference.

De Morgan was born in Madura, India, where his father was employed by the East India Company. He became blind in one eye not long after birth, and after his family returned to England his fellow students often taunted him and played cruel tricks on him because of his disability. When he was ten, his father died coming home from another trip to India. This left the boy under the influence of his mother, a devout Anglican who wanted her son to become an Anglican priest.

De Morgan obtained a BA from Trinity College, Cambridge, and might have received a master's degree but for the fact that Cambridge then required all candidates to take a theological test. Because of his commitment to the ideal of religious neutrality, De Morgan refused to take this test. Perhaps in rebellion against his mother's influence, he developed a lifelong habit of avoiding churches, claiming that he could not bear hearing sermons. Following his refusal to take the exam, he continued his studies at University College London, a new institution founded on the principle of religious neutrality. At age twenty-two, he became the first professor of mathematics there.

Three years into his professorship, De Morgan became involved in a disagreement with the administration regarding its treatment of a colleague. De Morgan led a faculty protest, and in the end he resigned his position on the faculty. Five years later, he returned to his former position after his replacement accidentally

Hulton Archive/Getty Images

drowned. He remained there for thirty years, until, at age sixty, he became involved in another administrative dispute—this time over a decision that De Morgan considered to be in violation of the university's stated policy of religious neutrality. He again resigned in protest, bringing his academic career to an end. Though active in academic politics, he curiously abstained from all involvement in national politics. An acquaintance once remarked that "he never voted in an election, and never visited the House of Commons."

De Morgan was proud of his son, George, who became a distinguished mathematician in his own right, and he was disconsolate at his son's untimely death, which occurred when De Morgan was sixty-two. The death of a daughter, during that same period, compounded his grief, and De Morgan died three years later, possibly owing to grief and stress.

De Morgan was known for his sense of humor and his interest in odd facts. He produced an almanac of full moons spanning a 4,000-year period. A lunar crater is named after him. He liked to point out that he was x years old in the year x^2 (43 in 1849). He also enjoyed composing bits of verse in imitation of famous poets—for example, "Great fleas have little fleas upon their backs to bite 'em, and little fleas have lesser fleas, and so *ad infinitum*" (after Jonathan Swift).

MindTap® Strengthen your understanding of the topic with the section's **Video Lecture.**

I. When possible, compute the truth values of the simple components in the following compound propositions. If no truth value can be computed, write a question mark (?) under the letter or letters with unknown truth value.

★1. $K \lor D$
    F T

2. $Q \supset N$
      T

3. $B \equiv D$
    T F

★4. $N \supset G$
    T T

5. $S \supset B$
    T F

6. $K \cdot B$
      T

★7. $C \lor A$
    T F

8. $S \equiv E$
      T

9. $M \supset R$
    T T

★10. $H \lor J$
     T T

11. $E \equiv P$
    T F

12. $H \lor S$
     T

★13. $C \supset P$
     F

14. $G \cdot B$
     F

15. $S \equiv Q$
    T F

★16. $G \lor K$
     F

17. $N \supset \sim P$
    T T

18. $\sim A \equiv D$
    F T

★19. $\sim L \supset M$
     T F

20. $E \supset \sim M$
    T   F

21. $\sim N \equiv R$
    F F

★22. $\sim (H \lor B)$
     T

23. $Q \supset (R \cdot S)$
    T F

24. $K \supset \sim (S \equiv M)$
    T F   F

★25. $A \lor \sim (C \cdot \sim R)$
    F T

II. Use indirect truth tables to determine whether the following arguments are valid or invalid.

★1. $B \supset C$
   $\dfrac{\sim C}{\sim B}$

2. $\sim E \lor F$
   $\dfrac{\sim E}{\sim F}$

3. $P \supset (Q \cdot R)$
   $R \supset S$
   ___
   $P \supset S$

★4. $\sim(I \equiv J)$
   ___
   $\sim(I \supset J)$

5. $W \supset (X \supset Y)$
   $X \supset (Y \supset Z)$
   ___
   $W \supset (X \supset Z)$

6. $A \supset (B \lor C)$
   $C \supset (D \cdot E)$
   $\sim B$
   ___
   $A \supset \sim E$

★7. $G \supset H$
   $H \supset I$
   $\sim J \supset G$
   $\sim I$
   ___
   J

8. $J \supset (\sim L \supset \sim K)$
   $K \supset (\sim L \supset M)$
   $(L \lor M) \supset N$
   ___
   $J \supset N$

9. $P \cdot (Q \lor R)$
   $(P \cdot R) \supset \sim(S \lor T)$
   $(\sim S \lor \sim T) \supset \sim(P \cdot Q)$
   ___
   $S \equiv T$

★10. $(M \lor N) \supset O$
   $O \supset (N \lor P)$
   $M \supset (\sim Q \supset N)$
   $(Q \supset M) \supset \sim P$
   ___
   $N \equiv O$

11. $(A \lor B) \supset (C \cdot D)$
   $(\sim A \lor \sim B) \supset E$
   ___
   $(\sim C \lor \sim D) \supset E$

12. $F \supset G$
   $\sim H \lor I$
   $(G \lor I) \supset J$
   $\sim J$
   ___
   $\sim(F \lor H)$

★13. $(A \lor B) \supset (C \cdot D)$
   $(X \lor \sim Y) \supset (\sim C \cdot \sim W)$
   $(X \lor Z) \supset (A \cdot E)$
   ___
   $\sim X$

14. $\sim G \supset (\sim H \cdot \sim I)$
   $J \supset H$
   $K \supset (L \cdot M)$
   $K \lor J$
   ___
   $L \cdot G$

15. $N \lor \sim O$
   $P \lor O$
   $P \supset Q$
   $(N \lor Q) \supset (R \cdot S)$
   $S \supset (R \supset T)$
   $O \supset (T \supset U)$
   ___
   U

III. Use indirect truth tables to determine whether the following groups of statements are consistent or inconsistent.

★1. $K \equiv (R \lor M)$
   $K \cdot \sim R$
   $M \supset \sim K$

2. $F \equiv (A \cdot \sim P)$
   $A \supset (P \cdot S)$
   $S \supset \sim F$
   $A \cdot \sim F$

3. $(G \lor \sim Q) \supset (F \lor B)$
   $\sim(F \lor Q)$
   $B \supset N$
   $(F \lor N) \supset Q$

★4. $(N \lor C) \equiv E$
   $N \supset \sim(C \lor H)$
   $H \supset E$
   $C \supset H$

5. $P \vee \sim S$
   $S \vee \sim T$
   $T \vee \sim X$
   $X \vee \sim J$
   $J \vee \sim P$

6. $(Q \vee K) \supset C$
   $(C \cdot F) \supset (N \vee L)$
   $C \supset (F \cdot \sim L)$
   $Q \cdot \sim N$

★7. $S \supset (R \equiv A)$
   $A \supset (W \cdot \sim R)$
   $R \equiv (W \vee T)$
   $S \cdot U$
   $U \supset T$

8. $(E \vee H) \supset (K \cdot D)$
   $D \supset (M \cdot B)$
   $B \supset \sim E$
   $\sim (H \vee K)$
   $D \supset B$

9. $G \supset P$
   $P \supset (A \cdot \sim G)$
   $(R \vee T) \supset G$
   $Y \supset R$
   $B \supset T$
   $Y \vee B$

★10. $A \vee Z$
   $A \supset (T \cdot F)$
   $Z \supset (M \cdot Q)$
   $Q \supset \sim F$
   $T \supset \sim M$
   $M \supset A$

IV. Create a group of four compound statements, similar to Exercise 6.5, III, 2, such that: (1) the compound statements as a whole contain at least four simple statements, (2) one of the compound statements is a conjunction, (3) at least two compound statements have three or more simple components, and (4) each compound statement shares a simple statement in common with another compound statement in the group. Use an indirect truth table to test the group of compound statements for consistency. If the compound statements are consistent, construct a similar group of compound statements that turns out inconsistent, and vice versa.

MindTap   Master concepts and improve outcomes with Aplia, at the end of the chapter, in the Aplia folder.

6.6   Argument Forms and Fallacies

HOW LOGICAL ARE YOU? Suppose you are watching two politicians debate universal health care. One of them makes this argument: If we raise taxes, then we can afford to fund a universal health-care system. But we won't raise taxes. Therefore, we can't afford to fund a universal health-care system. Do you spot a flaw in this argument? If so, what is it?

Find the answer on MindTap.

Many of the arguments that occur in propositional logic have forms that bear specific names and can be immediately recognized as either valid or invalid. The first two parts of this section present some of the more common ones and explain how they are recognized. The third part discusses ways of refuting two of these forms, constructive and destructive dilemmas. The fourth part presents a word of caution relating to invalid forms. Finally, the fifth part applies to real-life arguments some of the principles developed in the first two parts.

Six Valid Argument Forms

In Section 6.2 we defined a statement form as an arrangement of statement variables and operators such that the uniform substitution of statements in place of the variables results in a statement. An example of a statement form is $p \cdot q$, where p and q are statement variables. Analogously, an **argument form** is an arrangement of statement variables and operators such that the uniform substitution of statements in place of the variables results in an *argument*. The resulting argument is said to be a **substitution instance** of its related argument form. For example, the following arrangement of statement variables and an operator is an argument form:

$$\frac{p \cdot q}{p}$$

If the statements A (Alice is a chemist.) and B (Barbara is a biologist.) are uniformly substituted in place of the p and q of the argument form, we obtain the following substitution instance, which is an argument:

$A \cdot B$	Alice is a chemist and Barbara is a biologist.
A	Alice is a chemist.

We can think of the relationship between an argument and its form as analogous to the relationship between an animal and its skeleton. Just as a skeleton can carry a lot of flesh, so can an argument form, so to speak. The following argument has the form we just considered.

$$\frac{[G \supset (J \vee K)] \cdot [(H \vee N) \supset L]}{[G \supset (J \vee K)]}$$

A *valid* argument form is an argument form that satisfies the truth-table test.

The first valid argument form we consider is called ***modus ponens*** ("asserting mode"). It consists of a conditional premise, a second premise that asserts the antecedent of the conditional premise, and a conclusion that asserts the consequent:

Modus ponens (MP):

$$\frac{\begin{array}{l} p \supset q \\ p \end{array}}{q}$$

Any argument having the form of *modus ponens* is a valid argument. Example:

If twelve million children die yearly from starvation, then something is wrong with food distribution.	$T \supset S$
Twelve million children die yearly from starvation.	T
Therefore, something is wrong with food distribution.	S

Closely associated with *modus ponens* is **modus tollens** ("denying mode"). *Modus tollens* is a valid argument form consisting of one conditional premise, a second premise that denies the consequent of the conditional premise, and a conclusion that denies the antecedent. It is defined as follows:

Modus tollens (MT):

$$p \supset q$$
$$\underline{\sim q}$$
$$\sim p$$

Although a little harder to understand than *modus ponens*, *modus tollens* can be understood by the following reasoning process: The conclusion states that we do not have *p*, because if we did have *p*, then (by the first premise) we would have *q*, and we do not have *q* (by the second premise). Any argument that has the form of *modus tollens* is a valid argument. Example:

If Japan cares about endangered species, then it has stopped killing whales.	$C \supset S$
Japan has not stopped killing whales.	$\sim S$
Therefore, Japan does not care about endangered species.	$\sim C$

The next valid argument form we consider is **pure hypothetical syllogism**. It consists of two premises and one conclusion, all of which are hypothetical (conditional) statements, and is defined as follows:

Pure hypothetical syllogism (HS):

$$p \supset q$$
$$\underline{q \supset r}$$
$$p \supset r$$

Any argument that has the form of a pure hypothetical syllogism (that is, any argument that can be produced by uniformly substituting statements in place of the variables in the form) is a valid argument. Example:

If world population continues to grow, then cities will become hopelessly overcrowded.	$W \supset C$
If cities become hopelessly overcrowded, then pollution will become intolerable.	$C \supset P$
Therefore, if world population continues to grow, then pollution will become intolerable.	$W \supset P$

The validity of a pure hypothetical syllogism is grounded in the fact that the premises link together like a chain. In the population argument, the consequent of the first premise is identical to the antecedent of the second. If the premises fail to link together in this way, the argument may be invalid. Example:

If Kevin Bacon is a man, then Kevin Bacon is a human being.	$M \supset H$
If Kevin Bacon is a woman, then Kevin Bacon is a human being.	$W \supset H$
Therefore, if Kevin Bacon is a man, then Kevin Bacon is a woman.	$M \supset W$

The premises of this argument are true, and the conclusion is false. Thus, the argument is invalid.

The next valid form we consider is called **disjunctive syllogism**. It consists of a disjunctive statement and another statement that negates the left-hand disjunct.

Disjunctive syllogism (DS):

$$p \lor q$$
$$\frac{\sim p}{q}$$

The validity of this form can be easily checked by a truth table. Now, given that validity is purely a function of the form of an argument, any argument produced by uniformly substituting statements in place of the variables in this argument form is a valid argument. Such an argument is said to *have* the form of a disjunctive syllogism. The following argument was produced in this way and is therefore valid:

Either Harvard or Princeton is in New Jersey.	$H \lor P$
Harvard is not in New Jersey.	$\sim H$
Therefore, Princeton is in New Jersey.	P

The validity of a disjunctive syllogism arises from the fact that one of the premises presents two alternatives and the other premise eliminates one of those alternatives, leaving the other as the conclusion. This so-called "method of elimination" is essential to the validity of a disjunctive syllogism. If one premise should present two alternatives and the other premise should *affirm* one of those alternatives, the argument is invalid (unless the conclusion is a tautology). Example:

Either Harvard or Amherst is in Massachusetts.	$H \lor A$
Harvard is in Massachusetts.	H
Therefore, Amherst is not in Massachusetts.	$\sim A$

Since both Harvard and Amherst are in Massachusetts, the premises are true and the conclusion is false. Thus, the argument is invalid. Because the wedge symbol designates inclusive disjunction, the disjunctive premise includes the possibility of both disjuncts being true. Thus, for the argument to be valid, the other premise must eliminate one of the disjuncts.

A **constructive dilemma** is a valid argument form that consists of a conjunctive premise made up of two conditional statements, a disjunctive premise that asserts the antecedents in the conjunctive premise (like *modus ponens*), and a disjunctive conclusion that asserts the consequents of the conjunctive premise. It is defined as follows:

Constructive dilemma (CD):

$$(p \supset q) \cdot (r \supset s)$$
$$\underline{p \vee r}$$
$$q \vee s$$

Any argument that has the form of a constructive dilemma is a valid argument. Example:

If we choose nuclear power, then we increase the risk of a nuclear accident; but if we choose conventional power, then we add to the greenhouse effect.	$(N \supset I) \cdot (C \supset A)$
We must choose either nuclear power or conventional power.	$\underline{N \vee C}$
Therefore, we either increase the risk of a nuclear accident or add to the greenhouse effect.	$I \vee A$

The **destructive dilemma** is also a valid argument form. It is similar to the constructive dilemma in that it includes a conjunctive premise made up of two conditional statements and a disjunctive premise. However, the disjunctive premise denies the consequents of the conditionals (like *modus tollens*), and the conclusion denies the antecedents:

Destructive dilemma (DD):

$$(p \supset q) \cdot (r \supset s)$$
$$\underline{\sim q \vee \sim s}$$
$$\sim p \vee \sim r$$

Any argument that has the form of a destructive dilemma is a valid argument. Example:

If we are to reverse the greenhouse effect, then we must choose nuclear power; but if we are to lower the risk of a nuclear accident, then we must choose conventional power.	$(R \supset N) \cdot (L \supset C)$
We will either not choose nuclear power or not choose conventional power.	$\underline{\sim N \vee \sim C}$
Therefore, we will either not reverse the greenhouse effect or not lower the risk of a nuclear accident.	$\sim R \vee \sim L$

Two Invalid Argument Forms

The invalid forms we will consider are closely associated with *modus ponens* and *modus tollens*. These are called **affirming the consequent** and **denying the antecedent**. Affirming the consequent consists of one conditional premise, a second premise that asserts the consequent of the conditional, and a conclusion that asserts the antecedent:

Affirming the consequent (AC):

$p \supset q$
$\underline{q}$
p

Any argument that has the form of affirming the consequent is an invalid argument.* The following argument has this form and is therefore invalid:

If Napoleon was killed in a plane crash, then Napoleon is dead.	$K \supset D$
Napoleon is dead.	$\underline{D}$
Therefore, Napoleon was killed in a plane crash.	K

Given that this argument has true premises and a false conclusion, it is clearly invalid.

Denying the antecedent consists of a conditional premise, a second premise that denies the antecedent of the conditional, and a conclusion that denies the consequent:

Denying the antecedent (DA):

$p \supset q$
$\underline{\sim p}$
$\sim q$

Any argument that has the form of denying the antecedent is an invalid argument. Example:

If Napoleon was killed in a plane crash, then Napoleon is dead.	$K \supset D$
Napoleon was not killed in a plane crash.	$\underline{\sim K}$
Therefore, Napoleon is not dead.	$\sim D$

Again, this argument has true premises and a false conclusion, so it is clearly invalid.

Refuting Constructive and Destructive Dilemmas

Now that we are familiar with several argument forms in propositional logic, we may return for a closer look at two of them, constructive and destructive dilemmas. Arguments having these forms occur frequently in public debate, where an arguer may use them to trap an opponent. Since both forms are valid, the only direct mode of defense available to the opponent is to prove the dilemma unsound. This can be done by proving at least one of the premises false. If the conjunctive premise (otherwise called the "horns of the dilemma") is proven false, the opponent is said to have "grasped the dilemma by the horns." This, of course, may be done by proving either one of the conditional statements false. If, on the other hand, the disjunctive premise is proven false, the opponent is said to have "escaped between the horns of the dilemma." The latter strategy often involves

---

*See "Note on Invalid Forms" later in this section.

finding a third alternative that excludes the two that are given in the disjunctive premise. If such a third alternative can be found, both of the given disjuncts will be proved false. Consider the following constructive dilemma:

> If taxes increase, the economy will suffer, and if taxes decrease, needed government services will be curtailed. Since taxes must either increase or decrease, it follows that the economy will suffer or that needed government services will be curtailed.

It is easy to escape between the horns of this dilemma by arguing that taxes could be kept as they are, in which case they would neither increase nor decrease.

Some dilemmas, however, do not allow for the possibility of escaping between the horns. Consider the following constructive dilemma:

> If we encourage competition, we will have no peace, and if we do not encourage competition, we will make no progress. Since we must either encourage competition or not encourage it, we will either have no peace or make no progress.

Since the disjunctive premise of this dilemma is a tautology, it cannot be proven false. This leaves the strategy of grasping the dilemma by the horns, which may be done by proving either of the conditional statements in the conjunctive premise false. One debater might want to attack the first conditional and argue that competition and peace can coexist, while another might want to attack the second and argue that progress can be achieved through some means other than encouraging competition.

The strategy to be followed in refuting a dilemma is therefore this: Examine the disjunctive premise. If this premise is a tautology, attempt to grasp the dilemma by the horns by attacking one or the other of the conditional statements in the conjunctive premise. If the disjunctive premise is not a tautology, then either escape between the horns by, perhaps, finding a third alternative, or grasp the dilemma by the horns—whichever is easier.

A third, indirect strategy for refuting a dilemma involves constructing a counterdilemma. This is typically done by changing either the antecedents or the consequents of the conjunctive premise while leaving the disjunctive premise as it is, so as to obtain a different conclusion. If the dilemma in question is a constructive dilemma, the consequents of the conjunctive premise are changed. Here are possible counterdilemmas for the two dilemmas just presented:

> If taxes increase, needed government services will be extended, and if taxes decrease, the economy will improve. Since taxes must either increase or decrease, it follows that needed government services will be extended or the economy will improve.

If we encourage competition, we will make progress, and if we do not encourage competition, we will have peace. Since we must either encourage competition or not encourage it, we will either make progress or have peace.

Constructing a counterdilemma falls short of a refutation of a given dilemma because it merely shows that a different approach can be taken to a certain problem. It does not cast any doubt on the soundness of the original dilemma. Yet the strategy is often effective because it testifies to the cleverness of the debater who can accomplish it successfully. In the heat of debate the attending audience is often persuaded that the original argument has been thoroughly demolished.

Note on Invalid Forms

Throughout this text we have seen that any substitution instance of a valid argument form is a valid argument. For example, consider *modus ponens:*

$$p \supset q$$
$$\underline{p\qquad}$$
$$q$$

Literally any two statements uniformly substituted in the place of p and q will result in a valid argument. Thus, the following symbolized arguments both have the form of *modus ponens,* and are accordingly valid:

$$S \supset T \qquad\qquad (K \vee B) \supset (N \cdot R)$$
$$\underline{S\qquad} \qquad\qquad \underline{K \vee B\qquad\qquad}$$
$$T \qquad\qquad\qquad N \cdot R$$

In the first argument S and T are uniformly substituted in the place of p and q, and in the second argument $K \vee B$ and $N \cdot R$ are uniformly substituted in the place of p and q.

However, this result does not extend to invalid argument forms. Consider, for example, affirming the consequent:

$$p \supset q$$
$$\underline{q\qquad}$$
$$p$$

Sometimes the uniform substitution of statements in the place of p and q results in an invalid argument, and sometimes it does not. Both of the following symbolized arguments are substitution instances of affirming the consequent, but the one on the left is invalid while the one on the right is valid:

$$G \supset N \qquad\qquad (F \vee D) \supset (F \cdot D)$$
$$\underline{N\qquad} \qquad\qquad \underline{F \cdot D\qquad\qquad}$$
$$G \qquad\qquad\qquad F \vee D$$

To deal with this problem we adopt a convention about when an argument will be said to *have* an invalid form. We will say that an argument has an invalid form if it is a substitution instance of that form *and* it is not a substitution instance of any valid form.

According to this convention only the argument on the left has the form of affirming the consequent. The argument on the right does not have this form because it is a substitution instance of the following valid form:

$$(p \lor q) \supset (p \cdot q)$$
$$\underline{p \cdot q}$$
$$p \lor q$$

The validity of this form results from the fact that the conclusion follows from the second premise alone, without any involvement of the first premise. This fact may be easily checked with a truth table.

Here is another invalid form:

$$p \supset q$$
$$\underline{r \supset q}$$
$$p \supset r$$

Both of the following symbolized arguments are substitution instances of this form, but only the one on the left is invalid:

$K \supset L$	$\sim C \supset A$
$\underline{R \supset L}$	$\underline{(C \supset E) \supset A}$
$K \supset R$	$\sim C \supset (C \supset E)$

The argument on the right is valid because its conclusion is a tautology. Accordingly, only the argument on the left will be said to have the invalid form in question.

The point of this discussion is that when we attempt to determine the validity of arguments through mere inspection, we have to exert caution with invalid forms. The mere fact that an argument is a substitution instance of an invalid form does not guarantee that it is invalid. Before judging it invalid we must make sure that it is not valid for some other reason, such as its conclusion being a tautology. However, as concerns the exercises at the end of this section, all of the arguments that are substitution instances of invalid forms are invalid. In other words, none of them is like either of the right-hand examples considered in these paragraphs.

Summary and Application

Any argument having one of the following forms is valid:

$p \supset q$	*modus ponens*	$p \supset q$	*modus tollens*
$\underline{p}$	(MP)	$\underline{\sim q}$	(MT)
q		$\sim p$	
$p \supset q$	pure hypothetical	$p \lor q$	disjunctive
$\underline{q \supset r}$	syllogism (HS)	$\underline{\sim p}$	syllogism
$p \supset r$		q	(DS)
$(p \supset q) \cdot (r \supset s)$	constructive	$(p \supset q) \cdot (r \supset s)$	destructive
$\underline{p \lor r}$	dilemma	$\underline{\sim q \lor \sim s}$	dilemma (DD)
$q \lor s$	(CD)	$\sim p \lor \sim r$	

Any argument having either of the following forms is invalid:

$$p \supset q \qquad \text{affirming the} \qquad\qquad p \supset q \qquad \text{denying the}$$
$$\underline{q} \qquad\qquad \text{consequent (AC)} \qquad \underline{\sim p} \qquad\qquad \text{antecedent (DA)}$$
$$p \qquad\qquad\qquad\qquad\qquad\qquad\quad \sim q$$

In identifying arguments as having these argument forms, use the following procedure. First symbolize the argument, using uppercase letters for the simple propositions. Then see whether the symbolized argument fits the pattern of one of these forms. For example, the following symbolized argument has the form of *modus ponens,* and is therefore valid:

$$K \supset R$$
$$\underline{K}$$
$$R$$

If K and R are substituted respectively in place of p and q in the *modus ponens* form, we obtain the symbolized argument in question.

However, not every attempt at argument recognition is as simple as this. For more-complicated cases it helps to keep two points in mind:

> The order of the premises never affects the argument's form.
>
> Negated letters can be substituted in place of the $p, q, r,$ and s of an argument form just as can non-negated letters.

In regard to the first point, consider these symbolized arguments:

$$N \qquad\qquad\qquad \sim S$$
$$\underline{N \supset B} \qquad\qquad \underline{S \vee F}$$
$$B \qquad\qquad\qquad F$$

The argument on the left is *modus ponens,* and the one on the right is a disjunctive syllogism. To see this more clearly, simply switch the order of the premises.

In regard to the second point (involving negated letters), consider these examples:

$$\sim G \supset \sim H \qquad\qquad \sim K \supset \sim M$$
$$\underline{\sim G} \qquad\qquad\qquad\quad \underline{\sim \sim M}$$
$$\sim H \qquad\qquad\qquad\quad \sim \sim K$$

The argument on the left is *modus ponens,* and the one on the right is *modus tollens.* To produce the argument on the left, substitute $\sim G$ in the place of p in the *modus ponens* form, and $\sim H$ in the place of q. For the argument on the right, substitute $\sim K$ in the place of p in the *modus tollens* form, and $\sim M$ in the place of q.

Another problem that complicates the task of argument recognition arises from the fact that many arguments can be translated in alternate ways. Consider, for example, this argument:

> Either the witness lied or Bob is guilty.
> The witness told the truth.
> Therefore, Bob is guilty.

If we select L to represent "The witness lied," then the argument can be translated into symbols as follows:

$L \lor B$
$\underline{\sim L}$
B

This symbolized argument is clearly an instance of disjunctive syllogism.

On the other hand, if we select T to represent "The witness told the truth," then we have this translation:

$\sim T \lor B$
$\underline{T}$
B

Technically this is not an instance of disjunctive syllogism, because the second premise, T, is not preceded by a tilde. To avoid this kind of difficulty in connection with alternative translations, we introduce two rules. They should be obvious, but if there is any doubt about them they can be proved using truth tables. The rules are as follows:

p is logically equivalent to $\sim\sim p$.   (Double Negation)
$p \lor q$ is logically equivalent to $q \lor p$.   (Commutativity)

According to the first rule, double tildes may be either inserted or deleted prior to any statement, and according to the second rule the order of the components in a disjunctive statement may be reversed. Applying the double-negation rule to the second premise of the symbolized argument above, we have

$\sim T \lor B$
$\underline{\sim\sim T}$
B

After this change, the argument is now an instance of disjunctive syllogism.

For examples of how the commutativity rule is applied, consider these symbolized arguments:

$M \lor E$ $(R \supset L) \cdot (T \supset K)$
$\underline{\sim E}$ $\underline{T \lor R}$
M $L \lor K$

Technically the argument on the left is not an instance of disjunctive syllogism because the letters in the first premise are in the wrong order, and the argument on the right is not an instance of constructive dilemma because the letters in the second premise are in the wrong order. We can reverse the order of these letters by applying the commutativity rule:

$E \lor M$ $(R \supset L) \cdot (T \supset K)$
$\underline{\sim E}$ $\underline{R \lor T}$
M $L \lor K$

After these changes, the argument on the left is now clearly an instance of disjunctive syllogism, and the one on the right is an instance of constructive dilemma.

Here are some additional examples. In some cases the symbolized argument must be rewritten using double negation or commutativity before it fits the pattern of the argument form indicated.

$\sim A \supset \sim B$			$A \supset \sim B$	
$\sim B \supset C$	HS—valid		$B \supset \sim C$	invalid
$\overline{\sim A \supset C}$			$\overline{A \supset \sim C}$	

$\sim A \supset \sim B$			$\sim A \supset B$	
B	MT—valid		A	DA—invalid
$\overline{A}$			$\overline{\sim B}$	

$\sim A \vee \sim B$			$\sim A \vee B$	
A	DS—valid		$\sim A$	invalid
$\overline{\sim B}$			$\overline{B}$	

$(A \supset \sim B) \cdot (\sim C \supset D)$			$(\sim A \supset B) \cdot (C \supset \sim D)$	
$A \vee \sim C$	CD—valid		$B \vee \sim D$	invalid
$\overline{\sim B \vee D}$			$\overline{A \vee \sim C}$	

$A \vee \sim B$			$A \supset \sim B$	
B	DS—valid		$\sim B$	AC—invalid
$\overline{A}$			$\overline{A}$	

A			$A \vee C$	
$A \supset B$	MP—valid		$(A \supset B) \cdot (C \supset D)$	CD—valid
$\overline{B}$			$\overline{B \ \vee D}$	

Let us now see how the argument forms presented in this section can be used to interpret the structure of some real-life arguments. Consider the following letter to the editor of a newspaper:

> If U.S. servicemen are indeed being held in Southeast Asia, what is the motivation of their captors? No government there has asked for anything in return, as might be expected if they were deliberately holding Americans.
>
> (Norm Oshrin)

This argument is enthymematic; in other words, it is missing certain parts. The author intends to prove that U.S. servicemen are not being held in Southeast Asia—because if they were, their captors would be demanding something for their return. The argument can thus be structured as a *modus tollens*:

> If U.S. servicemen are being held in Southeast Asia, then their captors have demanded something for their return.
> Their captors have not demanded something for their return.
> Therefore, U.S. servicemen are not being held in Southeast Asia.

Here is another example:

> In a time when an entire nation believes in Murphy's law (that if anything can go wrong, it surely will) and has witnessed serious accidents in the highly regulated, supposedly

fail-safe nuclear industry, it's fascinating that people can persist in the fantasy that an error will not occur in the area of nuclear weaponry.

(Burk Gossom, *Newsweek*)

Although this argument allows for more than one analysis, clearly the arguer presents two main reasons why we can expect an accident in the area of nuclear weaponry: "Murphy's law" (which everyone believes to be true) dictates it, and accidents have occurred in the area of nuclear power (which is presumed fail-safe). Thus, at the very least, we can extract two *modus ponens* arguments from this selection:

If everyone believes Murphy's law, then we can expect accidents in nuclear weaponry.
Everyone believes Murphy's law.
Therefore, we can expect accidents in nuclear weaponry.

If accidents have occurred in nuclear power, then we can expect accidents in nuclear weaponry.
Accidents have occurred in nuclear power.
Therefore, we can expect accidents in nuclear weaponry.

Many arguments that we encounter in ordinary life can be interpreted as instances of valid argument forms. After being so interpreted, however, not all will turn out sound. The invalid forms (denying the antecedent and affirming the consequent) should be reserved for the relatively few arguments that are clearly invalid as originally expressed.

6

MindTap® Strengthen your understanding of the topic with the section's **Video Lectures.**

EXERCISE 6.6

I. Interpret the following symbolized arguments in light of the eight argument forms presented in this section. In some cases a symbolized argument must be rewritten using commutativity or double negation before it becomes an instance of one of these forms. Those not having a named form are invalid.

★1. $N \supset C$
$\dfrac{\sim C}{\sim N}$

2. $S \supset F$
$\dfrac{F \supset \sim L}{S \supset \sim L}$

3. $A \vee \sim Z$
$\dfrac{\sim Z}{A}$

★4. $(S \supset \sim P) \cdot (\sim S \supset D)$
$\dfrac{S \vee \sim S}{\sim P \vee D}$

MindTap® Complete exercises online for immediate feedback.

5. ~N
~N ⊃ T
—————
T

6. M ∨ ~B
~M
—————
~B

★7. (E ⊃ N) • (~L ⊃ ~K)
~N ∨ K
————————————————
~E ∨ L

8. W ⊃ ~M
~M
—————
W

9. ~B ⊃ ~L
G ⊃ ~B
—————
G ⊃ ~L

★10. F ⊃ O
~F
—————
~O

11. (K ∨ B) • (N ∨ Q)
K ∨ N
————————————
B ∨ Q

12. X
X ⊃ ~E
—————
~E

★13. P ∨ ~S
S
—————
P

14. B • T
T
—————
~B

15. ~R ∨ ~Q
(G ⊃ Q) • (H ⊃ R)
————————————
~G ∨ ~H

★16. ~G ⊃ H
H
—————
~G

17. K ⊃ ~C
C
—————
~K

18. (I ⊃ M) • (~O ⊃ A)
~O ∨ I
————————————
M ∨ A

★19. X ⊃ ~F
W ⊃ ~F
—————
W ⊃ X

20. ~L ⊃ U
L
—————
~U

II. Translate the following arguments into symbolic notation and then interpret them in light of the eight argument forms presented in this section. In some cases a symbolized argument must be rewritten using commutativity or double negation before it becomes an instance of one of these forms. Those not having a named form are invalid. The letters to be used in translating the statements are given in parentheses.

★1. A Boeing 757 crashed into the Pentagon on 9/11 only if two giant engines were found outside the building. It is not the case that two giant engines were found outside the building. Therefore, a Boeing 757 did not crash into the Pentagon on 9/11. (B, G)

2. If Michelangelo painted the ceiling of the Sistine Chapel, then he was familiar with stories from the Old Testament. Michelangelo was familiar with stories from the Old Testament. Therefore, Michelangelo painted the ceiling of the Sistine Chapel. (M, F)

3. If you enter the teaching profession, you will have no money for vacations; and if you do not enter the teaching profession, you will have no time for vacations.

Since you must either enter or not enter the teaching profession, it follows that either you will have no money or no time for vacations. (E, M, T)

★4. Either the wealthiest people are the happiest, or it is not the case that money can buy everything. The wealthiest people are not the happiest. Therefore, money cannot buy everything. (W, M)

5. Either drivers are forbidden to send text messages, or the highways will not become safer. Drivers are forbidden to send text messages. Therefore, the highways will become safer. (D, H)

6. If the sun is a variable star, then its energy will drop drastically at some point in the future. If the sun's energy drops drastically at some point in the future, then the earth will become a giant ice ball. Therefore, if the sun is a variable star, then the earth will become a giant ice ball. (S, E, G)

★7. Nano-thermite is present in the debris from the World Trade Center. But if that is so, then the buildings were brought down by controlled demolition. Therefore, the buildings were brought down by controlled demolition. (N, B)

8. If TV viewing provides genuine relaxation, then TV enhances the quality of life. But TV viewing does not provide genuine relaxation. Therefore, TV does not enhance the quality of life. (G, E)

9. If high school clinics are to stem the tide of teenage pregnancy, then they must dispense birth-control devices; but if they want to discourage illicit sex, then they must not dispense these devices. Since high school clinics must either dispense or not dispense birth-control devices, either they will not stem the tide of teenage pregnancy, or they will not discourage illicit sex. (S, D, I)

★10. If limits are imposed on medical-malpractice suits, then patients will not be adequately compensated for their injuries; but if the cost of malpractice insurance continues to rise, then physicians will be forced out of business. Limits will not be imposed, and the cost of malpractice insurance will not continue to rise. Therefore, patients will be adequately compensated and physicians will not be forced out of business. (L, A, C, F)

11. If Prohibition succeeded in the 1920s, then the war on drugs will succeed today. But Prohibition did not succeed in the 1920s. Therefore, the war on drugs will not succeed today. (P, W)

12. If life is always better than death, then people do not commit suicide. People do commit suicide. Therefore, life is not always better than death. (L, C)

★13. If we want to arrest criminals, then police must engage in high-speed chases; but if we want to protect motorists, then police must not engage in high-speed chases. Since police must either engage or not engage in high-speed chases, either we will not arrest criminals or not protect motorists. (A, E, P)

14. Either industrial pollutants will be more stringently controlled, or air quality will continue to fall. Industrial pollutants will be more stringently controlled. Therefore, air quality will not continue to fall. (I, A)

15. Insurance companies contribute millions of dollars to political campaigns. But if that is so, then meaningful insurance reform is impossible. Therefore, meaningful insurance reform is impossible. (*I, M*)

★**16.** If Mexico does not get its population growth under control, then its unemployment problem will never be solved. Mexico's unemployment problem will never be solved. Therefore, Mexico will not get its population growth under control. (*M, U*)

17. Either the dinosaurs were not cold blooded or they were not the ancestors of modern birds. The dinosaurs were the ancestors of modern birds. Therefore, the dinosaurs were not cold blooded. (*C, A*)

18. If coal burning continues, then heavy metals will be released into the atmosphere. If heavy metals are not released into the atmosphere, then nervous-system damage will decrease. Therefore, if coal burning does not continue, then nervous-system damage will decrease. (*C, H, N*)

★**19.** If sea levels rise twenty feet worldwide, then coastal cities from New York to Sydney will be inundated. If the ice sheets on Antarctica slip into the sea, then sea levels will rise twenty feet worldwide. Therefore, if the ice sheets on Antarctica slip into the sea, then coastal cities from New York to Sydney will be inundated. (*S, C, I*)

20. If tax credits are given for private education, then the government will be supporting religion; but if tax credits are not given for private education, then some parents will end up paying double tuition. Either tax credits will or will not be given for private education. Therefore, either the government will be supporting religion, or some parents will end up paying double tuition. (*T, G, P*)

III. Identify the following dilemmas as either constructive or destructive. Then suggest a refutation for each by escaping between the horns, grasping by the horns, or constructing a counterdilemma.

★**1.** If Melinda spends the night studying, she will miss the party; but if she does not spend the night studying, she will fail the test tomorrow. Melinda must either spend the night studying or not studying. Therefore, she will either miss the party or fail the test. (*S, M, F*)

2. If we build our home in the valley, it will be struck by floods; and if we build it on the hilltop, it will be hit by lightning. Since we must either build it in the valley or on the hilltop, our home will either be struck by floods or hit by lightning. (*V, F, H, L*)

3. If psychotherapists respect their clients' right to confidentiality, then they will not report child abusers to the authorities; but if they have any concern for the welfare of children, then they will report them. Psychotherapists must either report or not report child abusers to the authorities. Therefore, psychotherapists either have no respect for their clients' right to confidentiality or no concern for the welfare of children. (*C, R, W*)

★4. If corporations are to remain competitive, then they must not spend money to neutralize their toxic waste; but if the environment is to be preserved, then corporations must spend money to neutralize their toxic waste. Corporations either will or will not spend money to neutralize their toxic waste. Therefore, either they will not remain competitive, or the environment will be destroyed. (*C*, *S*, *E*)

5. If physicians pull the plug on terminally ill patients, then they risk being charged with murder; but if they do not pull the plug, they prolong their patients' pain and suffering. Since physicians with terminally ill patients must do one or the other, either they risk being charged with murder or they prolong their patients' pain and suffering. (*P*, *M*, *S*)

6. If the Mitchells get a divorce, they will live separately in poverty; but if they stay married, they will live together in misery. Since they must either get a divorce or stay married, they will either live separately in poverty or together in misery. (*D*, *S*, *M*, *T*)

★7. If college students want courses that are interesting and rewarding, then they must major in liberal arts; but if they want a job when they graduate, then they must major in business. College students will either not major in liberal arts, or they will not major in business. Therefore, either they will not take courses that are interesting and rewarding, or they will not have a job when they graduate. (*C*, *L*, *J*, *B*)

8. If merchants arrest suspected shoplifters, then they risk false imprisonment; but if they do not arrest them, they risk loss of merchandise. Merchants must either arrest or not arrest suspected shoplifters. Therefore, they will either risk false imprisonment or loss of merchandise. (*A*, *F*, *L*)

9. If women threatened with rape want to avoid being maimed or killed, then they must not resist their assaulter; but if they want to ensure successful prosecution of the assailant, they must resist him. Since women threatened with rape must do one or the other, either they will risk being maimed or killed or they will jeopardize successful prosecution of the assailant. (*A*, *R*, *E*)

★10. If we prosecute suspected terrorists, then we risk retaliation by other terrorists; but if we release them, then we encourage terrorism. Since we must either prosecute or release suspected terrorists, we either risk retaliation by other terrorists or we encourage terrorism. (*P*, *R*, *T*, *E*)

IV. The following dialogue contains at least fifteen arguments. Translate each into symbolic notation, and then interpret them in light of the eight argument forms presented in this section.

A Little Help from a Friend

"I can only talk for a minute," Liz says to her friend Amy. "I have this bio midterm tomorrow, and I'm afraid I'm going to fail it."

"Okay," Amy replies. "I'll cut out after a minute or two. But why are you so afraid?"

"Because I really haven't studied at all. I figure if I don't pull an all-nighter, I'll fail the test. But I can't fail the test, so I must pull the all-nighter."

"I don't envy you," says Amy, digging in her purse. "But I have this little tablet of Adderall that might get you through. As I see it, either you take the tab or you'll fall asleep by midnight. But you can't fall asleep, so you must take the tab."

Liz stares at the little orange pill. "Adderall is for attention deficit disorder. You don't have that, do you?"

"No," says Amy. "I got the tab from my boyfriend, Zach, who talked the health clinic out of a whole bottle by faking ADD."

"Wow," says Liz. "Do you think it's safe for me to take it?"

"Of course," replies Amy. "Zach takes it all the time when he needs an extra spurt of energy, and he's had no adverse reactions. I've even tried it once or twice. If it's safe for Zach, then it's safe for me, and if it's safe for me, then it's safe for you. The conclusion is obvious."

"And do you really think the Adderall will help me pass the test?" asks Liz.

"Absolutely," says Amy. "If you take it, you'll be totally focused for the test, and you must be focused. Hence, you take it, girl."

"I don't know," Liz says as she takes a closer look at the little pill. "If I take it, then I'll feel like an athlete who takes performance-enhancing drugs. I'll feel like I'm putting myself at an unfair advantage over the other students. I don't want to do that, so maybe I shouldn't take it."

She thinks for a moment and sighs. "Either I take the Adderall or I don't. If I take it, I'll feel like I cheated, but if I don't take it, I'll fail the test. Thus, I'll feel like I cheated, or I'll fail the test. Either way, I lose."

Amy smiles. "There's another way of looking at it. Either you take the Adderall or you don't. If you take it, you'll pass the test, and if you don't take it, you'll have a clear conscience. Thus, you'll either pass the test or you'll have a clear conscience. Either way, you win."

"Very clever," says Liz, "but that really doesn't solve my problem."

"Okay," says Amy. "But maybe your problem isn't as bad as you think. Consider this: Older people take drugs all the time to help their memory and their sex lives. If it's okay for them to take those drugs—and it is—then it's okay for you to take the Adderall. You shouldn't sweat it."

"That's true," says Liz, "but those older people suffer from a medical condition. If I had ADD, I'd be justified in taking the Adderall, but I don't. So I'm not justified."

"Let's look at it another way," says Amy. "You could get through the night with lots of coffee and Red Bull. If it's okay to drink coffee and Red Bull—and it is—then it's okay to take the Adderall. The conclusion is clear."

"Not quite," says Liz. "Coffee and Red Bull aren't really comparable to Adderall—at least not if it's as good as you say it is. Suppose that I'm faced with this option: Either I drink lots of coffee and Red Bull, or I take the Adderall. I would say no to the coffee and Red Bull because it's less effective, and it leaves me frazzled. Thus, I would take the Adderall. See, the two are not the same."

"Maybe not," says Amy, "but think about it this way. We take advantage of new technology every day without giving it a second thought. We use smartphones instead of landlines because they're more convenient. We use lightbulbs instead of candles because we see better with them. And we use Adderall instead of coffee because it makes us sharper. If it's ethically okay to use smartphones, then it's okay to use Adderall; and it's certainly okay to use smartphones—just as it's okay to use lightbulbs. Hence, it's okay to use Adderall."

"The problem with that line of reasoning," Liz observes, "is that using lightbulbs and smartphones doesn't put anyone at a competitive advantage. Everyone uses them, so we're all on an equal footing. But not every student uses Adderall to pass a test. If everyone used it, I would have no problem with it. But not everyone uses it, so I do have a problem."

"I can see your point," Amy says. "At fifteen or twenty bucks a pop on the underground market, not every student can afford Adderall. If it were cheap, then everyone would use it. But it's not cheap, so many students don't."

Amy smiles again at her friend. "Messy stuff," she says. "So, what do you think you'll do?"

"I don't know." Liz groans and puts her face in her hands. "But leave that tab on my desk. I'll see how it goes. . . . I'll give myself until midnight."

V. The following selections were taken from letters-to-the-editor newspaper columns. Each contains one or more arguments, but the exact form of the argument may be hidden or ambiguous. Use the argument forms presented in this section to structure the selections as specifically named arguments.

★1. There is a simple way to put a big dent in the national human-organ shortage: Allocate organs first to the people who have agreed to donate their own. Giving organs first to registered donors would persuade more people to register, and that would make the allocation system fairer. People who aren't willing to share the gift of life should go to the end of the waiting list.

(David J. Undis)

2. Okay, I've tried it for a week again this year, but I still don't like daylight saving time. My grass is brown enough already—it doesn't need another hour of daylight each day. Let's turn the clocks back to the way God intended—standard time.

(Jim Orr)

3. The religious right, in its impassioned fervor to correct our alleged moral wrongs and protect the rights of our unborn "children," may one day realize its ultimate goal of a constitutional amendment banning abortion. And what will the punishment be for those caught performing or receiving an abortion? The death penalty, of course.

(David Fisher)

★4. Most educators believe math instructors ought to emphasize group problem solving. If *group* problem solving is so important (and I think it is), why do we place such emphasis on individual testing? The national math test is a mistake.

(Frederick C. Thayer)

5. If voluntary school prayer for our children is going to make them more moral, then just think what mandatory church attendance on Sunday could do for the rest of us.

(Roderick M. Boyes)

6. A country that replaces the diseased hearts of old white men but refuses to feed schoolchildren, pay women adequately, educate adolescents, or care for the elderly—that country is doomed. We are acting as if there is no tomorrow. Where is our shame?

(Robert Birch)

★7. We cannot afford to close the library at Central Juvenile Hall. These young people, in particular, need to have access to ideas, dreams, and alternative ways of living. It can make the difference for many students who might become interested in reading for the first time in their lives while in Juvenile Hall.

(Natalie S. Field)

8. If the death penalty deters one person from becoming a murderer, it is effective. There are also some other important reasons for having the death penalty. First, the families and friends of innocent victims have the right to see effective retribution. Second, terminating the life of a killer is more economical than keeping him in jail at the taxpayer's expense. Third, everyone will have greater respect for the judicial system when justice is carried out.

(Doug Kroker)

9. Regarding the bill to require parental consent for a minor's abortion, I would like to point out that the pious platitudes about parental authority quickly fall by the wayside when the minor wants to keep the baby and the parents say, "Don't be silly! You have an abortion and finish your education." If the parents can veto a minor's abortion, shouldn't they also be able to require one? Better the choice, either pro or con, be left to the girl/woman herself.

(Jane Roberts)

★10. More than a million adult videos are rented each week. Nor, as the propagandists would have you believe, does viewing such material lead to violent sex crimes. If it did, there would be over one million such crimes per week.

(Lybrand P. Smith)

VI. Create the following arguments:

1. A *modus ponens* about social media

2. A *modus tollens* relating to sports

3. A disjunctive syllogism concerning political parties

4. A pure hypothetical syllogism dealing with the Middle East

5. A constructive dilemma about health care

6. A destructive dilemma concerning the minimum wage

7. An affirming the consequent relating to North Korea

8. A denying the antecedent about privacy rights

MindTap® Master concepts and improve outcomes with Aplia, at the end of the chapter, in the Aplia folder.

Summary

Propositional Logic:
- The fundamental units are whole statements (propositions).
- Simple statements are represented by uppercase letters (A, B, C, etc.).
- These are combined via logical operators to form compound statements.
- The logical operators:
  - Tilde ($\sim$) forms negations ("not," "it is not the case that").
  - Dot ($\bullet$) forms conjunctions ("and," "also," "moreover," etc.).
  - Wedge ($\vee$) forms disjunctions ("or," "unless").
  - Horseshoe ($\supset$) forms conditionals ("if . . . then," "only if," etc.).
  - Triple bar ($\equiv$) forms biconditionals ("if and only if," etc.).

Truth Table:
- An arrangement of truth values that shows in every possible case how the truth value of a compound statement is determined by the truth values of its components.
- Used to define the meaning of the five logical operators:
  - $\sim p$ is true only when p is false.
  - $p \bullet q$ is true only when both p and q are true.
  - $p \vee q$ is false only when both p and q are false.
  - $p \supset q$ is false only when p is true and q is false.
  - $p \equiv q$ is true only when p and q have the same truth value.
- Used to classify individual compound statements:
  - Tautologous: Truth values under main operator are all true.
  - Self-contradictory: Truth values under main operator are all false.
  - Contingent: Under main operator: at least one true, at least one false.
- Used to compare one compound statement with another:
  - Logically equivalent: Truth values under main operators are the same on each line.
  - Contradictory: Truth values under main operators are opposite on each line.
  - Consistent: There is at least one line under main operators where all of the truth values are true.
  - Inconsistent: There is no line under main operators where all of the truth values are true.
- Used to test arguments for validity:
  - Invalid: There is a line on which all the premises are true and the conclusion false.
  - Valid: There is no such line.

Indirect Truth Table: A usually shorter truth table constructed by first assigning truth values to the main operators and then working backward to the simple components.
- Used to test arguments for validity:
  - Begin by assuming the premises true and the conclusion false.
  - Valid: Assumption necessarily leads to a contradiction.
  - Invalid: Assumption does not necessarily lead to a contradiction.

6

MindTap Need help? See the Learning Logic folder at the end of the chapter: the self-paced tutorial walks you through any section.
Prepare for exams with the Chapter Test.

- Used to test a series of statements for consistency:
  - Begin by assuming all of the statements true.
  - Inconsistent: Assumption necessarily leads to a contradiction.
  - Consistent: Assumption does not necessarily lead to a contradiction.

Argument Forms and Fallacies:

- Valid forms:
  - *Modus ponens:* $p \supset q / p // q$
  - *Modus tollens:* $p \supset q / \sim q // \sim p$
  - Pure hypothetical syllogism: $p \supset q / q \supset r // p \supset r$
  - Disjunctive syllogism: $p \vee q / \sim p // q$
  - Constructive dilemma: $(p \supset q) \cdot (r \supset s) / p \vee r // q \vee s$
  - Destructive dilemma $(p \supset q) \cdot (r \supset s) / \sim q \vee \sim s // \sim p \vee \sim r$

- Invalid forms (fallacies):
  - Affirming the consequent: $p \supset q / q // p$
  - Denying the antecedent: $p \supset q / \sim p // \sim q$

- Logical equivalencies:
  - p is logically equivalent to $\sim\sim p$.
  - $p \vee q$ is logically equivalent to $q \vee p$.

6

7 Natural Deduction in Propositional Logic

7.1 Rules of Implication I

7.2 Rules of Implication II

7.3 Rules of Replacement I

7.4 Rules of Replacement II

7.7 Proving Logical Truths

7.1   Rules of Implication I

HOW LOGICAL ARE YOU? Suppose you discover a canister containing nerve gas in a crowded enclosed space. The attached timer says the gas will be released in one minute. You call the anti-terrorist hotline, and the agent tells you, among other things, that if the black wire is wrapped around the yellow wire, then you must cut the green wire. In the end, you do not cut the green wire. What does this tell you about the black wire?

Find the answer on MindTap.

Natural deduction is a method for deriving the conclusion of valid arguments expressed in the symbolism of propositional logic. The method consists in using sets of **rules of inference** (valid argument forms) to derive either a conclusion directly, or a series of intermediate conclusions that links the premises of an argument with the stated conclusion. Natural deduction gets its name from the fact that it resembles the ordinary step-by-step reasoning process people use in daily life. It also resembles the method used in geometry to derive theorems relating to lines and figures; but whereas each step in a geometrical proof depends on some mathematical principle, each step in a logical proof depends on a rule of inference.

Natural deduction is similar in some respects to the truth-table method for testing arguments. Both methods can be used to prove a valid argument valid; but natural deduction is largely useless for invalid arguments, so we still need truth tables. However,

MindTap® Read, study, reflect, and prepare for exams online, anytime, anywhere.

the method of natural deduction is more illuminating than truth tables are. Natural deduction shows how a conclusion "comes out" of the premises, whereas truth tables show nothing of the sort. Also, while truth tables are relatively automatic and mechanical, natural deduction requires insight and creativity. As a result, most students find that natural deduction is challenging and fun, while truth tables can be tedious, especially for long arguments.

The first eight rules of inference are called **rules of implication** because they consist of simple, valid argument forms whose premises *imply* their conclusions. The first four rules of implication should be familiar from Section 6.6. They are listed together with an illustration of their use as follows.

1. *Modus ponens (MP)*

$p \supset q$
$\underline{p}$
q

If Su Lin is a panda, then Su Lin is cute.
Su Lin is a panda.
Su Lin is cute.

2. *Modus tollens (MT)*

$p \supset q$
$\underline{\sim q}$
$\sim p$

If Koko is a koala, then Koko is cuddly.
Koko is not cuddly.
Koko is not a koala.

3. Pure hypothetical syllogism (HS)

$p \supset q$
$\underline{q \supset r}$
$p \supset r$

If Leo is a lion, then Leo roars.
If Leo roars, then Leo is fierce.
If Leo is a lion, then Leo is fierce.

4. Disjunctive syllogism (DS)

$p \lor q$
$\underline{\sim p}$
q

Scooter is either a mouse or a rat.
Scooter is not a mouse.
Scooter is a rat.

Modus ponens says that given a conditional statement and its antecedent on lines by themselves, we can assert its consequent on a line by itself. *Modus tollens* says that given a conditional statement and the negation of its consequent on lines by themselves, we can assert the negation of its antecedent on a line by itself. **Pure hypothetical syllogism** ("hypothetical syllogism" for short) says that given two conditional statements on lines by themselves such that the consequent of one is identical with the antecedent of the other, we can assert on a line by itself a conditional statement whose antecedent is the antecedent of the first conditional and whose consequent is the consequent of the second conditional. Note in the rule that the two premises hook together like links of a chain.

Disjunctive syllogism says that given a disjunctive statement and the negation of the left-hand disjunct on lines by themselves, we can assert the right-hand disjunct on a line by itself. Because of the way this rule is written, only the right-hand disjunct can be asserted as the conclusion. However, once we are supplied with the commutativity rule (see Section 7.3), we will be able to switch the order of the disjuncts in the first line, and this will allow us to assert what was originally the left-hand disjunct as the conclusion. Disjunctive syllogism is otherwise called the method of elimination. The short premise eliminates one of the alternatives in the disjunctive premise, leaving the other as the conclusion.

These four rules will be sufficient to derive the conclusion of many simple arguments in propositional logic. Further, once we are supplied with all eighteen rules together with conditional proof, the resulting system will be sufficient to derive the conclusion of any valid argument in propositional logic. Conversely, since each rule is a valid argument form unto itself, any conclusion derived from their correct use results in a valid argument.

> To understand the rules of inference, it may help to visualize the components as spatial objects. For example, *modus ponens* and disjunctive syllogism might be visualized as follows:

> Any two statements can be uniformly substituted in place of the circle and square to convert the illustration into an argument.

Applying the rules of inference rests on the ability to visualize more- or less-complex arrangements of simple propositions as substitution instances of the rules. For a fairly simple substitution instance of *modus ponens*, consider the following:

1. ~A ⊃ B	p ⊃ q
2. ~A	p
3. B	q

When ~A and B are mentally substituted, respectively, in place of the p and q of the *modus ponens* rule, then you should be able to see that the argument on the left is an instance of the rule. The fact that A is preceded by a tilde is irrelevant.

Here is a more complex example:

1. (A • B) ⊃ (C ∨ D)	p ⊃ q
2. A • B	p
3. C ∨ D	q

In this case, if you mentally substitute A • B and C ∨ D, respectively, in place of p and q in the rule, you can see that the argument on the left is an instance of *modus ponens*. This example illustrates the fact that any pair of compound statements can be uniformly substituted in place of p and q to produce a substitution instance of the rule.

Finally, the order of the premises never makes a difference:

1. A	p
2. A ⊃ (B ⊃ C)	p ⊃ q
3. B ⊃ C	q

In this case, if you mentally substitute A and $B \supset C$ in place of p and q, you can see, once again, that the argument on the left is an instance of *modus ponens*. The fact that the order of the premises is reversed makes no difference.

These arguments are all instances of **modus ponens** (MP):

$\sim F \supset (G \equiv H)$	$(A \vee B) \supset \sim(C \cdot D)$	$K \cdot L$
$\sim F$	$A \vee B$	$(K \cdot L) \supset [(R \supset S) \cdot (T \supset U)]$
$G \equiv H$	$\sim(C \cdot D)$	$(R \supset S) \cdot (T \supset U)$

Now let us use the rules of inference to construct a proof. Such a proof consists of a sequence of propositions, each of which is either a premise or is derived from preceding propositions by application of a rule of inference and the last of which is the conclusion of the original argument. Let us begin with the following example:

> If the Astros switch leagues, then the Braves will not win the pennant.
> If the Cubs retain their manager, then the Braves will win the pennant.
> The Astros will switch leagues. Therefore, the Cubs will not retain their manager.

The first step is to symbolize the argument, numbering the premises and writing the intended conclusion to the right of the last premise, separated by a slash mark:

1. $A \supset \sim B$
2. $C \supset B$
3. A / $\sim C$

The next step is to derive the conclusion through a series of inferences. But before writing the first line, it is important to keep two points in mind. First, always begin by trying to "find" the conclusion in the premises, and second, always look at the main operator of the conclusion for a clue about how to derive it. In this particular proof, the first point is most helpful. The conclusion to be derived is $\sim C$, and we see that C appears in the antecedent of line 2. We could derive $\sim C$ from line 2 by *modus tollens* if we had $\sim B$, so now we look for $\sim B$. Turning our attention to line 1, we see that we could derive $\sim B$ by *modus ponens* if we had A, and we do have A on line 3. Thus, we have now thought through the entire proof, and we can begin to write it out. First, we derive $\sim B$ by *modus ponens* from lines 1 and 3:

1. $A \supset \sim B$
2. $C \supset B$
3. A / $\sim C$
4. $\sim B$ 1, 3, MP

The justification for line 4 is written to the right, directly beneath the slash mark. If you have trouble understanding how line 4 was derived, imagine substituting A and $\sim B$ in place of p and q in the *modus ponens* rule. Then you can see that lines 1, 3, and 4 constitute a substitution instance of that rule.

7

The final step is to derive ~C from lines 2 and 4 by *modus tollens*:

1. $A \supset \sim B$
2. $C \supset B$
3. A / ~C
4. $\sim B$ 1, 3, MP
5. $\sim C$ 2, 4, MT

The proof is now complete. The justification for line 5 is written directly beneath the justification for line 4.

These arguments are all instances of ***modus tollens*** (MT):

$(D \lor F) \supset K$	$\sim G \supset \sim(M \lor N)$	$\sim T$
$\sim K$	$\sim\sim(M \lor N)$	$[(H \lor K) \cdot (L \lor N)] \supset T$
$\sim(D \lor F)$	$\sim\sim G$	$\sim[(H \lor K) \cdot (L \lor N)]$

The next example is already translated into symbols:

1. $A \supset B$
2. $\sim A \supset (C \lor D)$
3. $\sim B$
4. $\sim C$ / D

Once again, to derive the conclusion, always begin by trying to "find" it in the premises. The intended conclusion is *D*, and after inspecting the premises we find *D* in line 2. If we had the consequent of that line, $C \lor D$, on a line by itself, we could derive *D* by disjunctive syllogism if we had $\sim C$. And we do have $\sim C$ on line 4. Also, we could derive $C \lor D$ by *modus ponens* if we had $\sim A$, so now we look for $\sim A$. Turning our attention to line 1, we see that we could derive $\sim A$ by *modus tollens* if we had $\sim B$, and we do have $\sim B$ on line 3. Thus, we have now thought through the entire proof, and we can write it out:

1. $A \supset B$
2. $\sim A \supset (C \lor D)$
3. $\sim B$
4. $\sim C$ / D
5. $\sim A$ 1, 3, MT
6. $C \lor D$ 2, 5, MP
7. D 4, 6, DS

As usual, the justification for each line is written directly beneath the slash mark preceding the intended conclusion. If you have trouble understanding line 6, imagine substituting $\sim A$ and $C \lor D$ in place of *p* and *q* in the *modus ponens* rule. Then you can see that lines 2, 5, and 6 constitute a substitution instance of that rule.

These arguments are all instances of **pure hypothetical syllogism** (HS):

$A \supset (D \cdot F)$	$\sim M \supset (R \supset S)$	$(L \supset N) \supset [(S \lor T) \cdot K]$
$(D \cdot F) \supset \sim H$	$(C \lor K) \supset \sim M$	$(C \equiv F) \supset (L \supset N)$
$A \supset \sim H$	$(C \lor K) \supset (R \supset S)$	$(C \equiv F) \supset [(S \lor T) \cdot K]$

Here is another example.

1. $F \supset G$
2. $F \lor H$
3. $\sim G$
4. $H \supset (G \supset I)$ / $F \supset I$

The intended conclusion is $F \supset I$. When we attempt to find it in the premises, we see no such statement. This tells us that we should turn to the second point mentioned earlier, which is to look at the main operator of the conclusion for a clue about how to derive it. In this case the main operator is a horseshoe, so we ask: What rule gives us a horseshoe—that is, a conditional statement? The answer is: pure hypothetical syllogism.

Having tentatively settled on pure hypothetical syllogism for deriving the conclusion, we now look for two conditional statements, which, when combined, will yield $F \supset I$. In line 1 we find $F \supset G$ and in line 4 we find $G \supset I$, but before we can apply pure hypothetical syllogism, we must obtain $G \supset I$ on a line by itself. Examining line 4, we see that $G \supset I$ could be derived by *modus ponens*, if we had H on a line by itself, and examining line 2, we see that H could be derived by disjunctive syllogism if we had $\sim F$ on a line by itself. Turning to line 1, we see that $\sim F$ could be derived by *modus tollens* if we had $\sim G$ on a line by itself, and we do have $\sim G$ on line 3. Thus, we have now thought through the entire proof, and we can write it out:

1. $F \supset G$
2. $F \lor H$
3. $\sim G$
4. $H \supset (G \supset I)$ / $F \supset I$
5. $\sim F$ 1, 3, MT
6. H 2, 5, DS
7. $G \supset I$ 4, 6, MP
8. $F \supset I$ 1, 7, HS

In addition to showing how useful it is to begin a proof by looking at the main operator of the conclusion, this proof teaches another important lesson about every proof. Every line in a proof can be used multiple times. In line 5, we used line 1 in conjunction with the *modus tollens* rule, and in line 8 we used that same line again in conjunction with pure hypothetical syllogism. Any line can be used as many times as we need it.

These arguments are all instances of **disjunctive syllogism** (DS):

$U \lor \sim(W \bullet X)$	$\sim(E \lor F)$	$\sim B \lor [(H \supset M) \bullet (S \supset T)]$
$\sim U$	$(E \lor F) \lor (N \supset K)$	$\sim\sim B$
$\sim(W \bullet X)$	$N \supset K$	$(H \supset M) \bullet (S \supset T)$

The next example is more complex:

1. $\sim(A \bullet B) \lor [\sim(E \bullet F) \supset (C \supset D)]$
2. $\sim\sim(A \bullet B)$
3. $\sim(E \bullet F)$
4. $D \supset G$ / $C \supset G$

Again, when we attempt to find the intended conclusion in the premises, we see no such statement. But then we notice that the main operator of the conclusion is a horseshoe, and we find $C \supset D$ on line 1 and $D \supset G$ on line 4. We could derive the conclusion by pure hypothetical syllogism if we could obtain $C \supset D$ on a line by itself. Examining line 1, we see that we could derive $C \supset D$ by *modus ponens* if we could obtain both $\sim(E \bullet F) \supset (C \supset D)$ and $\sim(E \bullet F)$ on lines by themselves, and we see that $\sim(E \bullet F)$ appears on line 3. Also, examining line 1, we see that we could derive $\sim(E \bullet F) \supset (C \supset D)$ by disjunctive syllogism if we had $\sim\sim(A \bullet B)$ on a line by itself, and we do have it on line 2. Thus, we can now write out the proof:

1. $\sim(A \bullet B) \lor [\sim(E \bullet F) \supset (C \supset D)]$
2. $\sim\sim(A \bullet B)$
3. $\sim(E \bullet F)$
4. $D \supset G$ / $C \supset G$
5. $\sim(E \bullet F) \supset (C \supset D)$ 1, 2, DS
6. $C \supset D$ 3, 5, MP
7. $C \supset G$ 4, 6, HS

If you have trouble seeing how lines 5 and 6 are derived, for line 5 imagine substituting $\sim(A \bullet B)$ and $\sim(E \bullet F) \supset (C \supset D)$, in place of the p and q of the disjunctive syllogism rule. Then you can see that lines 1, 2, and 5 constitute a substitution instance of that rule. For line 6, imagine substituting $\sim(E \bullet F)$ and $(C \supset D)$ in place of p and q in the *modus ponens* rule. Then you can see that lines 5, 3, and 6 constitute a substitution instance of that rule.

In applying the four rules of inference introduced in this section, we have noted that various expressions first had to be obtained on lines by themselves. If this procedure is not followed, the resulting proof will likely be invalid. For an example of an invalid application of *modus ponens*, consider the following:

1. $A \supset (B \supset C)$
2. B
3. C 1, 2, MP (invalid)

This inference is invalid because $B \supset C$ must first be obtained on a line by itself. In deriving the conclusion of an argument we always assume the premises are true. But if we assume line 1 of this proof is true, this does not entail that $B \supset C$ is true. What line 1 says is that *if* A is true, then $B \supset C$ is true. Thus, $B \supset C$ cannot be treated as a premise. We do not know if it is true or false.

Here are some additional examples of invalid inferences:

1. $A \lor B$
2. A
3. $\sim B$ 1, 2, HS (invalid—line 2 must negate A in line 1, not assert it)

1. $A \supset B$
2. B
3. A 1, 2, MP (invalid—line 2 must assert the antecedent of line 1, not the consequent)

1. $A \supset B$
2. $A \supset C$
_____
3. $B \supset C$ 1, 2, HS (invalid—the consequent of one conditional must be identical with the antecedent of the other)

1. $A \supset B$
2. $\sim A$
_____
3. $\sim B$ 1, 2, MT (invalid—line 2 must negate the consequent of line 1, not the antecedent)

1. $(A \supset B) \supset C$
2. $\sim B$
_____
3. $\sim A$ 1, 2, MT (invalid—$A \supset B$ must first be obtained on a line by itself)

1. $A \supset (B \supset C)$
2. $C \supset D$
_____
3. $B \supset D$ 1, 2, HS (invalid—$B \supset C$ must first be obtained on a line by itself)

1. $(A \lor B) \supset C$
2. $\sim A$
_____
3. B 1, 2, DS (invalid—$A \lor B$ must first be obtained on a line by itself)

We conclude this section with some strategies for applying the first four rules of inference.

Strategy 1: Always begin by attempting to "find" the conclusion in the premises. If the conclusion is not present in its entirety in the premises, look at the main operator of the conclusion. This will provide a clue as to how the conclusion should be derived.

Strategy 2: If the conclusion contains a letter that appears in the consequent of a conditional statement in the premises, consider obtaining that letter via *modus ponens:*

1. $A \supset B$
2. $C \lor A$
3. A / B
4. B 1, 3, MP

Strategy 3: If the conclusion contains a negated letter and that letter appears in the antecedent of a conditional statement in the premises, consider obtaining the negated letter via *modus tollens:*

1. $C \supset B$
2. $A \supset B$
3. $\sim B$ / $\sim A$
4. $\sim A$ 2, 3, MT

Strategy 4: If the conclusion is a conditional statement, consider obtaining it via pure hypothetical syllogism:

1. $B \supset C$
2. $C \supset A$
3. $A \supset B$ / $A \supset C$
4. $A \supset C$ 1, 3, HS

Strategy 5: If the conclusion contains a letter that appears in a disjunctive statement in the premises, consider obtaining that letter via disjunctive syllogism:

1. $A \supset B$
2. $A \lor C$
3. $\sim A$ / C
4. C   2, 3, DS

Of course, these strategies apply to deriving any line prior to the conclusion, just as they apply to deriving the conclusion.

I. For each of the following lists of premises, derive the conclusion and supply the justification for it. There is only one possible answer for each problem.

★(1)
1. $G \supset F$
2. $\sim F$
3. _____ ____

(2)
1. S
2. $S \supset M$
3. _____ ____

(3)
1. $R \supset D$
2. $E \supset R$
3. _____ ____

★(4)
1. $B \lor C$
2. $\sim B$
3. _____ ____

(5)
1. N
2. $N \lor F$
3. $N \supset K$
4. _____ ____

(6)
1. $\sim J \lor P$
2. $\sim J$
3. $S \supset J$
4. _____ ____

★(7)
1. $H \supset D$
2. $F \supset T$
3. $F \supset H$
4. _____ ____

(8)
1. $S \supset W$
2. $\sim S$
3. $S \lor N$
4. _____ ____

(9)
1. $F \supset \sim A$
2. $N \supset A$
3. $\sim F$
4. $\sim A$
5. _____ ____

★(10)
1. $H \supset A$
2. A
3. $A \lor M$
4. $G \supset H$
5. _____ ____

(11)
1. $W \lor B$
2. W
3. $B \supset T$
4. $W \supset A$
5. _____ ____

(12)
1. $K \supset \sim R$
2. $\sim R$
3. $R \lor S$
4. $R \supset T$
5. _____ ____

MindTap Complete exercises online for immediate feedback.

7

★(13) 1. ~C ⊃ ~F
2. L ⊃ F
3. ~~F
4. F ∨ ~L
5. _____ ____

(14) 1. N ⊃ ~E
2. ~~S
3. ~E ∨ ~S
4. ~S ∨ N
5. _____ ____

(15) 1. ~R ⊃ ~T
2. ~T ∨ B
3. C ⊃ ~R
4. ~C
5. _____ ____

★(16) 1. ~K
2. ~K ⊃ ~P
3. ~K ∨ G
4. G ⊃ Q
5. _____ ____

(17) 1. F ∨ (A ⊃ C)
2. A ∨ (C ⊃ F)
3. A
4. ~F
5. _____ ____

(18) 1. (R ⊃ M) ⊃ D
2. M ⊃ C
3. D ⊃ (M ∨ E)
4. ~M
5. _____ ____

★(19) 1. (S ∨ C) ⊃ L
2. ~S
3. ~L
4. S ⊃ (K ⊃ L)
5. _____ ____

(20) 1. (A ∨ W) ⊃ (N ⊃ Q)
2. Q ⊃ G
3. ~A
4. (Q ⊃ G) ⊃ (A ∨ N)
5. _____ ____

II. The following symbolized arguments are missing a premise. Write the premise needed to derive the conclusion (last line), and supply the justification for the conclusion. Try to construct the simplest premise needed to derive the conclusion.

★(1) 1. B ∨ K
2. _____
3. K   ____

(2) 1. N ⊃ S
2. _____
3. S   ____

(3) 1. K ⊃ T
2. _____
3. ~K   ____

★(4) 1. C ⊃ H
2. _____
3. R ⊃ H   ____

(5) 1. F ⊃ N
2. N ⊃ T
3. _____
4. ~F   ____

(6) 1. W ∨ T
2. A ⊃ W
3. _____
4. A ⊃ T   ____

★(7) 1. M ⊃ B
2. Q ⊃ M
3. _____
4. M   ____

(8) 1. C ∨ L
2. L ⊃ T
3. _____
4. L   ____

(9) 1. E ⊃ N
2. T ∨ ~E
3. S ⊃ E
4. _____
5. E   ____

7

★(10) 1. $H \supset A$
2. $S \supset H$
3. $\sim M \lor H$
4. _____
5. $\sim H$ ____

(11) 1. $T \supset N$
2. $G \supset T$
3. $H \lor T$
4. _____
5. $F \supset T$ ____

(12) 1. $G \supset C$
2. $M \lor G$
3. $T \lor \sim G$
4. _____
5. G ____

★(13) 1. $\sim S \supset \sim B$
2. $R \lor \sim B$
3. $\sim B \supset \sim S$
4. _____
5. $\sim \sim B$ ____

(14) 1. $\sim R \supset D$
2. $\sim J \supset \sim R$
3. $N \lor \sim R$
4. _____
5. $\sim F \supset \sim R$ ____

(15) 1. $\sim S \lor \sim P$
2. $\sim K \supset P$
3. $\sim P \supset F$
4. _____
5. $\sim P$ ____

★(16) 1. $J \supset E$
2. $B \lor \sim J$
3. $\sim Z \supset J$
4. _____
5. J ____

(17) 1. $(H \supset C) \supset A$
2. $N \supset (F \supset K)$
3. $(E \cdot R) \supset K$
4. _____
5. $H \supset K$ ____

(18) 1. $(S \supset M) \supset G$
2. $S \supset (M \cdot G)$
3. $G \supset (R \supset \sim S)$
4. _____
5. $\sim S$ ____

★(19) 1. $(W \lor \sim F) \supset H$
2. $(H \lor G) \supset \sim F$
3. $T \supset (F \supset G)$
4. _____
5. $\sim F$ ____

(20) 1. $(H \cdot A) \lor T$
2. $\sim S \supset (P \supset T)$
3. $(N \lor T) \supset P$
4. _____
5. T ____

III. Use the first four rules of inference to derive the conclusions of the following symbolized arguments.

★(1) 1. $\sim C \supset (A \supset C)$
2. $\sim C$ / $\sim A$

(2) 1. $F \lor (D \supset T)$
2. $\sim F$
3. D / T

(3) 1. $(K \cdot B) \lor (L \supset E)$
2. $\sim (K \cdot B)$
3. $\sim E$ / $\sim L$

★(4) 1. $P \supset (G \supset T)$
2. $Q \supset (T \supset E)$
3. P
4. Q / $G \supset E$

(5) 1. $\sim W \supset [\sim W \supset (X \supset W)]$
2. $\sim W$ / $\sim X$

(6) 1. $J \supset (K \supset L)$
2. $L \lor J$
3. $\sim L$ / $\sim K$

★(7) 1. $\sim S \supset D$
2. $\sim S \vee (\sim D \supset K)$
3. $\sim D$ / K

(8) 1. $A \supset (E \supset \sim F)$
2. $H \vee (\sim F \supset M)$
3. A
4. $\sim H$ / $E \supset M$

(9) 1. $\sim G \supset (G \vee \sim A)$
2. $\sim A \supset (C \supset A)$
3. $\sim G$ / $\sim C$

★(10) 1. $N \supset (J \supset P)$
2. $(J \supset P) \supset (N \supset J)$
3. N / P

(11) 1. $G \supset [\sim O \supset (G \supset D)]$
2. $O \vee G$
3. $\sim O$ / D

(12) 1. $\sim M \vee (B \vee \sim T)$
2. $B \supset W$
3. $\sim \sim M$
4. $\sim W$ / $\sim T$

★(13) 1. $R \supset (G \vee \sim A)$
2. $(G \vee \sim A) \supset \sim S$
3. $G \supset S$
4. R / $\sim A$

(14) 1. $(L \equiv N) \supset C$
2. $(L \equiv N) \vee (P \supset \sim E)$
3. $\sim E \supset C$
4. $\sim C$ / $\sim P$

(15) 1. $\sim J \supset [\sim A \supset (D \supset A)]$
2. $J \vee \sim A$
3. $\sim J$ / $\sim D$

★(16) 1. $(B \supset \sim M) \supset (T \supset \sim S)$
2. $B \supset K$
3. $K \supset \sim M$
4. $\sim S \supset N$ / $T \supset N$

(17) 1. $H \vee (Q \vee F)$
2. $R \vee (Q \supset R)$
3. $R \vee \sim H$
4. $\sim R$ / F

(18) 1. $\sim A \supset (B \supset \sim C)$
2. $\sim D \supset (\sim C \supset A)$
3. $D \vee \sim A$
4. $\sim D$ / $\sim B$

★(19) 1. $\sim G \supset [G \vee (S \supset G)]$
2. $(S \vee L) \supset \sim G$
3. $S \vee L$ / L

(20) 1. $H \supset [\sim E \supset (C \supset \sim D)]$
2. $\sim D \supset E$
3. $E \vee H$
4. $\sim E$ / $\sim C$

(21) 1. $\sim B \supset [(A \supset K) \supset (B \vee \sim K)]$
2. $\sim J \supset K$
3. $A \supset \sim J$
4. $\sim B$ / $\sim A$

★(22) 1. $(C \supset M) \supset (N \supset P)$
2. $(C \supset N) \supset (N \supset M)$
3. $(C \supset P) \supset \sim M$
4. $C \supset N$ / $\sim C$

(23) 1. $(R \supset F) \supset [(R \supset \sim G) \supset (S \supset Q)]$
2. $(Q \supset F) \supset (R \supset Q)$
3. $\sim G \supset F$
4. $Q \supset \sim G$ / $S \supset F$

(24) 1. $\sim A \supset [A \vee (T \supset R)]$
2. $\sim R \supset [R \vee (A \supset R)]$
3. $(T \vee D) \supset \sim R$
4. $T \vee D$ / D

★(25) 1. $\sim N \supset [(B \supset D) \supset (N \vee \sim E)]$
2. $(B \supset E) \supset \sim N$
3. $B \supset D$
4. $D \supset E$ / $\sim D$

IV. Translate the following arguments into symbolic form and use the first four rules of inference to derive the conclusion of each. The letters to be used for the simple statements are given in parentheses after each exercise. Use these letters in the order in which they are listed.

★1. If OxyContin is addictive, then either the pharmaceutical industry has stopped making it or thousands of patients are becoming addicted to it. The pharmaceutical industry has not stopped making OxyContin. Also, OxyContin is addictive. Therefore, thousands of patients are becoming addicted to it. (*O, P, T*)

2. If poor people live as long as rich people, then longevity is unaffected by wealth. Either the less affluent have stopped smoking or it is not the case that longevity is unaffected by wealth. It is not the case that the less affluent have stopped smoking. Therefore, poor people do not live as long as rich people. (*P, L, S*)

3. If quotas are imposed on textile imports only if jobs are not lost, then the domestic textile industry will modernize only if the domestic textile industry is not destroyed. If quotas are imposed on textile imports, the domestic textile industry will modernize. The domestic textile industry will modernize only if jobs are not lost. Therefore, if quotas are imposed on textile imports, the domestic textile industry will not be destroyed. (*Q, J, M, D*)

★4. If teachers are allowed to conduct random drug searches on students only if teachers are acting in loco parentis, then if teachers are acting in loco parentis, then students have no Fourth Amendment protections. Either students have no Fourth Amendment protections or if teachers are allowed to conduct random drug searches on students, then teachers are acting in loco parentis. It is not the case that students have no Fourth Amendment protections. Therefore, teachers are not allowed to conduct random drug searches on students. (*R, L, F*)

5. Either funding for nuclear fusion will be cut or if sufficiently high temperatures are achieved in the laboratory, nuclear fusion will become a reality. Either the supply of hydrogen fuel is limited, or if nuclear fusion becomes a reality, the world's energy problems will be solved. Funding for nuclear fusion will not be cut. Furthermore, the supply of hydrogen fuel is not limited. Therefore, if sufficiently high temperatures are achieved in the laboratory, the world's energy problems will be solved. (*C, H, R, S, E*)

6. Either the continents are not subject to drift or if Antarctica was always located in the polar region, then it contains no fossils of plants from a temperate climate. If the continents are not subject to drift, then Antarctica contains no fossils of plants from a temperate climate. But it is not the case that Antarctica contains no fossils of plants from a temperate climate. Therefore, Antarctica was not always located in the polar region. (*D, L, F*)

★7. If terrorists take more hostages, then terrorist demands will be met if and only if the media give full coverage to terrorist acts. Either the media will voluntarily limit the flow of information or if the media will recognize they are being exploited by terrorists, they will voluntarily limit the flow of information. Either the media will recognize they are being exploited by terrorists or terrorists will take more hostages. The media will not voluntarily limit the flow of information. Therefore, terrorist demands will be met if and only if the media give full coverage to terrorist acts. (*H, D, A, V, R*)

8. Either we take recycling seriously or we will be buried in garbage. If we incinerate our garbage only if our health is jeopardized, then we do not take recycling

seriously. If our landfills are becoming exhausted, then if we incinerate our garbage, then toxic ash will be produced. If toxic ash is produced, then our health is jeopardized. Our landfills are becoming exhausted. Therefore, we will be buried in garbage. (R, B, I, H, L, T)

9. If the drug interdiction program is strengthened only if heroin becomes more readily available, then either the number of addicts is decreasing or the war on drugs is failing. If the drug interdiction program is strengthened, then smugglers will shift to more-easily concealable drugs. If smugglers shift to more-easily concealable drugs, then heroin will become more readily available. Furthermore, the number of addicts is not decreasing. Therefore, the war on drugs is failing. (D, H, N, W, S)

★10. If the death penalty is not cruel and unusual punishment, then either it is cruel and unusual punishment or if society is justified in using it, then it will deter other criminals. If the death penalty is cruel and unusual punishment, then it is both cruel and unusual and its use degrades society as a whole. It is not the case that both the death penalty is cruel and unusual and its use degrades society as a whole. Furthermore, the death penalty will not deter other criminals. Therefore, society is not justified in using the death penalty. (C, J, D, U)

V. Create four symbolized arguments consisting of at least three premises each, and whose proof requires at least two of the rules introduced in this section. The arguments should look like those in Part III of this section. Then derive the conclusion of each.

MindTap® Master concepts and improve outcomes with Aplia, at the end of the chapter, in the Aplia folder.

7.2   Rules of Implication II

HOW LOGICAL ARE YOU? Suppose that you and a friend are planning a dinner party. The two of you decide that if you serve fish, then you will also serve carrots. And if you serve chicken, then you will also serve broccoli. You decide that you will serve either fish or chicken. Does this decision tell you which veggie you will serve?

Find the answer on MindTap.

Four additional rules of implication are listed here. Constructive dilemma should be familiar from Chapter 6. The other three are new. They are listed together with an illustration of their use as follows.*

Some textbooks include a rule called absorption *by which the statement form* p ⊃ (q • p) *is deduced from* p ⊃ q. *This rule is necessary only if conditional proof is not presented. This volume opts in favor of conditional proof, to be introduced shortly.*

5. Constructive dilemma (CD)

$(p \supset q) \cdot (r \supset s)$

$p \lor r$
_____

$q \lor s$

If Oscar is a dog, then you'll have fleas, and
   if Oscar is a cat, then you'll have fur balls.
Oscar is either a dog or a cat.
_____

You'll have either fleas or fur balls.

6. Simplification (Simp)

$p \cdot q$
_____

p

Eliza has long legs and runs fast.
_____

Eliza has long legs.

7. Conjunction (Conj)

p

q
_____

$p \cdot q$

Roxy has big eyes.

Roxy has a tail.
_____

Roxy has big eyes and a tail.

8. Addition (Add)

p
_____

$p \lor q$

Theo has spots.
_____

Theo has either spots or stripes.

Like the previous four rules, these are fairly easy to understand, but if there is any doubt about them their validity may be proven by means of a truth table.

Constructive dilemma can be understood as involving two *modus ponens* steps. The first premise states that if we have p then we have q, and if we have r then we have s. But since, by the second premise, we do have either p or r, it follows by *modus ponens* that we have either q or s. Constructive dilemma is the only form of dilemma that will be included as a rule of inference. By the rule of transposition, which will be presented in Section 7.4, any argument that is a substitution instance of the destructive dilemma form can be easily converted into a substitution instance of constructive dilemma. Destructive dilemma, therefore, is not needed as a rule of inference.

> These arguments are both instances of **constructive dilemma** (CD):
>
> $\sim M \lor N$
>
> $(\sim M \supset S) \cdot (N \supset \sim T)$
> _____
>
> $S \lor \sim T$
>
> $[(K \supset T) \supset (A \cdot B)] \cdot [(H \supset P) \supset (A \cdot C)]$
>
> $(K \supset T) \lor (H \supset P)$
> _____
>
> $(A \cdot B) \lor (A \cdot C)$

Simplification states that if two propositions are given as true on a single line, then each of them is true separately. According to the strict interpretation of the simplification rule, only the left-hand conjunct may be stated in the conclusion. Once the commutativity rule for conjunction has been presented, however (see Section 7.3), we will be justified in replacing a statement such as $H \cdot K$ with $K \cdot H$. Once we do this, the K will appear on the left, and the appropriate conclusion is K.

> These arguments are all instances of **simplification** (Simp):
>
> $\sim F \cdot (U \equiv E)$
> _____
>
> $\sim F$
>
> $(M \lor T) \cdot (S \supset R)$
> _____
>
> $M \lor T$
>
> $[(X \supset Z) \cdot M] \cdot (G \supset H)$
> _____
>
> $(X \supset Z) \cdot M$

Conjunction states that two propositions—for example, H and K—asserted separately on different lines may be conjoined on a single line. The two propositions may be conjoined in whatever order we choose (either $H \cdot K$ or $K \cdot H$) without appeal to the commutativity rule for conjunction.

These arguments are all instances of **conjunction** (Conj):

$$\begin{array}{lll}
\sim E & C \supset M & R \supset (H \cdot T) \\
\underline{\sim G} & \underline{D \supset N} & \underline{K \supset (H \cdot O)} \\
\sim E \cdot \sim G & (C \supset M) \cdot (D \supset N) & [R \supset (H \cdot T)] \cdot [K \supset (H \cdot O)]
\end{array}$$

Addition states that whenever a proposition is asserted on a line by itself it may be joined disjunctively with any proposition we choose. In other words, if G is asserted to be true by itself, it follows that $G \vee H$ is true. This may appear somewhat puzzling at first, but once one realizes that $G \vee H$ is a much weaker statement than G by itself, the puzzlement should disappear. The new proposition must, of course, always be joined disjunctively (not conjunctively) to the given proposition. If G is stated on a line by itself, we are *not* justified in writing $G \cdot H$ as a consequence of addition.

These arguments are all instances of **addition** (Add):

$$\begin{array}{lll}
S & (C \cdot D) & W \equiv Z \\
\underline{} & \underline{} & \underline{} \\
S \vee \sim T & (C \cdot D) \vee (K \cdot \sim P) & (W \equiv Z) \vee [A \supset (M \supset O)]
\end{array}$$

The use of these four rules may now be illustrated. Consider the following argument:

1. $A \supset B$
2. $(B \vee C) \supset (D \cdot E)$
3. A / D

As usual, we begin by looking for the conclusion in the premises. D appears in the consequent of the second premise, which we can derive via simplification if we first obtain $B \vee C$. This expression as such does not appear in the premises, but from lines 1 and 3 we see that we can derive B by itself via *modus ponens*. Having obtained B, we can derive $B \vee C$ via addition. The proof has now been thought through and can be written out as follows:

1. $A \supset B$
2. $(B \vee C) \supset (D \cdot E)$
3. A / D
4. B 1, 3, MP
5. $B \vee C$ 4, Add
6. $D \cdot E$ 2, 5, MP
7. D 6, Simp

Another example:

1. $K \supset L$
2. $(M \supset N) \cdot S$
3. $N \supset T$
4. $K \lor M$ / $L \lor T$

Seeing that $L \lor T$ does not appear as such in the premises, we look at the main operator of the conclusion, which is a wedge. This makes us think of constructive dilemma and addition, each of which would give us a statement containing a wedge. Finding L and T as the consequents of two distinct conditional statements causes us to think that the conclusion can be derived via constructive dilemma. If a constructive dilemma can be set up, it will need a disjunctive statement as its second premise, and such a statement appears on line 4. Furthermore, each of the components of this statement, K and M, appears as the antecedent of a conditional statement, exactly as they both should for a dilemma. The only statement that is missing now is $M \supset T$. Inspecting line 2 we see that we can obtain $M \supset N$ via simplification, and putting this together with line 3 gives us $M \supset T$ via hypothetical syllogism. The completed proof may now be written out:

1. $K \supset L$
2. $(M \supset N) \cdot S$
3. $N \supset T$
4. $K \lor M$ / $L \lor T$
5. $M \supset N$ 2, Simp
6. $M \supset T$ 3, 5, HS
7. $(K \supset L) \cdot (M \supset T)$ 1, 6, Conj
8. $L \lor T$ 4, 7, CD

Another example:

1. $\sim M \cdot N$
2. $P \supset M$
3. $Q \cdot R$
4. $(\sim P \cdot Q) \supset S$ / $S \lor T$

When we look for $S \lor T$ in the premises we find S in the consequent of line 4 but no T at all. This signals an important principle: Whenever the conclusion of an argument contains a letter not found in the premises, addition must be used to introduce the missing letter. Addition is the *only* rule of inference that can introduce new letters. To introduce T by addition, however, we must first obtain S on a line by itself. S can be derived from line 4 via *modus ponens* if we first obtain $\sim P \cdot Q$. This, in turn, can be derived via conjunction, but first $\sim P$ and Q must be obtained individually on separate lines. Q can be derived from line 3 via simplification and $\sim P$ from line 2 via *modus tollens*, but the latter step requires that we first obtain $\sim M$ on a line by itself. Since this can be derived from line 1 via simplification, the proof is now complete. It may be written out as follows:

1. $\sim M \cdot N$
2. $P \supset M$

3. $Q \cdot R$
4. $(\sim P \cdot Q) \supset S$ / $S \vee T$
5. $\sim M$ 1, Simp
6. $\sim P$ 2, 5, MT
7. Q 3, Simp
8. $\sim P \cdot Q$ 6, 7, Conj
9. S 4, 8, MP
10. $S \vee T$ 9, Add

Addition is used together with disjunctive syllogism to derive the conclusion of arguments having inconsistent premises. As we saw in Chapter 6, such arguments are always valid. The procedure is illustrated as follows:

1. S
2. $\sim S$ / T
3. $S \vee T$ 1, Add
4. T 2, 3, DS

With arguments of this sort the conclusion is always introduced via addition and then separated via disjunctive syllogism. Since addition can be used to introduce any letter or arrangement of letters we choose, it should be clear from this example that inconsistent premises validly entail any conclusion whatever.

To complete this presentation of the eight rules of implication, let us consider some of the typical ways in which they are *misapplied*. Examples are as follows:

1. $P \vee (S \cdot T)$
2. S 1, Simp (invalid—$S \cdot T$ must first be obtained on a line by itself)

1. K
2. $K \cdot L$ 1, Add (invalid—the conclusion must be a disjunctive statement)

1. $M \vee N$
2. M 1, Simp (invalid—simplification is possible only with a conjunctive premise; line 1 is a disjunction)

1. $G \supset H$
2. $G \supset (H \vee J)$ 1, Add (improper—J must be added to the whole line, not just to the consequent of line 1)

1. $L \supset M$
2. $L \supset N$
3. $M \cdot N$ 1, 2, Conj (invalid—M and N must first be obtained on lines by themselves)

1. $\sim(P \cdot Q)$
2. $\sim P$ 1, Simp (invalid—parentheses must be removed first)

1. $\sim(P \vee Q)$
2. $\sim P$
3. Q 1, 2, DS (invalid—parentheses must be removed first)

The use of addition in the $G \supset H$ example is called "improper" because the letter that is added is not added to the whole line. It turns out, however, that even though the addition rule is not correctly applied here, the inference is still valid. Hence, this inference is not called "invalid," as the others are. As for the last two examples, a rule will be presented in the next section (De Morgan's rule) that will allow us to remove parentheses preceded by negation signs. But even after the parentheses have been removed from these examples, the inferences remain invalid.

Like the previous section, this one ends with a few strategies for applying the last four rules of implication:

Strategy 6: If the conclusion contains a letter that appears in a conjunctive statement in the premises, consider obtaining that letter via simplification:

```
1. A ⊃ B
2. C • B
3. C ⊃ A        / C
4. C            2, Simp
```

Strategy 7: If the conclusion is a conjunctive statement, consider obtaining it via conjunction by first obtaining the individual conjuncts:

```
1. A ⊃ C
2. B
3. ~C           / B • ~C
4. B • ~C       2, 3, Conj
```

Strategy 8: If the conclusion is a disjunctive statement, consider obtaining it via constructive dilemma or addition:

```
1. (A ⊃ B) • (C ⊃ D)
2. B ⊃ C
3. A v C        / B v D
4. B v D        1, 3, CD
```

```
1. A v C
2. B
3. C ⊃ D        / B v D
4. B v D        2, Add
```

Strategy 9: If the conclusion contains a letter not found in the premises, addition *must* be used to introduce that letter.

Strategy 10: Conjunction can be used to set up constructive dilemma:

```
1. A ⊃ B
2. C ⊃ D
3. A v C              / B v D
4. (A ⊃ B) • (C ⊃ D)  1, 2, Conj
5. B v D              3, 4, CD
```

I. For each of the following lists of premises, derive the indicated conclusion and complete the justification. In problems 4 and 8 you can add any statement you choose.

★(1) 1. $S \vee H$
    2. $B \cdot E$
    3. $R \supset G$
    4. ____ ____, Simp

(2) 1. $(N \supset T) \cdot (F \supset Q)$
    2. $(N \supset R) \vee (F \supset M)$
    3. $N \vee F$
    4. _____ ____, CD

(3) 1. D
    2. W
    3. ____ ____, Conj

★(4) 1. H
    2. ____ ____, Add

(5) 1. $R \cdot (N \vee K)$
    2. $(G \cdot T) \vee S$
    3. $(Q \cdot C) \supset (J \cdot L)$
    4. _____ ____, Simp

(6) 1. $\sim R \vee P$
    2. $(P \supset \sim D) \cdot (\sim R \supset S)$
    3. $(\sim R \supset A) \cdot (P \supset \sim N)$
    4. _____ ____, CD

★(7) 1. $(Q \vee K) \cdot \sim B$
    2. $(M \cdot R) \supset D$
    3. $(W \cdot S) \vee (G \cdot F)$
    4. _____ ____, Simp

(8) 1. $E \cdot G$
    2. _____ ____, Add

(9) 1. $\sim B$
    2. $F \vee N$
    3. ____ ____, Conj

★(10) 1. $S \vee \sim C$
    2. $(S \supset \sim L) \cdot (\sim C \supset M)$
    3. $(\sim N \supset S) \cdot (F \supset \sim C)$
    4. _____ ____, CD

II. In the following symbolized arguments, derive the line needed to obtain the conclusion (last line), and supply the justification for both lines.

★(1) 1. $G \supset N$
    2. $G \cdot K$
    3. _____ ____
    4. $G \vee T$ ____

(2) 1. $\sim A$
    2. $A \vee E$
    3. _____ ____
    4. $\sim A \cdot E$ ____

(3) 1. $B \supset N$
    2. $B \vee K$
    3. $K \supset R$
    4. ____ ____
    5. $N \vee R$ ____

★(4) 1. T
    2. $T \supset G$
    3. $(T \vee U) \supset H$
    4. _____ ____
    5. H ____

(5) 1. $S \supset E$
    2. $E \vee (S \cdot P)$
    3. $\sim E$
    4. _____ ____
    5. S ____

(6) 1. N
    2. $N \supset F$
    3. $(N \supset A) \cdot (F \supset C)$
    4. _____ ____
    5. $A \vee C$ ____

★(7) 1. J
    2. $\sim L$
    3. $F \supset L$
    4. _____ ___
    5. $\sim F \cdot J$ ___

(8) 1. $(E \supset B) \cdot (Q \supset N)$
    2. $K \supset E$
    3. $B \supset K$
    4. _____ ___
    5. $E \supset K$ ___

(9) 1. $G \vee N$
    2. $\sim G$
    3. $\sim G \supset (H \cdot R)$
    4. _____ ___
    5. H ___

★(10) 1. M
    2. $(M \cdot E) \supset D$
    3. E
    4. _____ ___
    5. D ___

III. Use the first eight rules of inference to derive the conclusions of the following symbolized arguments:

★(1) 1. $\sim M \supset Q$
    2. $R \supset \sim T$
    3. $\sim M \vee R$ / $Q \vee \sim T$

(2) 1. $N \supset (D \cdot W)$
    2. $D \supset K$
    3. N / $N \cdot K$

(3) 1. $E \supset (A \cdot C)$
    2. $A \supset (F \cdot E)$
    3. E / F

★(4) 1. $(H \vee \sim B) \supset R$
    2. $(H \vee \sim M) \supset P$
    3. H / $R \cdot P$

(5) 1. $G \supset (S \cdot T)$
    2. $(S \vee T) \supset J$
    3. G / J

(6) 1. $(L \vee T) \supset (B \cdot G)$
    2. $L \cdot (K \equiv R)$ / $L \cdot B$

★(7) 1. $(\sim F \vee X) \supset (P \vee T)$
    2. $F \supset P$
    3. $\sim P$ / T

(8) 1. $(N \supset B) \cdot (O \supset C)$
    2. $Q \supset (N \vee O)$
    3. Q / $B \vee C$

(9) 1. $(U \vee W) \supset (T \supset R)$
    2. $U \cdot H$
    3. $\sim R \cdot \sim J$ / $U \cdot \sim T$

★(10) 1. $(D \vee E) \supset (G \cdot H)$
    2. $G \supset \sim D$
    3. $D \cdot F$ / M

(11) 1. $(B \vee F) \supset (A \supset G)$
    2. $(B \vee E) \supset (G \supset K)$
    3. $B \cdot \sim H$ / $A \supset K$

(12) 1. $(P \supset R) \supset (M \supset P)$
    2. $(P \vee M) \supset (P \supset R)$
    3. $P \vee M$ / $R \vee P$

★(13) 1. $(C \supset N) \cdot E$
    2. $D \vee (N \supset D)$
    3. $\sim D$ / $\sim C \vee P$

(14) 1. $F \supset (\sim T \cdot A)$
    2. $(\sim T \vee G) \supset (H \supset T)$
    3. $F \cdot O$ / $\sim H \cdot \sim T$

(15) 1. $(\sim S \vee B) \supset (S \vee K)$
    2. $(K \vee \sim D) \supset (H \supset S)$
    3. $\sim S \cdot W$ / $\sim H$

★(16) 1. $(C \vee \sim G) \supset (\sim P \cdot L)$
    2. $(\sim P \cdot C) \supset (C \supset D)$
    3. $C \cdot \sim R$ / $D \vee R$

(17) 1. $[A \vee (K \cdot J)] \supset (\sim E \cdot \sim F)$
    2. $M \supset [A \cdot (P \vee R)]$
    3. $M \cdot U$ / $\sim E \cdot A$

(18) 1. $\sim H \supset (\sim T \supset R)$
    2. $H \vee (E \supset F)$
    3. $\sim T \vee E$
    4. $\sim H \cdot D$ / $R \vee F$

★(19) 1. $(U \cdot \sim \sim P) \supset Q$
    2. $\sim O \supset U$
    3. $\sim P \supset O$
    4. $\sim O \cdot T$ / Q

(20) 1. $(M \lor N) \supset (F \supset G)$
2. $D \supset \sim C$
3. $\sim C \supset B$
4. $M \cdot H$
5. $D \lor F$ / $B \lor G$

(21) 1. $(F \cdot M) \supset (S \lor T)$
2. $(\sim S \lor A) \supset F$
3. $(\sim S \lor B) \supset M$
4. $\sim S \cdot G$ / T

★(22) 1. $(\sim K \cdot \sim N) \supset$
    $[(\sim P \supset K) \cdot (\sim R \supset G)]$
2. $K \supset N$
3. $\sim N \cdot B$
4. $\sim P \lor \sim R$ / G

(23) 1. $(\sim A \lor D) \supset (B \supset F)$
2. $(B \lor C) \supset (A \supset E)$
3. $A \lor B$
4. $\sim A$ / $E \lor F$

(24) 1. $(J \supset K) \cdot (\sim O \supset \sim P)$
2. $(L \supset J) \cdot (\sim M \supset \sim O)$
3. $\sim K \supset (L \lor \sim M)$
4. $\sim K \cdot G$ / $\sim P$

★(25) 1. $(\sim M \cdot \sim N) \supset [(\sim M \lor H) \supset (K \cdot L)]$
2. $\sim M \cdot (C \supset D)$
3. $\sim N \cdot (F \equiv G)$ / $K \cdot \sim N$

(26) 1. $(P \lor S) \supset (E \supset F)$
2. $(P \lor T) \supset (G \supset H)$
3. $(P \lor U) \supset (E \lor G)$
4. P / $F \lor H$

(27) 1. $(S \supset Q) \cdot (Q \supset \sim S)$
2. $S \lor Q$
3. $\sim Q$ / $P \cdot R$

★(28) 1. $(D \supset B) \cdot (C \supset D)$
2. $(B \supset D) \cdot (E \supset C)$
3. $B \lor E$ / $D \lor B$

(29) 1. $(R \supset H) \cdot (S \supset I)$
2. $(\sim H \cdot \sim L) \supset (R \lor S)$
3. $\sim H \cdot (K \supset T)$
4. $H \lor \sim L$ / $I \lor M$

(30) 1. $(W \cdot X) \supset (Q \lor R)$
2. $(S \lor F) \supset (Q \lor W)$
3. $(S \lor G) \supset (\sim Q \supset X)$
4. $Q \lor S$
5. $\sim Q \cdot H$ / R

IV. Translate the following arguments into symbolic form and use the first eight rules of inference to derive the conclusion of each. Use the letters in the order in which they are listed.

★1. If topaz is harder than quartz, then it will scratch quartz and also feldspar. Topaz is harder than quartz and it is also harder than calcite. Therefore, either topaz will scratch quartz or it will scratch corundum. (T, Q, F, C, O)

2. If clear-cutting continues in primary forests and the Endangered Species Act is not repealed, then either the Endangered Species Act will be repealed or thousands of animal species will become extinct. Clear-cutting continues in primary forests. The Endangered Species Act will not be repealed. Therefore, thousands of animal species will become extinct. (C, E, T)

3. If either executive salaries are out of control or exorbitant bonuses are paid, then either shareholders will be cheated or ordinary workers will be paid less. Executive salaries are out of control and the rich are getting richer. If shareholders are cheated, then future investors will stay away; also, if ordinary workers are paid less, then consumer spending will decline. If either future investors stay away or consumer spending declines, then the economy will suffer. Therefore, the economy will suffer. (S, B, C, P, R, F, D, E)

★4. Either animals are mere mechanisms or they feel pain. If either animals feel pain or they have souls, then they have a right not to be subjected to needless pain and humans have a duty not to inflict needless pain on them. It is not the case that animals are mere mechanisms. Therefore, animals have a right not to be subjected to needless pain. (*M, P, S, R, D*)

5. If half the nation suffers from depression, then if either the insurance companies have their way or the psychiatrists have their way, then everyone will be taking antidepressant drugs. If either half the nation suffers from depression or sufferers want a real cure, then it is not the case that everyone will be taking antidepressant drugs. Half the nation suffers from depression. Therefore, it is not the case that either the insurance companies or the psychiatrists will have their way. (*H, I, P, E, W*)

6. If either parents get involved in their children's education or the school year is lengthened, then if the children learn phonics, their reading will improve and if they are introduced to abstract concepts earlier, their math will improve. If either parents get involved in their children's education or nebulous subjects are dropped from the curriculum, then either the children will learn phonics or they will be introduced to abstract concepts earlier. Parents will get involved in their children's education, and writing lessons will be integrated with other subjects. Therefore, either the children's reading or their math will improve. (*P, S, L, R, I, M, N, W*)

★7. If either manufacturers will not concentrate on producing a superior product or they will not market their product abroad, then if they will not concentrate on producing a superior product, then the trade deficit will worsen. Either manufacturers will concentrate on producing a superior product or the trade deficit will not worsen. Manufacturers will not concentrate on producing a superior product. Therefore, today's business managers lack imagination. (*C, M, T, B*)

8. If either medical fees or malpractice awards escape restrictions, then health-care costs will soar and millions of poor will go uninsured. If the lawyers get their way, then malpractice awards will escape restrictions. If the doctors get their way, then medical fees will escape restrictions. Either the doctors or the lawyers will get their way, and insurance companies will resist reform. Therefore, health-care costs will soar. (*F, A, H, P, L, D, I*)

9. If we are less than certain the human fetus is a person, then we must give it the benefit of the doubt. If we are certain the human fetus is a person, then we must accord it the right to live. If either we must give the fetus the benefit of the doubt or accord it the right to live, then we are not less than certain the fetus is human and it is not merely a part of the mother's body. Either we are less than certain the human fetus is a person or we are certain about it. If we are certain the human fetus is a person, then abortion is immoral. Therefore, abortion is immoral. (*L, G, C, A, M, I*)

★10. If the assassination of terrorist leaders violates civilized values and also is not effective in the long run, then if it prevents terrorist atrocities, then it is effective in the long run. If the assassination of terrorist leaders violates civilized values, then it is not effective in the long run. The assassination of terrorist leaders violates civilized values and is also illegal. If the assassination of terrorist leaders is not effective in the long run, then either it prevents terrorist atrocities or it justifies acts of revenge by terrorists. Therefore, the assassination of terrorist leaders justifies acts of revenge by terrorists and also is not effective in the long run. (*V, E, P, I, J*)

V. Create four symbolized arguments consisting of at least three premises each, and whose proof requires at least two of the rules introduced in this section. The arguments should look like those in Part III of this section. Then derive the conclusion of each.

MindTap Master concepts and improve outcomes with Aplia, at the end of the chapter, in the Aplia folder.

7.3 Rules of Replacement I

HOW LOGICAL ARE YOU? Suppose you tell a friend that after graduation you will either travel to Europe or move in with your parents. Later you say that after graduation you will either look for a job or travel to Europe. What you're telling me, your friend says, is that after graduation you will either travel to Europe or move in with your parents and look for a job. Has your friend understood you correctly?

Find the answer on MindTap.

Unlike the rules of implication, which are basic argument forms, the ten **rules of replacement** are expressed in terms of pairs of logically equivalent statement forms, either of which can replace the other in a proof sequence. To express these rules, a new symbol, called a **double colon** (::), is used to designate logical equivalence. This symbol is a *metalogical* symbol in that it makes an assertion not about things but about symbolized statements: It asserts that the expressions on either side of it have the same truth value regardless of the truth values of their components. Underlying the use of the rules of replacement is an **axiom of replacement**, which asserts that within the context of a proof, logically equivalent expressions may replace each other. The first five rules of replacement are as follows:

9. De Morgan's rule (DM):
   $\sim(p \cdot q) :: (\sim p \lor \sim q)$
   $\sim(p \lor q) :: (\sim p \cdot \sim q)$

10. Commutativity (Com):
    $(p \lor q) :: (q \lor p)$
    $(p \cdot q) :: (q \cdot p)$

11. Associativity (Assoc):

$$[p \lor (q \lor r)] :: [(p \lor q) \lor r]$$
$$[p \bullet (q \bullet r)] :: [(p \bullet q) \bullet r]$$

12. Distribution (Dist):

$$[p \bullet (q \lor r)] :: [(p \bullet q) \lor (p \bullet r)]$$
$$[p \lor (q \bullet r)] :: [(p \lor q) \bullet (p \lor r)]$$

13. Double negation (DN):

$$p :: \sim\sim p$$

De Morgan's rule (named after the nineteenth-century logician Augustus De Morgan) was discussed in Section 6.1 in connection with translation. There it was pointed out that "Not both p and q" is logically equivalent to "Not p or not q," and that "Not either p or q" is logically equivalent to "Not p and not q." When applying De Morgan's rule, one should keep in mind that it holds only for conjunctive and disjunctive statements (not for conditionals or biconditionals). The rule may be summarized as follows: When moving a tilde inside or outside a set of parentheses, a dot switches with a wedge and vice versa.

Commutativity asserts that the truth value of a conjunction or disjunction is unaffected by the order in which the components are listed. In other words, the component statements may be commuted, or switched for one another, without affecting the truth value. The validity of this rule should be immediately apparent. You may recall from arithmetic that the commutativity rule also applies to addition and multiplication and asserts, for example, that $3 + 5$ equals $5 + 3$, and that 2×3 equals 3×2. However, it does *not* apply to division; $2 \div 4$ does not equal $4 \div 2$. A similar lesson applies in logic: The commutativity rule applies only to conjunction and disjunction; it does *not* apply to implication.

Associativity states that the truth value of a conjunctive or disjunctive statement is unaffected by the placement of parentheses when the same operator is used throughout. In other words, the way in which the component propositions are grouped, or associated with one another, can be changed without affecting the truth value. The validity of this rule is quite easy to see, but if there is any doubt about it, it may be readily checked by means of a truth table. You may recall that the associativity rule also applies to addition and multiplication and asserts, for example, that $3 + (5 + 7)$ equals $(3 + 5) + 7$, and that $2 \times (3 \times 4)$ equals $(2 \times 3) \times 4$. But it does *not* apply to division: $(8 \div 4) \div 2$ does not equal $8 \div (4 \div 2)$. Analogously, in logic, the associativity rule applies only to conjunctive and disjunctive statements; it does *not* apply to conditional statements. Also note, when applying this rule, that the order of the letters remains unchanged; only the placement of the parentheses changes.

Distribution, like De Morgan's rule, applies only to conjunctive and disjunctive statements. When a proposition is conjoined to a disjunctive statement in parentheses or disjoined to a conjunctive statement in parentheses, the rule allows us to put that proposition together with each of the components inside the parentheses, and also to go in the reverse direction. In the first form of the rule, a statement is distributed through a disjunction, and in the second form, through a conjunction. While the rule may not be immediately obvious, it is easy to remember: The operator that is at first outside the parentheses goes inside, and the operator that is at first inside the parentheses goes outside. Note also how distribution differs from commutativity and associativity. The latter two rules apply only when the *same* operator (either a dot or a wedge) is used throughout a statement. Distribution applies when a dot and a wedge appear *together* in a statement.

Double negation is fairly obvious and needs little explanation. The rule states simply that pairs of tildes immediately adjacent to one another may be either deleted or introduced without affecting the truth value of the statement.

There is an important difference between the rules of implication, treated in the first two sections of this chapter, and the rules of replacement. The rules of implication derive their name from the fact that each is a simple argument form in which the premises imply the conclusion. To be applicable in natural deduction, certain lines in a proof must be interpreted as substitution instances of the argument form in question. Stated another way, the rules of implication are applicable only to *whole lines* in a proof. For example, step 3 in the following proof is not a legitimate application of *modus ponens*, because the first premise in the *modus ponens* rule is applied to only a *part* of line 1.

1. $A \supset (B \supset C)$
2. B
3. C 1, 2, MP (invalid)

The rules of replacement, on the other hand, are not rules of implication but rules of logical equivalence. Since, by the axiom of replacement, logically equivalent statement forms can always replace one another in a proof sequence, the rules of replacement can be applied either to a whole line or to any part of a line. Step 2 in the following proof is a quite legitimate application of De Morgan's rule, even though the rule is applied only to the consequent of line 1:

1. $S \supset \sim(T \cdot U)$
2. $S \supset (\sim T \vee \sim U)$ 1, DM (valid)

Another way of viewing this distinction is that the rules of implication are "one-way" rules, whereas the rules of replacement are "two-way" rules. The rules of implication allow us to proceed only from the premise lines of a rule to the conclusion line, but the rules of replacement allow us to replace either side of an equivalence expression with the other side.

Application of the first five rules of replacement may now be illustrated. Consider the following argument:

1. $A \supset \sim(B \cdot C)$
2. $A \cdot C$ / $\sim B$

Examining the premises, we find B in the consequent of line 1. This leads us to suspect that the conclusion can be derived via *modus ponens*. If this is correct, the tilde would then have to be taken inside the parentheses via De Morgan's rule and the resulting $\sim C$ eliminated by disjunctive syllogism. The following completed proof indicates that this strategy yields the anticipated result:

1. $A \supset \sim(B \cdot C)$
2. $A \cdot C$ / $\sim B$
3. A 2, Simp

4. ~(B • C)	1, 3, MP
5. ~B ∨ ~C	4, DM
6. C • A	2, Com
7. C	6, Simp
8. ~~C	7, DN
9. ~C ∨ ~B	5, Com
10. ~B	8, 9, DS

The rationale for line 6 is to get *C* on the left side so that it can be separated via simplification. Similarly, the rationale for line 9 is to get ~*C* on the left side so that it can be eliminated via disjunctive syllogism. Line 8 is required because, strictly speaking, the negation of ~*C* is ~ ~*C*—not simply *C*. Thus, *C* must be replaced with ~ ~*C* to set up the disjunctive syllogism. If your instructor permits it, you can combine commutativity and double negation with other inferences on a single line, as the following shortened proof illustrates. However, we will avoid this practice throughout the remainder of the book.

1. A ⊃ ~(B • C)	
2. A • C	/ ~B
3. A	2, Simp
4. ~(B • C)	1, 3, MP
5. ~B ∨ ~C	4, DM
6. C	2, Com, Simp
7. ~B	5, 6, Com, DN, DS

Another example:

1. D • (E ∨ F)	
2. ~D ∨ ~F	/ D • E

The conclusion requires that we get *D* and *E* together. Inspection of the first premise suggests distribution as the first step in achieving this. The completed proof is as follows:

1. D • (E ∨ F)	
2. ~D ∨ ~F	/ D • E
3. (D • E) ∨ (D • F)	1, Dist
4. (D • F) ∨ (D • E)	3, Com
5. ~(D • F)	2, DM
6. D • E	4, 5, DS

Some proofs require that we use distribution in the reverse manner. Consider this argument:

1. (G • H) ∨ (G • J)	
2. (G ∨ K) ⊃ L	/ L

The conclusion can be obtained from line 2 via *modus ponens* if we first obtain *G* ∨ *K* on a line by itself. Since *K* does not occur in the first premise at all, it must be introduced by addition. Doing this requires in turn that we obtain *G* on a line by itself. Distribution applied to line 1 provides the solution:

1. $(G \cdot H) \vee (G \cdot J)$
2. $(G \vee K) \supset L$ $/ L$
3. $G \cdot (H \vee J)$ 1, Dist
4. G 3, Simp
5. $G \vee K$ 4, Add
6. L 2, 5, MP

Application of the associativity rule is illustrated in the next proof:

1. $M \vee (N \vee O)$
2. $\sim O$ $/ M \vee N$
3. $(M \vee N) \vee O$ 1, Assoc
4. $O \vee (M \vee N)$ 3, Com
5. $M \vee N$ 2, 4, DS

Before *O* can be eliminated via disjunctive syllogism from line 1, it must be moved over to the left side. Associativity and commutativity together accomplish this objective.

In some arguments the attempt to "find" the conclusion in the premises is not immediately successful. When confronted with such an argument, one should often begin by "deconstructing" the conclusion using the rules of replacement. In other words, one should first apply the rules of replacement to the conclusion to see how it is put together. After this is done, how the premises entail the conclusion may be evident. This procedure is justified by the fact that the rules of replacement are two-way rules. As a result, after the conclusion is deconstructed, it can be derived by using the same rules in reverse order. Here is an example of such an argument:

1. $K \supset (F \vee B)$
2. $G \cdot K$ $/ (F \cdot G) \vee (B \cdot G)$

If immediate inspection does not reveal how the conclusion should be derived, we may begin by applying the rules of replacement to the conclusion. The form of the conclusion suggests the distribution rule, but first we must use commutativity to move the *G*'s to the left-hand side. The deconstruction proceeds as follows:

$(F \cdot G) \vee (B \cdot G)$
$(G \cdot F) \vee (B \cdot G)$ Com
$(G \cdot F) \vee (G \cdot B)$ Com
$G \cdot (F \vee B)$ Dist

Now we see that if we can obtain *G* on a line by itself, and *F* ∨ *B* on a line by itself, we can combine them on a single line via the conjunction rule. We can then derive the conclusion via distribution and commutativity. Inspection of the premises reveals that *G* can be derived from line 2 of the premises by simplification, and *F* ∨ *B* can be derived from line 1 by *modus ponens*. The completed proof is as follows:

Willard Van Orman Quine 1908–2000

Prior to his death in the year 2000, Willard Van Orman Quine was widely considered to be, as Stuart Hampshire put it, "the most distinguished and influential of living philosophers." At that time, over 2,000 scholarly articles had been written about his work.

Quine was born in Akron, Ohio, in 1908 to a father who founded a heavy equipment company and a mother who taught elementary school. He earned his bachelor's degree in mathematics from Oberlin College, where he graduated *summa cum laude* in 1930. He then entered Harvard University, where he switched to philosophy so he could study under Alfred North Whitehead. He earned his PhD in a record two years. Except for four years during World War II, when he served in the Navy decoding messages from German submarines, Quine remained affiliated with Harvard for the remainder of his life.

Quine wrote twenty-two books, the first five of which dealt with mathematical logic. One of the goals of the earlier books was to show how the foundations of mathematics could be laid out in less than a fourth of the space taken by Whitehead and Russell's *Principia Mathematica.* One of his most famous publications was "Two Dogmas of Empiricism," which shook the pillars of analytic philosophy by undermining the sacrosanct distinction between analytic and synthetic statements. As a result of this work, even the truths of logic and mathematics became subject to the dictates of empirical experience.

As a boy, Quine had a fascination with collecting stamps and drawing maps, which, as an adult, he translated into a zest for world travel. He visited 118 countries, became fluent in six different languages, delivered lectures all over the world, and was awarded the first Schock Prize (Stockholm, 1993) and the Kyoto Prize (Tokyo, 1996). He was married twice, raised two children from each marriage, loved Dixieland jazz, and played the banjo, mandolin, and piano. He was singularly unpretentious, had an unfailing curiosity about a vast range of topics, and delighted in teaching freshman logic as well as advanced courses in philosophy. He died in Boston at the age of ninety-two.

AP Images/Julia Malakia

7

1. $K \supset (F \lor B)$	
2. $G \cdot K$	/ $(F \cdot G) \lor (B \cdot G)$
3. G	2, Simp
4. $K \cdot G$	2, Com
5. K	4, Simp
6. $F \lor B$	1, 5, MP
7. $G \cdot (F \lor B)$	3, 6, Conj
8. $(G \cdot F) \lor (G \cdot B)$	7, Dist
9. $(F \cdot G) \lor (G \cdot B)$	8, Com
10. $(F \cdot G) \lor (B \cdot G)$	9, Com

Here are some strategies for applying the first five rules of replacement. Most of them show how these rules may be used together with other rules.

Strategy 11: Conjunction can be used to set up De Morgan's rule:

```
1.  ~A
2.  ~B
3.  ~A • ~B          1, 2, Conj
4.  ~(A ∨ B)         3, DM
```

Strategy 12: Constructive dilemma can be used to set up De Morgan's rule:

```
1.  (A ⊃ ~B) • (C ⊃ ~D)
2.  A ∨ C
3.  ~B ∨ ~D          1, 2, CD
4.  ~(B • D)         3, DM
```

Strategy 13: Addition can be used to set up De Morgan's rule:

```
1.  ~A
2.  ~A ∨ ~B          1, Add
3.  ~(A • B)         2, DM
```

Strategy 14: Distribution can be used in two ways to set up disjunctive syllogism:

```
1.  (A ∨ B) • (A ∨ C)
2.  ~A
3.  A ∨ (B • C)      1, Dist
4.  B • C            2, 3, DS
```

```
1.  A • (B ∨ C)
2.  ~(A • B)
3.  (A • B) ∨ (A • C)   1, Dist
4.  A • C               2, 3, DS
```

Strategy 15: Distribution can be used in two ways to set up simplification:

```
1.  A ∨ (B • C)
2.  (A ∨ B) • (A ∨ C)   1, Dist
3.  A ∨ B               2, Simp
```

```
1.  (A • B) ∨ (A • C)
2.  A • (B ∨ C)         1, Dist
3.  A                   2, Simp
```

Strategy 16: If inspection of the premises does not reveal how the conclusion should be derived, consider using the rules of replacement to deconstruct the conclusion. (See the final example in this section.)

MindTap® Strengthen your understanding of the topic with the section's **Video Lecture**.

I. For each of the following lists of premises, derive the indicated conclusion and complete the justification. For double negation, avoid the occurrence of triple tildes. Exercise 6 has two possible answers.

★(1) 1. $\sim(E \supset H)$
    2. $\sim(N \vee G)$
    3. $\sim A \vee D$
    4. _____ ____, DM

(2) 1. $G \supset (N \supset K)$
    2. $R \vee (D \supset F)$
    3. $S \cdot (T \vee U)$
    4. _____ ____, Dist

(3) 1. $M \vee (G \vee T)$
    2. $P \cdot (S \supset N)$
    3. $D \cdot (R \vee K)$
    4. _____ ____, Assoc

★(4) 1. $B \supset W$
    2. $G \equiv F$
    3. $S \cdot A$
    4. _____ ____, Com

(5) 1. $\sim \sim R \vee T$
    2. $\sim N \vee \sim B$
    3. $\sim A \supset \sim H$
    4. _____ ____, DN

(6) 1. $(F \vee N) \supset (K \cdot D)$
    2. $(H \cdot Z) \vee (H \cdot W)$
    3. $(P \supset H) \vee (P \supset N)$
    4. _____ ____, Dist

★(7) 1. $\sim(G \cdot \sim Q)$
    2. $\sim(K \equiv \sim B)$
    3. $\sim T \supset \sim F$
    4. _____ ____, DM

(8) 1. $G \supset (\sim L \supset T)$
    2. $L \equiv (\sim R \supset \sim C)$
    3. $J \supset (S \vee \sim N)$
    4. _____ ____, Com

7

MindTap® Complete exercises online for immediate feedback.

(9) 1. $S \supset (M \supset D)$
   2. $(K \cdot G) \lor B$
   3. $(E \cdot H) \cdot Q$
   4. _____ _____, Assoc

★(10) 1. $\sim R \lor \sim P$
    2. $\sim F \supset \sim W$
    3. $G \cdot \sim A$
    4. _____ _____, DM

(11) 1. $\sim B \lor E$
   2. $\sim E \cdot \sim A$
   3. $\sim C \supset \sim R$
   4. _____ _____, DN

(12) 1. $\sim G \cdot (S \supset A)$
   2. $\sim S \supset (B \cdot K)$
   3. $\sim Q \lor (T \cdot R)$
   4. _____ _____, Dist

★(13) 1. $F \supset (\sim S \lor M)$
    2. $H \supset (\sim L \cdot \sim D)$
    3. $N \supset (\sim G \supset \sim C)$
    4. _____ _____, DM

(14) 1. $F \supset (P \supset \sim E)$
   2. $C \lor (S \cdot \sim B)$
   3. $M \cdot (R \cdot \sim T)$
   4. _____ _____, Assoc

(15) 1. $(D \lor \sim K) \cdot (D \lor \sim W)$
   2. $(S \lor \sim Z) \lor (P \lor \sim T)$
   3. $(Q \supset \sim N) \cdot (Q \supset \sim F)$
   4. _____ _____, Dist

II. In the following symbolized arguments, derive the line needed to obtain the conclusion (last line), and supply the justification for both lines.

★(1) 1. $K \lor C$
   2. $\sim C$
   3. _____ ____
   4. K ____

(2) 1. $G \supset (R \lor N)$
   2. $\sim R \cdot \sim N$
   3. _____ _____
   4. $\sim G$ ____

(3) 1. $H \cdot T$
   2. _____ ____
   3. T ____

★(4) 1. $(L \cdot S) \cdot F$
   2. _____ ____
   3. L ____

(5) 1. $\sim B \lor K$
   2. _____ ____
   3. $\sim (B \cdot \sim K)$ ____

(6) 1. $C \supset \sim A$
   2. A
   3. _____ ____
   4. $\sim C$ ____

★(7) 1. $(D \cdot M) \lor (D \cdot N)$
2. _____ _____
3. D _____

(8) 1. $(U \lor T) \supset R$
2. $T \lor U$
3. _____ _____
4. R _____

(9) 1. $\sim L \lor M$
2. L
3. _____ _____
4. M _____

★(10) 1. $D \lor (N \cdot H)$
2. _____ _____
3. $D \lor N$ _____

(11) 1. $(K \lor E) \cdot (K \lor G)$
2. $\sim K$
3. _____ _____
4. $E \cdot G$ _____

(12) 1. $(N \supset T) \cdot (F \supset Q)$
2. $F \lor N$
3. _____ _____
4. $T \lor Q$ _____

★(13) 1. $(M \lor G) \lor T$
2. $\sim M$
3. _____ _____
4. $G \lor T$ _____

(14) 1. $(\sim A \supset T) \cdot (\sim S \supset K)$
2. $\sim (A \cdot S)$
3. _____ _____
4. $T \lor K$ _____

(15) 1. $\sim R$
2. _____ _____
3. $\sim (R \cdot T)$ _____

III. Use the first thirteen rules of inference to derive the conclusions of the following symbolized arguments:

★(1) 1. $(\sim M \supset P) \cdot (\sim N \supset Q)$
2. $\sim (M \cdot N)$ / $P \lor Q$

(2) 1. $\sim S$ / $\sim (F \cdot S)$

(3) 1. $J \lor (K \cdot L)$
2. $\sim K$ / J

★(4) 1. $\sim (N \cdot T)$
2. T / $\sim N$

(5) 1. $H \supset \sim A$
2. A / $\sim (H \lor \sim A)$

(6) 1. $R \supset \sim B$
2. $D \lor R$
3. B / D

★(7) 1. $T \supset (B \lor E)$
2. $\sim E \cdot T$ / B

(8) 1. $(O \lor M) \supset S$
2. $\sim S$ / $\sim M$

(9) 1. $Q \lor (L \lor C)$
2. $\sim C$ / $L \lor Q$

★(10) 1. $(K \cdot H) \lor (K \cdot L)$
2. $\sim L$ / H

(11) 1. $\sim (\sim E \cdot \sim N) \supset T$
2. $G \supset (N \lor E)$ / $G \supset T$

(12) 1. $H \cdot (C \cdot T)$
2. $\sim (\sim F \cdot T)$ / F

★(13) 1. $(E \cdot I) \lor (M \cdot U)$
2. $\sim E$ / $\sim (E \lor \sim M)$

(14) 1. $\sim (J \lor K)$
2. $B \supset K$
3. $S \supset B$ / $\sim S \cdot \sim J$

(15) 1. $(G \cdot H) \lor (M \cdot G)$
2. $G \supset (T \cdot A)$ / A

★(16) 1. $(Q \cdot N) \lor (N \cdot T)$
2. $(Q \lor C) \supset \sim N$ / T

(17) 1. $\sim (U \lor R)$
2. $(\sim R \lor N) \supset (P \cdot H)$
3. $Q \supset \sim H$ / $\sim Q$

(18) 1. $\sim (F \cdot A)$
2. $\sim (L \lor \sim A)$
3. $D \supset (F \lor L)$ / $\sim D$

★(19) 1. $[(I \lor M) \lor G] \supset \sim G$
2. $M \lor G$ / M

(20) 1. $E \supset \sim B$
2. $U \supset \sim C$
3. $\sim(\sim E \cdot \sim U)$ / $\sim(B \cdot C)$

(21) 1. $\sim(K \lor F)$
2. $\sim F \supset (K \lor C)$
3. $(G \lor C) \supset \sim H$ / $\sim(K \lor H)$

★(22) 1. $S \lor (I \cdot \sim J)$
2. $S \supset \sim R$
3. $\sim J \supset \sim Q$ / $\sim(R \cdot Q)$

(23) 1. $(J \lor F) \lor M$
2. $(J \lor M) \supset \sim P$
3. $\sim F$ / $\sim(F \lor P)$

(24) 1. $(K \cdot P) \lor (K \cdot Q)$
2. $P \supset \sim K$ / $Q \lor T$

★(25) 1. $E \lor \sim(D \lor C)$
2. $(E \lor \sim D) \supset C$ / E

(26) 1. $A \cdot (F \cdot L)$
2. $A \supset (U \lor W)$
3. $F \supset (U \lor X)$ / $U \lor (W \cdot X)$

(27) 1. $(T \cdot R) \supset P$
2. $(\sim P \cdot R) \cdot G$
3. $(\sim T \lor N) \supset H$ / H

★(28) 1. $P \lor (I \cdot L)$
2. $(P \lor I) \supset \sim(L \lor C)$
3. $(P \cdot \sim C) \supset (E \cdot F)$ / $F \lor D$

(29) 1. $B \lor (S \cdot N)$
2. $B \supset \sim S$
3. $S \supset \sim N$ / $B \lor W$

(30) 1. $(\sim M \lor E) \supset (S \supset U)$
2. $(\sim Q \lor E) \supset (U \supset H)$
3. $\sim(M \lor Q)$ / $S \supset H$

★(31) 1. $(\sim R \lor D) \supset \sim(F \cdot G)$
2. $(F \cdot R) \supset S$
3. $F \cdot \sim S$ / $\sim(S \lor G)$

(32) 1. $\sim Q \supset (C \cdot B)$
2. $\sim T \supset (B \cdot H)$
3. $\sim(Q \cdot T)$ / B

(33) 1. $\sim(A \cdot G)$
2. $\sim(A \cdot E)$
3. $G \lor E$ / $\sim(A \cdot F)$

★(34) 1. $(M \cdot N) \lor (O \cdot P)$
2. $(N \lor O) \supset \sim P$ / N

(35) 1. $(T \cdot K) \lor (C \cdot E)$
2. $K \supset \sim E$
3. $E \supset \sim C$ / $T \cdot K$

IV. Translate the following arguments into symbolic form and then use the first thirteen rules of inference to derive the conclusion of each. Use the translation letters in the order in which they are listed.

★1. Either health-care costs are skyrocketing and they are attributable to greedy doctors, or health-care costs are skyrocketing and they are attributable to greedy hospitals. If health-care costs are skyrocketing, then both the government should intercede and health care may have to be rationed. Therefore, health-care costs are skyrocketing and health care may have to be rationed. (S, D, H, I, R)

2. Either the ancient Etruscans were experienced city planners and they invented the art of writing or they were highly skilled engineers and they invented the art of writing. If the ancient Etruscans were bloodthirsty numskulls (as scholars once thought), they did not invent the art of writing. Therefore, the ancient Etruscans were not bloodthirsty numskulls (as scholars once thought). (C, I, H, B)

3. It is not the case that either the earth's molten core is stationary or that it contains no iron. If it is not the case that both the earth's molten core is stationary

and has a regular topography, then either the earth's core contains no iron or the direction of the earth's magnetic field is subject to change. Therefore, the direction of the earth's magnetic field is subject to change. (S, C, R, D)

★4. Either mosquito genes can be cloned or mosquitoes will become resistant to all insecticides and the incidence of encephalitis will increase. If either mosquito genes can be cloned or the incidence of encephalitis increases, then mosquitoes will not become resistant to all insecticides. Therefore, either mosquito genes can be cloned or mosquitoes will multiply out of control. (G, R, E, M)

5. Protein engineering will prove to be as successful as genetic engineering, and new enzymes will be developed for producing food and breaking down industrial wastes. If protein engineering proves to be as successful as genetic engineering and new enzymes are developed for breaking down industrial wastes, then it is not the case that new enzymes will be developed for producing food but not medicines. Therefore, protein engineering will prove to be as successful as genetic engineering and new enzymes will be developed for producing medicines. (E, P, B, M)

6. If workers have a fundamental right to a job, then unemployment will be virtually nonexistent but job redundancy will become a problem. If workers have no fundamental right to a job, then production efficiency will be maximized but job security will be jeopardized. Workers either have or do not have a fundamental right to a job. Therefore, either unemployment will be virtually nonexistent or production efficiency will be maximized. (F, U, R, P, S)

★7. If China is to reduce its huge trade surplus, then it must either convince its citizens to spend more or it must move its manufacturing facilities to other countries. It is not the case that China will either increase its imports or convince its citizens to spend more. Furthermore, it is not the case that China will either allow foreign construction companies to compete on an equal footing or move its manufacturing facilities to other countries. Therefore, China will not reduce its huge trade surplus. (R, C, M, I, A)

8. If women are by nature either passive or uncompetitive, then it is not the case that there are lawyers who are women. If men are by nature either insensitive or without the ability to nurture, then it is not the case that there are kindergarten teachers who are men. There are lawyers who are women and kindergarten teachers who are men. Therefore, it is not the case that either women by nature are uncompetitive or men by nature are without the ability to nurture. (P, U, L, I, W, K)

9. It is not the case that either the sun's interior rotates faster than its surface or Einstein's general theory of relativity is wrong. If the sun's interior does not rotate faster than its surface and eccentricities in the orbit of Mercury can be explained by solar gravitation, then Einstein's general theory of relativity is wrong. Therefore, eccentricities in the orbit of Mercury cannot be explained by solar gravitation. (S, E, M)

★10. Either school dropout programs are not as effective as they could be, or they provide basic thinking skills and psychological counseling to their students.

7

Either school dropout programs are not as effective as they could be, or they adequately prepare their students for getting a job and working effectively with others. Either school dropout programs do not provide psychological counseling to their students or they do not provide adequate preparation for working effectively with others. Therefore, school dropout programs are not as effective as they could be. (E, B, P, G, W)

V. The following dialogue contains eight arguments. Translate each into symbolic form and then use the first thirteen rules of inference to derive the conclusion of each.

New Cradle

Chloe, with youngster in tow, is strolling across campus when she bumps into her friend Dylan. "Hi," she says. "You must be coming from class."

"Yes, I am," he says. "Social psychology. And who is the little one?"

"This is my niece Ashley. She was three last month. Ashley, say "Hi" to Dylan. We're heading over to the campus day-care center. Do you want to join us?"

"Sure," he says. "At least as far as the cafeteria."

"You know, kids are really a kick in the pants," she says. "That's why my heart goes out to a same-sex couple I know."

"And why is that?" Dylan asks.

"They're trying to adopt a baby, but the only adoption agency in this small town refuses to help them because the agency is religiously affiliated. I'm talking about the New Cradle agency. Those people at New Cradle think same-sex marriage is sinful."

"Well, in light of this religious freedom legislation that's been coming down the pike lately, the people at New Cradle may be within their rights."

"How is that?" Chloe asks.

"It goes like this," he says. "If religious freedom is a right, then the people at New Cradle have a right to practice it as they choose. And if they have a right to practice it as they choose, then if they think same-sex marriage violates their religion, then they can refuse to help same-sex couples adopt a baby. Now religious freedom is a right and those people think same-sex marriage violates their religion. Hence they can refuse to help same-sex couples adopt a baby."

"But wait just a minute," Chloe says. "New Cradle is engaged in a commercial activity, just like a restaurant, and some of its babies come from out of state. So I would offer you this argument. If New Cradle receives government support or is engaged in interstate commerce, then if it discriminates against same-sex couples, then it violates those couple's civil rights. Now if New Cradle refuses to help same-sex couples adopt, then it discriminates. New Cradle is engaged in interstate commerce and it refuses to help same-sex couples adopt. Thus, New Cradle violates those couples' civil rights."

"I can see that New Cradle faces a dilemma," Dylan replies. "If it helps same-sex couples adopt a baby, then it will violate its own principles; but if it does not help them, then it will violate constitutional principles. And if New Cradle abandons its own principles, then it will close up shop and lay off its employees. But New Cradle will never lay off its employees, and it will either help same-sex couples adopt a baby or not help them. Therefore, New Cradle will violate constitutional principles."

"Another point we must not forget," Chloe adds, "is that same sex couples now have the right to marry. And, if that is the case, they have a right to raise a family. And if they have a right to raise a family and they have good parenting skills, then if New Cradle can refuse to help them adopt a baby, then religion is misappropriated and the public good is subverted. Same-sex couples do have good parenting skills, and the public good will not be subverted. Therefore, New Cradle cannot refuse to help them adopt a baby."

"I think you're right," says Dylan, "that equality plays a big role in this issue. Our country is based on the principle of equality. If straight couples have a right to the services of an adoption agency, and obviously they do, then either same-sex couples have such a right or they are not equal to straight couples. And if same-sex couples have a right to the services of an adoption agency, then New Cradle must change its policy and other religiously affiliated agencies must do the same. Now if our country is based on the principle of equality, then same-sex couples are equal to straight couples. Thus, as you say, New Cradle must change its policy."

"Yet," Dylan continues, "up till now we've said nothing about the welfare of the baby who will be adopted. If New Cradle helps same-sex couples adopt a baby, then it's important that the baby grow up well adjusted. But if the baby is to be well adjusted, then it must have both a male role model and a female role model. If the parents are both men, then the baby will not have a female role model. If they are both women, then it will not have a male role model. If the couple is a same-sex couple, then the parents will be either both men or both women, and the couple is a same-sex couple. Therefore, New Cradle must not help same-sex couples adopt a baby."

"I think your reasoning is a bit shortsighted," Chloe replies. "Let's suppose a same-sex couple adopts a baby. If a same-sex couple adopts a baby, then the parents will be either both men or they will be both women. This much I grant you. But if they are both men, then surely they will have close female friends. And if that is so, then there will be both male and female role models. If the parents are both women, then surely they will have close male friends. And if that is so, then there will be both male and female role models. If there are both male and female role models, then the baby will be well adjusted. And if the baby will be well adjusted, then New Cradle should help with the adoption. Thus, the conclusion follows, that New Cradle should help with the adoption."

"Interesting point," Dylan says. "But I wonder if those surrogate role models would be as effective as male and female parents. Anyway, here's where I get off. See you again soon, I hope."

"Yeah, me too," says Chloe.

"Bye-bye, Ashley. It was nice meeting you."

"G'bye," she says, waving her hand.

VI. Create four symbolized arguments consisting of at least three premises each, and whose proof requires at least two of the rules introduced in this section. The arguments should look like those in Part III of this section. Then derive the conclusion of each.

7.4 Rules of Replacement II

The remaining five rules of replacement are as follows:

14. Transposition (Trans):
    $(p \supset q) :: (\sim q \supset \sim p)$

15. Material implication (Impl):
    $(p \supset q) :: (\sim p \vee q)$

16. Material equivalence (Equiv):
    $(p \equiv q) :: [(p \supset q) \bullet (q \supset p)]$
    $(p \equiv q) :: [(p \bullet q) \vee (\sim p \bullet \sim q)]$

17. Exportation (Exp):
    $[(p \bullet q) \supset r] :: [p \supset (q \supset r)]$

18. Tautology (Taut):
    $p :: (p \vee p)$
    $p :: (p \bullet p)$

Transposition asserts that the antecedent and consequent of a conditional statement may switch places if and only if tildes are inserted before both or tildes are removed from both. The rule is fairly easy to understand and is easily proved by a truth table.

Material implication is less obvious than transposition, but it can be illustrated by substituting actual statements in place of the letters. For example, the statement "If you bother me, then I'll punch you in the nose" ($B \supset P$) is logically equivalent to "Either you stop bothering me or I'll punch you in the nose" ($\sim B \vee P$). The rule states that a horseshoe may be replaced by a wedge if the left-hand component is negated, and the reverse replacement is allowed if a tilde is deleted from the left-hand component.

Material equivalence has two formulations. The first is the same as the definition of material equivalence given in Section 6.1. The second formulation is easy to remember through recalling the two ways in which $p \equiv q$ may be true. Either p and q are both true or p and q are both false. This, of course, is the meaning of $[(p \bullet q) \vee (\sim p \bullet \sim q)]$.

Exportation is also fairly easy to understand. It asserts that the statement "If we have both p and q, then we have r" is logically equivalent to "If we have p, then if we have q, then we have r." As an illustration of this rule, the statement "If Bob and Sue told the truth, then Jim is guilty" is logically equivalent to "If Bob told the truth, then if Sue told the truth, then Jim is guilty."

Tautology, the last rule introduced in this section, is obvious. Its effect is to eliminate redundancy in disjunctions and conjunctions.

The following proofs illustrate the use of these five rules.

1. $\sim A$ / $A \supset B$

In this argument the conclusion contains a letter not found in the premise. Obviously, addition must be used to introduce the B. The material implication rule completes the proof:

1. ~A   / A ⊃ B
2. ~A ∨ B   1, Add
3. A ⊃ B   2, Impl

Here is another example:

1. F ⊃ G
2. F ∨ G   / G

To derive the conclusion of this argument, some method must be found to link the two premises together and eliminate the F. Hypothetical syllogism provides the solution, but first the second premise must be converted into a conditional. Here is the proof:

1. F ⊃ G
2. F ∨ G   / G
3. ~ ~F ∨ G   2, DN
4. ~F ⊃ G   3, Impl
5. ~F ⊃ ~ ~G   4, DN
6. ~G ⊃ F   5, Trans
7. ~G ⊃ G   1, 6, HS
8. ~ ~G ∨ G   7, Impl
9. G ∨ G   8, DN
10. G   9, Taut

Another example:

1. J ⊃ (K ⊃ L)   / K ⊃ (J ⊃ L)

The conclusion can be obtained by simply rearranging the components of the single premise. Exportation provides the simplest method:

1. J ⊃ (K ⊃ L)   / K ⊃ (J ⊃ L)
2. (J • K) ⊃ L   1, Exp
3. (K • J) ⊃ L   2, Com
4. K ⊃ (J ⊃ L)   3, Exp

Another example:

1. M ⊃ N
2. M ⊃ O   / M ⊃ (N • O)

As with the F and G example, some method must be found to link the two premises together. In this case, however, hypothetical syllogism will not work. The solution lies in setting up a distribution step:

1. M ⊃ N
2. M ⊃ O   / M ⊃ (N • O)
3. ~M ∨ N   1, Impl
4. ~M ∨ O   2, Impl
5. (~M ∨ N) • (~M ∨ O)   3, 4, Conj
6. ~M ∨ (N • O)   5, Dist
7. M ⊃ (N • O)   6, Impl

Another example:

1. $P \supset Q$
2. $R \supset (S \cdot T)$
3. $\sim R \supset \sim Q$
4. $S \supset (T \supset P)$ / $P \equiv R$

The conclusion is a biconditional, and there are only two ways that a biconditional can be obtained from such premises—namely, via the two formulations of the material equivalence rule. The fact that the premises are all conditional statements suggests the first formulation of this rule. Accordingly, we must try to obtain $P \supset R$ and $R \supset P$. Again, the fact that the premises are themselves conditionals suggests hypothetical syllogism to accomplish this. Premises 1 and 3 can be used to set up one hypothetical syllogism; premises 2 and 4 provide the other. Here is the proof:

1. $P \supset Q$
2. $R \supset (S \cdot T)$
3. $\sim R \supset \sim Q$
4. $S \supset (T \supset P)$ / $P \equiv R$
5. $Q \supset R$ 3, Trans
6. $P \supset R$ 1, 5, HS
7. $(S \cdot T) \supset P$ 4, Exp
8. $R \supset P$ 2, 7, HS
9. $(P \supset R) \cdot (R \supset P)$ 6, 8, Conj
10. $P \equiv R$ 9, Equiv

As we saw in Section 7.3, if it is not readily apparent how the conclusion should be derived, we can use the rules of replacement to deconstruct the conclusion. This will usually provide insight on how best to proceed. Again, this technique is justified because the rules of replacement are two-way rules. As a result, they can be applied in reverse order in the completed proof. Here is an example:

1. $\sim S \supset K$
2. $S \supset (R \vee M)$ / $\sim R \supset (\sim M \supset K)$

In deconstructing the conclusion, the form of the conclusion suggests exportation, and the result of this step suggests De Morgan's rule. For further insight, we apply transposition to the latter step. Each step follows from the one preceding it:

$\sim R \supset (\sim M \supset K)$
$(\sim R \cdot \sim M) \supset K$ Exp
$\sim (R \vee M) \supset K$ DM
$\sim K \supset \sim \sim (R \vee M)$ Trans
$\sim K \supset (R \vee M)$ DN

Now, examining the premises in light of the deconstruction suggests that we begin by setting up a hypothetical syllogism. This will give us the last step in the deconstruction.

We can then obtain the conclusion by repeating the deconstruction steps in reverse order. The completed proof is as follows:

1. $\sim S \supset K$
2. $S \supset (R \lor M)$ $/ \sim R \supset (\sim M \supset K)$
3. $\sim K \supset \sim\sim S$ 1, Trans
4. $\sim K \supset S$ 3, DN
5. $\sim K \supset (R \lor M)$ 2, 4, HS
6. $\sim(R \lor M) \supset \sim\sim K$ 5, Trans
7. $\sim(R \lor M) \supset K$ 6, DN
8. $(\sim R \cdot \sim M) \supset K$ 7, DM
9. $\sim R \supset (\sim M \supset K)$ 8, Exp

Here is another example:

1. $K \supset M$
2. $L \supset M$ $/ (K \lor L) \supset M$

In deconstructing the conclusion, the form of the premises suggests that we use some procedure that will combine M separately with K and L. This, in turn, suggests distribution; but before we can use distribution, we must eliminate the horseshoe via material implication. The deconstruction is as follows:

$(K \lor L) \supset M$
$\sim(K \lor L) \lor M$ Impl
$(\sim K \cdot \sim L) \lor M$ DM
$M \lor (\sim K \cdot \sim L)$ Com
$(M \lor \sim K) \cdot (M \lor \sim L)$ Dist
$(\sim K \lor M) \cdot (M \lor \sim L)$ Com
$(\sim K \lor M) \cdot (\sim L \lor M)$ Com
$(K \supset M) \cdot (\sim L \lor M)$ Impl
$(K \supset M) \cdot (L \supset M)$ Impl

Now, examining the premises in light of the last line of the deconstruction suggests that we begin by joining the premises together via the conjunction rule. The conclusion can then be obtained by reversing the steps of the deconstruction:

1. $K \supset M$
2. $L \supset M$ $/ (K \lor L) \supset M$
3. $(K \supset M) \cdot (L \supset M)$ 1, 2, Conj
4. $(\sim K \lor M) \cdot (L \supset M)$ 3, Impl
5. $(\sim K \lor M) \cdot (\sim L \lor M)$ 4, Impl
6. $(M \lor \sim K) \cdot (\sim L \lor M)$ 5, Com
7. $(M \lor \sim K) \cdot (M \lor \sim L)$ 6, Com
8. $M \lor (\sim K \cdot \sim L)$ 7, Dist
9. $(\sim K \cdot \sim L) \lor M$ 8, Com
10. $\sim(K \lor L) \lor M$ 9, DM
11. $(K \lor L) \supset M$ 10, Impl

Note that whenever we use this strategy of working backward from the conclusion, the rules of replacement are the *only* rules we may use. We may not use the rules of implication, because these rules are one-way rules.

This section ends with some strategies that show how the last five rules of replacement can be used together with various other rules.

Strategy 17:   Material implication can be used to set up hypothetical syllogism:

1.	~A ∨ B	
2.	~B ∨ C	
3.	A ⊃ B	1, Impl
4.	B ⊃ C	2, Impl
5.	A ⊃ C	3, 4, HS

Strategy 18:   Exportation can be used to set up *modus ponens*:

1.	(A • B) ⊃ C	
2.	A	
3.	A ⊃ (B ⊃ C)	1, Exp
4.	B ⊃ C	2, 3, MP

Strategy 19:   Exportation can be used to set up *modus tollens*:

1.	A ⊃ (B ⊃ C)	
2.	~C	
3.	(A • B) ⊃ C	1, Exp
4.	~(A • B)	2, 3, MT

Strategy 20:   Addition can be used to set up material implication:

1.	A	
2.	A ∨ ~B	1, Add
3.	~B ∨ A	2, Com
4.	B ⊃ A	3, Impl

Strategy 21:   Transposition can be used to set up hypothetical syllogism:

1.	A ⊃ B	
2.	~C ⊃ ~B	
3.	B ⊃ C	2, Trans
4.	A ⊃ C	1, 3, HS

Strategy 22:   Transposition can be used to set up constructive dilemma:

1.	(A ⊃ B) • (C ⊃ D)	
2.	~B ∨ ~D	
3.	(~B ⊃ ~A) • (C ⊃ D)	1, Trans
4.	(~B ⊃ ~A) • (~D ⊃ ~C)	3, Trans
5.	~A ∨ ~C	2, 4, CD

Strategy 23:   Constructive dilemma can be used to set up tautology:

1.	(A ⊃ C) • (B ⊃ C)	
2.	A ∨ B	
3.	C ∨ C	1, 2, CD
4.	C	3, Taut

Strategy 24: Material implication can be used to set up tautology:

1. $A \supset \sim A$
2. $\sim A \lor \sim A$ 1, Impl
3. $\sim A$ 2, Taut

Strategy 25: Material implication can be used to set up distribution:

1. $A \supset (B \cdot C)$
2. $\sim A \lor (B \cdot C)$ 1, Impl
3. $(\sim A \lor B) \cdot (\sim A \lor C)$ 2, Dist

MindTap® Strengthen your understanding of the topic with the section's **Video Lectures**.

EXERCISE 7.4

I. For each of the following lists of premises, derive the indicated conclusion and complete the justification. For tautology, derive a conclusion that is simpler than the premise.

★(1)   1. $H \lor F$
        2. $N \lor \sim S$
        3. $\sim G \lor Q$
        4. _____ _____, Impl

(2)   1. $R \supset (S \supset N)$
      2. $T \supset (U \lor M)$
      3. $K \cdot (L \supset W)$
      4. _____ _____, Exp

(3)   1. $G \equiv R$
      2. $H \supset P$
      3. $\sim F \lor T$
      4. _____ _____, Trans

★(4)   1. $(B \supset N) \cdot (N \supset B)$
        2. $(R \lor F) \cdot (F \lor R)$
        3. $(K \supset C) \lor (C \supset K)$
        4. _____ _____, Equiv

(5)   1. $E \lor \sim E$
      2. $A \lor A$
      3. $G \cdot \sim G$
      4. _____ _____, Taut

MindTap® Complete exercises online for immediate feedback.

(6) 1. $S \lor \sim M$
2. $\sim N \cdot \sim T$
3. $\sim L \supset Q$
4. _____ ____, Trans

★(7) 1. $\sim C \supset \sim F$
2. $D \lor \sim P$
3. $\sim R \cdot Q$
4. _____ ____, Impl

(8) 1. $E \supset (R \cdot Q)$
2. $(G \cdot N) \supset Z$
3. $(S \supset M) \supset P$
4. _____ ____, Exp

(9) 1. $(D \cdot H) \lor (\sim D \cdot \sim H)$
2. $(F \supset J) \cdot (\sim F \supset \sim J)$
3. $(N \lor T) \cdot (\sim N \lor \sim T)$
4. _____ ____, Equiv

★(10) 1. $L \supset (A \supset A)$
2. $K \supset (R \lor \sim R)$
3. $S \supset (G \cdot G)$
4. _____ ____, Taut

(11) 1. $K \cdot (S \lor B)$
2. $\sim F \supset \sim J$
3. $\sim E \lor \sim M$
4. _____ ____, Trans

(12) 1. $H \supset (K \cdot J)$
2. $(N \lor E) \supset B$
3. $C \supset (H \supset A)$
4. _____ ____, Exp

★(13) 1. $(A \supset \sim C) \cdot (C \supset \sim A)$
2. $(W \supset \sim T) \cdot (\sim T \supset W)$
3. $(M \supset \sim E) \cdot (\sim M \supset E)$
4. _____ ____, Equiv

(14) 1. $(\sim K \lor M) \equiv S$
2. $T \lor (F \cdot G)$
3. $R \equiv (N \cdot \sim H)$
4. _____ ____, Impl

(15) 1. $(S \lor S) \supset D$
2. $K \supset (T \cdot \sim T)$
3. $(Q \supset Q) \supset M$
4. _____ ____, Taut

II. In the following symbolized arguments, derive the line needed to obtain the conclusion (last line), and supply the justification for both lines.

★(1) 1. ~J ∨ M
　　 2. M ⊃ B
　　 3. _____ ____
　　 4. J ⊃ B ____

(2) 1. (J • F) ⊃ N
　　 2. J
　　 3. _____ ____
　　 4. F ⊃ N ____

(3) 1. C ⊃ A
　　 2. A ⊃ C
　　 3. _____ ____
　　 4. C ≡ A ____

★(4) 1. (G ⊃ K) • (T ⊃ K)
　　 2. G ∨ T
　　 3. _____ ____
　　 4. K ____

(5) 1. (G ⊃ B) • (~C ⊃ ~H)
　　 2. G ∨ H
　　 3. _____ ____
　　 4. B ∨ C ____

(6) 1. J ⊃ (M ⊃ Q)
　　 2. J • M
　　 3. _____ ____
　　 4. Q ____

★(7) 1. H ⊃ (~C ∨ R)
　　 2. _____ ____
　　 3. (H • C) ⊃ R ____

(8) 1. ~G ⊃ ~T
　　 2. G ⊃ N
　　 3. _____ ____
　　 4. T ⊃ N ____

(9) 1. K ⊃ (A ⊃ F)
　　 2. ~F
　　 3. _____ ____
　　 4. ~(K • A) ____

★(10) 1. H ⊃ ~H
　　 2. _____ ____
　　 3. ~H ____

(11) 1. ~S
　　 2. _____ ____
　　 3. S ⊃ K ____

(12) 1. M ⊃ (M ⊃ D)
　　 2. _____ ____
　　 3. M ⊃ D ____

★(13) 1. (N ⊃ A) • (~N ⊃ ~A)
　　 2. _____ ____
　　 3. N ≡ A ____

(14) 1. E • R
　　 2. _____ ____
　　 3. E ≡ R ____

(15) 1. Q ⊃ (~W ⊃ ~G)
　　 2. _____ ____
　　 3. (Q • G) ⊃ W ____

III. Use the eighteen rules of inference to derive the conclusions of the following symbolized arguments.

★(1) 1. (S • K) ⊃ R
　　 2. K 　　　　　 / S ⊃ R

(2) 1. T ⊃ (F ∨ F)
　　 2. ~(F • F) 　　 / ~T

(3) 1. G ⊃ E
　　 2. H ⊃ ~E 　　 / G ⊃ ~H

★(4) 1. S ≡ Q
　　 2. ~S 　　　　 / ~Q

(5) 1. ~N ∨ P
　　 2. (N ⊃ P) ⊃ T 　 / T

(6) 1. $F \supset B$
    2. $B \supset (B \supset J)$ / $F \supset J$

★(7) 1. $(B \supset M) \cdot (D \supset M)$
     2. $B \lor D$ / M

(8) 1. $Q \supset (F \supset A)$
    2. $R \supset (A \supset F)$
    3. $Q \cdot R$ / $F \equiv A$

(9) 1. $T \supset (\sim T \lor G)$
    2. $\sim G$ / $\sim T$

★(10) 1. $(B \supset G) \cdot (F \supset N)$
      2. $\sim (G \cdot N)$ / $\sim (B \cdot F)$

(11) 1. $(J \cdot R) \supset H$
     2. $(R \supset H) \supset M$
     3. $\sim (P \lor \sim J)$ / $M \cdot \sim P$

(12) 1. T / $S \supset T$

★(13) 1. $K \supset (B \supset \sim M)$
      2. $D \supset (K \cdot M)$ / $D \supset \sim B$

(14) 1. $(O \supset C) \cdot (\sim S \supset \sim D)$
     2. $(E \supset D) \cdot (\sim E \supset \sim C)$ / $O \supset S$

(15) 1. $\sim (U \cdot W) \supset X$
     2. $U \supset \sim U$ / $\sim (U \lor \sim X)$

★(16) 1. $T \supset R$
      2. $T \supset \sim R$ / $\sim T$

(17) 1. $S \lor \sim N$
     2. $\sim S \lor Q$ / $N \supset Q$

(18) 1. $M \supset (U \supset H)$
     2. $(H \lor \sim U) \supset F$ / $M \supset F$

★(19) 1. $\sim R \lor P$
      2. $R \lor \sim P$ / $R \equiv P$

(20) 1. $\sim H \supset B$
     2. $\sim H \supset D$
     3. $\sim (B \cdot D)$ / H

(21) 1. $J \supset (G \supset L)$ / $G \supset (J \supset L)$

★(22) 1. $S \supset (L \cdot M)$
      2. $M \supset (L \supset R)$ / $S \supset R$

(23) 1. $F \supset (A \cdot K)$
     2. $G \supset (\sim A \cdot \sim K)$
     3. $F \lor G$ / $A \equiv K$

(24) 1. $(I \supset E) \supset C$
    2. $C \supset \sim C$ $/ I$

★(25) 1. $T \supset G$
    2. $S \supset G$ $/ (T \lor S) \supset G$

(26) 1. $H \supset U$ $/ H \supset (U \lor T)$

(27) 1. $Q \supset (W \cdot D)$ $/ Q \supset W$

★(28) 1. $P \supset (\sim E \supset B)$
    2. $\sim (B \lor E)$ $/ \sim P$

(29) 1. $(G \supset J) \supset (H \supset Q)$
    2. $J \cdot \sim Q$ $/ \sim H$

(30) 1. $I \lor (N \cdot F)$
    2. $I \supset F$ $/ F$

★(31) 1. $K \equiv R$
    2. $K \supset (R \supset P)$
    3. $\sim P$ $/ \sim R$

(32) 1. $C \supset (\sim L \supset Q)$
    2. $L \supset \sim C$
    3. $\sim Q$ $/ \sim C$

(33) 1. $(E \supset A) \cdot (F \supset A)$
    2. $E \lor G$
    3. $F \lor \sim G$ $/ A$

★(34) 1. $(F \cdot H) \supset N$
    2. $F \lor S$
    3. H $/ N \lor S$

(35) 1. $T \supset (H \cdot J)$
    2. $(H \lor N) \supset T$ $/ T \equiv H$

(36) 1. $T \supset \sim (A \supset N)$
    2. $T \lor N$ $/ T \equiv \sim N$

★(37) 1. $(D \supset E) \supset (E \supset D)$
    2. $(D \equiv E) \supset \sim (G \cdot \sim H)$
    3. $E \cdot G$ $/ G \cdot H$

(38) 1. $(O \supset R) \supset S$
    2. $(P \supset R) \supset \sim S$ $/ \sim R$

(39) 1. $(L \lor P) \supset U$
    2. $(M \supset U) \supset I$
    3. P $/ I$

★(40) 1. $A \equiv W$
    2. $\sim A \lor \sim W$
    3. $R \supset A$ $/ \sim (W \lor R)$

(41) 1. $(S \lor T) \supset (S \supset {\sim}T)$
  2. $(S \supset {\sim}T) \supset (T \supset K)$
  3. $S \lor T$ / $S \lor K$

(42) 1. $G \equiv M$
  2. $G \lor M$
  3. $G \supset (M \supset T)$ / T

★**(43)** 1. $O \supset (Q \cdot N)$
  2. $(N \lor E) \supset S$ / $O \supset S$

(44) 1. $H \equiv I$
  2. $H \supset (I \supset F)$
  3. ${\sim}(H \lor I) \supset F$ / F

★**(45)** 1. $P \supset A$
  2. $Q \supset B$ / $(P \lor Q) \supset (A \lor B)$

IV. Translate the following arguments into symbolic form and then use the eighteen rules of inference to derive the conclusion of each. Use the translation letters in the order in which they are listed.

★1. If sports-shoe manufacturers decline to use kangaroo hides in their products, then Australian hunters will cease killing millions of kangaroos yearly. It is not the case that both Australian hunters will cease killing millions of kangaroos yearly and the kangaroo will not be saved from extinction. Therefore, if sports-shoe manufacturers decline to use kangaroo hides in their products, then the kangaroo will be saved from extinction. (*D, C, S*)

2. If there is a direct correlation between what a nation spends for health care and the health of its citizens, then America has the lowest incidence of disease and the lowest mortality rates of any nation on Earth. But America does not have the lowest mortality rates of any nation on Earth. Therefore, there is not a direct correlation between what a nation spends for health care and the health of its citizens. (*C, D, M*)

3. It is not the case that strict controls exist on either the manufacture or the sale of handguns. Therefore, if strict controls exist on the sale of handguns, then the use of handguns in the commission of crimes has decreased. (*M, S, U*)

★4. If birth-control devices are made available in high school clinics, then the incidence of teenage pregnancy will decrease. Therefore, if both birth-control information and birth-control devices are made available in high school clinics, then the incidence of teenage pregnancy will decrease. (*D, P, I*)

5. If Congress enacts a law that either establishes a religion or prohibits the free exercise of religion, then that law is unconstitutional. Therefore, if Congress enacts a law that establishes a religion, then that law is unconstitutional. (*E, P, U*)

6. If selecting a Supreme Court justice creates intense political upheaval and extreme efforts are expended to block judicial candidates, then Supreme Court

rulings are contaminated with political bias. Selecting a Supreme Court justice creates intense political upheaval. Therefore, if extreme efforts are expended to block judicial candidates, then Supreme Court rulings are contaminated with political bias. (S, E, C)

★7. If grade-school children are assigned daily homework, then their achievement level will increase dramatically. But if grade-school children are assigned daily homework, then their love for learning may be dampened. Therefore, if grade-school children are assigned daily homework, then their achievement level will increase dramatically but their love for learning may be dampened. (G, A, L)

8. If two black holes collide, then Einstein's general theory is proven true and gravitational waves are propagated throughout the universe. Either two black holes collide, or space-time is distorted and Einstein's general theory is proven true. Therefore, Einstein's general theory is proven true. (T, E, G, S)

9. If parents are told that their unborn child has Tay–Sachs disease, then if they go ahead with the birth, then they are responsible for their child's pain and suffering. Therefore, if parents are not responsible for their child's pain and suffering, then if they go ahead with the birth, then they were not told that their unborn child had Tay–Sachs disease. (T, G, R)

★10. Vitamin E is an antioxidant and a useless food supplement if and only if it does not reduce heart disease. It is not the case either that vitamin E does not reduce heart disease or is not an antioxidant. Therefore, vitamin E is not a useless food supplement. (A, U, R)

V. The following dialogue contains ten arguments. Translate each into symbolic form and then use the eighteen rules of inference to derive the conclusion of each.

Is This the End?

Brian and Molly are at the memorial service of a mutual friend who had died suddenly the week before. "I'm still shocked to think that Karl is gone," Molly says.

"I know you were quite close to him," Brian says. "But do you think in some sense Karl could still be with us? I mean do you think there could be such a thing as postmortem persistence of consciousness—life after death, as most people say?"

"I wish there were," Molly replies, "and that's what makes death so tragic. As I see it, the mind is totally dependent on the brain, and if that's so, when the brain dies, the mind dies. If the mind dies, then consciousness dies, too. Thus, if the brain dies, then consciousness dies—which means there's no life after death."

"But what makes you think that the mind is totally dependent on the brain?" Brian asks.

"Our day-to-day experience provides lots of evidence," Molly replies. "If you drink alcohol, your mind is affected. If you smoke marijuana, your mind is affected. If your mind is affected by these things, then you have firsthand experience that the mind is dependent on the brain. Thus, if you either smoke marijuana or drink alcohol, then you have firsthand experience that the mind is dependent on the brain."

"So the mind is affected by the brain. Anyone with ordinary sensation knows that," Brian retorts. "If your eye receives a visual stimulus, then that stimulus is sent to the brain and your mind is affected. If your ear receives an auditory stimulus, then your mind is affected. Thus, if either your eye or your ear receives a stimulus, then your mind is affected. But that doesn't prove that the mind is *necessarily* dependent on the brain. And there are lots of reasons for saying that it isn't."

"What reasons are those?" Molly asks.

"Well, we learned about Plato in Introduction to Philosophy," Brian replies. "And Plato held that the mind can conceive ideal objects such as perfect justice and perfect triangularity. Now, if either of these concepts came through the senses, then perfect ideals exist in nature. But no perfect ideals exist in nature. And if the concept of triangularity did not come through the senses, then the mind produced it independently of the brain. But if that is the case or the concept of triangularity is innate, then the mind is not necessarily dependent on the brain. I'll leave the conclusion up to you."

"Very interesting," Molly replies, "but I question whether the mind is really capable of conceiving ideal objects such as perfect justice and perfect triangularity. For me, these things are just words. But there are other reasons for thinking that the mind is *necessarily* dependent on the brain. Consider the visual cortex. The visual cortex is part of the brain. If the visual cortex isn't stimulated, there is no visual sensation. But if visual sensation occurs only if the visual cortex is stimulated, and if the visual cortex is part of the brain, then visual sensation is dependent on the brain. And if that is true and visual sensation is a function of the mind, then the mind is necessarily dependent on the brain. Therefore, if visual sensation is a function of the mind, then the mind is necessarily dependent on the brain."

"Furthermore," Molly continues, "there are many cases where strokes have caused loss of memory, and also loss of speech. But if remembering is a mental function, then if the mind is not necessarily dependent on the brain, then strokes do not cause loss of memory. Therefore, if remembering is a mental function, then the mind is necessarily dependent on the brain."

"It may indeed be the case," Brian replies, "that memory—or at least certain kinds of memory—are dependent on the brain. And the same may be true of sensation. But that doesn't prove that consciousness as such is brain dependent. It seems to me that consciousness as such is a nonmaterial process, and that it can occur only in a nonmaterial entity, such as a soul. And if those two claims are true and the soul is immortal, then consciousness survives the death of the body. Thus, if the soul is immortal, then consciousness survives the death of the body."

"If memory goes with the brain," Molly replies, "then I wonder if the consciousness you speak of is in any way *your* consciousness. But setting that aside, are there any reasons for thinking that the soul is immortal?"

"I think there are," Brian replies. "If the soul is nonmaterial, then it has no parts, and if it has no parts, then it can't come 'a-part'—in other words it can't disintegrate. And if it can't disintegrate, then if nothing can destroy it, then it is immortal. But the soul can be destroyed only if God destroys it, and God does not destroy souls. Therefore, if the soul is nonmaterial, then it is immortal. I think Leibniz invented that argument."

"Fine," Molly says. "But what makes you think that you have a nonmaterial soul in the first place?"

"Well," Brian replies, "according to Descartes, I am essentially either a mind or a body. But if I can doubt that I have a body, then I am not essentially a body. And I can doubt that I have a body. For example I can imagine that I am in *The Matrix*, and that all of my sensations are illusions. If I am essentially a mind, then if the essence of mind is to be nonextended, then I am a nonextended substance. But the essence of mind, being different from the essence of body, is to be nonextended. And if I am a nonextended substance, then I am (or have) a nonmaterial soul. Therefore, I am (or have) a nonmaterial soul."

"Your argument is so abstruse that I don't find it very persuasive," says Molly, as she scratches her head. "I think the evidence is overwhelming that humans are the product of biological evolution, and if that is true and humans have souls, then there is a point in the course of evolution where humans either received or developed a soul. But there is no evidence that humans ever received a soul. Also, there is no evidence that humans ever developed a soul. Therefore, humans do not have souls."

"Wow, that sounds pretty far out," Brian replies. "Well, it looks like the service is ready to start, so we'll have to hang this up. But maybe we can continue it at a later date."

"Maybe we can," Molly replies.

VI. Create four symbolized arguments consisting of at least three premises each, and whose proof requires at least two of the rules introduced in this section. The arguments should look like those in Part III of this section. Then derive the conclusion of each.

MindTap Master concepts and improve outcomes with Aplia, at the end of the chapter, in the Aplia folder.

7.5 Conditional Proof

HOW LOGICAL ARE YOU? Suppose a theft has been committed by an unknown assailant. As the chief investigator, you suspect that Sneaky Sam did it. But if Sam did it, then fingerprint evidence will link him to the crime. But if that happens, then Sam will be tried. But if that happens, then Sam will be convicted. But if that happens, then Sam will go to jail. Write out the single conditional statement that sums up this reasoning process.

Find the answer on MindTap.

Conditional proof is a method for deriving a conditional statement (either the conclusion or some intermediate line) that offers the usual advantage of being both shorter and simpler to use than the direct method. Moreover, some arguments have conclusions that cannot be derived by the direct method, so some form of conditional proof must be used on them. Conditional proof may thus be seen as completing the rules of inference. The method consists of assuming the antecedent of the required conditional statement on one line, deriving the consequent on a subsequent line, and then "discharging" this sequence of lines in a conditional statement that exactly replicates the one that was to be obtained.

Any argument whose conclusion is a conditional statement is an immediate candidate for conditional proof. Consider the following example:

1. $A \supset (B \cdot C)$
2. $(B \lor D) \supset E$ / $A \supset E$

Using the direct method to derive the conclusion of this argument would require a proof having at least twelve lines, and the precise strategy to be followed in constructing it might not be immediately obvious. Nevertheless, we need only give cursory inspection to the argument to see that the conclusion does indeed follow from the premises. The conclusion states that if we have A, we then have E. Let us suppose, for a moment, that we do have A. We could then derive $B \cdot C$ from the first premise via *modus ponens*. Simplifying this expression we could derive B, and from this we could get $B \lor D$ via addition. E would then follow from the second premise via *modus ponens*. In other words, if we assume that we have A, we can get E. But this is exactly what the conclusion says. Thus, we have just proved that the conclusion follows from the premises.

The method of conditional proof consists of incorporating this simple thought process into the body of a proof sequence. A conditional proof for this argument requires only eight lines and is substantially simpler than a direct proof:

1. $A \supset (B \cdot C)$
2. $(B \lor D) \supset E$ / $A \supset E$
   | 3. A ACP
   | 4. $B \cdot C$ 1, 3, MP
   | 5. B 4, Simp
   | 6. $B \lor D$ 5, Add
   | 7. E 2, 6, MP
8. $A \supset E$ 3–7, CP

Lines 3 through 7 are indented to indicate their hypothetical character: They all depend on the assumption introduced in line 3 via ACP (assumption for conditional proof). These lines, which constitute the conditional proof sequence, tell us that if we assume A (line 3), we can derive E (line 7). In line 8 the conditional sequence is discharged in the conditional statement $A \supset E$, which simply reiterates the result of the conditional sequence. Since line 8 is not hypothetical, it is written adjacent to the original margin, under lines 1 and 2. A vertical line is added to the conditional sequence to emphasize the indentation.

The first step in constructing a conditional proof is to decide what should be assumed on the first line of the conditional sequence. While any statement whatsoever *can* be assumed on this line, only the right statement will lead to the desired result. The clue is always provided by the conditional statement to be obtained in the end. The antecedent of this statement is what must be assumed. For example, if the statement to be obtained is $(K \cdot L) \supset M$, then $K \cdot L$ should be assumed on the first line. This line is always indented and tagged with the designation "ACP." Once the initial assumption has been made, the second step is to derive the consequent of the desired conditional statement at the end of the conditional sequence. To do this, we simply apply the ordinary rules of inference to any previous line in the proof (including the assumed line), writing the

eminentlogicians
Gottlob Frege 1848–1925

Pictorial Press Ltd/Alamy Stock Photo

The German mathematician, logician, and philosopher Gottlob Frege (pronounced fray-ga) was born in Wismar, a small town in northern Germany on the Baltic Sea. His parents taught at a private girls' school, which his father had helped to found. Frege attended the local gymnasium, where he studied mathematics, and then the University of Jena, where he studied mathematics, philosophy, and chemistry. After two years he transferred to the University of Göttingen, earning a doctor's degree in mathematics at age twenty-four. He then returned to the University of Jena, where he taught until retiring in 1917. While there he married Margaret Liesburg, who bore him at least two children. The children died young, but years later the couple adopted a son, Alfred.

Frege spent his entire life analyzing the concept of number, developing theories of logic and language, and attempting to reduce arithmetic to logic. In 1879 he published the *Begriffsschrift* ("Concept-Script"), a work written in the tradition of Leibniz that develops a purely formal symbolic language to express any proposition in any area of human discourse. Five years later he published *Die Grundlagen der Arithmetik* ("The Foundations of Arithmetic"), a less technical work containing few symbols that outlined his goal of reducing arithmetic to logic. Then, nine years later he published Volume 1 of *Grundgesetze der Arithmetik* ("Basic Laws of Arithmetic"), which attempted to accomplish the first phase of this reduction.

None of these works were well received, for several reasons: They were ahead of their time, the symbolic notation of the technical works struck readers as bizarre, and they were written in German, whereas most of the new work in logic was being done by English speakers. In fact, the last of these works was so badly reviewed that Frege was forced to publish Volume 2 at his own expense. To make matters worse, in 1902, while Volume 2 was in proof, Frege received a letter from Bertrand Russell that left him "thunderstruck." He was later to remark that it had destroyed his entire life's work.

Basic Law 5 of the *Grundgesetze* provides for the creation of classes of things merely by describing the properties of their members. So Russell invited Frege to create the class of all classes that are not members of themselves, and he then asked whether this very class is a member of itself. If it is a member of itself, then it is one of those classes that are not members of themselves; but if is not a member of itself, then, again, it is one of those classes, and it is a member of itself. The derivation of this contradiction (which has come to be called Russell's paradox) meant that the axioms of the *Grundgesetze* were fatally inconsistent. Frege attempted a last-minute modification of his system, but the change proved unworkable.

Despite this setback, Frege is universally recognized today as one of the most important logicians and philosophers of all time. Single-handedly he developed quantification theory and predicate logic, and his analysis of the concept of number led to a general theory of meaning that introduced the important distinction between *Sinn* ("sense") and *Bedeutung* ("reference"). Also, his work on concept clarification initiated the current movement known as analytic philosophy.

7

result directly below the assumed line. The third and final step is to discharge the conditional sequence in a conditional statement. The antecedent of this conditional statement is whatever appears on the first line of the conditional sequence, and the consequent is whatever appears on the last line. For example, if $A \lor B$ is on the first line and $C \cdot D$ is on the last, the sequence is discharged by $(A \lor B) \supset (C \cdot D)$. This discharging line is always written adjacent to the original margin and is tagged with the designation "CP" (conditional proof) together with the numerals indicating the first through the last lines of the sequence.

Conditional proof can also be used to derive a line other than the conclusion of an argument. The following proof, which illustrates this fact, incorporates two conditional sequences one after the other within the scope of a single direct proof:

1.	$G \supset (H \cdot I)$	
2.	$J \supset (K \cdot L)$	
3.	$G \lor J$	/ $H \lor K$
4.	G	ACP
5.	$H \cdot I$	1, 4, MP
6.	H	5, Simp
7.	$G \supset H$	4–6, CP
8.	J	ACP
9.	$K \cdot L$	2, 8, MP
10.	K	9, Simp
11.	$J \supset K$	8–10, CP
12.	$(G \supset H) \cdot (J \supset K)$	7, 11, Conj
13.	$H \lor K$	3, 12, CD

The first conditional proof sequence gives us $G \supset H$, and the second $J \supset K$. These two lines are then conjoined and used together with line 3 to set up a constructive dilemma, from which the conclusion is derived.

This proof sequence provides a convenient opportunity to introduce an important rule governing conditional proof. The rule states that after a conditional proof sequence has been discharged, no line in the sequence may be used as a justification for a subsequent line in the proof. If, for example, line 5 in the proof just given were used as a justification for line 9 or line 12, this rule would be violated, and the corresponding inference would be invalid. Once the conditional sequence is discharged, it is sealed off from the remaining part of the proof. The logic behind this rule is easy to understand. The lines in a conditional sequence are hypothetical in that they depend on the assumption stated in the first line. Because no mere assumption can provide any genuine support for anything, neither can any line that depends on such an assumption. When a conditional sequence is discharged, the assumption on which it rests is expressed as the antecedent of a conditional statement. This conditional statement *can* be used to support subsequent lines because it makes no claim that its antecedent is true. The conditional statement merely asserts that *if* its antecedent is true, then its consequent is true, and this, of course, is what has been established by the conditional sequence from which it is obtained.

Just as a conditional sequence can be used within the scope of a direct proof to derive a desired statement, one conditional sequence can be used within the scope of another to derive a desired statement. The following proof provides an example:

1. $L \supset [M \supset (N \lor O)]$
2. $M \supset {\sim}N$ $/ \; L \supset ({\sim}M \lor O)$
    3. L ACP
    4. $M \supset (N \lor O)$ 1, 3, MP
      5. M ACP
      6. $N \lor O$ 4, 5, MP
      7. ${\sim}N$ 2, 5, MP
      8. O 6, 7, DS
    9. $M \supset O$ 5–8, CP
   10. ${\sim}M \lor O$ 9, Impl
11. $L \supset ({\sim}M \lor O)$ 3–10, CP

The rule introduced in connection with the previous example applies unchanged to examples of this sort. No line in the sequence 5–8 could be used to support any line subsequent to line 9, and no line in the sequence 3–10 could be used to support any line subsequent to line 11. Lines 3 or 4 could, of course, be used to support any line in the sequence 5–8.

One final reminder regarding conditional proof is that every conditional proof must be discharged. It is absolutely improper to end a proof on an indented line. If this rule is ignored, any conclusion one chooses can be derived from any set of premises. The following invalid proof illustrates this mistake:

1. P $/ \; Q \supset R$
  2. ${\sim}Q$ ACP
  3. ${\sim}Q \lor R$ 2, Add
  4. $Q \supset R$ 2, Impl

7

EXERCISE 7.5

I. Use conditional proof and the eighteen rules of inference to derive the conclusions of the following symbolized arguments. Having done so, attempt to derive the conclusions without using conditional proof.

★(1) 1. $N \supset O$
      2. $N \supset P$ $/ \; N \supset (O \cdot P)$

(2) 1. $F \supset E$
     2. $(F \cdot E) \supset R$ $/ \; F \supset R$

MindTap® Complete exercises online for immediate feedback.

(3) 1. $G \supset T$
2. $(T \lor S) \supset K$ / $G \supset K$

★**(4)** 1. $(G \lor H) \supset (S \cdot T)$
2. $(T \lor U) \supset (C \cdot D)$ / $G \supset C$

(5) 1. $A \supset \sim(A \lor E)$ / $A \supset F$

(6) 1. $J \supset (K \supset L)$
2. $J \supset (M \supset L)$
3. $\sim L$ / $J \supset \sim(K \lor M)$

★**(7)** 1. $M \lor (N \cdot O)$ / $\sim N \supset M$

(8) 1. $P \supset (Q \lor R)$
2. $(P \supset R) \supset (S \cdot T)$
3. $Q \supset R$ / T

(9) 1. $H \supset (I \supset N)$
2. $(H \supset \sim I) \supset (M \lor N)$
3. $\sim N$ / M

★**(10)** 1. $C \supset (A \cdot D)$
2. $B \supset (A \cdot E)$ / $(C \lor B) \supset A$

(11) 1. $M \supset (K \supset L)$
2. $(L \lor N) \supset J$ / $M \supset (K \supset J)$

(12) 1. $F \supset (G \cdot H)$ / $(A \supset F) \supset (A \supset H)$

★**(13)** 1. $R \supset B$
2. $R \supset (B \supset F)$
3. $B \supset (F \supset H)$ / $R \supset H$

(14) 1. $(F \cdot G) \equiv H$
2. $F \supset G$ / $F \equiv H$

(15) 1. $C \supset (D \lor \sim E)$
2. $E \supset (D \supset F)$ / $C \supset (E \supset F)$

★**(16)** 1. $Q \supset (R \supset S)$
2. $Q \supset (T \supset \sim U)$
3. $U \supset (R \lor T)$ / $Q \supset (U \supset S)$

(17) 1. $N \supset (O \cdot P)$
2. $Q \supset (R \cdot S)$ / $(P \supset Q) \supset (N \supset S)$

(18) 1. $E \supset (F \supset G)$
2. $H \supset (G \supset I)$
3. $(F \supset I) \supset (J \lor \sim H)$ / $(E \cdot H) \supset J$

★**(19)** 1. $P \supset [(L \lor M) \supset (N \cdot O)]$
2. $(O \lor T) \supset W$ / $P \supset (M \supset W)$

(20) 1. $A \supset [B \supset (C \cdot \sim D)]$
    2. $(B \lor E) \supset (D \lor E)$ / $(A \cdot B) \supset (C \cdot E)$

II. Translate the following arguments into symbolic form, using the letters in the order in which they are listed. Then use conditional proof and the eighteen rules of inference to derive the conclusion of each. Having done so, attempt to derive the conclusion without using conditional proof.

★1. If high-tech products are exported to Russia, then domestic industries will benefit. If the Russians can effectively utilize high-tech products, then their standard of living will improve. Therefore, if high-tech products are exported to Russia and the Russians can effectively utilize them, then their standard of living will improve and domestic industries will benefit. (H, D, U, S)

2. If the police take you into custody, then if they inform you that you have the right to remain silent, then whatever you say will be used against you. If the police inform you that you have the right to remain silent, then if whatever you say will be used against you, then you should not say anything. Therefore, if the police take you into custody, then if they inform you that you have the right to remain silent, then you should not say anything. (P, I, W, S)

3. A doctor must disconnect a dying patient from a respirator if and only if the fact that patients are self-determining implies that the doctor must follow the patient's orders. If a dying patient refuses treatment, then the doctor must disconnect the patient from a respirator and the patient will die peacefully. Patients are self-determining. Therefore, if a dying patient refuses treatment, then the doctor must follow the patient's orders. (D, S, F, R, P)

★4. If jails are overcrowded, then dangerous suspects will be released on their own recognizance. If jails are overcrowded and dangerous suspects are released on their own recognizance, then crime will increase. If no new jails are built and crime increases, then innocent victims will pay the price of increased crime. Therefore, if jails are overcrowded, then if no new jails are built, then innocent victims will pay the price of increased crime. (J, D, C, N, I)

5. If astronauts attempt interplanetary space travel, then heavy shielding will be required to protect them from solar radiation. If massive amounts of either fuel or water are carried, then the spacecraft must be very large. Therefore, if heavy shielding is required to protect the astronauts from solar radiation only if massive amounts of fuel are carried, then if astronauts attempt interplanetary space travel, then the spacecraft must be very large. (A, H, F, W, L)

III. Create two symbolized arguments consisting of at least two premises each, and which invite conditional proof to derive the conclusion. The arguments should look like those in Part I of this section. Then derive the conclusion of each.

MindTap Master concepts and improve outcomes with Aplia, at the end of the chapter, in the Aplia folder.

Indirect Proof

Indirect proof is a technique similar to conditional proof that can be used on any argument to derive either the conclusion or some intermediate line leading to the conclusion. It consists of assuming the negation of the statement to be obtained, using this assumption to derive a contradiction, and then concluding that the original assumption is false. This last step, of course, establishes the truth of the statement to be obtained. The following proof sequence uses indirect proof to derive the conclusion:

1. $(A \lor B) \supset (C \cdot D)$		
2. $C \supset {\sim}D$	/ ${\sim}A$	
3. A	AIP	
4. $A \lor B$	3, Add	
5. $C \cdot D$	1, 4, MP	
6. C	5, Simp	
7. ${\sim}D$	2, 6, MP	
8. $D \cdot C$	5, Com	
9. D	8, Simp	
10. $D \cdot {\sim}D$	7, 9, Conj	
11. ${\sim}A$	3–10, IP	

The indirect proof sequence (lines 3–10) begins by assuming the negation of the conclusion. Since the conclusion is a negated statement, it shortens the proof to assume A instead of ${\sim}{\sim}A$. This assumption, which is tagged "AIP" (assumption for indirect proof), leads to a contradiction in line 10. Since any assumption that leads to a contradiction is false, the indirect sequence is discharged (line 11) by asserting the negation of the assumption made in line 3. This line is then tagged with the designation "IP" (indirect proof) together with the numerals indicating the scope of the indirect sequence from which it is obtained.

Indirect proof can also be used to derive an intermediate line leading to the conclusion. Example:

1. $E \supset [(F \lor G) \supset (H \cdot J)]$	
2. $E \cdot {\sim}(J \lor K)$	/ ${\sim}(F \lor K)$
3. E	2, Simp
4. $(F \lor G) \supset (H \cdot J)$	1, 3, MP
5. ${\sim}(J \lor K) \cdot E$	2, Com
6. ${\sim}(J \lor K)$	5, Simp

7. ~J • ~K	6, DM
8. F	AIP
9. F ∨ G	8, Add
10. H • J	4, 9, MP
11. J • H	10, Com
12. J	11, Simp
13. ~J	7, Simp
14. J • ~J	12, 13, Conj
15. ~F	8–14, IP
16. ~K • ~J	7, Com
17. ~K	16, Simp
18. ~F • ~K	15, 17, Conj
19. ~(F ∨ K)	18, DM

The indirect proof sequence begins with the assumption of *F* (line 8), leads to a contradiction (line 14), and is discharged (line 15) by asserting the negation of the assumption. One should consider indirect proof whenever a line in a proof appears difficult to obtain.

As with conditional proof, when an indirect proof sequence is discharged, no line in the sequence may be used as a justification for a subsequent line in the proof. In reference to the last proof, this means that none of the lines 8–14 could be used as a justification for any of the lines 16–19. Occasionally, this rule requires certain priorities in the derivation of lines. For example, for the purpose of deriving the contradiction, lines 6 and 7 could have been included as part of the indirect sequence. But this would not have been advisable, because line 7 is needed as a justification for line 16, which lies outside the indirect sequence. If lines 6 and 7 had been included within the indirect sequence, they would have had to be repeated after the sequence had been discharged to allow ~K to be derived on a line outside the sequence.

Just as a conditional sequence may be constructed within the scope of another conditional sequence, so a conditional sequence may be constructed within the scope of an indirect sequence, and, conversely, an indirect sequence may be constructed within the scope of either a conditional sequence or another indirect sequence. The next example illustrates the use of an indirect sequence within the scope of a conditional sequence:

1. L ⊃ [~M ⊃ (N • O)]	
2. ~N • P	/ L ⊃ (M • P)
3. L	ACP
4. ~M ⊃ (N • O)	1, 3, MP
5. ~M	AIP
6. N • O	4, 5, MP
7. N	6, Simp
8. ~N	2, Simp
9. N • ~N	7, 8, Conj
10. ~~M	5–9, IP
11. M	10, DN
12. P • ~N	2, Com
13. P	12, Simp
14. M • P	11, 13, Conj
15. L ⊃ (M • P)	3–14, CP

The indirect sequence (lines 5–9) is discharged (line 10) by asserting the negation of the assumption made in line 5. The conditional sequence (lines 3–14) is discharged (line 15) in the conditional statement that has the first line of the sequence as its antecedent and the last line as its consequent.

Indirect proof provides a convenient way for proving the validity of an argument having a tautology for its conclusion. In fact, the only way in which the conclusion of many such arguments can be derived is through either conditional or indirect proof. For the following argument, indirect proof is the easier of the two:

1. S / $T \lor \sim T$
   2. $\sim(T \lor \sim T)$ AIP
   3. $\sim T \cdot \sim\sim T$ 2, DM
4. $\sim\sim(T \lor \sim T)$ 2–3, IP
5. $T \lor \sim T$ 4, DN

Here is another example of an argument having a tautology as its conclusion. In this case, since the conclusion is a conditional statement, conditional proof is the easier alternative:

1. S / $T \supset T$
   2. T ACP
   3. $T \lor T$ 2, Add
   4. T 3, Taut
5. $T \supset T$ 2–4, CP

The similarity of indirect proof to conditional proof may be illustrated by returning to the first example presented in this section. In the proof that follows, conditional proof—not indirect proof—is used to derive the conclusion:

1. $(A \lor B) \supset (C \cdot D)$
2. $C \supset \sim D$ / $\sim A$
   3. A ACP
   4. $A \lor B$ 3, Add
   5. $C \cdot D$ 1, 4, MP
   6. C 5, Simp
   7. $\sim D$ 2, 6, MP
   8. $D \cdot C$ 5, Com
   9. D 8, Simp
   10. $D \lor \sim A$ 9, Add
   11. $\sim A$ 7, 10, DS
12. $A \supset \sim A$ 3–11, CP
13. $\sim A \lor \sim A$ 12, Impl
14. $\sim A$ 13, Taut

This example illustrates how a conditional proof can be used to derive the conclusion of *any* argument, whether or not the conclusion is a conditional statement. Simply begin by assuming the negation of the conclusion, derive contradictory statements on separate lines, and use these lines to set up a disjunctive syllogism yielding the negation of the assumption as the last line of the conditional sequence. Then, discharge the sequence and use tautology to derive the negation of the assumption outside the sequence.

Indirect proof can be viewed as a variety of conditional proof in that it amounts to a modification of the way in which the indented sequence is discharged, resulting in an overall shortening of the proof for many arguments. The indirect proof for the argument just given is repeated as follows, with the requisite changes noted in the margin:

1. $(A \lor B) \supset (C \cdot D)$	
2. $C \supset \sim D$	/ $\sim A$
3. A	AIP
4. $A \lor B$	3, Add
5. $C \cdot D$	1, 4, MP
6. C	5, Simp
7. $\sim D$	2, 6, MP
8. $D \cdot C$	5, Com
9. D	8, Simp
10. $D \cdot \sim D$	7, 9, Conj ⎫
11. $\sim A$	3–10, IP ⎬ _____ changed

The reminder at the end of the previous section regarding conditional proof pertains to indirect proof as well: It is essential that every indirect proof be discharged. No proof can be ended on an indented line. If this rule is ignored, indirect proof, like conditional proof, can produce any conclusion whatsoever. The following invalid proof illustrates such a mistake:

1. P	/ Q
2. Q	AIP
3. $Q \lor Q$	2, Add
4. Q	3, Taut

EXERCISE 7.6

I. Use either indirect proof or conditional proof (or both) and the eighteen rules of inference to derive the conclusions of the following symbolized arguments. Having done so, attempt to derive the conclusions without using indirect proof or conditional proof.

★(1) 1. $(S \lor T) \supset \sim S$ / $\sim S$

(2) 1. $(K \supset K) \supset R$

    2. $(R \lor M) \supset N$ / N

MindTap® Complete exercises online for immediate feedback.

(3) 1. $(C \cdot D) \supset E$
    2. $(D \cdot E) \supset F$ $/ (C \cdot D) \supset F$

★(4) 1. $H \supset (L \supset K)$
     2. $L \supset (K \supset \sim L)$ $/ \sim H \vee \sim L$

(5) 1. $S \supset (T \vee \sim U)$
    2. $U \supset (\sim T \vee R)$
    3. $(S \cdot U) \supset \sim R$ $/ \sim S \vee \sim U$

(6) 1. $\sim A \supset (B \cdot C)$
    2. $D \supset \sim C$ $/ D \supset A$

★(7) 1. $(E \vee F) \supset (C \cdot D)$
     2. $(D \vee G) \supset H$
     3. $E \vee G$ $/ H$

(8) 1. $\sim M \supset (N \cdot O)$
    2. $N \supset P$
    3. $O \supset \sim P$ $/ M$

(9) 1. $(R \vee S) \supset T$
    2. $(P \vee Q) \supset T$
    3. $R \vee P$ $/ T$

★(10) 1. K $/ S \supset (T \supset S)$

(11) 1. $(A \vee B) \supset C$
     2. $(\sim A \vee D) \supset E$ $/ C \vee E$

(12) 1. $(K \vee L) \supset (M \cdot N)$
     2. $(N \vee O) \supset (P \cdot \sim K)$ $/ \sim K$

★(13) 1. $[C \supset (D \supset C)] \supset E$ $/ E$

(14) 1. F $/ (G \supset H) \vee (\sim G \supset J)$

(15) 1. $B \supset (K \cdot M)$
     2. $(B \cdot M) \supset (P \equiv \sim P)$ $/ \sim B$

★(16) 1. $(N \vee O) \supset (C \cdot D)$
     2. $(D \vee K) \supset (P \vee \sim C)$
     3. $(P \vee G) \supset \sim (N \cdot D)$ $/ \sim N$

(17) 1. $(R \cdot S) \equiv (G \cdot H)$
     2. $R \supset S$
     3. $H \supset G$ $/ R \equiv H$

(18) 1. $K \supset [(M \vee N) \supset (P \cdot Q)]$
     2. $L \supset [(Q \vee R) \supset (S \cdot \sim N)]$ $/ (K \cdot L) \supset \sim N$

★(19) 1. $A \supset [(N \vee \sim N) \supset (S \vee T)]$
     2. $T \supset \sim (F \vee \sim F)$ $/ A \supset S$

(20) 1. $F \supset [(C \supset C) \supset G]$
     2. $G \supset \{[H \supset (E \supset H)] \supset (K \cdot {\sim}K)\}$ / ${\sim}F$

II. Translate the following arguments into symbolic form, using the letters in the order in which they are listed. Then use indirect proof and the eighteen rules of inference to derive the conclusion of each. Having done so, attempt to derive the conclusion without using indirect proof.

★1. If government deficits continue at their present rate and a recession sets in, then interest on the national debt will become unbearable and the government will default on its loans. If a recession sets in, then the government will not default on its loans. Therefore, either government deficits will not continue at their present rate or a recession will not set in. (C, R, I, D)

2. If either the sea turtle population continues to decrease or rescue efforts are commenced to save the sea turtle from extinction, then nesting sanctuaries will be created and the indiscriminate slaughter of these animals will be halted. If either nesting sanctuaries are created or poachers are arrested, then if the indiscriminate slaughter of these animals is halted, then the sea turtle population will not continue to decrease. Therefore, the sea turtle population will not continue to decrease. (C, R, N, I, P)

3. If asbestos workers sue their employers, then if punitive damages are awarded, then their employers will declare bankruptcy. If asbestos workers sue their employers, then punitive damages will be awarded. If asbestos workers contract asbestosis, then either they will sue their employers or their employers will declare bankruptcy. Therefore, either asbestos workers will not contract asbestosis or their employers will declare bankruptcy. (S, P, B, C)

★4. If astronauts spend long periods in zero gravity only if calcium is resorbed in their bodies, then astronauts on a Mars voyage will arrive with brittle bones. If astronauts attempt a voyage to Mars only if they spend long periods in zero gravity, then astronauts on a Mars voyage will arrive with brittle bones. Therefore, astronauts on a Mars voyage will arrive with brittle bones. (Z, C, B, V)

5. Either deposits should be required on beer and soft-drink containers, or these containers will be discarded along highways and the countryside will look like a dump. If these containers will be discarded either in parks or along highways, then deposits should be required on soft-drink containers. Therefore, deposits should be required on soft-drink containers. (B, S, H, C, P)

III. Create two symbolized arguments consisting of at least two premises each, and which invite indirect proof to derive the conclusion. The arguments should look like those in Part I of this section. Then derive the conclusion of each.

MindTap® Master concepts and improve outcomes with Aplia, at the end of the chapter, in the Aplia folder.

Both conditional and indirect proof can be used to establish the truth of a logical truth (tautology). Tautological statements can be treated as if they were the conclusions of arguments having no premises. Such a procedure is suggested by the fact that any argument having a tautology for its conclusion is valid regardless of what its premises are. As we saw in the previous section, the proof for such an argument does not use the premises at all but derives the conclusion as the exclusive consequence of either a conditional or an indirect sequence. Using this strategy for logical truths, we write the statement to be proved as if it were the conclusion of argument, and we indent the first line in the proof and tag it as being the beginning of either a conditional or an indirect sequence. In the end, this sequence is appropriately discharged to yield the desired statement form.

Tautologies expressed in the form of conditional statements are most easily proved via a conditional sequence. The following example uses two such sequences, one within the scope of the other:

$$/ \ P \supset (Q \supset P)$$

1.	P	ACP
2.	Q	ACP
3.	$P \lor P$	1, Add
4.	P	3, Taut
5.	$Q \supset P$	2–4, CP
6.	$P \supset (Q \supset P)$	1–5, CP

Notice that line 6 restores the proof to the original margin—the first line is indented because it introduces the conditional sequence.

Here is a proof of the same statement using an indirect proof. The indirect sequence begins, as usual, with the negation of the statement to be proved:

$$/ \ P \supset (Q \supset P)$$

1.	$\sim[P \supset (Q \supset P)]$	AIP
2.	$\sim[\sim P \lor (Q \supset P)]$	1, Impl
3.	$\sim[\sim P \lor (\sim Q \lor P)]$	2, Impl
4.	$\sim\sim P \cdot \sim(\sim Q \lor P)$	3, DM
5.	$P \cdot \sim(\sim Q \lor P)$	4, DN
6.	$P \cdot (\sim\sim Q \cdot \sim P)$	5, DM
7.	$P \cdot (\sim P \cdot \sim\sim Q)$	6, Com
8.	$(P \cdot \sim P) \cdot \sim\sim Q$	7, Assoc
9.	$P \cdot \sim P$	8, Simp

| 10. $\sim\sim[P \supset (Q \supset P)]$ | 1–9, IP |
| 11. $P \supset (Q \supset P)$ | 10, DN |

More-complex conditional statements are proved by merely extending the technique used in the first proof. In the following proof, notice how each conditional sequence begins by asserting the antecedent of the conditional statement to be derived:

	/ $[P \supset (Q \supset R)] \supset [(P \supset Q) \supset (P \supset R)]$
1. $P \supset (Q \supset R)$	ACP
2. $P \supset Q$	ACP
3. P	ACP
4. $Q \supset R$	1, 3, MP
5. Q	2, 3, MP
6. R	4, 5, MP
7. $P \supset R$	3–6, CP
8. $(P \supset Q) \supset (P \supset R)$	2–7, CP
9. $[P \supset (Q \supset R)] \supset [(P \supset Q) \supset (P \supset R)]$	1–8, CP

Tautologies expressed as equivalences are usually proved using two conditional sequences, one after the other. Example:

	/ $P \equiv [P \bullet (Q \supset P)]$
1. P	ACP
2. $P \lor \sim Q$	1, Add
3. $\sim Q \lor P$	2, Com
4. $Q \supset P$	3, Impl
5. $P \bullet (Q \supset P)$	1, 4, Conj
6. $P \supset [P \bullet (Q \supset P)]$	1–5, CP
7. $P \bullet (Q \supset P)$	ACP
8. P	7, Simp
9. $[P \bullet (Q \supset P)] \supset P$	7–8, CP
10. {line 6} $\bullet$ {line 9}	6, 9, Conj
11. $P \equiv [P \bullet (Q \supset P)]$	10, Equiv

7

EXERCISE 7.7

I. Use conditional proof or indirect proof and the eighteen rules of inference to establish the truth of the following tautologies.

★1. $P \supset [(P \supset Q) \supset Q]$

2. $(\sim P \supset Q) \lor (P \supset R)$

3. $P \equiv [P \lor (Q \bullet P)]$

★4. $(P \supset Q) \supset [(P \cdot R) \supset (Q \cdot R)]$

5. $(P \lor \sim Q) \supset [(\sim P \lor R) \supset (Q \supset R)]$

6. $P \equiv [P \cdot (Q \lor \sim Q)]$

★7. $(P \supset Q) \lor (\sim Q \supset P)$

8. $(P \supset Q) \equiv [P \supset (P \cdot Q)]$

9. $[(P \supset Q) \cdot (P \supset R)] \supset [P \supset (Q \cdot R)]$

★10. $[\sim(P \cdot \sim Q) \cdot \sim Q] \supset \sim P$

11. $(P \supset Q) \lor (Q \supset P)$

12. $[P \supset (Q \supset R)] \equiv [Q \supset (P \supset R)]$

★13. $(P \supset Q) \supset [(P \supset \sim Q) \supset \sim P]$

14. $[(P \supset Q) \supset R] \supset [(R \supset \sim R) \supset P]$

15. $(\sim P \lor Q) \supset [(P \lor \sim Q) \supset (P \equiv Q)]$

★16. $\sim[(P \supset \sim P) \cdot (\sim P \supset P)]$

17. $P \supset [(Q \cdot \sim Q) \supset R]$

18. $[(P \cdot Q) \lor R] \supset [(\sim R \lor Q) \supset (P \supset Q)]$

★19. $P \equiv [P \lor (Q \cdot \sim Q)]$

20. $P \supset [Q \equiv (P \supset Q)]$

II. Create a symbolized tautology (logical truth). Then use conditional proof or indirect proof to prove it.

MindTap° Master concepts and improve outcomes with Aplia, at the end of the chapter, in the Aplia folder.

Summary

Natural Deduction in Propositional Logic:

- A step-by-step method for proving the validity of propositional type arguments.
- Shows exactly how the conclusion "comes out" of the premises.
- Consists in applying eighteen rules of inference to the premises and deriving the conclusion as the last line in a sequence of lines.
- Success in using this method requires much practice.

MindTap° Need help? See the Learning Logic folder at the end of the chapter: the self-paced tutorial walks you through any section.

Prepare for exams with the Chapter Test.

Rules of Inference:

- Rules of implication ("one-way" rules):

  - The premise(s) can be used to derive the conclusion.
  - The conclusion cannot be used to derive the premise(s).

- Rules of replacement ("two-way" rules):

  - Expressed as logical equivalencies.
  - Either side of the equivalence can replace the other.
  - Can be used to "deconstruct" the conclusion for insight into how to derive it.

Conditional Proof:

- A method for deriving a conditional statement.
- Assume the antecedent of the desired conditional on an indented line.
- Derive the consequent of the desired conditional statement.
- Discharge the indented sequence in a conditional statement having the first line of the sequence as the antecedent and the last line as the consequent.
- This method can greatly simplify many proofs.

Indirect Proof:

- A method for deriving any kind of statement.
- Assume the negation of the desired statement (often this is the conclusion) on an indented line.
- Derive a contradiction.
- Any assumption that necessarily leads to a contradiction is false.
- Discharge the indented sequence in a statement consisting of the negation of the first line of the sequence.

Proving Logical Truths (Tautologies):

- Use conditional proof to derive conditionals and biconditionals.

  - Assume the antecedent of the conditional statement on an indented line.
  - Derive the consequent.
  - Discharge the indented sequence in the usual way.
  - Biconditionals require two indented sequences.

- Use indirect proof to derive any logical truth:

  - Assume the negation of the logical truth on an indented line.
  - Derive a contradiction.
  - Discharge the indented sequence in the usual way.

7

8 Predicate Logic

8.1 Symbols and Translation

HOW LOGICAL ARE YOU? Suppose that you are playing a game that requires you to rephrase categorical propositions as conditional statements. You are given the statement "All humans are mammals." How would you rephrase this proposition as a conditional statement?

Find the answer on MindTap.

Techniques were developed in earlier chapters for evaluating two basically different kinds of arguments. The chapter on categorical syllogisms dealt with arguments such as the following:

> All episodes of amnesia are neurological disorders.
> No cases of leukemia are neurological disorders.
> Therefore, no episodes of amnesia are cases of leukemia.

In such arguments the fundamental components are *terms*, and the validity of the argument depends on the arrangement of the terms within the premises and conclusion.

The chapter on propositional logic, on the other hand, dealt with arguments such as this:

> If chronic stress is reduced, then relaxation increases and health improves.
> If health improves, then people live longer.
> Therefore, if chronic stress is reduced, then people live longer.

MindTap Read, study, reflect, and prepare for exams online, anytime, anywhere.

In such arguments the fundamental components are not terms but *statements*. The validity of these arguments depends not on the arrangement of the terms within the statements but on the arrangement of the statements themselves as simple units.

Not all arguments, however, can be assigned to one or the other of these two groups. There is a third type that is a kind of hybrid, sharing features with both categorical syllogisms and propositional arguments. Consider, for example, the following:

> Kate Middleton is rich and beautiful.
> If a woman is either rich or famous, she is happy.
> Therefore, Kate Middleton is happy.

The validity of this argument depends on both the arrangement of the terms and the arrangement of the statements. Accordingly, neither syllogistic logic nor propositional logic alone is sufficient to establish its validity. What is needed is a third kind of logic that combines the distinctive features of syllogistic logic and propositional logic. This third kind is called **predicate logic**.

The fundamental component in predicate logic is the **predicate**, symbolized by uppercase letters ($A, B, C, \ldots X, Y, Z$), called **predicate symbols**. Here are some examples of bare predicates:

English predicate	Symbolic predicate
____ is a rabbit	R __
____ is gigantic	G __
____ is a doctor	D __
____ is helpless	H __

The blank space immediately following the predicate letter is not part of the predicate; rather, it indicates the place for some lowercase letter that will represent the subject of the statement. Depending on what lowercase letter is used, and on the additional symbolism involved, symbolic predicates may be used to translate three distinct kinds of statements: singular statements, universal statements, and particular statements.

A **singular statement**, you may recall from Section 4.7, is a statement that makes an assertion about a specifically named person, place, thing, or time. Translating a singular statement involves writing a lowercase letter corresponding to the subject of the statement to the immediate right of the uppercase letter corresponding to the predicate. The letters that are allocated to serve as abbreviated names of individuals are the first twenty-three letters of the alphabet ($a, b, c, \ldots u, v, w$). These letters are called **individual constants**. Here are some examples of translated statements:

Statement	Symbolic translation
Socrates is mortal.	Ms
Tokyo is populous.	Pt
The *Sun-Times* is a newspaper.	Ns
King Lear is not a fairy tale.	$\sim Fk$
Berlioz was not a German.	$\sim Gb$

Compound arrangements of singular statements may be translated by using the familiar connectives of propositional logic. Here are some examples:

Statement	Symbolic translation
If Paris is beautiful, then Andre told the truth.	$Bp \supset Ta$
Irene is either a doctor or a lawyer.	$Di \lor Li$
Senator Wilkins will be elected only if he campaigns.	$Ew \supset Cw$
General Motors will prosper if either Nissan is crippled by a strike or Subaru declares bankruptcy.	$(Cn \lor Ds) \supset Pg$
Indianapolis gets rain if and only if Chicago and Milwaukee get snow.	$Ri \equiv (Sc \cdot Sm)$

Recall from Chapter 4 that a **universal statement** is a statement that makes an assertion about every member of its subject class. Such statements are either affirmative or negative, depending on whether the statement affirms or denies that the members of the subject class are members of the predicate class. The key to translating universal statements is provided by the Boolean interpretation of these statements (see Section 4.3):

Statement form	Boolean interpretation
All S are P.	If anything is an S, then it is a P.
No S are P.	If anything is an S, then it is not a P.

According to the Boolean interpretation, universal statements are translated as conditionals. We have a symbol (the horseshoe) to translate conditional statements, so we may use it to translate universal statements. What is still needed, however, is a symbol to indicate that universal statements make an assertion about *every* member of the S class. This symbol is called the **universal quantifier**. It is formed by placing a lowercase letter in parentheses, (x), and is translated as "for any x." The letters that are allocated for forming the universal quantifier are the last three letters of the alphabet (x, y, z). These letters are called **individual variables**. They can stand for any item at random in the universe, and they have individual constants as substitution instances.

The horseshoe operator and the universal quantifier are combined to translate universal statements as follows:

Statement form	Symbolic translation	Verbal meaning
All S are P.	$(x)(Sx \supset Px)$	For any x, if x is an S, then x is a P.
No S are P.	$(x)(Sx \supset \sim Px)$	For any x, if x is an S, then x is not a P.

Because an individual variable can stand for any item at random in the universe, the expression $(x)(Sx \supset Px)$ means "If anything is an S, then it is a P." Also $(x)(Sx \supset \sim Px)$ means "If anything is an S, then it is not a P." The fact that these expressions are equivalent to the Boolean interpretation of universal statements may be seen by recalling how the Boolean interpretation is represented by Venn diagrams (see Section 4.3). The Venn diagrams corresponding to the two universal statement forms are as follows:

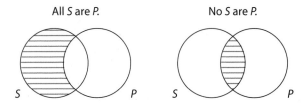

All *S* are *P*.   No *S* are *P*.

Where shading designates emptiness, the diagram on the left asserts that if anything is in the *S* circle, it is also in the *P* circle, and the one on the right asserts that if anything is in the *S* circle, it is not in the *P* circle. This is exactly what is asserted by the symbolic expressions just given. These symbolic expressions may therefore be taken as being exactly synonymous with the Boolean interpretation of universal statements.

A possible source of confusion at this point concerns the fact that both *S* and *P* in the symbolic expressions are predicates, whereas in the original statement forms *S* is the subject and *P* is the predicate. Any problem in this regard vanishes, however, once one understands what happens when universal statements are converted into conditionals. When so converted, *S* becomes the predicate of the antecedent and *P* becomes the predicate of the consequent. In other words, in the conditional "If anything is an *S*, then it is a *P*," both *S* and *P* are predicates. Thus, using predicate symbolism to translate universal statements leads to no difficulties. When translating these statements, the point to remember is simply this: The subject of the original statement is represented by a capital letter in the antecedent, and the predicate by a capital letter in the consequent. Here are some examples:

Statement	Symbolic translation
All skyscrapers are tall.	$(x)(Sx \supset Tx)$
No frogs are birds.	$(x)(Fx \supset {\sim}Bx)$
All ambassadors are statesmen.	$(x)(Ax \supset Sx)$
No diamonds are rubies.	$(x)(Dx \supset {\sim}Rx)$

In these examples, the expressions $Sx \supset Tx$, $Fx \supset {\sim}Bx$, and so on are called statement functions. A **statement function** is the expression that remains when a quantifier is removed from a statement. It is a mere pattern for a statement. It makes no definite assertion about anything in the universe, has no truth value, and cannot be translated as a statement. The variables that occur in statement functions are called **free variables** because they are not bound by any quantifier. In contrast, the variables that occur in statements are called **bound variables**.

In using quantifiers to translate statements, we adopt a convention similar to the one adopted for the tilde operator. That is, the quantifier governs only the expression immediately following it. For example, in the statement $(x)(Ax \supset Bx)$ the universal quantifier governs the entire statement function in parentheses—namely, $Ax \supset Bx$. But

8

in the expression $(x)Ax \supset Bx$, the universal quantifier governs only the statement function Ax. The same convention is adopted for the existential quantifier, which will be introduced presently.

Recall from Chapter 4 that a **particular statement** is a statement that makes an assertion about one or more unnamed members of the subject class. As with universal statements, particular statements are either affirmative or negative, depending on whether the statement affirms or denies that members of the subject class are members of the predicate class. Also, as with universal statements, the key to translating particular statements is provided by the Boolean interpretation:

Statement form	Boolean interpretation
Some S are P.	At least one thing is an S and it is also a P.
Some S are not P.	At least one thing is an S and it is not a P.

In other words, particular statements are translated as conjunctions. Since we are already familiar with the symbol for conjunction (the dot), the only additional symbol that we need in order to translate these statements is a symbol for existence. This is provided by the **existential quantifier**, formed by placing a variable to the right of a backward E in parentheses, thus: $(\exists x)$. This symbol is translated "there exists an x such that." The existential quantifier is combined with the dot operator to translate particular statements as follows:

Statement form	Translation	Symbolic verbal meaning
Some S are P.	$(\exists x)(Sx \cdot Px)$	There exists an x such that x is an S and x is a P.
Some S are not P.	$(\exists x)(Sx \cdot {\sim}Px)$	There exists an x such that x is an S and x is not a P.

As in the symbolic expression of universal statements, the letter x is an individual variable, which can stand for any item in the universe. Accordingly, the expression $(\exists x)(Sx \cdot Px)$ means "Something exists that is both an S and a P," and $(\exists x)(Sx \cdot {\sim}Px)$ means "Something exists that is an S and not a P." To see the equivalence of these expressions with the Boolean (and Aristotelian) interpretation of particular statements, it is again useful to recall how these statements are represented by Venn diagrams:

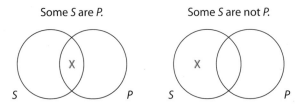

Some S are P. Some S are not P.

Where the X designates at least one existing item, the diagram on the left asserts that something exists that is both an S and a P, and the one on the right asserts that something exists that is an S and not a P. In other words, these diagrams assert exactly the same thing as the symbolic expressions just given. These symbolic expressions, therefore, exactly express the Boolean (and Aristotelian) interpretation of particular statements. Here are some examples:

Statement	Symbolic translation
Some men are paupers.	$(\exists x)(Mx \cdot Px)$
Some diseases are not contagious.	$(\exists x)(Dx \cdot \sim Cx)$
Some jobs are boring.	$(\exists x)(Jx \cdot Bx)$
Some vehicles are not motorcycles.	$(\exists x)(Vx \cdot \sim Mx)$

The general rule to follow in translating statements in predicate logic is always to make an effort to understand the meaning of the statement to be translated. If the statement makes an assertion about every member of its subject class, a universal quantifier should be used to translate it; but if it makes an assertion about only one or more members of this class, an existential quantifier should be used.

Many of the principles developed in syllogistic logic (see Section 4.7) may be carried over into predicate logic. Specifically, it should be understood that statements beginning with the words *only* and *none but* are exclusive propositions. When these statements are translated, the term occurring first in the original statement becomes the consequent in the symbolic expression, and the term occurring second becomes the antecedent. One of the few differences in this respect between predicate logic and syllogistic logic concerns singular statements. In syllogistic logic, singular statements are translated as universals, while in predicate logic, as we have seen, they are translated in a unique way. Here are some examples of a variety of statements:

Statement	Symbolic translation
There are happy marriages.	$(\exists x)(Mx \cdot Hx)$
Every pediatrician loses sleep.	$(x)(Px \supset Lx)$
Animals exist.	$(\exists x)Ax$
Unicorns do not exist.	$\sim(\exists x)Ux$ or $(x)\sim Ux$
Anything is conceivable.	$(x)Cx$
Sea lions are mammals.	$(x)(Sx \supset Mx)$
Sea lions live in these caves.	$(\exists x)(Sx \cdot Lx)$
Egomaniacs are not pleasant companions.	$(x)(Ex \supset \sim Px)$
A few egomaniacs did not arrive on time.	$(\exists x)(Ex \cdot \sim Ax)$
Only close friends were invited to the wedding.	$(x)(Ix \supset Cx)$
None but citizens are eligible to vote.	$(x)(Ex \supset Cx)$
It is not the case that every Girl Scout sells cookies.	$\sim(x)(Gx \supset Sx)$ or $(\exists x)(Gx \cdot \sim Sx)$
Not a single psychologist attended the convention.	$\sim(\exists x)(Px \cdot Ax)$ or $(x)(Px \supset \sim Ax)$

8

As these examples illustrate, the general procedure in translating statements in predicate logic is to render universal statements as conditionals preceded by a universal quantifier, and particular statements as conjunctions preceded by an existential quantifier. However, as the third and fifth examples indicate, there are exceptions to this procedure. A statement that makes an assertion about literally everything in the universe is translated in terms of a single predicate preceded by a universal quantifier, and a statement that asserts that some class of things simply exists is translated in terms of a single predicate preceded by an existential quantifier. The last two examples illustrate that a particular statement is equivalent to a negated universal, and vice versa. The first of these is equivalent to "Some Girl Scouts do not sell cookies" and the second to "No psychologists attended the convention." Actually, any quantified statement can be translated using either a universal or an existential quantifier, provided that one of them is negated. The equivalence of these two forms of expression will be analyzed further in Section 8.3.

More-complex statements may be translated by following the basic rules just presented. Examples:

Statement	Symbolic translation
Only snakes and lizards thrive in the desert.	$(x)[Tx \supset (Sx \lor Lx)]$
Oranges and lemons are citrus fruits.	$(x)[(Ox \lor Lx) \supset Cx]$
Ripe apples are crunchy and delicious.	$(x)[(Rx \cdot Ax) \supset (Cx \cdot Dx)]$
Azaleas bloom if and only if they are fertilized.	$(x)[Ax \supset (Bx \equiv Fx)]$
Peaches are edible unless they are rotten.	$(x)[Px \supset (\sim Rx \supset Ex)]$ or $(x)[Px \supset (Ex \lor Rx)]$
Cats and dogs bite if they are frightened or harassed.	$(x)\{(Cx \lor Dx) \supset [(Fx \lor Hx) \supset Bx]\}$

Notice that the first example is translated in terms of the disjunction $Sx \lor Lx$ even though the English statement reads "snakes *and* lizards." If the translation were rendered as $(x)[Tx \supset (Sx \cdot Lx)]$ it would mean that anything that thrives in the desert is both a snake and a lizard (at the same time). And this is surely *not* what is meant. For the same reason, the second example is translated in terms of the disjunction $Ox \lor Lx$ even though the English reads "oranges *and* lemons." If the statement were translated $(x)[(Ox \cdot Lx) \supset Cx]$, it would mean that anything that is simultaneously an orange and a lemon (and there are none of these) is a citrus fruit. The same principle is used in translating the sixth example, which, incidentally, reads "If anything is a cat or a dog, then if it is frightened or harassed, it bites." The third example employs the conjunction $Rx \cdot Ax$ to translate ripe apples. This, of course, is correct, because such a thing is both ripe and an apple at the same time. The fifth example illustrates the fact that "unless" may be translated as either "if not" or "or."

The operators of propositional logic can be used to form compound arrangements of universal and particular statements, just as they can be used to form compound arrangements of singular statements. Here are some examples:

Statement	Symbolic translation
If Elizabeth is a historian, then some women are historians.	$He \supset (\exists x)(Wx \cdot Hx)$
If some cellists are music directors, then some orchestras are properly led.	$(\exists x)(Cx \cdot Mx) \supset (\exists x)(Ox \cdot Px)$
Either everything is alive or Bergson's theory is not correct.	$(x)Ax \vee \sim Cb$
All novels are interesting if and only if some Steinbeck novels are not romances.	$(x)(Nx \supset Ix) \equiv (\exists x)[(Nx \cdot Sx) \cdot \sim Rx]$
Green avocados are never purchased unless all the ripe ones are expensive.	$(x)[(Gx \cdot Ax) \supset \sim Px] \vee (x)[(Rx \cdot Ax) \supset Ex]$

We have seen that the general procedure is to translate universal statements as conditionals preceded by a universal quantifier, and to translate particular statements as conjunctions preceded by an existential quantifier. Let us see what happens to these translations when they are preceded by the wrong quantifier. Consider the false statement "No cats are animals." This is correctly translated $(x)(Cx \supset \sim Ax)$. If, however, it were translated $(\exists x)(Cx \supset \sim Ax)$, the symbolic statement would turn out to be true. This may be seen as follows. $(\exists x)(Cx \supset \sim Ax)$ is equivalent via material implication to $(\exists x)(\sim Cx \vee \sim Ax)$, which in turn is equivalent via De Morgan's rule to $(\exists x)\sim(Cx \cdot Ax)$. The latter statement, however, merely asserts that something exists that is not both a cat and an animal—for example, a dog—which is true. Again, consider the true statement "Some cats are animals." This is correctly translated $(\exists x)(Cx \cdot Ax)$. If, however, it were translated $(x)(Cx \cdot Ax)$, the symbolic statement would assert that everything in the universe is both a cat and an animal, which is clearly false. Thus, as these examples illustrate, it is imperative that the two quantifiers not be confused with each other.

One final observation needs to be made. It was mentioned earlier that the letters x, y, and z are reserved for use as variables for translating universal and particular statements. In accord with this convention, the other twenty-three lowercase letters (a, b, c, ... u, v, w) may be used as names for translating singular statements. Thus, for example, "Albert is a scientist" is translated Sa. But a question naturally arises with statements such as "Xerxes was a king." Should this statement be translated Kx? The answer is no. Some other letter, for example the second letter in the name, should be selected instead of x. Maintaining this alphabetical convention will help us avoid mistakes in the next section when we use natural deduction to derive the conclusions of arguments.

8

EXERCISE 8.1

I. Translate the following statements into symbolic form. Avoid negation signs preceding quantifiers. The predicate letters are given in parentheses.

★1. Elaine is a chemist. (C)

2. Nancy is not a sales clerk. (S)

MindTap Complete exercises online for immediate feedback.

3. Neither Wordsworth nor Shelley was Irish. (*I*)

★4. Rachel is either a journalist or a newscaster. (*J, N*)

5. Intel designs a faster chip only if Micron does. (*D*)

6. Belgium and France subsidize the arts only if Austria or Germany expand museum holdings. (*S, E*)

★7. All maples are trees. (*M, T*)

8. Some grapes are sour. (*G, S*)

9. No novels are biographies. (*N, B*)

★10. Some holidays are not relaxing. (*H, R*)

11. If Gertrude is correct, then the Taj Mahal is made of marble. (*C, M*)

12. Gertrude is not correct only if the Taj Mahal is made of granite. (*C, G*)

★13. Tigers exist. (*T*)

14. Anything that leads to violence is wrong. (*L, W*)

15. There are pornographic art works. (*A, P*)

★16. Not every smile is genuine. (*S, G*)

17. Every penguin loves ice. (*P, L*)

18. There is trouble in River City. (*T, R*)

★19. Whoever is a socialite is vain. (*S, V*)

20. Any caring mother is vigilant and nurturing. (*C, M, V, N*)

21. Terrorists are neither rational nor empathic. (*T, R, E*)

★22. Nobody consumed by jealousy is happy. (*C, H*)

23. Everything is imaginable. (*I*)

24. Ghosts do not exist. (*G*)

★25. A thoroughbred is a horse. (*T, H*)

26. A thoroughbred won the race. (*T, W*)

27. Not all mushrooms are edible. (*M, E*)

★28. Not any horse chestnuts are edible. (*H, E*)

29. A few guests arrived late. (*G, A*)

30. None but gentlemen prefer blondes. (*G, P*)

★31. A few cities are neither safe nor beautiful. (*C, S, B*)

32. There are no circular triangles. (*C, T*)

33. Snakes are harmless unless they have fangs. (*S, H, F*)

★34. Some dogs bite if and only if they are teased. (*D, B, T*)

35. An airliner is safe if and only if it is properly maintained. (*A, S, P*)

36. Some companies go bankrupt if sales decline. (*C, B, S*)

★37. Some children act up only if they are tired. (*C, A, T*)

38. The only musicians that are available are trombonists. (*M, A, T*)

39. Only talented musicians perform in the symphony. (*T, M, P*)

★40. Any well-made car runs smoothly. (*W, C, R*)

41. Not every foreign car runs smoothly. (*F, C, R*)

42. A good violin is rare and expensive. (*G, V, R, E*)

★43. Violins and cellos are stringed instruments. (*V, C, S, I*)

44. A room with a view is available. (*R, V, A*)

45. A room with a view is expensive. (*R, V, E*)

★46. Some French restaurants are exclusive. (*F, R, E*)

47. Some French cafés are not recommended. (*F, C, R*)

48. Hurricanes and earthquakes are violent and destructive. (*H, E, V, D*)

★49. Taylor is guilty if and only if all the witnesses committed perjury. (*G, W, C*)

50. If any witnesses told the truth, then either Parsons or Harris is guilty. (*W, T, G*)

51. If all mysteries are interesting, then *Rebecca* is interesting. (*M, I*)

★52. If there are any interesting mysteries, then *Rebecca* is interesting. (*M, I*)

53. Skaters and dancers are energetic individuals. (*S, D, E, I*)

54. Swiss watches are not expensive unless they are made of gold. (*S, W, E, M*)

★55. If all the buildings in Manhattan are skyscrapers, then the Chrysler building is a skyscraper. (*B, M, S*)

56. Experienced mechanics are well paid only if all the inexperienced ones are lazy. (*E, M, W, L*)

57. Balcony seats are never chosen unless all the orchestra seats are taken. (*B, S, C, O, T*)

★58. Some employees will get raises if and only if some managers are overly generous. (*E, R, M, O*)

59. The physicists and astronomers at the symposium are listed in the program if they either chair a meeting or read a paper. (*P, A, S, L, C, R*)

60. If the scientists and technicians are conscientious and exacting, then some of the mission directors will be either pleased or delighted. (*S, T, C, E, M, P, D*)

II. Create five statements relating to social media. Then translate them into the symbolism of predicate logic.

MindTap Master concepts and improve outcomes with Aplia, at the end of the chapter, in the Aplia folder.

8.2 Using the Rules of Inference

The chief reason for using truth-functional operators (the dot, wedge, horseshoe, and so on) in translating statements into the symbolism of predicate logic is to allow for the application of the eighteen rules of inference to derive the conclusion of arguments via natural deduction. Since, however, the first eight of these rules are applicable only to whole lines in an argument, as long as the quantifier is attached to a line these rules of inference cannot be applied—at least not to the kind of arguments we are about to consider. To provide for their application, four additional rules are required to remove quantifiers at the beginning of a proof sequence and to introduce them, when needed, at the end of the sequence. These four rules are called universal instantiation, universal generalization, existential instantiation, and existential generalization. The first two are used to remove and introduce universal quantifiers, respectively, and the second two to remove and introduce existential quantifiers.

Let us first consider **universal instantiation**. As an illustration of the need for this rule, consider the following argument:

All economists are social scientists.
Paul Krugman is an economist.
Therefore, Paul Krugman is a social scientist.

This argument, which is clearly valid, is symbolized as follows:

1. $(x)(Ex \supset Sx)$
2. Ep / Sp

As the argument now stands, none of the first eight rules of inference can be applied; as a result, there is no way in which the two premises can be combined to derive the conclusion. However, if the first premise could be used to derive a line that reads $Ep \supset Sp$, this statement could be combined with the second premise to yield the conclusion via *modus ponens*. Universal instantiation serves exactly this purpose.

The first premise states that for any item x in the universe, if that item is an E, then it is an S. But since Paul Krugman is himself an item in the universe, the first premise implies that if Paul Krugman is an E, then Paul Krugman is an S. A line stating exactly this can be derived by universal instantiation (UI). In other words, universal instantiation provides us with an *instance* of the universal statement $(x)(Ex \supset Sx)$. In the completed proof, which follows, the p in line 3 is called the **instantial letter**:

1. $(x)(Ex \supset Sx)$
2. Ep / Sp
3. $Ep \supset Sp$ 1, UI
4. Sp 2, 3, MP

At this point the question might arise as to why *modus ponens* is applicable to lines 2 and 3. In Chapter 7 we applied *modus ponens* to lines of the form $p \supset q$, but are we justified in applying it to a line that reads $Ep \supset Sp$? The answer is yes, because Ep and Sp are simply alternate ways of symbolizing simple statements. As so understood, these symbols do not differ in any material way from the p and q of propositional logic.

We may now give a general definition of instantiation. *Instantiation* is an operation that consists in deleting a quantifier and replacing every variable bound by that quantifier with the same instantial letter. For an example of an operation that violates the rule expressed in this definition, consider line 3 of the foregoing proof. If this line were instantiated as $Ep \supset Sx$, it would not be correct because the x in Sx was not replaced with the instantial letter p.

Let us now consider **universal generalization**. The need for this rule may be illustrated through reference to the following argument:

All psychiatrists are doctors.
All doctors are college graduates.
Therefore, all psychiatrists are college graduates.

This valid argument is symbolized as follows:

1. $(x)(Px \supset Dx)$
2. $(x)(Dx \supset Cx)$ / $(x)(Px \supset Cx)$

Once universal instantiation is applied to the two premises, we will have lines that can be used to set up a hypothetical syllogism. But then we will have to reintroduce a universal quantifier to derive the conclusion as written. This final step is obtained by universal generalization (UG). The justification for such a step lies in the fact that both premises are universal statements. The first states that if *anything* is a P, then it is a D, and the second states that if *anything* is a D, then it is a C. We may therefore conclude that if *anything* is a P, then it is a C. But because of the complete generality of this reasoning process, there is a special way in which we must perform the universal instantiation step. Instead of selecting a *specifically named* instance, as we did in the previous example, we must select a *variable* that can range over every instance in the universe. The variables at our disposal, you may recall from the previous section, are x, y, and z. Let us select y. The completed proof is as follows:

1. $(x)(Px \supset Dx)$
2. $(x)(Dx \supset Cx)$ / $(x)(Px \supset Cx)$
3. $Py \supset Dy$ 1, UI
4. $Dy \supset Cy$ 2, UI
5. $Py \supset Cy$ 3, 4, HS
6. $(x)(Px \supset Cx)$ 5, UG

As noted earlier, the expressions in lines 3, 4, and 5 are called *statement functions*. As such, they are mere patterns for statements; they have no truth value and cannot be translated as statements. Yet if we take certain liberties, we might characterize line 5 as saying "If *it* is a *P*, then *it* is a *C*, where "it" designates any item at random in the universe. Line 6 can then be seen as reexpressing this sense of line 5.

As the two previous examples illustrate, we have two ways of performing universal instantiation. On the one hand, we may instantiate with respect to a *constant*, such as *a* or *b*, and on the other, with respect to a *variable*, such as *x* or *y*. The exact way in which this operation is to be performed depends on the kind of result intended. If we want some part of a universal statement to match a singular statement on another line, as in the first example, we instantiate with respect to a constant. But if, at the end of the proof, we want to perform universal generalization over some part of the statement we are instantiating, then we *must* instantiate by using a variable. This latter point leads to an important restriction governing universal generalization—namely, that we cannot perform this operation when the instantial letter is a constant. Consider the following *erroneous* proof sequence:

1. *Ta*
2. (*x*)*Tx* 1, UG (invalid)

If *Ta* means "Albert is a thief," then on the basis of this information, we have concluded (line 2) that everything in the universe is a thief. Clearly, such an inference is invalid. This illustrates the fact that universal generalization can be performed only when the instantial letter (in this case *a*) is a variable.

Let us now consider **existential generalization**. The need for this operation is illustrated through the following argument:

> All tenors are singers.
> Andrea Bocelli is a tenor.
> Therefore, there is at least one singer.

This argument is symbolized as follows:

1. (*x*)(*Tx* ⊃ *Sx*)
2. *Ta*   / (∃*x*)*Sx*

If we instantiate the first line with respect to *a*, we can obtain *Sa* via *modus ponens*. But if it is true that Andrea Bocelli is a tenor, then it certainly follows that there is at least one singer (namely, Andrea Bocelli). This last step is accomplished by existential generalization (EG). The proof is as follows:

1. (*x*)(*Tx* ⊃ *Sx*)
2. *Ta*   / (∃*x*)*Sx*
3. *Ta* ⊃ *Sa* 1, UI
4. *Sa*   2, 3, MP
5. (∃*x*)*Sx* 4, EG

There are no restrictions on existential generalization, and the operation can be performed when the instantial letter is either a constant (as in the Bocelli example) or a variable. As an instance of the latter, consider the following sequence:

1. $(x)(Px \supset Qx)$
2. $(x)Px$ / $(\exists x)Qx$
3. $Py \supset Qy$ 1, UI
4. Py 2, UI
5. Qy 3, 4, MP
6. $(\exists x)Qx$ 5, EG

Line 5 states in effect that everything in the universe is a Q. From this, the much weaker conclusion follows (line 6) that *something* is a Q. If you should wonder how an existential conclusion can be drawn from universal premises, the answer is that predicate logic assumes that at least one thing exists in the universe. Hence, line 2, which asserts that everything in the universe is a P, entails that at least one thing is a P. Without this assumption, universal instantiation in line 4 would not be possible.

We may now construct a definition of generalization that covers both varieties. *Generalization* in the inclusive sense is an operation that consists in (1) introducing a quantifier immediately prior to a statement, a statement function, or another quantifier, and (2) replacing one or more occurrences of a certain instantial letter in the statement or statement function with the same variable that appears in the quantifier. For universal generalization, *all* occurrences of the instantial letter must be replaced with the variable in the quantifier, and for existential generalization, *at least one* of the instantial letters must be replaced with the variable in the quantifier. Thus, both of the following cases of existential generalization are valid (although the one on the left is by far the more common version):

1. $Fa \cdot Ga$
2. $(\exists x)(Fx \cdot Gx)$ 1, EG

1. $Fa \cdot Ga$
2. $(\exists x)(Fx \cdot Ga)$ 1, EG

On the other hand, only one of the following cases of universal generalization is valid:

1. $Fx \supset Gx$
2. $(y)(Fy \supset Gy)$ 1, UG

1. $Fx \supset Gx$
2. $(y)(Fy \supset Gx)$ 1, UG (invalid)

The inference on the right is invalid because the x in Gx was not replaced with the variable in the quantifier (that is, y).

Of course, it may happen that the instantial letter is the same as the variable that appears in the quantifier. Thus, the operation "Gx, therefore $(x)Gx$" counts as a generalization. Cases of generalization where a quantifier is introduced prior to another quantifier will be presented in Section 8.6.

The need for **existential instantiation** can be illustrated through the following argument:

All attorneys are college graduates.
Some attorneys are golfers.
Therefore, some golfers are college graduates.

The symbolic formulation is as follows:

1. $(x)(Ax \supset Cx)$
2. $(\exists x)(Ax \cdot Gx)$ / $(\exists x)(Gx \cdot Cx)$

If both quantifiers can be removed, the conclusion can be derived via simplification, *modus ponens*, and conjunction. The universal quantifier can be removed by universal instantiation, but to remove the existential quantifier we need existential instantiation. Line 2 states that there is *something* that is both an *A* and a *G*. Existential instantiation consists in giving this something a *name*, for example, "David." We will call this name an "existential name" because it is obtained through existential instantiation. The completed proof is as follows:

1. $(x)(Ax \supset Cx)$
2. $(\exists x)(Ax \cdot Gx)$ / $(\exists x)(Gx \cdot Cx)$
3. $Ad \cdot Gd$ 2, EI
4. $Ad \supset Cd$ 1, UI
5. Ad 3, Simp
6. Cd 4, 5, MP
7. $Gd \cdot Ad$ 3, Com
8. Gd 7, Simp
9. $Gd \cdot Cd$ 6, 8, Conj
10. $(\exists x)(Gx \cdot Cx)$ 9, EG

Examination of this proof reveals an immediate restriction that must be placed on existential instantiation. The name that we have assigned to the particular something in line 2 that is both an *A* and a *G* is a hypothetical name. It would be a mistake to conclude that this something really has that name. Accordingly, we must introduce a restriction that prevents us from ending the proof with some line that includes the letter *d*. If, for example, the proof were ended at line 9, we would be concluding that the something that is a *G* and a *C* really does have the name *d*. This, of course, would not be legitimate, because *d* is an arbitrary name introduced into the proof for mere convenience. To prevent such a mistake, we require that the name selected for existential instantiation not appear to the right of the slanted line adjacent to the last premise that indicates the conclusion to be derived. Since the last line in the proof must be identical to this line, such a restriction prevents us from ending the proof with a line that contains the existential name.

    Further examination of this proof indicates another important restriction on existential instantiation. Notice that the line involving existential instantiation is listed before the line involving universal instantiation. There is a reason for this. If the order were reversed, the existential instantiation step would rest on the illicit assumption that the something that is both an *A* and a *G* has the *same* name as the name used in the earlier universal instantiation step. In other words, it would involve the assumption that the something that is both an *A* and a *G* is the very same something named in the line $Ad \supset Cd$. Of course, no such assumption is legitimate. To keep this mistake from happening, we introduce the restriction that the name introduced by existential instantiation be a new name not occurring earlier in the proof sequence. The following defective proof illustrates what can happen if this restriction is violated:

8

1. $(\exists x)(Fx \cdot Ax)$
2. $(\exists x)(Fx \cdot Ox)$ / $(\exists x)(Ax \cdot Ox)$
3. $Fb \cdot Ab$ 1, EI
4. $Fb \cdot Ob$ 2, EI (invalid)
5. $Ab \cdot Fb$ 3, Com
6. Ab 5, Simp
7. $Ob \cdot Fb$ 4, Com
8. Ob 7, Simp
9. $Ab \cdot Ob$ 6, 8, Conj
10. $(\exists x)(Ax \cdot Ox)$ 9, EG

To see that this proof is indeed defective, let *F* stand for fruits, *A* for apples, and *O* for oranges. The argument that results is:

> Some fruits are apples.
> Some fruits are oranges.
> Therefore, some apples are oranges.

Since the premises are true and the conclusion false, the argument is clearly invalid. The defect in the proof occurs on line 4. This line asserts that the something that is both an *F* and an *O* is the very same something that is both an *F* and an *A*. In other words, the restriction that the name introduced by existential instantiation be a new name not occurring earlier in the proof is violated.

The first restriction on existential instantiation requires that the existential name not occur in the line that indicates the conclusion to be derived, and the second restriction requires that this name be a new name that has not occurred earlier in the proof. These two restrictions can easily be combined into a single restriction that requires that the name introduced by existential instantiation be a new name that has not occurred in *any* previous line, including the line adjacent to the last premise that indicates the conclusion to be derived.

One further restriction that affects all four of these rules of inference requires that the rules be applied only to *whole lines* in a proof. The following sequence illustrates a violation of this restriction:

1. $(x)Px \supset (x)Qx$
2. $Py \supset Qy$ 1, UI (invalid)

In line 2 universal instantiation is applied to both the antecedent and consequent of the first line. To derive line 2 validly, the first line would have to read $(x)(Px \supset Qx)$. With this final restriction in mind, the four new rules of inference, developed on the previous pages, may now be summarized. In the formulation that follows, the symbols $\mathscr{F}x$ and $\mathscr{F}y$ represent any statement function—that is, any symbolic arrangement containing individual variables, such as $Ax \supset Bx$, $Cy \supset (Dy \vee Ey)$, or $Gz \cdot Hz$. The symbol $\mathscr{F}a$ represents any **statement**; that is, any symbolic arrangement containing individual constants (or names), such as $Ac \supset Bc$, $Cm \supset (Dm \vee Em)$, or $Gw \cdot Hw$. And the symbol $\mathscr{F}$ is a predicate variable that represents any predicate such as *F*, *G*, or *H*.[*]

---

[*]*Some textbooks use Greek letters such as φ (phi), χ (chi), and ψ (psi) in the place of $\mathscr{F}$ to express these and other rules.*

1. **Universal instantiation (UI):**

$$\frac{(x)\mathcal{F}x}{\mathcal{F}y} \qquad \frac{(x)\mathcal{F}x}{\mathcal{F}a}$$

2. **Universal generalization (UG):**

$$\frac{\mathcal{F}y}{(x)\mathcal{F}x} \qquad \text{not allowed:} \qquad \frac{\mathcal{F}a}{(x)\mathcal{F}x}$$

3. **Existential instantiation (EI):**

$$\frac{(\exists x)\mathcal{F}x}{\mathcal{F}a} \qquad \text{not allowed:} \qquad \frac{(\exists x)\mathcal{F}x}{\mathcal{F}y}$$

Restriction: The existential name *a* must be a new name that does not appear in any previous line (including the conclusion line).

4. **Existential generalization (EG):**

$$\frac{\mathcal{F}a}{(\exists x)\mathcal{F}x} \qquad \frac{\mathcal{F}y}{(\exists x)\mathcal{F}x}$$

The *not allowed* version of universal generalization recalls the already familiar fact that generalization is not possible when the instantial letter is a constant. In other words, the mere fact that the individual *a* is an $\mathcal{F}$ is not sufficient to allow us to conclude that everything in the universe is an $\mathcal{F}$. At present this is the only restriction needed for universal generalization. In Sections 8.4 and 8.6, however, two additional restrictions will be introduced. The *not allowed* version of existential instantiation merely recalls the fact that this operation is a naming process. Because variables (*x*, *y*, and *z*) are not names, they cannot be used as instantial letters in existential instantiation.

Let us now investigate some applications of these rules. Consider the following proof:

1. $(x)(Hx \supset Ix)$
2. $(x)(Ix \supset Hx)$ / $(x)(Hx \equiv Ix)$
3. $Hx \supset Ix$ 1, UI
4. $Ix \supset Hx$ 2, UI
5. $(Hx \supset Ix) \cdot (Ix \supset Hx)$ 3, 4, Conj
6. $Hx \equiv Ix$ 5, Equiv
7. $(x)(Hx \equiv Ix)$ 6, UG

Because we want to perform universal generalization on the last line of the proof, we instantiate lines 1 and 2 using a variable, not a constant. Notice that the variable selected for lines 3 and 4 is the same letter that occurs in lines 1 and 2. While a new letter (*y* or *z*) *could* have been selected, this is never necessary in such a step. It *is* necessary, however, since we want to combine lines 3 and 4, that the *same* variable be selected in deriving these lines. Another example:

1. $(x)[(Ax \lor Bx) \supset Cx]$
2. $(\exists x)Ax$ / $(\exists x)Cx$
3. Am 2, EI
4. $(Am \lor Bm) \supset Cm$ 1, UI
5. $Am \lor Bm$ 3, Add
6. Cm 4, 5, MP
7. $(\exists x)Cx$ 6, EG

In conformity with the restriction on existential instantiation, the EI step is performed *before* the UI step. The same letter is then selected in the UI step as was used in the EI step. In line 5, *Bm* is joined disjunctively via addition to *Am*. This rule applies in predicate logic in basically the same way that it does in propositional logic. Any statement or statement function we choose can be joined disjunctively to a given line.

Another example:

1. $(\exists x)Kx \supset (x)(Lx \supset Mx)$
2. $Kc \cdot Lc$ / Mc
3. Kc 2, Simp
4. $(\exists x)Kx$ 3, EG
5. $(x)(Lx \supset Mx)$ 1, 4, MP
6. $Lc \supset Mc$ 5, UI
7. $Lc \cdot Kc$ 2, Com
8. Lc 7, Simp
9. Mc 6, 8, MP

Since the instantiation (and generalization) rules must be applied to whole lines, it is impossible to instantiate line 1. The only strategy that can be followed is to use some other line to derive the antecedent of this line and then derive the consequent via *modus ponens*. Once the consequent is derived (line 5), it is instantiated using the same letter that appears in line 2.

The next example incorporates all four of the instantiation and generalization rules:

1. $(x)(Px \supset Qx) \supset (\exists x)(Rx \cdot Sx)$
2. $(x)(Px \supset Sx) \cdot (x)(Sx \supset Qx)$ / $(\exists x)Sx$
3. $(x)(Px \supset Sx)$ 2, Simp
4. $(x)(Sx \supset Qx) \cdot (x)(Px \supset Sx)$ 2, Com
5. $(x)(Sx \supset Qx)$ 4, Simp
6. $Py \supset Sy$ 3, UI
7. $Sy \supset Qy$ 5, UI
8. $Py \supset Qy$ 6, 7, HS
9. $(x)(Px \supset Qx)$ 8, UG
10. $(\exists x)(Rx \cdot Sx)$ 1, 9, MP
11. $Ra \cdot Sa$ 10, EI
12. $Sa \cdot Ra$ 11, Com
13. Sa 12, Simp
14. $(\exists x)Sx$ 13, EG

As with the previous example, line 1 cannot be instantiated. To instantiate the two conjuncts in line 2, they must first be separated (lines 3 and 5). Because UG is to be used in line 9, lines 3 and 5 are instantiated using a variable. On the other hand, a constant is used to instantiate line 10 because the statement in question is a particular statement.

Another example:

1. [(∃x)Ax • (∃x)Bx] ⊃ Cj
2. (∃x)(Ax • Dx)
3. (∃x)(Bx • Ex)   / Cj
4. Am • Dm   2, EI
5. Bn • En   3, EI
6. Am   4, Simp
7. Bn   5, Simp
8. (∃x)Ax   6, EG
9. (∃x)Bx   7, EG
10. (∃x)Ax • (∃x)Bx   8, 9, Conj
11. Cj   1, 10, MP

When line 2 is instantiated (line 4), a letter other than *j*, which appears in line 1, is selected. Then, when line 3 is instantiated (line 5), another new letter is selected. The conclusion is derived, as in earlier examples, via *modus ponens* by deriving the antecedent of line 1.

The following examples illustrate *invalid* or *improper* applications of the instantiation and generalization rules:

1. Fy ⊃ Gy
---
2. (x)(Fx ⊃ Gy)   1, UG   (invalid—every instance of *y* must be replaced with *x*)

1. (x)Fx ⊃ Ga
---
2. Fx ⊃ Ga   1, UI   (invalid—instantiation can be applied only to whole lines)

1. (x)Fx ⊃ (x)Gx
---
2. Fx ⊃ Gx   1, UI   (invalid—instantiation can be applied only to whole lines)

1. Fc
2. (∃x)Gx
---
3. Gc   2, EI   (invalid—*c* appears in line 1)

1. Fm ⊃ Gm
---
2. (x)(Fx ⊃ Gx)   1, UG   (invalid—the instantial letter must be a variable; *m* is a constant)

1. (∃x)Fx
2. (∃x)Gx
---
3. Fe   1, EI
4. Ge   2, EI   (invalid—*e* appears in line 3)

1. Fs • Gs
---
2. (∃x)Fx • Gs   1, EG   (improper—generalization can be applied only to whole lines)

1. ~(x)Fx
---
2. ~Fy   1, UI   (invalid—lines involving negated quantifiers cannot be instantiated; see Section 8.3)

I. Use the eighteen rules of inference to derive the conclusions of the following symbolized arguments. Do not use either conditional proof or indirect proof.

★(1) 1. $(x)(Ax \supset Bx)$
   2. $(x)(Bx \supset Cx)$ / $(x)(Ax \supset Cx)$

(2) 1. $(x)(Bx \supset Cx)$
   2. $(\exists x)(Ax \cdot Bx)$ / $(\exists x)(Ax \cdot Cx)$

(3) 1. $(x)(Ax \supset Bx)$
   2. $\sim Bm$ / $(\exists x)\sim Ax$

★(4) 1. $(x)(Ax \supset Bx)$
   2. $(y)(Ay \vee \sim By)$ / $(x)(Ax \equiv Bx)$

(5) 1. $(x)[Ax \supset (Bx \vee Cx)]$
   2. $Ag \cdot \sim Bg$ / Cg

(6) 1. $(x)[(Ax \vee Bx) \supset Cx]$
   2. $(\exists y)(Ay \cdot Dy)$ / $(\exists y)Cy$

★(7) 1. $(x)[Jx \supset (Kx \cdot Lx)]$
   2. $(\exists y)\sim Ky$ / $(\exists z)\sim Jz$

(8) 1. $(x)[Ax \supset (Bx \vee Cx)]$
   2. $(\exists x)(Ax \cdot \sim Cx)$ / $(\exists x)Bx$

(9) 1. $(x)(Ax \supset Bx)$
   2. $Am \cdot An$ / $Bm \cdot Bn$

★(10) 1. $(x)(Ax \supset Bx)$
   2. $Am \vee An$ / $Bm \vee Bn$

(11) 1. $(x)(Bx \vee Ax)$
   2. $(x)(Bx \supset Ax)$ / $(x)Ax$

(12) 1. $(\exists x)Ax \supset (y)(By \vee \sim Ay)$
   2. An / $(\exists y)By$

★(13) 1. $(x)[(Ax \cdot Bx) \supset Cx]$
   2. $(\exists x)(Bx \cdot \sim Cx)$ / $(\exists x)\sim Ax$

(14) 1. $(x)(Ax \supset Bx)$
   2. $(x)(Cx \supset Dx)$
   3. $Ae \vee Ce$ / $(\exists x)(Bx \vee Dx)$

(15) 1. $(\exists x)Ax \supset (x)(Bx \supset Cx)$
   2. $Am \cdot Bm$ / Cm

MindTap· Complete exercises online for immediate feedback.

★(16) 1. $(\exists x)Ax \supset (x)Bx$
2. $(\exists x)Cx \supset (\exists x)Dx$
3. $An \cdot Cn$ / $(\exists x)(Bx \cdot Dx)$

(17) 1. $(x)(Ax \cdot Bx)$
2. $Cr \vee \sim(x)Bx$ / $(\exists x)(Cx \cdot Ax)$

(18) 1. $(x)[Ax \supset (Bx \equiv Cx)]$
2. $An \cdot Am$
3. $Cn \cdot \sim Cm$ / $Bn \cdot \sim Bm$

★(19) 1. $(\exists x)Ax \supset (x)(Cx \supset Bx)$
2. $(\exists x)(Ax \vee Bx)$
3. $(x)(Bx \supset Ax)$ / $(x)(Cx \supset Ax)$

(20) 1. $(\exists x)Ax \supset (x)(Bx \supset Cx)$
2. $(\exists x)Dx \supset (\exists x)\sim Cx$
3. $(\exists x)(Ax \cdot Dx)$ / $(\exists x)\sim Bx$

(21) 1. $(\exists x)(Ax \cdot Bx) \supset (x)(Cx \cdot Dx)$
2. $(\exists x)Ax \supset (x)(Bx \cdot Cx)$
3. Ae / $(\exists x)(Dx \cdot Bx)$

★(22) 1. $(x)(Ax \cdot \sim Bx)$
2. $An \supset [\sim(\exists x)Cx \supset Bc]$
3. $Am \supset (x)(Cx \supset Dx)$ / $(\exists x)Dx$

(23) 1. $(x)(Ax \cdot Bx)$
2. $(x)Ax \supset (Ce \vee \sim Be)$
3. $(x)Bx \supset [(\exists x)Cx \supset (Dn \vee \sim An)]$ / $(\exists x)Dx$

(24) 1. $(\exists x)Ax \supset (x)[(Ax \vee Ex) \supset Dx]$
2. $(\exists x)Dx \supset (x)[Dx \supset (Cx \vee \sim Bx)]$
3. $An \cdot Bn$ / $(\exists x)Cx$

★(25) 1. $(\exists x)Ax \supset (x)(Ax \supset Bx)$
2. $(\exists x)Cx \supset (x)\sim(Dx \cdot Bx)$
3. $(\exists x)(Ax \cdot Cx)$ / $(\exists x)\sim Dx$

II. Translate the following arguments into symbolic form. Then use the eighteen rules of inference to derive the conclusion of each. Do not use conditional or indirect proof.

★1. Oranges are sweet. Also, oranges are fragrant. Therefore, oranges are sweet and fragrant. (O, S, F)

2. Tomatoes are vegetables. Therefore, the tomatoes in the garden are vegetables. (T, V, G)

3. Apples and pears grow on trees. Therefore, apples grow on trees. (A, P, G)

★4. Carrots are vegetables and peaches are fruit. Furthermore, there are carrots and peaches in the garden. Therefore, there are vegetables and fruit in the garden. (C, V, P, F, G)

5. Beans and peas are legumes. There are no legumes in the garden. Therefore, there are no beans in the garden. (B, P, L, G)

6. There are some cucumbers in the garden. If there are any cucumbers, there are some pumpkins in the garden. All pumpkins are vegetables. Therefore, there are some vegetables in the garden. (C, G, P, V)

★7. All gardeners are industrious people. Furthermore, any person who is industrious is respected. Therefore, since Arthur and Catherine are gardeners, it follows that they are respected. (G, I, P, R)

8. Some huckleberries are ripe. Furthermore, some boysenberries are sweet. If there are any huckleberries, then the boysenberries are edible if they are sweet. Therefore, some boysenberries are edible. (H, R, B, S, E)

9. If there are any ripe watermelons, then the caretakers performed well. Furthermore, if there are any large watermelons, then whoever performed well will get a bonus. There are some large, ripe watermelons. Therefore, the caretakers will get a bonus. (R, W, C, P, L, B)

★10. If the artichokes in the kitchen are ripe, then the guests will be surprised. Furthermore, if the artichokes in the kitchen are flavorful, then the guests will be pleased. The artichokes in the kitchen are ripe and flavorful. Therefore, the guests will be surprised and pleased. (A, K, R, G, S, F, P)

III. The following dialogue contains nine arguments. Translate each into symbolic form and then use the eighteen rules of inference to derive the conclusion of each. Some of them are quite challenging.

Where's the Beef?

"Have you decided what to order?" Paul says to Mindy, as he folds his menu and puts it on the table.

"I think I'll have the tofu stir-fry," she replies. "And you?"

"I'll have the rib steak," Paul says. "You know the rib steak is really good here, and so is the pork tenderloin."

"I'm a vegetarian," she says.

"Oh," Paul says. He smiles sheepishly.

Mindy smiles too. "First date," she says.

"Yeah," says Paul. "What made you decide to become a vegetarian?"

"For one thing," Mindy says, "I think a vegetarian diet is healthier. People who eat meat increase their intake of cholesterol and carcinogens. Those who increase their intake of cholesterol run a higher risk of heart attack, and those who increase their intake of carcinogens run a higher risk of cancer. Anyone who runs a higher risk of heart attack and cancer is less healthy. Thus, people who eat meat are less healthy.

"I might add that if people who eat meat are less healthy, then if parents are responsible, then they will refrain from feeding meat to children. All parents love their children, and if they do, then they are responsible. But if parents refrain from feeding meat to children, then children will grow up to be vegetarians. And if that happens, then nobody will eat meat in the future. Thus, we can look forward to a future where everyone is a vegetarian."

"Well, I won't hold my breath on that," Paul says, as he offers Mindy a slice of bread from the basket on the table. "If children and teenagers fail to eat meat, then they become deficient in zinc. And if children become deficient in zinc, then they risk a weakened immune system. And if that happens, then they are less healthy. Also, if elderly people fail to eat meat, then they become deficient in iron. And if elderly people become deficient in iron, then they risk becoming anemic, and if that happens, they are less healthy. Therefore, if children and elderly people fail to eat meat, then they are less healthy."

Mindy smiles. "That's what zinc tablets and iron supplements are for," she says. Anyway, there are also moral reasons for being a vegetarian. Consider this. Animals are sentient beings—they feel pain, fear, and joy—and they have an interest in preserving their lives. If animals are sentient, then if humans cause animals to suffer, then they act immorally. And if animals have an interest in preserving their lives, then if humans exploit animals, then they act immorally. But if humans kill animals for food, then they cause animals to suffer or they exploit them. Therefore, if humans kill animals for food, then they act immorally."

"I agree with you that animals should not be made to suffer," Paul responds. "But if animals are raised under humane conditions, and some of them are, then they will not be caused to feel pain or distress. And if animals are not caused to feel pain, then we are morally justified in eating them. Thus, we are morally justified in eating some animals."

"I disagree," says Mindy.

"That's because you think that animals have rights," Paul says. "If animals have rights, then they have moral judgment. And if animals have moral judgment, then they respect the rights of other animals. But every animal pursues its own self-interest to the exclusion of other animals, and if that's so, then it does not respect the rights of other animals. Therefore, animals have no moral judgment and they also have no rights."

"Well," Mindy replies, "by that line of reasoning infants and mentally challenged adults have no rights. But everyone recognizes that they do have rights. And if infants have rights, then some people who lack the capacity for moral judgment have rights. But if this is true, then animals have rights, and if they do, then surely they have the right to life. But if animals have the right to life, then if humans are moral, then they must respect that right and they cannot kill animals for food. Thus, if humans are moral, they cannot kill animals for food."

"The question of infants and mentally challenged adults raises an interesting point," Paul says. "I think what it comes down to is this: Something is considered to have rights if and only if it looks human. Infants and mentally challenged adults look human, so they are considered to have rights. But animals do not look human, so they are not considered to have rights."

"That sounds awfully arbitrary," says Mindy. "But I think what it really comes down to is power. Something is considered to have rights if and only if it has as much power as humans. Animals do not have as much power as humans, so animals are not considered to have rights. But that seems terribly wrong to me. It shouldn't be a question of power. Anyway, now that our food has arrived, how's your steak?"

Paul takes a bite. "It's great," he says. "And how's your stir-fry?"

"Great," Mindy says. She laughs. "And so is my conscience."

IV. Create two valid arguments relating to national parks. Then translate them into the symbolism of predicate logic and use the rules of inference to derive the conclusion of each.

MindTap Master concepts and improve outcomes with Aplia, at the end of the chapter, in the Aplia folder.

8.3 Quantifier Negation Rule

HOW LOGICAL ARE YOU? Given the statement "Everything is a surprise," does this mean the same thing as "It is not the case that something is not a surprise"? Given the statement "Something is a surprise," does this mean the same thing as "It is not the case that everything is not a surprise"?

Find the answer on MindTap.

The rules of inference developed thus far are not sufficient to derive the conclusion of every argument in predicate logic. For instance, consider the following:

$$\sim(\exists x)(Px \bullet \sim Qx)$$
$$\underline{\sim(x)(\sim Rx \vee Qx)}$$
$$(\exists x)\sim Px$$

Both premises have tildes preceding the quantifiers. As long as they remain, neither statement can be instantiated; and if these statements cannot be instantiated, the conclusion cannot be derived. What is needed is a rule that will allow us to remove the negation signs. This rule, which we will proceed to develop now, is called the **quantifier negation rule**.

As a basis for developing the quantifier negation rule, consider the following statements:

Everything is beautiful.
It is not the case that everything is beautiful.
Something is beautiful.
It is not the case that something is beautiful.

You should be able to see that these statements are equivalent in meaning to the following statements, respectively:

It is not the case that something is not beautiful.
Something is not beautiful.
It is not the case that everything is not beautiful.
Everything is not beautiful.

Alfred North Whitehead 1861–1947
Bertrand Russell 1872–1970

Alfred North Whitehead and Bertrand Russell collaborated in writing *Principia Mathematica*, which is generally considered the most important logical endeavor of the twentieth century. It represents an attempt to reduce all of mathematics to logic. Published in three volumes between 1910 and 1913, the manuscript was so huge that it required a "four wheeler" to transport it to the printer. The combined work comprises over 1,900 pages, nearly all of them filled with highly complex and technical notation. The American philosopher Willard Van Orman Quine described the *Principia* as "one of the great intellectual monuments of all time."

Whitehead was born the son of an Anglican minister in Ramsgate, England. He entered Trinity College, Cambridge, with a scholarship in mathematics, and after graduating, he was elected a Fellow of Trinity. While there he published *A Treatise on Universal Algebra*, for which he was elected to the prestigious Royal Society. Whitehead's most distinguished student at Trinity was Bertrand Russell. After Russell graduated he and Whitehead became close friends. At age thirty-one Whitehead married Evelyn Wade, and they had three children, two sons and a daughter.

In 1910 Whitehead left Cambridge for London, where he taught at University College London and later at the Imperial College of Science and Technology. While in London he wrote books in the areas of physics and the philosophy of science. Then, in 1924 he was appointed professor of philosophy at Harvard University, where he wrote *Process and Reality*. The book became a cornerstone of what would later be called process philosophy and process theology. Whitehead died at age eighty-six in Cambridge, Massachusetts.

Bertrand Russell, one of the world's best-known intellectuals, was born in Wales to aristocratic parents. Both died when he was very young, and although they had requested that their son be raised an agnostic, the young Russell was brought up by a staunchly Victorian grandmother who fed him a steady dose of religion. As he grew older he became an atheist (or at best an agnostic) who considered religion little better than superstition. At Trinity College Russell studied mathematics and philosophy and befriended Ludwig Wittgenstein and G. E. Moore, as well as Whitehead. After graduating he was elected fellow of Trinity College and later, fellow of the Royal Society. He was extremely prolific as a writer, and in 1950 he won the Nobel Prize in literature.

Russell was married four times, engaged in numerous love affairs with prominent women, was imprisoned for six months for opposing conscription in World War I, and was later imprisoned for opposing nuclear weapons. A staunch supporter of birth control, population control, democracy, free trade, and world government, he opposed communism, imperialism, and every form of mind control. He died at age ninety-seven at his home in Wales.

If we generalize these English equivalencies symbolically, we obtain:

$$
\begin{array}{lll}
(x)\mathscr{F}x & :: & \sim(\exists x)\sim\mathscr{F}x \\
\sim(x)\mathscr{F}x & :: & (\exists x)\sim\mathscr{F}x \\
(\exists x)\mathscr{F}x & :: & \sim(x)\sim\mathscr{F}x \\
\sim(\exists x)\mathscr{F}x & :: & (x)\sim\mathscr{F}x
\end{array}
$$

These four expressions constitute the quantifier negation rule (QN). Since they are stated as logical equivalences, they apply to parts of lines as well as to whole lines. They can be summarized as follows:

> One type of quantifier can be replaced by the other type if and only if immediately before and after the new quantifier:
>
> 1. Tilde operators that were originally present are deleted.
> 2. Tilde operators that were not originally present are inserted.

To see how the quantifier negation rule is applied, let us return to the argument at the beginning of this section. The proof is as follows:

1.	$\sim(\exists x)(Px \cdot \sim Qx)$	
2.	$\sim(x)(\sim Rx \lor Qx)$	/ $(\exists x)\sim Px$
3.	$(x)\sim(Px \cdot \sim Qx)$	1, QN
4.	$(\exists x)\sim(\sim Rx \lor Qx)$	2, QN
5.	$\sim(\sim Ra \lor Qa)$	4, EI
6.	$\sim(Pa \cdot \sim Qa)$	3, UI
7.	$\sim\sim Ra \cdot \sim Qa$	5, DM
8.	$\sim Pa \lor \sim\sim Qa$	6, DM
9.	$\sim Pa \lor Qa$	8, DN
10.	$\sim Qa \cdot \sim\sim Ra$	7, Com
11.	$\sim Qa$	10, Simp
12.	$Qa \lor \sim Pa$	9, Com
13.	$\sim Pa$	11, 12, DS
14.	$(\exists x)\sim Px$	13, EG

Before either line 1 or line 2 can be instantiated, the tilde operators preceding the quantifiers must be removed. In accordance with the quantifier negation rule, tilde operators are introduced immediately after the new quantifiers in the expressions on lines 3 and 4.

Another example:

1.	$(\exists x)(Hx \cdot Gx) \supset (x)Ix$	
2.	$\sim Im$	/ $(x)(Hx \supset \sim Gx)$
3.	$(\exists x)\sim Ix$	2, EG
4.	$\sim(x)Ix$	3, QN
5.	$\sim(\exists x)(Hx \cdot Gx)$	1, 4, MT
6.	$(x)\sim(Hx \cdot Gx)$	5, QN
7.	$(x)(\sim Hx \lor \sim Gx)$	6, DM
8.	$(x)(Hx \supset \sim Gx)$	7, Impl

The statement that m is not an I (line 2) intuitively implies that not everything is an I (line 4); but existential generalization and quantifier negation are needed to get the desired result. Notice that lines 7 and 8 are derived via De Morgan's rule and material implication, even though the quantifier is still attached. Since these rules are rules of replacement, they apply to parts of lines as well as to whole lines. The following example illustrates the same point with respect to the quantifier negation rule:

1. $(\exists x)Jx \supset {\sim}(\exists x)Kx$
2. $(x){\sim}Kx \supset (x){\sim}Lx$ / $(\exists x)Jx \supset {\sim}(\exists x)Lx$
3. $(\exists x)Jx \supset (x){\sim}Kx$ 1, QN
4. $(\exists x)Jx \supset (x){\sim}Lx$ 2, 3, HS
5. $(\exists x)Jx \supset {\sim}(\exists x)Lx$ 4, QN

The quantifier negation rule is applied to only the consequent of line 1, yielding line 3. Similarly, the quantifier negation rule is then applied to only the consequent of line 4, yielding line 5.

EXERCISE 8.3

I. Use the quantifier negation rule together with the eighteen rules of inference to derive the conclusions of the following symbolized arguments. Do not use either conditional proof or indirect proof.

★(1) 1. $(x)Ax \supset (\exists x)Bx$
      2. $(x){\sim}Bx$ / $(\exists x){\sim}Ax$

(2) 1. $(\exists x){\sim}Ax \lor (\exists x){\sim}Bx$
      2. $(x)Bx$ / ${\sim}(x)Ax$

(3) 1. ${\sim}(\exists x)Ax$ / $(x)(Ax \supset Bx)$

★(4) 1. $(\exists x)Ax \lor (\exists x)(Bx \cdot Cx)$
      2. ${\sim}(\exists x)Bx$ / $(\exists x)Ax$

(5) 1. $(x)(Ax \cdot Bx) \lor (x)(Cx \cdot Dx)$
      2. ${\sim}(x)Dx$ / $(x)Bx$

(6) 1. $(\exists x){\sim}Ax \supset (x)(Bx \supset Cx)$
      2. ${\sim}(x)(Ax \lor Cx)$ / ${\sim}(x)Bx$

★(7) 1. $(x)(Ax \supset Bx)$
      2. ${\sim}(x)Cx \lor (x)Ax$
      3. ${\sim}(x)Bx$ / $(\exists x){\sim}Cx$

(8) 1. $(x)Ax \supset (\exists x){\sim}Bx$
      2. ${\sim}(x)Bx \supset (\exists x){\sim}Cx$ / $(x)Cx \supset (\exists x){\sim}Ax$

(9) 1. $(\exists x)(Ax \vee Bx) \supset (x)Cx$
2. $(\exists x)\sim Cx$ / $\sim(\exists x)Ax$

★(10) 1. $\sim(\exists x)(Ax \cdot \sim Bx)$
2. $\sim(\exists x)(Bx \cdot \sim Cx)$ / $(x)(Ax \supset Cx)$

(11) 1. $\sim(\exists x)(Ax \cdot \sim Bx)$
2. $\sim(\exists x)(Ax \cdot \sim Cx)$ / $(x)[Ax \supset (Bx \cdot Cx)]$

(12) 1. $(x)[(Ax \cdot Bx) \supset Cx]$
2. $\sim(x)(Ax \supset Cx)$ / $\sim(x)Bx$

★(13) 1. $(x)(Ax \cdot \sim Bx) \supset (\exists x)Cx$
2. $\sim(\exists x)(Cx \vee Bx)$ / $\sim(x)Ax$

(14) 1. $(\exists x)\sim Ax \supset (x)\sim Bx$
2. $(\exists x)\sim Ax \supset (\exists x)Bx$
3. $(x)(Ax \supset Cx)$ / $(x)Cx$

(15) 1. $\sim(\exists x)(Ax \vee Bx)$
2. $(\exists x)Cx \supset (\exists x)Ax$
3. $(\exists x)Dx \supset (\exists x)Bx$ / $\sim(\exists x)(Cx \vee Dx)$

★(16) 1. $(\exists x)(Ax \cdot Bx) \supset (x)(Cx \cdot Dx)$
2. $(x)[(Ax \vee Ex) \cdot (Bx \vee Fx)]$
3. $\sim(x)Dx$ / $(x)(Ex \vee Fx)$

(17) 1. $(\exists x)(Ax \cdot Bx) \vee (\exists x)(Cx \vee Dx)$
2. $(\exists x)(Ax \vee Cx) \supset (x)Ex$
3. $\sim En$ / $(\exists x)Dx$

(18) 1. $(\exists x)Ax \supset [(\exists x)Bx \vee (x)Cx]$
2. $(\exists x)(Ax \cdot \sim Cx)$
3. $\sim(x)Cx \supset [(x)Fx \supset (x)\sim Bx]$ / $(\exists x)\sim Fx$

★(19) 1. $(\exists x)(Ax \cdot Bx) \supset (x)(Bx \supset Cx)$
2. $Bn \cdot \sim Cn$ / $\sim(x)Ax$

(20) 1. $(\exists x)Ax \supset \sim(\exists x)(Bx \cdot Ax)$
2. $\sim(x)Bx \supset \sim(\exists x)(Ex \cdot \sim Bx)$
3. An / $\sim(x)Ex$

II. Translate the following arguments into symbolic form. Then use the quantifier negation rule and the eighteen rules of inference to derive the conclusion of each. Do not use either conditional proof or indirect proof.

★1. If all the physicians are either hematologists or neurologists, then there are no cardiologists. But Dr. Frank is a cardiologist. Therefore, some physicians are not neurologists. (P, H, N, C)

2. Either Dr. Adams is an internist or all the pathologists are internists. But it is not the case that there are any internists. Therefore, Dr. Adams is not a pathologist. (I, P)

3. If some surgeons are allergists, then some psychiatrists are radiologists. But no psychiatrists are radiologists. Therefore, no surgeons are allergists. (*S*, *A*, *P*, *R*)

★4. Either some general practitioners are pediatricians or some surgeons are endocrinologists. But it is not the case that there are any endocrinologists. Therefore, there are some pediatricians. (*G*, *P*, *S*, *E*)

5. All physicians who did not attend medical school are incompetent. It is not the case, however, that some physicians are incompetent. Therefore, all physicians have attended medical school. (*P*, *A*, *I*)

6. It is not the case that some internists are not physicians. Furthermore, it is not the case that some physicians are not doctors of medicine. Therefore, all internists are doctors of medicine. (*I*, *P*, *D*)

★7. All pathologists are specialists and all internists are generalists. Therefore, since it is not the case that some specialists are generalists, it is not the case that some pathologists are internists. (*P*, *S*, *I*, *G*)

8. If some obstetricians are not gynecologists, then some hematologists are radiologists. But it is not the case that there are any hematologists or gynecologists. Therefore, it is not the case that there are any obstetricians. (*O*, *G*, *H*, *R*)

9. All poorly trained allergists and dermatologists are untrustworthy specialists. It is not the case, however, that some specialists are untrustworthy. Therefore, it is not the case that some dermatologists are poorly trained. (*P*, *A*, *D*, *U*, *S*)

★10. It is not the case that some physicians are either on the golf course or in the hospital. All of the neurologists are physicians in the hospital. Either some physicians are cardiologists or some physicians are neurologists. Therefore, some cardiologists are not on the golf course. (*P*, *G*, *H*, *N*, *C*)

III. Create two valid arguments relating to vacations. At least one of the premises of each argument must begin with the words "It is not the case that. . . ." Then translate the arguments into the language of predicate logic and derive the conclusion of each.

MindTap Master concepts and improve outcomes with Aplia, at the end of the chapter, in the Aplia folder.

8.4   Conditional and Indirect Proof

HOW LOGICAL ARE YOU? While musing about the benefits of exercise, the following thoughts come to mind: People who exercise are healthier. Healthier people are more engaged. More-engaged people are more successful. People who are more successful feel better about themselves and those people are more respected by others. What single conditional statement sums up this train of thoughts?

Find the answer on MindTap.

Many arguments with conclusions that are either difficult or impossible to derive by the conventional method can be handled with ease by using either conditional or indirect proof. The use of these techniques on arguments in predicate logic is basically the same as it is on arguments in propositional logic. Arguments having conclusions expressed in the form of conditional statements or disjunctions (which can be derived from conditional statements) are immediate candidates for conditional proof. For these arguments, the usual strategy is to put the antecedent of the conditional statement to be obtained in the first line of an indented sequence, to derive the consequent as the last line, and to discharge the conditional sequence in a conditional statement that exactly matches the one to be obtained. Here is an example of such a proof:

1. $(x)(Hx \supset Ix)$	/ $(\exists x)Hx \supset (\exists x)Ix$
2. $(\exists x)Hx$	ACP
3. Ha	2, EI
4. $Ha \supset Ia$	1, UI
5. Ia	3, 4, MP
6. $(\exists x)Ix$	5, EG
7. $(\exists x)Hx \supset (\exists x)Ix$	2–6, CP

In this argument the antecedent of the conclusion is a complete statement consisting of a statement function, Hx, preceded by a quantifier. This complete statement is assumed as the first line in the conditional sequence. The instantiation and generalization rules are used within an indented sequence (both conditional and indirect) in basically the same way as they are in a conventional sequence. When the consequent of the conclusion is derived, the conditional sequence is completed, and it is then discharged in a conditional statement having the first line of the sequence as its antecedent and the last line as its consequent.

The next example differs from the previous one in that the antecedent of the conclusion is a statement function, not a complete statement. With arguments such as this, only the statement function is assumed as the first line in the conditional sequence. The quantifier is added after the sequence is discharged.

1. $(x)[(Ax \lor Bx) \supset Cx]$	/ $(x)(Ax \supset Cx)$
2. Ax	ACP
3. $Ax \lor Bx$	2, Add
4. $(Ax \lor Bx) \supset Cx$	1, UI
5. Cx	3, 4, MP
6. $Ax \supset Cx$	2–5, CP
7. $(x)(Ax \supset Cx)$	6, UG

This example leads to an important restriction on the use of universal generalization. You may recall that the x in line 2 of this proof is said to be *free* because it is not bound by any quantifier. (In contrast, the x's in lines 1 and 7 are bound by quantifiers.) The restriction is as follows:

UG: $\dfrac{\mathscr{F}y}{(x)\mathscr{F}x}$ *Restriction:* UG must not be used within the scope of an indented sequence if the instantial variable y is free in the first line of that sequence.

The proof just given does not violate this restriction, because UG is not used within the scope of the indented sequence at all. It is used only after the sequence has been discharged, which is perfectly acceptable. If, on the other hand, UG had been applied to line 5 to produce a statement reading $(x)Cx$, the restriction would have been violated because the instantial variable x is free in the first line of the sequence.

To understand why this restriction is necessary, consider the following *defective* proof:

1. $(x)Rx \supset (x)Sx$	/ $(x)(Rx \supset Sx)$
2. Rx	ACP
3. $(x)Rx$	2, UG (invalid)
4. $(x)Sx$	1, 3, MP
5. Sx	4, UI
6. $Rx \supset Sx$	2–5, CP
7. $(x)(Rx \supset Sx)$	6, UG

If Rx means "x is a rabbit" and Sx means "x is a snake," then the premise translates "If everything in the universe is a rabbit, then everything in the universe is a snake." This statement is *true* because the antecedent is false; that is, it is *not* the case that everything in the universe is a rabbit. The conclusion, on the other hand, is *false*, because it asserts that all rabbits are snakes. The argument is therefore invalid. If the restriction on UG had been obeyed, UG could not have been used on line 3 and, as a result, the illicit conclusion could not have been derived.

It is interesting to see what happens when the premise and the conclusion of this defective argument are switched. The proof, which is perfectly legitimate, is as follows:

1. $(x)(Rx \supset Sx)$	/ $(x)Rx \supset (x)Sx$
2. $(x)Rx$	ACP
3. Rx	2, UI
4. $Rx \supset Sx$	1, UI
5. Sx	3, 4, MP
6. $(x)Sx$	5, UG
7. $(x)Rx \supset (x)Sx$	2–6, CP

Notice in this proof that UG *is* used within the scope of a conditional sequence, but the restriction is not violated because the instantial variable x is not free in the first line of the sequence.

Let us now consider some examples of *indirect* proof. We begin an indirect sequence by assuming the negation of the statement to be obtained. When a contradiction is derived, the indirect sequence is discharged by asserting the denial of the original assumption. In the examples that follow, the negation of the conclusion is assumed as the first line of the sequence, and the quantifier negation rule is then used to eliminate the tilde. When the resulting statement is then instantiated, a new letter, m, is selected that has not appeared anywhere in a previous line. The same letter is then selected for the universal instantiation of line 1:

1. $(x)[(Px \supset Px) \supset (Qx \supset Rx)]$ / $(x)(Qx \supset Rx)$
   2. $\sim(x)(Qx \supset Rx)$ AIP
   3. $(\exists x)\sim(Qx \supset Rx)$ 2, QN
   4. $\sim(Qm \supset Rm)$ 3, EI
   5. $(Pm \supset Pm) \supset (Qm \supset Rm)$ 1, UI
   6. $\sim(Pm \supset Pm)$ 4, 5, MT
   7. $\sim(\sim Pm \lor Pm)$ 6, Impl
   8. $\sim\sim Pm \cdot \sim Pm$ 7, DM
   9. $Pm \cdot \sim Pm$ 8, DN
10. $\sim\sim(x)(Qx \supset Rx)$ 2–9, IP
11. $(x)(Qx \supset Rx)$ 10, DN

The next example has a particular statement for its conclusion:

1. $(\exists x)Ax \lor (\exists x)Fx$
2. $(x)(Ax \supset Fx)$ / $(\exists x)Fx$
   3. $\sim(\exists x)Fx$ AIP
   4. $(\exists x)Fx \lor (\exists x)Ax$ 1, Com
   5. $(\exists x)Ax$ 3, 4, DS
   6. Ac 5, EI
   7. $Ac \supset Fc$ 2, UI
   8. Fc 6, 7, MP
   9. $(x)\sim Fx$ 3, QN
10. $\sim Fc$ 9, UI
11. $Fc \cdot \sim Fc$ 8, 10, Conj
12. $\sim\sim(\exists x)Fx$ 3–11, IP
13. $(\exists x)Fx$ 12, DN

Since indirect proof sequences are indented, they are subject to the same restriction on universal generalization as are conditional sequences. The following proof, which is similar to the previous one, violates this restriction because the instantial variable x is free in the first line of the sequence. The violation (line 4) allows a universal statement to be drawn for the conclusion, whereas only a particular statement is legitimate (as in the prior example):

1. $(\exists x)Ax \lor (\exists x)Fx$
2. $(x)(Ax \supset Fx)$ / $(x)Fx$
   3. $\sim Fx$ AIP
   4. $(x)\sim Fx$ 3, UG (invalid)
   5. $\sim(\exists x)Fx$ 4, QN
   6. $(\exists x)Fx \lor (\exists x)Ax$ 1, Com
   7. $(\exists x)Ax$ 5, 6, DS
   8. Ac 7, EI
   9. $Ac \supset Fc$ 2, UI
10. Fc 8, 9, MP
11. $\sim Fc$ 4, UI
12. $Fc \cdot \sim Fc$ 10, 11, Conj
13. $\sim\sim Fx$ 3–12, IP
14. Fx 13, DN
15. $(x)Fx$ 14, UG

To see that this argument is indeed invalid, let *Ax* stand for "*x* is an apple" and *Fx* for "*x* is a fruit." The first premise then reads "Either an apple exists or a fruit exists" (which is true), and the second premise reads "All apples are fruits" (which is also true). The conclusion, however, reads "Everything in the universe is a fruit," and this, of course, is false.

As in propositional logic, conditional and indirect sequences in predicate logic may include each other. The following proof uses an indirect sequence within the scope of a conditional sequence.

1. (x)[(Px ∨ Qx) ⊃ (Rx • Sx)]	/ (∃x)(Px ∨ Sx) ⊃ (∃x)Sx
2. (∃x)(Px ∨ Sx)	ACP
3. ~(∃x)Sx	AIP
4. (x)~Sx	3, QN
5. Pa ∨ Sa	2, EI
6. ~Sa	4, UI
7. Sa ∨ Pa	5, Com
8. Pa	6, 7, DS
9. Pa ∨ Qa	8, Add
10. (Pa ∨ Qa) ⊃ (Ra • Sa)	1, UI
11. Ra • Sa	9, 10, MP
12. Sa • Ra	11, Com
13. Sa	12, Simp
14. Sa • ~Sa	6, 13, Conj
15. ~~(∃x)Sx	3–14, IP
16. (∃x)Sx	15, DN
17. (∃x)(Px ∨ Sx) ⊃ (∃x)Sx	2–16, CP

8

The conditional sequence begins, as usual, by assuming the antecedent of the conditional statement to be derived. The objective, then, is to derive the consequent. This is accomplished by the indirect sequence, which begins with the negation of the consequent and ends (line 14) with a contradiction.

EXERCISE **8.4**

I. Use either indirect proof or conditional proof to derive the conclusions of the following symbolized arguments.

★(1) 1. (x)(Ax ⊃ Bx)
    2. (x)(Ax ⊃ Cx)   / (x)[Ax ⊃ (Bx • Cx)]

 (2) 1. (∃x)Ax ⊃ (∃x)(Bx • Cx)
    2. (∃x)(Cx ∨ Dx) ⊃ (x)Ex   / (x)(Ax ⊃ Ex)

MindTap Complete exercises online for immediate feedback.

(3) 1. $(\exists x)Ax \supset (\exists x)(Bx \cdot Cx)$
2. $\sim(\exists x)Cx$ / $(x)\sim Ax$

★(4) 1. $(x)(Ax \supset Cx)$
2. $(\exists x)Cx \supset (\exists x)(Bx \cdot Dx)$ / $(\exists x)Ax \supset (\exists x)Bx$

(5) 1. $(x)(Ax \supset Bx)$
2. $(x)[(Ax \cdot Bx) \supset Cx]$ / $(x)(Ax \supset Cx)$

(6) 1. $(\exists x)Ax \supset (x)Bx$
2. $An \supset \sim Bn$ / $\sim An$

★(7) 1. $(x)[(Ax \lor Bx) \supset Cx]$
2. $(x)[(Cx \lor Dx) \supset Ex]$ / $(x)(Ax \supset Ex)$

(8) 1. $(\exists x)(Ax \lor Bx) \supset \sim(\exists x)Ax$ / $(x)\sim Ax$

(9) 1. $(x)(Ax \supset Bx)$
2. $(x)(Cx \supset Dx)$ / $(\exists x)(Ax \lor Cx) \supset (\exists x)(Bx \lor Dx)$

★(10) 1. $(x)(Ax \supset Bx)$
2. $Am \lor An$ / $(\exists x)Bx$

(11) 1. $(x)[(Ax \lor Bx) \supset Cx]$
2. $(x)[(Cx \lor Dx) \supset \sim Ax]$ / $(x)\sim Ax$

(12) 1. $(\exists x)Ax \supset (x)(Bx \supset Cx)$
2. $(\exists x)Dx \supset (x)\sim Cx$ / $(x)[(Ax \cdot Dx) \supset \sim Bx]$

★(13) 1. $(\exists x)Ax \supset (x)(Bx \supset Cx)$
2. $(\exists x)Dx \supset (\exists x)Bx$ / $(\exists x)(Ax \cdot Dx) \supset (\exists x)Cx$

(14) 1. $(\exists x)Ax \lor (\exists x)(Bx \cdot Cx)$
2. $(x)(Ax \supset Cx)$ / $(\exists x)Cx$

(15) 1. $(\exists x)Ax \supset (\exists x)(Bx \cdot Cx)$
2. $(\exists x)Cx \supset (x)(Dx \cdot Ex)$ / $(x)(Ax \supset Ex)$

★(16) 1. $(x)[(Ax \lor Bx) \supset Cx]$
2. $(\exists x)(\sim Ax \lor Dx) \supset (x)Ex$ / $(x)Cx \lor (x)Ex$

(17) 1. $(x)Ax \equiv (\exists x)(Bx \cdot Cx)$
2. $(x)(Cx \supset Bx)$ / $(x)Ax \equiv (\exists x)Cx$

(18) 1. $(x)(Ax \equiv Bx)$
2. $(x)[Ax \supset (Bx \supset Cx)]$
3. $(\exists x)Ax \lor (\exists x)Bx$ / $(\exists x)Cx$

★(19) 1. $(x)[Bx \supset (Cx \cdot Dx)]$ / $(x)(Ax \supset Bx) \supset (x)(Ax \supset Dx)$

(20) 1. $(x)[Ax \supset (Bx \cdot Cx)]$
2. $(x)[Dx \supset (Ex \cdot Fx)]$ / $(x)(Cx \supset Dx) \supset (x)(Ax \supset Fx)$

(21) 1. $(\exists x)(Ax \lor Bx)$
2. $(\exists x)Ax \supset (x)(Cx \supset Bx)$
3. $(\exists x)Cx$ / $(\exists x)Bx$

8

★(22) 1. $(x)Ax \lor (x)Bx$ / $(x)(Ax \lor Bx)$

(23) 1. $(\exists x)(Ax \lor Ex) \supset (x)(Bx \cdot \sim Cx)$
2. $(\exists x)(Bx \lor Fx) \supset (x)(Cx \lor Dx)$ / $(x)(Ax \supset Dx)$

(24) 1. $(x)(Ax \supset Bx)$
2. $\sim(\exists x)Ax \supset (\exists x)(Cx \cdot Dx)$
3. $(\exists x)(Dx \lor Ex) \supset (\exists x)Bx$ / $(\exists x)Bx$

★(25) 1. $(\exists x)Ax \supset (x)(Bx \supset Cx)$
2. $(\exists x)Dx \supset (x)(Ex \supset \sim Bx)$
3. $\sim(\exists x)(Cx \cdot \sim Ex)$ / $(\exists x)(Ax \cdot Dx) \supset \sim(\exists x)Bx$

II. Translate the following arguments into symbolic form. Then use conditional or indirect proof to derive the conclusion of each.

★1. All ambassadors are wealthy. Furthermore, all Republicans are clever. Therefore, all Republican ambassadors are clever and wealthy. (A, W, R, C)

2. All senators are well liked. Also, if there are any well-liked senators, then O'Brien is a voter. Therefore, if there are any senators, then O'Brien is a voter. (S, W, V)

3. If all judges are wise, then some attorneys are rewarded. Furthermore, if there are any judges who are not wise, then some attorneys are rewarded. Therefore, some attorneys are rewarded. (J, W, A, R)

★4. All secretaries and undersecretaries are intelligent and cautious. All those who are cautious or vigilant are restrained and austere. Therefore, all secretaries are austere. (S, U, I, C, V, R, A)

5. All ambassadors are diplomats. Furthermore, all experienced ambassadors are cautious, and all cautious diplomats have foresight. Therefore, all experienced ambassadors have foresight. (A, D, E, C, F)

6. If there are any senators, then some employees are well paid. If there is anyone who is either an employee or a volunteer, then there are some legislative assistants. Either there are some volunteers or there are some senators. Therefore, there are some legislative assistants. (S, E, W, V, L)

★7. If there are any consuls, then all ambassadors are satisfied diplomats. If no consuls are ambassadors, then some diplomats are satisfied. Therefore, some diplomats are satisfied. (C, A, S, D)

8. If there are any voters, then all politicians are astute. If there are any politicians, then whoever is astute is clever. Therefore, if there are any voters, then all politicians are clever. (V, P, A, C)

9. Either no senators are present or no representatives are present. Furthermore, either some senators are present or no women are present. Therefore, none of the representatives who are present are women. (S, P, R, W)

★10. Either some governors are present or some ambassadors are present. If anyone is present, then some ambassadors are clever diplomats. Therefore, some diplomats are clever. (G, P, A, C, D)

III. Create two valid arguments relating to hobbies. Then translate the arguments into the symbolism of predicate logic; use conditional proof to derive the conclusion of one and indirect proof to derive the conclusion of the other.

MindTap® Master concepts and improve outcomes with Aplia, at the end of the chapter, in the Aplia folder.

8.5 Proving Invalidity

HOW LOGICAL ARE YOU? Suppose you create a design for a smartphone battery that recharges itself without energy input of any kind from outside the battery. In your laboratory in Seattle you work up a protype, but after weeks of testing the battery fails to recharge itself. You conclude that since the battery failed in Seattle, it would fail in every other region of the country. Would your reasoning be correct?

Find the answer on MindTap.

In the previous chapter we saw that natural deduction could not be used with any facility to prove invalidity in propositional logic. The same thing can be said about natural deduction in predicate logic. But in predicate logic there is no simple and automatic technique such as truth tables or Venn diagrams to fall back on. However, there are two methods for proving invalidity in predicate logic that are just as effective as these other techniques, even though they may not be as convenient. One is the method used in Chapter 1 to prove the invalidity of various kinds of syllogisms—namely, the counterexample method. The other is what we will call the finite universe method. Both appeal to the basic idea underlying most proofs of invalidity: Any argument is proved invalid if it is shown that it is possible for it to have true premises and a false conclusion. Both methods are aimed at disclosing a situation that fulfills this requirement.

Counterexample Method

Recall from Chapter 1 that applying the **counterexample method** consists in finding a substitution instance of a given invalid argument form (or, equally well, a given invalid symbolized argument) that has actually true premises and a false conclusion. For an example of its use, consider the following invalid symbolized argument:

$(\exists x)(Ax \cdot \sim Bx)$
$(x)(Cx \supset Bx)$ / $(\exists x)(Cx \cdot \sim Ax)$

In creating a substitution instance, beginning with the conclusion is often easiest. The conclusion is translated as "Some *C* are not *A*." Thus, to make this statement false, we need to find an example of a class (for *C*) that is included in another class (for *A*). Cats and animals will serve this purpose. A little ingenuity provides us with the following substitution instance:

> Some animals are not mammals.
> All cats are mammals.
> Therefore, some cats are not animals.

When we produce such a substitution instance, the premises must turn out to be indisputably true in the actual world, and the conclusion indisputably false. Statements involving the names of animal classes are convenient for this purpose, because everyone agrees about cats, dogs, mammals, fish, and so on. Also, several different substitution instances can usually be produced that suffice to prove the argument invalid. Finally, any substitution instance that results in true premises and a true conclusion (or any arrangement other than true premises and false conclusion) proves nothing.

Here is an example of an invalid symbolized argument that includes a singular statement:

> $(x)(Ax \supset Bx)$
> $\sim Ac$ / $\sim Bc$

This argument form commits the fallacy of denying the antecedent. Producing a substitution instance is easy:

> All cats are animals.
> Lassie is not a cat.
> Therefore, Lassie is not an animal.

In selecting the name of an individual for the second premise, it is again necessary to pick something that everyone agrees on. Since everyone knows that Lassie is a dog, this name serves our purpose. But if we had selected some other name, such as Trixie or Ajax, this would hardly suffice, because there is no general agreement as to what these names denote.

Here is a slightly more complex example:

> $(x)[Ax \supset (Bx \vee Cx)]$
> $(x)[Bx \supset (Cx \cdot Dx)]$ / $(x)(Ax \supset Dx)$

A little ingenuity produces the following substitution instance:

> All dogs are either sharks or animals.
> All sharks are animals that are fish.
> Therefore, all dogs are fish.

The counterexample method is effective with most fairly simple invalid arguments in predicate logic. Since its application depends on the ingenuity of the user, however, it is not particularly well suited for complex arguments. For those, the finite universe method is probably a better choice.

Finite Universe Method

The **finite universe method** can be used to establish the invalidity of any invalid argument expressed in terms of a single variable. It depends on the idea that a valid argument remains valid no matter how things in the actual universe might be altered. Accordingly, if we are given a valid argument, then that argument remains valid if it should happen that the universe is contracted so that it contains only a single member. On the other hand, if it should turn out that an argument has true premises and false conclusion in a universe consisting of only one or a few members, then that argument has been proved invalid.

To see how this method works, we need to understand what happens to the meaning of universal and particular statements when the universe is shrunk in size. Accordingly, let us imagine that the universe contains only one thing instead of the billions of things that it actually contains. Let us name that one thing "Abigail." The statement "Everything in the universe is perfect" is then equivalent to "Abigail is perfect" (because Abigail is all that there is), and the statement "Something in the universe is perfect" is also equivalent to "Abigail is perfect" (because Abigail is that "something").

To represent this equivalence symbolically, we need a new metalogical symbol that asserts that the expressions on either side of it necessarily have the same truth value given a universe of a designated size. Although this equivalence bears a close resemblance to logical equivalence, it is not identical to it because logical equivalence holds independently of any alterations in the universe. The concept that we need to represent is a kind of conditional logical equivalence. Accordingly, we will select the double colon superscribed with a "c" (for "conditional"). For our purpose here, $\overset{c}{::}$ has the same effect as :: does. Using the former symbol, we have for a universe consisting of one member:

$$(x)Px \overset{c}{::} Pa$$
$$(\exists x)Px \overset{c}{::} Pa$$

Proceeding, if we imagine that the universe contains exactly two things—let us name them "Abigail" and "Beatrice"—the statement "Everything in the universe is perfect" is equivalent to "Abigail is perfect *and* Beatrice is perfect." On the other hand, the statement "Something in the universe is perfect" is equivalent to "Abigail is perfect *or* Beatrice is perfect" (because "some" means at least one). In other words, the universal statement is equivalent to a *conjunction* of singular statements, and the particular statement is equivalent to a *disjunction* of singular statements. In symbols:

$$(x)Px \overset{c}{::} (Pa \cdot Pb)$$
$$(\exists x)Px \overset{c}{::} (Pa \lor Pb)$$

If the universe is increased to three—let us call the new member "Charmaine"—we have

$$(x)Px \overset{c}{::} (Pa \cdot Pb \cdot Pc)$$
$$(\exists x)Px \overset{c}{::} (Pa \lor Pb \lor Pc)$$

This equivalence continues indefinitely as more and more members are added to the universe.

Extending this treatment to the more typical kinds of universal and particular statements, we have, for a universe of three:

$(x)(Px \supset Qx)$ :: $[(Pa \supset Qa) \cdot (Pb \supset Qb) \cdot (Pc \supset Qc)]$
$(\exists x)(Px \cdot Qx)$ :: $[(Pa \cdot Qa) \vee (Pb \cdot Qb) \vee (Pc \cdot Qc)]$

For expressions involving combinations of quantified statements, each of the component statements is translated separately and the resulting statement groups are linked together by means of the connective appearing in the original statement. Here are two examples for a universe of three:

$[(x)Px \supset (\exists x)Qx]$ :: $[(Pa \cdot Pb \cdot Pc) \supset (Qa \vee Qb \vee Qc)]$
$[(x)(Px \supset Qx) \vee (\exists x)(Rx \cdot Sx)]$ :: $\{[(Pa \supset Qa) \cdot (Pb \supset Qb) \cdot (Pc \supset Qc)]$
$\vee [(Ra \cdot Sa) \vee (Rb \cdot Sb) \vee (Rc \cdot Sc)]\}$

The method for proving an argument invalid consists in translating the premises and conclusion into singular statements, as per the preceding examples, and then testing the result with an indirect truth table (see Section 6.5). First a universe of one is tried. If it is possible for the premises to be true and the conclusion false in this universe, the argument is immediately identified as invalid. If, on the other hand, a contradiction results from this assumption, a universe of two is then tried. If, in this second universe, it is possible for the premises to be true and the conclusion false, the argument is invalid. If not, a universe of three is tried, and so on.

Consider the following symbolized argument:

$(x)(Gx \supset Hx)$
$(\exists x)Hx$ / $(\exists x)Gx$

For a universe having one member—call this member "Abigail"—the argument translates into

$Ga \supset Ha$
Ha / Ga

Testing with an indirect truth table, we have

$Ga \supset Ha$ / Ha / / Ga
F T T   T   F

Because it is possible for the premises to be true and the conclusion false, the argument is invalid. Another example:

$(x)(Jx \supset Kx)$
$(\exists x)Jx$ / $(x)Kx$

For a universe having one member, the indirect truth table is as follows:

$Ja \supset Ka$ / Ja / / Ka
(T T F)   T   F

Since it is impossible for the premises to be true and the conclusion false for this universe, we try a universe having two members, *a* and *b*:

$(Ja \supset Ka) \bullet (Jb \supset Kb)$ / $Ja \lor Jb$ / / $Ka \bullet Kb$
T T T T F T F   T T F   T F F

Since it is possible for the premises to be true and the conclusion false for this universe, the argument is invalid.

Here is an example involving compound statements:

$(\exists x)Hx \supset (x)(Fx \supset Gx)$
$(\exists x)Fx$ $/(\exists x)Hx \supset (x)Gx$

The indirect truth table for a universe having one member is as follows:

$Ha \supset (Fa \supset Ga)$ / Fa / / $Ha \supset Ga$
T T T F F   T   T F F

A contradiction results, so we try a universe having two members. The resulting indirect truth table proves the argument invalid:

$(Ha \lor Hb) \supset [(Fa \supset Ga) \bullet (Fb \supset Gb)]$ / $Fa \lor Fb$ / / $(Ha \lor Hb) \supset (Ga \bullet Gb)$
   T   T   T T T T F T F   T T F   T   F T F F

The next example involves singular statements:

$(\exists x)Mx \bullet (\exists x)Nx$
Md $/ Nd$

The second premise asserts that something named *d* is an *M*. For this argument, the assumption that the universe contains only one member entails that this one member is named *d*. Here is the indirect truth table for such a universe:

$Md \bullet Nd$ / Md / / Nd
T T F   T   F

When the universe is expanded to include two members, we are free to give any name we wish to the second member. Let us call it *e*. The resulting indirect truth table, which follows, shows that the argument is invalid. Notice that the second premise and the conclusion remain the same:

$(Md \lor Me) \bullet (Nd \lor Ne)$ / Md / / Nd
T T   T F T T   T   F

The basic concept behind this method of proving invalidity rests on the fact that a valid argument is valid in all possible universes. Consequently, if an argument fails in a universe consisting of one, two, or any number of members, it is invalid.

While this method is intended primarily for proving arguments invalid, theoretically it can also be used to prove arguments valid. Several years ago a theorem was proved to the effect that an argument that does not fail in a universe of 2^n members, where *n* designates the number of different predicates, is valid.* According to this theorem,

---

*See Wilhelm Ackermann, Solvable Cases of the Decision Problem (*Amsterdam: North-Holland Publishing, 1954*), Chapter 4. This theorem, incidentally, holds only for monadic predicates.*

establishing the validity of an argument containing two different predicates requires a universe having four members, establishing the validity of an argument containing three different predicates requires a universe having eight members, and so on. For most arguments, however, a universe having four members is unwieldy at best, and a universe having eight members approaches the impossible (although a computer could handle it easily). Thus, while this method is usually quite convenient for proving invalidity, practical limitations impede its usefulness in establishing validity.

EXERCISE 8.5

I. Use the counterexample method to prove that the following symbolized arguments are invalid.

★(1) 1. $(x)(Ax \supset Bx)$
    2. $(x)(Ax \supset \sim Cx)$ / $(x)(Cx \supset Bx)$

(2) 1. $(\exists x)(Ax \cdot Bx)$
    2. $(x)(Cx \supset Ax)$ / $(\exists x)(Cx \cdot Bx)$

(3) 1. $(x)(Ax \supset Bx)$
    2. Bc / Ac

★(4) 1. $(\exists x)(Ax \cdot Bx)$
    2. $(\exists x)(Ax \cdot Cx)$ / $(\exists x)[Ax \cdot (Bx \cdot Cx)]$

(5) 1. $(x)[Ax \lor (Bx \lor Cx)]$ / $(x)Ax \lor [(x)Bx \lor (x)Cx]$

(6) 1. $(x)[Ax \supset (Bx \lor Cx)]$
    2. $(x)[(Bx \cdot Cx) \supset Dx]$ / $(x)(Ax \supset Dx)$

★(7) 1. $(\exists x)Ax$
    2. $(\exists x)Bx$
    3. $(x)(Ax \supset \sim Cx)$ / $(\exists x)(Bx \cdot \sim Cx)$

(8) 1. $(x)[(Ax \lor Bx) \supset Cx]$
    2. $(x)[(Cx \cdot Dx) \supset Ex]$ / $(x)(Ax \supset Ex)$

(9) 1. $(x)[(Ax \cdot Bx) \supset Cx]$
    2. $(x)[(Ax \cdot Cx) \supset Dx]$ / $(x)[(Ax \cdot Dx) \supset Cx]$

★(10) 1. $(\exists x)(Ax \cdot Bx)$
    2. $(\exists x)(Cx \cdot \sim Bx)$
    3. $(x)(Ax \supset Cx)$ / $(\exists x)[(Cx \cdot Bx) \cdot \sim Ax]$

II. Use the finite universe method to prove that the following symbolized arguments are invalid.

★(1) 1. $(x)(Ax \supset Bx)$
    2. $(x)(Ax \supset Cx)$ / $(x)(Bx \supset Cx)$

MindTap®   Complete exercises online for immediate feedback.

(2) 1. $(x)(Ax \lor Bx)$
2. $\sim An$ / $(x)Bx$

(3) 1. $(\exists x)Ax \lor (\exists x)Bx$
2. $(\exists x)Ax$ / $(\exists x)Bx$

★(4) 1. $(x)(Ax \supset Bx)$
2. $(\exists x)Ax$ / $(x)Bx$

(5) 1. $(x)[Ax \supset (Bx \lor Cx)]$
2. $(\exists x)Ax$ / $(\exists x)Bx$

(6) 1. $(\exists x)Ax$
2. $(\exists x)Bx$ / $(\exists x)(Ax \cdot Bx)$

★(7) 1. $(x)(Ax \supset Bx)$
2. $(\exists x)Bx \supset (\exists x)Cx$ / $(x)(Ax \supset Cx)$

(8) 1. $(\exists x)(Ax \cdot Bx) \equiv (\exists x)Cx$
2. $(x)(Ax \supset Bx)$ / $(x)Ax \equiv (\exists x)Cx$

(9) 1. $(\exists x)(Ax \cdot \sim Bx)$
2. $(\exists x)(Bx \cdot \sim Ax)$ / $(x)(Ax \lor Bx)$

★(10) 1. $(\exists x)(Ax \cdot Bx)$
2. $(\exists x)(\sim Ax \cdot \sim Bx)$ / $(x)(Ax \equiv Bx)$

III. Translate the following arguments into symbolic form. Then use either the counterexample method or the finite universe method to prove that each is invalid.

★1. Violinists who play well are accomplished musicians. There are some violinists in the orchestra. Therefore, some musicians are accomplished. (V, P, A, M, O)

2. Pianists and harpsichordists are meticulous. Alfred Brendel is a pianist. Therefore, everyone is meticulous. (P, H, M)

3. If there are any oboists, there are some bassoonists. If there are any clarinetists, there are some flutists. Amelia is both an oboist and a clarinetist. Therefore, some bassoonists are flutists. (O, B, C, F)

★4. All timpanists are haughty. If some timpanists are haughty, then some percussionists are overbearing. Therefore, all timpanists are overbearing. (T, H, P, O)

5. All cellists and violinists are members of the string section. Some violinists are not cellists. Also, some cellists are not violinists. Therefore, everyone is a member of the string section. (C, V, M)

IV. Create an invalid argument relating to parties—the fun kind, not the political sort. Then translate the argument into the symbolism of predicate logic and use both the counterexample method and the finite universe method to prove the argument invalid.

8

MindTap® Master concepts and improve outcomes with Aplia, at the end of the chapter, in the Aplia folder.

SECTION 8.5 PROVING INVALIDITY   **511**

Relational Predicates and Overlapping Quantifiers

Even the logical machinery developed thus far is not adequate for deriving the conclusions of a number of arguments. Consider, for example, the following:

> All dogs are animals. Therefore, whoever owns a dog owns an animal.

> If there are any butterflies, then if all butterflies are free, they are free. There are butterflies in the garden. Therefore, if all butterflies are free, something in the garden is free.

The first argument involves a relation—the relation of ownership—and we have yet to see how relations can be dealt with. The second argument, while not involving any relations, involves a quantifier that overlaps another quantifier. In this section the apparatus of predicate logic will be extended to cover examples such as these.

The predicates we have used thus far are called **monadic predicates**, or one-place predicates, because they are used to assign an attribute to individual things. A **relational predicate** (or relation) is a predicate that is used to establish a connection *between* or *among* individuals.

Relations occur in varying degrees of complexity, depending on the number of individuals related. The simplest, called *binary* (or *dyadic*) relations, establish a connection between two individuals. Some examples are the relation of being taller than, as expressed in the statement "Steve is taller than David," and the relation of being a friend, as expressed in "Sylvia is a friend of Olivia." *Trinary* (or *triadic*) relations establish a connection among three individuals: for example, the relation of being between, as in "St. Louis is between Chicago and New Orleans," and the relation of reading something to someone, as in "George read *Othello* to Madeline." *Quaternary* (or *tetradic*) relations link four individuals together—for example, the relation of reading something to someone at a certain time, as in "George read *Othello* to Madeline on Thursday." The complexity increases until we have what are called *n-ary* (or *n-adic*) relations, which link *n* things together. In this section we will restrict our attention to binary relations.

Translating Relational Statements

Relations are symbolized like other predicates except that two lowercase letters, representing the two related individuals, are written to the immediate right of the uppercase letter representing the relation. Here are some examples of relational statements involving specifically named individuals:

Statement	Symbolic translation
Anthony is married to Cynthia.	*Mac*
Deborah loves physics.	*Ldp*
The Willis Tower is taller than the Empire State Building.	*Twe*
Donald is the father of Jim.	*Fdj*

Notice that the order in which the lowercase letters are listed often makes a difference. If the third statement were translated *Tew*, the symbolic statement would read "The Empire State Building is taller than the Willis Tower," which is false. Quantifiers are attached to relational predicates in the same way they are to monadic predicates. Some examples of relational statements involving quantifiers are as follows:

Statement	Symbolic translation
Thomas knows everything.	$(x)Ktx$
Thomas knows something.	$(\exists x)Ktx$
Everything is different from everything.	$(x)(y)Dxy$
Something is different from something.	$(\exists x)(\exists y)Dxy$
Everything is different from something (or other).	$(x)(\exists y)Dxy$
Something is different from everything.	$(\exists x)(y)Dxy$

The last four statements involve **overlapping quantifiers**. We may read these symbols as follows:

$(x)(y)$	For all x and for all y ...
$(\exists x)(\exists y)$	There exists an x such that there exists a y such that ...
$(x)(\exists y)$	For all x there exists a y such that ...
$(\exists x)(y)$	There exists an x such that for all y ...

Applying this phraseology to the last statement given, for example, we have "There exists an x such that for all y, x is different from y"—which is simply another way of saying "Something is different from everything."

When two quantifiers of the same sort appear adjacent to each other, the order in which they are listed is not significant. In other words, the statement $(x)(y)Dxy$ is logically equivalent to $(y)(x)Dxy$, and $(\exists x)(\exists y)Dxy$ is logically equivalent to $(\exists y)(\exists x)Dxy$. A little reflection on the meaning of these statements should justify this equivalence. But when different quantifiers appear adjacent to each other, the order *does* make a difference, sometimes even when the statement function is nonrelational. Accordingly, $(x)(\exists y)Dxy$ is not logically equivalent to $(\exists y)(x)Dxy$. This fact can be seen more clearly in terms of a different example. If *Lxy* means "x loves y" and we imagine the universe of discourse restricted to people, then $(x)(\exists y)Lxy$ means "Everyone loves someone (or other)," while $(\exists y)(x)Lxy$ means "There is someone whom everyone loves." Clearly these two statements are not equivalent.

Relational predicates can be combined with ordinary predicates to translate statements having varying degrees of complexity. In the examples that follow, *Px* means "*x* is a person." The meaning of the other predicates should be clear from the context:

Any heavyweight can defeat any lightweight.
  $(x)[Hx \supset (y)(Ly \supset Dxy)]$

Some heavyweights can defeat any lightweight.
  $(\exists x)[Hx \bullet (y)(Ly \supset Dxy)]$

No heavyweight can defeat every lightweight.
  $(x)[Hx \supset (\exists y)(Ly \bullet \sim Dxy)]$
            or
  $\sim(\exists x)[Hx \bullet (y)(Ly \supset Dxy)]$

Everyone cares for someone (or other).
  $(x)[Px \supset (\exists y)(Py \bullet Cxy)]$

Someone does not care for anyone.
  $(\exists x)[Px \bullet (y)(Py \supset \sim Cxy)]$

Anyone who cares for someone is cared for himself.
  $(x)\{[Px \bullet (\exists y)(Py \bullet Cxy)] \supset (\exists z)(Pz \bullet Czx)\}$

Not everyone respects himself.
  $(\exists x)(Px \bullet \sim Rxx)$
          or
  $\sim(x)(Px \supset Rxx)$

Anyone who does not respect himself is not respected by anyone.
  $(x)[(Px \bullet \sim Rxx) \supset (y)(Py \supset \sim Ryx)]$

The same general rule applies in translating these statements as applies in translating any other statement in predicate logic: Universal quantifiers go with implications and existential quantifiers go with conjunctions. Every one of the eight symbolic expressions given here follows this rule. For example, in the first statement, both quantifiers are universal and both operators are horseshoes. In the second statement, the main quantifier is existential and the subordinate quantifier universal; accordingly, the main operator is a dot and the subordinate operator is a horseshoe. Among these statements, the sixth is the most complex. The symbolic translation of this statement reads, "For all *x*, if *x* is a person and there exists a *y* such that *y* is a person and *x* cares for *y*, then there exists a *z* such that *z* is a person and *z* cares for *x*." It should be clear that this is simply another way of expressing the original English statement.

Another important rule to keep in mind when translating statements of this kind is that every variable must be bound by some quantifier. If a variable is left dangling outside the scope of its intended quantifier, the translation is defective. For example, if the second statement were translated $(\exists x)Hx \bullet (y)(Ly \supset Dxy)$, then the *x* in *Dxy* would not be bound by the existential quantifier. As a result, the translation would be defective. Instead, in our example, brackets provide for the existential quantifier to range over *Dxy*.

The same techniques used to translate these eight statements are also used to translate certain statements involving monadic predicates throughout. Consider the following:

If anything is good and all good things are safe, then it is safe.

$(x)\{[Gx \bullet (y)(Gy \supset Sy)] \supset Sx\}$

If anything is good and some good things are dangerous, then it is dangerous.

$(x)\{[Gx \bullet (\exists y)(Gy \bullet Dy)] \supset Dx\}$

Since the "it" at the end of these statements refers to one of the "good" things mentioned at the beginning, the quantifier that binds the x in Gx must also bind the x in Sx and Dx. The set of braces in the symbolic expressions ensures this.

Another point to notice regarding statements such as these is that the quantified expression inside the brackets is expressed in terms of a *new* variable. This procedure is essential to avoiding ambiguity. If instead of y, x had been used, the variable in this expression would appear to be bound by two different quantifiers at the same time.

In other statements, the one or more individuals mentioned at the end are *not* necessarily the same ones mentioned at the beginning. In such cases the quantifier that binds the individuals at the beginning should *not* bind those at the end. Compare the next pair of statements with those we have just considered.

If anything is good and all good things are safe, then something is safe.

$[(\exists x)Gx \bullet (y)(Gy \supset Sy)] \supset (\exists z)Sz$

If anything is good and some good things are dangerous, then something is dangerous.

$[(\exists x)Gx \bullet (\exists y)(Gy \bullet Dy)] \supset (\exists z)Dz$

In these cases the "something" at the end is not necessarily one of the "good" things mentioned at the beginning. Accordingly, the quantifier that binds the x in Gx does *not* range all the way to the end of the statement. Furthermore, the quantifier in question is now an *existential* quantifier. In the previous pair of statements the quantifier had to be universal because it ranged over the main operator, which was a horseshoe. In the new pair, however, no quantifier ranges over the implication symbol. As a result, the sense of these statements has shifted to mean "If *something* is good . . ."

Note that, although a different variable is used to express each of the three different components in the pair of statements just given, this is not required. Because in this case no quantifier ranges over any other quantifier, it would be perfectly appropriate to use the same variable throughout.

The next pair of statements involve relational predicates. As in the previous pair, no single quantifier ranges over the entire statement, because the individuals mentioned at the end are not necessarily the same ones mentioned at the beginning:

If everyone helps himself, then everyone will be helped.

$(x)(Px \supset Hxx) \supset (x)[(Px \supset (\exists y)Hyx)]$

If someone helps himself, then someone will be helped.

$(\exists x)(Px \bullet Hxx) \supset (\exists x)(\exists y)(Px \bullet Hyx)$

This completes our explanation of how to translate statements involving relational predicates and overlapping quantifiers. You may, if you wish, proceed directly to Exercise 8.6 part I before completing the remainder of this section.

Using the Rules of Inference

Let us now see how the various quantifier rules apply to overlapping quantifiers. The quantifier negation rule is applied in basically the same way as it is with single quantifiers. The following short sequence illustrates its application:

1. $\sim(x)(\exists y)Pxy$
2. $(\exists x)\sim(\exists y)Pxy$ 1, QN
3. $(\exists x)(y)\sim Pxy$ 2, QN

As the tilde operator is moved past a quantifier, the quantifier in question is switched for its correlative. With the exception of a restriction on universal generalization, which we will introduce presently, the instantiation and generalization rules are also used in basically the same way as they are with single quantifiers. Example:

1. $(\exists x)(\exists y)Pxy$
2. $(\exists y)Pay$ 1, EI
3. Pab 2, EI
4. $(\exists x)Pxb$ 3, EG
5. $(\exists y)(\exists x)Pxy$ 4, EG

With each successive instantiation the outermost quantifier drops off. Generalization restores the quantifiers in the reverse order.

This proof demonstrates our earlier observation that the order of the quantifiers is not significant when the same kind of quantifier is used throughout. We also observed that the order does make a difference when different quantifiers appear together. Accordingly, the statement $(x)(\exists y)Pxy$ is not logically equivalent to $(\exists y)(x)Pxy$. As the instantiation and generalization rules now stand, however, it is quite possible, with a proof similar to the one just given, to establish the logical equivalence of these two expressions. Therefore, to keep this from happening we now introduce a new restriction on universal generalization:

UG: $\dfrac{\mathscr{F}y}{(x)\mathscr{F}x}$ *Restriction:* UG must not be used if the instantial variable y is free in any preceding line obtained by EI.

To see how this restriction applies, let us attempt to derive $(\exists x)(y)Mxy$ from $(y)(\exists x)Mxy$:

1. $(y)(\exists x)Mxy$
2. $(\exists x)Mxy$ 1, UI
3. May 2, EI
4. $(y)May$ 3, UG (invalid)
5. $(\exists x)(y)Mxy$ 4, EG

The proof fails on line 4 because the instantial variable y occurs free in line 3, which was obtained by EI. To see that line 4 is invalid, suppose that the universe of discourse is restricted to people, and that *Mxy* means "*x* is the mother of *y*." Then line 1 asserts that for every person *y* there exists a person *x* such that *x* is the mother of *y*—which means that every person has a mother. On line 2 we select one of these people at random, and on line 3 we give the name Abigail to the mother of that person. Then on line 4 we draw the conclusion that Abigail is the mother of everyone in the universe. This inference is clearly invalid. The new restriction on UG prevents this kind of inference from being drawn.

In summary, we now have two restrictions on universal generalization. The first concerns only conditional and indirect sequences and prevents UG from occurring within the scope of such a sequence when the instantial variable is free in the first line. The second restriction concerns only arguments involving overlapping quantifiers. With these two restrictions in hand, we may now proceed to examine the use of natural deduction in arguments involving relational predicates and overlapping quantifiers. The example that follows does not include any relational predicates, but it does involve overlapping quantifiers:

1. $(\exists x)Ax \supset (\exists x)Bx$ / $(\exists y)(x)(Ax \supset By)$
    2. Ax ACP
    3. $(\exists x)Ax$ 2, EG
    4. $(\exists x)Bx$ 1, 3, MP
    5. Bc 4, EI
6. $Ax \supset Bc$ 2–5, CP
7. $(x)(Ax \supset Bc)$ 6, UG
8. $(\exists y)(x)(Ax \supset By)$ 7, EG

Conditional and indirect proof are used in the same way with relational predicates and overlapping quantifiers as they are with monadic predicates and nonoverlapping quantifiers. The conditional proof just given begins, as usual, by assuming the antecedent of the conclusion. When line 7 is reached, we must be careful that neither of the restrictions against universal generalization is violated. While the instantial variable *x* is free in the first line of the conditional sequence, line 7 does not lie within that sequence, so the first restriction is obeyed. And while line 5 was obtained by EI, *x* is not free in that line. Thus, the second restriction is obeyed as well.

The next proof involves a relational predicate. The proof shows that while $(x)(\exists y)$ *Dxy* is not logically equivalent to $(\exists y)(x)Dxy$, it can be derived from that statement:

1. $(\exists y)(x)Dxy$ / $(x)(\exists y)Dxy$
2. $(x)Dxm$ 1, EI
3. Dxm 2, UI
4. $(\exists y)Dxy$ 3, EG
5. $(x)(\exists y)Dxy$ 4, UG

Notice that line 5 is derived by UG. Also notice that the instantial variable *x* occurs in line 2, which was derived by EI. However, *x* is not free in line 2. Thus, the second restriction on UG is obeyed.

The next example concludes with a line in which an individual is related to itself. Since there are no restrictions on universal instantiation, the procedure leading up to this line is perfectly legitimate. Notice in line 4 that tautology is used with relational predicates in the same way that it is with monadic predicates:

1. $(\exists y)(x)(Exy \lor Eyx)$ $/ (\exists z)Ezz$
2. $(x)(Exa \lor Eax)$ 1, EI
3. $Eaa \lor Eaa$ 2, UI
4. Eaa 3, Taut
5. $(\exists z)Ezz$ 4, EG

Sometimes the order in which instantiation steps are performed is critical. The following proof provides an example:

1. $(x)(\exists y)(Fxy \supset Gxy)$
2. $(\exists x)(y)Fxy$ $/ (\exists x)(\exists y)Gxy$
3. $(y)Fmy$ 2, EI
4. $(\exists y)(Fmy \supset Gmy)$ 1, UI
5. $Fmo \supset Gmo$ 4, EI
6. Fmo 3, UI
7. Gmo 5, 6, MP
8. $(\exists y)Gmy$ 7, EG
9. $(\exists x)(\exists y)Gxy$ 8, EG

Line 2 must be instantiated before line 1 because the step introduces a new existential name. For the same reason, line 4 must be instantiated before line 3.

The next proof involves an indirect sequence. Such sequences often make use of the quantifier negation rule, as this proof illustrates:

1. $(\exists x)(\exists y)(Jxy \lor Kxy) \supset (\exists x)Lx$
2. $(x)(y)(Lx \supset \sim Ly)$ $/ (x)(y)\sim Jxy$
3. $\sim(x)(y)\sim Jxy$ AIP
4. $(\exists x)\sim(y)\sim Jxy$ 3, QN
5. $(\exists x)(\exists y)\sim\sim Jxy$ 4, QN
6. $(\exists x)(\exists y)Jxy$ 5, DN
7. $(\exists y)Jmy$ 6, EI
8. Jmn 7, EI
9. $Jmn \lor Kmn$ 8, Add
10. $(\exists y)(Jmy \lor Kmy)$ 9, EG
11. $(\exists x)(\exists y)(Jxy \lor Kxy)$ 10, EG
12. $(\exists x)Lx$ 1, 11, MP
13. Lo 12, EI
14. $(y)(Lo \supset \sim Ly)$ 2, UI
15. $Lo \supset \sim Lo$ 14, UI
16. $\sim Lo$ 13, 15, MP
17. $Lo \cdot \sim Lo$ 13, 16, Conj
18. $\sim\sim(x)(y)\sim Jxy$ 3–17, IP
19. $(x)(y)\sim Jxy$ 18, DN

Because line 1 cannot be instantiated, the only strategy is to derive the antecedent of the conditional with the aim of deriving the consequent via *modus ponens*. This is

8

accomplished on line 11 via indirect proof. Notice on line 9 that addition is used with relational predicates in the same way that it is with monadic predicates.

A final word of caution is called for regarding universal instantiation and the two generalization rules. First, when UI is used to introduce variables into a proof, it is important that these variables end up free and that they not be captured in the process by other quantifiers. The following examples illustrate both correct and incorrect applications of this rule:

1. $(x)(\exists y)Pxy$		
2. $(\exists y)Pyy$	1, UI	(invalid—the instantial variable y has been captured by the existential quantifier)

1. $(x)(\exists y)Pxy$		
2. $(\exists y)Pxy$	1, UI	(valid—the instantial variable x is free)

1. $(x)(\exists y)Pxy$		
2. $(\exists y)Pzy$	1, UI	(valid—the instantial variable z is free)

An analogous caution applies to the two generalization rules. When UG and EG are used, it is important that the instantial letter be replaced by a variable that is captured by no previously introduced quantifier and that no other variables be captured by the newly introduced quantifier. The following examples illustrate both correct and incorrect applications of this rule:

1. $(\exists x)Pxy$		
2. $(x)(\exists x)Pxx$	1, UG	(invalid—the new x has been captured by the existential quantifier)

1. $(\exists x)Pxy$		
2. $(\exists x)(\exists x)Pxx$	1, EG	(invalid—the new x has been captured by the old existential quantifier)

1. $(\exists x)Pxy$		
2. $(\exists y)(\exists x)Pxy$	1, EG	(valid)

1. $(x)(\exists y)Lxy$		
2. $(\exists y)Lxy$	1, UI	
3. Lxa	2, EI	
4. $(\exists x)Lxx$	3, EG	(invalid—the quantifier has captured the x immediately adjacent to the L)

1. $(x)(\exists y)Lxy$		
2. $(\exists y)Lxy$	1, UI	
3. Lxa	2, EI	
4. $(\exists z)Lxz$	3, EG	(valid—the x remains free)

1. $(x)(y)Kxy$		
2. $(y)Kxy$	1, UI	
3. Kxx	2, UI	
4. $(x)Kxx$	3, UG	(valid)

To see that the fourth example is indeed invalid, let *Lxy* stand for "*x* is larger than *y*," and let the variables range over the real numbers. The statement $(x)(\exists y)Lxy$ then means that there is no smallest number—which is true. But the statement $(\exists x)Lxx$ means that there is a number that is larger than itself—which is false.

I. Translate the following statements into symbolic form.

★**1.** Charmaine read *Paradise Lost*. (*Rxy*: *x* read *y*)

2. Whoever reads *Paradise Lost* is educated. (*Rxy*: *x* reads *y*; *Ex*: *x* is educated)

3. James is a friend of either Ellen or Connie. (*Fxy*: *x* is a friend of *y*)

★**4.** If James has any friends, then Marlene is one of them. (*Fxy*: *x* is a friend of *y*)

5. Dr. Jordan teaches only geniuses. (*Txy*: *x* teaches *y*; *Gx*: *x* is a genius)

6. Dr. Nelson teaches a few morons. (*Txy*: *x* teaches *y*; *Mx*: *x* is a moron)

★**7.** Every person can sell something or other. (*Px*: *x* is a person; *Sxy*: *x* can sell *y*)

8. Some people cannot sell anything.

9. No person can sell everything.

★**10.** Some people can sell anything.

11. The Royal Hotel serves only good drinks. (*Sxy*: *x* serves *y*; *Gx*: *x* is good; *Dx*: *x* is a drink)

12. The Clark Corporation advertises everything it produces. (*Axy*: *x* advertises *y*; *Pxy*: *x* produces *y*)

★**13.** Peterson can drive some of the cars in the lot. (*Dxy*: *x* can drive *y*; *Cx*: *x* is a car; *Lx*: *x* is in the lot)

14. Jones can drive any car in the lot.

15. Sylvia invited only her friends. (*Ixy*: *x* invited *y*; *Fxy*: *x* is a friend of *y*)

★**16.** Christopher invited some of his friends.

17. Some people break everything they touch. (*Px*: *x* is a person; *Bxy*: *x* breaks *y*; *Txy*: *x* touches *y*)

18. Some people speak to whoever speaks to them. (*Px*: *x* is a person; *Sxy*: *x* speaks to *y*)

★**19.** Every person admires some people he or she meets. (*Px*: *x* is a person; *Axy*: *x* admires *y*; *Mxy*: *x* meets *y*)

MindTap® Complete exercises online for immediate feedback.

20. Some people admire every person they meet.

21. Some policemen arrest only traffic violators. (*Px*: *x* is a policeman; *Axy*: *x* arrests *y*; *Tx*: *x* is a traffic violator)

★22. Some policemen arrest every traffic violator they see. (*Px*: *x* is a policeman; *Axy*: *x* arrests *y*; *Tx*: *x* is a traffic violator; *Sxy*: *x* sees *y*)

23. If there are cheaters, then some cheaters will be punished. (*Cx*: *x* is a cheater; *Px*: *x* will be punished)

24. If there are any cheaters, then if all the referees are vigilant they will be punished. (*Cx*: *x* is a cheater; *Rx*: *x* is a referee; *Vx*: *x* is vigilant; *Px*: *x* will be punished)

★25. Every lawyer will represent a wealthy client. (*Lx*: *x* is a lawyer; *Rxy*: *x* will represent *y*; *Wx*: *x* is wealthy; *Cx*: *x* is a client)

26. Some lawyers will represent any person who will not represent himself. (*Lx*: *x* is a lawyer; *Px*: *x* is a person; *Rxy*: *x* represents *y*)

27. Some children in the third grade can read any of the books in the library. (*Cx*: *x* is a child; *Tx*: *x* is in the third grade; *Rxy*: *x* can read *y*; *Bx*: *x* is a book; *Lx*: *x* is in the library)

★28. All children in the fourth grade can read any of the books in the library.

29. If there are any safe drivers, then if none of the trucks break down they will be hired. (*Sx*: *x* is safe; *Dx*: *x* is a driver; *Tx*: *x* is a truck; *Bx*: *x* breaks down; *Hx*: *x* will be hired)

30. If there are any safe drivers, then some safe drivers will be hired.

II. Derive the conclusion of the following symbolized arguments. Use conditional proof or indirect proof as needed.

★(1) 1. $(x)[Ax \supset (y)Bxy]$
     2. Am / $(y)Bmy$

(2) 1. $(x)[Ax \supset (y)(By \supset Cxy)]$
    2. $Am \cdot Bn$ / Cmn

(3) 1. $(\exists x)[Ax \cdot (y)(By \supset Cxy)]$
    2. $(\exists x)Ax \supset Bj$ / $(\exists x)Cxj$

★(4) 1. $(x)(\exists y)(Ax \supset By)$ / $(x)Ax \supset (\exists y)By$

(5) 1. $(\exists x)Ax \supset (\exists y)By$ / $(\exists y)(x)(Ax \supset By)$

(6) 1. $(x)(y)(Ax \supset By)$
    2. $(\exists x)(y)(Ay \supset Cx)$ / $(x)(\exists y)[Ax \supset (By \cdot Cy)]$

★(7) 1. $(\exists x)[Ax \cdot (y)(Ay \supset Bxy)]$ / $(\exists x)Bxx$

(8) 1. $(\exists x)[Ax \cdot (y)(By \supset Cxy)]$
    2. $(x)(\exists y)(Ax \supset By)$ / $(\exists x)(\exists y)Cxy$

(9) 1. $(\exists x)(y)(Axy \supset Bxy)$
2. $(x)(\exists y)\sim Bxy$ / $\sim(x)(y)Axy$

★(10) 1. $(x)(\exists y)Axy \supset (x)(\exists y)Bxy$
2. $(\exists x)(y)\sim Bxy$ / $(\exists x)(y)\sim Axy$

(11) 1. $(\exists x)\{Ax \cdot [(\exists y)By \supset Cx]\}$
2. $(x)(Ax \supset Bx)$ / $(\exists x)Cx$

(12) 1. $(\exists x)(y)[(Ay \cdot By) \supset Cxy]$
2. $(y)(Ay \supset By)$ / $(y)[Ay \supset (\exists x)Cxy]$

★(13) 1. $(\exists x)\{Ax \cdot (y)[(By \vee Cy) \supset Dxy]\}$
2. $(\exists x)Ax \supset (\exists y)By$ / $(\exists x)(\exists y)Dxy$

(14) 1. $(x)\{Ax \supset [(\exists y)(By \cdot Cy) \supset Dx]\}$
2. $(x)(Bx \supset Cx)$ / $(x)[Ax \supset (Bx \supset Dx)]$

(15) 1. $(\exists x)(y)(Ayx \supset \sim Axy)$ / $\sim(x)Axx$

★(16) 1. $(x)(Ax \supset Bx)$
2. $(\exists x)Bx \supset \sim(\exists x)(\exists y)Cxy$ / $(\exists x)Ax \supset \sim Cmn$

(17) 1. $(\exists x)(y)(Axy \supset Byx)$
2. $(x)(\exists y)(Byx \supset \sim Axy)$ / $\sim(x)(y)Axy$

(18) 1. $(x)[Ax \supset (\exists y)(By \cdot Cxy)]$
2. $(\exists x)[Ax \cdot (y)(By \supset Dxy)]$ / $(\exists x)(\exists y)(Cxy \cdot Dxy)$

★(19) 1. $(\exists x)(y)Ayx \vee (x)(y)Bxy$
2. $(\exists x)(y)(Cy \supset \sim Byx)$ / $(x)(\exists y)(Cx \supset Axy)$

(20) 1. $(x)(y)[Axy \supset (Bx \cdot Cy)]$
2. $(x)(y)[(Bx \vee Dy) \supset \sim Axy]$ / $\sim(\exists x)(\exists y)Axy$

III. Translate the following arguments into symbolic form. Then derive the conclusion of each, using conditional proof or indirect proof when needed.

★1. Any professional can outplay any amateur. Jones is a professional but he cannot outplay Meyers. Therefore, Meyers is not an amateur. (*Px*: *x* is a professional; *Ax*: *x* is an amateur; *Oxy*: *x* can outplay *y*)

2. Whoever is a friend of either Michael or Paul will receive a gift. If Michael has any friends, then Eileen is one of them. Therefore, if Ann is a friend of Michael, then Eileen will receive a gift. (*Fxy*: *x* is a friend of *y*; *Rx*: *x* will receive a gift)

3. A horse is an animal. Therefore, whoever owns a horse owns an animal. (*Hx*: *x* is a horse; *Ax*: *x* is an animal; *Oxy*: *x* owns *y*)

★4. O'Brien is a person. Furthermore, O'Brien is smarter than any person in the class. Since no person is smarter than himself, it follows that O'Brien is not in the class. (*Px*: *x* is a person; *Sxy*: *x* is smarter than *y*; *Cx*: *x* is in the class)

5. If there are any honest politicians, then if all the ballots are counted they will be reelected. Some honest politicians will not be reelected. Therefore, some

ballots will not be counted. (*Hx*: *x* is honest; *Px*: *x* is a politician; *Bx*: *x* is a ballot; *Cx*: *x* is counted; *Rx*: *x* will be reelected)

6. Dr. Rogers can cure any person who cannot cure himself. Dr. Rogers is a person. Therefore, Dr. Rogers can cure himself. (*Px*: *x* is a person; *Cxy*: *x* can cure *y*)

★7. Some people are friends of every person they know. Every person knows someone (or other). Therefore, at least one person is a friend of someone. (*Px*: *x* is a person; *Fxy*: *x* is a friend of *y*; *Kxy*: *x* knows *y*)

8. If there are any policemen, then if there are any robbers, then they will arrest them. If any robbers are arrested by policemen, they will go to jail. There are some policemen and Macky is a robber. Therefore, Macky will go to jail. (*Px*: *x* is a policeman; *Rx*: *x* is a robber; *Axy*: *x* arrests *y*; *Jx*: *x* will go to jail)

9. If anything is missing, then some person stole it. If anything is damaged, then some person broke it. Something is either missing or damaged. Therefore, some person either stole something or broke something. (*Mx*: *x* is missing; *Px*: *x* is a person; *Sxy*: *x* stole *y*; *Dx*: *x* is damaged; *Bxy*: *x* broke *y*)

★10. If there are any instructors, then if at least one classroom is available they will be effective. If there are either any textbooks or workbooks, there will be instructors and classrooms. Furthermore, if there are any classrooms, they will be available. Therefore, if there are any textbooks, then some instructors will be effective. (*Ix*: *x* is an instructor; *Cx*: *x* is a classroom; *Ax*: *x* is available; *Ex*: *x* is effective; *Tx*: *x* is a textbook; *Wx*: *x* is a workbook)

IV. Create five statements involving the relational predicate "friend of." Then translate each statement into the language of predicate logic.

MindTap® Master concepts and improve outcomes with Aplia, at the end of the chapter, in the Aplia folder.

8

8.7   Identity

HOW LOGICAL ARE YOU? Consider the following facts: Any friend of Theo is a friend of Justine. Barbara is a friend of Theo. Barbara is also known as "Bopsie." All Justine's friends are English majors. Based on this information, do we know what Bopsie's major is? If so, what is it?

Find the answer on MindTap.

Many arguments in ordinary language involve a special relation called *identity*, and translating this relation requires special treatment. Consider, for example, the following argument:

The only friend I have is Elizabeth. Elizabeth is not Nancy. Nancy is a Canadian. Therefore, there is a Canadian who is not my friend.

The peculiar feature of this argument is that it involves special statements about individuals. To translate such statements, we adopt a symbol from arithmetic, the equal sign (=), to represent the identity relation. We can use this symbol to translate a large variety of statements, including simple identity statements, existential assertions about individuals, statements involving "only," "the only," "no . . . except," and "all except," and statements involving superlatives, numerical claims, and definite descriptions. After seeing how the identity relation is used to translate such statements, we will see how natural deduction is used to derive the conclusions of arguments involving identity.

Simple Identity Statements

The simplest statements involving identity are those asserting that a named individual is identical to another named individual. Here are some examples:

Samuel Clemens is Mark Twain.	$s = m$
LL Cool J is James Todd Smith.	$c = j$
Dr. Jekyll is Mr. Hyde.	$j = h$

The first statement asserts that Samuel Clemens is identically the same person as Mark Twain, the second that LL Cool J is the same person as James Todd Smith, and the third that Dr. Jekyll is the same person as Mr. Hyde. In other words, the statements claim that the names "Samuel Clemens" and "Mark Twain" designate the same person, "LL Cool J" and "James Todd Smith" designate the same person, and so on.

To translate a negated identity statement, we simply draw a slash through the identity symbol. Thus, "Beethoven is not Mozart" is translated $b \neq m$. The expression $b \neq m$ is just an abbreviated way of writing $\sim(b = m)$. Here are some additional examples:

William Wordsworth is not John Keats.	$w \neq j$
Natalie Portman is not Rosie O'Donnell.	$n \neq r$
Brian Williams is not Katie Couric.	$b \neq k$

The kinds of statements we will consider next are more complicated, and to facilitate their translation a set of conventions governing conjunctions, disjunctions, and simple identity statements will now be introduced. Many of our translations will involve lengthy strings of conjunctions, such as $Pm \cdot Km \cdot Pn \cdot Kn$. Instead of introducing parentheses and brackets into these expressions, we may simply write them as a string of conjuncts. Lengthy disjunctions may be treated the same way. In simple identity statements, the identity symbol controls only the letters to its immediate left and right. Accordingly, instead of writing $(c = n) \cdot (e = p) \cdot (s = t)$, we may write $c = n \cdot e = p \cdot s = t$, and instead of writing $P \supset (a = m)$, we may write $P \supset a = m$. Let us now use these conventions to translate some special kinds of statements involving identity.

"Only," "The Only," and "No . . . Except"

Section 4.7 explained that the words "only," "the only," and "no . . . except" signal an ordinary categorical proposition when the word that follows is a plural noun or pronoun. For example, the statement "Only relatives are invited" means simply "All invited people are relatives," and "The only animals in this canyon are skunks" means "All animals in this canyon are skunks." However, when the word that follows "only," "the only," or "no . . . except" designates an individual, something more is intended. Thus the statement "Only Nixon resigned the presidency" means (1) that Nixon resigned the presidency and (2) that if anyone resigned the presidency, that person is Nixon. Thus, the general form of such statements is that a designated individual has a stated attribute and anything having that attribute is identical to the designated individual. Here are some examples:

Only Nolan Ryan has struck out 5,000 batters.	$Sn \cdot (x)(Sx \supset x = n)$
The only opera written by Beethoven is *Fidelio*.	$Of \cdot Bf \cdot (x)[(Ox \cdot Bx) \supset x = f]$
No nation except Australia is a continent.	$Na \cdot Ca \cdot (x)[(Nx \cdot Cx) \supset x = a]$
The only presidents who were Whigs were Taylor and Fillmore.	$Pt \cdot Wt \cdot Pf \cdot Wf \cdot (x)[(Px \cdot Wx) \supset (x = t \lor x = f)]$

The first translation may be read as "Nolan Ryan has struck out 5,000 batters, and if anyone has struck out 5,000 batters, then he is identical to Nolan Ryan." The last part of the translation ensures that no other person has struck out 5,000 batters. The second translation may be read as "*Fidelio* is an opera, and *Fidelio* was written by Beethoven, and if anything is an opera written by Beethoven, then it is identical to *Fidelio*." Analogous remarks pertain to the other two statements. The third statement is equivalent to "The only nation that is a continent is Australia."

"All Except"

Statements beginning with "all except" are similar to those beginning with "the only" in that they, too, assert something about a designated individual (or individuals). For example, the statement "All presidents except Washington had a predecessor" means that Washington did not have a predecessor but all other presidents did. Thus, the general form of such statements is that a designated individual lacks a stated attribute and that anything not identical to the designated individual has the stated attribute. Examples:

All painters except Jackson Pollock make sense.	$Pj \cdot \sim Mj \cdot (x)[(Px \cdot x \neq j) \supset Mx]$
All continents except Antarctica are heavily populated.	$Ca \cdot \sim Ha \cdot (x)[(Cx \cdot x \neq a) \supset Hx]$
All states except Alaska and Hawaii are contiguous with their sister states.	$Sa \cdot \sim Ca \cdot Sh \cdot \sim Ch \cdot (x)[(Sx \cdot x \neq a \cdot x \neq h) \supset Cx]$

The first translation may be read as "Jackson Pollock is a painter who does not make sense, and every painter not identical to Jackson Pollock makes sense."

Kurt Gödel, generally considered to be the most important logician of the contemporary period, was born in what is today Brno, Czechoslovakia, to a father who managed a textile factory and a mother who was educated and cultured. After excelling at the gymnasium in Brno, Gödel entered the University of Vienna, where he studied mathematics, physics, and philosophy. On completing his undergraduate degree he commenced graduate work in mathematics, earning his doctorate at age twenty-four. Four years later Gödel began teaching at the university as a *Privatdozent*. However, when the Nazis annexed Austria they abolished his teaching position in favor of one that required a political test, and one year later they found him qualified for military service.

In 1940, under threat of being drafted into the German army, Gödel and his wife Adel (whom he had married two years earlier) left for the United States, where he accepted a position at the famous Institute for Advanced Studies, in Princeton, New Jersey. Soon after arriving, he became best of friends with Albert Einstein, with whom he took daily walks. Gödel became a permanent member of the institute in 1946, and five years later he received the first Albert Einstein Award. In 1974 he was awarded the National Medal of Science.

Gödel is most famous for developing incompleteness theorems that relate to the efforts by logicians to reduce arithmetic to logic. Ordinary arithmetic rests on a set of axioms (called the Peano axioms), and for many years logicians thought (or hoped) that all of the theorems of arithmetic could be reduced to those axioms. Such a system would be complete in that every theorem would be linked to the axioms by a logical proof sequence. Quite to the surprise of these logicians, Gödel showed that every axiom system adequate

Alfred Eisenstaedt/ Time Life Pictures/Getty Images

to support arithmetic contains at least one assertion that is neither provable nor disprovable from the axioms. A second incompleteness theorem showed that the consistency of such a system cannot be proved within the system itself.

As a philosopher Gödel was a Platonic realist and a Leibnizian rationalist. He thought that abstract concepts (such as number and figure) represented objects in an ideal realm that were perfect, changeless, and eternal. As a result he thought that mathematics is a science that describes this ideal realm, and not, as many think, a mere invention of the human mind. Following Leibniz, Gödel conceived the visible world as fundamentally beautiful, perfect, and thoroughly ordered. To complete this perfect world he developed his own ontological argument for the existence of God.

Tragically, from an early age, Gödel was troubled by emotional afflictions, including depression, and as he grew older he suffered from psychotic delusions. In the middle of the winter he would open wide all the windows of his house because he thought that malevolent forces intended to poison him with gas. He also feared they wanted to poison his food, so he ate only his wife's cooking. When Adel became incapacitated from illness, Gödel stopped eating altogether. At age seventy-one he died from malnutrition, at which point his body weighed only sixty-five pounds.

8

Superlatives

Statements containing superlative adjectives are yet another kind of statement that can be translated by using the identity relation. These are statements asserting that, of all the members of a class, something is the largest, tallest, smallest, heaviest, lightest, and so on. To translate these statements, first give the designated item the class attribute, and then say that, if anything else has that attribute, it is somehow exceeded by the designated item. Here are some examples:

The largest planet is Jupiter.	$Pj \cdot (x)[(Px \cdot x \neq j) \supset Ljx]$
The deepest lake is Ozero Baykal.	$Lo \cdot (x)[(Lx \cdot x \neq o) \supset Dox]$
The highest peak in North America is Mt. McKinley.	$Pm \cdot Nm \cdot (x)[(Px \cdot Nx \cdot x \neq m) \supset Hmx]$

The first translation may be read as "Jupiter is a planet, and if anything is a planet and not identical to Jupiter, then Jupiter is larger than it." The second may be read as "Ozero Baykal is a lake, and if anything is a lake and not identical to Ozero Baykal, then Ozero Baykal is deeper than it."

Numerical Statements

One of the more interesting uses of the identity symbol is to translate certain kinds of numerical statements, such as "There are three people in this room." In particular, the identity symbol allows us to translate such statements without the use of numerals. There are three types of numerical statements: those that assert a property of *at most n* items, those that assert a property of *at least n* items, and those that assert a property of *exactly n* items.

The first group does not assert that there actually are any items that have the stated property but only that, if there are any with the stated property, then the maximum number is *n*. Accordingly, for "at most" statements we use universal quantifiers. Here are some examples:

There is at most one god.	$(x)(y)[(Gx \cdot Gy) \supset x = y]$
There is at most one U.S. representative from Alaska.	$(x)(y)[(Ux \cdot Ax \cdot Uy \cdot Ay) \supset x = y]$
There are at most two superpowers.	$(x)(y)(z)[(Sx \cdot Sy \cdot Sz) \supset (x = y \lor x = z \lor y = z)]$
There are at most two cities in Kuwait.	$(x)(y)(z)[(Cx \cdot Kx \cdot Cy \cdot Ky \cdot Cz \cdot Kz) \supset (x = y \lor x = z \lor y = z)]$

It can be seen from these examples that to translate "at most *n*" is to say that, if there are *n* + 1 items that have the stated property, then at least one of them is identical to at least one of the "others." The result is to limit the number of such items to *n*. Thus, to translate "at most one," we need two quantifiers; to translate "at most two," we need three quantifiers; and so on. We could use this procedure to translate statements about any number of items, but because such translations become rather lengthy, this discussion is limited to statements about one or two items at most.

Unlike "at most" statements, statements that assert something about *at least n* items do claim that the items actually exist. Thus, to translate "at least" statements we need to use existential quantifiers. The number of quantifiers must be equal to the number of items asserted. Examples:

There is at least one city in Monaco. $(\exists x)(Cx \cdot Mx)$

There are at least two women in $(\exists x)(\exists y)(Wx \cdot Hx \cdot Wy \cdot Hy \cdot x \neq y)$
Hamlet.

There are at least three satellites $(\exists x)(\exists y)(\exists z)(Sx \cdot Sy \cdot Sz \cdot x \neq y \cdot x \neq z \cdot y \neq z)$
of Neptune.

The first of these examples merely asserts that some city is in Monaco. Thus, it is translated without any inclusion of the identity relation. When the stated number is greater than 1, however, the translation must incorporate one or more negative identity statements to ensure that the items referred to are distinct. Thus, in the second statement, if x and y should be identical, then there would actually be only one woman (at least) in *Hamlet*. To ensure that there are at least two distinct women, we must conjoin the assertion that x and y are not identical. Similarly, when we assert something about at least three items, we must conjoin the assertion that none of them is identical to either of the other two.

A statement about *exactly n* items can be seen to be the conjunction of a statement about at least *n* items and a statement about at most *n* items. For example, the statement "There are exactly three cars in the lot" means that there are at least three cars in the lot and at most three cars in the lot. Thus, a statement about exactly *n* items requires *n* existential quantifiers to ensure the existence of the items, one or more negated identity statements to ensure their distinctness (assuming *n* is greater than 1), and a universally quantified statement to limit the group to at most *n* items. Here are some examples:

There is exactly one city in Grenada. $(\exists x)\{Cx \cdot Gx \cdot (y)[(Cy \cdot Gy) \supset x = y]\}$

There are exactly two houses $(\exists x)(\exists y)\{Hx \cdot Hy \cdot x \neq y \cdot$
of Congress. $\quad (z)[Hz \supset (z = x \lor z = y)]\}$

There are exactly two sopranos in $(\exists x)(\exists y)\{Sx \cdot Lx \cdot Sy \cdot Ly \cdot x \neq y \cdot$
La Boheme. $\quad (z)[(Sz \cdot Lz) \supset (z = x \lor z = y)]\}$

Definite Descriptions

The last form of phraseology considered here is the definite description. A *definite description* is a group of words of the form "the such-and-such" that identifies an individual person, place, or thing. Here are some examples:

The author of *Evangeline*
The capital of Nebraska
The mother of John F. Kennedy

The first designates Henry Wadsworth Longfellow, the second the city of Lincoln, and the third Rose Fitzgerald Kennedy. Definite descriptions are like names in that they identify only one thing, but unlike names they do so by describing a situation or relationship that only that one thing satisfies.

Statements incorporating definite descriptions have given rise to disputes in logic, because alternate interpretations of such statements can lead to conflicts in truth value. Suppose, for example, we are given the statement "The queen of the United States is a woman." Should we consider this statement to be true, because every queen is a woman, or should we consider it to be false, because there is no queen of the United States? In response to this question, most logicians today accept an interpretation of definite descriptions originally proposed by Bertrand Russell. According to this interpretation, a statement that incorporates a definite description asserts three things: an item of a certain sort exists, there is only one such item, and that item has the attribute assigned to it by the statement. If we accept this interpretation, the statement about the queen of the United States is false, because no such person exists.

Here are some additional examples with their translations:

The inventor of the phonograph was an American.	$(\exists x)[Ixp \cdot (y)(Iyp \supset y = x) \cdot Ax]$
The author of *Middlemarch* was a Victorian freethinker.	$(\exists x)[Wxm \cdot (y)(Wym \supset y = x) \cdot Vx \cdot Fx]$
The painter of *The Starry Night* was Van Gogh.	$(\exists x)[Pxs \cdot (y)(Pys \supset y = x) \cdot x = v]$

The first translation may be read as "There is someone who invented the phonograph, and if anyone invented the phonograph, then that person is identical to the first, and the first person is an American." The second may be read as "There is someone who wrote *Middlemarch,* and if anyone wrote *Middlemarch,* then that person is identical to the first, and the first person is a Victorian freethinker." The third may be read as "There is someone who painted *The Starry Night,* and if anyone painted *The Starry Night,* then that person is identical to the first, and the first person is identical to Van Gogh."

This completes our explanation of how to translate statements involving the identity relation. At this point, you may, if you wish, proceed to Exercise 8.7 part I before completing the remainder of this section.

Using the Rules of Inference

Now that we have seen how to translate statements involving the identity relation, let us use natural deduction to derive the conclusions of arguments that include statements of this sort. Before doing so, however, some special rules governing the identity relation must be introduced. These rules, which are collectively designated "Id," are as follows:

$$\text{Id: (1)} \quad \frac{\text{Prem}}{x = x} \qquad (2) \quad x = y :: y = x \qquad (3) \quad \frac{\begin{array}{c}\mathscr{F}x \\ x = y\end{array}}{\mathscr{F}y}$$

These rules are expressed in terms of individual variables (*x* and *y*), so obviously they hold for any individual variables. But since any individual constant (such as *a* or *b*) is a substitution instance of any individual variable, these rules hold for individual constants as well. The first rule expresses the idea that anything is identical to itself; it asserts what is called the reflexive property of the identity relation. The rule allows us to insert a self-identity statement after any premise (that is, on any line in a proof).

The second rule is a rule of replacement; it expresses what is called the symmetric property of the identity relation. It states, very simply, that the letters on either side of the equal sign can be switched. An immediate use of this rule is to prove that $x \neq y$ is logically equivalent to $y \neq x$. Recall that $x \neq y$ is simply an abbreviation for $\sim(x = y)$. If we apply the rule to the latter expression, we obtain $\sim(y = x)$, which, in its abbreviated form, is $y \neq x$.

The third rule expresses the intuitively obvious idea that, if something is true of *x* and *x* is identical to *y*, then that something is true of *y*. This rule is the basis of what is called the transitive property of identity, which allows us to infer from $x = y$ and $y = z$ that $x = z$. If we suppose that the $\mathscr{F}$ in this rule stands for the expression "$x =$," that *x* is *y*, and that *y* is *z*, then the first line of the rule reads $x = y$, the second line reads $y = z$, and the conclusion is $x = z$. This inference is used often in the derivation of the conclusions of arguments.

In general, the rules of inference used earlier apply to arguments containing identity statements in the same way they apply to any other arguments. Also, conditional proof and indirect proof are used in the same way.

The following argument illustrates the first expression of the rule for identity.

> No biologists are identical to Isabel. Therefore, Isabel is not a biologist.

If we use *Bx* to translate "*x* is a biologist," and *i* for Isabel, this argument becomes

    1. $(x)(Bx \supset x \neq i)$ / $\sim Bi$

The fact that the conclusion contains *i* suggests that we instantiate line 1 with respect to that letter. The proof is as follows:

    1. $(x)(Bx \supset x \neq i)$ / $\sim Bi$
    2. $Bi \supset i \neq i$ 1, UI
    3. $i = i$ Id
    4. $\sim(i \neq i)$ 3, DN
    5. $\sim Bi$ 2, 4, MT

Line 3 comes merely from the first expression of the identity rule, which allows us to insert any self-identity statement after any premise. Thus, no numeral is included in the justification for that line. Also note that line 4 is simply another way of writing $\sim\sim(i = i)$.

Now let us return to the argument given at the beginning of this section:

> The only friend I have is Elizabeth. Elizabeth is not Nancy. Nancy is a Canadian. Therefore, there is a Canadian who is not my friend.

If we use *Fx* to translate "*x* is my friend" and *Cx* to translate "*x* is a Canadian," this argument may be translated as follows:

    1. $Fe \cdot (x)(Fx \supset x = e)$
    2. $e \neq n$
    3. Cn / $(\exists x)(Cx \cdot \sim Fx)$

Inspecting the second line, we see a negated identity statement involving e and n. This suggests that we instantiate the universal statement in the first line with respect to n. The proof is as follows:

1. $Fe \cdot (x)(Fx \supset x = e)$
2. $e \neq n$
3. Cn / $(\exists x)(Cx \cdot \sim Fx)$
4. $(x)(Fx \supset x = e) \cdot Fe$ 1, Com
5. $(x)(Fx \supset x = e)$ 4, Simp
6. $Fn \supset n = e$ 5, UI
7. $n \neq e$ 2, Id
8. $\sim Fn$ 6, 7, MT
9. $Cn \cdot \sim Fn$ 3, 8, Conj
10. $(\exists x)(Cx \cdot \sim Fx)$ 9, EG

Line 7 is justified by the second rule for identity. Also, since $n \neq e$ is simply an abbreviation for $\sim(n = e)$, line 8 follows directly from lines 6 and 7.

Here is another example:

The only person who invested is Ms. Snyder. Cathy is one of the people who lost money. Some people who invested did not lose money. Therefore, Cathy is not Ms. Snyder.

The translation is as follows:

1. $Ps \cdot Is \cdot (x)[(Px \cdot Ix) \supset x = s]$
2. $Pc \cdot Lc$
3. $(\exists x)(Px \cdot Ix \cdot \sim Lx)$ / $c \neq s$

Cursory inspection reveals no easy way to obtain the conclusion. This suggests indirect proof:

8

1. $Ps \cdot Is \cdot (x)[(Px \cdot Ix) \supset x = s]$
2. $Pc \cdot Lc$
3. $(\exists x)(Px \cdot Ix \cdot \sim Lx)$ / $c \neq s$
4. $c = s$ AIP
5. $Pa \cdot Ia \cdot \sim La$ 3, EI
6. $(x)[(Px \cdot Ix) \supset x = s] \cdot Ps \cdot Is$ 1, Com
7. $(x)[(Px \cdot Ix) \supset x = s]$ 6, Simp
8. $Pa \cdot Ia \supset a = s$ 7, UI
9. $Pa \cdot Ia$ 5, Simp
10. $a = s$ 8, 9, MP
11. $s = c$ 4, Id
12. $a = c$ 10, 11, Id
13. $\sim La \cdot Pa \cdot Ia$ 5, Com
14. $\sim La$ 13, Simp
15. $\sim Lc$ 12, 14, Id
16. $Lc \cdot Pc$ 2, Com
17. Lc 16, Simp
18. $Lc \cdot \sim Lc$ 15, 17, Conj
19. $c \neq s$ 4–18, IP

As usual, the existential statement is instantiated first, then the universal. Line 11 is derived by commuting line 4 by the second rule of identity, and line 12 is derived from lines 10 and 11 by applying the third rule of identity. Line 15 is derived by substituting c in the place of a in line 14 according to the third rule of identity. The indirect sequence is discharged in line 19 in the normal way.

In arguments involving identity, especially more-complicated ones, it is often difficult or impossible to see by mere inspection how to obtain the conclusion. A good general procedure is to begin with instantiation. Always instantiate the existential statements first, then the universals. When instantiating the universal statements, normally pick the letter (or one of the letters) used to instantiate the existential statement(s). If there are no existential statements, pick one of the letters appearing in the singular statements. If the conclusion is still not apparent, try indirect proof. In general, whenever the conclusion is a complicated statement, it is best to start out with indirect proof. Developing facility in proving arguments involving identity requires a little practice, but adequate skill should not take too long to acquire.

Translation hints

Only i is F.	$Fi \cdot (x)[Fx \supset x = i]$
The only F that is G is i.	$Fi \cdot Gi \cdot (x)[(Fx \cdot Gx) \supset x = i]$
No F except i is G.	$Fi \cdot Gi \cdot (x)[(Fx \cdot Gx) \supset x = i]$
All F except i are G.	$Fi \cdot {\sim}Gi \cdot (x)[(Fx \cdot x \neq i) \supset Gx]$
i is the F that is most so-and-so.	$Fi \cdot (x)[(Fx \cdot x \neq i) \supset i$ is more so-and-so than $x]$
There is at most one F.	$(x)(y)[(Fx \cdot Fy) \supset x = y]$
There are at least two F's.	$(\exists x)(\exists y)[Fx \cdot Fy \cdot x \neq y]$
There are exactly two F's.	$(\exists x)(\exists y)\{Fx \cdot Fy \cdot x \neq y \cdot (z)[Fz \supset (z = x \lor z = y)]\}$
The F is G.	$(\exists x)[Fx \cdot (y)(Fy \supset y = x) \cdot Gx]$

EXERCISE 8.7

I. Translate the following statements.

Simple identity statements

★1. Dr. Seuss is Theodore Geisel. (s, g)

2. Auguste Renoir is not Claude Monet. (r, m)

3. Marilyn Monroe is Norma Jean Baker. (*m, b*)

★**4.** Hermann Hesse is not André Gide. (*h, g*)

Statements involving "only," "the only," and "no . . . except"

★**5.** Only Linus Pauling has won two unshared Nobel prizes. (*Wx: x* has won two Nobel prizes; *p*: Linus Pauling)

6. Only Don Larsen has pitched a perfect World Series game. (*Px: x* has pitched a perfect World Series game; *l*: Don Larsen)

7. The only national park in Maine is Acadia. (*Nx: x* is a national park; *Mx: x* is in Maine; *a*: Acadia)

★**8.** The only nation having a maple-leaf flag is Canada. (*Nx: x* is a nation; *Mx: x* has a maple-leaf flag; *c*: Canada)

9. The only U.S. presidents who were Federalists were Washington and Adams. (*Ux: x* is a U.S. president; *Fx: x* is a Federalist; *w*: Washington; *a*: Adams)

10. No state except Hawaii is surrounded by water. (*Sx: x* is a state; *Wx: x* is surrounded by water; *h*: Hawaii)

★**11.** No sport except hockey uses a puck. (*Sx: x* is a sport; *Px: x* uses a puck; *h*: hockey)

Superlative statements

★**12.** Hydrogen is the lightest element. (*Ex: x* is an element; *Lxy: x* is lighter than *y*; *h*: hydrogen)

13. The smallest planet in our solar system is Mercury. (*Px: x* is a planet in our solar system; *Sxy: x* is smaller than *y*; *m*: Mercury)

14. Harvard is the oldest American university. (*Ax: x* is American; *Ux: x* is a university; *Oxy: x* is older than *y*; *h*: Harvard)

★**15.** Death Valley is the lowest region in North America. (*Rx: x* is a region; *Nx: x* is in North America; *Lyx: x* is lower than *y*; *d*: Death Valley)

Statements involving "all except"

★**16.** Every city except Istanbul is situated on a single continent. (*Cx: x* is a city; *Sx: x* is situated on a single continent; *i*: Istanbul)

17. Every U.S. president except Ford won a national election. (*Ux: x* is a U.S. president; *Wx: x* won a national election; *f*: Ford)

18. All metals except mercury are solids at room temperature. (*Mx: x* is a metal; *Sx: x* is a solid at room temperature; *m*: mercury)

★**19.** Every pitcher except Cy Young has won fewer than 500 games. (*Px: x* is a pitcher; *Wx: x* has won fewer than 500 games; *c*: Cy Young)

8

Numerical statements

★20. There is at most one city in Belize. (Cx: x is a city; Bx: x is in Belize)

21. There are at most two national parks in South Dakota. (Nx: x is a national park; Sx: x is in South Dakota)

22. There is at most one national holiday in July. (Nx: x is a national holiday; Jx: x is in July)

★23. There are at most two cities in Malta. (Cx: x is a city; Mx: x is in Malta)

24. There is at least one quarterback on a football team. (Qx: x is a quarterback; Fx: x is on a football team)

25. There are at least two atoms in a water molecule. (Ax: x is an atom; Wx: x is in a water molecule)

★26. There are at least three carbon allotropes. (Cx: x is a carbon allotrope)

27. There is exactly one U.S. Supreme Court. (Ux: x is a U.S. Supreme Court)

28. There is exactly one natural satellite of the earth. (Sx: x is a satellite of the earth; Nx: x is natural)

★29. There are exactly two bright stars in Gemini. (Sx: x is a star; Bx: x is bright; Gx: x is in Gemini)

Statements containing definite descriptions

★30. The author of *Vanity Fair* was born in India. (Wxy: x wrote y; Bx: x was born in India; v: *Vanity Fair*)

31. The wife of Othello is Desdemona. (Wxy: x is the wife of y; o: Othello; d: Desdemona)

32. The man who composed *The Nutcracker* was Russian. (Mx: x is a man; Cxy: x composed y; Rx: x was Russian; n: *The Nutcracker*)

★33. The artist who painted the *Allegory of Spring* was Botticelli. (Ax: x is an artist; Pxy: x painted y; a: the *Allegory of Spring*; b: Botticelli)

34. The capital of Georgia is not Savannah. (Cxy: x is the capital of y, g: Georgia; s: Savannah)

Assorted statements

★35. The smallest state is Rhode Island. (Sx: x is a state; Sxy: x is smaller than y; r: Rhode Island)

36. There is at least one newspaper in St. Louis. (Nx: x is a newspaper; Sx: x is in St. Louis)

37. Lady Gaga is Stefani Germanotta. (l: Lady Gaga; s: Stefani Germanotta)

★38. The only American president elected to a fourth term was Franklin D. Roosevelt. (Ax: x is an American president; Ex: x was elected to a fourth term; r: Franklin D. Roosevelt)

39. There are at least two cities in Qatar. (*Cx: x* is a city; *Qx: x* is in Qatar)

40. Only George Blanda has played twenty-six seasons of professional football games. (*Px: x* has played twenty-six seasons of professional football games; *b:* George Blanda)

★41. Hamlet had at most one sister. (*Sxy: x* is a sister of *y*; *h:* Hamlet)

42. No major league baseball player has hit seventy-three home runs in a single season except Barry Bonds. (*Mx: x* is a major league baseball player; *Hx: x* has hit seventy-three home runs in a single season; *b:* Barry Bonds)

43. There are at most two senators from New Hampshire. (*Sx: x* is a senator; *Nx: x* is from New Hampshire)

★44. Gustav Mahler is not Anton Bruckner. (*m:* Gustav Mahler; *b:* Anton Bruckner)

45. The explorer who discovered the North Pole was Admiral Peary. (*Ex: x* is an explorer; *Dxy: x* discovered *y*; *n:* the North Pole; *a:* Admiral Peary)

46. Hinduism is the oldest religion. (*Rx: x* is a religion; *Oxy: x* is older than *y*; *h:* Hinduism)

★47. There are exactly two tenors in *Carmen*. (*Tx: x* is a tenor; *Cx: x* is in *Carmen*)

48. Every Speaker of the House except Nancy Pelosi has been a man. (*Sx: x* is Speaker of the House; *Mx: x* is a man; *n:* Nancy Pelosi)

49. The person who discovered relativity theory was an employee in the Swiss patent office. (*Px: x* is a person; *Dxy: x* discovered *y*; *Ex: x* is an employee in the Swiss patent office; *r:* relativity theory)

★50. There are at least three stars in Orion. (*Sx: x* is a star; *Ox: x* is in Orion)

II. Derive the conclusion of the following symbolized arguments. Use conditional proof or indirect proof as needed.

★(1) 1. $(x)(x = a)$
    2. $(\exists x)Rx$ / Ra

(2) 1. Ke
    2. $\sim Kn$ / $e \neq n$

(3) 1. $(x)(x = c \supset Nx)$ / Nc

★(4) 1. $(\exists x)(x = g)$
    2. $(x)(x = i)$ / $g = i$

(5) 1. $(x)(Gx \supset x = a)$
    2. $(\exists x)(Gx \cdot Hx)$ / Ha

(6) 1. $(x)(Ax \supset Bx)$
    2. $Ac \cdot \sim Bi$ / $c \neq i$

★(7) 1. $(x)(x = a)$
    2. Fa / $Fm \cdot Fn$

8

(8) 1. $(x)(x = r)$
2. $Hr \cdot Kn$ / $Hn \cdot Kr$

(9) 1. $(x)(Lx \supset x = e)$
2. $(x)(Sx \supset x = i)$
3. $(\exists x)(Lx \cdot Sx)$ / $i = e$

★**(10)** 1. $(x)(Px \supset x = a)$
2. $(x)(x = c \supset Qx)$
3. $a = c$ / $(x)(Px \supset Qx)$

(11) 1. $(x)(y)(Txy \supset x = e)$
2. $(\exists x)Txi$ / Tei

(12) 1. $(x)[Rx \supset (Hx \cdot x = m)]$ / $Rc \supset Hm$

★**(13)** 1. $(x)(Ba \supset x \neq a)$
2. Bc / $a \neq c$

(14) 1. $(\exists x)Gx \supset (\exists x)(Kx \cdot x = i)$ / $Gn \supset Ki$

(15) 1. $(x)(Rax \supset \sim Rxc)$
2. $(x)Rxx$ / $c \neq a$

★**(16)** 1. $(x)[Nx \supset (Px \cdot x = m)]$
2. $\sim Pm$ / $\sim Ne$

(17) 1. $(x)(Fx \supset x = e)$
2. $(\exists x)(Fx \cdot x = a)$ / $a = e$

(18) 1. $(x)[Ex \supset (Hp \cdot x = e)]$
2. $(\exists x)(Ex \cdot x = p)$ / He

★**(19)** 1. $(x)(\exists y)(Cxy \supset x = y)$
2. $(\exists x)(y)(Cxy \cdot x = a)$ / Caa

(20) 1. $(x)[Fx \supset (Gx \cdot x = n)]$
2. $Gn \supset (\exists x)(Hx \cdot x = e)$ / $Fm \supset He$

III. Derive the conclusion of the following arguments. Use conditional proof or indirect proof as needed.

★**1.** Some of Jane Collier's novels are interesting. The only novel Jane Collier wrote is *The Cry*. Therefore, *The Cry* is interesting. (Nx: x is a novel; Wxy: x wrote y; Ix: x is interesting; j: Jane Collier; c: *The Cry*)

2. Ronald Reagan was the oldest U.S. president. Woodrow Wilson was a U.S. president. Woodrow Wilson is not Ronald Reagan. Therefore, Ronald Reagan was older than Woodrow Wilson. (Ux: x is a U.S. president; Oxy: x is older than y; r: Ronald Reagan; w: Woodrow Wilson)

3. The artist who painted the *Mona Lisa* was a Florentine. Leonardo is the artist who painted the *Mona Lisa*. Therefore, Leonardo was a Florentine. (Ax: x is an artist; Pxy: x painted y; Fx: x was a Florentine; m: the *Mona Lisa*; l: Leonardo)

8

★4. The novel on the table was written by Margaret Mitchell. The only novel Margaret Mitchell wrote is *Gone with the Wind*. Therefore, the novel on the table is *Gone with the Wind*. (*Nx*: *x* is a novel; *Tx*: *x* is on the table; *Wxy*: *x* wrote *y*; *m*: Margaret Mitchell; *g*: *Gone with the Wind*)

5. The author of *King Lear* was an English actor. John Milton was English but not an actor. Therefore, John Milton is not the author of *King Lear*. (*Wxy*: *x* wrote *y*; *Ex*: *x* is English; *Ax*: *x* is an actor; *k*: *King Lear*; *m*: John Milton)

6. The dog that bit the letter carrier is a large terrier. Ajax is a small dog. Therefore, Ajax did not bite the letter carrier. (*Dx*: *x* is a dog; *Bx*: *x* bit the letter carrier; *Lx*: *x* is large; *Tx*: *x* is a terrier; *a*: Ajax)

★7. Every member except Ellen sang a song. Every member except Nancy gave a speech. Ellen is not Nancy. Therefore, Ellen gave a speech and Nancy sang a song. (*Mx*: *x* is a member; *Sx*: *x* sang a song; *Gx*: *x* gave a speech; *e*: Ellen; *n*: Nancy)

8. The only person who ordered fish is Astrid. The only person who suffered indigestion is Ms. Wilson. Some person who ordered fish also suffered indigestion. Therefore, Astrid is Ms. Wilson. (*Px*: *x* is a person; *Ox*: *x* ordered fish; *Sx*: *x* suffered indigestion; *a*: Astrid; *w*: Ms. Wilson)

9. The highest mountain is in Tibet. Therefore, there is a mountain in Tibet that is higher than any mountain not in Tibet. (*Mx*: *x* is a mountain; *Hxy*: *x* is higher than *y*; *Tx*: *x* is in Tibet)

★10. The tallest building in North America is One World Trade Center. The tallest building in North America is located in New York City. If one thing is taller than another, then the latter is not taller than the former. Therefore, One World Trade Center is located in New York City. (*Bx*: *x* is a building in North America; *Txy*: *x* is taller than *y*; *Nx*: *x* is located in New York City; *o*: One World Trade Center.)

11. There are at least two philosophers in the library. Robert is the only French philosopher in the library. Therefore, there is a philosopher in the library who is not French. (*Px*: *x* is a philosopher; *Lx*: *x* is in the library; *Fx*: *x* is French; *r*: Robert)

12. The only dogs that barked were Fido and Pluto. Fido is not Pluto. Every dog except Fido ran on the beach. Therefore, exactly one barking dog ran on the beach. (*Dx*: *x* is a dog; *Bx*: *x* barked; *Rx*: *x* ran on the beach; *f*: Fido; *p*: Pluto)

★13. There are at least two attorneys in the office. All attorneys are professionals. There are at most two professionals in the office. Therefore, there are exactly two professionals in the office. (*Ax*: *x* is an attorney; *Ox*: *x* is in the office; *Px*: *x* is a professional)

14. There are at most two scientists in the laboratory. At least two scientists in the laboratory are Russians. No Russians are Chinese. Therefore, if Norene is a Chinese scientist, then she is not in the laboratory. (*Sx*: *x* is a scientist; *Lx*: *x* is in the laboratory; *Rx*: *x* is Russian; *Cx*: *x* is Chinese; *n*: Norene)

8

15. Every candidate except Mary was elected. The only candidate who was elected is Ralph. Mary is not Ralph. Therefore, there were exactly two candidates. (*Cx*: *x* is a candidate; *Ex*: *x* was elected; *m*: Mary; *r*: Ralph)

★16. Every student except Charles and Norman passed the course. The only student who was dismissed was Norman. Every student retook the course if and only if he or she was not dismissed and did not pass. Charles is not Norman. Therefore, exactly one student retook the course. (*Sx*: *x* is a student; *Px*: *x* passed the course; *Dx*: *x* was dismissed; *Rx*: *x* retook the course; *c*: Charles; *n*: Norman)

IV. Create an argument relating to cities that involves an identity expression. Then translate the argument into the symbolism of predicate logic and derive the conclusion using conditional proof or indirect proof as needed.

MindTap Master concepts and improve outcomes with Aplia, at the end of the chapter, in the Aplia folder.

Summary

Predicate Logic: Combines the use of these symbols:

- The five operators of propositional logic: $\sim, \bullet, \lor, \supset, \equiv$
- Symbols for predicates: $G\_, H\_, K\_$, etc.
- Symbols for universal quantifiers: $(x), (y), (z)$
- Symbols for existential quantifiers: $(\exists x), (\exists y), (\exists z)$
- Symbols for individual variables: x, y, z
- Symbols for individual constants: $a, b, c, \ldots u, v, w$

Statements:

- Singular statements combine predicate symbols with constants: $Ga, Hc \bullet Kc$, etc.
- Universal statements are usually translated as conditionals: $(x)(Px \supset Qx)$, etc.
- Particular statements are usually translated as conjunctions: $(\exists x)(Px \bullet Qx)$, etc.

Using the Rules of Inference (*modus ponens, modus tollens,* etc.):

- Rules are used in basically the same way as in propositional logic.
- Using the rules usually requires that quantifiers be removed or inserted:
  - Universal instantiation (UI): Removes universal quantifiers.
  - Universal generalization (UG): Introduces universal quantifiers.
  - Existential instantiation (EI): Removes existential quantifiers.
  - Existential generalization (EG): Introduces existential quantifiers.

MindTap Need help? See the Learning Logic folder at the end of the chapter: the self-paced tutorial walks you through any section.
Prepare for exams with the Chapter Test.

- Restrictions:
  - For EI, the existential name that is introduced must not appear in any previous line, including the conclusion line.
  - The instantiation and generalization rules can be applied only to whole lines—not parts of lines.

Quantifier Negation Rule:
- Is used to remove or insert tildes preceding quantifiers.
- The instantiation rules cannot be applied if a tilde precedes the quantifier.
- One type of quantifier can be replaced by the other type if and only if immediately before and after the new quantifier:
  - Tildes that were originally there are deleted, and
  - Tildes that were not originally there are inserted.

Conditional Proof and Indirect Proof:
- Used in basically the same way as in propositional logic.
- Restriction:
  - UG must not be used within an indented sequence if the instantial variable is free in the first line of that sequence.

Proving Invalidity:
- Counterexample method:
  - Produce a substitution instance of a symbolized argument that has indisputably true premises and an indisputably false conclusion.
- Finite universe method:
  - Reduce the universe of discourse to a finite number until an indirect truth table proves the resulting argument invalid.
  - Universal statements are rendered as conjunctions.
  - Particular statements are rendered as disjunctions.
  - Singular statements are kept as they are.

Relational Predicates:
- Symbols for relational predicates: $G\_\_, H\_\_, K\_\_\_$, etc.
- Are used to translate relational statements.
- Example: "Paul is taller than Cathy": Tpc

Overlapping Quantifiers:
- Quantifiers that fall within the scope of another quantifier.
- Example: $(\exists x)[Mx \bullet (y)(Wy \supset Txy)]$
- Restriction:
  - UG must not be used if the instantial variable is free in any preceding line obtained by EI.

Identity:
- The symbol for the identity relation is the equal sign: $=$
- Used to assert that one thing is identical to another.
- Used to translate statements involving "only," "the only," "no . . . except," and "all except" when these expressions are used with individuals.
- Used to translate superlative statements, numerical statements, and definite descriptions.
- The rule for identity (Id) allows the application of the other rules of inference.

9 Analogy and Legal and Moral Reasoning

9.1 Analogical Reasoning

9.2 Legal Reasoning

9.3 Moral Reasoning

HOW LOGICAL ARE YOU? Environmentalists argue that we owe it to our children to preserve the environment, so we should strive to reduce our carbon footprint. But that's like saying that I shouldn't buy a Porsche because my children won't inherit the money I would spend on the car. Now, clearly, I don't owe it to my kids to refrain from buying things I enjoy and can afford. So, the environmentalists are wrong in thinking we have obligations to our children. Does this argument convince you?

Find the answer on MindTap.

9.1 Analogical Reasoning

Analogical reasoning may be the most fundamental and the most common of all rational processes. It stands at the basis of many ordinary decisions in life. For example, a woman wanting to buy a can of soup might deliberate between Campbell's and Brand X and, after recalling that other varieties of Campbell's were good, decide in favor of that brand. A man contemplating a haircut might recall that a friend got an especially good cut at the Golden Touch and as a result decide to go there himself. A woman selecting a plant for her garden might observe that gardenias grow well at the house next door and conclude that gardenias would grow well at her house, too. A man thinking of reading a novel by Stephen King might recall that King's last three novels were thrilling and conclude that his latest novel would also be thrilling.

Analogical reasoning is reasoning that depends on a comparison of instances. If the instances are sufficiently similar, the decision reached in the end is usually a good

MindTap Read, study, reflect, and prepare for exams online, anytime, anywhere.

one; but if they are not sufficiently similar, the decision may not be good. When such a reasoning process is expressed in words, the result is an argument from analogy (see Chapter 1). Simple arguments from analogy have the following structure:

> Entity A has attributes $a, b, c,$ and z.
> Entity B has attributes a, b, c.
> Therefore, entity B probably has attribute z also.

If the attributes a, b, and c are connected in some important way to z (that is, are relevant to z), the argument is usually strong. If they are not so connected (that is, are irrelevant to z), the argument is usually weak.

Analogical arguments are closely related to generalizations. In a generalization, the arguer begins with one or more instances and proceeds to draw a conclusion about all the members of a class. The arguer may then apply the generalization to one or more members of this class that were not noted earlier. The first stage of such an inference is inductive, and the second stage is deductive. For example, the man thinking of reading the latest Stephen King novel might argue that because the last three novels by King were thrilling, all King novels are thrilling (inductive argument). Applying this generalization to the latest novel, he might then conclude that it too will be thrilling (deductive argument). In an argument from analogy, on the other hand, the arguer proceeds directly from one or more individual instances to a conclusion about another individual instance without appealing to any intermediate generalization. Such an argument is purely inductive. Thus, the arguer might conclude directly from reading three earlier King novels that the latest one will be thrilling.

In any argument from analogy, the items that are compared are called *analogues*. Thus, if one should argue that Rihanna's latest album is probably good because her two previous albums were good, the three albums are the analogues. The two earlier albums are called the *primary analogues*, and the latest album is called the *secondary analogue*. With these definitions in mind, we may now examine a set of principles that are useful for evaluating most arguments from analogy. They include (1) the relevance of the similarities shared by the primary and secondary analogues, (2) the number of similarities, (3) the nature and degree of disanalogy, (4) the number of primary analogues, (5) the diversity among the primary analogues, and (6) the specificity of the conclusion.

1. *Relevance of the similarities.* Suppose a certain person—let us call her Lucy—is contemplating the purchase of a new car. She decides in favor of a Chevrolet because she wants good fuel economy and her friend Tom's new Chevy gets good fuel economy. To support her decision, Lucy argues that both cars have a padded steering wheel, tachometer, fabric upholstery, tinted windows, premium sound system, and white paint. Lucy's argument is weak because these similarities are irrelevant to fuel economy. On the other hand, if Lucy bases her conclusion on the fact that both cars have the same-size engine, her argument is relatively strong, because engine size is relevant to fuel economy.

2. *Number of similarities.* Suppose, in addition to the same-size engine, Lucy notes further similarities between the car she intends to buy and Tom's car: curb weight, aerodynamic body, gear ratio, and tires. These additional similarities, all of which are relevant to fuel economy, tend to strengthen Lucy's argument. If, in addition, Lucy notes that she

and Tom both drive about half on city streets and half on freeways, her argument is strengthened even further.

3. *Nature and degree of disanalogy.* On the other hand, if Lucy's car is equipped with a turbocharger, if Lucy loves to make jackrabbit starts and screeching stops, if Tom's car has overdrive but Lucy's does not, and if Lucy constantly drives on congested freeways while Tom drives on relatively clear freeways, Lucy's argument is weakened. These differences are called *disanalogies.* Depending on how they relate to the conclusion, disanalogies can either weaken or strengthen an argument. If we suppose instead that Tom's car has the turbocharger, that Tom loves jackrabbit starts, and so on, then Lucy's argument is strengthened, because these disanalogies tend to reduce Tom's fuel economy.

4. *Number of primary analogues.* Thus far, Lucy has based her conclusion on the similarity between the car she intends to buy and only one other car—Tom's. Now suppose that Lucy has three additional friends, that all of them drive cars of the same model and year as Tom's, and that all of them get good fuel economy. These additional primary analogues strengthen Lucy's argument because they lessen the likelihood that Tom's good fuel economy is a freak incident. On the other hand, suppose that two of these additional friends get the same good fuel economy as Tom but that the third gets poor fuel economy. As before, the first two cases tend to strengthen Lucy's argument, but the third now tends to weaken it. This third case is called a *counteranalogy* because it supports a conclusion opposed to that of the original analogy.

5. *Diversity among the primary analogues.* Suppose now that Lucy's four friends (all of whom get good fuel economy) all buy their gas at the same station, have their cars tuned up regularly by the same mechanic, put the same friction-reducing additive in their oil, inflate their tires to the same pressure, and do their city driving on un-congested, level streets at a fuel-maximizing 28 miles per hour. Such factors would tend to reduce the probability of Lucy's conclusion, because it is possible that one or a combination of them is responsible for the good fuel economy and that this factor (or combination of them) is absent in Lucy's case. On the other hand, if Lucy's friends buy their gas at different stations, have their cars tuned up at different intervals by different mechanics, inflate their tires to different pressures, drive at different speeds on different grades, and have different attitudes toward using the oil additive, then it is less likely that the good fuel economy they enjoy is attributable to any factor other than the model and year of their car.

6. *Specificity of the conclusion.* Lucy's conclusion is simply that her car will get "good" fuel economy. If she now changes her conclusion to state that her car will get fuel economy "at least as good" as Tom's, then her argument is weakened. Such a conclusion is more specific than the earlier conclusion and is easier to falsify. Thus, if her fuel economy were only one-tenth of a mile per gallon less than Tom's, her conclusion would turn out to be false. Now suppose that Lucy changes her conclusion to state that her car will get exactly the same fuel economy as Tom's. This conclusion is even more specific than the "at least as good" conclusion, and it is easier still to falsify. Thus, such a con-clusion renders Lucy's argument much weaker than her original argument.

Summarizing these results, we have,

> The more relevant the similarities between primary and secondary analogues, the stronger the argument.
>
> The greater the number of similarities between primary and secondary analogues, the stronger the argument.
>
> Differences between primary and secondary analogues are disanalogies, which can either strengthen or weaken the argument.
>
> The greater the number of similar primary analogues, the stronger the argument; dissimilar primary analogues are counteranalogies, which weaken the argument.
>
> The more diverse the primary analogues, the stronger the argument.
>
> The more specific the conclusion, the weaker the argument.

Let us now use these six principles to evaluate an argument from analogy. Suppose that you want to shade a bedroom window from the intense western sun. To accomplish this purpose, you decide to plant some trees, but the trees must be narrow ones that will grow approximately 25 feet tall. Recalling that a friend has some Italian cypresses that are almost exactly 25 feet tall, you conclude that this variety of tree will do the job. Thus far, your argument is based on a single similarity, the species of the tree. Because this similarity is very relevant to height, your argument is fairly strong. Now if, in addition, it turns out that your friend lives in the same city and has the same kind of soil as you have, your argument is strengthened. However, if it happens that your friend has a knack for growing trees whereas you have a knack for killing them, your argument is weakened.

To this set of facts, suppose we add the observation that four of your neighbors have Italian cypresses and that all of their trees are approximately 25 feet tall. This fact tends to strengthen your argument. Also, if all four neighbors planted their trees in different years, use different kinds of fertilizers on them, and give them different amounts of water, your argument is further strengthened. Finally, should you broaden your conclusion to state that your trees will grow between 22 and 28 feet tall, your argument is strengthened even further. But if you narrow your conclusion to state that your trees will grow to between 24½ and 25½ feet tall, your argument is weakened.

9.2 Legal Reasoning

Many of the arguments used by lawyers in the United States and Canada to support a case at trial are analogical arguments. The reason is that the legal systems of these countries were derived many years ago from the English system, and an essential feature of the English system is its dependence on precedent. According to the requirement of precedent, similar cases must be decided similarly. Thus, in arguing a case, a lawyer will often attempt to show that the case is analogous to some earlier case that was decided in a favorable way. Sometimes, even today, these precedents go back to early English law.

For example, suppose you own a factory and one of your machines, a drill press, breaks down, causing the entire operation to come to a halt. Urgently you call a repair company and explain the whole situation. The spokesperson for the company promises to have the drill press back in operation within two days. Unfortunately, there are delays, and two weeks elapse before the drill press is repaired. In the meantime your company loses an additional $10,000 in profits. Because you relied on the spokesperson's assurance that the drill press would be fixed in two days, you demand that the repair company reimburse you for the additional lost profits. When the repair company refuses your demand, you file suit.

The lawyer who argues your case will probably make reference to a much earlier case, *Hadley v. Baxendale*, decided in Gloucester, England, in 1854. In that case the operation of a mill was halted because of a broken crankshaft, and the owner of the mill (Hadley) employed a shipping company (Baxendale) to return the crankshaft to the manufacturer. Hadley informed Baxendale that the broken crankshaft had interrupted the operation of the mill, and Baxendale replied that the broken crankshaft would be in the hands of the manufacturer within one day. As it turned out, the shipment was delayed by several days, and Hadley incurred lost profits from the additional time the mill was shut down. Hadley demanded reimbursement from Baxendale, and when Baxendale refused, Hadley filed suit. The court ruled that Baxendale should pay only if he foresaw when he agreed to do the work that delays would result in lost profits for Hadley.

Applying this result to the drill-press case, your lawyer will argue that because the repair company was informed that delays in repairing the drill press would result in lost profits, it should reimburse you for the losses incurred.

In the early days, much of English law resulted directly from judges' rendering decisions in particular cases. This judge-made law is otherwise called common law. However, today many of our laws are not the direct product of judges but rather of legislative bodies. These laws, called *statutes*, are codified in books that are periodically revised. Can it be said that precedent plays a central role in decisions involving statutory law in the same way that it does in decisions involving common law? The answer is a definite yes. Statutory laws are invariably phrased in relatively general language, and precedent is required to determine how the statutes should be interpreted and applied.

Consider, for example, a "law" that we are all familiar with, the First Amendment to the U.S. Constitution, which provides for freedom of speech and religious expression. Suppose that you decide, in reliance on the First Amendment, to pass out religious pamphlets on a downtown street corner. Suppose further that most of the people you hand your pamphlets to merely glance at them and then throw them on the street and that the gathering litter makes the area look like a garbage dump. To prevent the litter, the police tell you that you can hand out your pamphlets only in the vicinity of public garbage cans, so that those who do not want the pamphlets can properly dispose of them. You object that such a restriction violates your First Amendment rights, and you take the issue to court.

In presenting your case, your lawyer will argue that the case is analogous to other cases where the state attempted to limit not the content of religious expression, but the time, place, and manner of its expression. Next, your lawyer will note that in such cases the state is allowed to restrict the expression only if the restriction is "narrowly tailored" to serve a "significant government interest." Finally, your lawyer will attempt to show that your case is analogous to cases in which the government failed to prove that the restriction was so tailored.

As these examples illustrate, many of the arguments that occur in law are arguments from analogy, and the principles developed at the beginning of this section can be used to evaluate them. The first principle, which deals with the relevance of the similarities, has an obvious application to legal arguments. Suppose, for example, that two cases are similar in that each involves a burning building, the building in each case is located in Chicago, and in each case ten people died. The comparison is pointless if the issue in the first case is whether an insurance company is liable to pay damages whereas the issue in the second is whether somebody is guilty of arson.

The second and third principles, which deal with the number of similarities and the nature and degree of disanalogy, are also applicable. If a preceding case resembles the case at hand in virtually all important details, then the preceding case is said to be "on point" and, given certain other requirements (discussed shortly), will dictate the outcome of the case to be decided. As for the nature and degree of disanalogy, if a preceding case deals with fraud by a stockbroker while the case to be decided deals with fraud by a real estate broker, the precedent may be more or less controlling, depending on such circumstances as applicable statutory law.

As applied to legal analogies, the fourth principle (number of primary analogues) usually determines how well established a legal precedent is. If fifty previous courts have followed a certain rule, the precedent is stronger (everything else being equal) than if only two courts have followed that rule. The fifth principle (diversity among the primary analogues) is also applicable. If a certain rule turns up in a broad range of cases, it provides a stronger precedent (other things being equal) than a rule that turns up in a narrow range of cases. For example, the principle underlying the inadmissibility of hearsay testimony is well established because it appears in a broad cross section of cases.

Finally, the sixth principle states that the more specific a conclusion is, the weaker the argument becomes. Suppose, in an earlier case, a person is awarded half a million dollars for injuries inflicted by a surgeon who, during an appendix operation, left a stethoscope in the body opening. The argument that another person injured in the same way by another doctor should be awarded *exactly* the same amount of money is relatively weak in comparison with the argument that the person should be awarded *approximately* the same amount of money.

Analogical arguments that occur in law differ from the fairly simple analogies considered earlier in at least two important ways. In the analogy dealing with fuel economy, the modes of similarity that linked the analogues (number of engine cylinders, curb weight, and the like) were clearly defined by conventional thinking, and their relevance to the conclusion had been established by scientific principles. In law, however, clarity of this sort is seldom to be found. Modes of similarity between cases are often the result of highly creative thinking by lawyers and judges, and the relevance of these similarities to the proposed conclusion is nearly always debatable. These differences render analogical arguments in law considerably more elusive than those dealing with subjects such as fuel economy.

The other difference between simple analogical arguments and those found in law is that the primary analogues in law (earlier cases) do not all have equal weight. The reason is that our courts operate in different jurisdictions. The system of federal courts is totally separate from the system of state courts. As a result, a case that might have considerable weight as a precedent in one system might have little or no weight in the other. In addition, within these systems there are different circuits, and a case that is controlling in one circuit may not be in another. Lastly, within these systems, the courts exist on different levels. For example, within the federal system there are the district courts, courts of appeals, and the U.S. Supreme Court. A case that is binding on a lower court may not be binding on a higher court.

Let us now illustrate the process of legal reasoning with a hypothetical example. Suppose a certain vagrant—let us call him Blake—attempted to earn some pocket change by breaking into a soft-drink vending machine and stealing the cash. The police apprehended Blake in the act, and the district attorney charged him with burglary. Blake had one prior conviction for breaking into a soft-drink machine.

The first thing that any lawyer would do with this case is to recall the definition of "burglary." According to the traditional definition, "burglary" means "the trespassory breaking and entering of a dwelling house of another at night with the intent to commit a felony therein." Under many modern statutes, "dwelling house" has been replaced by "structure" and "at night" has been deleted.

There is little doubt that Blake has broken into a structure. The question is, is a soft-drink machine the kind of structure intended by the statute? A second question is, did Blake intend to commit a felony when he broke into the soft-drink machine? To answer these questions a lawyer would consult additional statutes and relevant cases. Let us suppose that our jurisdiction has a statute that defines felony theft as theft of $400 or more. Also, let us suppose that the cash box of this particular machine contained $450 but most similar machines can hold no more than $350.

As for cases, let us suppose that our jurisdiction has two controlling precedents. In *People v. Harris*, Harris broke into a warehouse with the intent of stealing its contents. The warehouse contained microwave ovens valued at $10,000, and Harris was found guilty of burglary. In *People v. Sawyer*, Sawyer broke into a newspaper vending machine with the intent to steal the cash in the cash box. The maximum capacity of the cash box was $20, and Sawyer was found not guilty of burglary.

Relying on these facts and preceding cases, the district attorney might present the following argument to the judge (or jury):

> In breaking into the soft-drink machine, Blake is guilty of burglary for the following reasons. In *People v. Harris*, the defendant was found guilty of burglary for breaking into a warehouse. A soft-drink vending machine is like a warehouse in that it contains goods stored for resale. Furthermore, like a warehouse, people's livelihoods depend on the goods stored therein. Also, the vending machine contained over $400, and Blake intended to steal this money. Stealing over $400 is a felony. Therefore, Blake intended to commit a felony when he broke into the machine. Also, by placing his hand into the machine, he "entered" it. A soft-drink machine differs from a newspaper machine in that it can hold goods valued much more than a stack of newspapers. Thus, all the requirements are met for conviction.

Defense counsel, on the other hand, might argue as follows:

In breaking into the soft-drink machine, Blake is not guilty of burglary, for the following reasons. The original crime of burglary extended only to dwelling houses because people live in dwelling houses and it is important that their lives be protected. Modern law has extended the kind of structure requisite for burglary to include warehouses because people work and live in them. A soft-drink machine is unlike a warehouse in that a person is not capable of working and living in it. Also, for the crime of burglary to be committed, the burglar must enter the structure. A soft-drink machine differs from a warehouse in that a person is not capable of entering it with his whole body.

On the contrary, a soft-drink vending machine is very similar to a newspaper vending machine in that it contains relatively small quantities of products for resale. In *People v. Sawyer*, the defendant was found not guilty of burglary in breaking into a newspaper vending machine. Finally, Blake was familiar with soft-drink machines (he broke into one once before), and he therefore knew that their cash boxes are usually limited to holding less than $400. Therefore, when he broke into this particular machine, Blake intended to steal less than $400, and therefore he did not intend to commit a felony.

In deciding whether Blake is guilty, the judge or jury will have to evaluate these analogical arguments by determining which analogies are the strongest.

Sometimes lawyers and judges are confronted with cases for which there is no clear precedent. Such cases are called *cases of first impression*, and the attempt to deal with them by appeal to analogous instances involves even more creativity than does the attempt to deal with ordinary cases. In deciding cases of first impression, judges often resort to moral reasoning, and they grope for any analogy that can shed light on the issue. The reasoning process in such a decision often involves a sequence of analogies followed by disanalogies and counteranalogies. These analogies present the issue in a continually shifting light, and the experience of coming to grips with them expands the outlook of the reasoner. New perspectives are created, attitudes are changed, and worldviews are altered.

9

9.3   Moral Reasoning

As in law, arguments from analogy are also useful in deciding moral questions. Such arguments often occur in the context of a dialogue. As an example of a dialogue that includes several arguments from analogy, consider the following one between two fictional characters, Jason and Deirdre. The dialogue deals with the morality and legality of fetal abuse.

"Jason, I read an article in this morning's newspaper about fetal abuse—you know, expectant mothers who take drugs or drink alcohol during pregnancy and cause damage to their fetus. The article said that eleven percent of all babies currently born in this country have traces of alcohol or illegal drugs in their blood. I think such women should be shot!"

"I can see that you're pretty worked up about this, Deirdre, but don't you think you're being a bit prudish? After all, what's so bad about a little alcohol or a few drugs?"

"I can't believe you said that!" Deirdre scolds. "The alcohol and drugs cause permanent brain damage to the fetus and leave the child maimed for life. Many of these kids will grow up mentally challenged, and many will become criminals and end up in jail. The burden on society will be incredible! Women who treat their unborn child in this way are utterly immoral, and they ought to be sent to jail."

"Let's take these claims one at a time," Jason responds. "First, why do you think feeding alcohol or drugs to a fetus is immoral, Deirdre?"

"Because I think the fetus has rights."

"But wait a minute," counters Jason. "According to *Roe v. Wade*, the mother can abort the fetus. That must mean the fetus has no right to life; and if it has no right to life, surely it has no rights at all."

Deirdre scratches her head. "It seems to me you're overlooking something," she says. "When a mother intends to abort her fetus, it's one thing. But when she intends to bring it to term, it's quite another thing. It's almost as if she has extended a contract to the fetus. Look, suppose I tell a house painter, 'You paint my house, and I'll pay you $1,000.' If the painter fulfills his end of the bargain but I refuse to pay, clearly I am doing something wrong. In the same way, the mother who intends to bear her child in effect tells the fetus, 'You agree to grow and develop in a normal way, and I'll provide you with a healthy environment.' If the fetus grows and develops normally and then the mother feeds it drugs, she reneges on the deal."

> Mom has a contract with her fetus.

"I agree with you about the house painter," Jason answers. "But it seems to me that you can only enter into contracts with human beings. You don't enter into contracts with dogs and cats, and you don't enter into contracts with fetuses, either."

"A fetus is very much like a complete human being, though," Deirdre replies. "It's made up of human flesh and blood, it has the same genetic code as a human being, and as it develops, it has the same organization of internal organs as a human being and it even looks like a human being. Isn't this enough?"

"And because of these similarities you think the fetus has rights?"

"Yes, I do."

"Well, I think your analogy is nice," Jason replies, "but I don't think the similarities you cite are relevant to your conclusion. The reason human beings have rights and can enter into contracts is because they are rational and have the power of speech. They demonstrate these powers by proving theorems in geometry and engaging in conversations. I've never seen a fetus do either of these things."

"No," replies Deirdre, "but neither do people when they're asleep. Do you think a sleeping person is not human? Would you take a sleeping person and sweep him out the door like a clump of dust because he wasn't at that moment demonstrating rational powers?"

"Of course not," Jason replies. "But unlike a sleeping person, a fetus has *never* demonstrated rational powers."

> When does a fetus become human?

"But neither has a newborn baby," Deirdre argues. "When do you think a newborn baby becomes human? Does it happen at the moment it's born? Was it not a human being one hour before birth? Isn't a tomato growing on a vine as much a tomato one day before it ripens as it is when it's ripe? Isn't an apple growing on a tree as much an apple when it's green as it is after it turns red?"

"That's a good analogy," says Jason.

"Also, even if a fetus can't be proved beyond any uncertainty to be fully human, don't you think it should be given the benefit of the doubt? When a person falls through the ice on a frozen lake, don't the rescuers who pull the person out rush him to a hospital even though no signs of life remain? Isn't the person, whether dead or alive, treated as if he were still alive? Similarly, shouldn't a fetus, who shows no signs of rationality, be treated as if it had rationality?"

"Perhaps," Jason answers, "but I have trouble attributing humanity or personhood to a mere lump of flesh. This wart on the back of my hand is made of human flesh and blood, and its cells carry the same genetic code as I do. Of course it's not shaped like a human being, but neither is a fetus in the early stages of development. Does this mean that I should consider this wart to be human or a person?"

"So what you're saying," Deirdre replies, "is that the fetus is just a part of its mother's body, like that wart is part of yours?"

"Exactly," he says. "And that means the fetus can have no rights or interests distinct from those of the mother, any more than someone's liver can have rights distinct from the person who has the liver. When an alcoholic abuses his liver by excessive alcohol consumption, we don't say that he is immoral and incarcerate him for liver abuse. Similarly, we don't say that smokers are immoral for abusing their lungs and put them in jail for lung abuse. Accordingly, we shouldn't call pregnant women immoral and put them in jail for fetal abuse."

"Your analogy has one fatal flaw," Deirdre answers with a smile. "If the fetus is merely part of its mother's body, then it would have exactly the same genetic code as the mother. Every ordinary body part—heart, liver, lungs, and so on—carries the same genes as the host organism. But the fetus has a unique genetic code. Also, it's meant to develop and separate from the body of its host, unlike a liver or a lung. Therefore, a fetus is not merely a part of the mother's body."

A fetus has its own genes.

"Well, perhaps you're right," Jason says. "But I have a better analogy. The fetus is like a seed planted in the ground or a group of cells growing in a petri dish. Imagine you were walking down the street and a little seed shouted up at you, 'Help! Get me out of this soil! It's too acidic!' What would you do? Would you reach down, lift the seedling up, and transplant it elsewhere? Of course not. You'd say to the seed, 'Be quiet! It's lucky you found any soil at all to grow in.' Isn't that what you'd say?"

"Maybe I would," she says, "but not if I expected the seed to grow into a human being. And incidentally, don't ever accuse me of anthropomorphizing! I think a far better analogy is that of someone who perpetrates a battery on another person. I was reading about a famous case where a man approached a woman in her sleep and gave her a kiss on the cheek. The man was someone the woman despised, and when she woke up and found out what had happened, she was so furious that she sued the man for battery—and she won. A battery, you know, is any intentionally produced harmful or offensive contact. The case establishes the principle that the target of a battery need not be aware of it at the time it happens. Now if a kiss can be a battery, how much more so is being drowned in drugs and booze? The fetus might not be able to sue till after it's born, but the battery was nevertheless committed before birth."

"Very clever," Jason responds. "However, I don't think you can say someone's asleep if that person has never been awake. A fetus has never been awake."

"I see you're still harping on whether the fetus has human thought processes," replies Deirdre. "Well, consider this. After the child is born, everyone agrees it's a full-fledged human being. When that child enters the world with drugs in its body, we can appropriately ask where those drugs came from. The answer, of course, is the mother. Thus, the mother has given drugs not to a mere fetus but to a real child. The situation would be exactly the same as if a common drug dealer had given drugs to the kid. Thus, the mother should be treated the same way as any drug dealer."

"I think you've got me there," Jason admits. "But your analogy holds only for kids who are actually born with drugs or alcohol in their system. What about fetuses who are fed drugs or alcohol weeks before birth but who are delivered without any trace of them?"

"Suppose," replies Deirdre, "a doctor who is treating a pregnant woman periodically injects cocaine into the fetus using a long hypodermic needle. Not only would everyone consider the doctor fiendish and immoral, but the doctor would be liable for civil and criminal sanctions. Is the mother who feeds cocaine to her fetus any different from this doctor?"

"Interesting point," says Jason. "I expect, however, that the doctor would be subject to liability for acting without the mother's consent—not for acting without the fetus's consent."

"I hope you're wrong," says Deirdre. "But you know how I feel about these fetal abusers? I see a child in a playpen near a window. Outside the window other kids are playing on the grass. The child in the playpen is excited and happy when it sees them and can't wait until it's big enough to go out and join them. Then one day the mother comes in with a baseball bat and smashes the child's legs, and the child is never able to walk from that day on. That's what fetal abuse does, as far as I'm concerned."

"Getting a little emotional, aren't we, Deirdre?"

"Maybe. But I don't think morality is something devoid of feeling. Morality concerns life and life is feeling, and the two can't be separated."

"Well, even if I agreed with you that fetal abuse is immoral, that doesn't mean I think it should be made illegal. I know our criminal laws are closely tied to public morality, but that's true only up to a point. I think making fetal abuse a crime might be going too far."

"Why is that?" asks Deirdre.

"Because it's so invasive," Jason responds. "Like a rapist, the state would be invading the most private aspects of a woman's life. Also, it would be patronizing. The state would be treating the pregnant woman like an errant, recalcitrant child who's done something wrong and needs to be punished."

"But there is a long history of state intervention in the lives of people who are a danger to themselves or others," Deirdre observes. "For example, people who attempt

suicide are sometimes institutionalized to prevent them from killing themselves. Also, mental deviants are often committed to mental institutions for their own benefit. The theory is that, if these people were in their right minds, they would want the state to do exactly that. Women who abuse their fetuses are very similar to mental deviants. If these women were in their right minds, they would want the state to intercede and prevent them from injuring their fetuses."

"Still," replies Jason, "I think a law criminalizing fetal abuse would be unenforceable. It would be just like the law against alcohol during prohibition. That law was eventually repealed because, among other things, it was impossible to enforce. A law against fetal abuse would suffer the same fate. It would require that police officers snoop into the homes and bedrooms of every pregnant woman reasonably suspected of abusing her fetus. Such action would violate one of our most cherished values, the right to privacy, and it would require massive additions to our police force."

"Yes," answers Deirdre, "but the problem is so significant that I think something must be done. You can look at the whole of society as a single human body grown large. Women who abuse their unborn children are like spiders who inject venom into the body of society. This venom creates a sore that lasts for seventy years or more. Now I ask you, what person threatened by such a spider would not go to any lengths to prevent its bite? What rational person would stand idle, let the spider inject its venom, and then tolerate the resulting canker for seventy years?"

"Yes," agrees Jason, "but unfortunately, getting rid of fetal abuse is harder than simply brushing off a spider. I think the solution is to stress educational programs and provide prenatal care for every expectant mother. After all, you catch more flies with honey than you do with vinegar. Such programs might reduce the problem of fetal abuse to a point where it becomes tolerable."

Honey catches more flies than vinegar.

"I think any amount of fetal abuse is intolerable," Deirdre replies.

"Society is like a water supply," Jason says. "Public-health officials test it for contaminants and find microscopic amounts of this and microscopic amounts of that. If these amounts are within acceptable limits, they pronounce the water supply potable. Yes, the thought of any fetal abuse is disturbing, but we can never eliminate it entirely. The best we can hope for is to reduce it to a point where it won't cripple society as a whole."

"Perhaps you're right," concludes Deirdre, "but the thought of that child in the playpen still bothers me."

This dialogue contains numerous analogies and counteranalogies. The modes of similarity between the many primary analogues and the secondary analogues (the fetus, women who commit fetal abuse, laws against fetal abuse, and so on) are never relevant beyond dispute, and the nature and degree of disanalogy rarely has undisputed consequences. However, the dialogue serves to illustrate the subtle effect that analogies have on our thought processes and the power they have to alter our attitudes and perspectives.

EXERCISE 9

I. Evaluate the arguments from analogy contained in the dialogue between Jason and Deirdre. First, identify the primary and secondary analogues in each analogy and counteranalogy. Next, list the similarities between the primary and secondary analogues and note their relevance to the conclusion. Add any additional similarities you can think of. Finally, identify the disanalogies associated with each analogy or counteranalogy and evaluate their effectiveness in destroying the original analogy.

II. Work the following problems.

★1. Jessica has long admired Rachel's near-perfect body, and she notes that Rachel works out on a Roboflex exercise machine. Jessica concludes that if she buys a Roboflex for herself, she will be able to duplicate Rachel's results. How do the following facts bear on Jessica's argument?

   a. Roboflex recently changed its corporate headquarters from Ohio to Illinois.

   b. Jessica and Rachel are siblings.

MindTap Complete exercises online for immediate feedback.

    c. Rachel is 25 years old, but Jessica is 32.

    d. Jessica is 40 pounds overweight, but Rachel was only 10 pounds overweight when she started using her Roboflex.

    e. Whenever Jessica makes up her mind to do something, she always sticks with it longer than Rachel does.

    f. Jessica knows of five other women who work out on a Roboflex, and these women all look as good as Rachel.

    g. These women are all between the ages of 24 and 26.

    h. Jessica discovers four additional women between the ages of 31 and 33 who work out on a Roboflex, and these women look nearly as good as Rachel.

    i. Jessica changes her conclusion to state that she will look almost as good as Rachel.

    j. Jessica changes her conclusion to state that she will look better than Rachel.

2. Harold needs to have his rugs cleaned, and his friend Veronica reports that Ajax Carpet Service did an excellent job on her rugs. From this, Harold concludes that Ajax will do an equally good job on his rugs. How do the following facts bear on Harold's argument?

    a. Veronica hired Ajax several times, and Ajax always did an excellent job.

    b. Veronica's rugs are wool, whereas Harold's are rayon.

    c. Veronica's carpets never had any stains on them before they were cleaned, but Harold's have several large stains.

    d. Veronica always had her rugs cleaned in mid-October, whereas Harold wants his done just a week before Easter.

    e. Harold knows of six additional people who have had their carpets cleaned by Ajax, and all six have been very pleased.

    f. All six own rugs made of different materials.

    g. All six additional people were born in Massachusetts.

    h. Ajax has recently undergone a change in management.

    i. The Environmental Protection Agency recently banned the cleaning solution Ajax has used for many years.

    j. Harold changes his conclusion to state that Ajax will get his carpets approximately as clean as it has gotten Veronica's.

3. Kristin is president of a corporation that operates a chain of clothing stores, and she faces the task of hiring a manager to replace a man who retired from one of the stores. The former manager increased sales by 15 percent every year for the past five years. Kristin concludes that Roger Benson, a recent graduate of Wharton School of Business, will duplicate the former manager's performance. How do the following facts bear on Kristin's argument?

a. The manager who retired was a graduate of Wharton.

b. The manager who retired liked tennis and drove a Jaguar, whereas Benson dislikes tennis and drives a BMW.

c. Unlike the manager who retired, Benson formerly managed a shoe store, where he increased sales 20 percent for each of the two years he was there.

d. A labor dispute has recently erupted in the store Benson will manage.

e. The manager who retired was an alcoholic, whereas Benson is a moderate drinker.

f. The government has approved a 10 percent increase in federal income taxes that takes effect at the beginning of the year.

g. Three additional stores owned by Kristin's company are managed by recent Wharton graduates, and all three managers have increased sales by 18 percent for each of the past three years.

h. These three stores are located in the city's three wealthiest suburbs.

i. The store Benson will manage is located in a neighborhood that has recently begun to decline.

j. Kristin changes her conclusion to state that Benson will increase sales by at least 10 percent for the first year.

★4. Sam has planned a one-day fishing trip in Alaska. He intends to fish off Rocky Point, where he fished last year. Because he caught five fish in a one-day outing last year, Sam concludes that he will catch five fish this year. How do the following facts bear on Sam's argument?

a. Last year Sam used a wooden boat, but this year he will use a fiberglass boat.

b. Sam used herring for bait last year, but this year he will use anchovies.

c. Sam fished with four friends last year, and each of them caught more than five fish on that day.

d. This year Sam will fish on July 15, but last year he fished on August 1.

e. Last year these four friends caught an average of five fish per day from July 15 to August 1.

f. These four friends are women.

g. These four friends used various kinds of bait—herring, squid, anchovies, and artificial lures.

h. It is now July 12. Yesterday, ten people fished off Rocky Point, and none caught any fish.

i. A fleet of commercial fishing boats has been fishing the area near Rocky Point for the first time.

j. Sam changes his conclusion to state that he will catch at least one fish.

5. Susan is considering a job as public relations specialist with the Chamber of Commerce. Her friend Terry took such a job one year ago, and within nine

months her annual salary was $50,000. Susan argues that if she takes this job, then her annual salary will be at least $50,000 within nine months. How do the following facts bear on Susan's argument?

a. Susan is beautiful and outgoing, whereas Terry is average looking and introverted.

b. Susan is a Democrat, but Terry is a Republican.

c. Like Terry, Susan is 5 feet 4 inches tall and has blonde hair.

d. Susan's parents are elementary school teachers, but Terry's parents are prominent businesspeople.

e. One year ago, Cindy, April, Elizabeth, and Jackie accepted jobs as public relations specialists with the Chamber of Commerce, and today all are earning $44,000.

f. April is a Republican, Cindy is a Democrat, Elizabeth is a Libertarian, and Jackie is a member of the Peace and Freedom Party.

g. Cindy, April, Elizabeth, and Jackie are beautiful and outgoing.

h. Susan has five years of experience as a public relations specialist, whereas Terry, when she was hired, had only two years of experience in that area.

i. There is a shortage of public relations specialists in the local job pool.

j. Susan changes her conclusion to state that after nine months she will be earning at least $47,000.

6. Paul is searching for a puppy that will grow up to be friendly with his children. His friend Barbara has an Airedale terrier that is good with her children. From this, Paul concludes that an Airedale puppy would make a good choice. How do the following facts bear on Paul's argument?

a. Barbara's dog is a female, but Paul plans to get a male.

b. Tim, Ed, and Irene have male Airedales that are friendly with their children.

c. Tim's, Ed's, and Irene's dogs all came from the same litter.

d. Fran, Penny, and Bob have Airedales that snap at their children.

e. Fran's, Penny's, and Bob's Airedales all came from different litters.

f. The puppy that Paul plans to get was born in the month of June, just as Barbara's was.

g. The puppy that Paul plans to get is of the same subspecies as Barbara's dog.

h. The puppy that Paul plans to get had a littermate that was vicious and had to be destroyed. Barbara's dog had no such littermates.

i. Paul plans to give his dog special training, but Barbara's dog received no such training.

j. Paul changes his conclusion to state that if he gets an Airedale puppy, it will grow up to at least tolerate children.

9

★7. Laura is considering taking Calculus I from Professor Rogers. Her friend Gina took Professor Rogers for this class and got an A. Laura concludes that she, too, will get an A from Professor Rogers. How do the following facts bear on Laura's argument?

 a. Gina earned straight A's in high school math, whereas Laura got B's.

 b. Laura took precalculus in high school, but Gina took no precalculus class.

 c. Laura is a Buddhist, whereas Gina is a Protestant.

 d. Kevin, Toni, and Samantha took precalculus in high school, and all of them received A's in Professor Rogers's Calculus I class.

 e. Kevin, Toni, and Samantha all have different majors.

 f. Kevin, Toni, and Samantha attended Franklin High School.

 g. Laura attended Roosevelt High School.

 h. Kevin, Toni, and Samantha took precalculus from different instructors.

 i. Laura and Gina earned equal scores on the college math entrance exam.

 j. Laura changes her conclusion to state that she will receive an A+ in Professor Rogers's class.

8. Andrew is thinking about buying stock in E-Tron, a new company that sells electronic equipment over the Internet. Six months ago, he bought shares in E-Boot, a new company that sells shoes over the Internet, and the price of the stock doubled in two months. Andrew argues that if he buys E-Tron, the stock will double in two months. How do the following facts bear on Andrew's argument?

 a. Stocks in Internet companies have been in a steep decline for the past two weeks, whereas they were rising six months ago.

 b. E-Tron will be run by the same management team that runs E-Boot.

 c. During the past year, the stock of five other new companies that sell over the Internet doubled within two months of their initial offering.

 d. These five companies market Swiss chocolates, tires, appliances, furniture, and luggage.

 e. A survey was taken of E-Boot customers, and 90 percent said they would not consider buying electronic equipment over the Internet.

 f. Two other companies that market jewelry and lingerie over the Internet have done poorly.

 g. Comcast, the most widely used Net service provider, just increased its monthly service charge by 50 percent.

 h. E-Boot is incorporated in New Jersey, whereas E-Tron is incorporated in Delaware.

 i. E-Boot introduced its products with a major ad campaign, whereas E-Tron plans no such campaign.

j. Andrew changes his conclusion to state that E-Tron stock will triple within the next two months.

9. According to the doctrine of adverse possession, a person occupying a piece of land in a way that is open, notorious, and hostile to the owner's rights can claim ownership of the land after a certain number of years of continuous occupancy. In this connection, Dr. Wacko, a mad scientist, hauled telescopes and radio antennas to the top of Mica Peak every night for twenty years to detect extraterrestrial life. At the end of the period he petitioned the court for a decree stating that he owned Mica Peak under the theory of adverse possession. Tom Bell, the owner of Mica Peak, attempts to defeat Dr. Wacko's petition.

Construct two arguments, one supporting Dr. Wacko's position, the other supporting Tom Bell's position. The statutory period for adverse possession in this jurisdiction is twenty years, and there are two controlling cases:

Crick v. Hoskins: Crick occupied a house in Centerville that was owned by Hoskins. She lived in the house continuously, mowed the lawn weekly, and parked her car in front. After twenty years she petitioned the court for a decree stating that she owned the property under the theory of adverse possession, and the court granted the decree against the objections of Hoskins.

Raymond v. McBride: Raymond set up a large tent on a piece of rural property owned by McBride and lived in it for nine months each year. During the remaining three months, heavy snow made the property inaccessible. After twenty years Raymond petitioned the court for a decree stating that he owned the property under the theory of adverse possession, and the court denied Raymond's petition.

★10. The Fourth Amendment to the U.S. Constitution prohibits unreasonable searches and seizures. A *search* is defined as a "violation of a person's reasonable expectation of privacy by the police." Legal issues dealing with searches often turn on the question of whether the person who was searched had a reasonable expectation of privacy at the time and place the search was conducted. In this connection, consider the following set of facts. Maxie was lining up drug contacts from his cell phone while he was driving on the freeway. Without obtaining a search warrant, federal agents intercepted one of his messages and used it to locate Maxie's car and arrest Maxie. Maxie argues that the federal agents violated his reasonable expectation of privacy, and the government denies it.

Your task is to construct two arguments, one supporting Maxie's position, the other supporting the position of the federal agents. There are three controlling cases in this jurisdiction:

U.S. v. Taylor: Federal agents suspected Taylor of illegal distribution of firearms. Without obtaining a search warrant, they planted a listening device on the phone in Taylor's home and used the evidence obtained to arrest Taylor. The court ruled that their action violated Taylor's reasonable expectation of privacy and disallowed the evidence.

U.S. v. Weber: Without obtaining a search warrant, federal agents operating inside U.S. borders intercepted a radio transmission from a plane flying over Mexico. The message mentioned drugs, and it disclosed the location of a landing strip inside the

United States. Using this information, the agents met the plane and arrested its pilot for drug smuggling. The court ruled that their action did not violate the pilot's reasonable expectation of privacy.

U.S. v. Robinson: Federal agents were using a telescope to conduct surveillance on the resident of a distant apartment building. Inadvertently they noticed some teenagers smoking crack in a car parked in the lot near the building, and they proceeded to arrest them. The court ruled that their action did not violate the teenagers' reasonable expectation of privacy.

11. The First Amendment to the U.S. Constitution states that Congress shall make no law abridging the freedom of speech or the right to peaceable assembly. This "law" applies to states (and cities) as a result of the adoption of the Fourteenth Amendment. In reliance on the First Amendment, a group of gays and lesbians apply for a permit to march on Gay Freedom Day. Similar parades in other cities have been calm and orderly, but the police chief denies a parade permit to this group.

Construct two arguments, one supporting the position of the group, the other supporting the position of the police chief. There are three controlling cases in this jurisdiction:

Lester v. City: Police seized an art collection displayed in a public park, because it depicted heterosexuals in nude poses. The court ruled that the display was protected by the First Amendment.

Byron v. City: Police denied a parade permit to a Nazi group that wanted to march on Hitler's birthday. The court ruled that the denial violated the group's rights under the First Amendment.

Stone v. City: Police closed down a theater showing an erotic gay film, because they claimed that the film promoted the spread of AIDS. The court ruled that the action of the police was allowed under the First Amendment.

12. *Constructive eviction* is a legal doctrine by which a landlord who substantially interferes with a tenant's and enjoyment of the premises will be considered to have evicted the tenant. Such a landlord cannot collect rent from the tenant. In this connection, Isabel signed a lease for an apartment owned by Carolyn. A clause in the lease stated that all tenants must keep noise to a minimum during evening hours. After moving in, Isabel found that another tenant played his stereo all night long at ear-splitting levels. Carolyn declined to enforce the noise clause in the lease. After one week without sleep, Isabel moved out, and Carolyn now sues Isabel for rent.

Construct two arguments, one supporting Isabel's position, the other supporting Carolyn's. There are two controlling cases in this jurisdiction:

Garvin v. Linder: Linder rented an apartment from Garvin, and the lease stated that Garvin would provide heat during the winter. When winter arrived, Garvin provided heat for only one hour per day, and the inside temperature sometimes dropped to 50°F. Linder moved out, and Garvin sued Linder for rent. The court ruled in favor of Linder.

Quincy v. Fulton: Fulton rented a tenth-floor apartment from Quincy. Shortly thereafter, Quincy decided to have repairs made on the elevator, causing it to be shut

9

down for a month. Because Fulton had arthritis, he had great difficulty climbing ten flights of stairs. Fulton moved out, and Quincy sued Fulton for rent. The court ruled in favor of Quincy.

★13. A negligent person who causes an injury to another person is liable for the latter's injuries. Because it is sometimes very difficult to determine the causal extent of a negligent action, courts have developed the theory of proximate cause, which limits the scope of liability. In this connection, Liz Shaffer negligently failed to maintain the brakes on her car, and as a result her car crashed into one driven by Mary Vassar. Mary was taken to the hospital for bumps and bruises, but while she was there, doctors mistakenly amputated her perfectly healthy leg. Mary sues Liz for loss of her leg.

Construct two arguments, one supporting Mary's position, the other supporting Liz's position. The only issue is whether Liz proximately caused the loss of the leg. There are two controlling cases in this jurisdiction:

Sacco v. Lane: Lane negligently used gasoline to light his barbecue in a strong wind. The flames from the barbecue ignited nearby trees and then spread to ten houses in the neighborhood, burning them to the ground. The court ruled that Lane was liable for damage to the houses.

Hunt v. Gomez: Hunt was a passenger in a taxi driven by Gomez. Gomez was drunk and negligently let Hunt out at the wrong corner. While Hunt was walking home, a worker dropped a brick from a building that was under construction, injuring Hunt. Hunt sued Gomez for injury resulting from the falling brick. The court ruled in favor of Gomez.

14. Lynn Dodd, age twenty, has become a member of New Age Enlightenment, a religious cult group. The group has convinced Lynn to sell all her worldly possessions and give the proceeds to the group. The group forbids any contact between Lynn and her relatives and friends. On one occasion Lynn's parents encountered Lynn on a street corner, and they tried to persuade her to leave the group and return home, but she refused. The parents fear that some form of mind control is being used to keep Lynn in the group, and they plan a rescue operation.

Write a dialogue, similar to the one presented in this chapter, examining the morality and legality of such an operation. Include in your dialogue analogies between the proposed rescue operation and the following: rescuing an adult who has been hypnotized by captors, kidnapping someone against his or her will, rescuing a child who has been kidnapped, spiriting away a novice who has joined a Jesuit seminary or Franciscan convent, coercing an alcoholic to enter a detoxification center, forcing a child to attend a certain school, preventing someone from committing suicide, forcing a child to attend a certain church, rescuing an eighteen-year-old from a Nazi youth group, removing one's daughter from the Girl Scouts, and any other pertinent analogy that comes to mind.

15. During fifteen years of marriage, James and Leslie Knox had not succeeded in having a baby. As a last resort, they tried in vitro fertilization. Doctors surgically removed nine eggs from Leslie and fertilized them with James's sperm. The embryos were then placed in a freezer until the proper time for them to be implanted in Leslie's womb. In the meantime, James and Leslie came

to realize that their marriage was going nowhere, and they decided to get a divorce. The couple has had no trouble arriving at a settlement concerning the house, cars, bank accounts, and other possessions, but they cannot agree on the disposition of the frozen embryos. James is adamant about not wanting to have any children by Leslie, and he wants the embryos destroyed. Leslie, on the other hand, realizing that she is getting older, thinks that the frozen embryos offer her the best chance of having a baby, and she wants them implanted.

Write a dialogue, similar to the one in this chapter, examining the moral and/or legal ramifications of this dispute. Include in your dialogue analogies between this situation and the following: killing a fetus, killing a baby, forcing your wife to have an abortion, having an abortion against the wishes of your husband, owning a dog or cat, owning a child, determining custody of a child upon divorce, dividing a bank account, determining ownership of a unique and valuable painting produced jointly by two people, implanting an embryo in a surrogate mother, and any other analogies that come to mind, including analogies that show that the embryos have or do not have rights and analogies that illustrate the investment that James and Leslie have in the embryos.

MindTap° Master concepts and improve outcomes with Aplia, at the end of the chapter, in the Aplia folder.

Summary

Argument from Analogy:

- An inductive argument that rests on a similarity between two things.
- The two things that are compared are called analogues.
  - Primary analogue: An analogue mentioned in the premise.
  - Secondary analogue: The analogue mentioned in the conclusion.

- Principles for evaluating arguments from analogy:
  - Relevance of the similarities
  - Number of similarities
  - Nature and degree of disanalogy
  - Number of primary analogues
  - Diversity among the primary analogues
  - Specificity of the conclusion

9

Legal Reasoning:

- Requirement of precedent: Similar cases are decided similarly.
- The six principles for evaluating arguments from analogy apply to legal arguments.

Moral Reasoning:

- Analogies are useful in constructing arguments about moral issues.

MindTap° Need help? See the Learning Logic folder at the end of the chapter: the self-paced tutorial walks you through any section.

10 Causality and Mill's Methods

10.1 "Cause" and Necessary and Sufficient Conditions
10.2 Mill's Five Methods
10.3 Mill's Methods and Science

HOW LOGICAL ARE YOU? Suppose, during a certain month, ten people were arrested for animal abuse. These people had different family backgrounds, different ethnicities, different ages, different employment histories, different levels of education, and were of different gender. The one feature that all of them shared in common was they had a childhood history of bullying other children. Does this show that being a childhood bully causes a person to engage in animal abuse?

Find the answer on MindTap.

10.1 "Cause" and Necessary and Sufficient Conditions

A knowledge of causal connections plays a prominent role in our effort to control the environment in which we live. We insulate our homes because we know insulation will prevent heat loss, we vaccinate our children because we know vaccination will protect them from polio and diphtheria, we practice the piano and violin because we know that by doing so we may become proficient on them, and we cook our meat and fish because we know that doing so will make them edible.

When the word "cause" is used in ordinary English, however, it is seriously affected by ambiguity. For example, when we say that sprinkling water on the flowers will cause them to grow, we mean that water is required for growth, not that water alone will do the job—sunshine and the proper soil are also required. On the other hand, when we say

MindTap Read, study, reflect, and prepare for exams online, anytime, anywhere.

560

that going for a swim on a hot summer day will cause us to cool off, we mean that the swim by itself *will* do the job; but we understand that other things will work just as well, such as taking a cold shower, entering an air-conditioned room, and so on.

To clear up this ambiguity affecting the meaning of "cause," adopting the language of sufficient and necessary conditions is useful. When we say that electrocution is a cause of death, we mean "cause" in the sense of *sufficient* condition. Electrocution is sufficient to produce death, but there are other methods equally effective, such as poisoning, drowning, and shooting. On the other hand, when we say that the presence of clouds is a cause of rain, we mean "cause" in the sense of *necessary* condition. Without clouds, rain cannot occur, but clouds alone are not sufficient. Certain combinations of pressure and temperature are also required.

Sometimes "cause" is used in the sense of necessary *and* sufficient condition, as when we say that the action of a force causes a body to accelerate or that an increase in voltage causes an increase in electrical current. For a body to accelerate, nothing more and nothing less is required than for it to be acted on by a net force; and for an electrical current to increase through a resistive circuit, nothing more and nothing less is required than an increase in voltage.

Thus, as these examples illustrate, the word "cause" can have any one of three different meanings:

1. Sufficient condition
2. Necessary condition
3. Sufficient and necessary condition

Sometimes the context provides an immediate clue to the sense in which "cause" is being used. If we are trying to *prevent* a certain phenomenon from happening, we usually search for a cause that is a necessary condition, and if we are trying to *produce* a certain phenomenon, we usually search for a cause that is a sufficient condition. For example, in attempting to prevent the occurrence of smog around cities, scientists try to isolate a necessary condition or group of necessary conditions that, if removed, will eliminate the smog. And in their effort to produce an abundant harvest, farmers search for a sufficient condition that, given sunshine and rainfall, will increase crop growth.

Another important point is that whenever an event occurs, at least *one* sufficient condition is present and *all* the necessary conditions are present. The conjunction of the necessary conditions *is* the sufficient condition that actually produces the event. For example, the necessary conditions for lighting a match are heat (produced by striking) and oxygen. Combining these two necessary conditions gives the sufficient condition. In other words, striking the match in the presence of oxygen is sufficient to ignite it. In cases where the sufficient condition is also a necessary condition, there is only one necessary condition, which is identical with the sufficient condition.

We can now summarize the meaning of cause in the sense of a sufficient condition and a necessary condition:

> *A* is a sufficient condition for *B*: *A*'s occurrence requires *B*'s occurrence.
> *A* is a necessary condition for *B*: *B*'s occurrence requires *A*'s occurrence.

According to these statements, if *A* occurs and *B* does not occur, then *A* is not a sufficient condition for *B*, and if *B* occurs and *A* does not occur, then *A* is not a necessary condition for *B*. Thus:

> *A* is not a sufficient condition for *B*: *A* is present when *B* is absent.
> *A* is not a necessary condition for *B*: *A* is absent when *B* is present.

These results will serve as important rules in the material that follows.

10.2 Mill's Five Methods

In his *System of Logic*, the nineteenth-century philosopher John Stuart Mill compiled five methods for identifying causal connections between events. These he called the method of agreement, the method of difference, the joint method of agreement and difference, the method of residues, and the method of concomitant variation. In the years that have elapsed since the publication of Mill's *Logic*, the five methods have received a good deal of philosophical criticism. Today most logicians agree that the methods fall short of the claims made for them by Mill, but the fact remains that the methods function implicitly in many of the inductive inferences we make in ordinary life.

In addition to criticizing these methods, modern logicians have introduced many variations that have multiplied their number beyond the original five. Some of these variations have resulted from the fact that Mill himself failed to distinguish causes that are sufficient conditions from causes that are necessary conditions. The account that follows introduces this distinction into the first three methods, but apart from that, it remains faithful to Mill's own presentation.

Method of Agreement

Suppose that five people eat dinner in a certain restaurant, and a short while later all five become sick. Suppose further that these people ordered an assortment of items from the menu, but the only food that all of them ordered was vanilla ice cream for dessert. In other words, all of the dinners were in agreement only as to the ice cream. Such a situation suggests that the ice cream caused the sickness. The **method of agreement** consists in a systematic effort to find a single factor (such as the ice cream) that is common to several occurrences for the purpose of identifying that factor as the cause of a phenomenon present in the occurrences (such as the sickness).

The method of agreement identifies a cause in the sense of a necessary condition. To see how this method works, let us develop the restaurant example a bit further.

> Five people eat dinner in a restaurant. Jack has salad, french fries, a hamburger, ice cream, and mixed vegetables; Bob has salad, french fries, soup, ice cream, fish, and mixed vegetables; Mary has a hamburger, soup, and ice cream; Tim has fish, mixed vegetables, ice cream, salad, and soup; and Gail has mixed vegetables, fish, ice cream, french fries, and salad. Afterwards, all of them became sick from something they ate. What food caused the sickness?

TABLE 10.1

Occurrence	Possible Necessary Conditions							Phenomenon (sickness)
	A	B	C	D	E	F	G	
1	*	—	*	*	—	*	*	*
2	*	*	*	—	*	*	*	*
3	—	*	—	*	—	*	—	*
4	*	*	—	—	*	*	*	*
5	*	—	*	—	*	*	*	*

If we let occurrences 1 through 5 stand for Jack, Bob, Mary, Tim, and Gail, respectively, and let A through G represent salad, soup, french fries, a hamburger, fish, ice cream, and mixed vegetables, respectively, we can construct a table that reflects what these five people ate (Table 10.1). In this table an asterisk means that a certain food was eaten, and a dash means that it was not eaten.

Now, since the method of agreement identifies a cause in the sense of a necessary condition, we begin by eliminating from this table the conditions that are not necessary for the occurrence of the phenomenon. In doing so, we use the rule that a condition is not necessary for the occurrence of a phenomenon if that condition is absent when the phenomenon is present. Thus, occurrence 1 eliminates condition B and condition E; occurrence 2 eliminates D; occurrence 3 eliminates A, C, E (again), and G; occurrence 4 eliminates C (again) and D (again); and occurrence 5 eliminates B (again) and D (again). This leaves only F (the ice cream) as a possible necessary condition. The conclusion is therefore warranted that the ice cream caused the sickness of the diners.

This conclusion follows only probably for two reasons. First, it is quite possible that some condition was overlooked in compiling conditions A through G. For example, if the ice cream was served with contaminated spoons, then the sickness of the diners could have been caused by that condition and not by the ice cream. Second, if more than one of the foods were contaminated (for example, both soup and french fries), then the sickness could have been caused by this combination of foods and not by the ice cream. Thus, the strength of the argument depends on the nonoccurrence of these two possibilities.

It is also important to realize that the conclusion yielded by Table 10.1 applies directly only to the five diners represented in the five occurrences, and not to everyone who may have eaten in the restaurant. Thus, if some food other than those listed in the table—for example, spaghetti—was contaminated, then only if they avoided both spaghetti and ice cream could the other diners be assured of not getting sick. But if, among all the foods in the restaurant, only the ice cream was contaminated, the conclusion would extend to the other patrons as well. This last point illustrates the fact that a conclusion reached by the method of agreement has limited generality. It applies directly only to those occurrences listed, and only indirectly, through a second inductive inference, to others.

Furthermore, because the conclusion yields a cause in the sense of a necessary condition, it does not assert that anyone who ate the ice cream would get sick. Many people

John Stuart Mill 1806–1873

John Stuart Mill, who would become the most important English-speaking philosopher of the nineteenth century, was born in London to the philosopher and historian James Mill and his wife, Harriet Barrow. From a very early age the father took charge of his son's education, imposing on him an unusually strict course of studies. The boy began studying Greek at age three; he began Latin, geometry, and algebra at eight; and by fourteen he had read most of the Latin and Greek classics. Also, by that time he had developed a thorough knowledge of history, scholastic and Aristotelian logic, and higher-level mathematics. At seventeen he accepted a position with the East India Company, a private corporation that virtually ruled all of India. He remained there for twenty-five years, eventually becoming chief examiner, which put him largely in charge of the company.

When he was twenty, Mill suffered an acute attack of depression that lasted for several months. Although he managed to continue his work, everything seemed worthless to him at that time. This condition was most likely brought on by the severity of his educational upbringing, which had attended to his intellect but left his emotional life a desert. Gradually he pulled himself out by reading the poetry of William Wordsworth. Four years later Mill met Harriet Taylor, with whom he became emotionally but not sexually intimate (she was married at that time). Taylor would exert a profound influence on him for the rest of his life. After the death of her husband, nineteen years after she and Mill first met, they were married.

Today John Stuart Mill is widely known for his essay "On Liberty" and his book *Utilitarianism*. The essay is a sustained argument in favor of freedom of speech and the maximization of individual liberty against the strictures of government. *Utilitarianism* further develops the ethical theory promoted by James Mill and Jeremy Bentham. As perfected by John Stuart Mill, this theory holds that we should always perform the action that produces

Library of Congress Prints and Photographs Division [Williams, Sophus/LC-USZ62-76491]

the greatest happiness for the greatest number of people. This work was important, among other reasons, for creating an ethical theory that was not based on any theology or religion. Mill also wrote extensively on women's rights, and when he was later elected to a three-year term in Parliament, he became the first member to urge that women receive the right to vote.

Mill's greatest work was his *System of Logic*, which went through eight editions during his lifetime. In that book Mill argues that deductive argumentation, far from being the paradigmatic form of reasoning most philosophers take it to be, is largely bereft of value because it never yields any new knowledge. Also, it is essentially dependent on induction. Thus, it is really induction that should be studied as the primary engine of scientific discovery.

In 1858 Harriet Taylor died from a lung infection while the couple were visiting Avignon, France. Nearly inconsolable, Mill bought a house there so he could be near her grave. He died in Avignon fifteen years later, and his body was buried alongside hers.

have a natural immunity to food poisoning. What the conclusion says is that patrons who did not eat the ice cream would not get sick—at least not from the food. Thus, the method of agreement has a certain limited use. Basically what it says, in reference to the example, is that the ice cream is a highly suspect factor in the sickness of the patrons, and if investigators want to track down the cause of the sickness, this is where they should begin.

An example of an actual use of the method of agreement is provided by the discovery of the beneficial effects of fluoride on teeth. It was noticed several decades ago that people in certain communities were favored with especially healthy teeth. In researching the various factors these communities shared, scientists discovered that all had a high level of natural fluoride in their water supply. The scientists concluded from this evidence that fluoride causes teeth to be healthy.

Method of Difference

For an example of how this method works, let us modify our earlier case of people becoming sick from eating food in a restaurant. Instead of five people, suppose that identical twins, who have identical susceptibilities to food poisoning, go to that restaurant for dinner. They both order identical meals except that one orders ice cream for dessert while the other does not. The ice cream is the only way that the two meals differ. Later the twin who ordered the ice cream gets sick, whereas the other twin does not. The natural conclusion is that the ice cream caused the sickness.

The **method of difference** consists in a systematic effort to identify a single factor that is present in an occurrence in which the phenomenon in question is present, and absent from an occurrence in which the phenomenon is absent. The method is confined to investigating exactly two occurrences, and it identifies a cause in the sense of a sufficient condition. For a clearer illustration of how this method works, let us add a few details to the twin example:

> A pair of twins, Jane and Jan, have dinner in a restaurant. The twins have identical susceptibilities to food poisoning. Jane orders soup, salad, chicken, carrots, rice, and ice cream. Jan orders soup, salad, chicken, carrots, rice, and no ice cream. Later, Jane gets sick from something she ate, but Jan does not. What food caused Jane's sickness?

If we let Jane and Jan stand for occurrences 1 and 2, respectively, and let A stand for the specific susceptibility to food poisoning shared by Jane and Jan, and B through G stand for soup, salad, chicken, carrots, rice, and ice cream, respectively, we can produce Table 10.2. Again, an asterisk indicates that a certain condition is present, and a dash indicates it is absent.

TABLE 10.2

Occurrence	Possible Sufficient Conditions							Phenomenon (sickness)
	A	B	C	D	E	F	G	
1	*	*	*	*	*	*	*	*
2	*	*	*	*	*	*	—	—

As with the method of agreement, we proceed to eliminate certain conditions, but in this case we use the rule that a condition is not sufficient for the occurrence of a phenomenon if it is present when the phenomenon is absent. Accordingly, occurrence 2 eliminates A, B, C, D, E, and F. This leaves only G as the sufficient condition for the phenomenon. Thus, G (ice cream) is the cause of Jane's sickness.

Since the result yielded by the method of difference applies to only the one occurrence in which the phenomenon is present (in this case, Jane), it is often less susceptible to generalization than is the method of agreement, which usually applies to several occurrences. Thus, the mere fact that the ice cream may have caused Jane to become sick does not mean that it caused other patrons who ate ice cream to get sick. Perhaps these other people have a higher resistance to food poisoning than does Jane or Jan. But given that the others are similar to Jane and Jan in relevant respects, the result can often be generalized to cover these others as well. At the very least, if others in the restaurant became sick, the fact that the ice cream is what made Jane sick suggests that this is where investigators should begin when they try to explain what made the others sick.

The conclusion yielded by the method of difference is only probable, however, even for the one occurrence to which it directly applies. The problem is that it is impossible for two occurrences to be literally identical in every respect but one. The mere fact that two occurrences occupy different regions of space, that one is closer to the wall than the other, amounts to a difference. Such differences may be insignificant, but therein lies the possibility for error. It is not at all obvious how insignificant differences should be distinguished from significant ones. Furthermore, it is impossible to make an exhaustive list of all the possible conditions; but without such a list there is no assurance that significant conditions have not been overlooked.

The objective of the method of difference is to identify a sufficient condition among those that are *present* in a specific occurrence. Sometimes, however, the *absence* of a factor can count as something positive that must be taken into account. Suppose, for example, that both of the twins who dined in the restaurant are allergic to dairy products, but they can avoid an allergic reaction by taking Lactaid tablets. Suppose further that both twins ordered ice cream for dessert, but only Jan took the tablets. After the meal, Jane got sick. We can attribute Jane's sickness to the absence of the Lactaid.

We can illustrate this situation by modifying Table 10.2 as follows. Let A stand for the allergy to dairy products, let B through G stand for the same foods as before, and let H stand for Lactaid tablets. Then ~H will stand for the *absence* of Lactaid (the symbol ~ means "not"). As before, let occurrence 1 stand for Jane, and occurrence 2 for Jan (see Table 10.3).

TABLE 10.3

Occurrence	Possible Sufficient Conditions								Phenomenon (sickness)
	A	B	C	D	E	F	G	~H	
1	*	*	*	*	*	*	*	*	*
2	*	*	*	*	*	*	*	—	—

Using the same rule for elimination as with Table 10.2, we see that occurrence 2 eliminates *A* through *G* as sufficient conditions. This leaves ~*H* (the absence of Lactaid) as the cause of Jane's sickness. In this case, the ice cream is not identified as the cause, because Jan (occurrence 2) ate ice cream (*G*) but did not get sick.

The method of difference has a wide range of applicability. For example, a farmer might fertilize one part of a field but not the other part to test the benefit of using fertilizer. If the fertilized part of the crop turns out to be fuller and healthier than the nonfertilized part, then the farmer can conclude that the improvement was caused by the fertilizer. On the other hand, a cook might leave some ingredient out of a batch of biscuits to determine the importance of that ingredient. If the biscuits turn out dry and crunchy, the cook can attribute the difference to the absence of that ingredient.

Joint Method of Agreement and Difference

To illustrate the joint method, we can once again modify the example of the diners who got sick by eating food in a restaurant. In place of the original five diners and the pair of twins, suppose that six people eat dinner in the restaurant. Among the first three, suppose that a variety of meals are eaten but that only ice cream is consumed by all, and later all three get sick. And among the other three, suppose that a variety of meals are eaten but that none of these diners eats any ice cream, and later none of them gets sick. The conclusion is warranted that the ice cream is what made the first three diners sick.

The **joint method of agreement and difference** consists of a systematic effort to identify a single condition that is present in two or more occurrences in which the phenomenon in question is present and that is absent from two or more occurrences in which the phenomenon is absent. In addition, the condition must never be present when the phenomenon is absent nor absent when the phenomenon is present. Stated briefly, the occurrence/nonoccurrence of the condition matches the occurrence/nonoccurrence of the phenomenon. When the phenomenon is present, so is the condition, and when the phenomenon is absent, so is the condition. This condition is then taken to be the cause of the phenomenon in the sense of a necessary and sufficient condition. To see more clearly how this method works, let us add some details to the example:

> Six people eat dinner in a restaurant. Liz has soup, a hamburger, ice cream, french fries, and mixed vegetables. Tom has salad, soup, fish, mixed vegetables, and ice cream. Andy has salad, a hamburger, french fries, and ice cream. Sue has french fries, a hamburger, and salad. Meg has fish and mixed vegetables. Bill has french fries, a hamburger, and soup. Later Liz, Tom, and Andy get sick from something they ate, but Sue, Meg, and Bill do not. What food made the first three diners sick?

Let occurrences 1 through 6 stand for Liz, Tom, Andy, Sue, Meg, and Bill, respectively. And let *A* through *G* stand for salad, soup, a hamburger, fish, ice cream, french fries, and mixed vegetables (see Table 10.4).

TABLE 10.4

| Occurrence | Possible Necessary or Sufficient Conditions | | | | | | | Phenomenon (sickness) |
	A	B	C	D	E	F	G	
1	—	*	*	—	*	*	*	*
2	*	*	—	*	*	—	*	*
3	*	—	*	—	*	*	—	*
4	*	—	*	—	—	*	—	—
5	—	—	—	*	—	—	*	—
6	—	*	*	—	—	*	—	—

In the first three occurrences the phenomenon is present, so we proceed by eliminating possible necessary conditions. Using the rule that a condition is not necessary if it is absent when the phenomenon is present, occurrence 1 eliminates *A* and *D*, occurrence 2 eliminates *C* and *F*, and occurrence 3 eliminates *B*, *D* (again), and *G*. This leaves only *E* as the necessary condition. Next, in the last three occurrences the phenomenon is absent, so we use the rule that a condition is not sufficient if it is present when the phenomenon is absent. Occurrence 4 eliminates *A*, *C*, and *F*; occurrence 5 eliminates *D* and *G*; and occurrence 6 eliminates *B*, *C* (again), and *F* (again). This leaves only *E* as the sufficient condition. Thus, condition *E* (ice cream) is the cause in the sense of both a necessary and sufficient condition of the sickness of the first three diners.

Students sometimes have difficulty understanding the joint method because its definition is a bit complicated. But this method is really easier to grasp than either the method of agreement or the method of difference. To understand the joint method, keep in mind that claims about something being a necessary and sufficient condition are equivalent to "if and only if" claims. Thus, in reference to Table 10.4, the phenomenon occurs if and only if *E* occurs. If *E* occurs then so does the phenomenon; if *E* does not occur, then neither does the phenomenon. So, to identify a cause in the sense of a necessary and sufficient condition, look for a column beneath the possible conditions that is identical to the column beneath the phenomenon. The column beneath *E* is *** – – –. The column beneath the phenomenon is also *** – – –. Thus, *E* is the cause in the sense of a necessary and sufficient condition.

Since the joint method yields a cause in the sense of both a necessary and sufficient condition, it is usually thought to be stronger than either the method of agreement by itself, which yields a cause in the sense of a necessary condition, or the method of difference by itself, which yields a cause in the sense of a sufficient condition. However, when any of these methods is used as a basis for a subsequent inductive generalization, the strength of the conclusion is proportional to the number of occurrences that are included. Thus, an application of the method of agreement that included, say, one hundred occurrences might offer stronger results than an application of the joint method that included, say, only six occurrences. By similar reasoning, multiple applications of the method of difference might offer stronger results than a single application of the joint method.

As with the other methods, the conclusion yielded by the joint method is only probable because some relevant condition may have been overlooked in producing the table.

10

If, for example, both salad and soup were contaminated, then the ice cream could not be identified as a necessary condition for the sickness, and if one of the last three diners was naturally immune, then the ice cream could not be identified as a sufficient condition. Obviously the attempt to extend the results of this example to other patrons of the restaurant who may have gotten sick is fraught with other difficulties.

Lastly, we note that even though the name of the joint method suggests that it results from a mere combination of the method of agreement with the method of difference, this is not the case. Such a combination would consist of one occurrence in which the phenomenon is present, one occurrence in which the phenomenon is absent and which differs from the former occurrence as to only one condition, and one occurrence in which the phenomenon is present and which agrees with the first occurrence in only one condition. However, according to Mill, the joint method requires "two or more" occurrences in which the phenomenon is present, and "two or more" occurrences in which the phenomenon is absent.* His further description of the method accords with the foregoing account.

Method of Residues

This method and the one that follows are used to identify a causal connection between two conditions without regard for the specific kind of connection. Both methods may be used to identify conditions that are sufficient, necessary, or both sufficient and necessary. The **method of residues** consists of separating from a group of causally connected conditions and phenomena those strands of causal connection that are already known, leaving the required causal connection as the "residue." Here is an example:

> After occupying his new house Mr. Smith found it drafty. He traced the source of the draft to three conditions: a broken window in the garage, a crack under the front door, and a broken damper in the fireplace. When the window was replaced he noticed an improvement, and a further improvement when weather stripping was installed on the door. He concluded that the draft that remained was caused by the broken damper in the fireplace.

The method of residues as illustrated in this example may be diagrammed as follows:

$$(A\ B\ C)\ \text{causes}\ (a\ b\ c.)$$

A causes a.

B causes b.

Therefore, C causes c.

In reference to the draft example, $(A\ B\ C)$ is the combination of possible conditions producing $(a\ b\ c)$, the total draft. When A (the broken window) is separated out, it is found to cause a (a portion of the draft). When B (the crack) is separated out, it is found to cause b (another portion of the draft). The conclusion is that C (the broken damper) causes c

---

*A System of Logic, Book 3, Chapter 8, Section 4, Third Canon.

(the remaining portion of the draft). The conclusion follows only probably because it is quite possible that a fourth source of the draft was overlooked. Here is another example:

> After realizing a loss of $100,000, a department store's chief accountant could suggest only three causes: an excessive number of clerks, increases in utility rates, and damage to merchandise caused by a flood. These expenses were estimated at $25,000, $30,000, and $10,000, respectively. Since no other ordinary sources could be found, the accountant attributed the remaining $35,000 to shoplifting.

In this case $(A\ B\ C\ D)$ is the combination of conditions consisting of the number of clerks, the utility rate increases, the flood, and shoplifting; and $(a\ b\ c\ d)$ is the total loss of $100,000. After A, B, and C are separated out, the conclusion is that D (shoplifting) caused d (the remaining loss). Because the estimates might have been incorrect and because additional sources of financial loss might have been overlooked, the conclusion is only probable.

Some procedures that, at least on the face of it, appear to use the method of residues come closer to being deductive than inductive. A case in point is the procedure used to determine the weight of the cargo carried by a truck. First, the empty truck is put on a scale and the weight recorded. Then the truck is loaded and the truck together with the cargo is put on the same scale. The weight of the cargo is the difference between the two weights. If, to this procedure, we add the rather unproblematic assumptions that weight is an additive property, that the scale is accurate, that the scale operator reads the indicator properly, that the truck is not altered in the loading process, and a few others, the conclusion about the weight of the cargo follows deductively.

To distinguish deductive from inductive uses of the method of residues, we must take into account such factors as the role of mathematics. If the conclusion depends on a purely arithmetical computation, the argument is probably best characterized as deductive. If not, then it is probably inductive.

Method of Concomitant Variation

The **method of concomitant variation** identifies a causal connection between two conditions by matching variations in one condition with variations in another. According to one formulation, increases are matched with increases and decreases with decreases. Example:

> In attempting to diagnose Mrs. Thompson's high blood pressure, a cardiologist noticed a correlation between fluctuations in blood pressure and certain brain waves. As the blood pressure increased, so did the intensity of the brain waves, and as the blood pressure decreased, the intensity of the brain waves decreased. The cardiologist concluded that the two conditions were causally related.

The method of concomitant variation as illustrated in this example may be diagrammed as follows:

$(A\ B\ C)$ is coincident with $(X\ Y\ Z.)$

$(A\ B+\ C)$ is coincident with $(X\ Y+\ Z.)$

$(A\ B-\ C)$ is coincident with $(X\ Y-\ Z.)$

Therefore, B is causally connected to Y.

Here, $\boxed{A\,B\,C}$ is a set of observable conditions such as cholesterol level, liver function, and basal metabolism, with B representing blood pressure; and $\boxed{X\,Y\,Z}$ is another set of observable conditions with Y representing certain brain waves. In the second and third rows, $B+$ and $B-$ represent increases and decreases in blood pressure, and $Y+$ and $Y-$ represent increases and decreases in the intensity of the brain waves. The conclusion asserts that either B causes Y, Y causes B, or B and Y have a common cause. Determining which is the case requires further investigation; of course, if B occurs earlier in time than Y, then Y does not cause B, and if Y occurs earlier in time than B, then B does not cause Y.

The blood pressure example matches increases in one condition with increases in another. For an example that matches increases in one condition with decreases in another, consider the following:

> A sociologist studying divorce noticed a correlation between changes in the national divorce rate and fluctuations in the gross domestic product (GDP). As the GDP increases, the divorce rate decreases, and when the GDP sags, the divorce rate goes up. The sociologist concluded that the two phenomena are causally connected.

This second version of the method of concomitant variation may be diagramed as follows:

$\boxed{A\;B\;C}$ is coincident with $\boxed{X\;Y\;Z.}$
$\boxed{A\;B+\;C}$ is coincident with $\boxed{X\;Y-\;Z.}$
$\boxed{A\;B-\;C}$ is coincident with $\boxed{X\;Y+\;Z.}$

Therefore, B is causally connected to Y.

In this example $\boxed{A\,B\,C}$ is a set of economic conditions such as stock-exchange indexes, interest rates, and commodity prices, with B representing gross domestic product; and $\boxed{X\,Y\,Z}$ is a set of social conditions such as birthrates, employment rates, and immigration numbers, with Y representing the national divorce rate. The conclusion is that B is somehow causally connected to Y. However, in this example an even stronger conclusion could probably be drawn—namely, that decreases in the GDP cause increases in the divorce rate, and not conversely. That changes in economic prosperity (which is indicated by GDP) should affect the divorce rate is quite plausible, but the converse is less so.

At this point we should note that the existence of a mere correlation between two phenomena is never sufficient to identify a causal connection. In addition, the causal connection suggested by the correlation must at least make sense. Consider the following example:

> After an in-depth study, researchers discovered a correlation between the price of pork-belly futures on the Chicago Mercantile Exchange and earthquake activity in Japan. As the number and intensity of the quakes increased, the futures prices also increased, and vice versa. The researchers concluded that the two phenomena were causally connected.

The argument is clearly weak. Because it is virtually inconceivable that either phenomenon could cause a change in the other, or that changes in both could have a common cause, it is most likely that the correlation is purely coincidental.

The method of concomitant variation is useful when it is impossible for a condition to be either wholly present or wholly absent, as was required for the use of the first three of Mill's methods. Many conditions are of this sort—for example, the temperature of the ocean, the price of gold, the incidence of crime, the size of a mountain glacier, a person's cholesterol level, and so on. If some kind of correlation can be detected between variations in conditions such as these, the method of concomitant variation asserts that the two are causally connected. The method has been used successfully in the past to help establish the existence of causal connections between smoking and lung cancer, nuclear radiation and leukemia, and alcohol consumption and cirrhosis of the liver.

10.3 Mill's Methods and Science

Mill's methods closely resemble certain scientific methods that are intended to establish causal connections and correlations. For example, the method of difference is virtually identical to the method of controlled experiment employed in such fields as biology, pharmacology, and psychology. A controlled experiment is one that involves two groups of subjects: an experimental group and a control group. The experimental group includes the subjects that receive a certain treatment, and the control group includes the subjects that do not receive the treatment but are otherwise subjected to the same conditions as the experimental group.

The simplest type of controlled experiment involves an experimental group and a control group each consisting of just one member. Example:

> Two mice were used in a controlled experiment to determine whether a certain substance was carcinogenic. The two mice had identical genes, were the same age, were placed in identical cages in the same location, were subjected to the same environmental conditions, and were fed the same food over the same period of time. One mouse was injected with the suspected carcinogen, and the other was not. After two months, the injected mouse developed cancerous tumors but the other mouse did not.

To summarize the results of this experiment we can construct a table just like the one for the method of difference. If we let occurrence 1 represent the injected mouse and occurrence 2 the mouse that was not injected, and let A through F represent the conditions common to the two mice (genes, age, cage, etc.) and G represent the injection, we have Table 10.5. Using the rule that a condition is not sufficient if it is present when the phenomenon is absent, occurrence 2 eliminates A through F, leaving G (the suspected carcinogen) as the cause of the phenomenon.

TABLE 10.5

| Occurrence | Possible Sufficient Conditions | | | | | | | Phenomenon (tumors) |
	A	B	C	D	E	F	G	
1	*	*	*	*	*	*	*	*
2	*	*	*	*	*	*	—	—

The principal drawback of this experiment is that the suspected carcinogen was given to only one mouse. As a result, the experiment offers relatively weak evidence that *any* mouse injected with this substance would develop tumors. Perhaps the injected mouse had some hidden defect that would have caused tumors even without the injection. Scientists address this problem by increasing the size of the experimental group and the control group. Thus, suppose the same experiment were performed on 100 mice, of which 50 were injected and 50 were not. Suppose that after two months all 50 injected mice developed tumors and none of the control subjects did. Such a result would constitute much stronger evidence that the injected substance was carcinogenic.

This expanded experiment can be considered to be a case of multiple uses of Mill's method of difference. Since the method of difference always involves just two occurrences, mouse #1 could be matched with mouse #51 for one use of the method, mouse #2 with mouse #52 for a second use of the method, and so on. Although this expanded experiment might look like a case of the joint method, it is not (at least not a successful one). Any successful application of the joint method includes occurrences in which certain conditions are absent when the phenomenon is present. Those conditions are then eliminated as possible necessary conditions. The expanded experiment with the mice includes no such occurrences.

This fact points to an important difference between Mill's joint method and his method of difference. The purpose of the method of difference is to determine whether a *preselected* condition is the cause of a phenomenon. This preselected condition is present in one of the two occurrences and absent from the other. On the other hand, the purpose of the joint method is to determine which condition, among a selected *class* of conditions, is a cause of a phenomenon. The joint method applies rules for sufficient conditions and necessary conditions to (one hopes) reduce the class of conditions to just one.

Returning to the expanded experiment with the mice, let us suppose that only forty of the mice in the experimental group developed tumors, and none of those in the control group did. From Mill's standpoint, this would be equivalent to forty uses of the method of difference yielding positive results and ten yielding negative results. On the basis of such an outcome, the experimenter might conclude that the likelihood of the suspected carcinogen producing tumors in mice was 80 percent ($40 \div 50$).

Controlled experiments such as the one involving 100 mice are often conducted on humans, but with humans it is never possible to control the circumstances to the degree that it is with mice. Humans cannot be put in cages or fed exactly the same food for any length of time, they are not genetically identical to other humans, and so forth. Also, humans react to their environment in ways that cannot be anticipated or controlled. To correct this deficiency, statistical methods are applied to the results to enable the drawing of a conclusion.

For example, an experiment could be conducted to test the effectiveness of some new drug on children with attention deficit/hyperactivity disorder (ADHD). Fifty children with ADHD could be selected, with twenty-five being placed at random in the experimental group and twenty-five in the control group. The children in the experimental group would be given the drug, probably in a classroom situation, and the children in the control group would be given a placebo (sugar pill). This could be done on a "double blind" basis, so that neither the children nor the people conducting the experiment would know in advance who was getting the drug. The objective is to

10

FIGURE 10.1

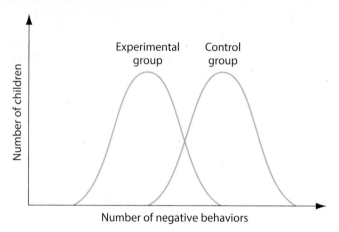

control the conditions as much as possible. Then the negative behavior of each of the fifty children would be recorded over a period, say, of an hour. Each time a child was out of his or her seat, disturbed others, fidgeted, failed to follow instructions, and so forth, the incident would be noted.

The results of such an experiment would be expected to follow what is called a normal probability distribution (bell-shaped curve). (Further discussion of normal probability distribution is presented in Chapter 12.) One curve would represent the experimental group, another curve the control group. Assuming the drug is effective, the two curves would be displaced from one another, but they would probably overlap in part, as indicated in Figure 10.1. This means that certain children in the experimental group exhibited more negative behaviors than certain children in the control group, but most of the children in the experimental group exhibited fewer negative behaviors than most of the children in the control group. Then statistical methods would be applied to the two curves to determine the effectiveness of the drug. Such an experiment is similar to Mill's method of difference except that instead of the phenomenon (negative behavior) being wholly present in some occurrences, it is present in varying degrees. In this sense, the experiment resembles the method of concomitant variation.

In some kinds of scientific research on humans, controlling the circumstances to any significant degree is nearly impossible. Such research includes investigations that cover a long period or investigations in which the health of the subjects is at issue and legal or moral restrictions come into play. Example:

> A nutritionist wanted to determine the effect of fifteen vitamin and mineral supplements on atherosclerosis (artery disease). Because the effect was expected to require several years to develop, the nutritionist ran an ad in a health publication for individuals who had ingested these substances on a regular basis for five years. Eighty people answered the ad and reported which substances they had taken and how much of each. These people were then examined. Some showed no evidence of the disease, while others manifested the disease in varying degrees. After analyzing the data, the nutritionist concluded that certain vitamins and minerals offer protection against atherosclerosis.

The procedure followed by the nutritionist is very similar to Mill's joint method of agreement and difference. The objective is to identify a cause among a preselected class of possible conditions, some of which are accompanied by the phenomenon (atherosclerosis), and some of which are not. The major difference between the nutritionist's procedure and Mill's joint method is that the nutritionist took account of varying degrees in which the conditions and the phenomenon were present in the eighty occurrences. In this sense, again, the nutritionist's procedure was similar to Mill's method of concomitant variation. However, the nutritionist may also have taken into account various combinations of conditions, a consideration that lies beyond the power of the joint method by itself.

The procedure illustrated in this example is not an experiment but a study. More precisely, it is a *retrospective study* because it examines subjects who have already fulfilled the requirements of the examination—as opposed to a *prospective study*, where the subjects are expected to fulfill the requirements in the future. For a prospective study, the nutritionist could select a group of subjects and follow their future vitamin and mineral intake for five years. Such a study, however, would be more costly, and if the nutritionist instructed the subjects to ingest certain vitamins and minerals and avoid others, the study could involve legal or moral implications.

Another kind of study found widely in the social sciences uses what is called the *correlational method*, which closely replicates Mill's method of concomitant variation. Example:

> A psychology professor was interested in the relationship between IQ scores and grade point average. The professor randomly selected 100 graduating seniors, obtained their GPAs from the registrar, and asked them to take an IQ test. All of them complied. Then the professor compared the scores of each student with his or her GPA. The professor found that, in general, higher IQ scores corresponded with higher GPAs.

The results of this study indicate a positive correlation between IQ score and GPA. If the study showed that students with higher IQs had, in general, lower GPAs, this would indicate a negative correlation. Once a study of this sort is done, the next step is to compute the *correlation coefficient*, which is a number between $+1.00$ and -1.00 that expresses the degree of correlation. If it turned out that the student with the highest IQ score also had the highest GPA, the student with the next highest IQ score had proportionately the next highest GPA, and so on, so that the IQ–GPA graph was a straight line, then the correlation coefficient would be $+1.00$. This would reflect a perfect positive correlation.

On the other hand, if it turned out that the student with the highest IQ score had the lowest GPA, the student with the next highest IQ score had proportionately the next lowest GPA, and so on, so that, once again, the IQ–GPA graph was a straight line, then the correlation coefficient would be -1.00. This would reflect a perfect negative correlation. A correlation coefficient of 0.00 would mean that no correlation exists, which would be the case if the IQ scores corresponded randomly with the GPAs. A correlation coefficient of, say, $+0.60$ would mean that in general higher IQ scores corresponded positively with higher GPAs.

The outcome of this study can also be indicated graphically, with IQ score representing one coordinate on a graph, and GPA the other coordinate. The result for each

FIGURE 10.2

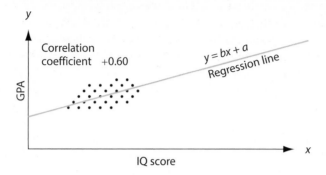

student would then correspond to a point on the graph, such as the one in Figure 10.2. The graph of all the points is called a *scatter diagram*. A line that "best fits" the data can then be drawn through the scatter diagram. This line is called the *regression line*, and it can be used to produce a linear equation, $y = bx + a$, that describes the approximate relation between IQ score (x) and GPA (y). This equation can then be used to predict future GPAs. For example, suppose that an entering freshman student has an IQ of 116. This student's future GPA could be predicted to be approximately $116b + a$.

Hundreds of studies such as this one have been conducted to detect correlations between such factors as TV violence and aggression in children, self-esteem and intelligence, motivation and learning time, exposure to classical music and retention ability, and marijuana use and memory. However, such studies often fall short of establishing a causal connection between the two factors. For example, a positive correlation between exposure to TV violence and aggression in children does not necessarily mean that exposure to TV violence causes aggression. It might be the case that children who tend to be violent are naturally attracted to violent TV shows. Or perhaps a third factor is the cause of both. But a positive correlation can at least suggest a causal connection.

Once a correlation is established, a controlled experiment can often be designed that will identify a causal connection. For example, in the case of TV violence, a group of children could be randomly divided into an experimental group and a control group. The experimental group could then be exposed to violent TV shows for a certain period, and the control group would be exposed to nonviolent shows for the same period. Later, the behavior of the children in both groups could be observed, with every act of aggression noted. If the experimental group displayed more acts of aggression than the control group, the conclusion might be drawn that TV violence causes aggression.

Experimental procedures resembling Mill's method of concomitant variation have also been used in the physical sciences to identify causal connections. For example, in the early part of the nineteenth century, Hans Christian Oerstead noticed that a wire carrying a current of electricity could deflect a nearby compass needle. As the current was increased, the amount of deflection increased, and as the current was decreased, the amount of deflection decreased. Also, if the current were reversed, the deflection would be reversed. Oerstead concluded that a current of electricity flowing through a wire causes a magnetic field to be produced around the wire.

Other applications of the method of concomitant variation have been used not so much to detect the existence of a causal connection (which may have already been known) as to determine the precise nature of a causal law. For example, in the latter part of the sixteenth century Galileo performed experiments involving spheres rolling down inclined planes. As the plane was incrementally lifted upward, the sphere covered greater and greater distances in a unit of time. Recognizing that the downward force on the sphere is proportional to the pitch of the plane, Galileo derived the law that the acceleration imparted to a body is directly proportional to the force acting on it. Galileo also noticed that whatever the angle of the plane, the distance covered by the ball increased exponentially with the time in which it was allowed to roll. For example, if the time was doubled, the distance was quadrupled. From this correlation he derived the law that the distance traveled by a falling body is proportional to the square of the time that it falls.

In the seventeenth century, Robert Boyle conducted experiments involving the pressure and volume of gases. Boyle constructed an apparatus that allowed him to compute the volume of a gas as he varied the pressure. He noted that as the pressure increased, the volume decreased, and as the pressure decreased, the volume increased. From this correlation he derived the law that the volume of a gas is inversely proportional to its pressure. A century later, Jacques Alexandre Charles observed a correlation between the temperature of a gas and its volume. As the temperature increased, the volume increased, and vice versa. This correlation provided the basis for Charles's law for gases.

Detecting correlations has also been important in astronomy. Early in the twentieth century, Henrietta Swan Leavitt recognized a correlation between the average brightness of certain variable stars, called Cepheids (pronounced sef'-ee-ids), and their periods of variation. Cepheids fluctuate in brightness over periods ranging from a day to several months, and Leavitt discovered that longer periods correspond with greater average brightness, and shorter periods with lesser average brightness. Once the distance of a few nearby Cepheids was determined, the distance of any Cepheid could then be computed from its average brightness and its period of variation. This correlation provided the first method available to astronomers for measuring the distance between our planet and galaxies other than our own.

EXERCISE 10   10

I. Identify the kind of causality intended by the following statements. Is the cause a sufficient condition, necessary condition, or both sufficient and necessary condition?

★1. Throwing a brick through a window causes the window to break.

2. Heating an iron rod causes it to expand.

MindTap Complete exercises online for immediate feedback.

3. Slashing an inflated automobile tire with a knife will cause it to go flat.

★4. Releasing the shutter of a digital camera causes an image to appear on the sensor.

5. Pulling the trigger of a gun causes it to fire.

6. Wetting litmus paper with an acid causes it to turn red.

★7. Pouring water on a wood fire will cause it to be extinguished.

8. Eating contaminated food will cause one to become ill.

9. Stretching a spring causes it to exert an opposing force.

★10. Flipping the wall switch to the "up" position causes the overhead lights to go on.

11. Spilling red wine on a white napkin causes a stain to appear.

12. Planting grass seed in the ground causes grass to grow.

★13. Getting proper exercise causes a person to be healthy.

14. Robbing a bank causes a person to be a criminal.

15. Getting at least five votes on an issue before the U.S. Supreme Court causes the issue to become law.

★16. Signing a personal check causes it to be negotiable.

17. Rubbing a knife on a whetstone causes it to be sharpened.

18. Increasing the temperature of a glass of ice water causes the ice cubes to melt.

★19. Picking up a bat causes a baseball player to hit a home run.

20. Heating the gas in a ridged, closed container causes the pressure of the gas to rise.

II. The following problems pertain to Mill's methods. Answer each as directed.

★1. To determine the effectiveness of an oil additive, a testing firm purchased two cars of the same make, year, and model, and drove each a distance of 30,000 miles using the same kind of gasoline, the same kind of oil, the same driver, under the same road conditions. The oil in one engine included the additive, whereas the oil in the other engine did not. At the end of the test, the engines of both cars were dismantled, and it was found that the engine that contained the additive had less wear. The testing firm concluded that the oil additive caused the reduced wear. Construct a table that supports this conclusion. Which one of Mill's methods did the testing firm use? What sense of causality is involved in the conclusion?

2. An eighth-grade teacher had five pupils who read very well. These pupils were distinguished by the following features. Tom came from a large family, had professional parents who were not wealthy, had training in phonics, read novels, lived close to a library, and watched educational TV. Andy came from a

family that was not large, had wealthy professional parents, watched educational TV, did not live close to a library, did not read novels, and had training in phonics. Cindy did not read novels, lived close to a library, had training in phonics, had wealthy professional parents, came from a large family, and did not watch educational TV. April had training in phonics, read novels, lived close to a library, watched educational TV, came from a large family, and had wealthy parents who were not professionals. Joe read novels, did not live close to a library, had professional parents who were not wealthy, had training in phonics, watched educational TV, and came from a large family. What can the teacher conclude caused these children to be good readers? Construct a table that supports this conclusion. Which one of Mill's methods did the teacher use? What sense of causality is involved in the conclusion?

3. An administrator for the Internal Revenue Service noticed that tax revenues for a certain year were down by 14 percent. Of this amount, the administrator attributed 6 percent to an economic slowdown that year, 3 percent to higher interest rates that led to higher write-offs, and 2 percent to changes in the tax code. Unable to attribute the remaining 3 percent to any lawful factor, the administrator concluded that it resulted from increased cheating by the taxpayers. Which one of Mill's methods did the administrator use?

★4. The repair manager for a manufacturer of desktop computers noticed that a large number of units were being returned for repairs. The manager selected a sample of seven returned units and noticed that these units were distinguished by the following characteristics. Units 1 and 3 had type X circuitry and were shipped to coastal regions. Units 2 and 7 were sold to business customers, were manufactured in the Kansas City plant, and were shipped to coastal regions. Units 4 and 5 were used to play computer games and were manufactured in the Kansas City plant. Units 6 and 7 were shipped to large cities and had type X circuitry. Unit 4 was shipped to a large coastal city. Units 2 and 3 were shipped to large cities. Unit 5 was shipped to a coastal region and had type X circuitry. Unit 3 was sold to a business customer who used it to play computer games. Unit 1 was used to play computer games and was manufactured in the Kansas City plant. Finally, Unit 6 was sold to a business customer in a coastal region. Among these six distinguishing characteristics the manager concluded that salty air caused the computers to break down. Construct a table that supports this conclusion. Which one of Mill's methods did the manufacturer use? What sense of causality is involved in the conclusion?

5. A manufacturer of fishing equipment conducted a test of its products by giving them to eight fishermen who used them with the following results. Ed and Flo used a Hot Spot lure and caught no fish. Dan and Amy used a Trusty rod with a Husky reel, and Amy caught fish but Dan did not. Jake used a Sure Catch lure, a Best Bet rod, a Spiffy reel, and caught fish. Bill and Tim used a Husky reel, but only Bill caught fish. Kat used a Best Bet rod with a Husky reel and caught fish. Amy and Kat used a Sure Catch lure, but only Kat used monofilament line. Bill used a Trusty rod, monofilament line, and a Sure Catch lure. Flo and Tim used

10

Best Bet rods, and both Tim and Dan used Dynamite lures. Finally, Flo used a Husky reel, Jake and Dan used monofilament line, and Ed used a Spiffy reel on a Trusty rod. What conclusion can the manufacturer draw about the power of this equipment to catch fish? Construct a table that supports this conclusion. Which one of Mill's methods did the manufacturer use? What sense of causality is involved in the conclusion?

6. Nancy was contemplating the purchase of a new oven for her kitchen, but she could not decide between an electric or a gas unit. Thus, she decided to conduct an experiment using the ovens—one gas, one electric—of two friends who live in adjoining apartments. She mixed up two identical batches of brownies under identical conditions of relative humidity and identical altitudes, put them into identical baking dishes, and cooked them at the same temperature for exactly the same time. The brownies cooked in the electric oven came out moist, while the brownies cooked in the gas oven came out relatively dry. Nancy concluded that baking in the electric oven caused the brownies to be moist. Construct a table that supports this conclusion. Which one of Mill's methods did Nancy use? What sense of causality is involved in the conclusion?

★7. Mrs. Wilkins sometimes has trouble sleeping. In order to determine the cause, she decided to take note of her pre-bedtime behavior over the course of a week. On Monday she drank chamomile tea, had a late dinner, took a hot bath, read from a book, took a walk, and slept well. On Tuesday she had a late dinner, read from a book, and slept poorly. On Wednesday she drank a glass of wine, got a massage, took a walk, and slept poorly. On Thursday she had a late dinner, drank a glass of wine, read from a book, took a hot bath, got a massage, and slept well. On Friday she read from a book, drank chamomile tea, got a massage, had a late dinner, took a walk, and slept well. On Saturday she drank a glass of wine, got a massage, took a walk, drank chamomile tea, took a hot bath, and slept well. On Sunday she read from a book, took a hot bath, drank chamomile tea, and slept poorly. What can Mrs. Wilkins conclude is the cause of sleeping well? Construct a table that supports this conclusion. Which one of Mill's methods did Mrs. Wilkins use? What sense of causality is involved in the conclusion?

8. From a comparison of statistics a criminologist detected what he thought was a correlation between fluctuations in the employment rate and in crimes of theft. For every 2 percent increase in the employment rate, the rate of theft decreased by 1 percent, and for every 2 percent decrease in the employment rate, the theft rate increased by 1 percent. The criminologist concluded that unemployment causes crimes of theft. Which one of Mill's methods did the criminologist use?

9. A man developed an allergic reaction to an unknown food. His doctor asked him about foods that often cause allergic reactions, and the man replied that he had eaten coconut, chocolate, nuts, milk products, shellfish, peppers, eggs, and wheat products prior to suffering the reaction. The doctor told him to eliminate all of these foods from his diet; when he had done so, the reaction disappeared. The doctor then told him to introduce each of these foods back

into his diet, one at a time. The man did so, and the reaction reappeared only when he ate milk products. The doctor concluded that milk products caused the allergic reaction. Construct a table that supports this conclusion. Which one of Mill's methods did the doctor use? What sense of causality is involved in the conclusion?

★10. A psychiatrist had six adult women patients who suffered blurred ego boundaries. These patients were distinguished by the following characteristics. Meg and Sue had been subjected to corporal punishment as children and both had siblings. Dot and Jane were adopted, had a male parent figure, and experienced sexual abuse. Lynn and Flo had siblings and a male parent figure, but only Flo had a domineering mother. Also, Lynn and Meg had experienced sexual abuse and were adopted, but only Meg had a domineering mother. Jane and Dot were uprooted often as children. Flo and Sue had experienced sexual abuse, but only Sue was raised in day-care centers. Jane and Dot each had a domineering mother, and each had been subjected to corporal punishment. Flo was uprooted often as a child and had been subjected to corporal punishment. Dot and Lynn were raised in day-care centers, Sue had a male parent figure, and Jane had siblings. What can the psychiatrist conclude is the cause of the blurred ego boundaries of these women? Construct a table that supports this conclusion. Which one of Mill's methods did the psychiatrist use? What sense of causality is involved in the conclusion?

11. A metallurgist added eight substances in various combinations to seven samples of molten aluminum for the purpose of producing aluminum alloys. The metallurgist was interested in producing an alloy that had a special resistance to corrosion. The samples were distinguished by the following characteristics. Samples 1, 2, and 3 contained both tin and copper, but only samples 1 and 2 were resistant. Samples 6 and 7 contained both silver and iron, but only sample 7 was resistant. Samples 4 and 5 contained sodium, but only sample 5 was resistant. In addition, samples 1 and 7 contained zinc, silicon, and nickel. Sample 2 contained sodium, iron, and silicon, and sample 5 contained silicon and copper. Finally, sample 3 contained nickel, and sample 4 contained zinc. Assuming no interaction occurs among these eight additives, what conclusion can the metallurgist draw about these additives? Construct a table that supports this conclusion. Which one of Mill's methods did the metallurgist use? What sense of causality is involved in the conclusion?

12. A doctor has five patients who suffer from an unusual form of cancer. The patients are distinguished by the following living conditions. Davis, Jones, and Ellis live in a smoggy area near high-voltage power lines, and Smith and Frank smoke cigarettes and live downwind from a company that produces chemical defoliants for the military. Frank also lives near the nuclear power plant. Davis, Smith, and Ellis eat red meat every day and live near the nuclear power plant. Jones smokes cigarettes and lives downwind from the chemical defoliant company. Smith lives in a smoggy area, and Davis and Ellis live downwind from the defoliant company. What can the doctor conclude is the cause

of the cancer? Construct a table that supports this conclusion. Which one of Mill's methods did the doctor use? What sense of causality is involved in the conclusion?

★13. Two of Mr. Andrews's rose bushes became infected with aphids. Mr. Andrews proceeded to spray one of the bushes with malathion insecticide but left the other bush untouched. The two bushes are both American Beauty, are five years old, have virtually identical locations, receive the same amount of water and sunlight, are planted in the same kind of soil, and receive the same degree of cultivation and the same amount of Bandini rose food. Within three days the aphids disappeared from the bush that was sprayed, but they continued to thrive on the other bush. Mr. Andrews concluded that the malathion killed the aphids on the bush that was sprayed. Construct a table that supports Mr. Andrews's conclusion. Which one of Mill's methods did Mr. Andrews use? What sense of causality is involved in the conclusion?

14. A sociologist conducted a study to determine if a correlation exists between grade point average at the time of graduation and income ten years after graduation. The sociologist visited the alumni office of a local university and obtained the names and addresses of those who had graduated ten years earlier. The sociologist then contacted those graduates and asked them to disclose their income and give permission for the university to disclose their graduating GPAs. Two hundred students replied to this inquiry. The sociologist then applied statistical methods to compute the correlation coefficient, which turned out to be +0.2. How does this study relate to Mill's methods? What does a correlation coefficient of +0.2 say about the correlation between GPA and income? Is such a study called a prospective study or a retrospective study? How do the two differ?

15. A cosmetics manufacturer tested a new cleansing cream on forty rabbits. The rabbits were virtually the same genetically and were the same age. Twenty of the rabbits were randomly placed in the experimental group and the other twenty were placed in the control group. A patch containing the cream was applied to the skin of each rabbit in the experimental group, and an identical patch containing a harmless substance was applied to the skin of each rabbit in the control group. Then, all forty rabbits were kept in the same room, at the same temperature, and under the same lighting conditions and were fed the same food. After five days, two of the rabbits in the experimental group developed a rash where the patch was applied, but none of the other rabbits did. The manufacturer concluded that there is a 10 percent likelihood that the cleansing cream will cause a rash on the skin of rabbits. How does this experiment relate to Mill's methods? What sense of causality is involved in the conclusion?

III. Identify the cause suggested by the information presented in the following tables. Is the cause a sufficient condition, necessary condition, or both sufficient and necessary condition? Can you identify the method?

★1.

Occurrence	Possible Conditions					Phenomenon
	A	B	C	D	E	
1	*	−	*	*	*	*
2	*	*	*	*	−	*
3	*	−	*	*	*	*
4	*	*	−	*	*	*
5	−	*	*	*	−	*

2.

Occurrence	Possible Conditions					Phenomenon
	A	B	C	D	E	
1	*	*	*	*	*	*
2	*	−	*	*	*	−

3.

Occurrence	Possible Conditions						Phenomenon
	A	B	C	D	E	F	
1	*	−	−	*	−	−	−
2	−	*	*	*	−	−	*
3	*	−	*	*	*	−	*
4	−	*	−	−	−	*	−
5	*	−	−	−	*	−	−
6	*	*	*	−	*	−	*

★4.

Occurrence	Possible Conditions					Phenomenon
	A	B	C	D	E	
1	*	*	*	*	−	*
2	−	−	*	−	*	*
3	*	−	−	−	*	−
4	−	*	−	*	*	*
5	*	*	−	−	−	−
6	−	*	*	−	−	−

5.

Occurrence	Possible Conditions					Phenomenon
	A	B	C	D	E	
1	—	—	*	—	*	—
2	—	*	*	—	*	*
3	*	*	—	*	*	*
4	—	*	—	—	*	—
5	*	—	*	*	—	—
6	*	*	*	—	—	*

IV. Identify three causal connections that are not mentioned in this book: One must be a sufficient condition, one must be a necessary condition, one must be a sufficient and necessary condition. Then explain why each causal connection fits the classification you have given it.

MindTap Master concepts and improve outcomes with Aplia, at the end of the chapter, in the Aplia folder.

Summary

Three Kinds of Cause:
- Sufficient condition
- Necessary condition
- Sufficient and necessary condition

Mill's Methods:
- Method of agreement: Identifies necessary conditions.
- Method of difference: Identifies sufficient conditions.
- Joint method of agreement and difference: Identifies sufficient and necessary conditions.
- Method of residues: Identifies generic causal connections.
- Method of concomitant variation: Identifies generic causal connections.

Mill's Methods and Science:
- The methods of agreement, difference, and concomitant variation resemble the methods used by scientists to identify causal connections.
- Controlled experiment and the method of difference.
- Experiment versus study (retrospective, prospective).
- Correlation versus causal connection.
- Scientists: Oerstead, Galileo, Boyle, Charles, Leavitt.

MindTap Need help? See the Learning Logic folder at the end of the chapter: the self-paced tutorial walks you through any section.

11 Probability

11.1 Theories of Probability

11.2 The Probability Calculus

HOW LOGICAL ARE YOU? You hope to go to Cancún, Mexico, for spring break, but your decision rests on two contingencies: You have applied for a bank loan to cover recent expenses, and there is a 70 percent chance you will get the loan. Secondly, meteorologists say there is a 35 percent chance that a hurricane will strike Cancún during that time. You will go only if the probability of getting the loan and there being no hurricane is greater than 50 percent. What do you do?

Find the answer on MindTap.

11.1 Theories of Probability

Probability is a topic that is central to the question of induction, but like causality, it has different meanings. Consider the following statements:

The probability of picking a spade from a full deck of cards is one-fourth.

The probability that a twenty-year-old man will live to age seventy-five is .63.

There is a high probability that Margaret and Peter will get married.

In each statement the word "probability" is used in a different sense. This difference stems from the fact that a different procedure is used in each case to determine or estimate the probability. To determine the probability of picking a spade from a deck of cards, a purely mathematical procedure is used. Given that there are fifty-two cards in a deck and thirteen are spades, thirteen is divided by fifty-two to obtain one-fourth. A different procedure is used to determine the probability that a twenty-year-old man will live to age seventy-five. For this, one must sample a large number of twenty-year-old men and count the number that live fifty-five more years. Yet a different procedure is used to determine the probability that Margaret and Peter will get married. This probability can only be estimated roughly, and doing so requires that we become acquainted with Margaret and Peter and with how they feel toward each other and toward marriage. These three procedures give rise to three distinct theories about probability: the classical theory, the relative frequency theory, and the subjectivist theory.

The **classical theory of probability** traces its origin to the work of the seventeenth-century mathematicians Blaise Pascal and Pierre de Fermat in determining the betting odds for a game of chance. The theory is otherwise called the *a priori theory of probability* because the computations are made independently of any sensory observation of actual events. According to the classical theory, the probability of an event *A* is given by the formula

$$P(A) = \frac{f}{n}$$

where *f* is the number of favorable outcomes and *n* is the number of possible outcomes. For example, in computing the probability of drawing an ace from a poker deck, the number of favorable outcomes is four (because there are four aces) and the number of possible outcomes is fifty-two (because there are fifty-two cards in the deck). Thus, the probability of that event is 4/52 or 1/13 (or .077).

It is important not to confuse the probability of an event's happening with the betting odds of its happening. For events governed by the classical theory, the fair betting odds that an event *A* will happen is given by the formula

$$odds(A) = f : u$$

where *f* is the number of favorable outcomes, and *u* is the number of unfavorable outcomes. For example, the fair betting odds of drawing an ace from a poker deck is 4 to 48, or 1 to 12, since there are four aces and 48 cards that are not aces. Or suppose that five horses are running a race; three are yours, two are your friend's, and there is an equal chance of any of the horses winning. The fair betting odds that one of your horses will win is 3 to 2, whereas the probability that one of your horses will win is 3/5.

Given that you and your friend accept these betting odds, if you bet $3 that one of your horses wins, and you win the bet, your friend must pay you $2. On the other hand, the odds that one of your friend's horses will win is 2 to 3, so if your friend bets $2 that one of her horses wins, and she wins the bet, then you must pay her $3.

Two assumptions are involved in computing probabilities and betting odds according to the classical theory: (1) that all possible outcomes are taken into account and (2) that all possible outcomes are equally probable. In the card example the first assumption entails that only the fifty-two ordinary outcomes are possible. In other words, it is assumed that the deck has not been altered, that the cards will not suddenly self-destruct or reproduce, and so forth. In the racing example, the first assumption entails that no other horses are running in the race, and that none of the horses will simply vanish.

The second assumption, which is otherwise called the **principle of indifference**, entails for the card example that there is an equal likelihood of selecting any card.

In other words, it is assumed that the cards are stacked evenly, that no two are glued together, and so on. For the horse-race example, the second principle entails that each of the horses has an equal chance of winning.

Whenever these two assumptions can be made about the occurrence of an event, the classical theory can be used to compute its probability or the odds of its happening. Here are some additional examples:

P(a fair coin turning up heads) $= 1/2$	odds $= 1:1$
P(drawing a face card) $= 12/52 = 3/13$	odds $= 12:40 = 3:10$
P(a single die coming up "3") $= 1/6$	odds $= 1:5$
P(a single die coming up even) $= 3/6 = 1/2$	odds $= 1:1$

Strictly speaking, of course, the two assumptions underlying the classical theory are never perfectly reflected in any actual situation. Every coin is slightly off balance, as is every pair of dice. As a result, the probabilities of the various outcomes are never exactly equal. Similarly, the outcomes are never strictly confined to the normal ones entailed by the first assumption. When tossing a coin, there is always the possibility that the coin will land on edge, and in rolling dice there is the analogous possibility that one of them might break in half. These outcomes may not be possible in the *practical* sense, but they are *logically* possible in that they do not involve any contradiction. Because these outcomes are so unusual, however, it is reasonable to think that for all practical purposes the two assumptions hold and that therefore the classical theory is applicable.

There are many events, however, for which the two assumptions required by the classical theory obviously do not hold. For example, in attempting to determine the probability of a sixty-year-old woman dying of a heart attack within ten years, it would be virtually impossible to take account of all the possible outcomes. She might die of cancer, pneumonia, or an especially virulent case of the flu. She might be incapacitated by a car accident, or she might move to Florida and buy a house on the beach. Furthermore, none of these outcomes is equally probable in comparison with the others. To compute the probability of events such as these we need the relative frequency theory.

The **relative frequency theory of probability** originated with the use of mortality tables by life insurance companies in the eighteenth century. In contrast with the classical theory, which rests upon a priori computations, the relative frequency theory depends on actual observations of the frequency with which certain events happen. The probability of an event A is given by the formula

$$P(A) = \frac{f_o}{n_o}$$

where f_o is the number of *observed* favorable outcomes and n_o is the total number of *observed* outcomes. For example, to determine the probability that a fifty-year-old man will live five more years, a sample of 1,000 fifty-year-old men could be observed. If 968 were alive five years later, the probability that a fifty-year-old man will live an additional five years is 968/1000 or .968.

Similarly, if one wanted to determine the probability that a certain irregularly shaped pyramid with different-colored sides would, when rolled, come to rest with the green side down, the pyramid could be rolled 1,000 times. If it came to rest with its green side down 327 times, the probability of this event happening would be computed to be .327.

The relative frequency method can also be used to compute the probability of the kinds of events that conform to the requirements of the classical theory. For example, the probability of a coin coming up heads could be determined by tossing the coin 100 times and counting the heads. If, after this many tosses, 46 heads have been recorded, one might assign a probability of .46 to this event. This leads us to an important point about the relative frequency theory: The results hold true only in the long run. It might be necessary to toss the coin 1,000 or even 10,000 times to get a close approximation. After 10,000 tosses one would expect to count close to 5,000 heads. If in fact only 4,623 heads have been recorded, one would probably be justified in concluding that the coin is off balance or that something was irregular in the way it had been tossed.

Strictly speaking, neither the classical method nor the relative frequency method can assign a probability to individual events. From the standpoint of these approaches only certain *kinds* or *classes* of events have probabilities. But many events in the actual world are unique—for example, Margaret's marrying Peter or Native Prancer's winning the fourth race at Churchill Downs. To interpret the probability of these events we turn to the subjectivist theory.

The **subjectivist theory of probability** rests on the degrees of belief that people have about the occurrence of some event or the truth of some proposition. Such beliefs are grounded in the knowledge we have about the world in which we live. Because this knowledge is incomplete and fluctuates from day to day as we acquire new knowledge and forget the knowledge we once had, the probabilities we assign to things are subject to change. Also, since the knowledge acquired by one person differs from the knowledge acquired by another (one person might know a lot about economics, another a lot about football), the probability that one person assigns to something will often differ from the probability that another assigns to it. The subjectivist theory is sometimes called the "epistemic theory of probability," after the Greek word *episteme*, which means knowledge.

For an example of how a probability can change from day to day, suppose you are rummaging in the attic of a deceased great-grandparent and you happen to come across an old violin. When you peer through one of the openings in the face of the violin you read "Strad 1691." You conclude with glee that the instrument is probably a Stradivarius. Then you do some investigating and find that "Strad 1691" means nothing at all, so you conclude that the violin is probably not a Stradivarius. After further research you discover that a true Stradivarius will have a circular logo bearing the initials of Antonio Stradivari beneath a cross. When you look through the other opening, you see "A$^+$S" inside a circle. So, the violin is probably a Strad after all. Then you check with an expert who tells you that the logo in a genuine Stradivarius has the initials inside a double circle, but yours is set within a single circle. In the end, you conclude that the violin you found is probably not a genuine Strad.

As for how different people can assign different probabilities to the same thing, consider the stock market. Every trade involves a buyer and a seller. The buyer believes at a certain moment in time that a certain stock is probably a good investment, but the seller believes at the same moment that the same stock is probably *not* a good investment. If the buyer and seller did not assign different probabilities, there would be no trade. In fact, if looked at in this way, the entire economy (and practically every decision in life) rests on people assigning probabilities according to the subjectivist theory. You buy a certain kind of laundry soap or can of tuna because you believe that the product is probably a good value, or probably more environmentally friendly, or probably more healthy than some alternate brand.

The subjectivist theory of probability differs in important ways from the classical theory and the relative frequency theory. Whereas the classical theory assigns probabilities independently of the actual state of the world, the subjectivist theory requires empirical knowledge. In fact, the more extensive the knowledge, the more accurate the probability assigned. The relative frequency theory deals with similar events that are repeatable in some relevant way. The great majority of events that the subjectivist theory addresses are not repeatable. Also, the first two theories yield probabilities that are highly precise, whereas the probabilities given by the subjectivist theory are often imprecise. Yet, the subjectivist theory is vastly more applicable than either of the other theories. Only the subjectivist theory can assign a probability to the claim that a certain person would make a good spouse, or the assertion that someone committed a crime, or the claim that one football team will defeat another.

The lack of precision affecting the subjectivist theory can sometimes be mitigated by averaging the probabilities that a large number of people assign to a given event. This is exactly what happens when people make bets on the outcome of a sporting event. For example, in horse racing, as the bets are placed, the odds of each horse winning are quickly computed. From these odds we can calculate what might be called the "true" probability that each horse will win. Similarly, the claim that the stock in some initial public offering is probably worth $10 per share is quickly settled once the stock begins trading. If no investors are willing to pay that amount, then the stock is probably worth less. Extending this idea, the probability that any product or service is worth a certain amount of money is arguably settled once that product or service is offered for sale in a free market.

The idea that probabilities can rest on people's beliefs requires a proviso: The beliefs must be rational (or "coherent," according to some accounts). But what is the meaning of *rational*? For an example of a belief that is not rational, suppose that a friend is willing to give you 7 to 4 odds that Ajax will win in the fifth race. This corresponds to a probability of 7/(7 + 4) or 7/11. At the same time your friend will give you 5 to 4 odds that Ajax will lose in that race, which corresponds to a probability of 5/9. Obviously your friend believes that Ajax will both win and lose the same race. Such a belief is not rational. Given the 7 to 4 odds that Ajax will win, the best odds your friend can give that Ajax will lose is 4/7. It has been proved that any assignment of probabilities that satisfies the rules of the probability calculus is rational.

11.2 The Probability Calculus

The three theories discussed thus far—the classical theory, the relative frequency theory, and the subjectivist theory—provide separate procedures for assigning a probability to an event (or class of events). Sometimes one theory is more readily applicable, sometimes another. But once individual events have been given a probability, the groundwork has been laid for computing the probabilities of compound arrangements of events. This is done by means of what is called the **probability calculus**. In this

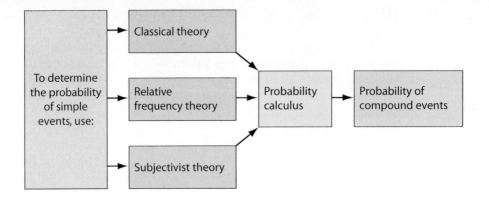

respect the probability calculus functions analogously to the set of truth-functional rules in propositional logic. Just as the truth-functional rules allow us to compute the truth values of compound propositions from the individual truth values of the simple components, the rules of the probability calculus allow us to compute the probability of compound events from the individual probabilities of the simple events.

Two preliminary rules of the probability calculus are (1) the probability of an event that must necessarily happen is taken to be 1, and (2) the probability of an event that necessarily cannot happen is taken to be 0. For example, the event consisting of it either raining or not raining (at the same time and place) has a probability of 1, and the event consisting of it both raining and not raining (at the same time and place) has a probability of 0. These events correspond to statements that are tautological and self-contradictory, respectively. Contingent events, on the other hand, have probabilities greater than 0 but less than 1. For example, the probability that the Dow Jones Industrial Average will end a certain week at least five points higher than the previous week would usually be around 1/2, the probability that the polar ice cap will melt away next year is very close to 0, and the probability that a traffic accident will occur somewhere tomorrow is very close to 1. Let us now consider six additional rules of the probability calculus.

1. Restricted Conjunction Rule

The **restricted conjunction rule** is used to compute the probability of two events occurring together when the events are *independent* of each other. Two events are said to be independent when the occurrence of one has no effect on the probability of the other one occurring. Examples include getting two heads from two tosses of a coin, drawing two hearts from a deck when the first is replaced before the second is drawn, and playing two sequential games of poker or roulette. The probability of two such events A and B occurring together is given by the formula

$$P(A \text{ and } B) = P(A) \times P(B)$$

For example, the probability of tossing two heads on a single throw of two coins is

$$P(H_1 \text{ and } H_2) = 1/2 \times 1/2 = 1/4$$

This result may be checked very easily by listing all the possible outcomes and comparing that number with the number of favorable outcomes:

Coin 1	Coin 2
H	H
H	T
T	H
T	T

Only one of the four possible outcomes shows both coins turning up heads.

Similarly, we may compute the probability of rolling two sixes with a pair of dice:

$$P(S_1 \text{ and } S_2) = 1/6 \times 1/6 = 1/36$$

Again, we may check the results by listing all the possible outcomes:

1-1	2-1	3-1	4-1	5-1	6-1
1-2	2-2	3-2	4-2	5-2	6-2
1-3	2-3	3-3	4-3	5-3	6-3
1-4	2-4	3-4	4-4	5-4	6-4
1-5	2-5	3-5	4-5	5-5	6-5
1-6	2-6	3-6	4-6	5-6	6-6

Since only one of the thirty-six possible outcomes shows two sixes together, the probability of this event is 1/36.

2. General Conjunction Rule

The **general conjunction rule** is used to compute the probability of two events occurring together whether or not the events are independent. When the events are independent, the general conjunction rule reduces to the restricted conjunction rule. Some examples of events that are not independent (that is, that are *dependent*) are drawing two spades from a deck on two draws when the first card drawn is not replaced, and selecting two or more window seats on an airplane. After the first card is drawn, the number of cards available for the second draw is reduced, and after one of the seats is taken on the plane, the number of seats remaining for subsequent choices is reduced. In other words, in both cases the second event is dependent on the first. The formula for computing the probability of two such events occurring together is

$$P(A \text{ and } B) = P(A) \times P(B \text{ given } A)$$

The expression $P(B$ given $A)$ is the probability that B will occur on the assumption that A has already occurred. Let us suppose, for example, that A and B designate the events of drawing two kings from a deck when the first card is not replaced before the second is drawn. If event A occurs, then only three kings remain, and the deck is also reduced to fifty-one cards. Thus, $P(B$ given $A)$ is 3/51. Since the probability of event A

is 4/52, the probability of both events happening is the product of these two fractions, or 12/2652 (= 1/221).

For another illustration, consider an urn containing five red balls, six green balls, and seven yellow balls. The probability of drawing two red balls (without replacement) is computed as follows:

$$P(R_1 \text{ and } R_2) = 5/18 \times 4/17 = 20/306 = 10/153$$

If a red ball is selected on the first draw, this leaves four red balls from a total of seventeen. Thus, the probability of drawing a second red ball if one has already been drawn is 4/17.

For another example, consider the same urn with the same contents, but let us compute the probability of drawing first a green ball and then a yellow ball (without replacement):

$$P(G \text{ and } Y) = 6/18 \times 7/17 = 42/306 = 7/51$$

If a green ball is selected on the first draw, this affects the selection of a yellow ball on the second draw only to the extent of reducing the total number of balls to seventeen.

3. Restricted Disjunction Rule

The **restricted disjunction rule** is used to compute the probability of either of two events occurring when the events are *mutually exclusive*—that is, when they cannot both occur. Examples of such events include picking either an ace or a king from a deck of cards on a single draw or rolling either a six or a one on a single roll of a die. The probability is given by the formula

$$P(A \text{ or } B) = P(A) + P(B)$$

For example, the probability of drawing either a king or a queen (of any suit) from a deck of cards on a single draw is

$$P(K \text{ or } Q) = 4/52 + 4/52 = 8/52 = 2/13$$

For another example, consider an urn containing six black balls, four white balls, and two red balls. The probability of selecting either a black or red ball on a single draw is

$$P(B \text{ or } R) = 6/12 + 2/12 = 8/12 = 2/3$$

When the event in question is one that must *necessarily* occur, the probability is, of course, 1. Thus, the probability of obtaining either heads or tails on a single toss of a coin is

$$P(H \text{ or } T) = 1/2 + 1/2 = 1$$

The restricted disjunction rule may be combined with the restricted conjunction rule to compute the probability of getting either a five or a six on each of two consecutive rolls of a single die:

$$
\begin{aligned}
P[(F \text{ or } S)_1 \text{ and } (F \text{ or } S)_2] &= P(F \text{ or } S)_1 \times P(F \text{ or } S)_2 \\
&= (1/6 + 1/6) \times (1/6 + 1/6) \\
&= 1/3 \times 1/3 \\
&= 1/9
\end{aligned}
$$

Since getting a five and getting a six on a single die are mutually exclusive events, $P(F \text{ or } S)_1$ is evaluated using the restricted disjunction rule. The same is true of $P(F \text{ or } S)_2$.

Then, since two rolls of a die are independent events, the conjunction of the two disjunctive events is evaluated by the restricted conjunction rule.

4. General Disjunction Rule

The **general disjunction rule** is used to compute the probability of either of two events whether or not they are mutually exclusive. The rule holds for any two events, but since its application is simplified when the events are independent, we will confine our attention to events of this kind. Examples of independent events that are not mutually exclusive include obtaining at least one head on two tosses of a coin, drawing at least one king from a deck on two draws when the first card is replaced before the second card is drawn, and getting at least one six when rolling a pair of dice. The formula for computing the probability of either of two such events is

$$P(A \text{ or } B) = P(A) + P(B) - P(A \text{ and } B)$$

If the events are independent, $P(A \text{ and } B)$ is computed using the restricted conjunction rule, and the general disjunction formula reduces to

$$P(A \text{ or } B) = P(A) + P(B) - [P(A) \times P(B)]$$

The general disjunction rule may be proved as follows. When A and B are nonexclusive, A occurs either with or without B, and B occurs either with or without A. Thus,

$$P(A) = P(A \text{ and } B) + P(A \text{ and not-}B)$$
$$P(B) = P(B \text{ and } A) + P(B \text{ and not-}A)$$

But A or B occurs in exactly three possible ways: A and not-B, B and not-A, and A and B. Thus,

$$P(A \text{ or } B) = P(A \text{ and not-}B) + P(B \text{ and not-}A) + P(A \text{ and } B)$$

Thus, when $P(A \text{ and } B)$ is subtracted from $P(A) + P(B)$, the difference is equal to $P(A \text{ or } B)$. [*Note*: $P(A \text{ and } B) = P(B \text{ and } A)$.]

For an example of the use of the general disjunction rule let us consider the probability of getting heads on either of two tosses of a coin. We have

$$\begin{aligned} P(H_1 \text{ or } H_2) &= 1/2 + 1/2 - (1/2 \times 1/2) \\ &= 1 - 1/4 \\ &= 3/4 \end{aligned}$$

For another example, consider the probability of getting at least one six when rolling a pair of dice. The computation is

$$\begin{aligned} P(S_1 \text{ or } S_2) &= 1/6 + 1/6 - (1/6 \times 1/6) \\ &= 2/6 - 1/36 \\ &= 11/36 \end{aligned}$$

The general disjunction rule may be combined with the restricted disjunction rule to compute the probability of getting either a three or a five when rolling a pair of dice.

This is the probability of getting either a three or a five on the first die or either a three or a five on the second:

$$P[(T \text{ or } F)_1 \text{ or } (T \text{ or } F)_2] = P(T \text{ or } F)_1 + P(T \text{ or } F)_2 - [P(T \text{ or } F)_1 \times P(T \text{ or } F)_2]$$
$$= (1/6 + 1/6) + (1/6 + 1/6) - [(1/6 + 1/6) \times (1/6 + 1/6)]$$
$$= 2/6 + 2/6 - 4/36$$
$$= 20/36$$
$$= 5/9$$

Since getting a three or getting a five on a single throw are mutually exclusive events, $P(T \text{ or } F)_1$ is equal to the sum of the separate probabilities. The same is true for $P(T \text{ or } F)_2$.

The general disjunction rule may be combined with the general conjunction rule to compute the probability of drawing first a red ball and then a black ball on pairs of draws from either of two urns (without replacement). Suppose that the first urn contains two red balls, two black balls, and one green ball, and that the second urn contains three red balls, one black ball, and one white ball. The probability, giving two draws per urn, is

$$P[(R \text{ and } B)_1 \text{ or } (R \text{ and } B)_2]$$
$$= P(R \text{ and } B)_1 + P(R \text{ and } B)_2 - [P(R \text{ and } B)_1 \times P(R \text{ and } B)_2]$$
$$= (2/5 \times 2/4) + (3/5 \times 1/4) - [(2/5 \times 2/4) \times (3/5 \times 1/4)]$$
$$= 4/20 + 3/20 - (4/20 \times 3/20)$$
$$= 7/20 - 12/400$$
$$= 8/25$$

5. Negation Rule

The **negation rule** is useful for computing the probability of an event when the probability of the event *not* happening is either known or easily computed. The formula is as follows:

$$P(A) = 1 - P(\text{not-}A)$$

The formula can be proved very easily. By the restricted disjunction rule the probability of A or not-A is

$$P(A \text{ or not-}A) = P(A) + P(\text{not-}A)$$

But since A or not-A happens necessarily, $P(A \text{ or not-}A) = 1$. Thus,

$$1 = P(A) + P(\text{not-}A)$$

Rearranging the terms in this equation gives us the negation rule. For an example of the use of this rule, consider the probability of getting heads at least once on two tosses of a coin. The probability of the event *not* happening, which is the probability of getting tails on both tosses, is immediately computed by the restricted conjunction rule to be 1/4. Then, applying the negation rule, we have

$$P(H_1 \text{ or } H_2) = 1 - 1/4$$
$$= 3/4$$

The negation rule may also be used to compute the probabilities of disjunctive events that are *dependent*. In presenting the general disjunction rule we confined our attention to *independent* events. Let us suppose we are given an urn containing two black balls and three white balls. To compute the probability of getting at least one black ball on two draws (without replacement), we first compute the probability of the event not happening. This event consists in drawing two white balls, which, by the general conjunction rule, has the probability

$$P(W_1 \text{ and } W_2) = 3/5 \times 2/4 = 6/20$$

Now, applying the negation rule, the probability of getting at least one black ball on two draws is

$$P(B_1 \text{ or } B_2) = 1 - 6/20$$
$$= 14/20$$
$$= 7/10$$

For an example that is only slightly more complex, consider an urn containing two white, two black, and two red balls. To compute the probability of getting either a white or black ball on two draws (without replacement) we first compute the probability of the event not happening. This is the probability of getting red balls on both draws, which is

$$P(R_1 \text{ and } R_2) = 2/6 \times 1/5 = 2/30 = 1/15$$

Now, by the negation rule the probability of drawing either a white or black ball is

$$P(W \text{ or } B) = 1 - 1/15$$
$$= 14/15$$

6. Bayes's Theorem

Bayes's theorem, named after the eighteenth-century English clergyman Thomas Bayes, is a useful rule for evaluating the conditional probability of two or more mutually exclusive and jointly exhaustive events. The conditional probability of an event is the probability of that event happening given that another event has already happened, and it is expressed $P(A \text{ given } B)$. You may recall that an expression of this form occurred in the formulation of the general conjunction rule. When the number of mutually exclusive and jointly exhaustive events is limited to two, which we will designate A_1 and A_2, Bayes's theorem is expressed as follows:

$$P(A_1 \text{ given } B) = \frac{P(A_1) \times P(B \text{ given } A_1)}{[P(A_1) \times P(B \text{ given } A_1)] + [P(A_2) \times P(B \text{ given } A_2)]}$$

This limited formulation of Bayes's theorem may be proved as follows. Applying the general conjunction rule to the events A_1 and B, we have

$$P(A_1 \text{ and } B) = P(A_1) \times P(B \text{ given } A_1)$$

Applying the same rule to the same events written in the reverse order, we have

$$P(B \text{ and } A_1) = P(B) \times P(A_1 \text{ given } B)$$

Now, since $P(A_1$ and $B)$ is equal to $P(B$ and $A_1)$, we may set the right-hand side of these two equations equal to each other:

$$P(B) \times P(A_1 \text{ given } B) = P(A_1) \times P(B \text{ given } A_1)$$

Dividing both sides of this equation by $P(B)$, we have

$$P(A_1 \text{ given } B) = \frac{P(A_1) \times P(B \text{ given } A_1)}{P(B)} \qquad (*)$$

Now, it can be easily proved using a truth table that B is logically equivalent to the expression $[(A_1$ and $B)$ or (not-A_1 and $B)]$. Furthermore, since A_1 and A_2 are mutually exclusive and jointly exhaustive, one and only one of them will happen. Thus, A_2 is simply another way of writing not-A_1. Accordingly, the former expression in brackets can be written $[(A_1$ and $B)$ or $(A_2$ and $B)]$, and since this expression is logically equivalent to B,

$$P(B) = P[(A_1 \text{ and } B) \text{ or } (A_2 \text{ and } B)]$$

Now, applying the general conjunction rule and the restricted disjunction rule to the right-hand side of this equation, we have

$$P(B) = [P(A_1) \times P(B \text{ given } A_1)] + [P(A_2) \times P(B \text{ given } A_2)]$$

Finally, substituting the right-hand side of this equation in place of $P(B)$ in the earlier equation marked (*), we have Bayes's theorem:

$$P(A_1 \text{ given } B) = \frac{P(A_1) \times P(B \text{ given } A_1)}{[P(A_1) \times P(B \text{ given } A_1)] + [P(A_2) \times P(B \text{ given } A_2)]}$$

For an illustration of the use of Bayes's theorem, suppose we are given one beige urn and four gray urns in a dimly lit room, so we cannot distinguish one color from the other. The beige urn contains eight red and two white balls, and each of the gray urns contains three red and seven white balls. Suppose that a red ball is drawn from one of these five urns. What is the probability that the urn was beige? In other words, we want to know the probability that the urn was beige given that a red ball was drawn. The events A_1 and A_2 in Bayes's theorem correspond to drawing a ball from either a beige urn or a gray urn. Substituting B and G for A_1 and A_2, respectively, we have

$$P(B \text{ given } R) = \frac{P(B) \times P(R \text{ given } B)}{[P(B) \times P(R \text{ given } B)] + [P(G) \times P(R \text{ given } G)]}$$

Now, since there are a total of five urns, the probability of randomly selecting the beige urn is 1/5, and the probability of randomly selecting one of the gray urns is 4/5. Finally, since each urn contains ten balls, the probability of drawing a red ball from the beige urn is 8/10, and the probability of drawing a red ball from the gray urn is 3/10. Thus, we have

$$P(B \text{ given } R) = \frac{1/5 \times 8/10}{(1/5 \times 8/10) + (4/5 \times 3/10)}$$

$$= \frac{8/50}{8/50 + 12/50} = \frac{8/50}{20/50} = 8/20 = .40$$

Bayes's theorem is quite practical because it allows us to change our probability estimates of ordinary events as new information is acquired. For an example of how Bayes's theorem is used for this purpose, consider the following example:

> Mr. Jones became seriously ill from ingesting defectively manufactured tablets of the painkiller novaprine. He intends to file a lawsuit against the most probable manufacturer of the tablets. After a brief investigation, he finds that 70 percent of the novaprine sold in this country is manufactured by Alpha Pharmaceuticals, and 30 percent is manufactured by Beta Pharmaceuticals.

From this information the probability that Alpha Pharmaceuticals manufactured the tablets is .70, in comparison with .30 for Beta Pharmaceuticals. Thus, Mr. Jones tentatively decides to file his lawsuit against Alpha. However, on further investigation Mr. Jones discovers the following:

> Of the novaprine manufactured by Alpha, 10 percent is sold on the East Coast and 90 percent on the West Coast, while 80 percent of Beta's novaprine is sold on the East Coast and 20 percent on the West Coast. Furthermore, Mr. Jones recalls that he purchased his novaprine on the East Coast.

Clearly this new information affects Mr. Jones's original probability estimate. We use Bayes's theorem to recompute the probability that Alpha manufactured the defective tablets given that the tablets were purchased on the East Coast as follows:

$$P(A \text{ given } E) = \frac{P(A) \times P(E \text{ given } A)}{[P(A) \times P(E \text{ given } A)] + [P(B) \times P(E \text{ given } B)]}$$

For $P(A)$ and $P(B)$ we use the original probabilities of .70 and .30, respectively. The probability that the tablets were purchased on the East Coast given that they were manufactured by Alpha is .10, and the probability that they were purchased on the East Coast given that they were manufactured by Beta is .80. Thus, we have

$$P(A \text{ given } E) = \frac{.70 \times .10}{(.70 \times .10) + (.30 \times .80)} = \frac{.07}{.07 + .24} = .07/.31 = .23$$

The new information that Mr. Jones acquired has significantly affected the probability that Alpha manufactured the defective tablets. The probability has dropped from .70 to .23. With this new information, it is more likely that Beta manufactured the tablets, so Mr. Jones should now file his lawsuit against Beta. The probability for Beta is $1 - .23$, or .77.

The earlier probability for Alpha (.70) is called the *prior* probability, and the later figure (.23) is called the *posterior* probability. If Mr. Jones should acquire even more information, the posterior probability becomes a new prior, and it is used as the value for $P(A)$ in a subsequent application of Bayes's theorem.

A relatively recent application of Bayes's theorem that garnered international attention was its use to search for the wreckage of Malaysia Airlines Flight 370. Two hundred thirty-nine people were on board when it disappeared without a trace while en route from Kuala Lumpur to Beijing in March 2014. In an effort to find the missing plane, all the known data, including flight path, fuel, wind speed, ocean flow, as well as areas that had been previously searched, were plugged into the theorem. The results were continually updated as additional data became available. However, the wreckage has yet to be found, probably owing to the scarcity of reliable and substantive data—even the direction the plane was flying at the moment it disappeared is an unknown.

Searchers had better luck three years earlier in finding the wreckage of Air France Flight 447, which disappeared over the ocean after departing Rio de Janeiro for Paris. The initial search, spanning two years, was fruitless; but six days after applying Bayes's theorem, the flight data recorder was found in 10,000 feet of water. Bayes's theorem was also used to locate German U-boats during World War II, a lost U.S. submarine in the 1960s, and a missing hydrogen bomb following the crash of a B-52 in Spain.

Additional Applications

Most of the examples considered thus far have used the classical theory to determine the probability of the component events. But as was mentioned earlier, the probability calculus can also be used in conjunction with the relative frequency theory and the subjectivist theory. If we apply the relative frequency theory to the mortality tables used by insurance companies, we find that the probability of a twenty-five-year-old man living an additional forty years is .82, and the probability of a twenty-five-year-old woman living the same number of years is .88. To compute the probability of such a man and woman both living that long, we use the restricted conjunction rule and obtain $.82 \times .88 = .72$. For the probability that either of these people would live that long, we use the general disjunction rule and obtain

$$.82 + .88 - (.82 \times .88) = .98$$

Let us suppose that these two people are married and both would give 9 to 1 odds on their staying married for forty years. This translates into a probability of $9/(9 + 1)$ or .90. Using the restricted conjunction rule, the probability of this event happening is the product of the latter figure and the probability of their both living that long, or .65.

For an example involving the subjectivist theory, if the Philadelphia Eagles are given 7 to 5 odds of winning the NFC championship, and the New England Patriots are given 3 to 2 odds of winning the AFC championship, the probability that at least one of these teams will win is computed using the general disjunction rule. The odds translate respectively into probabilities of 7/12 and 3/5, and so the probability of the disjunction is $7/12 + 3/5 - (7/12 \times 3/5) = 5/6$. The probability that the two teams will meet in the Super Bowl (that both will win their conference championship) is, by the restricted conjunction rule, $7/12 \times 3/5 = 21/60$, or 7/20. The probability that neither will play in the Super Bowl is, by the negation rule, $1 - 5/6 = 1/6$.

The probability calculus can also be used to evaluate the strength of inductive arguments. Consider the following:

> The Philadelphia Eagles are given 7 to 5 odds of winning the NFC championship. The New England Patriots are given 3 to 2 odds of winning the AFC championship. Therefore, the Eagles and the Patriots will meet in the Super Bowl.

On the assumption that the premises are true, that is, on the assumption that the odds are reported correctly, the conclusion follows with a probability of 7/20 or .35. Thus, the argument is not particularly strong. But if the odds given in the premises should increase, the strength of the argument would increase proportionately. The premises of the following argument give different odds:

> The Philadelphia Eagles are given 7 to 2 odds of winning the NFC championship. The New England Patriots are given 8 to 3 odds of winning the AFC championship. Therefore, the Eagles and the Patriots will meet in the Super Bowl.

In this argument, if the premises are assumed true, the conclusion follows with a probability of $7/9 \times 8/11 = 56/99$, or .57. Thus, the argument is at least moderately strong.

Lest this procedure be misinterpreted, however, we should recall a point raised in Chapter 1. The strength of an inductive argument depends not merely on whether the conclusion is probably true but on whether the conclusion follows probably from the premises. As a result, to evaluate the strength of an inductive argument it is not sufficient merely to know the probability of the conclusion on the assumption that the premises are true. One must also know whether the probability of the conclusion rests on the evidence given in the premises. If the probability of the conclusion does not rest on this evidence, the argument is weak regardless of whether the conclusion is probably true. The following argument is a case in point:

> All dogs are animals. Therefore, probably a traffic accident will occur somewhere tomorrow.

The conclusion of this argument is probably true independently of the premises, so the argument is weak.

In this connection the analogy between deductive and inductive arguments breaks down. As we saw in Chapter 6, any argument having a conclusion that is necessarily true is deductively valid regardless of the content of its premises. But any inductive argument having a probably true conclusion is not strong unless the probability of the conclusion rests on the evidence given in the premises.

A final comment is in order about the material covered in this chapter. Probability is one of those subjects about which there is little agreement among philosophers. Some philosophers defend each of the theories we have discussed as providing the only acceptable approach, and there are numerous views regarding the fine points of each. However, some philosophers argue that there are certain uses of "probability" that none of these theories can interpret. The statement "There is high probability that Einstein's theory of relativity is correct" may be a case in point. In any event, the various theories about the meaning of probability, as well as the details of the probability calculus, are highly complex subjects, and the brief account given here has merely scratched the surface.

EXERCISE 11   11

I. Compute probabilities or odds for the following simple events.

★1. What is the probability of rolling a five on a single roll of a die? What are the odds for this event?

MindTap Complete exercises online for immediate feedback.

2. From a sample of 9,750 Ajax trucks, 273 developed transmission problems within the first two years of operation. What is the probability that an Ajax truck will develop transmission problems within the first two years?

3. If the standard odds are 8 to 5 that the Chargers will beat the Lions, what is the probability that this event will happen?

★4. From a sample of 7,335 seventy-five-year-old women, 6,260 lived an additional five years. What is the probability that a seventy-five-year-old woman will live to age eighty?

5. What is the probability of picking a black jack from a poker deck (without jokers) on a single draw?

6. If the probability of the Red Sox beating the Tigers is 6/17, what are the odds for this event?

★7. Given an urn containing three red balls, four green balls, and five yellow balls, what is the probability of drawing a red ball on a single draw?

8. If the odds of the Broncos beating the Dolphins is 5 to 4, and you bet $10 on the Broncos, how much do you stand to win?

9. Given an urn containing four red balls, three green balls, and five yellow balls, what are the odds of drawing a red ball on a single draw?

★10. Suppose you give 1:6 odds that you can roll a "1" with a single fair die. If someone accepts your bet, how much could you expect to win after 100 rolls if you bet $1 on each roll?

11. Suppose four weather forecasters assign the following probabilities that it will rain tomorrow: 1/4, 1/5, 2/5, 1/3. What is the probability that this event will happen?

12. Given a regular dodecahedron (a twelve-sided solid in which each face is a regular pentagon that is congruent with each of the other faces): If this solid is rolled on a surface, what is the probability that a specifically named face will be in contact with the surface?

★13. Suppose three people enter a total of nine horses in a race. Bob enters two, Jane enters three, and Kate enters four. If each horse has an equal chance of winning, what is the probability that one of Kate's horses wins?

14. Over a ten-year period, in a given population, there were 5,491 births, and thirteen of the babies had a certain genetic disorder. What is the probability that one of the babies born during this period had the disorder?

15. Five bettors give the following odds that Black Mercury will win in the sixth race: 7 to 5, 2 to 1, 8 to 3, 5 to 2, and 7 to 4. Based on these odds, what is the probability that Black Mercury will win?

II. Compute probabilities for the following compound events:

★1. What is the probability of getting either a six or a one from a single roll of a die?

2. What is the probability of getting heads on three successive tosses of a coin?

3. What is the probability of drawing either a king or a queen from a poker deck (no jokers) on a single draw?

★4. What is the probability of drawing two aces from a poker deck in two draws

    a. If the first card is replaced before the second is drawn?
    b. If the first card is not replaced before the second is drawn?

5. What is the probability of drawing at least one ace from a poker deck on two draws if the first card is replaced before the second is drawn?

6. What is the probability of getting at least one head on three tosses of a coin?

★7. What is the probability of getting at least one six on three rolls of a die?

8. If a pair of dice are rolled, what is the probability that the points add up to

    a. five?
    b. six?
    c. seven?

9. Given two urns, one containing two red, three green, and four yellow balls, the other containing four red, two green, and three yellow balls, if a single ball is drawn from each urn, what is the probability that

    a. Both are red?
    b. At least one is green?
    c. One is red, the other yellow?
    d. At least one is either red or yellow?
    e. Both are the same color?

★10. Given an urn containing three red, four green, and five yellow balls, if two balls are drawn from the urn (without replacement), what is the probability that

    a. Both are red?
    b. One is green, the other yellow?
    c. One is either red or green?
    d. At least one is green?
    e. Both have the same color?

11. What is the probability of drawing either an ace or a king (or both) on three draws (without replacement) from a poker deck? (*Hint*: Use the negation rule.)

12. What is the probability of drawing an ace and a king on three draws (without replacement) from a poker deck? (*Hint*: Use the negation rule.)

★13. The probability of a twenty-year-old man living to age seventy is .74, and the probability of a twenty-year-old woman living to the same age is .82. If a recently married couple, both age twenty, give 8 to 1 odds on their staying married for fifty years, what is the probability that

    a. At least one will live to age seventy?
    b. They will celebrate their golden wedding anniversary?

14. Assign a numerical value to the strength of the following argument: The odds are 5 to 3 that the Indians will win the American League pennant and 7 to 5 that the Cardinals will win the National League pennant. Therefore, the Indians and the Cardinals will meet in the World Series.

15. Assign a numerical value to the strength of the following argument: The Wilson family has four children. Therefore, at least two of the children were born on the same day of the week.

★16. We are given three new urns each containing seven red, five green, and three white balls, and two old urns each containing five red, three green, and seven white balls. The urns are identical except for an old or new date stamped beneath the base. If a single red ball is randomly drawn from one of these urns, was it most probably drawn from an old urn or a new urn? (*Hint*: For this exercise and the ones that follow, use Bayes's theorem.)

17. Knowing that your friend Angella studies for her tests only 40 percent of the time, you place an even bet with a third party that Angella will not study for her upcoming test. Later, you just happen to hear that Angella passed the test. Should you retract your bet? Assume that Angella passes nine out of ten tests when she studies, and three out of ten when she does not.

18. A physician has diagnosed a patient as having either hepatitis or liver cancer (but not both). Statistics reveal that hepatitis occurs in the general population twice as frequently as liver cancer. Thus, the physician tentatively concludes that the patient probably has hepatitis. Later the physician conducts a test on the patient that turns out positive. On this test, nine out of ten cases of liver cancer trigger a positive outcome, and one out of six cases of hepatitis triggers a positive outcome. What is the new probability that the patient has liver cancer?

★19. Ms. Jones, a bookstore owner, wishes to send out an advertisement to potential customers. She estimates that 20 percent of the town's residents are recreational readers, and she knows that all of the residents are either recreational readers or TV addicts (but not both). Also, a media expert has told her that two of ten TV addicts are newspaper subscribers, and from a survey of her own customers she has learned that seven of ten recreational readers are newspaper subscribers. If Ms. Jones places an ad in the local newspaper, how effective will the ad be? (That is, what is the probability that a newspaper subscriber is a recreational reader?)

20. Mr. Andrews, a grape merchant, inquires about a certain wine that he tastes at a party. The host tells him that from a total of ten bottles of that wine, six came from the north vineyard and four came from the south vineyard. From this information, the merchant concludes that he should visit the north vineyard for a sample of the grapes. Later, he discovers that the wine in question came from a bottle labeled Classic Reserve, and 30 of 100 barrels of north vineyard wine were bottled with that label, while 130 of 200 barrels of south vineyard wine were bottled with that label. Given this new information, what is the probability that the wine came from the north vineyard?

III. Do some research and find an actual application of Bayes's theorem that is not mentioned in this book. Then write a paragraph on your findings.

Summary

Theories of Probability:

- Classical theory: Rests on a priori calculations.
- Relative frequency theory: Depends on empirical experimentation.
- Subjectivist theory: Rests on subjective beliefs of individual people.

Probability Calculus:

- Used to calculate the probability of compound events.
- Conjunction rule: Computes the probability of two events occurring together.
    - Restricted conjunction rule: The events are independent.
    - General conjunction rule: The events need not be independent.
- Disjunction rule: Computes the probability of either of two events occurring.
    - Restricted disjunction rule: The events are mutually exclusive.
    - General disjunction rule: The events need not be mutually exclusive.
- Negation rule: Computes the probability of an event not occurring.
- Bayes's theorem: Computes the conditional probability of two or more mutually exclusive and jointly exhaustive events.

12 Statistical Reasoning

HOW LOGICAL ARE YOU? Suppose you have a friend who is working as an intern for a local politician's reelection campaign. This friend says to you, "In the most recent poll, our candidate was favored by 58 percent of those who were polled, so it is very likely she will win the election." What would you need to know about the poll to have confidence in your friend's prediction?

Find the answer on MindTap.

12.1 Evaluating Statistics

In our day-to-day experience, all of us encounter arguments that rest on statistical evidence. The advertising industry is an especially prolific source of such arguments. We are constantly told that we ought to sign up with a certain mobile phone service because it has 30 percent fewer dropped calls, buy a certain kind of car because it gets 5 percent better fuel economy, and use a certain cold remedy because it is recommended by four out of five physicians. But the advertising industry is not the only source of these kinds of arguments. We often read in the newspapers that some union is asking for an increase in pay because its members earn less than the average, or that a certain region is threatened with floods because rainfall has been more than the average.

To evaluate such arguments, we must be able to interpret the statistics on which they rest, but doing so is not always easy. Statements expressing averages and percentages are often ambiguous and can mean a variety of things, depending on how the average or percentage is computed. These difficulties are compounded by the fact that statistics provide a highly convenient way for people to deceive one another. Such deceptions can be effective even

MindTap Read, study, reflect, and prepare for exams online, anytime, anywhere.

though they fall short of being outright lies. Thus, to evaluate arguments based on statistics one must be familiar not only with the ambiguities that occur in the language but with the devices that unscrupulous individuals use to deceive others.

This chapter touches on five areas that are frequent sources of such ambiguity and deception: problems in sampling, the meaning of "average," the importance of dispersion in a sample, the use of graphs and pictograms, and the use of percentages for the purpose of comparison. By becoming acquainted with these topics and with some of the misuses that occur, we improve our ability to determine whether a conclusion follows probably from a set of statistical premises.

12.2 Samples

Much of the statistical evidence presented in support of inductively drawn conclusions is gathered from analyzing samples. When a sample is found to possess a certain characteristic, it is argued that the group as a whole (the population) possesses that characteristic. For example, if we wanted to know what the student body at a certain university thought about a proposal to adopt an academic honor code, we could take a poll of 10 percent of the students. If the results of the poll showed that 80 percent of those sampled favored the code, we might draw the conclusion that 80 percent of the entire student body favored it. Such an argument would be classified as an inductive generalization.

The problem that arises with the use of samples has to do with whether the sample is representative of the population. Samples that are not representative are said to be **biased samples**. Depending on what the population consists of, whether machine parts or human beings, different considerations enter into determining whether a sample is biased. These considerations include (1) whether the sample is randomly selected, (2) the size of the sample, and (3) psychological factors.

A random sample is one in which every member of the population has an equal chance of being selected. The requirement that a sample be randomly selected applies to practically all samples, but sometimes it can be taken for granted. For example, when a physician draws a blood sample to test for blood sugar, there is no need to take a little bit from the finger, a little from the arm, and a little from the leg. Because blood is a circulating fluid, it can be assumed that it is homogenous in regard to blood sugar.

The randomness requirement demands more attention when the population consists of discrete units. Suppose, for example, that a quality-control engineer for a manufacturing firm needed to determine whether the components on a certain conveyor belt were within specifications. To do so, the engineer removed every tenth component for measurement. The sample obtained by such a procedure would not be random if the components were not randomly arranged on the conveyor belt. As a result of some malfunction in the manufacturing process it is quite possible that every tenth component was perfect and the rest were imperfect. If the engineer happened to select only the perfect ones, the sample would be biased. A selection procedure that would be more likely to ensure a random sample would be to roll a pair of dice and remove every component corresponding to a roll of ten. Since the outcome of a roll of dice is a random event, the selection would also be random. Such a procedure would be more likely to include defective components that turn up at regular intervals.

The randomness requirement presents even greater problems when the population consists of human beings. Suppose, for example, that a public-opinion poll is to be conducted on the question of excessive corporate profits. It would hardly do to ask such a question randomly of the people encountered on Wall Street in New York City. Such a sample would almost certainly be biased in favor of the corporations. A less biased sample could be obtained by randomly selecting phone numbers from the telephone directory, but even this procedure would not yield a completely random sample. Among other things, the time of day in which a call is placed influences the kind of responses obtained. Most people who are employed full-time are not available during the day, and even if calls are made at night, a large percentage of the population have unlisted landline and cell-phone numbers.

A poll conducted by mail based on the addresses listed in the city directory would also yield a fairly random sample, but this method, too, has shortcomings. Many apartment dwellers are not listed, and others move before the directory is printed. Furthermore, none of those who live in rural areas are listed. In short, it is both difficult and expensive to conduct a large-scale public-opinion poll that succeeds in obtaining responses from anything approximating a random sample of individuals.

A classic case of a poll that turned out to be biased in spite of a good deal of effort and expense occurred when the *Literary Digest* magazine undertook a poll to predict the outcome of the 1936 presidential election. The sample consisted of a large number of the magazine's subscribers together with other people selected from the telephone directory. Because four similar polls had picked the winner in previous years, the results of this poll were highly respected. As it turned out, however, the Republican candidate, Alf Landon, got a significant majority in the poll, but Franklin D. Roosevelt won the election by a landslide. The incorrect prediction is explained by the fact that the 1936 election occurred in the middle of the Depression, at a time when many people could afford neither a telephone nor a subscription to the *Digest*. These were the people who were overlooked in the poll, and they were also the ones who voted for Roosevelt.

A different kind of sampling bias can occur in clinical trials undertaken to disclose the negative side effects of a particular drug. If a participant in such a trial should suffer serious side effects, that participant might leave the trial altogether and never report any of the side effects to the doctors conducting the trial. As more and more participants drop out for the same reason, the sample would become increasingly biased. At the conclusion of such a trial, if a regulatory agency should grant approval for the drug to be sold to the public, the decision to approve would be based on a biased sample. A similar kind of bias can occur if the duration of a clinical trial is too short to allow for certain side effects to emerge. For example, cancer can take years to develop. If the clinical trial evaluating a particular drug is ended after a relatively short time, the possibility that the drug causes cancer might never be discovered. In effect, the sample consisting of the trial participants would be biased.

Size is also an important factor in determining whether a sample is representative. Given that a sample is randomly selected, the larger the sample, the more closely it replicates the population. In statistics, this degree of closeness is expressed in terms of sampling error. The **sampling error** is the difference between the relative frequency with which some characteristic occurs in the sample and the relative frequency with which the same characteristic occurs in the population. If, for example, a poll were taken of a labor union and 60 percent of the members sampled expressed their intention to vote for Smith for president but in fact only 55 percent of the whole union intended to vote for Smith, the sampling error would be 5 percent. If a larger sample were taken, the error would be smaller.

Just how large a sample should be is a function of the size of the population and of the degree of sampling error that can be tolerated. For a sampling error of, say, 5 percent, a population of 10,000 would require a larger sample than would a population of 100. However, the ratio is not linear. To obtain the same precision, the sample for the larger population need not be 100 times as large as the one for the smaller population. When the population is very large, the size of the sample needed to ensure a certain precision levels off at a constant figure. For example, a random sample of 500 will yield results that are just as accurate whether the population is 100,000 or 100 million.

When the population is very large, and the sample is random and less than 5 percent of the population, sampling error can be expressed in terms of a mathematical margin of error as per Table 12.1:

TABLE 12.1 Sample Size and Margin of Error

Sample Size	Margin of Error
9,604	±1%
2,401	±2%
1,067	±3%
600	±4%
384	±5%
267	±6%
196	±7%
96	±10%

The figures in this table are based on a 95 percent level of confidence, which means that we can be 95 percent certain that a sample will accurately reflect the whole population within the margin of error for that sample. Thus, if from a random poll of 9,604 people, 53 percent say they prefer Jones for governor, then we can be 95 percent certain that between 52 and 54 percent of the whole population prefers Jones. The figures in the table are based purely on mathematics and are not dependent on any empirical measurement. For a 95 percent confidence level, the margin of error is approximately equal to $.98/\sqrt{n}$, where n is the size of the sample. For a 99 percent confidence level, the margin of error is approximately equal to $1.29/\sqrt{n}$. Comparing these two expressions shows that as the confidence level increases, so does the margin of error.

In most polls, the margin of error is based on a 95 percent (or higher) confidence level. But if a much lower confidence level should be selected, and if this fact is not disclosed, then the results of a poll could be deceptive—even if the margin of error is stated. The reason for this is that the margin of error would be combined with a low

12

likelihood that it covered any actual discrepancy between the sample and the population. Also, of course, any poll that simply fails to disclose the margin of error can be deceptive. For example, if a poll should show Adams leading Baker for U.S. Senate by 55 to 45 percent, this means virtually nothing if neither the size of the sample nor the margin of error is given. If the margin of error should be as high as 10 percent, then it could be the case that it is Baker who leads Adams by 55 to 45 percent.

Even when the margin of error is stated, however, incorrect conclusions are often drawn when comparing the results of one poll with the results of another. Suppose a poll shows Adams leading Baker by 55 to 45 percent. After an article critical of Adams appears in the newspaper, a second poll is taken that shows Adams trailing Baker by 49 to 51 percent. Suppose further that the margin of error for both polls is 4 percent and the confidence level is 95 percent. From such polls people often draw the conclusion that Adams's lead over Baker has disappeared, when in fact no such conclusion is warranted. Taking into account the margin of error, it could be the case that in fact Adams's lead over Baker has remained constant at, say, 53 to 47 percent.

Statements of sampling error are often conspicuously absent from surveys used to support advertising claims. Marketers of products such as patent medicines have been known to take rather small samples until they obtain one that gives the "right" result. For example, several polls of twenty-five people might be taken inquiring about the preferred brand of aspirin. Even though the samples might be randomly selected, one will eventually be found in which twenty of the twenty-five respondents indicate their preference for Alpha brand aspirin. Having found such a sample, the marketing firm proceeds to promote this brand as the one preferred by four out of five of those sampled. The results of the other samples are, of course, discarded, and no mention is made of sampling error.

Psychological factors can also have a bearing on whether the sample is representative. When the population consists of inanimate objects, such as cans of soup or machine parts, psychological factors are usually irrelevant, but they can play a significant role when the population consists of human beings. If the people composing the sample think that they will gain or lose something by the kind of answer they give, their involvement will likely affect the outcome. For example, if the residents of a neighborhood were to be surveyed for annual income with the purpose of determining whether the neighborhood should be ranked among the fashionable areas in the city, we would expect the residents to exaggerate their answers. But if the purpose of the study were to determine whether the neighborhood could afford a special levy that would increase property taxes, we might expect the incomes to be underestimated.

The kind of question asked can also have a psychological bearing. Questions such as "How often do you brush your teeth?" and "How many books do you read in a year?" can be expected to generate responses that overestimate the truth, while "How many times have you been intoxicated?" and "How many extramarital affairs have you had?" would probably receive answers that underestimate the truth. Similar exaggerations can result from the way a question is phrased. For example, "Do you favor a reduction in welfare benefits as a response to rampant cheating?" would be expected to receive more affirmative answers than simply "Do you favor a reduction in welfare benefits?"

Another source of psychological influence is the personal interaction between the surveyor and the respondent. Suppose, for example, that a door-to-door survey were taken to determine how many people believe in God or attend church on Sunday. If the survey were conducted by priests and ministers dressed in clerical garb, one might expect a larger number of affirmative answers than if the survey were taken by nonclerics. The simple fact is that many people like to give answers that they think will please the questioner.

To prevent this kind of interaction from affecting the outcome, scientific studies are often conducted under "double-blind" conditions in which neither the surveyor nor the respondent knows what the "right" answer is. For example, in a double-blind study to determine the effectiveness of a drug, bottles containing the drug would be mixed with other bottles containing a placebo (sugar tablet). The contents of each bottle would be matched with a code number on the label, and neither the person distributing the bottles nor the person recording the responses would know what the code is. Under these conditions the people conducting the study would not be able to influence, by some smile or gesture, the response of the people to whom the drugs are given.

Most of the statistical evidence encountered in ordinary experience contains no reference to such factors as randomness, sampling error, or the conditions under which the sample was taken. In the absence of such information, the person faced with evaluating the evidence must use his or her best judgment. If either the organization conducting the study or the people composing the sample have something to gain by the kind of answer that is given, the results of the survey should be regarded as suspect. And if the questions that are asked concern topics that would naturally elicit distorted answers, the results should probably be rejected. In either event, the mere fact that a study *appears* scientific or is expressed in mathematical language should never intimidate a person into accepting the results. Numbers and scientific terminology are no substitute for an unbiased sample.

12.3 The Meaning of "Average"

In statistics the word "average" is used in three different senses: mean, median, and mode. In evaluating arguments and inferences that rest on averages, we often need to know in precisely what sense the word is being used.

The **mean** value of a set of data is the arithmetical average. It is computed by dividing the sum of the individual values by the number of values in the set. Suppose, for example, that we are given Table 12.2 listing the ages of a group of people. To compute the mean age, we divide the sum of the individual ages by the number of people:

TABLE 12.2

No. of People	Age
1	16
4	17
1	18
2	19
3	23

$$\text{mean age} = \frac{(1 \times 16) + (4 \times 17) + (1 \times 18) + (2 \times 19) + (3 \times 23)}{11} = 19$$

The **median** of a set of data is the middle point when the data are arranged in ascending order. In other words, the median is the point at which there is an equal number of data above and below. In Table 12.2 the median age is 18 because there are five people above this age and five below.

The **mode** is the value that occurs with the greatest frequency. Here the mode is 17, because there are four people of that age and fewer people of any other age.

TABLE 12.2 (Repeated)

Number of People	Age
1	16
4	17
1	18
2	19
3	23

In this example, the mean, median, and mode differ but are all fairly close together. The problem for induction occurs when a great disparity among these values occurs. This sometimes occurs in the case of salaries. Consider, for example, Table 12.3, which reports the salaries of a hypothetical architectural firm. Since there are twenty-one employees and a total of $1,365,000 is paid in salaries, the mean salary is $1,365,000/21, or $65,000. The median salary is $45,000 because ten employees earn less than this and ten earn more, and the mode, which is the salary that occurs most frequently, is $30,000. Each of these figures represents the "average" salary of the firm, but in different senses. Depending on the purpose for which the average is used, different figures might be cited as the basis for an argument.

For example, if the senior engineer were to request a raise in salary, the president could respond that the engineer's salary is already well above the average (in the sense of median and mode) and that therefore she or he does not deserve a raise. If the junior draftsmen were to make the same request, the president could respond that they are presently earning the firm's average salary (in the sense of mode), and that for draftsmen, to be earning the average salary is excellent. Finally, if someone from outside the firm were to allege that the firm pays subsistence-level wages, the president could respond that the average salary of the firm is a hefty $65,000. All of the president's responses would be true, but if the reader or listener were not sophisticated enough to distinguish the various senses of "average," he or she might be persuaded by the arguments.

In some situations, the mode is the most useful average. Suppose, for example, that you are in the market for a three-bedroom house. Suppose further that a real

TABLE 12.3

Capacity	Number of Personnel	Salary	
President	1	$275,000	
Senior architect	2	150,000	
Junior architect	2	80,000	
Senior engineer	1	65,000	← mean
Junior engineer	4	55,000	
Senior draftsman	1	45,000	← median
Junior draftsman	10	30,000	← mode

estate agent assures you that the houses in a certain complex have an average of three bedrooms and that therefore you will certainly want to see them. If the agent has used "average" in the sense of mean, it is possible that half the houses in the complex are four-bedroom, the other half are two-bedroom, and there are no three-bedroom houses at all. A similar result is possible if the agent has used average in the sense of median. The only sense of average that would be useful for your purposes is mode: If the modal average is three bedrooms, there are more three-bedroom houses than any other kind.

On other occasions a mean average is the most useful. Suppose, for example, that you have taken a job as a pilot on a plane that has nine passenger seats and a maximum carrying capacity of 1,350 pounds (in addition to yourself). Suppose further that you have arranged to fly a group of nine passengers over the Grand Canyon and that you must determine whether their combined weight is within the required limit. If a representative of the group tells you that the average weight of the passengers is 150 pounds, this by itself tells you nothing. If he means average in the sense of median, it could be the case that the four heavier passengers weigh 200 pounds and the four lighter ones weigh 145, for a combined weight of 1,530 pounds. Similarly, if the passenger representative means average in the sense of mode, it could be that two passengers weigh 150 pounds and that the others have varying weights in excess of 200 pounds, for a combined weight of over 1,700 pounds. Only if the representative means average in the sense of mean do you know that the combined weight of the passengers is 9 × 150 or 1,350 pounds.

Finally, sometimes a median average is the most meaningful. Suppose, for example, that you are a manufacturer of a product that appeals to people under age 35. To increase sales you decide to run an ad in a national magazine, but you want some assurance that the ad will be read by the right age group. If the advertising director of a magazine tells you that the average age of the magazine's readers is 35, you know virtually nothing. If the director means average in the sense of mean, it could be that 90 percent of the readers are over 35 and that the remaining 10 percent bring the average down to 35. Similarly, if the director means average in the sense of mode, it could be that 3 percent of the readers are exactly 35 and that the remaining 97 percent have ages ranging from 35 to 85. Only if the director means average in the sense of median do you know that half the readers are 35 or less.

12.4 Dispersion

Although averages often yield important information about a set of data, there are many cases in which merely knowing the average, in any sense of the term, tells us very little. The reason for this is that the average says nothing about how the data are distributed. For this, we need to know something about **dispersion**, which refers to how spread out the data are in regard to numerical value. Three important measures of dispersion are range, variance, and standard deviation.

Let us first consider the **range** of a set of data, which is the difference between the largest and the smallest values. For an example of the importance of this parameter, suppose that after living for many years in an intemperate climate, you decide to relocate in an area that has a more ideal mean temperature. On discovering that the annual mean temperature of Oklahoma City is 60°F you decide to move there, only

FIGURE 12.1*

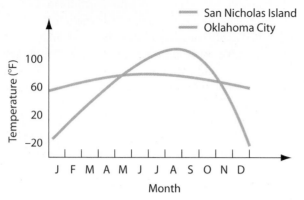

*This example is taken from Darrell Huff, *How to Lie with Statistics* (New York: Norton, 1954), 52.

to find that you roast in the summer and freeze in the winter. Unfortunately, you had ignored the fact that Oklahoma City has a temperature *range* of 130°, extending from a record low of −17° to a record high of 113°. In contrast, San Nicholas Island, off the coast of California, has a mean temperature of 61° but a range of only 40°, extending from 47° in the winter to 87° in the summer. The temperature ranges for these two locations are approximated in Figure 12.1.

Even granting the importance of the range of the data in this example, however, range really tells us relatively little because it comprehends only two data points, the maximum and minimum. It says nothing about how the other data points are distributed. For this we need to know the **variance**, or the **standard deviation**, which measure how every data point varies or deviates from the mean.

For an example of the importance of these two parameters in describing a set of data, suppose you have a four-year-old child and you are looking for a day-care center that will provide plenty of possible playmates about the same age as your child. After calling several centers on the phone, you narrow the search down to two: the Rumpus Center and the Bumpus Center. Both report that they regularly care for nine children, that the mean and median age of the children is four, and that the range in ages of the children is six. Unable to decide between these two centers, you decide to pay them a visit. Having done so, you see that the Rumpus Center will meet your needs better than the Bumpus Center. The reason is that the ages of the children in the two centers are distributed differently.

The ages of the children in the two centers are as follows:

  Rumpus Center: 1, 3, 3, 4, 4, 4, 5, 5, 7
  Bumpus Center: 1, 1, 2, 2, 4, 6, 6, 7, 7

To illustrate the differences in distribution, these ages can be plotted on a certain kind of bar graph, called a *histogram*, as shown in Figures 12.2a and 12.2b. Obviously the reason why the Rumpus Center comes closer to meeting your needs is that it has seven children within one year of your own child, whereas the Bumpus Center has only one such child. This difference in distribution is measured by the variance and the standard deviation. Computing the value of these parameters for the two centers is quite easy, but first we

12

FIGURE 12.2

(a)

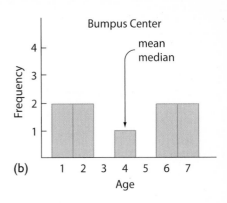

(b)

must introduce some symbols. The standard deviation is represented in statistics by the lowercase Greek letter σ (sigma), and the variance, which is the square of the standard deviation, is represented by σ². We compute the variance first, which is defined as follows:

$$\sigma^2 = \frac{\Sigma(x - \mu)^2}{n}$$

In this expression (which looks far more complicated than it is), Σ (uppercase sigma) means "the sum of," x is a variable that ranges over the ages of the children, the lowercase Greek letter μ (mu) is the mean age, and n is the number of children. Thus, to compute the variance, we take each of the ages of the children, subtract the mean age (4) from each, square the result of each, add up the squares, and then divide the sum by the number of children (9). The first three steps of this procedure for the Rumpus Center are reported in Table 12.4.

TABLE 12.4

x	$(x - \mu)$	$(x - \mu)^2$
1	−3	9
3	−1	1
3	−1	1
4	0	0
4	0	0
4	0	0
5	+1	1
5	+1	1
7	+3	9
		Total = 22

First, the column for x (the children's ages) is entered, next the column for $(x - \mu)$, and last the column for $(x - \mu)^2$. After adding up the figures in the final column, we obtain the variance by dividing the sum (22) by n (9):

$$\text{Variance} = \sigma^2 = \frac{22}{9} = 2.44$$

12

Finally, to obtain the standard deviation, we take the square root of the variance:

$$\text{Standard deviation} = \sigma = \sqrt{2.44} = 1.56$$

TABLE 12.5

x	$(x - \mu)$	$(x - \mu)^2$
1	−3	9
1	−3	9
2	−2	4
2	−2	4
4	0	0
6	+2	4
6	+2	4
7	+3	9
7	+3	9
		Total = 52

Next, we can perform the same operation on the ages of the children in the Bumpus Center. The figures are expressed in Table 12.5.

Now, for the variance, we have

$$\sigma^2 = \frac{52}{9} = 5.78$$

And for the standard deviation, we have

$$\sigma = \sqrt{5.78} = 2.40$$

These figures for the variance and standard deviation reflect the difference in distribution shown in the two histograms. In the histogram for the Rumpus Center, the ages of most of the children are clumped around the mean age (4). In other words, they vary or deviate relatively slightly from the mean, and this fact is reflected in relatively small figures for the variance (2.44) and the standard deviation (1.56). On the other hand, in the histogram for the Bumpus center, the ages of most of the children vary or deviate relatively greatly from the mean, so the variance (5.78) and the standard deviation (2.40) are larger.

One of the more important kinds of distribution used in statistics is called the **normal probability distribution**, which expresses the distribution of random phenomena in a population. Such phenomena include (approximately) the heights of adult men or women in a city, the useful life of a certain kind of tire or lightbulb, and the daily sales figures of a certain grocery store. To illustrate this concept, suppose that a certain college has 2,000 female students. The heights of these students range from 57 inches to 73 inches. If we divide these heights into one-inch intervals and express them in terms of a histogram, the resulting graph would probably look like the one in Figure 12.3a.

This histogram has the shape of a bell. When a continuous curve is superimposed on top of this histogram, the result appears in Figure 12.3b. This curve is called a normal curve, and it represents a normal distribution. The heights of all of the students fit under

12

FIGURE 12.3

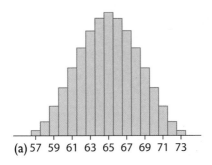

(a) 57 59 61 63 65 67 69 71 73

(b) 57 59 61 63 65 67 69 71 73

the curve, and each vertical slice under the curve represents a certain subset of these heights. The number of heights trails off toward zero at the extreme left and right ends of the curve, and it reaches a maximum in the center. The peak of the curve reflects the average height in the sense of mean, median, and mode.

The parameters of variance and standard deviation apply to normal distributions in basically the same way as they do for the histograms relating to the day-care centers. Normal curves with a relatively small standard deviation tend to be relatively narrow and pointy, with most of the population clustered close to the mean, while curves with a relatively large standard deviation tend to be relatively flattened and stretched out, with most of the population distributed some distance from the mean. This idea is expressed in Figure 12.4. As usual, σ represents the standard deviation, and μ represents the mean.

FIGURE 12.4

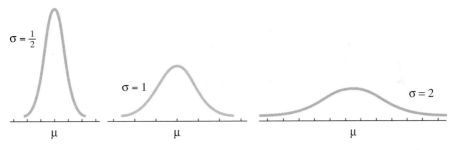

For a final example that illustrates the importance of dispersion, suppose that you decide to put your life savings into a business that designs and manufactures women's dresses. As corporation president you decide to save money by restricting production to dresses that fit the average woman. Because the average size in the sense of mean, median, and mode is 12, you decide to make only size 12 dresses. Unfortunately, you later discover that while size 12 is indeed the average, 95 percent of women fall outside this interval, as Figure 12.5 shows.

The problem is that you failed to take into account the standard deviation. If the standard deviation were relatively small, then most of the dress sizes would be clustered about the mean (size 12). But in fact the standard deviation is relatively large, so most of the dress sizes fall outside this interval.

FIGURE 12.5

Women who can wear size 12

Number of women

4 8 12 16 20

Dress size

Graphs and Pictograms

Graphs provide a highly convenient and informative way to represent statistical data, but they are also susceptible to misuse and misinterpretation. Here we will confine our attention to some of the typical ways in which graphs are misused.

First of all, if a graph is to represent an actual situation, it is essential that both the vertical and horizontal axes be scaled. Suppose, for example, that the profit level of a corporation is represented by a graph such as Figure 12.6. Such a graph is practically meaningless because it fails to show how much the profits increased over what period of time. If the curve represents a 10 percent increase over twenty years, then, of course, the picture is not very bright. Although they convey practically no information, graphs of this kind are used quite often in advertising. A manufacturer of vitamins, for example, might print such a graph on the label of the bottle to suggest that a person's energy level is supposed to increase dramatically after taking the tablets. Such ads often make an impression because they look scientific, and the viewer rarely bothers to check whether the axes are scaled, or precisely what the curve is supposed to signify.

FIGURE 12.6

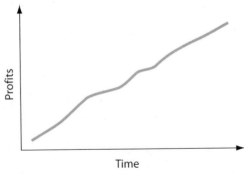

Profits

Time

A graph that more appropriately represents corporate profits is given in Figure 12.7 (the corporation is fictitious).

FIGURE 12.7

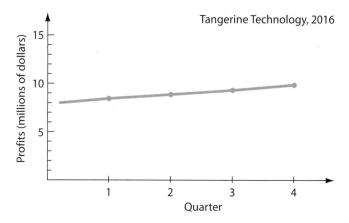

Inspection of the graph reveals that between January and December profits rose from $8 million to $10 million, which represents a respectable 25 percent increase. This increase can be made to *appear* even more impressive by chopping off the bottom of the graph and altering the scale on the vertical axis while leaving the horizontal scale as is (Figure 12.8). Again, strictly speaking, the graph accurately represents the facts, but if the viewer fails to notice what has been done to the vertical scale, he or she is liable to derive the impression that the profits have increased by something like a hundred percent or more. Most of the graphs shown on CNBC, a widely watched business channel, are of this sort.

FIGURE 12.8

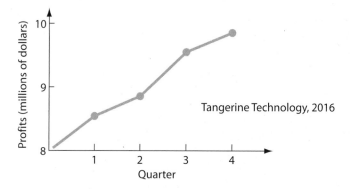

The same strategy can be used with bar graphs. The graphs in Figure 12.9 compare sales volume for two consecutive years, but the one on the right conveys the message more dramatically. Of course, if the sales volume has decreased, the corporate directors would probably want to minimize the difference, in which case the design on the left is preferable.

An even greater illusion can be created with the use of pictograms. A **pictogram** is a diagram that compares two situations through drawings that differ either in size or in the number of entities depicted. Consider Figure 12.10, which illustrates the increase in the milk production of a dairy between 2008 and 2016.

FIGURE 12.9

FIGURE 12.10

This pictogram accurately represents the increase because it unequivocally shows that the amount doubled between the years represented. But the effect is not especially dramatic. The increase in production can be exaggerated by representing the 2016 level with a milk storage container twice as tall (Figure 12.11).

FIGURE 12.11

Even though the actual production is stated adjacent to each drawing, this pictogram creates the illusion that production has much more than doubled. While the drawing on the right is exactly twice as high as the one on the left, it is also twice as wide. Thus, it occupies four times as much room on the page. Furthermore, when the viewer's three-dimensional judgment is called into play, the container on the right is perceived as having eight times the volume of the one on the left. Thus, when the third dimension is taken into account, the increase in consumption is exaggerated by 600 percent.

Percentages

The use of percentages to compare two or more situations or quantities is another source of illusion in statistics. A favorite of advertisers is to make claims such as "Zesty Cola has 20 percent fewer calories" or "The price of the new Vizio flat screen has been reduced by 15 percent." These claims are virtually meaningless. The question is, 20 percent less than *what*, and 15 percent reduced from *what*? If the basis of the comparison or reduction is not mentioned, the claim tells us nothing. Yet such claims are often effective because they leave us with the impression that the product is in some way superior or less expensive.

One ploy sometimes used by pharmaceutical companies in selling drugs, such as statins, to reduce the incidence of heart attacks, involves switching the base upon which percentages are computed. To see how this works, suppose a company sets up a clinical trial involving 200 people. One hundred are given the drug and 100 are given a placebo (sugar pill). By the end of the trial, suppose that one person in the treatment group suffered a heart attack and two people in the placebo group had a heart attack. That means that 1 percent of the treatment group had a heart attack and 2 percent of the placebo group had a heart attack. This is a 1 percent reduction in heart attacks. Projected into the future, if 100 people take the drug for two years we could expect one less heart attack than with 100 people who do not take the drug.

However, a 1 percent reduction in heart attacks will never sell anything. So the pharmaceutical company switches the numbers. The company figures that the drug reduced the incidence of heart attacks from 2 percent to 1 percent, which is a 50 percent reduction. Now it can claim in its advertising that the drug reduces heart attacks by 50 percent. This conveys the false impression that if 100 people take the drug for two years, there will be 50 fewer heart attacks than with 100 people who do not take the drug. Clearly this is not what the clinical trial suggests.

What the pharmaceutical company has done is to switch the base for the percentages. In the initial computation, the base is 100. In the revised computation, the base is two. One out of 100 is 1 percent; one out of two is 50 percent. The same strategy is sometimes used by nonprofits engaged in fund-raising. Suppose, for example, that you are a university president involved with a funding drive to increase the university's endowment. Suppose further that the endowment currently stands at $15 million and that the objective is to increase it to $20 million. To guarantee the success of the drive, you engage the services of a professional fund-raising organization. At the end of the allotted time the organization has increased the endowment to $16 million. They justify their effort by stating that, since $16 million of the $20 million has been raised, the drive was 80 percent successful ($16/20 \times 100\%$).

In fact, of course, the drive was nowhere near that successful. The objective was not to raise $20 million but only $5 million, and of that amount only $1 million has actually been raised. Thus, at best the drive was only 20 percent successful. Even this figure is probably exaggerated, though, because $1 million might have been raised without any special drive. The trick played by the fund-raising organization consisted in switching the numbers by which the percentage was to be computed.

This same trick, incidentally, was allegedly used by Joseph Stalin to justify the success of his first five-year plan.* Among other things, the original plan called for an increase in steel output from 4.2 million tons to 10.3 million. After five years the actual output rose to 5.9 million, whereupon Stalin announced that the plan was 57 percent successful (5.9/10.3 × 100%). The correct percentage, of course, is much lower. The plan called for an increase of 6.1 million tons and the actual increase was only 1.7 million. Thus, at best, the plan was only 28 percent successful.

Similar devices have been used by employers on their unsuspecting employees. When business is bad, an employer may argue that salaries must be reduced by 20 percent. Later, when business improves, salaries will be raised by 20 percent, thus restoring them to their original level. Such an argument, of course, is fallacious. If a person earns $10 per hour and that person's salary is reduced by 20 percent, the adjusted salary is $8. If that figure is later increased by 20 percent, the final salary is $9.60. The problem, of course, stems from the fact that a different base is used for the two percentages. The fallacy committed by such arguments is a variety of equivocation. Percentages are relative terms, and they mean different things in different contexts.

A different kind of fallacy occurs when a person attempts to add percentages as if they were cardinal numbers. Suppose, for example, that a baker increases the price of a loaf of bread by 50 percent. To justify the increase the baker argues that it was necessitated by rising costs: The price of flour increased by 10 percent, the cost of labor rose 20 percent, utility rates went up 10 percent, and the cost of the lease on the building increased 10 percent. This adds up to a 50 percent increase. Again, the argument is fallacious. If *everything* had increased by 20 percent, this would justify only a 20 percent increase in the price of bread. As it is, the justified increase is less than that. The fallacy committed by such arguments would probably be best classified as a case of missing the point (*ignoratio elenchi*). The arguer has failed to grasp the significance of his own premises.

Statistical variations of the suppressed evidence fallacy are also quite common. One variety consists in drawing a conclusion from a comparison of two different things or situations. For example, people running for political office sometimes cite figures indicating that crime in the community has increased by, let us say, 20 percent during the past three or four years. What is needed, they conclude, is an all-out war on crime. But they fail to mention that the population in the community has also increased by 20 percent during the same period. The number of crimes per capita, therefore, has not changed. Another example of the same fallacy is provided by the ridiculous argument that 90 percent more traffic accidents occur in clear weather than in foggy weather and that therefore it is 90 percent more dangerous to drive in clear than in foggy weather. The arguer ignores the fact that the vast percentage of vehicle miles are driven in clear weather, which accounts for the greater number of accidents.

A similar misuse of percentages is committed by businesses and corporations that, for whatever reason, want to make it appear that they have earned less profit than they actually have. The technique consists of expressing profit as a percentage of sales volume instead of as a percentage of investment. For example, during a certain year a corporation

---

*Stephen K. Campbell, Flaws and Fallacies in Statistical Thinking (Englewood Cliffs, NJ: Prentice-Hall, 1974), 8. The original reference is to Eugene Lyons's Workers' Paradise Lost.

might have a total sales volume of $100 million, a total investment of $10 million, and a profit of $5 million. If profits are expressed as a percentage of investment, they amount to a hefty 50 percent; but as a percentage of sales they are only 5 percent. To appreciate the fallacy in this procedure, consider the case of the jewelry merchant who buys one piece of jewelry each morning for $9 and sells it in the evening for $10. At the end of the year the total sales volume is $3,650, the total investment $9, and the total profit $365. Profits as a percentage of sales amount to only 10 percent, but as a percentage of investment they exceed 4,000 percent.

EXERCISE 12

I. Criticize the following arguments in light of the material presented in this chapter.

★1. To test the algae content in a lake, a biologist took a sample of the water at one end. The algae in the sample registered 5 micrograms per liter. Therefore, the algae in the lake at that time registered 5 micrograms per liter.

2. To estimate public support for a new municipality-funded convention center, researchers surveyed 100 homeowners in one of the city's fashionable neighborhoods. They found that 89 percent of those sampled were enthusiastic about the project. Therefore, we may conclude that 89 percent of the city's residents favor the convention center.

3. A quality-control inspector for a food-processing firm needed assurance that the cans of fruit in a production run were filled to capacity. He opened every tenth box in the warehouse and removed the can in the left front corner of each box. He found that all of these cans were filled to capacity. Therefore, it is probable that all of the cans in the production run were filled to capacity.

★4. When a random sample of 600 voters was taken on the eve of the presidential election, it was found that 51 percent of those sampled intended to vote for the Democrat and 49 percent for the Republican. Therefore, the Democrat will probably win the popular vote.

5. To determine the public's attitude toward TV soap operas, 1,000 people were contacted by telephone between 8:00 A.M. and 5:00 P.M. on weekdays. The numbers were selected randomly from the phone directories of cities across the nation. The researchers reported that 43 percent of the respondents said that they were avid viewers. From this we may conclude that 43 percent of the public watches TV soap operas.

6. To predict the results of a U.S. Senate race in New York State, two polls were taken. One was based on a random sample of 600 voters, the other on a random sample of 2,400 voters. Since the second sample was four times as large as the first, the results of the second poll were four times as accurate as the first.

12

MindTap® Complete exercises online for immediate feedback.

★7. In a survey conducted by the manufacturers of Ultrasheen toothpaste, 65 percent of the dentists randomly sampled preferred that brand over all others. Clearly, Ultrasheen is the brand preferred by most dentists.

8. To determine the percentage of adult Americans who have never read the U.S. Constitution, surveyors put this question to a random sample of 1,000 adults. Only 13 percent gave negative answers. Therefore, since the sampling error for such a sample is 3 percent, we may conclude that no more than 16 percent of American adults have not read the Constitution.

9. To determine the percentage of patients who follow the advice of their personal physician, researchers asked 200 randomly chosen physicians to put the question to their patients. Of the 2,400 patients surveyed, 98 percent replied that they did indeed follow their doctor's advice. We may therefore conclude that at least 96 percent of the patients across the nation follow the advice of their personal physician.

★10. Janet Ryan can afford to pay no more than $15 for a birthday gift for her eight-year-old daughter. Since the average price of a toy at General Toy Company is $15, Janet can expect to find an excellent selection of toys within her price range at that store.

11. Anthony Valardi, who owns a fish market, pays $2 per pound to fishermen for coho salmon. A certain fisherman certifies that the average size of the salmon in his catch of the day is 10 pounds, and that the catch numbers 100 salmon. Mr. Valardi is therefore justified in paying the fisherman $2,000 for the whole catch.

12. Pamela intends to go shopping for a new pair of shoes. She wears size 8. Since the average size of the shoes carried by the Bon Marche is size 8, Pamela can expect to find an excellent selection of shoes in her size at that store.

★13. Tim Cassidy, who works for a construction company, is told to load a pile of rocks onto a truck. The rocks are randomly sized, and the average piece weighs 50 pounds. Thus, Tim should have no trouble loading the rocks by hand.

14. The average IQ (in the sense of mean, median, and mode) of the students in Dr. Jacob's symbolic logic class is 120. Thus, none of the students should have any trouble mastering the subject matter.

15. An insecticide manufacturer prints the following graph on the side of its spray cans:

Obviously, the insecticide is highly effective at killing bugs, and it keeps working for a long time.

★16. A corporation's sales for two consecutive years are represented in a bar graph. Since the bar for the later year is twice as high as the one for the previous year, it follows that sales for the later year were double those for the previous year.

17. Forced to make cutbacks, the president of a manufacturing firm reduced certain costs as follows: advertising by 4 percent, transportation by 5 percent, materials by 2 percent, and employee benefits by 3 percent. The president thus succeeded in reducing total costs by 14 percent.

18. During a certain year, a grocery store chain had total sales of $100 million and profits of $10 million. The profits thus amounted to a modest 10 percent for that year.

★19. There were 20 percent more traffic accidents in 2016 than there were in 1995. Therefore, it was 20 percent more dangerous to drive a car in 2016 than it was in 1995.

20. An efficiency expert was hired to increase the productivity of a manufacturing firm and was given three months to accomplish the task. At the end of the period the productivity had increased from 1,500 units per week to 1,700. Since the goal was 2,000 units per week, the effort of the efficiency expert was 85 percent successful (1,700/2,000).

21. A pharmaceutical company claims that its new cholesterol drug reduces the likelihood of a heart attack by 50 percent. In a clinical trial consisting of 400 people, four people in the group not taking the drug suffered a heart attack, while only two people in the group taking the drug had a heart attack. This is a 50 percent reduction in the number of heart attacks.

II. Compute the answers to the following questions:

★1. What figures should be written in the left-hand column of Table 12.1, in the text, to produce a similar table based on a confidence level of 99 percent? For a confidence level of 99 percent, the margin of error is approximately equal to $1.29/\sqrt{n}$.

2. Given the following group of people together with their weights, what is the average weight in the sense of mean, median, and mode?

Number of people	Weight
2	150
4	160
3	170
1	180
1	190
1	200
1	220
2	230

3. Given the following group of people together with their salaries, what is the average salary in the sense of mean, median, and mode?

Number of people	Salary
1	$95,000
2	85,000
1	70,000
3	40,000
1	30,000
2	20,000
5	15,000

★4. A day-care center cares for ten children. Their ages are 1, 1, 2, 2, 2, 3, 3, 4, 6, 6. Construct a histogram that represents the distribution of ages. What is the mean age? What is the variance and standard deviation of these ages?

5. A small company has five employees who missed work during a certain month. The number of days missed were 1, 1, 2, 4, 7. What is the mean number of days missed? What is the variance and standard deviation of this set of data?

6. An instructor gave a ten-question multiple-choice quiz to twelve students. The scores were 10, 10, 9, 9, 8, 8, 8, 7, 7, 7, 7, 6. What is the mean score? What is the variance and standard deviation of these scores?

III. Answer "true" or "false" to the following statements:

★1. If a sample is very large, it need not be randomly selected.

2. If a population is randomly arranged, a sample obtained by selecting every tenth member would be a random sample.

3. If a sample is randomly selected, the larger the sample is, the more closely it replicates the population.

★4. To ensure the same precision, a population of 1 million would require a much larger random sample than would a population of 100,000.

5. In general, if sample A is twice as large as sample B, then the sampling error for A is one-half that for B.

6. When a sample consists of human beings, the purpose for which the sample is taken can affect the outcome.

★7. The personal interaction between a surveyor and a respondent can affect the outcome of a survey.

8. The mean value of a set of data is the value that occurs with the greatest frequency.

9. The median value of a set of data is the middle point when the data are arranged in ascending order.

12

★10. The modal value of a set of data is the arithmetical average.

11. If one needed to know whether a sizable portion of a group were above or below a certain level, the most useful sense of average would be mode.

12. Data reflecting the results of a random sample conform fairly closely to the normal probability distribution.

★13. If a set of data conforms to the normal probability distribution, then the mean, median, and mode have the same value.

14. Range, variance, and standard deviation are measurements of dispersion.

15. Statements about averages often present an incomplete picture, lacking information about the dispersion.

★16. Data reflecting the size of full-grown horses would exhibit greater dispersion than would data reflecting the size of full-grown dogs.

17. The visual impression made by graphs can be exaggerated by changing one of the scales while leaving the other unchanged.

18. Data reflecting a 100 percent increase in housing construction could be accurately represented by a pictogram of two houses, one twice as high as the other.

★19. If a certain quantity is increased by 10 percent and later decreased by 10 percent, the quantity is restored to what it was originally.

20. Expressing profits as a percentage of sales volume presents an honest picture of the earnings of a corporation.

IV. Do some research and find a way that people or corporations cheat with statistics. Write a paragraph describing what you found.

MindTap Master concepts and improve outcomes with Aplia, at the end of the chapter, in the Aplia folder.

Summary

Statistical Reasoning:

- Includes any kind of argumentation based on statistical measurement.
- Such arguments can be misleading for several reasons:
  - Biased samples:
    - ▶ Not randomly selected
    - ▶ Too small (note sampling error)
    - ▶ Psychological factors

12

MindTap Need help? See the Learning Logic folder at the end of the chapter: the self-paced tutorial walks you through any section.

- Different meaning for "average":
  - ▸ Mean (the numerical average)
  - ▸ Median (the midpoint)
  - ▸ Mode (the value that occurs with the greatest frequency)
- Failure to take dispersion into account:
  - ▸ Range (difference between largest and smallest values)
  - ▸ Variance (how much every data point varies from the mean)
  - ▸ Standard deviation (square root of the variance)
- Illusory graphs:
  - ▸ Failure to scale the axes
  - ▸ Chopping off the bottom of the graph
  - ▸ Altering the scale of the axes
- Illusory pictograms:
  - ▸ Illusions related to spatial dimensions
- Improper percentages:
  - ▸ Failure to state the base of the percentage
  - ▸ Slight-of-hand tricks with the base
  - ▸ Numerical errors

12

13 Hypothetical/Scientific Reasoning

HOW LOGICAL ARE YOU? Suppose, for the past six months, you have been dating a person whose parents live in the same city as you and the person you have been dating. The parents typically host a large family feast on Thanksgiving. You are disappointed when Thanksgiving Day arrives and you have not been invited to join the family in the holiday celebration. You invent several hypotheses to explain why you weren't invited. What are they?

Find the answer on MindTap.

13.1   The Hypothetical Method

Hypothetical reasoning is most immediately applied to the production of explanations. You will recall from Chapter 1 of this book that an explanation is a kind of expression that purports to shed light on some event. Many explanations are grounded in our immediate experience or background knowledge. For example, if someone should ask you why the *Titanic* sank, you would answer that it sank because it hit an iceberg. Why did you fail the calculus test? Because I didn't study. Why did President Kennedy die so young? Because he was assassinated. Why are you so jittery? Because I just drank three cups of coffee. No hypotheses are needed to produce explanations of this sort.

However, it often happens that the needed explanation is not so forthcoming. Suppose you are faced with questions such as these: Why is the suicide rate for young men four times the rate for young women? Why has the incidence of autism exploded in the past twenty years? Why is the universe expanding more rapidly today than it was a million years ago? Why do animals sleep? No appeal to immediate experience or background knowledge will supply an answer. Clearly a different approach is needed.

MindTap Read, study, reflect, and prepare for exams online, anytime, anywhere.

For a simpler example, suppose you try to open a window but find that it will not budge. Since it is impossible to see what is jamming it, you make a conjecture. Perhaps the window has been painted shut from the outside. If that is the case, then running a knife along the edge of the window from the outside should free it up. You do this, and the window opens. In solving the stuck-window problem, the informed conjecture that you made is a **hypothesis**, and the reasoning process you used to produce it, draw an implication, and test the implication is called **hypothetical reasoning**.

Hypothetical reasoning is used by nearly all of us in our day-to-day experience. The auto mechanic constructs hypotheses to determine why a vibration occurs at certain speeds, the motorist on the freeway or turnpike reasons hypothetically to determine why the traffic is backed up bumper-to-bumper even though it is not yet rush hour, the physician hypothesizes about the cause of a disease prior to prescribing medicine, the teacher hypothesizes about the best way to present a complicated subject in the classroom, and the prosecuting attorney suggests hypotheses to the jury in arguing about the motive for a crime. In all of these cases the evidence is not sufficient to indicate exactly what is going on, what lies behind the scene, or what approach to take, so hypotheses are constructed to make sense of the situation and to direct future action.

Hypothetical reasoning is used most explicitly in philosophical and scientific inquiry. Every scientific theory can be viewed as a hypothesis for unifying and rationalizing events in nature. The Ptolemaic and Copernican theories about the sun and planets, Dalton's atomic theory, Darwin's theory of evolution, and Einstein's theory of relativity are all hypotheses for making sense of the data of observation. The problem for the scientist is that the underlying structure of nature is hidden from view, and the data of observation by themselves are not sufficient to reveal this structure. In response, the scientist constructs hypotheses that provide ways of conceptualizing the data and that suggest specific questions to be answered through the design of controlled experiments.

Analogously, every philosophical system can be viewed as a grand hypothesis for interpreting the content of experience. Plato's theory of forms, Aristotle's theory of substance, Leibniz's monads, and Kant's theory about the mind are all hypotheses aimed at illuminating various aspects of experience. Just as the structure of nature is hidden from the scientist, the meaning of experience is hidden from the philosopher, and ordinary common sense will not provide the answer. In response, the philosopher constructs hypotheses that can be used to shed light on the content of experience and to provide suggestions for further analysis.

Whether it is applied in philosophy, science, or ordinary life, the hypothetical method involves four basic stages:

1. Occurrence of a problem
2. Formulating a hypothesis
3. Drawing implications from the hypothesis
4. Testing the implications

These four stages may be illustrated through the procedure used by a detective in solving a crime. Suppose that a woman has been murdered in her apartment. Initially, everything in the apartment is a potential clue: the empty wine glasses in the sink, the small container of cocaine on the coffee table, the automobile key found on the carpet, the strand of blond hair removed from the couch, and so on. To introduce an element of rationality into the situation, the detective formulates a hypothesis—let us say the hypothesis that the key found on the carpet fits the murderer's car.

From this hypothesis several implications can be drawn. Suppose that the key is the kind that fits only late-model Cadillacs. It follows that the murderer drives a late-model Cadillac. Furthermore, if the key is the only one the murderer owns, it follows that the car may be parked nearby. A third implication is that the murderer's name may be on record at the local Cadillac dealership. To test these implications, the detective conducts a search of the streets in the vicinity and contacts the local Cadillac dealer for the names of recent buyers.

This example illustrates three additional points about hypotheses. The first is that a hypothesis is not *derived* from the evidence to which it pertains but rather is *added* to the evidence by the investigator. A hypothesis is a free, albeit educated, creation of the mind used to structure the evidence and unveil the pattern that lies beneath the surface. It may be that the detective's hypothesis is completely false. Perhaps the key fits a car that was lent to the victim for the weekend. A wide variety of other possibilities are conceivable.

The second point is that a hypothesis directs the search for evidence. Without a hypothesis for guidance, all facts are equally relevant. The mineral content of moon rocks and the temperature in the Sahara would be as relevant as the cars parked on the street outside the apartment. The hypothesis tells the investigator what to look for and what to ignore.

The third point concerns the proof of hypotheses. Let us suppose that the detective finds a late-model Cadillac parked outside the apartment building and that the key fits the ignition. Such a discovery might lend credibility to the hypothesis, but it would not in any sense prove it. Concluding that a hypothesis is proven true by the discovery that one of its implications is true amounts to committing the fallacy of affirming the consequent (see Section 6.6). Where H stands for a hypothesis and I for an implication, such an argument has the invalid form

> If H, then I
> I
> ————————
> H

Let us suppose, on the other hand, that the murderer turns himself or herself in to the police and that the only car the murderer owns or drives is a Ford. Such a fact would prove the hypothesis false because it would falsify the implication that the murderer drives a Cadillac. The argument form involved in such an inference is *modus tollens*:

> If H, then I
> not I
> ————————
> not H

For the hypothesis to be proved true, the car that the key fits would have to be found and the owner would have to confess to the crime.

As we have just shown, hypotheses and hypothetical reasoning play an important role in many of life's endeavors—from philosophy, to science, to the solution of ordinary day-to-day problems. An important final question is, *How does the hypothetical reasoning that occurs in science differ from these other modes of hypothetical reasoning?* One answer

13

relates to the kinds of tests that scientific hypotheses are subjected to. Scientific tests always involve the measurement of something, and the results of that measurement are nearly always expressed in the language of mathematics.

For example, physics and chemistry test hypotheses by measuring physical quantities such as mass, force, distance, time, motion, pressure, pH levels, heat, and so on. For this purpose, instruments are nearly always used—meter sticks, clocks, balance scales, microscopes, thermometers, and such. These instruments automatically yield a mathematical expression of the measurement—10 centimeters, 4 minutes, 20 grams. Many of these same kinds of measurements are also used in biology. For example, a biologist wanting to test the hypothesis that water temperature affects the color of fish would use a thermometer to measure the temperature of the water and a color spectrometer or color chart to measure the color of the fish.

Social scientists also use measurements to test hypotheses. Suppose a psychologist wanted to test the hypothesis that playing violent video games causes children to exhibit aggressive behaviors. The psychologist might first develop a scale to measure the violence levels of the games, and then construct a chart of aggressive behaviors to measure the aggression levels of the children. Similarly, a sociologist wanting to test the hypothesis that drug use on a college campus is correlated with date rape might begin by accumulating statistics for the phenomena in question, and then use statistical methods to prove the correlation. Collecting the initial statistics for such research amounts to a measurement of the degree to which the phenomenon occurs in the community.

These types of test procedures differ from the kind of test undertaken in the stuck-window example, where a knife was used to cut through dried paint. Most hypotheses formed in connection with ordinary life problems are like this one and do not require measurements as a test. But in science, the lack of precise measurements would undermine the credibility of most test procedures.

13.2 Hypothetical Reasoning: Four Examples from Science

Some of the clearest illustrations of the hypothetical method of reasoning can be found in scientific discoveries. Four examples are the discovery of radium by Pierre and Marie Curie; the discovery of the planet Neptune by Adams, Leverrier, and Galle; the discovery of atmospheric pressure by Torricelli; and Pasteur's research concerning the spontaneous generation of life. Following is a consideration of each of these examples with special attention to the four stages of hypothetical inquiry.

Radium

In 1896 the French physicist Henri Becquerel discovered that crystals containing uranium had the power to expose photographic plates. He found that when these crystals were placed on top of an unexposed plate and left for a certain time, dark blotches appeared in their place when the plate was developed. Becquerel concluded that the crystals emitted certain rays that penetrated the opaque covering of the plates and reacted with the photosensitive material underneath. Further investigation showed that these rays were not as strong as X-rays, which could be used to photograph bone structure, and so Becquerel's interest in them lapsed.

A year later Marie Curie revived the question when she adopted it as the topic of her doctoral research at the University of Paris. In place of Becquerel's photographic plates she substituted an electrometer, which was better suited to measuring the intensity of the rays, and she proceeded to conduct various experiments with pure uranium to determine the source of the rays that the metal emitted. When none of these experiments proved fruitful, she shifted her attention to the question of whether other metals or minerals emitted the same kind of rays as uranium. She tested hundreds of metals, compounds, and ores, but the only one that proved interesting was pitchblende, a certain ore of uranium. Because pitchblende contained uranium, she anticipated that it would emit rays; however, because it also contained a number of impurities, she expected the rays to be weaker than they were for pure uranium. Instead, they turned out to be stronger. This problem caught Madame Curie's attention and provided the focus for her research in the months ahead.

In response to the problem, Madame Curie formulated the hypothesis that the impurities in the pitchblende somehow triggered the uranium to increase the emission of rays. One implication of this hypothesis was that mixing pure uranium with the kinds of impurities found in pitchblende would cause an increase in the emission of rays. To test this implication, Curie diluted pure uranium with various elements and measured the strength of the rays. The results were always the same: The emissions were always less than they were for pure uranium. Because of these results, she abandoned the hypothesis.

Madame Curie then formulated a second hypothesis: The intensified emissions were caused directly by some impurity in the pitchblende. The only other element besides uranium that was known to emit rays, however, was thorium, and the pitchblende that had been tested contained no thorium. Thus, an immediate implication of the hypothesis was that the increased rays were caused by an unknown element. A second implication was that this element could be separated from the pitchblende through a process of refinement. At this point Marie Curie was joined by her husband, Pierre, and they began a combined effort to isolate the unknown element.

Because the element was present in only the most minute quantities, separating a measurable amount from the other impurities required a great deal of effort. The Curies began by grinding up some pitchblende and dissolving it in acid. Finally, after numerous stages of filtration and the addition of other chemicals, they obtained a pinch of white powder. By weight, this material was found to be 900 times more radioactive than pure uranium, but since the primary component in the powder was barium, the unknown element still had not been isolated.

Rather than continue with additional stages of refinement, the Curies decided to attempt a spectrographic analysis of the powder. Such analysis, they hoped, would reveal the characteristic spectrum line of the unknown element. This proposal, which amounted to a third implication of the hypothesis, was put to the test. When the powder was burned in a spectrometer, a line appeared in the ultraviolet range that was different from that for any other element. From the combined evidence of the spectrum line and the intense radiation, the Curies announced in 1898 the discovery of a new element, which they called radium. After more processing and refinement, enough of the material was finally obtained to determine its atomic weight.

Neptune

In 1781 William Herschel discovered the planet Uranus. However, the production of a table giving the motion of the new planet had to wait until the gravitational interactions between Uranus, Jupiter, and Saturn had been worked out mathematically. The latter task was accomplished by Pierre Laplace in his *Mechanique Celeste*, and in 1820 Alexis Bouvard used this work to construct tables for all three planets. These tables predicted the orbital motions of Jupiter and Saturn very accurately, but within a few years Uranus was found to have deviated from its predicted path. A problem thus emerged: Why did the tables work for Jupiter and Saturn but not for Uranus?

In response to this problem, several astronomers entertained the hypothesis that an eighth planet existed beyond the orbit of Uranus and that the gravitational interaction between these two planets caused Uranus to deviate from its predicted position. Not until 1843, however, did John Couch Adams, a recent graduate of Cambridge, undertake the task of working out the mathematical implications of this hypothesis. After two years' work Adams produced a table of motions and orbital elements that predicted the location of the hypothetical planet, and his computations were so accurate that if anyone with a telescope had bothered to look, they would have found the new planet within two degrees of its predicted position. Unfortunately, no one looked for it.

At about the same time that Adams completed his work on the problem, the French astronomer U. J. J. Leverrier, working independently of Adams, reported a similar set of motions and orbital elements to the French Academy of Science. The close agreement between Adams's and Leverrier's predictions prompted a search for the planet, but because a rather broad section of sky was swept, the planet was missed.

Finally, Leverrier sent a copy of his figures to Johann Galle at the Berlin Observatory, where a set of star charts was being prepared. It was suggested that the region corresponding to Leverrier's computations be observed and the results matched against the charts. This was done, and a small starlike object was found that was not on the charts. The next night the same object was sighted, and it was found to have moved. The new planet was thus identified. It was named Neptune after most astronomers outside France objected to the original suggestion that it be called Leverrier.

Atmospheric Pressure

Originated by Aristotle, the principle that nature abhors a vacuum was used for centuries to explain the fact that in emptying a keg of wine an opening had to be made at the top as well as at the bottom. Because nature would not allow a vacuum to be created inside the keg, the wine would not drain from the bottom until air was let in at the top. It was thought that this principle held universally for all applications involving a vacuum, but in the sixteenth century it was found that suction pumps used to drain water from mine shafts would not work if the pump was situated over 30 feet above the water level.

13

This caused people to wonder whether nature's abhorrence of a vacuum, while holding true for kegs of wine, had certain limits for pumps.

In 1630 Giovanni Baliani of Genoa discovered a similar limitation in regard to siphons. When he attempted to siphon water from a reservoir over a 60-foot hill, he found that the siphon would not work. When the siphon was completely filled with water and the stoppers were removed from both ends, a vacuum seemed to be created in the uppermost parts of the pipe.

These findings were communicated to Gasparo Berti in Rome, who, around 1641, attempted to determine more scientifically whether a vacuum could actually be created. Berti designed an apparatus consisting of a spherical glass vessel attached to a pipe about 40 feet long. The apparatus was affixed upright to the side of a tower and after the valve at the lower end of the pipe was closed, water was poured through the upper opening in the glass vessel. When both the pipe and the glass vessel were completely filled, the opening in the vessel was sealed and the valve at the lower end of the pipe was opened. Immediately water rushed from the bottom of the pipe, creating a vacuum in the glass vessel. This experiment crystallized a problem that had been developing for many years: If nature abhorred a vacuum, why did it tolerate the creation of one in the glass vessel? Furthermore, why did the water always descend to the same level in the pipe?

The results of Berti's experiment were communicated to Evangelista Torricelli in Florence, who was at that time Galileo's assistant. Galileo himself thought that the water was supported in the pipe by the power of the vacuum, but after Galileo's death in 1642, Torricelli formulated his own hypothesis: The water was supported in the pipe by the pressure of the atmosphere. Torricelli reasoned that we live "at the bottom of an ocean of air" and that the pressure of the air pushing against the bottom of the pipe supported the water at a certain height in the pipe. A point of equilibrium was reached, he thought, when the weight of the water remaining in the pipe equaled the weight of the air pushing down from above.

From this hypothesis Torricelli derived several implications. One was that the pressure of the atmosphere would support a column of mercury about 29 inches high in a tube sealed at the top. This followed from the fact that the atmosphere supports a column of water 33 feet high, that mercury is 13.6 times as dense as water, and that $33/13.6 \times 12$ inches $= 29$ inches. A second implication was that such a tube filled with mercury could be used to measure fluctuations in atmospheric pressure. This second implication won Torricelli credit for formulating the theory of the barometer. Finally, Torricelli reasoned that if such a device were conveyed to a place where the air was more rarefied, such as on a mountaintop, the column of mercury would descend.

The first of these implications was tested by Torricelli's associate, Vincenzo Viviani. Viviani obtained a 4-foot section of glass tube sealed at one end, enough mercury to completely fill it, and a dish to hold more mercury. After pouring the mercury into the tube Viviani placed his thumb over the open end, inverted the tube, and placed the open end in the dish of mercury. After he released his thumb he watched the column of mercury descend to about 29 inches above the level of mercury in the dish. Thus was created the first barometer. Its successful use in measuring atmospheric pressure came later.

13

The test of Torricelli's third implication was taken up in 1647 by the French philosopher Blaise Pascal. Having received word of Torricelli's experiments with the barometer, Pascal constructed one for himself. He readily became convinced of the correctness of Torricelli's hypothesis, and to demonstrate its correctness in opposition to the vacuum principle, he requested that his brother-in-law, F. Perier, transport a barometer to the top of the Puy de Dôme, one of the highest mountains in Auvergne. A year later Perier was able to fulfill this request. He began the experiment by setting up two barometers in the monastery at the foot of the mountain. After noting that both columns of mercury rose to an identical height, he disassembled one of the barometers and instructed one of the friars to check the mercury level in the other throughout the day. Then Perier, accompanied by a group of witnesses, set off up the mountain with the other barometer. On reaching the summit, he assembled the second barometer and discovered to the amazement of all that the mercury level was more than 3 inches lower than it had been at the foot of the mountain. As a double check the barometer was taken apart and reassembled at five different spots on the summit. Each time the results were the same.

At the midpoint of his descent Perier reassembled the barometer once again. He found that the mercury level was about midway between where it was at the bottom and at the top of the mountain. Finally, on returning to the monastery, the friar who had been watching the barometer there was questioned about what he had observed. He reported that the mercury level had not changed since early that morning when the group had departed. Pascal announced the results of this experiment to the educated world, and the announcement succeeded in abolishing the principle that nature abhors a vacuum.

Spontaneous Generation

The theory of spontaneous generation holds that living beings arise spontaneously from lifeless matter. The roots of the theory extend into ancient times. Aristotle held that worms, the larvae of bees and wasps, ticks, fireflies, and other insects developed continually from the morning dew and from dry wood and hair. He also held that crabs and various mollusks developed from moist soil and decaying slime. Extensions of this theory prevailed throughout the Middle Ages and well into modern times. In the seventeenth century it was widely held that frogs were produced from the slime of marshes and eels from river water, and the physician Van Helmont thought that mice were produced from the action of human sweat on kernels of wheat. All one needed to do, according to Van Helmont, was toss a dirty shirt into a container of wheat, and in 21 days the container would be teeming with mice. Even Descartes and Newton accepted the theory of spontaneous generation. Descartes held that various plants and insects originated in moist earth exposed to sunlight, and Newton thought that plants were produced from emanations from the tails of comets.

The first systematic effort to abolish the belief in spontaneous generation was made by the Italian physician Francesco Redi. In response to the commonly held idea that worms were spontaneously generated in rotting meat, Redi hypothesized that the worms were caused by flies. An immediate implication was that if flies were kept away from the meat, the worms would not develop. To test this hypothesis Redi cut up a piece

13

of meat and put part of it in sealed glass flasks and the other part in flasks open to the air. Flies were attracted to the open flasks, and in a short time worms appeared; but no worms developed in the flasks that were sealed.

When Redi published his findings in 1668, they immediately affected the theory of spontaneous generation. Within a few years, though, the microscope came into common use, and it was discovered that even though meat sealed in glass containers produced no worms, it did produce countless microorganisms. The theory of spontaneous generation was thus reawakened on the microbial level.

By the middle of the nineteenth century the theory had received considerable refinement. It was thought that spontaneous generation resulted from the direct action of oxygen on lifeless organic nutrients. Oxygen was thought to be essential to the process because the technique of canning fruits and vegetables had come into practice, and people knew that boiling fruits and vegetables and sealing them in the absence of oxygen would cause them to be preserved. If they were left exposed to the air, however, microbes would develop in a short time.

One of the defenders of spontaneous generation at that time was the Englishman John Needham, an amateur biologist. Needham conducted an experiment in which flagons containing oxygen and a vegetable solution were buried in hot coals. The coals would have been expected to kill any life in the solution, but several days later the contents of the flagons were alive with microbes. Needham concluded that the oxygen acting alone on the nutrient solution caused the generation of the microbes. In response to this experiment, Lazzaro Spallanzani, an Italian physiologist, conducted a similar experiment. To ensure that the nutrient solution was lifeless he boiled it for an hour. Later, no microbes could be found. To this Needham objected that in boiling the solution for a full hour Spallanzani had destroyed its "vegetative force." In addition, Needham argued, he had polluted the small amount of oxygen in the containers by the fumes and heat. Thus, it was no wonder that microbes were not spontaneously generated.

To settle the issue once and for all, the French Academy of Science offered a prize for an experimental endeavor that would shed light on the question of spontaneous generation. This challenge drew Louis Pasteur into the controversy. Spontaneous generation presented a special problem for Pasteur because of his previous work with fermentation. He had discovered that fermentations, such as those involved in the production of wine and beer, required yeast; and yeast, as he also discovered, was a living organism. In view of these findings Pasteur adopted the hypothesis that life comes only from life. An immediate implication was that for life forms to develop in a sterile nutrient solution, they must first be introduced into the solution from the outside.

It was well known that life forms did indeed develop in sterile nutrient solutions exposed to the air. To account for this Pasteur adopted the second hypothesis that life forms are carried by dust particles in the air. To test this second hypothesis Pasteur took a wad of cotton and drew air through it, trapping dust particles in the fibers. Then he washed the cotton in a mixture of alcohol and examined drops of the fluid under a microscope. He discovered microbes in the fluid.

Returning to his first hypothesis, Pasteur prepared a nutrient solution and boiled it in a narrow-necked flask. As the solution boiled, the air in the neck of the flask was forced

13

out by water vapor, and as it cooled the water vapor was slowly replaced by sterilized air drawn through a heated platinum tube. The neck of the flask was then closed off with a flame and blowpipe. The contents of the flask thus consisted of a sterilized nutrient solution and unpolluted sterilized air—all that was supposedly needed for the production of life. Over time, however, no life developed in the flask. This experiment posed a serious threat to the theory of spontaneous generation.

Pasteur now posed the hypothesis that sterile nutrient solutions exposed to the air normally developed life forms precisely because these forms were deposited by dust particles. To test this third hypothesis Pasteur reopened the flask containing the nutrient solution, and, using a special arrangement of tubes that ensured that only sterilized air would contact the solution, he deposited a piece of cotton in which dust particles had been trapped. The flask was then resealed, and in due course microbes developed in the solution. This experiment proved not only that dust particles were responsible for the life but that the "vegetative force" of the nutrient solution had not been destroyed by boiling, as Needham was prone to claim.

Pasteur anticipated one further objection from the proponents of spontaneous generation: Perhaps the capacity of oxygen to generate life was destroyed by drawing it through a heated tube. To dispel any such notions Pasteur devised yet another experiment. He boiled a nutrient solution in a flask with a long, narrow gooseneck. As the solution boiled, the air was forced out, and as it cooled, the air returned very slowly through the long neck, trapping the dust particles on the moist inside surface. No microbes developed in the solution. Then, after a prolonged wait, Pasteur sealed the flask and shook it vigorously, dislodging the particles that had settled in the neck. In a short time the solution was alive with microbes.

When Pasteur reported these experiments to the Academy of Science in 1860, he was awarded the prize that had been offered a year earlier. The experiments dealt a mortal blow to the theory of spontaneous generation, and although the theory was not abandoned immediately, by 1900 it had very little support.

13.3 The Proof of Hypotheses

The four instances of hypothetical reasoning in science that we have investigated illustrate the use of two different kinds of hypotheses. The hypotheses involved in the discovery of Neptune and radium are sometimes called empirical hypotheses, and those relating to atmospheric pressure and spontaneous generation are sometimes called theoretical hypotheses. **Empirical hypotheses** concern the production of some thing or the occurrence of some event that can be observed. When radium had finally been obtained as a pure metal it was something that could be seen directly, and when Neptune was finally sighted through the telescope, it, too, had been observed. **Theoretical hypotheses**, on the other hand, concern how something should be conceptualized. When Galileo observed the water level rising in a suction pump, he conceived it as being *sucked* up by the vacuum. When Torricelli observed it, however, he conceived it as being *pushed* up by the atmosphere. Similarly, when Needham observed life emerging in a sterile nutrient solution, he conceived it as being spontaneously generated by the action of oxygen. But when Pasteur observed it, he conceived it as being implanted there by dust particles in the air.

The distinction between empirical and theoretical hypotheses has certain difficulties, which we will turn to shortly, but it sheds some light on the problem of the verification or confirmation of hypotheses. Empirical hypotheses are for all practical purposes *proved* when the thing or event hypothesized is observed. Today practically all of us would agree that the hypotheses relating to radium and Neptune have been established. Theoretical hypotheses, on the other hand, are never proved but are only *confirmed* to varying degrees. The greater the number of implications that are found to be correct, the more certain we can be of the hypothesis. If an implication is found to be incorrect, however, a theoretical hypothesis can be *disproved*. For example, if it should happen some day that life is produced in a test tube from inorganic materials, Pasteur's hypothesis that life comes only from life might be considered to be disproved.

The problem with the distinction between empirical and theoretical hypotheses is that observation is theory-dependent. Consider, for example, a man and a woman watching a sunrise. The man happens to believe that the sun travels around the earth, as Ptolemy held, and the woman that the earth travels around the sun, as Copernicus and Galileo contended. As the sun rises, the man thinks that he sees the sun moving upward, while the woman thinks she sees the earth turning. The point is that all of us have a tendency to see what we think is out there to be seen. As a result, it is sometimes difficult to say when something has or has not been observed.

In regard to the discovery of Neptune, the unknown planet was observed two times in 1795 by J. J. Lalande, fifty-one years before it was "discovered" by Adams, Leverrier, and Galle. Lalande noted that his observations of the position of the small starlike object were discordant, so he rejected one as erroneous. Because he thought he was observing a *star*, he received no credit for discovering a *planet*. Analogous remarks extend to Galle's observations of the *planet* Neptune in 1846. If Leverrier's computations had been erroneous, Galle might have seen what was really a comet. Thus, if we can never be sure that we really see what we think we see, is it ever possible for a hypothesis to be actually proved? Perhaps it is better to interpret the proof of empirical hypotheses as a high degree of confirmation.

Conversely, with theoretical hypotheses, would we want to say that Torricelli's hypothesis relating to atmospheric pressure has *not* been proved? Granted, we cannot observe atmospheric pressure directly, but might we not say that we observe it *instrumentally*? If barometers can be regarded as extensions of our sense organs, Torricelli's hypothesis has been proved. Another example is provided by Copernicus's hypothesis that the earth and planets move around the sun, instead of the sun and planets around the earth, as Ptolemy hypothesized. Can we consider this theoretical hypothesis to be proved? If a motion picture camera were sent outside the solar system and pictures were taken supporting the Copernican hypothesis, would we say that these pictures constituted proof? We probably would. Thus, while the distinction between theoretical and empirical hypotheses is useful, it is more a distinction in degree than in kind.

13

Charles Sanders Peirce 1839–1914

Charles Sanders Peirce (pronounced "purse") was born in Cambridge, Massachusetts. His father, Benjamin, was the leading mathematician of the day, and he took a special interest in his son's intellectual development. Under his direction Charles was reading college-level material, including logic, at age twelve, and Benjamin would challenge the boy with highly complex problems that Charles would solve on his own. Although his most significant education came from his father, Charles went on to attend Harvard University, where he received a BS in chemistry in 1863. Yet, he was not a successful student (he usually placed in the lower quarter of his class), partly because he showed disdain for his professors as inadequately qualified to teach him. This arrogance is likely the main reason Peirce lived a difficult life. He died in poverty at age seventy-four in the then-isolated town of Milford, Pennsylvania.

Throughout his life Peirce suffered a painful and debilitating neurological condition that may have been responsible for his detached, depressed, and sometimes violent behavior. It may also have been the reason he could not obtain a tenured university position. In 1879 he did secure a position as a lecturer at Johns Hopkins University, and in some ways, he proved himself a remarkable teacher—a collection of his students' essays is considered a key work in the development of logic. Yet, despite his teaching, Peirce was discharged from his faculty position. He had recently separated from his wife and had lived with another woman before his divorce was finalized. This "immoral" behavior and other supposed transgressions were probably the chief factors leading to his dismissal. After that he never held another academic position.

Without an academic base, Peirce continued to write copiously, producing some 80,000 pages of material; yet he did not complete a single book in logic or philosophy, which limited his influence while alive.

NOAA's People Collection

Beginning in the late 1930s, his writings were collected and published, bringing him the attention he missed during his lifetime. As the founder of pragmatism, America's only unique philosophy, Peirce is now considered to be America's greatest philosopher and probably its greatest logician as well. Peirce's own version of pragmatism took the form of a thoroughly scientific enterprise according to which the meaning of a concept depends on the practical effect it has on how we lead our lives and conduct our inquiries.

In logic Peirce is best known for his work in the logic of relations and quantification theory. The theory of quantification that Peirce developed is the one that led ultimately to the writing of *Principia Mathematica* by Whitehead and Russell, and it closely resembles the system used today in most logic courses. In the logic of relations, Peirce extended the work done by De Morgan by applying the concepts of Boolean algebra to relative terms such as "friend of" or "enemy of." This work has also significantly impacted the way we treat this subject today. In addition, Peirce was a leader in exploring the use of truth values, and he was the first to develop a three-valued logic incorporating true, false, and an intermediate or unknown value. In propositional logic Peirce succeeded in reducing all the connectives to one, and in inductive logic he rejected the subjectivist theory of probability in favor of an objectivist theory based on observed regularities.

The Tentative Acceptance of Hypotheses

A certain amount of time is required for a hypothesis to be proved or disproved. The hypotheses relating to the discovery of radium and Neptune required more than a year to prove. Theoretical hypotheses in science often take much longer, and theoretical hypotheses in philosophy may never be confirmed to the satisfaction of the majority of philosophers. During the period that intervenes between the proposal of a hypothesis and its proof, confirmation, or disproof, the question arises as to its tentative acceptability. Four criteria that bear on this question are (1) adequacy, (2) internal coherence, (3) external consistency, and (4) fruitfulness.

Adequacy is the extent to which a hypothesis fits the facts it is intended to unify or explain. A hypothesis is said to "fit" the facts when each fact can be interpreted as an instance of some idea or term in the hypothesis. For example, before the Neptune hypothesis was confirmed, every fluctuation in the position of Uranus could be interpreted as an instance of gravitational interaction with an unknown planet. Similarly, before Torricelli's hypothesis was confirmed, the fact that water would rise only 30 feet in suction pumps and siphons could be interpreted as an instance of equilibrium between the pressure of the water and the pressure of the atmosphere.

A hypothesis is inadequate to the extent that facts exist that the hypothesis cannot account for. The principle that nature abhors a vacuum was inadequate to explain the fact that water would rise no more than 30 feet in suction pumps and siphons. Nothing in the hypothesis could account for this fact. Similarly, Needham's hypothesis that life is generated by the direct action of oxygen on nutrient solutions was inadequate to account for the fact that life would not develop in Pasteur's flask containing a sterilized nutrient solution and sterilized oxygen.

In scientific hypotheses a second kind of adequacy is the *accuracy* with which a hypothesis accounts for the data. If one hypothesis accounts for a set of data with greater accuracy than another, then that hypothesis is more adequate than the other. For example, Kepler's hypothesis that the orbits of the planets were ellipses rather than circles, as Copernicus had hypothesized, accounted for the position of the planets with greater accuracy than the Copernican hypothesis. Similarly, Einstein's theory of relativity accounted for the precise time of certain eclipses with greater accuracy than Newton's theory did. For these reasons Kepler's and Einstein's theories were more adequate than the competing theories.

Internal coherence is the extent to which the component ideas of a hypothesis are rationally interconnected. The purpose of a hypothesis is to unify and interconnect a set of data and by so doing to *explain* the data. Obviously, if the hypothesis itself is not internally connected, there is no way that it can interconnect the data. After Adams and Leverrier had worked out the mathematical details of the Neptune hypothesis, it exhibited a great deal of internal coherence. The hypothesis showed how all the fluctuations in the position of Uranus could be rationally linked in terms of the gravitational interaction of an eighth planet. Similarly, Torricelli's hypothesis showed how the various fluid levels could be rationally interconnected in terms of the equilibrium of pressures.

13

Internal coherence is responsible for the features of elegance and simplicity that often attract scientists to a hypothesis.

An example of incoherence in science is provided by the theoretical interpretation of light, electricity, and magnetism that prevailed during the first half of the nineteenth century. During that period each of these phenomena was understood separately, but the interconnections between them were unknown. Toward the end of the century the English physicist James Clerk Maxwell showed how these three phenomena were interconnected in terms of his theory of the electromagnetic field. Maxwell's theory was thus more coherent than the ones that preceded it.

Similarly, in philosophy, Spinoza's metaphysical theory is more internally coherent than Descartes's. Descartes postulated the existence of two kinds of substance to account for the data of experience. He introduced extended, material substance to explain the data of the visible world, and nonextended, immaterial substance to explain the phenomena of the invisible world, including the existence and activity of the human soul. But Descartes failed to show how the two kinds of substance were interconnected. In the wake of this disconnection the famous mind–body problem arose, according to which no account could be given of how the human body acted on the mind through the process of sensation or how the mind acted on the body through the exercise of free choice. Spinoza, on the other hand, postulated only one substance to account for everything. Spinoza's theory is thus more internally coherent than Descartes's.

External consistency occurs when a hypothesis does not disagree with other, well-confirmed hypotheses. Adams's and Leverrier's hypothesis of an eighth planet was perfectly consistent with the nineteenth-century theory of the solar system, and it was rendered even more attractive by the fact that the seventh planet, Uranus, had been discovered only a few years earlier. Similarly, Marie Curie's hypothesis of the existence of a new element was consistent with Mendeleev's periodic table and with the general hypothesis that elements could emit penetrating rays. In 1890 Mendeleev's table had certain gaps that were expected to be filled in by the discovery of new elements, and two ray-emitting elements, thorium and uranium, had already been discovered.

The fact that a hypothesis is inconsistent with other, well-confirmed hypotheses does not, however, immediately condemn it to obscurity. It often happens that a new hypothesis arises in the face of another, well-confirmed hypothesis and that the two hypotheses compete for acceptance in the future. Which hypothesis will win is determined by an appeal to the other three criteria. For example, Torricelli's hypothesis was inconsistent with the ancient hypothesis that nature abhors a vacuum, and Pasteur's hypothesis was inconsistent with the equally ancient hypothesis of spontaneous generation. In the end, the newer hypotheses won out because they were more adequate, coherent, or fruitful than their competitors. For the same reason, the Copernican hypothesis eventually triumphed over the Ptolemaic, the theory of oxidation won out over the old phlogiston theory, and Einstein's theory of relativity won out over Newton's theory.

Fruitfulness is the extent to which a hypothesis suggests new ideas for future analysis and confirmation. Torricelli's hypothesis suggested the design of an instrument for measuring fluctuations in the pressure of the atmosphere. Similarly, Pasteur's hypothesis suggested changes in the procedures used to maintain sterile conditions in hospitals. After these latter changes were implemented, the death rate from surgical

13

operations decreased dramatically. The procedure of pasteurization, used to preserve milk, was another outgrowth of the hypothesis that life comes only from life.

Newton's theory of universal gravitation is an example of a hypothesis that proved especially fruitful. It was originated to solve the problem of falling bodies, but it also explained such things as the ebb and flow of the tides, the orbital motion of the moon and planets, and the fluctuations in planetary motion caused by a planet's interaction with other planets. Einstein's theory of relativity is another example. It was originated to account for certain features of Maxwell's theory of electricity and magnetism, but it ushered in the atomic age forty years later.

The factors of coherence and fruitfulness together account for the overall rationality and explanatory power of a hypothesis. Suppose, for example, that someone formulated the hypothesis that the water level in suction devices is maintained by the action of demons instead of by atmospheric pressure. Such a hypothesis would be neither coherent nor fruitful. It would not be coherent because it would not explain why the maximum water level in these devices is consistently about 30 feet, why the mercury level in barometers is much less, and why the mercury level in a barometer decreases when the instrument is carried to the top of a mountain. Do the demons decide to maintain these levels by free choice or according to some plan? Because there is no answer to this question, the hypothesis exhibits internal disconnectedness, which leaves it open to the charge of being irrational. As for the fourth criterion, the demon hypothesis is unfruitful because it suggests no new ideas that experimenters can put to the test. The hypothesis that nature abhors a vacuum is hardly any more fruitful, which accounts in part for why it was so suddenly abandoned in favor of Torricelli's hypothesis—it simply did not lead anywhere.

In summary, for any hypothesis to receive tentative acceptance it must cover the facts it is intended to interpret and it must rationally interconnect these facts—in other words, it must be adequate and coherent. After that, it helps if the hypothesis does not conflict with other, well-confirmed hypotheses. Finally, it is important that a hypothesis capture the imagination of the community to which it is posed. This it does by being fruitful—by suggesting interesting ideas and experiments to which members of the community can direct their attention in the years ahead.

EXERCISE 13

I. For each of the following situations, invent at least three hypotheses aimed at explaining what went wrong or at solving the problem. Then, for each hypothesis, describe one or more experiments or inquiries that would confirm or disconfirm the hypothesis.

1. Someone you have been dating has a birthday coming up, so you call a florist and order flowers for the occasion. Two days later the person is cold and distant.

MindTap Complete exercises online for immediate feedback.

13

2. After settling in a new location you buy some seeds for a flower garden. When the flowers come up, they are stunted and of poor quality.

3. After mailing your paycheck to the bank, you write a check to pay your rent. The rent check bounces.

4. On a windy day you pick up the phone to call a friend, but you find that the line is dead. You live in a house and share phone expenses with a housemate.

5. After driving for miles on a dusty road, you park your car near the bank of a river and take a hike through the woods. Soon you become lost. In one direction you see a small stream, and in the other, a trail.

6. A close friend calls you on the phone and confides a personal secret. That night you write the secret in your diary. A few days later your friend is furious with you because the friend overheard someone on campus talking about the secret.

7. On a rainy evening you return to your ground-floor apartment and discover that you have been burglarized. You can't believe it, because you are certain you locked the door when you went out. You share the apartment with a roommate.

8. You are a philosophy professor at a university, and while reading a set of term papers you discover that two of them are identical. Those two papers are also extremely well written.

9. You are a manager of a department store, and, although business has been brisk lately, your chief accountant informs you that the store is losing money.

10. A short time before final exams you lose your class notes. You recall having seen them four days ago. Use your own personal activities and movements during the past four days as the basis for formulating your hypotheses as to the whereabouts of the notes.

II. For the four scientific discoveries presented in this chapter, identify the problem, the hypotheses that were formulated, the implications that were drawn, and the test procedure that was used. Include an account of measurements that were taken and possible instruments that were used.

III. Write a short paper (3–5 pages) on one of the following scientific events. Discuss the problem, one or more hypotheses that were formulated, the implications that were drawn, and the test procedures that were used. Then evaluate the hypothesis in terms of adequacy, internal coherence, external consistency, and fruitfulness.

1. Isaac Newton: corpuscular theory of light

2. Christian Huygens: wave theory of light

3. Johannes Kepler: orbit of Mars

4. Nicolaus Copernicus: theory of the solar system

5. Count von Rumford: theory of heat

6. Charles Darwin: theory of natural selection

7. John Dalton: theory of atoms

8. William Harvey: circulation of the blood

9. Louis Pasteur: theory of vaccination

10. J. J. Thomson: discovery of the electron

11. André Marie Ampère: discovery of the electromagnet

12. Niels Bohr: structure of the atom

13. Alexander Fleming: discovery of penicillin

14. Henri Becquerel: radioactivity of uranium

15. Dmitri Mendeleev and Clemens Winkler: discovery of germanium

16. Amedeo Avogadro: Avogadro's law

17. Johann Balmer: theory of the spectrograph

18. Alfred Wegener: theory of continental drift

19. James Watson and Francis Crick: structure of the DNA molecule

20. John Bardeen: theory of superconductivity

21. Albert Einstein: theory of Brownian motion

22. Edwin Hubble: recession of the galaxies

23. Jean Baptiste Lamarck: inheritance of acquired characteristics

IV. Write a short paper (2–3 pages) analyzing one or more of the hypotheses formulated by Sherlock Holmes in one of the stories by Arthur Conan Doyle. Include a discussion of the problem, the hypothesis, the implications that were drawn, and the test procedures.

V. Answer "true" or "false" to the following statements:

★1. Hypothetical reasoning is useful when the evidence by itself does not provide the solution to the problem.

2. Hypotheses are derived directly from the evidence.

3. Hypotheses serve the purpose of directing the search for additional evidence.

★4. If the implications of a hypothesis are true, then we may conclude that the hypothesis is true.

5. If an implication of a hypothesis is false, then we may conclude that the hypothesis is false, at least in part.

6. In the episode pertaining to the discovery of radium, all of the hypotheses turned out to be true.

★7. In the Neptune episode, Adams and Leverrier deserve the credit for working out the implications of the hypothesis.

13

8. Torricelli's hypothesis was consistent with the hypothesis that nature abhors a vacuum.

9. In Pasteur's day, the theory of spontaneous generation held that life was produced by the direct action of oxygen on organic nutrients.

★10. The hypotheses relating to the discoveries of radium and Neptune may be classified as empirical hypotheses.

11. Torricelli's and Pasteur's hypotheses may be classified as theoretical hypotheses.

12. Theoretical hypotheses concern how something should be conceptualized.

★13. The problem with the distinction between empirical and theoretical hypotheses is that observation is dependent on theory.

14. The adequacy of a hypothesis has to do with how well the ideas or terms in the hypothesis are rationally interconnected.

15. The coherence of a hypothesis has to do with how well the hypothesis fits the facts.

★16. If a hypothesis is not externally consistent, then it must be discarded.

17. A hypothesis is fruitful to the extent that it suggests new ideas for future analysis and confirmation.

18. If a theory is incoherent, it is deficient in rationality.

★19. The theoretical interpretations of light, electricity, and magnetism during the first part of the nineteenth century illustrate a condition of inadequacy.

20. If a hypothesis gives rise to contradictory implications, it is incoherent.

MindTap® Master concepts and improve outcomes with Aplia, at the end of the chapter, in the Aplia folder.

Summary

Hypothetical Reasoning:
- Used to solve a problem when the solution is not readily apparent.
- Involves four basic stages:
  - Occurrence of a problem
  - Formulating a hypothesis
  - Drawing implications from the hypothesis
  - Testing the implications
- Four examples taken from science:
  - Discovery of radium by Marie Curie
  - Discovery of Neptune by Adams and Leverrier

MindTap® Need help? See the Learning Logic folder at the end of the chapter: the self-paced tutorial walks you through any section.

- Discovery of atmospheric pressure by Torricelli
- Refutation of spontaneous generation by Louis Pasteur
- Kinds of hypotheses:
  - Empirical:
    - Can be proved true or false.
  - Theoretical:
    - Can only be confirmed in varying degrees.
- Criteria that bear on the tentative acceptance of hypotheses:
  - Adequacy (Does the hypothesis fits the facts?)
  - Internal coherence (Are the component ideas interconnected?)
  - External consistency (Are there conflicts with other hypotheses?)
  - Fruitfulness (Are new ideas suggested for future analysis?)

13

14 Science and Superstition

HOW LOGICAL ARE YOU? Suppose a friend posts a chain letter on your social-media website. The letter promises good luck over the coming year if you forward the letter to ten of your friends, but very bad luck if you don't. You decide not to forward and, soon after, your car's engine burns up, your best friend emails you a hate letter, your boss fires you, and you fail an important exam. Do these calamities prove that you should have forwarded the letter?

Find the answer on MindTap.

14.1 Distinguishing Between Science and Superstition

The idea that the human mind is capable of operating on different levels in its effort to comprehend reality is as old as philosophy itself. Twenty-four centuries ago Plato drew a distinction between what he called opinion and knowledge. Opinion, he said, is a kind of awareness that is uncertain, confined to the particular, inexact, and subject to change, whereas knowledge is certain, universal, exact, and eternally true. Every human being starts out in life by operating on the level of opinion, and only through great struggle and effort can he or she escape it and rise to the level of knowledge. This struggle is called education, and it opens the eye of the mind to realities that cannot even be imagined from the standpoint of opinion.

Today's distinction between science and superstition is a modern equivalent of Plato's distinction between knowledge and opinion. Everyone recognizes that science has revealed wonderful truths about the world of nature. It has put men on the moon,

MindTap Read, study, reflect, and prepare for exams online, anytime, anywhere.

wiped out life-threatening diseases, and ushered in the computer age. Also, almost everyone recognizes that superstition is little better than foolishness. It leads people to fear walking under ladders, breaking mirrors, and spilling salt. Practically everyone agrees that if some claim is grounded in science, then it is probably worthy of belief, while if it is grounded in superstition, then it should probably be ignored. Where people do not agree, however, is in what constitutes science and what constitutes superstition. What one person calls science another calls superstitious nonsense.

Both science and superstition involve hypotheses, so the four criteria developed in Chapter 13 for evaluating hypotheses are relevant to the distinction between science and superstition: adequacy, internal coherence, external consistency, and fruitfulness. But the distinction between science and superstition also involves psychological and volitional elements. It involves such factors as how the observer's subjective states influence how he sees the world, and how his needs and desires play a role in the formation of his beliefs. Accordingly, to explore the distinction between science and superstition, we must introduce criteria that include these psychological and volitional elements. The criteria suggested here are evidentiary support, objectivity, and integrity. The following account of evidentiary support encompasses adequacy and fruitfulness, and the account of integrity encompasses adequacy, internal coherence, and external consistency.

Science and superstition are, in large measure, polar opposites. Where scientific activity recognizes the importance of evidentiary support, objectivity, and integrity, superstition ignores them. Accordingly, these criteria can be used as a kind of measuring stick for sizing up the various beliefs people have about the world. To the extent that those beliefs are supported by evidence, are objective, and arise from research that reflects integrity, the closer they come to the ideal of science, and the more justified they are. Conversely, to the extent that our beliefs do not share in these characteristics, the closer they come to the "ideal" of superstition, and the less justified they are.

Note, however, that to say a belief is justified is not to say it is true in any absolute sense. As we saw in Chapter 13, all beliefs that arise from science are tentative at best. But such beliefs are the best ones we can have for now. Also, to say that a belief is not justified is not to say it is absolutely false. It is quite possible that a belief grounded in superstition today could tomorrow be grounded in science. But such a belief is not worthy of assent today. An analogy can be found in rolling dice. No sensible person would bet even money that a pair of dice will come up "snake eyes" on the next roll, even though he realizes that tomorrow it might be discovered that the dice were loaded in favor of this outcome.

14.2 Evidentiary Support

In Chapter 13 we saw that hypotheses are conjectures—informed conjectures—but still conjectures. Before they can be believed by reasonable people they must be supported by evidence. We also saw that scientific evidence nearly always involves the measurement of something such as force, mass, levels of aggression, social affluence, and so on, and the result is expressed in the language of mathematics. Such measurement is nearly always accomplished through some kind of instrumentation. This requirement that scientific evidence includes measurements expressed mathematically is useful in distinguishing science from superstition.

For example, in the sixteenth century Copernicus formulated the hypothesis that the sun is the center of our planetary system and that the earth revolves around the sun—in opposition to the prevailing Ptolemaic hypothesis, which put the earth at the center. In the years that followed, the telescope was invented, and thousands of precise measurements confirmed the Copernican hypothesis and disconfirmed the Ptolemaic hypothesis. Without these measurements, the Copernican hypothesis would never have been adopted.

In contrast, consider the superstition that breaking a mirror will bring bad luck. No evidence has ever been collected in support of this hypothesis. No tests have been conducted and no experiments performed. Possibly on one occasion or other someone did break a mirror and later lost money on the stock exchange or was injured in a car accident, but surely it would be unreasonable to believe that breaking a mirror caused the loss or the accident. Such reasoning constitutes a classic case of the *post hoc ergo propter hoc* (false cause) fallacy. But in spite of the lack of evidence, many people believe the mirror hypothesis.

Before inquiring further into the need for evidence, however, we must first investigate what counts as evidence. Do books count as evidence? What about religious books such as the Torah, the Bhagavad Gita, the sutras of Buddhism, the Bible, and the Koran? If books

Do books count as evidence?

are credible reports of measurements expressed mathematically, then they can be accepted as the conveyance of evidence. But because religious books report no such measurements, they count neither as evidence nor as the conveyance of evidence for scientific purposes. This does not imply, of course, that the content of such books automatically falls under the rubric of superstition. It simply means that it cannot be used as a source for confirming or disconfirming scientific hypotheses.

Another kind of evidence that is considered unreliable is anecdotal evidence. Suppose that you have cancer and a friend advises you that eating garlic can cure it. You decide to take this advice, and after eating a clove of garlic every day for a year, the cancer goes into remission. Did the garlic cure the cancer? Evidence of this sort is called anecdotal, and science usually rejects it. The trouble with anecdotal evidence is that it is too isolated to establish any causal connection. Thus, the garlic evidence ignores the thousands of people with cancer who have eaten garlic and have not been cured, and it ignores the thousands of people who have experienced spontaneous remission of cancer and have not eaten any garlic. Also, there is no way to turn the clock back and try the experiment again.

One of the key features of scientific evidence gathering is that an experiment be replicable under controlled conditions. This means that the experiment must be repeatable by different scientists at different times and places. Replicability helps ensure that

Scientific experiments must be replicable.

the outcome of the experiment did not result from anything peculiar to one certain experimenter operating at a single place and time. Also, the controlled conditions are designed to eliminate the influence of extraneous factors. Perhaps, in reference to the garlic example, the cure was effected not by the garlic but by something else that was eaten, or by any one of a thousand other factors that occurred during this time, or by any combination of these factors.

The evidence offered in support of superstitious hypotheses is rarely replicable, and when it is, the outcome almost always fails to support the hypothesis. For example, the belief in ghosts is usually supported by what one or more individuals claim to have seen on some unique occasion. This occasion can never be repeated. And the belief in psychic phenomena such as extrasensory perception is sometimes claimed to be supported by experiments involving Zener cards: cards imprinted with crosses, circles, wavy lines, stars, and squares whose image an observer might "transmit" to a psychic receiver. But when these experiments have been repeated under carefully controlled conditions, the outcome has never been other than what would have been expected to occur through mere chance.

Another defect found in superstitious hypotheses is that they are often framed so vaguely that it is virtually impossible to provide any kind of unequivocal confirmation. For example, according to *feng shui* (pronounced "fung-shway"), an ancient Chinese system of magic, bad luck travels in straight lines, whereas good luck does not. As a result, one invites bad luck by living in a house or apartment that has two (or, what is worse, three) doors lined up in a row. But what, exactly, is the meaning of bad luck? What is interpreted as bad luck today may turn out to be good luck tomorrow. If a person loses $1,000 in the stock market today, that may lead her to be more cautious in the future, and that increased caution may save $10,000 later on.

In contrast, the hypotheses of science are often framed in the language of mathematics, or they can at least be translated into some mathematical expression. This fact provides for extremely accurate confirmations and is largely responsible for the extraordinary success science has enjoyed during the past 500 years. For example, in 1802 the French chemist Joseph Louis Gay-Lussac formulated the hypothesis that if the temperature is raised 1 degree Celsius in a closed container of gas—any gas—the pressure of the gas will increase by 0.3663 percent. The hypothesis has been tested thousands of times by chemists and students in chemistry labs, and it has been found to be correct.

Scientific hypotheses are phrased precisely.

Closely related to the problem of vagueness is the breadth with which a hypothesis is framed. If a hypothesis is framed so broadly and comprehensively that even contradictory evidence serves to confirm it, then the hypothesis is not really confirmed by anything. Suppose, for example, that a health-care practitioner should invent a hypothesis involving diet: Practicing this diet is guaranteed to make you feel great, but before it has this effect it may make you feel either rotten or the same as usual. After following this diet for six months you report that you feel the same as before. The practitioner replies that your experience confirms the hypothesis, because this is what the diet is supposed to do. On the other hand, suppose that after six months you feel great, or perhaps rotten. Again the practitioner will report that your experience confirms the hypothesis. Hypotheses of this sort are not genuinely scientific.

In 1919 the philosopher Karl Popper discovered this very problem concerning hypotheses. In response, he argued that any genuinely scientific hypothesis must be framed narrowly enough so that it forbids certain things from happening. In other words, the hypothesis must be falsifiable. In the years following its announcement, many philosophers criticized Popper's falsifiability criterion because, strictly speaking, hypotheses are rarely susceptible of being disproved. But, as we saw in Chapter 13, hypotheses can be disconfirmed (or rendered less plausible). Thus, we can retain Popper's basic insight by requiring that any genuinely scientific hypothesis be disconfirmable. This means that the hypothesis must be framed narrowly enough so that it is possible for evidence to count against it. Newton's gravitational hypothesis, for example, satisfies this criterion because the discovery of two large bodies that failed to attract each other would tend to disconfirm the hypothesis. But the dietary hypothesis just mentioned fails the disconfirmability criterion because no outcome could ever count against it.

A problem closely associated with excessively broad hypotheses arises in connection with what are called *ad hoc* modifications of hypotheses. For an example, suppose that you are a sociologist conducting research into alcoholism. You formulate a hypothesis that alcoholism is caused by cultural factors that present alcohol consumption in a favorable light. When you gather evidence to support this hypothesis, however, you find that relatively few people who come from such cultures are alcoholics. Thus, you modify the hypothesis to say that alcoholism is caused by cultural factors but only when a genetic predisposition exists. But then you find that many alcoholics drink to ease the pain of depression and other psychological problems. Thus, you modify the hypothesis once again to take this fact into account. Further research shows that parental drinking patterns play a role, so you add another modification. These changes are called ad hoc ("to this") modifications because they are introduced purely to cover some problem or anomaly that was not recognized when the hypothesis was first framed.

Ad hoc modifications can ruin hypotheses.

The problem with ad hoc modifications is that their purpose is to shore up a failure of evidentiary support in the original hypothesis. As more and more modifications are added, the hypothesis becomes self-supporting; it becomes a mere description of the phenomenon it is supposed to explain. For example, suppose that we introduce a certain hypothesis h to explain the occurrence of a certain phenomenon x among a group of entities A, B, C, D, E. As ad hoc modifications are added, we find that A has x because of some unique attribute a, B has x because of b, and so on. In the end our hypothesis states that anyone who has attributes a, b, c, d, e exhibits x. But the set of attributes a, b, c, d, e is simply a description of A, B, C, D, E. If we should ask *why* entity A has x, the answer is that A has x because of a, where a is just a unique something that A has. Applying this analysis to the alcoholism hypothesis, if we ask why a certain person (let us call him Smith) is an alcoholic, the answer is that Smith is an alcoholic because he has a certain attribute s that causes him to be an alcoholic. The explanation is vacuous.

Another problem with ad hoc modifications is that they result in hypotheses that are so complicated that applying them becomes difficult. Science has always favored simplicity over complexity. Given two hypotheses that explain the same phenomenon, the simpler of the two is always the preferable one. In part, this preference is aesthetic. The simpler hypothesis is more "beautiful" than the more complex one. But the preference for simplicity also results from the application of what has been called "Ockham's razor." This is a principle, introduced by the fourteenth-century philosopher William of Ockham, that holds that theoretical entities are not to be multiplied needlessly. Why settle for a complicated theory when a simpler one works equally well? Besides, the simpler one is easier to apply.

One consequence of Ockham's razor is that naturalistic explanations are preferable, at least at the outset, to supernatural ones. For example, over the years there have been numerous reports of statues depicting Jesus or the Virgin Mary that are said to weep tears of water, or oil, or blood. After viewing these statues, thousands of faithful come away convinced that they have seen a miracle. However, Ockham's razor says that we should look for naturalistic explanations first. Perhaps the tears came from condensation or from rainwater that may have leached into the statue from small surface cracks; another possible explanation could be that they are the work of pranksters. Scientists have shown how the appearance of such tears can be replicated by drilling a small hole in a statue's head, pouring a liquid into the hole, and then scratching away a bit of lacquer or paint from the corner of the eyes. The liquid will percolate down through the porous substance of the statue and escape through the scratches.

> Naturalistic explanations are preferred.

Another, closely related consequence of Ockham's razor is that explanations based on known realities are preferred to those based on the fantastic or the bizarre. For example, there is a region in Peru, high in the Andes mountains, known as the Nazca Desert. The floor of that desert features large drawings of geometrical figures and animals such as monkeys, hummingbirds, and lizards. The drawings were produced more than a thousand years ago by scraping away the iron oxide–coated pebbles that cover the land. But given their huge size, they can be recognized as coherent figures only from a position high above. One accepted explanation is that the Nazca Indians produced the drawings using simple tools and surveying equipment to impress the rain gods that dwell in the clouds. However, the best-selling author Erich von Däniken proposes that the lines represent landing strips for alien spacecraft, and it was those aliens who guided the Indians from overhead in producing the drawings. Given its far-fetched character, this explanation would seem to violate Ockham's razor.

Returning to the question of evidentiary support, one of the surest ways to know that our hypotheses are supported by evidence is that they lead to predictions that turn out to be true. Each true prediction represents a pillar of support for the hypothesis. But some predictions are better than others, and the best ones are those that reveal ways of viewing the world that would never have been dreamed of apart from the hypothesis. If a hypothesis leads to predictions of this sort, and if those predictions are confirmed by evidence, then the hypothesis has earned a very special kind of support. Such a hypothesis reveals hidden truths about nature that would never have been recognized without it.

A classic example of a prediction of this kind resulted from the hypothesis underlying Einstein's general theory of relativity. One of the consequences predicted by this hypothesis is that light is affected by gravity. In particular, the hypothesis predicted that a light ray coming from a star and passing by the sun would be bent in the direction of the sun. As a result, the position of the star with respect to other stars would appear to be different from what it was usually observed to be. Of course, testing such a prediction under normal circumstances would be impossible, because the light of the sun is so bright that it completely blocks out the light from stars. But it could be tested during a solar eclipse. Such an opportunity arose on May 29, 1919, and scientists took advantage of it. The prediction turned out to be true, and as

> Science is progressive; superstition is not.

a result Einstein's theory was quickly adopted. Within a few years the theory led to the discovery of atomic energy.

Hypotheses that yield striking, novel predictions are largely responsible for progress in science. And it is precisely these kinds of predictions, argues the philosopher Imre Lakatos, that distinguish science from pseudoscience. Of course, not every scientific hypothesis leads to such startling predictions as Einstein's, but this kind of hypothesis may at least be integrally connected to broader, umbrella hypotheses that have led to such predictions. In contrast, the hypotheses underlying astrology have been around for twenty-seven centuries, and they have produced not a single startling prediction that has been verified and not a single new insight into the course of human events. They have produced no master plan for future civilization and no hint about future discoveries in physics or medicine. This lack of progress over centuries is one reason that the philosopher Paul Thagard named astrology a pseudoscience.

14.3   Objectivity

Our beliefs about the world are objective to the extent that they are unaffected by conditions peculiar to the experiencing subject. Such conditions can be either motivational or observational. For example, a belief that is motivated by the emotions of the experiencing subject and that exists for the primary purpose of satisfying those emotions tends to lack objectivity. Also, a belief that is grounded in observations peculiar to the experiencing subject, such as visual hallucinations, lacks objectivity. Even though objectivity is an ideal that can never be completely attained, practically everyone would agree that beliefs are more trustworthy if their content is not distorted by the experiencing subject. The scientist constantly strives to avoid such distortions, but the superstitious mind either revels in them or, in the more tragic cases, succumbs to them.

All superstitions exist at least in part to satisfy the emotional needs of the experiencing subject. The chief emotions that give rise to superstitious beliefs are fear and anxiety, and they are often reinforced by a disposition to fantasy and mental laziness. Much of the fear

Superstitions exist to satisfy emotional needs.

and anxiety is generated by the fact that everyone dies. Death can come suddenly, as in a freeway accident, a fall from a roof, or an avalanche, or it can come as a result of cancer, heart failure, or stroke. Short of death, everyone is subject to injury with its attendant pain, and most people at some time experience the mental suffering that accompanies rejection, loneliness, and failure.

People have little control over these facts of life, and to relieve the anxiety they produce, many resort to charms and amulets, the rosary beads dangling from the rearview mirror or the talisman or medal worn around the neck. If nothing else will protect us from the terrors of life, perhaps these objects will. After all, science has failed to conquer disease and death, and it offers to the believer nothing but tentative truths that may change tomorrow. Besides, science is too hard to understand. Becoming competent requires years of serious study. To the person facing an uncertain future, dejection, or loneliness, it may seem more reasonable to contact a local psychic and buy a bit of immediate consolation than to trust in science.

A second element in the human condition that generates anxiety is freedom and the responsibility freedom entails. The idea that you, and you only, are in charge of your destiny can be an extremely frightening idea. Many people recoil from the thought and seek refuge in a leader or guru. They turn all their power of critical thinking over to this leader and blindly follow his or her instructions to the last detail. When the leader orders them to believe any form of nonsense, no matter how silly, they do so. The belief or practice ordered by the leader, they are told, is essential to their protection. But, following such orders can sometimes lead to tragedy, as it did in the Jonestown massacre in 1978 and the Heaven's Gate suicides in 1997.

A disposition to magical ways of thinking and mental laziness greatly facilitates the flight to superstition. Many people, if not most, are fascinated by the mysterious, the arcane, and the occult, and some would rather believe an explanation clothed in magic than they would a scientifically grounded one. The psychologists Barry F. Singer and Victor A. Benassi performed a series of experiments on their students in which they had a magician pose as a "psychic" and perform demonstrations of psychic feats. Before the demonstrations began, the students were told repeatedly in the clearest language that the magician was only pretending to be a psychic, and that what they were about to witness was really a series of conjurer's tricks. Nevertheless, in spite of these warnings, a majority of students concluded, in one experiment after another, that the magician was really a psychic. Furthermore, many concluded that the magician was an agent of Satan.

People are fascinated by the mysterious.

The disposition toward the magical and the fantastic is greatly reinforced by the media, particularly television and motion pictures. The media are slavishly subservient to the entertainment desires of their audience, so, given a widespread fascination with the magical, the media issue a constant stream of movies, miniseries, and "news" stories devoted to that subject. These programs touch everything from vampires and disembodied spirits to irrational conspiracies and the intervention of angels. This persistent attention to the fantastical increases the public's acceptance of superstitious explanations whenever realistic ones are not readily available, or even in the face of realistic explanations.

A disposition to mental laziness also assists in the formation of superstitious beliefs. It is, in fact, extremely difficult to ensure that one's beliefs are supported by evidence and that they pass the test of internal coherence. Sloppy logic is so easy it is no wonder people resort to it. Most of the informal fallacies treated in Chapter 3 can arise from sloppy thinking. After old Mrs. Chadwicke hobbled past the church, lightning struck the steeple and burned the church to the ground. Obviously old Mrs. Chadwicke is a witch (false cause). Furthermore, old Mrs. Chadwicke wears a black cape and a black hood. It must be the case that all witches wear such clothing (hasty generalization). And of course witches exist because everybody in the village believes in them (appeal to the people).

Superstitions are supported by sloppy thinking.

Another kind of sloppy thinking involves an appeal to what might be called false coherence. A farmer discovers that one of his cows has been killed. At the same time the farmer happens to read a story in a local tabloid saying that a satanic cult is operating in the vicinity. The cult practices its rites on the thirteenth day of each month. The cow was killed on the thirteenth. Thus, the farmer concludes that the cow was killed by Satan worshippers. This line of thinking involves many loose ends, but that rarely deters people from drawing a conclusion. Becoming a clear, critical thinker is one of the primary goals of education, but unfortunately becoming educated is no less of a struggle for students today than it was for students in Plato's day.

Thus far we have focused on emotions and dispositions in the experiencing subject that lead to superstitious beliefs. We now turn to some of the many ways that our observation of the world can be distorted. Such distortions constitute avenues in which conditions peculiar to the experiencing subject enter into the content of observation. When such distorted observations are combined with the emotions and dispositions mentioned earlier, superstitious beliefs are likely to arise. The distorted observations can occur in the same person who has the emotions and dispositions or they can be conveyed secondhand. In either case, the combination leads to superstition.

One well-documented phenomenon that influences our observation of our own bodily states is the so-called placebo effect. Recall that a placebo is any kind of "medicine" or procedure that provides no medicinal or therapeutic benefit by itself but that can effect a cure when the patient is told that it has such benefit. For example, patients with knee pain have been told that an operation will cure them, and after they undergo a minor incision that, by itself, has no therapeutic effect, the pain often disappears. Also, patients who suffer from nervous tension or depression have been told that a little colored pill (which consists of nothing but sugar) will cure them, and after they take the pill, the tension or depression disappears. Obviously in these cases it is not the placebo alone that effects the cure but the placebo together with the suggestion implanted in the patients' minds by their doctors.

Placebos can masquerade as cures.

The perceived efficacy of many treatments in Eastern medicine can probably be attributed to the placebo effect. For example, the widely held belief in China that tiger bones cure ulcers, malaria, and arthritis, and that rhinoceros horns cure fevers and convulsions and act as an aphrodisiac are almost certainly grounded in superstition. But they have led to the decimation of the tiger and rhino populations wherever these animals are found in the wild. Also, the belief that bear bile reduces fevers and improves eyesight is most likely an imagined cure, but it has led to the horribly inhumane treatment of bears in Asia.

Another well-documented effect that influences our observation of the world around us is called pareidolia. This is the effect by which we can look at clouds, smoke, or the textured coatings on walls and ceilings and see animals, faces, trees, and so on. We project familiar visual images onto vague, relatively formless sensory stimuli and "see" that image as if it were really there. Pareidolia is responsible for a good deal of religious superstition. For example, a few years ago a woman making burritos saw the face of Jesus in the skillet burns on a tortilla. She built a shrine to house the tortilla, and thousands of believers came to pray before it. More recently, a grilled cheese sandwich that believers thought bore the image of the Virgin Mary sold on eBay for $28,000. But incidents of this sort are not confined to the Christian world. Followers of Islam have seen the Arabic words for "Allah" and "Muhammad" in such media as fish scales, eggshells, and lamb's wool.

Closely related to pareidolia is the concept of the perceptual set, where "set" refers to our tendency to perceive events and objects in a way that our prior experience has led us to expect. The idea of perceptual set is a product of Gestalt psychology, according to which perceiving is a kind of problem solving. When we are confronted with a

Can you see the white triangle?
Is the white triangle really "there"?
(Taken from Kanizsa, 1979, 74.)

We perceive what we
expect to perceive.

problem, such as finding the solution to a riddle or puzzle, we enter into a state of mental incubation in which potential solutions are turned over in our minds. This state is followed by a flash of insight (assuming we are able to solve the puzzle), after which the solution seems obvious. When we consider the puzzle at a later time, the solution leaps into our minds. Such a solution is called a *gestalt*, from the German, for "form" or "configuration." Analogously, every act of perception involves solving the puzzle of organizing sensory stimuli into meaningful patterns. Each such pattern is a perceptual gestalt, or set, and once such a set is formed, it serves to guide the processing of future perceptions. As a result, we perceive what we expect to perceive.

In 1949 the psychologists Jerome S. Bruner and Leo J. Postman performed a famous experiment in which subjects were shown replicas of ordinary playing cards—but some of the cards had been altered by reversing their color. For example, in some groups of cards, the three of hearts was black and the six of spades was red. Of twenty-eight subjects, twenty-seven initially saw the altered cards as normal ones. One subject identified the black three of hearts as a three of spades on forty-four successive showings. This experiment clearly shows that we perceive what we expect to perceive and, indeed, this fact is familiar to nearly everyone. For example, we expect to receive a phone call, and while taking a shower we think we hear the phone ringing, only to be told by someone in the other room that the phone did not ring. Or, while driving, we might approach a red octagonal sign that reads ST_P (our view of the sign being partly blocked by a tree branch between the S and the P). However, we bring the car to a stop, because we perceived the sign to read STOP. In fact, what our sense of vision received was three consonants (S, T, P), meaningless until processed through perception.

Yet another factor that influences our sense of vision is the autokinetic effect. According to this effect a small, stationary light surrounded by darkness will often seem to move. One can prove the existence of this effect for oneself by looking at a bright star on a dark night, or by observing a small stationary point of light in a dark room. Psychologists speculate that the autokinetic effect results from small, involuntary motions of the eyeball of the observer, and they have shown that the effect is enhanced by the reports of other observers. If someone standing nearby says that she just saw the object move, others will often confirm this report. The autokinetic effect is thought to be responsible for many claims of UFO sightings.

Hallucinations of various sorts can also distort the content of perception. Two kinds of hallucination that affect many people in the drowsy moments between sleep and wakeful-

Hallucinations distort perception.

ness are hypnagogic and hypnopompic hallucinations (Hines, 1988, 61–62). The former occur just before drifting off to sleep, when the brain's alpha waves are switching to theta waves, and the latter occur just before awak-

ening. During these moments the subject may experience extremely vivid, emotionally charged images that seem very real. These hallucinations are thought to be responsible for the ghosts and other appearances that people sometimes see in bedrooms.

Collective hallucinations are another kind of perceptual distortion that can occur in large crowds of people. Before such hallucinations can happen, the crowd must be brought to a heightened emotional state, which may be brought on by the expectation of seeing something important or miraculous. An occurrence of this sort may have happened on October 13, 1917, when some 70,000 people gathered in the village of Fatima in Portugal expecting to see a miraculous sign from heaven. At midday, one of the children who was supposedly in contact with the Virgin Mary cried out to the people to look at the sun. They did so, whereupon thousands saw the sun swirl amid the clouds and plunge toward the earth. Of course, if the sun had actually moved, it would have triggered seismograph readings all over the globe. Also, many of the people there did not see anything unusual, but their reports were discounted. Neverthe-less, even to this day many of the faithful take this observation of the swirling sun as evidence of a miracle.

Finally, the operation of memory can distort the way we recall our observations. Human memory is not like the process whereby a computer recalls information from its hard drive with total accuracy. Rather, it is a creative process susceptible to many influences. When images are recalled from human memory, they are retrieved in bits

Confabulation produces false recollections.

and pieces. The brain then fills in the gaps through a process called con-fabulation. The brain naturally and unconsciously tries to produce a coherent account of what happened, but precisely how the gaps are filled

in depends on such things as one's feelings at the time of recall, other people's sug-gestions about the event recalled, and one's own successive reports of what happened. Given that memory recall is selective to begin with and that many details are inevitably left out, the final picture recalled may range anywhere from a fairly accurate representa-tion to a total fabrication.

These effects represent only a few of the ways the subjective state of the observer can influence human observation and memory. To avoid such distortions, scientific inquiry restricts human observation to circumstances in which known aberrations of perception and recall are least likely to occur. In the natural sciences, much if not most observation occurs through instruments, such as volt meters, Geiger counters, and tele-scopes, the behavior of which is well known and highly predictable. The results are then recorded on relatively permanent media such as photographic film, or digital storage devices. In the social sciences, techniques such as double-blind sampling and statistical analysis of data insulate the observer from the outcome of the experiment. Such procedures provide considerable assurance that the data are not distorted by the subjective state of the experimenter.

14.4 Integrity

Our efforts to understand the world in which we live have integrity to the extent that they involve honesty in gathering and presenting evidence and honest, logical thinking in responding to theoretical problems that develop along the way. Most forms of superstition involve elements of dishonesty in gathering evidence or a failure of logic in responding to theoretical problems. Such failures of logic can be found in the lack of response by the community of practitioners to problems involving the adequacy, coherence, or external consistency of the hypotheses related to their practices.

The most severe lack of integrity arises when the evidence is faked. One of the more striking examples of faked evidence is found in the case of the Israeli entertainer Uri

Practitioners of superstition fake the evidence.

Geller. Beginning in the early 1970s, Geller presented himself in numerous venues throughout the world as a psychic who could perform marvelous feats such as bending spoons, keys, nails, and other metal objects through the sheer power of his mind. Such objects would appear to bend when he merely stroked them with his finger, or even without his touching them at all. Scientists were called in to witness these feats, and many came away convinced of their authenticity. But in fact Geller was just a clever trickster who duped his audiences. Geller's trickery was exposed in large measure by the magician James Randi.

After watching videos of Geller's performances, Randi discovered how Geller performed his tricks, and in no time he was able to perform every one of them himself. Sometimes Geller would prepare a spoon or key beforehand by bending it back and

---

Donald Singleton, a reporter for the *New York Daily News,* was familiar with Uri Geller's alleged psychic ability to bend spoons and keys and identify handmade drawings that had been sealed inside two envelopes, one inside the other. He suspected that the latter trick was performed by holding the envelopes up to a strong light while the subject's attention was diverted. Prior to writing a story on Geller, Singleton performed the following test:

> I went to a locksmith and got a duplicate of the strongest, thickest key on my key ring. I tried with all my might and I couldn't bend it, even by pressing it against the corner of a steel desk. Then I made a simple drawing (of an eye), wrapped it in aluminum foil and put it into two envelopes.
>
> I went to see Geller the next afternoon.
>
> He tried for more than an hour, with me keeping the envelope in my sight every second, to get the drawing. And he failed.
>
> Then he made an effort to bend the key, again with me keeping it in view every second. Again, nothing happened. Uri said that he was terribly disappointed, that this simply had been an all-around bad day for him (Quoted in Randi, 1982b, 29).

forth several times to the point where it was nearly ready to break. Later, by merely stroking it gently, he could cause it to double over. On other occasions Geller, or his accomplices, would use sleight-of-hand maneuvers to substitute bent objects in the place of straight ones. In yet another trick, Geller claimed to be able to deflect a compass needle by merely concentrating his attention on it. As he would wave his hands over the compass, the needle would spin—and his hands had been thoroughly examined earlier for hidden magnets. But Geller had concealed a powerful magnet in his mouth, and as he bent over the compass, the needle would spin in tune with his head gyrations.

For another example of faked evidence, let us look at fire walking. Practitioners of this art claim that their self-help seminars can alter a person's body chemistry so as to allow him or her to walk barefoot over a bed of glowing coals without being burned. One of the leading gurus of this business is Tony Robbins of the Robbins Research Institute. Robbins uses what he calls "neurolinguistic programming" to cure all sorts of physical and psychological ailments, from irrational fears and impotence to drug addiction and tumors. As proof of the efficacy of this technique, he invites those who have taken his seminar to engage in a fire walk. By merely believing they will avoid burning their feet, he tells them, they will survive the ordeal unharmed.

The truth is that anyone, whether or not he has taken the seminar and regardless of what he believes, can, under controlled conditions, walk across burning coals and escape unharmed. The physicist Bernard J. Leikind proved this, at least to his own satisfaction, when he showed up at a Robbins seminar in the fall of 1984 (Frazier, 1991, 182–193). Even though he had not attended the sessions and he declined to think cool thoughts as per the instructions of the attendants, he found that he could perform the fire walk without even getting singed. He explained his success by noting certain basic laws of physics. In spite of their high temperature, wood coals contain a very low quantity of heat, and they conduct heat very poorly. Also, the foot is in contact with the coals for only a second at a time, thus allowing only a small quantity of heat energy to flow to the foot. As a result, the feet of fire walkers rarely sustain injury (or at least serious injury).

For a third example of faked evidence we need look no further than the thousands of fortune-tellers, palm readers, and mentalists who use the art of "cold reading" to divine all sorts of amazing truths about their clients' lives. Most people who engage the services of these "readers" do so because they have problems concerning love, health, or finances.

Cold readers deceive their clients.

The reader knows this and often begins the reading with a flattering spiel that is tailored to fit practically everybody. This recital is intended to put the client at ease and condition him or her to open up to the reader. All the while the reader is taking in every detail: the client's age, sex, weight, posture, speech patterns, grammar, eye contact, build, hands, clothing (style, age, neatness, and cost), hairstyle, jewelry, and whatever the client might be holding or carrying (books, car keys, etc.). All of these provide clues to the personality, intelligence, line of work, socioeconomic status, religion, education, and political affiliation of the client.

The reader uses this information to formulate hypotheses that are then presented to the client in the form of subtle questions. Depending on the client's reactions—facial expression, eye motion, pupil dilation, gestures—the reader can often tell if he or she is on the right track. Once the reader hits on something close to home, the client will usually react in amazement and begin revealing more personal details. After appropriate intervals, the reader will then rephrase this information in a different sequence and feed it back to the client, to the client's ever-increasing amazement. The client then provides even more details, which the reader weaves together with everything else learned to that point. The use of a crystal ball, satin cape, or tarot cards combined with a polished sense of confidence convey to the client that the reader can literally read the client's mind.

The psychologist Ray Hyman, who as a teenager read palms to supplement his income, has studied the art of cold reading in some depth. He relates a story about a young woman who visited a mind reader during the 1930s:

She was wearing expensive jewelry, a wedding band, and a black dress of cheap material. The observant reader noticed that she was wearing shoes that were currently being advertised for people with foot trouble. He assumed that this client came to see him, as did most of his female customers, because of a love or financial problem. The black dress and the wedding band led him to reason that her husband had died recently. The expensive jewelry suggested that she had been financially comfortable during marriage, but the cheap dress indicated that her husband's death had left her penniless. The therapeutic shoes signified that she was now standing on her feet more than she used to, implying that she was working to support herself since her husband's death.

The reader's shrewdness led him to the following conclusion—which turned out to be correct: The lady had met a man who had proposed to her. She wanted to marry the man to end her economic hardship. But she felt guilty about marrying so soon after her husband's death. The reader told her what she had come to hear—that it was all right to marry without further delay (Frazier, 1981, 85–86).

If the deceptive techniques of the magician who pretends to be a psychic, the neuro-linguistic programmer, and the cold reader are accepted at face value, they appear to constitute evidence that really supports the hypotheses underlying these activities. But faking the evidence is not the only way in which the practitioners of superstition lack integrity. The other way concerns the reaction of the community of practitioners to problems that arise in connection with the adequacy, coherence, and external consistency of those hypotheses.

Such problems arise in connection with scientific hypotheses no less often than they do with superstitious ones. When they arise in science, the community of scientists shifts to what the philosopher Thomas Kuhn (1970b) calls a puzzle-solving mode, and scientists work on them with great persistence until the problems are solved. This puzzle-solving activity occupies the attention of the vast majority of scientists for the greatest part of their careers, and it constitutes what Kuhn calls "normal science." Furthermore, it is precisely this puzzle-solving character of normal science, Kuhn argues, that distinguishes science from pseudoscience.

Scientists are puzzle solvers.

For example, after the Copernican hypothesis was introduced, a problem turned up in connection with stellar parallax. If, as the hypothesis held, the earth travels around the sun, then, in the course of its orbit, the farthest stars should appear to shift in position with respect to the nearer ones. An analogous phenomenon can be observed as you change your position in a room. The distant lamp, which originally appeared to the left of the chair in the foreground, now appears to the right of it. In the case of the stars, however, no parallax could be observed. The explanation given at the time was that the stars were too far away for any parallax to be detectable. Nevertheless, stellar parallax constituted an adequacy problem that the community of astronomers regarded as a puzzle, and they worked on it for 300 years. Eventually more-powerful telescopes were produced that did indeed detect a change in position of the stars as the earth orbited the sun.

In contrast, when an astrological prediction fails to materialize, the community of astrologers never sets to work to figure out what went wrong. Astrologers never recheck the location and birth time of the client or the exact position of the planets at the time of his birth. They merely charge forward and issue more predictions. Similarly, when the bumps on a person's head fail to indicate essential features of that person's personality, or when the lines on her palm fail to reveal features of her life, the community of phrenologists and the community of palm readers never try to account for the failures. They just ignore them and move on to the next batch of clients. Such a response reveals a lack of integrity on the part of these practitioners toward their respective hypotheses. Something is clearly wrong with the hypotheses or with the measurements, but no one cares enough to do anything about it.

A similar response occurs in connection with coherence problems. Most superstitions involve serious incoherencies, many of which arise from the lack of known causal connections. For example, if astrology claims that the planets influence our lives, then there must be some causal connection between the planets and individual humans. But what could this connection be? Is it gravity? If so, then astrologers need to show how infinitesimally small gravitational fluctuations can affect people's lives. On the other hand, if some other causal influence is at work, the astrologers need to pin it down. What kind of laws govern it? Is it an inverse square law, like the law of gravity, or some other kind of law? Analogously, if the lines on a person's palms indicate something about the person's life, then what form of causality is at work here? Do the lines influence the life, or is it the other way around? And what laws does this form of causality obey?

Any absence of a causal connection is a defect in coherence, because it signals the lack of a connection between ideas functioning in a hypothesis. However, such a lack of coherence need not be fatal to a hypothesis. Physicians from the time of Hippocrates knew that willow leaves, which contain the essential ingredient of aspirin, had the power to relieve pain, but they failed to understand the causal connection until relatively recently. What distinguishes the biomedical community from the community of astrologers lies in their respective reactions to such problems. The members of the biomedical community recognized the aspirin problem as a puzzle, and they worked on it until they found the solution, but members of the astrological community are unconcerned with identifying the causal mechanism by which the planets influence human lives. Similarly, members of the community of palm readers and members of the community of phrenologists care nothing about identifying the essential causal connections implied by their respective hypotheses.

An even more serious problem is posed by hypotheses that are inconsistent with established theories or laws. A case in point may be found in claims made by promoters of the Transcendental Meditation (TM) movement. The practice of TM was popularized in the 1960s by the late Maharishi Mahesh Yogi, and since then it has attracted thousands of adherents. It consists in the silent repetition of a mantra, which induces a mental state similar to self-hypnosis.

Levitation is a puzzle no one wants to solve.

For many who have tried it, the benefits are mental and physical relaxation leading to a sense of rejuvenation. But with further instruction in TM (at considerable cost to the student), longer and deeper trances can be induced that, the Maharishi claimed, allow the meditator to levitate—to hover in the air without any physical support. Thousands of disciples, he claimed, have learned how to do this, and he released photographs that purported to verify this claim. But of course if levitation actually occurs, it constitutes a violation of, or a suspension of, the law of gravity.

The inconsistency of the Maharishi hypothesis with such a well-confirmed theory as the law of gravity is probably sufficient reason to assign it to the category of superstition. But the reaction of the community of TM practitioners to this inconsistency leaves little room for doubt. In 1971 the Maharishi bought the grounds and buildings of what was formerly Parsons College in Fairfield, Iowa, and he converted the site into Maharishi International University. The university then became the home of the International Center for Scientific Research, which, one would think, would be the perfect forum for investigating levitation. Given the availability of scores of alleged levitators, the "scientists" in residence could conduct in-depth studies into this phenomenon. Their findings could develop the basis for interplanetary space travel, to say nothing of what they might do to achieve safer airplanes. However, from its inception, the International Center has conducted not a shred of research on levitation. No experiments have been performed and no scholarly papers have been written. This response is inconceivable for any bona fide center of scientific research.

14.5 Concluding Remarks

The foregoing observations about integrity should not be taken to imply that no scientist has ever faked the evidence. Fraud has occurred and it results chiefly from changes that have taken place in the last fifty years or so. First, science today is a multibillion-dollar industry funded by grants from the government, private foundations, and corporations. To get funding, scientists are under constant pressure to produce definitive results, and sometimes the "right" results. This pressure has led a number of scientists, particularly in the biomedical and life sciences, it seems, to fudge the data. Another motivation for fraud is the pressure in academia to "publish or perish." Without a solid publishing record, a graduate student in the sciences will never be awarded a PhD, never secure a postdoctoral appointment, and never hold down a position on a university faculty. Again, sometimes the pressure can be too much for some individuals.

A prime example of a scientist who has faked the evidence is Dr. Scott Reuben, former Professor of Anesthesiology at Tufts University and former chief of acute pain at Baystate Medical Center in Springfield, Massachusetts. Over a period of nearly thirteen years, Dr. Reuben wrote or co-wrote twenty-one articles that were published in scientific journals and that he claimed were supported by clinical trials, The so-called research had been funded by grants from the pharmaceutical company Pfizer and it reported favorable results for Pfizer's Bextra, Celebrex, and Lyrica, as well as Merck's Vioxx. Reuben's work led to the sale of billions of dollars of these drugs. After his work became suspect, Reuben admitted that every one of the clinical trials had been fabricated, the names of many patients invented, and the signatures of coauthors forged. In the end, Dr. Reuben was sentenced to prison for fraud and his practice of medicine was terminated.

Granted that some scientific work is tainted with fraud, the next question is, how extensive is this abuse? One way of approaching this question is to look at the number of articles in scientific journals that are retracted each year—that is, permanently withdrawn from the literature. The highly respected scientific journal *Nature* published such a study in its October 6, 2011, issue.* The author concluded that out of approximately 1,400,000 scientific articles published that year, perhaps 400 would be retracted, and half of those would involve some form of misconduct. That amounts to less than .02 percent.

Yet, there is a different, more insidious kind of dishonesty that is not measurable in terms of articles retracted from scientific journals that works to undermine scientific integrity no less than outright fraud. This kind of dishonesty results from the millions of dollars in grants that large corporations pour into colleges and universities for the purpose of influencing public opinion in regard to their products. For an example, consider the actions of the Monsanto Corporation in securing the cooperation of university science professors to influence public opinion in regard to its widely used herbicide, Roundup.

Monsanto is the world's largest seed producer, and it specializes in the genetic modification of seeds. The main purpose of such modification is to make the resulting plants immune to the effect of glyphosate, the active ingredient in their herbicide Roundup. The idea is that if farmers plant the genetically modified seeds, they can spray their fields with Roundup, causing the weeds to die but leaving the crop unscathed. Monsanto's marketing of Roundup-resistant seeds has been hugely profitable for several years, but recently the World Health Organization has identified glyphosate as a probable cause of cancer in humans. This has caused a major problem for Monsanto because glyphosate can likely be found in practically every processed food—bread, beer, pizza, pasta, cornflakes, salad dressing, mayonnaise—which for many consumers will lead to the question, "If I eat these foods, will I get cancer?"

To sway public opinion in its favor, Monsanto has paid university science professors to write articles and give speeches in support of the claim that glyphosate is harmless to humans. University professors have the reputation of being impartial and above the fray, so if they express their opinion on an issue the public tends to believe them. One such professor was Kevin Folta, chairman of the Horticultural Sciences Department at the University of Florida. Monsanto gave Folta an unrestricted grant of $25,000 in addition to paying his travel expenses to multiple conferences and gatherings. After receiving the grant, Folta said in an email to a Monsanto executive, "I am grateful for this opportunity and promise a solid return on the investment."[†]

It appears that the $25,000 grant to Professor Folta was originally intended to be secret, but somehow the word got out. However, in the vast majority of cases, the word

---

*For another article on this topic, see "Misconduct Accounts for the Majority of Retracted Scientific Publications." In Proceedings of the National Academy of Sciences, vol. 110, issue 3, p. 1137 (2013).

†Eric Lipton, "Food Industry Enlisted Academics in GMO Lobbying War, Emails Show," New York Times, September 5, 2015, www.nytimes.com/2015/09/06/us/food-industry-enlisted-academics-in-gmo-lobbying-war-emails -show.html?_r=0.

does not get out. And it is precisely this fact that renders the influence of corporate money on scientific research so insidious. When a scientist takes a public stand on some contested issue, is this stand based on unbiased scientific research, or does it reflect the influence of corporate money? The question has broad relevance. A notorious example, dating back as early as the 1940s, related to whether cigarettes are addictive and/or caused cancer. Of course, scientists (and physicians) in the pay of the tobacco companies claimed there was no scientific foundation for the connection between tobacco use and these illnesses. More recently, a handful of scientists have taken the position that climate change either does not exist or is not the result of human activity. Whether such claims are influenced by the fossil fuel industry's sponsorship of studies aimed at casting doubt on authentic scientifically based climate change research may be hard to prove.

Do the actions of Dr. Rueben, Professor Folta, and others similarly situated serve to erode the distinction between science and superstition? The answer can be found in the reaction of the scientific community to these incidents. As the case of Dr. Rueben illustrates, outright fraud is not tolerated. When fraud is discovered, the scientist is often fired—or worse. And if fraudulent research serves as the basis of a publication, the publication is retracted. Quite to the contrary, no astrologer has ever been sent to prison for casting fraudulent horoscopes, and no palm reader has ever been sanctioned for negligently interpreting the lines on a client's hands. Needless to say, no publication of a psychic has ever been retracted for fake predictions. In these endeavors, fraud is virtually meaningless.

Examined more closely, the case with Professor Folta is more complicated. It is possible that Folta would have defended Monsanto's use of glyphosate to the extent that he did even if he had not been given any money. However, the lack of transparency relating to Monsanto's grant and the monies and perks given to Folta certainly raises suspicions about the trustworthiness of Folta's opinion. At this point in time the scientific community has been largely silent on the question of whether university researchers should be allowed to accept grants from large corporations when such corporate sponsorship may be used to influence research results—and ultimately be used for the purpose of swaying public opinion in regard to that corporation's products. But a strong argument can be made that such a statement from all reputable scientists is imperative.

If the time should come when the general public believes that "truth" in science is whatever Monsanto, Koch Industries, or ExxonMobil says that it is, then any shred of integrity attaching to scientific research will have been eviscerated. That point has not been reached yet, but these recent incidents concerning university scientists are ominous.

Key ideas introduced in this chapter

anecdotal evidence	autokinetic effect
replicability	hypnagogic hallucinations
falsifiable/disconfirmable	hypnopompic hallucinations
ad hoc modifications	collective hallucinations
Ockham's razor	confabulation
placebo effect	scientific progress
pareidolia	striking predictions
perceptual set	vague hypotheses

In the foregoing discussion we have examined some features that are characteristic of scientific inquiry and some contrasting features that are characteristic of superstition. The purpose of this exposition has not been to provide the sufficient and necessary conditions for a bright demarcation line between science and superstition. Rather, the purpose has been the more modest one of setting forth a group of family resemblances that a fair-minded inquirer may use in rendering a judgment that a set of beliefs is more probably scientific or more probably superstitious.

To the extent that a set of beliefs rests on hypotheses that are coherent, precisely tailored, narrowly formulated, supported by genuine evidence, and productive of new insights, these beliefs can be considered scientifically grounded. This judgment is reinforced by the conscientious response of the scientific community to problems that develop concerning the adequacy, coherence, and external consistency of those hypotheses. But to the extent that a set of beliefs rests on hypotheses that are incoherent, inconsistent with well-established theories, vague, overly broad, motivated by emotional needs, and supported by evidence that fails to be trustworthy, as well as leading to no new insights, then those beliefs tend to be superstitious. Such a judgment is reinforced by a reaction of oblivious unconcern on the part of the community of practitioners to problems that arise in connection with the adequacy, coherence, and external consistency of those hypotheses.

EXERCISE 14

I. Engage in the following discussion exercises.

1. Discuss the evidentiary problems raised by the following questions:

   a. After drinking tea made from tarragon leaves every day for a year, your grandfather reports that his bunions cleared up. Does this prove that tarragon tea has the power to cure bunions?

   b. You go to a psychotherapist who diagnoses your emotional condition as resulting from suppressed Oedipal tendencies. When these tendencies rise to the surface they can cause outbursts of emotion, but when they are held in check your behavior may be either normal or overly placid. Is the psychotherapist's hypothesis a good one?

   c. Every time the star running back of your school's football team makes a touchdown, he kneels for a quick prayer in the end zone. Is God blessing this player's performance on the field?

   d. In 1998, Rose Creek Health Products began marketing a product it called "Vitamin O," for which it charged $10 per ounce. In newspaper and Internet ads the company published several testimonials from users. One of them, from a lung cancer victim, read, "Three days after starting the Vitamin O, I threw my cane away. In November we went to Arizona and I bought myself a bicycle." Another, about a man who had suffered severe headaches for twenty years stated, "The day he began taking Vitamin O his headaches disappeared." Yet another said that a man received "very significant relief from his emphysema." Do these testimonials prove that Vitamin O provides relief from disease and pain? In 2000 the Federal Trade Commission obtained an injunction against Rose Creek after proving that Vitamin O is nothing more than ordinary salt water. Rose Creek still sells Vitamin O without making any beneficial claims for it.

e. Shortly before drifting off to sleep, your roommate reports that she heard someone call out her name in a loud, clear voice. Since no one else was in the room at that time, does this mean that the voice came from a ghost?

f. In 2002, the Hubble Space Science Institute released new high-resolution photographs of the Cone Nebula that were taken by the recently refurbished Hubble Space Telescope. On viewing these images, hundreds of Christians thought they could see the face of Jesus in the nebula, which they renamed the Jesus Nebula (see www.skyimagelab.com/jesus-nebula.html). Do these images prove that Jesus is alive in the cosmos?

2. Discuss the meaning of the following selections:

a. The universe is a macrocosm of creative energy and power, and every man, woman, and child is the epitome of this totality of the cosmos. Within your individualized energy field, the microcosm called *you*, are twenty-two Causal Powers, or angels, that control your conscious behavior and govern the manifestation of all forms and experiences in your personal life.

(John Randolph Price, *The Angels Within Us*)

b. What is remarkable about the nervous system of the human species is that it can command this infinite organizing power through conscious intent. Intent in the human species is not fixed or locked into a rigid network of energy and information. It has infinite flexibility. In other words, as long as you do not violate the other laws of nature, through your intent you can literally command the laws of nature to fulfill your dreams and desires.

(Deepak Chopra, *The Seven Spiritual Laws of Success*)

c. Every plant has an aura, the invisible charge of energy that exists around all things. It is the refracted and reflected light from electrical impulses, heat, and vapor of the object. Or put another way, it is simply light dancing around, inside, and off all things.

(Laurie Cabot, *The Power of the Witch*)

d. The Pleiadians are back from the future to give us a broader perspective on "the absurd times" we live in. They explain how we are fragmented and cut off from our connection to the whole of life. The crucial test for us will be to shift from lineal thinking to a multidimensional perspective and expand our understanding of the frequency of love—the gateway to freeing ourselves.

(Advertisement for *Family of Light*, by Barbara Marciniak)

e. When advice from your angel is incorrect, it ain't your angel. Messages that prove misleading or untrue are due to desire or fear that was not released before you began talking with your heavenly helper. You're aware, of course, that any situation has the likelihood of multiple outcomes.

(Alma Daniel, Timothy Wyllie, and Andrew Ramer, *Ask Your Angels*)

3. Discuss the following reports from residents of Hong Kong (taken from "Hong Kong's *Feng Shui*: Popular Magic in a Modern Urban Setting," by Charles F. Emmons, *Journal of Popular Culture*, Summer 1992).

   a. I have a little restaurant in Aberdeen, a seafood place facing the sea. I used to be on the other side of the street and had very bad business. The *feng shui* man told me that it should face the sea. Now I have very good business.

   b. I am a guard at a dockyard. The Westerners there believe in *feng shui*. They changed the entrance to the place because the old one was unlucky. They also put out a [shiny] wok to deflect the bad luck, and a *fok dzi* [the Chinese Script character for good luck] upside down to bring luck in rather than out. All the workers there feel a lot better now and are in better health.

   c. There were a lot of car accidents on the slope we faced, and even a murder upstairs from there, so we put up a fork and mirror to eliminate the killing atmosphere. The mirror faced east and reflected the morning sun. A guy across from us came over and said he had been sick since we had put the mirror up, and asked us to take it down. We did, and then he said he had been well after that. But we moved to another place then.

   d. *Feng shui* is what causes radios to work better facing one way than another.

4. One of the early creationist theories advanced in opposition to Darwin's theory of natural selection was put forward by the nineteenth-century naturalist Philip Gosse. According to this theory, God created the world in about 4000 B.C., and he did so in exactly six days, per the account in Genesis. To reconcile this story with indications that the world is much older, Gosse argued that God created the world with the appearance of a history. Adam was created with a navel, trees were created with rings, and fossils were implanted in geologic formations and in sea beds. Is Gosse's theory plausible? Does his theory make God out to be a deceiver? Is a world with a fake history intrinsically better than one with no history? If we were to update Gosse's theory, we would have to add that God created the world complete with light rays that appear to have been emitted by distant galaxies more than 10 billion years ago, as well as with fossils having ratios of carbon-12 to carbon-14 that indicate (by carbon-dating techniques) the fossils are millions of years old. Given these provisions, is there any way of disproving Gosse's theory? In other words, is the theory disconfirmable? If not, does this fact make the theory unscientific?

5. The modern creationist theory, called "scientific creationism," propounded by Duane Gish and Henry Morris, accounts for geologic formations and fossils by appealing to the great flood of Noah. This flood allegedly killed numerous mammals, birds, fish, and insects, and their carcasses settled in different strata

amid the swirling waters, thus producing the fossils. But is it plausible that all the animals that populate the earth today were saved on Noah's ark? These would include 25,000 species of birds, 15,000 species of mammals, 2,500 species of amphibians, 6,000 species of reptiles, including dinosaurs, and a million species of insects. How large must the ark have been, in comparison, say, with the *Titanic*, to house these animals together with sufficient food for a 300-day voyage? Based on the number of human hours it took to build the *Titanic* (do some research on this), how long do you think it would have taken Noah, his wife, and three sons to build the ark? Assuming the ark was made of wood, approximately how many board feet of lumber would have been needed to build it (include enough wood for walls and floors between the animals)? How long would it have taken Noah and his family to collect and load the animals on the ark? How much time would it have taken to provide one meal for the animals? Is scientific creationism a plausible theory?

6. Suppose you are a fortune-teller. You have a small shop in Milwaukee complete with a crystal ball, beads hanging in the doorway, incense, and a shelf of books devoted to the dark arts. At about 4:00 in the afternoon in early March a couple in their mid-thirties comes into your shop. They are apparently healthy, and both are well dressed and wearing slightly worn gold wedding bands. They are obviously affectionate, and as they take a seat on your couch, the woman gives the man a quick kiss. You notice that their faces and arms are well tanned, and the man is holding a key ring with two keys. One is stamped with the word "Porsche." When you glance through the front window, you notice a small, two-seat sports car of that make parked on the street. You introduce yourself as a fortune-teller famous throughout the world, and as you gaze into your crystal ball, you say, "I see . . ." (Do a cold reading of this couple.)

   At about 10:00 the next morning a woman in her mid-forties comes through the front door. She looks tired, her makeup is slightly smeared, and behind dark glasses you notice that her eyes look puffy. Her clothing is rumpled, and you detect a slight scent of alcohol on her breath. As she takes a seat on your couch, you notice that she is agitated and nervous, and she fidgets with the wedding ring on her finger. In a subdued tone of voice she says that she wants her fortune told. You reply that she has come to the right place, and as you wave your hands over your crystal ball, you begin with the words "I see . . ." (Do a cold reading of this woman.)

7. Psychic phenomena include psychokinesis, telepathy, clairvoyance, and precognition. Psychokinesis is the ability to move objects through the direct power of the mind, telepathy is the power to perceive the thoughts of others without the use of the senses, clairvoyance is the ability to perceive distant objects without the use of the senses, and precognition is the ability to see the future without the use of the senses.

   The psychologist Terence Hines (Hines, 1988, 83) argues that gambling casinos and government-run lotteries provide a real-world test for the existence of psychic phenomena. Every roll of a pair of dice, every spin of a roulette wheel, every game of poker or blackjack, and every purchase of a lottery ticket is an opportunity for the operation of psychokinesis, telepathy, clairvoyance, or precognition. If these phenomena actually occurred, then one would expect that the earnings of casinos and lotteries would be affected. But in fact these earnings are exactly as the laws of chance predict. Does this fact provide a fair test for the existence of psychic phenomena? Some defenders of psychic phenomena argue that psychic powers cannot be used for personal gain. Does this argument amount to an ad hoc modification of the hypothesis underlying psychic phenomena? Is the argument plausible?

8. In 1975 James Randi offered $10,000 (later increased to $1,000,000) to any person who could perform a paranormal feat (including any demonstration of psychic power) in his presence under controlled conditions. (This offer was still open as of the printing of this edition, but certain restrictions were placed in effect as of September 1, 2015.) Since that time, hundreds of people have tried to win the prize, but not a single one has succeeded. Does the failure of such people to collect the prize constitute a fair test of the existence of psychic phenomena?

   During the past hundred years, thousands of experiments have been performed to demonstrate unequivocally the existence of psychic phenomena, but thus far none has succeeded. To account for the negative results of some of these experiments, Gertrude Schmeidler invented the "sheep-goat" hypothesis, according to which such experiments are influenced by the attitudes of the experimenters. If the experimenters doubt the existence of psychic phenomena, then the experiment is doomed to failure; but if the experimenters are believers, then the experiment will succeed. Is this hypothesis believable? Does it qualify as an ad hoc modification? How might the attitude of the experimenters affect the outcome of the experiment? Could James Randi's presence account for the inability of performers such as Uri Geller to demonstrate their alleged psychic powers? (G. R. Schmeidler, "Separating the Sheep from the Goats," *Journal of the American Society for Psychical Research*, 39, no. 1 [1945], 47–50.)

9. In 1970, the physicist David Simpson and his colleague Norman Foxwell performed an experiment involving a group of UFO buffs in England. On a Saturday evening about thirty of these individuals had gathered on a remote hilltop where they thought there was a good chance of sighting a UFO. Simpson positioned himself on another hilltop, about three-quarters of a mile away, and he pointed a purple spotlight, connected to a 12-volt battery, in the direction of the group. At 11:00 P.M. he switched on the light for 5 seconds, and after a 5-second pause he switched it on again for 25 seconds. Mr. Foxwell, Simpson's accomplice, was stationed among the observers, and to enhance the emotional effect, shortly after the purple light was sighted, Foxwell switched on a buzzer that was attached to a bogus magnetic-field sensor. According to UFO lore, UFOs are supposed to generate intense magnetic fields, so the buzzer signaled to the crowd that a UFO was operating nearby. To further enhance the effect, Foxwell had loaded a camera with a roll of film, two frames of which had been doctored with a fake latent image of a UFO. Foxwell proceeded to take two additional snapshots in the general direction of the purple light (which by then had been turned off), and he then gave the film to one of the members of the group for processing.

When the film was developed, sure enough, a tiny image of what appeared to be a UFO was visible on two frames. But those two frames (which were taken a year earlier) also contained geographic features that were inconsistent with the other two (genuine) frames. These inconsistencies were so glaring that anyone who examined all four frames closely would detect that at least two of them had been faked. However, when the photographs were examined in the laboratory of the *Flying Saucer Review*, an international publication devoted to UFO sightings, the experts announced that the negatives were "genuine beyond all doubt." Later, the director of research at the Astrophysical Institute of the French National Centre for Scientific Research published a "tentative interpretation" of the photographs, stating "In my opinion there is no question of the object photographed being in any possible way the result of faking."

Four months after the sighting, a report of the incident was published in the *Flying Saucer Review*. As you read the following selection from the report, remember that the purple light was turned on for a total of 30 seconds, that it was absolutely stationary, and that it was located on the horizon, at zero degrees of elevation from the observers:

At 11:02 P.M. an object was seen at an elevation of approximately 20 degrees in the eastern sky. The object appeared very suddenly as if it came through the clouds, and appeared to the eye as a very bright ovoid light—purple in colour with a periphery of white. Two members of my group who observed the object through binoculars both remarked they could see a crimson light in the centre; this was also attested to by witnesses with good vision.

The object remained stationary for approximately 30 seconds, during which time Mr. Foxwell was able to take the first of his photographs. The object then moved slowly to the right—towards the town—and lost a little altitude in the process. At one stage in the movement it dimmed considerably as though obscured by a low cloud. The object continued moving for approximately 20 to 30 seconds, and then stopped again. The light then increased considerably in intensity, though we could not be sure if the object was moving directly toward the observation point, or if it remained stationary. At this point the alarm of a detector sounded and a witness ran to switch it off. After 10 to 20 seconds the light dimmed and went out as though concealed by a cloud. However we were all certain that the object had not moved once more. The sighting had lasted for approximately one to one and a half minutes.

Why do you think the observers saw the purple light move? Was it because they associated the light with the faked UFO images (the second of which appeared slightly below and to the right of the first)? Why did the observers see the light as elevated 20 degrees off the horizon? (The faked UFO images appeared approximately on the horizon.) Do you think that the expectations of the observers affected what they reportedly saw? Do you think that confabulation played a role in the report? How about the autokinetic effect? Or perceptual sets? Why do you think the specialists who examined the photographs failed to detect the inconsistencies? Could emotions have played a role in this oversight? (From "A Controlled UFO Hoax: Some Lessons," by David I. Simpson, in Frazier, 1981.)

10. On the basis of a person's natal chart (horoscope cast according to the person's date, time, and place of birth), astrologers claim to be able to analyze that person's character and personality and make predictions about his or her life course. To test the claims of astrology about character analysis, UCLA physicist Shawn Carlson conducted a study involving thirty American and European astrologers considered by their peers to be among the best in the field. To complete the study Carlson selected 116 "clients," who were then given the California Personality Inventory (CPI), a widely used and scientifically accepted test that measures personality traits. The results of the CPI were then used to compile a personality profile for each of the clients. The astrologers were informed about the nature of the CPI, and to prevent any anti-astrology bias, many of their suggestions were incorporated into the study.

The astrologers were then given each client's natal chart together with three personality profiles. One of the profiles matched the client in question, and the other two were chosen at random from a separate batch of personality profiles composed in the same way as the true one. No astrologer was able to confront any client face-to-face, and the study was done on a double-blind basis so that neither the astrologer nor the experimenters knew which profile corresponded with which natal chart. The astrologers predicted that they would be able to match a chart with the correct profile at least 50 percent of the time. However, as it turned out, only one out of three matches was correct—exactly what would be expected by chance. The results of Carlson's study were published in the widely respected scientific journal *Nature*.

Do you think that Carlson's study tends to disprove the claim that astrology can analyze personality features? Do you think that if the astrologers were allowed to meet the clients face-to-face, the results would have been different? Why? (From "Double-Blind Test of Astrology . . ." in Frazier, 1991.)

Astrologers also claim the ability to make predictions. In 1978, R. N. Hunter and J. S. Durr of the U.S. Geological Survey invited astrologers to submit predictions about earthquakes. Hunter and Durr analyzed 240 predictions made by 27 astrologers and found that their accuracy was worse than would have been the case had they simply guessed. Also, in 1985, G. Chatillon analyzed 30 predictions for North America made by Huguette Hirsig, one of Montreal's most famous astrologers. Only two were found to be correct. Do studies of this sort tend to disprove the claims that astrologers are able to make true predictions?

11. The first step in providing an astrological reading is to cast the chart. This is followed by an analysis of interacting chart factors, which in turn is followed by the astrologer's interpretation of these factors. In regard to the third step, D. Hamblin, former chairman of the United Kingdom Astrological Association, wrote:

If I find a very meek and unaggressive person with five planets in Aries, this does not cause me to doubt that Aries means aggression. I may be able to point to his Pisces Ascendant, or to his Sun conjunct Saturn, or to his ruler in the twelfth house; and if none of these alibis are available, I can simply say that he has not yet fulfilled his Aries potential. Or I can argue (as I have heard argued) that, if a person has an *excess* of planets in a particular sign, he will tend to suppress the characteristics of that sign because he is scared that, if he reveals them, he will carry them to excess. But if on the next day I meet a very aggressive person who also has five planets in Aries, I will change my tune: I will say that he *had* to be like that because of his planets in Aries.

Does this statement indicate that the step involving chart interpretation is not subject to disconfirmation and is therefore unscientific? Is Hamblin saying here that the interpretation is not of the chart but of the face-to-face encounter with the client? (From "Does Astrology Need to Be True?" by Geoffrey Dean, in Frazier, 1991.)

12. In 1955, the psychologist N. D. Sundburg gave the Minnesota Multiphasic Personality Inventory, a commonly used personality test, to forty-four students. Next he had two highly experienced psychologists draw up personality sketches for each student based on the results of the test. He then presented the individualized personality sketch to each student, together with a universal faked sketch—one provided for all the men and another for all the women. Fifty-nine percent of the students picked the faked sketch as describing their true personality. What do these findings imply about self-knowledge and the accuracy of personal validation? Are people prone to accept descriptions of themselves that are flattering? Do people tend to find some specific feature in their makeup that fits any generalization?

Specifically, Sundburg found that the following sketch was acceptable as describing the majority of college men:

You are a person who is very normal in his attitudes, behavior and relationships with people. You get along well without effort. People naturally like you, and you are not overly critical of them or yourself. You are neither overly conventional nor overly individualistic. Your prevailing mood is one of optimism and constructive effort, and you are not troubled by periods of depression, psychosomatic illness, or nervous symptoms.

The following sketch was found to be acceptable as describing the majority of college women:

You appear to be a cheerful, well-balanced person. You may have some alternation of happy and unhappy moods, but they are not extreme now. You have few or no problems with your health. You are sociable and mix well with others. You are adaptable to social situations. You tend to be adventurous. Your interests are wide. You are fairly confident and usually think clearly.

Do you find that either of these descriptions fits you fairly well? If so, what implications does this have for the astrologer, the tarot-card reader, or the fortune-teller?

13. On June 24 and 26, 1981, six children in the little village of Medjugorje in Bosnia (former Yugoslavia) claimed to have had a vision of the Virgin Mary. In the days and weeks that followed, more alleged visions occurred, and reports began to attract visitors anxious for a vision of their own. From 1981 until 2010, approximately 30 million people, many from the United States,

visited Medjugorje, and many reported that their hopes were fulfilled. By the time these visits began, claims of visions were popping up everywhere, to the obvious glee of the charismatic pastor of the local church. However, not everyone accepted the authenticity of these visions. Among the detractors was the local bishop, Pavao Zanic, who, on July 25, 1987, issued a declaration that included the following:

> The Madonna, they say, started to appear on the Podbrdo [a hamlet] of the Mountain Crnica, but when the militia forbade going there, she came into homes, into forests, fields, vineyards and tobacco fields; she appeared in the church, on the altar, in the sacristy, in the choir loft, on the roof, on the church steeple, on the roads, on the way to Cerno, in a car, on buses, in classrooms, in several places in Mostar and Sarajevo, in monasteries in Zagreb, Verazdin, Switzerland, Italy, once again in the Podbrdo, atop Krizevac, in the parish, in the rectory, etc. It is certain that not even half of the alleged places where the apparitions have taken place have been mentioned. . . .

In 1991, after a lengthy inquiry, the Yugoslavian Bishops Conference issued a statement that nothing miraculous had occurred at Medjugorje; nevertheless, thousands of pilgrims continue to stream into the village even to this day. Also, the original six visionaries continue to claim apparitions of the Virgin.

How do you think all these visions are best explained? Do you think they are evidence of miracles? Or, could collective hallucination be responsible? Do people see what they want to see? What is your estimate of the average annual economic benefit that 30 million visitors would bring to a small village over a span of twenty-nine years? Do you think that this benefit has anything to do with the motives of the original six visionaries? Do you think that the pilgrims to Medjugorje are prone to superstition?

The philosopher Paul Kurtz suggests that religion, with its emphasis on miracles and the supernatural, sensitizes people to believe in the superstitious and the paranormal. Do you think that Kurtz is correct in this assessment? Is there any essential difference between the miraculous and the superstitious? If so, is there any evidence to support this difference? (Paul Kurtz, "Reflections on the 'Transcendental Temptation,'" in Frazier, 1991, 13–16.)

II. Design or perform the following experiments, as directed.

1. Psychic phenomena include psychokinesis, telepathy, clairvoyance, and precognition (see Exercise I, 7). Design an experiment to test for the existence of one or more forms of these phenomena. The experiment might use Zener cards, dice, remote-viewing tests, or Ganzfield (sensory deprivation) conditions. (For Ganzfield studies, see Frazier, 1991, 143–148.) Be sure to build sufficient precautions into the experiment to prevent cheating.

2. Iridology is a diagnostic procedure that depends on the hypothesis that each organ of the body is represented by a specific part of the iris. By examining the eyes of a patient, the iridologist is supposed to be able to detect disease. Design an experiment to test this hypothesis. Employ proper restrictions to prevent cheating.

3. Dowsing involves the use of a forked tree branch ("dowsing rod") to find underground water. Sometimes a pair of metal rods are used, and sometimes oil, minerals, and metal objects are claimed to have been found. When the dowser feels sudden jerks from the dowsing rod, he knows he is standing over a source of water (or oil, etc.). The practice depends on the hypothesis that water exerts some kind of magnetic influence over the rod or engages the psychic abilities of the dowser (or both). Design an experiment to test for the existence of this phenomenon. (See the references to dowsing in Randi, 1982a.)

4. Try your hand at cold reading. Have an assistant select some "clients" who are willing to come in for a reading. They should be told in advance that you have genuine abilities in this area. In preparation read Ray Hayman's article in Frazier, 1981, 79–96.

5. Set up an experiment to test for the autokinetic effect. The experiment might involve a small point of light in a large, dark room, or a flashlight some distance away on a dark night. Select a small group of observers for this experiment, and include a test for the claim that one observer's insistence that the light is moving influences what the others see.

6. Design an experiment to test whether people are prone to believing fantastical explanations of things they do not understand (including conjurer's tricks.) Consider repeating the experiment (described in the text) that Singer and Benassi performed.

7. Design an experiment to test the claims of astrology. You might begin by selecting ten "clients"; obtain the exact time and location of their births and have an astrologer do a reading for each. Then see if the clients can recognize which reading (out of, say, a total of five) pertains to them. Or, alternately, for each reading you might prepare a "reverse reading" in which the character description is the exact reverse of the "true" reading. Then give each client a copy of both readings (true and reverse) and see if he or she can distinguish the true one. (See Geoffrey Dean's two articles in Frazier, 1991, 279–319.)

III. After researching one of the following topics, write an essay of eight to ten pages evaluating the plausibility of the underlying hypothesis.

1. The existence of UFOs

2. Extraterrestrial abductions

3. Scientific creationism

4. Darwin's theory of natural selection

5. Biorhythms

6. Phrenology

7. Séances and channeling

MindTap Master concepts and improve outcomes with Aplia, at the end of the chapter, in the Aplia folder.

Summary

Criteria that bear on the distinction between science and superstition:

- Evidentiary support:
  - Superstitious hypotheses tend to lack supporting evidence.
  - Evidence is based on measurements expressed in mathematical terms.
  - Anecdotal evidence is usually not acceptable.
  - Experiments must be replicable at other times and places.
  - Hypotheses must be framed in precise language.
  - Hypotheses must be disconfirmable.
  - Ad hoc modifications must be avoided.
  - Simple explanations are better than complex ones.
  - The best hypotheses lead to predictions that turn out to be true.
  - Superstitious hypotheses never lead to striking, new insights that turn out to be true.
- Objectivity:
  - Beliefs grounded in emotion are not well founded.
  - Well-founded beliefs are not rooted in the preachings of a guru.
  - Mental laziness and magical thinking must be avoided.
  - The media are complicit in reinforcing magical thinking.
  - The placebo effect is responsible for many apparent cures.
  - Perceptions are affected by expectations.
  - Hallucinations can distort the content of perception.
  - Confabulation can distort the content of memory.
- Integrity:
  - Superstition often rests on faked evidence.
  - Practitioners of superstition ignore bad predictions that arise in connection with their practice.
  - Practitioners of superstition ignore coherence problems in their hypotheses.
  - Practitioners of superstition ignore conflicts between their hypotheses and other, well-confirmed hypotheses.
  - Scientists work on such problems until they are solved.
- Concluding Remarks:
  - Fraudulent work occurs occasionally in science, but it is not sufficient to erode the distinction between science and superstition.
  - Distinguishing science from superstition is crucial to the future of civilization.

Selected Readings

Best, John B. 1986. *Cognitive Psychology*. St. Paul, MN: West Publishing.

Bruner, Jerome S., and Leo J. Postman. 1973. "On the Perception of Incongruity: A Paradigm." In *Beyond the Information Given*, by Jerome S. Bruner. New York: W. W. Norton.

Feyerabend, Paul. 1975. *Against Method*. London: New Left Books.

MindTap Need help? See the Learning Logic folder at the end of the chapter: the self-paced tutorial walks you through any section.

Frazier, Kendrick (ed.). 1981. *Paranormal Borderlines of Science*. Buffalo, NY: Prometheus Books.

———— (ed.). 1991. *The Hundredth Monkey, and Other Paradigms of the Paranormal*. Buffalo, NY: Prometheus Books.

Gardner, Martin. 1957. *Fads and Fallacies in the Name of Science*. New York: Dover.

Guthrie, Stewart. 1993. *Faces in the Clouds: A New Theory of Religion*. Oxford, UK: Oxford University Press.

Hines, Terence. 1988. *Pseudoscience and the Paranormal*. Amherst, NY: Prometheus Books.

Kanizsa, Gaetano. 1979. *Organization in Vision*. New York: Praeger Publishers.

Kitcher, Philip. 1982. *Abusing Science: The Case Against Creationism*. Cambridge, MA: MIT Press.

Kuhn, Thomas S. 1970a. "Logic of Discovery or Psychology of Research." In *Criticism and the Growth of Knowledge*. Edited by Imre Lakatos and Alan Musgrave. Cambridge, UK: Cambridge University Press, 4–10.

————. 1970b. *The Structure of Scientific Revolutions*, 2nd ed. Chicago: University of Chicago Press.

Lakatos, Imre. 1977. *Philosophical Papers*, Vol. 1. Cambridge, UK: Cambridge University Press.

Popper, Karl. 1963. *Conjectures and Refutations*. London: Routledge and Kegan Paul.

Radner, Daisie, and Michael Radner. 1982. *Science and Unreason*. Belmont, CA: Wadsworth.

Randi, James. 1982a. *Flim Flam*. Buffalo, NY: Prometheus Books.

————. 1982b. *The Truth About Uri Geller*. Buffalo, NY: Prometheus Books.

Schick, Theodore, and Lewis Vaughn. 1995. *How to Think About Weird Things*. Mountain View, CA: Mayfield Publishing Co.

Singer, Barry, and Victor A. Benassi. 1980–81. "Fooling Some of the People All of the Time." *The Skeptical Inquirer*, Winter, 17–24.

Thagard, Paul. 1978. "Why Astrology Is a Pseudoscience." In *Proceedings of the Philosophy of Science Association*, Vol. 1, 223–234.

Answers

to Selected Exercises

Exercise 1.1

I.

1. P: Carbon monoxide molecules happen to be just the right size and shape, and happen to have just the right chemical properties, to fit neatly into cavities within hemoglobin molecules in blood that are normally reserved for oxygen molecules.
   C: Carbon monoxide diminishes the oxygen-carrying capacity of blood.
4. P: When individuals voluntarily abandon property, they forfeit any expectation of privacy in it that they might have had.
   C: A warrantless search and seizure of abandoned property is not unreasonable under the Fourth Amendment.
7. P_1: We need sleep to think clearly, react quickly, and create memories.
   P_2: Studies show that people who are taught mentally challenging tasks do better after a good night's sleep.
   P_3: Other research suggests that sleep is needed for creative problem solving.
   C: It really does matter if you get enough sleep.
10. P_1: Punishment, when speedy and specific, may suppress undesirable behavior.
    P_2: Punishment cannot teach or encourage desirable alternatives.
    C: It is crucial to use positive techniques to model and reinforce appropriate behavior that the person can use in place of the unacceptable response that has to be suppressed.
13. P_1: Private property helps people define themselves.
    P_2: Private property frees people from mundane cares of daily subsistence.
    P_3: Private property is finite.
    C: No individual should accumulate so much property that others are prevented from accumulating the necessities of life.

16. P_1: The nations of planet earth have acquired nuclear weapons with an explosive power equal to more than a million Hiroshima bombs.
    P_2: Studies suggest that explosion of only half these weapons would produce enough soot, smoke, and dust to blanket the earth, block out the sun, and bring on a nuclear winter that would threaten the survival of the human race.
    C: Radioactive fallout isn't the only concern in the aftermath of nuclear explosions.
19. P_1: Antipoverty programs provide jobs for middle-class professionals in social work, penology, and public health.
    P_2: Such workers' future advancement is tied to the continued growth of bureaucracies dependent on the existence of poverty.
    C: Poverty offers numerous benefits to the nonpoor.
22. P: Take the nurse who alleges that physicians enrich themselves in her hospital through unnecessary surgery; the engineer who discloses safety defects in the braking systems of a fleet of new rapid-transit vehicles; the Defense Department official who alerts Congress to military graft and overspending: All know that they pose a threat to those whom they denounce and that their own careers may be at risk.
    C: The stakes in whistle-blowing are high.
25. P_1: It is generally accepted that by constantly swimming with its mouth open, the shark is simply avoiding suffocation.
    P_2: This assures a continuous flow of oxygen-laden water into the shark's mouth, over its gills, and out through the gill slits.
    C: Contrary to the tales of some scuba divers, the toothy, gaping grin on the mouth of an approaching shark is not necessarily anticipatory.
28. P_1: Anyone familiar with our prison system knows that there are some inmates who behave little better than brute beasts.

MindTap All answers to the exercise sets are available online.

676

P$_2$: If the death penalty had been truly effective as a deterrent, such prisoners would long ago have vanished.

C: The very fact that these prisoners exist is a telling argument against the efficacy of capital punishment as a deterrent.

II.

1. College sports are as much driven by money as are professional sports.
4. Business majors are robbing themselves of the true purpose of collegiate academics, a sacrifice that outweighs the future salary checks.
7. A person cannot reject free will and still insist on criminality and codes of moral behavior.
10. Protecting the environment requires that we limit population growth.

Exercise 1.2

I.

1. Nonargument; explanation.
4. Nonargument; illustration.
7. Argument (conclusion: If stem-cell research is restricted, then people will die prematurely).
10. Nonargument; report.
13. Nonargument; illustration.
16. Nonargument; piece of advice.
19. Argument (conclusion: For organisms at the sea surface, sinking into deep water usually means death).
22. Argument (conclusion: Atoms can combine to form molecules whose properties generally are very different from those of the constituent atoms).
25. Nonargument; explanation.
28. Argument (conclusion: A person never becomes truly self-reliant).
31. This passage could be both an argument and an explanation (conclusion: In areas where rats are a problem, it is very difficult to exterminate them with bait poison).
34. Nonargument; loosely associated statements.

II.

1. Nonargument.
4. Nonargument.
7. Argument (conclusion: Creating a third political party—the independent party—is a good idea).
10. Argument (conclusion: Strong anti-bullying programs are needed to provide a means to report bullying anonymously, to train all school personnel to take reports of bullying seriously, and to offer workshops for children on how to respond to being bullied).

VI.

1. Sufficient: If something is a tiger, then it is an animal.
4. Necessary: If a person has no racket, then he/she cannot play tennis. Or, If a person plays tennis, then he/she has a racket.
7. Sufficient: If leaves burn, then smoke is produced.
10. Necessary: If a person does not intend to deceive someone, then he or she does not tell a lie. Or, If a person tells a lie, then he or she intends to deceive someone.

Exercise 1.3

I.

1. Deductive (argument based on mathematics; also, conclusion follows necessarily from the premises).
4. Deductive (categorical syllogism; also, conclusion follows necessarily from the premises).
7. Inductive (causal inference; also, conclusion follows only probably from the premise).
10. Inductive (argument from analogy; also, conclusion follows only probably from the premise).
13. Inductive (argument from authority; also, conclusion follows only probably from the premise).
16. Deductive (conclusion follows necessarily from the premise).
19. Inductive (causal inference; also, conclusion follows only probably from the premises).
22. Deductive (conclusion follows necessarily from the premise; this example might also be interpreted as an argument from definition—the definition of "refraction").
25. Inductive (causal inference: The dog's familiarity with the visitor caused the dog to be silent).
28. Inductive (causal inference; also, the word "may" suggests a probabilistic inference).

Exercise 1.4

I.

1. Valid, unsound; false premises, false conclusion.
4. Valid, sound; true premises, true conclusion.
7. Invalid, unsound; true premise, true conclusion.
10. Valid, unsound; false premise, false conclusion.
13. Invalid, unsound; true premises, true conclusion.

II.

1. Strong, cogent; true premise, probably true conclusion.
4. Weak, uncogent; true premise, probably false conclusion.
7. Strong, uncogent; false premise, probably true conclusion.

10. Strong, cogent; true premise, probably true conclusion.

13. Weak, uncogent; true premises, probably false conclusion.

III.

1. Deductive, valid.
4. Deductive, valid.
7. Inductive, weak.
10. Deductive, invalid.
13. Inductive, weak.
16. Deductive, invalid.
19. Inductive, strong.

Exercise 1.5

I.

1. All *G* are *S*. _All Q are S._ All *G* are *Q*.	All cats are animals. (T) _All dogs are animals. (T)_ All cats are dogs. (F)
4. No *U* are *P*. _Some U are not F._ Some *F* are not *P*.	No fish are mammals. (T) _Some fish are not cats. (T)_ Some cats are not mammals. (F)
7. No *P* are *H*. _No C are H._ No *P* are *C*.	No dogs are fish. (T) _No mammals are fish. (T)_ No dogs are mammals. (F)
10. Some *S* are not *O*. _Some G are not O._ Some *S* are not *G*.	Some dogs are not fish. (T) _Some animals are not fish. (T)_ Some dogs are not animals. (F)
13. Some *I* are not *E*. _All C are E._ Some *C* are not *I*.	Some animals are not mammals. (T) _All cats are mammals. (T)_ Some cats are not animals. (F)

II.

1. If *A* then *E*.
   Not *A*.
   Not *E*.
   If George Washington was assassinated, then George Washington is dead. (T)
   George Washington was not assassinated. (T)
   George Washington is not dead. (F)
4. If *E*, then either *D* or *C*.
   If *D*, then *I*.
   If *E*, then *I*.
   If Tom Cruise is a man, then he is either a mouse or a human. (T)
   If Tom Cruise is a mouse, then he has a tail. (T)
   If Tom Cruise is a man, then he has a tail. (F)
7. All *C* with *L* are either *S* or *I*.
   All *C* are *I*.
   All cats with fur are either mammals or dogs. (T)
   All cats are dogs. (F)

10. All *R* that are *F* are either *L* or *H*.
    All *R* are *H*.
    All *F* are *L*.
    All cats that are mammals are either dogs or animals. (T)
    All cats are animals. (T)
    All mammals are dogs. (F)

Exercise 1.6

I.

1.

4.

7.

10.

13.

II.

1.

4.

7.

10.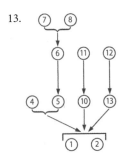

Note: Possible variations exist for ⑤, ⑥, and ⑦.

13.

⑦ ⑧
⑥ ⑪ ⑫
④ ⑤ ⑩ ⑬
① ②

Exercise 2.1

II.

1. In dog sled races the dogs are tortured.
Torturing animals is morally wrong.
Therefore, dog sled races are morally wrong.

4. Free ownership of guns is as noble as belief in God and intestinal fortitude.
Belief in God and intestinal fortitude made our country great and free.
Continued belief in God and intestinal fortitude are necessary to keep our country the way it is.
Free ownership of guns is no less important than God and intestinal fortitude.
Therefore, gun control is wrong.

7. The celebration of cultural diversity causes social fragmentation.
The celebration of cultural diversity is symptomatic of a split personality.
The people who set this country up framed one nation, indivisible.
The celebration of cultural diversity works against the intention of these people.
The celebration of cultural diversity erodes national identity.
Therefore, the celebration of cultural diversity is wrong.

10. Liberalism has excessively enlarged the welfare system.
Liberalism has made welfare recipients indolent and irresponsible.
The liberals refuse to acknowledge or correct the defects in this system.
Liberalism has made the criminal justice system too sensitive to the criminal and too insensitive to the victim of crime.
Liberalism has given more rights to the criminal than to the ordinary citizen.
Liberalism has promoted sex and violence in the school system.
Liberals have opposed prayer in the schools.
Therefore, liberalism is bad.

III.

1. Probably verbal; ambiguity. Does "sound" designate a subjective perception or an objective disturbance of the air (or some other medium)?

4. Probably verbal; ambiguity. By "violence" do we mean intentional hostility exerted by one human against another, or the operation of blind physical forces? Possibly a combination of verbal and factual. Is human violence caused by the operation of physical forces just as other physical events are?

7. Factual. Did Paul go to Knoxville or Nashville?

10. Factual. When was the Battle of Trafalgar fought, and when did Nelson die?

13. Probably a combination of verbal (ambiguity) and factual. First, does "freedom" mean the absence of external constraint only, or the absence of both internal and external constraint? Second, given the former, is it appropriate to punish the perpetrator of evil acts even though those acts might be internally compelled?

16. Verbal; vagueness. What is the meaning of "overpaid"?

19. Verbal; vagueness. What is the meaning of "poverty"?

Exercise 2.2

I.

4a. Plant, tree, conifer, spruce, Sitka spruce.

Exercise 2.3

I.

1. Precising definition.
4. Lexical definition.
7. Persuasive definition.
10. Theoretical definition.
13. Stipulative definition.
16. Persuasive definition.
19. Lexical definition.

22. Precising definition.
25. Stipulative definition.

Exercise 2.4

I.

1. Definition by subclass.
4. Enumerative definition.
7. Demonstrative definition.
10. Operational definition.
13. Definition by genus and difference.
16. Etymological definition.
19. Enumerative definition.
22. Synonymous definition.
25. Definition by subclass.
28. Definition by genus and difference.

II.

1a. "Skyscraper" means the Empire State Building, Chrysler Building, Willis Tower, and so on. Nonsynonymous term: building.
3a. "Animal" means a horse, bear, lion, and so on. Nonsynonymous term: mammal.
5a. "Intersection" means crossing.
6a. A person is a "genius" if and only if that person can earn a score of 140 on an IQ test.
7a. "Drake" means a male duck.
8a. "Morphology" is derived from the Greek words *morphe*, meaning "form," and *logos*, meaning reason, speech, or account. The morphology of something (such as an animal or a plant) gives an account or explanation of the form or structure of that thing.

Exercise 2.5

I.

1. Rule 3: too narrow; the definiens excludes images made of bronze, wood, plaster, and so on.
4. Rule 6: figurative language.
7. Rule 5: negative.
10. Rule 7: affective terminology.
13. Rule 1: improper grammar.
16. Rule 4: circular.
19. Rule 6: vague.
22. Rule 1: improper grammar; Rule 6: vague; Rule 3: too broad (the definiens also includes ketches, sloops, and yawls).
25. Rule 3: too broad (the definiens also describes violins, violas, and string basses).
28. Rule 2: fails to convey the essential meaning; the definition says nothing about the purpose of a clock, which is to tell the time; also too narrow: the definiens

excludes twenty-four-hour clocks and clocks without twelve numerals on their face.
31. Rule 7: affective terminology.
34. Rule 3: both too narrow and too broad; the definiens excludes instruments used for writing on canvas, glass, metal, plastic, and so on, and it includes pencils, crayons, and so on.

Exercise 3.1

I.

1. Formal fallacy.
4. Informal fallacy.
7. Informal fallacy.
10. Formal fallacy.

Exercise 3.2

I.

1. Appeal to pity.
4. Accident.
7. Appeal to force.
10. *Tu quoque* (you, too).
13. Red herring.
16. *Ad hominem* circumstantial.
19. Straw man.
22. Appeal to the people, indirect variety.
25. Missing the point.

Exercise 3.3

I.

1. Hasty generalization (converse accident).
4. Slippery slope.
7. Appeal to ignorance.
10. Appeal to unqualified authority.
13. Weak analogy.

III.

1. Hasty generalization.
4. *Ad hominem* circumstantial.
7. False cause (gambler's fallacy).
10. Straw man.
13. Red herring.
16. Missing the point.
19. Weak analogy.
22. No fallacy.
25. Appeal to ignorance.
28. False cause.

Exercise 3.4

I.

1. False dichotomy.
4. Amphiboly.
7. Begging the question.
10. Equivocation.
13. Composition.
16. Suppressed evidence.
19. Division.
22. Complex question.
25. Begging the question.

III.

1. *Ad hominem* circumstantial.
4. Equivocation.
7. Begging the question.
10. Division.
13. False cause (oversimplified cause).
16. Appeal to unqualified authority.
19. Composition.
22. Weak analogy.
25. Straw man.
28. Accident.
31. Red herring.
34. Amphiboly.
37. False cause (gambler's fallacy).
40. Begging the question.
43. Missing the point or suppressed evidence.
46. Hasty generalization.
49. Composition.

Exercise 3.5

I.

1. Missing the point or begging the question.
4. Composition.
7. No fallacy? Weak analogy?
10. Appeal to unqualified authority. The statement "Only a fool . . ." involves an *ad hominem* abusive.
13. False cause, suppressed evidence, begging the question. There is little or no evidence of any causal connection between malpractice suits and the decision of some obstetricians to leave the field. An unmentioned factor is the inconvenience of being on call twenty-four hours per day waiting for patients to deliver. There is also little or no evidence of any genuine "lawsuit crisis."
16. Begging the question? (Strange argument!)
19. Slippery slope.
22. False cause? No fallacy?
25. False cause.
28. Suppressed evidence? Weak analogy? Begging the question? No fallacy? The Commerce Clause of the U.S. Constitution and pertinent federal legislation prohibit unfair trade practices between states. No equivalent regulations exist for international trade.
31. Appeal to the people (direct variety). Also appeal to pity?
34. Appeal to the people (direct variety)?
37. False dichotomy? No fallacy?
40. Appeal to unqualified authority, slippery slope.
43. Several cases of weak analogy. Also, a possible case of *ad hominem* abusive.
46. Begging the question; straw man.
49. Appeal to unqualified authority. The last paragraph suggests a hasty generalization.
52. Hasty generalization. *Ad hominem* abusive? Also, begging the question or red herring?
55. Weak analogy.
58. Weak analogy? No fallacy?

Exercise 4.1

I.

1. *Quantifier*: some; *subject term*: executive pay packages; *copula*: are; *predicate term*: insults to ordinary workers.
4. *Quantifier*: some; *subject term*: preachers who are intolerant of others' beliefs; *copula*: are not; *predicate term*: television evangelists.
7. *Quantifier*: no; *subject term*: sex education courses that are taught competently; *copula*: are; *predicate term*: programs that are currently eroding public morals.
10. *Quantifier*: no; *subject term*: fast-food restaurants; *copula*: are; *predicate term*: establishments that promote public health.
13. *Quantifier*: all; *subject term*: animal-rights activists; *copula*: are; *predicate term*: individuals motivated by empathy.
16. *Quantifier*: some; *subject term*: presidential candidates; *copula*: are not; *predicate term*: threats to the establishment.

Exercise 4.2

I.

1. **E** proposition, universal, negative, subject and predicate terms are distributed.
4. **O** proposition, particular, negative, subject term undistributed, predicate term distributed.
7. **I** proposition, particular, affirmative, subject and predicate terms undistributed.

II.

1. No drunk drivers are threats to others on the highway.
4. Some CIA operatives are champions of human rights.
7. Some stay-at-home moms are workers who deserve Social Security.

III.

1. Some owners of pit bull terriers are people who can expect expensive lawsuits.
4. No residents of Manhattan are people who can afford to live there.
7. Some prescription medicines are substances hazardous to human health.

IV.

1. Some oil spills are not events catastrophic to the environment.
4. All corporate lawyers are people with a social conscience.
7. Some economic forums are venues for airing financial fears.

Exercise 4.3

I.

1.

L   H

4.

R   F

7.

H   C

II.

1. Invalid.   10. Valid.
4. Valid.   13. Invalid.
7. Invalid.

III.

1. No S are B.

S   B

All S are B.
(invalid)

S   B

4. All M are C.

M   C

False: Some
M are not C.
(valid)

M   C

7. No F are S.

F   S

False: All F are S.
(invalid, existential fallacy)

F   S

10. No V are A.

V   A

False: Some V are A.
(valid)

V   A

13. False: Some S are
not O.

S   O

Some S are O.
(invalid,
existential fallacy)

S   O

Exercise 4.4

I.

1. No non-B are A. (true)
4. All non-B are A. (false)
7. Contraposition. (undetermined)
10. Obversion. (false)

II.

1a. All storms intensified by global warming are hurricanes. (not logically equivalent)
2a. No radically egalitarian societies are societies that
preserve individual liberties. (logically equivalent)
3a. All physicians eligible to practice are physicians with
valid licenses. (logically equivalent)

III.

1. Invalid (illicit conversion).
4. Invalid (illicit contraposition).
7. Valid.
10. Valid.
13. Invalid (illicit conversion).
16. Invalid (illicit contraposition).
19. Valid.

Exercise 4.5

I.

1. (a) False, (b) True, (c) False.
4. (a) Undetermined, (b) True, (c) Undetermined.
7. (a) False, (b) Undetermined, (c) Undetermined.

II.

1. Valid.
4. Invalid (existential fallacy).
7. Invalid (illicit contrary).
10. Invalid (illicit subcontrary).
13. Invalid (existential fallacy).

III.

1. Valid, unsound.
4. Valid, sound.
7. Invalid, unsound (existential fallacy).
10. Invalid, unsound (illicit subcontrary).

IV.

1. All non-*B* are *A*. (true)
4. Some non-*A* are *B*. (undetermined)
7. No non-*A* are *B*. (false)
10. Some non-*A* are not non-*B*. (true)
13. Obversion. (false)
16. Contradiction. (true)
19. Contrary. (undetermined)

V.

1. Valid.
4. Invalid (illicit contraposition).
7. Valid.
10. Invalid (illicit contrary).
13. Invalid (illicit subcontrary).

VI.

1. All *I* are *C*.
   Some *I* are *C*. (subalternation)
   Some *C* are *I*. (conversion)
4. All *E* are *A*.
   False: No *E* are *A*. (contrary)
   False: No *A* are *E*. (conversion)
   False: All *A* are non-*E*. (obversion)
7. Some *P* are not non-*S*.
   Some *P* are *S*. (obversion)
   Some *S* are *P*. (conversion)
   False: No *S* are *P*. (contradiction)
10. False: Some *F* are not *A*.
    False: No *F* are *A*. (subalternation)
    False: No *A* are *F*. (conversion)
    False: All *A* are non-*F*. (obversion)

Exercise 4.6

I.

1. Some *A* are not *B*.

   No *A* are *B*.
   (invalid)

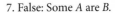

4. All *A* are *B*.

   False: No *A* are *B*.
   (invalid, Boolean; conditionally
   valid, Aristotelian)

7. False: Some *A* are *B*.

   No *A* are *B*.
   (valid, Boolean)

10. No *A* are *B*.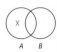

    Some *A* are not *B*.
    (invalid, Boolean; conditionally
    valid, Aristotelian)

II.

1. No *S* are *B*.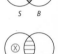

   False: Some *S* are *B*.
   (valid, Boolean)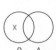

4. False: Some *D* are *A*.

   Some *D* are not *A*.
   (invalid, Boolean; valid, Aristotelian;
   existential fallacy, Boolean)

7. All *P* are *F*.

   False: No *P* are *F*.
   (invalid; existential fallacy,
   Boolean and Aristotelian)

10. False: Some *T* are *Q*.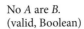

    All *T* are *Q*.
    (invalid)

13. False: Some *P* are *T*.

False: All *P* are *T*.
(invalid, Boolean; valid, Aristotelian;
existential fallacy, Boolean)

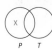

Exercise 4.7

I.

1. All banks that make too many risky loans are banks that will fail.
4. All substances identical to bromine are substances extractable from seawater.
7. No halogens are chemically inert elements.
10. All ships that fly the Jolly Roger are pirate ships.
13. All bachelors are unmarried men.
16. Some organic silicones are things used as lubricants.
19. Some giant stars are things in the Tarantula Nebula. *Or* All things identical to the Tarantula Nebula are things that contain a giant star.
22. All people who require insulin treatments are diabetics.
25. All cities identical to Berlin are cities that were the setting for the 1936 Olympic Games. *Or* All events identical to the 1936 Olympic Games are events that took place in Berlin.
28. All places there is smoke are places there is fire.
31. All ores identical to pitchblende are radioactive ores.
34. All novels written by John Grisham are novels about lawyers.
37. All times a rainbow occurs are times the sun is shining.
40. Some corporate raiders are people known for their integrity, and some corporate raiders are not people known for their integrity.
43. All people identical to me are people who like strawberries. *Or* All things identical to strawberries are things I like.
46. All places Cynthia wants to travel are places Cynthia travels.
49. No physicists are people who understand the operation of superconductors.
52. All measures that increase efficiency are measures that improve profitability.
55. Some picnics are events entirely free of ants, and some picnics are not events entirely free of ants.
58. Some contestants are people who won prizes.

II.

1. Some figure skating finalists are performers who may win medals.
4. No downhill skiers who suffer from altitude sickness are effective competitors.
7. No matadors are performers who succumb easily to fear.
10. All hungry crocodiles are dangerous animals.

III.

1. No flu vaccines are completely effective medicines. Therefore, some flu vaccines are not completely effective medicines. (valid)
4. All dates who spend every minute texting are dates who are bad dinner companions. Therefore, all dates who are bad dinner companions are dates who spend every minute texting. (invalid, illicit conversion; contrapose premise and conclusion)
7. No tax cuts are measures that please everyone. Therefore, all tax cuts are measures that please everyone. (invalid, illicit contrary)
10. Some fake artworks are items sold on eBay. Therefore, some items sold on eBay are fake artworks. (valid, convert either the premise or the conclusion)

Exercise 5.1

I.

1. *Major term:* things that produce intense gravity.
   Minor term: extremely dense objects.
   Middle term: neutron stars.
   Mood, figure: **AAA**-3; invalid.
4. *Major term:* good witnesses.
   Minor term: hypnotized people.
   Middle term: people who mix fact with fantasy.
   Mood, figure: **EIO**-1; valid, Boolean.

II.

1. All *B* are *D*.
   No *R* are *D*.
   ─────────────
   No *R* are *B*.
       AEE-2
       valid, Boolean
4. No *M* are *F*.
   All *M* are *I*.
   ─────────────
   Some *I* are not *F*.
       EAO-3
       invalid, Boolean;
       valid, Aristotelian
7. All *P* are *E*.
   All *L* are *P*.
   ─────────────
   Some *L* are *E*.
       AAI-1
       invalid
10. Some *O* are not *C*.
   All *S* are *O*.
   ─────────────
   Some *S* are *C*.
       OAI-1
       invalid

III.

1. Some *M* are not *P*.
   All *M* are *S*.
   No *S* are *P*.
4. Some *M* are *P*.
   All *S* are *M*.
   No *S* are *P*.
7. All *M* are *P*.
   All *S* are *M*.
   All *S* are *P*.
10. Some *P* are not *M*.
    No *M* are *S*.
    All *S* are *P*.

IV.

1. No dogmatists are scholars who encourage free thinking.
   Some theologians are scholars who encourage free thinking.
   Some theologians are not dogmatists.
4. Some viruses are not things capable of replicating by themselves.
   All viruses are structures that invade cells.
   Some structures that invade cells are not things capable of replicating by themselves.

Exercise 5.2

I.

1. All *C* are *U*.
   Some *U* are *I*.
   Some *I* are *C*.
   AII-4
   invalid

4. All *H* are *D*.
   Some *D* are not *P*.
   Some *P* are not *H*.
   AOO-4
   invalid

7. No *P* are *I*.
   All *F* are *I*.
   No *F* are *P*.
   EAE-2
   valid, Boolean

10. No *C* are *O*.
    Some *D* are not *O*.
    Some *D* are not *C*.
    EOO-2
    invalid

13. No *P* are *W*.
    All *D* are *P*.
    No *D* are *W*.
    EAE-1
    valid, Boolean

16. All *C* are *G*.
    All *G* are *E*.
    Some *E* are *C*.
    AAI-4
    invalid

19. No *T* are *R*.
    All *T* are *G*.
    Some *G* are not *R*.
    EAO-3
    invalid, Boolean;
    valid, Aristotelian

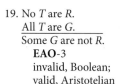

II.

1.

Conclusion: No *S* are *P*.

4.

Conclusion: Some *S* are not *P*.

7.

Conclusion: All *S* are *P*.

10.

Conclusion: None.

Exercise 5.3

I.

1. All *M* are *P*.
   All *M* are *S*.
   All *S* are *P*.
      invalid;
      illicit minor

4. All *P* are *M*.
   All *S* are *M*.
   Some *S* are *P*.
      invalid;
      undistributed middle

7. No *M* are *P*.
   All *S* are *M*.
   All *S* are *P*.
      invalid;
      drawing affirmative
      conclusion from
      negative premise

10. Some *M* are *P*.
    All *M* are *S*.
    Some *S* are not *P*.
       invalid;
       illicit major;
       drawing negative
       conclusion from
       affirmative premises

13. All *P* are *M*.
    No *M* are *S*.
    No *S* are *P*.
       valid, Boolean;
       no rules broken

16. No *M* are *P*.
    No *S* are *M*.
    No *S* are *P*.
       invalid;
       exclusive premises

19. All *P* are *M*.
    Some *S* are not *M*.
    Some *S* are not *P*.
       valid, Boolean;
       no rules broken

II.

1. Some *N* are *C*.
   Some *C* are *O*.
   Some *O* are *N*.
      invalid;
      undistributed middle

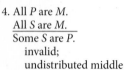

4. Some *C* are not *M*.
   No *C* are *I*.
   Some *I* are not *M*.
      invalid;
      exclusive premises

7. No *S* are *V*.
   Some *W* are *V*.
   Some *W* are not *S*.
      valid, Boolean;
      no rules broken

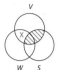

10. All *S* are *M*.
    All *M* are *P*.
    Some *P* are *S*.
       invalid, Boolean;
       valid, Aristotelian;
       existential fallacy,
       Boolean

Exercise 5.4

I.

1. Some non-*T* are *M*. (convert, obvert)
   All non-*I* are non-*M*. (contrapose)
   Some *I* are *T*.
   Some *M* are not *T*.
   All *M* are *I*.
   Some *I* are *T*.
      invalid; drawing affirmative conclusion
      from negative premise

4. Some *I* are *C*.
   All *C* are non-*P*.
   Some non-*I* are not *P*. (contrapose)
   Some *I* are *C*.
   All *C* are non-*P*.
   Some non-*P* are not *I*.
      invalid; illicit major

7. All non-*M* are non-*E*. (contrapose)
   Some *P* are not *M*.
   Some *P* are non-*E*. (obvert)
   All *E* are *M*.
   Some *P* are not *M*.
   Some *P* are not *E*.
      valid

10. Some *F* are non-*D*. (obvert)
    No *D* are *V*.
    Some non-*V* are *F*. (convert, obvert)
    Some *F* are not *D*.
    No *D* are *V*.
    Some *F* are not *V*.
       invalid; exclusive premises

Exercise 5.5

I.

1. All scientists who theorize about the nature of time are physicists.
   All people identical to Stephen Hawking are scientists who theorize about the nature of time.
   All people identical to Stephen Hawking are physicists.
   valid

4. All people who wrote the Declaration of Independence are people who had a big impact on civilization.
   All people identical to Thomas Jefferson are people who had a big impact on civilization.
   All people identical to Thomas Jefferson are people who wrote the Declaration of Independence.
   invalid, undistributed middle

7. Some songs Miranda Lambert sings are country songs.
   All songs Miranda Lambert wants to sing are songs Miranda Lambert sings.
   Some songs Miranda Lambert wants to sing are country songs.
   invalid, undistributed middle

10. All TV viewers who receive scrambled signals are viewers with a decoder.
    All people who receive digital satellite signals are TV viewers who receive scrambled signals.
    All people who receive digital satellite signals are viewers with a decoder.
    valid

13. All diseases carried by recessive genes are diseases that can be inherited by offspring of two carriers.
    All diseases identical to cystic fibrosis are diseases carried by recessive genes.
    All diseases identical to cystic fibrosis are diseases that can be inherited by offspring of two carriers.
    valid

Exercise 5.6

I.

1. Premise missing: Some police chiefs fix parking tickets.

4. Conclusion missing: A few fraternities have no legitimate role in campus life.

7. Conclusion missing: Some text messages are not from friends.

10. Premise missing: Whenever administrative salaries have exploded, attempts to reduce tuition have failed.

13. Premise missing: No one who thinks that everything is governed by deterministic laws believes in free will.

II.

1. All people who fix parking tickets are people who undermine the evenhanded enforcement of the law.
   Some police chiefs are people who fix parking tickets.
   Some police chiefs are people who undermine the evenhanded enforcement of the law.
   valid

4. No groups that have dangerous initiation rites are groups that have a legitimate role in campus life.
   Some fraternities are groups that have dangerous initiation rites.
   Some fraternities are not groups that have a legitimate role in campus life.
   valid

7. All messages from friends are welcome messages.
   Some text messages are not welcome messages.
   Some text messages are not messages from friends.
   valid

10. All times administrative salaries have exploded are times attempts to reduce tuition have failed.
    All recent years are times administrative salaries have exploded.
    All recent years are times attempts to reduce tuition have failed.
    valid

13. No people who think that everything is governed by deterministic laws are people who believe in free will.
    All mechanistic materialists are people who think everything is governed by deterministic laws.
    No mechanistic materialists are people who believe in free will.
    valid

III.

1. No organizations that make alcohol readily available and acceptable are organizations that are serious about fighting alcohol abuse.
   All organizations identical to the Defense Department are organizations that make alcohol readily available and acceptable.
   No organizations identical to the Defense Department are organizations that are serious about fighting alcohol abuse.

4. All efforts to ban books are efforts that ensure those books will be read.
   All efforts by the fundamentalist families in Church Hill, Tennessee, to remove *Macbeth*, etc. from the libraries are efforts to ban books.
   All efforts by the fundamentalist families in Church Hill, Tennessee, to remove *Macbeth*, etc. from the libraries are efforts that ensure those books will be read.

7. All policies that promote more college graduates tomorrow are policies that result in higher tax revenues tomorrow.

5

All policies that offer financial aid to college students today are policies that promote more college graduates tomorrow.

All policies that offer financial aid to college students today are policies that result in higher tax revenues tomorrow.

and

All policies that result in higher tax revenues tomorrow are good investments in the future.

All policies that offer financial aid to college students today are policies that result in higher tax revenues tomorrow.

All policies that offer financial aid to college students today are good investments in the future.

10. All people who act in ways that decrease their chances of survival are people who will die out through natural selection.

All smokers who continue smoking are people who act in ways that decrease their chances of survival.

All smokers who continue smoking are people who will die out through natural selection.

and

All people who act in ways that increase their chances of survival are people who will survive through natural selection.

All smokers who quit are people who act in ways that increase their chances of survival.

All smokers who quit are people who will survive through natural selection.

V.

1. All average childless couples are couples who experience higher levels of emotional well-being.
All couples who experience higher levels of emotional well-being are happier couples.
Therefore, all average childless couples are happier couples.

Exercise 5.7

I.

1. All *A* are *B.*
No *B* are *C.*
Some *D* are *C.*
No *C* are *A.*

Some *D* are not *A.*
   valid

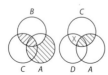

4. No *K* are *N.*
Some *T* are *K.*
All *T* are *C.*
Some *C* are *Q.*
Some *T* are not *N.*
Some *C* are not *N.*

Some *Q* are not *N.*
   invalid

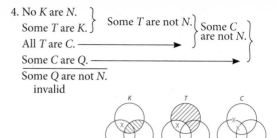

7. After contraposing the first premise, obverting the second premise and the conclusion, and rearranging the premises, we have

No *X* are *W.*
All *U* are *W.*
All *V* are *U.*
All *V* are *Y*
No *U* are *X.*
No *V* are *X.*

No *Y* are *X.*
   invalid

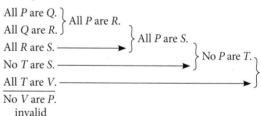

10. After converting and obverting the second and fourth premises, obverting the third and fifth premises and the conclusion, and rearranging the premises, we have

All *P* are *Q.*
All *Q* are *R.*
All *R* are *S.*
No *T* are *S.*
All *T* are *V.*
All *P* are *R.*
All *P* are *S.*
No *P* are *T.*

No *V* are *P.*
   invalid

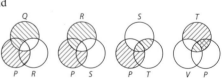

II.

1. Valid—no rules broken.
4. Invalid—breaks Rule 1: *C* is undistributed in both premises.
7. Invalid—breaks Rule 2: *Y* is distributed in the conclusion but not in the premise.
10. Invalid—breaks Rule 2: *V* is distributed in the conclusion but not in the premise.

III.

1. All things that produce oxygen are things that support human life.
   All rain forests are things that produce oxygen.
   No things that support human life are things that should be destroyed.

   No rain forests are things that should be destroyed.
   After rearranging the premises, we have

   All O are S.
   All R are O.
   No S are D.
   No R are D.

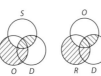

   No R are D.
      no rules broken

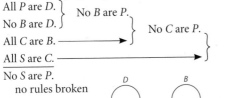

4. No brittle things are ductile things.
   All superconductors are ceramics.
   All things that can be pulled into wires are ductile things.
   All ceramics are brittle things.

   No superconductors are things that can be pulled into wires.
   After rearranging the premises, we have

   No B are D.
   All S are C.
   All P are D.
   All C are B.
   No S are P.

   No S are P.
      no rules broken

7. All people who give birth to crack babies are people who
   increase future crime rates.
   Some pregnant women are pregnant crack users.
   All people who increase future crime rates are criminals.
   No pregnant crack users are people who fail to give birth to crack babies.

   Some pregnant women are criminals.
   After obverting the fourth premise and rearranging the premises, we have

   All B are I.
   Some P are U.
   All I are C.
   No U are non-B.
   Some P are C.

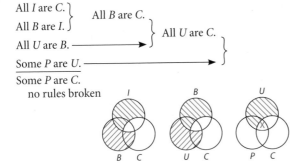

   Some P are C.
      no rules broken

5

10. All things that promote skin cancer are things that cause death.
    All things that preserve the ozone layer are things that prevent the release of CFCs.
    No things that resist skin cancer are things that increase UV radiation.
    All things that do not preserve the ozone layer are things that increase UV radiation.
    Some packaging materials are things that release CFCs.
    No things that cause death are things that should be legal.
    _____
    Some packaging materials are things that should not be legal.
    After contraposing the second premise, converting and obverting the third premise, and obverting the conclusion, we have

All S are C.
All O are non-R.
No non-S are U.
All non-O are U.
Some M are R.
No C are L.
_____
Some M are non-L.

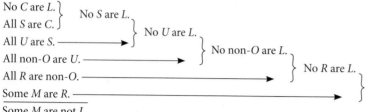

No C are L. }
All S are C. } No S are L.
All U are S. ⟶ } No U are L.
All non-O are U. ⟶ } No non-O are L.
All R are non-O. ⟶ } No R are L.
Some M are R. ⟶ }

Some M are not L.
    no rules broken

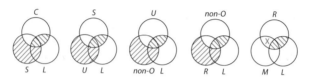

C   S   U   non-O   R
S   L   U   L   non-O   L   R   L   M   L

IV.

1. No ducks are waltzers.
   No officers are non-waltzers.
   All poultry of mine are ducks.
   _____
   No poultry of mine are officers.
   After obverting the second premise and rearranging the premises, we have

No D are W.
No O are non-W.
All P are D.
_____
No P are O.

All O are W. }
No D are W. } No D are O.
All P are D. ⟶ }

No P are O.
    no rules broken

W   D
D   O   P   O

4. All hummingbirds are richly colored birds.
   No large birds are birds that live on honey.
   All birds that do not live on honey are birds that are dull in color.
   _____
   All hummingbirds are small birds.

All H are R.
No L are O.
All non-O are non-R.
All H are non-L.

After contraposing the third premise, obverting the conclusion, and rearranging the premises, we have

No *L* are *O*. ⎱
All *R* are *O*. ⎰ No *L* are *R*. ⎱
All *H* are *R*. ⟶ ⎰

No *H* are *L*.
   no rules broken

7. All books in this library that I do not recommend are books that are unhealthy in tone.
   All the bound books are well-written books.
   All the romances are books that are healthy in tone.
   All the unbound books are books in this library that I do not recommend.
   All the romances are well-written books.
   After contraposing the first and fourth premises, we have

All non-*R* are non-*H*.
All *B* are *W*.
All *O* are *H*.
All non-*B* are non-*R*.
All *O* are *W*.

All *B* are *W*. ⎱
All *R* are *B*. ⎰ All *R* are *W*. ⎱
All *H* are *R*. ⟶ ⎰ All *H* are *W*. ⎱
All *O* are *H*. ⟶ ⎰

All *O* are *W*.
   no rules broken

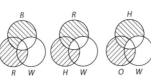

10. All animals that belong to me are animals I trust.
   All dogs are animals that gnaw bones.
   All animals I admit to my study are animals that beg when told to do so.
   All the animals in the yard are animals that belong to me.
   All animals I trust are animals I admit into my study.
   All animals that are willing to beg when told to do so are dogs.
   All the animals in the yard are animals that gnaw bones.
   After rearranging the premises, we have

All *A* are *T*.
All *D* are *G*.
All *S* are *B*.
All *Y* are *A*.
All *T* are *S*.
All *B* are *D*.
All *Y* are *G*.

All *D* are *G*. ⎱
All *B* are *D*. ⎰ All *B* are *G*. ⎱
All *S* are *B*. ⟶ ⎰ All *S* are *G*. ⎱
All *T* are *S*. ⟶ ⎰ All *T* are *G*. ⎱
All *A* are *T*. ⟶ ⎰ All *A* are *G*. ⎱
All *Y* are *A*. ⟶ ⎰

All *Y* are *G*.
   no rules broken

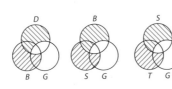

Exercise 6.1

I.

1. ~C
4. H • B
7. M ≡ P
10. P ⊃ A
13. M • (E ∨ D)
16. ~J • ~P
19. ~(F ∨ M) or ~F • ~M
22. (B ⊃ C) ⊃ R
25. ~R ∨ (M ⊃ P)
28. (~P • ~C) ⊃ M
31. (T • B) ∨ (~Z • ~K)
34. S • [N ⊃ (C ∨ J)]
37. M ⊃ [N ⊃ (S • T)]
40. ~[(L ∨ K) • (T ∨ M)]
43. I ≡ P
46. ~[(W ⊃ T) • (C ⊃ K)]
49. [(C • J) ≡ K] ⊃ ~(B ∨ S)

II.

1. R ∨ F
4. ~(H ∨ S)
7. S ⊃ G
10. A ⊃ (~N ⊃ M)
13. (C • K) ≡ P
16. [(T • L) ⊃ H] • (H ⊃ I)
19. (B ⊃ M) • [(M • F) ⊃ (C • P)]

Exercise 6.2

I.

1. Dot.
4. Triple bar.
7. Horseshoe.
10. Wedge.

II.

1. ~ H
   Ⓕ T
4. H • ~ N
   T Ⓕ F T
7. W ⊃ E
   F Ⓣ F
10. H ⊃ (C ∨ E)
    T Ⓣ T T F
13. ~ (E ∨ F) ⊃ (H • L)
    T F F F Ⓣ T T T

III.

1. A • X
   T Ⓕ F
4. ~ C ∨ Z
   F T Ⓕ F
7. ~ X ⊃ Z
   T F Ⓕ F
10. ~ (A • ~ Z)
    Ⓕ T T T F
13. (A • Y) ∨ (~ Z • C)
    T F F Ⓣ T F T T
16. (C ≡ ~ A) ∨ (Y ≡ Z)
    T F F T Ⓣ F T F
19. ~ [~ (X ⊃ C) ≡ ~ (B ⊃ Z)]
    Ⓣ F F T T F T T F F
22. ~ [(A ≡ X) ∨ (Z ≡ Y)] ∨ [(~ Y ⊃ B) • (Z ⊃ C)]
    F T F F T T F Ⓣ T F T T T F T T
25. (Z ⊃ C) ⊃ {[(~ X ⊃ B) ⊃ (C ⊃ Y)] ≡
    F T T Ⓣ T F T T F T F F T
    [(Z ⊃ X) ⊃ (~ Y ⊃ Z)]}
    F T F F T F F F

IV.

1. A ∨ P
   T Ⓣ ?
4. Q • A
   ? Ⓣ T
7. A ⊃ P
   T Ⓣ ?
10. (P ⊃ A) ≡ (Q ⊃ B)
    ? T T Ⓣ ? T T
13. ~ (Q • Y) ≡ ~ (Q ∨ A)
    T ? F F Ⓕ F ? T T

Exercise 6.3

I.

1. N ⊃ (N ⊃ N)
   T [T] T T T
   F [T] F T F
   tautologous
4. [(E ⊃ F) ⊃ F] ⊃ E
   T T T T T [T] T
   T F F T F [T] T
   F T T T T [F] F
   F T F F F [T] F
   contingent
7. [(Z ⊃ X) • (X ∨ Z)] ⊃ X
   T T T T T T T [T] T
   T F F F F T T [T] F
   F T T T T T F [T] T
   F T F F F F F [T] F
   tautologous

10. [G ⊃ (N ⊃ ~ G)] • [(N ≡ G) • (N ∨ G)]

```
T F  T F F T  [F]  T T T T T T T
T T  F T F T  [F]  F F T F F T T
F T  T T T F  [F]  T F F F T T F
F T  F T T F  [F]  F F T F F F F
```
self-contradictory

13. [U • (T ∨ S)] ≡ [(~ T ∨ ~ U) • (~ S ∨ ~ U)]

```
T T  T T T  [F]  F T F F T  F F T F F T
T T  T T F  [F]  F T F F T  F T F T F T
T T  F T T  [F]  T F T F T  F F T F F T
T F  F F F  [F]  T F T F T  T T F T F T
F F  T T T  [F]  F T T T F  T F T T T F
F F  T T F  [F]  F T T T F  T T F T T F
F F  F T T  [F]  T F T T F  T F T T T F
F F  F F F  [F]  T F T T F  T T F T T F
```
self-contradictory

II.

1. ~ D ∨ B   ~ (D • ~ B)

```
F T [T] T     [T] T F F T
F T [F] F     [F] T T T F
T F [T] T     [T] F F F T
T F [T] F     [T] F F T F
```
logically equivalent

4. R ∨ ~ S   S • ~ R

```
T [T] F T     T [F] F T
T [T] T F     F [F] F T
F [F] F T     T [T] T F
F [T] T F     F [F] T F
```
contradictory

7. (E ⊃ C) ⊃ L   E ⊃ (C ⊃ L)

```
T T T [T] T     T [T] T T T
T T T [F] F     T [F] T F F
T F F [T] T     T [T] F T T
T F F [T] F     T [T] F T F
F T T [T] T     F [T] T T T
F T T [F] F     F [T] T F F
F T F [T] T     F [T] F T T
F T F [F] F     F [T] F T F
```
consistent

10. W ≡ (B • T)   W • (T ⊃ ~ B)

```
T [T] T T T     T [F] T F F T
T [F] T F F     T [T] F T F T
T [F] F F T     T [T] T T T F
T [F] F F F     T [T] F T T F
F [F] T T T     F [F] T F F T
F [T] T F F     F [F] F T F T
F [T] F F T     F [F] T T T F
F [T] F F F     F [F] F T T F
```
inconsistent

13. H • (K ∨ J)   (J • H) ∨ (H • K)

```
T [T] T T T     T T T [T] T T T
T [T] T T F     F F T [T] T T T
T [T] F T T     T T T [T] T F F
T [F] F F F     F F T [F] T F F
F [F] T T T     T F F [F] F F T
F [F] T T F     F F F [F] F F T
F [F] F T T     T F F [F] F F T
F [F] F F F     F F F [F] F F F
```
logically equivalent

III.

1. Carlson's prediction is false (self-contradictory).

4. It is possible that both astronomers are correct. If they are, a supernova will not occur within 10 light years of the earth.

7. It is possible that both stockbrokers are correct. If they are, then Datapro will cut back its workforce. We can conclude nothing about Netmark and Compucel.

10. It is possible that Nicole's philosophy makes sense. If it does, then the mind is not identical to the brain, personal freedom exists, and humans are responsible for their actions.

Exercise 6.4

I.

1. N ⊃ S // ~ N ⊃ ~ S

```
T T T    F T T F T
T F F    F T T T F
F (T) T    T F (F) F T
F T F    T F T T F
```
invalid

4. D ⊃ W / D // W

```
T T T   T   T
T F F   T   F
F T T   F   T
F T F   F   F
```
valid

7. Invalid (fails on first line).

10. Valid.

II.

1. Valid. 4. Valid.

7. Invalid (fails on fourth line).

10. Invalid (fails on fourth and sixth lines).

13. Valid.

16. Invalid (fails on third line).   19. Valid.

22. Invalid (fails on eighth line). 25. Valid.

Exercise 6.5

I.

1. D = True
4. N = Unknown
7. C = True
10. J = Unknown
13. C = True, P = False
16. G = False, K = False
19. L = True
22. H = False, B = False
25. C = Unknown, R = Unknown

II.

Note: Truth values may vary depending on how the problem is done.

1. $B \supset C \; / \sim C \; / / \sim B$
   T T F   T F   F T
   valid

4. $\sim (I \equiv J) \; / / \sim (I \supset J)$
   T T F F   F T F F
   T F F T   F F T T
   invalid

7. $G \supset H \; / \; H \supset I \; / \sim J \supset G \; / \sim I \; / / \; J$
   T T T   T T T   T F T T   T T   F
   valid

10. $(M \lor N) \supset O \; / \; O \supset (N \lor P) \; / \; M \supset (\sim Q \supset N) \; / \; (Q \supset M) \supset \sim P \; / / \; N \equiv O$
    T T T F   T   T   T   T F F
        T T T T F T T   F T   T F F T F T   F F T
    invalid

13. $(A \lor B) \supset (C \bullet D) \; / \; (X \lor \sim Y) \supset (\sim C \bullet \sim W) \; / \; (X \lor Z) \supset (A \bullet E) \; / / \sim X$
    T T T F F   T T   T T F T T F   T T   T T T T   F T
    valid

III.

1. $K \equiv (R \lor M) \; / \; K \bullet \sim R \; / \; M \supset \sim K$
   T T F T T   T T T F   T T F T
   inconsistent

4. $(N \lor C) \equiv E \; / \; N \supset \sim (C \lor H) \; / \; H \supset E \; / \; C \supset H$
   F T T T T   F T F T T T   T T T   T T T
                                          F T T
                                          F T F
   consistent

7. $S \supset (R \equiv A) \; / \; A \supset (W \bullet \sim R) \; / \; R \equiv (W \lor T) \; / \; S \bullet U \; / \; U \supset T$
   T T T T F   F T   F F T   T T   T T   T T T   T T T
   inconsistent

10. $A \lor Z \; / \; A \supset (T \bullet F) \; / \; Z \supset (M \bullet Q) \; / \; Q \supset \sim F \; / \; T \supset \sim M \; / \; M \supset A$
    T T T   T T F F F   T T T T T   T T T F   F T F T   T T T
    T T F   T T T T T   F T F F F   F T F T   T T T F   F T T
                                                             F T F
    consistent

Exercise 6.6

I.

1. MT—valid.
4. CD—valid.
7. DD—valid.
10. DA—invalid.
13. DS—valid.
16. AC—invalid.
19. Invalid.

Numbers 7 and 13 must be rewritten as follows:

7. $(E \supset N) \bullet (\sim L \supset \sim K)$
$$\frac{\sim N \vee \sim\sim K}{\sim E \vee \sim\sim L}$$

13. $\sim S \vee P$
$$\frac{\sim\sim S}{P}$$

II.

1. $B \supset G$
$$\frac{\sim G}{\sim B} \qquad \text{MT—valid}$$

4. $W \vee \sim M$
$$\frac{\sim W}{\sim M} \qquad \text{DS—valid}$$

7. N
$$\frac{N \supset B}{B} \qquad \text{MP—valid}$$

10. $(L \supset \sim A) \bullet (C \supset F)$
$$\frac{\sim L \bullet \sim C}{A \bullet \sim F} \qquad \text{invalid}$$

13. $(A \supset E) \bullet (P \supset \sim E)$
$$\frac{E \vee \sim E}{\sim A \vee \sim P}$$
rewritten:
$$(A \supset E) \bullet (P \supset \sim E)$$
$$\frac{\sim E \vee \sim\sim E}{\sim A \vee \sim P} \qquad \text{DD—valid}$$

16. $\sim M \supset U$
$$\frac{U}{\sim M} \qquad \text{AC—invalid}$$

19. $S \supset C$
$$\frac{I \supset S}{I \supset C} \qquad \text{HS—valid}$$

III.

1. $(S \supset M) \bullet (\sim S \supset F)$
$$\frac{S \vee \sim S}{M \vee F} \qquad \text{CD}$$

Since the second premise is a tautology, it is impossible to escape between the horns. The two available strategies are therefore grasping by the horns and constructing a counterdilemma. If Melinda

adequately prepares for the test before the party, then she does not spend the party night studying and she does not fail the test. This would falsify the right-hand conjunct of the first premise, thus falsifying the entire premise. Here is a counterdilemma:

> If Melinda spends the night studying, she will pass the test tomorrow; and if she doesn't spend the night studying, she will go to the party. She will either spend the night studying or not studying. Therefore, she will either pass the test or go to the party.

4. $(C \supset \sim S) \bullet (E \supset S)$
$$\frac{S \vee \sim S}{\sim C \vee \sim E}$$
rewritten:
$$(C \supset \sim S) \bullet (E \supset S)$$
$$\frac{\sim\sim S \vee \sim S}{\sim C \vee \sim E} \qquad \text{DD}$$

The second premise is a tautology, so it is impossible to escape between the horns. One could grasp the dilemma by the horns by arguing that corporations could share the cost of neutralizing toxic waste, thus preserving the competitive edge. Here is a constructive counterdilemma:

> If corporations spend money to neutralize their toxic waste, then the environment will be preserved; but if corporations do not spend money to neutralize their toxic waste, then they will remain competitive. Corporations will do one or the other. Therefore, either the environment will be preserved or corporations will remain competitive.

7. $(C \supset L) \bullet (J \supset B)$
$$\frac{\sim L \vee \sim B}{\sim C \vee \sim J} \qquad \text{DD}$$

Here the second premise is not a tautology, so it is possible to escape between the horns. Perhaps students could take a double major in liberal arts and business. One could also grasp the dilemma by the horns by arguing that students could major in a liberal arts field where a job *would* be available upon graduation. Here is a constructive counterdilemma:

> If students major in liberal arts, then they will take courses that are interesting and rewarding; but if they major in business, then they will have a job when they graduate. Students will either major in liberal arts or business. Therefore, either they will take courses that are interesting and rewarding or they will have a job when they graduate.

10. $(P \supset R) \bullet (T \supset E)$
$$\frac{P \vee T}{R \vee E} \qquad \text{CD}$$

The second premise is not a tautology, so it is at least possible to escape between the horns. If we instructed counterterrorist squads to execute terrorists on the spot, we would neither prosecute them nor release them. Can you think of a way to grasp the dilemma by the horns? Here is a counterdilemma:

> If we prosecute suspected terrorists, then we discourage terrorism; but if we release them, then we avoid the risk of retaliation by other terrorists. We must either prosecute or release suspected terrorists. Therefore, either we will discourage terrorism or we will avoid the risk of retaliation by other terrorists.

V.

1. If human organs are given first to registered donors, then more people will register as donors. If more people register as donors, then the supply of organs will increase. Therefore, if human organs are given first to registered donors, then the supply of organs will increase. (HS)

4. If group problem solving is important, then we should not emphasize individual testing. Group problem solving is important. Therefore, we should not emphasize individual testing. (MP)

   If we should not emphasize individual testing, then the national math test is a mistake. We should not emphasize individual testing. Therefore, the national math test is a mistake. (MP)

7. If we close the library at Central Juvenile Hall, then delinquents will be deprived of an opportunity to read. If delinquents are deprived of an opportunity to read, then they will not have access to ideas, dreams, and alternative ways of living. Therefore, if we close the library at Central Juvenile Hall, then delinquents will not have access to ideas, dreams, and alternative ways of living. (HS)

   If we close the library at Central Juvenile Hall, then delinquents will not have access to ideas, dreams, and alternative ways of living. Delinquents must have access to ideas, dreams, and alternative ways of living. Therefore, we must not close the library at Central Juvenile Hall. (MT)

10. If viewing adult videos led to violent sex crimes, then there would be over a million violent sex crimes per week. It is not the case that there are over a million violent sex crimes per week. Therefore, viewing adult videos does not lead to violent sex crimes. (MT)

Exercise 7.1

I.

1. $\sim G$	1, 2, MT
4. C	1, 2, DS
7. $F \supset D$	1, 3, HS
10. $G \supset A$	1, 4, HS
13. $\sim\sim C$	1, 3, MT
16. $\sim P$	1, 2, MP
19. $\sim(S \vee C)$	1, 3, MT

II.

1. $\sim B$	
4. $R \supset C$	1, 2, DS
7. Q	1, 2, HS
10. $\sim A$	2, 3, MP
13. $\sim\sim S$	1, 4, MT
16. $\sim Z$	3, 4, MT
19. $H \vee G$	3, 4, MP
	2, 4, MP

III.

(1)
1.	$\sim C \supset (A \supset C)$	
2.	$\sim C$	/ $\sim A$
3.	$A \supset C$	1, 2, MP
4.	$\sim A$	2, 3, MT

(4)
1.	$P \supset (G \supset T)$	
2.	$Q \supset (T \supset E)$	
3.	P	
4.	Q	/ $G \supset E$
5.	$G \supset T$	1, 3, MP
6.	$T \supset E$	2, 4, MP
7.	$G \supset E$	5, 6, HS

(7)
1.	$\sim S \supset D$	
2.	$\sim S \vee (\sim D \supset K)$	
3.	$\sim D$	/ K
4.	$\sim\sim S$	1, 3, MT
5.	$\sim D \supset K$	2, 4, DS
6.	K	3, 5, MP

(10)
1.	$N \supset (J \supset P)$	
2.	$(J \supset P) \supset (N \supset J)$	
3.	N	/ P
4.	$J \supset P$	1, 3, MP
5.	$N \supset J$	2, 4, MP
6.	$N \supset P$	4, 5, HS
7.	P	3, 6, MP

(13)
1.	$R \supset (G \vee \sim A)$	
2.	$(G \vee \sim A) \supset \sim S$	
3.	$G \supset S$	
4.	R	/ $\sim A$
5.	$G \vee \sim A$	1, 4, MP
6.	$\sim S$	2, 5, MP
7.	$\sim G$	3, 6, MT
8.	$\sim A$	5, 7, DS

(16)
1.	$(B \supset \sim M) \supset (T \supset \sim S)$	
2.	$B \supset K$	
3.	$K \supset \sim M$	
4.	$\sim S \supset N$	/ $T \supset N$
5.	$B \supset \sim M$	2, 3, HS
6.	$T \supset \sim S$	1, 5, MP
7.	$T \supset N$	4, 6, HS

(19)
1.	$\sim G \supset [G \vee (S \supset G)]$	
2.	$(S \vee L) \supset \sim G$	
3.	$S \vee L$	/ L

4. ~G   2, 3, MP
5. G ∨ (S ⊃ G)   1, 4, MP
6. S ⊃ G   4, 5, DS
7. ~S   4, 6, MT
8. L   3, 7, DS

(22) 1. (C ⊃ M) ⊃ (N ⊃ P)
2. (C ⊃ N) ⊃ (N ⊃ M)
3. (C ⊃ P) ⊃ ~M
4. C ⊃ N   / ~C
5. N ⊃ M   2, 4, MP
6. C ⊃ M   4, 5, HS
7. N ⊃ P   1, 6, MP
8. C ⊃ P   4, 7, HS
9. ~M   3, 8, MP
10. ~C   6, 9, MT

(25) 1. ~N ⊃ [(B ⊃ D) ⊃ (N ∨ ~E)]
2. (B ⊃ E) ⊃ ~N
3. B ⊃ D
4. D ⊃ E   / ~D
5. B ⊃ E   3, 4, HS
6. ~N   2, 5, MP
7. (B ⊃ D) ⊃ (N ∨ ~E)   1, 6, MP
8. N ∨ ~E   3, 7, MP
9. ~E   6, 8, DS
10. ~D   4, 9, MT

IV.

(1) 1. O ⊃ (P ∨ T)
2. ~P
3. O   / T
4. P ∨ T   1, 3, MP
5. T   2, 4, DS

(4) 1. (R ⊃ L) ⊃ (L ⊃ ~F)
2. ~F ∨ (R ⊃ L)
3. ~~F   / ~R
4. R ⊃ L   2, 3, DS
5. L ⊃ ~F   1, 4, MP
6. ~L   3, 5, MT
7. ~R   4, 6, MT

(7) 1. H ⊃ (D ≡ A)
2. V ∨ (R ⊃ V)
3. R ∨ H
4. ~V   / D ≡ A
5. R ⊃ V   2, 4, DS
6. ~R   4, 5, MT
7. H   3, 6, DS
8. D ≡ A   1, 7, MP

(10) 1. ~C ⊃ [C ∨ (J ⊃ D)]
2. C ⊃ (C • U)
3. ~(C • U)
4. ~D   / ~J
5. ~C   2, 3, MT
6. C ∨ (J ⊃ D)   1, 5, MP
7. J ⊃ D   5, 6, DS
8. ~J   4, 7, MT

Exercise 7.2

I.

1. B   2
4. H ∨ F   1
7. Q ∨ K   1
10. ~L ∨ M   1, 2

II.

1. G   2, Simp
                              3, Add
4. T ∨ U   1, Add
                              3, 4, MP
7. ~F   2, 3, MT
                              1, 4, Conj
10. M • E   1, 3, Conj
                              2, 4, MP

III.

(1) 1. ~M ⊃ Q
2. R ⊃ ~T
3. ~M ∨ R   / Q ∨ ~T
4. (~M ⊃ Q) • (R ⊃ ~T)   1, 2, Conj
5. Q ∨ ~T   3, 4, CD

(4) 1. (H ∨ ~B) ⊃ R
2. (H ∨ ~M) ⊃ P
3. H   / R • P
4. H ∨ ~B   3, Add
5. R   1, 4, MP
6. H ∨ ~M   3, Add
7. P   2, 6, MP
8. R • P   5, 7, Conj

(7) 1. (~F ∨ X) ⊃ (P ∨ T)
2. F ⊃ P
3. ~P   / T
4. ~F   2, 3, MT
5. ~F ∨ X   4, Add
6. P ∨ T   1, 5, MP
7. T   3, 6, DS

(10) 1. (D ∨ E) ⊃ (G • H)
2. G ⊃ ~D
3. D • F   / M
4. D   3, Simp
5. D ∨ E   4, Add
6. G • H   1, 5, MP
7. G   6, Simp
8. ~D   2, 7, MP
9. D ∨ M   4, Add
10. M   8, 9, DS

(13) 1. (C ⊃ N) • E
2. D ∨ (N ⊃ D)
3. ~D   / ~C ∨ P

4.	$N \supset D$	2, 3, DS
5.	$\sim N$	3, 4, MT
6.	$C \supset N$	1, Simp
7.	$\sim C$	5, 6, MT
8.	$\sim C \lor P$	7, Add
(16) 1.	$(C \lor \sim G) \supset (\sim P \bullet L)$	
2.	$(\sim P \bullet C) \supset (C \supset D)$	
3.	$C \bullet \sim R$	$/ D \lor R$
4.	C	3, Simp
5.	$C \lor \sim G$	4, Add
6.	$\sim P \bullet L$	1, 5, MP
7.	$\sim P$	6, Simp
8.	$\sim P \bullet C$	4, 7, Conj
9.	$C \supset D$	2, 8 MP
10.	D	4, 9, MP
11.	$D \lor R$	10, Add
(19) 1.	$(U \bullet \sim \sim P) \supset Q$	
2.	$\sim O \supset U$	
3.	$\sim P \supset O$	
4.	$\sim O \bullet T$	$/ Q$
5.	$\sim O$	4, Simp
6.	U	2, 5, MP
7.	$\sim \sim P$	3, 5, MT
8.	$U \bullet \sim \sim P$	6, 7, Conj
9.	Q	1, 8, MP
(22) 1.	$(\sim K \bullet \sim N) \supset [(\sim P \supset K) \bullet (\sim R \supset G)]$	
2.	$K \supset N$	
3.	$\sim N \bullet B$	
4.	$\sim P \lor \sim R$	$/ G$
5.	$\sim N$	3, Simp
6.	$\sim K$	2, 5, MT
7.	$\sim K \bullet \sim N$	5, 6, Conj
8.	$(\sim P \supset K) \bullet (\sim R \supset G)$	1, 7, MP
9.	$K \lor G$	4, 8, CD
10.	G	6, 9, DS
(25) 1.	$(\sim M \bullet N) \supset [(\sim M \lor H) \supset (K \bullet L)]$	
2.	$\sim M \bullet (C \supset D)$	
3.	$\sim N \bullet (F \equiv G)$	$/ K \bullet \sim N$
4.	$\sim M$	2, Simp
5.	$\sim N$	3, Simp
6.	$\sim M \bullet \sim N$	4, 5, Conj
7.	$(\sim M \lor H) \supset (K \bullet L)$	1, 6, MP
8.	$\sim M \lor H$	4, Add
9.	$K \bullet L$	7, 8, MP
10.	K	9, Simp
11.	$K \bullet \sim N$	5, 10, Conj
(28) 1.	$(D \supset B) \bullet (C \supset D)$	
2.	$(B \supset D) \bullet (E \supset C)$	
3.	$B \lor E$	$/ D \lor B$
4.	$D \lor C$	2, 3, CD
5.	$B \lor D$	1, 4, CD
6.	$B \supset D$	2, Simp
7.	$D \supset B$	1, Simp
8.	$(B \supset D) \bullet (D \supset B)$	6, 7, Conj
9.	$D \lor B$	5, 8, CD

IV.

(1) 1.	$T \supset (Q \bullet F)$	
2.	$T \bullet C$	$/ Q \lor O$
3.	T	2, Simp
4.	$Q \bullet F$	1, 3, MP
5.	Q	4, Simp
6.	$Q \lor O$	5, Add
(4) 1.	$M \lor P$	
2.	$(P \lor S) \supset (R \bullet D)$	
3.	$\sim M$	$/ R$
4.	P	1, 3, DS
5.	$P \lor S$	4, Add
6.	$R \bullet D$	2, 5, MP
7.	R	6, Simp
(7) 1.	$(\sim C \lor \sim M) \supset (\sim C \supset T)$	
2.	$C \lor \sim T$	
3.	$\sim C$	$/ B$
4.	$\sim C \lor \sim M$	3, Add
5.	$\sim C \supset T$	1, 4, MP
6.	T	3, 5, MP
7.	$T \lor B$	6, Add
8.	$\sim T$	2, 3, DS
9.	B	7, 8, DS
(10) 1.	$(V \bullet \sim E) \supset (P \supset E)$	
2.	$V \supset \sim E$	
3.	$V \bullet I$	
4.	$\sim E \supset (P \lor J)$	$/ J \bullet \sim E$
5.	V	3, Simp
6.	$\sim E$	2, 5, MP
7.	$V \bullet \sim E$	5, 6, Conj
8.	$P \supset E$	1, 7, MP
9.	$\sim P$	6, 8, MT
10.	$P \lor J$	4, 6, MP
11.	J	9, 10, DS
12.	$J \bullet \sim E$	6, 11, Conj

Exercise 7.3

I.

1.	$\sim N \bullet \sim G$	2
4.	$A \bullet S$	3
7.	$\sim G \lor \sim \sim Q$	1
10.	$\sim (R \bullet P)$	1
13.	$H \supset \sim (L \lor D)$	2

II.

1.	$C \lor K$	1, Com
		2, 3, DS
4.	$L \bullet (S \bullet F)$	1, Assoc
		2, Simp
7.	$D \bullet (M \lor N)$	1, Dist
		2, Simp

10. $(D \lor N) \bullet (D \lor H)$ — 1, Dist
     2, Simp
13. $M \lor (G \lor T)$ — 1, Assoc
     2, 3, DS

III.

(1) 1. $(\sim M \supset P) \bullet (\sim N \supset Q)$
     2. $\sim (M \bullet N)$ — $/ P \lor Q$
     3. $\sim M \lor \sim N$ — 2, DM
     4. $P \lor Q$ — 1, 3, CD

(4) 1. $\sim (N \bullet T)$
     2. T — $/ \sim N$
     3. $\sim N \lor \sim T$ — 1, DM
     4. $\sim T \lor \sim N$ — 3, Com
     5. $\sim \sim T$ — 2, DN
     6. $\sim N$ — 4, 5, DS

(7) 1. $T \supset (B \lor E)$
     2. $\sim E \bullet T$ — $/ B$
     3. $T \bullet \sim E$ — 2, Com
     4. T — 3, Simp
     5. $B \lor E$ — 1, 4 MP
     6. $E \lor B$ — 5, Com
     7. $\sim E$ — 2, Simp
     8. B — 6, 7, DS

(10) 1. $(K \bullet H) \lor (K \bullet L)$
     2. $\sim L$ — $/ H$
     3. $K \bullet (H \lor L)$ — 1, Dist
     4. $(H \lor L) \bullet K$ — 3, Com
     5. $H \lor L$ — 4, Simp
     6. $L \lor H$ — 5, Com
     7. H — 2, 6, DS

(13) 1. $(E \bullet I) \lor (M \bullet U)$
     2. $\sim E$ — $/ \sim (E \lor \sim M)$
     3. $\sim E \lor \sim I$ — 2, Add
     4. $\sim (E \bullet I)$ — 3, DM
     5. $M \bullet U$ — 1, 4, DS
     6. M — 5, Simp
     7. $\sim \sim M$ — 6, DN
     8. $\sim E \bullet \sim \sim M$ — 2, 7, Conj
     9. $\sim (E \lor \sim M)$ — 8, DM

(16) 1. $(Q \bullet N) \lor (N \bullet T)$
     2. $(Q \lor C) \supset \sim N$ — $/ T$
     3. $(N \bullet Q) \lor (N \bullet T)$ — 1, Com
     4. $N \bullet (Q \lor T)$ — 3, Dist
     5. N — 4, Simp
     6. $\sim \sim N$ — 5, DN
     7. $\sim (Q \lor C)$ — 2, 6, MT
     8. $\sim Q \bullet \sim C$ — 7, DM
     9. $\sim Q$ — 8, Simp
     10. $(Q \lor T) \bullet N$ — 4, Com
     11. $Q \lor T$ — 10, Simp
     12. T — 9, 11, DS

(19) 1. $[(I \lor M) \lor G] \supset \sim G$
     2. $M \lor G$ — $/ M$
     3. $(M \lor G) \lor I$ — 2, Add
     4. $I \lor (M \lor G)$ — 3, Com

     5. $(I \lor M) \lor G$ — 4, Assoc
     6. $\sim G$ — 1, 5, MP
     7. $G \lor M$ — 2, Com
     8. M — 6, 7, DS

(22) 1. $S \lor (I \bullet \sim J)$
     2. $S \supset \sim R$
     3. $\sim J \supset \sim Q$ — $/ \sim (R \bullet Q)$
     4. $(S \lor I) \bullet (S \lor \sim J)$ — 1, Dist
     5. $(S \lor \sim J) \bullet (S \lor I)$ — 4, Com
     6. $S \lor \sim J$ — 5, Simp
     7. $(S \supset \sim R) \bullet (\sim J \supset \sim Q)$ — 2, 3, Conj
     8. $\sim R \lor \sim Q$ — 6, 7, CD
     9. $\sim (R \bullet Q)$ — 8, DM

(25) 1. $E \lor \sim (D \lor C)$
     2. $(E \lor \sim D) \supset C$ — $/ E$
     3. $E \lor (\sim D \bullet \sim C)$ — 1, DM
     4. $(E \lor \sim D) \bullet (E \lor \sim C)$ — 3, Dist
     5. $E \lor \sim D$ — 4, Simp
     6. C — 2, 5, MP
     7. $(E \lor \sim C) \bullet (E \lor \sim D)$ — 4, Com
     8. $E \lor \sim C$ — 7, Simp
     9. $\sim C \lor E$ — 8, Com
     10. $\sim \sim C$ — 6, DN
     11. E — 9, 10, DS

(28) 1. $P \lor (I \bullet L)$
     2. $(P \lor I) \supset \sim (L \lor C)$
     3. $(P \bullet \sim C) \supset (E \bullet F)$ — $/ F \lor D$
     4. $(P \lor I) \bullet (P \lor L)$ — 1, Dist
     5. $P \lor I$ — 4, Simp
     6. $\sim (L \lor C)$ — 2, 5, MP
     7. $\sim L \bullet \sim C$ — 6, DM
     8. $\sim L$ — 7, Simp
     9. $(P \lor L) \bullet (P \lor I)$ — 4, Com
     10. $P \lor L$ — 9, Simp
     11. $L \lor P$ — 10, Com
     12. P — 8, 11, DS
     13. $\sim C \bullet \sim L$ — 7, Com
     14. $\sim C$ — 13, Simp
     15. $P \bullet \sim C$ — 12, 14, Conj
     16. $E \bullet F$ — 3, 15, MP
     17. $F \bullet E$ — 16, Com
     18. F — 17, Simp
     19. $F \lor D$ — 18, Add

(31) 1. $(\sim R \lor D) \supset \sim (F \bullet G)$
     2. $(F \bullet R) \supset S$
     3. $F \bullet \sim S$ — $/ \sim (S \lor G)$
     4. $\sim S \bullet F$ — 3, Com
     5. $\sim S$ — 4, Simp
     6. $\sim (F \bullet R)$ — 2, 5, MT
     7. $\sim F \lor \sim R$ — 6, DM
     8. F — 3, Simp
     9. $\sim \sim F$ — 8, DN
     10. $\sim R$ — 7, 9, DS
     11. $\sim R \lor D$ — 10, Add
     12. $\sim (F \bullet G)$ — 1, 11, MP
     13. $\sim F \lor \sim G$ — 12, DM
     14. $\sim G$ — 9, 13, DS

7

15.	$\sim S \cdot \sim G$	5, 14, Conj
16.	$\sim(S \vee G)$	15, DM

(34)
1.	$(M \cdot N) \vee (O \cdot P)$	
2.	$(N \vee O) \supset \sim P$	/ N
3.	$[(M \cdot N) \vee O] \cdot [(M \cdot N) \vee P]$	1, Dist
4.	$(M \cdot N) \vee O$	3, Simp
5.	$O \vee (M \cdot N)$	4, Com
6.	$(O \vee M) \cdot (O \vee N)$	5, Dist
7.	$(O \vee N) \cdot (O \vee M)$	6, Com
8.	$O \vee N$	7, Simp
9.	$N \vee O$	8, Com
10.	$\sim P$	2, 9, MP
11.	$[(M \cdot N) \vee P] \cdot [(M \cdot N) \vee O]$	3, Com
12.	$(M \cdot N) \vee P$	11, Simp
13.	$P \vee (M \cdot N)$	12, Com
14.	$M \cdot N$	10, 13, DS
15.	$N \cdot M$	14, Com
16.	N	15, Simp

IV.

(1)
1.	$(S \cdot D) \vee (S \cdot H)$	
2.	$S \supset (I \cdot R)$	/ S • R
3.	$S \cdot (D \vee H)$	1, Dist
4.	S	3, Simp
5.	$I \cdot R$	2, 4, MP
6.	$R \cdot I$	5, Com
7.	R	6, Simp
8.	$S \cdot R$	4, 7, Conj

(4)
1.	$G \vee (R \cdot E)$	
2.	$(G \vee E) \supset \sim R$	/ G v M
3.	$(G \vee R) \cdot (G \vee E)$	1, Dist
4.	$(G \vee E) \cdot (G \vee R)$	3, Com
5.	$G \vee E$	4, Simp
6.	$\sim R$	2, 5, MP
7.	$G \vee R$	3, Simp
8.	$R \vee G$	7, Com
9.	G	6, 8, DS
10.	$G \vee M$	9, Add

(7)
1.	$R \supset (C \vee M)$	
2.	$\sim(I \vee C)$	
3.	$\sim(A \vee M)$	/ ~R
4.	$\sim I \cdot \sim C$	2, DM
5.	$\sim A \cdot \sim M$	3, DM
6.	$\sim C \cdot \sim I$	4, Com
7.	$\sim C$	6, Simp
8.	$\sim M \cdot \sim A$	5, Com
9.	$\sim M$	8, Simp
10.	$\sim C \cdot \sim M$	7, 9, Conj
11.	$\sim(C \vee M)$	10, DM
12.	$\sim R$	1, 11, MT

(10)
1.	$\sim E \vee (B \cdot P)$	
2.	$\sim E \vee (G \cdot W)$	
3.	$\sim P \vee \sim W$	/ ~E
4.	$(\sim E \vee B) \cdot (\sim E \vee P)$	1, Dist
5.	$(\sim E \vee P) \cdot (\sim E \vee B)$	4, Com
6.	$\sim E \vee P$	5, Simp
7.	$(\sim E \vee G) \cdot (\sim E \vee W)$	2, Dist
8.	$(\sim E \vee W) \cdot (\sim E \vee G)$	7, Com
9.	$\sim E \vee W$	8, Simp
10.	$(\sim E \vee P) \cdot (\sim E \vee W)$	6, 9, Conj
11.	$\sim E \vee (P \cdot W)$	10, Dist
12.	$(P \cdot W) \vee \sim E$	11, Com
13.	$\sim(P \cdot W)$	3, DM
14.	$\sim E$	12, 13, DS

Exercise 7.4

I.

1.	$G \supset Q$	3
4.	$B \equiv N$	1
7.	$\sim\sim C \vee \sim F$	1
10.	$S \supset G$	3
13.	$W \equiv \sim T$	2

II.

1.	$J \supset M$	1, Impl
		2, 3, HS
4.	$K \vee K$	1, 2, CD
		3, Taut
7.	$H \supset (C \supset R)$	1, Impl
		2, Exp
10.	$\sim H \vee \sim H$	1, Impl
		2, Taut
13.	$(N \supset A) \cdot (A \supset N)$	1, Trans
		2, Equiv

III.

(1)
1.	$(S \cdot K) \supset R$	
2.	K	/ S ⊃ R
3.	$(K \cdot S) \supset R$	1, Com
4.	$K \supset (S \supset R)$	3, Exp
5.	$S \supset R$	2, 4, MP

(4)
1.	$S \equiv Q$	
2.	$\sim S$	/ ~Q
3.	$(S \supset Q) \cdot (Q \supset S)$	1, Equiv
4.	$(Q \supset S) \cdot (S \supset Q)$	3, Com
5.	$Q \supset S$	4, Simp
6.	$\sim Q$	2, 5, MT

(7)
1.	$(B \supset M) \cdot (D \supset M)$	
2.	$B \vee D$	/ M
3.	$M \vee M$	1, 2, CD
4.	M	3, Taut

(10)
1.	$(B \supset G) \cdot (F \supset N)$	
2.	$\sim(G \cdot N)$	/ ~(B • F)
3.	$\sim G \vee \sim N$	2, DM
4.	$(\sim G \supset \sim B) \cdot (F \supset N)$	1, Trans
5.	$(\sim G \supset \sim B) \cdot (\sim N \supset \sim F)$	4, Trans
6.	$\sim B \vee \sim F$	3, 5, CD
7.	$\sim(B \cdot F)$	6, DM

(13) 1. $K \supset (B \supset \sim M)$
2. $D \supset (K \cdot M)$ / $D \supset \sim B$
3. $K \supset (\sim\sim M \supset \sim B)$ 1, Trans
4. $K \supset (M \supset \sim B)$ 3, DN
5. $(K \cdot M) \supset \sim B$ 4, Exp
6. $D \supset \sim B$ 2, 5, HS

(16) 1. $T \supset R$
2. $T \supset \sim R$ / $\sim T$
3. $\sim\sim R \supset \sim T$ 2, Trans
4. $R \supset \sim T$ 3, DN
5. $T \supset \sim T$ 1, 4, HS
6. $\sim T \vee \sim T$ 5, Impl
7. $\sim T$ 6, Taut

(19) 1. $\sim R \vee P$
2. $R \vee \sim P$ / $R \equiv P$
3. $R \supset P$ 1, Impl
4. $\sim P \vee R$ 2, Com
5. $P \supset R$ 4, Impl
6. $(R \supset P) \cdot (P \supset R)$ 3, 5, Conj
7. $R \equiv P$ 6, Equiv

(22) 1. $S \supset (L \cdot M)$
2. $M \supset (L \supset R)$ / $S \supset R$
3. $(M \cdot L) \supset R$ 2, Exp
4. $(L \cdot M) \supset R$ 3, Com
5. $S \supset R$ 1, 4, HS

(25) 1. $T \supset G$
2. $S \supset G$ / $(T \vee S) \supset G$
3. $\sim T \vee G$ 1, Impl
4. $\sim S \vee G$ 2, Impl
5. $G \vee \sim T$ 3, Com
6. $G \vee \sim S$ 4, Com
7. $(G \vee \sim T) \cdot (G \vee \sim S)$ 5, 6, Conj
8. $G \vee (\sim T \cdot \sim S)$ 7, Dist
9. $(\sim T \cdot \sim S) \vee G$ 8, Com
10. $\sim(T \vee S) \vee G$ 9, DM
11. $(T \vee S) \supset G$ 10, Impl

(28) 1. $P \supset (\sim E \supset B)$
2. $\sim(B \vee E)$ / $\sim P$
3. $\sim(E \vee B)$ 2, Com
4. $\sim(\sim\sim E \vee B)$ 3, DN
5. $\sim(\sim E \supset B)$ 4, Impl
6. $\sim P$ 1, 5, MT

(31) 1. $K \equiv R$
2. $K \supset (R \supset P)$
3. $\sim P$ / $\sim R$
4. $(K \cdot R) \vee (\sim K \cdot \sim R)$ 1, Equiv
5. $(K \cdot R) \supset P$ 2, Exp
6. $\sim(K \cdot R)$ 3, 5, MT
7. $\sim K \cdot \sim R$ 4, 6, DS
8. $\sim R \cdot \sim K$ 7, Com
9. $\sim R$ 8, Simp

(34) 1. $(F \cdot H) \supset N$
2. $F \vee S$
3. H / $N \vee S$
4. $(H \cdot F) \supset N$ 1, Com
5. $H \supset (F \supset N)$ 4, Exp

6. $F \supset N$ 3, 5, MP
7. $\sim N \supset \sim F$ 6, Trans
8. $\sim\sim F \vee S$ 2, DN
9. $\sim F \supset S$ 8, Impl
10. $\sim N \supset S$ 7, 9, HS
11. $\sim\sim N \vee S$ 10, Impl
12. $N \vee S$ 11, DN

(37) 1. $(D \supset E) \supset (E \supset D)$
2. $(D \equiv E) \supset \sim(G \cdot \sim H)$
3. $E \cdot G$ / $G \cdot H$
4. E 3, Simp
5. $E \vee \sim D$ 4, Add
6. $\sim D \vee E$ 5, Com
7. $D \supset E$ 6, Impl
8. $E \supset D$ 1, 7, MP
9. $(D \supset E) \cdot (E \supset D)$ 7, 8, Conj
10. $D \equiv E$ 9, Equiv
11. $\sim(G \cdot \sim H)$ 2, 10, MP
12. $\sim G \vee \sim\sim H$ 11, DM
13. $\sim G \vee H$ 12, DN
14. $G \cdot E$ 3, Com
15. G 14, Simp
16. $\sim\sim G$ 15, DN
17. H 13, 16, DS
18. $G \cdot H$ 15, 17, Conj

(40) 1. $A \equiv W$
2. $\sim A \vee \sim W$
3. $R \supset A$ / $\sim(W \vee R)$
4. $(A \cdot W) \vee (\sim A \cdot \sim W)$ 1, Equiv
5. $\sim(A \cdot W)$ 2, DM
6. $\sim A \cdot \sim W$ 4, 5, DS
7. $\sim A$ 6, Simp
8. $\sim R$ 3, 7, MT
9. $\sim W \cdot \sim A$ 6, Com
10. $\sim W$ 9, Simp
11. $\sim W \cdot \sim R$ 8, 10, Conj
12. $\sim(W \vee R)$ 11, DM

(43) 1. $O \supset (Q \cdot N)$
2. $(N \vee E) \supset S$ / $O \supset S$
3. $\sim O \vee (Q \cdot N)$ 1, Impl
4. $(\sim O \vee Q) \cdot (\sim O \vee N)$ 3, Dist
5. $(\sim O \vee N) \cdot (\sim O \vee Q)$ 4, Com
6. $\sim O \vee N$ 5, Simp
7. $O \supset N$ 6, Impl
8. $\sim(N \vee E) \vee S$ 2, Impl
9. $(\sim N \cdot \sim E) \vee S$ 8, DM
10. $S \vee (\sim N \cdot \sim E)$ 9, Com
11. $(S \vee \sim N) \cdot (S \vee \sim E)$ 10, Dist
12. $S \vee \sim N$ 11, Simp
13. $\sim N \vee S$ 12, Com
14. $N \supset S$ 13, Impl
15. $O \supset S$ 7, 14, HS

(45) 1. $P \supset A$
2. $Q \supset B$ / $(P \vee Q) \supset (A \vee B)$
3. $\sim P \vee A$ 1, Impl
4. $\sim Q \vee B$ 2, Impl

5. $(\sim P \lor A) \lor B$	3, Add
6. $(\sim Q \lor B) \lor A$	4, Add
7. $\sim P \lor (A \lor B)$	5, Assoc
8. $(A \lor B) \lor \sim P$	7, Com
9. $\sim Q \lor (B \lor A)$	6, Assoc
10. $\sim Q \lor (A \lor B)$	9, Com
11. $(A \lor B) \lor \sim Q$	10, Com
12. $[(A \lor B) \lor \sim P] \cdot [(A \lor B) \lor \sim Q]$	8, 11, Conj
13. $(A \lor B) \lor (\sim P \cdot \sim Q)$	12, Dist
14. $(\sim P \cdot \sim Q) \lor (A \lor B)$	13, Com
15. $\sim(P \lor Q) \lor (A \lor B)$	14, DM
16. $(P \lor Q) \supset (A \lor B)$	15, Impl

IV.

(1)
1. $D \supset C$	
2. $\sim(C \cdot \sim S)$	$/ D \supset S$
3. $\sim C \lor \sim\sim S$	2, DM
4. $C \supset \sim\sim S$	3, Impl
5. $C \supset S$	4, DN
6. $D \supset S$	1, 5, HS

(4)
1. $D \supset P$	$/ (I \cdot D) \supset P$
2. $(D \supset P) \lor \sim I$	1, Add
3. $\sim I \lor (D \supset P)$	2, Com
4. $I \supset (D \supset P)$	3, Impl
5. $(I \cdot D) \supset P$	4, Exp

(7)
1. $G \supset A$	
2. $G \supset L$	$/ G \supset (A \cdot L)$
3. $\sim G \lor A$	1, Impl
4. $\sim G \lor L$	2, Impl
5. $(\sim G \lor A) \cdot (\sim G \lor L)$	3, 4, Conj
6. $\sim G \lor (A \cdot L)$	5, Dist
7. $G \supset (A \cdot L)$	6, Impl

(10)
1. $(A \cdot U) \equiv \sim R$	
2. $\sim(\sim R \lor \sim A)$	$/ \sim U$
3. $[(A \cdot U) \supset \sim R] \cdot [\sim R \supset (A \cdot U)]$	1, Equiv
4. $(A \cdot U) \supset \sim R$	3, Simp
5. $\sim\sim R \cdot \sim\sim A$	2, DM
6. $\sim\sim R$	5, Simp
7. $\sim(A \cdot U)$	4, 6, MT
8. $\sim A \lor \sim U$	7, DM
9. $\sim\sim A \cdot \sim\sim R$	5, Com
10. $\sim\sim A$	9, Simp
11. $\sim U$	8, 10, DS

Exercise 7.5

I.

(1)
1. $N \supset O$	
2. $N \supset P$	$/ N \supset (O \cdot P)$
3. N	ACP
4. O	1, 3, MP
5. P	2, 3, MP
6. $O \cdot P$	4, 5, Conj
7. $N \supset (O \cdot P)$	3–6, CP

(4)
1. $(G \lor H) \supset (S \cdot T)$	
2. $(T \lor U) \supset (C \cdot D)$	$/ G \supset C$
3. G	ACP
4. $G \lor H$	3, Add
5. $S \cdot T$	1, 4, MP
6. $T \cdot S$	5, Com
7. T	6, Simp
8. $T \lor U$	7, Add
9. $C \cdot D$	2, 8, MP
10. C	9, Simp
11. $G \supset C$	3–10, CP

(7)
1. $M \lor (N \cdot O)$	$/ \sim N \supset M$
2. $\sim M$	ACP
3. $N \cdot O$	1, 2, DS
4. N	3, Simp
5. $\sim M \supset N$	2–4, CP
6. $\sim N \supset \sim\sim M$	5, Trans
7. $\sim N \supset M$	6, DN

(10)
1. $C \supset (A \cdot D)$	
2. $B \supset (A \cdot E)$	$/ (C \lor B) \supset A$
3. $C \lor B$	ACP
4. $[C \supset (A \cdot D)] \cdot [B \supset (A \cdot E)]$	1, 2, Conj
5. $(A \cdot D) \lor (A \cdot E)$	3, 4, CD
6. $A \cdot (D \lor E)$	5, Dist
7. A	6, Simp
8. $(C \lor B) \supset A$	3–7, CP

(13)
1. $R \supset B$	
2. $R \supset (B \supset F)$	
3. $B \supset (F \supset H)$	$/ R \supset H$
4. R	ACP
5. B	1, 4, MP
6. $B \supset F$	2, 4, MP
7. F	5, 6, MP
8. $F \supset H$	3, 5, MP
9. H	7, 8, MP
10. $R \supset H$	4–9, CP

(16)
1. $Q \supset (R \supset S)$	
2. $Q \supset (T \supset \sim U)$	
3. $U \supset (R \lor T)$	$/ Q \supset (U \supset S)$
4. Q	ACP
5. U	ACP
6. $R \supset S$	1, 4, MP
7. $T \supset \sim U$	2, 4, MP
8. $\sim\sim U$	5, DN
9. $\sim T$	7, 8, MT
10. $R \lor T$	3, 5, MP
11. $T \lor R$	10, Com
12. R	9, 11, DS
13. S	6, 12, MP
14. $U \supset S$	5–13, CP
15. $Q \supset (U \supset S)$	4–14, CP

(19)
1. $P \supset [(L \lor M) \supset (N \cdot O)]$	
2. $(O \lor T) \supset W$	$/ P \supset (M \supset W)$
3. P	ACP
4. M	ACP

5.	$(L \lor M) \supset (N \bullet O)$	1, 3, MP
6.	$M \lor L$	4, Add
7.	$L \lor M$	6, Com
8.	$N \bullet O$	5, 7, MP
9.	$O \bullet N$	8, Com
10.	O	9, Simp
11.	$O \lor T$	10, Add
12.	W	2, 11, MP
13.	$M \supset W$	4–12, CP
14.	$P \supset (M \supset W)$	3–13, CP

II.

(1)

1.	$H \supset D$	
2.	$U \supset S$	/ $(H \bullet U) \supset (S \bullet D)$
3.	$H \bullet U$	ACP
4.	H	3, Simp
5.	D	1, 4, MP
6.	$U \bullet H$	3, Com
7.	U	6, Simp
8.	S	2, 7, MP
9.	$S \bullet D$	5, 8, Conj
10.	$(H \bullet U) \supset (S \bullet D)$	3–9, CP

(4)

1.	$J \supset D$	
2.	$(J \bullet D) \supset C$	
3.	$(N \bullet C) \supset I$	/ $J \supset (N \supset I)$
4.	J	ACP
5.	N	ACP
6.	D	1, 4, MP
7.	$J \bullet D$	4, 6, Conj
8.	C	2, 7, MP
9.	$N \bullet C$	5, 8, Conj
10.	I	3, 9, MP
11.	$N \supset I$	5–10, CP
12.	$J \supset (N \supset I)$	4–11, CP

Exercise 7.6

I.

(1)

1.	$(S \lor T) \supset {\sim}S$	/ ${\sim}S$
2.	S	AIP
3.	$S \lor T$	2, Add
4.	${\sim}S$	1, 3, MP
5.	$S \bullet {\sim}S$	2, 4, Conj
6.	${\sim}S$	2–5, IP

(4)

1.	$H \supset (L \supset K)$	
2.	$L \supset (K \supset {\sim}L)$	/ ${\sim}H \lor {\sim}L$
3.	$H \bullet L$	AIP
4.	H	3, Simp
5.	$L \supset K$	1, 4, MP
6.	$L \bullet H$	3, Com
7.	L	6, Simp
8.	$K \supset {\sim}L$	2, 7, MP
9.	K	5, 7, MP
10.	${\sim}L$	8, 9, MP
11.	$L \bullet {\sim}L$	7, 10, Conj

12.	${\sim}(H \bullet L)$	3–11, IP
13.	${\sim}H \lor {\sim}L$	12, DM

(7)

1.	$(E \lor F) \supset (C \bullet D)$	
2.	$(D \lor G) \supset H$	
3.	$E \lor G$	/ H
4.	${\sim}H$	AIP
5.	${\sim}(D \lor G)$	2, 4, MT
6.	${\sim}D \bullet {\sim}G$	5, DM
7.	${\sim}D$	6, Simp
8.	${\sim}D \lor {\sim}C$	7, Add
9.	${\sim}C \lor {\sim}D$	8, Com
10.	${\sim}(C \bullet D)$	9, DM
11.	${\sim}(E \lor F)$	1, 10, MT
12.	${\sim}E \bullet {\sim}F$	11, DM
13.	${\sim}E$	12, Simp
14.	G	3, 13, DS
15.	${\sim}G \bullet {\sim}D$	6, Com
16.	${\sim}G$	15, Simp
17.	$G \bullet {\sim}G$	14, 16, Conj
18.	${\sim}{\sim}H$	4–17, IP
19.	H	18, DN

(10)

1.	K	/ $S \supset (T \supset S)$
2.	S	ACP
3.	$S \lor {\sim}T$	2, Add
4.	${\sim}T \lor S$	3, Com
5.	$T \supset S$	4, Impl
6.	$S \supset (T \supset S)$	2–5, CP

(13)

1.	$[C \supset (D \supset C)] \supset E$	/ E
2.	C	ACP
3.	$C \lor {\sim}D$	2, Add
4.	${\sim}D \lor C$	3, Com
5.	$D \supset C$	4, Impl
6.	$C \supset (D \supset C)$	2–5, CP
7.	E	1, 6, MP

(16)

1.	$(N \lor O) \supset (C \bullet D)$	
2.	$(D \lor K) \supset (P \lor {\sim}C)$	
3.	$(P \lor G) \supset {\sim}(N \bullet D)$	/ ${\sim}N$
4.	N	AIP
5.	$N \lor O$	4, Add
6.	$C \bullet D$	1, 5, MP
7.	$D \bullet C$	6, Com
8.	D	7, Simp
9.	$D \lor K$	8, Add
10.	$P \lor {\sim}C$	2, 9, MP
11.	C	6, Simp
12.	${\sim}C \lor P$	10, Com
13.	${\sim}{\sim}C$	11, DN
14.	P	12, 13, DS
15.	$P \lor G$	14, Add
16.	${\sim}(N \bullet D)$	3, 15, MP
17.	${\sim}N \lor {\sim}D$	16, DM
18.	${\sim}{\sim}N$	4, DN
19.	${\sim}D$	17, 18, DS
20.	$D \bullet {\sim}D$	8, 19, Conj
21.	${\sim}N$	4–20, IP

(19)

1.	$A \supset [(N \lor {\sim}N) \supset (S \lor T)]$	
2.	$T \supset {\sim}(F \lor {\sim}F)$	/ $A \supset S$

7

3. $A \cdot \sim S$	AIP
4. A	3, Simp
5. $(N \lor \sim N) \supset (S \lor T)$	1, 4, MP
6. N	ACP
7. $N \lor N$	6, Add
8. N	7, Taut
9. $N \supset N$	6–8, CP
10. $\sim N \lor N$	9, Impl
11. $N \lor \sim N$	10, Com
12. $S \lor T$	5, 11, MP
13. $\sim S \cdot A$	3, Com
14. $\sim S$	13, Simp
15. T	12, 14, DS
16. $\sim(F \lor \sim F)$	2, 15, MP
17. $\sim F \cdot \sim\sim F$	16, DM
18. $\sim(A \cdot \sim S)$	3–17, IP
19. $\sim A \lor \sim\sim S$	18, DM
20. $\sim A \lor S$	19, DN
21. $A \supset S$	20, Impl

II.

(1)
1. $(C \cdot R) \supset (I \cdot D)$
2. $R \supset \sim D$ / $\sim C \lor \sim R$

3. $C \cdot R$	AIP
4. $I \cdot D$	1, 3, MP
5. $D \cdot I$	4, Com
6. D	5, Simp
7. $R \cdot C$	3, Com
8. R	7, Simp
9. $\sim D$	2, 8, MP
10. $D \cdot \sim D$	6, 9, Conj
11. $\sim(C \cdot R)$	3–10, IP
12. $\sim C \lor \sim R$	11, DM

(4)
1. $(Z \supset C) \supset B$
2. $(V \supset Z) \supset B$ / B

3. $\sim B$	AIP
4. $\sim(Z \supset C)$	1, 3, MT
5. $\sim(\sim Z \lor C)$	4, Impl
6. $\sim\sim Z \cdot \sim C$	5, DM
7. $\sim\sim Z$	6, Simp
8. $\sim(V \supset Z)$	2, 3, MT
9. $\sim(\sim V \lor Z)$	8, Impl
10. $\sim\sim V \cdot \sim Z$	9, DM
11. $\sim Z \cdot \sim\sim V$	10, Com
12. $\sim Z$	11, Simp
13. $\sim Z \cdot \sim\sim Z$	7, 12, Conj
14. $\sim\sim B$	3–13, IP
15. B	14, DN

Exercise 7.7

I.

(1)   / $P \supset [(P \supset Q) \supset Q]$

1. P	ACP
2. $P \supset Q$	ACP

3. Q	1, 2, MP
4. $(P \supset Q) \supset Q$	2–3, CP
5. $P \supset [(P \supset Q) \supset Q]$	1–4, CP

(4)   / $(P \supset Q) \supset [(P \cdot R) \supset (Q \cdot R)]$

1. $P \supset Q$	ACP
2. $P \cdot R$	ACP
3. P	2, Simp
4. Q	1, 3, MP
5. $R \cdot P$	2, Com
6. R	5, Simp
7. $Q \cdot R$	4, 6, Conj
8. $(P \cdot R) \supset (Q \cdot R)$	2–7, CP
9. $(P \supset Q) \supset [(P \cdot R) \supset (Q \cdot R)]$	1–8, CP

(7)   / $(P \supset Q) \lor (\sim Q \supset P)$

1. $\sim[(P \supset Q) \lor (\sim Q \supset P)]$	AIP
2. $\sim(P \supset Q) \cdot \sim(\sim Q \supset P)$	1, DM
3. $\sim(P \supset Q)$	2, Simp
4. $\sim(\sim P \lor Q)$	3, Impl
5. $\sim\sim P \cdot \sim Q$	4, DM
6. $P \cdot \sim Q$	5, DN
7. P	6, Simp
8. $\sim(\sim Q \supset P) \cdot \sim(P \supset Q)$	2, Com
9. $\sim(\sim Q \supset P)$	8, Simp
10. $\sim(\sim\sim Q \lor P)$	9, Impl
11. $\sim(Q \lor P)$	10, DN
12. $\sim Q \cdot \sim P$	11, DM
13. $\sim P \cdot \sim Q$	12, Com
14. $\sim P$	13, Simp
15. $P \cdot \sim P$	7, 14, Conj
16. $\sim\sim[(P \supset Q) \lor (\sim Q \supset P)]$	1–15, IP
17. $(P \supset Q) \lor (\sim Q \supset P)$	16, DN

(10)   / $[\sim(P \cdot \sim Q) \cdot \sim Q] \supset \sim P$

1. $\sim(P \cdot \sim Q) \cdot \sim Q$	ACP
2. $\sim(P \cdot \sim Q)$	1, Simp
3. $\sim P \lor \sim\sim Q$	2, DM
4. $\sim P \lor Q$	3, DN
5. $\sim Q \cdot \sim(P \cdot \sim Q)$	1, Com
6. $\sim Q$	5, Simp
7. $Q \lor \sim P$	4, Com
8. $\sim P$	6, 7, DS
9. $[\sim(P \cdot \sim Q) \cdot \sim Q] \supset \sim P$	1–8, CP

(13)   / $(P \supset Q) \supset [(P \supset \sim Q) \supset \sim P]$

1. $P \supset Q$	ACP
2. $P \supset \sim Q$	ACP
3. $\sim\sim Q \supset \sim P$	2, Trans
4. $Q \supset \sim P$	3, DN
5. $P \supset \sim P$	1, 4, HS
6. $\sim P \lor \sim P$	5, Impl
7. $\sim P$	6, Taut
8. $(P \supset \sim Q) \supset \sim P$	2–7, CP
9. $(P \supset Q) \supset [(P \supset \sim Q) \supset \sim P]$	1–8, CP

(16)   / $\sim[(P \supset \sim P) \cdot (\sim P \supset P)]$

1. $(P \supset \sim P) \cdot (\sim P \supset P)$	AIP
2. $(\sim P \lor \sim P) \cdot (\sim P \supset P)$	1, Impl
3. $\sim P \cdot (\sim P \supset P)$	2, Taut
4. $\sim P \cdot (\sim\sim P \lor P)$	3, Impl

	5. $\sim P \cdot (P \vee P)$	4, DN
	6. $\sim P \cdot P$	5, Taut
	7. $P \cdot \sim P$	6, Com
	8. $\sim[(P \supset \sim P) \cdot (\sim P \supset P)]$	1–7, IP
(19)		/ $P \equiv [P \vee (Q \cdot \sim Q)]$
	1. P	ACP
	2. $P \vee (Q \cdot \sim Q)$	1, Add
	3. $P \supset [P \vee (Q \cdot \sim Q)]$	1–2, CP
	4. $P \vee (Q \cdot \sim Q)$	ACP
	5. $\sim P$	AIP
	6. $Q \cdot \sim Q$	4, 5, DS
	7. $\sim \sim P$	5–6, IP
	8. P	7, DN
	9. $[P \vee (Q \cdot \sim Q)] \supset P$	4–8, CP
	10. {line 3} • {line 9}	3, 9, Conj
	11. $P \equiv [P \vee (Q \cdot \sim Q)]$	10, Equiv

Exercise 8.1

I.

1. Ce
4. $Jr \vee Nr$
7. $(x)(Mx \supset Tx)$
10. $(\exists x)(Hx \cdot \sim Rx)$
13. $(\exists x)Tx$
16. $(\exists x)(Sx \cdot \sim Gx)$
19. $(x)(Sx \supset Vx)$
22. $(x)(Cx \supset \sim Hx)$
25. $(x)(Tx \supset Hx)$
28. $(x)(Hx \supset \sim Ex)$
31. $(\exists x)[Cx \cdot \sim(Sx \vee Bx)]$
34. $(\exists x)[Dx \cdot (Bx \equiv Tx)]$
37. $(\exists x)[Cx \cdot (Ax \supset Tx)]$
40. $(x)[(Wx \cdot Cx) \supset Rx]$
43. $(x)[(Vx \vee Cx) \supset (Sx \cdot Ix)]$
46. $(\exists x)[(Fx \cdot Rx) \cdot Ex]$
49. $Gt \equiv (x)(Wx \supset Cx)$
52. $(\exists x)(Ix \cdot Mx) \supset Ir$
55. $(x)[(Bx \cdot Mx) \supset Sx] \supset Sc$
58. $(\exists x)(Ex \cdot Rx) \equiv (\exists x)(Mx \cdot Ox)$

Exercise 8.2

I.

(1)	1. $(x)(Ax \supset Bx)$	
	2. $(x)(Bx \supset Cx)$	/ $(x)(Ax \supset Cx)$
	3. $Ax \supset Bx$	1, UI
	4. $Bx \supset Cx$	2, UI
	5. $Ax \supset Cx$	3, 4, HS
	6. $(x)(Ax \supset Cx)$	5, UG
(4)	1. $(x)(Ax \supset Bx)$	
	2. $(y)(Ay \vee \sim By)$	/ $(x)(Ax \equiv Bx)$
	3. $Ax \supset Bx$	1, UI
	4. $Ax \vee \sim Bx$	2, UI

	5. $\sim Bx \vee Ax$	4, Com
	6. $Bx \supset Ax$	5, Impl
	7. $(Ax \supset Bx) \cdot (Bx \supset Ax)$	3, 6, Conj
	8. $Ax \equiv Bx$	7, Equiv
	9. $(x)(Ax \equiv Bx)$	8, UG
(7)	1. $(x)[Jx \supset (Kx \cdot Lx)]$	
	2. $(\exists y) \sim Ky$	/ $(\exists z) \sim Jz$
	3. $\sim Km$	2, EI
	4. $Jm \supset (Km \cdot Lm)$	1, UI
	5. $\sim Km \vee \sim Lm$	3, Add
	6. $\sim(Km \cdot Lm)$	5, DM
	7. $\sim Jm$	4, 6, MT
	8. $(\exists z) \sim Jz$	7, EG
(10)	1. $(x)(Ax \supset Bx)$	
	2. $Am \vee An$	/ $Bm \vee Bn$
	3. $Am \supset Bm$	1, UI
	4. $An \supset Bn$	1, UI
	5. $(Am \supset Bm) \cdot (An \supset Bn)$	3, 4, Conj
	6. $Bm \vee Bn$	2, 5, CD
(13)	1. $(x)[(Ax \cdot Bx) \supset Cx]$	
	2. $(\exists x)(Bx \cdot \sim Cx)$	/ $(\exists x) \sim Ax$
	3. $Bm \cdot \sim Cm$	2, EI
	4. $(Am \cdot Bm) \supset Cm$	1, UI
	5. $\sim Cm \cdot Bm$	3, Com
	6. $\sim Cm$	5, Simp
	7. $\sim(Am \cdot Bm)$	4, 6, MT
	8. $\sim Am \vee \sim Bm$	7, DM
	9. Bm	3, Simp
	10. $\sim \sim Bm$	9, DN
	11. $\sim Bm \vee \sim Am$	8, Com
	12. $\sim Am$	10, 11, DS
	13. $(\exists x) \sim Ax$	12, EG
(16)	1. $(\exists x)Ax \supset (x)Bx$	
	2. $(\exists x)Cx \supset (\exists x)Dx$	
	3. $An \cdot Cn$	/ $(\exists x)(Bx \cdot Dx)$
	4. An	2, Simp
	5. $(\exists x)Ax$	4, EG
	6. $(x)Bx$	1, 5, MP
	7. $Cn \cdot An$	3, Com
	8. Cn	7, Simp
	9. $(\exists x)Cx$	8, EG
	10. $(\exists x)Dx$	2, 9, MP
	11. Dm	10, EI
	12. Bm	6, UI
	13. $Bm \cdot Dm$	11, 12, Conj
	14. $(\exists x)(Bx \cdot Dx)$	13, EG
(19)	1. $(\exists x)Ax \supset (x)(Cx \supset Bx)$	
	2. $(\exists x)(Ax \vee Bx)$	
	3. $(x)(Bx \supset Ax)$	/ $(x)(Cx \supset Ax)$
	4. $Am \vee Bm$	2, EI
	5. $Bm \supset Am$	3, UI
	6. $\sim \sim Am \vee Bm$	4, DN
	7. $\sim Am \supset Bm$	6, Impl
	8. $\sim Am \supset Am$	5, 7, HS
	9. $\sim \sim Am \vee Am$	8, Impl
	10. $Am \vee Am$	9, DN

8

11. *Am*   10, Taut
12. $(\exists x)Ax$ 11, EG
13. $(x)(Cx \supset Bx)$ 1, 12, MP
14. $Cx \supset Bx$ 13, UI
15. $Bx \supset Ax$ 3, UI
16. $Cx \supset Ax$ 14, 15, HS
17. $(x)(Cx \supset Ax)$ 16, UG

(22) 1. $(x)(Ax \cdot \sim Bx)$
2. $An \supset [\sim(\exists x)Cx \supset Bc]$
3. $Am \supset (x)(Cx \supset Dx)$ / $(\exists x)Dx$
4. $An \cdot \sim Bn$ 1, UI
5. An 4, Simp
6. $\sim(\exists x)Cx \supset Bc$ 2, 5, MP
7. $Am \cdot \sim Bm$ 1, UI
8. Am 7, Simp
9. $(x)(Cx \supset Dx)$ 3, 8, MP
10. $Ac \cdot \sim Bc$ 1, UI
11. $\sim Bc \cdot Ac$ 10, Com
12. $\sim Bc$ 11, Simp
13. $\sim\sim(\exists x)Cx$ 6, 12, MT
14. $(\exists x)Cx$ 13, DN
15. Cs 14, EI
16. $Cs \supset Ds$ 9, UI
17. Ds 15, 16, MP
18. $(\exists x)Dx$ 17, EG

(25) 1. $(\exists x)Ax \supset (x)(Ax \supset Bx)$
2. $(\exists x)Cx \supset (x)\sim(Dx \cdot Bx)$
3. $(\exists x)(Ax \cdot Cx)$ / $(\exists x)\sim Dx$
4. $An \cdot Cn$ 3, EI
5. An 4, Simp
6. $Cn \cdot An$ 4, Com
7. Cn 6, Simp
8. $(\exists x)Ax$ 5, EG
9. $(\exists x)Cx$ 7, EG
10. $(x)(Ax \supset Bx)$ 1, 8, MP
11. $An \supset Bn$ 10, UI
12. Bn 5, 11, MP
13. $(x)\sim(Dx \cdot Bx)$ 2, 9, MP
14. $\sim(Dn \cdot Bn)$ 13, UI
15. $\sim Dn \vee \sim Bn$ 14, DM
16. $\sim Bn \vee \sim Dn$ 15, Com
17. $\sim\sim Bn$ 12, DN
18. $\sim Dn$ 16, 17, DS
19. $(\exists x)\sim Dx$ 18, EG

II.

(1) 1. $(x)(Ox \supset Sx)$
2. $(x)(Ox \supset Fx)$ / $(x)[Ox \supset (Sx \cdot Fx)]$
3. $Ox \supset Sx$ 1, UI
4. $Ox \supset Fx$ 2, UI
5. $\sim Ox \vee Sx$ 3, Impl
6. $\sim Ox \vee Fx$ 4, Impl
7. $(\sim Ox \vee Sx) \cdot (\sim Ox \vee Fx)$ 5, 6, Conj
8. $\sim Ox \vee (Sx \cdot Fx)$ 7, Dist
9. $Ox \supset (Sx \cdot Fx)$ 8, Impl
10. $(x)[Ox \supset (Sx \cdot Fx)]$ 9, UG

(4) 1. $(x)(Cx \vee Vx) \cdot (x)(Px \supset Fx)$
2. $(\exists x)(Cx \cdot Gx) \cdot$ / $(\exists x)(Vx \cdot Gx) \cdot$
    $(\exists x)(Px \cdot Gx)$ $(\exists x)(Fx \cdot Gx)$
3. $(\exists x)(Cx \cdot Gx)$ 2, Simp
4. $Cm \cdot Gm$ 3, EI
5. $(\exists x)(Px \cdot Gx) \cdot (\exists x)(Cx \cdot Gx)$ 2, Com
6. $(\exists x)(Px \cdot Gx)$ 5, Simp
7. $Pn \cdot Gn$ 6, EI
8. $(x)(Cx \supset Vx)$ 1, Simp
9. $Cm \supset Vm$ 8, UI
10. Cm 4, Simp
11. Vm 9, 10, MP
12. $Gm \cdot Cm$ 4, Com
13. Gm 12, Simp
14. $Vm \cdot Gm$ 11, 13, Conj
15. $(\exists x)(Vx \cdot Gx)$ 14, EG
16. $(x)(Px \supset Fx) \cdot$ 1, Com
    $(x)(Cx \supset Vx)$
17. $(x)(Px \supset Fx)$ 16, Simp
18. $Pn \supset Fn$ 17, UI
19. Pn 7, Simp
20. Fn 18, 19, MP
21. $Gn \cdot Pn$ 7, Com
22. Gn 21, Simp
23. $Fn \cdot Gn$ 20, 22, Conj
24. $(\exists x)(Fx \cdot Gx)$ 23, EG
25. $(\exists x)(Vx \cdot Gx) \cdot$ 15, 24, Conj
    $(\exists x)(Fx \cdot Gx)$

(7) 1. $(x)[Gx \supset (Ix \cdot Px)]$
2. $(x)[(Ix \cdot Px) \supset Rx]$
3. $Ga \cdot Gc$ / $Ra \cdot Rc$
4. $Gx \supset (Ix \cdot Px)$ 1, UI
5. $(Ix \cdot Px) \supset Rx$ 2, UI
6. $Gx \supset Rx$ 4, 5, HS
7. $(x)(Gx \supset Rx)$ 6, UG
8. $Ga \supset Ra$ 7, UI
9. Ga 3, Simp
10. Ra 8, 9, MP
11. $Gc \supset Rc$ 7, UI
12. $Gc \cdot Ga$ 3, Com
13. Gc 12, Simp
14. Rc 11, 13, MP
15. $Ra \cdot Rc$ 10, 14, Conj

(10) 1. $(x)[(Ax \cdot Kx) \supset Rx] \supset (x)(Gx \supset Sx)$
2. $(x)[(Ax \cdot Kx) \supset Fx] \supset (x)(Gx \supset Px)$
3. $(x)[(Ax \cdot Kx) \supset (Rx \cdot Fx)]$ / $(x)[Gx \supset (Sx \cdot Px)]$
4. $(Ax \cdot Kx) \supset (Rx \cdot Fx)$ 3, UI
5. $\sim(Ax \cdot Kx) \vee (Rx \cdot Fx)$ 4, Impl
6. $[\sim(Ax \cdot Kx) \vee Rx] \cdot$ 5, Dist
    $[\sim(Ax \cdot Kx) \vee Fx]$
7. $\sim(Ax \cdot Kx) \vee Rx$ 6, Simp
8. $[\sim(Ax \cdot Kx) \vee Fx] \cdot$ 6, Com
    $[\sim(Ax \cdot Kx) \vee Rx]$
9. $\sim(Ax \cdot Kx) \vee Fx$ 8, Simp
10. $(Ax \cdot Kx) \supset Rx$ 7, Impl
11. $(Ax \cdot Kx) \supset Fx$ 9, Impl
12. $(x)[(Ax \cdot Kx) \supset Rx]$ 10, UG

13. $(x)[(Ax \cdot Kx) \supset Fx]$ 11, UG
14. $(x)(Gx \supset Sx)$ 1, 12, MP
15. $(x)(Gx \supset Px)$ 2, 13, MP
16. $Gx \supset Sx$ 14, UI
17. $Gx \supset Px$ 15, UI
18. $\sim Gx \lor Sx$ 16, Impl
19. $\sim Gx \lor Px$ 17, Impl
20. $(\sim Gx \lor Sx) \cdot (\sim Gx \lor Px)$ 18, 19, Conj
21. $\sim Gx \lor (Sx \cdot Px)$ 20, Dist
22. $Gx \supset (Sx \cdot Px)$ 21, Impl
23. $(x)[Gx \supset (Sx \cdot Px)]$ 22, UG

Exercise 8.3

I.

(1) 1. $(x)Ax \supset (\exists x)Bx$
    2. $(x)\sim Bx$ $/ (\exists x)\sim Ax$
    3. $\sim(\exists x)Bx$ 2, QN
    4. $\sim(x)Ax$ 1, 3, MT
    5. $(\exists x)\sim Ax$ 4, QN
(4) 1. $(\exists x)Ax \lor (\exists x)(Bx \cdot Cx)$
    2. $\sim(\exists x)Bx$ $/ (\exists x)Ax$
    3. $(x)\sim Bx$ 2, QN
    4. $\sim Bx$ 3, UI
    5. $\sim Bx \lor \sim Cx$ 4, Add
    6. $\sim(Bx \cdot Cx)$ 5, DM
    7. $(x)\sim(Bx \cdot Cx)$ 6, UG
    8. $\sim(\exists x)(Bx \cdot Cx)$ 7, QN
    9. $(\exists x)(Bx \cdot Cx) \lor (\exists x)Ax$ 1, Com
    10. $(\exists x)Ax$ 8, 9, DS
(7) 1. $(x)(Ax \supset Bx)$
    2. $\sim(x)Cx \lor (x)Ax$
    3. $\sim(x)Bx$ $/ (\exists x)\sim Cx$
    4. $(\exists x)\sim Bx$ 3, QN
    5. $\sim Bm$ 4, EI
    6. $Am \supset Bm$ 1, UI
    7. $\sim Am$ 5, 6, MT
    8. $(\exists x)\sim Ax$ 7, EG
    9. $\sim(x)Ax$ 8, QN
    10. $(x)Ax \lor \sim(x)Cx$ 2, Com
    11. $\sim(x)Cx$ 9, 10, DS
    12. $(\exists x)\sim Cx$ 11, QN
(10) 1. $\sim(\exists x)(Ax \cdot \sim Bx)$
    2. $\sim(\exists x)(Bx \cdot \sim Cx)$ $/ (x)(Ax \supset Cx)$
    3. $(x)\sim(Ax \cdot \sim Bx)$ 1, QN
    4. $(x)\sim(Bx \cdot \sim Cx)$ 2, QN
    5. $\sim(Ax \cdot \sim Bx)$ 3, UI
    6. $\sim(Bx \cdot \sim Cx)$ 4, UI
    7. $\sim Ax \lor \sim\sim Bx$ 5, DM
    8. $\sim Ax \lor Bx$ 7, DN
    9. $\sim Bx \lor \sim\sim Cx$ 6, DM
    10. $\sim Bx \lor Cx$ 9, DN
    11. $Ax \supset Bx$ 8, Impl
    12. $Bx \supset Cx$ 10, Impl
    13. $Ax \supset Cx$ 11, 12, HS
    14. $(x)(Ax \supset Cx)$ 13, UG

(13) 1. $(x)(Ax \cdot \sim Bx) \supset (\exists x)Cx$
    2. $\sim(\exists x)(Cx \lor Bx)$ $/ \sim(x)Ax$
    3. $(x)\sim(Cx \lor Bx)$ 2, QN
    4. $\sim(Cx \lor Bx)$ 3, UI
    5. $\sim Cx \cdot \sim Bx$ 4, DM
    6. $\sim Cx$ 5, Simp
    7. $(x)\sim Cx$ 6, UG
    8. $\sim(\exists x)Cx$ 7, QN
    9. $\sim(x)(Ax \cdot \sim Bx)$ 1, 8, MT
    10. $(\exists x)\sim(Ax \cdot \sim Bx)$ 9, QN
    11. $\sim(Am \cdot \sim Bm)$ 10, EI
    12. $\sim Am \lor \sim\sim Bm$ 11, DM
    13. $\sim Am \lor Bm$ 12, DN
    14. $\sim Bx \cdot \sim Cx$ 5, Com
    15. $\sim Bx$ 14, Simp
    16. $(x)\sim Bx$ 15, UG
    17. $\sim Bm$ 16, UI
    18. $Bm \lor \sim Am$ 13, Com
    19. $\sim Am$ 17, 18, DS
    20. $(\exists x)\sim Ax$ 19, EG
    21. $\sim(x)Ax$ 20, QN
(16) 1. $(\exists x)(Ax \cdot Bx) \supset (x)(Cx \cdot Dx)$
    2. $(x)[(Ax \lor Ex) \cdot (Bx \lor Fx)]$
    3. $\sim(x)Dx$ $/ (x)(Ex \lor Fx)$
    4. $(\exists x)\sim Dx$ 3, QN
    5. $\sim Dn$ 4, EI
    6. $\sim Dn \lor \sim Cn$ 5, Add
    7. $\sim Cn \lor \sim Dn$ 6, Com
    8. $\sim(Cn \cdot Dn)$ 7, DM
    9. $(\exists x)\sim(Cx \cdot Dx)$ 8, EG
    10. $\sim(x)(Cx \cdot Dx)$ 9, QN
    11. $\sim(\exists x)(Ax \cdot Bx)$ 1, 10, MT
    12. $(x)\sim(Ax \cdot Bx)$ 11, QN
    13. $\sim(Ax \cdot Bx)$ 12, UI
    14. $\sim Ax \lor \sim Bx$ 13, DM
    15. $(Ax \lor Ex) \cdot (Bx \lor Fx)$ 2, UI
    16. $(\sim\sim Ax \lor Ex) \cdot (Bx \lor Fx)$ 15, DN
    17. $(\sim\sim Ax \lor Ex) \cdot (\sim\sim Bx \lor Fx)$ 16, DN
    18. $(\sim Ax \supset Ex) \cdot (\sim\sim Bx \lor Fx)$ 17, Impl
    19. $(\sim Ax \supset Ex) \cdot (\sim Bx \supset Fx)$ 18, Impl
    20. $Ex \lor Fx$ 14, 19, CD
    21. $(x)(Ex \lor Fx)$ 20, UG
(19) 1. $(\exists x)(Ax \cdot Bx) \supset (x)(Bx \supset Cx)$
    2. $Bn \cdot \sim Cn$ $/ \sim(x)Ax$
    3. $(\exists x)(Bx \cdot \sim Cx)$ 2, EG
    4. $(\exists x)(\sim\sim Bx \cdot \sim Cx)$ 3, DN
    5. $(\exists x)\sim(\sim Bx \lor Cx)$ 4, DM
    6. $(\exists x)\sim(Bx \supset Cx)$ 5, Impl
    7. $\sim(x)(Bx \supset Cx)$ 6, QN
    8. $\sim(\exists x)(Ax \cdot Bx)$ 1, 7, MT
    9. $(x)\sim(Ax \cdot Bx)$ 8, QN
    10. $\sim(An \cdot Bn)$ 9, UI
    11. $\sim An \lor \sim Bn$ 10, DM
    12. $\sim Bn \lor \sim An$ 11, Com
    13. Bn 2, Simp
    14. $\sim\sim Bn$ 13, DN

15. ~An   12, 14, DS
16. (∃x)~Ax   15, EG
17. ~(x)Ax   16, QN

II.

(1) 1. (x)[Px ⊃ (Hx ∨ Nx)] ⊃ ~(∃x)Cx
    2. Cf   / (∃x)(Px • ~Nx)
    3. (∃x)Cx   2, EG
    4. ~~(∃x)Cx   3, DN
    5. ~(x)[Px ⊃ (Hx ∨ Nx)]   1, 4, MT
    6. (∃x)~[Px ⊃ (Hx ∨ Nx)]   5, QN
    7. ~[Pm ⊃ (Hm ∨ Nm)]   6, EI
    8. ~[~Pm ∨ (Hm ∨ Nm)]   7, Impl
    9. ~~Pm • ~(Hm ∨ Nm)   8, DM
    10. Pm • ~(Hm ∨ Nm)   9, DN
    11. Pm • (~Hm • ~Nm)   10, DM
    12. Pm   11, Simp
    13. (Pm • ~Hm) • ~Nm   11, Assoc
    14. ~Nm • (Pm • ~Hm)   13, Com
    15. ~Nm   14, Simp
    16. Pm • ~Nm   12, 15, Conj
    17. (∃x)(Px • ~Nx)   16, EG

(4) 1. (∃x)(Gx • Px) ∨ (∃x)(Sx • Ex)
    2. ~(∃x)Ex   / (∃x)Px
    3. (x)~Ex   2, QN
    4. ~Ex   3, UI
    5. ~Ex ∨ ~Sx   4, Add
    6. ~Sx ∨ ~Ex   5, Com
    7. ~(Sx • Ex)   6, DM
    8. (x)~(Sx • Ex)   7, UG
    9. ~(∃x)(Sx • Ex)   8, QN
    10. (∃x)(Sx • Ex) ∨ (∃x)(Gx • Px)   1, Com
    11. (∃x)(Gx • Px)   9, 10, DS
    12. Gm • Pm   11, EI
    13. Pm • Gm   12, Com
    14. Pm   13, Simp
    15. (∃x)Px   14, EG

(7) 1. (x)(Px ⊃ Sx) • (x)(Ix ⊃ Gx)
    2. ~(∃x)(Sx • Gx)   / ~(∃x)(Px • Ix)
    3. (x)~(Sx • Gx)   2, QN
    4. ~(Sx • Gx)   3, UI
    5. ~Sx ∨ ~Gx   4, DM
    6. (x)(Px ⊃ Sx)   1, Simp
    7. (x)(Ix ⊃ Gx) • (x)(Px ⊃ Sx)   1, Com
    8. (x)(Ix ⊃ Gx)   7, Simp
    9. Px ⊃ Sx   6, UI
    10. Ix ⊃ Gx   8, UI
    11. ~Sx ⊃ ~Px   9, Trans
    12. ~Gx ⊃ ~Ix   10, Trans
    13. (~Sx ⊃ ~Px) • (~Gx ⊃ ~Ix)   11, 12, Conj
    14. ~Px ∨ ~Ix   5, 13, CD
    15. ~(Px • Ix)   14, DM
    16. (x)~(Px • Ix)   15, UG
    17. ~(∃x)(Px • Ix)   16, QN

(10) 1. ~(∃x)[Px • (Gx ∨ Hx)]
    2. (x)[Nx ⊃ (Px • Hx)]
    3. (∃x)(Px • Cx) ∨ (∃x)(Px • Nx)   / (∃x)(Cx • ~Gx)
    4. (x)~[Px • (Gx ∨ Hx)]   1, QN
    5. ~[Px • (Gx ∨ Hx)]   4, UI
    6. ~Px ∨ ~(Gx ∨ Hx)   5, DM
    7. ~Px ∨ (~Gx • ~Hx)   6, DM
    8. (~Px ∨ ~Gx) • (~Px ∨ ~Hx)   7, Dist
    9. ~Px ∨ ~Gx   8, Simp
    10. (~Px ∨ ~Hx) • (~Px ∨ ~Gx)   8, Com
    11. ~Px ∨ ~Hx   10, Simp
    12. ~(Px • Hx)   11, DM
    13. Nx ⊃ (Px • Hx)   2, UI
    14. ~Nx   12, 13, MT
    15. ~Nx ∨ ~Px   14, Add
    16. ~Px ∨ ~Nx   15, Com
    17. ~(Px • Nx)   16, DM
    18. (x)~(Px • Nx)   17, UG
    19. ~(∃x)(Px • Nx)   18, QN
    20. (∃x)(Px • Nx) ∨ (∃x)(Px • Cx)   3, Com
    21. (∃x)(Px • Cx)   19, 20, DS
    22. Pm • Cm   21, EI
    23. (x)(~Px ∨ ~Gx)   9, UG
    24. ~Pm ∨ ~Gm   23, UI
    25. Pm   22, Simp
    26. ~~Pm   25, DN
    27. ~Gm   24, 26, DS
    28. Cm • Pm   22, Com
    29. Cm   28, Simp
    30. Cm • ~Gm   27, 29, Conj
    31. (∃x)(Cx • ~Gx)   30, EG

Exercise 8.4

I.

(1) 1. (x)(Ax ⊃ Bx)
    2. (x)(Ax ⊃ Cx)   / (x)[Ax ⊃ (Bx • Cx)]
      3. Ax   ACP
      4. Ax ⊃ Bx   1, UI
      5. Ax ⊃ Cx   2, UI
      6. Bx   3, 4, MP
      7. Cx   3, 5, MP
      8. Bx • Cx   6, 7, Conj
    9. Ax ⊃ (Bx • Cx)   3–8, CP
    10. (x)[Ax ⊃ (Bx • Cx)]   9, UG

(4) 1. (x)(Ax ⊃ Cx)
    2. (∃x)Cx ⊃ (∃x)(Bx • Dx)   / (∃x)Ax ⊃ (∃x)Bx
      3. (∃x)Ax   ACP
      4. Am   3, EI
      5. Am ⊃ Cm   1, UI
      6. Cm   4, 5, MP
      7. (∃x)Cx   6, EG
      8. (∃x)(Bx • Dx)   2, 7, MP
      9. Bn • Dn   8, EI
      10. Bn   9, Simp
      11. (∃x)Bx   10, EG
    12. (∃x)Ax ⊃ (∃x)Bx   3–11, CP

(7) 1. $(x)[(Ax \lor Bx) \supset Cx]$
   2. $(x)[(Cx \lor Dx) \supset Ex]$ / $(x)(Ax \supset Ex)$
      3. Ax ACP
      4. $(Ax \lor Bx) \supset Cx$ 1, UI
      5. $(Cx \lor Dx) \supset Ex$ 2, UI
      6. $Ax \lor Bx$ 3, Add
      7. Cx 4, 6, MP
      8. $Cx \lor Dx$ 7, Add
      9. Ex 5, 8, MP
  10. $Ax \supset Ex$ 3–9, CP
  11. $(x)(Ax \supset Ex)$ 10, UG

(10) 1. $(x)(Ax \supset Bx)$
    2. $Am \lor An$ / $(\exists x)Bx$
      3. $\sim(\exists x)Bx$ AIP
      4. $(x)\sim Bx$ 3, QN
      5. $Am \supset Bm$ 1, UI
      6. $An \supset Bn$ 1, UI
      7. $(Am \supset Bm) \cdot (An \supset Bn)$ 5, 6, Conj
      8. $Bm \lor Bn$ 2, 7, CD
      9. $\sim Bm$ 4, UI
    10. Bn 8, 9, DS
    11. $\sim Bn$ 4, UI
    12. $Bn \cdot \sim Bn$ 10, 11, Conj
  13. $\sim\sim(\exists x)Bx$ 3–12, IP
  14. $(\exists x)Bx$ 13, DN

(13) 1. $(\exists x)Ax \supset (x)(Bx \supset Cx)$
    2. $(\exists x)Dx \supset (\exists x)Bx$ / $(\exists x)(Ax \cdot Dx) \supset (\exists x)Cx$
      3. $(\exists x)(Ax \cdot Dx)$ ACP
      4. $Am \cdot Dm$ 3, EI
      5. Am 4, Simp
      6. $(\exists x)Ax$ 5, EG
      7. $(x)(Bx \supset Cx)$ 1, 6, MP
      8. $Dm \cdot Am$ 4, Com
      9. Dm 8, Simp
    10. $(\exists x)Dx$ 9, EG
    11. $(\exists x)Bx$ 2, 10, MP
    12. Bn 11, EI
    13. $Bn \supset Cn$ 7, UI
    14. Cn 12, 13, MP
    15. $(\exists x)Cx$ 14, EG
  16. $(\exists x)(Ax \cdot Dx) \supset (\exists x)Cx$ 3–15, CP

(16) 1. $(x)[(Ax \lor Bx) \supset Cx]$
    2. $(\exists x)(\sim Ax \lor Dx) \supset (x)Ex$ / $(x)Cx \lor (x)Ex$
      3. $\sim[(x)Cx \lor (x)Ex]$ AIP
      4. $\sim(x)Cx \cdot \sim(x)Ex$ 3, DM
      5. $\sim(x)Cx$ 4, Simp
      6. $(\exists x)\sim Cx$ 5, QN
      7. $\sim Cm$ 6, EI
      8. $(Am \lor Bm) \supset Cm$ 1, UI
      9. $\sim(Am \lor Bm)$ 7, 8, MT
    10. $\sim Am \cdot \sim Bm$ 9, DM
    11. $\sim Am$ 10, Simp
    12. $\sim Am \lor Dm$ 11, Add
    13. $(\exists x)(\sim Ax \lor Dx)$ 12, EG
    14. $(x)Ex$ 2, 13, MP
    15. $\sim(x)Ex \cdot \sim(x)Cx$ 4, Com
    16. $\sim(x)Ex$ 15, Simp
    17. $(x)Ex \cdot \sim(x)Ex$ 14, 16, Conj
  18. $\sim\sim[(x)Cx \lor (x)Ex]$ 3–17, IP
  19. $(x)Cx \lor (x)Ex$ 18, DN

(19) 1. $(x)[Bx \supset (Cx \cdot Dx)]$ / $(x)(Ax \supset Bx) \supset (x)(Ax \supset Dx)$
    2. $(x)(Ax \supset Bx)$ ACP
      3. Ax ACP
      4. $Ax \supset Bx$ 2, UI
      5. Bx 3, 4, MP
      6. $Bx \supset (Cx \cdot Dx)$ 1, UI
      7. $Cx \cdot Dx$ 5, 6, MP
      8. $Dx \cdot Cx$ 7, Com
      9. Dx 8, Simp
    10. $Ax \supset Dx$ 3–9, CP
  11. $(x)(Ax \supset Dx)$ 10, UG
  12. $(x)(Ax \supset Bx) \supset (x)(Ax \supset Dx)$ 2–11, CP

(22) 1. $(x)Ax \lor (x)Bx$ / $(x)(Ax \lor Bx)$
    2. $\sim(x)(Ax \lor Bx)$ AIP
    3. $(\exists x)\sim(Ax \lor Bx)$ 2, QN
    4. $(\exists x)(\sim Ax \cdot \sim Bx)$ 3, DM
    5. $\sim An \cdot \sim Bn$ 4, EI
    6. $\sim An$ 5, Simp
    7. $(\exists x)\sim Ax$ 6, EG
    8. $\sim(x)Ax$ 7, QN
    9. $(x)Bx$ 1, 8, DS
    10. Bn 9, UI
    11. $\sim Bn \cdot \sim An$ 5, Com
    12. $\sim Bn$ 11, Simp
    13. $Bn \cdot \sim Bn$ 10, 12, Conj
  14. $\sim\sim(x)(Ax \lor Bx)$ 2–13, IP
  15. $(x)(Ax \lor Bx)$ 14, DN

(25) 1. $(\exists x)Ax \supset (x)(Bx \supset Cx)$
    2. $(\exists x)Dx \supset (x)(Ex \supset \sim Bx)$
    3. $\sim(\exists x)(Cx \cdot \sim Ex)$ / $(\exists x)(Ax \cdot Dx) \supset \sim(\exists x)Bx$
      4. $(\exists x)(Ax \cdot Dx)$ ACP
      5. $An \cdot Dn$ 4, EI
      6. An 5, Simp
      7. $(\exists x)Ax$ 6, EG
      8. $(x)(Bx \supset Cx)$ 1, 7, MP
      9. $Dn \cdot An$ 5, Com
    10. Dn 9, Simp
    11. $(\exists x)Dx$ 10, EG
    12. $(x)(Ex \supset \sim Bx)$ 2, 11, MP
    13. $(x)\sim(Cx \cdot \sim Ex)$ 3, QN
    14. $\sim(Cx \cdot \sim Ex)$ 13, UI
    15. $\sim Cx \lor \sim\sim Ex$ 14, DM
    16. $\sim Cx \lor Ex$ 15, DN
    17. $Cx \supset Ex$ 16, Impl
    18. $Bx \supset Cx$ 8, UI
    19. $Bx \supset Ex$ 17, 18, HS
    20. $Ex \supset \sim Bx$ 12, UI
    21. $Bx \supset \sim Bx$ 19, 20, HS
    22. $\sim Bx \lor \sim Bx$ 21, Impl

23. ~Bx   22, Taut
24. (x)~Bx   23, UG
25. ~(∃x)Bx   24, QN
26. (∃x)(Ax • Dx) ⊃ ~(∃x)Bx   4–25, CP

II.

(1) 1. (x)(Ax ⊃ Wx)
    2. (x)(Rx ⊃ Cx)   / (x)[(Rx • Ax) ⊃
                                              (Cx • Wx)]
       3. Rx • Ax   ACP
       4. Rx   3, Simp
       5. Ax • Rx   3, Com
       6. Ax   5, Simp
       7. Ax ⊃ Wx   1, UI
       8. Rx ⊃ Cx   2, UI
       9. Cx   4, 8, MP
      10. Wx   6, 7, MP
      11. Cx • Wx   9, 10, Conj
   12. (Rx • Ax) ⊃ (Cx • Wx)   3–11, CP
   13. (x)[(Rx • Ax) ⊃ (Cx • Wx)]   12, UG
(4) 1. (x)[(Sx ∨ Ux) ⊃ (Ix • Cx)]
    2. (x)[(Cx ∨ Vx) ⊃ (Rx • Ax)]   / (x)(Sx ⊃ Ax)
       3. Sx   ACP
       4. Sx ∨ Ux   3, Add
       5. (Sx ∨ Ux) ⊃ (Ix • Cx)   1, UI
       6. Ix • Cx   4, 5, MP
       7. Cx • Ix   6, Com
       8. Cx   7, Simp
       9. Cx ∨ Vx   8, Add
      10. (Cx ∨ Vx) ⊃ (Rx • Ax)   2, UI
      11. Rx • Ax   9, 10, MP
      12. Ax • Rx   11, Com
      13. Ax   12, Simp
   14. Sx ⊃ Ax   3–13, CP
   15. (x)(Sx ⊃ Ax)   14, UG
(7) 1. (∃x)Cx ⊃ (x)[Ax ⊃ (Sx • Dx)]
    2. (x)(Cx ⊃ ~Ax) ⊃ (∃x)(Dx • Sx)   / (∃x)(Dx • Sx)
       3. ~(∃x)(Dx • Sx)   AIP
       4. ~(x)(Cx ⊃ ~Ax)   2, 3, MT
       5. (∃x)~(Cx ⊃ ~Ax)   4, QN
       6. ~(Cm ⊃ ~Am)   5, EI
       7. ~(~Cm ∨ ~Am)   6, Impl
       8. ~~Cm • ~~Am   7, DM
       9. Cm • ~~Am   8, DN
      10. Cm • Am   9, DN
      11. Cm   10, Simp
      12. (∃x)Cx   11, EG
      13. (x)[Ax ⊃ (Sx • Dx)]   1, 12, MP
      14. Am ⊃ (Sm • Dm)   13, UI
      15. Am • Cm   10, Com
      16. Am   15, Simp
      17. Sm • Dm   14, 16, MP
      18. Dm • Sm   17, Com
      19. (∃x)(Dx • Sx)   18, EG
      20. (∃x)(Dx • Sx) •   3, 19, Conj
          ~(∃x)(Dx • Sx)

21. ~~(∃x)(Dx • Sx)   3–20, IP
22. (∃x)(Dx • Sx)   21, DN
(10) 1. (∃x)(Gx • Px) ∨ (∃x)(Ax • Px)
     2. (∃x)Px ⊃ (∃x) [Ax • (Cx • Dx)]   / (∃x)(Dx • Cx)
        3. ~(∃x)Px   AIP
        4. (x)~Px   3, QN
        5. ~Px   4, UI
        6. ~Px ∨ ~Gx   5, Add
        7. ~Gx ∨ ~Px   6, Com
        8. ~(Gx • Px)   7, DM
        9. (x)~(Gx • Px)   8, UG
       10. ~(∃x)(Gx • Px)   9, QN
       11. (∃x)(Ax • Px)   1, 10, DS
       12. Am • Pm   11, EI
       13. Pm • Am   12, Com
       14. Pm   13, Simp
       15. ~Pm   4, UI
       16. Pm • ~Pm   14, 15, Conj
    17. ~~(∃x)Px   3–16, IP
    18. (∃x)Px   17, DN
    19. (∃x)[Ax • (Cx • Dx)]   2, 18, MP
    20. An • (Cn • Dn)   19, EI
    21. (Cn • Dn) • An   20, Com
    22. Cn • Dn   21, Simp
    23. Dn • Cn   22, Com
    24. (∃x)(Dx • Cx)   23, EG

Exercise 8.5

I.

1. All cats are animals.
   No cats are dogs.
   No dogs are animals.

4. Some mammals are dogs.
   Some mammals write books.
   Some mammals are dogs that write books.

7. There are flowers.
   There are dogs.
   No flowers are animals.
   Some dogs are not animals.

10. Some mammals are felines.
    Some animals are not felines.
    All mammals are animals.
    Some feline animals are not mammals.

II.

(1) 1. (x)(Ax ⊃ Bx)
    2. (x)(Ax ⊃ Cx)   / (x)(Bx ⊃ Cx)
       For a universe consisting of one member, we have
       Aa ⊃ Ba / Aa ⊃ Ca // Ba ⊃ Ca
       F T T   F T F   T F F

(4) 1. $(x)(Ax \supset Bx)$
   2. $(\exists x)Ax$ / $(x)Bx$

For a universe consisting of two members, we have
$(Aa \supset Ba) \cdot (Ab \supset Bb)$ / $Aa \lor Ab$ // $Ba \cdot Bb$
 T T T T F T F   T T F   T F F

(7) 1. $(x)(Ax \supset Bx)$
   2. $(\exists x)Bx \supset (\exists x)Cx$ / $(x)(Ax \supset Cx)$

For a universe consisting of two members, we have
$(Aa \supset Ba) \cdot (Ab \supset Bb)$ / $(Ba \lor Bb) \supset (Ca \lor Cb)$ // $(Aa \supset Ca) \cdot (Ab \supset Cb)$
 T T T T T T T   T T T T T T F   T T T F T F F

(10) 1. $(\exists x)(Ax \cdot Bx)$
    2. $(\exists x)(\sim Ax \cdot \sim Bx)$ / $(x)(Ax \equiv Bx)$

For a universe consisting of one member, we have
$Aa \cdot Ba$ / $\sim Aa \cdot \sim Ba$ // $Aa \equiv Ba$
 T T   &boxed{F T T}   F

For a universe consisting of two members, we have
$(Aa \cdot Ba) \lor (Ab \cdot Bb)$ / $(\sim Aa \cdot \sim Ba) \lor (\sim Ab \cdot \sim Bb)$ // $(Aa \equiv Ba) \cdot (Ab \equiv Bb)$
 T T T T T F F   F T &boxed{F F T T F T F} T F   T T T F T F F

For a universe consisting of three members, we have
$(Aa \cdot Ba) \lor [(Ab \cdot Bb) \lor (Ac \cdot Bc)]$ / $(\sim Aa \cdot \sim Ba) \lor [(\sim Ab \cdot \sim Bb) \lor (\sim Ac \cdot \sim Bc)]$
 T T T T T F F F T F F F   F T F F T T   F T F T F T T F T T F

// $(Aa \equiv Ba) \cdot [(Ab \equiv Bb) \cdot (Ac \equiv Bc)]$
   T T T F   T F F F   F F T F

III.

(1) 1. $(x)[(Vx \cdot Px) \supset (Ax \cdot Mx)]$
   2. $(\exists x)(Vx \cdot Ox)$ / $(\exists x)(Mx \cdot Ax)$

For a universe consisting of one member, we have

$(Va \cdot Pa) \supset (Aa \cdot Ma)$ / $Va \cdot Oa$ // $Ma \cdot Aa$
 T F F T F F T   T T T   T F F

(4) 1. $(x)(Tx \supset Hx)$
   2. $(\exists x)(Tx \cdot Hx) \supset (\exists x)(Px \cdot Ox)$ / $(x)(Tx \supset Ox)$

For a universe consisting of two members, we have
$(Ta \supset Ha) \cdot (Tb \supset Hb)$ / $[(Ta \cdot Ha) \lor (Tb \cdot Hb)] \supset [(Pa \cdot Oa) \lor (Pb \cdot Ob)]$
 T T T T T T T   T T T T T T T   T   F F F T T T

// $(Ta \supset Oa) \cdot (Tb \supset Ob)$
   T F F F T T T

Exercise 8.6

I.

  1. Rcp
  4. $(\exists x)Fxj \supset Fmj$
  7. $(x)[Px \supset (\exists y)Sxy]$
 10. $(\exists x)[Px \cdot (y)Sxy]$
 13. $(\exists x)[(Cx \cdot Lx) \cdot Dpx]$
 16. $(\exists x)(Fxc \cdot Icx)$
 19. $(x)\{Px \supset (\exists y)[Py \cdot (Mxy \supset Axy)]\}$
 22. $(\exists x)\{Px \cdot (y)[(Ty \cdot Sxy) \supset Axy]\}$
 25. $(x)\{Lx \supset (y)[(Wy \cdot Cy) \supset Rxy]\}$
 28. $(x)\{(Cx \cdot Fx) \supset (y)[(By \cdot Ly) \supset Rxy]\}$

II.

(1) 1. $(x)[Ax \supset (y)Bxy]$
   2. Am / $(y)Bmy$
   3. $Am \supset (y)Bmy$ 1, UI
   4. $(y)Bmy$ 2, 3, MP

(4) 1. $(x)(\exists y)(Ax \supset By)$ / $(x)Ax \supset (\exists y)By$
     | 2. $(x)Ax$ ACP
     | 3. Ax 2, UI
     | 4. $(\exists y)(Ax \supset By)$ 1, UI
     | 5. $Ax \supset Bm$ 4, EI
     | 6. Bm 3, 5, MP
     | 7. $(\exists y)By$ 6, EG
   8. $(x)Ax \supset (\exists y)By$ 2-7, CP

(7) 1. $(\exists x)[Ax \cdot (y)(Ay \supset Bxy)]$ / $(\exists x)Bxx$
   2. $Am \cdot (y)(Ay \supset Bmy)$ 1, EI
   3. Am 2, Simp
   4. $(y)(Ay \supset Bmy) \cdot Am$ 2, Com
   5. $(y)(Ay \supset Bmy)$ 4, Simp
   6. $Am \supset Bmm$ 5, UI
   7. Bmm 3, 6, MP
   8. $(\exists x)Bxx$ 7, EG

8

(10) 1. $(x)(\exists y)Axy \supset (x)(\exists y)Bxy$
2. $(\exists x)(y)\sim Bxy$ / $(\exists x)(y)\sim Axy$
3. $(\exists x)\sim(\exists y)Bxy$ 2, QN
4. $\sim(x)(\exists y)Bxy$ 3, QN
5. $\sim(x)(\exists y)Axy$ 1, 4, MT
6. $(\exists x)\sim(\exists y)Axy$ 5, QN
7. $(\exists x)(y)\sim Axy$ 6, QN

(13) 1. $(\exists x)\{Ax \cdot (y)[(By \vee Cy) \supset Dxy]\}$
2. $(\exists x)Ax \supset (\exists y)By$ / $(\exists x)(\exists y)Dxy$
3. $Am \cdot (y)[(By \vee Cy) \supset Dmy]$ 1, EI
4. Am 3, Simp
5. $(\exists x)Ax$ 4, EG
6. $(\exists y)By$ 2, 5, MP
7. Bn 6, EI
8. $(y)[(By \vee Cy) \supset Dmy] \cdot Am$ 3, Com
9. $(y)[(By \vee Cy) \supset Dmy]$ 8, Simp
10. $(Bn \vee Cn) \supset Dmn$ 9, UI
11. $Bn \vee Cn$ 7, Add
12. Dmn 10, 11, MP
13. $(\exists y)Dmy$ 12, EG
14. $(\exists x)(\exists y)Dxy$ 13, EG

(16) 1. $(x)(Ax \supset Bx)$
2. $(\exists x)Bx \supset \sim(\exists x)(\exists y)Cxy$ / $(\exists x)Ax \supset \sim Cmn$
> 3. $(\exists x)Ax$ ACP
> 4. Ae 3, EI
> 5. $Ae \supset Be$ 1, UI
> 6. Be 4, 5, MP
> 7. $(\exists x)Bx$ 6, EG
> 8. $\sim(\exists x)(\exists y)Cxy$ 2, 7, MP
> 9. $(x)\sim(\exists y)Cxy$ 8, QN
> 10. $(x)(y)\sim Cxy$ 9, QN
> 11. $(y)\sim Cmy$ 10, UI
> 12. $\sim Cmn$ 11, UI
13. $(\exists x)Ax \supset \sim Cmn$ 3–12, CP

(19) 1. $(\exists x)(y)Ayx \vee (x)(y)Bxy$
2. $(\exists x)(y)(Cy \supset \sim Byx)$ / $(x)(\exists y)$
                                  $(Cx \supset Axy)$
> 3. Cx ACP
> 4. $(y)(Cy \supset \sim Bym)$ 2, EI
> 5. $Cx \supset \sim Bxm$ 4, UI
> 6. $\sim Bxm$ 3, 5, MP
> 7. $(\exists y)\sim Bxy$ 6, EG
> 8. $(\exists x)(\exists y)\sim Bxy$ 7, EG
> 9. $(\exists x)\sim(y)Bxy$ 8, QN
> 10. $\sim(x)(y)Bxy$ 9, QN
> 11. $(x)(y)Bxy \vee (\exists x)(y)Ayx$ 1, Com
> 12. $(\exists x)(y)Ayx$ 10, 11, DS
> 13. $(y)Ayn$ 12, EI
> 14. Axn 13, UI
15. $Cx \supset Axn$ 3–14, CP
16. $(\exists y)(Cx \supset Axy)$ 15, EG
17. $(x)(\exists y)(Cx \supset Axy)$ 16, UG

III.

(1) 1. $(x)[Px \supset (y)(Ay \supset Oxy)]$
2. $Pj \cdot \sim Ojm$ / $\sim Am$

3. $Pj \supset (y)(Ay \supset Ojy)$ 1, UI
4. Pj 2, Simp
5. $(y)(Ay \supset Ojy)$ 3, 4, MP
6. $Am \supset Ojm$ 5, UI
7. $\sim Ojm \cdot Pj$ 2, Com
8. $\sim Ojm$ 7, Simp
9. $\sim Am$ 6, 8, MT

(4) 1. Po
2. $(x)[(Px \cdot Cx) \supset Sox]$
3. $(x)(Px \supset \sim Sxx)$ / $\sim Co$
> 4. Co AIP
> 5. $(Po \cdot Co) \supset Soo$ 2, UI
> 6. $Po \cdot Co$ 1, 4, Conj
> 7. Soo 5, 6, MP
> 8. $Po \supset \sim Soo$ 3, UI
> 9. $\sim Soo$ 1, 8, MP
> 10. $Soo \cdot \sim Soo$ 7, 9, Conj
11. $\sim Co$ 4–10, IP

(7) 1. $(\exists x)\{Px \cdot (y)[(Py \cdot Kxy) \supset Fxy]\}$
2. $(x)[Px \supset (\exists y)(Py \cdot Kxy)]$ / $(\exists x)(\exists y)$
                                  $[(Px \cdot Py) \cdot Fxy]$
3. $Pm \cdot (y)[(Py \cdot Kmy) \supset Fmy]$ 1, EI
4. $Pm \supset (\exists y)(Py \cdot Kmy)$ 2, UI
5. Pm 3, Simp
6. $(\exists y)(Py \cdot Kmy)$ 4, 5, MP
7. $Pn \cdot Kmn$ 6, EI
8. $(y)[(Py \cdot Kmy) \supset Fmy] \cdot Pm$ 3, Com
9. $(y)[(Py \cdot Kmy) \supset Fmy]$ 8, Simp
10. $(Pn \cdot Kmn) \supset Fmn$ 9, UI
11. Fmn 7, 10, MP
12. Pn 7, Simp
13. $Pm \cdot Pn$ 5, 12, Conj
14. $(Pm \cdot Pn) \cdot Fmn$ 11, 13, Conj
15. $(\exists y)[(Pm \cdot Py) \cdot Fmy]$ 14, EG
16. $(\exists x)(\exists y)[(Px \cdot Py) \cdot Fxy]$ 15, EG

(10) 1. $(x)\{Ix \supset [(\exists y)(Cy \cdot Ay) \supset Ex]\}$
2. $[(\exists x)Tx \vee (\exists x)Wx] \supset [(\exists x)Ix \cdot (\exists x)Cx]$
3. $(x)(Cx \supset Ax)$ / $(\exists x)Tx \supset (\exists x)(Ix \cdot Ex)$
> 4. $(\exists x)Tx$ ACP
> 5. $(\exists x)Tx \vee (\exists x)Wx$ 4, Add
> 6. $(\exists x)Ix \cdot (\exists x)Cx$ 2, 5, MP
> 7. $(\exists x)Ix$ 6, Simp
> 8. Im 7, EI
> 9. $Im \supset [(\exists y)(Cy \cdot Ay) \supset Em]$ 1, UI
> 10. $(\exists y)(Cy \cdot Ay) \supset Em$ 8, 9, MP
> 11. $(\exists x)Cx \cdot (\exists x)Ix$ 6, Com
> 12. $(\exists x)Cx$ 11, Simp
> 13. Cn 12, EI
> 14. $Cn \supset An$ 3, UI
> 15. An 13, 14, MP
> 16. $Cn \cdot An$ 13, 15, Conj
> 17. $(\exists y)(Cy \cdot Ay)$ 16, EG
> 18. Em 10, 17, MP
> 19. $Im \cdot Em$ 8, 18, Conj
> 20. $(\exists x)(Ix \cdot Ex)$ 19, EG
21. $(\exists x)Tx \supset (\exists x)(Ix \cdot Ex)$ 4–20, CP

8

Exercise 8.7

I.

1. $s = g$
4. $h \neq g$
5. $Wp \bullet (x)(Wx \supset x = p)$
8. $Nc \bullet Mc \bullet (x)[(Nx \bullet Mx) \supset x = c]$
11. $Sh \bullet Ph \bullet (x)[(Sx \bullet Px) \supset x = h]$
12. $Eh \bullet (x)[(Ex \bullet x \neq h) \supset Lhx]$
15. $Rd \bullet Nd \bullet (x)[(Rx \bullet Nx \bullet x \neq d) \supset Ldx]$
16. $Ci \bullet \sim Si \bullet (x)[(Cx \bullet x \neq i) \supset Sx]$
19. $Pc \bullet \sim Wc \bullet (x)[(Px \bullet x \neq c) \supset Wx]$
20. $(x)(y)[(Cx \bullet Bx \bullet Cy \bullet By) \supset x = y]$
23. $(x)(y)(z)[(Cx \bullet Mx \bullet Cy \bullet My \bullet Cz \bullet Mz) \supset$
    $(x = y \lor x = z \lor y = z)]$
26. $(\exists x)(\exists y)(\exists z)(Cx \bullet Cy \bullet Cz \bullet x \neq y \bullet x \neq z \bullet y \neq z)$
29. $(\exists x)(\exists y)\{Sx \bullet Bx \bullet Gx \bullet Sy \bullet By \bullet Gy \bullet x \neq y \bullet$
    $(z)[(Sz \bullet Bz \bullet Gz) \supset (z = x \lor z = y)]\}$
30. $(\exists x)[Wxv \bullet (y)(Wyv \supset y = x) \bullet Bx]$
33. $(\exists x)\{Ax \bullet Pxa \bullet (y)[(Ay \bullet Pya) \supset y = x] \bullet x = b\}$
35. $Sr \bullet (x)[(Sx \bullet x \neq r) \supset Srx]$
38. $Ar \bullet Er \bullet (x)[(Ax \bullet Ex) \supset x = r]$
41. $(x)(y)[(Sxh \bullet Syh) \supset x = y]$
44. $m \neq b$
47. $(\exists x)(\exists y)\{Tx \bullet Cx \bullet Ty \bullet Cy \bullet x \neq y \bullet (z)[(Tz \bullet Cz) \supset$
    $(z = x \lor z = y)]\}$
50. $(\exists x)(\exists y)(\exists z)(Sx \bullet Ox \bullet Sy \bullet Oy \bullet Sz \bullet Oz \bullet x \neq y \bullet$
    $x \neq z \bullet y \neq z)$

II.

(1) 1. $(x)(x = a)$
    2. $(\exists x)Rx$ / Ra
    3. Ri 2, EI
    4. $i = a$ 1, UI
    5. Ra 3, 4, Id

(4) 1. $(\exists x)(x = g)$
    2. $(x)(x = i)$ / $g = i$
    3. $n = g$ 1, EI
    4. $n = i$ 2, UI
    5. $g = n$ 3, Id
    6. $g = i$ 4, 5, Id

(7) 1. $(x)(x = a)$
    2. Fa / $Fm \bullet Fn$
    3. $m = a$ 1, UI
    4. $a = m$ 3, Id
    5. Fm 2, 4, Id
    6. $n = a$ 1, UI
    7. $a = n$ 6, Id
    8. Fn 2, 7, Id
    9. $Fm \bullet Fn$ 5, 8, Conj

(10) 1. $(x)(Px \supset x = a)$
    2. $(x)(x = c \supset Qx)$
    3. $a = c$ / $(x)(Px \supset Qx)$

    4. Px ACP
    5. $Px \supset x = a$ 1, UI
    6. $x = a$ 4, 5, MP
    7. $x = c$ 3, 6, Id
    8. $x = c \supset Qx$ 2, UI
    9. Qx 7, 8, MP
    10. $Px \supset Qx$ 4–9, CP
    11. $(x)(Px \supset Qx)$ 10, UG

(13) 1. $(x)(Ba \supset x \neq a)$
    2. Bc / $a \neq c$
    3. $a = c$ AIP
    4. $c = a$ 3, Id
    5. Ba 2, 4, Id
    6. $Ba \supset c \neq a$ 1, UI
    7. $c \neq a$ 5, 6, MP
    8. $c = a \bullet c \neq a$ 4, 7, Conj
    9. $a \neq c$ 3–8, IP

(16) 1. $(x)[Nx \supset (Px \bullet x = m)]$
    2. $\sim Pm$ / $\sim Ne$
    3. Ne AIP
    4. $Ne \supset (Pe \bullet e = m)$ 1, UI
    5. $Pe \bullet e = m$ 3, 4, MP
    6. Pe 5, Simp
    7. $e = m \bullet Pe$ 5, Com
    8. $e = m$ 7, Simp
    9. Pm 6, 8, Id
    10. $Pm \bullet \sim Pm$ 2, 9, Conj
    11. $\sim Ne$ 3–10, IP

(19) 1. $(x)(\exists y)(Cxy \supset x = y)$
    2. $(\exists x)(y)(Cxy \bullet x = a)$ / Caa
    3. $(y)(Cny \bullet n = a)$ 2, EI
    4. $(\exists y)(Cay \supset a = y)$ 1, UI
    5. $Cam \supset a = m$ 4, EI
    6. $Cnm \bullet n = a$ 3, UI
    7. Cnm 6, Simp
    8. $n = a \bullet Cnm$ 6, Com
    9. $n = a$ 8, Simp
    10. Cam 7, 9, Id
    11. $a = m$ 5, 10, MP
    12. $m = a$ 11, Id
    13. Caa 10, 12, Id

III.

(1) 1. $(\exists x)(Nx \bullet Wjx \bullet Ix)$
    2. $Nc \bullet Wjc \bullet (x)[(Nx \bullet Wjx) \supset$
       $x = c]$ / Ic
    3. $Na \bullet Wja \bullet Ia$ 1, EI
    4. $(x)[(Nx \bullet Wjx) \supset x = c] \bullet$
       $Nc \bullet Wjc$ 2, Com
    5. $(x)[(Nx \bullet Wjx) \supset x = c]$ 4, Simp
    6. $(Na \bullet Wja) \supset a = c$ 5, UI
    7. $Na \bullet Wja$ 3, Simp
    8. $a = c$ 6, 7, MP
    9. $Ia \bullet Na \bullet Wja$ 3, Com
    10. Ia 9, Simp
    11. Ic 8, 10, Id

(4) 1. $(\exists x)\{Nx \cdot Tx \cdot$
       $(y)[(Ny \cdot Ty) \supset y = x] \cdot Wmx\}$
    2. $Ng \cdot Wmg \cdot$ $/ (\exists x)\{Nx \cdot Tx \cdot$
       $(x)[(Nx \cdot Wmx) \supset x = g]$ $(y)[(Ny \cdot Ty) \supset y = x] \cdot$
                                 $x = g\}$
    3. $Na \cdot Ta \cdot$
       $(y)[(Ny \cdot Ty) \supset y = a] \cdot$
       Wma 1, EI
    4. $(x)[(Nx \cdot Wmx) \supset x = g] \cdot$
       $Ng \cdot Wmg$ 2, Com
    5. $(x)[(Nx \cdot Wmx) \supset x = g]$ 4, Simp
    6. $(Na \cdot Wma) \supset a = g$ 5, UI
    7. Na 3, Simp
    8. $Wma \cdot Na \cdot Ta \cdot$
       $(y)[(Ny \cdot Ty) \supset y = a]$ 3, Com
    9. Wma 8, Simp
   10. $Na \cdot Wma$ 7, 9, Conj
   11. $a = g$ 6, 10, MP
   12. $Na \cdot Ta \cdot$
       $(y)[(Ny \cdot Ty) \supset y = a]$ 3, Simp
   13. $Na \cdot Ta \cdot (y)[(Ny \cdot Ty) \supset$
       $y = a] \cdot a = g$ 11, 12, Conj
   14. $(\exists x)\{Nx \cdot Tx \cdot (y)[(Ny \cdot Ty) \supset$
       $y = x] \cdot x = g\}$ 13, EG

(7) 1. $Me \cdot \sim Se \cdot$
       $(x)[(Mx \cdot x \neq e) \supset Sx]$
    2. $Mn \cdot \sim Gn \cdot (x)[(Mx \cdot x \neq n) \supset Gx]$
    3. $e \neq n$ $/ Ge \cdot Sn$
    4. $(x)[(Mx \cdot x \neq e) \supset Sx] \cdot$
       $Me \cdot \sim Se$ 1, Com
    5. $(x)[(Mx \cdot x \neq e) \supset Sx]$ 4, Simp
    6. $(Mn \cdot n \neq e) \supset Sn$ 5, UI
    7. Mn 2, Simp
    8. $n \neq e$ 3, Id
    9. $Mn \cdot n \neq e$ 7, 8, Conj
   10. Sn 6, 9, MP
   11. $(x)[(Mx \cdot x \neq n) \supset Gx] \cdot$
       $Mn \cdot \sim Gn$ 2, Com
   12. $(x)[(Mx \cdot x \neq n) \supset Gx]$ 11, Simp
   13. $(Me \cdot e \neq n) \supset Ge$ 12, UI
   14. Me 1, Simp
   15. $Me \cdot e \neq n$ 3, 14, Conj
   16. Ge 13, 15, MP
   17. $Ge \cdot Sn$ 10, 16, Conj

(10) 1. $Bw \cdot (x)[(Bx \cdot x \neq w) \supset Twx]$
     2. $(\exists x)\{Bx \cdot (y)[(By \cdot y \neq x) \supset Txy] \cdot Cx\}$
     3. $(x)(y)(Txy \supset \sim Tyx)$ $/ Cw$
     4. $Ba \cdot (y)[(By \cdot y \neq a) \supset$
        $Tay] \cdot Ca$ 2, EI
     5. $(x)[(Bx \cdot x \neq w) \supset Twx] \cdot Bw$ 1, Com
     6. $(x)[(Bx \cdot x \neq w) \supset Twx]$ 5, Simp
     7. $(Ba \cdot a \neq w) \supset Twa$ 6, UI
        8. $a \neq w$ AIP
        9. Ba 4, Simp
       10. $Ba \cdot a \neq w$ 8, 9, Conj
       11. Twa 7, 10, MP

   12. $(y)[(By \cdot y \neq a) \supset$
       $Tay] \cdot Ca \cdot Ba$ 4, Com
   13. $(y)[(By \cdot y \neq a) \supset Tay]$ 12, Simp
   14. $(Bw \cdot w \neq a) \supset Taw$ 13, UI
   15. Bw 1, Simp
   16. $w \neq a$ 8, Id
   17. $Bw \cdot w \neq a$ 15, 16, Conj
   18. Taw 14, 17, MP
   19. $(y)(Tay \supset \sim Tya)$ 3, UI
   20. $Taw \supset \sim Twa$ 19, UI
   21. $\sim Twa$ 18, 20, MP
   22. $Twa \cdot \sim Twa$ 11, 21, Conj
23. $\sim(a \neq w)$ 8–22, IP
24. $a = w$ 23, DN
25. $Ca \cdot Ba \cdot (y)[(By \cdot y \neq a) \supset Tay]$ 4, Com
26. Ca 25, Simp
27. Cw 24, 26, Id

(13) 1. $(\exists x)(\exists y)(Ax \cdot Ox \cdot Ay \cdot Oy \cdot x \neq y)$
     2. $(x)(Ax \supset Px)$
     3. $(x)(y)(z)[(Px \cdot Ox \cdot Py \cdot Oy \cdot Pz \cdot$
        $Oz) \supset (x = y \lor x = z \lor y = z)]$
                 $/ (\exists x)(\exists y)\{Px \cdot Ox \cdot Py \cdot Oy \cdot x \neq y \cdot$
                     $(z)[(Pz \cdot Oz) \supset (z = x \lor z = y)]\}$
     4. $(\exists y)(Aa \cdot Oa \cdot Ay \cdot Oy \cdot a \neq y)$ 1, EI
     5. $Aa \cdot Oa \cdot Ab \cdot Ob \cdot a \neq b$ 4, EI
     6. $Aa \supset Pa$ 2, UI
     7. Aa 5, Simp
     8. Pa 6, 7, MP
     9. $Ab \supset Pb$ 2, UI
    10. $Ab \cdot Ob \cdot a \neq b \cdot Aa \cdot Oa$ 5, Com
    11. Ab 10, Simp
    12. Pb 9, 11, MP
    13. $Oa \cdot Ab \cdot Ob \cdot a \neq b \cdot Aa$ 10, Com
    14. Oa 13, Simp
    15. $Ob \cdot a \neq b \cdot Aa \cdot Oa \cdot Ab$ 5, Com
    16. Ob 15, Simp
    17. $a \neq b \cdot Aa \cdot Oa \cdot Ab \cdot Ob$ 5, Com
    18. $a \neq b$ 17, Simp
    19. $Pa \cdot Oa \cdot Pb \cdot Ob \cdot a \neq b$ 8, 14, 12, 16,
                                      18, Conj

    20. $\sim(z)[(Pz \cdot Oz) \supset$
        $(z = a \lor z = b)]$ AIP
    21. $(\exists z)\sim[(Pz \cdot Oz) \supset$
        $(z = a \lor z = b)]$ 20, QN
    22. $\sim[(Pc \cdot Oc) \supset (c = a \lor c = b)]$ 21, EI
    23. $\sim[\sim(Pc \cdot Oc) \lor (c = a \lor c = b)]$ 22, Impl
    24. $\sim\sim(Pc \cdot Oc) \cdot \sim(c = a \lor c = b)$ 23, DM
    25. $Pc \cdot Oc \cdot \sim(c = a \lor c = b)$ 24, DN
    26. $(y)(z)[(Pa \cdot Oa \cdot Py \cdot Oy \cdot Pz \cdot Oz) \supset$
        $(a = y \lor a = z \lor y = z)]$ 3, UI
    27. $(z)[(Pa \cdot Oa \cdot Pb \cdot Ob \cdot Pz \cdot Oz) \supset$
        $(a = b \lor a = z \lor b = z)]$ 26, UI
    28. $(Pa \cdot Oa \cdot Pb \cdot Ob \cdot Pc \cdot Oc) \supset$
        $(a = b \lor a = c \lor b = c)$ 27, UI
    29. $Pc \cdot Oc$ 25, Simp
    30. $Pa \cdot Oa \cdot Pb \cdot Ob$ 19, Simp

31. $Pa \cdot Oa \cdot Pb \cdot Ob \cdot Pc \cdot Oc$ 29, 30, Conj
32. $a = b \lor a = c \lor b = c$ 28, 31, MP
33. $a = c \lor b = c$ 18, 32, DS
34. $\sim(c = a \lor c = b) \cdot Pc \cdot Oc$ 25, Com
35. $\sim(c = a \lor c = b)$ 34, Simp
36. $\sim(a = c \lor c = b)$ 35, Id
37. $\sim(a = c \lor b = c)$ 36, Id
38. $(a = c \lor b = c) \cdot \sim(a = c \lor b = c)$ 33, 37, Conj

39. $\sim\sim(z)[(Pz \cdot Oz) \supset z = a \lor z = b)]$ 20–38, IP
40. $(z)[(Pz \cdot Oz) \supset (z = a \lor z = b)]$ 39, DN
41. $Pa \cdot Oa \cdot Pb \cdot Ob \cdot a \neq b \cdot$
    $(z)[(Pz \cdot Oz) \supset (z = a \lor z = b)]$ 19, 40, Conj
42. $(\exists y)\{Pa \cdot Oa \cdot Py \cdot Oy \cdot a \neq y \cdot$
    $(z)[(Pz \cdot Oz) \supset (z = a \lor z = y)]\}$ 41, EG
43. $(\exists x)(\exists y)\{Px \cdot Ox \cdot Py \cdot Oy \cdot x \neq y \cdot$
    $(z)[(Pz \cdot Oz) \supset (z = x \lor z = y)]\}$ 42, EG

(16) 1. $Sc \cdot \sim Pc \cdot Sn \cdot \sim Pn \cdot$
    $(x)[(Sx \cdot x \neq c \cdot x \neq n) \supset Px]$
2. $Sn \cdot Dn \cdot (x)[(Sx \cdot Dx) \supset x = n]$
3. $(x)\{Sx \supset [Rx \equiv (\sim Dx \cdot \sim Px)]\}$
4. $c \neq n$ / $(\exists x)\{Sx \cdot Rx \cdot (y)[(Sy \cdot Ry) \supset y = x]\}$
5. Sc 1, Simp
6. $Sc \supset [Rc \equiv (\sim Dc \cdot \sim Pc)]$ 3, UI
7. $Rc \equiv (\sim Dc \cdot \sim Pc)$ 5, 6, MP
8. $[Rc \supset (\sim Dc \cdot \sim Pc)] \cdot$
    $[(\sim Dc \cdot \sim Pc) \supset Rc]$ 7, Equiv
9. $[(\sim Dc \cdot \sim Pc) \supset Rc] \cdot$
    $[Rc \supset (\sim Dc \cdot \sim Pc)]$ 8, Com
10. $(\sim Dc \cdot \sim Pc) \supset Rc$ 9, Simp
11. $(x)[(Sx \cdot Dx) \supset x = n] \cdot Sn \cdot Dn$ 2, Com
12. $(x)[(Sx \cdot Dx) \supset x = n]$ 11, Simp
13. $(Sc \cdot Dc) \supset c = n$ 12, UI
14. $\sim(Sc \cdot Dc)$ 4, 13, MT
15. $\sim Sc \lor \sim Dc$ 14, DM
16. $\sim\sim Sc$ 5, DN
17. $\sim Dc$ 15, 16, DS
18. $\sim Pc \cdot Sn \cdot \sim Pn \cdot$
    $(x)[(Sx \cdot x \neq c \cdot x \neq n) \supset Px] \cdot Sc$ 1, Com
19. $\sim Pc$ 18, Simp
20. $\sim Dc \cdot \sim Pc$ 17, 19, Conj
21. Rc 10, 20, MP
22. $Sc \cdot Rc$ 5, 21, Conj
23. $\sim(y)[(Sy \cdot Ry) \supset y = c]$ AIP
24. $(\exists y)\sim[(Sy \cdot Ry) \supset y = c]$ 23, QN
25. $\sim[(Sa \cdot Ra) \supset a = c]$ 24, EI
26. $\sim[\sim(Sa \cdot Ra) \lor a = c]$ 25, Impl
27. $\sim\sim(Sa \cdot Ra) \cdot a \neq c$ 26, DM
28. $Sa \cdot Ra \cdot a \neq c$ 27, DN
29. $Sa \supset [Ra \equiv (\sim Da \cdot \sim Pa)]$ 3, UI
30. Sa 28, Simp
31. $Ra \equiv (\sim Da \cdot \sim Pa)$ 29, 30, MP
32. $[Ra \supset (\sim Da \cdot \sim Pa)] \cdot$
    $[(\sim Da \cdot \sim Pa) \supset Ra]$ 31, Equiv
33. $Ra \supset (\sim Da \cdot \sim Pa)$ 32, Simp
34. $Ra \cdot a \neq c \cdot Sa$ 28, Com
35. Ra 34, Simp

36. $\sim Da \cdot \sim Pa$ 33, 35, MP
37. $(x)[(Sx \cdot x \neq c \cdot x \neq n) \supset Px] \cdot$
    $Sc \cdot \sim Pc \cdot Sn \cdot \sim Pn$ 1, Com
38. $(x)[(Sx \cdot x \neq c \cdot x \neq n) \supset Px]$ 37, Simp
39. $(Sa \cdot a \neq c \cdot a \neq n) \supset Pa$ 38, UI
40. $(Sa \cdot a \neq c) \supset (a \neq n \supset Pa)$ 39, Exp
41. $a \neq c \cdot Sa \cdot Ra$ 28, Com
42. $a \neq c$ 41, Simp
43. $Sa \cdot a \neq c$ 30, 42, Conj
44. $a \neq n \supset Pa$ 40, 43, MP
45. $\sim Pa \cdot \sim Da$ 36, Com
46. $\sim Pa$ 45, Simp
47. $\sim(a \neq n)$ 44, 46, MT
48. $a = n$ 47, DN
49. $n = a$ 48, Id
50. $Dn \cdot (x)[(Sx \cdot Dx) \supset x = n] \cdot$
    Sn 2, Com
51. Dn 50, Simp
52. Da 49, 51, Id
53. $\sim Da$ 36, Simp
54. $Da \cdot \sim Da$ 52, 53, Conj
55. $\sim\sim(y)[(Sy \cdot Ry) \supset y = c]$ 23–54, IP
56. $(y)[(Sy \cdot Ry) \supset y = c]$ 55, DN
57. $Sc \cdot Rc \cdot (y)[(Sy \cdot Ry) \supset y = c]$ 22, 56, Conj
58. $(\exists x)\{Sx \cdot Rx \cdot$
    $(y)[(Sy \cdot Ry) \supset y = x]\}$ 57, EG

Exercise 9

II.

1. a. Has no effect.
   b. Strengthens.
   c. Weakens.
   d. Weakens.
   e. Strengthens.
   f. Strengthens.
   g. Weakens.
   h. Strengthens.
   i. Strengthens.
   j. Weakens.

4. a. Has no effect.
   b. Weakens.
   c. Strengthens.
   d. Weakens.
   e. Strengthens.
   f. Has no effect.
   g. Strengthens.
   h. Weakens.
   i. Weakens.
   j. Strengthens.

7. a. Weakens.
   b. Strengthens.
   c. Has no effect.
   d. Strengthens.
   e. Strengthens.
   f. Weakens.
   g. Weakens.
   h. Strengthens.
   i. Strengthens.
   j. Weakens.

10. *Hint:* For Maxie's argument, concentrate on the similarities between a home and a car (a car is an extended living space with heating, air conditioning, stereo, comfortable seating, and so on), the dissimilarities between a plane and a car (greater difficulty in controlling, ease of crossing international borders, greater danger in operating, and so on). Also, people outside U.S. borders are not accorded the same constitutional protections as people inside, and a phone message normally suggests greater privacy than a radio message. In

9

addition, the teenagers parked in the lot were acting in plain view, and a telescope only enhances ordinary sense perception (so there was no search). Maxie, on the other hand, was talking while speeding down the freeway and was thus not acting in plain view (in the same sense), and a radio receiver (used by the agents) does not enhance ordinary sense perception.

For the agents' argument, concentrate on the similarities between a car and a plane (both are means of transportation, both can cross state lines, both are relatively hard to keep track of, and so on) and the dissimilarities between a car or plane and a house (houses do not move, so it will stay in place while a search warrant is obtained). Also, cell phones use radio transmitters just like planes, both the cell phone message and the radio message from the plane were received inside U.S. borders, and the cell phone message was received inadvertently, just as the radio message from the plane and the image through the telescope were (thus making it impossible to plan ahead for a search warrant). Also, in a sense, Maxie *was* acting in plain view: A lip reader traveling in an adjacent car might interpret his message. Lastly, controlling illicit drugs is a high priority for the government.

13. *Hint:* Couch your arguments in terms of foreseeability.

For Liz's argument note that there were several events that intervened between the car accident and the amputation: Mary's being taken to the hospital, Mary's being treated by doctors for bumps and bruises, Mary's apparent mix-up with some other patient scheduled for leg amputation, the doctors' failure to check Mary's proper identity before operating, etc. Liz did not directly control any of these events, and therefore she could not have foreseen them. Liz could not have foreseen what hospital Mary would be taken to, the fact that Mary would be mixed up with another patient, etc. Because Liz should not be held liable for an event utterly unforeseen to her, she should not be liable for Mary's amputated leg. The facts are similar to those in *Gomez v. Hunt*, where Gomez could not foresee the exact route that Hunt would take when walking home, the fact that a worker would drop a brick, the fact that the brick would strike Hunt, etc. The facts are dissimilar to those in *Sacco v. Lane*, where Lane was in direct control over the flames in the barbecue, and it was those very same flames that spread to the houses.

For Mary's argument note that Liz initiated a chain of events that flowed naturally from the car accident to the amputation. Once the car accident occurred, it was foreseeable that Mary would be taken to the hospital; once Mary was in the hospital it was foreseeable that mix-ups would occur (after all, mix-ups occur in hospitals every day); given the nature of these mix-ups, it was foreseeable that Mary's leg would be amputated. Granted, Liz might not have been able to foresee each event in the chain, but once an event occurred, someone familiar with it could have foreseen the next event. Therefore, given that each event was foreseeable by *someone*—at least some hypothetical person—Liz should be held liable. The events are similar to those in *Sacco v. Lane*. When the flames were leaping from the barbecue, it was foreseeable that they would ignite the trees; once the trees were aflame, it was foreseeable that a house would be ignited, then another house, etc. Lane would not have been able to foresee the whole chain of events at the time he was tending the barbecue, but once one event occurred, the next was foreseeable. Also, even though the wind constituted an intervening event, Lane was still held liable. Finally, the facts are dissimilar to those in *Gomez v. Hunt*. When Hunt was walking home, he was in complete control over his own actions. He freely chose to walk past the building under construction, and he should have been on the lookout for falling objects. The fact that he was struck by a falling brick was partly the result of his own failure to observe. On the contrary, from the time of the accident until the amputation, Mary was in the hands of others: the person who took her to the hospital, nurses in the hospital, etc. In no sense was the amputation the result of Mary's free choices.

Exercise 10

I.

1. Sufficient condition. The window can also be broken by throwing a stone or baseball through it.
4. Necessary condition. For an image to appear on the sensor the camera must also be focused and there must be sufficient light.
7. Sufficient condition. The fire will also be extinguished if it is smothered.
10. Necessary condition. Electricity must also be supplied from the main lines.
13. Necessary condition. Without exercise a person cannot be healthy, but other things are needed such as proper nutrition.
16. Necessary condition. The check must also be dated and the payee must be named.
19. Necessary condition. If the batter does not pick up the bat, he/she cannot hit a home run. But the batter must also hit the ball.

II.

1. A = a certain make, B = a certain year, C = a certain model, D = driven 30,000 miles, E = a certain gasoline, F = a certain oil, G = a certain driver, H = certain road conditions, I = the additive.

| | Possible Conditions | | | | | | | | | Phenomenon |
Occurrence	A	B	C	D	E	F	G	H	I	(less wear)
1	*	*	*	*	*	*	*	*	*	*
2	*	*	*	*	*	*	*	*	—	—

Method of difference, sufficient condition.

4. A = type X circuitry, B = shipped to a coastal region, C = sold to a business customer, D = manufactured in the Kansas City plant, E = used to play computer games, F = shipped to a large city.

| | Possible Conditions | | | | | | Phenomenon |
Occurrence	A	B	C	D	E	F	(returned)
1	*	*	—	*	*	—	*
2	—	*	*	*	—	*	*
3	*	*	*	—	*	*	*
4	—	*	—	*	*	*	*
5	*	*	—	*	*	—	*
6	*	*	*	—	—	*	*
7	*	*	*	*	—	*	*

Coastal region (salty air) is the cause in the sense of a necessary condition.
Method of agreement.

7. A = camomile tea, B = late dinner, C = hot bath, D = read book, E = walk, F = wine, G = massage.

| | Possible Conditions | | | | | | | Phenomenon |
Occurrence	A	B	C	D	E	F	G	(slept well)
Mon	*	*	*	*	*	—	—	*
Tu	—	*	—	*	—	—	—	—
Wed	—	—	—	—	*	*	*	—
Th	—	*	*	*	—	*	*	*
Fri	*	*	—	*	*	—	*	*
Sat	*	—	*	—	*	*	*	*
Sun	*	—	*	*	—	—	—	—

None of the possible conditions is a cause of the phenomenon.
Joint method of agreement and difference.

10. A = corporal punishment, B = siblings, C = adopted, D = male parent figure, E = sexual abuse, F = domineering mother, G = uprooted often, H = day-care center.

| | Possible Conditions | | | | | | | | Phenomenon |
Occurrence	A	B	C	D	E	F	G	H	(blurred bound)
Meg	*	*	*	—	*	*	—	—	*
Sue	*	*	—	*	*	—	—	*	*
Dot	*	—	*	*	*	*	*	*	*
Jane	*	*	*	*	*	*	*	—	*
Lynn	—	*	*	*	*	—	—	*	*
Flo	*	*	—	*	*	*	*	—	*

Sexual abuse is the cause of the phenomenon in the sense of a necessary condition. Method of agreement.

13. A = malathion, B = American Beauty, C = five years old, D = a certain location, E = a certain amount of water, F = a certain amount of sun, G = a certain kind of soil, H = a certain amount of cultivation, I = a certain amount of Bandini rose food.

Occurrence	Possible Conditions								Phenomenon (no aphids)
	A	B	C	D	E	F	G	H	
1	*	*	*	*	*	*	*	*	*
2	−	*	*	*	*	*	*	*	−

Method of difference, sufficient condition.

III.

1. By the method of agreement, D is the cause in the sense of a necessary condition.
4. By an unnamed method, D is the cause in the sense of a sufficient condition.

Exercise 11

I.

1. 1/6
4. .853
7. 1/4 or .25
10. Approximately $17
13. 4/9

II.

1. $P(6 \text{ or } 1) = P(6) + P(1) = 1/6 + 1/6 = 2/6 = 1/3$
4. a. $P(A_1 \text{ and } A_2) = P(A_1) \times P(A_2)$
   $= 4/52 \times 4/52$
   $= 1/169 = .0059$
   b. $P(A_1 \text{ and } A_2) = P(A_1) \times P(A_2 \text{ given } A_1)$
   $= 4/52 \times 3/51$
   $= 1/221 = .0045$
7. First compute the probability of getting no sixes:
   $P(\text{no sixes}) = 5/6 \times 5/6 \times 5/6$
   $= 125/216$
   Then use the negation rule:
   $P(\text{at least one six}) = 1 − P(\text{no sixes})$
   $= 1 − 125/216$
   $= 91/216 = .4213$
10. a. $P(R_1 \text{ and } R_2) = P(R_1) \times P(R_2 \text{ given } R_1)$
   $= 3/12 \times 2/11$
   $= 6/132 = .045$

b. $P(Y \text{ and } G) = P(Y_1 \text{ and } G_2) + P(G_1 \text{ and } Y_2)$
   $= (5/12 \times 4/11) + (4/12 \times 5/11)$
   $= 20/132 + 20/132$
   $= 10/33 = .303$
c. $P(R \text{ or } G) = 1 − P(Y_1 \text{ and } Y_2)$
   $= 1 − (5/12 \times 4/11)$
   $= 1 − 20/132$
   $= 28/33 = .848$
d. $P(G_1 \text{ or } G_2) = 1 − P(\text{not } G)$
   $= 1 − [P(R_1 \text{ and } R_2) + P(R_1 \text{ and } Y_2)$
   $+ P(Y_1 \text{ and } R_2) + P(Y_1 \text{ and } Y_2)]$
   $= 1 − [(3/12 \times 2/11) + (3/12 \times 5/11) + (5/12 \times 3/11) + (5/12 \times 4/11)]$
   $= 1 − [6/132 + 15/132 + 15/132 + 20/132]$
   $= 1 − 56/132$
   $= 19/33 = .57$
e. $P(\text{same color}) = P(R_1 \text{ and } R_2) + P(G_1 \text{ and } G_2) + P(Y_1 \text{ and } Y_2)$
   $= (3/12 \times 2/11) + (4/12 \times 3/11) + (5/12 \times 4/11)$
   $= 6/132 + 12/132 + 20/132$
   $= 19/66 = .288$

13. a. $P(M \text{ or } W) = P(M) + P(W) − P(M \text{ and } W)$
   $= .74 + .82 − (.74 \times .82)$
   $= .95$
b. $P(M \text{ and } W \text{ and } S) = P(M) \times P(W) \times P(S)$
   $= .74 \times .82 \times 8/9$
   $= .54$

16. $P(N \text{ given } R) = \dfrac{P(N) \times P(R \text{ given } N)}{[P(N) \times P(R \text{ given } N)] + [P(O) \times P(R \text{ given } O)]}$

$= \dfrac{3/5 \times 7/15}{[3/5 \times 7/15] + [2/5 \times 5/15]} = \dfrac{21/75}{21/75 + 10/75}$

$= \dfrac{21/75}{31/75} = 21/31 = .68$

Answer: new urn.

19. $P(R \text{ given } N) = \dfrac{P(R) \times P(N \text{ given } R)}{[P(R) \times P(N \text{ given } R)] + [P(T) \times P(N \text{ given } T)]}$

$= \dfrac{.2 \times .7}{(.2 \times .7) + (.8 \times .2)} = \dfrac{.14}{.14 + .16} = .14/.30 = .47$

Exercise 12

I.

1. Since the water in the lake might not be circulating, the algae content of the water at one end might not be representative of the whole lake. Thus, the sample might be biased.
4. According to Table 12.1, the margin of error for a random sample of 600 is ± 5 percent. Since the sample taken indicates a difference of only 2 percent, the results of the sample are inconclusive.
7. Since no mention is made of the size of the sample or of the expected sampling error, the sample might be biased. The manufacturer might have taken 25 separate samples consisting of ten dentists per sample and reported the results of only the most favorable one.
10. The problem concerns the meaning of "average." If the average is a mean, most of the toys could be over $15, and a few very cheap toys could bring the average down to $15. If the average is a mode, there might be a few toys priced at $15, and all the other toys might have varying prices exceeding $15. Only if the average is a median can one be assured that half the toys are $15 or less.
13. Since no mention is made of the dispersion, the argument is weak. The rock pile might consist of several pieces weighing 500 pounds and enough weighing only 4 or 5 pounds to bring the average down to 50 pounds. If the range were only 10 pounds or so, the conclusion would follow.
16. If the scale on the vertical axis does not begin at zero, the conclusion does not follow.
19. Since there were many more cars on the road in 2016 than there were in 1995, the comparison is faulty.

II.

1. Margin of error $= 1.29/\sqrt{n}$
   Solving for n, $n = (1.29/\text{margin of error})^2$
   For 1%, $n = (1.29/.01)^2 = 129^2 = 16,641$

For 2%, $n = (1.29/.02)^2 = 64.5^2 = 4,160$
For 3%, $n = (1/29/.03)^2 = 43^2 = 1,849$
For 4%, $n = (1.29/.04)^2 = 32.25^2 = 1,040$
For 5%, $n = (1.29/.05)^2 = 25.8^2 = 666$
For 6%, $n = (1.29/.06)^2 = 21.5^2 = 462$
For 7%, $n = (1.29/.07)^2 = 18.43^2 = 340$
For 10%, $n = (1.29/.1)^2 = 12.9^2 = 166$

4.

Mean age = 3, variance = 3, standard deviation = 1.73.

III.

1. False.
4. False.
7. True.
10. False.
13. True.
16. False.
19. False.

Exercise 13

V.

1. True.
4. False.
7. True.
10. True.
13. True.
16. False.
19. False.

13

Glossary/Index

Double negation: A valid rule of inference that allows the introduction or deletion of pairs of negation signs, 391, 427–429

Drawing an affirmative/negative conclusion from negative/affirmative premises: A formal fallacy that occurs in a categorical syllogism when an affirmative conclusion is drawn from a negative premise or a negative conclusion is drawn from affirmative premises, 298–299

Duns Scotus, 152

E proposition: A categorical proposition having the form "No *S* are *P*," 210–211

Edmonstone, Susanna Carnegie, 284

Einstein, Albert, 33, 526, 628, 639–640, 651–652

"Either," 334

Eminent logicians, *See* Logicians

Emotional disposition and avoiding fallacies, 190, 193

Emotive meaning: The meaning by which terminology expresses or evokes feelings, 82–84

Empirical hypotheses: Hypotheses that concern the production of some thing or the occurrence of some event that can be observed, 636–637

Empty extension: The extension of a term that denotes something that does not exist; the null class, 94

Empty intension, 94

Enthymeme: A categorical syllogism that is missing a premise or conclusion, 312–314; an argument that is missing a premise or conclusion, 23n, 312–314

Enumerative definition: A definition that assigns a meaning to a word by naming the members of the class that the word denotes, 107–108, 113

Equivalence. *See* Biconditional statement; Logically equivalent statements; Material equivalence

Equivocation: An informal fallacy that occurs because some word or group of words is used either implicitly or explicitly in two different senses, 165, 173–174, 192, 620; division and, 179

Escaping between the horns of a dilemma, 386–387

Essential meaning, definitions and, 118

Etymological definition: A definition that assigns a meaning to a word by disclosing the word's ancestry in both its own language and other languages, 109–110, 113

Everest, Mary, 218

Evidentiary support, 647–652

Exceptive propositions, 266; in predicate logic, 525; syllogisms containing, 310

Exclusive disjunction, 330, 343–344, 348

Exclusive premises: A formal fallacy that occurs when both premises of a categorical syllogism are negative, 298

Exclusive propositions, 265; in predicate logic, 475–476, 524–525

Existential fallacy: A fallacy that occurs whenever an argument is invalid merely because the premises lack existential import, 225–226, 243–245, 256–257, 299–301

Existential generalization: A rule of inference that introduces existential quantifiers, 480, 482–483, 486–488, 516, 519; improper or invalid applications of, 488, 519

Existential import: An attribute of a categorical proposition by which it implies that one or more things denoted by the subject term actually exist, 216–217, 226–227

Existential instantiation: A rule of inference that removes existential quantifiers, 480, 483–486, invalid applications of, 485, 488; restrictions on, 484–488

Existential names, 484–485

Existential quantifier: The quantifier used to translate particular statements in predicate logic, 474–477

Explanandum: The component of an explanation that describes the event or phenomenon to be explained, 20–21

Explanans: The component of an explanation that explains the event or phenomenon indicated by the explanandum, 20–21

Explanation: An expression that purports to shed light on some event or phenomenon, 20–22

Exportation: A valid rule of inference that allows conditional statements having conjunctive antecedents to be replaced with conditional statements having conditional consequents, and vice versa, 440–444

Expository passage: A kind of discourse that begins with a topic sentence followed by one or more sentences that develop the topic sentence, 18–19

Extended arguments, 67–72

Extensional (denotative) definition: A definition that assigns a meaning to a term by indicating the members of the class that the term denotes, 107–109, 118

Extensional meaning (extension): The members of the class that a term denotes, 93–95, 107; empty, 94

External consistency: The extent to which a hypothesis agrees with other, well-confirmed hypotheses, 639–641, 647, 659, 664

Exxon Mobil, 663

Factual disputes, 86

Fallacies of ambiguity: A group of informal fallacies that occur because of an ambiguity in the premises or conclusion, 165–166, 173–176

Fallacies of categorical syllogisms, 296–301

Fallacies of illicit transference: A group of informal fallacies that involves the incorrect transference of an attribute from the parts of something onto the whole, or from the whole onto the parts, 166, 176–179

Fallacies of presumption: A group of informal fallacies that occur when the premises of an argument presume what they purport to prove, 165–173

Fallacies of relevance: A group of informal fallacies that occur because the premises of an argument are irrelevant to the conclusion, 128–141

Fallacies of weak induction: A group of informal fallacies that occur because the connection between the premises and conclusion is not strong enough to support the conclusion, 147–158

Fallacy: A defect in an argument that arises from a mistake in reasoning or the creation of an illusion that makes a bad argument appear good, 125. *See also* Fallacies (of various kinds); Formal fallacy; Informal fallacy

False cause: An informal fallacy that occurs when the conclusion of an argument depends on some imagined causal connection that probably does not exist, 153–155, 190–191, 193, 648, 653; and appeal to the people, 133

False dichotomy: An informal fallacy that is committed when an arguer presents two nonjointly exhaustive alternatives as if they were jointly exhaustive and then eliminates one, leaving the other as the conclusion, 165, 170–171, 189–190

Falsifiability criterion, 649–650

Feng shui, 649

Fermat, Pierre de, 586

"Few," "a few," 263–264

Figurative definitions, 119–120

Figure: An attribute of a categorical syllogism that specifies the location of the middle term, 276–277

Finite universe method: A method for proving invalidity in predicate logic that consists in reducing the universe to a single object and then sequentially increasing it until one is found in which the premises of an argument turn out true and the conclusion false, 507–510

Folta, Kevin, 662–663

"For the reason that," 3

"For this reason," 3

Form of a categorical syllogism, 276–277

Form of an argument, 59–62, 382–386, 388–392; invalid, 385–386, 388–392

Formal fallacy: A fallacy that can be identified by merely examining the form or structure of an argument, 125–126. *See also* Fallacies (of various kinds)

Free variable: A variable that is not bound by a quantifier, 473

Frege, Gottlob, 7, 15, 455

Fruitfulness: The extent to which a hypothesis suggests new ideas for future analysis and confirmation, 639–641, 647

Fulbert, 101

Galen, 6

Galilei, Galileo, 577, 633, 636–637

Galle, Johann, 630, 632, 637

Gambler's fallacy, 154

Gay-Lussac, Joseph Luis, 649

Geller, Uri, 658

General conjunction rule: In probability theory, a rule for computing the probability of two events occurring together whether or not they are independent, 591–592, 594

General disjunction rule: In probability theory, a rule for computing the probability of either of two events whether or not they are mutually exclusive, 593–594, 598

Liesburg, Margaret, 455

Literary Digest poll, 606

Logic: The science that evaluates arguments, 1; history of, 5–7

Logical operators, definitions of, 341–345

Logically equivalent statements: (1) Statements that necessarily have the same truth value, 230, 233, 235; (2) statements having the same truth value on each line under their main operators, 359–361; consistency and, 361

Logically false statement: A statement that is necessarily false, a self-contradictory statement, 358–359

Logically true statement: A statement that is necessarily true; a tautology, 358–359; proving, 358–359, 466–467

Logically undetermined truth value: A condition that exists when a certain statement is not necessarily either true or false, given the truth value of some related statement, 221, 231, 235–237, 241–242, 254–255

Logicians (biographies): Abelard, 101; Ambrose, 208; Aristotle, 15; Boole, 218; Byron, 366; Chrysippus, 54; De Morgan, 378; Frege, 455; Gödel, 526; Kripke, 306; Leibniz, 335; Marcus, 34; Mill, 564; Ockham, 152; Peirce, 638; Quine, 431; Russell, 494; Venn, 284; Whitehead, 494

Loosely associated statements: Statements that are about the same general subject and that lack an inferential relationship, 17

Ludwig of Bavaria, 152

Lyons, Eugene, 620n

McCarthy, Joseph, 132

Maharishi Mahesh Yogi, 660–661

Main operator: The operator (connective) in a compound statement that has as its scope everything else in the statement, 330, 346, 358–359

Major premise: In a categorical syllogism, the premise that contains the major term, 275

Major term: In a standard-form categorical syllogism, the predicate of the conclusion, 275

Marcus, Jules Alexander, 34

Marcus, Ruth Barcan, 34

Margin of Error, 607–608

Material equivalence: (1) The relation expressed by a truth-functional biconditional, 328–329, 333; comparison with ordinary language, 350; truth-functional definition of, 345; (2) a valid rule of inference that allows an equivalence statement to be replaced by a conjunctive statement or a disjunctive statement, 440–442

Material implication: (1) The relation expressed by a truth-functional conditional, 328–329, 332; comparison with ordinary language, 348–350; truth-functional definition of, 344; (2) a valid rule of inference that allows an implication sign to be replaced by a disjunction sign if and only if the antecedent is negated, 440–445

Maxwell, James Clerk, 640–641

Mean: The arithmetical average, 609–611, 613, 615

Meaning, 81–86, 92; cognitive, 82, 84–86; emotive, 82–84; extensional, 93–95, 108–109; intensional, 93–95 109; varieties of, 81–86

Median: The middle point when data are arranged in ascending order, 609–611, 615

Mendeleev, Dmitri, 640

Mental carelessness, 190, 192

Mention of a word, 93

Method of agreement: A method for identifying a causal connection between an effect and a single factor that is present in several occurrences in which the effect is present, 562–563, 565

Method of concomitant variation: A method for identifying a causal connection between two conditions by matching variations in one condition with variations in another, 570–572, 575–577

Method of difference: A method for identifying a causal connection between an effect and a single factor that is present in an occurrence in which the effect is present and absent from an occurrence in which the effect is absent, 565–567, 573–575

Method of residues: A method of identifying a causal connection by subtracting already-known strands of causal connection from a compound causal connection, 569–570

Michael of Cesena, 152

Middle term: In a standard-form categorical syllogism, the term that occurs only in the premises, 275–276; of a sorites, 319–321

Milbanke, Annabella, 366

Mill, James, 564

Mill, John Stuart, 7, 284, 562, 564

Mill's methods and science, 572–577

Mill's methods of induction, 284, 562–577

Minor premise: In a categorical syllogism, the premise that contains the minor term, 275

Minor term: In a standard-form categorical syllogism, the subject of the conclusion, 275

Missing the point: An informal fallacy that occurs when the premise of an argument entails one particular conclusion but a completely different conclusion is actually drawn, 139–141, 190, 193, 620

Mnemonic device, for distribution, 213; for sufficient conditions, necessary conditions, 332

Mob mentality, 131–134

Modal logic: A kind of logic that deals with concepts such as possibility, necessity, belief, and doubt, 5, 7, 306

Mode: The value that occurs with the greatest frequency in a set of data, 609–611, 615

Modern square of opposition: A diagram that illustrates the necessary relations that prevail between the four kinds of standard-form categorical propositions as interpreted from the Boolean standpoint, 221–222

Modus ponens: A valid argument form/ rule of inference: "If *p* then *q* / *p* // *q*," 36, 382–383, 388–390, 392–393, 404–410; in predicate logic, 480–481

Modus tollens: A valid argument form/rule of inference: "If *p* then *q* / not *q* // not *p*," 383, 385–386, 389–390, 392, 404–410, 629

Monadic predicate: A predicate used to assign an attribute to individual things, 512

Monsanto, 662–663

Mood: An attribute of a categorical syllogism that specifies the kind of statements (**A, E, I, O**) that make it up, 276–277

Moore, G. E., 494

Moral reasoning, 547–551

Multiple conclusion, 69–70

Mutually exclusive events, 592

Names, 92, 94–95; existential, 484–485

Narrow definitions, 118

Natural deduction: A method for deriving the conclusion of a valid argument in which each step is justified by a rule of inference, 403–404; in predicate logic, 480–539; in propositional logic, 403–469

Necessary and sufficient condition, 332; causality and, 561–563, 565, 567–568

Necessary condition: The condition represented by the consequent in a conditional statement, 24, 332; causality and, 560–563, 565, 568

Needham, John, 635–637, 639

Negation: A statement having a tilde as its main operator, 328–329; truth-functional definition of, 342

Negation rule: A rule for computing the probability of an event from the probability of the event *not* happening, 594–595, 598

Negative definitions, 119

Negative proposition/statement: A proposition/statement that denies class membership, 210–211, 213–214

"Neither . . . nor," 334

Neptune, discovery of, 632, 636–637, 639–640

Newton, Isaac, 634, 639–641, 650

"No . . . except," 265, 524–525

Non causa pro causa, 153

Non sequitur, 125

Nonarguments, typical kinds of, 16–25

"None but," 265; in predicate logic, 475

"None except," 265

Nonstandard quantifiers, 263–264

Nonstandard verbs, translation of, 260–261

Normal probability distribution: A distribution of random phenomena that has the shape of a bell, 574, 614–616

"Not both," 334

"Not either," 334

Numerical statement, 527–528

O proposition: A categorical proposition having the form "Some *S* are not *P*," 210–211

Objectivity, 647, 652–657

Obscure definitions, 119–120

Obverse, 231–234, 236

Obversion: An operation that consists of changing the quality of a standard-form categorical proposition and replacing the predicate term with its term complement, 231–234, 236, 245–246; to reduce the number of terms in a syllogism, 305–307

Ockham, William of, 6, 152, 650

Restricted disjunction rule: In probability theory, a rule for computing the probability of either of two mutually exclusive events, 592–593

Retrospective study, 575

Reuben, Scott, 661–663

Rice, N. L., 156

Robbins, Tony, 658

Root, Elihu, 132

Rule of implication: A rule consisting of a basic argument form by means of which the conclusion of an argument is derived from the premises, 403–411, 416–421

Rule of inference: A rule by means of which the conclusion of an argument is derived from the premises, 403–411, 416–421, 426–432, 440–445; for identity, 529–532; for relational predicates and overlapping quantifiers, 516–520; in predicate logic, 480–489; misapplications of, 409–410, 420–421

Rule of replacement: A rule consisting of two logically equivalent statement forms by means of which the conclusion of an argument is derived from the premises, 426–432, 440–445

Rules for categorical syllogisms, 296–301

Rules for sorites, 320–321

Russell, Bertrand, 7, 15, 208, 378, 431, 455, 494, 638

Russell's paradox, 455

Samples, 605–609

Sampling error: The difference between the relative frequency with which some characteristic occurs in a sample and the relative frequency with which the same characteristic occurs in the population, 607–608

Scatter diagram, 576

Science and superstition, 646–664

Scientific arguments, 38–39

Scientific progress, 651–652

Scientific reasoning, 627–645

Secondary analogue, 541, 543

Self-contradictory statement: A statement that is necessarily false, a logically false statement, 358–359; and inconsistency, 359–361

Seneca, 54

Sense, 93

Shannon, Claude, 218

Sherwood, William of, 6

Shirt-collar model, 276–277

Sidgwick, Henry, 284

Simple identity statements, 524

Simple noninferential passages, 16–18

Simple statement: A statement that does not contain any other statement as a component, 328

Simplification: A valid rule of inference, "*p* and *q* // *p*," 417–421, 432

"Since," 3, 16

Singer, Barry F., 653

Singleton, Donald, 657

Singular proposition/statement: A proposition/statement that makes an assertion about a specifically named person, place, thing, or time, 261–262; in predicate logic, 471

Size of sample, 606–609

Slippery slope: An informal fallacy that occurs when the conclusion of an argument rests on an alleged chain reaction, and there is not sufficient reason to think that the chain reaction will actually take place, 155–157, 190

"Some," 63, 207, 217n

Sorites: A chain of categorical syllogisms in which the intermediate conclusions have been left out, 318–321; Aristotelian, 319n; Goclenian, 319n; rules for, 320–321; standard form of, 319, Venn diagrams for, 319–320

Sound argument: A deductive argument that is valid and has all true premises, 48, 53, 245

Spallanzani, Lazzaro, 635

Species, 111

Specific difference, 111

Spinoza, Benedict, 640

Spontaneous generation, 634–636

Square of opposition. *See* Modern square of opposition; Traditional square of opposition

Stalin, Joseph, 620

Standard deviation: In statistics, a measure of how far the data vary or deviate from the mean value; the square root of the variance, 612–615

Standard-form categorical proposition: A proposition that has one of the following forms: "All *S* are *P*," "No *S* are *P*," "Some *S* are *P*," "Some *S* are not *P*," 207

Standard-form categorical syllogism: A categorical syllogism in which all three statements are standard-form categorical propositions, the two occurrences of each term are identical, each term is used in the same sense throughout the argument, and the major premise is listed first, the minor premise second, and the conclusion last, 275

Standard-form sorites: A sorites in which each of the component propositions is in standard form, each term occurs twice, the predicate of the conclusion is in the first premise, and each successive premise has a term in common with the preceding one, 319

Statement: (1) A sentence that is either true or false, 2, 53; (2) in predicate logic, an expression involving bound variables or constants throughout, 471–477, 485. *See also* Compound statement; General statement; Numerical statement; Particular statement; Simple statement; Singular proposition; Superlative statement; Universal statement

Statement form: An arrangement of statement variables and operators such that the uniform substitution of statements in place of the variables results in a statement, 342

Statement function: In predicate logic, the expression that remains when a quantifier is removed from a statement, 473, 481–482, 485

Statement of belief: A kind of nonargument composed of statements that express the personal conviction of a speaker or writer without giving any evidence in support of that conviction, 17

Statement variable: A lowercase letter, such as *p* or *q*, that can represent any statement, 342

Statistical reasoning, 604–626

Stellar parallax, 659–660

Stipulative definition: A definition that assigns a meaning to a word for the first time, 98–99, 103, 108, 113

Stipulative use of a word, 98

Stoicism, 54

Straw man: A fallacy that occurs when the arguer misinterprets an opponent's position for the purpose of more easily attacking it, demolishes the misinterpreted argument, and then proceeds to conclude that the original argument has been demolished, 138–139, 141, 188–190

Striking predictions, 652

Strong inductive argument: An inductive argument in which it is improbable that the conclusion be false given that the premises are true 48–53

Study, 575

Subalternation relation: The relation by which a true **A** or **E** statement necessarily implies a true **I** or **O** statement, respectively, and by which a false **I** or **O** statement necessarily implies a false **A** or **E** statement, respectively, 226, 240–246, 255

Subcontrary relation: The relation that exists between two statements that are necessarily not both false, 241–244, 254

Subject, 208

Subject term: In a standard-form categorical proposition, the term that comes immediately after the quantifier, 206–208

Subjectivist theory of probability: The theory according to which probabilities are computed from the odds that people would accept on a bet, 586, 588–589, 590, 598

Subjunctive biconditionals, 350

Subjunctive conditionals, 350

Substitution instance: An argument or statement that has the same form as a given argument form or statement form; of an argument form, 59–65, 382–385, of a statement form, 342

Sufficient and necessary condition, 332; causality and, 561–562, 567–569

Sufficient condition: The condition represented by the antecedent in a conditional statement, 24, 332; causality and, 561–562, 565–569

Superfluous distribution rule, 300, 320

Superlative statement, 527

Superstition, 646–664

Suppressed evidence: A fallacy that occurs when the arguer ignores relevant evidence that outweighs the presented evidence and entails a very different conclusion, 165, 171–173, 189–190, 620

Syllogism: A deductive argument consisting of two premises and one conclusion, 36, 274. *See also* Categorical syllogism; Disjunctive syllogism; Hypothetical syllogism; Pure hypothetical syllogism

Syllogistic logic: The logic that deals with categorical propositions and categorical syllogisms, 5; predicate logic and, 470–471

Guide to Important Rules & Argument Forms

Traditional Square of Opposition

Logically Equivalent Statement Forms

Conversion	*Given statement*	*Converse*
	E: No *S* are *P.*	No *P* are *S.*
	I: Some *S* are *P.*	Some *P* are *S.*
Obversion	*Given statement*	*Obverse*
	A: All *S* are *P.*	No *S* are non-*P.*
	E: No *S* are *P.*	All *S* are non-*P.*
	I: Some *S* are *P.*	Some *S* are not non-*P.*
	O: Some *S* are not *P.*	Some *S* are non-*P.*
Contraposition	*Given statement*	*Contrapositive*
	A: All *S* are *P.*	All non-*P* are non-*S.*
	O: Some *S* are not *P.*	Some non-*P* are not non-*S.*

Valid Syllogistic Forms

Unconditionally Valid Forms

Figure 1	Figure 2	Figure 3	Figure 4
AAA	EAE	IAI	AEE
EAE	AEE	AII	IAI
AII	EIO	OAO	EIO
EIO	AOO	EIO	

Conditionally Valid Forms

Figure 1	Figure 2	Figure 3	Figure 4	Required condition
AAI	AEO		AEO	*S* exist
EAO	EAO			
		AAI	EAO	*M* exist
		EAO		
			AAI	*P* exist

Rules for Categorical Syllogisms

Rule 1: The middle term must be distributed at least once.
Fallacy: Undistributed middle

Rule 2: If a term is distributed in the conclusion, then it must be distributed in a premise.
Fallacy: Illicit major; illicit minor

Rule 3: Two negative premises are not allowed.
Fallacy: Exclusive premises

Rule 4: A negative premise requires a negative conclusion, and a negative conclusion requires a negative premise.
Fallacy: Drawing an affirmative conclusion from a negative premise; drawing a negative conclusion from affirmative premises

Rule 5: If both premises are universal, the conclusion cannot be particular.
Fallacy: Existential fallacy

NOTE: If only Rule 5 is broken, the syllogism is valid from the Aristotelian standpoint if the critical term denotes actually existing things.

CENGAGE Learning®

Rules of Implication

1. Modus ponens (MP)
$$p \supset q$$
$$\underline{p}$$
$$q$$

2. Modus tollens (MT)
$$p \supset q$$
$$\underline{\sim q}$$
$$\sim p$$

3. Pure hypothetical syllogism (HS)
$$p \supset q$$
$$\underline{q \supset r}$$
$$p \supset r$$

4. Disjunctive syllogism (DS)
$$p \vee q$$
$$\underline{\sim p}$$
$$q$$

5. Constructive dilemma (CD)
$$(p \supset q) \bullet (r \supset s)$$
$$\underline{p \vee r}$$
$$q \vee s$$

6. Simplification (Simp)
$$\underline{p \bullet q}$$
$$p$$

7. Conjunction (Conj)
$$p$$
$$\underline{q}$$
$$p \bullet q$$

8. Addition (Add)
$$\underline{p}$$
$$p \vee q$$

Rules of Replacement

9. De Morgan's rule (DM)
$$\sim(p \bullet q) :: (\sim p \vee \sim q)$$
$$\sim(p \vee q) :: (\sim p \bullet \sim q)$$

10. Commutativity (Com)
$$(p \vee q) :: (q \vee p)$$
$$(p \bullet q) :: (q \bullet p)$$

11. Associativity (Assoc)
$$[p \vee (q \vee r)] :: [(p \vee q) \vee r]$$
$$[p \bullet (q \bullet r)] :: [(p \bullet q) \bullet r]$$

12. Distribution (Dist)
$$[p \bullet (q \vee r)] :: [(p \bullet q) \vee (p \bullet r)]$$
$$[p \vee (q \bullet r)] :: [(p \vee q) \bullet (p \vee r)]$$

13. Double negation (DN)
$$p :: \sim\sim p$$

14. Transposition (Trans)
$$(p \supset q) :: (\sim q \supset \sim p)$$

15. Material implication (Impl)
$$(p \supset q) :: (\sim p \vee q)$$

16. Material equivalence (Equiv)
$$(p \equiv q) :: [(p \supset q) \bullet (q \supset p)]$$
$$(p \equiv q) :: [(p \bullet q) \vee (\sim p \bullet \sim q)]$$

17. Exportation (Exp)
$$[(p \bullet q) \supset r] :: [p \supset (q \supset r)]$$

18. Tautology (Taut)
$$p :: (p \vee p)$$
$$p :: (p \bullet p)$$

Truth Tables for the Propositional Operators

p	q	$\sim p$	$p \bullet q$	$p \vee q$	$p \supset q$	$p \equiv q$
T	T	F	T	T	T	T
T	F	F	F	T	F	F
F	T	T	F	T	T	F
F	F	T	F	F	T	T

Rules for Removing and Introducing Quantifiers

($a, b, c, \ldots u, v, w$ are individual constants; x, y, z are individual variables)

1. Universal instantiation (UI)

$$\frac{(x)\mathscr{F}x}{\mathscr{F}y} \qquad \frac{(x)\mathscr{F}x}{\mathscr{F}a}$$

2. Universal generalization (UG)

$$\frac{\mathscr{F}y}{(x)\mathscr{F}x} \qquad not\ allowed: \frac{\mathscr{F}a}{(x)\mathscr{F}x}$$

Restrictions: *(conditional and indirect proof)* (1) UG must not be used within the scope of an indented sequence if the instantial variable y is free in the first line of that sequence.

(overlapping quantifiers) (2) UG must not be used if the instantial variable y is free in any preceding line obtained by EI.

3. Existential instantiation (EI)

$$\frac{(\exists x)\mathscr{F}x}{\mathscr{F}a} \qquad not\ allowed: \frac{(\exists x)\mathscr{F}x}{\mathscr{F}y}$$

Restriction: The existential name a must be a new name that does not appear in any previous line (including the conclusion line).

4. Existential generalization (EG)

$$\frac{\mathscr{F}a}{(\exists x)\mathscr{F}x} \qquad \frac{\mathscr{F}y}{(\exists x)\mathscr{F}x}$$

Quantifier Negation Rule

$$(x)\mathscr{F}x :: \sim(\exists x)\sim\mathscr{F}x \qquad (\exists x)\mathscr{F}x :: \sim(x)\sim\mathscr{F}x$$
$$\sim(x)\mathscr{F}x :: (\exists x)\sim\mathscr{F}x \qquad \sim(\exists x)\mathscr{F}x :: (x)\sim\mathscr{F}x$$

Conditional Proof

$$p \qquad\qquad /\underline{} \quad ACP$$
$$\underline{}$$
$$q$$
$$p \supset q \qquad\qquad CP$$

Indirect Proof

$$p \qquad\qquad /\underline{} \quad AIP$$
$$\underline{}$$
$$q \bullet \sim q$$
$$\sim p \qquad\qquad IP$$

Rules for the Probability Calculus

1. $P(A \text{ or not } A) = 1$
2. $P(A \text{ and not } A) = 0$
3. $P(A \text{ and } B) = P(A) \times P(B)$ (when A and B are independent)
4. $P(A \text{ and } B) = P(A) \times P(B \text{ given } A)$
5. $P(A \text{ or } B) = P(A) + P(B)$ (when A and B are mutually exclusive)
6. $P(A \text{ or } B) = P(A) + P(B) - P(A \text{ and } B)$
7. $P(A) = 1 - P(\text{not } A)$

Identity Rules

1. Prem.
$$x = x$$

2. $x = y :: y = x$

3.
$$\mathscr{F}x$$
$$\underline{x = y}$$
$$\mathscr{F}y$$

Conditional Proof			Indirect Proof		
—			—		
—			—		
—	$/\_\_$		—	$/\_\_$	
p	ACP		p	AIP	
—			—		
—			—		
q			$q \cdot \sim q$		
$p \supset q$	CP		$\sim p$	IP	

Rules for Removing and Introducing Quantifiers

$(a, b, c, \ldots u, v, w$ are individual constants; x, y, z are individual variables)

1. Universal instantiation (UI)
$$\frac{(x)\mathscr{F}x}{\mathscr{F}y} \qquad\qquad \frac{(x)\mathscr{F}x}{\mathscr{F}a}$$

2. Universal generalization (UG)
$$\frac{\mathscr{F}y}{(x)\mathscr{F}x} \quad \begin{array}{c}not\\allowed:\end{array} \quad \frac{\mathscr{F}a}{(x)\mathscr{F}x}$$

Restrictions: (1) UG must not be used within the scope of an indented
(conditional and sequence if the instantial variable y is free in the first
indirect proof) line of that sequence.

(overlapping (2) UG must not be used if the instantial variable y is free in
quantifiers) any preceding line obtained by EI.

3. Existential instantiation (EI)
$$\frac{(\exists x)\mathscr{F}x}{\mathscr{F}a} \quad \begin{array}{c}not\\allowed:\end{array} \quad \frac{(\exists x)\mathscr{F}x}{\mathscr{F}y}$$

Restriction: The existential name a must be a new name that does not appear in any previous line (including the conclusion line).

4. Existential generalization (EG)
$$\frac{\mathscr{F}a}{(\exists x)\mathscr{F}x} \qquad\qquad \frac{\mathscr{F}y}{(\exists x)\mathscr{F}x}$$

Quantifier Negation Rule

$$(x)\mathscr{F}x :: \sim(\exists x)\sim\mathscr{F}x \qquad (\exists x)\mathscr{F}x :: \sim(x)\sim\mathscr{F}x$$
$$\sim(x)\mathscr{F}x :: (\exists x)\sim\mathscr{F}x \qquad \sim(\exists x)\mathscr{F}x :: (x)\sim\mathscr{F}x$$

Identity Rules

1. $\dfrac{\text{Prem.}}{x = x}$ 　　　 **2.** $x = y :: y = x$ 　　　 **3.** $\mathscr{F}x$
$$x = y$$
$$\mathscr{F}y$$